D1592860

PUBLIC PAPERS OF THE PRESIDENTS
OF THE
UNITED STATES

PUBLIC PAPERS OF THE PRESIDENTS
OF THE
UNITED STATES

George W. Bush

2003

(IN TWO BOOKS)

BOOK II—JULY 1 TO DECEMBER 31, 2003

UNITED STATES GOVERNMENT PRINTING OFFICE
WASHINGTON : 2006

Published by the
Office of the Federal Register
National Archives and Records Administration

For sale by the Superintendent of Documents, U.S. Government Printing Office
• Internet: bookstore.gpo.gov • Phone: (202) 512–1800 • Fax: (202) 512–2250
• Mail: Stop SSOP, Washington, DC 20401

Foreword

This volume collects my speeches and papers from the second half of 2003.

These months brought significant legislative accomplishments in Washington. In December, after months of bipartisan work by Members of Congress, I signed into law the "Medicare Prescription Drug, Improvement, and Modernization Act of 2003." This new law gave seniors prescription drug coverage, as well as better choices and more control over their health care. It also established tax-free Health Savings Accounts, so more Americans could save for health care expenses and more small businesses could secure health insurance for their workers. During this period, we also showed our Nation's compassion and good heart by creating the American Dream Downpayment Fund, to help low-income citizens afford the down payment on homes of their own. To promote a culture of life, we banned the brutal practice of partial-birth abortion, and we also passed new incentives for the adoption of older children in foster care.

Meanwhile, the American economy continued to gain strength from the tax relief we passed in 2001, 2002, and May 2003—creating almost 400,000 new jobs during the final 4 months of the year. In the third quarter of 2003, our economy grew at a rate of 7.2 percent, the fastest quarterly growth rate since before the attacks of September 11, 2001. To build on this progress, I signed free trade agreements into law with Chile and Singapore, opening new markets for American workers, farmers, and entrepreneurs. I also continued to urge the Congress to exercise spending restraint, pass legal and regulatory reforms, and reduce America's dependence on foreign sources of energy.

During the latter half of 2003, I made several trips abroad to reaffirm America's commitment to advancing liberty, human dignity, and peace. In July, I began my week-long trip to Africa by visiting Senegal's Goree Island, where slaves once departed for American shores. I noted there that our Nation's history had taught us that "freedom is not the possession of one race" or "one nation," and that "this belief leads America into the world"—including Africa, where it motivates our efforts to help the people of that great continent overcome the challenges of HIV/AIDS, poverty, and civil war.

In November, I visited the United Kingdom to reaffirm the strong alliance between our two nations and thank Prime Minister Tony Blair and the British people for their sacrifices and commitment in the War on Terror. In my speech at Whitehall Palace in London, I said that America was now pursuing a "forward strategy of freedom" in the Middle East: "We will consistently challenge the enemies of reform and confront the allies of terror. We will expect a higher standard from our friends in the region—and we will meet our responsibilities in Afghanistan and in Iraq by finishing the work of democracy we have begun."

During these months, our Government worked tirelessly to meet this commitment to protect the American people and spread the blessings of freedom. We continued to hunt down al-Qaida leaders and associates around the world. In a strong bipartisan vote, the Congress approved $87 billion in supplemental spending to support our troops in Afghanistan and Iraq and to help those nations rebuild. In Iraq, Coalition forces worked with the newly free Iraqi people to destroy remnants of the old regime and various extremist networks. Uday and Qusay Hussein were killed by American forces in July. In December, Coalition forces captured Saddam Hussein—ensuring that he would answer for his many crimes. At the same time, the Coalition Provisional Authority worked to rebuild schools, reopen hospitals, and restore damaged water, electrical, and communications systems in Iraq. The Iraqi people took a crucial step in July, when they formed a governing council that would draft an interim constitution to prepare for free elections.

We also continued our efforts beyond Iraq and Afghanistan to keep the world's deadliest weapons out of the hands of terrorists and dangerous regimes. In the fall, American and British intelligence tracked a cargo ship bound for Libya that was carrying parts for nuclear centrifuges. We alerted German and Italian authorities, who intercepted the ship—and in December, Libya pledged to disclose and dismantle all of its weapons of mass destruction programs.

The heaviest burdens in our War on Terror fell on our Armed Forces and our intelligence services. These brave men and women faced the enemy abroad so we would not face them here at home. On Thanksgiving Day, I had the honor of visiting some of these fine Americans in Baghdad, where I expressed the gratitude of our entire country for their skill, courage, and sacrifice. In 2003, these men and women advanced the cause of freedom—and their fellow Americans were safer because of it.

Preface

This book contains the papers and speeches of the 43d President of the United States that were issued by the Office of the Press Secretary during the period July 1–December 31, 2003. The material has been compiled and published by the Office of the Federal Register, National Archives and Records Administration.

The material is presented in chronological order, and the dates shown in the headings are the dates of the documents or events. In instances when the release date differs from the date of the document itself, that fact is shown in the textnote. Every effort has been made to ensure accuracy: Remarks are checked against a tape recording, and signed documents are checked against the original. Textnotes and cross references have been provided by the editors for purposes of identification or clarity. At the request of the Office of the Press Secretary, the Bush property known as Prairie Chapel Ranch in Crawford, Texas, is referred to simply as the Bush Ranch. Speeches were delivered in Washington, DC, unless indicated. The times noted are local times. All materials that are printed full-text in the book have been indexed in the subject and name indexes, and listed in the document categories list.

The Public Papers of the Presidents series was begun in 1957 in response to a recommendation of the National Historical Publications Commission. An extensive compilation of messages and papers of the Presidents covering the period 1789 to 1897 was assembled by James D. Richardson and published under congressional authority between 1896 and 1899. Since then, various private compilations have been issued, but there was no uniform publication comparable to the Congressional Record or the United States Supreme Court Reports. Many Presidential papers could be found only in the form of mimeographed White House releases or as reported in the press. The Commission therefore recommended the establishment of an official series in which Presidential writings, addresses, and remarks of a public nature could be made available.

The Commission's recommendation was incorporated in regulations of the Administrative Committee of the Federal Register, issued under section 6 of the Federal Register Act (44 U.S.C. 1506), which may be found in title 1, part 10, of the Code of Federal Regulations.

A companion publication to the Public Papers series, the Weekly Compilation of Presidential Documents, was begun in 1965 to provide a broader range of Presidential materials on a more timely basis to meet the needs of the contemporary reader. Beginning with the administration of Jimmy Carter, the Public Papers series expanded its coverage to include additional material as printed in the Weekly Compilation. That coverage provides a listing of the President's daily schedule and meetings, when announced, and other items of general interest issued by the Office of the Press Secretary. Also included are lists of the President's nominations submitted to the Senate, materials released by the Office of the Press Secretary that are not printed full-text in the book, and proclamations, Executive orders, and other Presidential documents released by the Office of the Press Secretary and published in the *Federal Register*. This information appears in the appendixes at the end of the book.

Volumes covering the administrations of Presidents Herbert Hoover, Harry S. Truman, Dwight D. Eisenhower, John F. Kennedy, Lyndon B. Johnson, Richard Nixon, Gerald R. Ford, Jimmy Carter, Ronald Reagan, George Bush, and William J. Clinton are also included in the Public Papers series.

The Public Papers of the Presidents publication program is under the direction of Frances D. McDonald, Managing Editor, Office of the Federal Register. The series is produced by the Presidential and Legislative Publications Unit, Gwendolyn J. Henderson, Chief. The Chief Editor of this book was Stacey A. Mulligan, assisted by William K. Banks, Loretta F. Cochran, Kathleen M. Fargey, Stephen J. Frattini, Alfred Jones, and Michael J. Sullivan.

The frontispiece and photographs used in the portfolio were supplied by the White House Photo Office. The typography and design of the book were developed by the Government Printing Office under the direction of Bruce R. James, Public Printer.

Raymond A. Mosley
Director of the Federal Register

Allen Weinstein
Archivist of the United States

Contents

Cabinet

Secretary of State .... Colin L. Powell

Secretary of the Treasury .... John Snow

Secretary of Defense .... Donald H. Rumsfeld

Attorney General .... John Ashcroft

Secretary of the Interior .... Gale A. Norton

Secretary of Agriculture .... Ann M. Veneman

Secretary of Commerce .... Donald L. Evans

Secretary of Labor .... Elaine L. Chao

Secretary of Health and Human
Services .... Tommy G. Thompson

Secretary of Housing and Urban
Development .... Mel R. Martinez

Secretary of Transportation .... Norman Y. Mineta

Secretary of Energy .... Spencer Abraham

Secretary of Education .... Roderick R. Paige

Secretary of Veterans Affairs .... Anthony J. Principi

Secretary of Homeland Security .... Tom Ridge

Chief of Staff .... Andrew H. Card, Jr.

Administrator of the Environmental
Protection Agency .... Michael O. Leavitt

United States Trade Representative .... Robert B. Zoellick

Director of the Office of Management
and Budget .... Joshua B. Bolten

Director of National Drug Control
Policy .... John P. Walters

Administration of George W. Bush

2003

Letter to Congressional Leaders Transmitting a Report on the National Emergency With Respect to Libya
June 30, 2003

Dear Mr. Speaker: *(Dear Mr. President:)*

Consistent with section 401(c) of the National Emergencies Act, 50 U.S.C. 1641(c), section 204(c) of the International Emergency Economic Powers Act, 50 U.S.C. 1703(c), and section 505(c) of the International Security and Development Cooperation Act of 1985, 22 U.S.C. 2349aa-9(c), I am transmitting a 6-month periodic report prepared by my Administration on the national emergency with respect to

Libya that was declared in Executive Order 12543 of January 7, 1986.

Sincerely,

GEORGE W. BUSH

NOTE: Identical letters were sent to J. Dennis Hastert, Speaker of the House of Representatives, and Richard B. Cheney, President of the Senate. This letter was released by the Office of the Press Secretary on July 1.

Remarks at the KIPP DC: KEY Academy
July 1, 2003

Thank you all very much. Thanks for coming. Please be seated. Thanks for coming. I'm honored that—I'm honored you'd have me—[*laughter*]—here at KIPP Academy. Susan, thanks for your hospitality.

I know something about KIPP Academy, the network. The reason I do is, when I was the Governor of Texas, I went to a school in Houston that was called KIPP Academy. Nobody had ever heard of it. I think Steve—is that you back there, Steve? No, it's not. I thought Steve was here. You look like Steve. [*Laughter*] And they said—the principal—and they said, "Come by the school." And it was full of kids that were not supposed to be able to learn. You know, our State at that time was suffering what I call the soft bigotry of low expectations. Perhaps that's happening in places in the District as well. You see, when you lower the bar, that's what you get, low results. So they had la-

beled these kids, you know, unable to learn, difficult to learn.

So I go to this KIPP Academy. And first of all, I was overwhelmed by the spirit of the kids, the involvement of the parents, the dedication of the teachers, and the entrepreneurial spirit of the principal. And then I said, "Well, are you making any progress here at KIPP Academy with these so-called hard to educate?" And the answer was, "Yes. They're the best middle school in the city of Houston." The reason we knew is because we measured. We wouldn't have known that had we not measured.

The KIPP Academy sets high standards. It's got the absolute right attitude for education, in my judgment. First of all, it says, "Every child can learn. We refuse to condemn any child to mediocrity and failure. We have high standards; we have high expectations; and we're going to meet those high standards and high expectations with a curriculum which works."

And so I want to congratulate you, Susan, and the KIPP Academy entrepreneurs who are challenging mediocrity on a daily basis and raising standards for those who in some communities have been condemned to failure. Thanks for having us here, and thanks for the bright example you've set.

What we're really here is to talk about how do we make sure that the education system works for everybody. That's why the act that we passed out of Congress, the law, was called the No Child Left Behind Act. And the reason why it was called the No Child Left Behind Act, it set out a goal for the country that every child deserves a good education. And it said no child should be left behind, which means we'd better understand whether any—we'd better answer the question, "Is every child learning?"

But that wasn't the case oftentimes in America, public schools. We didn't know whether or not we were achieving what we expected. And so we passed this law. And the law basically said, in return for Federal dollars, the Federal Government will finally start asking the question, "What are the results?"—that we expect to spend money, and as a matter of fact, we set record levels of expenditure for elementary and secondary education programs and Title I programs. That's an obligation of the Federal Government. We met the obligation with the largest budget increases in our history. But instead of just spending money, we're starting to ask the question, "What's happening in the classrooms?" And if things are good, we want to praise the schools that are working, like KIPP Academy. But if we find things are lousy and children are being left behind, instead of just accepting the status quo, it is now time for our society to challenge failure. And that's what we're doing.

And I'm proud of Washington, DC. Washington, DC, is willing to challenge

failure and to praise success. This is not an easy issue for some in the political process. It is hard to take on the established order, particularly when you have to blow the whistle on failure. Nobody likes to have the whistle blown. But for the sake of our children, we need to be blowing whistles. And so I appreciate very much the Mayor. Mayor Williams has stood strong, along with the Councilman Chavous. And I appreciate my friend David being here as well, for standing strong and making sure that the children—we focus on results, not process.

I want to thank very much my friend Rod Paige. When I hired—hired—I asked Rod to join me. I didn't hire him. [*Laughter*] He gets hired by school boards, not by Presidents. [*Laughter*] I was interested in somebody that actually had been on the frontlines of public school education. He had a tough job in Texas. He was running the Houston Independent School District, which is a heck of a lot tougher than being President. [*Laughter*] And the results in Houston were exceptional because Rod challenged the soft bigotry of low expectations and raised the bar. And he understands you've got to hold people accountable in life. And so he's doing a fine job for our country.

And Peggy, I appreciate you being here, too. Peggy is the head of the school board. That is a tough job. That's a tough job, and I thank you for taking it on.

I appreciate the Members of Congress coming. Tom, I'm glad you're here. I'm honored you're here. He's the chairman of the House Government Reform Committee. He is concerned about making sure DC functions well, its schools function well. He's going to work closely with the Mayor. And Rodney Frelinghuysen is here as well. He's the House Appropriations Subcommittee on the District of Columbia. I'm sure he and the Mayor spend a lot of time talking and coming up with the amount of money the Mayor thinks is appropriate to run this important city. My only admonition is to make sure the potholes in front of the White House are full. [*Laughter*]

But I want to thank you guys for coming here today. We're going to talk about an extremely important initiative that will make a difference in the lives of children here in the city. And I want to describe it a little bit, this Federal initiative that is going to serve as a model for the rest of the country. I want my second home to become a model of excellence so that when people see the educational entrepreneurial spirit alive and well in DC, they realize they can do the same in their own communities.

Father McCarrick, thank you for coming, too, sir. I appreciate the—I appreciate your presence. I appreciate the excellence of the Catholic school system, not only here in Washington but around the country. I think it's very important for our fellow citizens to see the Catholic school system as a model of what is possible, how to provide a high-quality education at a reasonable cost per student. And it's an interesting— these Catholic schools can serve not only as an interesting go-by but as a model as well for other schools in the District.

Listen, the No Child Left Behind Act understands that there must be accountability, and the way you achieve accountability is you measure. And so now we're measuring a lot. We're measuring annually to determine whether or not the children can read and write and add and subtract. We've got to know that. The first fundamental question in terms of achieving educational excellence is to measure and to provide the test and to see whether or not the children have got the basics—and if they do, recognize that the curriculum being used is working; if they don't, recognize something has got to change.

See, the measurement is not meant to punish; it is meant to remedy. It is meant to serve as a diagnostic tool. No one ever wants to measure, to hold a good teacher up and say, "You know, gosh, you've got

a good heart, but you're doing a lousy job. Therefore, you're a failure." That's not the reason you measure. The reason you measure is you say to a teacher, "You've got a great heart, but you need to fine-tune what you're doing because it's not working right now."

You've also got to measure in order to begin to effect change that's just more— when there's more than talk, there's just actual—a paradigm shift. That's what measurement does. It provides the foundations for significant change.

Accountability is important. But accountability without consequences means nothing. So in other words, if you measure and find success, there needs to be—something needs to happen, which is praise. And parents will say, "Well, gosh, if that's successful, I think we'll continue sending my child to that school." But if parents don't have any options other than a public school system, there's no accountability—really no accountability. In other words, if there's nothing else can happen, if you find failure and you're stuck, why measure? And so one of the things that we're going to talk about today is making sure that any accountability system has got—has got some oomph to it, by trusting parents to make the right decision for their particular child.

The District of Columbia needs to improve. Let me just put it bluntly. [*Laughter*] There are some great schools in the District, and there are some lousy schools in the District. There has been a recent measurement to determine how the District schools do relative to other schools around the country. Ninety—in grades four and eight—those were the two grades tested— the District of Columbia scored below every single State in the Union in terms of basic skills. And that's unacceptable. It's unacceptable to the Mayor. It's unacceptable to the City Council. It's unacceptable to Peggy. It's unacceptable, most importantly, to the parents. And we need to do something about it.

And the Mayor and the City Council and Peggy have started by invigorating a—having a vigorous charter school program. See, charter schools say to the world, "If you've got a better idea, show up and show us whether or not you can do a better job of challenging the status quo, if the status quo is failing." And that's what's happening in Washington, and I want to applaud the city for being on the front edge of the charter school initiative.

I'm going to work with Congress—and I appreciate the Members of Congress being here to—we need to boost our budget for charter schools. I proposed $320 million for charter schools. I want to work specifically with the city of Washington, DC. The Mayor and I have—I answer the Mayor's calls, and he occasionally answers mine. [*Laughter*] And one of the things that he likes to talk about is the need to make sure that the charter school system here is—receives good Federal attention. After all, the Federal Government has got a lot to do with how the schools in Washington, DC, are funded. So we're committed to a charter school program in my administration. I think it's one of the options that ought to be made available to parents.

KIPP Academy is a charter school. The money follows the child, and that makes sense. The problem is that oftentimes there's not enough charter schools in certain communities to meet the demand. And there is big demand here in Washington, DC, for alternatives other than the status quo. And so I've got an idea that I want to share with you today about how to meet that demand. And that is, I'm going to request $75 million from the Congress for what we call a choice incentive fund. This will be basically scholarships for students to be able to use the money as they see fit, public or private. Obviously, private is where you're going to require tuition.

Fifteen million of that dollars will stay here in Washington. It is the beginning of a school choice program funded by the Federal Government for students here in Washington, DC. The scholarships will range up to $7,500 per student. If the private school charges less than that, then the remainder, the difference between $7,500 and the tuition, goes back into the pot so that more children will be funded. We think this will affect a couple of thousand children here in Washington, DC. It is the beginning of an experiment that will show whether or not private school choice makes a difference in quality education in public schools. I happen to believe it will.

I do believe that competition will serve its purpose, and that will—other schools will say, "Wait a minute. We're losing folks. We better try something differently. The accountability system says we're not doing so well. We need to remember the customer." The customer happens to be the parent and the student. And I believe the change will cause folks to want to invigorate their own curriculum and to figure out what's going right or wrong. It will certainly shake the system up. And it sounds like to me the system needs to be shaken up if you're not doing as well as you should be here in Washington, DC.

People say, "Well, gosh, if you're going to do that, then there will be no accountability." Of course, if a school receives a scholarship, then the school needs to be held accountable as well. The same accountability system applies to the recipient school as it does to the public schools in Washington. We want there to be accountability throughout the system. Father McCarrick wouldn't mind that at all. He runs a system that is anxious to be held accountable. And so if a private scholarship ends up in a Catholic school, people will be held to account. After all, it's taxpayers' money. We want to know. We want to know whether it—in a public school or a private school, whether or not the children are learning.

Now, if there—if we run out of—if there's more applicants than scholarships, then people will say, "What's going to happen?" Well, there needs to be a lottery. I mean, there needs to be a fair way—this isn't—to make sure that everybody has got an equal shot. And then, of course, the Congress is going to want to know whether or not the program is working, just like the President will want to know. And so therefore, what we'll end up doing is, Rod will measure and then submit a report to the Congress on an annual basis, so that people will begin to see firsthand whether or not what we're attempting to do in Washington, DC, has got the positive effect that a lot of us think it will have.

Look, what we're trying to do is to give parents more options. Step one was to measure. Step two was to post the results so everybody knows, so they can compare school to school. Step three is to say, "In any accountability system, there has to be consequences." And the consequences, when it comes to education, for failure is the parent says, "I've had it. I'm going to a different option for my particular child."

The other thing that's important is we've got to have the philosophical notion that we cannot have a two-tiered education system in America, one tier for those who can afford a certain type of school and one tier for those who can't. And so this plan is an attempt to say: The two-tiered deal is over with; we're starting to a new tier.

And there's a demand for this, by the way, in Washington. The Washington Scholarship Fund is an interesting idea where people came together—I presume from the business community and others—and put up money to help children. There are 1,000 applications last year for 100 slots. It's a measurement, a data point, a measurement of demand, where people are interested in doing something differently.

Virginia Walden-Ford, who I met, is the executive director of the DC Parents for School Choice. She says that hundreds of calls come in each week to her organization. Parents are wondering, "Do I have

a choice? Is there something else I can do? I'm frustrated."

Virginia is a good person to be running the program. She—mom of three—her youngest son looked like he was a—I guess the best way to describe it would be a train wreck. He wasn't doing well in the public school system. He might say the system quit on him, but he certainly quit on the system. And Virginia pulled him up and got him into a Catholic school. The ninth grade on, he became a student. He was challenged. It raised his standards. He's now a United States Marine. He's preparing to go to the college. It's a wonderful story about Archbishop Carroll High School. More importantly, it's a wonderful story about a mom who never gave up.

So she's taking that experience and is now trying to help other parents who are frustrated and other parents who are looking for different options for a particular child. I want to thank her for that very much. Here's what she said. She said, "Low-income parents don't want handouts. They just want the same opportunities to send their children to schools that meet their children's needs." And I appreciate that comment, and I appreciate you working on this.

I appreciate meeting Valarie Garland today. We had a very emotional meeting. Valarie is concerned, frustrated, worried. We had a—we shed a tear or two about the future. Valarie is a single mom—which, by the way, is the toughest job in America. It's really hard to be a single mom in our country. And then she's a single mom who is worried about the education system, on top. And her emotions came forth, and we had a good visit about trying to provide a hopeful future for Valarie's child. And I believe we can get the Congress to move on this. It will make a difference in a lot of people's lives here in Washington.

Let me summarize by saying, first of all, there's a lot of great teachers in America. There's a lot of great teachers right here in Washington, DC. There's a lot of good, hard-working folks. And we need to always keep in mind the need to praise our teachers and to praise people on the frontlines of education.

Sometimes, however, the system, the curriculum, whatever it may be, it becomes stagnant. And wherever we find mediocrity, this society has an obligation to challenge that. And that's what we're talking about today. We're talking about making sure no child gets left behind by focusing on each child. And the best way to focus on each child is to look at results and then remember the decisionmaker, who the decisionmaker is in society. The decisionmaker is the mom or the dad.

The District of Columbia is setting a bright example of what is possible in education reform. And I'm here to praise the public school system of Washington, DC, and for those who are working hard to make it better. I'm here to praise the elected officials of Washington, DC, for your willingness to step out and to confront failure when you see it and to praise success when you see it as well.

And I'm here to say to the parents of Washington, DC: We care about your children. Each child matters. We believe every child can learn. We're going to challenge the soft bigotry of low expectations in the Nation's Capital and around the country, because we know a more hopeful America depends on this Nation's capacity to educate each and every child.

I want to thank you for coming, and may God bless America.

NOTE: The President spoke at 10:05 a.m. in a classroom at the school. In his remarks, he referred to Susan Schaeffler, principal, KIPP DC: KEY Academy; Mayor Anthony A. Williams of Washington, DC; Kevin Chavous and David Catania, members, District of Columbia City Council; Peggy Cooper Cafritz, president, DC Board of Education; Representative Tom Davis; and Theodore E. Cardinal McCarrick, Archbishop of Washington.

Remarks at a Reenlistment Ceremony on the 30th Anniversary of the All-Volunteer Force
July 1, 2003

Please be seated. Welcome. Thank you all very much. Welcome to the White House. We're joined today by 30 men and women who have chosen to reenlist in the United States Armed Forces. Each of them decided years ago to serve and defend our country. Today they reaffirm their commitment and take the oath again.

Like many thousands of other soldiers, sailors, airmen, coast guardsmen, and marines who will reenlist this year, these men and women are answering the highest call of citizenship. They have stood between the American people and the dangers of the world, and we are glad they are staying on duty.

I want to thank Paul Wolfowitz, the Deputy Secretary of Defense, for joining us, and members of the defense team. I want to thank Richard Myers, Chairman of the Joint Chiefs, and Pete Pace, the Vice Chairman of the Joint Chiefs. I want to thank James Roche, the Secretary of the Air Force, Les Brownlee, the Acting Secretary of the Army, H.T. Johnson, the Acting Secretary of the Navy, for being with us today.

I appreciate Admiral Vernon Clark, the Chief of Naval Operations, for being here; General Michael W. Hagee, the Commandant of the Marine Corps; General John M. Keane, Acting Chief of Staff for the Army. I appreciate Terry D. Scott,

Master Chief Petty Officer of the Navy, for being with us today, John L. Estrada, Sergeant Major of the Marine Corps, Frank A. Welch, Master Chief Petty Officer of the Coast Guard, members of the Armed Forces, and our fellow Americans.

Before the draft ended on July 1st, 1973, generations of men entered military service by the decision of others. And during two World Wars and in Korea and in Vietnam, they served nobly, and they served well. Yet in the past 30 years, we have seen the great advantages of a military in which all serve by their own decision. Our country's all-volunteer force attracts idealistic and committed young Americans. They stay in service longer because they have chosen the military life. The result is a military with the highest levels of training, experience, motivation, and professionalism.

The military life is rewarding. Yet, even at its best, that life is difficult, often involving separation and danger. Those who willingly make these sacrifices and the families who share their hardships have the respect and the gratitude of their fellow Americans.

All in our military are serving in one of history's critical hours. Less than 2 years ago, determined enemies of America entered our country, committed acts of murder against our people, and made clear their intentions to strike again. As long as terrorists and their allies plot to harm America, America is at war. We did not choose this war. Yet, with the safety of the American people at stake, we will continue to wage this war with all our might.

From the beginning, we have known the effort would be long and difficult and that our resolve would be tested. We know that sacrifice is unavoidable. We have seen victories in the decisive defeat of two terror regimes and in the relentless pursuit of a global terror network. Yet the war on terror goes on. We will not be distracted, and we will prevail.

Of those directly involved in organizing the September the 11th attacks, almost all are now in custody or confirmed dead. Of the senior Al Qaida leaders, operational managers, and key facilitators we have been tracking, 65 percent have been captured or killed.

Still, we recognize that Al Qaida has trained thousands of foot soldiers in many nations and that new leaders may emerge. And we suspect that some Al Qaida deserters will attach themselves to other terrorist groups in order to strike American targets. Terrorists that remain can be certain of this: We will hunt them by day and by night in every corner of the world until they are no longer a threat to America and our friends.

At this moment, American and allied forces continue the work of fighting terrorists and establishing order in Afghanistan. When we removed the Taliban from power, surviving Al Qaida members fled from most of that country. However, many terrorists sought sanctuary along the Afghanistan-Pakistan border, and some are still hiding there. These Al Qaida and Taliban holdouts have attacked allied bases with unguided rockets, conducted ambushes, and fired upon border posts. In close cooperation with the Afghan and Pakistani Governments, America is engaged in operations to find and destroy these terrorists.

Since the beginning of Operation Enduring Freedom, it is important for our fellow citizens to know that Pakistan has apprehended more than 500 terrorists, including hundreds of members of Al Qaida and the Taliban.

As this fight continues, the people of Afghanistan are moving forward with the reconstruction of their country and the founding of a democratic government. They have selected a President. They're building a national army, and they are now in the final stages of drafting a new constitution.

America and other countries continue to provide humanitarian aid and assistance in building clinics and schools and roads. Joined by other nations, we are deploying the first group of provincial reconstruction teams to various cities in Afghanistan, groups of experts who are working with local officials to improve public safety, promote reconstruction, and solidify the authority of elected governments.

Afghanistan still has many challenges, but that country is making progress, and its people are a world away from the nightmare they endured under the Taliban. Pakistan and Afghanistan are among many governments that understand the threat of terror and are determined to root it out.

After the terrible attacks in Riyadh on May the 12th, the Government of Saudi Arabia has intensified its longstanding efforts against the Al Qaida network. Recently, Saudi's security services apprehended Abu Bakr, believed to be a central figure in the Riyadh bombing, and killed a major Al Qaida operational planner and fundraiser, a man known in terrorist circles as "Swift Sword." Saudi authorities have also uncovered terrorist operations in the holy city of Mecca, demonstrating once again that terrorists hold nothing sacred and have no home in any religion. America and Saudi Arabia face a common terrorist threat, and we appreciate the strong, continuing efforts of the Saudi Government in fighting that threat.

The war on terror also continues in Iraq, where coalition forces are engaging remnants of the former regime as well as members of terrorist groups. We met the major combat objectives in Operation Iraqi Freedom. We ended a regime that possessed weapons of mass destruction, harbored and supported terrorists, suppressed human rights, and defied the just demands of the United Nations and the world.

The true monuments of Saddam Hussein's rule have been brought to light, the mass graves, the torture chambers, the jail cells for children. And now we are moving forward with the reconstruction of that country by restoring basic services, maintaining order, searching for the hidden weapons, and helping Iraqis to establish a representative government.

The rise of Iraq as an example of moderation and democracy and prosperity is a massive and long-term undertaking. And the restoration of that country is critical to the defeat of terror and radicalism throughout the Middle East. With so much in the balance, it comes as no surprise that freedom has enemies inside of Iraq. The looting and random violence that began in the immediate aftermath of war remains a challenge in some areas. A greater challenge comes from former Ba'ath Party and security officials who will stop at nothing to regain their power and their privilege. But there will be no return to tyranny in Iraq. And those who threaten the order and stability of that country will face ruin, just as surely as the regime they once served.

Also present in Iraq are terrorist groups seeking to spread chaos and to attack American and coalition forces. Among these terrorists are members of Ansar Al Islam, which operated in Iraq before the war and is now active in the Sunni heartland of the country. We suspect that the remnants of a group tied to Al Qaida associate Al Zarqawi are still in Iraq, waiting for an opportunity to strike. We're also beginning to see foreign fighters enter Iraq.

These scattered groups of terrorists, extremists, and Saddam loyalists are especially active to the north and west of Baghdad, where they have destroyed electricity lines and towers, set off explosions at gas pipelines, and ignited sulfur fires. They have attacked coalition forces, and they're trying to intimidate Iraqi citizens. These groups believe they have found an opportunity to harm America, to shake our resolve in the war on terror, and to cause us to leave Iraq before freedom is fully established. They are wrong, and they will not succeed.

Those who try to undermine the reconstruction of Iraq are not only attacking our coalition; they are attacking the Iraqi people. And we will stand with the Iraqi people strongly as they build a hopeful future. Having liberated Iraq as promised, we will help that country to found a just and representative government as promised. Our goal is a swift transition to Iraqi control of their own affairs. People of Iraq will be secure, and the people of Iraq will run their own country.

At present, 230,000 Americans are serving inside or near Iraq. Our whole Nation, especially their families, recognizes that our people in uniform face continuing danger. We appreciate their service under difficult circumstances and their willingness to fight for American security and Iraqi freedom. As Commander in Chief, I assure them, we will stay on the offensive against the enemy. And all who attack our troops will be met with direct and decisive force.

As America fights our war against terror, we will continue to depend on the skill and the courage of our volunteer military. In these last 22 months, our Armed Forces have been tested and tested again. In every case, in every mission, America's service men and women have brought credit to the uniform, to our flag, and to our country. We have needed you, and you have never let us down.

I want to thank you for keeping your pledge of duty to America and thank you for renewing that demanding pledge today.

And now, General Myers will administer the oath of enlistment in the Armed Forces of the United States. May God bless you.

NOTE: The President spoke at 2 p.m. in the East Room at the White House. In his remarks, he referred to President Hamid Karzai of Afghanistan; senior Al Qaida associates Abu Bakr Al Azdi and Abu Musab Al Zarqawi; Al Qaida operational planner and fundraiser Yousif Salih Fahad Al-Ayeeri, also known as "Swift Sword," who was killed on May 31; and former President Saddam Hussein of Iraq. The Office of the Press Secretary also released a Spanish language transcript of these remarks.

Letter to Congressional Leaders Transmitting a Report on Peacekeeping Operations
July 1, 2003

Dear Mr. Chairman:

I transmit herewith the 2002 Annual Report to the Congress on Peacekeeping, prepared by my Administration, consistent with section 4 of the United Nations Participation Act (Public Law 79–264), as amended.

United Nations and other peacekeeping operations around the world helped the United States protect our interests, and ensured that other nations shared with us the burdens, risks, and costs of maintaining international stability. In 2002, my Administration worked closely with the United Nations and key member states to promote sound peacekeeping policies, realistic mandates, and appropriately sized missions.

I will continue to work with the Congress to ensure that peacekeeping, under the right circumstances, remains a viable option for maintaining international peace and security.

Sincerely,

GEORGE W. BUSH

NOTE: Identical letters were sent to Richard G. Lugar, chairman, Senate Committee on Foreign Relations, John W. Warner, chairman, Senate Committee on Armed Services, Ted Stevens, chairman, Senate Committee on Appropriations, Henry J. Hyde, chairman, House Committee on International Relations, C.W. Bill Young, chairman, House Committee on Appropriations, and Duncan Hunter, chairman, House Committee on Armed Services.

Letter to Congressional Leaders Reporting on Sanctions Under the Foreign Narcotics Kingpin Designation Act
July 1, 2003

Dear Mr. Chairman:

I hereby report, pursuant to section 804(d) of the Foreign Narcotics Kingpin Designation Act, 21 U.S.C. 1903(d) (the "Kingpin Act"), on the status of sanctions imposed upon significant foreign narcotics traffickers designated this year.

On May 29, 2003, I designated the following seven foreign persons and entities as appropriate for sanctions, and subsequently imposed sanctions against them, under the Kingpin Act:

Juan Jose Esparragoza Moreno
Jose Albino Quintero Meraz
Hector Luis Palma Salazar
United Wa State Army
Leonardo Dias Mendonca
Revolutionary Armed Forces of Colombia (Fuerzas Armadas Revolucionarias de Colombia, "FARC")
United Self-Defense Forces of Colombia (Autodefensas Unidas de Colombia, "AUC")

Attached is individual background information on each of the above foreign persons and entities. Each individual and entity is now subject to all of the sanctions authorized under the Kingpin Act. As a result, United States persons are prohibited from engaging in financial transactions and conducting business with these individuals. In addition, any assets within the United States or within the possession or control of United States persons that are owned or controlled by significant foreign narcotics traffickers are blocked. Finally, significant foreign narcotics traffickers and immediate family members who have knowingly benefited from their illicit activity will be denied visas for entry into the United States. While all of the sanctions are currently in effect, to date I have not been notified of any specific enforcement action taken since the date of their imposition.

The Department of the Treasury, in consultation with the Departments of Justice, Defense, and State, the Central Intelligence Agency, the Federal Bureau of Investigation, and the Drug Enforcement Administration, continues to work toward identifying derivative designations for these newly designated individuals pursuant to the powers granted under section 805(b) of the Kingpin Act, 21 U.S.C. 1904(b).

In addition to the foregoing actions, the Department of the Treasury, in consultation with the Departments of Justice, Defense, and State, the Central Intelligence Agency, the Federal Bureau of Investigation, and the Drug Enforcement Administration, continues to research potential foreign persons for future recommendations for designation as kingpins.

Enclosed is a classified table reflecting expenses incurred and projected for fiscal year 2003. Other than certain intelligence expenses reflected in the enclosed table, total reportable expenses incurred by Federal agencies in fiscal year 2002 are approximately $1,022,115. These expenses are those directly attributable to the imposition of the Kingpin Act sanctions. The personnel costs portion, $591,562, is centered principally in the Department of the Treasury. The remaining $430,553 of the $1,022,115 total was for resource expenditures.

Sincerely,

GEORGE W. BUSH

NOTE: Identical letters were sent to Porter J. Goss, chairman, House Permanent Select Committee on Intelligence, and Pat Roberts, chairman, Senate Select Committee on Intelligence. This letter was released by the Office of the Press Secretary on July 2.

Remarks Announcing the Nomination of Randall Tobias To Be Global AIDS Coordinator and an Exchange With Reporters
July 2, 2003

The President. Thank you all. Please be seated. I appreciate very much our Secretary of State for joining us, and Tommy Thompson, the Department of Health and Human Services Secretary. I want to thank Andrew Natsios, who's the Administrator of USAID. I want to thank Joe O'Neill, who is the Office of National AIDS Policy, for joining us. I want to thank Elias Zerhouni, who is the Director of the NIH. Where are you, Elias? There you are. Thank you for coming, Doctor. And Tony Fauci is here as well. Honored you're here, Tony. It's good to see Richard Lee Armitage, who is the Deputy Secretary of the Department of State. Thank you for coming, Rich.

I appreciate the Tobias family for joining us. Marianne, thanks for coming, and Paige and Tim and Todd and Amy, I'm honored you all are here as well.

Five weeks ago I signed into law the Emergency Action Plan for AIDS Relief. It's one of the largest humanitarian undertakings in our history. The plan will provide $15 billion over the next 5 years to fight AIDS abroad. Millions of lives depend on the success of this effort, and we are determined to succeed.

To direct this mission, I have chosen a superb leader who knows a great deal about lifesaving medicines and who knows how to get results. I'm pleased to announce my nomination of Randall Tobias to serve as the Global AIDS Coordinator.

Randy is one of America's most talented and respected executives. He was vice chairman of AT&T and chairman of ATT International, guiding the firm through immense organizational challenges. He went to head Eli Lilly and Company, one of our Nation's largest and most innovative pharmaceutical companies. He is a highly regarded civic leader and philanthropist in his home State of Indiana. Throughout his

career, Randy has shown the ability to manage complex organizations and to navigate government bureaucracies. He has earned a reputation as an executive of great energy, resourcefulness, good judgment, and integrity.

As Global AIDS Coordinator, Randy will have the rank of Ambassador and will report directly to Secretary of State Powell. He will coordinate all of our international HIV/AIDS activities for all of our Government departments and agencies. He will oversee all resources of this program. And he will work with the faith-based and community groups to get the job done. He will report regularly to Congress on the progress and effectiveness of our efforts.

Randy Tobias has a mandate directly from me to get our AIDS initiative up and running as soon as possible. We'll work quickly to get help to the people who need it most, by purchasing low-cost antiretroviral medications and other drugs that are needed to save lives. We will set up a broad and efficient network to deliver drugs to the farthest reaches of Africa, even by motorcycle or bicycle.

We will train doctors and nurses and other health care professionals so they can treat HIV/AIDS patients. Our efforts will ensure that clinics and laboratories will be built or renovated and then equipped. Childcare workers will be hired and trained to care for AIDS orphans, and people living with AIDS will get home-based care to ease their suffering.

Throughout all regions of the targeted countries, we will provide HIV testing. We will support abstinence-based prevention education. Faith-based and community organizations will have our help as they provide treatment and prevention and support services in communities affected by HIV/AIDS. And we're developing a system to monitor and evaluate this entire program, so we can be sure we're getting the job done.

Next week I will go to Africa to meet with leaders of African countries and with some of the heroic men and women who are caring for the sick and are saving lives. They deserve our praise. They deserve our help without delay, and they will have our help.

When I visit Africa, I will reaffirm our Nation's commitment to helping Africans fight this disease. America makes this commitment for a clear reason directly rooted at our founding: We believe in the value and dignity of every human life. We're putting that belief into practice.

We have a lot of work ahead of us, and we're eager to get started. I'm hopeful that the Senate will act quickly to confirm Randall Tobias as our Global AIDS Coordinator and that the United States Congress will fully fund my request for this lifesaving initiative. I'm also hopeful that other nations of the world will join us to combat the AIDS pandemic.

I want to thank you very much for coming. May God bless our work, and may God bless the work of Randy Tobias.

[*At this point, Mr. Tobias made brief remarks.*]

The President. Thank you, Randy. Good job.

I'll answer a couple of questions here today. Let me start off with Deb [Deb Riechmann, Associated Press].

Multinational Forces for Iraq

Q. Mr. President, a posse of small nations like the Ukraine and Poland are materializing to help keep the peace in Iraq. But with the attacks on U.S. forces and the casualty rates rising, what is the administration doing to get larger powers like France and Germany and Russia to join the American occupation there?

The President. Well, first of all, we'll put together a force structure to meets the

threats on the ground. And we've got a lot of forces there ourselves. And as I said yesterday, anybody who wants to harm American troops will be found and brought to justice. There are some who feel like that if they attack us, that we may decide to leave prematurely. They don't understand what they're talking about, if that's the case.

Let me finish. There are some who feel like that the conditions are such that they can attack us there. My answer is: Bring them on. We've got the force necessary to deal with the security situation. Of course we want other countries to help us. Great Britain is there. Poland is there. Ukraine is there, you mentioned. Anybody who wants to help, we'll welcome the help. But we've got plenty tough force there right now to make sure the situation is secure. We always welcome help. We're always glad to include others in. But make no mistake about it—and the enemy shouldn't make any mistake about it—we will deal with them harshly if they continue to try to bring harm to the Iraqi people.

I also said yesterday an important point, that those who blow up the electricity lines really aren't hurting America. They're hurting the Iraq citizens. Their own fellow citizens are being hurt. But we will deal with them harshly as well.

Holland [Steve Holland, Reuters].

Liberia

Q. Sir, Liberians are hopeful the U.S. will send peacekeepers. What's the likelihood of that, and how soon will you decide?

The President. Yes.

Q. And is there a danger of U.S. forces being stretched too thin?

The President. Well, look, we're looking at all options. I've tasked the Secretary of State to talk to Kofi Annan on how best to deal with Liberia. And we're concerned when we see suffering; there's people who are suffering there. They've got the—the political instability is such that people are panicking.

But the good news is, there's a cease-fire in place now. And one of the things that Colin is going to do is to work closely with the United Nations to see how best to keep the cease-fire in place. We're exploring all options as to how to keep the situation peaceful and stable.

One thing has to happen: Mr. Taylor needs to leave the country. And Colin has made that a—I made it clear publicly. I've just made it clear again. He made it clear to Kofi Annan. In order for there to be peace and stability in Liberia, Charles Taylor needs to leave now.

And—but we're looking at all options, Steve, and—but Colin has got the diplomatic initiative taking place.

Dick [Richard Keil, Bloomberg News].

Conversation With President Putin

Q. Mr. President, we understand you talked with President Putin this morning.

The President. I did. He wished me a happy birthday. [*Laughter*]

Q. It was a birthday phone call?

The President. I expect you to do the same thing. [*Laughter*]

Q. Happy birthday to you, a few days early.

The President. Thank you, sir. It's not until the 6th, however. [*Laughter*]

Q. You can never be too early with these things.

The President. That's right. [*Laughter*]

Q. But did you discuss the situation in Iran——

The President. Yes, we did.

Q. ——and did you discuss the situation in Liberia?

The President. No, we did not discuss the situation in Liberia. We did discuss the situation in Iran. I thanked him for keeping the pressure on the Iranian Government to dismantle any notions they might have of building a nuclear weapon.

And we're making progress on that front. Not only does Vladimir Putin understand

our concerns and shares the concerns; the EU, for example, has sent out a very strong statement to the Iranians that the world expects them to conform with the IAEA, to cooperate with the IAEA, and to get rid of any plans to develop a nuclear weapon.

We also talked about North Korea. And I appreciate his understanding that the best way to deal with North Korea is to do so in a multinational forum, where the United States and China and South Korea and Japan and, hopefully, Russia all sit down with the North Koreans and make it clear that the world expects them to dismantle a nuclear weapons program and, at the same time, will be willing to help the starving North Korean people.

We're making progress on both fronts, and it's helpful to be able to cooperate with Russia in dealing with matters of international security.

Yes, Terry [Terry Moran, ABC News].

Definition of Marriage

Q. Mr. President, do you support or do you oppose a Federal constitutional amendment that would define marriage as a union between a man and a woman?

The President. I don't know if it's necessary yet. Let's let the lawyers look at the full ramifications of the recent Supreme Court hearing. What I do support is the notion that marriage is between a man and a woman.

Any other questions? I'm willing to exhaust questions today. I feel like I'm on a roll. [*Laughter*]

Q. I've got——

The President. Yes, Steve.

Middle East Peace Process

Q. There's been some recent good news out of the Middle East. Would you like to comment on that? What do you expect the parties to do now, the Palestinians and Israelis?

The President. Well, we're pleased with——

Q. And when is Prime Minister Abbas coming?

The President. I don't know that yet.

Q. Okay.

The President. We are pleased with the progress in the Middle East. I want to thank the parties in the Middle East for willing to take a risk for peace. I am pleased with the hard work that our Secretary of State has done, along with Ambassador Wolf, who has been shuttling back and forth between parties, reminding people of the commitments they made to our Government—me personally—the commitments they made to me personally in Jordan.

I am optimistic, but I also recognize the nature of the Middle East. I mean, there are people there who still hate. They hate Israel. They hate the idea of peace. They can't stand the thought of a peaceful state existing side by side with Israel. And they are willing to—may be willing to attack. And what we must continue to do is to reject that kind of thought. That's why we spoke out clearly. I spoke out, the Secretary of State has spoken out, on Hamas. Hamas is not a peaceful organization when they're willing to blow people up and destroy innocent life. And so we are making progress, but the progress will be ultimately made when the world, particularly that part of the world, firmly and finally rejects terrorist activities.

The other thing that needs to happen, Steve, is that institutions that will enable a Palestinian state to emerge need to be—continue to be fostered and put in place. There needs to be a constitution. There needs to be a capable security force. There needs to be economic hope. The Palestinian people must know that by accepting a peaceful government, by embracing the Prime Ministership of Abu Mazen, that there is a better day ahead for them when it comes to making a living. And so we will work with all parties to promote economic development in a secure environment.

And so we're making progress. I'm pleased. I think we're all—the best way to describe it is, we're really happy with what we've seen so far. But we're realists in this administration. We understand that there has been years of hatred and distrust. And we'll continue to keep the process moving forward.

I talked to President Mubarak and King Abdullah of Jordan today. I praised them for their efforts. I continue to—I urged them to continue to stay involved in the process, that we all must continue to reject terror, that we must call terrorists what they—by their real name. We must condemn terror in all instances. We must cut off money to terrorist organizations in order to keep this progress moving.

Yes, Terry.

Iraqi Weapons of Mass Destruction

Q. On weapons of mass destruction, is it fair to say now, after 2 months of looking for them, that there is a discrepancy between what the intelligence community and you and your top officials described as the threat from Saddam Hussein, and what was actually there on the ground?

The President. No, Saddam Hussein had a weapons program. Remember, he used them. He used chemical weapons on his own people. Saddam Hussein is no longer a threat to the United States, because we removed him. But he was a threat, such a threat that my predecessor, using the same intelligence, in 1998 ordered a bombing of Iraq. I mean, so, no, he was a threat. He's not a threat now. And the world is more peaceful by virtue of the fact that he is not in power.

See, we've been there, what, how many days? You're counting the days since we've been there? Because I'm not. Eighty, ninety? Frankly, it wasn't all that long ago that we started military operations. And we got rid of him much faster than a lot of people thought. And so we're bringing some order to the country, and we're beginning to learn the truth.

But he played his hand, Terry—he, Saddam Hussein—when he used chemical weapons. And then he played his hand by not letting people come in and inspect for the weapons. He had them, and it's just a matter of time. It's a matter of time. The man was a threat to America. He's not a threat today.

But what we're really finding out as well is the threat he posed to the Iraqi people. I mean, we have uncovered some unbelievable scenes. I have not seen them myself. They've been described to me, what it means to see mass graves opened up, with the remains of men and women and children murdered by that regime.

Yes, he was a threat to America. He was a threat to freedom-loving countries. He was a threat in the Middle East. But what we're finding out is the nature of this man when it came to how he dealt with the Iraqi people as well. And it was—it's unbelievable what he did. And I—when it comes to—like the AIDS initiative, we believe in human dignity; we also believe that everybody ought to live in free societies too.

And so we'll stay the course in Iraq. You know, as I said, there's people there that would like to run us out of there, create the conditions where we get nervous and decide to leave. We're not going to get nervous, and we're not leaving until we accomplish the task. And that task is going to be a free country run by the Iraqi people. And that in turn will help the peace in the Middle East. That in turn will bring stability in a part of the world that needs stability. And I am—I'm optimistic about achieving this objective because I believe that people want to be free. I believe it's in the nature of the individual to love freedom and embrace freedom.

And so it has been a great honor to lead our Nation in not only the cause of humanitarian relief through an AIDS initiative but also to lead our Nation to free people from the clutches of what history will show was an incredibly barbaric regime.

Thank you all very much.

NOTE: The President spoke at 10:59 a.m. in the Roosevelt Room at the White House. In his remarks, he referred to Anthony Fauci, Director, National Institute of Allergy and Infectious Diseases, National Institutes of Health; Mr. Tobias' wife, Marianne Williams Tobias, and his children, Paige T. Button and Todd C. Tobias; Secretary-General Kofi Annan of the United Nations; President Charles Taylor of Liberia; President Vladimir Putin of Russia; Prime Minister Mahmoud Abbas (Abu Mazen) of the Palestinian Authority; Assistant Secretary of State for Nonproliferation John S. Wolf; President Hosni Mubarak of Egypt; King Abdullah II of Jordan; and former President Saddam Hussein of Iraq. The transcript released by the Office of the Press Secretary also included the remarks of Mr. Tobias.

Interview With African Print Journalists
July 3, 2003

The President. Thank you all for coming. What I thought I would do is make a couple of opening comments about the upcoming trip and answer some questions, maybe go around the horn a couple of times and give everybody a chance to fire away.

First, I'm really looking forward to the trip. I have been to the continent of Africa twice, but I've never been as President, nor have I been on as extensive a tour as the one we are going on.

I'll be carrying a message to the African people that, first, America cares about the future of Africa. It's in our national interests that Africa become a prosperous place. It's in our interest that people will continue to fight terror together. It's in our interest that when we find suffering, we deal with it.

I've laid out some initiatives that I'll be further describing to the African people and African nations: an AIDS initiative; the Millennium Challenge Account; our education initiative, where we'll be spending now $600 million over a 5-year period of time; a $100 million to fight terrorism in east Africa. In other words, just a series of specific initiatives behind a well-intentioned administration. And it's important for the leaders to understand precisely what I mean when I talk about these different initiatives.

And so when we go to Senegal, we'll be talking to not only my friend President Wade but other leaders from western Africa. When I go to South Africa, of course, it'll be a significant platform from which to speak to leaders in the southern region of Africa. I'll be going to Botswana as well and then up to Nigeria and, finally, Uganda and then home. So it's an extensive trip, and it's an important trip, and I'm very much looking forward to it.

And I'll be glad to answer any questions. Why don't we start with you, Mr. Babou.

President's Upcoming Visit to Senegal

Q. Thank you very much. Mr. President, when will you be going to Senegal and how long will you stay?

The President. We're leaving Monday night from here, flying all night long and arriving in Senegal in the morning, and we'll be there for about a half a day. I'll be meeting with President Wade in a bilateral meeting, and then we'll be meeting with—I'm not sure how many western African leaders have RSVP'd yet; maybe Jendayi knows.

African Affairs Senior Director Jendayi Frazer. Seven.

The President. Seven other leaders. And then we'll be going to Goree Island, where I'll be giving a speech about race, race in the world, race as it relates to Africa and America. And we're in the process of writing it. I can't give you any highlights of the speech yet because I, frankly, haven't seen it. But I'll be fine-tuning the speech. It's an important speech for me to give, and it's one I'm looking forward to giving.

I look forward to seeing President Wade on his home turf, because I admire him. I admire his leadership. He is a man who believes in the same principles I believe in. He believes in the dignity of each life. He believes in democracy. He believes in open markets. He understands trade. And in our discussions—and we've had quite a few discussions with President Wade—he has constantly talked about the need for infrastructure development to link markets.

So he's got a—he cares deeply about the people of Senegal, but he's also got a regional vision that makes sense. He is a leader, he is one of the leaders of—every time we meet at, like, the G–8, President Wade is one of the representatives of the African nations, because he believes in the principles of NEPAD, and he is a good fellow. I'm looking forward to seeing him at home.

Yes, sir.

Situation in Zimbabwe

Q. Thank you, sir. On Zimbabwe, Mr. President, in recent days there has been several references from yourself and Secretary Powell to Zimbabwe once again.

The President. Yes, there has been.

Q. Now, beyond President Mbeki and President Obasanjo's efforts in the past to get Mugabe and Tsvangirai to sit down together, which has not been very successful, what more do you think they should do? Or what more——

The President. Well, that's a good question; I appreciate that. Yes, we have been outspoken on the subject because we believe that a democracy in Zimbabwe will improve the lives of all the citizens of that important country.

Listen, one of the things that we must—this country cares about is the plight of each human. And when we see and hear about suffering because of lack of food in sub-Saharan Africa, part of our attention is focused on places where there's political instability. And there's no reason why Zimbabwe is not capable of feeding not only herself but others in the region.

And the reason why now is because of political instability created by a lack of adherence to the principles of democracy. So when you hear me speak out or when you hear Colin speak out, we're speaking out for principles. And the answer to what more can be done, the world needs to speak with common voice in insisting that the principles of democracy are adhered to by the ruling party in Zimbabwe.

Zimbabwe—the economy of Zimbabwe at one time was a powerful economy for the region. It was a successful economy. People grew food in plentiful supply. Now the people of that country are starving. This country is putting up a billion dollars of money to help people who are starving. Then we're also—I'm asking Congress to put up what they call a $200-million fast reaction—or a fund for fast reaction to confront famine. We need that so that the flexibility—sometimes the appropriators like to put strings on appropriations, so it makes it hard for the executive branch to move with speed. I would like to have more capacity to move with speed when it comes to dealing with emergencies. The reason I bring that up is that it would be incredibly helpful for the continent of Africa to have its countries that are able to feed people prosperous and whole.

The other issue I want to bring up, now that I brought up the issue of food, is genetically modified crops. I think it is essential that throughout the continent of Africa, nations be encouraged to develop—use the technologies that have been developed to deal with pestilence and drought. And I

have been very outspoken on that subject as well, not to be putting thoughts in your mind that you didn't want to hear about, but I've got the mike. [*Laughter*]

But I do want to emphasize, and I will emphasize on the continent of Africa, the need for our agricultural economies on the continent of Africa to adjust with modern technology so that in places where there is drought or likelihood of drought, there can be drought-resistance crops being given a chance to succeed. Where there's pests that some agriculture economy has not been able to deal with, we use pest-resistant crop, and they're available. The problem, of course, we have is that much of the enthusiasm for what we believe is scientifically proven safe crops have been condemned by the refusal of some countries and/or accumulation of countries to accept exports into their markets from countries that use genetically modified crop.

That's a very long answer to a short question. Yes, sir.

Q. Mr. President, sir——

The President. Where is The Guardian based?

Q. In Nigeria.

The President. Very good.

U.S. Policy Toward Africa

Q. I'd like to know what's your reaction to people who say that the major driving force for your interest in Africa is oil and that, you know, what you are trying to do, essentially, is to shift the focus from Saudi—with first your relationship between Saudi and U.S. now to Africa. Now, how much of that——

The President. Saudi Arabia?

Q. Yes. So I'd like to know how much of that is actually for instance, in your interest in Africa?

The President. Well, conspiracy theorists about everywhere, I guess. That's one of the most amazing conspiracies I've heard. Heck, no one has ever made that connection, and so I would say—well, first, look, I have been talking about Africa since I was sworn in as President. I've met with 22, I believe it is, heads of state here. And I have met with President Obasanjo, gosh, I would say—I better be careful, because every number I put out there, people scrutinize—a lot, maybe five times——

Dr. Frazer. Five times, yes, sir.

The President. ——President Wade, several times in the Oval Office, several times in overseas meetings, President Mbeki, quite a few. In other words, Africa has been on the—we've been thinking about Africa ever since I've been sworn in.

Secondly, the initiatives I've laid out are bold initiatives. The Millennium Challenge Account is a very bold initiative. We're going to increase our basic developmental aid by 50 percent, with a new approach which basically says we'll reward those countries which make correct choices on behalf of the people of the countries, countries which are not corrupt, countries which focus on the health and education of the people, countries which adopt market-oriented policies which will enable a country to more likely grow in a prosperous fashion, which would then benefit the people.

I spoke out early on free trade with Africa. Certainly, the AGOA initiative was not my administration's initiative. I readily understand that. But we built on the AGOA initiative because I believe in free trade and, as a matter of fact, took the free trade argument to the Halls of Congress and got trade promotion authority, which was not an easy vote, by the way. It was a tough vote. There's a protectionist element in our country that works beneath the political surface. But I feel strongly that trade is an engine of opportunity for developing countries.

These are all initiatives I spoke about prior to—during the war on terror, I guess. I wasn't in office very long before the war on terror became evident here in America.

We've got good relations with Saudi. I gave a speech—just to put it in context, I gave a speech—I swore in some folks the other day to reenlist in our military.

I pointed out that the relationship with Saudi Arabia, when it comes to tracking down terrorists, is strong. I reminded our citizens that Abu Bakr, who is a key operative, and "Swift Sword" are no longer issues for America and Saudi Arabia because of the cooperation that is an ongoing cooperation inside the Kingdom.

And anyway, no, listen, let me speak specifically to Nigeria. I have got good relations with President Obasanjo. Every time we have visited, it has been a very cordial, up-front way. I appreciate his cooperation on the U.S.' desire to work with countries such as Nigeria to train troops necessary to be able to handle some of the difficult situations on the continent. As a matter of fact, I believe the United States in working with Nigeria has trained five battalions of Nigerian troops, preparing them for issues such as Liberia or other areas on the continent. And we will continue that relationship with the President of Nigeria. And I appreciate his leadership on that issue.

Mr. Cobb.

Uganda/Liberia

Q. Yes, sir. You're going at least in two of the regions of Africa. You're going to West Africa and—well, Uganda being next door to the Congo.

The President. Right.

Q. There's a fair amount of tumult in those regions. First, I have two specific questions related to that and your trip. Will you make a decision about U.S. troops in Liberia before you go? Or will you be bringing some message about these U.S. troops in Liberia when you visit in Senegal?

Secondly, what will you tell Mr. Museveni, whom I know you admire in terms of his work with HIV/AIDS and his economic policy, with regard to the role of militias that he created and are responsible for much of the violence in eastern Congo?

The President. Right, let me start with that. I also talked to him about ongoing democracy in Uganda. We talked about transfer of power. We talked about the fact that he's been a remarkably good leader on many fronts and that we would hope that he would adhere to the concept of having any democracy with a peaceful transfer of power at the appropriate time.

We did talk about that part of the region. I spoke very clearly about the need for all countries to recognize the peace agreements that we have been involved with—we're not the lead country on, but we're very much supportive of the peace agreements. And he listened very carefully to our admonition that we expect for people to honor the agreements that are being forged. And I will continue to discuss that with him when I go to Uganda.

As well as Uganda, it's important to—one reason why one would go to Uganda is to make sure that people around the world, and particularly on the continent of Africa, understand that dealing with HIV/AIDS is possible. In other words, you can deal with it in a positive way, and it's a remarkable record of Mr. Museveni and his Government in dealing with the pandemic of AIDS. It's essential that—we're fixing to spend $15 billion—I believe Congress will respond and keep the pressure on as, you know—and that this trip will also help create an awareness of the issue in America.

And it's important for our fellow citizens to realize that while we live a relative luxurious life throughout our society, there is a pandemic taking place that's destroying a lot of people, ruining families. You know, the idea of a 14-year-old little girl raising three brothers and sisters without parents is something that's just—it's sad. It is tragic. It needs to be dealt with. And I want to use this trip to say: Here's an example of what is possible, and let's make sure we follow our hearts as a society.

In terms of Liberia, I am in the process of gathering the information necessary to make a rational decision as to how to bring a—how to enforce the cease-fire, keep the

cease-fire in place. I said yesterday—I said a while back and I said it again yesterday, "Mr. Taylor must go." A condition for any progress in Liberia is his removal, in removing himself. And that's the message Colin has taken to the United Nations and to Kofi Annan.

Secondly, that today there is a meeting with ECOWAS, and we had a representative at the—you probably knew this before I did, Mr. Cobb—but we had a meeting there with our military thinkers to determine feasibility, to look at different options. And they have yet to report back to the White House. Maybe the information has gone to the Pentagon at this point in time.

So I'm gathering information in order to make a decision that will achieve a—that will allow me to make a proper decision as to how to bring stability to that country.

Look, I recognize the United States has got a—has had a, you know, unique history with Liberia. And therefore, it's created a certain sense of expectations. But I also want to make sure that there are certain expectations met as well. And one expectation is Mr. Taylor has got to leave. And that message is clear, and I can't make it any more clear.

As to whether or not—look, once the strategy is in place, I will let people know whether or not I'm airborne or not. In other words, I'm not trying to make any—I don't need to dramatize the decision. It's getting plenty of attention here at home. But we've got—and look, I'm just gathering enough information to be rational in what we do.

You know, you read all kinds of things, of course, in American newspapers—it's sport here. I'm sure it is elsewhere as well. The gathering of the speculator, the leaker, the whatever—what do you call them? The source—[*laughter*]—people speaking out loud, "The President has done this. The President is thinking this." And what I am thinking about is how to bring some stability to the country in a way that will be effective.

And there's no question, step one of any effective policy, whether we are involved or not, is for Charles Taylor to leave.

Yes, sir. Around the horn again. We call it going around the horn.

Temporary Protective Status for Senegalese

Q. We understand that many African countries, like many countries in the world, get a lot of help from their immigrants living in the United States.

The President. Yes.

Q. And in the South America, at one point there were some special programs for immigrants, illegal immigrants, living here from Nicaragua, from El Salvador. Will you consider supporting a special program for countries that are fighting for a democracy—for the——

The President. Temporary protective status, we call that TPS. We analyze that on a case-by-case basis. TPS generally is granted for those who are fleeing a very difficult political situation. In Senegal's case, the situation doesn't look very—it looks the opposite of difficult political situation. It's a very stable political situation. But we'll analyze any TPS requests.

National Security Adviser Condoleezza Rice. ——remittances.

The President. Are you talking about remittances, people sending money from here to there?

Q. No, what I'm saying is like a TPS, to support democracy in countries because they can't on that—the Senegalese here sent about $80 million a year to their country.

The President. So it's a combination of status and money being remitted, yes.

Well, we look at that. Of course, you know—TPS recognizes that, first of all, illegal immigration is an issue that we've got to deal with. And nobody wants anything illegal happening. But we recognize people come to our country not legally and that sometimes they come for political reasons. And that's why we have the TPS exceptions. And we'll look at it case by case.

Yes, sir.

South Africa

Q. Mr. President, you mentioned in the efforts of Americans to support peacekeeping in countries like Nigeria. What about South Africa——

The President. Same.

Q. ——presently engaged in the Congo and Burundi?

The President. No, very much so. I should have—I brought it up only in the context of Nigeria. I feel the very same way about—I will not count this as a question, because I should have mentioned South Africa. You're absolutely right. South Africa has been a leader. President Mbeki is a leader. When you think about the continent of Africa, you think about leadership, you think about President Mbeki. He's taking strong positions along with President Obasanjo, and providing troops—the South African.

I will be visiting, by the way, a training base there in South Africa. I look forward to doing so. The South African Army is a very sophisticated, well-trained army. And President Mbeki has been a leader in peace.

And so now you get a question.

U.S. Support for African Peacekeeping Forces

Q. Along the same lines, do you foresee increased aid from the United States for peacekeeping, like training, equipment?

The President. Yes, I do. I do. We've been active in training up to now. We've trained seven battalions for potential peacekeeping missions. I think this is a very important use of U.S. assets. I think the American people would understand and support the notion of training others to take care of their business in their own neighborhood. And that is a—I say, take care of their business, bring peace is what I mean by that. And yes, I do see continued activity on that front.

Yes, sir.

President's Upcoming Visit to Nigeria

Q. Currently, there is a nationwide strike going on in Nigeria. Does that put a—do you have any—how does that affect your planned trip?

The President. It does not affect it at all. And I've been briefed on the strike. I obviously hope it gets settled in a peaceful way. If I have to, I'll make my own bed at the hotel. [*Laughter*] But I'm going. [*Laughter*]

I'm looking forward to it. It's going to be a very interesting trip. It's a local issue, one that—when I go to different countries, sometimes there's local issues that pop up, not because of my trip, just because of the normal course of business. And this happens to be what's happening in the country. So I'm not changing my mind.

Yes, sir.

War on Terror in Africa

Q. I'm curious, how big a factor—are you concerned about international terrorism on this trip? We've seen the numbers drop very sharply in terms of sympathy towards the United States. In the aftermath of the Iraq war, there were the strains between the United States and South Africa over this issue, and a Pew report, in fact, that said that 44 percent of Nigerians believe that they serve a—believe that Usama bin Laden would do the right thing in world affairs.

The President. Well, I would have to say obviously there needs to be an education program, because Usama bin Laden is nothing but a killer who has hijacked a great religion. And he doesn't care about innocent life. And so I would be glad to have that debate with anybody, anywhere. And I would be glad to take those who believe that he is of some kind of remedial value, to his point of view, to the World Trade Center and introduce them to families who lost life for no reason other than the fact that he is a killer.

Secondly, parts of Africa are—they've got ongoing terrorist threats. And the good news is we are working closely with those governments to deal with those threats. We've got very good intelligence-sharing. We are—the law enforcement officials of these countries where there is a direct threat are moving rapidly upon the—when we enrich the intelligence, when we calibrate the intelligence.

Kenya is a great country, and it has been a place where there's been threats. Everybody knows that. Not only threats, there's been an attack in the past. And the Government of Kenya has been very responsive. And we are—we are helping them. We're helping other countries in Africa. Djibouti comes to mind. There is country after country after country where we're working with their governments when we—or they—they ask for help, and/or we provide information that we have been able to pick up.

Did you ask whether or not the threats are going down?

Q. No, I was saying that the admiration of the United States in surveys has dropped in the aftermath of the Iraq war, particularly in Nigeria.

The President. No, I got what you're saying. Yes, yes, I beg your pardon.

Well, look, it depends upon what the people are being told sometimes. I mean, if there's a constant effort to describe America as a non-caring country, then the people are going to have a bad attitude about us.

But when they know the truth, when the truth comes out, which is that we care deeply about the plight of the African citizen, that we're not only trading partners—and by the way, most nations, I think, would really like to trade with America—that we not only care deeply about the pandemic of AIDS but that we hear the cries of those who are sick and tired of corruption on the continent of Africa. And therefore, we are—we've got a new approach to foreign aid. I think people, when they know the facts, will say, "Well, this is a great country."

And the other thing is that no one likes war, and what you heard—there was kind of attachment to the word "America" with war. What they're going to find out, the word "freedom" and "America" are synonymous. That's what we believe. We believe in freedom. And we believe everybody desires freedom. And that when it's all said and done in Iraq, the world will wake up and say, "Now we understand what a free Iraq means to peace and stability."

And so I—if I conducted our foreign policy based upon polls and focus groups, we would be stumbling all over ourselves. That's not the way I do things. I base our foreign policy based upon deep-seated principles.

And this is a peroration to what's been a very, hopefully, constructive dialog for you. It has been for me. My message to the African people is, we come as a nation that believes in the future of Africa. We believe that people want to be free. We will work with those who embrace the habits of freedom, that when this Nation sees suffering, we will not turn away.

There is tremendous suffering on the continent of Africa. And we will put a strategy in place that effectively spends $15 billion over 5 years to help ease the suffering from HIV/AIDS. When we see starvation, we don't turn our back. We act. We care about the people of the continent. And there are—we've got great relations with leaders and countries on the continent of Africa, relations which will not only make—help enable people to realize their dreams but also make the world more safe.

And that is my message. And I am proud to carry the message on behalf of a great nation to a very important, great continent.

Thank you all for your time.

NOTE: The interview began at 10:30 a.m. in the Roosevelt Room at the White House. In his remarks, the President referred to President Abdoulaye Wade of Senegal; Jendayi E. Frazer, Special Assistant to the President and Senior Director for African Affairs at the National Security Council; President Olusegun Obasanjo of Nigeria; President Thabo Mbeki of South Africa; Abu Bakr Al Azdi, senior Al Qaida associate responsible for the May 12 bombing in Riyadh, Saudi Arabia; President Yoweri Kugata Museveni of Uganda; President Charles Taylor of Liberia; Secretary-General Kofi Annan of the United Nations; and Usama bin Laden, leader of the Al Qaida terrorist organization. A journalist referred to President Robert Mugabe of Zimbabwe and Morgan Tsvangirai, leader of Zimbabwe's opposition party, Movement for Democratic Change. Journalists participating in the interview were: Dame Babou, Sud Quotidien; Charlie Cobb, AllAfrica.com; Lalou Akande, The Guardian; and Deon Lamprecht, Media 24/Naspers. A tape was not available for verification of the content of this interview.

Interview With the South African Broadcasting Corporation
July 3, 2003

Liberia

Simon Marks. Mr. President, thank you very much indeed for talking to us here today. Let me start by seeing if we can perhaps make a little bit of news.

Liberia: Many West African leaders have asked you to send U.S. peacekeeping troops to join a multinational stabilization force in Liberia. Are you going to? If so, how many and for how long?

The President. We're in the process of determining the course of action necessary to see that peace and stability reign in Liberia. And some of our military people are meeting with ECOWAS leaders today. And I haven't made a decision yet.

Mr. Marks. Are you closing in on a decision?

The President. Yes. Every day that goes by is closer to a decision. But I need—before I make decisions, I like to have facts, and I'm gathering the facts necessary to determine what is necessary, who's willing to participate.

The one thing that must happen is, Charles Taylor has got to leave. A condition for any kind of operation that stabilizes the country is for Mr. Taylor to leave the country, and hopefully, we can achieve that objective diplomatically. Colin Powell is working closely with Kofi Annan and others at the United Nations to prepare the groundwork, if possible, for Mr. Taylor's departure.

Zimbabwe

Mr. Marks. Let me switch countries, if I may, and ask you about Zimbabwe. A short while ago your Secretary of State, Colin Powell, wrote in the New York Times that "South Africa can and should play a stronger and more sustained role in resolving matters in Zimbabwe." Specifically, what would you like to see President Thabo Mbeki do in Zimbabwe that he's not already doing?

The President. Insist that there be elections. Insist that democracy rule. Insist that the conditions necessary for that country to become prosperous again are in place.

I agree with the Secretary of State. I certainly don't want to put any pressure on my friend, but Zimbabwe has not been a good case study for democracy in a very important part of the world. And we hope that not only Mr. Mbeki but other leaders convince the current leadership to promote democracy.

Mr. Marks. Do you think quiet diplomacy can work?

The President. I hope any kind of diplomacy can work. So far, diplomacy hasn't worked. That's part of the problem. You

know, it's an interesting question. I guess writing an article may not be viewed as quiet diplomacy, since it was quite public. But I also have spoken out on Zimbabwe. It's a bad example.

Let me give you one reason why. There's a lot of starving people in sub-Sahara Africa; yet, Zimbabwe used to be able to grow more than it needed, to help deal with the starvation. We're a nation that is interested in helping people that are starving. We're going to spend a billion dollars this year on programs to help the hungry. It would be really helpful if Zimbabwe's economy was such that they would become a breadbasket again, a capacity to grow more food that's needed so that we could help—they could help deal with the hunger. And yet, the country is in such that, you know, in such a condition that the agricultural sector of its economy is in shambles right now.

HIV/AIDS Initiative/Debt Relief

Mr. Marks. On HIV, you surprised many in Washington by the vigor with which you've embraced the battle to combat HIV/AIDS. Some say you could do even more by more enthusiastically embracing debt relief for Africa. You favor it enthusiastically for Iraq; why not more enthusiastically for Africa?

The President. Well, let me start with the HIV program. I mean, enthusiasm is to the tune of $15 billion—that's pretty darn enthusiastic—to deal with the pandemic. And I also have agreed to increase the direct developmental aid grants from the United States by 50 percent. However, we expect countries, whether they be in Africa or anywhere else, that are applying for this money to embrace the habits of a free country, like transparency, anticorruption, making sure the people are educated and receive health care. So we're doing a lot in America.

There is a program in place for debt relief. And I would like to see that program implemented in full. I also called for the

World Bank to give more grants rather than loans. And so our program across the board is compassionate, in my judgment, because we care about Africa and we care about the people of Africa.

Nelson Mandela

Mr. Marks. And as you head to Africa, you are obviously aware that there are a large number of people on the continent who disagree with many of your policies, particularly your decision to move into Iraq, some of them very prominent personalities. When a statesman like former South African President Nelson Mandela says the very personal things about you that he has said in the past and continues to say even this week, that's got to hurt.

The President. No. I did the right thing. My job is to make sure America is secure. And if some don't like the tactics, that's the nature of a free world, where people can express their opinion.

I admire Nelson Mandela. As a matter of fact, my administration was the one that gave him the Medal of Freedom because of his courage and bravery. I just happen to disagree with him on his view of how best to secure America.

But you can be rest assured that if I think America is threatened, I will act. And you know, I understand criticism. I mean, look, but I'm not the kind of person that runs around trying to take a poll to determine what to do. If I believe it's necessary for my country, I will act.

I also believe it's necessary, when we see people enslaved, to work on behalf of their freedom, because this country believes that freedom is the desire of every human heart. And one of the great benefits of our action in Iraq is not only going to make America more secure, but it's going to make the Iraqi people more free. And you know, these mass graves we're finding is just the tip of the iceberg about what these poor people had to suffer at the hands of Saddam Hussein. And it's that kind of suffering that troubles me. And I believe the use of—proper use of power by America will make the world more peaceful, America more secure, and as importantly, people more free.

Mr. Marks. Mr. President, bon voyage.

The President. Thank you, sir.

NOTE: The interview was taped at 1:17 p.m. in the Map Room at the White House for later broadcast. In his remarks, the President referred to President Charles Taylor of Liberia; Secretary-General Kofi Annan of the United Nations; President Thabo Mbeki of South Africa; and former President Saddam Hussein of Iraq. A tape was not available for verification of the content of this interview.

Interview With the Voice of America
July 3, 2003

Liberia

Vincent Makori. Mr. President, if the U.S. was to send a peacekeeping force to Liberia, what role will it play and what limitations will you have?

The President. I haven't made up my mind, Vincent, whether we are going to send a so-called peacekeeping force. I have made up my mind there needs to be stability in Liberia, and one of the conditions for a peaceful and stable Liberia is for Mr. Charles Taylor to leave the country.

And so we're working the issue now. And I say "we," it's my—of course, the Secretary of State, the very capable Colin Powell, is working with Kofi Annan, who is also working with others on the continent to facilitate that type of move.

As well, there was a meeting today with ECOWAS leadership as to what the nature of a so-called peacekeeping force might look like. And that's very important information for me, the decisionmaker on this issue, to understand what the recommendations might be. I have yet to get those recommendations, but I expect I will in the next couple of days.

Mr. Makori. Mr. President, you have asked Mr. Charles Taylor to step down for the sake of peace. What will be your response to him if he does not heed your advice?

The President. Oh, I think we'll have to wait, Vincent, on that. You know, I suspect he will, and so therefore, I'm an optimistic person. I'm not going to take "no" for an answer. My hope is—it's not only my voice. It's the voice of a lot of others saying the same thing, and I think it's very important for us to be positive about having a good outcome.

Mr. Makori. And given the historical ties between the United States and Liberia, does the U.S. have a moral obligation to intervene in Liberia?

The President. Well, there's no question there is a—it is a unique relationship between Liberia and the United States, and I suspect that's why we're—I don't suspect; I know—that's why we're very much engaged in the discussions about how to bring a peaceful and secure Liberia to be. I mean, it's—yes, there is a unique history between the United States and Liberia.

Democracy in Africa

Mr. Makori. Mr. President, because all this boils down to leadership, what is the best thing the U.S. can do to discourage despotic and dictatorial rulerships in Africa and promote democracy, true democracy?

The President. Well, I appreciate that question. One thing is, we can help deal with the AIDS pandemic. A society which is ravished by AIDS is a society which is likely to be unstable. And therefore, if we can bring good health care to the millions who suffer and love to the orphans whose parents might have died from AIDS, it makes it easier to have a stable platform for growth.

Secondly, trade: I'm a big backer of what they call AGOA, which is trade agreements between African countries and the United States. Trade is more likely to make societies prosperous. Our aid program needs to promote the habits necessary for the evolution of a free society. In other words, we're not going to give money to corrupt rulers, and we're not going to give money to nontransparent societies. The American taxpayer and this American President believes that in return for aid—and we've got a generous amount of aid available—we expect people to take care of their people by educating them and creating good health care. We expect there to be market-oriented economies growing. And we expect the rulers to be thoughtful and mindful of who they represent, and that is the people of their country, not themselves or their ruling elite.

War on Terror in Africa

Mr. Makori. Mr. President, on the area of terrorism, which parts of Africa do you consider the hotspots for terrorism, and what role is the U.S. playing, especially with the regional leaders, to ensure that you are achieving the desired result?

The President. Well, unfortunately, a hotspot now is your country, Kenya. And we're very closely working with the Government there. And I will tell you, the Kenyan Government is very strong when it comes to fighting terror. The best thing we can do is share intelligence, is to work closely with the intelligence services of a particular country and then, when we find information, provide that information and encourage the Government to act. And Kenya has done a good job of working with the United States to protect Kenya. And that's what we want. We want people to be able to defend themselves against terror.

And unfortunately, some terrorists have been—and this has all come to light recently—obviously, there was a bombing in Kenya, and now it looks like there may be some action there as well. But the Government is making some very strong moves.

Mr. Makori. Thank you very much, Mr. President.

The President. Vincent, thank you, sir.

NOTE: The interview was taped at 1:25 p.m. in the Map Room at the White House for later broadcast. In his remarks, the President referred to President Charles Taylor of Liberia; and Secretary-General Kofi Annan of the United Nations. A tape was not available for verification of the content of this interview.

Interview With CNN International
July 3, 2003

Tomi Makagabo. Mr. President, thank you very much for speaking with us, and welcome to South Africa.

The President. Thanks. Thanks for having me.

Liberia

Ms. Makagabo. If we could begin with the issue of Liberia, President Charles Taylor in particular. You said he needs to step down; he needs to leave the country. The U.S., along with other west African countries, are busy negotiating the whole issue. What are the discussions and options that are being put on the table?

The President. Well, I'm glad you brought up the departure of Charles Taylor. In our judgment, he needs to go in order to create the conditions necessary for a peaceful solution to this difficult situation occurs.

You know, look, we're talking to ECOWAS countries right now to determine whether or not the—what the nature of a peacekeeping force might look like. I'm the kind of person that likes to know all the facts before I make a decision. We've got special ties to Liberia. There are historical ties to the United States. That's why we are involved in this issue, and I am going to look at all the options to determine how best to bring peace and stability.

One thing has to happen. That's Mr. Taylor needs to leave, and I've been outspoken on that. Mr. Colin Powell has been outspoken on that. And I think most of the people involved with this issue understand that that's important, that he do leave.

Ms. Makagabo. You said that he needs to leave. Does that mean that if those negotiations fail and President Charles Taylor refuses to go, that you will send troops to remove him from office and——

The President. Well, first of all, I refuse to accept the negative. I understand it's your job to try to put that forth. I believe he'll listen. And until he doesn't listen, then we can come back and talk about the issue. In other words, I hope he does listen, and I'm convinced he will listen.

Ms. Makagabo. And should he not?

The President. No, you—I'm convinced he will listen and make the decision—the right decision, if he cares about his country.

President's Upcoming Visit to Africa

Ms. Makagabo. Let's talk about, then, your trip to Africa. It hasn't necessarily—it has only recently become more apparent, this particular administration's interest in African affairs and involvement in what's going on in the country.

The President. Yes, can I stop you there? That's not true. As a matter of fact, from the very beginning of my administration, I've been very much involved with African affairs. I've met over 22 African leaders. And I just want to make—correct the record before——

Ms. Makagabo. Absolutely.

The President. ——disabuse you of that misinformation, because Africa has been a very important part of my administration's foreign policy.

Ms. Makagabo. However, many people will say that has only become more apparent to them, perhaps not necessarily to the administration, but more apparent, outwardly, that this administration is becoming involved in African affairs. My question to you, then, is if that is the case and looking at the history which you've pointed out, why now? Why this visit now?

The President. Why am I going now? I thought it was important to go before my first term was over to show the importance of Africa to my administration's foreign policy. And besides going on a trip— I mean, trips are fine, but what's more important is policy.

And I proposed a Millennium Challenge Account, which will, in my judgment, affect the lives of African citizens in an incredibly positive way, which says that in return for aid—and we're increasing the amount of aid available—governments actually have to make decisions which will be positive on behalf of their people, such as educating their people or providing health care for their people, not to steal the money; in other words, don't focus on elite but focus on the people themselves, create the conditions necessary for market growth.

I promoted AGOA. Now, I didn't invent AGOA; that happened in my predecessor's time. But I promoted the extension of AGOA, which was the trade agreements between the African Continent and the United States, which has been incredibly beneficial for a lot of countries and a lot of people on the African Continent.

I proposed an AIDS initiative because I believe it's very important for the United States to not only show its muscle to the world but also its heart. And the AIDS initiative, in our judgment, when implemented, will help affect the lives of thousands of people who are suffering from an incredibly—a pandemic that is actually destroying life. And it is—it's sad for us.

And so my administration is not only, you know, good on trips and meetings but more important, fundamental policy. And I think that's important.

Iraqi Weapons of Mass Destruction

Ms. Makagabo. One policy that your administration hasn't necessarily agreed on with many African countries is the question of Iraq and the war in Iraq. Can you give us a sense of how close the administration feels you are to finding those weapons of mass destruction and banned weapons?

The President. Oh, sure. Yes, there's no doubt in my mind he had a weapons program. He was—he used them. Remember, he was the guy that gassed his own people. Those were weapons of mass destruction he used on his own people. No doubt. We found a biological lab, the very same lab that had been banned by the United Nations. It will be a matter of time.

Let me talk about Iraq, and I appreciate you bringing it up. If I think something that needs to be done to enhance the security of the American people, I'll do it. You see, that's my most important job, is to protect the security of America.

Secondly, I believe in freedom for people, and I suffer when I hear the stories of what took place inside of Iraq, the mass graves that have been discovered, the torture chambers, the jails for children. And the Iraqi people are going to benefit mightily from the actions of the United States and a lot of other nations, because they'll be free. And we've been there for about 90 days. And the world is such that they expect democracy to have occurred yesterday. It's going to take a while for a free, democratic Iraq to evolve. But it's going to happen. And history will show you what a—it will show you or the skeptics that we are actually correct in our assessment of Mr. Saddam Hussein.

Ms. Makagabo. All right, Mr. President. I think that's where I'm going to have to leave it.

The President. Thank you very much for coming. Hope to see you in South Africa.

NOTE: The interview was taped at 1:33 p.m. in the Map Room at the White House for later broadcast. In his remarks, the President referred to former President Saddam Hussein of Iraq. A tape was not available for verification of the content of this interview.

Statement on Signing the Strengthen AmeriCorps Program Act
July 3, 2003

Today I have signed into law S. 1276, the "Strengthen AmeriCorps Program Act." The Act clarifies the methods by which the Corporation for National and Community Service (CNCS) records obligations to the National Service Trust for volunteer educational awards by authorizing the use of estimating methodology similar to other comparable programs. In order to ensure appropriate accountability hereafter, the Act also provides for annual independent audits of the Trust.

Section 2(b)(2) of the Act purports to require the CNCS to consult the Director of the Congressional Budget Office (CBO), a legislative agent, in executing section 2(b)(1)(B) of the Act relating to determination of a formula for calculating certain obligations for recordation. Because section 191 of the National and Community Service Act of 1990 (NCSA) (42 U.S.C. 12651) assigns to the CNCS the Executive function to "administer the programs established under the national service laws," and because the CNCS is an "Executive agency"

under section 105 of title 5 of the United States Code by virtue of the provisions of section 191 of the NCSA and section 103 of title 5, the CNCS is plainly part of the unitary executive branch.

Since a statute cannot constitutionally require the executive branch to involve a legislative agent in executive decision-making, the executive branch shall construe section 2(b)(2) as requiring the CNCS only to notify the Director of the CBO with regard to the matters addressed by the provision. At the same time, the Chief Executive Officer (CEO) of the CNCS shall, as a matter of comity between the executive and legislative branches, seek and consider the views of the Director of CBO in this matter as the CEO deems appropriate.

GEORGE W. BUSH

The White House,
July 3, 2003.

NOTE: S. 1276, approved July 3, was assigned Public Law No. 108–45.

Message on the Observance of Independence Day, 2003
July 3, 2003

On July 4, 1776, our Founders adopted the Declaration of Independence, creating a great Nation and establishing a hopeful vision of liberty and equality that endures today. This Independence Day, we express gratitude for our many blessings and we celebrate the ideals of freedom and opportunity that our Nation holds dear.

America's strength and prosperity are testaments to the enduring power of our founding ideals, among them, that all men are created equal, and that liberty is God's gift to humanity, the birthright of every individual. The American creed remains powerful today because it represents the universal hope of all mankind.

On the Fourth of July, we are grateful for the blessings that freedom represents and for the opportunities it affords. We are thankful for the love of our family and friends and for our rights to think, speak, and worship freely. We are also humbled in remembering the many courageous men and women who have served and sacrificed throughout our history to preserve, protect, and expand these liberties. In liberating oppressed peoples and demonstrating honor and bravery in battle, the members of our Armed Forces reflect the best of our Nation.

We also recognize the challenges that America now faces. We are winning the war against enemies of freedom, yet more work remains. We will prevail in this noble mission. Liberty has the power to turn hatred into hope.

America is a force for good in the world, and the compassionate spirit of America remains a living faith. Drawing on the courage of our Founding Fathers and the resolve of our citizens, we willingly embrace the challenges before us.

Laura joins me in sending our best wishes for a safe and joyous Independence Day. May God bless you, and may God continue to bless America.

GEORGE W. BUSH

NOTE: An original was not available for verification of the content of this message.

Letter to Congressional Leaders Transmitting a Report on the National Emergency With Respect to the Proliferation of Weapons of Mass Destruction
July 3, 2003

Dear Mr. Speaker: *(Dear Mr. President:)*
Consistent with section 204(c) of the International Emergency Economic Powers Act, 50 U.S.C. 1703(c), and section 401(c) of the National Emergencies Act, 50 U.S.C. 1641(c), I transmit herewith a 6-month periodic report prepared by my Administration on the national emergency with respect to the proliferation of weapons of mass destruction that was declared in Executive Order 12938 of November 14, 1994.

Sincerely,

GEORGE W. BUSH

NOTE: Identical letters were sent to J. Dennis Hastert, Speaker of the House of Representatives, and Richard B. Cheney, President of the Senate.

Letter to Congressional Leaders Transmitting a Report on Benchmarks for a Sustainable Peace Process in Bosnia and Herzegovina
July 3, 2003

Dear Mr. Speaker: (Dear Mr. President:)

Consistent with the Levin Amendment to the 1998 Supplemental Appropriations and Rescissions Act (section 7(b) of Public Law 105–174) and section 1203(a) of the Strom Thurmond National Defense Authorization Act for Fiscal Year 1999 (Public Law 105–261), I am providing a report prepared by my Administration on progress made toward achieving benchmarks for a sustainable peace process in Bosnia and Herzegovina.

This eighth report, which also includes supplemental reporting consistent with section 1203(a) of Public Law 105–261, provides an updated assessment of progress on the benchmarks covering the period January 1 to June 30, 2003.

Sincerely,

GEORGE W. BUSH

NOTE: Identical letters were sent to J. Dennis Hastert, Speaker of the House of Representatives, and Richard B. Cheney, President of the Senate.

Letter to Congressional Leaders Transmitting Proposed Legislative Changes To Implement the United States-Singapore Free Trade Agreement
July 3, 2003

Dear Mr. Speaker: (Dear Mr. President:)

On May 6, 2003, I signed the United States-Singapore Free Trade Agreement. Consistent with section 2105(a)(1)(B) of the Trade Act of 2002 (Public Law 107–210), I am submitting a description of the changes to existing laws, prepared by my Administration, that would be required to bring the United States into compliance with that Agreement.

I look forward to working with the Congress in developing legislation to implement this important Free Trade Agreement.

Sincerely,

GEORGE W. BUSH

NOTE: Identical letters were sent to J. Dennis Hastert, Speaker of the House of Representatives, and Richard B. Cheney, President of the Senate.

Letter to Congressional Leaders Transmitting Proposed Legislative Changes To Implement the United States-Chile Free Trade Agreement
July 3, 2003

Dear Mr. Speaker: (Dear Mr. President:)

On June 6, 2003, the United States Trade Representative signed the United

States-Chile Free Trade Agreement on behalf of the United States. Consistent with section 2105(a)(1)(B) of the Trade Act of

2002 (Public Law 107–210), I am submitting a description of the changes to existing laws, prepared by my Administration, that would be required to bring the United States into compliance with that Agreement.

I look forward to working with the Congress in developing legislation to implement this important Free Trade Agreement.

Sincerely,

GEORGE W. BUSH

NOTE: Identical letters were sent to J. Dennis Hastert, Speaker of the House of Representatives, and Richard B. Cheney, President of the Senate.

Remarks on the 100th Anniversary of Flight in Dayton, Ohio
July 4, 2003

The President. Thank you all very much. Thanks for the warm welcome. Want to be seated? Be seated. [*Laughter*] It's kind of a long speech. [*Laughter*] Thanks for coming. It's great to be in the great State of Ohio. I am proud to be at Wright-Patt, the birthplace, the home, and the future of aerospace.

I had the honor of meeting Amanda Wright Lane and Steve Wright, descendants of the Wright brothers. They were quick to remind me that Dayton is where the Wright brothers first drew up the plans for their flying machine. I wonder what Wilbur and Orville would have thought if they'd have seen that flying machine that I came in on today. [*Laughter*]

I'm truly honored to join you in celebrating the 227th anniversary of our Nation's independence. The Fourth of July, 2003, finds our country facing many challenges, and we're rising to meet them. Today and every day, the people of this land are grateful for our freedom, and we are proud to call ourselves citizens of the United States of America.

I want to thank Governor Bob Taft and the First Lady of Ohio for their friendship and their leadership for the State of Ohio.

I appreciate so very much my friends Senator George Voinovich and Senator Mike DeWine for coming out to greet with me today and to be here with you all.

They're great United States Senators. I want to thank Congressman Michael Turner, Congressman David Hobson, and Congressman John Boehner for their service to the State of Ohio.

I was so honored that a great American, former Senator John Glenn, and his wife, Annie, came out to say hello at the airport, and I'm honored they are here today. I want to thank them for coming.

I appreciate members of the State government: The Lieutenant Governor, Jennette Bradley, is with us today; Treasurer Joe Deters; and Doug White, the senate president. I want to thank the mayor of the city of Dayton, Mayor McLin, for coming today as well and all those involved with city government.

I appreciate the generals on this base that make this fantastic base function so well, starting with Les Lyles, the commander. I want to thank Brad Tillson, who is the chairman of Inventing Flight Commission, and John Barry, who is chairman of the Air Force Museum Foundation.

Today when I landed, I had the opportunity to meet a fellow citizen named Becky Lundy.

Audience member. Yeah!

The President. Somebody has heard of her. [*Laughter*] Becky Lundy is the spouse of a active duty Air Force member. What makes her unique is she's a volunteer at the Family Support Center at Wright-Patterson Air Force Base. She takes time out of her day to comfort those who need comfort. She understands that service to our country means helping somebody in need.

Listen, we're a strong and powerful nation because we've got a great military. But we're also strong because we're a nation of fine hearts. If those of you are looking for some way to serve your country, go to usafreedomcorps.gov on your Internet. Look up a place to help a neighbor in need. Join the armies of compassion, just as Becky Lundy does. We are changing America one heart, one soul, one conscience at a time, and we need your help.

But most of all, I want to thank you all for coming today. I appreciate the families from this base and citizens from all across the State of Ohio who have come to celebrate our Independence Day. During the last year, people at this base have met hardships together. You looked out for each other. You've given strength and support to our men and women in uniform. Like military communities across the country, you have played a vital part in our Nation's cause, and America is grateful.

Every year on this date, we take special pride in the founding generation, the men and women who waged a desperate fight to overcome tyranny and live in freedom. Centuries later, it is hard to imagine the Revolutionary War coming out any way other than it—how it came out. Yet victory was far from certain and came at great cost. Those brave men and women were certain only of the cause they served, the belief that freedom is the gift of God and the right of all mankind.

Six years passed from the fighting at Concord Bridge to the victory at Yorktown, 6 years of struggle and hardship for American patriots. By their courage and perseverance, the Colonies became a country. The land of 13 States and fewer than 4 million people grew and prospered. And today, all who live in tyranny and all who yearn for freedom place their hopes in the United States of America.

For more than two centuries, Americans have been called to serve and sacrifice for the ideals of our founding, and the men and women of our military have never failed us. They have left many monuments along the way, an undivided Union, a liberated Europe, the rise of democracy in Asia, and the fall of an evil empire. Millions across the world are free today because of the unselfish courage of American veterans. And today we honor our veterans.

And today we honor the current generation of our military, which is answering the call to defend our freedom and to bring freedom to others. The 23,000 men and women of Wright-Patt, military and civilian, have been crucial to our victories in Afghanistan and in Iraq.

Research done at this base has helped give America the finest Air Force in history. The Predator drone, which is serving us so well overseas, was developed right here. Doctors and specialists from this base cared for wounded soldiers and for wounded prisoners. Many critical medical evacuations were carried out by the skillful pilots and crews of the mighty 445th Wing of Wright-Patt. C–141s from this base transported troops and equipment to serve in both Operation Enduring Freedom and in Operation Iraqi Freedom. And B–1 bombers supported from this base made their presence known in Baghdad, striking the dictator's regime until the regime was no more.

Our United States military is meeting the threats of a new era. People in every branch of the service and thousands of Guard and Reserve members called to active duty have carried out their missions with all the skill and the honor we expect of them. This Nation is grateful to the men and women who wear our Nation's uniform.

And on this Fourth of July, we also remember the brave Americans we have lost. We honor each one for their courage and for their sacrifice. We think of the families who miss them so much. And we are thankful that this Nation produces such fine men and women who are willing to defend us all. May God rest their souls.

Our Nation is still at war. The enemies of America plot against us, and many of our fellow citizens are still serving and sacrificing and facing danger in distant places. Many military families are separated. Our people in uniform do not have easy duty, and much depends on their success. Without America's active involvement in the world, the ambitions of tyrants would go unopposed, and millions would live at the mercy of terrorists. With Americans' active involvement in the world, tyrants learn to fear, and terrorists are on the run.

By killing innocent Americans, our enemies made their intentions clear to us. And since that September day, we have made our own intentions clear to them. The United States will not stand by and wait for another attack or trust in the restraint and good intentions of evil men. We are on the offensive against terrorists and all who support them. We will not permit any terrorist group or outlaw regime to threaten us with weapons of mass murder. We will act whenever it is necessary to protect the lives and the liberty of the American people.

America's work in the world does not end with the removal of grave threats. The Declaration of Independence holds a promise for all mankind. Because Americans believe that freedom is an unalienable right, we value the freedom of every nation. Because we are committed to the God-given worth of every life, we work for human dignity. We protect our friends, and we raise up former enemies to be our friends.

We bring food and disaster relief to the nations of the world in times of crisis. And in Africa, where I'll go next week, the United States is leading the effort to fight AIDS and save millions of lives with the healing power of medicine.

Just as our enemies are coming to know the strong will of America, people across the Earth are seeing the good and generous heart of America. Americans are a generous people because we realize how much we have been given. On the Fourth of July, we can be grateful for the unity of our country in meeting great challenges, for the renewal of patriotism that adversity has brought, and for the valor we have seen in those who defend the United States.

In recent events, we have learned the names of some exceptional young men and women who have shown the strength and character of America. At a hospital in Washington, I met Master Gunnery Sergeant Guadalupe Denogean, an immigrant from Mexico who has served in the Marine Corps for 25 years. In March, he was wounded in combat in Basra and sent back to America for treatment. When I asked if he had any requests, the Master Gunnery Sergeant had just two. He wanted a promotion for the colonel who rescued him, and he wanted to be an American citizen.

I was there the day that Guadalupe Denogean took the oath of citizenship. From the hospital where he was recovering, this son of Mexico raised his right hand and pledged to support and defend the Constitution of the United States of America. He had kept that oath for decades before he took it. I'm proud to call him a fellow American.

To be an American, whether by birth or choice, is a high privilege. As citizens of this good Nation, we can all be proud of our heritage and confident in our future. The ideals of July 4th, 1776, still speak to all humanity. And the Revolution declared that day goes on. On July the 4th, 2003, we still placed our trust in divine providence. We still pledge our lives and honor to freedom's defense. And we will always believe that freedom is the hope and the future of every land.

May God continue to bless the United States of America.

NOTE: The President spoke at 12:13 p.m. outside the U.S. Air Force Museum at Wright-Patterson Air Force Base. In his remarks, he referred to Gov. Bob Taft of Ohio and his wife, Hope; Mayor Rhine McLin of Dayton, OH; Gen. Les Lyles, USAF, commander, Air Force Materiel Command; and former President Saddam Hussein of Iraq.

The President's Radio Address
July 5, 2003

Good morning. Every Fourth of July, we take special pride in the first generation of Americans, the men and women who waged a desperate fight to overcome tyranny and live in freedom. Centuries later, it is hard to imagine the Revolutionary War coming out any other way. Yet victory was far from certain and came at great cost.

Six years passed from the fighting at Concord Bridge to the victory at Yorktown, 6 years of struggle and hardship for American patriots. By their courage and perseverance, the Colonies became a country. That land of 13 States and fewer than 4 million people grew and prospered. And today, all who live in tyranny and all who yearn for freedom place their hopes in the United States of America.

For more than two centuries, Americans have been called to serve and sacrifice for the ideals of our founding, and the men and women of our military have never failed us. They have left many monuments along the way, an undivided Union, a liberated Europe, the rise of democracy in Asia, and the fall of an evil empire. Millions across the world are free today because of the unselfish courage of America's veterans.

The current generation of our military is meeting the threats of a new era and fighting new battles in the war on terror. People in every branch of the service and thousands of Guard and Reserve members called to active duty have carried out their missions with all the skill and honor we expect of them. This Nation is grateful to our men and women in uniform.

On this Fourth of July weekend, we also remember the brave Americans we've lost in Afghanistan and Iraq. We honor each one for their courage and sacrifice. We think of the families who miss them so much. And we are thankful that this Nation produces such fine men and women who are willing to defend us all.

At this hour, many are still serving, sacrificing, and facing danger in distant places. Many military families are still separated. Our people in uniform do not have easy duty, and much depends on their success. Without America's active involvement in the world, the ambitions of tyrants would go unopposed, and millions would live at the mercy of terrorists. With America's active involvement in the world, tyrants have learned to fear, and terrorists are on the run.

This Nation is acting to defend our security, yet our mission in the world is broader. The Declaration of Independence holds a promise for all mankind. Because Americans believe that freedom is an unalienable right, we value the freedom of every nation. Because we are committed to the God-given worth of every life, we work for human dignity in every land. We protect our friends and raise up former enemies to be our friends. We bring food and disaster relief to the nations of the world in times of crisis. And in Africa, where I will go next week, the United States of America is leading the effort to fight AIDS and save millions of lives with the healing power of medicine. Just as our enemies are going to know the strong will of America, people across this Earth are seeing the good and generous heart of America.

As citizens of this good Nation, we can be proud of our heritage and confident in our future. The ideals of July 4th, 1776, still speak to all humanity, and the Revolution declared that day goes on. As we celebrate our independence in 2003, we still place our trust in divine providence. We still pledge our lives and honor to freedom's defense. And we will always believe that freedom is the hope and the future of every land.

May God continue to bless the United States of America. Thank you for listening.

NOTE: The address was recorded at 11:01 a.m. on July 3 in the Cabinet Room at the White House for broadcast at 10:06 a.m. on July 5. The transcript was made available by the Office of the Press Secretary on July 4 but was embargoed for release until the broadcast. The Office of the Press Secretary also released a Spanish language transcript of this address.

Remarks at Highland Park Elementary School in Landover, Maryland
July 7, 2003

Thank you all. Thanks for coming. Please. Windy, thank you very much. I'm proud of you. I'm proud of your dedication. It is a great country where Windy can come from a Head Start program and is now a leader in the movement to make sure Head Start fulfills the promise of the program.

First, I want to thank the good folks here at Highland Park Elementary School for letting me come by and see a program which works. I don't know if the people in the State of Maryland know this—I know the Governor does—that the teachers here and the program here uses a strategy, what they call a Center for Improving Readiness for Children, Learning, and Education, C.I.R.C.L.E., which is a model program. It's a program that incorporates profound and simple reading lessons necessary to lay the foundation for future readers. And it's a program that's working. There is a strong emphasis on learning. There is obviously the continued Head Start focus on good nutrition and health care. This program also works well because the parents are involved.

So, I've really come to say a couple of things. One, I want to thank the good folks

at this learning institution for your focus and dedication. I also want to say that this is possible, this program is possible, to be spread around the country. I mean, this is what we need to do. That's what we're here to talk about. We're really here to talk about how to make sure Head Start works.

I'll never forget the lady in Houston, Texas, who stood up at one time and she said, "Reading is the new civil right." Her point was, is that if you can't read, it is hard to access the greatness of America. And if reading is the new civil right, a good place to start with civil rights is at the Head Start programs all across the country.

And that's what we're here to talk about, how to make then work better. They're working okay. We want better than okay in America. We want excellence. Windy understands that, and I want to thank her for working with my Secretary for the Department of Health and Human Services, Tommy Thompson. I appreciate you coming, Tommy.

And I appreciate my friend Rod Paige. He's the Secretary of Education. If you noticed, the two Secretaries are here, Health and Human Services and Education. The idea is to combine both focuses, both Departments into one when it comes to Head Start. The Head Start program will stay under Tommy's purview, but we want it to become an Education Department as well.

I mean, after all, you've got a million kids gathered together at one time during the day. If you've got a million kids that may be, as they call them in the education world, at-risk readers, let's get it right early then. That's what we're saying. And that's what this initiative is attempting to do.

I appreciate Bob Ehrlich, the Governor of this great State. He knows what he's doing when it comes to education. He's got a great wife, the first lady, Kendel, with us as well. Governor Ehrlich sets high standards. He challenges what I call the soft bigotry of low expectations. He understands if you lower the bar, assign certain kids to failure based upon demographics, that's precisely what you'll get in the State of Maryland. So he said, "We ought to raise the bar." He believes every child can learn. And so does the Lieutenant Governor, Michael Steele. They understand that high standards will yield high results. And the best place to start in achieving high standards is with the littlest of children.

I want to thank very much Congressman John Boehner for coming today. The Congressman is not from Maryland; he's from Ohio. But he's an important figure since he's the chairman of the House Education Committee which is marking up legislation which will help us spread excellence to the Head Start programs all across the country. Congressman, thanks for coming. I look forward to continuing to work with him.

He also is one of the authors of what we call the No Child Left Behind Act, which I'll talk about a little bit later. But the No Child Left Behind Act essentially says we expect every child to learn, and there is going to be high standards and strong accountability measures to every

State in the Union. In return for increased Title I funding and in return for an increase in the Federal budget of elementary and secondary schools act money, we expect results. You see, we're not going to just spend money and hope something positive happens. We're going to spend money and see results.

Well, if you believe in high standards and accountability, then it's really important to get the young kids up to the starting line at the same time. And that's why the Head Start reforms we're going to talk about are important, the reforms which John and his committee are carrying to the floor of the House relatively soon.

I want to thank Nancy Grasmick, who is the State superintendent of schools in Maryland. I'm honored that you're here. Thank you for coming, and thank you for taking on a tough job. I appreciate Andre Hornsby as the superintendent of schools, an even tougher job. Government closest to the people is sometimes government that's the hardest. And I want to thank Guylaine Richard, who is the program director for the Head Start. I appreciate, Guylaine, you opening up this chance for me to come and see a program which works.

I want to thank Lori Ellis, the principal. When we leave, she can take a deep breath and relax and say, "Thank goodness the entourage has departed." [*Laughter*] I appreciate the—Tonya Riggins, who is the Highland Park Head Start Center coordinator. I want to thank Lisa Dunmore and Alice Williams, the two fine teachers we had to meet. For the teachers who are here, thank you for doing what you're doing. You're a part of a noble profession, an incredibly important profession for the future of this country. You know what I know, that reading is the key to all learning. It's where you've got to start.

And the research—I see some of my friends from the National Research Council, National Institutions of Child Health who are here. Reid Lyon is an expert. He's not a political person. He's a scientist. He understands how the brain works, and he's spent a lot of time analyzing what works and what doesn't work. He caught my attention when I was the Governor of Texas. I would ask him a question, "Are you sure we can teach kids, you know, the so-called impossible-to-teach?" He said, "Sure, I know it. I'm absolutely certain." And so he started doing research to convince the people about the real future. And he says that—he and his fellow researchers—that preschoolers can learn much more than we ever thought possible about words and sounds.

In other words, society limited how much a certain—how much a preschooler could learn. At least our imaginations weren't very open. It kind of felt like certain things were impossible to—certain knowledge was impossible to impart to our children, particularly the young.

And so I want to thank Reid and the good folks who are focusing on science, who have opened up a tremendous realm of possibility now to achieve that which we want, a literate America. He also says there—he and other researchers say, and this is just as important, kids love to learn. They love to learn to read. Even the youngest child can learn that we read words and letters from left to right or that letters are associated with sounds; even the youngest of toddlers can figure that out over time.

In one exercise, children clapped for each syllable in a word. They can trace letters on the page to begin to understand the movements we use to write. They can play word games and learn rhymes and songs that help them to develop their own vocabulary. That sounds like a simple curriculum, but it is research-based, all aimed at laying the foundation for children to become good readers. These are what we call the building blocks, and these building blocks need to be a part of Head Start programs all across America. That's the mission. That's the goal.

Research also shows that if children do not develop these skills before they reach kindergarten, they will struggle to achieve success in their lives. Now, we need to listen to that kind of research in America. If the scientists come together and say, "If we fail in our mission to give children the foundation necessary for reading, they will fall behind and may not be able to develop the skills necessary, so they have to struggle in life," we got a—this is an opportunity that we better not miss.

We cannot let our children down. Now look, Head Start is a great opportunity to provide the foundation for reading. And first, I just want everybody to understand, Head Start does a good job of giving children nutrition and medical care. That has been primarily the focus, and the program needs to be applauded for meeting that goal. And nobody in this room wants Head Start to change that focus. We just want an additional focus to Head Start, and the Head Start focus is teaching the basics for reading and math. That's the new focus, along with health and nutrition.

The Department of Health and Human Services did a report, and here is what it said: "Even though most children in Head Start make some educational progress, most of them still leave the program with skills and knowledge levels that are far below what we expect." Now, in my line of work, if you see a problem, you address it. And I see that as a problem. If we're not meeting expectations, if we're not challenging the soft bigotry of low expectations, let's start right now in America. We want Head Start to set higher ambitions for the million children it serves.

And so I laid out a plan. Every Head Start center must prepare children to succeed by teaching the basics of learning and literacy. That's the cornerstone of the plan. And every Head Start teacher must have the skills necessary to do so.

And so we started last year when we launched the Strategic Teacher Education Program, STEP, to train 3,300 Head Start teachers and supervisors in the C.I.R.C.L.E. program, which is used right here at this school. In other words, it's a go-by. It is a curriculum. It's easy to understand. It's easy to teach. It's easy to implement. It is not a difficult chore for a teacher to take the basic learning from the C.I.R.C.L.E. program developed by the scientists and implement it at the Head Start program in which he or she teaches.

Tonya Riggins, the assistant Head Start supervisor at Highland Park, was one of the teachers in the program. Tonya and thousands of other trained teachers went back to train other teachers at the program. So it's going to—we started with 3,300. Those 3,300 went back to their local communities and talked to teachers with whom they teach how to teach a basic curriculum. It is a—and by the way, as new teachers are added, they too will be given the tools necessary to teach the program.

Now, in order to make sure that the C.I.R.C.L.E. program is—and other curriculums which work—are being used, is working, I believe there needs to be an evaluation program. And after all, if we're spending a lot of taxpayers' money, which we are, it makes sense to determine whether or not these programs are, in fact, laying the foundation for reading.

Now, I fully understand a 4-year-old child is not going to take a standardized test. That would be absurd. That we would—we would be defeating the purpose of accountability before we even began if we said, "Okay, we'll give standardized tests to 4-year-olds." But we can have children assessed by asking simple questions. You know, words go left to right. Are you able to identify certain sounds? Are they developed by—developing the key skills necessary?

And I think what needs to happen is— and I hope Congress agrees—that the simple evaluations at the beginning of the year and the end of the year will tell us whether or not progress is being made in developing a curriculum necessary to teach children

how to read. And if they are, we ought to be praising the programs, and if they're not, something else ought to happen. We cannot miss the opportunity much longer in America. Otherwise, children will be left behind.

And so Boehner is here because his committee and the Congress is considering legislation that would put a new emphasis on language skills and literacy skills in Head Start programs. In other words, we're going to codify into law that which we have started through the teacher training program.

The legislation will require Head Start providers to teach language, reading, and writing skills, as well as early math skills. In other words, it now becomes a part— when they pass the law that says the Head Start mission is further defined as an educational mission. And those programs that are used must be proven by scientific research. The legislation would hold Head Starts accountable for getting the job done.

Now look, as I mentioned before, the No Child Left Behind Act says every child can learn. We're going to have high standards. We're going to trust the local people to develop the curriculum, but in return for Federal money, we want you to measure to tell us whether or not children are learning to read and write. And that's a heavy lift for some communities, because there hasn't been a proper focus on the little children.

And therefore, we're asking people to develop an accountability system without everybody being at the same starting position. And that's why it's so important for preschool programs to be focused on literacy, so that when the accountability systems kick in in Maryland or Texas or anybody else, we can truthfully say that every child has been given the tools necessary to be at the starting line at the same time, so that we have true accountability, true measurement. And that's why the Head Start program is important.

Now, there's Governors around the State, the country that have said, "Look, give us the flexibility to be able to dovetail the Head Start program into our preschool programs so that all students—so we have a better control over whether or not the students are given the skills necessary so that when you hold us to account, we can achieve that which we want to achieve, which is excellence in the classroom."

I appreciate the desire for flexibility. I support the Governors' desire for flexibility so long as, one, Federal monies going to the States are used only for Head Start. In other words, what we really don't want to do is say we're going to focus on Head Start; the Head Start money goes for, you know, a prison complex. I know that won't happen with Governor Ehrlich, but there needs to be a guarantee that the Federal money spent on Head Start only go to Head Start.

Secondly, States and local governments must put money into the program, which would lock in the Head Start money for Head Start. So, in other words, the flexibility given to the State would not allow the States budget flexibility. It's management flexibility to be able to take the Head Start program, dovetail into the preschool program, then the kindergarten program, and then into the elementary school program.

Governors ought to have that flexibility to—hope that Congress will provide that flexibility so that when the accountability systems kick in, fully kick in, that a Governor can truthfully say, "Well, I've had the tools necessary to make sure the Head Start program fits into an overall comprehensive plan for literacy and math for every child in the State of Maryland," in Governor Ehrlich's case.

This is a very important initiative I'm talking about. It is—it seems like to me a fantastic opportunity for the country to make sure that the desires of this country are met, and that is, every child become a good reader. If reading is the new civil right and human dignity and freedom is

what this country is all about, let's make sure every child learns to read.

So I want to thank you for giving me a chance to come today. We know what works. We've got the pros and the experts that have laid out a curriculum that will help us achieve a goal. We've got a million kids anxious to learn, showing up on a daily basis at Head Start programs all across the country. We've got teachers who want to teach. We're writing the checks for the local governments and the local Head Start programs. Let's combine it all into a comprehensive strategy that will allow us all to say, "We have done our duty for future generations of children by laying the most important foundation of all, and that is the ability for each child to learn to read." I know it can happen. There's no doubt in my mind.

I want to thank those of you who are working on the frontlines of education. I appreciate your willingness to accept a new mission to be incorporated with the old mission. And I appreciate your willingness to work hard, to see to it that not one single child in America is left behind.

May God bless your work. And may God continue to bless America. Thank you.

NOTE: The President spoke at 11 a.m. at the Head Start Center. In his remarks, he referred to Windy M. Hill, associate commissioner, Head Start Bureau, Administration for Children and Families, Department of Health and Human Services; Andre J. Hornsby, chief executive officer, Prince George's County Public Schools; Guylaine Richard, program supervisor, and Tonya Riggins, acting assistant program supervisor, Head Start, Prince George's County Public Schools; and G. Reid Lyon, branch chief, Child Development and Behavior, National Institute of Child Health and Human Development, National Institutes of Health. The Office of the Press Secretary also released a Spanish language transcript of these remarks.

Letter to the Speaker of the House of Representatives Transmitting Emergency Supplemental Appropriations Requests
July 7, 2003

Dear Mr. Speaker:

I ask the Congress to consider expeditiously the enclosed requests, totaling $1.9 billion, for emergency FY 2003 supplemental appropriations. I hereby designate the specific proposals in the amounts requested herein as emergency requirements.

The details of these requests are set forth in the enclosed letter from the Director of the Office of Management and Budget.

Sincerely,

GEORGE W. BUSH

Exchange With Reporters in Dakar, Senegal
July 8, 2003

Liberia

Q. Can we ask you about Liberia, sir?

The President. We had a good discussion about Liberia.

Q. Have you made a decision?

The President. The President of Ghana is the leader of ECOWAS. I told him we'd participate with ECOWAS. We're now in the process to determine the extent of our participation. And I really appreciate the President's leadership on this issue. Charles Taylor must leave. The United Nations is going to be involved. The United States will work with ECOWAS. The leaders of ECOWAS were at the table, all of whom are concerned about Liberia, as are we, and are concerned about a peaceful western Africa.

Q. Does that mean you'll send troops?

The President. We're in the process of determining what is necessary to maintain the cease-fire and to allow for a peaceful transfer of power. We're working very closely with ECOWAS. The President of ECOWAS is with us today, the President of Ghana. He and I had a good discussion. I assured him we'll participate in the process. And we're now in the process of determining what that means.

Q. Do you have to wait until Mr. Taylor is gone?

The President. We're in the process of determining what that means.

NOTE: The exchange began at 9:48 a.m. at the Presidential Palace. In his remarks, the President referred to President John Agyekum Kufuor of Ghana; and President Charles Taylor of Liberia. A tape was not available for verification of the content of this exchange.

Remarks at Goree Island, Senegal
July 8, 2003

Mr. President and Madam First Lady, distinguished guests and residents of Goree Island, citizens of Senegal, I'm honored to begin my visit to Africa in your beautiful country.

For hundreds of years on this island, peoples of different continents met in fear and cruelty. Today we gather in respect and friendship, mindful of past wrongs and dedicated to the advance of human liberty.

At this place, liberty and life were stolen and sold. Human beings were delivered and sorted and weighed and branded with the marks of commercial enterprises and loaded as cargo on a voyage without return. One of the largest migrations of history was also one of the greatest crimes of history.

Below the decks, the Middle Passage was a hot, narrow, sunless nightmare, weeks and months of confinement and abuse and confusion on a strange and lonely sea. Some refused to eat, preferring death to any future their captors might prepare for them. Some who were sick were thrown over the side. Some rose up in violent rebellion, delivering the closest thing to justice on a slave ship. Many acts of defiance and bravery are recorded; countless others, we will never know.

Those who lived to see land again were displayed, examined, and sold at auctions across nations in the Western Hemisphere. They entered societies indifferent to their anguish and made prosperous by their unpaid labor. There was a time in my country's history when one in every seven human beings was the property of another. In law, they were regarded only as articles of commerce, having no right to travel or to marry or to own possessions. Because families were often separated, many were denied even the comfort of suffering together.

For 250 years, the captives endured an assault on their culture and their dignity. The spirit of Africans in America did not break; yet, the spirit of their captors was corrupted. Small men took on the powers and airs of tyrants and masters. Years of unpunished brutality and bullying and rape produced a dullness and hardness of conscience. Christian men and women became blind to the clearest commands of their faith and added hypocrisy to injustice. A republic founded on equality for all became a prison for millions. And yet in the words of the African proverb, "No fist is big enough to hide the sky." All the generations of oppression under the laws of man could not crush the hope of freedom and defeat the purposes of God.

In America, enslaved Africans learned the story of the Exodus from Egypt and set their own hearts on a promised land of freedom. Enslaved Africans discovered a suffering Saviour and found He was more like themselves than their masters. Enslaved Africans heard the ringing promises of the Declaration of Independence and asked the self-evident question, "Then why not me?"

In the year of America's founding, a man named Olaudah Equiano was taken in bondage to the New World. He witnessed all of slavery's cruelties, the ruthless and the petty. He also saw beyond the slaveholding piety of the time to a higher standard of humanity. "God tells us," wrote Equiano, "that the oppressor and the oppressed are both in His hands. And if these are not the poor, the brokenhearted, the blind, the captive, the bruised which our Saviour speaks of, who are they?"

Down through the years, African Americans have upheld the ideals of America by exposing laws and habits contradicting those ideals. The rights of African Americans were not the gift of those in authority. Those rights were granted by the Author of Life and regained by the persistence and courage of African Americans, themselves.

Among those Americans was Phyllis Wheatley, who was dragged from her home here in West Africa in 1761, at the age of 7. In my country, she became a poet and the first noted black author in our Nation's history. Phyllis Wheatley said, "In every human breast, God has implanted a principle which we call love of freedom. It is impatient of oppression and pants for deliverance." That deliverance was demanded by escaped slaves named Frederick Douglass and Sojourner Truth, educators named Booker T. Washington and W.E.B. Du Bois, and ministers of the Gospel named Leon Sullivan and Martin Luther King, Jr.

At every turn, the struggle for equality was resisted by many of the powerful. And some have said we should not judge their failures by the standards of a later time. Yet in every time, there were men and women who clearly saw this sin and called it by name.

We can fairly judge the past by the standards of President John Adams, who called slavery "an evil of colossal magnitude." We can discern eternal standards in the deeds of William Wilberforce and John Quincy Adams and Harriet Beecher Stowe and Abraham Lincoln. These men and women, black and white, burned with a zeal for freedom, and they left behind a different and better nation. Their moral vision caused Americans to examine our hearts, to correct our Constitution, and to teach our children the dignity and equality of every person of every race. By a plan known only to Providence, the stolen sons and daughters of Africa helped to awaken the conscience of America. The very people traded into slavery helped to set America free.

My Nation's journey toward justice has not been easy, and it is not over. The racial bigotry fed by slavery did not end with slavery or with segregation. And many of the issues that still trouble America have roots in the bitter experience of other times. But however long the journey, our destination is set: liberty and justice for all.

In the struggle of the centuries, America learned that freedom is not the possession of one race. We know with equal certainty that freedom is not the possession of one nation. This belief in the natural rights of man, this conviction that justice should reach wherever the Sun passes, leads America into the world.

With the power and resources given to us, the United States seeks to bring peace where there is conflict, hope where there is suffering, and liberty where there is tyranny. And these commitments bring me and other distinguished leaders of my Government across the Atlantic to Africa.

African peoples are now writing your own story of liberty. Africans have overcome the arrogance of colonial powers, overturned the cruelties of apartheid, and made it clear that dictatorship is not the future of any nation on this continent. In the process, Africa has produced heroes of liberation, leaders like Mandela, Senghor, Nkrumah, Kenyatta, Selassie, and Sadat. And many visionary African leaders, such as my friend, have grasped the power of economic and political freedom to lift whole nations and put forth bold plans for Africa's development.

Because Africans and Americans share a belief in the values of liberty and dignity, we must share in the labor of advancing those values. In a time of growing commerce across the globe, we will ensure that the nations of Africa are full partners in the trade and prosperity of the world. Against the waste and violence of civil war, we will stand together for peace. Against the merciless terrorists who threaten every nation, we will wage an unrelenting campaign of justice. Confronted with desperate hunger, we will answer with human compassion and the tools of human technology. In the face of spreading disease, we will join with you in turning the tide against AIDS in Africa.

We know that these challenges can be overcome, because history moves in the direction of justice. The evils of slavery were accepted and unchanged for centuries. Yet eventually, the human heart would not abide them. There is a voice of conscience and hope in every man and woman that will not be silenced, what Martin Luther King called "a certain kind of fire that no water could put out." That flame could not be extinguished at the Birmingham jail. It could not be stamped out at Robben Island prison. It was seen in the darkness here at Goree Island, where no chain could bind the soul. This untamed fire of justice continues to burn in the affairs of man, and it lights the way before us.

May God bless you all.

NOTE: The President spoke at 11:47 a.m. In his remarks, he referred to President Abdoulaye Wade of Senegal and his wife, Viviane.

Remarks to U.S. Embassy Personnel in Dakar
July 8, 2003

I thank you all very much for coming out to say hello. Laura and I are honored to be here with you all. I'm also, as you can see, traveling with quite distinguished company; our great Secretary of State Colin Powell is with us as well. I want to thank Ambassador Roth and his wife, Carol, for their service to our country.

I'm here to thank our fellow citizens who are serving a great land. Thank you for your dedication and your love of country. I want to thank the foreign nationals who are helping our fellow citizens make sure the Embassy runs so well.

This is an historic trip—oh, there's the Ambassador. But we are so honored to start our trip to this continent here in Senegal. I had the opportunity to go out to Goree Island and talk about what slavery meant to America. It's very interesting when you think about it, the slaves who left here to go to America, because of their steadfast— and their religion and their belief in freedom, helped change America. America is what it is today because of what went on

in the past. Yet when I looked out over the sea, it reminded me that we've always got to keep history in mind. And one of the things that we've always got to know about America is that we love freedom, that we love people to be free, that freedom is God's gift to each and every individual. That's what we believe in our country.

I'm here to spread that message of freedom and peace. Where we see suffering, America will act. Where we find the hungry, we will act. We're here not only on a mission of mercy; we're also here on a mission of alliance. And I want to thank you all for helping make that come true.

May God bless you all. And may God continue to bless Senegal and America. Thank you all very much.

NOTE: The President spoke at approximately 1 p.m. at Leopold Sedar Senghor International Airport. In his remarks, he referred to U.S. Ambassador to Senegal Richard Allan Roth and his wife, Carol.

Statement on House of Representatives Action on the Department of Defense Appropriations Bill
July 8, 2003

I commend the House for passing the Department of Defense Appropriations bill. The House action will help strengthen and

transform our military to keep America safe from the threats of this new era. The bill also continues my long-term commitment to improving the quality of life for our troops and their families through higher pay and good benefits. I am pleased the House has acted quickly and in a fiscally responsible manner, and I look forward to continuing to work with the Congress to ensure that we have the resources necessary to support our troops.

The President's News Conference With President Thabo Mbeki of South Africa in Pretoria, South Africa
July 9, 2003

President Mbeki. Good morning, ladies and gentlemen, and welcome. I'm very pleased indeed to welcome President Bush and his delegation, Mrs. Bush, and young Barbara. We are very pleased indeed, Mr. President, that you were able to come. It's very important for us because of the importance of the United States to our future and the United States to the future of our continent.

We've had very good discussions with the President, able to cover quite a wide field. We're very pleased with the development of the bilateral relations, strong economic links, growing all the time. Continued attention by the U.S. corporate world on South Africa is very critically important for us. AGOA has had a very big impact in terms of the development of our economy, and we continue to work on all of these matters.

It also gave us a chance to convey our thanks to the President for the support with regards to meeting the African continental challenges. That includes questions of peace and security, the NEPAD processes, again, very important for the future of our continent. That, of course, also gave an opportunity to discuss some of the specific areas of conflict around the continent.

I must say, President, that at the end of these discussions, we, all of us, feel enormously strengthened by your very, very firm and clear commitment to assist us to meet the challenges that we've got to meet domestically and on the African Continent. And therefore, President, thank you very much indeed for coming. We—the visit will certainly result in strengthened bilateral relations and strengthened cooperation to meet these other challenges that we face together.

But welcome, President.

President Bush. Mr. President, thanks. Gosh, we're honored to be here. Thank you for your wonderful hospitality. Thank Mrs. Mbeki as well for her gracious hospitality. It's a pleasure to be in South Africa.

Your Nation's recent history is a great story of courage and persistence in the pursuit of justice. This is a country that threw off oppression and is now the force of freedom and stability and a force for progress throughout the continent of Africa.

I appreciate our strong relationship, and it is a vital relationship. And Mr. President, I want to thank you very much for working hard to make it a vital and strong relationship. We've met quite a few times in the recent past, and every time we've met, I've—I feel refreshed and appreciate very much your advice and counsel and your leadership.

I appreciate the President's dedication to openness and accountability. He is advancing these principles in the New Partnership for African Development, the leader in that effort. The President and I believe that the partnership can help extend democracy and free markets and transparency across the continent of Africa. President Mbeki has shown great leadership in this initiative, and our country will support the leaders who accept the principles of reform, and we'll work with them. So thank you, Mr. President.

South Africa is playing a critical role in promoting regional security in Africa, and we discussed the President's leadership, for example, in Burundi. South Africa has helped achieve the peaceful inauguration of a new President. Or in the Congo, South Africa brokered an agreement on the creation of a transitional government. And in Zimbabwe, I've encouraged President Mbeki and his Government to continue to work for the return of democracy in that important country.

I also discussed with the President the importance of the continued cooperation in the global war on terror. The United States and South Africa are working together to strengthen this nation's border security and law enforcement. And we're devoting $100 million to help countries in eastern Africa increase their counterterror efforts. We are determined to fight and to join our friends to fight terrorists throughout this continent, throughout the world.

We're also committed to helping African nations achieve peace. In Liberia, the United States strongly supports the ceasefire agreement signed last month. President Taylor needs to leave Liberia so that his country can be spared further grief and bloodshed. Yesterday, I talked with President Kufuor of Ghana, who leads ECOWAS. I shared with the President our conversation. I assured him the United States will work closely with ECOWAS and the United Nations to maintain the ceasefire and to enable a peaceful transfer of power.

We're also pressing forward to help end Africa's long-running civil war in Sudan. My Special Envoy, Senator Jack Danforth, is returning to the region. We're making progress there. And his message is that there's only one option, and that's going to be peace. And his efforts are making good progress.

The President also discussed our action to combat HIV/AIDS. South Africa has re-

cently increased its budget to fight the disease, and we noticed and we appreciate that. America is now undertaking a major new effort to help governments and private groups combat AIDS. Over the next 5 years, we will spend $15 billion in the global fight against AIDS. People across Africa had the will to fight this disease but often not the resources, and the United States of America is willing to put up the resources to help in the fight.

We're committed to helping the people of Africa defeat hunger. We provided more than 500,000 metric tons of food aid to southern Africa over the past 18 months. This year we'll provide nearly $1 billion to address food emergencies. We care when we see people who are hungry. We look forward to working with Mr. President to alleviate suffering.

We're also working to expand trade, which I believe is the key to Africa's economic future. The African Growth and Opportunity Act is creating jobs and stimulating investment across the continent. Right here in South Africa, exports to the United States under AGOA have increased by 45 percent in the last year alone—significant progress. We're working with five nations of the Southern African Customs Union on a free trade agreement to help expand the circle of prosperity even wider.

Mr. President, our countries have many common interests. We also share a fundamental commitment to the spread of peace and human rights and liberty. By working in close partnership, we're serving both the interests of the people of South Africa and the United States.

I want to thank you for your friendship, appreciate the hospitality. It's been a great honor to be in your country.

President Mbeki. Thank you very much, President.

I understand that two U.S. journalists and two South African journalists will pose some questions.

HIV/AIDS Initiative

Q. Thank you, Mr. President. I'd like to direct the question to both Presidents, and it does concern the issue of HIV/AIDS and the $15 billion grant. Did you manage to reach some kind of understanding or consensus on the issue of how South Africa will access that money, on what terms South Africa will be able to access that money?

And President Bush, did you give any undertakings in terms of using your influence to ensure that there will be cheaper access—access to cheaper drugs and medicines?

And to President Mbeki, sir, did you——

President Mbeki. How many questions——

President Bush. Yes, I was going to say— [*laughter*].

Q. This is the last part.

President Bush. This is the ultimate five-part question. [*Laughter*]

Q. Did you give any undertaking in terms of the running out of the national treatment plan? Thank you.

President Mbeki. Well, as the President had indicated, we did indeed discuss this. The situation is that we received a request from the U.S. Government to say, can we make proposals as to how to access the fund, for what purposes—a program, a program that we would present. So we are working on that. We want to respond to that request from the United States Government as quickly as is possible. We will do that and convey it. So it will be out of that process of discussion that will result, out of that proposal between the U.S. Government and ourselves, that then will come a program, a particular concrete kind of action, with the necessary costing when we get to that stage. So that's where we are.

So the matter will be discussed in that way. And President Bush had indicated in our discussions that of course the U.S. Government is taking a comprehensive approach to this, which would, therefore, include questions of awareness, questions of health infrastructure, questions of treatment, and so on. So we will look at the totality of those and—in the proposal that we would make.

President Bush. We just named Tobias to be the Ambassador, nominated him to be the Ambassador, and he's—upon confirmation—will be working with the countries such as South Africa to develop a strategy—is what we need. We need a commonsense strategy to make sure that the money is well-spent. And the definition of "well-spent" means lives are saved, which means good treatment programs, good prevention programs, good programs to develop health infrastructures in remote parts of different countries so that we can actually get antiretroviral drugs to those who need help.

The cost of antiretroviral drugs has dropped substantially. But we did talk about the pharmaceutical union in a broader context. As you may know, the United States supported a moratorium on the enforcement of patent laws concerning those drugs related to diseases that were causing pandemics. And we will continue to work with South Africa as well as other countries to see if we can't reach a commonsense policy that, on the one hand, protects intellectual property rights and, on the other hand, makes, you know, lifesaving drugs or treatment drugs for, in some cases, lifesaving, in some cases that are proper for treatment, more widely available at reasonable costs.

But one reason I felt emboldened to ask the Congress for a substantial amount of new money for the AIDS Initiative was because of the cost of antiretrovirals, and it's significantly lower than it was a couple of years ago.

So we're making good progress. And I look forward to working with the President on putting together a sound strategy that saves lives. That's what our country is interested in. We're interested in dealing with this pandemic in a practical way.

Tom [Tom Raum, Associated Press]. But whatever you do, don't fall into that bad habit of asking both of us three or four questions. [*Laughter*] How about keeping it to one.

Liberia/Deployment of U.S. Troops Worldwide

Q. Mr. President, you have an assessment team in Liberia now to help you decide whether to send in U.S. troops as part of a peacekeeping effort.

President Bush. Right.

Q. U.S. troops are getting shot at increasingly in Iraq every day. We have troops in Kosovo, Bosnia, Afghanistan, Korea. What do you say to critics who suggest that our forces may be spread too thinly now to engage in further initiatives?

And to President Mbeki, do you think that the United States should play a more active role in peacekeeping, specifically in Liberia?

President Bush. Well, first, my answer to people is that we won't overextend our troops, period.

Secondly, we have made a commitment that we will work closely with the United Nations and ECOWAS to enforce the cease-fire, see to it that Mr. Taylor leaves office, so that there can be a peaceful transition in Liberia. We've made that commitment. I've said it clearly more than one time, like yesterday in Senegal, for example. So nothing has changed from about 12 hours ago on that question.

We do have assessment teams there to assess what is necessary to help with the transition. And the President brought up the question, and he can answer it his own way. But he asked whether or not we'd be involved, and I said, "Yes, we'll be involved." And we're now determining the extent of our involvement.

President Mbeki. Yes, certainly, we discussed this question with the President many years ago and agreed that it's critically important that we as Africans should, indeed, take responsibility for the future

of peace and stability on the continent. So that is a principal obligation that falls on us as Africans.

So as you would know, the West African states, ECOWAS, have agreed to send in troops into Liberia. And they are trying to move that process forward as quickly as is possible.

We appreciate very much the point that was made by the President of the commitment of the United States to lend support—the assessment teams are there to assess that—to lend support to those processes, processes of restoration of peace, making sure people don't starve, making sure that there's a restoration of democracy in Liberia.

So the U.S. will cooperate with the African troops that will go there. So it's not—we're not saying that this is a burden that just falls on the United States. It really ought to principally fall on us as Africans. Of course, we need a lot of support, logistics-wise and so on, to do that, but the will is there.

President Bush. Just one quick followup on that—violating of the one-answer policy. [*Laughter*] I think our money has helped train seven battalions of peacekeepers amongst African troops. And it's a sensible policy for us to continue that training mission, so that we never do get overextended.

And so one of the things you'll see us do is invigorate this—reinvigorate the strategy of helping people help themselves by providing training opportunities. I think we've trained five Nigerian battalions, if I'm not mistaken, one Senegalese. So we've got—but it's in our interest that we continue that strategy, Tom, so that we don't ever get overextended.

President Mbeki. Thanks.

Zimbabwe

Q. During the past week, the two Presidents or the Governments of—the Government of the U.S. and South Africa have expressed sharp differences about the best way to deal with the Zimbabwean question.

President Bush. Yes.

Q. And having met this morning, I wonder if the two Presidents have found the best approach or have agreed about the best approach to deal with Zimbabwe. I see that it has come up. Can we get from the smiles that you now have a formula to deal best with Zimbabwe? [*Laughter*]

President Mbeki. I didn't know, President, that we'd expressed sharp differences.

President Bush. That's right. [*Laughter*]

President Mbeki. No. We are absolutely of one mind, the two Governments and President Bush and myself are absolutely of one mind about the urgent need to address the political and economic challenges of Zimbabwe. It's necessary to resolve this matter as quickly as is possible.

We have said, as you would know, for a long time that the principle is rooted—principal responsibility for the resolution of these problems rests with the people of Zimbabwe and, therefore, have urged them—both the ruling party and the opposition, the Government and the opposition—to get together and seriously tackle all of these issues.

I did tell the President that, indeed, the Government—ZANU-PF and the MDC are indeed discussing. They are engaged in discussions on all of the matters that would be relevant to the resolution of these political and economic problems. So that process is going on. We have communicated the message to both sides that—indeed, as we agreed with the President—that it is very, very important that they should move forward with urgency to find a resolution to these questions.

Of course, again, as the President was saying, that apart from these important political issues about democrats and so on, you actually have ordinary people who are hungry in an economy which can't cope with them, and you can't allow that kind of situation to go on forever. So they are discussing.

We had discussed this matter earlier, sometime back, with the U.S. Government

that we have to find—we've got to find a way of getting a political solution, and we would indeed count very much on such economic, financial support as would come from the United States afterwards, in order to address the urgent challenges that face Zimbabwe.

So we didn't fight about any of what I've just said. [*Laughter*]

President Bush. We were smiling because we were certain a clever reporter would try to use the Zimbabwe issue as a way to maybe create tensions which don't exist.

Look, Zimbabwe is an important country for the economic health of Africa. A free, peaceful Zimbabwe has got the capacity to deliver a lot of goods and services which are needed on this continent in order to help relieve suffering. And it's a very sad situation that's taken place in that country.

Look, we share the same objective. The President is the person most involved. He represents a mighty country in the neighborhood who's, because of his position and his responsibility, is working the issue. And I'm not—not any intention of second-guessing his tactics. We share the same outcome. And I think it's important for the United States, whether it be me or my Secretary of State, to speak out when we see a situation where somebody's freedoms have been taken away from them and they're suffering. And that's what we're going to continue to do.

The President is the point man on this important subject. He is working it very hard. He's in touch with the parties involved. He is—he's making—he believes, making good progress. And the United States supports him in this effort.

Last question. Randy [Randall Mikkelsen, Reuters].

Intelligence on Iraq/Zimbabwe

Q. Yes, Mr. President. Do you regret that your State of the Union accusation that Iraq was trying to buy nuclear materials in Africa is now fueling charges that you and Prime Minister Blair misled the public?

And then, secondly, following up on Zimbabwe, are you willing to have a representative meet with a representative of the Zimbabwe opposition leader, who sent a delegation here and complained that he did not think Mr. Mbeki could be an honest broker in the process?

President Bush. Well, I think Mr. Mbeki can be an honest broker, to answer the second question.

The first question is—look, there is no doubt in my mind that Saddam Hussein was a threat to the world peace. And there's no doubt in my mind the United States, along with allies and friends, did the right thing in removing him from power. And there's no doubt in my mind, when it's all said and done, the facts will show the world the truth. There's absolutely no doubt in my mind. And so there's going to be a lot of, you know, attempts to try to rewrite history, and I can understand that. But I am absolutely confident in the decision I made.

Q. Do you still believe they were trying to buy nuclear materials in Africa?

President Bush. Right now?

Q. No, were they? I mean, the statement you made——

President Bush. One thing is for certain, he's not trying to buy anything right now. If he's alive, he's on the run. And that's to the benefit of the Iraqi people. But look,

I am confident that Saddam Hussein had a weapons of mass destruction program. In 1991, I will remind you, we underestimated how close he was to having a nuclear weapon. Imagine a world in which this tyrant had a nuclear weapon. In 1998, my predecessor raided Iraq based upon the very same intelligence. And in 2003, after the world had demanded he disarm, we decided to disarm him. And I'm convinced the world is a much more peaceful and secure place as a result of the actions.

Thank you all very much.

President Mbeki. Thanks a lot.

NOTE: The President's news conference began at 11:47 a.m. at the Presidential Guest House. In his remarks, President Bush referred to Zanele Dlamini, wife of President Mbeki; President Domitien Ndayizeye of Burundi; President Charles Taylor of Liberia; President John Agyekum Kufuor of Ghana; former Senator John C. Danforth, Special Envoy for Peace in the Sudan; Randall Tobias, nominee to be Global AIDS Coordinator, Department of State; and former President Saddam Hussein of Iraq. President Mbeki referred to the Zimbabwe African National Union Patriotic Front (ZANU-PF), political party of President Robert Mugabe of Zimbabwe, and the Movement for Democratic Change (MDC), the opposition party.

Statement on the Senate's Failure To Pass Medical Liability Reform Legislation
July 9, 2003

I am disappointed that the Senate has failed to pass medical liability reform legislation. The Nation's medical liability system is badly broken, and access to quality health care for Americans is endangered by frivolous and abusive lawsuits.

The medical liability crisis is driving good doctors out of medicine and leaving pa-

tients in many communities without access to both basic and specialty medical services. The American people want and deserve access to doctors in their own communities, yet the number of physicians has decreased in States without reasonable litigation reforms. The liability crisis, particularly the use of defensive medicine, also imposes substantial costs on the Federal Government and all Americans.

This is a national problem that deserves a national solution. The House of Representatives has already acted. For the sake of all Americans, it is time for the Senate to pass meaningful medical reform liability legislation and get it to my desk.

Message to the Congress Transmitting the District of Columbia's Fiscal Year 2004 Budget Request
July 9, 2003

To the Congress of the United States:

Consistent with my constitutional authority and sections 202(c) and (e) of the District of Columbia Financial Management and Responsibility Assistance Act of 1995 and section 446 of the District of Columbia Self-Governmental Reorganization Act as amended in 1989, I am transmitting the District of Columbia's Fiscal Year 2004 Budget Request Act.

The proposed Fiscal Year 2004 Budget Request Act reflects the major programmatic objectives of the Mayor and the Council of the District of Columbia. For Fiscal Year 2004, the District estimates total revenues and expenditures of $5.6 billion.

GEORGE W. BUSH

The White House,
July 9, 2003.

Remarks Following Discussions With President Festus Gontebanye Mogae of Botswana and an Exchange With Reporters in Gaborone, Botswana
July 10, 2003

President Mogae. Ladies and gentlemen of the press, honorable Ministers, you are probably wondering what we have been talking between the President and I. And I was just thanking him for, first of all, visiting us, but above all, for the generous assistance we have been receiving.

As you know, we are the country in southern Africa that is most seriously affected by HIV/AIDS, and we are receiving generous assistance from the United States Government, who are helping us with the testing and counseling centers and in which we are spending about $8 million U.S. a year, which is about 40 million pula in our own currency.

They have also responded to a request for human resources assistance, and they have restored the Peace Corps program. We are collaborating with our own private sector, the foundations in the United States—the Bill and Melinda Gates Foundation, the Merck Corporation Foundation—for providing us with antiretrovirals and also with assistance for mounting of our prevention campaign. That program is going very well.

I mention that—it is the most important—but also we are very grateful for AGOA, on behalf of ourselves, on behalf of Africa as a whole, because most African countries have benefited by AGOA. I was telling the President that in my view, AGOA is perhaps the most significant thing that United States has done for sub-Saharan Africa in recent decades.

As some of us—some of you will know, initially Namibia and us—and Botswana were left out of AGOA I, as a result of the level of our—[inaudible]—and we have since been included under AGOA II. And so the only issue is that the dispensation, that concession should be maintained, therefore, as long as AGOA remains, because like the President, we believe in trade. Of course, we believe in aid too— [laughter]—so both aid and trade and co-operation.

So that's what we have been talking about—of course, other things. But of course, there are a whole range of issues on which we consulted, reaching across the region, performance of our economy but the region of the south—of southern Africa and then sub-Saharan Africa as a whole.

President Bush. Mr. President, thanks. Listen, we're so honored that you invited us here. We're thrilled to be here. You have been a very strong leader. First, I want to commend you for your leadership. I appreciate your commitment to democracy and freedom, to rule of law and transparency. I want to congratulate you for serving your country so very well.

We did talk a lot of issues. We talked about the regional issues. We talked about the war on terror. We've got a great friend in the war on terror. We both understand that we must work together to share intelligence, to cut off money, to forever deny terrorists a chance to plot and plan and hurt those of us who love freedom.

I talked—spent some time on the HIV/AIDS issue. Botswana, as a result of the President's leadership, has really been on the forefront of dealing with this serious problem by, first and foremost, admitting that there is a problem and then by working to put a strategy in place to prevent and treat and to provide help for those who suffer.

And Mr. President, the United States of America stands squarely with you——

President Mogae. Thank you.

President Bush. ——with you and your Health Minister and your administration to help put together a strategy that will save lives.

We talked about the shortage of food in parts of Africa. We had a wide-ranging discussion. And President Mogae is a strong, visionary leader who I'm proud to call friend.

So thank you, Mr. President, for your hospitality.

We'll be glad to answer a couple of questions. If you'd like to call on somebody from your press corps first——

President Mogae. Does anyone want to ask——

President Bush. That's not the way we do it in—[laughter].

Zimbabwe

Q. To the U.S. President, yesterday when you met President Mbeki of South Africa, the MDC leader in Zimbabwe was not very excited about that. He feels you were misled. What are your views on that? Did you have any plans for Zimbabwe, and did you shelve them because of what you heard yesterday or are you still going to go ahead with them?

President Bush. Well, thank you very much. I made it very clear publicly, the position of this administration, and that is that we expect there to be democracy in Zimbabwe in order for the people of that country to advance. We did speak about Zimbabwe here. I explained why the Secretary of State and myself have been very outspoken on the subject. And we had a frank discussion with President Mbeki on Zimbabwe as well.

It is—it's a shame that that economy has gotten so weak and soft—it's a shame for Botswana; it's a shame for southern Africa—and that the weakness in the economy is directly attributable to bad governance. And therefore, we will continue to speak out for democracy in Zimbabwe.

Ryan of Bloomberg [Ryan Donmoyer, Bloomberg News]. There he is. Hi, Ryan. How are you?

Agricultural Subsidies

Q. Mr. President, in Evian you and the Europeans talked about maybe reducing agricultural subsidies. Is this something that has come up in your meeting today? And what assurances can you give to your African counterparts that this is something that the U.S. is serious about?

President Bush. Yes, that's a very good question. Absolutely, the subject of agricultural subsidies came up here today; it came up yesterday. I suspect—and it came up in Senegal. It will come up in every country we come to, because African leaders are worried that subsidies, agricultural subsidies, are undermining their capacity to become self-sufficient in food. That's part of the problem.

The other part of the problem is the lack of technological development in agriculture. And we talked about the need for genetically modified crops throughout the continent of Africa.

I told them the reality of the situation, that we have proposed a very strong reduction in agricultural subsidies. However, in order to make that come to be, there needs to be reciprocation from Europe and Japan in order to make the policy effective. We're committed to a world that trades in freedom, and we will work toward that through the Doha Round of the World Trade Organization.

African Growth and Opportunity Act

Q. To President Festus Mogae——
President Mogae. Yes, yes. Okay.
President Bush. This is a bad precedent, where the same person gets to ask two questions. [*Laughter*]

Q. There was a sentiment that Your Honor was going to ask the U.S. President if AGOA, the lifespan of AGOA, could be extended. Was that done today?
President Mogae. You bet. [*Laughter*]

President Bush. In plain English.
President Mogae. Yes.
Q. And for how long?
President Bush. Well, I've asked Congress to extend AGOA to '08, 2008. And the President, of course, said, "Well, fine, if that extension takes place, make sure we're a part of it." And he made his case very explicitly. Everybody in the delegation heard him clearly. And my response was, "We will work closely with you to see if that can't happen."

Tamara [Tamara Lipper], Newsweek.

Iraq/HIV/AIDS Initiative

Q. Thank you, Mr. President. I'm going to try for two questions as well.
President Bush. No, no, please don't do that. It may be the last question you get if you try. [*Laughter*] Go ahead.

Q. On this trip you've highlighted a lot of different success stories in Africa, the countries that have been successful in fighting AIDS or on trade. What do you hope Americans who are watching you take from your trip here?

And then secondly, on Iraq, given the sort of day-to-day challenges facing American soldiers there, how important—or is it increasingly important to find Saddam Hussein, and any updates on a hunt for him to really convince people he might be gone for good?

President Bush. Well, let me start with Iraq. Having talked to Jerry Bremer, the man in charge of the civilian operations there, he believes that the vast majority of Iraqi citizens are thrilled that Saddam Hussein is no longer in power. Secondly, there's no question we've got a security issue in Iraq, and we're just going to have to deal with person by person. We're going to have to remain tough.

Now, part of the issue that we've got to make clear is that any terrorist acts on infrastructure by former Ba'athists, for example, really are attacks on the Iraqi people. And therefore, the more involved the Iraqi citizens become in securing their own infrastructure and the more involved Iraqi citizens are in the transitional government, the more likely it is the average citizen will understand that once again the apologists for Saddam Hussein are bringing misery on their country.

The world will see eventually as freedom spreads that—what Saddam Hussein did to the mentality of the Iraqi people. I mean, we've discovered torture chambers where people, citizens, were tortured just based upon their beliefs. We've discovered mass graves, graves for not only men and women but graves for children. We discovered a prison for children—all aimed at—for Saddam Hussein to intimidate the people of Iraq. And slowly but surely, the people of Iraq are learning the responsibility that comes with being a free society.

We haven't been there long, I mean, relatively speaking. We've been there for 90 to 100 days—I don't have the exact number. But I will tell you, it's going to take more than 90 to 100 days for people to recognize the great joys of freedom and the responsibilities that come with freedom. We're making steady progress. A free Iraq will mean a peaceful world. And it's very important for us to stay the course, and we will stay the course.

The first question was about what I want Americans to know. The first thing I wanted the leadership in Africa to know is the American people care deeply about the pandemic that sweeps across this continent, the pandemic of HIV/AIDS, that we're not

only a powerful nation, we're also a compassionate nation.

You know, I laid out a very strong initiative on helping countries in the continent of Africa deal with AIDS. It's a—to me, it's an expression of the great, good heart of the American people. It doesn't matter what political party or what the ideology of the American citizen, the average citizen cares deeply about the fact that people are dying in record numbers because of HIV/AIDS. We cry for the orphan. We care for the mom who is alone. We are concerned about the plight and, therefore, will respond as generously as we can.

That's really the story that I want the people of Africa to hear. And I want the people of America to know that I'm willing to take that story to this continent and talk about the goodness of our country. And I believe we'll be successful, when it's all said and done, of making our intentions well-known.

Listen, thank you all.

NOTE: The President spoke at approximately 11:43 a.m. at the Gaborone International Convention Centre. In his remarks, he referred to Minister of Health Joy Phumaphi of Botswana; President Thabo Mbeki of South Africa; L. Paul Bremer III, Presidential Envoy to Iraq; and former President Saddam Hussein of Iraq. A tape was not available for verification of the content of these remarks.

Remarks at a Luncheon Hosted by President Mogae in Gaborone
July 10, 2003

President Mogae. The President of the United States, Mr. George W. Bush, and First Lady, Mrs. Laura Welch Bush; Your Lordship, the Chief Justice and Mrs. Nganunu; the Honorable Deputy Speaker of the National Assembly and Mrs.

Temane; honorable members of the Cabinet from the United States and from Botswana; distinguished ladies and gentlemen.

I'm delighted to once again welcome you to Botswana, Mr. President, and members of your high delegation. It is an honor and privilege on behalf of the Government and people of Botswana to thank you for honoring us with a visit and for your pro-African initiatives on AIDS and trade.

This visit, the second of its kind by a President of the United States, is indeed a welcome gesture of the friendship that exists between our countries. The United States and Botswana have enjoyed many years of fruitful and beneficial relations.

Recently, when Botswana appealed to the United States for help in the fight against HIV/AIDS, you not only increased the funding for the BOTUSA testing and counseling program, but also restored the Peace Corps program to mitigate the human resources constraints.

Our country, together with Namibia, has also been given special treatment under the Africa Growth and Opportunity Act, AGOA. In spite of the fact that Botswana graduated from the least-developed-country status several years ago, you, Mr. President, gave us a special dispensation which allows us to use third-country fabrics to produce textile goods for export to the U.S. market.

I am happy to say that, as in many other African countries, many jobs have been created for Botswana. We deeply appreciate your decision and are determined to maximize the benefits under this dispensation.

The assistance and cooperation we have received clearly demonstrates that in the United States, Botswana has a true and dependable partner. Mr. President, we also welcome your administration's encouragement of and collaboration with your country's private sector in the fight against the HIV/AIDS pandemic in sub-Saharan Africa as a whole and in Botswana in particular.

Distinguished ladies and gentlemen, may I now ask you to join me in drinking a toast to the continued good health and happiness of the President of the United States, Mr. George W. Bush, and First Lady, Mrs. Laura Bush, to continued friendship and cooperation between Botswana and the United States of America,

and of course, to international peace and security for which the President stands.

To the President.

[*At this point, the participants drank a toast.*]

President Mogae. Pula!
Audience members. Pula!
President Mogae. Pula!
Audience members. Pula!
President Bush. Well, thank you very much, Mr. President, for your warm words of welcome and for your friendship and your hospitality. And thank you, Madam First Lady, as well for the hospitality that you've shown Laura and me. We're delighted to make our first visit to Botswana and to see the vast and rich beauty of your country.

The United States and Botswana share many beliefs. We believe that democratic government provides the best protections for human dignity. We believe that political and economic liberty go together and that prosperity is another word for economic freedom. Botswana is known for the strength of your democracy and for the vigor of your economy. And that's a tribute to the leadership of President Mogae and his administration. You have demonstrated, sir, sound economic management and fiscal discipline and a commitment to free market principles. You have shown that you can build a nation's prosperity and transform the lives of its people. And your trade policies, Mr. President, are also ensuring strong commerce between Botswana and the United States, which will only grow in years ahead.

Botswana is also directly confronting HIV/AIDS and taking bold steps to overcome this crisis. We applaud your leadership. The people of this nation have the courage and the resolve to defeat this disease, and you will have a partner in the United States of America. My country is acting to help all of Africa in turning the tide against AIDS. This is the deadliest enemy Africa has ever faced, and you will not face this enemy alone.

Together, our two nations are determined to build an Africa that is growing in peace, in prosperity, and in hope. So let us toast to the enduring friendship between the United States and the Republic of Botswana.

Mr. President, to your health and to your country's success.

NOTE: The President spoke at approximately 12:30 p.m. at the Gaborone International Convention Centre. In his remarks, he referred to Barbara Mogae, wife of President Mogae. President Mogae referred to Chief Justice Julian Nganunu of Botswana's High Court; and Deputy Speaker of the Botswana National Assembly Bahiti Temane.

Remarks Following Discussions With President Yoweri Kaguta Museveni of Uganda and an Exchange With Reporters in Entebbe, Uganda
July 11, 2003

President Museveni. So here is your chance to see the heart of Africa, because from where we are to Cape Town is about 5½ hours by plane. From here to Alexandria is 5 hours. From here to Senegal is 7 hours by plane. From here to the Indian Ocean is 3 hours. To reach the center of the continent is only 2 hours. And no tour will be complete—[*inaudible*].

But we are most grateful that—[*inaudible*]—support, the financial support. But most important, the opening of the markets, because when somebody buys what I produce, he is giving me a little support. Why? First of all, he is giving me money—[*inaudible*]—because once I produce is a great example.

So we are very, very grateful you are helping, United States. Thank you so much.

President Bush. Thank you, sir. Mr. President, thank you for your hospitality. We have come at your invitation to herald your leadership. You have been a strong advocate of free trade because you understand the benefits of trade. My administration supports AGOA and the promises and opportunities that AGOA brings. You have been a strong leader in helping to resolve regional disputes. I want to thank you for that leadership.

And your country, as you noted, is strategically located in the heart of Africa. And therefore, you're drawn into a lot disputes. And you've done an excellent job of using your prestige and your position to help resolve those disputes. And we—I will continue to work with you to bring peace on the continent.

And finally, Mr. President, you have been a world leader, not just a leader on the continent of Africa but a world leader in the fight against HIV/AIDS. You have shown the world what is possible in terms of reducing infection rates. You have been honest and open about the AIDS pandemic and, therefore, have led your people to seek prevention and treatment and help and love.

And so Mr. President, we come to herald your leadership and to assure you and to assure the people of Uganda that when it comes to the struggle against hopelessness and poverty and disease, that you've got a friend in the United States. Thank you very much, sir.

President Museveni. Thank you.

Assistant Press Secretary Reed Dickens. Thank you all.

Q. Mr. President, can you take a question, sir, on the——

Assistant Press Secretary Dickens. Thank you all.

Ugandan Spokesperson. Those—you had the statements from our two Presidents. And actually we are asking you that you report what you've seen here. So we are pleased, really——

State of the Union Address

Q. With all due respect, Mr. President, can you take a question, sir?

President Bush. Sure.

Q. Why—can you explain how an erroneous piece of intelligence on the Iraq-Niger connection got into your State of the Union speech? Are you upset about it, and should somebody be held accountable, sir?

President Bush. I gave a speech to the Nation that was cleared by the intelligence services. And it was a speech that detailed to the American people the dangers posed by the Saddam Hussein regime. And my Government took the appropriate response to those dangers. And as a result, the world is going to be more secure and more peaceful.

NOTE: The President spoke at approximately 3 p.m. at the Imperial Botanical Beach Hotel. In his remarks, he referred to former President Saddam Hussein of Iraq. A tape was not available for verification of the content of these remarks.

Remarks at The AIDS Support Organisation Centre in Entebbe
July 11, 2003

Thank you all. Please be seated, unless you don't have a chair. [*Laughter*] Thank you so much for the gracious welcome. And I want to thank the people of Uganda for such a warm welcome for Laura and me. We love being here. I'm really glad we came.

I want to thank the President for his hospitality, and the First Lady, I want to thank you for your hospitality as well.

This is such a land of hope in the heart of Africa, is the best way to describe it. And I bring with me the good wishes of the American people to the citizens of Uganda.

I'm especially thankful to the staff and volunteers of TASO. I appreciate you, Dr. Alex. Thank you for your tour and your hospitality. You know, it's one thing to hear about the ravages of AIDS or to read about them; it's another thing to see them first-hand.

I oftentimes talk about the armies of compassion in my own country. There's no doubt in my mind, today I met generals in the armies—in the worldwide army of compassion. And I want to thank all of you who are involved in the fight to deal with this terrible pandemic.

A small place, a small house, you're doing great works of compassion. And the influence of TASO is bigger than you think. You have worldwide influence here because you've provided a model of care for Uganda. You've shown what can work here in this country. And Uganda, by confronting AIDS aggressively and directly, is giving hope to peoples all across the continent of Africa. We know what it takes to fight AIDS because TASO clinics and others like them are showing the way.

People who come through these doors need medical treatment, and you provide it. People who come here needing to learn about AIDS prevention; you give them important information. Men and women sometimes come to this place with terrible fears and a broken spirit. You receive them with kindness. You help them gain skills.

You care for their families. You encourage them to go forward with life.

The AIDS virus does its worst harm in an atmosphere of secrecy and unreasoning fear. TASO is speaking the truth. The President of Uganda speaks the truth. And therefore you're overcoming the stigma of the disease, and you're lifting despair. You're welcoming lonely, isolated people as brothers and sisters. You treat every soul with respect and dignity, because that's the only way to treat a child of God.

The disease of AIDS is fought with knowledge and medical skill. It also is fought with decent and loving hearts. TASO began here 16 years ago because of the vision of one woman. It's been my honor and Laura's honor to meet Noerine. Noerine, thank you. Noerine is a catalyst for change, a remarkable soul who acted when she lost her husband, Charles, to AIDS. Here's what Noerine said. She said, "I used to ask him, when he was ill, 'As you are lying there, what is the most precious thing?'" And he would say, "Just touching me, holding my hand, just being there." "And," says Noerine, "you don't have to be a doctor to do that."

The caring people of TASO have transformed so many lives, as Agnes told us. Agnes, we appreciate your testimony, and we appreciate your love. Her husband died in 1992 of AIDS, and TASO counselors encouraged her to get tested. She discovered she also had HIV and feared she did not have long to live. The clinic gave her treatment. Counselors brought food to her family and paid the school fees for one of her daughters.

In 1994, Agnes started volunteering to help at TASO by teaching children and counseling other women who have lost their husbands. She says that when people hear her story, they begin to think different: They get courage; they have the will to live.

Others here at TASO have shown the courage that turns loss and fear into something positive and good. Godfrey Monda

has worked here for a decade. In addition to supporting his own children, he cares for six children left by his two sisters who died of AIDS. Godfrey is a counselor to about 300 people in his region. Every 3 months, he and several coworkers take a boat to Goosie Island on Lake Victoria, where they train volunteers to combat AIDS and provide AIDS education with a drama group. Because of this good man's work, others will be spared from the grief his family has known.

And that is the kind of devotion and unselfish effort that turning the tide against AIDS requires all across the continent of Africa and all across the world. You're leading the way here in Uganda.

To win this fight, governments must also act with compassion and purpose. Governments have got to lead. And Mr. President, you're leading, and so is your administration. And I've been honored to meet the ministers of health, the AIDS coordinator, people of your Cabinet who understand when President Museveni says we must deal with the issue honestly and openly and compassionately.

President Museveni and Uganda have pursued a direct and comprehensive anti-AIDS strategy. They emphasize abstinence and marital fidelity as well as condoms to prevent HIV transmissions. They developed a strategy. They're implementing the strategy for the whole world to see, and the results have been magnificent.

Their approach has reduced the HIV infection rate to 5 percent in this country, the most dramatic decline in the world. For many in Uganda, the value of this achievement is beyond measure. Men and women are gaining years of life. More Ugandan children are growing up with mothers and fathers, and this country is reclaiming its future. Life by life, village by village, Uganda is showing that AIDS can be defeated across Africa.

However, the current efforts to oppose the disease are simply not equal to the need. And America understands that. Nearly 30 million people on this continent are living with HIV/AIDS, including 3 million children under the age of 15. More than 4 million people require immediate drug treatment, but just 1 percent of them are receiving the medicine they require.

Africa has the will to fight AIDS, but it needs the resources as well. And this is my country's pledge to the people of Africa and the people of Uganda: You are not alone in this fight. America has decided to act. Over the next 5 years, my country will spend $15 billion on the fight—to fight AIDS around the world, with special focus here on the continent of Africa. We'll work with governments and private groups and faith-based organizations to put in place a comprehensive system to prevent, to diagnose, and to treat AIDS. We will support abstinence-based education for young people in schools and churches and community centers. We will provide comprehensive services to treat millions of new infections.

Throughout all regions of targeted countries, we'll provide HIV testing. We'll purchase antiretroviral medications and other drugs that are needed to extend lives. We will help establish broad and efficient networks to deliver drugs, including by motorcycle, just as you did here in Uganda. We will help build and renovate and equip clinics and laboratories. We will prepare doctors and nurses and other health care professionals to treat AIDS more effectively.

The resources our country provides will help to hire and train childcare workers, to look after orphans, and to provide care at home to many AIDS patients. In other words, we want to join you in the war against the pandemic of AIDS. We want to be on your side in a big way.

This is the proper place for me to summarize the initiative that I've laid out before Congress. Because there's no doubt about it, in order to be effective, there has to be a willingness on the part of the people of the country, and you've got a willingness here in Uganda. You've got good leadership. You've got good leadership in your religious institutions. You've got good leadership throughout your Government. You've got fantastic doctors. You've got the people themselves that are willing to rise up and to confront the disease.

You know, I believe God has called us into action. I believe we have a responsibility—my country has got a responsibility. We are a great nation; we're a wealthy nation. We have a responsibility to help a neighbor in need, a brother and sister in crisis. And that's what I'm here to talk about. And I want to thank you for giving me the chance. I want to thank you for giving me the chance to come and share the compassion of my country for the people who suffer. We look forward to working with you. We look forward to being on the forefront of saying that when history called, we responded.

So, Mr. President, I'm honored that you would receive us. Laura and I are thrilled to be spending time in your beautiful country. I want to thank those who have provided witness and provided music. I want to thank you all for your hospitality. May God bless the people of Uganda. May God continue to bless the United States of America.

Thank you very much.

NOTE: The President spoke at 4:10 p.m. In his remarks, he referred to President Yoweri Kaguta Museveni of Uganda and his wife, Janet; and Alex G. Coutinho, director, and Noerine Kaleeba, founder, The AIDS Support Organisation.

Remarks Prior to Discussions With President Olusegun Obasanjo of Nigeria and an Exchange With Reporters in Abuja, Nigeria
July 12, 2003

President Obasanjo. Mr. President——

President Bush. Here, I'll stand up with you.

President Obasanjo. Is that what you want?

President Bush. Oh, absolutely. I want to be over here. [*Laughter*]

President Obasanjo. It is, indeed, a matter of general honor and pleasure for me to welcome you, Mr. President, to our country, Nigeria. On behalf of all the people of Nigeria, I sincerely extend to you our warmest greetings on this historic visit to our continent of Africa in general and to Nigeria in particular.

President has generally acknowledged that much has changed in the world since the end of the cold war. There's no doubt there is an emerging new world order, with new realities of nations and people throughout the world—their international outlooks, seek new friends and confirm old realities in the bid to find fresh places for global peace, harmony, and security.

In this imagined new world order, Mr. President, the rest of the world acknowledges that the United States of America will remain a key player politically, economically, and militarily. Thus we appreciate your visit to our continent as indication that Africa is to be reckoned with in the emerging world order. We salute your visit to so many African countries—four of them—and now Nigeria, in particular, as an expression that Africa should not be sidelined or even detached from the—of the emerging world order.

We in Africa realize the extent to which we are ultimately responsible for our own development and that we are the architects of our fortune or misfortune. Nevertheless, this is also generally true that hardly any country has transformed its fortunes without external support from friends and well-wishers. That is why we acknowledge with deepest appreciation the role that the United States has played and continues to play, particularly within the G–8, in supporting the vision of the New Partnership for African Development, NEPAD. As you are well aware, Mr. President, NEPAD is our vision as well as our blueprint for making our continent great.

Through the NEPAD, African leaders have made a commitment to the African peoples and to the world to work together in developing the continent by consolidating democracy, good governance, and implementing such general social, economic development programs. Implicit in the NEPAD program are all the universal values, such as democracy, human rights, rule of law, eradication of corruption, conflict resolution, and fight against terrorism. We are hopeful that NEPAD will strengthen Africa's position in the emerging world order.

Here in Nigeria, we are making bold strides to consolidate democracy and reform our Government structures as well as the national economy. We also have continuing and new regional responsibilities, especially in the area of maintaining security. These areas require global understanding, cooperation, and substantial financial support. You will agree with me that sustainable national reforms are central to regional and global transformation and for development.

Thank you, Mr. President.

President Bush. Thank you, friend.

It's my honor, Mr. President, to be here as your guest. Gosh, we've met three or four times already. You keep telling me to come to your country—finally made it. And I'm glad we're here. It's been a— it's an honor.

Listen, Nigeria is a very important country on the continent of Africa. And because of your forthrightness and your style and your commitment, you're a very important leader on this continent, and I'm honored to be here with you.

I appreciate very much your commitment to trade and markets, and we look forward to being an active trading partner with Nigeria. I appreciate your commitment to regional peace, and we will work with Nigeria and ECOWAS on issues such as Liberia. I appreciate very much your focus on education, and the United States stands ready to help.

But most of all, Mr. President, I appreciate your honesty and openness and forthrightness when it comes to battling the pandemic of AIDS. You're truly an international leader on this issue. And the United States of America, when Congress acts, will stand side by side with leaders such as yourself to fight the pandemic of AIDS to save lives.

So Mr. President, it's an honor to be here. I've been looking forward to this visit for a long time. I appreciate your leadership, and I appreciate your friendship. Thank you very much.

Director of Central Intelligence/State of the Union Address

Q. Mr. President, do you have faith in your CIA Director?

President Bush. Yes, I do, absolutely. I've got confidence in George Tenet. I've got confidence in the men and women who work at the CIA, and I continue to—I look forward to working with them and—as we win this war on terror.

Q. Mr. President——

Assistant Press Secretary Reed Dickens. Thank you all. Thank you.

Q. Is the matter over then?

Q. Mr. Bush, what about——

Q. Do you consider the matter over, sir, that——

President Bush. I do.

Liberia

Q. What about Liberia? Is America sending troops to Liberia?

President Bush. The President and I just talked about Liberia, and we are—our assessment teams are still in place. We need to know exactly what is necessary to achieve our objectives. The first objective, of course, is for Mr. Taylor to leave the country, which he said he is—do. And I want to thank the President for his leadership on that issue. It's been a tough issue, but he's led. And the world is grateful for that.

Secondly, we've got a commitment to the cease-fire. And therefore, we need to know exactly what it means to keep the cease-fire in place. Thirdly, we got a commitment to relieve human suffering, and we need to know what that has required. And so, we're still in the process of assessing. And I told the President we would be active. And the definition of that will be made known when we're—when we understand all the parameters.

Q. See a decision next week, sir?

Assistant Press Secretary Dickens. Thank you all very much. Thank you——

President Bush. I'm not sure yet when, Randy [Randall Mikkelsen, Reuters].

Assistant Press Secretary Dickens. Pool, let's go.

Q. Thank you, sir.

President Bush. Thank you.

NOTE: The President spoke at approximately 10:58 a.m. at Aso Presidential Villa. In his remarks, he referred to President Charles Taylor of Liberia. A tape was not available for verification of the content of these remarks.

Remarks at the Leon H. Sullivan Summit in Abuja
July 12, 2003

Thank you all. Thank you very much. Thanks a lot. Please be seated—please. J.C., thank you for that warm introduction. I thought you might have lost your touch—[*laughter*]—as a retired Member of Congress, but you didn't. I'm proud to be introduced by my friend. And I want to thank you all very much for such a warm welcome.

This the last day of our journey through Africa. And each of us is drawn to this summit by the vision of the late Leon Sullivan. And I'm so honored to be in the presence of Mrs. Grace Sullivan. It's great to see you again, Mrs. Sullivan.

We believe that relationship between America and Africa will benefit both our people. Work of the summit to promote commerce and understanding across the Atlantic is important work, and I'm determined that the American Government will do its part. We will help nations on this continent to achieve greater health and education and trade with the world. Working together, we can help make this a decade of rising prosperity and expanding peace across Africa.

We've got a great visit here, thanks to the hospitality of the President, my friend. Mr. President, thank you for your friendship. Thank you for your leadership. I appreciate the President's leadership on crucial issues. I particularly appreciate the fact that he's willing to confront the HIV/AIDS epidemic head on, with an honest approach.

Madam First Lady, thank you very much for your hospitality as well. Laura and I have enjoyed getting to be with you. I thank the Vice President and all the members of the Government who are here.

I'm particularly pleased to be traveling with such good company in Colin Powell and Condi Rice and Andy Card and other members of my administration. I want to thank Congressman William Jefferson from the State of Louisiana for being here. And I understand that Rodney Slater is here as well. Rodney, thank you for coming. Rodney, good to see you.

I appreciate so much the Sullivan Summit leadership: Hope Sullivan and Carl Masters and, of course, one the great public servants in America—America's history, Andy Young. Thank you all.

Dave O'Reilly understands the definition of corporate responsibility, and I appreciate the leadership of Dave and Chevron. Their job is not only to make a return for their shareholders; their job is to show compassion as well. And I appreciate your leadership, Dave.

I'm especially thankful to all the citizens of Nigeria for such a warm welcome, such gracious hospitality. Nigeria is a nation of great diversity and great promise. My country deeply appreciates the friendship of Nigeria.

This has been a wonderful week for Laura and me. We have seen the rich culture and resources of Africa as well as the continuing challenges of Africa. We have met really fine people. I have confidence in Africa's future because I believe in the goodness and the compassion and the enterprise of the men and women on this continent. With greater opportunity, the peoples of Africa will build their own future of hope. And the United States will help this vast continent of possibilities to reach its full potential.

I began my trip in Senegal, where I met with President Wade and seven other leaders of West Africa. These leaders are committed to the spread of democratic institution and democratic values throughout Africa. Yet those institutions and values are threatened in some parts of Africa by terrorism and chaos and civil war. To extend liberty on this continent, we must build security and peace on this continent.

Several African governments face particular dangers from terrorists, and the United States is working closely with those nations to fight terror, and we will do more. I proposed a new $100-million initiative to help those governments in east Africa protect their people and to fight terrorist networks. The United States is also supporting the efforts of good friends all across this continent, friends such as Mauritania. We will not allow terrorists to threaten African peoples or to use Africa as a base to threaten the world.

America is also committed to helping end Africa's regional wars, including those in Sudan and Congo, the Ivory Coast, and Liberia. In Liberia, the United States strongly supports the cease-fire that was signed last month. President Taylor needs to leave Liberia so that his country can be spared further grief and bloodshed.

In Dakar this week, I met with President Kufuor of Ghana. He also leads ECOWAS. I assured him the United States will work closely and in concert with the United Nations and ECOWAS to maintain the cease-fire and to allow a peaceful transfer of power.

This week, I've also seen the dedicated efforts of Africans who are fighting hunger and famine, illiteracy, and a deadly preventable disease. At the TASO clinic in Entebbe and here at the National Hospital, I saw the heroic efforts of African doctors and nurses and volunteers who are devoted to saving and extending lives. I also heard from men and women who are living with AIDS and continue to lead productive and hopeful lives. The progress we are already seeing in parts of Africa is proof that AIDS can be defeated in Africa.

The people of Africa are fighting HIV/AIDS with courage. And I'm here to say, you will not be alone in your fight. In May, I signed a bill that authorizes $15 billion for the global fight on AIDS. This week, a committee of the House of Representa-

tives took an important step to fund the first year of the authorization bill, and the Senate is beginning to take up debate. The House of Representatives and the United States Senate must fully fund this initiative for the good of the people on this continent of Africa.

On this journey, I've also seen the economic potential of Africa. Botswana is a model of economic reform and has one of the highest sustained economic growth rates in the world. Yet, far too many Africans still live in poverty. And providing effective and promoting—providing effective aid, promoting free markets and the rule of law, and encouraging greater trade, we will help millions of Africans find more opportunity and a chance for better life.

To be effective, development aid requires progrowth policies and strong reforms in the nations that receive the aid. The Millennium Challenge Account I have proposed would direct resources to countries with governments that rule justly, root out corruption, encourage entrepreneurship, and invest in the health and education of their people.

Countries making these changes will gain more help from America. They will gain more foreign investment, more trade, and more jobs. And I call upon the United States Congress to finalize the MCA legislation and to fully fund the first year of this initiative.

One specific obstacle to development in many countries is the lack of access to capital. Many Africans find it impossible to get a loan for a business or a home, and this makes it far difficult for people to build equity or to borrow money to start a business. The United States has some of the most effective mortgage markets in the world. We understand the flow of capital, and we want to share this knowledge with the nations of Africa.

So I've asked Secretary of the Treasury John Snow to work with experts in America and Africa and with financial institutions like Fannie Mae and the Overseas Private

Investment Corporation to help strengthen and broaden capital markets on this continent. With the ability to borrow money to buy homes and start businesses, more Africans will have the tools to achieve their dreams.

My travels this week underscore the critical importance of trade to the economic future of Africa. Open trade has proven its ability to increase the standards of living and to create new jobs and to encourage the habits of freedom and enterprise.

In Botswana, I visited one of our new Hubs for Global Competitiveness that is helping African businesses sell their products into the United States and on global markets. I have seen—and I know you have seen—how the African Growth and Opportunity Act, AGOA, is bringing jobs and investment and opportunity to sub-Sahara Africa. And to help give businesses the confidence to make long-term investments in Africa, Congress must extend AGOA beyond 2008.

Our Nation will work to complete a free trade agreement with the nations of the Southern African Customs Union to create new opportunities for farmers and workers and entrepreneurs all across Africa. To achieve our goals of a more peaceful, hopeful, and prosperous Africa, we need a partnership of our governments. We also need partnerships among our people, our businessmen and doctors and bankers and teachers and clergy. These are the kinds of bridges that Leon Sullivan dedicated his life to building. And you're continuing that good work, and I thank you for that.

Eight years ago at the Sullivan Summit, delegates launched the MedHelp Foundation, which is training and equipping physicians in Senegal. This foundation has also assembled a team of American medical professionals in Senegal that has conducted more than 150 operations, including 88 open-heart surgeries.

Another group established by Reverend Sullivan is the International Foundation For Education and Self-Help. Over the past 10 years, the foundation has helped build more than 182 rural schools in Africa, placed 820 American teachers in African schools. Today I'm pleased to announce that the United States Agency for International Development will give a new $5-million grant to the foundation, resources that will help send 90 American teachers to Africa to train more than 14,000 African educators. In these and many other ways, you are doing more than fulfilling the dreams of one man; you're helping to unlock the potential of an entire continent.

At Goree Island earlier this week, I spoke of how the struggles of African Americans against the injustices of slavery and segregation helped to redeem the promise of America's founding. Today, you are carrying the same passion for liberty and justice from America to Africa. Americans believe that people in every culture and in every land have the right to live in freedom and deserve the chance to improve their lives. And we know that the people of Africa, when given their rights and given their chance, will achieve great things on this continent of possibilities.

May God bless Africa, and may God continue to bless America.

NOTE: The President spoke at 1:35 p.m. at Congress Hall. In his remarks, he referred to former Representative J.C. Watts; Rev. Leon H. Sullivan's wife, Grace Sullivan, and daughter, Hope L. Sullivan, summit president; Andrew J. Young, summit chairman; Carl Masters, summit vice chairman; President Olusegun Obasanjo of Nigeria and his wife, Stella; Vice President Atiku Abubakar of Nigeria; Rodney Slater, board member, Leon H. Sullivan Foundation; David J. O'Reilly, chairman of the board and chief executive officer, ChevronTexaco Corp., summit corporate sponsor; President Abdoulaye Wade of Senegal; President Charles Taylor of Liberia; and President John Agyekum Kufuor of Ghana.

The President's Radio Address
July 12, 2003

Good morning. I've spent this week visiting Africa, a continent of great challenge and promise. Throughout this journey and in meetings with leaders of more than 10 countries, I have reaffirmed America's strong commitment to a more peaceful and prosperous future for all the peoples of Africa.

America supports democratic and economic reforms in Africa because we know the power of freedom to lift whole nations and bring new opportunities to millions. And in a time of growing commerce across the globe, we are working to ensure that the nations of Africa are full partners in the trade and prosperity of the world.

Progress in Africa depends on peace and stability, so America is standing with friends and allies to help end regional wars. And against the murderous ambitions of terrorists, the United States and African countries are working in common purpose. We will not permit terrorists to threaten African peoples or to use Africa as a base to threaten the world.

The United States is also committed to helping African peoples overcome one of the gravest dangers they have ever faced, the spread of HIV/AIDS. And the need is urgent. Across the continent today, nearly 30 million people are living with HIV/AIDS, including 3 million children under the age of 15. In Botswana alone, where I visited on Thursday, nearly 40 percent of the adult population has HIV.

People in Africa are waging a courageous fight against this disease. In another nation on my trip, Uganda, urban and rural clinics are providing vital medical care, counseling, sound and honest information on AIDS prevention. Thanks to caring people and wise government policies, Uganda has dramatically reduced its infection rate. More Ugandan children are growing up with mothers and fathers, and Uganda is reclaiming its future.

The tremendous progress in Uganda is showing that AIDS can be defeated across Africa. Yet current efforts to oppose the disease are simply not equal to the need. More than 4 million people require immediate drug treatment, but just 1 percent of them are receiving the medicine they require. Africa has the will to fight AIDS, but it needs the resources as well.

Over the next 5 years, the United States Congress has authorized $15 billion to fight AIDS around the world, with a special focus on 14 nations in Africa and the Caribbean. Working with governments and private groups and faith-based organizations, we will build on the progress in Uganda by establishing a comprehensive system to prevent, diagnose, and treat AIDS.

We will support abstinence-based education for young people and provide comprehensive services to prevent millions of new infections. We will provide HIV testing and purchase antiretroviral medications and other drugs that are needed to extend lives. We will help establish broad and efficient networks to deliver drugs. We will help build, renovate, and equip clinics and laboratories. We'll prepare doctors, nurses, and other health care professionals to treat AIDS more effectively. And the resources America provides will also help to hire and train childcare workers to look after orphans and provide care at home to many AIDS patients.

This week, a committee of the House of Representatives took an important step to fund the first year of this effort. I ask the Senate to move quickly as well. And I urge the entire Congress to fully fund my request for the Emergency Plan for AIDS Relief so that America can help turn the tide against AIDS in Africa.

All of our actions in Africa—from fighting AIDS to promoting security and prosperity across the continent—represent the ideals that have always guided America in the world. The United States is committed to the success of Africa, because the peoples of Africa deserve to live in freedom and dignity and to share in the progress of our times.

Thank you for listening.

NOTE: The address was recorded at approximately 8:15 a.m., local time, on July 11 at the Sheraton Pretoria Hotel and Towers in Pretoria, South Africa, for broadcast at 10:06 a.m., e.d.t., on July 12. The transcript was made available by the Office of the Press Secretary on July 11 but was embargoed for release until the broadcast. Due to the 6-hour time difference, the radio address was broadcast after completion of all other Presidential activities for July 12. The Office of the Press Secretary also released a Spanish language transcript of this address.

Statement Welcoming the New Leadership of the African Union
July 12, 2003

I congratulate President Joaquim Alberto Chissano of Mozambique on his appointment as the new President of the African Union. I also extend congratulations to President Konare of Mali on his appointment as the new Chair of the Commission of the African Union. I am confident that the African Union—and the people of Africa—will be well-served by the experience and vision these two leaders bring to these important posts.

Africa is a place of both great potential and daunting challenges. The United States shares the hopes of peoples across the African Continent for a future of greater peace, greater freedom, and greater development. And America will work in partnership with all African nations committed to these great goals.

The African Union has the mandate and the responsibility to respond effectively to Africa's challenges, including instability, terrorist threats, challenges to the effective rule of law, HIV/AIDS, poverty, and humanitarian emergencies. I look forward to the African Union continuing to play a vital role in shaping Africa's future under its dynamic new leadership.

Remarks Following Discussions With Secretary-General Kofi Annan of the United Nations and an Exchange With Reporters
July 14, 2003

President Bush. I'm so honored that Kofi Annan has come back to the Oval Office. We've had a great discussion. I briefed him on my trip to Africa, his native continent, and I told him that I was most impressed with the possibilities of the continent. I saw the potential, and I also saw many of the problems. And I want to thank the Secretary-General for his work on hunger and HIV/AIDS. We're going to work closely with him to help defeat the pandemic.

And the other thing we talked about was Liberia. I assured him that our Government's position is a strong position. We want to enable ECOWAS to get in and help create the conditions necessary for the cease-fire to hold, that Mr. Taylor must leave, that we'll participate with the troops. We're in the process, still, of determining what is necessary, what ECOWAS can bring to the table, when they can bring it to the table, what is the timetable, and be able to match the necessary U.S. help to expediting the ECOWAS' participation.

I told the Secretary-General that we want to help, that there must be a U.N. presence, quickly, into Liberia. He and I discussed how fast it would take to blue-helmet whatever forces arrived, other than our own, of course. We would not be blue-helmeted. We would be there to facilitate and then to leave. And we had a good discussion. And I think we had a meeting of minds on that subject.

We talked about Iraq. And I told him and assured him that the United States would stay the course because we believe freedom is on its way to the Iraqi people. And by that I mean that the Iraqi people are beginning to assume more and more responsibility in their society. Free society requires a certain kind of responsible behavior. And we're seeing more and more of that amongst the Iraqi citizens. Our deep desire is to make sure that the infrastructure is repaired, that people are educated, and health care delivery systems are good.

I was honest in my appraisal when I told him that I recognize certain elements of the former regime are interested in keeping the infrastructure blown up because of— for pure power reasons, and that—I told him, and I will continue to speak as clearly as I can that an attack on the Iraqi infrastructure by the Ba'athists are—is an attack on the Iraqi people. And it's those Iraqis who are causing the continued suffering, where there's suffering in Iraq.

But we're making good progress. I'm proud of Jerry Bremer's work. And then the—we also talked about other issues that are on his mind and my mind. The long and short of it is we had a great discussion.

Mr. Secretary-General, I'm honored you're here.

Secretary-General Annan. Thank you very much, Mr. President. I think it is fair to say that it's wonderful that I should be meeting the President soon after the return—his return from Africa, my own continent. We weren't too far away. I was in Mozambique when he was in South Africa and Botswana.

But I would want to thank the President for the interest in the continent and his determination to help defeat the AIDS pandemic. I think it is a tragedy that is not only taking away the future of Africa; it is really destroying the present.

And it's a disease that takes parents away from children, teachers away from students, doctors away from hospitals. So the effort that is going in is absolutely worthwhile. And at the African Union Summit, this topic was very much on everyone's mind.

We also discussed, as the President has indicated, the situation in Liberia. And I'm satisfied with the discussions we've had and the approach the U.S. Government is taking. And of course, there is an assessment team in west Africa, but we have more or less agreed to a general approach on the Liberian issue, and I'm very pleased with that.

We talked about at least where the President's leadership has made a difference. Over the past couple of weeks, things are going in the right direction. We have bumps in the road, but I think, with the determination of the leaders and the support of the international community, we will make progress on this very difficult issue.

In Iraq, we were encouraged to see the formation of the Governing Council yesterday. And I must say that my special representative, Sergio de Mello, and Mr. Bremer are working very well together.

And on the Hill, I indicated that regardless of the differences that existed between nations before the war, now we have a challenge. The challenge is to stabilize Iraq, to help Iraq to become a peaceful, stable, and prosperous state. And I think everyone needs to help. An Iraq that is at peace with itself and its neighbors is in the interest of the neighbors and the entire international community.

So I would want to see the entire community, international community, come together to assist the Iraqi people and to help us stabilize a region.

President Bush. Thank you, Kofi.

Quality of Intelligence/Iraqi Weapons of Mass Destruction

Q. Mr. President, thank you. On Iraq, what steps are being taken to ensure that questionable information like the Africa uranium material doesn't come to your desk and wind up in your speeches?

President Bush. Well, let me first say that, you know, I think the intelligence I get is darn good intelligence. And the speeches I have given were backed by good intelligence. And I am absolutely convinced today, like I was convinced when I gave the speeches, that Saddam Hussein developed a program of weapons of mass destruction and that our country made the right decision.

We worked with the United Nations—as Kofi mentioned, not all nations agreed with the decision, but we worked with the United Nations. And Saddam Hussein did not comply. And it's the same intelligence, by the way, that my predecessor used to make the decision he made in 1998.

We are in the process now of interrogating people inside of Iraq to—and looking at documents, exploring documents to determine the extent that—what we can find as quickly as possible. And I believe, firmly believe, that when it's all said and done, the people of the United States and the world will realize that Saddam Hussein had a weapons program.

Steve [Steve Holland, Reuters].

Liberia

Q. On Liberia, are you now telling us that you will send U.S. troops to Liberia, and how many, and when will this happen?

President Bush. Yes, see, that's—what I'm telling you is that we want to help ECOWAS. It may require troops, but we don't know how many yet. And therefore, it's hard for me to make a determination until I've seen all the facts. And as Kofi mentioned, there's still—or the Secretary-General mentioned, excuse me—[laughter]—there's still—a little informal here. They are still—our teams, our military is assessing ECOWAS' strength, how soon, how quick, what kind of troops, who they are, to determine what is necessary from our side to fulfill the commitment I have made that we will help maintain the ceasefire.

By the way, this is conditional upon Mr. Taylor leaving. He's got to leave. I think everybody understands that. We discussed that, by the way, in Nigeria, with President Obasanjo, who clearly understands that as well. But we're still, Steve, determining the facts. It is very difficult for me to make a decision until I see the facts.

Q. Well, when do you think——

President Bush. Well, I don't know. That's an interesting question. We asked that question today at a national security briefing. And as soon as we can get it, there is—the Secretary-General has been very helpful in urging nations to move forward with those plans. We hear numbers all the time as to—you know, Nigeria may be able to contribute this, or so and so may be able to contribute that. Maybe you'd like to answer the question—I mean, as soon as possible is the answer. We'd like to get the assessment teams. There has been two such teams out and about, and we'd like to get the information as soon as possible.

Secretary-General Annan. And Jacques Klein is going to be the special representative—the gentleman with the red tie—in

Liberia. So you'll be seeing a lot of him, and you can talk to him.

Q. No long-term commitments——

President Bush. Correct. I think everybody understands any commitment we had would be limited in size and limited in tenure. Our job would be to help facilitate an ECOWAS presence which would then be converted into a U.N. peacekeeping mission.

Secretary-General Annan. Maybe I should add something here. The understanding which is emerging now is for the ECOWAS forces to send in a vanguard of about 1,000 to 1,500 troops. And I think this is something that they have worked out amongst themselves and now discussing in Accra with the—also with the U.S. team. After that, from what I gather, Taylor— President Taylor will leave Liberia, and then the force will be strengthened, hopefully with U.S. participation and additional troops from the west African region. And eventually, the U.N. blue helmets will be set up to stabilize the situation, along the lines that we've done in Sierra Leone, and once the situation is calmer and stabilized, the U.S. would leave and the U.N. peacekeepers would carry on the operation.

President Bush. Yes, Dana [Dana Bash, CNN], one last question.

State of the Union Address

Q. Mr. President, back on the question of Iraq and that specific line that has been in question——

President Bush. Can you cite the line? [*Laughter*]

Q. Really? I could, if you gave me time.

President Bush. When I gave the speech, the line was relevant.

Q. So even though there has been some question about the intelligence—the intelligence community knowing beforehand that perhaps it wasn't, you still believe that when you gave it——

President Bush. Well, the speech that I gave was cleared by the CIA. And look, I mean, the thing that's important to realize is that we're constantly gathering data. Subsequent to the speech, the CIA had some doubts. But when I gave the—when they talked about the speech and when they looked at the speech, it was cleared. Otherwise, I wouldn't have put it in the speech. I'm not interested in talking about intelligence unless it's cleared by the CIA. And as Director Tenet said, it was cleared by the CIA.

The larger point is, and the fundamental question is, did Saddam Hussein have a weapons program? And the answer is: Absolutely. And we gave him a chance to allow the inspectors in, and he wouldn't let them in. And therefore, after a reasonable request, we decided to remove him from power, along with other nations, so as to make sure he was not a threat to the United States and our friends and allies in the region. I firmly believe the decisions we made will make America more secure and the world more peaceful.

Thank you.

NOTE: The President spoke at 2:11 p.m. in the Oval Office at the White House. In his remarks, he referred to President Charles Taylor of Liberia; L. Paul Bremer III, Presidential Envoy to Iraq; former President Saddam Hussein of Iraq; and President Olusegun Obasanjo of Nigeria. Secretary-General Annan referred to Sergio Vieira de Mello, U.N. Special Representative for Iraq; and Ambassador Jacques Klein, U.N. Special Representative for Liberia.

Statement on the Establishment of the Iraqi Governing Council
July 14, 2003

The establishment of the Iraqi Governing Council is an important step forward in the ongoing transition from ruthless dictatorship to a free and democratic Iraq with Iraqis determining their own future. We look forward to working with the Council as it moves toward a democratic and prosperous Iraq, at peace with its neighbors.

Statement on Signing Legislation To Provide Bill Emerson and Mickey Leland Hunger Fellowships
July 14, 2003

Today I am signing into law H.R. 2474, which would permit the Congressional Hunger Center to spend up to $3 million in funds appropriated for each of fiscal years 2003 and 2004 to provide Bill Emerson and Mickey Leland Hunger Fellowships.

Upon signing the Farm Security and Rural Investment Act of 2002 on May 13, 2002, I stated that the method of appointing members to the Board of Trustees for the Hunger Fellowship Program runs afoul of the Appointments Clause of the Constitution. The current legislation does not adequately address this constitutional problem, in that it simply provides that the Hunger Fellowship Program will be administered for 2 years by a private, nonprofit corporation, the Congressional Hunger Center. Again, I remain prepared to work with the Congress on legislation that will provide a long-term solution for this constitutional infirmity. To avoid any constitutional concerns stemming from the provision of funds to the Congressional Hunger Center, I instruct the head of the department to whose agency these funds are appropriated to treat the money as a grant and ensure the Center's compliance with the terms of its grant.

GEORGE W. BUSH

The White House,
July 14, 2003.

NOTE: H.R. 2474, approved July 14, was assigned Public Law No. 108–58. An original was not available for verification of the content of this statement.

Message to the Congress Transmitting Proposed Legislation To Implement the United States-Chile Free Trade Agreement
July 15, 2003

To the Congress of the United States:

I am pleased to transmit legislation and supporting documents to implement the United States-Chile Free Trade Agreement (FTA). The Agreement will further open Chile's markets for U.S. manufactured goods, agricultural products, services, and investors. It will increase competition and consumer choice. The FTA will enhance prosperity in the United States and Chile, serve the interest of expanding U.S. commerce, and advance our overall national interest.

The U.S.-Chile FTA is the first United States free trade agreement with a South American country. We hope the FTA will add momentum to Chile's continued implementation of the free market economic policies that have made Chile a model for its Latin American neighbors. This Agreement will also encourage other countries in the Western Hemisphere to follow Chile's path, furthering our efforts to establish a Free Trade Area of the Americas.

My Administration is strongly committed to securing a level playing field for America's workers, farmers, and businesses. The Congress helped advance that policy by passing Trade Promotion Authority in the Trade Act of 2002 (the "Trade Act"). The Congress can help us take another important step by approving this Agreement and the implementing legislation. United States workers and businesses are currently at a competitive disadvantage in the Chilean market. Chile is an associate member in Mercosur and has FTAs with many other countries, including Canada, Mexico, and the 15 members of the European Union. Securing an FTA with Chile will ensure that U.S. workers and businesses will receive treatment in the Chilean market that is as good as or better than their competitors.

In negotiating this FTA, my Administration was guided by the negotiating objectives set out in the Trade Act. More than 85 percent of trade in consumer and industrial goods between the United States and Chile will be free of duties immediately upon implementation, and most remaining tariffs on U.S. exports to Chile will be eliminated within 4 years after that. More than three-quarters of U.S. farm goods will enter Chile duty free within 4 years and all duties on such goods will be phased out over 12 years. At the same time, the Agreement includes measures to ensure

that U.S. firms and farmers have an opportunity to adjust to imports from Chile.

This Agreement opens opportunities for our services businesses, which now account for nearly 65 percent of our gross domestic product and more than 80 percent of employment in the United States. Chile will grant substantial market access to U.S. firms across nearly the entire spectrum of services, including banking, insurance, securities and related financial services, express delivery services, professional services, and telecommunications.

This Agreement provides for state-of-the-art intellectual property protection and recognizes the importance of trade in the digital age by including significant commitments on trade in digital products. In addition, it ensures that electronic commerce will stay free of duties and discriminatory rules.

United States citizens and businesses that invest in Chile will have significant increased protections. This Agreement promotes rule of law and enhances transparency and openness in order to foster a more secure environment for trade and investment. Furthermore, Chile will provide U.S. investors with important substantive protections that Chilean investors already enjoy in the United States.

The United States and Chile have also agreed to cooperate on environment and labor issues and to establish mechanisms to support those efforts. A number of important cooperative projects that will promote environmental protection are identified for future work. The FTA encourages the adoption of high labor and environmental standards, obligates each country to enforce its own labor and environmental laws, and makes clear that domestic labor and environmental protections may not be reduced in order to encourage trade or investment. The Agreement also preserves our right to pursue other legitimate domestic objectives, including the protection of health and safety, consumer interests, and national security.

Trade and openness contribute to development, the rule of law, economic growth, and international cooperation. Chile is a close partner of the United States, and this Agreement will strengthen those ties.

With the approval of this Agreement and passage of the implementing legislation by the Congress, we will advance U.S. economic and political interests, while encouraging others to work with us to expand free trade around the world.

GEORGE W. BUSH

The White House,
July 15, 2003.

Message to the Congress Transmitting Proposed Legislation To Implement the United States-Singapore Free Trade Agreement
July 15, 2003

To the Congress of the United States:

I am pleased to transmit legislation and supporting documents to implement the United States-Singapore Free Trade Agreement (FTA). The Agreement will further open Singapore's markets and increase competition and consumer choice. This is America's first FTA with an Asian-Pacific nation, and we hope it will serve as a benchmark for future free trade agreements with other nations in the region. The Agreement will enhance prosperity in the United States and Singapore, serve the interest of expanding U.S. commerce, and advance our overall national interest.

My Administration is strongly committed to securing a level playing field for America's workers, farmers, and businesses. The Congress helped advance that policy by passing Trade Promotion Authority in the Trade Act of 2002 (the "Trade Act"). The Congress can help us take another important step by approving this Agreement and the implementing legislation. Without this Agreement, U.S. workers and businesses could be placed at a competitive disadvantage, because Singapore has signed or is currently working on free trade agreements with Japan, Canada, Australia, Mexico, and India.

In negotiating this FTA, my Administration was guided by the negotiating objectives set out in the Trade Act. The Agreement locks in tariff-free access for all U.S. goods, including textile and agriculture products, and addresses other barriers to trade. It opens opportunities for our services businesses, which now account for nearly 65 percent of our gross domestic product and more than 80 percent of employment in the United States. Through this FTA, Singapore will grant substantial additional market access to U.S. firms across a broad spectrum of services, including banking, insurance, securities and related financial services, express delivery services, professional services, and telecommunications. The Agreement also incorporates commitments on regulatory transparency that will be of special help to services business.

This Agreement provides state-of-the-art intellectual property protection, including significant commitments on trade in digital products. It ensures that electronic commerce will stay free of duties and discriminatory rules. In addition, Singapore will accede to international treaties dealing with copyright and access issues for the Internet.

United States citizens and businesses that invest in Singapore will have significant increased protections. This Agreement enhances transparency and openness in order to foster a more secure environment for trade and investment. Furthermore, Singapore will provide U.S. investors with important substantive protections that Singaporean investors already enjoy in the United States.

Singapore and the United States have also agreed to cooperate on the environment and labor issues and to establish mechanisms to support those efforts. The FTA obligates each country to enforce its own labor and environmental laws and makes clear that domestic labor or environmental protections may not be reduced in order to encourage trade or investment. The Agreement also preserves our right to pursue other legitimate domestic objectives, including the protection of health and safe-

ty, consumer interests, and national security.

Trade and openness contribute to development, the rule of law, economic growth, and international cooperation. Singapore is a close partner of the United States, and this Agreement will strengthen those ties.

With the approval of this Agreement and passage of the implementing legislation by the Congress, we will advance U.S. economic, security, and political interests, while encouraging others to work with us to expand free trade around the world.

GEORGE W. BUSH

The White House,
July 15, 2003.

Letter to the Speaker of the House of Representatives Transmitting Requests To Change Appropriations Law and a Fiscal Year 2004 Budget Amendment
July 15, 2003

Dear Mr. Speaker:
I ask the Congress to consider the enclosed requests to change FY 2003 appropriations law and an FY 2004 budget amendment for the Department of Veterans Affairs, none of which will affect budget levels.

The details of these requests are set forth in the enclosed letter from the Director of the Office of Management and Budget.

Sincerely,

GEORGE W. BUSH

NOTE: This letter was released by the Office of the Press Secretary on July 16. An original was not available for verification of the content of this letter.

Remarks to Urban Leaders
July 16, 2003

I thank you all for coming. I'm joined by some pretty distinguished company up here. I want to thank my friends the social entrepreneurs of America—[*laughter*]—for standing up here today. I want to talk about a couple of subjects.

First, I want to introduce Condoleezza Rice, my National Security Adviser, who, as I understand it, is going to stay afterwards and answer some questions about our trip, that I appreciate you doing.

Let's talk about the values that make our country unique and different. We love freedom here in America. We believe freedom is God's gift to every single individual, and we believe in the worth of each individual. We believe in human dignity, and we believe where we find hopelessness and suffering, we shall not turn our back. That's what we believe.

And there are—in this land of plenty, there are people who hurt, people who wonder whether or not the American experience, what they call the American Dream, is meant for them. And I believe the American Dream is meant for everybody. And when we find there's doubt, we've got to bring light and hope, and so that's what we're here to talk about today. And the men up here represent a representative sample of what we call the faith community in America, people who first and foremost have been called because of a calling much higher than government.

I say "social entrepreneurs" because in many of our faith institutions, we find people who are willing to reach out in the neighborhood in which they exist to help those who hurt and those who are in need. They're willing to take a new tack, a tack based upon faith, to heal hearts and provide hope and provide inspiration, so that the American Dream is available in every corner in America. And where we find those programs which are effective, society ought to support those programs.

What I'm saying is, we ought not to fear faith. We ought not to discriminate against faith-based programs. We ought to welcome what I call neighborhood healers in the compassionate delivery of help so that people can experience the greatness of our country.

Of course, that then leads to the question of public money, taxpayers' money. My attitude is, taxpayers' money should and must fund effective programs, effective faith-based programs, so long as those services go to anybody in need. We ought to focus on—we ought to ask the question in our society, "Is the faith-based program working," not focus on the fact that it's a faith-based program.

The Government, as it gives support, as it provides help to the faith-based program and in return asks for help for solving social problems, as it does that, it should never discriminate. It should never cause the faith-based program to lose its character or to compromise the mission. That's the basic principles of the Faith-Based Initiative which you've heard a lot about. Really what we're doing is, we're signing up the armies of compassion which already exist and saying, "What can we do to help you fulfill your calling and your mission?" That's really what we're doing.

I signed an Executive order banning discrimination against faith-based charities by Federal agencies. We waited for Congress to act. They couldn't act on the issue. So I just went ahead and signed an Executive order which will unleash—which says the Federal agencies will not discriminate against faith-based programs. They ought to welcome the armies of compassion as opposed to turning them away.

I know you've heard from some of my key Cabinet Secretaries. Within their secretariat are offices designed to speak up for, defend, and empower faith-based groups, specially created within the bureaucracy.

Look, I fully understand the issue, the frustration some face. And it's a frustration based upon a long practice here at the Federal level, and that is, there's no place for faith-based programs and trying to help people in need. And therefore, we'll discriminate, shove out of the way, not deal with, make it hard for, create barriers to entry. And my administration is absolutely committed to reducing those barriers to entry. And we've created these offices whose sole function it is to, one, recognize the power of faith and, two, recognize there are fantastic programs all throughout the country on a variety of subjects, all based upon faith, all changing lives, all making American life better, and therefore, folks would be enlisted in making sure the American Dream extends throughout our society.

And let me give you some examples, particularly those who might be tuning in to this moment. People—"What do you mean by faith-based discrimination?" Well, in Seattle, there was an earthquake, and the Federal Emergency Management Agency gave disaster relief funds to schools but denied them to the Seattle Hebrew Academy. In other words, schools—public schools got the funds from FEMA, but not a religious school. And so we've changed that rule. That's the kind of discrimination that I— that may make some sense to people who are not exactly sure what I'm talking about.

Another interesting example is, in Boston, the Old North Church, the famous historic landmark, needed preservation funds; yet it was denied Federal help because it was a church. And that's not right. That's not right. It makes no sense, and therefore, we're changing those kinds of rules.

And we're also making sure that Federal monies are available. It's one thing to talk about a Faith-Based Initiative, but there needs to be money in the system available for the faith-based programs in order for— to make it work. And that's money that's coming out of these agencies already. I mean, there's—we spend a lot of money here in Washington, and that—monies ought to be accessible to effective faith-based programs which heal people from all walks of life. It's—money is not going to proselytize; money is going to save lives.

And let me give you some examples of what is working today, maybe examples that you already have heard about, particularly when you go to the White House conferences as we try to describe how to access the system.

In Columbus, Ohio, St. Stephen's Community House—faith-based program—is using a—nearly $1 million from the Department of Education to expand its afterschool program. There's kind of an inter-

esting use of education dollars that will help faith-based programs fulfill their mission.

The Frederick Douglass Community Development Corporation, started by the Memorial AME Zion Church in Rochester, New York, has received more than $5 million from HUD to build low-income houses for seniors. The AME Church decided to do something about the housing issue, as far as the seniors go in their congregation, and accessed Federal money and put together a housing project. Now a lot of people don't—when they think about the AME Church or any church for that matter, they don't think housing. Except I know some social entrepreneurs from my State—right, Evans?—[*laughter*]—who have used their facilities, their skills to go ahead and to build homes.

The Operation New Hope and City Center Ministries in Jacksonville, Florida, and the Exodus Transitional Community in East Harlem went to the Department of Labor, and they received labor funds for job training programs for ex-offenders. A person gets out of prison, checks in at the church, and the church says, "Wait, we want to help you get back into society; not only will there be some lessons to be learned, but also, here's some training money. Here's a training course." So it's a practical application of taxpayers' money to meet societal needs. And one of the greatest societal needs is—we have is to make sure our—you know, a guy who's spent time in the pen not only receives spiritual guidance and love, but spiritual guidance and love can only go so far. And it's also helpful to have him be trained in a job which exists. In other words, there's practical application of taxpayers' money that we want to get into the hands of our faith-based organizations all throughout our society.

People say, "Well, we're already doing that." Now, what's happening is that the same programs are being funded over and over and over again. In other words, there's kind of a rut. And that doesn't encourage the entrepreneurial spirit that we're interested in.

So one of the things we've done here in the White House to deal with this issue is we've started—and Jim Towey is—we've got an office dedicated, by the way, to the Faith-Based Initiative. And we've started White House conferences to explain to people how the process works. And Towey handed me this book when I came in. These are the different pots of money, if you will, that are accessible to the faith community so that you can help fund the programs.

Now, look, we've got to do a better job of making sure that we explain what we mean by the Faith-Based Initiative. I understand that. It requires education. People can read everything they want into it. When they hear "Faith-Based Initiative," they—that all of a sudden opens everybody's imagination in the world to vast possibilities, some which exist and some which don't. [*Laughter*]

And so therefore we're reaching out to explain to people the practical applications. The Compassion—Capital Compassion Fund, which Congress has funded—I've asked for $100 million; they gave it 30 million and 35 million over the last 2 years—but that money goes to help smaller charities learn how to fill out grants, learn what it means to access Federal monies.

It's one thing for people, however, to learn how to fill out a grant. It's another thing to have the grant fall on deaf ears. So we're also changing habits here in Washington, DC. And that's what the office of the—within these departments are all designed to do, to facilitate, to make it easier for people to access, to make sure that we really do tap the heart and soul of our country.

Evans—Tony Evans first kind of woke me up to this. We were in Greenville, Texas, together, and he said, "The best welfare programs already exist on the street corners of inner-city Dallas," in this case. "They're open 24 hours a day. They've got

a fantastic guidebook"—[*laughter*]—"been around a long time." [*Laughter*] "The motto of the workforce is clear: Love your neighbor." And it dawned on me how true he is. There's no need to reinvent. We've got it in place. And so therefore, when I lay out an initiative that talks about saving the lives of drug offenders, really what I'm saying is, is that I understand that when you change a person's heart, you can change their habits. So let's enlist it, the faith community, on the goal of saving people's lives who happen to be hooked on drugs.

Six hundred million dollars over 3 years—I would hope that the faith community gets very much involved when Congress funds this. And by the way, part of this mission is for me to remind Congress they need to fund it. But once funded, it's very important for the faith community to be involved. The 10-step program is a faith initiative, when you really think about the—how it works. And I know many of you who run churches and synagogues and mosques in America are worried about addiction in your neighborhoods. And we want to help because we believe—we know—that some of the most effective programs are those that work when a heart is changed.

I've also laid out a mentoring initiative. I would love to have every child who has a mother or dad in prison to have a mentor. The most vulnerable of our population are those who may have a mom or a dad incarcerated. And they need love. They need a lot of love. And the best way to provide love is to find somebody who's willing to love them through a mentoring program.

I went to the Amachi program in Philadelphia—perhaps you all know about it—out of the Bright Hope Baptist Church, saw the program that works. There's a lot of initiatives around from the faith-based program that track the child who needs to be mentored. And the best place to find mentors, of course, is you can find them every Sunday. But we need help to make sure the program works. And so Congress I've asked to get this program moving.

My point is, we've got some Federal initiatives, job training, education, addiction. We've got a housing initiative here, by the way, that I'm deeply concerned about, what they call a minority gap in America. Too many—relative to the Anglo community, too many minorities don't own their own homes. I believe in an ownership society. I know when somebody owns their home, they've got such a fantastic stake in the future.

The faith community can help in homeownership. The Federal Government's got to help a lot here. We've got to make sure there is more affordable homes. We've got to provide tax incentives for people to build homes in inner cities. We've got to have downpayment help. And we've got to make sure that the contracts—I can understand somebody, a first-time homebuyer, getting a little nervous when they pull up the contract and the print's about that big, and nobody understands what's in the print. And a lot of people don't want to sign something they're not sure what it's about. And so we've got education programs through our housing institutions to teach people what it means to buy a home and how to help them access the downpayment help and also to make sure the contracts are clear and understandable.

This is a mission at home, is to help people. And you know, Government can help. I like to say, Government can pass out money, but it cannot put hope in people's hearts or purpose in people's lives. And that's why it's vital for our country to count on those who can put hope in people's hearts and a sense of purpose in people's lives, and that's our faith community.

You know, we will accomplish a lot here at home if we use all the resources available to our communities. And I will tell— continue to tell the American people, one of the great untapped resources for Gov-

ernment is to work side by side with the faith community. And I want to thank you all for your—hearing the call.

Now, look, before I end, I do want to also remind you that we will not turn our back on people who suffer in the world as well. I have just come from Africa, and I'd like to share some thoughts, if you don't mind.

First—and Condi was traveling with me, of course. I don't dare go overseas without her. [*Laughter*] At Goree Island, we stood at the Point of No Return, and it was a moving moment for our entire delegation. I went to Auschwitz earlier, and then I went to here, and it reminded me of the capacity for mankind to be cruel.

But the interesting thing that I've come to realize, that I spoke at Goree Island, was, those who were sent to America as slaves and their ancestors who lived in a segregated society stood strong, never gave up faith, and in fact, helped America find her soul and her conscience.

It's an interesting historical twist, when you think about it. Those who were chained, sent in those ships, separated from their families, those who were really beaten down, never lost their spirit, never lost their desire for freedom and hope, stood strong in the face of the oppressor, finally made the oppressor feel guilty, and in fact made us realize what it meant, "liberty and justice for all."

South Africa and Botswana and Uganda and Nigeria—and by the way, it took a long time to fly from Senegal to South Africa. [*Laughter*] It took longer to fly from Senegal to South Africa than it took from America to Senegal, which means we're covering a lot of country. [*Laughter*]

It's a continent of vast potential, is the way I'd like to describe it, a continent of possibility. And it's in our national interest that Africa do well. Africa has got to deal with a lot of issues. And first of all, the policy of this Government is to understand Africans are plenty capable of dealing with issues themselves; they just need help.

So for example, when it comes to helping deal with regional conflicts, one of the things we've got to do is help train their militaries so that they've got the capacity to move in and separate warring factions. One of the problems Africa faces, of course, is there is—every time there's a civil war, there's a lot of hurt, death, displacement. It makes it awfully hard for a society to function that is at war with itself, as you know.

In those countries, I was struck by its potential and struck by the issues that are faced, one—education issues and health issues of course—no bigger issue in my judgment, however, than the pandemic of HIV/AIDS. And we live in an amazing world, and yet in the midst of our world, there's a lot of folks who are dying and will die. And it's time for the United States of America to act and act in a big way, which is what we're going to do.

Reverend Rivers went over just to make sure that I fulfilled my promise. He was watching my every move. [*Laughter*] I asked for 15 billion. Now let me just give you a quick update; then Condi will be glad to answer any other questions you have about the trip.

Some countries are prepared for our aid. As a matter of fact, a lot of countries are. And that was a very important question to ask. If in fact we fund—and we will fund, and I want to thank you for your help in convincing Congress that they've got to fund the initiative. As you know, we have authorized it. Now they've got to write the check. And we will—we will. But it was very important for us to see whether or not the—for example, the capacity to distribute antiretrovirals was in place. Nothing worse than stockpiling medicines that never get distributed to the actual people. We're not interested in helping organizations. We're interested in helping organizations actually get the medicine to the people.

And we saw a good infrastructure. The Catholic Church, for example, in Uganda is fully prepared to pave the way for distribution of antiretrovirals, at the same time help with education and prevention.

The first step, by the way, is for leadership to stand up and admit there is an issue. You've got to admit there's a problem. And most of the societies that we saw admitted there's a significant problem, starting with the leaders. You know, President Museveni of Uganda and President Obasanjo of Nigeria are very strong and said, "We've got an issue. Forget stigma. We've got a health issue that we must deal with as a society."

And so, in America, the first thing we do is look for willingness to participate, and we saw some strong leadership, which is really important. The attitudes are changing on the continent.

Secondly, we're looking for infrastructure, people who understand what works. You, know, there's an interesting effect with the antiretroviral drugs. It's called the Lazarus effect. And if we can get those antiretrovirals out, and people begin to—out in the country and in the cities, of course—people begin to improve, and all of a sudden, somebody sees a neighbor improving: "Well, maybe I've got hope." So hope begins to rise.

And so we've got to get these medicines out, and we've got to get a strategy out and a plan out. And what I'm telling you is, we saw some good strategies and some good plans proposed by strong leaders, which is a very heartening thing. Our taxpayers have got to know that when we spend that money, it's going to go to save lives.

The other key component, interestingly enough, in Africa that's going to make a huge difference is the faith-based community. The faith-based community from all religions, all walks of life, are interested in being a part of this—solving this pandemic.

And the other issue is hunger. Our country puts a billion a year up to help feed the hungry. And we're by far the most generous nation in the world when it comes to that, and I'm proud to report that. This isn't a contest of who's the most generous. I'm just telling you as an aside. [*Laughter*] We're generous. We shouldn't be bragging about it. But we are. We're very generous.

However, one of the things it seems like we've got to do is help Africa feed herself. There is no reason in the world why the great continent of Africa can't be self-sustaining in food, and not only self-sustaining; how about being—the capacity to help others eat. And it's got a great potential.

So that's the mission. The mission at home is to help those who hurt and make the vast potential of America available to every citizen. The mission abroad is to use our good heart and good conscience and not turn our back away when we see suffering.

It has been a—it's a huge honor to represent our country overseas. It is a—I am a proud American. I'm proud of what we stand for. I'm proud of our heritage. I understand we've had tough times in our history. But the thing about it is, we never get stuck in history. We always move beyond. We're always trying to improve. And we base it, our history and our decision-making, our future, on solid values. The first value is, we're all God's children.

May God bless you. Thank you for your time.

NOTE: The President spoke at 1:27 p.m. in Room 450 of the Dwight D. Eisenhower Executive Office Building. In his remarks, he referred to Rev. Tony Evans, Oakcliff Baptist Church, Dallas, TX; Rev. Eugene F. Rivers III, Azusa Christian Community, Dorchester, MA; President Yoweri Kaguta Museveni of Uganda; and President Olusegun Obasanjo of Nigeria.

Statement on House of Representatives Action on the "Project BioShield Act of 2003"
July 16, 2003

In my State of the Union Address, I outlined a major research and production effort called Project BioShield to better protect the American people against possible bioterrorist attacks. I commend the House for passing the "Project BioShield Act of 2003." This legislation will help spur the development and availability of next generation countermeasures against biological, chemical, nuclear, and radiological weapons. I urge the Senate to act on this very important legislation.

Letter to Congressional Leaders on Review of Title III of the Cuban Liberty and Democratic Solidarity (LIBERTAD) Act of 1996
July 16, 2003

Dear _____ :

Consistent with section 306(c)(2) of the Cuban Liberty and Democratic Solidarity (LIBERTAD) Act of 1996 (Public Law 104–114), (the "Act"), I hereby determine and report to the Congress that suspension for 6 months beyond August 1, 2003, of the right to bring action under title III of the Act is necessary to the national interests of the United States and will expedite a transition to democracy in Cuba.

Sincerely,

GEORGE W. BUSH

NOTE: Identical letters were sent to Richard G. Lugar, chairman, and Joseph R. Biden,

Jr., ranking member, Senate Committee on Foreign Relations; Ted Stevens, chairman, and Robert C. Byrd, ranking member, Senate Committee on Appropriations; Henry J. Hyde, chairman, and Tom Lantos, ranking member, House Committee on International Relations; and C.W. Bill Young, chairman, and David R. Obey, ranking member, House Committee on Appropriations.

The President's News Conference With Prime Minister Tony Blair of the United Kingdom
July 17, 2003

President Bush. Good afternoon. It is, once again, a pleasure to welcome the Prime Minister, Tony Blair, and Cherie Blair to the White House. Mr. Prime Minister, fabulous speech. Congratulations.

In his address to Congress this afternoon, Prime Minister Blair once again showed the qualities that have marked his entire career. Tony Blair is a leader of conviction, of passion, of moral clarity, and eloquence. He is a true friend of the American people. The United Kingdom has produced some of the world's most distinguished statesmen, and I'm proud to be standing with one of them today.

The close partnership between the United States and Great Britain has been and remains essential to the peace and security of all nations. For more than 40 years of the cold war, we stood together to ensure that the conflicts of Europe did not once again destroy the peace of the world. The duties we accepted were demanding, as we found during the Berlin blockade and other crises. Yet British and American leaders held firm, and our cause prevailed.

Now we are joined in another great and difficult mission. On September the 11th, 2001, America, Britain, and all free nations saw how the ideologies of hatred and terror in a distant part of the world could bring

violence and grief to our own citizens. We resolved to fight these threats actively, wherever they gather, before they reach our shores. And we resolved to oppose these threats by promoting freedom and democracy in the Middle East, a region that has known so much bitterness and resentment.

From the outset, the Prime Minister and I have understood that we are allies in this war, a war requiring great effort and patience and fortitude. The British and American peoples will hold firm once again, and we will prevail.

The United States and Great Britain have conducted a steady offensive against terrorist networks and terror regimes. We're dismantling the Al Qaida network, leader by leader, and we're hunting down the terrorist killers, one by one.

In Afghanistan, we removed the cruel and oppressive regime that had turned that country into a training camp for Al Qaida, and now we are helping the Afghan people to restore their nation and regain self-government.

In Iraq, the United States, Britain, and other nations confronted a violent regime that armed to threaten the peace, that cultivated ties to terror and defied the clear demands of the United Nations Security Council. Saddam Hussein produced and possessed chemical and biological weapons and was trying to reconstitute his nuclear weapons program. He used chemical weapons in acts of murder against his own people.

The U.N. Security Council, acting on information it had acquired over many years, passed more than a dozen resolutions demanding that the dictator reveal and destroy all of his prohibited weapons. A final Security Council resolution promised serious consequences if he continued his defiance. The former dictator of Iraq chose his course of action, and for the sake of peace and security, we chose ours.

The Prime Minister and I have no greater responsibility than to protect the lives and security of the people we serve. The regime of Saddam Hussein was a grave and growing threat. Given Saddam's history of violence and aggression, it would have been reckless to place our trust in his sanity or his restraint. As long as I hold this office, I will never risk the lives of American citizens by assuming the good will of dangerous enemies.

Acting together, the United States, Great Britain, and our coalition partners enforced the demands of the world. We ended the threat from Saddam Hussein's weapons of mass destruction. We rid the Middle East of an aggressive, destabilizing regime. We liberated nearly 25 million people from decades of oppression, and we are now helping the Iraqi people to build a free nation.

In Iraq as elsewhere, freedom and self-government are hated and opposed by a radical and ruthless few. American, British, and other forces are facing remnants of a fallen regime and other extremists. Their attacks follow a pattern. They target progress and success. They strike at Iraqi police officers who have been trained to enforce order. They sabotage Iraqi power grids that we're rebuilding. They are the enemies of the Iraqi people.

Defeating these terrorists is an essential commitment on the war on terror. This is a duty we accept. This is a fight we will win. We are being tested in Iraq. Our enemies are looking for signs of hesitation. They're looking for weakness. They will find none. Instead, our forces in Iraq are finding these killers and bringing them to justice.

And we will finish the task of helping Iraqis make the challenging transition to democracy. Iraq's governing council is now meeting regularly. Soon the council will nominate ministers and propose a budget. After decades of tyranny, the institutions of democracy will take time to create. America and Britain will help the Iraqi people as long as necessary. Prime Minister Blair and I have the same goal: The Government and the future of Iraq will be in the hands of the people of Iraq.

The creation of a strong and stable Iraqi democracy is not easy, but it's an essential part on the war against terror. A free Iraq will be an example to the entire Middle East, and the advance of liberty in the Middle East will undermine the ideologies of terror and hatred. It will help strengthen the security of America and Britain and many other nations.

By helping to build and secure a free Iraq, by accepting the risks and sacrifice, our men and women in uniform are protecting our own countries, and they're giving essential service in the war on terror. This is the work history has given us, and we will complete it.

We're seeing movement toward reform and freedom in other parts of the Middle East. The leadership and courage of Prime Minister Abbas and Prime Minister Sharon are giving their peoples new hope for progress. Other nations can add to the momentum of peace by fighting terror in all its forms. A Palestinian state will be built upon hope and reform, not built upon violence.

Terrorists are the chief enemies of Palestinian aspirations. The sooner terrorism is rooted out by all the governments in the region, the sooner the Palestinian flag will rise over a peaceful Palestinian state.

The spread of liberty in Afghanistan and Iraq and across the Middle East will mark a hopeful turn in the history of our time. Great Britain and America will achieve this goal together. And one of the reasons I'm confident in our success is because the character and the leadership of Prime Minister Tony Blair.

Mr. Prime Minister.

Prime Minister Blair. Thank you, Mr. President. And first of all, as I did a short time ago, I would like to pay tribute to your leadership in these difficult times, because ever since September the 11th, the task of leadership has been an arduous one, and I believe that you have fulfilled it with tremendous conviction, determination, and courage.

President Bush. Thank you, sir.

Prime Minister Blair. And I think it's as well that we understand how this has all come about. It came about because we realized that there was a new source of threat and insecurity in our world that we had to counter. And as I was saying in my speech to Congress, this threat is sometimes hard for people to understand, because it's of such a different nature than the threats we have faced before, but September the 11th taught us it was real.

And when you lead countries, as we both do, and you see the potential for this threat of terrorism and weapons of mass destruction to come together, I really don't believe that any responsible leader could ignore the evidence that we see or the threat that we face. And that's why we've taken the action that we have, first in Afghanistan and now in Iraq.

And in Afghanistan, we acted to remove the Taliban, and we still pursue the Al Qaida terrorist network there and in other parts of the world. But there is no doubt at all that but for that action, Al Qaida would have retained its central place of command and control which now is denied to it.

And in respect to Iraq, we should not forget Resolution 1441 that was passed in the United Nations, in which the entire international community accepted the threat that Iraq constituted.

I think it's just worth pointing out, in these last few days, Iraq has had a governing council established, with the help of the United Nations representative, Sergio de Mello, and in the last 2 weeks, the United Nations has spoken about the numbers of missing people and mass graves. And that number, just on the present count, is round about 300,000 people.

So let us be clear: We have been dealing with a situation in which the threat was very clear and the person, Saddam Hussein, wielding that threat, someone of total brutality and ruthlessness, with no compunction about killing his own people or those of another nation.

And of course, it's difficult to reconstruct Iraq. It's going to be a hard task. We never expected otherwise. But as the President has said to you a moment or two ago, the benefit of that reconstruction will be felt far beyond the territory of Iraq. It is, as I said earlier today, an indispensable part of bringing about a new settlement in the whole of the Middle East.

And I would also pay tribute to the President's leadership in the Middle East and in rekindling the prospect of the Middle East peace process. If I can remind people, I think many people were cynical as to whether this could ever be rekindled. Many people doubted whether the commitment was there, to fairness for Palestinian people as well as to the state of Israel. And yet the President has stated very clearly the goal of a two-state solution. And now we actually have the first steps, albeit tentative, towards achieving that.

And when I met Prime Minister Sharon in London a few nights ago, I was more than ever convinced that if we could provide the right framework within which these tentative steps are made, then we do genuinely have the prospect of making progress there.

And then, again, as I was saying earlier, the commitment that America has now given, that the President has given, in respect of Africa, in tackling some of the poorest parts of our world, is again a sign of hope. And all these things are changing our world. And however difficult the change may be, I genuinely believe it is change for the better.

So I am honored once again to be here in the White House with you, Mr. President. As I said earlier, we are allies, and we are friends. And I believe that the work that we are embarked upon is difficult but is essential, and so far as we are concerned, we shall hold to it, ride the way through.

President Bush. We'll take a couple of questions. Tom [Tom Raum, Associated Press].

Responsibility for the War on Terror/ Coalition in Iraq

Q. Mr. President, others in your administration have said your words on Iraq and Africa did not belong in your State of the Union Address. Will you take personal responsibility for those words? And the both of you, how is it that two major world leaders such as yourselves have had such a hard time persuading other major powers to help stabilize Iraq?

President Bush. First, I take responsibility for putting our troops into action. And I made that decision because Saddam Hussein was a threat to our security and a threat to the security of other nations.

I take responsibility for making the decision, the tough decision, to put together a coalition to remove Saddam Hussein because the intelligence, not only our intelligence but the intelligence of this great country, made a clear and compelling case that Saddam Hussein was a threat to security and peace.

I say that because he possessed chemical weapons and biological weapons. I strongly believe he was trying to reconstitute his nuclear weapons program. And I will remind the skeptics that in 1991, it became clear that Saddam Hussein was much closer to developing a nuclear weapon than anybody ever imagined. He was a threat. I take responsibility for dealing with that threat.

We are in a war against terror, and we will continue to fight that war against terror. We're after Al Qaida, as the Prime Minister accurately noted, and we're dismantling Al Qaida. The removal of Saddam Hussein is an integral part of winning the war against terror. A free Iraq will make it much less likely that we'll find violence in that immediate neighborhood. A free Iraq will make it more likely we'll get a Middle Eastern peace. A free Iraq will have incredible influence on the states that could potentially unleash terrorist activities on us. And yes, I take responsibility for making the decisions I made.

Q. Mr. President——

President Bush. Hold on for a second, please.

Prime Minister Blair. Sorry. First of all, before I answer the question you put to me about other countries helping us, let me just say this on the issue to do with Africa and uranium. The British intelligence that we had we believe is genuine. We stand by that intelligence. And one interesting fact I think people don't generally know, in case people should think that the whole idea of a link between Iraq and Niger was some invention, in the 1980s we know for sure that Iraq purchased round about 270 tons of uranium from Niger. So I think we should just factor that into our thinking there.

As for other countries, actually, other countries are coming in. We have with us now round about nine other countries who will be contributing or are contributing literally thousands of troops. I think I'm right in saying the Poles in their sector have somewhere in the region of 20 different countries offering support. And I have no doubt at all we will have international support in this. Indeed, to be fair, even to those countries that opposed the action, I think they recognize the huge importance of reconstructing Iraq.

And it's an interesting thing, I was at a European meeting just a couple of weeks ago, where, as you know, there were big differences between people over the issue of Iraq. And yet, I was struck by the absolutely unanimous view that whatever people felt about the conflict, it was obviously good that Saddam was out, and most people now recognize that the important thing is that we all work together to reconstruct Iraq for the better so that it is a free and stable country.

Adam [Adam Boulton, Sky News].

Guantanamo Bay Detainees/Andrew Gilligan

Q. I wonder if I could ask you both about one aspect of Iraq and freedom and justice which, as you know, is causing a great deal of concern in Britain and the British Parliament, that is what happens now in Guantanamo Bay to the people detained there, particularly whether there's any chance that the President will return the British citizens to face British justice, as John Walker Lindh faced regular American justice?

And just on a quick point, could the Prime Minister react to the decision of the Foreign Affairs Committee tonight that the BBC reporter Andrew Gilligan is a "unsatisfactory witness?"

President Bush. You probably ought to comment on that one. [*Laughter*]

Prime Minister Blair. Can I just say to you on the first point, obviously, this is an issue that we will discuss when we begin our talks tonight, and we will put out a statement on that tomorrow for you.

President Bush. We will work with the Blair Government on this issue. And we're about to—after we finish answering your questions, we're going to go upstairs and discuss the issue.

Q. Do you have concerns they're not getting justice, the people detained there?

President Bush. No, the only thing I know for certain is that these are bad people, and we look forward to working closely with the Blair Government to deal with the issue.

Prime Minister Blair. On your other point, Adam, the issue here is very, very simple. The whole debate for weeks revolved around a claim that either I or a member of my staff had effectively inserted intelligence into the dossier we put before the British people against the wishes of the intelligence services. Now, that is a serious charge. It never was true. Everybody now knows that that charge is untrue. And all we are saying is, those who made that charge should simply accept that it is untrue. It's as simple as that.

President Bush. Patsy [Patricia Wilson], Reuters.

Iraqi Weapons of Mass Destruction

Q. In his speech to Congress, the Prime Minister opened the door to the possibility that you may be proved wrong about the threat from Iraq's weapons of mass destruction.

President Bush. Yes.

Q. Do you agree, and does it matter whether or not you find these weapons?

President Bush. Well, you might ask the Prime Minister that. We won't be proven wrong——

Prime Minister Blair. No.

President Bush. I believe that we will find the truth. And the truth is, he was developing a program for weapons of mass destruction.

Now, you say, why didn't it happen all of a sudden? Well, there was a lot of chaos in the country, one; two, Saddam Hussein has spent over a decade hiding weapons and hiding materials; three, we're getting—we're just beginning to get some cooperation from some of the high-level officials in that administration or that regime.

But we will bring the weapons, and of course we will bring the information forward on the weapons when they find them. And that will end up—end all this speculation. I understand there has been a lot of speculation over in Great Britain—we've got a little bit of it here—about whether or not the—whether or not the actions were based upon valid information. We can debate that all day long until the truth shows up, and that's what's going to happen.

And we based our decisions on good, sound intelligence. And the—our people are going to find out the truth, and the truth will say that this intelligence was good intelligence. There's no doubt in my mind.

Prime Minister Blair. And—yes, if I can just correct you on one thing. I certainly did not say that I would be proved wrong. On the contrary, I said with every fiber of instinct and conviction, I believe that we are right. And let me just say this one other thing to you, because sometimes, again, in the debate in the past few weeks, it's as if, prior to the early part of this year, the issue of Saddam Hussein and weapons of mass destruction were some sort of unknown quantity, and on the basis of some speculative intelligence, we go off and take action.

The history of Saddam Hussein and weapons of mass destruction is a 12-year history and is a history of him using the weapons, developing the weapons, and concealing the weapons and not complying with the United Nations inspectors who were trying to shut down his programs. And I simply say, which is why I totally agree with the President, it's important we wait for the Iraq Survey Group to complete their work. Because the proposition that actually he was not developing such weapons and such programs rests on this rather extraordinary proposition that, having for years obstructed the United Nations inspectors and concealed his programs, having finally effectively got rid of them in December '98, he then took all the problems and

sanctions and action upon himself, voluntarily destroyed them, but just didn't tell anyone. I don't think that's very likely as a proposition. I really don't.

Right, Nick.

Guantanamo Bay Detainees

Q. Nick Robinson, ITV News. Mr. President, do you realize that many people hearing you say that we know these are "bad people" in Guantanamo Bay will merely fuel their doubts that the United States regards them as innocent until proven guilty and due a fair, free, and open trial?

President Bush. Well, yes—let me just say these were illegal combatants. They were picked up off the battlefield aiding and abetting the Taliban. I'm not trying to try them in front of your cameras or in your newspaper.

But we will talk with the Prime Minister about this issue. He's asked. Prior to his arrival, he said, "I want to talk about this in a serious way. Can we work with you?" And the answer is, absolutely. I understand the issue. And we will. We'll have a very good discussion about it, right after he finishes answering this aspect of your question.

Prime Minister Blair. I just think you should realize—I mean, of course, as I said a moment or two ago, we will discuss this together, and we'll put out a statement for you tomorrow. But I think, again, it's important just to realize the context in which all this arises, without saying anything about any specific case at all. And the context was a situation in which the Al Qaida and the Taliban were operating together in Afghanistan against American and British forces. So, as I say, we will discuss this issue. We will come back to it. You will have a statement tomorrow.

But I want to say just in concluding, once again, that the conviction that this threat of terrorism and weapons of mass destruction is the security threat our world faces has never left me. It's with me now, and I believe it to be the threat that we have to take on and defeat. I really do.

President Bush. Good job. Thank you. I appreciate your coming. [*Inaudible*]

Thank you all.

NOTE: The President's news conference began at 5:29 p.m. in the Cross Hall at the White House. In his remarks, he referred to Cherie Blair, wife of Prime Minister Blair; former President Saddam Hussein of Iraq; Prime Minister Mahmoud Abbas (Abu Mazen) of the Palestinian Authority; and Prime Minister Ariel Sharon of Israel. Prime Minister Blair referred to Sergio Vieira de Mello, U.N. Special Representative for Iraq. A reporter referred to John Walker Lindh, convicted American Taliban fighter.

Statement on the Death of Celia Cruz
July 17, 2003

Celia Cruz was an international artist whose voice and talent entertained audiences around the world. Her success in the years following her departure from her beloved Cuba was a tribute to her perseverance, compassion, and love for life. Laura joins me in sending our thoughts and prayers to her family and friends.

NOTE: The Office of the Press Secretary also released a Spanish language transcript of this statement.

Remarks on the HealthierUS Initiative in Dallas, Texas
July 18, 2003

Thanks a lot. Please be seated. Thanks. It is nice to be home.

I am honored to be here at Lakewest YMCA. I've got to tell you, the facility is overwhelming. It is a beautiful facility, and I appreciate so very much the hospitality and the dedicated staff here.

Listen, we're here to talk about a health care plan that makes a lot of sense. And it's a health care plan that says if you exercise and eat healthy food, you will live longer. I mean, there is a lot of talk about treating chronic diseases and finding treatments and research and development. And that's great, and the country is on the leading edge of all kinds of new discoveries. But we've already discovered what works. And what works is to encourage people to exercise on a regular basis and to eat good foods. It's called preventative medicine. An integral part of any health care plan is to encourage people to adapt the habits necessary to avoid disease in the first place. And that's what we're here to talk about, and that is what the YMCA does, and I'm grateful for that.

And there's no better place to start in encouraging healthy choices and exercise than with our children. And so Lynn and I were honored to go to the—some of these exercise classes and were pleased to see little youngsters doing jumping jacks— with enthusiasm, I might add—[*laughter*]— counting out the number of stretches.

I mean, look, the YMCA is an integral part of a healthy America by encouraging our youngsters to exercise, to have fun, to get outside, to learn to eat good foods. We're really here to thank the Y, thank the Y here in west Dallas and thank the

YMCAs all across America for being an integral part of a healthy United States of America.

Ken Gladish is the president and CEO of YMCA of the entire United States. We've got the President of the United States of the Ys with us. [*Laughter*] Thank you for coming. I'm honored you're here. Gordon Echtenkamp is the president and CEO of YMCA Metropolitan Dallas. Thank you, Gordon, appreciate you being here. Jo Harris is the executive director of the Lakewest Family YMCA. Thank you, Jo, for being here.

I hope this entourage of mine didn't over-stress the organization. [*Laughter*] Turns out we don't travel lightly these days. [*Laughter*] But thanks a lot to you and your staff for opening up this facility for us to discuss health.

I'm honored that the Governor is here, Governor Rick Perry. I ran as Governor; he runs as Governor. He'll be running faster than I ran as Governor, soon. But he understands what I know: There's a lot of stress in certain jobs. I guess every job could have stress to it. There's nothing like exercise to relieve the stress, and I know Rick works out a lot, and I thank you for setting a good example for the State of Texas, friend. Thanks for coming.

And I want to thank Congressman Sam Johnson and Congressman Michael Burgess, both here from the State of Texas, for joining us. Thank you all for coming. I'm honored you're here.

In the midst of some of those Ranger losing streaks, I would get all anxious, and I would go over and visit with my friend Ken Cooper, who's got a fantastic facility which promotes exercise. He'd just say, "Run until it doesn't hurt anymore." [*Laughter*] And I'm honored you're here, Ken. Thanks for setting such a good example for—see, he's on the leading edge of research. He's determined a lot of simple facts. One of them is, is that if you exercise, like, 20 minutes a day, the incident of heart disease drops dramatically. That doesn't

seem like much of a challenge, does it, to convince people to exercise 20 minutes a day? And that's what we're here to do.

And so I put together a group of really strong American citizens who understand the value of exercise, understand the value of health for our society, to help spread the message. And the Chairman of that, of course, is a fabulous person who happened to be a very good football player named Lynn Swann. And I appreciate you, Lynn.

And I appreciate so very much, Lynn, because he's a busy guy, and he's got a lot to do. And for him to volunteer, along with others on the Council, to help to make America a healthy place really speaks to the character of the person. And I'm honored to be associated with him, just like I'm honored to be associated with Dr. Dot Richardson, Olympic gold medalist, surgeon, and Vice Chairwoman. Doc, thanks for coming.

As I say, we put together a really good Council, people who are out in the communities putting the word out. One guy who is here is a guy who I know has put the word out for running. Austin, Texas, is one of the greatest running cities in the country. And one of the reasons why is because Paul Carrozza, who is an entrepreneur, a business entrepreneur, started with nothing—except a good pair of legs—[*laughter*]—and started what they call RunTex. I know him well, and he'd probably like me to say, if you're interested in a pair of shoes in the Austin area, drop by. [*Laughter*] But he has organized a lot of running clubs and really has convinced a lot of people who never would think about running or exercise to get out on Town Lake and run. And I know we've got the same type of folks here in Dallas, but Paul, thank you for your dedication to a fit America.

President of Trek Bicycle Corp. is John Burke. John is with us, been introduced now twice. But John is an entrepreneur as well who cares a lot about fitness. He recognizes there's other ways to stay fit than running, for example, like getting on a bicycle. That also counts, by the way. And I appreciate you coming, John. Thank you for being here, as well as Dr. Ted Mitchell. He works at the Cooper Clinic. He works for the Cooper Clinic Wellness Program. They take the research at Cooper Clinic and implement it into programs to get people to stay fit. And I want to thank all of you all for joining this Council, and thanks for coming. Good to see you, Doc. How's the fastball?

I appreciate Dennis Roberson, who is here with us today. Dennis is a active volunteer. The reason I like to talk about volunteers, this country of ours has got a lot of muscle, and we're strong. And we, by the way, stay strong in order to keep the peace. We will stay strong in order to promote freedom. But the truth of the matter is, the great strength of America is the heart and soul of the American citizen, people who are willing to dedicate time to make somebody else's life better, people who are willing to volunteer. And this guy, Dennis Roberson, comes here and volunteers to help teach children healthy lifestyles, to teach children how to use the computer, to teach children how to access the Internet, to teach children that a healthy body and a healthy mind will lead to a strong future.

And I want to thank you, Dennis, for setting a good example for volunteers all across the Metroplex, all across our State, and all across our Nation. One of the things—my jobs is to call people to a higher calling. And there's nothing higher than to loving a neighbor just like you would like to be loved yourself and volunteering your time to help somebody in need. Thank you, sir.

We have a problem when people don't exercise and eat bad food. Obesity can cause serious health problems, like heart disease and diabetes. And it adds to the cost of health care in America; that is a fact. In 2000 alone, obesity costs totaled

the country an estimated cost of $117 billion. Since 1980, rates of obesity have doubled among children, tripled among adolescents. Now, that is a problem, and the Nation must do something about it for the sake of our future.

We must reverse the trend, and we know how to do it. It's exercise and good dieting. Good foods and regular exercise will reverse the trend and save our country a lot of money but, more importantly, save lives.

The local Ys is a great place to start, and that's why we're here. There are other programs across the country, by the way, that encourage exercise, no doubt about it. The YMCA is on the forefront. I remember being a loyal Y member in Midland, Texas, playing basketball with a bunch of 45-year-olds. [*Laughter*] It was like full-court karate. [*Laughter*]

But here at this Y, they hook youngsters on exercise. And Andrew Simpson just gave us a tour, gave Lynn Swann and me a tour. He's a good guide. He tells me exercise not only gives him energy but, as importantly, confidence. He's a more confident person as a result of the program. He said he was always tired of being the little guy, and so he decided to work out. He's not a little guy anymore. [*Laughter*] He's a man who understands that when you make right choices in life, you'll have a healthier future.

The thing that I like to see, and the Y is good at this, and other programs need to understand, exercise doesn't need to be drudgery. It can be fun. It can be a fun way for people to spend their day. I love the idea of a day camp. I asked how long the day camp is. I think it's, like, 10 weeks. It's a really good idea. It's a good idea to help build up the spirit of the community. It's a good idea to give the kids something smart to do. It's a good idea to instill the habits necessary for a healthy future.

And so we saw the problem in this administration, and we decided to do something about it and started what I call the HealthierUS Initiative. Washington has got to have initiatives, and so this is a HealthierUS Initiative. [*Laughter*] And here's the—we came up with four basic guidelines which make a lot of sense. And so our job of the Council and me and others, the Governors, the mayors, hopefully, is to focus on these four guidelines.

First, be physically active every day, not just once a week or a couple times a week and say, "Gosh, I've met the goal." It's every day, try to get some physical activity. And moms and dads, by the way, need to stay physically active as well, just not the sons or daughters.

Secondly, develop good eating habits. It's been estimated that dietary changes can reduce cancer deaths in the United States by a third. Well, that's—given that potential, it seems like to make a lot of sense for all of us to figure out what we're going to eat. Listen, I'd be the first to admit to the kids here, I didn't like vegetables when I was young. I've learned to like them because I understand that they're good for you. That means not only vegetables but fruits, wise choices, not grease—[*laughter*]—but fruits and vegetables.

Third, take advantage of preventative screenings. This is more, obviously, applicable to older Americans. Ken Cooper insists that I have preventative screenings on an annual basis. And it is important for us to do this, I mean, for example, like check your blood pressure. It can be an indicator that something might go wrong. I hope the Y—I don't know if you do or not, it would make sense if you did, a neighborhood screening—you do; that's good—to help provide screening for citizens in each community, so people can be able to detect early whether or not they may have a potential problem. A lot of disease can be picked up through a simple test.

And fourth, make healthy choices. That not only means food, but no cigarettes, no excessive drinking, no drugs, no underage drinking. Those are the kind of healthy— you hear people say "healthy choices," that is what we're talking about. And if our

country, old and young alike, followed the four steps and measures, we'd be a much healthier nation. It would be, really, one of the best health care plans we could possibly implement in America.

To promote this program, as I mentioned, I talked Lynn into doing this job. It's called—and we're setting a fitness challenge today. And he and I are going to spend a lot of time working on the fitness challenge. I probably will spend most time by trying to set the example. It turns out, when a President shows up, cameras show up. And I like to exercise, and I want people to see their President exercising. Today I knocked off about 30 minutes' worth of exercise and feel better for it.

But our goal is to get 20 million additional Americans to exercise for at least 30 minutes a day, 5 days a week. That is a noble goal, and it's an important goal. Americans will feel better if they accept the challenge. America will be better off when Americans accept the challenge. It's easy to get started in this, and so we've set up a web page, as Lynn mentioned, and John is responsible for the web page. It's presidentschallenge.org.

And it's an interesting opportunity for people. If you need a little discipline in your life—in other words, if you need— so you can check on yourself, a self-policing mechanism, call up the web page and follow the instructions, and there's a go-by to help you get involved with an exercise program. And I can assure you, and Lynn can assure you, the Governor assure you, once you get hooked on exercise, it is hard to get off. Once you get started, once you realize the benefits, once you understand how great you feel, once you understand that it's easier to go to sleep at night after a good day of exercise, you're not going to quit.

And so our job as a country, at the Federal level, the State level, and the local level is to get people started and realize the great benefits of exercise. And so we've set up this web page, trying to take advantage of the new technologies. So if people are interested, please go to presidentschallenge.org.

Now, the other thing is, I do think there is a role for the Federal Government to help. I proposed $125 million for community monies to help different organizations like the Y to start promoting awareness. It's to facilitate an awareness campaign, to make people aware of what it's like to exercise, to make people aware of opportunities available in the communities, and to make people aware that—what good nutrition and good exercise will do for their long-term health.

The funds would be available to target obesity and diabetes and asthma. It also could be used to encourage preventative screenings. In other words, it's a part of a larger process throughout our society to get this initiative going. And I hope Congress takes a good, solid look at it.

The other thing we're going to try to do at the Federal—not "try to do"—will do at the Federal level, is provide incentives for local schools to focus on better nutrition and eating habits. As you know, the Federal Government is involved with the school programs. The U.S. Department of Agriculture is integrally involved, and it makes sense to me, since we've got a lot of kids eating food around the country once the schools are in, that we have better nutrition. And the Federal Government must encourage better nutrition at the local school level, which we will do.

One of the things I talk a lot about is the need to really work on cultural change in America to encourage a culture of personal responsibility, to encourage people to be responsible for the decisions they make in life. I like to talk about, if you're a mother or a dad, reminding people you're responsible for loving your child and really making sure your child understands the difference between right and wrong and what it means to make right choices in life. If you're involved, if you're worried about

your public school system, you're responsible for getting involved with it, as opposed to hoping somebody far away gets involved. You're responsible for getting involved with your schools.

You're responsible if you're a CEO, by the way, in America, for telling the truth to your shareholders and your employees. You're responsible for loving a neighbor like you'd like to be loved yourself. The Initiative, the HealthierUS Initiative, really speaks to personal responsibility, doesn't it? It says that we are responsible for our own health. By making the right choices, we can make the right choice for our future. By making healthy choices, we can do the right things for our future.

Moms and dads, by working on healthy choices not only for themselves but their kids, are doing their job as a parent. By exercising every day, by finding time, by carving out time, no matter how busy you may seem or how boring exercise may seem initially, it's a part of a responsibility culture. And I appreciate giving it—being given the chance to come and talk about this.

We'll work on health care matters. We're working on Medicare reform. That's—we need to work on Medicare reform. And we're working on how to make sure the working uninsured get insurance. But the truth of the matter is, one of the best reforms in America for health care is a strong, preventative health care program that starts with each American being responsible for what he or she eats, what he or she drinks, what he or she doesn't smoke, and is responsible for whether or not they get out and exercise on a regular basis. I encourage my fellow citizens to exercise.

Thank you all very much. Thanks for coming, and may God bless.

NOTE: The President spoke at 2:04 p.m. in the gymnasium at the Lakewest Family

YMCA. In his remarks, he referred to Chairman Lynn C. Swann, Vice Chairman Dorothy G. "Dot" Richardson, and Council Members Paul R. Carrozza, John P. Burke, and Dr. Teddy L. Mitchell, President's Council on Physical Fitness and Sports; Kenneth L. Gladish, national executive director and chief executive officer, YMCA of the USA; Gov. Rick Perry of Texas; Kenneth H. Cooper, the President's personal physician; and Andrew Simpson, youth volunteer, Lakewest Family YMCA. The Office of the Press Secretary also released a Spanish language transcript of these remarks.

Statement on the Inauguration of the Transitional Government in the Democratic Republic of the Congo
July 18, 2003

I congratulate President Joseph Kabila and the Congolese people on the installation of the new transitional Government in the Democratic Republic of the Congo. I also extend congratulations to Vice Presidents Jean-Pierre Bemba, Abdoulaye Yerodia, Azarias Ruberwa, and Z'Ahidi Ngoma. The arrival of former rebel leaders in Kinshasa and their participation with former opposition parties in the new Government is a major achievement that sets the country on a course toward peace and democratic elections. I am confident that the Congolese people will be well served by the experience and vision these five leaders bring to these important posts.

The United States will work closely with President Kabila and the transitional Government to promote peace, prosperity, and democracy for all Congolese. I call upon neighboring countries to join us in supporting Congo's new Government during this crucial time.

Remarks at a Bush-Cheney Reception in Dallas
July 18, 2003

Thank you all very much. Laura and I are thrilled to be here. It is great to be home. It's really fun for us to see a lot of our old buddies—some of our young buddies too. [*Laughter*] This is our first trip back to Texas since I got back from Africa. You may remember we were over there, and we went to a park in Botswana. That's where we learned a lot about our party's mascot. [*Laughter*]

I want to thank you all for your help. Thanks a lot. It means a lot to Laura and me. We love Texas, and we love our friends, and we want to thank our friends for helping us. You're laying the foundation for what is going to be a great victory in November of 2004.

I'm getting ready, loosening up. [*Laughter*] But I'm going to have to count on you to energize the grassroots and to make the phone calls and to put up the signs and to address the envelopes and remind everybody that our message is so positive and hopeful for every citizen of this State and this country.

The political season will come in its own time. But right now, I'm focused on the people's business in our Nation's Capital. I have a job to do, and we have a lot on our agenda. And I will continue to work hard to earn the confidence of all America by keeping this Nation strong and secure, free, and prosperous.

I am thrilled that Laura's here. She is a fabulous First Lady, and I love her dearly. She is just a steady rock and has been a great comforter for a lot of Americans during some of our difficult times.

I appreciate our Governor. I want to thank him for his introduction. I thank him for his introduction; more importantly, I thank him for his great leadership for the State of Texas. He is Governor during some tough times for this State, and he has led with courage and vision. And the State of Texas is better off with Rick Perry as the Governor.

I know we've got quite a few of the mighty Texas congressional delegation with us today. And I'm going to tell you something: It's really good to have steady support in the House of Representatives from our fellow Texans, Texans like Joe Barton and Michael Burgess and Kay Granger and Jeb Hensarling and Sam Johnson. I want to thank all of them for their service to our State and to our Nation.

I know our able Lieutenant Governor is here, and I want to thank David Dewhurst for his service to the State of Texas, and the speaker of the house, my fellow Midland, Texan, citizen Tommy Craddick; I want to thank Tom for his service. Thank you, Tom and Nadine. I saw Marchant and Branch out there, two fine members of the Texas House. It's good to see you all.

I appreciate so very much my close personal friend Mercer Reynolds. He's the national finance chairman for the Bush-Cheney '04 campaign. I want to thank Mercer for his hard work. I want to thank my close friend Fred Meyer for being the Texas State finance chairman. I thank Jeanne Johnson Phillips and Roger Williams for being the finance vice chairmen for our campaign here. I want to thank all of you who worked hard to raise this money. I appreciate your help.

Finally, I want to thank the Gatlin boys for bringing their mother. [*Laughter*]

In the last 2½ years, our Nation has acted decisively to confront great challenges. I came to this office to solve problems, not to pass them on to future Presidents and future generations. I came to seize opportunities, instead of letting them slip away. We are meeting the tests of our time.

Terrorists declared war on the United States of America, and war is what they got. We have captured or killed many leaders of Al Qaida, and the rest of them know we're on their trail. In Afghanistan and Iraq, we gave ultimatums to terror regimes. Those regimes chose defiance, and those regimes are no more. Fifty million people in those two countries once lived under tyranny, and now they live under freedom.

Two-and-a-half years ago, our military was not receiving the resources it needed, and morale was beginning to suffer. We increased the defense budget to prepare for the threats of a new era. And today, no one in the world can question the skill and the strength and the spirit of the United States military.

Two-and-a-half years ago, we inherited an economy in recession. And then the attacks happened on our country, and there were corporate scandals and war. All affected the people's confidence. But we acted. We passed tough new laws to hold corporate criminals to account. And to get the economy going again, we have twice led the United States Congress to pass historic tax relief for the people of this country.

We know that when Americans have more take-home pay to spend, to save, or to invest, the whole economy grows, and people are more likely to find a job. We understand whose money we spend in Washington, DC. It is not the Government's money. It is the people's money.

We're returning more money to people to help them raise their families. We're reducing taxes on dividends and capital gains to encourage investment. We are giving small businesses incentives to expand and to hire people. With all these actions, we have laid the foundation for greater prosperity and more jobs, so that every single American in our country can realize the great hope of the American Dream.

Two-and-a-half years ago, there was a lot of talk about education reform, but there wasn't much action. So I called for and Congress passed the No Child Left Behind Act. With a solid bipartisan majority, we delivered the most dramatic education reforms in a generation. We're bringing high standards and strong accountability measures to every public school in America. We believe and strongly believe that every child can learn the basics of reading and math, and we expect every school to teach the basics of reading and math. We are challenging the soft bigotry of low expectations. The days of excuse-making are over. We expect results in every classroom, so that not one single child in America is left behind.

We reorganized the Government and created the Department of Homeland Security to safeguard our borders and ports and to better protect the American people. We passed trade promotion authority to open up new markets for our entrepreneurs and farmers and ranchers and manufacturers. We passed a budget agreement that is helping to maintain spending discipline in Washington, DC. On issue after issue, this administration has acted on principle, has kept its word, and has made progress on behalf of the American people.

The United States Congress has shared in these great achievements. I appreciate the leadership of Speaker Hastert and Leader Frist. I want to thank the hard work of many Members of the Congress. We're going to continue to work together to change the tone in Washington, DC, and to focus on results.

And those are the kind of—the nature of the men and women I have asked to serve in my administration. I have put together a fantastic team on behalf of America. These are people who understand their job is to serve all Americans. Our country has had no finer Vice President than Dick Cheney—although Mother may have a different opinion. [*Laughter*]

In 2½ years, we have come far, but we're only beginning. I have set great goals worthy of this great Nation. First, America is committed to expanding the realm of freedom and peace for our own security and for the benefit of the world. And second, in our own country, we must work for a society of prosperity and compassion, so that every citizen has a chance to work, to succeed, and to realize the promise of our country.

It is clear that the future of freedom and peace depend upon the actions of America. This Nation is freedom's home and freedom's defender. We welcome this charge of history, and we are keeping it. Our war on terror continues. The enemies of freedom are not idle, and neither are we. This country will not rest; we will not tire; we will not stop until this danger to civilization is removed.

Yet, our national interest involves more than eliminating aggressive threats to our safety. Our greatest security comes from the advance of human liberty because free nations do not support terror, free nations do not attack their neighbors, free nations do not threaten the world with weapons of mass terror. Americans believe that freedom is the deepest need and the deepest hope of every human heart, and we believe that freedom is the right of every person and the future of every nation.

America also understands that unprecedented influence brings tremendous responsibilities. We have duties in the world, and when we see disease and starvation and hopelessness, we will not turn away. Laura and I just came from Africa. America is now committed to bringing the healing power of medicine to millions of men and women and children who suffer with AIDS. This great, strong, compassionate Nation is leading the world in this incredibly important work of human rescue.

We face challenges here at home, and our actions will prove that we are equal to those challenges. I will continue to work on our economy until everybody who wants to work and is not working today can find a job.

We have a duty to keep our commitment to America's seniors by strengthening and modernizing Medicare. Recently, the Congress took historic action to improve the lives of our older Americans. For the first time since the creation of Medicare, the House and the Senate have passed reforms to increase choices for seniors and to provide prescription drug coverage. The next step is for both Houses to come together to iron out the details and to get a good bill to my desk.

And for the sake of our health care system, we need to cut down on the frivolous lawsuits which increase the cost of medicine. I want to thank Governor Perry and the Lieutenant Governor and the Speaker for passing meaningful, real medical liability reform. People who have been harmed by a bad doctor deserve their day in court. Yet, the system should not reward lawyers who are simply fishing for rich settlements. Because frivolous lawsuits drive up the cost of health care at the national level, medical liability reform is a national issue that requires a national solution. The House of Representatives has passed a good bill. It is stalled in the Senate. For the sake of a good health care system, the United States Senate must act.

I have a responsibility as the President to make sure the judicial system runs well, and I have met that duty. I have nominated superb men and women like Priscilla Owen for our Federal courts, good people who will interpret the law, not legislate from the bench. Yet, some Members of the Senate are trying to keep my nominees off the bench by blocking up-or-down votes. Every judicial nominee deserves a fair hearing and an up-or-down vote on the Senate

floor. It is time for some Members of the United States Senate to stop playing politics with American justice.

This Congress needs to pass a comprehensive energy plan. Our Nation must promote energy efficiency and conservation. We must develop cleaner technology. We must explore in environmentally friendly ways. Yet, for the sake of economic security and national security, we need to become less dependent on foreign sources of energy.

Our strong and prosperous Nation must be a compassionate nation. I will continue to advance our agenda of compassionate conservatism, applying the best and most innovative ideas to the task of helping our fellow citizens in need.

There are still millions of men and women who want to end their dependence on Government and become independent through hard work. We must build on the success of welfare reform to bring work and dignity into the lives of more of our fellow citizens.

Congress should complete the "Citizen Service Act" so that more Americans can serve their communities and their country. And both Houses should reach agreement on my Faith-Based Initiative to support the armies of compassion that are mentoring children, that are caring for the homeless, that are offering hope to the addicted.

A compassionate society must promote opportunity for all, including the independence and dignity that come from ownership. This administration will constantly strive to promote an ownership society in America. We want more of our citizens owning their own home. We want people to own and manage their own health care account and their own retirement account. We want more people to own their small business, because we understand when an American owns something, he or she has a vital stake in the future of our country.

In a compassionate society, people respect one another and take responsibility for the decisions they make. We're changing the culture of America from one that says, "If it feels good, do it," and "If you've got a problem, blame somebody else," to a culture in which each of us understands we are responsible for the decisions we make in life. If you're fortunate to be a mom or a dad, you're responsible for your child. If you're concerned about the quality of the education in your community, you are responsible for doing something about it. If you're a CEO in America, you are responsible to tell the truth to your employees and your shareholders. And in this new responsibility society, each of us is responsible for loving our neighbor just like we'd like to be loved ourself.

We can see the culture of service and responsibility growing around us. I started the USA Freedom Corps to encourage Americans to extend a compassionate hand to neighbors in need, and the response has been very strong. Our charities and our faith-based institutions are strong and vibrant all across our country. They're helping people who cry out for help. Policemen and firefighters and people who wear our Nation's uniform are reminding us what it means to sacrifice for something greater than yourself. Once again, the children of America believe in heroes because they see them every day.

In these challenging times, the world has seen the resolve and the courage of America, and I have been privileged to see the compassion and the character of the American people. All the tests of the last 2½ years have come to the right nation.

We are a strong country, and we use our strength to defend the peace. We're an optimistic country, confident in ourselves and in ideals bigger than ourselves. Abroad, we seek to lift whole nations by spreading freedom. At home, we seek to lift up lives by spreading opportunity to every corner of America. This is the work that history has set before us. We welcome it, and we know that for our country and for our cause, better days lie ahead.

Thank you for coming. May God bless.

NOTE: The President spoke at 6:16 p.m. at the Wyndham Anatole Hotel. In his remarks, he referred to Gov. Rick Perry and Lt. Gov. David Dewhurst of Texas; Texas House of Representatives Speaker Tom Craddick and his wife, Nadine; Texas State Representatives Kenny Marchant and Dan Branch; Jeanne Johnson Phillips, Texas State vice chairman, and J. Roger Williams, north Texas chairman, Bush-Cheney '04, Inc.; country music entertainers the Gatlin Brothers, and their mother, Billie; and Priscilla Owen, nominee to be U.S. Circuit Judge for the Fifth Circuit.

The President's Radio Address
July 19, 2003

Good morning. Next week, the United States Treasury will begin printing and mailing more than 25 million child tax credit checks, putting over $12 billion back into the hands of American families. These rebates are the result of the Jobs and Growth Act I recently signed into law, which increases the child tax credit from $600 to $1,000 per child. And because this new law reduced income tax rates, businesses earlier this month lowered tax withholding for worker paychecks. Now, those workers and their families have a lighter tax bill and more take-home pay.

With the child tax credit rebates and the lower tax rates taking effect, America's families will have more of their own money to make purchases, pay their bills, save for their children's education, and invest in a new home or business. There are hopeful signs that our actions are contributing to economic growth. Individual investors are showing greater confidence, leading to a significant rise in the stock market. And thanks to our efforts to reduce taxes on stock dividends, dozens of major companies have announced plans to either increase their existing dividend payout or pay dividends for the first time, putting billions of dollars in cash into shareholders' pockets.

Earlier this week, I met with leading private economists who see a faster rate of economic growth in the coming year-and-a-half. The U.S. housing market is robust, strengthened by low mortgage rates and rising after-tax incomes. Inflation is low. Retail sales have been rising, and productivity growth, the most important indicator of economic strength, remains high.

My administration remains focused on faster economic growth that will translate into more jobs. Now that Americans can keep more of what they earn, we can expect to see rising demand for goods and services. And as demand increases, companies will need more workers to meet it.

We will continue to take action on a broad agenda for more growth and jobs. We are pressing the Senate to join the House of Representatives in passing an energy bill to assure stable and affordable energy supplies. And we're pressing the Senate on litigation reform, so small businesses and manufacturers can focus on creating jobs instead of fighting frivolous lawsuits. I'm asking both Houses of Congress to create reemployment accounts for those seeking jobs, so they can pay for job training

and child care and other costs of finding work.

Faster economic growth will bring the added benefit of higher revenues for our Government, and those new revenues, combined with spending discipline in Washington, DC, are the surest way to bring down the deficit. My budget for fiscal year 2004 calls for a modest increase in discretionary spending of only 4 percent, or about the same increase as the average American household budget. I urge Congress to make spending discipline a priority, so that we can cut the deficit in half over the next 5 years.

Government does not create prosperity. Government can, however, create the conditions that make prosperity possible. The Jobs and Growth Act of 2003 was based on the fundamental faith in the energy and creativity of the American people. With hard work and daily determination, entrepreneurs and workers are moving this economy forward. The American economy is headed in the right direction, and we can be confident of better days ahead.

Thank you.

NOTE: The address was recorded at 10:50 a.m. on July 17 in the Cabinet Room at the White House for broadcast at 10:06 a.m. on July 19. The transcript was made available by the Office of the Press Secretary on July 18 but was embargoed for release until the broadcast. The Office of the Press Secretary also released a Spanish language transcript of this address.

Remarks at a Bush-Cheney Reception in Houston, Texas
July 19, 2003

Thank you all very much. It's such an honor to be here. Laura and I are glad to be home. First, let me say it's great to see so many familiar faces. A couple

of them scolded me when I was a kid. I see old—[*inaudible*]—over there. [*Laughter*] A lot of the people in this room worked hard to see to it that I became the Governor, and I want to thank you all for your continued friendship and your support. I want to thank you for your loyalty to our country. I want to thank you for coming tonight.

This is the first time we've been back to Texas since our trip to Africa. You may recall, we went to a park in Botswana. It's where I learned a lot about our party's mascot. [*Laughter*]

I want to thank you for all your help. You see, you're laying the groundwork for what is going to be a great national victory in November of 2004. And we're going to need your help. We're going to need your help at the grassroots level. We're going to need you to talk to your neighbors and send out the flyers and put up the signs and turn out the vote and remind people that this message—the message of this administration is hopeful for every single person who lives in this country.

And I'm getting ready, and I'm loosening up. [*Laughter*] But the truth of the matter is, there's plenty of time for politics. Right now, I'm focused on the people's business in Washington, DC. We have a lot on the agenda. We will continue to work hard to earn the confidence of all Americans by keeping this Nation secure and strong and prosperous and free.

And I'm glad Laura is here tonight. In my book, she's a fabulous First Lady. And I love her a lot, and I hope she loves me a lot for dragging her out of Texas.

I'm also honored to be introduced by Rick Perry. He is the right guy to be Governor of Texas. They had a good session, because he watched the people's money very closely. He's a good Governor, and I'm proud to call him friend. And I appreciate you, Rick.

I want to thank Fred Meyer, the Texas State finance chairman, and Jeanne Johnson Phillips and Nancy Kinder for putting on this party tonight. You all did a fantastic job.

I want to thank all who helped. This is a fantastic turnout, and I know it requires a lot of effort to get people to come, particularly on a Saturday night. [*Laughter*] So I want to thank all those who worked hard, and I really appreciate your support.

I want to thank my friend Tom DeLay for being here. Congressman DeLay is a leader in the House of Representatives. I'm pleased that our Lieutenant Governor, David Dewhurst, is here—thank you, David, for your leadership—and the speaker of the house, from Midland, Texas, Tommy Craddick. Thanks, Tom. And I know we've got two State senators with us, Teel Bivins and Kyle Janek, and State Representative Joe Nixon. I appreciate you all coming.

And finally, I want to thank the Houston Children's Chorus for lending their beautiful voices to this event.

In the last 2½ years, our Nation has acted decisively to confront great challenges. I came to this office to solve problems, not to pass them on to future Presidents and future generations. I came to seize opportunities, instead of letting them slip away. We are meeting the tests of our time.

Terrorists declared war on the United States of America, and war is what they got. We have captured or killed many key leaders of Al Qaida, and the rest of them know we're on their trail. In Afghanistan and in Iraq, we gave ultimatums to terror regimes. Those regimes chose defiance, and those regimes are no more. Fifty million people in those two countries once lived under tyranny. Today, they live in freedom.

Two-and-a-half years ago, our military was not receiving the resources it needed, and morale was beginning to suffer. We increased the defense budget to prepare for the threats of a new era. And today, no one in the world can question the skill and the strength and the spirit of the United States military.

Two-and-a-half years ago, we inherited an economy in recession. And then the attacks on our country and scandals in corporate America and war affected the people's confidence. But we acted. We passed tough new laws to hold corporate criminals to account. And to get the economy going again, we have twice led the United States Congress to pass historic tax relief for the American people.

We know that when Americans have more take-home pay to spend, to save, or to invest, the whole economy grows, and people are more likely to find a job. We understand whose money we spend in Washington, DC. It is not the Government's money. It is the people's money.

We are returning more money to the people to help them raise their families. We are reducing taxes on dividends and capital gains to encourage investment. We're giving small businesses incentives to expand and hire new people. With all these actions, we are laying the foundation for greater prosperity and more jobs across America, so that every single person in this country can realize the American Dream.

Two-and-a-half years ago, there was a lot of talk about education reform, but there wasn't much action. So I called for and Congress passed the No Child Left Behind Act. With a solid bipartisan majority, we delivered the most dramatic education reforms in a generation. We're bringing high standards and strong accountability measures to every single public school in America. We believe that every child can learn the basics of reading and math, and we expect every school to teach the basics of reading and math. We are challenging the soft bigotry of low expectations. The days of excuse-making are over. We expect results in every classroom, so that not one single child in America is left behind.

We reorganized the Government and created a Department of Homeland Security to safeguard our borders and ports and to better protect the American people. We passed trade promotion authority to open new markets for America's entrepreneurs and farmers and ranchers. We passed a budget agreement that is helping to maintain spending discipline in Washington, DC. On issue after issue, this administration has acted on principle, has kept its word, and has made progress for the American people.

The United States Congress has shared in these great achievements, and I appreciate the hard work of the Members of the Congress. I appreciate being able to work with Speaker Hastert and Leader DeLay and Senator Frist. And we will continue to work together to change the tone in Washington, DC, by focusing on the people's business and by focusing on results.

And that's the nature of the men and women I have asked to serve in my administration. I have put together a really fine administration on behalf of the American people. Our country has had no finer Vice President than Dick Cheney. Mother may have a different thought. [*Laughter*]

In 2½ years we have come far, but our work is only beginning. We have great goals worthy of this Nation. First, America is committed to extending the realm of freedom and peace for our own security and for the benefit of the world. And second, in our own country, we must work for a society of prosperity and compassion, so that every citizen has a chance to work and succeed and realize the great promise of our country.

It is clear that the future of freedom and peace depend on the actions of America. This Nation is freedom's home and freedom's defender. We welcome this charge of history, and we are keeping it. Our war on terror continues. The enemies of freedom are not idle, and neither are we. This country will not rest; we will not tire; and we will not stop until this danger to civilization is removed.

Yet, our national interest involves more than eliminating aggressive threats to our security. Our greatest security comes from the advance of human liberty because free nations do not support terror, free nations do not attack their neighbors, free nations do not threaten the world with weapons of mass terror. Americans believe that freedom is the deepest need and hope of every human heart, and we believe that freedom is the right of every person and the future of every nation.

America also understands that unprecedented influence brings tremendous responsibilities. We have duties in the world, and when we see disease and starvation and hopeless poverty, we will not turn away. On the continent of Africa, America is now bringing the healing power of medicine to millions of men and women and children now suffering with AIDS. This great land is leading the world in this incredibly important work of human rescue.

We face challenges at home as well. And our actions will prove that we are equal to those challenges. I will continue to work on our economy until everybody who wants to work and who cannot find a job today is able to do so.

We have a duty to keep our commitment to America's seniors by strengthening and modernizing Medicare. Recently, the Congress took historic action to improve the lives of older Americans. For the first time since the creation of Medicare, the House and the Senate have passed reforms to increase choices for our seniors and to provide coverage for prescription drugs. The next step is for both Houses to work out their differences and to get a good bill to my desk as soon as possible.

For the sake of our health care system, we need to cut down on the frivolous lawsuits which increase the cost of medicine. I appreciate the very fine work of the Governor and the Lieutenant Governor and the speaker for passing real, meaningful medical liability reform here in the State of Texas. The State Representative Nixon, who is here with us today, was the author of that bill, and I appreciate your hard work, Joe.

Look, we understand a person who has been harmed by a bad doctor deserves his or her day in court. Yet, the system should not reward lawyers who are fishing for rich settlements. Because frivolous lawsuits drive up the cost of health care, they affect the Federal budget. Therefore, medical liability reform is a national issue that requires a national solution. The House of Representatives has passed a fine bill. It is stuck in the United States Senate. The Senate must act on behalf of the American citizens.

I have a responsibility as President to make sure the judicial system runs well. And I have met that duty. I have nominated superb men and women like Priscilla Owen to the Federal courts, people who will interpret the law, not legislate from the bench.

Some Members of the Senate are trying to keep my nominees off the bench by blocking up-or-down votes. Every judicial nominee deserves a fair hearing and an up-or-down vote in the Senate floor. It is time for some of those Members in the Senate to stop playing politics with American justice.

The Congress needs to pass a comprehensive energy plan. Our Nation must promote energy efficiency and conservation and continue to develop technology so we can explore in a more environmentally friendly way. But for the sake of our economic security and for the sake of our national security, we must be less dependent on foreign sources of energy.

Our strong and prosperous Nation must also be a compassionate nation. I will continue to advance our agenda of compassionate conservatism, applying the best and most innovative ideas to the task of helping our fellow citizens in need. There are still millions of men and women who want to end their dependence on Government and become independent through hard work. We must build on the success of welfare reform to bring work and dignity into the lives of more of our fellow citizens.

Congress should complete the "Citizen Service Act" to encourage more Americans to serve their communities and their country. And both Houses should reach agreement on my Faith-Based Initiative to support the armies of compassion that are mentoring our children and caring for the homeless and offering hope to the addicted.

A compassionate society must promote opportunity for all, including the independence and dignity that come from ownership. My administration will constantly strive to promote an ownership society in America. We want more people owning their own home. We want our fellow citizens to own and manage their own health care plan and to own and manage their own retirement accounts. We want more of our citizens, our entrepreneurs, to own their own small business. We understand that when a person owns something, he or she has a vital stake in the future of our country.

In a compassionate society, people respect one another and take responsibilities for the decisions they make. We're changing the culture of America from one that has said, "If it feels good, do it," and "If you've got a problem, blame somebody else," to one in which each of us understands we are responsible for the decisions we make in life. If you are a mom or a dad, if you're fortunate enough to be a mom or a dad, it is you who is responsible for loving your child. If you're concerned about the quality of the education in the community in which you live, you're responsible for doing something about it. If you're a CEO in America, you have the responsibility to tell the truth to your shareholders and your employees. And in this new responsibility society, each of us is responsible for loving a neighbor just like we'd like to be loved ourself.

We can see the culture of service and responsibility growing around us. I started the USA Freedom Corps to encourage Americans to extend a compassionate hand to neighbors in need, and the response has been fantastic. As I travel our country, I also see the vibrancy of many of the faith-based organizations, the neighborhood healers that are concerned about saving lives. I also know that policemen and firefighters and people who wear our Nation's uniform are reminding us once again what it means to sacrifice for something greater than ourselves. Our children believe in heroes because they see them every day.

In these challenging times, the world has seen the resolve and the courage of America, and I've been privileged to see the compassion and character of the American people. All the tests of the last 2½ years have come to the right nation.

We are a strong country, and we use that strength to defend the peace. We're an optimistic country, confident in ourselves and in ideals bigger than ourselves. Abroad, we seek to lift whole nations by spreading freedom. At home, we seek to lift up lives by spreading opportunity to every corner of America. This is the work that history has set before us. We welcome it. And we know that for our country and for our cause, the best days lie ahead.

May God bless America. Thank you all.

NOTE: The President spoke at 5:55 p.m. at the Westin Galleria. In his remarks, he referred to Texas House of Representatives Speaker Tom Craddick; and Fred Meyer, Texas State finance chairman, Jeanne Johnson Phillips, Texas State finance vice chairman, and Nancy Kinder, fundraiser, Bush-Cheney '04, Inc.

The President's News Conference With Prime Minister Silvio Berlusconi of Italy in Crawford, Texas
July 21, 2003

President Bush. Thank you for coming. I'm honored to host my friend the Prime Minister of Italy, Silvio Berlusconi. It's such an honor for us to welcome—I say "us"; Laura welcomes him as well as I to our ranch. We welcome the Prime Minister as a good friend, and he represents a country which is a strong ally to America. Welcome.

Prime Minister Berlusconi. Thank you.

President Bush. I want to thank him for being such a gracious host during our trips overseas, and we're really pleased to return the hospitality.

Last year, on America's Memorial Day, Prime Minister Berlusconi visited a American military cemetery in Italy to honor our service members who gave their lives defending freedom in Europe. His actions touched me personally. He understands the history and the values that our two countries share. The people of the United States and Italy love freedom, and we know that freedom must be defended.

We also understand that defending freedom requires costs and sacrifice. And the United States is grateful for Italy's willingness to bear the burdens with us. Italy and America stood together through nearly a half a century of cold war. Over the past decade, we have stood together against oppression and hatred in the Balkans. And in the months since September the 11th, 2001, Italy and America have stood side by side against tyranny and global terror.

The war on terror continues. We will see it through to victory. Global terrorist networks are a threat to America, to Italy, and to all peaceful nations. And we are disrupting and destroying those networks. The proliferation of weapons of mass destruction is a threat to America, to Italy, and to all peaceful nations. We will persevere until that threat is removed. Radicalism and ideologies of hatred are a threat to America, to Italy, and to all peaceful nations. And we are determined to spread liberty and progress and hope.

My country is especially grateful to the Italian troops and police who are serving with skill and courage in Afghanistan and Iraq. Our efforts to work for freedom and stability in these countries and throughout the entire region are an integral part of the war on terror. And we will make both our nations safer and advance the peace of the world.

The Prime Minister and I are both encouraged by signs of progress toward a great goal in the Middle East: two states, Palestine and Israel, living side by side in peace and security. Both Prime Minister Abbas and Prime Minister Sharon are showing leadership and courage. Now it is time for governments across the Middle East to support the efforts of these two men by fighting terror in all its forms. This includes the Governments of Syria and Iran. This behavior is—today, Syria and Iran continue to harbor and assist terrorists. This behavior is completely unacceptable, and states that support terror will be held accountable.

Supporting and harboring terrorists undermines the prospects for peace in the Middle East and betrays the true interests of the Palestinian people. Terrorism is the greatest obstacle to the emergence of a Palestinian state, and all leaders who seek this goal have an obligation to back up their words in real actions against terror. And leaders who are interested in a peaceful solution in the Middle East must support the efforts of Prime Minister Abbas to build a democratic Palestine and ease the hardships faced by the Palestinian people.

The Prime Minister and I are in complete agreement that Europe and America are both more secure and more effective when we act together. I'm pleased that Prime Minister Berlusconi is now serving as the President of the European Union. And I'm confident that under his leadership of the EU, Europe and America will continue to meet the great challenges before us.

Mr. Prime Minister, thank you for your leadership, your wise counsel, and your friendship, and welcome to Crawford, Texas.

Prime Minister Berlusconi. Thank you, Mr. President. Thank you for hosting me, and thank you for inviting me here to visit a country which I love very much to talk about our common concerns: that is, freedom, democracy, and justice and development.

Thank you very much for welcoming me in your home, making me feel as a member of your family. Please let me say so, this is again a chance for me to talk to you and tell you about the gratitude I have, the gratitude I personally have, my country has for you, for a country which allowed us to enjoy our freedom and our welfare and well-being and to enjoy all of this.

This morning I attended one of your meetings, work meetings, and I was strongly impressed by the burden of responsibilities that you take on yourself and on your country. And I really thought that it was extremely important for the citizens in the West to know with what attention and care and with what spirit of sacrifice and generosity the United States and its President follow the developments all over the world which might bring about danger and threat and hurt any country in the world.

He already mentioned the subjects we discussed in our meeting and already said that we have a common vision on all of these issues, with no exception. I'll go back to Italy and Europe with a belief which I already had but which was strengthened by my visit here. My belief is that we really need to support and develop the culture of union and cohesion and certainly not nurture the culture of division. Selfishness,

narcissism, and division shall never win. We need to revive the huge strength of cohesion. And this has to be a vital force, able to plan and build something. And this is the message which I'm going to bring back to my European allies as President of the European Union.

Once again, thank you, Mr. President, for the friendship of your people to my country and for your personal friendship and esteem.

President Bush. Thank you, sir. Before the Prime Minister and I take a tour of the ranch, we'll answer a couple of questions.

Deb, AP [Deb Riechmann, Associated Press].

Liberia

Q. Mr. President, a mortar shell has hit the U.S. Embassy in Liberia. The U.S. has sent a contingent of Marines there to protect its interests. What about the civilians being killed? There were some civilians dragged in front of the Embassy this morning. Sir, my question is, can the U.S. stand by and watch the violence spiral out of control, and what about sending U.S. peacekeepers?

President Bush. Well, you're right, we just sent a group of troops in to protect our interests, and we're concerned about our people in Liberia. We'll continue to monitor the situation very closely. We're working with the United Nations to effect policy necessary to get the cease-fire back in place. We are working with ECOWAS to determine when they will be prepared to move in the peacekeeper troops that I have said we'd be willing to help move into Liberia. We're monitoring the situation very carefully.

You call on somebody.

Prime Minister Berlusconi. [*Inaudible*]

President Bush. No, you get to call on somebody.

Prime Minister Berlusconi. Si, si. Prego.

Iraq

Q. The question, if possible, could be answered by both of you—that is, the situation in Iraq. Did you discuss the possibility of having Italian troops taking over and replacing the—taking over the peacekeeping operations and taking over from the U.S. military? And did you talk about reconstruction of Iraq? And did you also mention the possibility that countries which did not participate in the coalition can have the same role and the same share in the reconstruction of Iraq?

President Bush. No, we didn't talk about Italy replacing the United States as peacekeepers. Yes, we did discuss how to broaden the coalition to bring more security to Iraq.

It's very important for our citizens of both countries to understand that this extension of hostility is really a part of the war to liberate Iraq. There are people in Iraq who hate the thought of freedom. There are Saddam apologists who want to try to stay in power through terrorist activity. And I explained to the Prime Minister, we're patient, we're strong, we're resolute, and we will see this matter through. And obviously, the more help we can get, the more we appreciate it. And we are continuing to work with other nations to ask their help and advice. And we appreciate the leadership of the Prime Minister.

Secondly, the answer to your question about reconstruction efforts, the answer is, who can do the best job for the Iraqi people? The reconstruction effort shouldn't be viewed as a political exercise. It shouldn't be viewed as an international grab bag. It shouldn't be viewed as a special opportunity.

The answer to your question is, how best to improve the lives of the Iraqi people, how best to quickly establish electricity and clean water and hospitals and schools, all the things necessary for a free society to develop. And so if that can be—if that question can be answered positively by somebody who didn't necessarily agree with the decision, that's fine. We're interested—mostly interested in the Iraqi people.

Okay, Adam [Adam Entous, Reuters].

Q. Thank you, Mr. President.

Prime Minister Berlusconi. I share——

President Bush. You want to answer that? Sure.

Prime Minister Berlusconi. No, no, I completely share what the President just said.

President Bush. Then why don't you ask the Prime Minister a question so he can answer a question.

Q. Mr. President.

President Bush. Yes, Adam.

North Korea

Q. New evidence suggests North Korea may have built a second, secret site to process plutonium. How concerned are you? Are you going to let this stand? Also, are you still hopeful of making progress in talks through the Chinese?

President Bush. Well, I appreciate you bringing up the latter, because I do believe we can solve this issue diplomatically by encouraging the neighborhood—the Chinese, the South Koreans, and the Japanese to join us with a single voice that says to Mr. Kim Chong-il, "A decision to develop a nuclear arsenal is one that will alienate you from the rest of the world."

The desire by the North Koreans to convince the world that they're in the process of developing a nuclear arsenal is nothing new. We've known that for a while. And therefore, we must continue to work with the neighborhood to convince Kim Chong-il that his decision is an unwise decision. And we will do just that.

Iraq

Q. Under what condition would you accept a new United Nation resolution about Iraq? You know that some countries are asking.

President Bush. Well, we're in close consultation with the U.N. We believe that

1483 empowers countries to make a proper decision to get involved in Iraq. Let me talk about the U.N. in relations to Iraq in general. Mr. de Mello is doing a very fine job. He is working very closely with Bremer. They've got a fine relationship, and that bodes well for future discussions. Fourteen eighty-three is a very strong resolution and a very adequate resolution.

But we're constantly in touch with U.N. officials. And Kofi Annan was in my office the other day, discussing a lot of different issues, and one of the issues was Iraq. The more people involved in Iraq, the better off we will be. And that's exactly what our intention is, to encourage people to participate in the—making Iraq more secure and more free. A free Iraq is a crucial part of winning the war on terror.

And now I'm going to go see to it that the Prime Minister is well fed. We're going to feed him some chicken.

Thank you, sir. I appreciate it very much. Thank you all.

NOTE: The President's news conference began at 11:13 a.m. at the Bush Ranch. In his remarks, he referred to Prime Minister Mahmoud Abbas (Abu Mazen) of the Palestinian Authority; Prime Minister Ariel Sharon of Israel; former President Saddam Hussein of Iraq; Chairman Kim Chong-il of North Korea; Secretary-General Kofi Annan and Special Representative for Iraq Sergio Vieira de Mello of the United Nations; and L. Paul Bremer III, Presidential Envoy to Iraq. Prime Minister Berlusconi spoke in Italian, and some reporters asked their questions in Italian, and their remarks were translated by an interpreter.

Letter to Congressional Leaders on Continued Operations of United States Forces in Bosnia and Herzegovina
July 22, 2003

Dear Mr. Speaker: (Dear Mr. President:)

In my report to the Congress of January 21, 2003, I provided information on the deployment of combat-equipped U.S. Armed Forces to Bosnia and Herzegovina and other states in the region in order to participate in and support the North Atlantic Treaty Organization (NATO)-led Stabilization Force (SFOR). The SFOR began its mission and assumed authority from the NATO-led Implementation Force on December 20, 1996. I am providing this supplemental report, prepared by my Administration and consistent with the War Powers Resolution (Public Law 93–148), to help ensure that the Congress is kept fully informed on continued U.S. contributions in support of peacekeeping efforts in the former Yugoslavia.

The U.N. Security Council authorized Member States to continue SFOR for a period of 12 months in U.N. Security Council Resolution 1491 of July 11, 2003. The mission of SFOR is to provide a focused military presence in order to deter hostilities, stabilize and consolidate the peace in Bosnia and Herzegovina, contribute to a secure environment, and provide, within its means and capabilities, selective support to key tasks and key civil implementation organizations.

The U.S. force contribution to SFOR in Bosnia and Herzegovina is approximately 1,800 personnel. United States personnel comprise approximately 15 percent of the total SFOR force of approximately 12,000 personnel. During the first half of 2003, 17 NATO nations and 11 others provided military personnel or other support to

SFOR. Most U.S. forces in Bosnia and Herzegovina are assigned to Multinational Brigade, North, headquartered near the city of Tuzla. The U.S. forces continue to support SFOR efforts to apprehend persons indicted for war crimes and to conduct counter-terrorism operations. In the last 6 months, U.S. forces have not sustained any combat-related fatalities.

I have directed the participation of U.S. Armed Forces in these operations pursuant to my constitutional authority to conduct U.S. foreign relations and as Commander in Chief and Chief Executive.

I am providing this report as part of my efforts to keep the Congress fully informed about developments in Bosnia and Herzegovina. I will continue to consult closely with the Congress regarding our efforts to foster peace and stability in the former Yugoslavia.

Sincerely,

GEORGE W. BUSH

NOTE: Identical letters were sent to J. Dennis Hastert, Speaker of the House of Representatives, and Ted Stevens, President pro tempore of the Senate.

Message to the Congress Transmitting a Progress Report on Spending in Support of Plan Colombia
July 22, 2003

To the Congress of the United States:

Consistent with section 3204(e), Public Law 106–246, I am providing a report prepared by my Administration detailing the progress of spending by the executive branch during the first two quarters of Fiscal Year 2003 in support of Plan Colombia.

GEORGE W. BUSH

The White House,
July 22, 2003.

Remarks on Coalition Activities in Iraq
July 23, 2003

It is my pleasure to welcome Ambassador Paul Bremer back to the White House. I'm also pleased to be joined by Secretary Rumsfeld and General Myers. Thank you all for coming.

Ambassador Bremer is doing a fine job in an essential cause. The nations in our coalition are determined to help the Iraqi people recover from years of tyranny. And we are determined to help build a free and sovereign and democratic nation.

The coalition provisional authority, led by Ambassador Bremer, has a comprehensive strategy to move Iraq toward a future that is secure and prosperous. We are carrying out that strategy for the good of Iraq, for the peace of the region, and for the security of the United States and our friends.

Saddam Hussein's regime spent more than three decades oppressing Iraq's people, attacking Iraq's neighbors, and threatening the world's peace. The regime tortured at home, promoted terror abroad, and armed in secret. Now, with the regime of Saddam Hussein gone forever, a few remaining holdouts are trying to prevent the advance of order and freedom. They are targeting our success in rebuilding Iraq;

they're killing new police graduates; they're shooting at people that are guarding the universities and powerplants and oil facilities.

These killers are the enemies of Iraq's people. They operate mainly in a few areas of the country. And wherever they operate, they are being hunted, and they will be defeated. Our military forces are on the offensive. They're working with the newly free Iraqi people to destroy the remnants of the old regime and their terrorist allies.

Yesterday, in the city of Mosul, the careers of two of the regime's chief henchmen came to an end. Saddam Hussein's sons were responsible for torture, maiming, and murder of countless Iraqis. Now more than ever, all Iraqis can know that the former regime is gone and will not be coming back.

As our work continues, we know that our coalition forces are serving under difficult circumstances. Our Nation will give those who wear its uniform all the tools and support they need to complete their mission. We are eternally grateful for the bravery of our troops, for their sacrifice, and for the sacrifices of their families. The families of our service men and women can take comfort in knowing that their sons and daughters and moms and dads are serving a cause that is noble and just and vital to the security of the United States.

A free, democratic, peaceful Iraq will not threaten America or our friends with illegal weapons. A free Iraq will not be a training ground for terrorists or a funnel of money to terrorists or provide weapons to terrorists who would willingly use them to strike our country or our allies. A free Iraq will not destabilize the Middle East. A free Iraq can set a hopeful example to the entire region and lead other nations to choose freedom. And as the pursuits of freedom replace hatred and resentment and terror in the Middle East, the American people will be more secure.

America has assumed great responsibilities for Iraq's future. Yet, we do not bear these responsibilities alone. Nineteen nations are providing more than 13,000 troops to help stabilize Iraq, and additional forces will soon arise—arrive. More than two dozen nations have pledged funds that will go directly towards relief and reconstruction efforts. Every day, we are renovating schools for the new school year. We're restoring the damaged water, electrical, and communication systems. And when we introduce a new Iraqi currency later this year, it will be the first time in 12 years that the whole country is using the same currency.

Our greatest ally in the vital work of stabilizing and rebuilding a democratic and prosperous Iraq is the Iraqi people themselves. Our goal is to turn over authority to Iraqis as quickly as possible. Coalition authorities are training Iraqi police forces to help patrol Iraqi cities and villages. Ambassador Bremer and General Abizaid are working to establish as quickly as possible a new Iraqi civilian defense force to help protect supply convoys and powerplants and ammunition depots. Offices have been established in major Iraqi cities to recruit soldiers for a new Iraqi army that will defend the people of Iraq instead of terrorizing them.

Most importantly, 10 days ago, Iraqis formed a new Governing Council. The Council represents all of Iraq's diverse groups, and it has given responsible positions to religious authorities and to women. The Council is naming ministers to establish control over Iraq's ministries, and the Council is drawing up a new budget. The process of drafting a constitution will soon be underway, and this will prepare the way for elections.

Yesterday in New York, members of Iraq's Governing Council participated in a meeting of the United Nations Security Council. They heard a report from U.N. Secretary-General Annan which welcomed the establishment of the Iraqi Governing Council as a broadly representative Iraqi partner with whom the U.N. and the international community can engage to build Iraq's future.

Now that we have reached this important milestone, I urge the nations of the world to contribute militarily and financially towards fulfilling Security Council Resolution 1483's vision of a free and secure Iraq. The U.N. report also urges a swift return to full Iraqi sovereignty.

And this morning, Ambassador Bremer briefed me on our strategy to accelerate progress toward this goal. He outlined a comprehensive plan for action for bringing greater security, essential services, economic development, and democracy to the Iraqi people. The plan sets out ambitious timetables and clear benchmarks to measure progress and practical methods for achieving results.

Rebuilding Iraq will require a sustained commitment. America and our partners kept our promise to remove the dictator and the threat he posed not only to the Iraqi people but to the world. We also keep our promise to destroy every remnant of that regime and to help the people of Iraq

to govern themselves in freedom. In the 83 days since I announced the end of major combat operations in Iraq, we have made progress, steady progress, in restoring hope in a nation beaten down by decades of tyranny.

Ambassador Bremer is showing great skill and resourcefulness and is demonstrating fine leadership and the great values of our country. Mr. Ambassador, thank you for what you're doing for America. I appreciate you.

NOTE: The President spoke at 10:16 a.m. in the Rose Garden at the White House. In his remarks, he referred to L. Paul Bremer III, Presidential Envoy to Iraq; Uday and Qusay Hussein, sons of former President Saddam Hussein of Iraq, who were killed July 22 by U.S. military forces in Mosul, Iraq; Gen. John P. Abizaid, USA, combatant commander, U.S. Central Command; and Secretary-General Kofi Annan of the United Nations. The Office of the Press Secretary also released a Spanish language transcript of these remarks.

Remarks on Presenting the Presidential Medal of Freedom
July 23, 2003

The President. Good afternoon, and welcome to the White House. Laura and I are really glad you all are here. We're especially pleased to welcome the distinguished guests we honor today and their proud families and friends.

I appreciate former Secretary of State Madeleine Albright for joining us today. Madam Secretary, thank you for coming.

I'm honored that Kay Bailey Hutchison from the great State of Texas is here with us today. I appreciate the ambassadors who have joined us. I appreciate former Presidential Medal of Freedom recipients and their families who are here: Zbigniew

Brzezinski is with us today; Liz Moynihan is the widow of Senator Moynihan; and Irving Kristol. I thank you all for coming.

The Presidential Medal of Freedom is America's highest civil award. It is conferred upon men and women of high achievement in the arts and entertainment, public service, science, education, athletics, business, and other fields. For most recipients, this award is a special distinction added to many prior honors.

Some recipients are no longer with us but are still highly regarded and fondly remembered. All who receive the Presidential

Medal of Freedom have the continued respect of their peers and the lasting admiration of the American people.

Julia Child already holds the highest distinction of the French Government. She was awarded the Legion of Honor for sharing with millions of Americans the appreciation and artistry of French cooking.

Before Julia Child came along, no one imagined it could be so interesting to watch a meal being prepared. [*Laughter*] The reason, of course, is Julia herself, her friendly way, her engaging conversation, and her eagerness to teach. American cuisine and American culture have been enriched for decades by the unmistakable voice and the presence of Julia Child.

Americans are not always in the mood for exquisite meals. Sometimes all we want is a hamburger at the drive-up window. [*Laughter*] And a lot of those windows are at places named for the daughter of Dave Thomas. The late founder of Wendy's left school without a diploma to begin working at a very young age.

His great success as a restauranteur allowed Dave to fulfill other ambitions in his life. He became a benefactor of good causes, especially the cause of adoption. Dave himself was orphaned at an early age, and many young men and women today can thank Dave Thomas for helping to join them with loving parents.

At the height of his career, Dave Thomas went back to school and earned a GED. His classmates voted him "most likely to succeed." [*Laughter*] And today his country honors the hard work behind his success and the great generosity Dave Thomas showed others.

Van Cliburn was last here in 2001 as one of the Kennedy Center honorees. His life of honor started early, as the 23-year-old winner of the Tchaikovsky Competition in Moscow. In the years since, he has even further refined the gifts of a prodigy with the discipline and consistency of a true master. He has lived up to the high standards of the music teacher who first inspired

him, his mother, Rildia Bee Cliburn. Today, throughout America and across the world, musicians find inspiration in his example, and all of us associate the name Van Cliburn with grace and the perfect touch at the piano.

Like Van, the scholar Jacques Barzun now lives in Texas. He began his life 95 years ago in France. He became an American citizen in 1933 and joined the faculty at Columbia University and gained a reputation as a thinker of great discernment and integrity. From his first book, published 71 years ago, to his latest, a bestseller published in 2000, Jacques Barzun has influenced generations of serious readers. Few academics of the last century have equaled his output and his influence, and today he has the profound gratitude of his adopted country.

Charlton Heston is known for his portrayals of the most compelling dramatic figures: Moses, Judah Ben-Hur, Michelangelo, General Andrew Jackson, and Captain George Taylor. In the process, Charlton Heston himself has become one of the great names in film history. Over more than half a century, his talent and intensity have proven big enough to fill any role.

The largeness of character that comes across the screen has also been seen throughout his life, during Charlton Heston's service in World War II, his leadership of a labor union, his activism on behalf of civil rights, and his principled defense of the Bill of Rights. Charlton Heston has left his mark on our country as an artist, as a citizen, and as a patriot, and we're honored he is with us today.

We're also honored as well by the presence of an artist whose life brought two experiences he never could have expected, that of a prisoner and that of a President. In the days of Communist rule over Czechoslovakia, Vaclav Havel ridiculed the pretensions of an oppressive government and was viewed as an enemy of the state. The most subversive act of this playwright was telling the truth about tyranny, and when the truth finally triumphed in a "kindhearted revolution," the people elected this dignified, charming, humble, determined man to lead their country. Unintimidated by threats, unchanged by political power, this good man has suffered much in the cause of liberty, and he has become one of liberty's great heroes.

When liberty was threatened by nazism, a young Hungarian scientist named Edward Teller left Europe and found his way to the United States. Within a decade, the German Reich was at war with America and in search of the most terrible weapons. Dr. Teller joined the Manhattan Project and applied his disciplined mind to the most urgent task America had ever faced, to develop the atom bomb before Hitler.

Dr. Teller contributed to the success of that mission and helped us to meet other great national security challenges during the cold war. In recent decades, he has turned his efforts to the great scientific and moral task of building a defense against ballistic missiles. For a long life of brilliant achievement and patriotic service, America is in debt to Dr. Edward Teller.

Professor James Q. Wilson may be the most influential political scientist in America since the White House was home to Professor Woodrow Wilson. Throughout his career, he has demonstrated the best virtues of the academic profession. His theories and ideas are drawn from actual human experience and therefore have great practical value in addressing social problems. He writes with authority on a range of subjects, from the workings of government to the causes and prevention of crime. Whatever his subject, James Q. Wilson writes with intellectual rigor, with moral clarity, to the appreciation of a wide and growing audience. And it is my honor to congratulate Professor James Q. Wilson.

Of the 108 Americans who have served on the Supreme Court of the United States, only one is also in the College Football Hall of Fame. Justice Byron White was a rare kind of person who seemed to excel at everything he attempted. Whether playing football or earning a Bronze Star in World War II or enforcing civil rights as Deputy Attorney General, Byron White was tough, and he was determined.

When he was nominated, his close friend at the Supreme Court, President John F. Kennedy, called Byron White a man of "character, experience, and intellectual force." Over the next three decades, Justice White showed those qualities in majority opinions of great depth and in dissenting opinions of great wisdom and courage. When he passed away last year, people across our country felt that loss of a superb judge and a great American.

John Wooden is also a Hall of Famer, one of the only two enshrined both as basketball player and basketball coach. In a legendary career, Coach Wooden led his teams to 885 victories with only 203 losses. His players included some of the alltime greats: Kareem Abdul-Jabbar and Bill Walton and Gail Goodrich, to name a few.

But all his players will tell you the most important man on their team was not on the court. He was the man who taught generations of basketball players the fundamentals of hard work and discipline, patience, and teamwork. Coach Wooden remains a part of their lives as a teacher of the game and as an example of what a good man should be. Nell Wooden, the coach's wife of 53 years, would be incredibly proud of him again. Coach Wooden, it's wonderful to see you with us today.

Another recipient this afternoon would have been 69 years old next month. Millions of Americans remember hearing the news that Roberto Clemente had been lost on a mission to help the people of Nicaragua after an earthquake. His full name was Roberto Clemente Walker, and in an era of Mays and Mantle and Aaron, he ranked as one of the greats.

He was a young man with a quick bat, a rifle arm, and a gentle heart. In the words of one baseball executive, "I never saw any ballplayer like him. No, sir. Whenever anybody signs a big contract these days, we always wonder how many millions Clemente would be worth." As a former team owner, it would be a lot. [*Laughter*] Yet the true worth of this man, seen in how he lived his life and how he lost his life, cannot be measured in money. And all these years later, his family can know that America cherishes the memory of Roberto Clemente.

Our country and our world have been improved by the lives of the men and women we honor today. And now it is my honor to present the awards, and I ask the military aide to read the citations.

[*At this point, Lt. Col. John Newell, USAF, Air Force Aide to the President, read the citations, and the President presented the medals.*]

The President. Thank you all for coming. And Laura and I would now like to invite you to join us for a reception to honor these great Americans and great member of the Czech Republic, our great friend.

Thank you all for coming. God bless.

NOTE: The President spoke at 3:05 p.m. in the East Room at the White House. In his remarks, he referred to Senator Kay Bailey Hutchison of Texas.

Letter to the Speaker of the House of Representatives on Reallocation of Funds Previously Transferred From the Emergency Response Fund
July 23, 2003

Dear Mr. Speaker:

In order to continue the necessary and critical responses to the September 11 terrorist attacks, I am notifying the Congress of my intent to reallocate funds previously transferred from the Emergency Response Fund (ERF).

At this time, $5 million of ERF funds will be transferred to the Food and Drug Administration to support activities to improve the security of the food supply.

The details of this action are set forth in the enclosed letter from the Director of the Office of Management and Budget.

Sincerely,

GEORGE W. BUSH

Remarks Following a Roundtable Discussion in Philadelphia, Pennsylvania
July 24, 2003

Thank you all. Please be seated. Thank you all very much for allowing us to come. John, thanks for your leadership. He's doing a fabulous job as the Secretary of Treasury, and I'm so glad he decided to join my administration.

I want to thank you for the warm welcome, and I want to thank you all for helping us keep a commitment to the American people. We promised tax reductions for the good of American families and for the good of our economy. And we delivered on that promise. And soon the mail carrier will be delivering the checks that we promised to the American people. Twelve billion dollars in tax relief is on its way to more than 25 million American families.

And this is an appropriate place to come and talk about checks being mailed to American families, here at the Financial

Management Service. The reason why is because here and at other facilities, these checks are being printed, and the checks will be mailed. And I want to thank you all very much for working as hard as you are to make sure that the promise that the Government has made is being kept.

I know a lot of you are putting in weekend shifts. I know a lot of you are working really hard. And I am grateful, but more importantly, the American people should be grateful for the work you do right here. Thank on behalf of—[*applause*].

I have traveled today with two really fine men and great United States Senators, Arlen Specter and Rick Santorum. I want to thank you all for coming. I want to thank you for—I want to thank Mike Colarusso and Bob Mange for leading this fine group of folks. Thank you all for your hospitality.

I want to thank those good workers who allowed me and the press corps to come and see you doing your job. It's not easy to do your job with a distraction, and I must confess that sometimes the Presidential entourage can be distracting. [*Laughter*] But we want to thank you all for your hospitality and, most of all, thank you for being such great Americans and working so hard on behalf of the American people.

Today when I landed in Philadelphia, I met a lady named Valerie Christy. She's what we call USA—there's Valerie, right there. I'm sure you don't know who Valerie is, but you're about to, because Valerie is a person who has taken time out of her life to make somebody else's life better. She is a volunteer. One of the things she's done is she has participated in the Philadelphia Cares Day, which helps to paint and repair public schools in Philadelphia. She also volunteers twice a month in what they call Partners in Technology to help seniors and other special needs residents learn to use the technological change—learn to adapt to the technological changes of our society.

In other words, and the reason I bring this up is, much has been made about the great strength and might of America, and we are strong, and we are mighty, and we'll remain that way. But the true strength of our country is the heart and soul of our citizens, and Valerie represents that. She represents those who have heard the call to love a neighbor like you'd like to be loved yourself.

And the reason I bring this up is I want to continue to remind our fellow citizens that the way to change America for the better, and the way to make sure the great promise of our country exists for every single citizen, is that when we see somebody in need, we must act. If you're worried about children not being able to read, mentor a child. If you have a shut-in in your neighborhood who is lonely, provide comfort and love to that person. See, each of us can make a difference in America. America changes one heart, one soul, one conscience at a time. And each of us must be that some person trying to help make that change when we find somebody who hurts. Valerie, thank you for the example you set for our fellow citizens.

You know, this country has faced a lot of challenges in the past few years. And I believe those challenges have brought out the best in America. On September the 11th, 2001, a date I will not forget so long as I'm on this Earth, America's enemies declared war on this country. That's what happened on that day. It was a declaration of war by people who hate what America stands for, and war is what they got.

We are dismantling the Al Qaida network leader by leader. We are finding these killers one by one, and they will be brought to justice. We also acted in decisive ways to uphold doctrine. One of the doctrines said, "If you harbor a terrorist, you're just as guilty as the terrorist." And so in Afghanistan, we recognized that there was a cruel and oppressive regime that had turned a nation into training camps. And so we removed that regime, and the people of Afghanistan are free.

In Iraq, a dictator was arming to threaten the peace, and he defied the demands of the world. He didn't defy just the demands of the United States; he defied the demands of the United Nations Security Council, not once but many times. And so for peace and for the security of the free world, we removed that regime, and the Iraqi people are now free.

Our military is still facing danger from elements of the fallen regime and other extremists. These folks hate the thought of Iraq being free. And we're finding those people, and we're bringing them to justice. Two days ago in the city of Mosul, the careers of two of the regime's chief henchmen came to an end. Saddam Hussein's sons were responsible for torture, for maiming innocent citizens, and for the murder of countless Iraqis. And now, more than ever, the Iraqis can know that the former regime is gone and is not coming back.

Our people in uniform, our brave soldiers, are doing essential work in the war on terror. What they're doing in Iraq is an integral part on winning the war on terror. You see, a free and democratic and peaceful Iraq will not threaten America or our friends with illegal weapons. A free Iraq will not provide weapons to terrorists or money to terrorists who threaten the American people. A free Iraq will not destabilize the Middle East. A free Iraq can set a hopeful example for the entire region. And so the pursuits of freedom—and as the pursuits of freedom replace hatred and terror in the Middle East, America and our friends will be more secure.

Our Nation is incredibly grateful for the men and women who defend us, for the men and women who serve the cause of peace and security, and we are incredibly proud of those who wear our Nation's uniform.

We have risen to challenges abroad, and we are rising to challenges at home as well.

When I took office, when my administration came into office, the stock market had been falling for months and the economy was sliding into recession. And so we acted, and we passed tax relief, which made the recession one of the most shallow in history. We found that we had some of our corporate executives—we found they weren't telling the truth. [*Laughter*] They were being dishonest, not only to their shareholders but their employees, and we acted. We'll punish those who violate the law, and we're working together with Congress—and we worked together with Congress, and I signed the most historic corporate's governors reforms in a long period of time.

Last year, we saw that our economy was still not growing fast enough or creating jobs we need. So we acted. We passed meaningful, real tax relief. We expanded the child credit from $600 to $1,000 per child. We made that change retroactive to January 1st of this year, which is why the checks are going out of this facility soon. In other words, we said, "If we've got a problem, let's get the money to the people as quickly as possible." In the Jobs and Growth Act—that was the tax relief act—all aimed at increasing the capacity for our fellow citizens to find work. We brought down the marriage penalty. You see, we believe we ought to encourage marriage, not discourage marriage in the Tax Code.

We reduced all tax rates so our fellow citizens have got more take-home pay. That's good for the economy when people have more take-home pay. You see, by cutting individual tax relief, we passed tax relief as well for millions of small businesses, because most small businesses are what they call a sole proprietorship or Subchapter S, which means they pay taxes at the individual income tax rates. So in other words, the tax relief not only helped our families and our citizens, but it also helped the small-business sector of our economy.

And the benefits for this tax relief will be spread throughout all the economy.

That's what's important for people to know; it's widespread benefits. You see, because when people have more of their own money, more money in their pocket, they will demand a good or a service. And when somebody demands a good or a service in our system, somebody will produce the good or a service. And when somebody produces that good or a service, it means it's much more likely, as demand increases, that somebody will be able to find a job.

And that's what we're interested in. We're interested in creating jobs so our fellow citizens can find work. More than a million Pennsylvania families will benefit from the increased child tax credit. And earlier I had a chance to talk with some of the families who have joined us today. See, I think it's very important for our fellow citizens to understand, we're not just talking theory. When people get checks, it changes—it helps them with their lives.

The Lonabergers are with us. Barry says he wants to start saving more for his retirement and for the college education of his two sons, Kyle and Brandon, who are with us today. Where's Kyle? There they are, back there. He will get $800 soon, because of the increased child credit. His tax burden will drop by—be cut by 29 percent because of the tax relief.

He—so what does Barry say? He said, "Look, I'm interested in saving for my kids." He also said, "This extra money will help on a summer vacation." And he wants to renovate the kitchen in his home. So— and he told me he's going on a vacation. See, that makes it more likely that somebody is going to find a job at the motel in the place where he's going. [*Laughter*] And I'm sure he's going to eat when he gets there. So he'll take some of the money, and he'll buy food. And that's good for the person who owns the restaurant and for the people that serve the food or cook the food.

And when he renovates his kitchen, he's going to have to buy some equipment to help renovate it, which means somebody is going to have to manufacture the equipment that he buys to help renovate his— or the paint, for that matter. In other words, it has an effect throughout our economy. Increasing the child credit helps Barry. But it also is going to help those who deliver the goods and services that he now demands as a result of having extra money in his pocket.

Brian Peffley is here today. Brian and his wife, Heather, have three sons, Caleb, Joshua, Noah. And they have got to make sacrifices. Every family makes sacrifices. And one of the things he wants to do is to obviously have more money for back-to-school expenses. People are beginning to think about what it means to send their child back to school.

One of the sacrifices he was going to make in order to make sure he could— he and his family could purchase back-to-school expenses was he was going to delay taking a course he needed to get his bachelor's degree. And so what this means is, when he gets his check for $1,200, it will mean that he now can do both. And that's important. First of all, purchasing school supplies means the school supply manufacturer or school supply salesman has got a little extra business. But also, one of the things that's important in our workforce is for people to continually upgrade their education, so that they can be more productive and find a better job that pays better pay.

One of the things we want to encourage is additional education, and I appreciate the fact that Brian wants to go back to school. Here's what he said. He said, "This tax relief has eased the burden on us, and it will continue to allow us to achieve our goals and dreams." And that's what we want. We want people to have dreams in America and make it easier for them to realize their dreams.

Jeanette Luna is with us today. She, by the way, has the hardest job in America. She is a single mom. Adley is with us today. Eric is not here. But she earns a modest salary, and thanks to the tax relief, her refund will go from $600 to more than $1,100. And that will help pay for the school supplies. She's made the decision to send her child to a Catholic school, and that will help with tuition payments, which is important. It will help her buy clothes.

One of the things that's important is that tax relief helps people from all walks of life. And one of the things I've asked Congress to do, by the way, is to help low-income families like Jeanette's by making more of the child credit refundable. The benefits of the Jobs and Growth Act should be as broad as possible, should be widespread throughout our society. The House and the Senate have passed different versions of extending the child credit. They've got to resolve their differences and get it to my desk as quickly as possible, so people can get additional help.

Now, as John mentioned, the benefits of tax relief are positive. Economists—a lot of economists expect growth to pick up over the next 18 months. In other words, we've overcome a lot, and we've laid the foundation for growth. And I'll tell you why they believe that. First of all, home sales are rising, and that's positive. We want, by the way, more people owning their own home. That's one of—a grand objective for our economy. We've got a downpayment plan to help people do that. We're trying to simplify the contracts so people don't get discouraged by the fine print. But the best thing that's happening is, is that low mortgage rates have encouraged people to buy a home. And when you couple that with rising after-tax incomes, that's a positive foundation for home growth.

The other thing is people have refinanced their homes. In other words, lower mortgages mean that you can refinance and put a little extra money in your pocket for savings or needed purchases. Inflation is low, and that's positive. That's part of the foundation for economic vitality. Retail sales are rising, and that's good. Productivity amongst our workers is the highest

it's been in a long while, and that's positive. We're a more productive society.

Investors are showing more confidence. The stock market seems to be trending upwards. That's a positive sign. Since we're an ownership society, more and more people have got different retirement plans, and they count on the markets as part of their assets for retirement.

We've reduced taxes on stock dividends, and now companies have announced plans to increase their dividend payout. And some companies are going to pay dividends for the first time. And that's positive for our economy because billions of dollars in cash will now go directly to shareholders and back into the economy.

And so we're making progress. The other thing we've done is, as I mentioned, small businesses get relief from tax relief, which is vital. And what's really important for—to invigorate small-business growth is, most new jobs are created by small businesses in America, and therefore, it makes sense to have a policy that enhances the entrepreneurial spirit of America.

And so we did not only reduce taxes, but we also allowed for certain expensing of new equipment to encourage people to purchase new equipment. In other words, if there's an incentive for some small business to purchase a new piece of equipment, and they do, somebody's got to make the equipment. And when somebody makes the equipment, it is all part of making sure that there's job stability and job growth throughout our economy.

And so we've—there are hopeful signs, good progress. But there is more to do. And one of the things we've got to do is to make sure that—you know, we've got lawsuit reform. Listen, businesses are fighting a lot of frivolous litigation, and it's costly to our economy. And the House has taken up the reform of class-action—the class-action system, and the Senate has not. In my judgment, in order to enhance economic vitality, the Senate must act on fair and balanced tort reform legislation, starting with class-action lawsuits.

We need a comprehensive energy bill. We've got to have a policy, a comprehensive energy policy if we want our economy to grow. I'm concerned about the costs of natural gas. The demand is strong for natural gas, and supplies are not as plentiful for natural gas, which means there's price pressure. The House has acted on this important piece of legislation; the Senate hasn't. We need an energy bill that promotes conservation, that applies new and cleaner technologies, but one that improves national security by making us less dependent on foreign sources of energy.

We need to expand trade so our farmers and ranchers and manufacturers have got new markets. Listen, if you're good at something, you want to be able to sell what you're good at all around the world. And we're really good at a lot of things, and we ought to be encouraging markets to open up for United States products. That's important for job creation.

The other thing is that as we create new job opportunities, we've got to help the people be prepared to fill those job vacancies. And so I proposed what we call reemployment accounts. It gives Americans a chance, particularly those who are having the greatest difficulty finding work, to realize their dream of work. People get $3,000 to use in their job search. Now, that $3,000 should be used according to the needs of the people, not according to what the Government thinks the needs are. So if a person needs child care, they ought to be able to use that money. If a person needs transportation, they ought to be able to use that money. If a person needs extra training, they ought to be able to use that money. If a person finds a job in another part of the State, they ought to be able to use that money to help them move.

In other words, this is focus money, called reemployment accounts, to help people get ahead. If we want to expand this economy, we've got to recognize that some people need training and help to enter in that workforce.

And the other thing I said, if a worker believes—a worker can find work within 13 weeks, and there's still money left over of the $3,000, they can put it in their pocket as a reemployment bonus. Congress needs to look at this idea, need to act. They've got to understand that as we expand the economy, some of our citizens need some focus and some help.

And one of the things you hear talk about is the deficit, and we've got a deficit. We've got a deficit because revenues to the Treasury have dropped as a result of recession. And we've got a deficit as well because I'm spending the money necessary to win the war. My attitude is, when we put our troops in harm's way, they deserve the best. When we've got people overseas defending us—*[applause]*. I also firmly believe that as the economy—I know as the economy grows, there's going to be more revenue coming into the Treasury. And the tax relief, as I've described to you, will help the economy grow.

The best, surest way to make sure we deal with the deficit is to make sure we don't overspend in Washington, is we have a reasonable increase in discretionary spending. And I proposed Congress stay within a 4-percent increase of discretionary spending. It's about the same amount that the average American household budget will increase this year. It seems to make sense to me. If it's good enough for American families, it ought to be good enough for the appetite of the Congress.

The good news is they voted for that number, and now we expect them to hold the line. And I believe with economic growth and spending discipline, we can cut the deficit in half over the next 5 years, and that's progress.

What I hope you come away with is that I believe in the future of this Nation, and I believe the economy is strengthening, is going to be strong, because I know the character of the American people. In 22 months—think about this—in 22 months, our Nation has been tested by a national emergency, by corporate scandals, by a recession, and by war. And time after time, this country has responded effectively to each challenge we've faced. Time after time, we have shown firm resolve and unshakable faith in our country.

And the basis of the Jobs and Growth Act, the kind of fundamental principle of the Jobs and Growth Act, is that I've got faith in the American people, in the strength and the enterprise and the creativity of the American people. And I believe with hard work and determination, this economy is going to be strong. We're headed in the right direction. Better days are ahead for our citizens.

Listen, thank you for letting me come. May God bless. Thank you all.

NOTE: The President spoke at 11:14 a.m. at the Treasury Department's Philadelphia Financial Management Service regional center. In his remarks, he referred to Mike Colarusso, Regional Director, Philadelphia Financial Management Service Center; former President Saddam Hussein of Iraq; and Uday and Qusay Hussein, sons of former President Hussein, who were killed July 22 by U.S. military forces in Mosul, Iraq. The Office of the Press Secretary also released a Spanish language transcript of these remarks.

Remarks in Livonia, Michigan
July 24, 2003

Thank you for the warm welcome. Thanks for letting me come by to say hello. First, let me just say I appreciate the hardworking folks here at Beaver Aerospace for making sure that Air Force One functions properly. [*Laughter*] Otherwise, it might have been a long flight. [*Laughter*] I appreciate what you do for America's defense. I appreciate your hard work. I appreciate your talent. I appreciate you helping make this country strong.

I want to thank Bill Phillips and his family for inviting me. You know, one of the great things about America is the entrepreneurial spirit of our country, and Mr. Phillips is an entrepreneur. And one of the things we've got to do in America is keep that entrepreneurial spirit alive and well. And Mr. Phillips knows what I know: You can be an entrepreneur, but without good workers, good, dedicated, hard-working people willing to run the machines and show up on time and work hard, the entrepreneurial spirit is kind of empty. And so,

first of all, I want to not only thank the Phillips folks, I want to thank the people who work here in this facility. Thanks for making America go.

And I am interested in making sure every one of our fellow citizens who wants to work can find a job, and that's what I want to talk about today. I want to talk about how to make sure this economy is strong and vibrant so our citizens can work and families can be hopeful for the future.

First, I want to thank the Secretary of Commerce, Don Evans, my long-time friend. I appreciate his service. He's part of my economic team that is staying focused on economic vitality and growth.

I appreciate so very much Jack Kirksey. He's the mayor here. Mr. Mayor, you've got a tougher job than I do. [*Laughter*] You've got to empty the garbage and fill the potholes. [*Laughter*]

I appreciate the State attorney general, Mike Cox, for joining us today. He's right here from Livonia. I want to thank members of the legislative body, Senator Laura Toy and John Pastor, who have joined us today. I want to thank the chief of police, who's with us. I want to thank the president of the city council that's with us. I want to thank you all for coming. We've got quite a distinguished group.

I want to share the name of one person you've probably never heard of. It's a fellow I just met when I landed at the airport, and his name is Walter Piper. Walter is right there. Walter has been an active member of what they call SCORE, which is Service Corps of Retired Executives. That should tell you two things or three things about Walter: One, he is retired— [*laughter*]—two, he was an executive, and three, he is in service. And what he has done is he's decided to provide counsel and advice to people who want to start their own small business. He is volunteering his time to try to make the community in which he lives a better place.

The reason I bring that up is there's a lot made about how strong we are militarily. And we are strong militarily, and we will remain strong militarily. But the true strength of America is found in the hearts and souls of our fellow citizens. The true strength of our country is found in those hearts and souls that have heard the universal call to love a neighbor just like you'd like to be loved yourself. No, the strength of our country is the compassion of our fellow citizens, people like Walter who are willing to dedicate their time and talents to make somebody else's life better.

My call to you is when you see a neighbor in need, when you see somebody who's hurt, don't turn your back but love them just like you'd like to be loved yourself.

This country of ours has faced many challenges over the last couple of years, and I believe those challenges have brought out the best in America. Terrorists declared war on us. On September the 11th, a date we will not forget, people who hated our country, hate it for what we stand for,

hated the fact that we love freedom, declared war on the United States of America, and war is what they got. We are hunting down the killers one at a time. We are slowly but surely dismantling the Al Qaida network, and we will continue to find them and to bring them to justice. We owe that to this generation of Americans and future generations to come.

In Afghanistan, a cruel regime, a brutal regime, had turned that country into a training camp for terrorists. I declared as clearly as I could, "If you harbor a terrorist, you're just as guilty as the terrorists." So we removed the Taliban from power and freed people from the clutches of a barbaric regime.

In Iraq, a brutal dictator was arming to threaten the peace. This brutal dictator defied the demands of the free world. For years, he thumbed his nose at the United Nations Security Council, time and time again. We gave him plenty of time to disclose and disarm. He chose defiance, and the regime of Saddam Hussein is no more.

Our brave troops still face danger in Iraq because there are people there who hate the thought of a free society. They can't stand freedom, and they're dangerous. But we're finding these terrorists as well, and we're bringing them to justice. As you know, earlier this week, two of the favorite henchmen of Saddam Hussein were brought to justice. They were discovered, and their violent careers ended in justice. These two sons of Saddam Hussein were responsible for hundreds and hundreds of people being tortured and maimed and murdered. And now the Iraqi people have seen clearly the intent of the United States to make sure that they are free and to make sure that the Saddam regime never returns again to Iraq.

Our brave men and women serving to free—make sure Iraq is free are serving as well in the war on terror. A free and democratic and peaceful Iraq will not threaten America and our friends with illegal weapons. A free Iraq will not provide harbor and money to terrorist organizations which would like to hurt America. A free Iraq will not destabilize the Middle East. A free Iraq can set a hopeful example for the entire region. And as the pursuits of freedom replace hatred and resentment and terror in the Middle East, the American people will be more secure, and the world will be more peaceful. We owe a significant debt of gratitude to the men and women who wear the uniform of the United States of America.

Our Nation has responded to challenges here at home as well. Think about what we've been through. As I was showing up into office, the stock market had been falling for nearly a year, and the country was headed into recession. And then after the recession came the attacks of September the 11th, a significant attack on our homeland. It caused the economy to sputter. It significantly affected our capacity to generate jobs.

And then we found out that some of our fellow citizens forgot what it means to assume responsibility. They didn't tell the truth. Corporate CEOs around this country didn't tell the truth to their shareholders and their employees, and that shook the confidence of America. And then, of course, the drumbeat of war shook the— began to affect the ability for this economy to grow strong.

We've overcome a lot because we acted. First and foremost, in 2001, I worked with Congress to pass tax relief, and history will show that the recession we're in is one of the shallowest recessions our country has had. We passed tough laws that say to a corporate criminal, if you lie, cheat, or steal, you will be held to account.

Last year, when it looked like the economy was still sputtering and wasn't strong enough, when we realized too many Americans were still struggling to find work and too many families were having trouble meeting their monthly bills or saving for their child's education, we acted again, and

I convinced the Congress to pass the Jobs and Growth Act.

And that's a significant development in terms of economic vitality, because the more money people have in their pockets, the more they will demand a good or a service. And when somebody demands a good or a service, in this economy of ours, somebody will produce a good or a service. And when somebody produces that good or a service, it means somebody is more likely to find work.

The jobs-and-growth plan came at the exact right time in our history. Part of that jobs-and-growth plan is to increase the child credit from $600 to $1,000 per child. But I thought it was necessary to act quickly, so I asked Congress to make it retroactive to January 1st of this year, and they agreed.

Today I went to Philadelphia. I saw firsthand the checks that are being printed, that are fixing to be sent to the people who have got children who qualify for the child credit. That is, $13 billion is going out the door to be in the pockets of our fellow citizens; $13 billion for more money for people to save or to spend but to do with it which you want to do with it. After all, we're talking about your money, not the Government's money.

Part of the Jobs and Growth Act continue to bring down the marriage penalty. Seems like to me that the Tax Code ought to encourage marriage, not discourage marriage. I don't know why you want to penalize marriage. But part of the Jobs and Growth Act also reduced the overall tax rates people pay. It cut the individual tax rates across the board. You're going to have more money in your pocket. That's what we want. That's part of the economic jobs-and-growth plan.

The interesting thing about reducing taxes as well, it helped a lot of small businesses. And the cornerstone of any good jobs plan is to encourage small-business growth. A lot of small businesses pay tax at the individual tax rate. They're Subchapter S's, or they're what they call sole proprietorships. And so when you hear us talking about rate reduction, I also want you to think about your neighbor who is a small-business owner. And their taxes are going down, and that will have a positive effect on economic vitality and growth.

We also changed the policy on taxes on dividends and capital gains. And let me talk about what that means. It means many companies have now decided to pay a dividend to the people who own the company, the thousands of shareholders all across our country. Many others have increased their dividend. And as a result, there are billions of dollars of cash now going into the economy, to the people, to the shareholders, large and small, and that will encourage savings and investment and spending.

Now, let me talk about the jobs act in terms of small business. Not only will it affect small businesses by reducing the income taxes on small businesses, we allowed small businesses to deduct more money up front when they buy new equipment. And that's important. We want people to buy more equipment. You know why? Because somebody has got to make the equipment. When there's an incentive for small businesses across the country to buy a new piece of machinery to make their business more productive, it means somebody has got to make that machine. And when somebody makes that machine, it means somebody is going to be working, making the machine.

Here at Beaver, you're going to save about $70,000 on taxes, and that means more money that goes into research to develop new products. And that's important. If I were a worker here, I'd want to be on the cutting edge of new products. I'd want the people who run this company being—thinking about how best can I use my talent and my skills to build a new product to stay competitive. As Bill Phillips said, "It gives us the money to do some research."

But he also said, "It gives us some money to build new products." He's already hired 14 workers this year. He says to me, the tax relief will enable him to hire 10 more workers. That's 10 more people working. There are small businesses—see, we're not talking about just this company here. There are companies all across the country like this company. And if you have 10 hired here and 10 hired there and 10 hired over there, and all of a sudden those 10 start adding up and our fellow citizens are getting back to work. And that's what we're here to talk about, how to get Americans back to work.

Mike Gendich is here with us. I had a chance to visit with Mike. He owns a company called Metalmite. He makes parts for Beaver Aerospace. He had a backlog of orders of only 2½ weeks over the past 3 years. His orders are picking up. That's a good sign. See, when the small-business guy's orders begin to pick up, he begins to get a little confidence, a little bounce in his step. And the backlog is now 2½ months. He's added three workers in the last 2 months. And now, with $22,000 of tax relief, he's decided he can afford a vertical milling machine to keep those three workers busy, to make sure they're more productive.

But somebody has got to build that vertical milling machine. And so there's some person out there whose job is more secure, or perhaps a new job, thanks to the fact that Mike is taking advantage of the tax relief. And that's what's important for our fellow citizens to know. There's a ripple effect throughout our economy. And as people make decisions, whether you're a consumer or whether you're a small-business owner trying to buy a machine, it affects economic vitality and growth. It affects more than just one life. And that's the whole purpose of the tax plan, was to have a ripple effect throughout the economy that's positive and far-reaching.

Nevin Groce is with us. He's from Grand Rapids. He owns L&G Industrial Products.

He said times are a little slow. But all of a sudden, he's beginning to see action being taken, and he sees a better future for his company. He's going to save $20,000 under the 2003 tax relief act.

He says that what he's thinking about doing is buying a large industrial saw. In other words, here's a guy whose business isn't quite the way he wants it to be, but he's getting optimistic because he's got a little more money in his pocket—more than a little money, $20,000, which is a lot of money for a small business. And so he's thinking positively. He's thinking about making new investments.

Dennis Orlewicz is here. He's a small-business owner, Magnum Manufacturing. He's an S corp. That means he pays taxes at the individual income tax rate. We've reduced the taxes on his business by $3,500. It will save him $8,000—individually and then $8,000 in his business, excuse me. He's thinking about buying a $250,000 machine. His quote is, "Tax relief makes investment more enticing."

Here's what I'm telling you. We've got to focus on small businesses, first and foremost. Most new jobs in America are created by entrepreneurs and small-business people. The plan I'm describing to you creates incentive for people to make investments to make their small business more competitive, to make their workers more productive. And when they make investment, it helps somebody else who has to make the machine in the first place. The jobs-and-growth bill is important for economic vitality in America.

I want to make sure the jobs-and-growth bill extend to all our citizens. The child credit must be given to low-income Americans as well. They passed a bill in the Senate. They passed a bill in the House. They need to get the differences resolved and to my desk. I want the benefits of tax relief all across the spectrum of our society. Economists were saying this economy is picking up. They're feeling positive about America and its economic future. They

know what I know: We've been through a lot, and we're strong.

Interest rates are down. That makes it easier for a person to buy their house. If you got your house and interest rates are down, it means it makes it profitable to refinance your house, put a little extra money in your pocket. Inflation is low, which is positive. Productivity is up. No, signs after sign after sign says we're poised for growth so people can find work.

But there is more to do. I want to share some other thoughts with you. First, we need an energy policy in America. We need a policy that recognizes we can do a better job of conservation, that we can do a better job of developing technologies that will enable us to develop energy sources in a cleaner way. But I'm worried about natural gas. See, the demand for natural gas is going up but the supply isn't, which means it's going to start affecting people's pocketbooks. We've got to do something about that. We need an energy plan. We need to be less dependent on foreign sources of energy. The House passed a bill; the Senate—is stuck in the Senate. They need to get moving and get a bill to my desk.

We need to make sure that we have—diminish the number of frivolous lawsuits in our society—pushing hard for class-action reform. The House passed a bill. The Senate has got to act. It's junk lawsuits that are affecting the cost of your health care. Listen, if you got hurt by a bad doc, you've got to have your day in court. But what we don't need is lawyers fishing for a rich settlement all across the country, which means you're either driving up the cost of health care or you're driving the docs out of business. One of the things we ought to make sure in America is health care is affordable and accessible.

When you're good at something, you ought to make the environment such that you can move product. If you're good at manufacturing, you want to sell it all around the world. If you're good at growing crops, we want to be able to sell our crops around the world. If you're good at growing cows, we ought to be selling our cows around the world. One way to make sure that we can increase jobs is to get some of these countries to open up their markets to United States' products. We're competitive. We've got the best workers in the world.

Well, these are some of the things we can do to make sure this economy grows. I'm interested in helping people find work. I want it so that everybody in America who wants to work and can't find a job today can work. I also know that we've got to help people who are trying to find work. Sometimes technology races ahead of the workforce. Sometimes people can't find work, even though they want to.

So what I proposed to the Congress is they create what they call unemployment accounts for people that are seeking jobs that are hard to find a job. This basically says that you get $3,000 to help yourself find a—to help find a job. If you need— and you can use the money the way you see fit. For example, if you need child care, it will help you pay for the child care or if you need extra job training or if you need to move to a community in which there's a job. And part of the incentive in there is that if you can find a job within 13 months, you get to keep the balance of the money from what you've spent to help yourself find a job and the $3,000 as a reemployment bonus. We've got to help our workers be ready to work and find work.

Now, I know you've heard talk about the deficit in Washington, DC. Yes, we've got a deficit. We've got a deficit for a couple of reasons. The main reason is, is that when you're in a recession, less money is coming into the Treasury. When the economy slows down, there's less tax revenue coming into the U.S. Treasury, and we've been going through slow economic times.

Another reason we've got a deficit, because I asked Congress to spend enough money to make sure our troops had the best equipment necessary to fight and win war. Any time this Nation puts one of our youngsters into harm's way, we'd better— and we will—make sure they get the best training, the best equipment, the best possible support.

And so we got a deficit. But I've got a plan to cut the deficit in half over the next 5 years. It starts with making sure this economy grows. First thing you want to do in trimming the deficit is to make sure you get more revenues into the Treasury. The best way to get more revenues in the Treasury is not raise taxes, slowing down the economy; it's cut taxes to create more economic growth. That's how you get more money into the U.S. Treasury.

And the other way is you make sure Washington doesn't overspend, that there be fiscal discipline. I got the Congress to support a 4-percent increase in discretionary spending. That's about the size of the average household budget will increase this year. If it's good enough for the households in America, it ought to be good enough for the House of Representatives. They agreed to the budget of a 4-percent increase in discretionary spending, and now we intend to make them—hold them to their word. There's going to be budget discipline in Washington. That's how you deal with the deficit.

The main—my main focus is making sure our citizens can find a job, and I believe it's going to happen. See, I believe in the future of the country in all aspects because I know the character of our people. This country has been through emergencies and scandals and war and recession, and we have responded. We're a strong country because we're full of strong people. We've got people of character. We've got determined people. We've got people who understand values. We've got people who understand service to something greater than yourself. This is a fabulous land, and I am so honored to be the President of the greatest country on the face of the Earth.

Thank you for coming. Thank you for giving me a chance. May God bless. Thank you all.

NOTE: The President spoke at 3:29 p.m. at Beaver Aerospace and Defense, Inc. In his remarks, he referred to William T. Phillips, chairman, Phillips Service Industries, Inc.; State Attorney General Mike Cox, State Senator Laura M. Toy, and State Representative John Pastor of Michigan; Mayor Jack E. Kirksey, Chief of Police Peter Kunst, and City Council President Jack Engebretson of Livonia, MI; and Uday and Qusay Hussein, sons of former President Saddam Hussein of Iraq, who were killed July 22 by U.S. military forces in Mosul, Iraq.

Statement on the Report of the Joint Inquiry Into the Terrorist Attacks of September 11, 2001
July 24, 2003

I welcome today's release of the final report of the Congressional Joint Inquiry into the terrorist attacks of September 11, 2001.

Since September 11, 2001, my administration has transformed our Government to pursue terrorists and prevent terrorist attacks. We established the Department of Homeland Security and carried out the most fundamental reorganization of the U.S. Government in half a century. We significantly expanded our foreign intelligence partnerships with countries across the globe and established the Terrorist Threat Integration Center so that all threat information can be integrated and analyzed in a single location. Our law enforcement and intelligence agencies are working together more closely than ever and are using new tools to intercept, disrupt, and prevent terrorist attacks.

The best way to prevent future attacks is to hunt down the terrorists before they strike again. America and our allies have continued the relentless pursuit of the global terror network. Many of those directly involved in organizing the September 11 attacks are confirmed dead or now in custody. We will not relent until Al Qaida is completely dismantled.

I appreciate the hard work and careful thought that went into today's report. My administration looks forward to working with the Congress and continuing to protect the American people.

NOTE: The report of December 2002 was entitled "Joint Inquiry Into Intelligence Community Activities Before and After the Terrorist Attacks of September 11, 2001."

Message to the Congress Transmitting a Report on the National Emergency With Respect to Terrorists Who Threaten To Disrupt the Middle East Peace Process
July 24, 2003

To the Congress of the United States:

Consistent with section 401(c) of the National Emergencies Act, 50 U.S.C. 1641(c), and section 204(c) of the International Emergency Economic Powers Act, 50 U.S.C. 1703(c), I transmit herewith a 6-month periodic report, prepared by my Administration, on the national emergency with respect to terrorists who threaten to disrupt the Middle East peace process that was declared in Executive Order 12947 of January 23, 1995.

GEORGE W. BUSH

The White House,
July 24, 2003.

Remarks at a Bush-Cheney Reception in Dearborn, Michigan
July 24, 2003

The President. Thank you all very much.

Audience members. Four more years! Four more years! Four more years!

The President. Thank you. I accept. Thank you for the warm welcome. I want to thank Betsy DeVos for her leadership and for her friendship and for her kind words. I appreciate all she's done for the children of this great State of Michigan. She's a fine soul, fine person.

I want to thank you all for coming tonight. You see, you're laying the groundwork for what will be a great victory in November of 2004. I appreciate so very much your coming tonight. I want you to know that I'm going to count on you during the course of the election. I'm going to count on you to energize the grassroots, to talk to your neighbors, to put signs in the yard, to mail the letters, and to remind people that our message is one that is hopeful and optimistic for every citizen who lives in this country.

I'm getting ready—[*laughter*]—and I'm loosening up. [*Laughter*] But the political season will come in its own time. Right now I'm focused on the people's business in Washington, DC. We have a lot on the agenda, and I will continue to work hard to earn the confidence of all America by keeping this Nation secure and strong and prosperous and free.

My only regret tonight is that Laura is not with me. I know, you drew the short straw. [*Laughter*] She is a fabulous First Lady, a great wife, and I love her dearly.

I want to thank all those who helped. I want to thank Michael Kojaian and the entire team who has put together this fantastic fundraiser. I appreciate so very much my very close friend Mercer Reynolds, who is the national finance chairman for this campaign. I want to thank Terri Lynn Land, who is the secretary of state, and Michael Cox, the State attorney general, for being here tonight.

I particularly want to thank Eric Childress, the student from the Cornerstone School. I visited the Cornerstone in May of 2000. I saw the good works of the teachers there and the administrators, all the hard work that goes to prepare the students for success in high school and beyond. I appreciate so very much the high standards set in that school. And I want to thank Eric for coming. But most of all,

I want to thank you all for your friendship and your support. It means an awful lot.

You know, in the last 2½ years, our Nation has acted decisively to confront great challenges. I came to this office to solve problems, not to pass them on to future Presidents and future generations. I came to seize opportunities instead of letting them slip away, and we are meeting the tests of our time.

Terrorists declared war on the United States of America, and war is what they got. We have captured or killed many key leaders of Al Qaida, and the rest of them know we're on their trail. In Afghanistan and in Iraq, we gave ultimatums to terror regimes. Those regimes chose defiance, and those regimes are no more. Fifty million people—50 million people in those two countries once lived under tyranny, and now they live in freedom.

Two-and-a-half years ago, our military was not receiving the resources it needed, and morale was beginning to suffer. We increased the defense budget to prepare for the threats of a new era. And today, no one in the world can question the skill and the strength and the spirit of the United States military.

Two-and-a-half years ago, we inherited an economy in recession. Then the attacks on our country came. We had scandals in corporate America and war—all affected the people's confidence. But we acted. We passed up new laws to hold corporate criminals to account. And to get the economy going again, we have twice led the Congress in—to pass historic tax relief on behalf of the American people.

We know this, that when people have more money in their pockets, when they have more take-home pay to spend, to save, or to invest, the whole economy grows and people are more likely to find a job. I understand whose money we spend in Washington, DC. It is not the Government's money. It is the people's money. We're returning more money to people to help them raise their families. We're reducing taxes on dividends and capital gains to encourage investment. We're giving small businesses incentives to expand and to hire new people.

With all these actions, we're laying the foundations for greater prosperity and more jobs across America, so that every single person in this country has a chance to realize the great American Dream.

Two-and-a-half years ago, there was a lot of talk about education reform, but there wasn't much action. So I called for and Congress passed the No Child Left Behind Act. With a solid bipartisan majority, we delivered the most dramatic education reform in a generation. We bring high standards and strong accountability measures to every public school in America. We believe that every child can learn the basics of reading and math, and we expect every school to teach the basics of reading and math. We are challenging the soft bigotry of low expectations. The days of excuse-making are over. We expect results in every single classroom across America, so that not one single child is left behind.

We reorganized the Government and created the Department of Homeland Security to safeguard our borders and ports and to protect the American people. We passed trade promotion authority to open up new markets for America's entrepreneurs and manufacturers and farmers and ranchers. We passed a budget agreement that is helping to maintain much needed spending discipline in Washington, DC. On issue after issue, this administration has acted on principle, has kept its word, and has made progress for the American people.

The United States Congress has shared in these great achievements. I appreciate the leadership of Speaker Hastert and Leader Frist. I will continue to work with Members of the Congress to change the tone in Washington, DC, by focusing on the people's business and by focusing on results. That's the kind of person I've attracted to my administration. I have put together a fantastic team of great Americans to serve the American people.

We have had no finer Vice President than Dick Cheney. Mother may have a different opinion. [*Laughter*]

In 2½ years, we have come far, but our work is only beginning. I have set great goals worthy of this great Nation. First, America is committed to expanding the realm of freedom and peace, not only for our own security but for the benefit of the world. And second, in our own country, we must work for a society of prosperity and compassion, so that every citizen has a chance to work and succeed and to realize the promise of our country.

It is clear that the future of freedom and peace depends on the actions of America. The Nation is freedom's home and freedom's defender. We welcome this charge of history, and we are keeping it.

Our war on terror continues. The enemies of freedom are not idle, and neither are we. This country will not rest; we will not tire; we will not stop until this danger to civilization is removed.

Yet our national interest involves more than eliminating aggressive threats to our security. Our greatest security comes from the advance of human liberty because free nations do not support terror, free nations do not attack their neighbors, free nations do not threaten the world with weapons of mass terror. Americans believe that freedom is the deepest need and hope of every human heart. And we believe that freedom is the right of every person and the future of every nation.

America also understands that unprecedented influence brings tremendous responsibilities. We have duties in the world. And when we see disease and starvation and hopeless poverty, we will not turn away. On the continent of Africa, America is now committed to bringing the healing power of medicine to millions of men and women and children now suffering with AIDS. This great land is leading the world in the incredibly important work of human rescue.

We face challenges at home, and our actions prove that we are equal to those challenges. I will continue to work on our economy until everybody who wants to work and who cannot find a job today will be able to find a job.

We have a duty to keep our commitment to America's seniors by strengthening and modernizing Medicare. Recently, the Congress took historic action to improve the lives of older Americans. For the first time since the creation of Medicare, the House and the Senate have passed reforms to increase the choices for our seniors and to provide coverage for prescription drugs. It is now time for both Houses to come together and to get a good bill to my desk as soon as possible.

For the sake of our health care system, we need to cut down on frivolous lawsuits which increase the cost of medicine. People who have been harmed by a bad doc deserve their day in court. Yet the system should not reward lawyers who are fishing for rich settlements. Because frivolous lawsuits drive up the cost of health care, they affect the Federal budget. Medical liability reform is a national issue that requires a national response. No one has ever been healed by a frivolous lawsuit.

I have a responsibility as President to make sure the judicial system runs well. And I have met that duty. I have nominated superb men and women for the Federal courts, people who interpret the law, not legislate from the bench. Yet some Members of the United States Senate are trying to keep my nominees off the bench by blocking up-or-down votes.

Here in Michigan, for example, I have nominated four outstanding individuals to serve on the Sixth Circuit Court of Appeals. Yet all four have been waiting more than a year for a vote. These kinds of delays create judicial vacancies that harm our legal system. Every judicial nominee deserves a fair hearing and an up-or-down vote on the

Senate floor. It is time for some of the Members of the United States Senate to stop playing politics with American justice.

The Congress needs to pass a comprehensive energy plan. Our Nation must promote energy efficiency and conservation and develop cleaner technologies to help us explore for more energy in an environmentally friendly way. Yet, for the sake of our economic security and for the sake of our national security, we must be less dependent on foreign sources of energy.

Our strong and prosperous Nation must also be a compassionate nation. I will continue to advance our agenda of compassionate conservatism, applying the best and most innovative ideas to the task of helping our fellow citizens in need. There's still millions of men and women who want to end their dependence on Government and become independent through hard work. We must build on the success of welfare reform to bring work and dignity into the lives of more of our fellow citizens.

Congress should complete the "Citizen Service Act" so more Americans can serve their communities and their country. And both Houses should reach agreement on my Faith-Based Initiative to support the armies of compassion that are mentoring our children, that are caring for the homeless, and that are offering hope to the addicted.

A compassionate society must promote opportunity for all, including the independence and dignity that come from ownership. This administration will constantly strive to promote an ownership society in America. We want more citizens owning their own home. We want our citizens owning and controlling their health care plans. We want our citizens owning and controlling their retirement plans. We want more people to own their own small business, because I understand that when people own something, they own a stake in the future of this great country.

In a compassionate society, people respect one another and take responsibility for the decisions they make. We're changing the culture of America from one that has said, "If it feels good, do it," and "If you've got a problem, blame somebody else"—[*laughter*]—to a culture in which each of us understands that we are responsible for the decisions we make in life.

If you are fortunate enough to be a mother or a father, you're responsible for loving your child. If you are concerned about the quality of the education in the community in which you live, you're responsible for doing something about it. If you're a CEO in America, you have the responsibility to tell the truth to your shareholders and your employees. And in the new responsibility society, each of us is responsible for loving our neighbor just like we'd like to be loved ourself.

We can see the culture of service and responsibility growing around us. I started the USA Freedom Corps to encourage Americans to extend a compassionate hand to a neighbor in need, and the response has been great.

I also know that our faith-based programs and our charities are strong and vibrant all across America. We have neighborhood healers who are performing miracles on a daily basis by helping people change their hearts and their lives. Policemen and firefighters and people who wear our Nation's uniform are reminding us what it means to sacrifice for something greater than yourself. Once again, the children of America believe in heroes, because they see them every day.

In these challenging times, the world has seen the resolve and the courage of America. And I have been privileged to see the compassion and the character of the American people. All the tests of the last 2½ years have come to the right nation. We're a strong country, and we use that strength to defend the peace. We're an optimistic country, confident in ourselves and in ideals bigger than ourselves.

Abroad, we seek to lift up whole nations by spreading freedom. At home, we seek to lift up lives by spreading opportunity to every corner of America. This is the work that history has set before us. We welcome it. And we know that for our country and for our cause, the best days lie ahead.

May God bless you all, and may God bless America. Thank you all.

NOTE: The President spoke at 7:01 p.m. in the Presidential Ballroom at the Ritz-Carlton Hotel. In his remarks, he referred to Betsy DeVos, chairman, Michigan Republican Party, who introduced the President; and Michael Kojaian, Michigan State finance chairman, and Mercer Reynolds, national finance chairman, Bush-Cheney '04, Inc.

Remarks at the Korean War Memorial
July 25, 2003

I'm here to honor those who served in Korea. There is a very profound statement here at this moving memorial. It says, "Freedom is not free." And today we honor those—this weekend we honor those who served in the cause of freedom in the Korean war.

This memorial is—and those who served in Korea also remind us of the challenges we face today, and it gives us a chance to reflect on the sacrifices that are being made on behalf of freedom today. And our Nation will be eternally grateful for the men and women who serve today, as we are for those who have served in the past.

NOTE: The President spoke at 7:10 a.m. A tape was not available for verification of the content of these remarks.

The President's News Conference With Prime Minister Mahmoud Abbas of the Palestinian Authority
July 25, 2003

President Bush. Good day. I'm honored to welcome Prime Minister Abbas to the White House. It is such an honor to have you here, sir.

Prime Minister Abbas. Thank you.

President Bush. To break through old hatreds and barriers to peace, the Middle East needs leaders of vision and courage and a determination to serve the interest of their people. Mr. Abbas is the first Palestinian Prime Minister, and he is proving to be such a leader.

We had a good meeting today about the way forward on the roadmap to Middle Eastern peace. Prime Minister Abbas and I share a common goal, peace in the Holy Land between two free and secure states, Palestine and Israel.

Reaching this goal will require all sides to meet their responsibilities. We made a good progress last month at the Red Sea Summit in Aqaba. The Government of Israel recognized that Israel's own interests would be served when the Palestinians govern themselves in their own state, a peaceful, democratic state where the forces of terror have been replaced by the rule of law.

Prime Minister Abbas committed to a complete end to violence and terrorism, and he recognized that terror against

Israelis, wherever they might be, is a dangerous obstacle to the achievement of a Palestinian state.

I committed to both sides that the United States will strive to see that promises are kept and monitor the parties' progress on this difficult journey.

To meet the goal we have set, we must improve the daily lives of ordinary Palestinians. For just this purpose, I recently approved a grant of $20 million directly to the Palestinian Authority.

Today I'm also pleased to announce that the United States and Palestinian Authority will establish a joint Palestine Economic Development Group. This group of American and Palestinian officials will meet regularly and be charged with finding practical ways to bring jobs and growth and investment to the Palestinian economy.

In addition, I'm sending Treasury Secretary John Snow and Commerce Secretary Don Evans to the region early this fall. I'll ask them to report back to me on the steps we need to take to build a solid economic foundation for a free and sovereign Palestinian state.

In our talks this morning, Prime Minister Abbas and I covered a range of issues. We discussed the impact on the Palestinian people of the limits on their freedom of movement and the need to reduce the network of checkpoints and barriers. Prime Minister Abbas shared his concerns about Israeli settlements, confiscation of land, and the building of a security fence. He also expressed his strong desire to see the release of many more Palestinian prisoners.

We will continue to address these issues. We will address them carefully and seriously with Palestinian and Israeli officials. We will work to seek solutions.

We've seen important progress towards peace over the last 13 months, and we see even more progress today, here in Washington and in the region as well. Today the Government of Israel announced that it will be taking down more of the checkpoints that are making it difficult for Pal-

estinians to travel to their jobs and schools. In addition, Israel will consider ways to reduce the impact of the security fence on the lives of the Palestinian people.

And Israel has helped—has also pledged to transfer to the Palestinian Authority security responsibility for two additional cities in the West Bank and to make further progress in removing settlement outposts. Like Prime Minister Abbas, Prime Minister Sharon is demonstrating that he's a partner committed to reaching a peace settlement.

I welcome these announcements from Israel, and I look forward to seeing Prime Minister Sharon on his visit to Washington next week. Together, these leaders can bring a bright future to both their people.

This is the time of possibility in the Middle East. And the people of the region are counting on the leaders to seize opportunities for peace and progress. Too many years and lives have been squandered by resentment and violence. The Palestinian people, like people everywhere, deserve freedom. They deserve an honest government, and they deserve peace.

I thank Prime Minister Abbas for his hard work. I thank him for his service to his people and for carrying their cause here to Washington, DC.

Welcome, Mr. Prime Minister.

Prime Minister Abbas. Thank you. Thank you very much. Mr. President, allow me to start by thanking you to your invitation and for the fruitful meeting we have just had and for the bilateral support we have received from you. We are particularly grateful for the $20 million of direct assistance to Palestinian Authority. And we hope that this assistance increases and is, in turn, in legislation.

Allow me to also express my appreciation to you for your relentless efforts in pursuit of peace and your intensive engagement in resolving the conflict between us and the Israelis.

Mr. President, we remain committed to the roadmap, and we are implementing our security and reform obligations. Security for all Palestinians and Israelis is an essential element in progress, and we will achieve security based on the rule of law. We have succeeded significantly where Israel, with its military might, has failed in reducing violence, and we will continue.

Reform and institution-building are an internal Palestinian priority. We do not merely seek a state, but we seek for a state that is built on the solid foundations of the modern constitution, democracy, transparency, the rule of law, and the market economy.

We continue to negotiate with Israel on the implementation of its obligations. Some progress has been made, but movement needs to be made in terms of freeing prisoners, lifting the siege on President Arafat, Israeli withdrawal from Palestinian areas, and easing up freedom of movement to Palestinians.

A transformation in the human conditions on the ground must occur. As you have said many times, Mr. President, attacks on the dignity of the Palestinians must end. Palestinians must be able to move, go to their jobs and schools, and conduct a normal life. Palestinians must not be afraid for their lives, property, or livelihood. Some steps have been taken by Israel so far, but these steps remain hesitant. The new era of peace requires the courageous logic of peace, not the suspicious logic of conflict.

The outcome must correspond with your vision, Mr. President, achieving a peace that will end the occupation that started in 1967; the establishment of a sovereign, independent Palestinian state, with East Jerusalem as its capital; and a just, agreed solution of the refugee question on the basis of the U.N. Resolution 194.

This vision cannot be realized if Israel continues to grab Palestinian land. If the settlement activities in Palestinian land and construction of the so-called "separation wall" on confiscated Palestinian land continue, we might soon find ourselves at a situation where the foundation of peace,

a free Palestine state living side by side in peace and security in Israel, is a factual impossibility. Nothing less than a full settlement freeze will do, because nothing less than a full settlement freeze will work. For the sake of peace and for the sake of future Palestinian and Israeli generations, all settlement activities must be stopped now, and the wall must come down.

Mr. President, in conclusion, allow me to thank you again for all your efforts, to reiterate our commitment to peace and security for all, and to express my hope for a solid, fruitful relations between our Governments and our peoples. Thank you.

President Bush. Good job, Mr. Prime Minister.

Prime Minister Abbas. Thank you very much.

Q. Mr. President——

President Bush. Hold on for a second, please. We'll have two questions a side, alternating, starting first with Barry of AP [Barry Schweid, Associated Press].

Liberia

Q. Thank you, Mr. President. On Liberia, if I may.

President Bush. Liberia, yes.

Q. How many U.S. troops will be going in? What is their role? How long might they stay?

President Bush. As the statement says that we put out, that U.S. troops will be there to help ECOWAS go in and serve as peacekeepers, necessary to create the conditions so that humanitarian aid can go in and help the people in Liberia. We're deeply concerned that the condition of the Liberian people is getting worse and worse and worse. Aid can't get to the people. We're worried about the outbreak of disease. And so our commitment is to enable ECOWAS to go in, and the Pentagon will make it clear over time what that means.

Secondly, it is very important for Charles Taylor to leave the country.

Third, we want to—in order to expedite aid and help, in order to make the conditions such that NGOs can do what they want to do, which is to help people from suffering, that the cease-fire must be in place.

And finally, we're working very closely with the United Nations. They will be responsible for developing a political solution, and they will be responsible for relieving the U.S. troops in short order. And so we're working all these pieces right now. But today I did order for our military in limited numbers to head into the area, to help prepare ECOWAS' arrival to relieve human suffering.

Palestinian Prisoners/Settlements/War on Terror

Q. Mr. President, how do you perceive the settlements as obstacle to your vision, to implementation of your vision? Thank you.

President Bush. Yes——

Q. And to the Prime Minister——

President Bush. Okay, good, yes. This is the old two-question trick. It's an international trick, I see. [*Laughter*] Very good job, yes. You learned from the guy to your left. Both of them from your left are pros at that too, I might add. [*Laughter*]

Q. Various officials in the administration yesterday indicated that they are having difficulties understanding the Palestinian situation when it comes to the issue of prisoners. In your meeting today with the President, did you discuss that, and did any progress happen on the U.S. understanding?

Prime Minister Abbas. We always raise this issue, that it is basically an important and sensitive issue for us. This is the issue of prisoners. We look at the prisoners as the true constituency for peace. And we have raised this issue. We believe that they will support the peace process. Today we did discuss this issue, and we see understanding coming from the administration about this humanitarian and fair issue.

President Bush. As to the settlements, I've constantly spoken out for the need to end the settlements. I—and we'll continue to work with both sides on this very sensitive issue.

Let me make something—let me say this—this is necessary. It is necessary for this good man to continue to fight off the terrorist activity that creates the conditions of insecurity for not only Israel but for the peaceful Palestinian people. In order for us to be able to make progress on a lot of difficult issues, there has to be a firm and continued commitment to fight terror.

One reason I'm willing to stand with the Prime Minister is because I believe that he has that commitment. He understands what I understand, that terrorists, every time, every place, will thwart the desires of those who want peace and freedom. And the commitment to fight terror and the results in fighting terror will make it a lot easier to deal with difficult issues, including the settlement issue.

Steve [Steve Holland]. That would be Steve of Reuters.

Palestinian Prisoners/Israeli Security Fence

Q. Would you like to see Israel release the political prisoners, and would you like to see them stop building this barrier wall?

President Bush. I think—first of all, on the wall. Let me talk about the wall. I think the wall is a problem, and I discussed this with Ariel Sharon. It is very difficult to develop confidence between the Palestinians and the Israel—Israel—with a wall snaking through the West Bank. And I will continue to discuss this issue very clearly with the Prime Minister. As I said in my statement today, he has issued a statement saying he is willing to come and discuss that with us. And I appreciate the—willing to discuss it.

On the prisoners, I think it's very important to have a frank discussion on the prisoners. We ought to look at the prisoner issue on a case-by-case basis. Surely nobody wants to let a coldblooded killer out of prison that would help derail the process. I mean, after all, it doesn't make any sense if you've got somebody who is bent upon destroying lives and killing people in prison to—if you were to let him out, it would make it harder to achieve the peace we all want. And so I think it's very important to analyze the prisoner situation on a case-by-case basis.

I fully understand the Prime Minister's desire. I fully understand his request. And I have—and therefore, we'll talk to—continue to talk to both sides on this issue. But I would never ask anybody in any society to let a prisoner out who would then commit terrorist actions. And I think that's logical and clear.

And so—but these are all difficult issues. By the way, we're discussing them now in a frank way, which is progress unto itself. These are issues where there had been no discussion before. And now we're putting them on the table, and we're making progress. And as people get more confidence—listen, I'm gaining confidence in the Palestinian Prime Minister and in his great cabinet.

I had the Finance Minister in to discuss issues with me. He told me he would put the budget of the Palestinian Authority on the web page. And he did, which means he's a man of his word. The Security Chief, Dahlan, and I have had some discussions. He's a good, solid leader. And so I gain confidence in them, because they're people who do what they say. And the more confidence we gain, the more easy it's going to be to tackle these very difficult issues.

Final question from the Palestinians.

Terrorism and Resolution of Issues

Q. Mr. President, Mr. President——
Q. Mr. President, Mr. President——
President Bush. Wait, wait, wait. It's best if we only have one question at a time.
Q. Mr. President, do you think that——
Q. Do you think that——
President Bush. Ladies first.

Prime Minister Abbas. Ladies first, okay. [*Laughter*]

Q. When you speak to Palestinians, they're saying that the biggest problems they have now are the 160 Israel checkpoints that are suffocating the Palestinian community. Did you get any guarantees from Mr. President that he will pressure Israel in removing these checkpoints?

And Mr. President, you said the settlements are an obstacle for peace. Will you pressure Israel to stop the settlement activity? When and how?

President Bush. Well, let me start, and then you can end.

Prime Minister Abbas. Please.

President Bush. We'll let my guest end. I just told you that we brought this issue up. I've constantly spoken out about the end of settlements. I have done so consistently. It's very important for us to continue to earn the confidence of each other. And I'm going to tell you pointblank that we must make sure that any terrorist activity is rooted out in order for us to be able to deal with these big issues.

Nobody is going to accept a situation in which they become less secure, whether it be the Palestinian people or the Israeli people. Security is the essential roadblock to achieving the roadmap to peace. And the reason I'm confident that we can achieve substantial progress and achieve the vision of two states living by side by side in peace is because I believe that the Prime Minister and his team is interested in routing out terror.

And so to answer your question, the more progress there's made on terror, the more progress there will be made on difficult issues.

Prime Minister Abbas. The issue of the checkpoints between various Palestinian towns and villages was one of the issues that basically was discussed with the President. As he mentioned, we discussed a wide variety of issues. We discussed issues of settlements, the issue of the wall, the issue of prisoners, and others, including the checkpoints. We feel that the President is paying attention to all these issues, and we believe that he will raise those issues with the upcoming visit of Prime Minister Sharon.

President Bush. Thank you all very much.

Q. We need three questions—we're making a news conference.

President Bush. Thank you very much.

That's Bill Plante of CBS, an old veteran, constantly willing to express his opinion.

Thank you for your opinion.

NOTE: The President's news conference began at 12:05 p.m. in the Rose Garden at the White House. In his remarks, he referred to Prime Minister Ariel Sharon of Israel; President Charles Taylor of Liberia; and Finance Minister Salam Fayyad and Minister of State for Security Affairs Mohammed Dahlan of the Palestinian Authority. During the question-and-answer session, some reporters asked their questions in Arabic, and Prime Minister Abbas responded in Arabic, and their remarks were translated by an interpreter.

Statement on the Death of Colin McMillan
July 25, 2003

Laura and I are saddened by the death of our good friend Colin McMillan. Colin was a public servant and patriot who served his country and State as a marine, State legislator, Assistant Secretary of Defense, community leader, and successful businessman. We send our condolences and prayers to his wife, children, and friends.

The President's Radio Address
July 26, 2003

Good morning. This weekend marks the 13th anniversary of the Americans With Disability Act, one of the great compassionate acts of American Government. Since becoming law, the ADA has helped to improve the quality of life for more than 50 million Americans with physical and mental disabilities. As a result, it is easier today for people with disabilities to find a job, to enter public buildings, and to live more independently in their communities. These are all welcome changes in American life.

Many citizens have dedicated themselves to serving the interests of persons with disabilities, and some of them are here with me at the White House. I am joined by members of the President's Committee on Mental Retardation. The men and women on this committee include people with disabilities as well as parents, teachers, health care workers, and advocates. They recently voted to change the committee's name to the President's Committee for People with Intellectual Disabilities, and I was pleased to sign an Executive order instituting that change.

There is much more we can do to assure that Americans with disabilities are treated with dignity and respect. In 2001, I announced the New Freedom Initiative to further promote the full participation of people with disabilities in all areas of society. As part of the New Freedom Initiative, we're giving States funding to help people with disabilities commute to work or purchase equipment that allows them to work

from home. We are promoting homeownership for people with disabilities and educating builders about the need for more
accessible rental housing.

We are working with Congress to provide
record levels of funding for special education programs and to make sure the
money is used to provide the most help
to the most children. And we are making
Government web sites more accessible to
people with disabilities so that they can
more easily find information about services
and programs of the Federal Government.
We're also focused on providing better care
to people with mental illness. I'm committed to making sure people get the treatment and support they need and don't fall
through the cracks.

My administration continues to work
with States to ensure full implementation
of the Supreme Court's *Olmstead* decision.
That decision rightly mandates that individuals with disabilities who can receive support and treatment in a community setting
should be given an opportunity to live close

to their families and friends whenever possible.

People with disabilities now have more
freedom to do productive work and live
independent lives. We're making good
progress toward ensuring that persons with
disabilities know the American Dream is
meant for them. With changes in old ways
of thinking, the development of new technologies, and the Federal Government's
firm commitment to equality, more and
more people with disabilities continue to
become full participants in the American
life.

Thank you for listening.

NOTE: The address was recorded at 2 p.m.
on July 25 in the Cabinet Room at the White
House for broadcast at 10:06 a.m. on July
26. The transcript was made available by the
Office of the Press Secretary on July 25 but
was embargoed for release until the broadcast. The Office of the Press Secretary also
released a Spanish language transcript of this
address.

Remarks at Andrews Air Force Base, Maryland, on the Death of Bob Hope
July 28, 2003

Today America lost a great citizen. We
mourn the passing of Bob Hope. Bob Hope
made us laugh, and he lifted our spirits.
Bob Hope served our Nation when he went
to battlefields to entertain thousands of
troops from different generations. We extend our prayers to his family, and we

mourn the loss of a good man. May God
bless his soul.

Thank you all.

NOTE: The President spoke at 9:50 a.m. prior
to departure for Pittsburgh, PA. A tape was
not available for verification of the content
of these remarks.

Remarks to the National Urban League Conference in Pittsburgh, Pennsylvania
July 28, 2003

Thanks for the warm welcome. Thanks for your kind invitation. But most importantly, thanks for your service to your fellow Americans. The Urban League has always stood for justice and hope and healing. It's stood for opportunity for all our citizens. I'm honored to be at such an organization.

I appreciate the chance as well to come to Pittsburgh. It's a city that's rich in civil rights, the history of civil rights. In the 1800s, the Underground Railroad here delivered thousands out of slavery and into freedom. In the 1930s and 1940s, Pittsburgh's Urban League led successful protests against schools and department stores that refused to hire African Americans. And today in this city, community leaders are showing what good people can accomplish by working together. I now know why they call it the Renaissance City, and I want to thank you for your hospitality.

The work of the National Urban League represents one of the basic commitments of this country. See, we believe in opportunity for all, a society where every person can dream and work and realize his or her potential. We're dedicated to bringing economic hope to every neighborhood, a good education to every child, and comfort and compassion to the afflicted. And our Nation has come a long way, and we have a long way to go. And we will not stop, we will not tire until we extend the great promise of America to every neighborhood in America. And that's what I want to talk about today.

I want to thank Mr. President, President Marc Morial, for his kind invitation and his willingness to lead this important American institution. He replaces a good man in Hugh Price, who has ably led the Urban League for nearly a decade. And there's no doubt in my mind that Marc Morial will do a great job on behalf of America. Thank you, Mr. Mayor. As he said, we grew up right around the corner from each other. And I know what he was—what New Orleans was like when he was the mayor of that important city. Bourbon Street was never more alive when—[*laughter*]—never mind. [*Laughter*]

I'm honored that the Secretary of Education is with us today, Rod Paige. He is a good friend and a good man.

I appreciate so very much Michael Critelli, who is the chairman of the board of the National Urban League, a businessman that understands corporate responsibility. It means you've got to help somebody else as well as watching the bottom line. Mike, thank you for being here.

I'm honored that members from the Pennsylvania congressional delegation are with us today, Senators Specter and Santorum and Congressman Tim Murphy. I appreciate them coming. A couple of them jumped on Air Force One. [*Laughter*] I'm not suggesting that's why they came. [*Laughter*] There's not a lot of air raids on Air Force One. [*Laughter*] But I'm glad to have them.

I see Reverend Jackson is with us today. Jesse Jackson, it's good to see you. Congressman Cummings—I'm honored to see you, Congressman. Thank you for being here. I appreciate so very much my friend Mayor Jim Garner, who's the president of the U.S. Conference of Mayors, who is with us today. Mr. Mayor, thank you for coming.

I know that Mike Fisher, the State attorney general, is with us today. And the Allegheny County chief executive, Jim Roddey, is with us today. And I'm honored that they have come. I want to thank all the elected officials. I want to thank the board of the National Urban League. And I want to thank the delegates for giving me a chance to come by and say hello.

Today I had the honor, when I landed at the airport, of meeting a board member of the Urban League of Pittsburgh, a fellow named Xavier Williams. He came to see me because one of the things I try to do is herald the great strength of the country, which happens to be the heart and soul of our citizens. You see, Xavier works for a—it's called INROADS. It's a nonprofit organization which matches minority youth with successful businesses and corporations to try to help them have the skills necessary to realize the entrepreneurial spirit of America. Xavier knows what I know, that the best way to serve your country is to love a neighbor just like you'd like to be loved yourself. And I appreciate the example that Xavier Williams sets for not only the good folks here in Pittsburgh but for people all around the country. Thank you, Xavier, for your service to our country.

Every generation of Americans must rise to its own challenges, and this generation is rising to meet ours. We will never forget the lessons of September the 11th, 2001. Great oceans no longer protect us from dangers that gather far from home. And the other lesson is that there are people who can't stand what America stands for and desire to conflict great harm on the American people. In the 22 months since that day, we have put those who hate America on notice: Wherever they plot, wherever they plan, they will find no place to hide from American justice.

The Al Qaida terrorists still threaten our country, but they're on the run. The regime in Afghanistan, the Taliban regime, inflicted great harm on the citizens of that country and protected the terrorists. But that regime is no more. Afghanistan is now free.

And our current mission in Iraq is essential to the broader war on terror; it's essential to the security of the American people. You see, a free, democratic, peaceful Iraq will not threaten America or our friends with weapons. A free Iraq will not be a training ground for terrorists or a funnel of money to terrorists or provide weapons to terrorists who would willingly use them to strike our country. A free Iraq will not destabilize the Middle East. A free Iraq can set a hopeful example to the entire region and lead other nations to choose freedom. And as the pursuits of freedom replace hatred and resentment and terror in the Middle East, the American people will be more secure.

Our men and women in uniform are serving our Nation and the cause of security and peace. We're proud of them. We appreciate their progress. We appreciate their dedication to the country called America.

This Nation has got another great challenge. While we stand for freedom and opportunity abroad, we must make those same values real in the lives of all Americans. This Nation has got work to do. There are citizens who can't find jobs. There are citizens looking for homes for their families. There are students who go to school that are letting them down every day and don't seem to improve. There are children who need mentors in their lives, people struggling with addiction who need to know they don't face that struggle alone.

To make the promise of America real for everyone, we need active citizens who help their neighbors; we need active churches and active communities; and we need active government. We can make a difference in people's lives with creative, innovative policies that focus on results.

Greater opportunity and hope begins with a growing economy. The stock market started to decline in March of 2000. And then we had recession in the first quarter of 2001. So we acted. We provided historic tax relief for families. And then as the economy was beginning to come back, we found out some of our citizens, corporate CEOs, forgot what it means to be a responsible citizen, and they did not tell the truth to shareholder and employee alike. So we acted, and we're now holding corporate criminals to account.

Last year, we saw too many Americans were still struggling to find a job, so we acted again. We brought the marriage penalty down. It doesn't make any sense, by the way, to penalize marriage in the Tax Code. It seems like the Tax Code ought to encourage marriage, not penalize it. We reduced income tax rates. We expanded the child credit from $600 to $1,000 per child, and we made the change retroactive to January 1st of this year, so the checks are in the mail. And as a matter of fairness, Congress should make the child credit refundable—low-income families need help as well during these economic slow times.

To add more jobs to the economy, we're also focusing a lot on small businesses, because small businesses create the most new jobs in an economy. Most small businesses are sole proprietorships or Subchapter S's, so when you reduce the income tax rates, you help small businesses. They pay tax at the individual rates. We're also allowing higher expense deduction for small businesses, which will make it easier for small businesses to buy new equipment and to hire new people. We're working through the Small Business Administration and Minority Business Development Agency to ensure that minority businesses get access to Federal contracting and financing and technical assistance for startups, because we understand small businesses are the path to the American Dream, and this path must be more open to all our citizens.

You hear a lot of talk about tax relief. Let me tell you my belief. When a person has got more money in his or her pocket, he or she is likely to demand an additional good or a service. And when somebody demands a good or a service in our society, somebody is going to produce the good or a service. And when somebody produces that good or a service, it means somebody is more likely find a job. The tax relief we packaged is good for helping people find work in America.

Now, we've been through a lot: recession, war, emergencies, and corporate scandals. But I'm optimistic about the future. I'm optimistic about the future, because I see hopeful signs. Home sales are strong, and people are refinancing their mortgages to put more money in their pockets. Inflation is low. Retail sales have begun to show growth. Productivity is high. And the good news is, a lot of the economists are beginning to forecast a better tomorrow, which is important for making sure that people have hope in our society.

No, we're dealing with the economy. We saw a problem, and we dealt with it straight up.

And as the economy expands, we've got to help Americans who find the greatest difficulty finding work. So I proposed what we call reemployment accounts. The jobseeker would have an account up to $3,000 for job training or child care or transportation or relocating to get a new job in a new city. If a worker finds a new job quickly, within 13 weeks, he or she gets to keep the balance of the cash as a reemployment account. Congress needs to put this plan in effect. Congress needs to help those who are having trouble finding work.

Congress also needs to understand, we need a sound energy policy in America. We need to cut down on frivolous litigation, which inhibits economic growth. We need a trade policy that opens up new markets for American products.

We also need good housing policy. A good way to make sure this economy remains strong is a housing policy which closes the minority homeownership gap in America. We need greater tax incentives for people to build homes in inner cities. I believe our Government should provide downpayment assistance to people who want to buy a home but need a little extra help. I understand there's a lot of fine print when it comes to mortgages, so we need to help people understand what's in the fine print. We need grant programs to help counsel low- and moderate-income folks across our country, to teach them what it means to buy a home and to make sure that the fine print is understood by all. No, we've got a goal in America of helping 5½ million more minority citizens become homeowners by the end of this decade.

The truth of the matter is, the future of our economy and our country depend upon good schools in all our neighborhoods. Equal education is one of the most pressing civil rights of our day. Nearly half a century after *Brown* v. *Board of Education*, there's still an achievement gap in America. On the most recent National Assessment of Educational Progress, on the reading test, 41 percent of white fourth graders were proficient and better readers, but only 12 percent of African Americans met that standard. That means we've got a problem. Both numbers are too low. I think too many of our schools are leaving too many of our children unprepared.

And so we acted. I worked with Congress to pass what we call the No Child Left Behind Act. It says every child can learn; we must have high standards for every child; and we must hold people to account to make sure children do learn. We must challenge the soft bigotry of low expectations, and you know what I'm talking about. And as Rod Paige will brief you, States are beginning to respond. We said, "In return for record levels of education spending at the Federal level, we expect results."

You see, if you believe every child can learn, then you ought to be asking the question to those who are spending our money, "Are you teaching the child?" That's what we ought to be asking all across America. And now there's accountability plans being put in place in 50 States plus Puerto Rico and the District. I know people are concerned about testing. I've heard this debate a lot. They say it's discriminatory to measure and compare results. I say it is discriminatory not to measure. I think it's important to know whether or not our schools are succeeding. We simply have got to stop shuffling our children from grade to grade without asking the question, have they been taught to learn to read and write and add and subtract?

I believe it is those who believe certain children can't learn that are willing to shuffle them through. And the No Child Left Behind Act ends that. In return for record levels of money, you've got to show us whether or not the children can read and write and add and subtract. And when schools don't measure up, parents must have more options. It's one thing to measure, but there has to be consequences for failing schools. So in that act, parents are able to send their children to a different public school or a charter school or get special tutorial help.

I also believe it makes sense to explore private school choices, so I'm working with the leadership in Washington, DC. This isn't a Democrat issue or Republican issue. This is an issue that focuses on children.

I know setting high standards works. I know measuring and using the measurement system as a way to diagnose problems so you can focus on the problems works. In my State, 73 percent of the white students passed the math test in 1994, while only 38 percent of the African American students passed it. So we made that the point of reference. We had people focused on the results for the first time—not process but results. And because teachers rose to the challenge, because the problem became clear, that gap has now closed to 10 points. Because every child can learn, you've just got to focus the attention and the resources when necessary. Accountability tells you what's going right, and it tells you what's going wrong, and it shows you where the emphasis needs to be. We're having the same results in North Carolina. In States that measure, you'll find that the achievement gap is closing dramatically.

Our opportunity society must also be a compassionate society. As Americans, when we see hopelessness and suffering and injustice, we will not turn our backs. And one of the best ways to build hope is to recognize where some of the great works of compassion are done. You see, Government can hand out money—sometimes we do a pretty good job of it—but what it can't do is put hope in people's hearts or a sense of purpose in people's lives. That happens when people who have been called to love a neighbor interface with a neighbor in need.

See, every day across America, faith-based and community groups are touching people's lives in profound ways—give shelter to the homeless and provide safety for battered women; they bring compassion to lonely seniors. America's neighborhood healers have long experience and deep understanding of the problems that many face, and many of them have something extra besides experience. They have inspiration, as they carry God's love to people in need. I like to call the neighborhood healers America's social entrepreneurs. And they need the support of foundation America and corporate America. They need the support of individuals and, of course, congregations. And when appropriate, they deserve the support of the Government.

Government has no business endorsing a religious creed or directly funding religious worship. But for too long, Government treated people of faith like second-class citizens in the grantmaking process. Government can and should support effective social services provided by religious people, as long as those services go to anyone in need. And when Government gives that support, faith-based institutions should not be forced to change the character of their service or compromise their principles.

Neighborhood healers have not been treated well by the Federal Government, so I signed an Executive order banning discrimination against faith-based charities by Federal agencies. I created special offices in my key Cabinet departments to speak up for faith-based groups and to help them access Government funding. I've asked the departments to report to me on a regular

basis to make sure the old days are gone, to make sure we challenge and harness the great strength of the country, the heart and soul of our citizens. We're changing the focus of Government from process to results. Instead of asking the question, "Is this a faith-based program," we're now asking the question, "Does the program work," and if so, it deserves our support.

And the support is making a difference. Here in Pittsburgh, the North Hills Community Outreach, an interfaith human services agency, uses about $76,000 from the Department of Health and Human Services to help people get through tough times. In other words, we're using taxpayers' money to help support programs that use the faith component to help change lives and save lives.

A fellow named Royal Patterson went to this program. He was a painter for 27 years, and then he was unable to climb up a ladder. So he goes to North Hills. They gave him food. They gave him bus passes. They helped him to get a new job. But what he said was—most important— he said, "It was so uplifting. You figure nobody cares, but they care."

There's a lot of programs around based on faith that care for people, and our Government must recognize their potential in our society if we want to heal lives all across America.

I've asked Congress to fund $100 million for the Compassionate Capital Fund. That's a fancy word for providing money for organizations like the Urban League to teach some of these small faith programs how to apply for grants, how to help manage and train their staffs. In other words, I fully recognize that some of the programs in some of the neighborhoods need management help. They need guidance. And I would hope that Marc would take advantage of this program to help some faith programs all around the country be fully prepared to do what they're called to do, which is love somebody in need.

I've asked Congress for $600 million over 3 years to extend drug and alcohol treatment to 300,000 Americans and that faith-based providers must be allowed to compete for these funds. Sometimes when a person changes their heart, they change their habits. And our Congress must recognize that and provide opportunity for faith-based programs such as the Sojourner House, named after Sojourner Truth, right here in Pittsburgh, Pennsylvania.

This is a program which helps mothers with drug and alcohol problems. A child can live in a loving environment while a mom works to break free from addiction. They help the people get on their feet. They help people see themselves as a worthy child of God. That may not sound like your average Government program. But we're no longer asking, "Is it a faith-based program?" We're asking, "Does it work?" The Sojourner House works, and this country of ours ought to support programs like the Sojourner House.

It's important for our Nation to recognize that too many young people are growing up without enough caring adults in their lives. Too many people wonder whether anybody loves them. We need more mentors, committed adults to serve as role models to help shepherd children through the early years of their life.

Congress—I called upon Congress to spend 450 million over 3 years to bring more mentors to more than a million disadvantaged children. We've got a goal, mentors for a million children—junior high children who are making life decisions, as well as the children of prisoners who face so many problems through no fault of their own, and they need somebody to surround them with some love.

Faith communities are a great source for mentors, and we must make sure that faith-based groups have a chance to participate in this program as well. More Americans volunteer through their houses of worship than any other organization, and Congress must recognize that. Our Government should not fear faith; we ought to welcome it as an equal partner in helping people who need help.

Now, we believe in the value and possibility of every life. And we'll help those who need help here at home, and we must help those who need help abroad as well.

I have recently seen for myself the great possibilities of Africa and the great needs of Africa. That continent's economic future depends upon trade. We'll continue to help African countries become full partners in trade and prosperity. Many African people struggle with hunger. You need to know your Government and your country is the most generous country in the world for providing aid and help for those who are hungry.

America's progress—Africa's progress is threatened by terrorism and civil wars, and so we're working with African governments to rid that continent of regional conflict and terrorist violence.

They're suffering in Liberia today. I directed the Secretary of Defense to position appropriate military capabilities off the coast of Liberia in order to support the deployment of an ECOWAS force. We're committed to working with ECOWAS to create the conditions in which lives can be saved and aid can be delivered.

We're also helping Africa overcome one of the deadliest enemies it has ever faced, the spread of HIV/AIDS. Over the next 5 years, the United States has pledged $15 billion to fight AIDS around the world, with special focus on nations in Africa and the Caribbean. We are working with governments and private groups and faith-based organizations to help with prevention and to provide much needed antiretroviral drugs for treatment. We are determined to turn the tide against AIDS in Africa.

Recently, on my trip to Africa, I visited Goree Island in Senegal, where for centuries men and women were delivered and sorted and branded and shipped. It's a haunting place, a reminder of mankind's capacity for cruelty and injustice.

Yet Goree Island is also a reminder of the strength of the human spirit and the capacity for good to overcome evil. The men and women who boarded slave ships on that island and wound up in America endured the separation of their families, the brutality of their oppressors, and the indifference of laws that regarded them only as articles of commerce. Still, the spirit of Africans in America did not break. All the generations of oppression under the laws of man could not crush the hope of freedom. And by a plan only known to providence, the stolen sons and daughters of Africa helped to awake the conscience of America. The very people traded into slavery helped to set America free.

The moral vision of African Americans and of groups like the Urban League caused Americans to examine our hearts, to correct our Constitution, and to teach our children the dignity and equality of every person of every race.

Our journey toward justice has not been easy, and it is not over. Yet I am confident that we will reach our destination. We have been called to great work in our time, and we will answer that call. We will defend our freedom, and we will lead the world toward peace. And we will unite America behind the great goals of opportunity for all and for compassion for those in need.

I want to thank each of you for serving this cause in your own lives. May God bless your work, may God bless the Urban League, and may God continue to bless the United States of America.

NOTE: The President spoke at 11:17 a.m. at the David Lawrence Convention Center. In his remarks, he referred to Rev. Jesse L. Jackson, Sr., founder and president, Rainbow/PUSH Coalition; and Mayor James A. Garner of Hempstead, NY.

Statement on the International Initiative To Help Developing Countries Stop Illegal Logging
July 28, 2003

Today my administration has announced a new international initiative to help developing countries stop illegal logging. Illegal logging destroys biodiversity and hundreds of thousands of acres of forest habitat annually. It releases millions of tons of greenhouse gases into the atmosphere. Last year, I directed Secretary Powell to develop a plan to address this serious issue. I thank him for his efforts in establishing this initiative. Working with the private sector, nongovernmental organizations, and other na-

tions, the United States will help identify and reduce threats to protected forest areas and other high-value conservation forests. These efforts will serve as a foundation for future actions to eliminate illegal logging, corruption in the forest sector, and the sale—including for export—of illegally harvested timber products. They will also help us protect forests and the livelihoods that depend upon them.

Statement on Signing the Burmese Freedom and Democracy Act of 2003 and the Accompanying Executive Order
July 28, 2003

Today I have signed into law the Burmese Freedom and Democracy Act of 2003 and an Executive order sending a clear signal to Burma's ruling junta that it must release Nobel Peace Laureate Aung San Suu Kyi, along with all other political prisoners, and move down the path toward democracy. These measures reaffirm to the people of Burma that the United States stands with them in their struggle for democracy and freedom.

The Burmese Freedom and Democracy Act is the result of close cooperation between my administration and Members of Congress on both sides of the aisle, especially Senator Mitch McConnell and Representative Tom Lantos. Among other measures, the legislation bans the import of Burmese products. The Executive order freezes the assets of senior Burmese officials and bans virtually all remittances to Burma. By denying these rulers the hard currency they use to fund their repression, we are providing strong incentives for democratic change and human rights in Burma.

In May of this year, the Burmese Government tightened its grip on the people of Burma when it organized an attack on the motorcade of Aung San Suu Kyi, the leader of the National League for Democracy (NLD). Since then, Burmese officials have ignored requests from around the world to release Aung San Suu Kyi and other members of the NLD and to reopen NLD offices.

The repression of the Burmese regime contributes to problems that spill across Burma's borders, including refugee flows, narcotics trafficking, and the spread of HIV/AIDS and other diseases. These problems affect Burma's neighbors, and these nations must play an important role in resolving the current crisis. I urge the Association of South-East Asian Nations (ASEAN) to continue to make clear to the regime that its behavior is inconsistent with ASEAN's standards and goals. Burma should not be permitted to tarnish ASEAN's record as a positive force for progress. I also welcome the measures taken by the European Union and Japan to bring about democratic change in Burma.

The United States will not waver from its commitment to the cause of democracy and human rights in Burma. The United States has raised the situation in Burma at the United Nations Security Council and will do so again as developments warrant. The world must make clear—through word and deed—that the people of Burma, like people everywhere, deserve to live in dignity and freedom under leaders of their own choosing.

NOTE: H.R. 2330, approved July 28, was assigned Public Law No. 108–61. The Executive order of July 28 is listed in Appendix D at the end of this volume.

Letter to Congressional Leaders Reporting on the Burmese Freedom and Democracy Act of 2003 and the Accompanying Executive Order
July 28, 2003

Dear Mr. Speaker: *(Dear Mr. President:)*

Consistent with section 204(b) of the International Emergency Economic Powers Act, 50 U.S.C. 1703(b) (IEEPA) and section 301 of the National Emergencies Act, 50 U.S.C. 1631, I hereby report that I have issued an Executive Order (the "Order") that expands the sanctions against Burma currently in place pursuant to the national emergency with respect to Burma declared in Executive Order 13047 of May 20, 1997. Further, I hereby provide the notification to the Congress required by section 3(b) of the Burmese Freedom and Democracy Act of 2003 (the "Act") regarding my exercise of the waiver authorities provided in that section.

In 1997, the United States put in place a prohibition on new investment in Burma in response to the Government of Burma's large scale repression of the democratic opposition in that country. Since that time, the Government of Burma has rejected our efforts and the efforts of others in the international community to end its repressive activities. In May of this year, that rejection manifested itself in a brutal and organized attack on the motorcade of Aung San Suu Kyi, a Nobel Peace Prize winner and leader of the peaceful democratic opposition party in Burma, the National League for Democracy. The Government of Burma has continued to ignore our requests for her to be released from confinement, for the other National League for Democracy leaders who were jailed before and after the attack to be released, and for the offices of the National League for Democracy to be allowed to reopen.

I have now determined that this continued and increasing repression by the Government of Burma warrants an expansion of the sanctions against that government. I applaud the Congress' efforts to address the Government of Burma's action. The prohibitions contained in my Order implement sections 3 and 4 of the Burmese Freedom and Democracy Act of 2003 and supplement that Act with additional restrictions.

The Order blocks all property and interests in property of the State Peace and Development Council of Burma, the Myanma Foreign Trade Bank, the Myanma Investment and Commercial Bank (MICB), and the Myanma Economic Bank as well as all property and interests in property of persons determined by the Secretary of the Treasury, in consultation with the Secretary of State, to be senior officials of the Government of Burma, the State Peace and Development Council of Burma, the Union Solidarity and Development Association of Burma, or any successor entity to any of the foregoing; or to be owned or controlled by, or acting or purporting to act for or on behalf of, directly or indirectly, any of the foregoing. The Order also prohibits the exportation or re-exportation of financial services to Burma either from the United States or by any United States person and, 30 days from the effective date of the Order, the importation into the United States of any article that is a product of Burma.

The Department of the Treasury, in consultation with the Department of State, will implement a remittance program authorizing limited personal transfers of funds and will authorize most transactions relating to humanitarian, educational, and official United States Government activities. Additionally, the Order grandfathers any activity, or trans-actions incident to any activity, other than the import of any products of Burma, undertaken pursuant to any agreement that was entered into by a United States person with the Government of

Burma or a nongovernmental entity in Burma prior to May 21, 1997, the effective date of Executive Order 13047.

I have determined that the waiver of the prohibitions described in section 3 of the Burmese Freedom and Democracy Act of 2003 with respect to any or all articles that are a product of Burma is in the national interest of the United States to the extent that prohibiting the importation of such articles would conflict with the international obligations of the United States under the Vienna Convention on Diplomatic Relations, the Vienna Convention on Consular Relations, the United Nations Headquarters Agreement, and other legal instruments providing equivalent privileges and immunities. In addition, in the exercise of my constitutional authorities under Article II of the Constitution to conduct the foreign relations of the United States, I will construe the Act in a manner that will in no way impair the existing ability of United States diplomatic and consular officials to import articles that are a product of Burma that are necessary to the performance of their functions as United States Government officials in Burma.

The Secretary of the Treasury, in consultation with the Secretary of State, is authorized to issue regulations in the exercise of authorities under the International Emergency Economic Powers Act and sections 3(a) and 4 of the Burmese Freedom and Democracy Act of 2003, other than the authority to make the determinations and certification to the Congress that Burma has met the conditions described in section 3(a)(3), to implement the measures provided in the Order. The Secretary of State is also authorized to exercise the functions and authorities conferred upon the President by section 3(b) of the Burmese Freedom and Democracy Act of 2003. All Federal agencies are directed to take actions within their authority to carry out the provisions of the Order.

I have enclosed a copy of the Executive Order I have issued. This Order becomes effective at 12:01 a.m. eastern daylight time on July 29, 2003.

Sincerely,

GEORGE W. BUSH

NOTE: Identical letters were sent to J. Dennis Hastert, Speaker of the House of Representatives, and Richard B. Cheney, President of the Senate. H.R. 2330, approved July 28, was assigned Public Law No. 108–61. The Executive order of July 28 is listed in Appendix D at the end of this volume.

The President's News Conference With Prime Minister Ariel Sharon of Israel
July 29, 2003

President Bush. Good day. I'm pleased to welcome Prime Minister Ariel Sharon back to the White House. I think you said this is our eighth meeting——

Prime Minister Sharon. Eighth meeting here.

President Bush. Eighth meeting in Washington. That should indicate to everybody that our nations have a deep and abiding friendship. America is firmly committed to the security of Israel as a Jewish state, and we are firmly committed to the safety of the Israeli people. We have now a tremendous opportunity to add to Israeli security and safety and add to the hopes of the average Palestinian citizen by making tangible progress towards two states living side by side in peace.

Last month's Red Sea Summits in Egypt and Jordan gave momentum to that progress. I'm encouraged by the positive steps that Israel has taken since then to further the cause of peace, including prisoner releases. Prime Minister Sharon is now meeting regularly with Prime Minister Abbas, and that's positive. Israeli and Palestinian cabinet and security officials are meeting as well. Israel has recently taken steps to make it easier for Palestinians to work in Israel and to travel to their jobs and schools and families, and I thank the Prime Minister for these important actions.

Much hard work remains to be done by Israelis and Palestinians and by their neighbors. If we are ever to reach our common goal of two states living side by side in peace and security, leaders must assume responsibility. The Prime Minister is assuming responsibility.

All parties agree that a fundamental obstacle to peace is terrorism, which can never be justified by any cause. Last month in Aqaba, Prime Minister Abbas committed to a complete end to violence and terrorism. The Palestinian Authority must undertake sustained, targeted, and effective operations to confront those engaged in terror and to dismantle terrorist capabilities and infrastructure. We're determined to help Prime Minister Abbas as he works to end terror and establish the rule of law that will protect Israelis and Palestinians alike.

Today I urge Arab states to follow through on the pledges made in Sharm el-Sheikh to actively contribute to these efforts and to reject the culture of extremism and violence from whatever source or place. The rise of a peaceful Palestinian state and the long-term security of the Israeli people both depend on defeating the threat of terrorist groups and ending incitement and hatred.

In our discussions, I encouraged the Prime Minister to take further steps to improve the daily conditions faced by Palestinians. Israelis and Palestinians deserve the same chance to live normal lives, free from fear, free from hatred and violence, and free from harassment. I also urged the Prime Minister to carefully consider all the consequences of Israel's actions as we move forward on the road to peace.

The United States of America will continue to act in the interests of peace. We will continue to be a firm warrior against terrorism wherever it is found. We will encourage all parties to keep their promises and monitor the progress that is made. We will also help the parties find solutions to legitimate concerns. As we head down the road to peace, my commitment to the security of Israel is unshakable, as is the enduring friendship of our countries. I want to thank Ariel for all he's done to contribute to that friendship, for his leadership, and his willing to make tough decisions in the cause of peace.

Mr. Prime Minister.

Prime Minister Sharon. Mr. President, it is a great privilege for me to be here at the White House for the eighth time. I am always pleased to visit and feel that I am among friends, true friends of the state and the people of Israel.

Mr. President, I congratulate you on the impressive victory in the Iraqi campaign and for removing Saddam Hussein from power, one of the most ruthless and tyrannical leaders in history. For 30 years, the free world has witnessed the recklessness and brutality of this dictator. Only you, Mr. President, have shown the courage, determination, and leadership needed to spearhead the successful campaign to oust this ruthless, merciless despot, his dynasty, and evil regime.

For the first time since World War II, the freedom- and peace-seeking democratic world had the wisdom to go after murderers and evil rulers and bring them to justice. I have no doubt, Mr. President, that thanks to you, any villain in any corner of the world knows that the long arm of justice will reach them. So many will owe their lives to you and the great nation of America. I'm confident, Mr. President, that the lessons learned by the nations of the world and the region on the courageous action of the United States in Iraq will serve to advance the peace process between Israel and the Palestinians and the entire Arab world.

Your latest statement regarding the threats emanating from Syria and Iran prove once again the seriousness of your intentions to continue leading the fight against terror. It must be made clear to these countries that their evil deeds cannot continue. There can be no compromise with terror and evil.

The people of Israel, Mr. President, are greatly thankful and appreciative of your activity, unrelenting commitment to Israel's security and the safety of its citizens, and your determination to advance the peace process between us and the Palestinians.

We are currently at an important juncture in our relations with our Palestinian neighbors. While relative quiet currently prevails in Israel, terror has not yet completely ceased. This relative calm was achieved, first and foremost, through the uncompromising activity of the Israeli security forces and as a result of your personal effort and the actions taken by the United States among Arab and European countries. We are thankful for every hour of increased quiet and less terrorism and for every drop of blood that is spared. At the same time, we are concerned that this welcome quiet will be shattered any minute as a result of the continued existence of terror organizations which the Palestinian Authority is doing nothing to eliminate or dismantle.

Mr. President, I am confident that you, as the leader of the free world in this war against terror, will act to ensure that the Palestinians put a complete stop to the threat of Palestinian terrorism so that it will never rear its head again. I wish to move forward with a political process with our Palestinian neighbors. And the right way to do that is only after a complete cessation of terror, violence, and incitement, full dismantlement of terror organiza-

tions, and completion of the reform process in the Palestinian Authority.

We had a useful talk today, where we examined ways to advance the peace process between us and our Palestinian neighbors. In this context, a number of issues came up: the security fence which we are forced to construct in order to defend our citizens against terror activities; the removal of unauthorized outposts; and the freezing of settlements in Judea and Samaria.

I listened to your statement on this subject and assured you, Mr. President, that I would address them. The security——

President Bush. It's stuck.

Prime Minister Sharon. As you can see, we need your help. [*Laughter*]

The security fence will continue to be built with every effort to minimize the infringement on the daily life of the Palestinian population. Unauthorized outposts will be removed, as required in a law-abiding country. We'll continue to discuss all these issues both directly and through our bureaus, which maintain close contact.

Mr. President, we also discussed a series of issues which could serve to promote the peace process. In a statement published on my behalf last Friday, we listed a long series of steps to accommodate the Palestinians. If calm prevails and we witness the dismantlement of terror organizations, Israel will be able to take additional steps.

I wish to thank you again, George, for your friendship and understanding toward the state and people of Israel and for your contribution and personal involvement in the effort to turn the Middle East into a place where the peoples of the region can live in peace and security and guarantee a better life for our children and generations to come.

Thank you, George.

Q. Mr. President——

President Bush. Hold on a second, please. I'll call upon two members of our press corps. We'll alternate. First, Barry [Barry Schweid, Associated Press].

Report of the Joint Inquiry Into the September 11, 2001, Terrorist Attacks

Q. Mr. President, will the decision to not declassify the entire 9/11 report affect relations with Saudi Arabia, do you think? Might it have an impact on what they are doing to counter terrorism? Do you have any qualms?

President Bush. About not declassifying? No, absolutely have no qualms at all, because there's an ongoing investigation into the 9/11 attacks, and we don't want to compromise that investigation. If people are being investigated, it doesn't make sense for us to let them know who they are.

Secondly, we have an ongoing war against Al Qaida and terrorists, and the declassification of that part of a 900-page document would reveal sources and methods that will make it harder for us to win the war on terror. Now, perhaps at some point in time down the road, after the investigations are fully complete and if it doesn't jeopardize our national security, perhaps we can declassify the 27 of the hundreds of pages in the document. But it makes no sense to declassify when we've got an ongoing investigation; that could jeopardize that investigation. And it made no sense to declassify during the war on terror because it would help the enemy if they knew our sources and methods.

Israeli Security Fence

Q. Mr. President, what do you accept Israel to do in practical terms in regarding the separation fence that you call the wall? Due to the fact that this is one of the most effective measure against terrorism, can you clarify what do you oppose, the concept of the separation fence or only its roots?

And with your permission——

[*At this point, the reporter asked a second question in Hebrew, and no translation was provided.*]

President Bush. ——an international problem. [*Laughter*]

[*The reporter continued in Hebrew.*]

President Bush. Me? Okay. First, the most effective way to fight terror is to dismantle terrorist organizations. I fully recognize that. And we will continue to work with all parties to do just that. I mean, I fully understand that the most effective campaign to enhance the security of Israel, as well as the security of peace-loving people in the Palestinian territories, is to get after organizations such as Hamas, the terrorist organizations that create the conditions where peace won't exist. And therefore, I would hope in the long term a fence would be irrelevant.

But look, the fence is a sensitive issue, I understand. And the Prime Minister made it very clear to me that it was a sensitive issue. And my promise to him is, we'll continue to discuss and to dialog how best to make sure that the fence sends the right signal that not only is security important, but the ability for the Palestinians to live a normal life is important as well.

Q. Why do you criticize, Mr. President——

President Bush. No, no, no. Hold on. Not you. Steve [Steve Holland, Reuters]. Maybe some other time, but not now.

Q. All right. Thank you.

Ending Terrorism in the Middle East

Q. Thanks, sir. How are both of you going to get the Palestinian militants to extend the cease-fire?

President Bush. Do what now?

Q. How are both of you going to get the Palestinian militants to extend the cease-fire?

President Bush. Let me—look, the important message that should have come out of the meeting with Prime Minister Abbas and, of course, with Prime Minister Sharon, is that the—those who want to destroy the peace process through terrorist activities must be dealt with. There will be no peace if terrorism flourishes. There's no peace. It's a contradiction in terms. Terrorists are against peace. Terrorists kill innocent life to prevent peace from happening. The way to make sure peace happens is for all of us to work to dismantle those who would like to kill. Those are called terrorists.

And the positive news is that Prime Minister Abbas made a public declaration that we would work together to dismantle terrorist organizations. And that's exactly what's going to happen. For those who want peace—I mean, all around the world—have got to understand very clearly, if you're interested in peace in the Middle East, then all of us must work together to dismantle terrorist organizations, to cut off money to terrorist organizations, to prevent the few from damaging the aspirations of the many.

Q. Mr. President——

President Bush. Answer his question first, though. We don't want to hurt your feelings.

[Prime Minister Sharon answered the question in Hebrew, and no translation was provided.]

President Bush. Okay.

Palestinian Prisoners

Q. Mr. President, why do you expect Israeli Government to set free Palestinian prisoners, while you don't order to set free the Israeli civilian Jonathan Pollard?

President Bush. Yes, well, I said very clearly at the press conference with Prime Minister Abbas, I don't expect anybody to release somebody from prison who will go kill somebody. That doesn't make any sense. I mean, if we're trying to fight off terror and we're interested in a peaceful settlement, it doesn't make any sense to release somebody who is going to get out of prison and start killing.

I do hope that the Prime Minister continues to work with the Palestinian Author-

ity to release those prisoners that won't create the conditions of terror.

And I believe that Prime Minister Abbas wants peace. I know that the—his cabinet is interested in developing the institutions necessary for a Palestinian state to emerge in a peaceful way. I've been impressed by the Finance Minister of the Palestinian Authority, who's willing to put the Palestinian budget up on the web page. In other words, he believes in transparency. And the reason I bring that up is that I also know that those same Palestinians who are working for the institutions necessary for a peaceful state to evolve know that terrorists would like to derail those plans and, therefore, are willing to work to rout out terrorist organizations. And look, we don't want to put people back into society that will make that task more complicated.

Listen, thank you all very much.

Q. Mr. President, Senator Shelby says 95 percent of the redaction has nothing to do with sources and methods, sir. Is he wrong?

President Bush. Sorry.

[A reporter asked a final question in Hebrew, and Prime Minister Sharon answered in Hebrew, and no translation was provided.]

President Bush. Let's go have lunch.

NOTE: The President's news conference began at noon in the Rose Garden at the White House. In his remarks, he referred to Prime Minister Mahmoud Abbas (Abu Mazen) and Minister of Finance Salam Fayyad of the Palestinian Authority. Prime Minister Sharon referred to former President Saddam Hussein of Iraq. A reporter referred to former civilian U.S. Navy intelligence analyst Jonathan Pollard, convicted of treason and espionage in 1987.

Letter to Congressional Leaders Transmitting the Executive Order Implementing the Clean Diamond Trade Act
July 29, 2003

Dear Mr. Speaker: (Dear Mr. President:)

Consistent with section 204(b) of the International Emergency Economic Powers Act, 50 U.S.C. 1703(b), and section 301 of the National Emergencies Act, 50 U.S.C. 1631, I hereby report that I have issued an Executive Order (copy attached) to implement the Clean Diamond Trade Act, Public Law 108–19 (the "Act"), which authorizes the President to take steps to implement the Kimberley Process Certification Scheme (KPCS) for rough diamonds in the United States. In addition, my Executive Order amends Executive Orders 13194 and 13213 to harmonize those orders with the Act and to reflect recent developments in Sierra Leone and Liberia. The prohibitions in section 1 and 3 of the order take effect at 12:01 a.m. eastern daylight time on July 30, 2003, and the remaining provisions of the order take effect immediately.

On January 18, 2001, the President issued Executive Order 13194 taking into account United Nations Security Council Resolution (UNSCR) 1306 of July 5, 2000. That order declared a national emergency in response to the role played by the illicit trade in diamonds in fueling conflict and human rights violations in Sierra Leone and prohibited the importation into the United States of rough diamonds from Sierra Leone that were not controlled by the Government of Sierra Leone through its Certificate of Origin regime.

On May 22, 2001, I issued Executive Order 13213 taking into account UNSCR 1343 of March 7, 2001. That order expanded the scope of the national emergency declared in Executive Order 13194 to respond to, among other things, the Government of Liberia's complicity in the illicit trade in rough diamonds through Liberia. Executive Order 13213 prohibited the direct or indirect importation into the United States of all rough diamonds from Liberia, whether or not such diamonds originated in Liberia, except to the extent provided in regulations, orders, directives, or licenses issued pursuant to the order.

The United Nations ban against the importation of rough diamonds from Sierra Leone without a certificate of origin, imposed by UNSCR 1306 and renewed by UNSCR 1446 of December 4, 2002, expired on June 4, 2003. The United Nations Security Council decided not to renew the measure in light of the Government of Sierra Leone's increased efforts to control and manage its diamond industry and ensure proper control over diamond mining areas, as well as the Government's full participation in the KPCS. Although the hostilities fueled by and funded with conflict diamonds have ceased in Sierra Leone, the attendant peace and stability are tentative, fragile, and jeopardized by ongoing illicit diamond production and smuggling. In addition, the Security Council, through UNSCR 1478 of May 6, 2003, renewed for 1 year the absolute import ban on rough diamonds from Liberia based on evidence that the Government of Liberia continues to breach the measures imposed by UNSCR 1343.

In a related development, representatives of the United States and numerous other countries, including Sierra Leone, announced in the Interlaken Declaration of November 5, 2002, the launch of the KPCS. Participants in the KPCS are expected to prohibit the importation of rough diamonds from, or the exportation of rough diamonds to, a non-Participant and to require that shipments of rough diamonds from or to a Participant be controlled through the KPCS. The Clean Diamond Trade Act, which I signed on April 25,

2003, enables the United States to implement the KPCS by providing that, when the Act is in effect, the President shall, subject to certain waiver authorities, prohibit the importation into, or exportation from, the United States of any rough diamond, from whatever source, that has not been controlled through the KPCS.

My Executive Order will implement the Clean Diamond Trade Act and amend Executive Orders 13194 and 13213 to harmonize those orders with the Act and to reflect recent developments in Sierra Leone and Liberia. Section 1 of the Executive Order puts in place, as of July 30, 2003, the prohibitions of section 4(a) of the Clean Diamond Trade Act. Section 2 of my Executive Order assigns various functions of the President under the Act to the Secretary of State and the Secretary of the Treasury, including authorizing the Secretary of the Treasury to issue implementing regulations.

Section 3 of my Executive Order amends Executive Orders 13194 and 13213 in the following ways. Executive Order 13194 is revised to control rough diamonds from Sierra Leone through the KPCS, rather than through the Certificate of Origin regime of the Government of Sierra Leone. Executive Order 13213 is revised to remove, consistent with section 4(a) of the Clean Diamond Trade Act, licensing and other authorities with respect to rough diamonds from Liberia.

Finally, section 4 of my Executive Order provides that for the purposes of the order and Executive Order 13194, the definitions set forth in section 3 of the Act shall apply, and that the term "Kimberley Process Certification Scheme" shall not be construed to include any changes to the KPCS after April 25, 2003.

My Executive Order demonstrates the U.S. commitment to exclude conflict diamonds from international trade, while promoting the legitimate trade in rough diamonds that is so vital to many nations in Africa and elsewhere.

Sincerely,

GEORGE W. BUSH

NOTE: Identical letters were sent to J. Dennis Hastert, Speaker of the House of Representatives, and Richard B. Cheney, President of the Senate. The Executive order of July 29 is listed in Appendix D at the end of this volume.

Letter to Congressional Leaders on Waiver Certification To Implement the Clean Diamond Trade Act
July 29, 2003

Dear Mr. Speaker: (Dear Mr. President:)

The Clean Diamond Trade Act (Public Law 108–19) (the "Act") authorizes the President to prohibit the importation into, or exportation from, the United States of any rough diamond that has not been "controlled through the Kimberley Process Certification Scheme." Section 15 of the Act provides that the Act shall take effect on the date on which the President certifies to the Congress that (1) an applicable waiver that has been granted by the World Trade Organization (WTO) is in effect, or (2) an applicable decision in a resolution adopted by the United Nations Security Council pursuant to Chapter VII of the Charter of the United Nations is in effect. Section 15 further provides that the Act shall thereafter remain in effect during those periods in which, as certified by the President to the Congress, such an applicable waiver or decision is in effect.

On May 15, 2003, the WTO General Council (copy attached) adopted a waiver decision pursuant to Article IX of the Marrakesh Agreement Establishing the World Trade Organization (WTO Agreement) concerning the Kimberley Process Certification Scheme for rough diamonds (Certification Scheme). The decision waives the following provisions of the WTO Agreement's General Agreement on Tariffs and Trade 1994: paragraph 1 of Article I, paragraph 1 of Article XI, and paragraph 1 of Article XIII, for measures taken consistent with the Certification Scheme that are necessary to prohibit the export of rough diamonds to, or import of rough diamonds from, non-Participants in the Certification Scheme. The decision further provides that the waiver applies to the United States and other WTO members that requested the waiver and to any WTO member that notifies the WTO of its desire to be covered by the waiver. The waiver has retroactive effect to January 1, 2003, and will remain in effect until December 31, 2006.

Exercising my discretion under the Act, I hereby certify that an applicable waiver, within the meaning of section 15 of the Clean Diamond Trade Act, granted by the World Trade Organization is in effect and will remain in effect until December 31, 2006.

Sincerely,

GEORGE W. BUSH

NOTE: Identical letters were sent to J. Dennis Hastert, Speaker of the House of Representatives, and Richard B. Cheney, President of the Senate. The related Executive order of July 29 is listed in Appendix D at the end of this volume.

Letter to Congressional Leaders Transmitting a Report on the National Emergency With Respect to Sierra Leone and Liberia
July 29, 2003

Dear Mr. Speaker: *(Dear Mr. President:)*

Consistent with section 401(c) of the National Emergencies Act, 50 U.S.C. 1641(c), and section 204(c) of the International Emergency Economic Powers Act, 50 U.S.C. 1703(c), I am transmitting a 6-month periodic report prepared by my Administration on the national emergency declared with respect to Sierra Leone and Liberia in Executive Order 13194 of January 18, 2001, as expanded in scope in Executive Order 13213 of May 22, 2001.

Sincerely,

GEORGE W. BUSH

NOTE: Identical letters were sent to J. Dennis Hastert, Speaker of the House of Representatives, and Richard B. Cheney, President of the Senate.

The President's News Conference
July 30, 2003

The President. Thank you. Good morning. I was hoping it would be a little hotter here to prepare the traveling team for the Crawford experience this August. But thank you for coming.

I'm looking forward to going down to Texas, and I know the Members will be going back to their districts. As I travel around the country from Crawford, I'm going to be focused on two vital concerns for our country: first, the safety of the American people, and the economic security of the American people.

On national security front, it has been 90 days since the end of the major combat operations in Iraq. The nation has been liberated from tyranny and is on the path to self-government and peace. The Iraqi Governing Council is meeting regularly. Local police forces are now being trained. And citizens are being recruited into a new Iraqi military, a military that will protect the Iraqi people instead of intimidating them. Soon, representatives of the people will begin drafting a new constitution, and free elections will follow. After decades of oppression, the people of Iraq are reclaiming their country and are reclaiming their future.

Conditions in most of Iraq are growing more peaceful. Some areas, however, the violent remnants of Saddam Hussein's regime, joined by terrorists and criminals, are making a last attempt to frighten the Iraqi people and to undermine the resolve of our coalition. They will fail. Our coalition forces are taking the fight to the enemy in an unrelenting campaign that is bringing daily results. Saddam Hussein's sons did not escape the raids, and neither will other members of that despicable regime.

By taking the offensive against desperate killers, Americans in uniform are assuming great risks for our country. The American people are proud of our Armed Forces, and we are grateful for their sacrifice and their service in fighting the war on terror. We also appreciate the military families who share in the hardship and uncertainties of this essential mission.

The rise of a free and peaceful Iraq is critical to the stability of the Middle East, and a stable Middle East is critical to the security of the American people. As the blanket of fear is lifted, as Iraqis gain confidence that the former regime is gone for-

ever, we will gain more cooperation in our search for the truth in Iraq.

We know that Saddam Hussein produced and possessed chemical and biological weapons and has used chemical weapons. We know that. He also spent years hiding his weapons of mass destruction programs from the world. We now have teams of investigators who are hard at work to uncover the truth.

The success of a free Iraq will also demonstrate to other countries in that region that national prosperity and dignity are found in representative government and free institutions. They are not found in tyranny, resentment, and for support of terrorism. As freedom advances in the Middle East, those societies will be less likely to produce ideologies of hatred and produce recruits for terror.

The United States and our allies will complete our mission in Iraq, and we'll complete our mission in Afghanistan. We'll keep our word to the peoples of those nations. We'll wage the war on terror against every enemy who plots against our forces and our people. I will never assume the restraint and good will of dangerous enemies when lives of our American citizens are at risk.

My administration is also acting to ensure the economic security of the American people. Paychecks are already reflecting the reduction in income tax rates, which is providing relief to millions of taxpayers and small businesses. American families have begun to receive checks from a $400-per-child increase in the child tax credit. This time, when we say the check's in the mail, we mean it.

Through our higher expense deduction, small businesses have an incentive to speed up purchases of new equipment. We're beginning to see hopeful signs of faster growth in the economy, which over time will yield new jobs. Yet the unemployment rate is still too high. And we will not rest until Americans looking for work can find a job.

To strengthen the economic security of the people, Congress needs to pass a sound energy bill to make sure that our households and businesses have a reliable, affordable supply of energy. Congress needs to pass legal reforms to cut down on the frivolous lawsuits that provide a drag to our economy. Congress needs to approve reemployment accounts to help citizens who have the toughest time finding work. Congress needs to make sure that the child credit is refundable for lower-income families. We must continue pursuing an aggressive, progrowth strategy that creates jobs throughout our economy.

Economic security for America's seniors is threatened by the rising cost of prescription drugs. I'm pleased that both Houses of Congress have responded by passing separate bills providing prescription drug coverage under Medicare. It's absolutely essential that the House and the Senate resolve their differences and enact a piece of legislation I can sign. The lack of coverage for prescription drugs and many preventative treatments is a major gap in Medicare that denies some of our seniors the latest and best medicine. We must keep the promise of Medicare by giving our seniors better coverage and better choices.

I congratulate the House and the Senate on a productive legislative session—so far. I also look forward to working with the Members this coming fall on the priorities for the American people.

And now I'll be glad to answer some questions. Tom [Tom Raum, Associated Press], and we'll work our way around. There's no need for any unrestrained yelling. [*Laughter*]

Military Operations in Iraq

Q. Thank you, Mr. President. Mr. President, now with the deaths of the sons of Saddam Hussein and the capture of his chief bodyguard, what can you tell us about how close we might be to actually capturing or killing Saddam himself? And how important would that be to ending the war and

stopping the violence against American troops? And what do you say to those troops who fought long and hard and now are eager to come home, given the fact that it's hard to find other countries to send in troops that could serve as replacements?

The President. Okay. Tom, I'm getting a little older, so when you ask four or five questions, it's hard for me to remember every question.

First, we do have a good rotation plan in place now for our troops. The 3d ID, which has conducted a lot of the major military operations at the beginning of the war, has now got a definite time in which they are coming home. And that in itself is a positive development. There was some concern amongst family members of the 3d ID that they were getting mixed signals, and I understand that. And now it's clear as to their rotation plan.

And by the way, as we rotate, we'll be changing the nature of the military configuration to be more of a—to have more of a—the capacity to move very quickly and to strike quickly, because our intelligence is getting better on the ground as we're able to pick targets, able to enrich targets and move quickly on the targets.

What other aspects of the—I told you— I warned you, I'm getting older.

Deaths of Uday and Qusay Hussein

Q. I asked you how close we are to catching——

The President. Catching Saddam Hussein, that's right. Yes.

Q. ——and how important it is to——

The President. Listen—right, thank you. Of course, it's important that the—that Saddam's sons were brought to justice. It changes attitudes in Iraq. People didn't believe that the Ba'athist regime was going to be gone forever. They felt like they— you would hear reports of Ba'athists, former Ba'athist officials saying to Iraqi citizens, "Listen, the Americans will grow stale and tired. They'll leave and, by the way, we'll come back. And when we come back, we'll come back with a vengeance if you help in the reconstruction of the country." So, needless to say, when two of the most despicable henchmen of the Saddam Hussein regime met their fate, the Ba'athist claim that at least these two will come back and haunt the citizen is—rings hollow.

I don't know how close we are to getting Saddam Hussein. You know, I—it's closer than we were yesterday, I guess. All I know is we're on the hunt. It's like if you had asked me right before we got his sons how close we were to get his sons, I'd say I don't know, but we're on the hunt.

And so we're making progress. It's slowly but surely making progress of bringing the—those who terrorize their fellow citizens to justice and making progress about convincing the Iraqi people that freedom is real. And as they become more convinced that freedom is real, they'll begin to assume more responsibilities that are required in a free society.

Steve [Steve Holland, Reuters].

War on Terror/Possible Terrorist Attacks

Q. Thank you, sir. Homeland Security is warning against possible hijackings this summer. How serious is this threat, and what can you do about it? How can Americans feel safe?

The President. Yes. Well, first of all, the war on terror goes on, as I continually remind people. In other words, there are still Al Qaida remnants that have designs on America. The good news is that we are, one, dismantling the Al Qaida organization, and two, we're learning more information about their plans as we capture more people.

And the threat is a real threat. It's a threat that where—we obviously don't have specific data; we don't know when, where, what. But we do know a couple of things. We do know that Al Qaida tends to use the methodologies that worked in the past. That's kind of their mindset. And we have got some data that indicates that they

would like to use flights, international flights, for example.

Now, what we can do is we can be—obviously, at home, continue to be diligent on the inspection process of baggage as well as making sure those who board aircraft are properly screened. And obviously, we're talking to foreign governments and foreign airlines to indicate to them the reality of the threat. We're conscious° of folks flying—getting lists of people flying into our country and matching them now with a much improved database. International flights coming into America must have hardened cockpit doors, which is a positive development.

Being on alert means that we contact all who are responsible, who have got positions of responsibility. And so we're focusing on the airline industry right now. And we've got reason to do so. And I'm confident we will thwart the attempts.

You know, let me talk about Al Qaida just for a second. I made the statement that we're dismantling senior management, and we are. Our people have done a really good job of hauling in a lot of the key operators: Khalid Sheikh Mohammed, Abu Zubaydah, Ramzi—Ramzi al-Shibh or whatever the guy's name was—*[laughter]*—sorry, Ramzi, if I got it wrong—*[laughter]*—bin al-Shibh, excuse me. "Swift Sword" is dead, thanks to the Saudis. Abu Bakr is now captured by the Saudis. We're dismantling the operating—decisionmakers.

We've got more to do. And the American people need to know we're not stopping. We've got better intelligence-gathering, better intelligence-sharing, and we're on the hunt. And we will stay on the hunt. The threat that you asked about, Steve, reminds us that we need to be on the hunt, and—because the war on terror goes on.

John [John King, Cable News Network].

° White House correction.

*Report of the Joint Inquiry Into the
September 11, 2001, Terrorist Attacks*

Q. Mr. President, thank you. You met yesterday with the Saudi Foreign Minister, who wants the administration to declassify these 27 or 28 pages about his Government in this report on 9/11. Many Members of Congress, including several Republicans, say they see nothing—or at least most of the materials, in their view, could be made public. Can you tell us, is there any compromise in sight on this, and could you at least summarize the material in that classified document? Is there, as some Members of Congress say, material that you could read and have an incriminating view of the Saudi Government when it comes to 9/11?

The President. John, the Foreign Minister did come and speak to me. And I told him this: I said we have an ongoing investigation about what may or may not have taken place prior to September the 11th. And therefore, it is important for us to hold this information close so that those who are being investigated aren't alerted.

I also told him, in the document, that if we were to reveal the content of the document—by the way, 29 pages of a near 900-page report—it would reveal sources and methods. By that I mean it would show people how we collect information and on whom we're collecting information, which, in my judgment and in the judgment of senior law enforcement officials in my administration, would be harmful on the war against terror.

I just described to you that there is a threat to the United States. And I also said, we're doing a better job of sharing intelligence and collecting data so we're able to find—able to anticipate. And what we really don't want to do, it doesn't make sense to me—doesn't seem like to me, is to reveal those sources and methods.

Now, at some point in time, as we make progress on the investigation and as a threat to our national security diminishes, perhaps we can put out the document. But in my judgment, now is not the time to do so.

And I made that clear to him. And I will be glad—I'm making it clear to Members of Congress. I want to remind you that—sure, some have spoken out, but others have agreed with my position, like the chairman of the House Intelligence Committee. So there's a different point of view. My point of view, however, since I'm in charge of fighting the war on terror, is that we won't reveal sources and methods that will compromise our efforts to succeed.

Campbell [Campbell Brown, NBC News].

Saddam Hussein's Links to Al Qaida

Q. Saddam Hussein's alleged ties to Al Qaida were a key part of your justification for war. Yet, your own intelligence report, the NIE, defined it as, quote, "low confidence that Saddam would give weapons to Al Qaida." Were those links exaggerated to justify war? Or can you finally offer us some definitive evidence that Saddam was working with Al Qaida terrorists?

The President. Yes. I think, first of all, remember, I just said we've been there for 90 days since the cessation of major military operations. Now, I know in our world where news comes and goes and there's this kind of instant news, and you must have done this, you must do this yesterday, that there's a level of frustration by some in the media. I'm not suggesting you're frustrated. You don't look frustrated to me at all. But it's going to take time for us to gather the evidence, the—analyze the mounds of evidence, literally, the miles of documents that we have uncovered.

David Kay came to see me yesterday. He's going to testify in closed hearing tomorrow, which in Washington may not be so closed, as you know. And he was telling me the process that they were going through to analyze all the documentation. And that's not only to analyze the documentation on the weapons programs that

Saddam Hussein had but also the documentation as to terrorist links.

And it's just going to take a while, and I'm confident the truth will come out. And there is no doubt in my mind, Campbell, that Saddam Hussein was a threat to the United States security and a threat to peace in the region. And there's no doubt in my mind that a free Iraq is important. It's got strategic consequences for not only achieving peace in the Middle East, but a free Iraq will help change the habits of other nations in the region who will make it—which will make America much more secure.

John [John Roberts, CBS News].

Decision To Go to War in Iraq

Q. Thank you, Mr. President. Building sort of on that idea, it's impossible to deny that the world is a better place in the region, certainly a better place without Saddam Hussein. But there's a sense here in this country and a feeling around the world that the U.S. has lost credibility by building the case for Iraq upon sometimes flimsy or, some people have complained, nonexistent evidence. I'm just wondering, sir, why did you choose to take the world to war in that way?

The President. Yes. You know, look, in my line of work, it's always best to produce results, and I understand that. The—for a while the questions were, "Could you conceivably achieve a military victory in Iraq? You know, the dust storms have slowed you down." And I was a patient man, because I realized that we would be successful in achieving our military objective.

Now, of course, the question is, will Iraq ever be free, and will it be peaceful? And I believe it will. I remind some of my friends that it took us a while to go from the Articles of Confederation to the United States Constitution. Even our own experiment with democracy didn't happen overnight. I never have expected Thomas Jefferson to emerge in Iraq in a 90-day period.

And so this is going to take time. And the world will see what I mean when I say a free Iraq will help peace in the Middle East, and a free Iraq will be important for changing the attitudes of the people in the Middle East. A free Iraq will show what is possible in a world that needs freedom, in a part of the world that needs freedom.

Let me finish for a minute, John, please. Just getting warmed up. I'm kind of finding my feet. [*Laughter*]

Saddam Hussein was a threat. The United Nations viewed him as a threat. That's why they passed 12 resolutions. Predecessors of mine viewed him as a threat. We gathered a lot of intelligence. That intelligence was good, sound intelligence on which I made a decision.

And in order to placate the critics and the cynics about intentions of the United States, we need to produce evidence. And I fully understand that. And I'm confident that our search will yield that which I strongly believe, that Saddam had a weapons program. I want to remind you, he actually used his weapons program on his own people at one point in time, which is pretty tangible evidence. But I'm confident history will prove the decision we made to be the right decision.

Q. [*Inaudible*]

The President. Hold on for a second. You're through, John.

Homosexuality/Definition of Marriage

Q. Thank you, sir. Mr. President, many of your supporters believe that homosexuality is immoral. They believe that it's been given too much acceptance in policy terms and culturally. As someone who's spoken out in strongly moral terms, what's your view on homosexuality?

The President. Yes. I am mindful that we're all sinners, and I caution those who may try to take a speck out of their neighbor's eye when they got a log in their own. I think it's very important for our society to respect each individual, to welcome those with good hearts, to be a welcoming country. On the other hand, that does not mean that somebody like me needs to compromise on an issue such as marriage. And that's really where the issue is headed here in Washington, and that is the definition of marriage. I believe in the sanctity of marriage. I believe a marriage is between a man and a woman. And I think we ought to codify that one way or the other. And we've got lawyers looking at the best way to do that.

Stevenson [Richard Stevenson, New York Times].

Tax Cuts/National Economy

Q. Thank you, sir. Since taking office, you've signed into law three major tax cuts, two of which have had plenty of time to take effect, the third of which, as you pointed out earlier, is taking effect now. Yet, the unemployment rate has continued rising. We now have more evidence of a massive budget deficit that taxpayers are going to be paying off for years or decades to come. The economy continues to shed jobs. What evidence can you point to that tax cuts, at least of the variety that you have supported, are really working to help this economy? And do you need to be thinking about some other approach?

The President. Yes. No, to answer the last part of your question. First of all, let me—just a quick history, recent history. The stock market started to decline in March of 2000. Then the first quarter of 2001 was a recession. And then we got attacked in 9/11. And then corporate scandals started to bubble up to the surface, which created a lack of confidence in the system. And then we had the drumbeat to war. Remember on our TV screens— I'm not suggesting which network did this—but it said, "march to war" every day from last summer until the spring—"march to war, march to war." That's not a very conducive environment for people to take risk, when they hear "march to war" all the time.

And yet our economy is growing. In other words, what I'm telling you is, is that we had a lot of obstacles to overcome. The '01 tax cuts affected the recession this way: It was a shallow recession. That's positive, because I care about people being able to find a job. Someone said, "Well, maybe the recession should have been deeper in order for the rebound to be quicker." My attitude is, a deeper recession means more people would have been hurt. And I view the actions we've taken as a jobs program, job creation program.

Secondly, there are hopeful signs. I mean, most economists believe that over the next 18 months we'll see positive economic growth. Interest rates are low. Housing starts are strong. Manufacturing indexes are improving.

There are other things we can do in Washington. As I said, we need an energy bill. We certainly need tort reform. I think the class action reform that's moved out of the House and into the Senate is something that can be done, and it ought to be done quickly. In other words, what I'm saying to you is, is that there's still work to do. But I'm optimistic about the future, and I believe you'll see more jobs created, and that's going to be good for the country.

Yes. Jim Rosen [James Rosen, FOX News].

North Korea

Q. Thank you, sir. You just explained that your approach to your job is to try to produce results. It has been roughly a year since North Korea apprised the United States Government that it is seeking to reactivate its nuclear weapons program. In that year, you and your aides have repeatedly said that you seek a diplomatic approach to that problem. And yet, over that year, all we've seen from the North Koreans are more bellicose statements and more steps taken to add to their stockpile of nuclear weapons that they already have. What can you point to in the record over the last year by your administration for Americans to look at and say this President has produced results?

The President. Yes. I think that one of the things that is important to understand in North Korea is that the past policy of trying to engage bilaterally didn't work. In other words, the North Koreans were ready to engage, but they didn't keep their word on their engagement. And that ought to be a clear signal to policymakers of what to expect with North Korea.

Secondly, in my judgment, the best way to convince the North Koreans to change their attitude about a nuclear weapon program is to have others in the neighborhood assume responsibility alongside the United States. So this morning, interesting enough—I'm glad you asked that question, because I can tell you that I talked to Hu Jintao this morning—not anticipation of your question, but as part of an ongoing process to encourage him to stay involved in the process of discussions with Mr. Kim Chong-il, all attempting to say to him that it is a—it is not in his nation's interest to continue developing these weapons and we would like to see him dismantle those weapons programs.

As well as—I told President Hu that I think it's very important for us to get Japan and South Korea and Russia involved as well. So the progress that is being made is, we're actually beginning to make serious progress about sharing responsibility on this issue in such a way that I believe will lead to an attitudinal change by Kim Chong-il, which will be very positive for peace in the region.

State of the Union Address

Q. Thank you, Mr. President——

The President. Kate [Kate Snow, ABC News].

Q. That's right. Thank you, Mr. President.

The President. How long have you been—how long have you been in the press corps? You look like you just came.

Q. Last week was my first week.

The President. Yes, congratulations.

Q. Thank you.

The President. Be careful whose company you're keeping, though. [*Laughter*]

Q. Mr. President, you often speak about the need for accountability in many areas. I wonder then, why is Dr. Condoleezza Rice not being held accountable for the statement that your own White House has acknowledged was a mistake in your State of the Union Address regarding Iraq's attempts to purchase uranium? And also, do you take personal responsibility for that inaccuracy?

The President. I take personal responsibility for everything I say, of course. Absolutely. I also take responsibility for making decisions on war and peace. And I analyzed a thorough body of intelligence—good, solid, sound intelligence that led me to come to the conclusion that it was necessary to remove Saddam Hussein from power.

We gave the world a chance to do it. We had—remember there's—again, I don't want to get repetitive here, but it's important to remind everybody that there was 12 resolutions that came out of the United Nations because others recognized the threat of Saddam Hussein. Twelve times the United Nations Security Council passed resolutions in recognition of the threat that he posed. And the difference was, is that some were not willing to act on those resolutions. We were, along with a lot of other countries, because he posed a threat.

Dr. Condoleezza Rice is an honest, fabulous person, and America is lucky to have her service. Period.

Michael Allen [Washington Post].

2004 Campaign

Q. Mr. President, with no opponent, how can you spend $170 million or more on your primary campaign?

The President. Just watch. [*Laughter*] Keep going.

Q. Yes, sir. And with 15 fundraisers scheduled between—for the summer months, do you worry about the perception that you're unduly attentive to the interests of people who can afford to spend $2,000 to see you?

The President. Michael, I think American people, now that they've realized I'm going to seek reelection, expect me to seek reelection. They expect me to actually do what candidates do. And so, you're right, I'll be spending some time going out and asking the American people to support me. But most of my time, as I say in my speeches—as I'm sure you've been bored to tears listening to—is that there is a time for politics, and that's going to be later on. I've got a lot to do. And I will continue doing my job, and my job will be to work to make America more secure.

Steve asked a question about this Al Qaida possible attack. Every day I am reminded that our Nation is still vulnerable. Every day I'm reminded about what 9/11 means to America. That's a lesson, by the way, I'll never forget, the lesson of 9/11, because—and I remember right after 9/11 saying that this will be a different kind of war, but it's a war, and sometimes there will be action, and sometimes there won't, but we're still threatened. And I see that almost every day, Mike. And therefore, that is a major part of my job.

And the other part of my job that I talked about is the economic security of the American people. And I spend a lot of time on the economy, going out and talking to the American people about the economy, and will continue to do so.

But no, listen, since I've made the decision to run, of course I'm going to do what candidates do. And we're having pretty good success, which is—it's kind of an interesting barometer, early barometer, about the support we're garnering.

Keil [Richard Keil, Bloomberg News], Jeanne [Jeanne Cummings, Wall Street Journal], and then Larry [Larry McQuillan, USA Today]. Keil. Stretch. Super Stretch.

Federal Deficit/National Economy

Q. Thank you, Mr. President. As you said just a few moments ago and say frequently in your speeches, the deficit was caused variously by the war, by recession, by corporate scandals, the 9/11 attacks. But just a couple of weeks ago, on July 15th, the Office of Management and Budget put out a report saying that without the tax cuts that Congress passed, the budget would be back in surplus by 2008, but with those tax cuts factored in, we have deficits that year and further years out of at least $200 billion, to use the phrase, as far as the eye can see. Aren't tax cuts in part responsible for the deficits, and does that fact concern you? Are we now in a period where we have deficits as far as the eye can see?

The President. We would have had deficits with or without tax cuts, for this reason: The slowdown in the economy, the decline in the stock market starting March of 2000, plus the recession, reduced the amount of revenues coming into the Federal Treasury. Secondly, we spent money on the war, and we spent money on homeland security. My attitude is, if we're going to put our troops into harm's way, they must have the very best. And there's no doubt we increased our budgets on defense and homeland security. So there would be recessions.

And so, given the—I mean, there would be deficits. So given the fact that we're in a recession, which had it gone on longer than it did could have caused even more revenues to be lost to the Treasury, I had a policy decision to make. And I made the decision to address the recession by a tax cut. And so part of the deficit, no question, was caused by taxes—about 25 percent of the deficit, the other 75—50 percent caused by lack of revenues, and 25 percent caused by additional spending on the war on terror.

Now, we have laid out a plan which shows that the deficit will be cut in half over the next 5 years. And that's good progress toward deficit reduction. That's assuming Congress holds the line on spending. I presented them with a 4-percent increase in the discretionary budget to help them hold the line on spending. They passed the budget. Now they've got to meet the budget in their appropriations process.

My first concern, Dick, was for those folks who couldn't find a job. And I addressed unemployment and addressed economic stagnancy with a tax cut that affected growth or the lack of growth in a positive way. And I'm optimistic about our economy. But I'm not going to stop working until people can find a job who are looking for work.

Jeanne.

Workforce and Technology

Q. Thank you, Mr. President. Staying with that theme, although there are some signs of improvement in the economy, there are sectors in the workforce who feel like they're being left behind. They're concerned about jobs going overseas, that technology is taking over jobs. And these people are finding difficulty finding work. And although you're recommitted yourself to your tax cut policy, do you have any ideas or any plans within the administration of what you might do for these people who feel like there are fundamental changes happening in the workforce and in the economy?

The President. Sure. Listen, I fully understand what you're saying. In other words, as technology races through the economy, a lot of times worker skills don't keep up with technological change. And that's a significant issue that we've got to address in the country.

I think my idea of reemployment accounts makes a lot of sense. In essence, it says that you get $3,000 from the Federal Government to help you with training, daycare, transportation, perhaps moving to another city. And if, within a period of

time, you're able to find a job, you keep the balance as a reemployment bonus.

I know the community colleges provide a very important role in worker training, worker retraining. I look forward to working with our community colleges through the Department of Education, coordinate closely with States, particularly in those States in which technology is changing the nature of the job force. I've always found the community college—and this is from my days as the Governor of Texas—found the community college to be a very appropriate place for job training programs because they're more adaptable; their curriculums are easier to change; they're accessible. Community colleges are all over the place.

And—but you're right. I mean, I think we need to make sure that people get the training necessary to keep up with the nature of the jobs as jobs change.

Laurence, USA Today.

Middle East Peace Process

Q. Mr. President, you've been involved now in the Mideast peace process and have certainly learned firsthand how developments like creation of a fence can complicate progress. Based on that, when you stood there about a year ago and proposed your roadmap, you spoke about a Palestinian state in 2005. I mean, do you think that goal is still realistic, or is it likely to slide just because it's so hard to make headway?

The President. I do think it's realistic. I also know when we start sliding goals, it makes progress less realistic. Absolutely, I think it's realistic, and I think we're making pretty good progress in a short period of time.

I'm impressed by Prime Minister Abbas' vision of a peaceful Palestinian state. I believe him when he says that we must rout out terror in order for a Palestinian state to exist. I believe he's true. I think Mr. Dahlan, his security chief, also recognizes that.

And we've got to help those two leaders in a couple of ways to realize that vision of a peaceful Palestinian state. One is to provide help and strategy to Mr. Dahlan so that he can lead Palestinian security forces to the dismantlement of bomb-making factories, rocket-making factories inside Gaza and the West Bank. That's going to be a very important part of earning the confidence of the world, for that matter. We've also got to recognize that there are things that can happen on the ground that will strengthen Mr. Abbas' hand, relative to the competition, moving—for example, movement throughout the country.

So I spent time talking to Prime Minister Sharon yesterday about checkpoints. We discussed the difference between a checkpoint for security purposes and a checkpoint that might be there that's—that isn't—there for inconvenience purposes, let me put it to you that way. We talked about all the thorny issues.

But the most important thing is that we now have an interlocutor in Mr. Abbas who is committed to peace and who believes in the aspirations of the Palestinian people.

One of the most interesting visits I've had on this issue took place in the Oval Office there with the Finance Minister of the Palestinian Authority. I was pleased to discover that he—I think he received a degree from the University of Texas, which gave me even more confidence when he spoke. But he is a—he talked about how a free state, free country, will flourish when the Palestinians are just given a chance.

See, he believes in the Palestinian people to the point where he's willing to take risks for peace. As I understand it, he's put the Palestinian budget on the web page. That's—that's what we call transparency in the diplomatic world. It means that he's willing to show the finances to make it clear they're not stealing money—is another way to put it. That's a positive development, Larry.

So I—what I first look at is attitudes. I also believe Prime Minister Sharon is committed to a peaceful Palestinian state. He's committed because he understands that I will in no way compromise the security of the Israeli people—or the Palestinian people, for that matter—to terror, that he knows when I say we're willing to fight terror, we mean it, because we proved it.

I thought it was interesting yesterday, by the way, that he spoke clearly about Iraq and the importance of Iraq in terms of Middle Eastern peace as well. And I believe he's right on that. I believe that a free Iraq will make it easier to achieve peace in that part of the world. I also know that we've got to get others in the neighborhood to continue to remind certain countries that it will be frowned upon if they destabilize the process.

The stated objective of Iran is the destruction of Israel, for example. And we've got to work in a collective way with other nations to remind Iran that they shouldn't develop a nuclear weapon. It's going to require more than one voice saying that, however. It's going to require a collective effort of the Europeans, for example, to recognize the true threat of an armed Iran to achieving peace in the Middle East. And—but I'm pleased by the attitudes.

You know, when I was in Aqaba, I don't know if you remember, but I asked Prime Minister Sharon and Prime Minister Abbas to go outside. I wanted to watch the body language, first and foremost, just to make sure we weren't fooling ourselves, that when leaders commit to being able to work with each other, you can get a pretty good sense of that commitment.

What was also interesting on the outside meeting—I mean, it was a very cordial discussion, and there was the desire for these leaders to talk. And they have talked since the Aqaba meeting, and that's a positive development. But what was also interesting, as Condi reported to me later, to watch the discussions between the different—both Cabinets. And we were watching carefully to determine if there's the will for peace. We have found a person who has got the will to work for peace, and that's Prime Minister Abbas.

We'll work through the issues that are nettlesome. And there will be some big issues that come along. But the first thing that has to happen is, the Palestinian people have got to realize there's hope in a free society. And if they choose the leader that is most likely to—choose to back the leader that is most likely to deliver that hope.

Carl [Carl Cannon, National Journal].

HIV/AIDS Initiative

Q. I want to ask you about something else in your State of the Union.

The President. Okay.

Q. You spoke and got great applause from both sides of the aisle about a new initiative in Africa for AIDS and mentioned the figure, $15 billion over 3 years. When the AIDS community and some of the activists got into the budget, they said when they saw your budget, they said it was really a little less than that. And these conversations have gone back and forth, and they said, really more like $10 billion in new money. And then somebody told me it was really more like $400 million for the first year. I want to ask you here, in the Rose Garden, will you reiterate that $15 billion figure and make sure, personally, that it's really delivered to Africa?

The President. Yes, I will, Carl, absolutely, $15 billion. Now, that's not new money. The person who said it's $15 billion on top of that which we're already—$10 billion on top of that which we're already spending equals the $15 billion. Secondly, there is some discussion about the first-year budget. In other words, we didn't send up a budget—$15 billion over 5—we didn't send up $3 billion. We sent up something less than $3 billion, because we didn't think the program could ramp up fast enough to absorb that amount of money early.

So it's not—people then say, "Well, wait a minute. He doesn't believe what he said." Well, that's just simply not true. As a mat-

ter of fact, after my trip to Africa, I know we're doing the right thing, even more.

But the OMB came up with a plan that allows for a smaller amount in the beginning. I think it's about a little less than $2.5 billion initially, and it ramps up more in the out-years as the program is capable of absorbing a lot of money.

You know, one of the things we looked for over there in Africa was whether or not countries could absorb money. In other words, whether—for example, was the distribution system for antiretrovirals in place? It doesn't make any sense to load up on antiretrovirals if the distribution system won't get them out. In other words, there's some things some countries have to do to prepare for the arrival of a lot of money, and we recognize that, Carl.

The commitment is there, absolutely. And a matter of fact, we're doing the right thing in Africa. The American people have got to understand that we're a blessed country, and when we find the kind of suffering that exists in Africa, we will help. And we are.

Liberia

Q. Liberia question?

The President. You want to ask a Liberian question? Please do.

Q. Thank you. Do you expect American troops to be landing in any large force in Liberia soon? And how far can the U.S. go in other international conflicts? When are we stretched too thin?

The President. Yes, very good question. First of all, the conditions that I laid out for the Liberian rescue mission still exist. Charles Taylor must go; the cease-fire must be in place; and we will be there to help ECOWAS. And so we're working to get those conditions in place. And we will continue working to get them in place until they are in place, at which point we will then take the necessary steps to get ECOWAS in place so that we can deliver aid and help to suffering Liberians.

I also want to remind you, I also said the troop strength will be limited and the timeframe will be limited. And we're working on that. The idea, of course, is to go in, stabilize the situation, get the NGOs moving back in to—to their positions to be able to help deliver aid, and then work immediately with the United Nations to provide blue helmets—maybe blue helmets, some of the ECOWAS forces in place, provide other blue helmets, and that the United Nations would then take up the peacekeeping mission as well as the political mission in order to provide the framework for a transition to democracy. And hopefully, that will help stabilize the situation. I think it will.

Hutch [Ron Hutcheson, Knight Ridder].

Iran

Q. I wanted to ask you about Iran, one of your other countries in the axis of evil. One of the things we learned from that march to war is that when you start warning countries, they better pay attention. Are we now in the early stages of a march to war in Iran? Or are they more like in the category of North Korea?

The President. No, I—look, Hutch, I remember right after Iraq the first thing that happened out of—out of some writers' pens was that, "Oh, no, they're getting ready to attack either Syria or Iran." You know, the march to war is a campaign that's just going to march everywhere.

I—all options remain on the table. I believe that the best way to deal with the Iranians at this point in time is to convince others to join us in a clear declaration that the development of a nuclear weapon is not in their interests. I believe a free Iraq will affect the lives of Iranians. I want to thank the diaspora here in the United States, particularly in L.A.—which reminds me, my last question is going to Ed [Ed Chen, Los Angeles Times]. And—so you can prepare for it, Ed. We've got a lot of our fellow citizens who are in e-mail contact, phone contact with people who live

throughout Iran. And I want to thank them for that.

Interestingly enough, there's a TV station that I think has been—people have read about that is broadcast out of L.A. by one of our citizens. He's—he or she has footed the bill. It's widely watched. The people of Iran are interested in freedom, and we stand by their side. We stand on the side of those who are desperate for freedom in Iran. We understand their frustrations in living in a society that is totalitarian in nature. And now is the time for the world to come together, Ron, to send a clear message.

And so I spent time with Prime Minister Berlusconi on the ranch, and I talked to him about the need for the EU to send a very clear message, along with the United States. As you know—some of you have been on the trips with me to Russia, and you remember me talking with my friend Vladimir Putin about the need to be mindful of the Iranians' desire to have a nuclear weapon. We're making progress there. I really believe that we can solve this issue peacefully, but this is an issue that's going to require a concerted effort by nations around the world to work with the United States, particularly in Europe, to speak clearly to the Iranian administration.

The other thing that's interesting about Iran is that they do have Al Qaida. They've admitted they got Al Qaida. Now, that's positive, that the Al Qaida is not talking to anybody. I mean, I would rather them be held somewhere other than out moving around, plotting and planning. And I would just hope the Iranians would listen to the request of countries in their neighborhood to turn them over. In other words, some of the countries of origin for these Al Qaida operatives have asked for those Al Qaida detainees to be sent back to the country of origin. It would be very helpful for the Iranians to make that decision.

Ed, last question.

Q. Mr. President——

The President. Hold on for a minute, please. Ed.

California Recall Campaign

Q. Good morning, Mr. President. Since California is on your mind, I'd like to ask you about the recall campaign. Since you're not only the leader of this country, but as someone who came into office under extraordinarily partisan circumstances, do you view this recall, which was funded almost entirely by one wealthy Republican who would like to be Governor, as a legitimate, democratic exercise? And do you have a candidate in this fight, since one of the potential successors is somebody you've backed before?

The President. Ed, let me tell you how I view it. I've got a lot of things on my mind, and I view it like a interested political observer would view it. You know, it's kind of a—we're not used to recalls in Texas, for example, thankfully. I think that—I think the most important opinion is not mine, but it's the people of California. Their opinion is what matters on a recall. It's their decision to decide whether or not there will be a recall, which they decided. Now they get to decide who the Governor is going to be. And that's really my only comment I've got.

Listen, thank you all very much for giving me a chance to come and answer some of your questions. For those of you who are traveling to Crawford, gosh, did you luck out. And we look forward to seeing you there. [*Laughter*] Thank you.

NOTE: The President's news conference began at 10:33 a.m. in the Rose Garden at the White House. In his remarks, he referred to former President Saddam Hussein of Iraq; Uday and Qusay Hussein, sons of former President Hussein, who were killed July 22 by U.S. military forces in Mosul, Iraq; Khalid Sheikh Mohammed, senior Al Qaida leader responsible for planning the September 11, 2001, terrorist attack, who was captured in Pakistan on March 1; Abu Zubaydah, a leader of the Al Qaida terrorist organization who was captured on March 28; Ramzi bin al-Shibh, an Al Qaida operative suspected of helping to plan the September 11, 2001, terrorist attack, who was captured in Karachi, Pakistan; Al Qaida operational planner and fundraiser Yousif Salih Fahad Al-Ayeeri, also known as "Swift Sword," who was killed on May 31; Abu Bakr Al Azdi, senior Al Qaida associate responsible for the May 12 bombing in Riyadh, Saudi Arabia; Foreign Minister Saud al-Faysal al Saud of Saudi Arabia; former United Nations weapons inspector David Kay; President Hu Jintao of China; Chairman Kim Chong-il of North Korea; Prime Minister Mahmoud Abbas (Abu Mazen), Minister of State for Security Affairs Mohammed Dahlan, and Finance Minister Salam Fayyad of the Palestinian Authority; Prime Minister Ariel Sharon of Israel; President Charles Taylor of Liberia; Prime Minister Silvio Berlusconi of Italy; and President Vladimir Putin of Russia.

Remarks on the 38th Anniversary of Medicare
July 30, 2003

Thank you all for coming. Welcome to the people's house. We're thrilled you're here. Tommy is right; 38 years ago, Lyndon Johnson signed the Medicare Act. What I found interesting was that he had the ceremony in Independence, Missouri, so that former President Harry Truman could be there, because Truman had set out the vision of Medicare many years before that. A few minutes after 3 o'clock, Medicare became law, and President Johnson handed the first Medicare card to Harry Truman.

Health insurance for elderly and disabled Americans was one of the greatest, most compassionate legislative achievements of the 20th century. It spared millions of seniors from needless worry and hardship. Since 1965, every President and every Congress has had the responsibility to uphold the promise of Medicare, and we will uphold our promise. We will do our duty.

The 38th anniversary of Medicare is a time for action. The purpose of the Medicare system is to deliver modern medicine to America's seniors. That's the purpose. And in the 21st century, delivering modern medicine requires coverage for prescription drugs.

Both Houses of Congress have passed Medicare improvements that include prescription coverage. Now the House and Senate must iron out the remaining differences and send me a bill. For the sake of our seniors, for the sake of future retirees, we must strengthen and modernize Medicare this year.

I appreciate Tommy Thompson taking the lead on this issue for this administration. He—I knew him when he was a Governor. I figured he'd make a pretty good Cabinet Secretary—[*laughter*]—and he proved me right. He's doing a fabulous job. He is the point man on the Hill on this complex, important legislation.

And we've got two of the Members from the Senate who have worked really hard to see to it that the legislation came to fruition and passed the Senate and are working hard to get a good bill out of the conference, and that's—starting with the majority leader of the United States Senate, Bill Frist from Tennessee; the ranking member on the Finance Committee from the State of Montana, that would be Max Baucus, Senator Baucus. For those of you who don't follow politics—[*laughter*]—Frist is a Republican—[*laughter*]—Baucus is a Democrat—[*laughter*]—both of them willing to put aside party to focus on what's

doing right for the seniors. And I appreciate their leadership of both these Senators. Thank you all for coming. You set a good example for the body you represent.

I appreciate Tom Scully, who is with us. He is the Administrator for the Centers for Medicare and Medicaid Services. That is a long title for a very tough job. And I appreciate Scully's knowledge on this issue. He too, along with Secretary Thompson, is working the Hill, along with members of my staff, working hard with Senators and Congressmen from both parties to come up with a bill that will stand the test of time.

I want to thank top docs in my administration who are traveling the country to talk about the benefits of Medicare reform. Rich Carmona is the Surgeon General of the United States. Thank you for coming, Doc. Dr. Julie Gerberding directs the Center for Disease Control and Prevention. It's a tough and important job. Mark McClellan is the Commissioner of the FDA, the Food and Drug Administration. Elias Zerhouni is the Director of the National Institute of Health—all four great Americans, all four fine doctors, all four doing a really good job on behalf of the American citizens.

On a piece of legislation like this, there's a—it obviously attracts the attention of advocates, people who are willing to get involved in the process, people who work hard on behalf of the constituents they represent. Today we've got Jim Parkel and Bill Novelli. Jim is the president, Bill Novelli is the director and CEO of AARP. I'm honored you all are here. Thanks. Thanks for providing such good leadership for all.

There's a group involved in the process called United Seniors Association. It's headed by Charlie Jarvis. He's the chairman and CEO, and Charlie is with us today. Thank you for coming, Charlie. Representing the 60 Plus Association is my long-time friend, Jim Martin. Thank you for coming. I'm glad you're here.

I want to thank those of you who are here today for your interest. I want to thank our fellow citizens who may be watching this on C–SPAN, if it happens to be on C–SPAN—seems like everything is on C–SPAN these days—[*laughter*]—for your interest in this very important issue.

You know, for a long time Medicare was called "Medi-scare," and it meant that political people weren't supposed to touch it for fear of losing an election, that when you talked about reforming Medicare, then all of a sudden you were supposed to lose because people would bang you over the head on the issue. I think we're beyond that, and that's a very positive development. A lot of you in this room have helped us get beyond that, and I want to thank you for that. Now we've got hard work to do to get this process across the line.

I'm joined onstage, by the way, by some of our fellow citizens, who I'll talk about in a little bit about how the current Medicare plan as envisioned by a lot of us will help in their daily lives. But let me start by telling you this: For four decades, it's important for our citizens to know that Medicare has done exactly what it was created to do, which is pretty unusual for an act of Congress—[*laughter*]—in all due respect. [*Laughter*] Under Medicare, older Americans have access to good quality health care in a system of private medicine. That what it was intended to do, and that's what it has done. Seniors and people with disabilities have greater peace of mind knowing that Medicare will always be there. It was the initial intent of the law, and that's what it has done.

Medicare coverage has helped protect the savings of our seniors and shielded their families from costs they may not be able to afford. Medicare is an important national achievement, and it is a continuing moral responsibility of our Federal Government. Americans are proud of our Medicare program. We must make sure that Medicare fits the needs of our seniors today. It has done what it was supposed to do. Our task is to make sure it continues to do what it was supposed to do.

It was created at a time when medicine consisted mostly of house calls and surgery and long hospital stays. Now modern medicine includes preventative care, outpatient procedures, and at-home care. Medicine is changing. Many invasive surgeries are now unnecessary because of the miraculous new prescription drugs being developed. Most Americans have coverage for all this new medicine, yet seniors relying exclusively on Medicare do not have coverage for most prescription drugs.

No one intended for Medicare to develop these major gaps in coverage. That was not the initial intent of the law. There are gaps in coverage now. Medicine has changed. Medicare hadn't. We must fill those gaps. Medicare must be modernized.

Let me give you a couple of examples by what I mean when I talk about modernization. Medicare today will pay for extended hospital stays for ulcer surgery at a cost of up to $28,000 per patient. This is important coverage. Yet Medicare will not pay for drugs that eliminate the cause of most ulcers, drugs that cost about $500 a year. Medicare will pay for the cost to treat a stroke, including bills from the hospital and rehab center, doctors, home health aides, and outpatient care. That's what Medicare pays for. Those costs can total up to $100,000. This is essential coverage; it's vital coverage. Yet Medicare does not cover the blood-thinning drugs that prevent strokes in the first place, drugs that cost less than $1,000 a year.

The Medicare system has got a lot of strengths, no question about it. Yet it is often slow to respond to the dramatic changes in medicine, and that's what we've got to address. That's what we are addressing.

The best way to provide our seniors with prescription drug coverage and better preventative care is to give them better choices under Medicare. If seniors have choices, health plans will compete for their business by offering better coverage at affordable prices.

Both Houses of Congress have passed bills that follow the framework of reform that I suggested and others have suggested. Under either bill, seniors who want to stay in current Medicare have that option plus a new prescription drug benefit. Seniors who want enhanced benefits, such as coverage for extended hospital stays and protection against high out-of-pocket expenses, will have that choice as well. Seniors who like managed-care plans will have that option as well. All low-income seniors will receive extra help so that all seniors will have the ability to choose a Medicare option that includes a prescription drug benefit.

Many retirees depend on employer-sponsored health plans for their prescription drug coverage. That's a reality in today's society. Medicare legislation—the legislation that these two good Senators are working hard on—should encourage employers to continue to provide those benefits while extending drug coverage to millions of Medicare beneficiaries who now lack it. It's important that those who have assumed the responsibility—corporate responsibility of providing prescription drugs for their retirees keep providing that benefit. And I know the Senators are working on that important part of the Medicare legislation.

Every Member of Congress gets to choose a health coverage plan that makes the most sense for them, and so does their staff. So does every Federal employee, and so should every senior have that choice. See, choice is good. It makes sense. I can understand why Members of Congress have said, "Well, look, give me more than one option, if you don't mind. I'm plenty capable of choosing for myself. I'd like to see what's available. As a matter of fact, I'd like to have my demand be listened to. I'd like to have plans begin to tailor their services to what I think is necessary for me." And seniors should have that same option, it seems like to me. Seniors are plenty capable of making decisions for what's best for them.

For seniors without any drug coverage now, these reforms will help a lot. Let me tell you what I mean by that. In return for a monthly premium of about $35 or about a dollar a day, seniors now without coverage will see their drug bills cut roughly in half. That's the good work that these Senators have done. They've heard the call, and they're responding with a piece of legislation that will help seniors save money.

A senior with a monthly drug cost of $200 will save between $1,300 and $1,800 on drug costs each year. That's under the bills that have been passed now. A senior with a monthly drug cost of $800—monthly cost of $800 would save between $5,700 a year and $6,100 each year on drug costs. That's some pretty good change.

The House and the Senate have got to work out their differences, and they're going to. This is—I believe that there's a spirit of cooperation and a can-do attitude amongst the conferees. But in either version of their bills, seniors who currently lack drug coverage will see real savings, and that's a positive reform for a lot of our fellow citizens.

As we move toward this system, we will provide seniors with a drug discount card that saves them 10 to 25 percent off the cost of all drugs, so they'll start seeing savings immediately as well. The conferees, I know, are working on the drug discount card now to make sure we can iron out any differences, and I was briefed on that today by our staffers who are working close with the conferees.

We have some seniors, as I mentioned, with us today—some citizens with us today that would like to see the legislation move forward for practical reasons. A lot of times in Washington we talk about statistics and laws and hearings, and I always like to bring the human element to the front so people get to see how these bills will actually affect people's lives in a positive way.

Mary Jane Jones from Midlothian, Virginia, is with us today. She's a Medicare recipient. She's 69 years old. She'd like to be retired for good. [*Laughter*] But she has to work 20 hours a week just to make sure she can afford her nearly $500-a-month bill for prescription drugs and insulin. Sometimes, she says, she uses her insulin needles 3 or 4 times to save money. That's a story I'm confident that those who have held hearings in Congress or members of groups up here hear from their members.

Mary Jane says that getting about half her drug cost covered would be a big help. That way, she says, she wouldn't have to work constantly. Seniors like Mary Jane have made their plans. This bill will help them enjoy their retirement.

Refa Ryan is with us from Warrenton, Virginia. She has Medicare. She doesn't have drug coverage, and she pays $120 to $200 a month for medicine. Three years ago, when she was having a hard time making payments on her drugs, rather than asking someone for help, she was ready to sell her engagement ring. Fortunately, Denise found out about it and bought the ring so it stayed in the family. Refa says she appreciates what Congress is trying to do to add drug coverage to Medicare.

"I wouldn't be anxious all the time," she said. "I wouldn't have to worry all the time." See, this bill will help our seniors not have to worry all the time. And that's why there's momentum toward getting something done.

I also fully recognize that there are some that are beginning to think about what Medicare means when they retire. I might be one of them. [*Laughter*] There's some baby boomers that are beginning to look out and say, "Medicare isn't going to be there. Is it going to be modern when we get ready?"

In support of what I know the Senators are doing and Members of the House are doing, the conferees are doing, is that they're thinking not only to make sure the system works for our seniors today but make sure that seniors—I mean, that the seniors-to-be have got a plan available for them and that most of us in the baby boomer era, we like the idea of choices. We want to be able to pick and choose to help meet our needs. We want to make sure that the system is—kind of listens to the demand of the citizen.

Richard Kamenitzer is with us. Richard and I are of the same generation. It says in here he and his wife, Rose Marie, are in their fifties. Well, Laura and I are in our fifties too. He's from Stroudsburg, Pennsylvania. He's a self-employed guy. He's a part of the entrepreneurial class here in America. He's a small-business man, and he and his wife take about seven medications a day right now. Now, he's probably beginning to wonder, after he retires, how can he afford seven medications—he and his wife—a day? Who's going to pay for it?

He said—here's what he says, with drug coverage and Medicare, about the new plans that we're trying to get done. He said, "I'd have a fighting chance"—that is, "I would have a fighting chance to enjoy retirement. Without it, I don't know what I'd do. Retirement, in a sense, may be out of the question, because I won't be able to afford the prescriptions I desperately need."

See, not only are we talking about helping the seniors today who are on Medicare; we're talking about the ones getting ready to get on Medicare too. And that's why these folks are thinking beyond just the immediate. We want a plan that stands the test of time. Remember, the plan that Lyndon Johnson signed was pretty effective for four decades. We have a chance to do the same thing here in Washington, DC.

I know that Congress is listening to the voices of the retired and near-retired. And I appreciate that very much. I appreciate the willingness throughout all the Federal Government to give our seniors and those living with disabilities the kind of options they deserve, the kind of hearing that they want. We should not let another Medicare anniversary go by without modernizing the system, without giving our seniors—[*applause*].

The Senate, I think, is getting ready to go out on the August vacation. We're certainly pulling for you to go out. [*Laughter*] The House is already gone. They're in their districts. They'll be listening to the people, and I know Americans who are concerned about this issue will want to make their voices heard. And we, of course, urge you to do so. We urge you to contact your Member of your House and your Senators and let them know your thoughts on Medicare reform. Let them know that we expect to plow through the doubts and the obstacles and get a good bill to the President's desk. My pen is ready. I'm ready to sign a good bill.

I know that this August, staff members of the conference will be working. And for those staff members who are here, I want to thank you for grinding through a complex piece of legislation and working out your differences. And then when the Members come back, we'll have some heavy lifting to do. But I want to be there to help you carry the load.

We've all come to Washington, those of us who have been elected to office, to serve something greater than ourself. And we have a duty and a call to not only describe a problem but to address it. And in this case, when we do, the lives of our fellow citizens will be improved.

I want to thank you for your interest in this really important subject, thank the two Senators who have joined us today. I want to thank the members of my Cabinet who are here.

May God bless you all, and may God continue to bless the United States of America.

NOTE: The President spoke at 2:45 p.m. in the East Room at the White House. The Office of the Press Secretary also released a Spanish language transcript of these remarks.

Statement on the Earth Observation Summit
July 31, 2003

The United States is pleased to host more than 30 nations at the Earth Observation Summit. The Summit participants will discuss plans for achieving the goal of building a better integrated Earth observation system in the next 10 years, an objective established by the G–8 heads of state in Evian, France, in June 2003. An integrated Earth observation system will benefit people around the world, particularly those in the Southern Hemisphere. Working together, our nations will develop and link observation technologies for tracking weather and climate changes in every corner of the world, which will allow us to make more informed decisions affecting our environment and economies. Our cooperation will enable us to develop the capability to predict droughts, prepare for weather emergencies, plan and protect crops, manage coastal areas and fisheries, and monitor air quality.

Letter to Congressional Leaders on Continuation of the National Emergency With Respect to Iraq
July 31, 2003

Dear Mr. Speaker: *(Dear Mr. President:)*

Section 202(d) of the National Emergencies Act (50 U.S.C. 1622(d)) provides for the automatic termination of a national emergency unless, prior to the anniversary date of its declaration, the President publishes in the *Federal Register* and transmits to the Congress a notice stating that the emergency is to continue in effect beyond the anniversary date. Consistent with this provision, I have sent the enclosed notice, stating that the Iraq emergency is to continue in effect beyond August 2, 2003, to the *Federal Register* for publication. The most recent notice continuing this emergency was published in the *Federal Register* on August 1, 2002, (67 *Fed. Reg.* 50341).

The crisis that led to the declaration of a national emergency on August 2, 1990, has not been fully resolved. The United States, along with its coalition partners, continues to work to stabilize Iraq, identify and dismantle Iraq's weapons of mass destruction, capture former regime leaders, and locate and return Iraqi assets overseas for the benefit of the Iraqi people. As part of the Coalition Provisional Authority, the United States is providing for the temporary governance of Iraq, including the establishment of a process to lead to a new internationally recognized government. For these reasons, I have determined that it is necessary to continue the national emergency declared with respect to Iraq.

Sincerely,

GEORGE W. BUSH

NOTE: Identical letters were sent to J. Dennis Hastert, Speaker of the House of Representatives, and Richard B. Cheney, President of the Senate. The notice of July 31 is listed in Appendix D at the end of this volume.

Letter to Congressional Leaders Transmitting a Report on the National Emergency With Respect to Iraq
July 31, 2003

Dear Mr. Speaker: *(Dear Mr. President:)*

Consistent with section 401(c) of the National Emergencies Act, 50 U.S.C. 1641(c), and section 204(c) of the International Emergency Economic Powers Act, 50 U.S.C. 1703(c), I am providing a 6-month periodic report prepared by my Administration on the national emergency with respect to Iraq that was declared in Executive Order 12722 of August 2, 1990.

Sincerely,

GEORGE W. BUSH

NOTE: Identical letters were sent to J. Dennis Hastert, Speaker of the House of Representatives, and Richard B. Cheney, President of the Senate.

Letter to the Speaker of the House of Representatives on Reallocation of Funds Previously Transferred From the Emergency Response Fund
July 31, 2003

Dear Mr. Speaker:

In order to continue responses necessary as a result of the September 11th terrorist attacks, I am notifying the Congress of my intent to reallocate funds previously transferred from the Emergency Response Fund (ERF).

At this time, $1.2 million of ERF funds will be transferred to the United States Trade Representative to support increased security at international trade negotiations.

The details of this action are set forth in the enclosed letter from the Director of the Office of Management and Budget.

Sincerely,

GEORGE W. BUSH

NOTE: An original was not available for verification of the content of this letter.

Remarks Following a Cabinet Meeting and an Exchange With Reporters
August 1, 2003

The President. We had a good Cabinet meeting, talked about a lot of issues. The Secretary of State and Defense brought us up to date about our desires to spread freedom and peace around the world. And the economics team of Secretary Snow, Evans, and Chao, who have been traveling the country, reported back that there's a positive feeling in America about our economy.

And my attitude is, is that even though some of the numbers are good, there are still too many people looking for work, and so we're going to keep working on the economy until people can find a job.

We took some strong action in the past. We reduced taxes on the working people, and those tax reductions will be reflected in their paychecks soon. Expansion of the child tax credit is helpful to people because checks are now in the mail. Both of those events will enhance demand for goods and services, which will make it more likely somebody will find work.

There is more to do here in Washington. I'm pleased that the House of Representatives and the Senate both have now passed energy bills. It's time for them to reconcile their differences, when they get back from their August breaks, and get a bill to my desk.

We need tort reform in America so that our entrepreneurs are more likely to focus on capital formation than lawsuits, frivolous lawsuits. We need to make sure we get a Medicare bill passed; that's going to be helpful for workers today to help plan for their future, to know there's a modern Medicare system.

I appreciate the fact that the Congress has passed trade agreements with Singapore and Chile, which means there will be more markets available for American entrepreneurs and farmers and ranchers. The more places for us to sell products, the more likely it is somebody is going to be able to find a job.

And so even though there's been some progress made in terms of numbers, this administration focuses on lives. And when there are people looking for work and they can't find a job, it means we're going to continue to try to put progrowth, expansive policies in place.

So I want to thank the Cabinet members who are focusing on these—this very important part of our agenda, and I appreciate your upbeat report.

Let me—I'll answer a couple of questions. Tom [Tom Raum, Associated Press] and Patsy [Patricia Wilson, Reuters]. Tom and Patsy will be asking questions this morning, and then you won't be asking questions. [Laughter]

National Economy

Q. Mr. President, are you surprised, and can you explain why 3 huge tax cuts and 12 rate cuts by the Fed have not done more in creating jobs to this point? And do you think that we're in a jobless recovery?

The President. I think—I think it's important to remember the history of the last couple of years. In March of 2000, the stock market began a precipitous decline. That was in March of 2000. And then the country went into a recession, which would be the first quarter of 2001, and we acted. We called the Congress together and passed a significant tax cut. Economic historians would say that the recession of 2001 was one of the more shallow recessions. Some would probably say, "Well, maybe you shouldn't have acted, and let the recession go deeper, which would have made—may have made for a more speedy recovery." Our attitude is that we're worried about people's lives; a deep recession would have meant more people would have been out of work. We want people to work in America; it's in our country's interest they do so.

Then as the economy kind of got going again, the enemy attacked us. September the 11th had a significant impact on our economy. And then we discovered some of our corporate CEOs forgot to tell the truth, and that affected confidence. And then, as you may remember, Tom, we had the steady drumbeat to war. As I mentioned in my press conference the other day, on our TV screens there was a—on some TV screens—there was a constant reminder for the American people, "march to war." War is not a very pleasant subject in people's minds. It's not conducive for the investment of capital.

In spite of all those obstacles and because this administration has acted firmly, our economy is growing. And we're confident that over time, people will be able to find a job. But we're not going to rest, and there's more to do. We need an energy policy. We need tort reform. We need Congress to join with the administration to promote progrowth policies. But this economy is vibrant and strong, just like our country is vibrant and strong. We've overcome a lot, but there's more to do. And there's no question there's more to do. And we will do it.

Patsy.

North Korea

Q. Thank you, sir. Does your offer still stand for assistance to North Korea if they give up their nuclear program? And how can you deal with someone like Kim Chong-il, a man you don't trust?

The President. Yes. Thank you for bringing that question up, because we had some—what we think as positive developments. As you know, we were very concerned about trying to enter into a bilateral agreement with Kim Chong-il because of the fact that he didn't tell the truth to previous administrations. And so we took a new tack, and that was to work with our—with China, primarily China, initially, to engage China in the process so that there is more than one voice speaking to Mr. Kim Chong-il.

And thanks to the Chinese leadership—and we do applaud Hu Jintao and his administration for agreeing to be a responsible party in the neighborhood in which they live—it looks like we'll have a multinational forum. What that really means is that more than the United States and China will show up to have a meaningful discussion with Mr. Kim Chong-il. That means

Japan will be there. After all, Japan is an important part of the neighborhood. South Korea will be there. They've had a vested interest in having discussions and dialogs with Kim Chong-il. And Russia has agreed to join, which means there are now five nations in North Korea sitting at a table, all aimed at convincing—the discussions will be all aimed at convincing Mr. Kim Chong-il to change his attitude about nuclear weaponry.

In the past, it was the lone voice of the United States speaking clearly about this. Now we'll have other parties who have got a vested interest in peace on the Korean Peninsula. And so I would say the progress is being—is good progress. And we're upbeat about the fact that others are assuming responsibility for peace besides the United States of America. And we'll see how the dialog goes. We fully understand the past. We are hopeful, however, that Mr. Kim Chong-il, because he's hearing other voices, will make the decision to totally dismantle his nuclear weapons program, that he will allow there to be complete transparency and verifiability. And we're optimistic that that can happen.

Listen, thank you all for coming. For those of you in Crawford, I will see you—going to Crawford, I will see you soon. As you can tell, I got my summer buzz. [*Laughter*] I'm ready to get down there and enjoy the weather.

NOTE: The President spoke at 11:20 a.m. in the Cabinet Room at the White House. In his remarks, he referred to Chairman Kim Chong-il of North Korea; and President Hu Jintao of China.

Statement on Senate Action To Block Votes on Judicial Nominations
August 1, 2003

This week, a minority of Senators continued to filibuster highly qualified judicial nominees who enjoy the support of a majority of Senators. These obstructionist tactics are unprecedented, unfair, and unfaithful to the Senate's constitutional responsibility to vote on judicial nominees.

These highly qualified nominees have stellar records that represent the mainstream of American law and values and strong bipartisan support from those who know them best. Instead of allowing an up-or-down vote, a minority of Senators have been filibustering Miguel Estrada for nearly 5 months and Priscilla Owen for 3 months and are now obstructing the nomination of Bill Pryor. The failure to hold votes on these nominations not only is inconsistent with the Senate's constitutional responsibility but also has caused extended judicial vacancies that are harmful to the American judicial system.

Every judicial nominee should receive an up-or-down vote in the full Senate, no matter who is President or which party controls the Senate. It is time to move past the partisan politics of the past and do what is right for the American legal system and the American people. Let each Senator vote how he or she thinks best, but give the nominees a vote.

NOTE: The statement referred to Miguel A. Estrada, nominee to be U.S. Circuit Judge for the District of Columbia Circuit; Priscilla Owen, nominee to be U.S. Circuit Judge for the Fifth Circuit; and William H. Pryor, Jr., nominee to be U.S. Circuit Judge for the Eleventh Circuit.

The President's Radio Address
August 2, 2003

Good morning. This week, we received some encouraging news on the economy. The Nation's economy grew faster than expected in the second quarter. Manufacturers are receiving more orders, and their inventories need to be replenished. Homebuilders are busy meeting near-record demand, and retailers report that consumers are buying more goods. Many economists expect that growth will accelerate in the coming months.

Yet this week's employment report also shows that many Americans who want to work are still having trouble finding a job. My administration is acting to promote faster growth to encourage the creation of new jobs. The key to job growth is higher demand for goods and services. With higher demand, businesses are more likely to hire new employees.

The best way to promote growth and job creation is to leave more money in the pockets of households and small businesses instead of taxing it away. So we lowered income tax rates, cut taxes on dividends and capital gains, reduced the marriage penalty, and increased the child tax credit. This week, the checks for up to $400 per child started arriving in the mailboxes of American families. That money will help American families move the economy forward.

We have also taken action to help small businesses, who are the job creators of America. We increased tax incentives for equipment purchases, giving small businesses an additional reason to invest. More orders for machinery and equipment means more jobs, and more business investment can lead to greater worker productivity, which helps raise worker wages.

We are starting to see results from our actions. My administration's economists believe that if we had not passed tax relief, our unemployment rate would have been nearly one percentage point higher, and as many as 1.5 million Americans would not have the jobs they have today.

This week, three members of my Cabinet—Treasury Secretary John Snow, Commerce Secretary Don Evans, and Labor Secretary Elaine Chao—visited business owners and their workers in the Midwest. They received reports that the economy is picking up.

Last month, I met with Mike Gendich, who owns a part-making company in Michigan called Metalmite. Mike's customers are keeping him busier than he has been in 3 years, giving him reason to hire three new workers. Tax relief has given him reason to invest in new equipment to keep those workers productive. In Mike's words, tax relief "can be the difference between making an investment or not." When small-business owners like Mike make new investments, that can also be the difference between someone finding work or not.

Tax relief is one part of my aggressive, progrowth agenda for America's economy. We're negotiating free trade agreements with countries to create new markets for products made in America. Congress needs to pass a sound energy bill to ensure our Nation has reliable, affordable supplies of energy. And Congress needs to let small businesses join together to purchase affordable health insurance for their employees. We need legal reform to stop the frivolous lawsuits that are a drag on our economy. We have pushed Congress to make the child credit refundable for lower income families. And we're working to control spending in Washington, DC, so that Government spending does not rise any faster than the average household budget is expected to grow this year.

America's economy has challenges, and I will not be satisfied until every American looking for work can find a job. By steady, persistent action, we are preparing the way for vigorous growth and more jobs. I have confidence in our economic future because I have confidence in the people whose effort and creativity make this economy run, the workers and the entrepreneurs of America.

Thank you for listening.

NOTE: The address was recorded at 11:53 a.m. on August 1 in the Cabinet Room at the White House for broadcast at 10:06 a.m. on August 2. The transcript was made available by the Office of the Press Secretary on August 1 but was embargoed for release until the broadcast. The Office of the Press Secretary also released a Spanish language transcript of this address.

Memorandum on Provision of Atomic Information to the Czech Republic, the Republic of Hungary, the Republic of Poland, and Spain
August 4, 2003

Memorandum for the Secretary of Defense

Subject: Provision of Atomic Information to the Czech Republic, the Republic of Hungary, the Republic of Poland, and Spain

In your memorandum to me of July 18, 2003, you recommended that I approve pursuant to sections 123 and 144 b. of the Atomic Energy Act of 1954, as amended, an agreement for cooperation within the context of the North Atlantic Treaty Organization (NATO) as between the Government of the United States and the following four members of NATO: the Czech Republic, the Republic of Hungary, the Republic of Poland, and Spain, hereinafter the "New Parties." The subject agreement is the Agreement between the Parties to the North Atlantic Treaty for Co-operation Regarding Atomic Information, including a technical annex and security annex (hereinafter collectively referred to as the ATOMAL Agreement), which entered into force on March 12, 1965, with respect to

the United States and the other members of NATO at that time.

Having considered your recommendations and the cooperation provided for in the ATOMAL Agreement with respect to the New Parties, in accordance with sections 123 and 144 b. of the Atomic Energy Act of 1954, as amended, I hereby:

a. Determine that the performance of the ATOMAL Agreement, including the proposed cooperation and the proposed communication of Restricted Data thereunder, with respect to the New Parties, will promote the common defense and security, and will not constitute an unreasonable risk to those interests.

b. Approve the ATOMAL Agreement with respect to the New Parties.

c. Authorize the Department of Defense to cooperate with the New Parties to the ATOMAL Agreement in the context of NATO upon satisfaction of the requirements of section 123 of the Atomic Energy Act of 1954, as amended.

GEORGE W. BUSH

Letter to Congressional Leaders Transmitting the Agreement Between the Parties to the North Atlantic Treaty for Co-operation Regarding Atomic Information, With Respect to the Czech Republic, Hungary, Poland, and Spain
August 4, 2003

Dear Mr. Speaker: (Dear Mr. President:)

I am pleased to transmit to the Congress, consistent with sections 123 and 144 b. of the Atomic Energy Act, as amended (42 U.S.C. 2153 and 2164(b)), the text of the Agreement between the Parties to the North Atlantic Treaty for Co-operation Regarding Atomic Information, including a technical annex and security annex (hereinafter collectively referred to as the ATOMAL Agreement), as a proposed agreement for cooperation within the context of the North Atlantic Treaty Organization (NATO) between the United States of America and each of the following four members of NATO: the Czech Republic, the Republic of Hungary, the Republic of Poland, and Spain, hereinafter the "New Parties." I am also pleased to transmit my written approval, authorization and determination concerning the ATOMAL Agreement with respect to the New Parties. The ATOMAL Agreement entered into force on March 12, 1965, with respect to the United States and the other NATO members at that time. The New Parties have signed this agreement and have indicated their willingness to be bound by it. The ATOMAL Agreement with respect to the New Parties meets the requirements of the Atomic Energy Act of 1954, as amended. While the ATOMAL Agreement continues in force with respect to its original parties, for the United States it will not become effective as an agreement for cooperation authorizing the exchange of atomic information with respect to the New Parties until completion of procedures prescribed by sections 123 and 144 b. of the Atomic Energy Act of 1954, as amended.

For more than 35 years, the ATOMAL Agreement has served as the framework within which NATO and the other NATO members party to this agreement have received the information that is necessary to an understanding and knowledge of and participation in the political and strategic consensus upon which the collective military capacity of the Alliance depends. This agreement permits only the transfer of atomic information, not weapons, nuclear material or equipment. Participation in the ATOMAL Agreement will give the Czech Republic, the Republic of Hungary, the Republic of Poland, and Spain the same standing within the Alliance with regard to nuclear matters as that of the other NATO members. This is important for the cohesiveness of the Alliance and will enhance its effectiveness.

I have considered the views and recommendations of the Department of Defense and other interested agencies in reviewing the ATOMAL Agreement and have determined that its performance, including the proposed cooperation and the proposed communication of Restricted Data thereunder, with respect to the New Parties will promote, and will not constitute an unreasonable risk to, the common defense and security. Accordingly, I have approved the ATOMAL Agreement with respect to the New Parties and authorized the Department of Defense to cooperate with the New Parties in the context of NATO upon satisfaction of the requirements of section 123 of the Atomic Energy Act of 1954, as amended.

In accordance with the Atomic Energy Act of 1954, as amended, I am submitting to each house of Congress an authoritative copy of the ATOMAL Agreement as signed by each of the New Parties, together with a copy of the letter from the Secretary of Defense recommending my approval of the ATOMAL Agreement with respect to the New Parties and a copy of my approval letter. The 60-day continuous session period provided for in section 123 begins upon receipt of this submission.

Sincerely,

GEORGE W. BUSH

NOTE: Identical letters were sent to J. Dennis Hastert, Speaker of the House of Representatives, and Richard B. Cheney, President of the Senate.

Letter to Congressional Leaders Transmitting the Final Report on the National Emergency With Respect to Angola
August 4, 2003

Dear Mr. Speaker: (Dear Mr. President:)
Consistent with section 401(c) of the National Emergencies Act, 50 U.S.C. 1641(c), and section 204(c) of the International Emergency Economic Powers Act, 50 U.S.C. 1703(c), I am transmitting a final report prepared by my Administration on the national emergency with respect to the National Union for the Total Independence of Angola (UNITA) that was declared in Executive Order 12865 of September 26,

1993, and terminated in Executive Order 13298 of May 6, 2003.
Sincerely,

GEORGE W. BUSH

NOTE: Identical letters were sent to J. Dennis Hastert, Speaker of the House of Representatives, and Richard B. Cheney, President of the Senate. This letter was released by the Office of the Press Secretary on August 5.

Remarks Following a Meeting With Secretary of State Colin L. Powell and an Exchange With Reporters in Crawford, Texas
August 6, 2003

The President. First, it's been my real privilege and honor to welcome the Secretary of State back to Crawford. He and Dick Armitage came, and we spent yesterday evening and this morning talking about our country's desire to promote peace and freedom, our obligations as a prosperous and strong nation to help the less fortunate. And we had a good strategy session, and now we're about to go out and brand some cows—well, not exactly. [*Laughter*]

Liberia
Q. Sir, what are your thoughts——
The President. Let me answer a couple of questions and let's—a little more order here to this particular press coverage, because this is Crawford.
Q. I'm sorry.
Q. Thanks, Mr. President. You sent an advance force—or you're authorizing an advance force in Liberia. Does this signal the start of a larger force in Liberia?
The President. This is all part of determining what is necessary to help

ECOWAS—now called ECOMIL—to go in and provide the conditions necessary for humanitarian relief to arrive, whether it be by sea or by air. And it's part of what we said we would do.

Q. Do you still want Taylor out? Is that still a condition, a hard condition?

The President. Yes, we would like Taylor out. And the Secretary may want to comment on this; he's working hard with the— you know, the U.N. and others to insist that Mr. Taylor leave.

Secretary Powell. We still expect President Taylor to leave. I'm pleased at what ECOWAS has been able to do. The Nigerians showed up in good order; more forces are arriving; and they're starting to establish a sense of security and I think put hope back in the hearts of the Liberian people. And we want to support them and assist them, as the President said.

The President. Patsy [Patricia Wilson, Reuters].

Q. Sir——

Q. I'm sorry, what do you want from the American troops?

The President. [*Inaudible*]—you seem to be dominating here. [*Laughter*]

Q. Sir, do you want the—sorry.

The President. It's okay; it's good; it's very aggressive. Your editors appreciate it.

Israeli Security Fence

Q. Do you want the Israelis to stop construction of the fence or just reroute it? And will you use loan guarantees to persuade them?

The President. We're talking to Israel about all aspects of the fence. I made it clear I thought the fence was a problem, and so we're talking with them, and we'll continue to work on this issue as well as other issues. I do believe we're making progress. The key for a peace to happen is for both parties to assume their necessary obligations and responsibilities to create the conditions so that people have confidence, that people know that their lives will be

safe, and that prosperity can break out. And we're making progress there.

Stretch [Richard Keil, Bloomberg News], and then we'll go to you, John, and then Elizabeth. You've got to speak above the train.

Tax Relief/National Economy

Q. I'm competing here with the train. Do you think you've done enough at this point to stimulate the economy? Is it a matter of just kind of letting things that you've put into place take effect, take hold, or is there more that needs to be done?

The President. Look, there's no question that the tax relief——

[*At this point, a passing train whistled.*]

The President. First, we've got to have better rail transportation. [*Laughter*]

The tax cuts will help a lot. And the second round of tax relief is now ending up in the pockets of our fellow citizens. The child tax credit checks are now being mailed. And that's going to help. But there needs to be more. And there needs to be an energy plan. There needs to be good litigation reform. I believe we can get a good class action lawsuit out of the Senate if we continue to work the issue. I also know that we need to make sure we continue this notion of reminding the investors and consumers alike that we're going to have fiscal discipline in Washington, DC. So yes, there's more we can do and will do.

Secretary Powell's Tenure

Q. Sir, you've seen the report that Secretary Powell and Secretary Armitage are going to leave at the end of this administration. Do you expect them to stay on if there is a second Bush administration? Would you like them to?

The President. Well, first things first: We hope there is a second Bush administration. And I will work hard to convince the American people that their confidence in me is justified. And we'll deal with it at the right time.

Listen, this guy has done a fabulous job. And I—Washington, particularly in August, is a dangerous period—a dangerous time because there's a lot of speculation. And all I can tell you is, the man flies to Crawford, and we've spent a good 24 hours talking about how we're going to work together to make the world a better place.

Q. But, Mr. President, you said, "We'll deal with it"——

The President. Yes, Elizabeth.

Q. "We'll deal with it at the right time." That isn't "yes."

The President. Deal with what at the right time?

Q. With whether Secretary Powell will serve in a second term. Is that "yes" or "no"? I mean, are you going to offer him a spot in the second term?

Secretary Powell. I don't have a term. I serve the President. [*Laughter*]

Q. No, the President——

The President. Elizabeth, look, first things first, and that is, we've got a year and a while during my first term to make the world a more peaceful place, and we'll deal with it. Washington loves speculation.

Clearly, you love speculation. You love it. You love to speculate about——

Q. It wasn't my story. [*Laughter*]

The President. Let me finish, please. You love to speculate about whether so-and-so is going to be a part of the administration or not. And I understand the game. But I have got to do my job, and I'm going to do it. And I'm going to do it with the Secretary of State. And the fact that he is here in Crawford, Texas, talking about issues of importance, should say loud and clear to the American people that he's completely engaged in doing what he needs to do, and that is serve as a great Secretary of State.

Q. Do you want to serve more than 4 years, Mr. Secretary?

Secretary Powell. I serve at the pleasure of the President, and this is all August speculation with no basis in fact. There was no basis for this story to begin with, and we're doing our jobs together.

The President. All right. We're going to get a burger. Thank you.

NOTE: The President spoke at 11:45 a.m. at the Coffee Station restaurant. In his remarks, he referred to President Charles Taylor of Liberia.

Letter to Congressional Leaders on Continuation of the National Emergency With Respect to the Lapse of the Export Administration Act of 1979
August 7, 2003

Dear Mr. Speaker: (Dear Mr. President:)

Section 202(d) of the National Emergencies Act (50 U.S.C. 1622(d)), provides for the automatic termination of a national emergency unless, prior to the anniversary date of its declaration, the President publishes in the *Federal Register* and transmits to the Congress a notice stating that the emergency is to continue in effect beyond the anniversary date. In accordance with

this provision, I have sent the enclosed notice, stating that the emergency caused by the lapse of the Export Administration Act of 1979, as amended, is to continue in effect beyond August 17, 2003, to the *Federal Register* for publication.

Sincerely,

GEORGE W. BUSH

NOTE: Identical letters were sent to J. Dennis Hastert, Speaker of the House of Representatives, and Richard B. Cheney, President of the Senate. The notice of August 7 is listed in Appendix D at the end of this volume.

Remarks Following a Meeting With Secretary of Defense Donald H. Rumsfeld and an Exchange With Reporters in Crawford, Texas
August 8, 2003

The President. We've had a fascinating discussion on a variety of subjects with Secretary Rumsfeld and Chairman Dick Myers. Of course, the Vice President is here. As an aside, the Vice President and I went fishing; we threw our first lure at about 6:20 a.m. this morning. Looks like—turns out the fish like cooler weather than hot weather; probably the press corps feels the same way.

Turns out this is our 100th day since major military operations have ended, ended in Iraq. And since then, we've made good progress. Iraq is more secure. The economy of Iraq is beginning to improve. I was interested to note that banks are now opening up and the infrastructure is improving. In a lot of places, the infrastructure is as good as it was at pre-war levels, which is satisfactory, but it's not the ultimate aim. The ultimate aim is for the infrastructure to be the best in the region. And the political process is moving toward democracy, which is a major shift of system in that part of the world.

And we're pleased with the progress, but we know we've got a lot more work to do. And the Secretary was briefing me on the ongoing security operations and the status of our forces. But I can say—and I think he can say—progress is being made not only in Iraq but in Afghanistan as well.

And then we spent time making sure that our military is configured in such a way as to represent the modern era, which means it will be more likely that the world will be peaceful. A modern, strong, light, active military will make it easier to keep the peace, and after all, that's the objective of the administration, is to promote freedom and peace. And the Secretary and his team are doing a really good job for the American people.

Welcome back to the ranch, Mr. Secretary. We're thrilled you're here.

Secretary Rumsfeld. Thank you, sir.

The President. We'll be glad to answer a few questions. Let's start with the wires, of course.

Iraq

Q. Thanks, Mr. President. You talked about progress, but there's some unfinished business in Iraq also.

The President. Yes——

Q. No Saddam——

The President. ——that's what I also said, we've got more to do.

Q. To be specific: No Saddam; no weapons; 56 soldiers have died in this 100 days——

The President. Right.

Q. ——including one last night. What can you tell the American people about how many more soldiers will die? And also, your commander in Iraq said yesterday, "Two years, absolute minimum." Is that an assessment you share?

The President. Well, first of all, we suffer when we lose life. I mean, our country is a country that grieves with those who sacrifice, and our heartfelt sympathies and appreciation go to the loved ones of any soldier who's willing to defend the security of the United States, and that's what they're doing in Iraq. It's very important to people to understand that this is a part of the war on terror, that we're dealing with terrorists today.

We learned a lesson on September the 11th, and that is, our Nation is vulnerable to attack. And we're doing everything we can to protect the homeland by making the Homeland Defense Department effective in securing the borders. But the best way to secure America is to get the enemy before they get us, and that's what's happening in Iraq. And we're grateful for the sacrifices of our soldiers.

I said, Scott [Scott Lindlaw, Associated Press], right after September the 11th, that this war on terror is a different kind of war, and it's going to take a while to win the war on terror. However long it takes to win the war on terror, this administration is committed to doing that, because our most solemn obligation is the protection of the American people.

And as I said, the Secretary and I discussed what's happening inside of Iraq, and we've got a lot of brave soldiers slowly but surely demolishing the elements of the Ba'athist regime, those foreign terrorists who feel like they can use Iraq as a place to arm up and inflict casualty or perhaps gain strength to come and attack Americans elsewhere.

We've been there 100 days. We've made a lot of progress in 100 days, and I am pleased with the progress we've made but fully recognize we've got a lot more work to do.

Do you want to add to that, Mr. Secretary?

Secretary Rumsfeld. No, sir. [*Laughter*]

Q. Should the American people expect 2 more years, at least?

The President. The American people should suspect that this administration will do what is necessary to win the war on terror. That's my pledge to the American people. They have got to understand that I will not forget the lessons of September the 11th. And those lessons are loud and clear that there are people who want to inflict harm on the American people. We lost 3,000-plus on that fateful day. And you know, I made the pledge to the American people and the families and those who grieved that we will hunt down the terrorists wherever they are and bring them to justice. And that's what we're going to do.

Steve [Steve Holland, Reuters].

California Gubernatorial Candidate Arnold Schwarzenegger

Q. What do you think of Arnold Schwarzenegger, and would you consider campaigning for him?

The President. I will never arm-wrestle Arnold Schwarzenegger. [*Laughter*] No matter how hard I try, I'll never lift as much weight as he does.

I think it's interesting. You know, I'm a follower of American politics. I find what's going on in the State of California very interesting, and I'm confident the citizens of California will sort all this out for the good of the citizenry.

Q. Would he be a good Governor?

The President. As I say, I'm interested in the process. It's fascinating to see who's in and who's out, and yes, I think he'd be a good Governor.

Israeli Security Fence

Q. Mr. President, there are reports today that Israel is willing, perhaps, to reroute the security fence it's been building. Is that enough of a concession by the Israelis, or should they abandon construction of the fence altogether?

The President. Well, Dick [Richard Keil, Bloomberg News], let me put the fence and these issues into a larger perspective, if I might. In order for a Palestinian state to emerge, a couple of things must happen. First, the Palestinians, the people in the neighborhood, must deal with terror, must rout out those who would like to destroy the process.

The fence, by the way, is a reaction to days when there were terror. I've said the fence is a problem because the fence is, you know, kind of meanders around the West Bank, which makes it awfully hard to develop a contiguous state over time. And so I've said we'd talk to the Israelis, and we are, about the fence. But we must have the fence in the context of the larger issue, and the larger issue is, will the conditions be such that a state can emerge? It's important for a Palestinian state to emerge, in our judgment, because the world will be more peaceful. Israel will be more secure, and more—or as importantly, the Palestinians will have hope. But all parties must work against those who would make it very difficult to achieve the vision.

Q. Are you regarding it as a step forward, a sign of progress?

The President. Well, as I said—look, the Israelis are willing to work with us. They've said, "We'd consult." We're consulting. In order for there to be the progress that needs to be made, there needs to be security. The fence was a reaction to—in some ways, a reaction to the days of the *intifada.* And the more secure Israel feels, the more likely there will be a peaceful state. The more secure the region is, the more likely institutions necessary for the development of a Palestinian state will emerge.

And so on all these issues, we'll deal, of course, with both parties. We're staying very active. Ambassador Wolf is doing a fine job there. But it's important to put all these issues in the larger context of what is necessary to achieve what we think— what I think will be great for the region: That is a peaceful Palestinian state.

Larry [Larry McQuillan, USA Today].

Iraq

Q. Mr. President, you've given us an update on Iraq and progress in stabilization there. At this point, are you able to give us even a ballpark estimate of what it may cost, say, in the next fiscal year? And will Americans be the ones who bear most of the cost of that?

The President. Two points there: One, we generally don't do our estimates on the

back of an envelope. In other words, by that I mean the commanders in the field will be dealing with the Secretary of Defense. Jerry Bremer will be bringing recommendations. And of course, we'll go to the Congress in order to fund any requests, and the requests will be well thought out, based upon some variables. And one of the key variables is how much money we can get other nations to contribute to the reconstruction efforts of Iraq or how many other nations are willing to contribute forces.

So therefore, this is a—you know, the budgeting process is one that's ongoing. It's an iterative process, I guess is the best way to put it. "Iterative" is the right word, do you think?

Secretary Rumsfeld. Yes.

The President. In other words——

Q. Is it too fluid, then? I mean, you're saying, because until we know how many people are going to help——

The President. No, at some point in time, Larry—no, it's fluid up to a point, but obviously we're going to have to make a request. And when we do, it will be a request based upon sound judgment. It will be a well thought out request. It will be one where the Congress will be able to ask legitimate questions like you're asking and will be answered. And they're now in the process of coming up with a—the basis for a request to the United States Congress.

You know, I remember, by the way, the initial stages of the war in Iraq. And the questions were, "How long is it going to take?" I think it kind of echoes the question that Scott asked: "How long will you be there? How long will it take?" And I can remember saying, "As long as necessary." Remember? I don't know if you remember the offensive stage of the war. You were doing an interesting job of trying to get us to make absolute predictions. And what is necessary is to achieve an overall strategy, and whatever it takes to achieve the strategy, this administration is committed to.

Q. But you know, going into that, sir, you actually gave a pretty accurate prediction of what that would cost.

The President. Well, going into it, right, and we'll give you an accurate projection of what it's going to cost next year at the appropriate time. But also going into it, there was the timetable question, which also relates to spending. And that is, "Why won't you tell us how long it's going to take?" My answer was, "How long? However necessary is how long it will take." And that's the way we feel now. And we are working hard to bring other nations to bear responsibility in Iraq.

I want to say something about Afghanistan. Germany has taken a very active role in Afghanistan, and we're very thankful for that. As NATO steps forward, Germany has assumed a big responsibility. And we really appreciate the German participation. And the reason I bring that up is, is that that's a change from 6 months ago. And not only is Germany's participation important, it's robust, more robust than we would have anticipated. I look forward to thanking Chancellor Schroeder for that.

And Larry, the point there is, is that things do change. And we will have a budget that is as accurate as it can possibly be when we go to the Congress, because we understand the questions our planners and operators will receive. And they will come with good, sound data.

Dana [Dana Bash, Cable News Network], and then Mark [Mark Knoller, CBS Radio]. We've got to get in before we have a heat stroke—[*laughter*]—before you have a heat stroke, excuse me. [*Laughter*]

Iran

Q. Mr. President, for you and for Secretary Rumsfeld, please. Secretary Rumsfeld, did you authorize Pentagon officials to hold some secret talks with Iran-*contra* figure Manucher Ghorbanifar in order to push for a regime change in Iran? And Mr. President, do you think that's a good idea, and is the new policy—official policy regime change in Iran?

Secretary Rumsfeld. I had not had a chance to see these articles—or an article that I guess exists. I did get briefed by Condi and Larry DiRita here a minute ago. And my understanding is that some—one or two Pentagon people were approached by some people who had information about Iranians that wanted to provide information to the United States Government, that a meeting did take place—this is more than a year ago—that such a meeting did take place and the information was moved around the interagency process to all the departments and agencies. And it's dropped. That is to say, the—as I understand it, there wasn't anything there that was of substance or of value that needed to be pursued further.

Q. But it's your understanding that this wasn't intended to sort of go around any other talks that have been going on; these are unofficial talks with the Iranians?

Secretary Rumsfeld. Oh, absolutely not. I mean, everyone on the interagency process, I'm told, was apprised of it, and it went nowhere. It was just—this happens, of course, frequently. People come in offering suggestions or information or possible contacts, and sometimes they are pursued. Obviously, if it looks as though something might be interesting, it's pursued. If it isn't, it isn't.

The President. Well, we support the aspirations of those who desire freedom in Iran.

Mark.

Democratic Presidential Candidates/Iraq

Q. Mr. President, what's your response to the Democrats, including Al Gore yesterday and some of the Democratic Presidential candidates, who say that the American people were misled in advance of the war about the reasons for going to war—that you said disarming Iraq was the main purpose, but since then, no weapons of mass destruction have been found?

The President. I say it's pure politics.

Listen, thank you all. Have a beautiful day.

Q. Do you want to say more than that?

The President. No, it's just pure politics. We've got a lot of people running for President, and it's pure politics. The American people know that we laid out the facts. We based the decision on sound intelligence, and they also know we've only been there for 100 days. And we're making progress. A free Iraq is necessary for a—is an integral part of the war on terror. And as far as all this political noise, it's going to get worse as time goes on, and I fully understand that. And that's just the nature of democracy. Sometimes pure politics enters into the rhetoric.

Thank you all.

European Union-U.S. Relations

Q. One on Germany? Do you think that signals a shift that Europe might be coming around to helping out in Iraq now?

The President. Oh, I think that we're getting—I mean, look, Great Britain has been helping out in Iraq for a long period of time. Poland has been helping out in Iraq. I mean, we've got a lot of people helping out in Iraq. And I thought that the German decision in Afghanistan was an important decision, and we're grateful for that.

Listen, thank you all.

U.S. Troop Strength

Q. Would you mind if I just asked about the meeting you had?

The President. Sure, go ahead and ask about the meeting.

Q. I mean, I know that's unusual, but——

The President. Beautiful meeting. [*Laughter*]

Q. But you know, are you now satisfied that maybe after reviewing our force strength that American forces are not stretched too thin by the war on terrorism or maybe potentially could be down the road?

The President. I'm satisfied.

Secretary Rumsfeld. We discussed that in the meeting, and it's a fair question. Needless to say, when you have a spike in activity, a crisis in Iraq, it is important to review those questions. Dick Myers and his folks in the military review them continuously.

We have found there are literally two or three—well, about two dozen things we can do that we reduce stress on the force, and the cost of adding end strength is significant. The time it takes to bring them in, recruit them, train them, equip them means there is a significant lag. So it's not something one does quickly. And as a result, we've got a major effort going on to take advantage of all the things we can do to increase the kinds of ways we can relieve that stress on the force. And it looks to me like we're going to be able to do that.

And on the other hand, our country can afford to pay for forces at the level that can help defend and protect us. And to the extent at any point it looks as though an end-strength increase is appropriate, we obviously would recommend it, but we certainly don't see the evidence of that at the present time.

The President. Thank you.

President's Vacation

Q. Any new 100-degree club members?

The President. Yesterday we added one.

Q. Do we know him?

The President. A Secret Service agent.

Q. Are you going running today?

The President. No, I'm not.

Q. Did Dick Cheney catch anything?

The President. Dick Cheney—he's a great fly fisherman. [*Laughter*]

NOTE: The President spoke at 11:47 a.m. at the Bush Ranch. In his remarks, he referred to Assistant Secretary of State for Nonproliferation John S. Wolf; L. Paul Bremer

III, Presidential Envoy to Iraq; and Chancellor Gerhard Schroeder of Germany. Secretary Rumsfeld referred to Acting Assistant Secretary of Defense for Public Affairs Larry DiRita. A reporter referred to former Vice President Al Gore. A portion of these remarks could not be verified because the tape was incomplete.

Letter to Congressional Leaders Transmitting a Report on the Extension of Normal Trade Relations Status for Certain Former Eastern Bloc States
August 8, 2003

Dear Mr. Speaker: *(Dear Mr. President:)*

I hereby submit an updated report to the Congress, prepared by my Administration, consistent with sections 402(b) and 409(b) of the Trade Act of 1974, as amended (19 U.S.C. 2432(b) and 2439(b)), concerning the emigration laws and policies of Armenia, Azerbaijan, Kazakhstan, Moldova, the Russian Federation, Tajikistan, Turkmenistan, Ukraine, and Uzbekistan. The report indicates continued compliance of these countries with international standards concerning freedom of emigration, with the exception of Turkmenistan. In light of new developments, I am submitting a waiver for Turkmenistan.

Sincerely,

GEORGE W. BUSH

NOTE: Identical letters were sent to J. Dennis Hastert, Speaker of the House of Representatives, and Richard B. Cheney, President of the Senate.

Letter to Congressional Leaders Transmitting a Waiver on the Extension of Normal Trade Relations Status for Turkmenistan
August 8, 2003

Dear Mr. Speaker: *(Dear Mr. President:)*

I hereby transmit the document referred to in subsection 402(c)(2) of the Trade Act of 1974, as amended, with respect to a waiver of the application of subsections 402(a) and (b) of that Act to Turkmenistan.

I report in that document my determination that such a waiver will substantially promote the objectives of section 402. I have instructed the Secretary of State to provide a copy of that determination to the Speaker of the House of Representatives and President of the Senate. I have also provided a separate report, prepared by my Administration, indicating that I have received the assurances with respect to the emigration practices of Turkmenistan required by section 402(c) (2)(B) of the Act.

Sincerely,

GEORGE W. BUSH

NOTE: Identical letters were sent to J. Dennis Hastert, Speaker of the House of Representatives, and Richard B. Cheney, President of the Senate. The Executive order and Presidential determination of August 8 with respect to Turkmenistan are listed in Appendix D at the end of this volume.

The President's Radio Address
August 9, 2003

Good morning. Friday of this week was the 100th day since the end of major combat operations in Iraq. For America and our coalition partners, these have been 100 days of steady progress and decisive action against the last holdouts of the former regime. And for the people of Iraq, this has been a period like none other in the country's history, a time of change and rising hopes after decades of tyranny.

Every day, we are working to make Iraq more secure. Coalition forces remain on the offensive against the Ba'ath Party loyalists and foreign terrorists who are trying to prevent order and stability. More and more Iraqis are coming forward with specific information as to the whereabouts of these violent thugs, enabling us to carry out raids to round them up and seize stockpiles of weapons.

We are working with Iraqis to establish a new Iraqi army and a new civil defense corps. In the city of Baghdad, 6,000 Iraqi police are patrolling the streets and protecting citizens. More than 20,000 more police are on duty in other towns and cities across Iraq.

Every day, Iraq is making progress in rebuilding its economy. In Baghdad, the banks have opened, and other banks will open across the country in the coming months. This fall, new banknotes will be issued, replacing the old ones bearing the former dictator's image. And Iraq's energy industry is once again serving the interests of the Iraqi people. More than a million barrels of crude oil and over 2 million gallons of gasoline are being produced daily.

Every day, Iraq draws closer to the free and functioning society its people were long denied. We're recovering hundreds of millions of dollars from the old regime and are using those funds to pay civil servants. Teachers, health care workers, police, and others performing essential services are also receiving salaries from our coalition. In fact, teacher pay is four times higher than under the old regime.

Life is returning to normal for the Iraqi people. Hospitals and universities have opened, and in many places, water and other utility services are reaching pre-war levels. Across Iraq, nearly all schoolchildren have completed their exams. And for the first time in many years, a free press is at work in Iraq. Across that country today, more than 150 newspapers are publishing regularly.

Most important of all, the Iraqi people are taking daily steps toward democratic government. The Iraqi Governing Council, whose 25 members represent all of that diverse country, is meeting regularly, naming ministers, and drawing up a budget for the country. Soon, representatives of the people will begin drafting a new constitution, and free elections will follow.

At the local level, all major Iraqi cities and most towns have municipal councils. Freedom is taking hold in that country as people gain confidence that the former regime is never coming back.

One hundred days is not enough time to undo the terrible legacy of Saddam Hussein. There is difficult and dangerous work ahead that requires time and patience. Yet all Americans can be proud of what our military and provisional authorities have achieved in Iraq.

Our country and the nations of the Middle East are now safer. We're keeping our word to the Iraqi people by helping them to make their country an example of democracy and prosperity throughout the region. This long-term undertaking is vital to peace in that region and to the security of the United States. Our coalition and the people of Iraq have made remarkable progress in a short time, and we will complete the great work we have begun.

Thank you for listening.

NOTE: The address was recorded at 9:45 a.m. on August 8 at the Bush Ranch in Crawford, TX, for broadcast at 10:06 a.m. on August 9. The transcript was made available by the Office of the Press Secretary on August 8 but was embargoed for release until the broadcast. In his remarks, the President referred to former President Saddam Hussein of Iraq. The Office of the Press Secretary also released a Spanish language transcript of this address.

Remarks on the Healthy Forests Initiative in Summerhaven, Arizona
August 11, 2003

Thank you all. Please be seated. Thanks a lot. Good morning. Thanks for welcoming me to this beautiful part of the world that has been scarred by nature. Senator McCain and I drove up the hill and he was saying, "You know, this part of Arizona is a lot prettier than anywhere in Texas." [*Laughter*] I didn't believe it at first— [*laughter*]—but it is beautiful. And all of us are sorry that fire has devastated life in the countryside here.

I want to thank the people for Summerhaven for allowing us to come up to visit your beautiful part of the world. You know, any time a community has been devastated like Summerhaven has been devastated, you could determine the character of the people. And the character of the people of Summerhaven and this part of Arizona have been tested, and you've met the test, and our Nation admires your courage and strength.

Too many communities like this have known too many hardships that fire causes. We've got a problem in the country, a problem which has built up over decades, and a problem we better fix before more people go through the griefs the people of Summerhaven have gone through, or the people that were affected by the Rodeo fires in northern Arizona.

See, our job as policy people and Members of Congress—have got to fix problems when we see them. They don't ignore problems. They don't hope the problems go away. We come up with commonsense solutions to the problems that affect the daily lives of our citizens, and that's what we're here to talk about today.

One of the people I've tasked with coming up with solutions to the problems we face is Secretary Ann Veneman. She's done a fabulous job on behalf of the people of the United States. She is a commonsense purpose—person. She asks the practical questions about how do we solve problems in America. She's also done a fine job of running the Forest Service. And I appreciate Dale Bosworth being here. He's the Chief of the Forest Service. And thank you for coming, Chief. I appreciate your commonsense policy. And I want to thank all the Forest Service employees, not only here in this part of Arizona but all across the country, for your dedication and service. Thank you, sir.

I appreciate Big Dan being with us. He is a firefighter's firefighter. The Senator and I and Madam Secretary had a chance to hear him talk about the courage and valor of the firefighters in this part of the State of Arizona as well as the others he commands. He and his partner, Larry, who I met last year, are just solid commanders. They're guys who set the course, set the strategy, and encourage the people to get after it.

And Dan, I want to thank you for your service to our country as well. I'm honored that you've given us a tour. I appreciate your service. I'm glad Ron called you into action—sad you had to come, but he called you into action because you're the best at what you do, and that's great for our country that you are. Thanks, Chief. Thank you and your wife for your service to America.

Ron, I want to thank you for your hospitality, and I want to thank all the good folks who work here in this park, in this park area, for working hard to make sure the environment is safe and sound and secure and that this park remains a beautiful part of the country.

I want to thank John McCain for being with us. He's a commonsense conservative who understands that we can do a better job of managing our national resources. I also want to thank Ben Nighthorse Campbell, who is over from the great State of Colorado. Colorado has also faced a lot of fire, too many fire. And he understands we need better policy.

Jim Kolbe is with us today; he's the Congressman from this area. I asked the county commissioner here, I said, "Has the response been good?" His first—right off, he said, "McCain and Kolbe have been incredibly responsive to the people of this part of the world." And I want to—and Kyl, he didn't show up, so he doesn't get any credit. [Laughter] Kyl is a good man. He deserves credit.

But I do want to thank the Senators and the Member of Congress for responding so quickly to the needs of the people here. I also want to thank other members of the congressional delegation from Arizona: Jeff Flake and Trent Franks, Big J.D. Hayworth and Rick Renzi, all fine Members of the United States Congress. All represent their State and their district with distinction and class, and I want to thank you all for joining us on this event.

I appreciate Janice Brewer, the secretary of state of the great State of Arizona, for being here. All the members of the legislature and the State senate who are here, the county commissioner, our fellow citizens, thank you for coming by to give us a chance to say hello.

I particularly want to thank the "hot shot" fire crews, the men and women who wear yellow, the people who put their lives on the line, those who respond to emergencies. The forest-fire crews have been put to incredible tests recently. A lot of it has to do with failed policy, backward policy, when it comes to maintaining the health of our forests.

Last year alone, it's important for our fellow citizens all across America to know that catastrophic wildfires burned about 7 million acres of land. And in trying to protect the natural resources and the people affected by those fires, we lost 23 firefighters, men and women who served our country with distinction. Our Nation is grateful for those who are willing to take risk on somebody else's behalf, and we extend our deepest sympathies to the loved ones who still mourn the lives of those which were lost.

Last month, the people of this beautiful part of America saw the devastating effects of the Aspen fire, which consumed over 85,000 acres. It destroyed hundreds of homes and buildings. We flew over Summerhaven. We saw the devastation. We saw the effects of a fire run wild, not only on the hillsides but also in the communities—burnt buildings, lives turned upside down because of the destruction of fire.

We also were able to see—I was able to hear the fact that our Government responded quickly, and that's important. In June, shortly after the fire began, FEMA issued a fire management assistance grant, granting millions of aid to the State of Arizona to cover a significant portion of the firefighting costs. That is a legitimate role of the Federal Government. And I will remind the House of Representatives and Members of the Senate that we have an obligation to help people fight fires in America.

The disaster declaration I signed authorized Federal assistance to the State and

Pima County for rebuilding public infrastructure and facilities. The SBA is providing low-interest loans to help small-business people in Summerhaven get their feet back on the ground and get the businesses started again. The Forest Service is putting down seed and hay to prevent soil erosion. We got to see some of the project, the hay project, on the hill right over there, right behind us.

The Federal Government has acted, and we need to act. But there's more we can do with good, sound policy. That's what we need to do at the Federal level. The University of Arizona Steward Observatory and the surrounding trees on Mount Lemmon are still standing today because of good, sound forest management practices. They didn't have fires in the area because there wasn't enough fuel to burn through the area, like that happened here.

There are campgrounds still intact, campgrounds used by church groups and scout troops which exist today because of good forest management. Forest-thinning projects make a significant difference about whether or not wildfires will destroy a lot of property. We need to thin our forests in America.

Our citizens must understand there are millions of acres of forest around this country that are vulnerable to catastrophic fire because of brush and small trees have been collecting for decades. As Senator McCain reminded me, it has taken decades for this problem to develop, and therefore, it's going to take a while to solve the problem. And we better get after it now with good, sound forest management projects.

It's important for people who don't know anything about forests and forest fires to understand that overgrowth chokes off nutrients to older and taller trees. It provides breeding grounds for insects and disease, which weaken our forests and make them more susceptible to fire. The kindling can turn small fires into large, raging fires that burn with such intensity that the trees literally explode. The devastation of a fire destroys not only trees but wildlife and its habitat. It causes flooding and soil erosion. It can ruin water supplies. Catastrophic fires burn so hot that it is incredibly hard to put them out. The kindling on the ground, the decades of neglect, the decades of failed policy have meant that our forest fires are incredibly hot, incredibly catastrophic. If you don't believe me, ask people like Dan who make a living fighting these fires.

And so we've listened to the people who are the frontline of making sure our forests are preserved and healthy. See, we listen to them because we have an obligation in America to preserve our forests. Our forests are treasures that must be preserved for future generations. It's important that we have good, sound forest policy. And the best way to do so is to listen to the experts who understand that by thinning out our forests, we risk—we reduce the risk of catastrophic fire, that we can and we should have good, sound forest management policy all across the United States of America.

And that's why I outlined what I called a Healthy Forests Initiative. The forest policies of the past operated to discourage efforts to thin forests. And unfortunately, well-meaning people proposed—put policy in place that made the health of the forests at risk, not better off.

And so the initiative said we're going to take a new approach. I called upon Ann and the Secretary of Interior and the Chairman of the Council on Environmental Quality to cut through bureaucratic redtape so that we can get urgently needed thinning projects moving. See, when you hear "redtape," that means there's a lot of rules and regulations that generally are in place to prevent something from happening. And our job is to slice through the redtape to get thinning projects moving forward.

We're speeding up the process of environmental assessment and consultations required now by current law, while considering both the health of the forest and our obligation to protect endangered species.

We're expediting the administrative appeals process, so that disputes over projects are resolved quickly. In other words, not everybody agrees with thinning; there will be objections. But we want those objections heard, of course. Every citizen needs to hear a voice, but we want the process to work quickly so we can get on about the business of saving our forests.

We believe in bringing people together to try to reach agreement on forest projects. We believe all voices should be heard. But we want to expedite the process to avoid the legal wrangling and the delays that take place in our courts. Delays in our courts prevent us from doing the job necessary to maintain healthy forests.

We're working with the western Governors, most of—a lot of the problems exist in—out West, and we understand that. This is a place for good, sound policy to take place—out West on the Federal lands. Above all, we will continue to rely upon the informed judgment of the forest professionals and those who fight the fires.

Any skeptic about what I'm talking about ought to come and talk to the people who know what they're talking about, who make a living fighting fires, who understand the devastation that is caused by backward forest policy. Every forest will be treated according to its unique circumstances. Federal policy must be flexible to be able to deal with the problems in each particular part of our country.

Saving millions of acres of forest through better management will require a lot of hard work in a lot of States and, interestingly enough, will not only save our forests but will create jobs. You see, not all the work of thinning will be done by Government. In order to meet some of the goals we've proposed, we have to rely upon local contractors who will clear away and be able to sell smaller trees, the trees that provide the kindling. And this way, the work of thinning overgrown forests improves public safety, will save taxpayers' money, and will help local economies.

This initiative that I outlined, the Healthy Forests Initiative, is producing results. Last year, we treated 2¼ million acres of overgrown forests. That's a million acres more than were treated in the year 2000, and that's good. By the end of the fiscal year in September, we will have treated more than 2.6 million acres of forest and range land, and that's important. In Arizona, we're treating 224,000 acres this year, about twice as many acres as were treated in 2001.

We're making progress, but current law makes it very difficult to expedite the thinning of forests. Laws on the books make it very difficult for us to set priorities, to listen to those who manage our forests and fight the fires, and to get after the thinning that is necessary to prevent catastrophic fires from occurring in the first place.

All too often, the litigation process delays forest projects for years and years, and that's a reality. Our forests remain unprotected; our communities are vulnerable. So I asked Congress to reform the review process for forest projects. The "Healthy Forest Restoration Act" now pending in Congress will do just that. It directs courts to consider long-term threats to forest health that could result if thinning projects are delayed. In other words, it says to the courts, the health of our forests is a national goal. It makes forest health the priority when it comes to the courts resolving disputes. It places reasonable time limits on the litigation process, after the public has had an opportunity to comment and a decision has been made.

For the sake of our forests, the Congress must act. The House of Representatives has passed a bill which includes these reforms, and I want to thank the Members from the great State of Arizona for their leadership. A bill—such a bill has passed the Senate Agriculture Committee. And now it's time for us in the administration and for Members in the Senate who agree with this policy to reach across the partisan divide and get a good bill out of the United States Senate.

The issue I speak about is not a political issue. It's not a partisan issue. This is an American issue that requires consensus to do what is smart and right about preserving and protecting our national forests. I look forward to working with members of both parties to get a good bill out of the United States Senate.

Within sight of where we stand are the results of wise forest policy and the ruins of unwise forest policy. For those who live here, it's the difference between lives surrounded by natural beauty and lives disrupted by natural disaster. We can serve the interests of this country by working together, by listening to people who know what they're talking about, and putting together commonsense policy to preserve our forests, to make them healthy so that when we step back after our time and service, people will say, "Job well done."

Thanks for coming. May God bless those who suffer, may God bless those who serve our country, and may God continue to bless America.

NOTE: The President spoke at 10:55 a.m. at Inspiration Rock. In his remarks, he referred to Dan Oltrogge and Larry Humphrey, incident commanders, Type 1 Southwest Area Incident Management Teams; Ron Senn, Santa Catalina District Ranger, U.S. Forest Service; Senator Ben Nighthorse Campbell of Colorado; and Senator Jon Kyl of Arizona.

Remarks Announcing the Nomination of Governor Michael O. Leavitt To Be Environmental Protection Agency Administrator in Aurora, Colorado
August 11, 2003

The President. Good afternoon. First, I want to make a comment about some foreign policy. Today's departure of Charles Taylor from Liberia is an important step toward a better future for the Liberian people. The United States will work with the Liberian people and with the international community to achieve a lasting peace after more than a decade of turmoil and suffering.

The United States will help ECOWAS and the humanitarian relief organizations to get aid to those who need it. I appreciate the efforts of many African leaders, most especially Nigerian President Obasanjo, Ghanaian President Kufuor, South African President Mbeki, Mozambican President Chissano. Their continued leadership will be needed in the weeks and months ahead as a new government is formed and the Liberian people seek to chart a future of peace and stability.

Earlier today, I spoke in Arizona about the urgent need to safeguard America's forests from wildfire. It's one of the many environmental challenges that face our Nation. Those challenges go beyond our forests. We must also be vigilant in protecting the air and soil and waters around us.

This is the primary responsibility of our Environmental Protection Agency, and today I am pleased to introduce my nominee to lead that Agency, Governor Mike Leavitt of Utah. I appreciate so very much Jackie being here, as well as Michael, Taylor, Anne Marie, Westin, and Chase, who's not with us. The Leavitt family is a great American family, primarily because Dixie and Anne, the mom and dad of the Governor, worked hard to make it such, and I'm honored they are here as well. Thank you all for coming.

I also appreciate the fact that the leader of the house and the senate from Utah have joined us today.

I selected Mike Leavitt because he is a trusted friend, a capable executive, and a man who understands the obligations of environmental stewardship. With the Senate's approval, Mike Leavitt will lead an agency with 18,000 dedicated employees in offices all across our country. The work of the EPA is vital and reflects a national consensus on the importance of good stewardship.

During the last three decades, we've seen extraordinary progress in cleaning our air and protecting our land and making our water more pure. The quality of our air is far better than it was in the 1970s. Many more of our lakes and rivers are safe for fishing and swimming. Toxic emissions have declined, and we're bringing new resources and programs to reduce runoff and erosion. We're making real progress protecting endangered species and helping them recover.

Mike Leavitt will come to the EPA with a strong environmental record and a strong desire to improve on what has taken place during the last three decades. He served for over a decade as Governor of an important State. As cochair of the Western Regional Air Partnership, Governor Leavitt has been a leader in applying high standards in air quality, and he understands the importance of clear standards in every environmental policy. He respects the ability of State and local governments to meet those standards, rejects the old ways of command and control from above. He was twice reelected by the people of Utah, in part because he leads by consensus and focuses on results instead of process.

In Utah and beyond, he has gained wide respect for handling environmental issues in a spirit of openness and bipartisanship. These qualities and his experience will make Mike Leavitt a fine addition to my administration. I will count on him to continue the good work begun by former Administrator Whitman and Acting Administrator Horinko.

He will join my Cabinet with a full agenda and with my full confidence. Mike, I appreciate your willingness to serve. I thank the people of Utah as you leave office to take on this incredibly important assignment in our Nation's Capital.

[At this point, Governor Leavitt made brief remarks.]

The President. Great job. Thank you. Thank you all. Good job, Michael.

NOTE: The President spoke at 3:34 p.m. at the Marriott Hotel. In his remarks, he referred to former President Charles Taylor of Liberia; President Olusegun Obasanjo of Nigeria; President John Agyekum Kufuor of Ghana; President Thabo Mbeki of South Africa; President Joaquim Alberto Chissano of Mozambique; Jacalyn S. Leavitt, wife of Gov. Leavitt, and their children Michael, Taylor, Anne Marie, Westin, and Chase; Martin R. Stephens, speaker, Utah State House of Representatives; and L. Alma "Al" Mansell, president, Utah State Senate. The transcript released by the Office of the Press Secretary also included the remarks of Gov. Leavitt.

Remarks at a Bush-Cheney Dinner in Denver, Colorado
August 11, 2003

The President. Thank you all very much. I appreciate you coming. Thanks for the warm welcome. There is nothing like heading west.

I spent a little time on our ranch in Crawford—get to see more cows than I do the press corps. [*Laughter*] Seems like the cows are handling the heat a little better too. [*Laughter*]

But I want to thank you all very much for your help. I appreciate your strong support. I want to thank all those who made this fundraiser a record-setting fundraiser. I appreciate what you're doing. You're laying the foundation for what is going to be a great victory in November of '04.

I'm here to not only thank you; I'm here to tell you I'm going to need your support in energizing the grassroots of the great State of Colorado. I need your help in putting up signs. I need you to make the phone calls. I need you to mail the letters. I need you to remind people of this State—Republican, Democrat, independent, don't care—that our message is one that is hopeful for every single citizen who lives in this State.

I'm loosening up. I'm getting ready—[*laughter*]—cutting a lot of cedar—[*laughter*]—running a lot of miles, getting ready for the contest. But the political season will come in its own time. For me, now is not the time for politics. You see, I've got a job to do. I'm staying focused on the people's business. I'm doing what you expect me to do in Washington, DC, and I'll continue to work to earn the confidence of every American by keeping this Nation secure and strong and prosperous and free.

I want to thank my friend the Governor of the great State of Colorado. He is—he's done a fabulous job as your Governor. He does what he says he's going to do, which is nice, to have somebody in public office—[*laughter*]—who says something and means it. And like me, he married above himself. I'm honored to be here with the First Lady of the State of Colorado as well.

I just called Laura and said that I'm fixing to go see a lot of our friends from the State of Colorado. I said, "How's—what's it like down there?" She said, "It's only 103." [*Laughter*] I said, "Well, if that's

the case, it feels like winter here." [*Laughter*]

I can't tell you how great it is to be married to such a fine woman as Laura Bush. She is a great First Lady for our country.

I appreciate the two Senators from the State of Colorado. Senator Wayne Allard, who's—turns out to be my State cochair, along with working with the Governor here. He's a great Senator, and so is Ben Nighthorse Campbell. I'm going to tell you, it's important to put this man back into the United States Senate. And if you've got a little something left in the wallet after tonight—[*laughter*]—and looking for a good man to help, somebody who can use your help, it's Senator Ben Nighthorse Campbell. He's a fine representative of the great State of Colorado, and I'm proud to call him friend.

Two members of the U.S. congressional delegation are with us. First, Bob Beauprez; Congressman Beauprez, thank you for coming. We didn't exactly landslide them last time—[*laughter*]—but neither did I. [*Laughter*] I know you're back home working hard in your district to tell the people of that district they made the right choice in putting Bob Beauprez in the U.S. Congress. He's a fine man. And I appreciate Tom Tancredo being here as well. Thank you, Congressman, for coming. I'm honored you're here.

I want to thank the Lieutenant Governor, Jane Norton, for being here tonight. I want to thank the treasurer for the great State of Colorado, Mike Coffman, for being here tonight. I appreciate the president of the State senate and the speaker of the house, Senator John Andrews and Lola Spradley, for coming as well. Governor, I know it's a pretty good deal to be working with a Republican speaker and a senate leader. I kind of like it myself. [*Laughter*]

I want to thank very much our party chairman, Ted Halaby. I want to thank Bruce Benson for putting this event on and for being the finance chairman. I want to thank all those who helped raise the money. I thank my friend Mercer Reynolds, who is the national finance chairman. But most of all, I want to thank you all for your friendship, for your prayers, for your support, for getting ready to get to work on behalf of this reelection campaign.

You know, in the last 2½ years, our Nation has acted decisively to confront great challenges. I came to this office to solve problems, not to pass them on to future Presidents and future generations. I came to seize opportunities instead of letting them slip away. We are meeting the tests of our time.

Terrorists declared war on the United States of America, and war is what they got. We've captured or killed many of the leaders of Al Qaida, and the rest of them know we're on their trail. In Afghanistan and Iraq, we gave ultimatums to terror regimes. Those regimes chose defiance, and those regimes are no more. Fifty million people—50 million people—in those two countries once lived under tyranny, and now they live in freedom. And the world is better off for it.

Two-and-a-half years ago, our military was not receiving the resources it needed, and morale was beginning to suffer. We increased the defense budget to prepare for the threats of a new era. And today, no one in the world can question the skill and the strength and the spirit of the United States military.

Two-and-a-half years ago, we inherited an economy in recession. Then the attacks happened on our country, and scandals in corporate America, as well as the war—it all affected the people's confidence. People began to lose confidence, but we acted. We passed tough new laws to hold corporate criminals to account.

To get the economy going, I have twice led the United States Congress to pass historic tax relief for the American people. Here's what I believe, and here's what we know, that when Americans have more take-home money to spend or to save, to

invest, the whole economy begins to grow, and people are more likely to find a job. And I understand whose money we spend in Washington, DC. It is not the Government's money we spend in Washington; it is the people's money.

Now we're returning more money to the American people to help them raise their families, reducing taxes on dividends and capital gains to encourage investment. We're giving small businesses proper incentives to encourage them to expand and to hire new people. With all these actions, we're laying the foundation for greater prosperity and more jobs across America so every one of our citizens can realize the great promise of our country.

I want you to remember, 2½ years ago there was a lot of talk about education reform, but there wasn't much action in Washington, DC. So I called for and our Congress passed the No Child Left Behind Act. With a solid bipartisan majority, we delivered the most dramatic education reforms in a generation.

We're bringing high standards and strong accountability measures to every public school in America. See, we believe every child can learn the basics of reading and math. And we expect every school to teach the basics of reading and math. I am challenging the soft bigotry of low expectations. The days of excuse-making are over. In return for Federal money, we expect results so that not one single child in America is left behind.

We've done a lot in 2½ years. We reorganized the Government and created the Department of Homeland Security to better strengthen our borders to protect the American people. We passed trade promotion authority to open up new markets for Colorado's entrepreneurs and farmers and ranchers. We passed budget agreements that helps maintain spending discipline in Washington, DC. On issue after issue, I want you to remind the skeptics and the undecideds that this administration has acted on principle, has kept its word, and has made progress on behalf of all the American people.

Of course, we didn't do this alone. A lot of the credit goes to Members of the United States Congress. We've got a fabulous Speaker of the House, Denny Hastert, a great majority leader of the United States Senate, Bill Frist. I appreciate so very much working with them and the folks from the great State of Colorado.

And the difference now in Washington is, is that we're focusing on results, not process. We're working to change the tone in Washington so we can get the people's business done. And by the way, those are the kind of people I've asked to serve in my administration. I put together a strong team to work on behalf of the American people.

Our country has had no finer Vice President than Dick Cheney. Mother may have a second opinion. [*Laughter*]

Audience member. I agree with you. [*Laughter*]

The President. Thank you.

In 2½ years, we have come far, but you know, we're only just beginning. We've great goals worthy of this great Nation. The job of the President is to set our sights high. A great nation requires great goals.

And here are the goals I've set: First, America is committed to expanding the realm of freedom and peace for our own security and for the benefit of the world; and secondly, in our own country, we must work for a society of prosperity and compassion so that every citizen—every single citizen—has a chance to work and to succeed and realize the American Dream.

It is clear that the future of freedom and peace depend on the actions of America. This Nation is freedom's home; it is freedom's defender. And this Nation welcomes this charge of history, and we are keeping this charge of history. The war on terror continues. See, the enemies of freedom are not idle, and neither are we. This country will not rest. We will not tire, and

we will not stop until this danger to civilization is removed.

Yet, our national interest involves more than eliminating aggressive threats to our safety. Our greatest security comes from the advance of human liberty, because free nations do not support terror. Free nations do not attack their neighbors. Free nations do not develop weapons of mass terror. Our country believes that freedom is the deepest need and hope of every human heart. And we believe that freedom is the right of every person. And we believe that freedom is the future of every single nation.

America also understands that unprecedented influence brings tremendous responsibilities. We have duties in the world. When we see disease and starvation and hopeless poverty, we will not turn away. On the continent of Africa, this great Nation is committed to bringing the healing power of medicine to millions of men and women and children who are now suffering with AIDS. This great land, this land for which I am so proud, is leading the world in the incredibly important work of human rescue.

We face big challenges abroad, and we won't shirk from those challenges. And we face big challenges here at home. I will continue to work on our economy. I'll continue to make sure the entrepreneurial spirit is strong. I will continue to try to lay the conditions for capital formation, so that anybody who wants to work and can't find a job today will be able to do so.

I will continue to work to make sure we meet our commitments to America's seniors by modernizing Medicare. A few weeks ago, the United States Congress took historic action to improve the lives of older Americans. I want you to remember this: For the first time—first time—since the creation of Medicare, the House and Senate have passed reforms to modernize the system, to give seniors more choices, and to provide coverage for prescription drugs for our seniors. The next step is for both bodies to iron out their differences and to get a bill to my desk so I can sign it on behalf of the elderly of the United States of America. We have a solemn obligation, an obligation which I will continue to call upon the Congress to keep.

For the sake of our health care system, we need to cut down on the frivolous lawsuits which increase the cost of medicine all across our country. I fully understand that people who have been harmed by a bad doctor deserve their day in court. Yet, the system should not reward lawyers who are simply fishing for rich settlements. Because frivolous lawsuits drive up the cost of health care, they affect the Federal budget. They affect the Medicare budget, the Medicaid budget, the veterans budgets. I view medical liability reform as a national issue which requires a national solution. The House of Representatives passed a good bill to reform medical liability. It's stuck in the Senate. The Senate must act. No one has ever been healed by a frivolous lawsuit. We need medical liability reform now.

I have a responsibility as President to make sure the judicial system runs well, and I have met that duty. I have nominated superb men and women to the Federal bench, people who interpret the law, not legislate from the bench. Yet, some Members of the United States Senate are trying to keep my nominees off the bench by blocking up-or-down votes. Every judicial nominee deserves a fair hearing and an up-or-down vote on the Senate floor. It is time for some of the Members of the United States Senate to stop playing politics with American justice.

The Congress needs to complete work on a comprehensive energy plan. Our Nation has got to promote energy conservation and efficiency and develop cleaner technology so we can explore in more environmentally sensitive areas. Yet, for the sake of our economic security and for the sake of our national security, we must be less dependent on foreign sources of energy.

Our strong and prosperous Nation must also be a compassionate nation. I will continue to advance the agenda of compassionate conservatism, which really means applying the best and most innovative ideas to helping our fellow citizens who hurt and who are in need.

See, there are still millions of men and women in this land who want the independence and dignity that come from work. We must build on the success of welfare reform to bring work to the lives of more of our fellow citizens. Congress ought to complete the "Citizen Service Act" so more Americans can serve their community and their country. Both Houses should finally reach agreement on the Faith-Based Initiative to support the armies of compassion that are mentoring our children and caring for the homeless, healing hearts, and helping the addicted.

A compassionate society must also be a society which promotes opportunity for all, including the independence and dignity that come from ownership. This administration will constantly strive to promote an ownership society in America. We want more people to own their homes. I'm troubled by the fact we have a minority home-ownership gap in America, and I put forth policies—constructive, smart policies to encourage more homeownership all across America.

We want people to own and manage their own health care plan. We want people to own and manage their own retirement accounts. We want the entrepreneurial spirit to be strong in America so that people feel confident in investing in their own small business.

Now, I understand an ownership society is one in which people have more hope for the future. In a compassionate society, people respect one another, and they take responsibility for the decisions they make in life. We're changing the culture of America, slowly but surely, from one that has said, "If it feels good, just go ahead and do it," and "If you've got a problem, blame somebody else," to a culture in which each of us understands that we are responsible for the decisions we make in life.

If you're fortunate enough to be a mother or father, you're responsible for loving your child with all your heart and all your soul. If you're concerned about the quality of the education in the community in which you live, you're responsible for doing something about it. If you happen to be a CEO in corporate America, you're responsible for telling the truth to your employees and your shareholders. And in the new responsibility society, each of us is responsible for loving our neighbor just like we'd like to be loved ourself.

We can see that culture of respect, the culture of change and service growing around us here in America today. You know, I started what they call the USA Freedom Corps. It's an opportunity for Americans to help neighbors in need, and the response has been fantastic. Got people signing up for all kinds of ways to help in their community, and I'm grateful.

Our faith-based charities are strong, and they're vibrant, which is important to bring hope to those who hurt. Our policemen and firefighters and people who wear our Nation's uniform are reminding us what it means to sacrifice for something greater than themselves in life—sacrifice for peace,

sacrifice for freedom, sacrifice for safe streets. And once again, the children of America believe in heroes because they see them every day in America.

In these challenging times, the world has seen the resolve and the courage of America. I've been privileged to see the compassion and the character of the American people. The tests of the last 2½ years have come to the right nation. We're a strong country, and we use that strength to defend the peace. We're an optimistic country, confident in ourselves and in ideals bigger than ourselves. Abroad, we seek to lift up whole nations by spreading freedom. And at home, we seek to lift up lives by spreading opportunity to every corner of our country. This is the work that history has set before us, and we welcome it. And we know that for our country and for our cause, the best days lie ahead.

Thank you for coming. May God bless. Thank you all.

NOTE: The President spoke at 5:44 p.m. at Wings Over the Rockies Air and Space Museum. In his remarks, he referred to Gov. Bill Owens of Colorado and his wife, Frances; Ted Halaby, chairman, and Bruce Benson, former chairman, Colorado Republican Party; and Mercer Reynolds, national finance chairman, Bush-Cheney '04, Inc.

Remarks Following a Meeting With Economic Advisers and an Exchange With Reporters in Crawford, Texas
August 13, 2003

The President. Good morning. As you can see, my economic team came down. We've had some great briefings. Let me summarize by saying that this administration is optimistic about job creation. We believe strongly that the tax relief plan that was approved by Congress in '01 and most recently in '03 is going to have a very posi-

tive effect on economic growth and vitality. We believe it is more likely in the upcoming year that people are going to be able to find a job, and that's exactly what—where we focused our policy.

But I also know there's more that can be done. I think one thing is certain, and we've spent a lot of time discussing this:

There needs to be a strong message to Congress not to overspend, set priorities, and hold the line on the priorities. As well, we need an energy policy, and we need good tort reform. And I appreciate the fact that the House has passed a good energy bill and the Senate passed an energy bill. Now is the time to get together and reconcile their differences and get a bill to my desk. I also appreciate the fact that the House passed good class-action reform, and the Senate now needs to follow suit.

And I also look forward to working with the Congress to get associated health care plans passed, which will make it easier for small businesses to be able to write affordable health care for their employees. So there's some things we can do to make sure that the economy continues to grow and so people can find work. If you'll remember, the tax relief plan that was passed was called the jobs plan, the growth-and-jobs creation plan. That's what we're interested in. We're interested in people being able to work in America, and we're upbeat about the chances for our fellow citizens who are looking for work to be able to find a job.

I'll answer some questions, starting with Scott [Scott Lindlaw, Associated Press].

Liberia/Former President Charles Taylor

Q. Thanks, Mr. President. President Taylor has met your demand to leave Liberia. You've got a west African peacekeeping force in there. Is the time right to send in those 4,500 marines and sailors? And should Nigeria turn President Taylor over to the war crimes tribunal?

The President. They can work that out with—how they deal with Taylor. One, I'm glad he's gone. But my focus now is on making sure that humanitarian relief gets to the people who are suffering in Liberia. And one of the things I have said all along was that we are there to help ECOMIL do its job by providing the conditions necessary for the arrival of relief. And that's why we've got an assessment team on the ground that's dealing with the Nigerian who's in charge of ECOMIL, to determine what is necessary to help ECOMIL do its job. They are in the lead, and we are there to support and help.

Obviously, one place we've got to make sure is secure and open is the port. And so we're working with ECOMIL, and I will again take recommendations from the Defense Department as to what is necessary to fulfill the mission.

Q. What's your timetable, if I may?

The President. My timetable of listening——

Q. Making a decision on whether to send those 4,500 in.

The President. Well, I've already made the decision, Scott. And I said this from day one. The decision is for us to help ECOMIL do its job of getting humanitarian relief to the people in Liberia. I've made that decision, and nothing's changed.

Yes.

Hemant Lakhani/Homeland Security

Q. Yesterday there was a sting operation that netted a Brit believed to be trying to sell surface-to-air missiles to someone they believed who was Al Qaida, highlighting the danger to airlines. Also yesterday, there were three lost fisherman who came onshore to JFK Airport, breaching security.

Your Democratic opponents are trying to use homeland security as an issue in the campaign, saying that the administration is not doing enough to protect the American people. What is your assessment in light of what happened yesterday?

The President. My assessment is people are going to say the darnedest thing when they run for office, in terms of just the politics. The American people know the difference between politics and reality, and the reality is we're doing everything we can to protect the homeland.

And the fact that we were able to sting this guy is a pretty good example of what we're doing in order to protect the American people. And our homeland security is focused on airport security. And today, the airports are much more secure than they were prior to September the 11th. America is a safe place for people to fly, precisely because we're working hard to make sure that our homeland security is strong.

The other way to make sure the homeland stays strong is to hunt terrorists down before they come to America. And that's why we're on the global hunt. That's why we've got troops around in places like Afghanistan and Iraq dealing with potential terrorists, bringing them to justice, finding them before they hurt us.

Yes, Elisabeth [Elisabeth Bumiller, New York Times].

Tax Policy

Q. Are you going to go for a new round of tax cuts this fall?

The President. Elisabeth, we are discussing a lot of things. And we believe that the tax relief plan we have in place is robust enough to encourage job growth.

Q. So is that a "no"?

The President. Well, as of this moment—you see, things change in the economy, as you know—but as of this moment, we feel like the plans we have in place are robust enough to create jobs.

Q. Is there any discussion——

The President. Please. The other thing that's necessary is to make sure we've got spending discipline in Washington, to make sure that Congress doesn't overspend. And that will—because that will affect the psychology of those who are—risk capital in order to create the job base.

You had a followup, I take it.

Q. Yes, I was just going to ask you: The discussions in the administration, maybe not at the White House level, about a—perhaps a business tax credit, that you would get a tax credit if you hired somebody to sort of——

The President. Well, thus far, we—in the discussions today, we feel like the tax relief

plans that we have passed will be robust enough to create the conditions necessary for economic growth, and therefore, people will find a job. If we change our opinion, we will let you know. You may not be the first to know, but you'll be one of the first to know.

Yes, sir.

North Korea

Q. Thank you. Russia has proposed a multilateral security pact to end the standoff with North Korea. Are you willing to offer incentives before North Korea dismantles its nuclear weapons program?

The President. Here's what we're going to do. We're going to continue the dialog with North Korea, to make it clear to them that not only does the United States feel strongly that the Peninsula ought to be nuclear-free, but other countries which live in the neighborhood feel the same way. And remember, the policy has evolved from one of bilateral—you know, pressure to negotiate bilaterally with the North Koreans. That's what we did in the past, and that policy unfortunately failed because the North Koreans didn't keep their word about whether or not they would enrich uranium.

And so now we've taken another tact, which is to—first of all, to convince the Chinese to be an active participant in a dialog to make sure that the Korean Peninsula is nuclear-free. By the way, the first stage of that happened right here in Crawford when Jiang Zemin came to visit, and he stated clearly after that visit that it was in China's interest that the Korean Peninsula be nuclear-weapons-free. And we're just continuing that policy. It's very helpful that the Russians are involved with the dialog with the North Koreans. It is also very helpful that the South Koreans and the Japanese will be involved. And I think we can deal with this issue in a peaceful way, and we're making good progress.

Carl [Carl Cannon, National Journal].

National Economy

Q. Mr. President, you said that candidates say the darnedest things when they're running for office. One of the things they're saying is that there are fewer jobs now than when you took office.

The President. Yes.

Q. A year from now, you are going to be standing for reelection yourself. Do you think there will be as many jobs as when you took office? And when will we start to see a significant decrease in the unemployment rate?

The President. Right. Let me remind the listeners here about what our country has gone through. We—the stock market started to change in March of 2000. And there was a precipitous decline in March of 2000. And that began to affect savings and money and attitude. And then the country went into a recession. The first three quarters of 2001 was a recession. And we dealt with that by passing tax relief, which made the recession one of the shallowest in history.

Now, people said, "Well, maybe you shouldn't have done that. Maybe you shouldn't have had tax relief. Maybe you should have let the recession run its course." But my attitude about that is, is that a deep recession would have caused more people to lose work. And I'm more worried about families finding a job and putting food on the table than I am about economic theory and economic numbers, and so the recession was shallow.

And as the economy was beginning to recover, the enemy hit us on September the 11th, and that affected our economy in a big way. And then we had corporate scandals which we've dealt with. And then, of course, you remember the march to war. I've reminded people—I think this isn't the first time I've said this—that some would put on their TV screens that we were "marching to war." As a matter of fact, it was a year ago we began the march to war. During the August vacation, as I recall, there was the march to war. It's hard to have a upbeat view of the world when you're marching to war. I mean, war is not exactly a positive thought, particularly when it comes to people willing to take risk, and consumer confidence.

But nevertheless, we dealt with that issue. And so now the economy is—having overcome those obstacles, is beginning to recover. And yes, I think people are going to go back to work, and I firmly believe that what we have done was the absolute right course of action in order to help people find a job.

Mark [Mark Knoller, CBS Radio], you've got a question?

Q. I do.

The President. I'm being very generous today, as you can see.

Q. Yes, you are. Thank you, sir.

The President. My pleasure.

Federal Deficit

Q. If a Democrat were President and running for——

The President. Wait a minute. Let me stop you there.

Q. Yes.

The President. They say the silliest things during the political season. And sometimes people ask the silliest questions.

Q. *[Inaudible]*——try not to do that, sir.

The President. Now, be careful. Be careful. *[Laughter]*

Q. With that in mind, if a Democrat were President——

The President. Are you adjusting? *[Laughter]*

Q. ——and were running a $455 billion deficit, as are you, all other things being equal, wouldn't you be upset about it?

The President. Let me tell you something, the deficit was caused by a recession which we inherited and did something about. The deficit was caused because we spent more money on fighting a war, and the American people expect a President to do what is necessary to win a war. And so I look forward to taking this debate on. I really do. We did the right thing when it came to tax relief. We inherited a tough situation.

But most importantly, the American people know that I'm not afraid to lead and to make a tough decision. And I made a tough decision, a series of tough decisions, one, to make America more secure, a tough decision to make the world more peaceful, and I made tough decisions when it comes to making sure our economy grows.

And I believe that we've laid the foundation for good economic growth and vitality. I think people are going to be more likely to find a job in the upcoming year.

Thank you all for coming.

California Gubernatorial Candidate Arnold Schwarzenegger

Q. Are you going to do anything for Arnold? You say he'll be a good Governor. You're spending 2 days in California.

The President. I'm going to campaign for George W., as you know.

Q. Will he get a plug in the speech, a mention?

The President. I think I've answered the question, and yes, he would be a good Governor, as would others running for Governor of California. And like you, I'm most interested in seeing how the process evolves. It's a fascinating bit of political drama evolving in the State—in the country's largest State.

Q. It's also the biggest political story in the country. Is it hard to go in there and say nothing about it?

The President. It is the biggest political story in the country? That's interesting. That says a lot. That speaks volumes.

Q. You don't agree?

The President. It's up to—I don't get to decide the biggest political story. You decide the biggest political story. But I find it interesting that that is the biggest political story in the country, as you just said.

Q. You don't think it should be?

The President. Oh, I think there's maybe other political stories. Isn't there, like, a Presidential race coming up? [*Laughter*] Maybe that says something. It speaks volumes, if you know what I mean. But yes, it's an interesting story; it really is. And I'm looking forward, like you are, to seeing the outcome of the interesting story.

But no, I'm going to go, I'm going to talk about—now that you've asked, are you going on the trip?

Q. Yes, sir.

The President. Good. Well, you'll see me speak to marines and their families, thanking them for their service to our country, reminding them that what's taking place in Iraq is essential to U.S. security. Then I'm going to go to a national park, talking about the fact that we believe parks ought to be revitalized and talk about the initiatives that I've laid out to do that. And then, of course, I'll be doing a little spadework for the '04 campaign. One of the most important political stories—[*laughter*].

Have a great day. Thank you all.

NOTE: The President spoke at 11:44 a.m. at the Bush Ranch. In his remarks, he referred to Brig. Gen. Festus Okonkwo, Nigerian commander of ECOMIL forces in Liberia; Hemant Lakhani, arms dealer charged with selling missiles to U.S. agents posing as terrorists; and former President Jiang Zemin of China.

Letter to Congressional Leaders on the Further Deployment of United States Military Forces in Liberia
August 13, 2003

Dear Mr. Speaker: *(Dear Mr. President:)*

In my report to the Congress of June 9, 2003, I provided information on the deployment of combat-equipped U.S. Armed Forces to Liberia. I am providing this additional report, consistent with the War Powers Resolution, to help ensure that the Congress is kept fully informed on U.S. military activities in Liberia.

Shortly after my initial report, additional U.S. combat-equipped, military personnel from the U.S. European Command deployed to Monrovia, Liberia, to augment the U.S. Embassy security forces and to aid in the evacuation of U.S. citizens from Liberia if required, raising the total of such personnel to 56.

On August 1, 2003, United Nations Security Council Resolution 1497 was adopted. It authorized member states to establish a Multinational Force in Liberia to support the implementation of the June 17, 2003, ceasefire, including establishing conditions for initial stages of disarmament, demobilization, and reintegration activities; establishing security; and securing the environment for the delivery of humanitarian assistance and the introduction of a longer term U.N. stabilization force. Soon thereafter, approximately 4,350 U.S. military personnel on board U.S. warships deployed into the area of operations off the coast of Liberia in preparation to assist the Eco-nomic Community of West African States Mission in Liberia (ECOMIL) forces in the conduct of initial humanitarian and stability operations in the vicinity of Monrovia, Liberia. On August 11, 2003, these combat-equipped forces entered the territorial waters of Liberia timed to coincide with the resignation and departure of President Taylor, which was the stated prerequisite before deploying U.S. Armed Forces in support of ECOMIL.

It is anticipated that U.S. forces will redeploy when ECOMIL forces have transitioned to the follow-on U.N. stabilization operations.

I have taken this action pursuant to my constitutional authority to conduct U.S. foreign relations and as Commander in Chief and Chief Executive. I am providing this report as part of my efforts to keep the Congress informed, consistent with the War Powers Resolution.

I appreciate the support of the Congress in these actions in Liberia.

Sincerely,

GEORGE W. BUSH

NOTE: Identical letters were sent to J. Dennis Hastert, Speaker of the House of Representatives, and Ted Stevens, President pro tempore of the Senate. An original was not available for verification of the content of this letter.

Remarks at the Marine Corps Air Station in Miramar, California
August 14, 2003

Thank you all. Thank you all very much. Thanks for coming out to say hello. It's getting a little quiet on the ranch—[laugh-ter]—so I decided to pay a visit to the "devil dogs."

I'm honored to be in the presence of the men and women who wear our Nation's uniform. I'm proud of you, and I want to thank you for your service to our great country. Each of you serves in a crucial time in our Nation's history. And this Nation is grateful for the sacrifice and service you make.

Many of you have recently returned from Iraq, and it seems like you're happy to be home. More than 70,000 men and women from bases in southern California were deployed in Iraq. You served with honor; you served with skill; and you were successful.

Before you went in, Iraqis were an oppressed people, and the dictator threatened his neighbors, the Middle East, and the world. Today, the Iraqis are liberated people; the former regime is gone; and our Nation and the world is more secure.

This Nation is at war with people who hate what we stand for. We love freedom, and we're not going to change. Our country depends on you to protect our freedom, and every day, you depend on your families. This has been a challenging time for military families; I know that. During the last year, our families and our military have met hardships and met them together. You've supported and looked out for one another. You've been strong and faithful to the people you love. Military families make tremendous sacrifices for America, and our Nation is grateful for your service to our country.

I appreciate General Conway. This isn't the first time I met him. He looks you right in the eye. He's the kind of commander I'd like to serve under—it's just that, he just serves under me. [*Laughter*] I appreciate General Amos, General Gallinetti. I appreciate all those who are in command of forces here. I want to thank you for what you do.

We've got members of the California congressional delegation here. These are stalwarts when it comes to understanding the need to provide you the resources necessary to do your job. There's no finer Congressman when it comes to military affairs than Congressman Duncan Hunter. With

him, the Congressman from southern California as well; I call him "The Ace," because he was an ace in Vietnam, a great fighter pilot, Randy "Duke" Cunningham. Two other members of the delegation are here who are friends of mine, people who serve with distinction, Congressman Ed Royce and Congressman Darrell Issa. I'm honored you all are here. Thank you for coming.

The Marine Corps Air Station and the military bases of southern California have long, long been crucial to the defense of this country. We intend to keep it that way. Generations of marines and sailors and pilots have trained and served here. And for the veterans who are with us today, I thank you for your service to our country.

Now you have been called. This group of marines and sailors have been called to serve in the first war of the 21st century. The war began almost 2 years ago, on September the 11th, 2001, when this Nation was brutally attacked and thousands of our fellow citizens died. We were awakened to new dangers on that day.

On that morning, the threats that had gathered far across the world appeared suddenly in our own cities. The world changed on that day. The enemies of the United States showed the harm they can do and the evil they intend. Since that September morning, our enemies have also seen something: They have seen the will and the might of the United States military, and they are meeting the fate they chose for themselves.

Our Nation is waging a broad and unrelenting campaign against the global terror network, and we're winning. Wherever Al Qaida terrorists try to hide—from the caves and mountains of central Asia to the islands of the Philippines to the cities in Pakistan— we are finding them, and we are bringing them to justice.

In the last 2 days, we captured a major terrorist named Hambali. He's a known killer who was a close associate of September the 11th mastermind Khalid Sheikh

Mohammed. Hambali was one of the world's most lethal terrorists, who is suspected of planning major terrorist operations, including that which occurred in Bali, Indonesia, and other recent attacks. He is no longer a problem to those of us who love freedom, and neither are nearly two-thirds of known senior Al Qaida leaders, operational managers, and key facilitators who have been captured or have been killed.

Now, we're making progress. Slowly but surely, we're doing our duty to our fellow citizens. Now, Al Qaida is still active, and they're still recruiting, and they're still a threat because we won't cower. Its leaders and foot soldiers continue to plot against the American people. But every terrorist can be certain of this: Wherever they are, we will hunt them down one by one until they are no longer a threat to the people who live in the United States of America.

Many of you served in Operation Enduring Freedom, and we thank you for your service. You can be proud of help—to liberate the good people of Afghanistan from the thugs who turned that country into a training camp for Al Qaida terrorists. You enforced the doctrine which said, "If you harbor a terrorist, if you hide a terrorist, if you feed a terrorist, you're just as guilty as the terrorists." And the Taliban found out what we meant.

Afghanistan today is a friend of the United States of America. It is not a haven for America's terrorist enemies. As NATO assumes a leading role in keeping Afghanistan secure, we're helping with the reconstruction and the founding of a democratic government. We're making steady progress in Afghanistan. New roads are being built. Medical clinics are opening. There are new schools in Afghanistan where many young girls are now going to school for the first time, thanks to the United States of America.

We've also helped to build an Afghan national army. We want the Afghan people to defend themselves at some point in time.

This army launched its first major operation, called Warrior Sweep, which are hunting down the terrorists along with the help of the United States of America. Now, thanks to the United States and our fine allies, Afghanistan is no longer a haven for terror. The Taliban is history, and the Afghan people are free.

The war on terror also continues in Iraq. Make no mistake about it: Iraq is part of the war on terror. Our coalition forces are still engaged in an essential mission. We met the major combat objectives in Operation Iraqi Freedom by removing a regime that persecuted Iraqis, that supported terrorists, and that was armed to threaten the peace of the world. All the world is now seeing just how badly the Iraqi people suffered under this brutal dictator. The Iraqi people themselves are seeing a new day, thanks to the brave men and women who came to liberate them.

Thanks to our military, Iraqi citizens do not have to fear a secret police, arbitrary arrests, or loved ones lost forever in mass graves. Thanks to our military, the torture chambers of a dictator are closed; the prison cells for children are empty. Thanks to our military, Saddam Hussein will never threaten anybody with a weapon of mass destruction.

Many members of the former regime challenged our military and had their day of reckoning, and the other ones still in there have a lot to worry about. Parts of Iraq are still dangerous because freedom has enemies inside of Iraq. Men loyal to the fallen regime, some joined by foreign terrorists, are trying to prevent order and stability.

We're on the offensive against these killers. We're going after them. We'll raid their hiding places, and we'll find them. The brave Americans who carry out these missions can know they will have every tool and every resource they need to defend themselves and to do the job they were sent to do.

The terrorists will meet their end, and in the meantime, the Iraqi people are making steady progress in building a stable society and beginning to form a democratic government. Iraq's new Governing Council represents the Nation's diverse groups. In the months ahead, Iraqis will begin drafting a new constitution, and this will prepare the way for elections. America and our coalition are training Iraqi civil defense and police forces so they can patrol their own cities and their own villages. We're training a new army, an army that defends the people instead of terrorizes them.

Life is returning to normal for a lot of citizens in Iraq. Hospitals and universities have opened. In many places, water and other utility services are reaching pre-war levels. For the first time, a free press is operating in Iraq. Across Iraq, nearly all schoolchildren have completed their exams. And now those children are receiving a real education without the hateful propaganda of Saddam Hussein.

By the hard efforts of our military, we are keeping our word to the world and to the Iraqi people. The illegal weapons hidden by the former regime will be found. The free and representative government Iraqis are building is there to stay.

A free and peaceful Iraq is an important part of winning the war on terror. A free Iraq will no longer be a training ground for terrorists, will no longer supply them with money or weapons. A free Iraq will help to rid the Middle East of resentment and violence and radicalism. A free Iraq will show all nations of the region that human freedom brings progress and prosperity. By working for peace and stability in the Middle East, we're making America and future generations of Americans more secure.

Our actions in Iraq are part of a duty we have accepted across the world. We're keeping our resolve, and we will stay focused on the war on terror. The United States will not stand by and wait for another attack. We will not trust the restraint or good intentions of evil people. We will oppose terrorists and all who support them. We will not permit any terrorist group or outlaw regime to threaten us with weapons of mass destruction. And when necessary, we will act decisively to protect the lives of our fellow citizens.

As our Nation confronts great challenges, we rely, as always, on the goodness and courage of the men and women of our military. Like all our men and women who continue to serve in Iraq, you've done hard duty far from home and family, and I know you'll never forget the people who fought at your side. As a major from Miramar said of his fellow marines who served in Iraq, "They are my brothers and sisters." Each of you recalls especially the ones who gave their lives for freedom of others. The United States will always honor their memory. And today we ask the Almighty's blessings on those who grieve here on Earth for their loved ones.

I know you're proud to wear the same uniform they wore. Each of you has chosen—you have made the choice to fill a great calling, to live by a code of honor, in service to your Nation, for the safety and security of your fellow citizens. You and I have taken an oath to defend America. We're meeting that duty together, and I am proud to be the Commander in Chief of such a fabulous group of men and women who wear our uniform.

May God bless you. May God bless you and your families. May God continue to bless the United States of America. *Semper fi.*

NOTE: The President spoke at 12:23 p.m. In his remarks, he referred to Lt. Gen. James T. Conway, USMC, commanding general, I Marine Expeditionary Force; Maj. Gen. James F. Amos, USMC, commanding general, 3d Marine Aircraft Wing; Maj. Gen. (Select) Jon A. Gallinetti, USMC, commander, Marine Corps Air Bases Western Area, and commanding general, Marine Corps Air Station Miramar; Nurjaman

Riduan Isamuddin (known as Hambali), Al Qaida's chief operational planner in Southeast Asia; Khalid Sheikh Mohammed, senior Al Qaida leader responsible for planning the September 11, 2001, terrorist attack, who was captured in Pakistan on March 1; and former President Saddam Hussein of Iraq.

Remarks on the Power Blackout in Portions of North America and an Exchange With Reporters in San Diego, California
August 14, 2003

The President. Today our country—a major portion of our country was affected by rolling blackout. Canada was affected; over 10 million people in Canada were affected as well. And I have been working with Federal officials to make sure the response to this situation was quick and thorough, and I believe it has been.

We're focused on two major things right now. One is to work with State and local authorities to manage the consequences of this rolling blackout. In my judgment, the Governors and mayors of the affected States and cities have responded very well. We've offered all the help they need to help people cope with this blackout. And they've—to this moment have said they've got the resources necessary to handle it. The emergency preparedness teams at the local level and the State level are responding very well.

I also want to thank the people in the affected cities and States for their calm response to this emergency situation. It has been remarkable to watch on television how resolved the people are about dealing with this situation, and it's—I'm grateful for that. And I know their neighbors are grateful as well for the proper and calm response.

The other thing, of course, we're working on is to get electricity up and running as quickly as possible. And Federal officials are working with State and local officials to get the electricity grid up and running. Our goal, of course, is to do this as quickly as possible. Obviously, the sooner we can get electricity up, the more normal people's lives will become.

One thing I think I can say for certain is that this was not a terrorist act. I've heard reports about a lightning strike in Niagara Falls, New York, and we're—Federal officials, of course, are investigating the veracity of that. We'll find out here what caused the blackout. But most importantly, what we now need to do is fix the problem and to get electricity up and running as quickly as possible.

I was pleased to hear that many of the airports up East are beginning to have flights leave, and that's good. So in other words, slowly but surely, we're coping with this massive national problem. Millions of people's lives are affected. I fully understand that their lives will not be normal for the short run and hope that they continue to cope with this in a manner that they have done so far. I'm confident we can get things up and running as quickly as possible, and people's lives will go back to normal.

Yes.

Security of the Power Grid

Q. Mr. President, does this suggest that, even with all the attention paid to homeland security, that the electrical grid is still vulnerable, should it have been a terrorist attack?

The President. Well, I think, you know, one of the things we'll have to do, of course, is take an assessment of why the cascade was so significant, why it was able to ripple so significantly throughout our system up East. And that'll be a very important part of the investigation once we deal with the immediate—and the immediate, of course, is to take care of people.

You know, for example, in New York City, Mayor Bloomberg has ordered out thousands of police officers on the street to help bring calm. Firefighters are working overtime. Emergency crews are out working well. My focus is to work with State and local authorities to help deal with the immediate problem. Of course, we'll have time to look at it and determine whether or not our grid needs to be modernized. I happen to think it does and have said so all along. But this will be—this is going to be an interesting lesson for our country, and we'll have to respond to it.

Cause of the Blackout

Q. Mr. President.

The President. Yes.

Q. Do we know why this happened?

The President. Well, as I say, I saw a preliminary report. But we'll find out why, and we'll deal with the problem.

Federal/State/Local Cooperation

Q. Mr. President, you said that the State and locals had said they have all the resources they need. Can you talk about what the Federal Government might do or might already be doing to help them out?

The President. Well, one thing, of course, we're doing is we're getting the airlines running. The FAA is—as I understand, has cleared flights out of LaGuardia and Newark, for example.

The organization of Homeland Security is aimed at quick communications with State and local authorities, and I think that that communication was quick and thorough. I talked to Secretary Ridge several times. Governors have been notified, and mayors have been notified, and we're prepared to do anything that we can upon request.

Q. But it doesn't sound like they've asked you yet to do very——

The President. Not much, because they're well prepared. I mean, the first thing that I think Americans ought to be pleased about is the fact that we're better organized today than we were 2½ years ago to deal with an emergency, and the system responded well. Secretary Ridge was telling me 30 minutes ago how quickly the local authorities responded and how good the communications were between the Federal Government, the State government, the local government.

It's a serious situation, but the people whose lives have been affected need to know there's a lot of people working to enable them to get on about their lives in a normal way. And hopefully, electricity will be restored soon. I can't tell you exactly when, but I know a lot of people are working overtime to get it done.

Thank you all.

NOTE: The President spoke at 5:24 p.m. at the Manchester Grand Hyatt. In his remarks, he referred to Mayor Michael Bloomberg of New York City.

Remarks at a Bush-Cheney Dinner in San Diego
August 14, 2003

The President. Thanks for the warm welcome. It's really great to be back in San Diego, California. What a fabulous city. I want to thank you for your help. You all have done a tremendous job of helping us get started in the campaign. The way I look at it is, you're laying the groundwork for what will be a great nationwide victory in November of '04.

I appreciate your generosity. But I'm going to warn you, I need your help in energizing the grassroots, for putting up the signs and making the phone calls and telling your fellow citizens—Republican, Democrat, independent, could care less—that ours is a message that is hopeful for every single person who lives in this country.

I'm loosening up—[laughter]—and I'm getting ready. But the political season will come in its own time, because I have a job to do for the American people. I'm focused on the people's business. We have a lot on our agenda, and over the next months I will continue to work hard to earn the confidence of our fellow Americans by making sure America is secure and strong and prosperous and free.

My only regret is that First Lady Laura Bush isn't here tonight too. She is visiting her mother in Midland, Texas.

Audience member. [Inaudible]

The President. You're right. [Laughter] I am really proud of her. She is a fabulous First Lady. But most important, she's a great mother and a great wife, and I love her dearly.

I want to thank my friend Brad Freeman. I thought for a minute he was going to announce for Governor, he spoke so long. [Laughter] He's been a longtime friend, just as has Gerry Parsky. Both of these friends are working hard in '04, just like they did—for the '04 election, just like they did in 2000. I'm proud to stand with them.

I also want to thank my friend Mercer Reynolds. Mercer is from Cincinnati, Ohio. He's dedicating a lot of time to make sure our national finance effort is as strong as I know it's going to be. I appreciate you, Mercer.

We've got members of the congressional delegation here today from the mighty State of California, Duncan Hunter and "Duke" Cunningham and Darrell Issa. I'm honored they're here.

I appreciate the Mayor, Dick Murphy, for greeting me. Mr. Mayor, thank you for your strong support. I want to thank the event cochairmen here from San Diego. You all have done a fantastic job. I'm proud to call you friends, and I thank you for your support.

In the last 2½ years, our Nation has acted decisively to confront great challenges. I came to this office to solve problems, not to pass them on to future Presidents and to future generations. I came to seize opportunities instead of letting them slip away, and we are meeting the tests of our time.

Terrorists declared war on the United States of America, and war is what they got. We have captured or killed many key leaders of the Al Qaida network, and the rest of them know we're on their trail. In Afghanistan and Iraq, we gave ultimatums to terror regimes. Those regimes chose defiance, and those regimes are no more. Fifty million people in those two countries once lived under tyranny, and now they live in freedom.

Two-and-a-half years ago, our military was not receiving the resources it needed, and morale was beginning to suffer. We increased the defense budget to prepare for the threats of a new era. And today, no one in the world can question the skill and the strength and the spirit of the United States military.

Two-and-a-half years ago, we inherited an economy in recession, and then our country was attacked. And scandals in corporate America became evident, and war began to affect the people's confidence. But we acted. We passed tough new laws to hold corporate criminals to account. And to get the economy going again, I have twice led the United States Congress to pass historic tax relief for the American people. Here is what I believe and here is what we know: When Americans have more take-home pay to spend, to save, or invest, the whole economy grows, and people are then more likely to find a job.

I also understand whose money we spend in Washington. It's not the Government's money; it's the people's money. We're returning more money to people to help them raise their families. We're reducing taxes on dividends and capital gains to encourage investment. We're giving small businesses incentives to expand and hire new people. With all these actions, we've laid the foundation for greater prosperity and more jobs across America, so that every single person in this country can realize the great American Dream.

Two-and-a-half years ago, there was a lot of talk about education reform, but there wasn't much action. So I called for and Congress passed the No Child Left Behind Act. With a solid bipartisan majority, we delivered the most dramatic education reforms in a generation. We bring high standards and strong accountability measures to every public school in America. See, we believe every child can learn the basics of reading and math, and we expect every school to teach the basics of reading and math. This administration is challenging the soft bigotry of low expectations. The days of excuse-making are over. We expect results in every classroom all across America so that not one single child is left behind.

We reorganized the Government and created the Department of Homeland Security to safeguard our borders and ports and to protect the American people. We passed trade promotion authority to open up new markets for California's manufacturers and entrepreneurs and ranchers and farmers. We passed a budget agreement that is helping to maintain spending discipline in Washington, DC. On issue after issue, this administration has acted on principle, has kept its word, and has made progress for the American people.

The United States Congress has shared these great achievements, and I appreciate the hard work of the Members of Congress. I enjoy a great relationship with Speaker Denny Hastert and Majority Leader Bill Frist. We're going to continue to work together to change the tone of Washington and focus on the people's business by focusing on results. And those are the kind of people I've asked to serve in my administration. I have put together a fantastic team of Americans to serve the American people.

We've got no finer Vice President in our history than Dick Cheney. Mother might have a different view. [*Laughter*]

In 2½ years, we have come far, but our work is only beginning. I have set great goals worthy of a great nation. First, America is committed to expanding the realm of freedom and peace for our own security and for the benefit of the world. And second, in our own country, we must work for a society of prosperity and compassion, so that every citizen has a chance to work and succeed and to realize the great promise of our country.

It is clear that the future of freedom and peace depends on the actions of America. This Nation is freedom's home and freedom's defender. We welcome this charge of history, and we're keeping it.

Our war on terror continues. The enemies of freedom are not idle, and neither are we. This country will not rest. We will not tire, and we will not stop until this danger to civilization is removed.

Yet, our national interest involves more than eliminating aggressive threats to our safety. Our greatest security comes from the advance of human liberty, because free nations do not support terror, free nations do not attack their neighbors, and free nations do not threaten the world with weapons of mass terror. Americans believe that freedom is the deepest need and hope of every human heart. We believe that freedom is the right of every person. And we believe that freedom is the future of every nation.

America also understands that unprecedented influence brings tremendous responsibilities. We have duties in the world. When we see disease and starvation and hopeless poverty, we will not turn away.

In the continent of Africa, this great, compassionate, strong Nation is committed to bringing the healing power of medicine to millions of men and women and children now suffering with AIDS. This great land is taking the lead. We are leading the world in this incredibly important work of human rescue.

We face challenges at home, and our actions will prove that we're equal to those challenges. I will continue to work to create a favorable condition for economic growth and vitality, until everybody who wants to work and can't find a job today will be able to find a job.

And we have a duty to keep our commitment to America's seniors by strengthening and modernizing Medicare. A few weeks ago, Congress took historic action to improve the lives of older Americans. For the first time since the creation of Medicare, the House and the Senate have passed reforms to increase the choices for our seniors and to provide coverage for prescription drugs. The next step is for both Houses to come together to iron out some details and to get a bill to my desk. We have an obligation to the seniors of America to modernize the Medicare system.

And for the sake of our health care system, we need to cut down on frivolous lawsuits, which increase the cost of medicine. People who have been harmed by a doctor deserve their day in court. Yet, the system should not reward lawyers who are simply fishing for rich settlements. Because frivolous lawsuits drive up the cost of health care, they affect the Federal budget. Medical liability reform is a national issue that requires a national solution. The House of Representatives has passed a good bill to reform the system. The bill is stuck in the Senate. The Senate must act on behalf of the American people. They must realize that nobody in America has ever been healed by a frivolous lawsuit.

I have a responsibility as President to make sure the judicial system runs well. And I've met that duty. I have nominated superb women and men for the Federal courts, people who will interpret the law, not legislate from the bench.

In California, I've nominated Carolyn Kuhl to the Ninth Circuit Court of Appeals. She has tremendous bipartisan support. She's respected as a State judge. Yet, some Senators are distorting Judge Kuhl's record, and they're threatening to block an up-or-down vote. And this is happening to too many of the judges I've nominated, and it is wrong. All the judicial nominees deserve a fair hearing and an up-or-down vote on the Senate floor. It is time for some Members of the United States Senate to stop playing politics with American justice.

The United States Congress needs to complete work on a comprehensive energy plan. Our Nation must promote energy efficiency and conservation. We must work to develop cleaner technology to help us explore for energy in an environmentally sensitive way. Yet, for the sake of economic security and for the sake of national security, we must be less dependent on foreign sources of energy.

Our strong and prosperous Nation must also be a compassionate nation. I will continue to advance our agenda of compassionate conservatism by applying the best and most innovative ideas to the task of helping fellow citizens in need.

There are still millions of men and women who want to end their dependence on Government and become independent through hard work. We must build on the success of welfare reform to bring work and dignity into the lives of more of our citizens. Congress should complete the "Citizen Service Act" so more Americans can serve their communities and their country. And both Houses should reach agreement on my Faith-Based Initiative to support the armies of compassion that are mentoring children, that are caring for the homeless, and that are offering hope to the addicted.

A compassionate society must promote opportunity for all, including the independence and dignity that come from ownership. This administration is firmly committed and will constantly strive to promote an ownership society in America. We want more people owning their home. We have a minority home ownership gap in America, and I have put forth a plan to solve it.

We want more people to manage and own their own health care accounts. We want people to own and manage their own retirement accounts. We want more people to own and operate their own small business, because, you see, we understand that when a person owns something in America, he or she has a vital stake in the future of our country.

In a compassionate society, people respect one another and take responsibility for the decisions they make. We're changing the culture of America from one that has said, "If it feels good, do it," and "If you've got a problem, blame somebody else," to a culture in which each of us understands we are responsible for the decisions we make in life. If you are fortunate enough to be a mom or a dad, you're responsible for loving your child with all your heart and all your soul. If you're concerned about the quality of education in your community, you're responsible for doing something about it. If you are a CEO in America, you're responsible for telling the truth to your shareholders and your employees. And in this new responsibility, each of us is responsible for loving our neighbor just like we'd like to be loved ourself.

Things are changing in America to the better. We can see a culture of service and responsibility growing around us. I started what we call the USA Freedom Corps to encourage Americans to extend a compas-sionate hand to neighbors in need. And the response has been fantastic. People are signing up. People want to serve something greater than themselves.

Our charities and our faith-based institutions are strong and they're vibrant, bringing important help to people who hurt. Policemen and firefighters and people who wear our Nation's uniform are reminding us what it means to sacrifice for something greater than yourself. Once again, the children of America believe in heroes, because they see them every day.

In these challenging times, the world has seen the resolve and the courage of America. And I've been privileged to see the compassion and the character of the American people. All the tests of the last 2½ years have come to the right nation. We're a strong country, and we use that strength to defend the peace. We're an optimistic country, confident in ourselves and in ideals bigger than ourselves.

Abroad, we seek to lift whole nations by spreading freedom. And at home, we seek to lift up lives by spreading opportunity to every corner of America. This is the work that history has set before us, and we welcome it. And we know that for our country and for our cause, the best days lie ahead.

Thank you for coming. May God bless.

NOTE: The President spoke at 6:30 p.m. at the San Diego Convention Center. In his remarks, he referred to Brad Freeman, California State finance chairman, and Mercer Reynolds, national finance chairman, Bush-Cheney '04, Inc.; Gerald Parsky, chairman, Team California, California Republican Party; and Mayor Dick Murphy of San Diego, CA.

Exchange With Reporters in Thousand Oaks, California
August 15, 2003

Q. Do you have time for a couple of questions?

The President. Yes, I'll answer a couple of questions.

North American Power Blackout/Energy Legislation

Q. Can you update us on the situation back East, what you've heard, whether there's been any progress toward finding out what possibly caused the blackout?

The President. Yes, it's going to take a while, I think. But we will find out what caused the blackout, and we'll deal with it. I view it as a wake-up call. You know, I've been concerned that our infrastructure—the delivery system is old and antiquated. And I think this is an indication of the fact that we need to modernize the electricity grid.

So it's a good opportunity for us to analyze what went wrong and to deal with it. We don't know yet what went wrong, but we will.

Q. There's a bill pending in Congress, the energy bill, that's pretty broad in scope. There's also a piece of that bill that's smaller that would fix this particular problem. Would you urge Congress to act on that?

The President. Yes, I think what we need to do is take a look at what went wrong, analyze the problem, and come up with a solution. And I think it's very important—I'm going to say this down here in the remarks—the people in New York and in the Northeast and in parts of the Midwest were—showed the great character of America in very difficult circumstances. The people responded in calm fashion. They worked hard to help their neighbors in need, and they showed the rest of the country and the world the true mettle of the American people.

As I said yesterday, I'm most pleased by the fact that we've got a—our emergency response was good. They acted well. And I doubt that would have happened—the response would have been this good—prior to September the 11th. But the creation of the Homeland Security Department, coupled with the modernization of communications between State and local and Federal officials, really enabled the system to work well. And now we've got to figure out how to make the electricity system have the redundancy necessary so that if there is an outage like there has been throughout our history, that it doesn't affect as many people as it did in the past.

Q. Sir, are you worried, though, that power still isn't restored to so many millions of people and may not be through the weekend?

The President. Well, I think, you know—listen, everybody is working hard to get it restored as quickly as possible. I think it's going to take a while to get 100 percent of the power up and running. And that's why it's important for our citizens who have got electricity in the Northeast and the Midwest would be wise about how they use the electricity. They must conserve, because the more conservation there is now, the more likely it is their neighbor is going to end up having electricity in a quicker fashion.

Q. In recent weeks, you have mentioned several times the need to pass your comprehensive energy plan. Is there anything in there that would have helped or mitigated this?

The President. Well, I think part of the plan recognizes that the grid needs to be modernized, the delivery systems need to be modernized. And obviously something like this isn't going to happen overnight. But it is—it begins to address the problem, that this particular incident has made abundantly clear to the American people that we've got an antiquated system, and now we've got to figure out what went wrong and how to address it. And I'm confident we will.

Q. You said yesterday that while you've made some offers of Federal assistance, the States and locals didn't really seem to need much help; they had it under control. Is that still the situation?

The President. Actually, as I understand it, as of this morning, at about 5:30 a.m. Pacific Coast time, there was a request for a generator by New York City from the Department of Defense, which we're now working on delivering.

Look, for example, Tommy Thompson started calling around to hospitals and ask-

ing, did everybody get what they need? And Tom Ridge was calling, which made it clear—abundantly clear—that where we had assets that could help, we're more than willing to help. This is a national problem, and the Federal Government has got a responsibility to help local and State officials. As far as I know, the one specific request to date was this generator.

Thank you all.

NOTE: The exchange began at 8:35 a.m. at the Santa Monica Mountains National Recreation Area. A tape was not available for verification of the content of this exchange.

Remarks at the Santa Monica Mountains National Recreation Area in Thousand Oaks, California
August 15, 2003

Thank you all for coming. This is a beautiful place to gather. It's a little different from Crawford—[*laughter*]—but the work is just as hard. If it looks like I'm kind of sweaty, it's because I am. [*Laughter*] I've been shoveling dirt to make sure the trails are maintained so people can use them.

Before I talk about our park system, I do want to say that the people of New York City and New York State and the people of the Northeast and Midwest who were affected by last night's blackout were—kept their calm, were decent to their neighbors, really showed the rest of the country and the world the true character of the American people. I want to thank all of them for how they dealt with a very difficult situation and assure them that Federal, State, and local authorities are working hard to get the power up and running to take care of the needs of the people. And at the same time, we'll figure out what went wrong, and we'll address it. We will view this rolling blackout as a wake-up call, a wake-up call for the need to

modernize our electricity delivery systems, and we'll respond.

And what we're here to talk about today is how do we make sure our national asset, the National Park System, has got a modern infrastructure system as well, so that the people who own the park, the American people, can use the parks. After all, the parks are owned by the people of this country, and we want the park system to work well, and we want there to be a modern infrastructure. We want the 80 million acres of national park land to be accessible and comfortable to use for the American people, and at the same time, we want to respect nature and honor God's great gift to our country by conserving these beautiful properties all across the country.

The responsibility to maintain our parks has not always been met in America. It's a problem that we will address, and helping me address the problem is the Secretary of the Interior, Gale Norton. You know, I picked somebody from the West to run the Interior Department because I felt like, in her case, she was sensitive to the needs of the people and to the needs of the land. And she's doing a heck of a good job on behalf of the American people. And I appreciate you being here.

And Fran Mainella is with us today. She's the Director of the National Park Service. Hi, Fran. When I tell you what we're going to do about maintaining our parks, really what I'm doing is telling you what she's going to do—[laughter]—in collaboration with the good folks who work for the Interior Department, the good folks who wear the hats, the people that are out on the frontline of maintaining our parks and making sure our parks are accessible to the American people, the park rangers, the dedicated employees who are—really make a difference in the people's lives. I want to thank you all for your hard work on behalf of the American people.

I had a chance to spend some quality time with such a person, Woody Smeck; he's the Superintendent of the Santa Monica Mountains. [Applause] Woody, it's a good sign when people who work with you cheer for you. [Laughter] I can see why. Woody cares a lot about the land. He cares deeply about the people who use the land. Woody has got a tough job. He manages the largest urban park in America, but it's a park that requires collaboration with State officials—and I want to thank the State officials who are here—requires cooperation with the local officials, and it requires collaboration with private property owners in order to make sure the park works the way we want it to work. And Woody, you're doing a heck of a good job, and I appreciate your service to our country.

We've got some mayors with us today, and I'm honored you all are here. Andy Fox and Greg Hill and James Bozajian are here with us. The local mayors of Thousand Oaks and Redondo Beach and Calabasas, California, are integral players in making sure the park system works. I asked the question, how are the local people—they were responding well to your initiatives that Woody has laid out? And he said, "Absolutely." He said the cooperation is fantastic. So Mayors, I want to thank you for coming, but more importantly, I want to thank you for doing your job in a way that makes your citizens proud.

I'm also am so proud that my friend Elton Gallegly is here with us. He is the congressman from this area. He cares a lot about this park. He cares a lot about the people who live in this congressional district. And Elton and I are going to work hard to make sure the appropriations process reflects our desire, our common desire, to maintain the park system of America. And Elton, thank you for coming.

One of the things that makes the park systems go and really function well is the volunteer effort all around our country, and you've got a fantastic volunteer effort here. I met two such people today. Melvin Caradine, he is a volunteer here. He leads tours. He shares his knowledge with the people who come to visit. And Ralph Waycott, he is the volunteer coordinator for the Rancho Sierra Vista Nursery. I don't know if Ralph was a botanist in college or not—[laughter]—but it sure sounded like it. [Laughter] He knows a lot about what he's talking about.

He and Melvin really represent the best of the country, when you think about it—people who are willing to take time out of their lives and to, in this case, make the park system work and make our fellow citizens feel comfortable and knowledgeable when they come to the parks. I'm told there's a couple hundred volunteers who come here on a regular basis to help make sure this park works, and I want to thank you. And I urge others that if you're interested in serving your community, interested in serving your country, volunteer at a park. Make it work better. Help restore it. Help the hard-working employees and dedicated folks that are in charge of our parks; help make their job easier. And so for those of you who are here who volunteer, thanks a lot for what you do.

What's interesting about this place is, there are over 33 million visitors who come here. That's a lot. [*Laughter*] There are a lot of people who use this park, and that's good. That's the way it should be. And I can see why they come. It's a beautiful spot. Fantastic trails—it's a good opportunity for people to care of their physiques—[*laughter*]—by taking off in the hills and a getting yourself a good walk on a daily basis. But 33 million people use this.

The truth of the matter is, God designed this park's beauty, but men and women make sure it remains beautiful. And that's an important part about conservation: It's man's ability to make sure that God's beauty is maintained and preserved and that when people use it, they use it in a respectful way. The park rangers and the landowners and the local businesses have made it so that people from all over the world can come here and use this place. Because of wise stewardship, this park has flourished. This is good for all of us, to understand what works.

You see, Gale mentioned we've got 388 national park areas. Now, this includes historic sites and battlefields and recreation areas and monuments and shores. But all of them are a point of pride for the local communities surrounding the particular site, and they need to be a point of pride for our country as well. And after all, our park system is the crown jewel of America's recreation system.

In the past, though, the sites have really, in some cases, been ignored. And that's the reality, and that's the truth. For many years, our Federal Government did not even have the basic information it needed to set priorities about what should be repaired or not repaired, because we had a haphazard system of dealing with the people's asset. We just kind of—as we say down there, catch as catch can, without

a national strategy to maintain this incredibly important asset.

And so I've set out to do something about it. And the first thing we've got to do is, we've got to get a commitment from the appropriators in Congress to spend enough money to maintain our parks. And so I'm calling on Congress to spend $5 billion over the next 5 years. I made that call 2 years ago. I've said, "If you're interested in helping us maintain the park system, put some money out there so that we can actually do the job." And Congress responded for the last 2 years by appropriating $1.8 billion to meet the needs to make sure our parks are modernized and maintained and get the needed repairs to make the parks accessible to the people. In this year's budget, this year's request, I put in $1.1 billion and then plan on asking 2.2 total for '05 and '06, so that we spend $5 billion on maintenance projects and repair projects in the park system all across the country.

And I expect Congress to respond. We've got a national asset that in some cases needs needed repairs, and now is the time to get after it on behalf of the American people. This is a problem, and now let's address the problem. And I think they'll respond.

In the first 2 years in my administration, under Gale and Fran's leadership, we've undertaken 900 park maintenance projects, and that's a good start. We're making progress. We'll do another 500 this year and 400 next year. Slowly but surely, we're beginning to deal with the backlog of much needed maintenance.

And these are projects that—I'll talk about some of them we're doing here, under Woody's supervision, but for example, there's repairs to a visitors center at Cape Cod National Seashore. I mean, when visitors show up for the Cape Cod National Seashore and its beauty, we want there to be a visitors center that's worth going into. We want the toilets to flush. [*Laughter*] We want the potholes to be taken out of the parking lot. Whatever the problem is, we need to address it so that the people, when it comes to using their own park, are able to do so in a comfortable way.

We've got a new wastewater system being developed at Yellowstone National Park, and that's important. We've got a new lighting and electrical systems on the U.S. *Arizona* Memorial at Pearl Harbor. At the Redwood National Park, we're removing abandoned roads to protect the park and to improve the watershed. There are just practical things that need to be done on a park-by-park basis in order to do our job on behalf of the American people.

In order to have a strategy, we felt it was important to develop a national system to take a national inventory so you can set priorities. If the information is scattered and haphazard, you'll have a haphazard and scattered response to a problem. And so I tasked Gale and Fran with the idea of setting up a national database that will track maintenance needs on a asset-by-asset basis. And so the Interior Department and the parks department have tasked the park superintendents to conduct an inventory of buildings and trails and monument roads and assets and let us know the condition on a park-by-park basis. And the data will be centralized in Washington. So far, 384 out of the 388 park superintendents have responded. We're chasing down the other four—[*laughter*]—to make sure we get inventories.

And then when you get an assessment of what is needed, we can set priorities. And when you set priorities, it is more likely that the $5 billion will be spent wisely on behalf of the American people to maintain their park system.

In the Santa Monica Mountains, Woody was telling me that—first of all, he was one of the first to apply to the system, first to input into the system. He determined that the buildings were in good shape but the trails were eroded and needed work. He sent out a priority list to Washington, DC. I think we've sent back

$2.4 million of trail maintenance money, if I'm not mistaken, which has improved a lot of the trails for the people who use the trails.

And as importantly, you've made it possible for people to see the beauty of the land, to access the beauty without destroying the land. The more modern the trail system, the more repaired our trail system is, the less likely it is that people will trample the beauty—that they'll stay on the trails, and so you'll be able to have people take wonderful hikes or bike rides throughout this beautiful countryside without the fear of damaging the countryside.

Woody accessed the system; he put out a plan; and the Government responded. And we expect other park superintendents to do so. And when Congress appropriates the money, which I'm confident they will, particularly after this moment—[*laughter*]—that we'll better spend the money on behalf of the people.

As Woody said, for the first time, we now have a system that moves us from reactive to proactive, and that's how we're able to track real improvements. And that's what we're going to be with America's park system: We're going to be proactive and doing what's right on behalf of the American people.

I mentioned the volunteers that make these parks work—and particularly, this park work. And I ran into some folks from Woodrow Wilson East High School in Los Angeles. Stan is with us. Stan is a teacher. Thank you, Stan, for being a teacher. Rosa Gomez and Susan Lam and Denise Sanchez are with us as well. Thank you all for coming. I see other students from Woodrow Wilson, as well, or Wilson—the Wilson Mules, I take it. [*Laughter*] But we were repairing the trails together. By the way, the three ladies I just mentioned are high school grads. They're going to college. A couple of them are the first time anybody in their family has ever gone to college, which is fabulous.

But I want to thank them for coming out and working hard on the trails. It's a—it's got to be a fantastic educational experience to get out in this beautiful part of our country and put something back into the system. After all, that's really what makes America great, when people realize that patriotism means serving something greater than yourself, serving the country you love, doing your part to make sure that the community in which you live is as good as it can possibly be, loving a neighbor just like you'd like to be loved yourself. Whether it be maintaining park roads or helping somebody who hurts, helping somebody who's addicted, we can all make a difference in changing our country.

And that's what the Harmans are doing. I ran into Terry and Holly Harman. Terry and Holly challenged me to a 6-mile run. [*Laughter*] I took one look at them; I said, "No thanks." [*Laughter*] But the Harmans are here. They love to use the park. They ride their bikes; they run. They've enjoyed this park for a lot of years, and part of their enjoyment is to make it a better place for other people. I want to tell you what Terry said. He said volunteering here has helped him feel ownership for the park. You're kind of protective. You realize, in his words, "This is my park too."

Well, it is your park. It's the park of every person who lives in America, and we've got to remember that. We're stewards of the people land. We have an obligation to leave this park a better place than when we found it. And there's no doubt in my mind, thanks to the hard work of the park employees, to the volunteers who come, thanks to a Congress that recognizes that we need to maintain this incredibly important asset for our country, we'll do our job.

Thanks for coming. May God continue to bless our country.

NOTE: The President spoke at 9:17 a.m. In his remarks, he referred to Stan Katase, teacher, Woodrow Wilson High School.

Remarks at a Bush-Cheney Luncheon in Irvine, California
August 15, 2003

Thank you very much. Thanks for the warm welcome. Thanks for the friendship. It's great to be back in the great State of California, and it's wonderful to see so many friends from Orange County. I'm honored you all are here. I appreciate the strong financial support you've given.

I want to thank those who have worked so hard to make this a major success. Really what we're doing is, we're laying the foundation for next year's campaign, putting the process in place and the foundation in place for what's going to be a great victory in November of '04.

And I need to count on you, particularly when it comes to energizing the vote, to making sure the grassroots gets our message. I want you to remind your Republican friends, your Democrat friends, your independent friends that this administration is one that is serving all the people of the United States of America.

I'm getting ready—[*laughter*]—and I'm loosening up. [*Laughter*] But the political season will come in its own time. See, I've got a job to do, and right now I'm focused on the people's business. We'll continue to work hard to earn the confidence of the American people by keeping this Nation strong and secure and prosperous and free.

I regret that our First Lady is not with us. I just talked to Laura. She's in Midland visiting her mother, and I'm going to see her tonight for dinner. But she sends her love, and I tell you, I love her a lot. She is a great lady.

I appreciate my friends Brad Freeman and Gerry Parsky and Mercer Reynolds for working so hard to organize what is going to be a great nationwide effort in terms of collecting the resources necessary to run a viable campaign.

I want to thank Duf Sundheim, the party chairman of the State of California, for his leadership. I'm honored that members of the mighty California congressional delegation are with us, friends of mine, people who work hard on behalf of the citizens of California: Congressmen David Dreier and Ed Royce and Ken Calvert and Congressman Chris Cox. I want to thank them for coming.

I appreciate John Campbell and Bob Pacheco, State reps, people who represented their districts well and who were strong supporters of mine in 2000.

But most of all, I thank you all for coming.

In the last 2½ years, our Nation has acted decisively to confront great challenges. I came to this office to solve problems, not to pass them on to future presidents or future generations. I came to seize opportunities instead of letting them slip away. We are meeting the test of our time.

Terrorists declared war on the United States of America, and war is what they got. We have captured or killed many key leaders of Al Qaida, and the rest of them know we're on their trail. In Afghanistan and Iraq, we gave ultimatums to terror regimes. Those regimes chose defiance, and those regimes are no more. Fifty million people in those two countries once lived under tyranny, and now they live in freedom.

Two-and-a-half years ago, our military was not receiving the resources it needed, and morale was beginning to suffer. We increased the defense budget to prepare for the threats of a new era. And today, no one in the world can question the skill and the strength and the spirit of the United States military.

Two-and-a-half years ago, we inherited an economy in recession. And then our country was attacked, and we found out that there were some CEOs in America who forgot to tell the truth. We had corporate scandals. War affected the people's confidence. But we acted. We passed tough new laws to hold corporate criminals to account. And to get the economy going again, I have twice led the United States Congress to pass historic tax relief for the American people.

I believe that when Americans have more take-home pay to spend, to save, or invest, the whole economy grows, and someone is more likely to find a job. And I understand whose money we spend in Washington. It is not the Government's money; it is the people's money. We're returning more money to people to help them raise their families. We're reducing taxes on dividends and capital gains to encourage investment. We're providing small businesses with incentives to expand so they can hire people. With all these actions, we are laying the foundation for greater prosperity and more jobs across America so that every single citizen in this country can realize the great promise of America.

Two-and-a-half years ago, there was a lot of talk about education reform, but there wasn't much action. So I called for and the Congress passed the No Child Left Behind Act. With a solid bipartisan majority, we delivered the most dramatic education reform in a generation. We're bringing high standards and strong accountability measures to every public school in America. We believe every child can learn the basics of reading and math, and we expect every school in America to teach the basics of reading and math. This administration is challenging the soft bigotry of low expectations. The days of excuse-making are over. We expect results in return for Federal money in every classroom in America so that not one child is left behind.

We reorganized our Government to create the Department of Homeland Security to better safeguard our borders and ports and to protect the American people. We passed trade promotion authority to open up new markets for California manufacturers and farmers and ranchers and entrepreneurs. We passed budget agreements to help maintain much needed spending discipline in Washington, DC.

On issue after issue, this administration has acted on principle, has kept its word, and has made progress for the American people.

The United States Congress has shared in these great achievements, and I appreciate their hard work. I've got a great relationship with Speaker Hastert and Leader Frist. I'll continue to work with them to change the tone in Washington, DC, and to focus on results as opposed to process and politics.

And those are the kind of people I've assembled in my administration. I have put together a great administration on behalf of the American people. We have no finer Vice President in our Nation's history than Dick Cheney. Mother might have a second opinion. [*Laughter*]

In 2½ years, we've come far, but our work is only beginning. I've set great goals worthy of this great Nation. First, America is committed to expanding the realm of freedom and peace for our own security and for the benefit of the world. And second, in our own country, we must work for a society of prosperity and compassion so that every single citizen, regardless of their background, regardless of their religion, regardless of their status, has a chance to work and to succeed and realize the great promise of our land.

It is clear that the future of freedom and peace depend on the actions of America. This Nation is freedom's home and freedom's defender. We welcome this charge of history, and we're keeping it.

Our war on terror continues. The enemies of freedom are not idle, and neither are we. This country will not rest; we will not tire; we will not stop until this danger to civilization is removed.

Yet, our national interest involves more than eliminating aggressive threats to our security. Our greatest security comes from the advance of human liberty. Free nations do not support terror. Free nations do not attack their neighbors. And free nations do not threaten the world with weapons of mass terror. Americans believe that freedom is the deepest need and hope of every human heart. And we believe that freedom is the right of every person. And we believe that freedom is the future of every nation.

America also understands that unprecedented influence brings tremendous responsibilities. We have duties in the world. And when we see disease and starvation and hopeless poverty, we will not turn away. On the continent of Africa, America is now committed to bringing the healing power of medicine to millions of men and women and children now suffering with AIDS. I'm so proud of our great land. We're leading the world in this incredibly important work of human rescue.

We face challenges at home, and our actions are equal to those challenges. I will continue to work to lay the foundation for economic growth, to make sure the entrepreneurial spirit is strong, to encourage job creation so that anybody who wants to work today and can't find a job will be able to do so.

And we have a duty to keep our commitment to America's seniors by strengthening and modernizing Medicare. A few weeks ago, the Congress took historic action to improve the lives of older Americans. For the first time—the first time—since the creation of Medicare, the House and Senate have passed reforms to increase the choices for our seniors and to provide coverage for prescription drugs. The next step is for both bodies to get together and iron out some details and get a bill to my desk. The sooner they finish the job, the sooner

Americans will get a modernized Medicare system.

And for the sake of our health care system, we need to cut down on the frivolous lawsuits which increase the cost of medicine. People who have been harmed by a bad doc deserve their day in court. Yet, the system should not reward lawyers who are simply fishing for a rich settlement. Because frivolous lawsuits drive up the cost of health care, they affect the Federal budget; they affect the Medicare budget, the Medicaid budget, the veterans health care budget. Medical liability reform is a national issue that requires a national solution. The House of Representatives passed a good bill to reform the Senate—the system. It is stuck in the Senate. It is now time for the United States Senate to act on behalf of the patients of America. No one has ever been healed by a frivolous lawsuit.

I have a responsibility as President to make sure the judicial system runs well, and I have met that duty. I have nominated superb men and women for the Federal courts, people who will interpret the law, not legislate from the bench.

In California, I nominated Carolyn Kuhl to the Ninth Circuit Court of Appeals. She is a—tremendous bipartisan support. She's respected as a State judge. Yet, some Senators are distorting her record; they're threatening to block an up-or-down vote. Unfortunately, she's not alone. They're doing that to too many of my nominees, and that is wrong. All judicial nominees deserve a fair hearing and an up-or-down vote on the Senate floor. It is time for some Members of the United States Senate to stop playing politics with American justice.

The Congress needs to complete work on a comprehensive energy plan that, among other things, will help us modernize our infrastructure around America. We must promote energy efficiency and conservation, develop cleaner—develop technology to help us explore for energy in environmentally sensitive ways. But for the sake of economic security and for the sake of national security, we need to become less dependent on foreign sources of energy.

Our strong and prosperous Nation must also be a compassionate nation. I will continue to advance our agenda of compassionate conservatism. We will apply the best and most innovative and effective ideas to the task of helping our fellow citizens in need. There are still millions of men and women who want to end their dependence on Government and become independent through hard work. We must build on the success of welfare reform to bring work and dignity into the lives of more of our fellow citizens.

Congress should complete the "Citizen Service Act" to encourage more Americans to serve their communities and their country. And both Houses should reach agreement on my Faith-Based Initiative so that we can support the armies of compassion which are mentoring children, caring for the homeless, and offering hope to the addicted.

A compassionate society must promote opportunity for every citizen, including the independence and dignity that come from ownership. This administration will constantly strive to promote an ownership society in America. We want more people owning their own home. We have a minority homeownership gap in America, and I've got a plan to close that gap. We want people owning their own retirement systems and managing their own retirement systems. We want people controlling their own health care systems. We want more people owning and operating their own small business in America, because we understand that when somebody owns something, he or she has a vital stake in the future in the United States of America.

In a compassionate society, people respect one another and take responsibility for the decisions they make. We're changing the culture of America from one that has said, "If it feels good, do it," and "If you've got a problem, blame somebody else," to a culture in which each of us understands we are responsible for the decisions we make in life.

If you're fortunate enough to be a mother or a father, you're responsible for loving your child with all your heart and all your soul. If you're concerned about the quality of education in your community, you're responsible for doing something about it. If you're a CEO in America, you have the responsibility to tell the truth to your shareholders and your employees.

And in the responsibility society, each of us is responsible for loving our neighbor just like we'd like to be loved ourself. And we can see the culture of responsibility and service growing around us here in America. I started what's called the USA Freedom Corps to encourage Americans to extend a compassionate hand to a neighbor in need, and the response has been strong. People from all walks of life are signing up to figure out how to help and do their duty as an American citizen.

Charities are strong and the faith-based organizations are vibrant, bringing hope and healing to citizens who hurt. Policemen and firefighters and people who wear our Nation's uniform are reminding us what it means to sacrifice for something greater than yourself in life. Once again the chil-

dren believe in heroes, because they see them every day in America.

In these challenging times, the world has seen the resolve and the courage of America. And I've been privileged to see the compassion and the character of the American people. All the tests of the last 2½ years have come to the right nation. We are a strong country, and we use that strength to defend the peace. We're an optimistic country, confident in ourselves and in ideals bigger than ourselves.

Abroad, we seek to lift whole nations by spreading freedom. At home, we seek to lift up lives by spreading opportunity to every corner of America. This is the work that history has set before us. We welcome it. And we know that for our country and for our cause, the best days lie ahead.

May God bless America.

NOTE: The President spoke at 12:57 p.m. at the Hyatt Regency Irvine Hotel. In his remarks, he referred to Brad Freeman, California State finance chairman, and Mercer Reynolds, national finance chairman, Bush-Cheney '04, Inc.; and Gerald L. Parsky, Team California chairman, and Duf Sundheim, party chairman, California Republican Party. A portion of these remarks could not be verified because the tape was incomplete.

Memorandum on the 2003 Combined Federal Campaign
August 15, 2003

Memorandum for the Heads of Executive Departments and Agencies

Subject: 2003 Combined Federal Campaign

I am delighted that the Secretary of Housing and Urban Development, Mel R. Martinez, has agreed to serve as the Chair of the 2003 Combined Federal Campaign (CFC) of the National Capital Area. I ask

you to enthusiastically support the CFC by personally chairing the campaign in your agency and appointing a top official as your Vice Chair.

The Combined Federal Campaign is an important way for Federal employees to support thousands of worthy charities. Public servants not only contribute to the campaign but also assume leadership roles to ensure its success.

Your personal support and enthusiasm will help positively influence thousands of

employees and will guarantee another successful campaign.

GEORGE W. BUSH

NOTE: This memorandum was released by the Office of the Press Secretary on August 16.

Letter to Congressional Leaders Transmitting a Report on Iraq
August 15, 2003

Dear Mr. Speaker: (*Dear Mr. President:*)
Consistent with the Authorization for Use of Military Force Against Iraq Resolution of 2002 (Public Law 107–243), the Authorization for the Use of Force Against Iraq Resolution (Public Law 102–1), and in order to keep the Congress fully informed, I am providing a report prepared by my Administration. This report includes matters relating to post-liberation Iraq

under section 7 of the Iraq Liberation Act of 1998 (Public Law 105–338).
Sincerely,

GEORGE W. BUSH

NOTE: Identical letters were sent to J. Dennis Hastert, Speaker of the House of Representatives, and Richard B. Cheney, President of the Senate. This letter was released by the Office of the Press Secretary on August 16.

The President's Radio Address
August 16, 2003

Good morning. This week, I traveled to Arizona and California to see some of America's forests and parks and to talk about my commitment to good stewardship of these natural treasures.

On Monday, I visited the Coronado National Forest in Arizona, where wildfires recently consumed thousands of acres of forest and destroyed hundreds of homes. Nearby, I also saw forests that remained largely intact thanks to wise forest-management policy. Fire professionals and forest and park rangers agree, by thinning overgrown forests we will reduce the risk of catastrophic fire and restore the health of forest ecosystems.

That is the purpose of my Healthy Forest Initiative. We're cutting through bureaucratic redtape to complete urgently needed forest-thinning projects. We are speeding up environmental assessments and consultations required by current law. And we're expediting the administrative appeals process to resolve disputes more quickly. By the end of this fiscal year in September, we will have treated more than 2.6 million acres of overgrowth, more than twice the acreage that was treated in the year 2000.

Under current law, however, litigation often delays projects, while some 190 million acres of forest remain at high risk of dangerous fires and nearby communities remain vulnerable. So I'm asking Congress to reform the review process for forest projects. The "Healthy Forests Restoration Act" would make forest health a high priority when courts are forced to resolve disputes, and it would place reasonable time limits on the litigation process after the public has had an opportunity to comment and a decision has been made. For the health of America's forests and for the safety and economic vitality of our communities, the Congress must complete work on this bill. The House has passed the legislation, and now the Senate must act.

As we protect America's forests, we must also preserve the beauty of America's nearly 80 million acres of national parkland. On Friday, I visited the Santa Monica Mountains National Recreation Area in southern California. It is one of America's 388 national park areas, including historic sites and battlefields, recreation areas, monuments, and shores. Every one of them is a point of pride for the Nation and for local communities.

Yet in the past, not all of these sites have been given the attention they require. Some of our national park areas are not in good condition. And for many years, Government did not even have the basic information about which places were most in need of repair or restoration. To meet this challenge, I pledge to spend $4.9 billion over 5 years on needed work and maintenance in our national park areas.

With the support of Congress, we're keeping that commitment. In the first 2 years of my administration, Congress provided nearly $1.8 billion for park maintenance and roads. And my request for the next three budgets will bring total funding for park maintenance and roads to more than $5 billion over 5 years.

With this funding, we've already undertaken approximately 900 park maintenance projects. This year, the Park Service is working on 500 more projects, and nearly 400 more are planned for next year. As we attend to needed repairs, we're also putting in place a new system of inventory and assessment to assure that America's parks stay in good condition. We have set a new course for our national parks, with better management and renewed investment in the care and protection. After all, the parks belong to the people.

I look forward to traveling next week to Oregon and Washington State, and I will be carrying the same message: Our system of national parks and forests is a trust given to every generation of Americans. By practicing good management and being faithful stewards of the land, our generation can show that we're worthy of that trust.

Thank you for listening.

NOTE: The address was recorded at 9:55 a.m. on August 14 at the Bush Ranch in Crawford, TX, for broadcast at 10:06 a.m. on August 16. The transcript was made available by the Office of the Press Secretary on August 15 but was embargoed for release until the broadcast. The Office of the Press Secretary also released a Spanish language transcript of this address.

Interview With the Armed Forces Radio and Television Service
August 14, 2003

Liberia

Q. Thank you for joining us today. We really appreciate you being here and taking time out to talk with us.

I'd like to start out with a topic that's in the news this morning, and that's Liberia. Two weeks ago, you authorized Secretary Rumsfeld to send a small contingency into that war-torn country to help out. And now this morning, we hear that a couple of hundred more U.S. forces are there to help out. What's the status there? Do you see this as a long-term deployment for our troops? Or do you think this is more short-term?

The President. No, I know it's short-term. Here's what I said. I said, look, we have a special obligation in Liberia to help with humanitarian aid, and therefore, we will. And I said, secondly, we will have a limited mission of limited duration and limited scope and that we will help what's called ECOMIL, which is the western African nations' militaries, go in and provide the conditions necessary for humanitarian aid to move.

We have yet to deploy anybody, really. Today you mentioned 200 troops. Those 200 troops will be the first really deployed, other than assessment teams, and their job is to help secure an airport and a port so food can be offloaded and the delivery process begun to help people in Monrovia. We'll be out of there by October the 1st. We've got U.N. blue-helmeted troops ready to replace our limited number of troops.

But our mission there is to help ECOWAS—help ECOMIL provide humanitarian aid.

Coalition Operations in Iraq

Q. I'd like to turn to Iraq now.

The President. Yes.

Q. On May 1st, you flew aboard the *Abraham Lincoln,* and you addressed the Nation, and you announced the end of combat operations.

The President. Actually, major military operations.

Q. Okay, I stand corrected.

The President. Because we still have combat operations going on.

Q. We do, sir; you're right. But as you say, duty there continues to be tough, dangerous work. But ironically, more of our troops have died since May 1st than during the main hostility. What do your advisers tell you about the security threat in Iraq

today? Is it getting better? Is it worse? Where do we stand?

The President. Well, it's certainly getting better on a day-by-day basis. And the reason why is because we're routing out former Ba'athists and some foreign terrorists from the country. These are people who can't stand the thought of a free Iraq.

Really, the way I'd like for your viewers to understand the Iraq theater is that the— Iraq is an integral part on the war on terror. See, Saddam Hussein was funding terrorist activities. He was providing money. Who knows what kind of armament he was providing. We know he had illegal weapons, and those weapons in the hands of terrorists would be very dangerous to the United States.

Iraq is in the middle of a part of the region that has produced terror and terrorists. And therefore, a free Iraq is an integral part of winning the war on terror, because a free Iraq is going to be one that will help—will have an amazingly positive effect on its neighborhood. A free Iraq will no longer be a threat to the United States and our friends and allies. And so what you're seeing now is a continuation on the battle for Iraq; it's just a different kind of battle. The first wave of military operations was to get rid of—the first major goal of military operations was to get rid of Saddam Hussein and his regime, and we have done that. And now it is to make the country secure enough for democracy to flourish. And it's a different kind of combat mission, but nevertheless, it's combat— just ask the kids that are over there killing and being shot at.

Listen, as Commander in Chief, I grieve for any loss of life. And I stand in—I send my deepest sympathies to the loved ones who grieve over the loss of a soldier, a loved one. But the cause is a good cause, because we will never forget the lessons of 9/11. This is part of the war on terror. And the effect of what we have done in Iraq and what we're doing in Iraq will be a very positive effect on future generations of Americans, and that's very important for people to understand.

Q. You talked about a democracy in Iraq. August 8th was the 100th day since the end of combat operations there. But we've got a lot of forces that are still there. I guess my question to you is, will U.S. forces continue to bear the brunt of the responsibility there? I believe down in Crawford you told the press that America was committed to staying in Iraq until they were free.

The President. Right.

Q. But will that responsibility continue to fall on U.S. forces, or will our coalition partners step up and give us some relief?

The President. Yes, I think what you'll find is, is that there will be a variety of different elements that will give relief to U.S. forces.

First of all, we will stay there until the job is done. If America pulls out, there's no telling what'll happen. It'll certainly embolden terrorists to think that we are going to a mission and don't complete it. But think about the following dynamics. First of all, Britain is still there. Polish troops are now moving in and will be in, I think, by September 4th of this year, which is in 2 weeks. That's a major Polish contingent. There will be other nations going in to support not only the Polish contingent but the British contingent.

We're developing an Iraq police force as well as an Iraqi army. And the idea is at some point in time, the Iraqi army is able to secure the powerlines and prevent the looting. See, what's happening there is there's a handful of people, an element of people who are willing to destroy the power grid as we rebuild it, in order to try to terrorize people. It would be helpful if other patrolled the power grid, other than our U.S. hunter-killer teams. And that's what's happening now. And this fall you'll see a lot of protective load, kind of the guarding role, being taken off the shoulders of U.S. troops and shared by coalition forces.

But you know, you mentioned 100 days. I want to put this in perspective. Saddam Hussein had 12 years or so, or more, to hide weapons and to fool the world. I say "12 years" because that's really the timeframe from '91, the last U.S. incursion, until today, but no telling what he was doing prior to '91. He has had years to terrorize people. This is the guy, if you disagreed with him, you're liable to be dead and your family would be tortured as well or killed as well.

And so we're dealing with a mindset and kind of a condition, an environment that has been in place for a long time, and yet we've only been there for 100 days. But we've done a lot in 100. In other words, my expectations aren't the democracy will flourish after 100 days. Of course, my expectations were that—I wasn't certain how long it was going to take for us to do an incredibly difficult, complex military operation. I knew that we had a good plan, because General Franks told me we had a good plan. But it happened a lot quicker than I thought.

So I don't—my point is, I don't tend to put time, artificial timelines; I try to be realistic, however, about how long it takes to accomplish a complex mission.

Afghanistan/War on Terror

Q. Mr. President, I'd like to talk about Afghanistan for a moment, formerly a hotbed of terrorist activity, and the first country to feel America's wrath and compassion in the war on terrorism after 9/11. But today, significant numbers of U.S. troops are still there helping to rebuild that country. My question for you is, is there a timetable for when U.S. forces will start to come home from there? Or is Afghanistan tied to Iraq?

The President. Well, listen, we've got about 10,000 troops there, which is down from, obviously, major combat operations. And they're there to provide security, and they're there to provide reconstruction help. But both those functions are being gradually replaced by other troops. Germany, for example, is now providing the troops for ISAF, which is the security force for Afghanistan under NATO control. In other words, more and more coalition forces and friends are beginning to carry a lot of the burden in Afghanistan.

We'll still have hunter-killer teams there to chase down remnants of Taliban and Al Qaida, because—we want, of course, Afghanistan to be a secure and democratic country. And we want to use—now that we're locked and loaded, as they say in the military, we want to chase down those who could eventually come back and harm America.

In other words, Afghanistan and Iraq—they're linked. They're linked because they're both integral theaters in the war on terror. And a free Afghanistan and a free Iraq will make America more secure, and that's, after all, the mission that we're after. Nine-eleven taught us a lesson, that we're vulnerable, and 9/11 reminded me that my obligation as the Commander in Chief is to hunt down an enemy and bring them to justice before they would ever harm America again. And that's what we're going to do, so long as I am the President.

North Korea

Q. I'd like to go to the other side of the world for a moment, if I could, to North Korea.

The President. Yes.

Q. What is the status on their weapons of mass destruction and their ability to use them? And most specifically, how concerned should U.S. forces in the Pacific theater be—South Korea, Japan—that North Korea would use nuclear weapons against them?

The President. Well, you know, we believe he has got a warhead. We know he's got rockets. And we know he's a dangerous man, and that's why we take his threats seriously. You know, the best thing to do, in my judgment, is to convince others to join us to convince Kim Chong-il to change his behavior.

In other words, we tried the bilateral approach, and it didn't work because he didn't tell the truth. And so now our strategy is to get the Chinese involved, which they are, and to get the Russians involved and the Japanese involved and the South Koreans involved, all of us involved to tell Kim Chong-il that we expect him to denuclearize the Korean Peninsula for the sake of peace. And that's where we're headed.

I'd like to solve this diplomatically, and I believe we can. It's going to take a lot of persuasion by countries besides the United States to convince him. He loves the idea of, you know, making people nervous and rattling sabers and getting the world all anxious. And my job is to tell others that let's speak with one voice and convince this man that developing a nuclear weapon on the Korean Peninsula is not in his interests.

Military Pay and Benefits/Military Families

Q. I'd like to talk about people for a minute. You've talked about them earlier, and nobody knows better than you the sacrifices that our servicemembers are making day in and day out on the war on terrorism, whether it's Iraq, Afghanistan, here at home. What can servicemembers look for in the way of benefits, pay, housing, health care, that kind of thing, to repay them for their unselfish sacrifice to the Nation?

The President. When I first came in, I made the commitment that help was on the way. I said that during the campaign to the military, help was on the way, and I've lived up to that commitment.

Pay is going up. I think if you talk to the servicemen, they do feel the pay increases that we've—that I proposed and Congress has passed. And when you couple that with two significant tax cuts, our servicemen have got more money in their pocket than before.

I ask the question all the time to troops. I don't know if I got—I hope I get the straight answer. You don't know; it must be a little awesome for a sergeant to talk to the Commander in Chief.

Q. It's very awesome, sir. [*Laughter*]

The President. And I turn to the guy and say, "Can you feel your pay raise?" And to a person, the answer is yes, they feel their pay raise, which is good. And that's what I want.

The other thing is that when you and I first met at Fort Stewart, Georgia, I was given a tour of substandard housing. And I went back and talked to Don Rumsfeld about that and said, "We've got to do something about that." Pay is one thing, and housing is another. And both of them are compatible; both of them are important for families in the military.

And I think you'll find that we have—we're living up to our commitment to have a full-scale housing program ongoing for our troops. And the housing issue is getting a lot—the housing condition is improving, compared to the way it was in the past, and so I'm mindful of it.

And health care is good for our troops. I think, again, if you ask the troops—that's who I ask, and they tell me they're pleased with the health care. And so the key is to continue the progress that we've made about making sure that the human condition in the military is excellent.

Q. One final question, Mr. President. The families of America's fighting forces, they make huge sacrifices in the name of freedom, just like the servicemembers. You touched on it earlier. You touched on it in your speech today. For months at a time, they give up their servicemembers. They don't know where they are. They don't hear from them. They don't know if they're safe. They don't know if they're dead or alive. What message do you have for the families today?

The President. Well, my message is that what your loved one is doing is the right thing for the country. We are called upon to defend the United States of America. I take that oath, and every soldier takes that oath. And on 9/11, our world changed, and we realized this country is vulnerable and we better do something about it. And the best way to secure the homeland is to get the enemy before he gets us. At least, that's my attitude. And so, I—first of all, the commitment that their loved ones have made, the families of the service ones have made, is in line with this business about winning and fighting war.

Every person is a volunteer in our military. They've chosen to defend the United States of America. And therefore, they need to get the best—if that's their attitude, and they made up their mind that's what they want to do, then my job is to get them the best equipment, the best pay, the best training possible, so that if we ever have to send them in, they'll be able to do the job.

And I hope their loved ones understand that, that this is a volunteer army and it requires sacrifice. Look, I understand what it must mean for the moms and dads and sons and daughters to wonder about their loved one. It must be a nerve-wracking experience. On the other hand, it's for a good cause.

I would tell you as well, as I think our military does is—I'm going to tell you two things I think the military does really well that will hopefully give comfort to people. One, there is a lot of communication that takes place with troops overseas and their loved ones at home. There are—there's e-mail efforts that go on, a lot of e-mail efforts. In other words, there's a capacity to communicate from afar, the likes of which our military has never had.

Secondly, I have visited our wounded. One of my jobs as the Commander in Chief is to try to comfort those who grieve and to comfort those who are wounded—those who grieve as a result of loss of life, and those—and to comfort those who have been wounded, and I do. I'm responsible for putting them into combat, and I know that. And so I go to hospitals on occasion, Walter Reed or Bethesda.

Ours is a country that can take a young, wounded soldier off the battlefield and have him in the best care in a number of days. I met many a troop that was wounded in Iraq and 3 days later was at Bethesda Naval Hospital getting the best possible treatment. And to me that speaks volumes about the commitment of our country to take care of our fighters and our soldiers and marines and sailors and airmen. If somebody gets hurt far from home, we will deliver the best care in the world in a rapid time. And I understand that doesn't replace an injured limb for a loved one, but it certainly should say loud and clear that this country cares deeply about those who are willing to sacrifice on its behalf.

Q. As you say, sir, freedom isn't free.

The President. That's right.

Q. Thank you, Mr. President, very much. I really appreciate the time.

The President. You bet. Thank you, sir. Good job.

NOTE: The interview began at 1:55 p.m. in Hangar Five at the Marine Corps Air Station in Miramar, CA, for later broadcast, and the transcript was released by the Office of the Press Secretary on August 18. In his remarks, the President referred to former President Saddam Hussein of Iraq; Gen. Tommy R. Franks, USA (Ret.), former combatant commander, U.S. Central Command; and Chairman Kim Chong-il of North Korea. A tape was not available for verification of the content of this interview.

Statement on Signing the Higher Education Relief Opportunities for Students Act of 2003
August 18, 2003

Today, I have signed into law H.R. 1412, the "Higher Education Relief Opportunities for Students Act of 2003." This Act permits the Secretary of Education to waive or modify Federal student financial assistance program requirements to help students and their families or academic institutions affected by a war, other military operation, or national emergency. The executive branch shall construe section 2(c) in a manner consistent with the President's authority under the Recommendations Clause of the Constitution to submit for the consideration of the Congress such measures as the President shall judge necessary or expedient.

GEORGE W. BUSH

The White House,
August 18, 2003.

NOTE: H.R. 1412, approved August 18, was assigned Public Law No. 108–76.

Remarks and an Exchange With Reporters in Crawford, Texas
August 19, 2003

Proposed Energy Legislation/Power Blackout

The President. Good morning, everybody. How are you? Last night I talked to Pete Domenici and Billy Tauzin. Pete is the chairman of the Senate committee dealing with energy and Billy is the chairman of the House committee dealing with energy. Pete believes they can get the conference up and running in 20 days to deal with this very important energy bill. Both Members are very optimistic about reaching agreement, obviously, on infrastructure modernization but, as importantly, other issues related to energy.

One thing is for certain. There is—very confident they'll have mandatory reliability standards in the energy bill. What that means is that companies transmitting energy will have to have strong reliability measures in place; otherwise, there will be a consequence for them. There will be incentives in the new bill to encourage investment in energy infrastructure.

So I'm very pleased with the attitude of the two Members, their desire to get a bill done quickly and get it to my desk. I have been calling for an energy bill for a long time. And now is the time for the Congress to move and get something done.

I also talked to Energy Secretary Abraham. Tomorrow the joint inquiry with the Canadians will begin. I don't know how long it's going to take to find out what went wrong, but I know it's not going to take long to get the meeting started to determine what went wrong.

I'll answer a couple of questions; then I've got to get moving.

Former Vice President Taha Yasin Ramadan of Iraq

Q. They've just captured Saddam's Vice President. Does that give you hope that we're closer to catching Saddam?

The President. Well, I don't know the facts of where he was, what was going on. I'm really pleased that we've captured the Vice President. Slowly but surely, we'll find who we need to find. It's just a matter of time. Listen, we've got a lot of brave people doing a lot of hard work in Iraq. And it's—because Iraq was terrorized and dominated by a dictator, it's going to take a while to get this country to understand what's necessary to be a free country. But we'll find him, and we'll bring him to justice.

Stevenson [Richard Stevenson, New York Times].

Proposed Energy Legislation

Q. Sir, I realize it's early to find out what went on with the blackout, but do you know enough at this point to be able to say whether there's anything new or different that you would like in the energy bill beyond what you proposed——

The President. Well, listen, I thought the energy bill was very comprehensive. We particularly liked the House—a lot of the House bill. The Senate, as you know, in order to get out of town, expedited a piece of legislation. The House bill is a very comprehensive bill. And I'm confident the two bodies can work out differences. If they do what's in the—if they do what's in the House bill, for example, and what's in the—a lot in the Senate bill, we'll get us a good bill.

Situation in the Middle East

Q. Sir, the cease-fire by the Palestinians runs out in a few weeks. Do you think it should be extended, and why?

The President. Well, you know, look, here's my view on cease-fires and—I'm happy there's calm, and I think that's important. But the most important thing is to—for the parties that care for their—for peace to dismantle terrorist organizations that want to kill. That's how we're going to achieve a peaceful settlement in the Middle East. Calm is good. The fact that people aren't dying is good. But the ultimate solution—and this can happen quickly, in my judgment—is to find those who would—who believe killing is the best approach to dealing with the very difficult problems in the Middle East.

Q. Sir, Israel has kind of eased off of their request for actual dismantling the terrorists, and they're putting their faith in the Palestinian Authority to contain these guys. Do you have——

The President. I don't want to put words in the Israelis' mouth, but I can assure you that they're interested in dismantling organizations such as Hamas.

Q. But do you think that the Palestinian Authority right now can contain these——

The President. I think that the Palestinian Authority needs to continue to work with the United States and others who are interested in dismantling terrorist organizations and ask for the help necessary so they can go and do what they need to do, which is dismantle and destroy organizations which are interested in killing innocent lives in order to prevent a peace process from going forward.

Tax Cuts/National Economy

Q. Mr. President, your budget director gave an interview to the Wall Street Journal suggesting that there won't be any corporate tax cuts to deal with this World Trade Organization trade dispute—about $100 billion in tax cuts making its way through Congress. Are we done with tax cuts for the foreseeable future?

The President. Well, we'll see. As I said the other day, as we stand right now, I believe the tax relief packages we have in place are doing their job. But I'm a flexible person. I want to make sure that the conditions for economic growth and vitality are strong. But we'll take a look and see. I'm pleased the markets have responded. I'm

pleased that there's economic vitality and growth. But until everybody finds a job who wants one—today—and can't find one, is able to work, then I'm going to continue working on the economy.

Coalition Operations in Iraq

Q. Sir, given the decreasing likelihood of there being another United Nations resolution on Iraq, should the American people be prepared for a longer and larger deployment of American forces there?

The President. Well, one of the things that's happening is that international forces are now coming into Iraq. There's a significant reconstruction effort going on in which other nations besides the United States and our initial coalition partners are participating.

In other words, there is an international effort going on that will help Iraq reconstruct itself and help Iraq develop into a peaceful, democratic country. And that's in our country's interest, that Iraq become a peaceful, free, democratic country. Part of the war on terror is to promote freedom in the Middle East. I like to remind people that a free Iraq will no longer serve as a haven for terrorists or as a place for terrorists to get money or arms. A free Iraq will make the Middle East a more peaceful place, and a peaceful Middle East is important to the security of the United States.

Listen, I've got to go. Thank you. I hope you all have a wonderful morning.

First Lady Laura Bush/President's Vacation

Q. How's the First Lady?

The President. She's great. Thanks. She actually suggested maybe bringing the press corps out to the ranch. Her idea.

Q. Good idea.

The President. What?

Q. Good idea.

The President. Well——

Q. What is she keeping busy with?

The President. You know, she's—you'll see, if you ever get out there, that she's got a lot of wildflowers. And she's restoring a lot of the area around the house, the native grasses. By the way, we've got quail back—bobwhite quail has now returned around our house. It wasn't there when we first bought the place. And because the grasses have been restored, we've got a nice little family of bobwhites. It's a fantastic experience to hear them call in the morning.

My friend Blossman caught about a 6-pound bass yesterday. So the bass are growing, and they're getting healthy. Life out there at the ranch is just fine. It gets a little toasty about 3:00 p.m. in the afternoon, though.

Thank you all.

NOTE: The President spoke at 6:40 a.m. at the Fina gas station. In his remarks, he referred to former President Saddam Hussein of Iraq; and Jack A. "Jay" Blossman, Jr., commissioner, Louisiana Public Service Commission. A reporter referred to Office and Management and Budget Director Joshua B. Bolten. A tape was not available for verification of the content of these remarks.

Remarks in Crawford on the Bombing of the United Nations Headquarters in Baghdad, Iraq
August 19, 2003

Today in Baghdad, terrorists turned their violence against the United Nations. The U.N. personnel and Iraqi citizens killed in the bombing were in that country on a purely humanitarian mission. Men and women in the targeted building were working on reconstruction, medical care for Iraqis. They were there to help with the distribution of food. A number have been killed or injured. And to those who suffer, I extend the sympathy of the American people.

A short time ago, I spoke with Ambassador Bremer and directed him to provide all possible assistance to the rescue and recovery effort at the United Nations headquarters. I also spoke to Secretary-General Kofi Annan about the personal loss the U.N. has suffered, about the assistance my country has offered, and about the vital work in Iraq that continues.

The terrorists who struck today have again shown their contempt for the innocent. They showed their fear of progress and their hatred of peace. They are the enemies of the Iraqi people. They are the enemies of every nation that seeks to help the Iraqi people. By their tactics and their targets, these murderers reveal themselves once more as enemies of the civilized world.

Every sign of progress in Iraq adds to the desperation of the terrorists and the remnants of Saddam's brutal regime. The civilized world will not be intimidated, and these killers will not determine the future of Iraq. The Iraqi people have been liberated from a dictator. Iraq is on an irreversible course toward self-government and peace. And America and our friends in the United Nations will stand with the Iraqi people as they reclaim their Nation and their future.

Iraqi people face a challenge, and they face a choice. The terrorists want to return to the days of torture chambers and mass graves. The Iraqis who want peace and freedom must reject them and fight terror. And the United States and many in the world will be there to help them.

All nations of the world face a challenge and a choice. By attempting to spread chaos and fear, terrorists are testing our will. Across the world, they are finding that our will cannot be shaken. We will persevere through every hardship. We will continue this war on terror until the killers are brought to justice, and we will prevail.

May God bless the souls who have been harmed in Iraq. Thank you very much.

NOTE: The President spoke at 11:05 a.m. at the Bush Ranch. In his remarks, he referred to L. Paul Bremer III, Presidential Envoy to Iraq; Secretary-General Kofi Annan of the United Nations; and former President Saddam Hussein of Iraq.

Statement on the Death of United Nations Special Representative for Iraq Sergio Vieira de Mello
August 19, 2003

I was deeply saddened to hear of Sergio Vieira de Mello's death at the hand of terrorists in Iraq. Special Representative Vieira de Mello committed his life to advancing the cause of human rights, most recently as U.N. High Commissioner for Human Rights. When Secretary-General Annan asked him to take a leave of absence from those duties to work in Iraq, he agreed without hesitation. Just as he selflessly coordinated international efforts in East Timor and Kosovo, Mr. de Mello was helping the Iraqi people move down the path towards a democratic country governed by the rule of law. My deepest condolences go to his family and to the people of Brazil, who have lost one of their finest public servants.

Remarks at a Bush-Cheney Luncheon in Portland, Oregon
August 21, 2003

Thank you all. Thanks for coming. Please be seated. Thanks for the warm welcome and the cool day. It seems the temperature is a little better here than it is in Crawford. [*Laughter*] But I want to thank you all for coming. I am so honored that we have set a record today, a record fundraiser, which indicates the depth of support here in Oregon, for which I am most grateful. I want to thank you for what you have done; I want to thank you for what you're going to do, which is to energize the grassroots all across this important State, to put up the signs and to mail out the mailers, but most importantly, to remind people that I have a vision that includes everybody, a vision that is hopeful and optimistic, a vision that believes in the best of America.

I want you to know that I'm getting ready for the coming campaign. I'm loosening up. [*Laughter*] But there's going to be ample time for politics, because I've got a job to do. I got a lot on the agenda. But I want you to know that I will continue to work hard to earn the confidence of every American by keeping this Nation secure and strong and prosperous and free.

My main regret for coming here is the fact that I'm not traveling with the First Lady. She is a great First Lady. I love her dearly. I'm proud to call her wife, and I already miss her. But she's in San Antonio, Texas, today. She's honoring a friend of ours, and she's working on a library event. But I'll be with her on the ranch Friday night and continuing our period of relaxation before we get back to the Nation's Capital. But it's a great comfort to have her by my side.

I'm also proud to call Gordon Smith friend. He's a great United States Senator. And I appreciate so much working with my friend Congressman Greg Walden as well.

After this event here, we're going to a different part of your beautiful State to talk about a Healthy Forest Initiative, a commonsense policy to do everything we can to thin out the forest beds so that we can prevent the catastrophic forest fires that seem to be occurring all over the West. I'm proud to have two commonsense conservatives with whom I can work to bring some sense to the forest policy of the United States of America.

I thank my friend Mercer Reynolds from Cincinnati, Ohio, who is with us today. He's the national finance chairman for this campaign. I appreciate Bill McCormick, who is the Oregon State chairman for the Bush-Cheney 2004 campaign. Sorry we're not using your restaurant. I appreciate Kevin Mannix, who is the chairman of the Republican Party here in the State of Oregon.

It was such an honor to be able to shake hands once again with a fine American, a great Oregonian, Senator Mark Hatfield. I appreciate you coming, Senator.

I want to thank so very much the leadership of the University of Portland for opening up this beautiful campus. But most of all, I want to thank you all for coming. I'm proud to have you as supporters. I'm proud that we're on the same team, working hard to do what's right for America.

See, I ran for office to solve problems, not to pass them on to future Presidents and future generations. I'm serving to seize opportunities, and that's what we're doing. I believe you can tell your neighbor that this administration is meeting the tests of our time.

Terrorists declared war on the United States of America, and war is what they got. We've captured or killed many key leaders of the Al Qaida network, and the rest of them know we're on their trail. In Afghanistan and Iraq, we gave ultimatums to terror regimes. Those regimes chose defiance, and those regimes are no more. Thanks to the United States of America and friends, 50 million people in those 2 countries once lived under tyranny, and today they live in freedom.

Two-and-a-half years ago, our military was not receiving the resources it needed, and morale was beginning to suffer. We increased the defense budget to prepare for the threats of a new era. And today, no one in the world can question the skill and the strength and the spirit of the United States military.

Two-and-a-half years ago, as Gordon mentioned, we inherited an economy in recession. And then we had attacks on our country and scandals in corporate America as well as a war, which affected—all affected the people's confidence. But we acted. We took action. We passed tough new laws to hold corporate criminals to account. And to get the economy going again, I have twice led the United States Congress to pass historic tax relief for the American people.

Here's what I believe, and here's what I know, that when Americans have more take-home pay to spend, to save, to invest, the whole economy will grow, and people are more likely to find a job.

I also understand whose money we spend in Washington, DC. It's not the Government's money. It's the people's money. We're returning more money to the people to help them raise their families. We're reducing taxes on dividends and capital gains to encourage investment. We're giving small businesses incentives to expand and to hire new people. With all these actions, we are laying the foundations for greater prosperity and more jobs across America so that every single person in this country—every person—has a chance to realize the American Dream.

Two-and-a-half years ago, there was a lot of talk about education reform, but there wasn't much action in Washington, DC, so I called for and the Congress passed the No Child Left Behind Act. With a solid bipartisan majority, we delivered the most dramatic education reform in a generation. We're bringing high standards and strong accountability measures to every public school in America. In return for Federal dollars, we now expect every school to teach the basics of reading and math. This administration is finally challenging the soft bigotry of low expectations. The days of excuse-making are over. We now expect results in every classroom so that not one single child in America is left behind.

We reorganized the Government and created a Department of Homeland Security to better safeguard our borders and ports and to protect the American people. We passed trade promotion authority to open new markets for Oregon's farmers and ranchers and entrepreneurs and manufacturers. We passed budget agreements that is helping to maintain much needed spending discipline in Washington, DC. On issue after issue, this administration has acted on principle, has kept its word, and has made progress for the American people.

And the United States Congress shares in this credit. I've got a great relationship with Speaker Denny Hastert and Majority Leader Bill Frist. I appreciate being able to work with them and, as I mentioned, Greg and Gordon. We'll continue to work hard to try to change the tone in Washington, DC, to focus on results, not petty politics.

And those are the kind of people I've attracted to my administration. I have assembled a great team of people to serve the American people. People in my administration are results-oriented people. They asked the question, what's best for the American people? And they're doing a great job. There has been no finer Vice President of the United States than Dick Cheney. Mother may have a different opinion. [Laughter]

In 2½ years, we've come far. In 2½ years, we've done a lot. But the work is only beginning. I have set great goals worthy of a great nation. First, America is committed to expanding the realm of freedom and peace for our own security and for the benefit of the world. And second, in our own country, we must work for a society of prosperity and compassion, so that every citizen has a chance to work and to succeed and to realize the great promise of this country.

It is clear that the future of freedom and peace depend on the actions of America. This Nation is freedom's home and freedom's defender, and we welcome—we welcome—this charge of history, and we are keeping it. Our war on terror continues. The enemies of freedom are not idle, and neither are we. This country will not rest; we will not tire; we will not stop until this danger to civilization is removed.

Yet our national interest involves more than eliminating aggressive threats to our safety. Our greatest security comes from the advance of human liberty, because free nations do not support terror. Free nations do not attack their neighbors, and free nations do not threaten the world with weapons of mass terror. Americans believe that freedom is the deepest need and hope of every human heart. And we believe that freedom is the right of every person, and we believe that freedom is the future of every nation.

America also understands that unprecedented influence brings tremendous responsibilities. We have duties in the world. When we see disease and starvation and hopeless poverty, we will not turn away. On the continent of Africa, this great, strong, and compassionate Nation is bringing the healing power to medicine to millions of men and women and children now suffering with AIDS. This great land, America, is leading the world in the incredibly important work of human rescue.

We face challenges at home as well, and our actions will prove that we're equal to those challenges. I understand there's a lot of people hurting in the State of Oregon. Your unemployment rate is too high. I will continue to try to create the conditions necessary for job creation, so long as there's anybody who's looking for work.

And we have a duty as well to keep our commitment to America's seniors by strengthening and modernizing Medicare. The Congress took historic action to improve the lives of older Americans. For the first time—for the first time—since the creation of Medicare, the House and the Senate have passed reforms to make the system work better, to give our seniors more choices, and to provide coverage of prescription drugs. It's now time for both Houses to iron out their differences and to get a bill to my desk as soon as possible, so that we can say to our seniors of today and those of us who are going to be seniors tomorrow, we have kept our commitment in Washington, DC.

And for the sake of our health care system, we need to cut down on the frivolous lawsuits which increase the cost of medicine. People who have been harmed by a bad doctor deserve their day in court, yet the system should not reward lawyers who are fishing for rich settlements. Because frivolous lawsuits drive up the cost of health care, they affect the Federal budget. Medical liability reform, therefore, is a national issue that requires a national solution. The House of Representatives have passed a good piece of legislation. The bill is stuck in the United States Senate. The Senate must act on behalf of the people. They must understand that no one has ever been healed by a frivolous or junk lawsuit. If Gordon has his way, he would unstick it in the Senate.

I have a responsibility as your President to make sure the judicial system runs well, and I have met that duty. I have nominated superb men and women for the Federal courts, people who will interpret the law,

not legislate from the bench. Yet, some Members of the United States Senate are trying to keep my nominees off the bench by blocking up-or-down votes. Every judicial nominee deserves a fair hearing and an up-or-down vote on the Senate floor. It is time for some of the Members of the United States Senate to stop playing politics with American justice.

The Congress needs to complete work on a comprehensive energy plan. We had a good bill pass the House, bill pass the Senate. They need to come together and get an energy plan, an energy bill to my desk as soon as possible, an energy bill which will encourage the modernization of the electricity infrastructure of America. I have proposed such a plan. We need an energy bill that will encourage energy efficiency and promote conservation, an energy bill which will encourage the use of technologies to help us explore for energy in environmentally sensitive ways. For the sake of economic security, for the sake of national security, this Nation must become less dependent on foreign sources of energy.

Our strong and prosperous Nation must also be a compassionate nation. I will continue to advance our agenda of compassionate conservatism, which means we'll apply the best and most innovative ideas to the task of helping our fellow citizens who hurt or fellow citizens in need.

There are still millions of men and women in our country who want to end their dependence on Government and to become independent through work. We must build on the success of welfare reform to bring work and dignity into the lives of more of our fellow citizens.

Congress should complete the "Citizen Service Act" to encourage more Americans to serve their communities and their country. Both Houses should finally reach agreement on my Faith-Based Initiative to support the armies of compassion that are mentoring our children, who are caring for the homeless, that offer hope to the addicted. This Nation of ours should not be fearful of faith. We ought to welcome faith to help solve many of the Nation's seemingly intractable problems.

A compassionate society must promote opportunity for all, including the independence and dignity that come from ownership. My administration will constantly strive to promote an ownership society all across America. We want more people owning a home. We have a minority home-ownership gap in America. I have laid before Congress a plan to solve it. We want people owning their own health care plan. We want people owning and managing their own retirement accounts. And we want more people owning a small business because, you see, we understand that when a person owns something, he or she has a vital stake in the future of the United States of America.

In a compassionate society, people respect one another, and they take responsibility for the decisions they make. You know, it seems like to me, I'm confident—not just seems like, I am confident that we're changing the culture of America from one that has said, "If it feels good, just go ahead and do it," and "If you've got a problem, blame somebody else," to a culture in which each of us understands that we are responsible for the decisions we make in life.

If you are fortunate enough to be a mom or a dad, you're responsible for loving your child with all your heart and all your soul. If you're concerned about the quality of the education in your community, you're responsible for doing something about it. If you're a CEO in America, you're responsible for telling the truth to your shareholders and your employees. And in this new responsibility society, each of us are responsible for loving our neighbor just like we'd like to be loved ourselves.

We can see the culture of service and responsibility growing around us, particularly after September the 11th, 2001. Shortly after September the 11th, I started what's called the USA Freedom Corps to encourage Americans to extend a compassionate hand to somebody who hurts. And the response has been terrific. Our faith-based groups and our charities are vibrant and strong, because people understand it's important to serve something greater than yourself in life. After all, that's what policemen and firefighters and people who wear our Nation's uniform remind us on a daily basis. Our children once again believe in heroes because they see them every day in America.

In these challenging times, the world has seen the resolve and the courage of America. I've been privileged to see the compassion and the character of the American people. All the tests of the last 2½ years have come to the right nation. We're a strong country, and we use that strength to defend the peace. We're an optimistic country, confident in ourselves and in ideals bigger than ourselves.

Abroad, we seek to lift whole nations by spreading freedom. At home, we seek to lift up lives by spreading opportunity to every corner of this country. This is the work that history has set before us. We welcome it. And we know that for our country and for our cause, the best days lie ahead.

May God bless you all.

NOTE: The President spoke at 12:08 p.m. in the Chiles Center at the University of Portland. In his remarks, he referred to former Senator Mark O. Hatfield of Oregon.

Remarks in Redmond, Oregon
August 21, 2003

Thank you. Please be seated. Thank you. You know you're in a pretty good country when you see a lot of cowboy hats out in the crowd—[*laughter*]—and when you got horses guarding the perimeter.

Thank you for your hospitality. It is like home, except the temperature seems to be a little cooler and a little more hospitable. But thanks for your hospitality. I'm thrilled to be in Deschutes County, Oregon. I've been planning to come for a while. I'm sad that I had to come to see another forest fire.

We just toured two fires that are burning in the area. It's hard to describe to our fellow citizen what it means to see a fire like we saw. It's the holocaust; it's devastating. We saw the big flames jumping from treetop to treetop, which reminds me about the brave men and women, what they have to face when they go in to fight the fires. I first want to start by thanking those who put their lives at risk to protect our communities, to protect our people, to protect our national treasures, the U.S. forests. I appreciate our firefighters. All those firefighters know something that I've come to realize, that we can thin our forests, that we can use commonsense policy to make the fires burn less hot and protect our forests.

And that's what I want to talk about here. Before I do so, I want to thank Secretary Ann Veneman, Secretary Gale Norton for doing a fine job on behalf of all Americans. I want you to notice that these two ladies are from the West. I appreciate Dale Bosworth, who's the Chief of the U.S. Forest Service. I also want to thank Leslie Weldon. Where are you, Leslie? Where? Oh, hi, Leslie. Thank you. Leslie is the Forest Supervisor of the Deschutes National Forest. She was our tour guide. She is a dedicated professional, just like the people she works with from the U.S. Forest Service. I want to thank those who work for the U.S. Forest Service, for the BLM, for serving your Nation in the communities in which you live. I appreciate the hard work you put in. I appreciate your dedication to the preservation and conservation of one of the greatest assets the United States has, which is our land and our forests.

I appreciate your Governor, Governor Kulongoski, who came with me today. I'm honored that he is here. It should say loud and clear to everybody that preserving and protecting our forests is not a political issue. It is not a partisan issue. It is a practical issue that we must come together and solve. So I'm very honored that the Governor is here.

I'm also honored to be with the two members of the legislative branch of our Government in Washington, DC—a great United States Senator, Gordon Smith, and a great Congressman, Greg Walden. I appreciate being able to work with these two fine men. You've just got to know they represent your interests well. They're constantly talking about the people of Oregon. Every time I'm around them, they bring you up. They say, "Let's have some commonsense policy in Washington, DC, to help people help themselves in our State. That's all we want. We just want the Federal Government to respond in a responsible way." And that's what we're here to talk about, how best to be able to do that.

I don't know if you know this, but today are the Waldens' 21st anniversary. Congratulations to you both. Eileen must be a patient soul—[*laughter*]—kind of like Laura. We both married above ourselves, Congressman. [*Laughter*]

Laura sends her love and her best, by the way. She's still in Texas and wasn't able to travel today, but I wish she could come and see how beautiful this country is. See, we both grew up in the desert of west Texas. This is really a beautiful part of the world.

I appreciate the mayors who are here today, Mayor Unger of Redmond, Mayor Teater of Bend, Mayor Allen, Mayor Uffelman, Mayor Elliott. I thank the mayors and the local authorities who have taken time to come and give me a chance to visit with you. I appreciate your service to your communities. I think mayor is a little tougher than being President because you've got to make sure the potholes are all full and the garbage is collected. [*Laughter*]

I appreciate Garland Brunoe, who is the Chairman of the Confederated Tribes of the Warm Springs, and I want to thank all the tribal members who are here with us today as well.

Today when I landed, I had the honor of meeting a fellow named Curtis Hardy. Curtis is sitting right there. The interesting thing about Curtis is, he's volunteered 5,000 hours over the last 10 years to the Deschutes National Forest. I asked Leslie if he was doing any good. [*Laughter*] She said, "Absolutely." She says it's people like Curtis Hardy that make her job easier. It's very important for people to know that they can take time out of their lives, if they care about their beautiful surroundings, and make a positive, significant difference. Curtis is doing that. Curtis, thank you for setting such a good example, and I appreciate your service.

Ann was right: I was here a year ago. Unfortunately, when I came a year ago, I witnessed the effects of fires. I saw the Biscuit fire and the Squires Peak fire. Both of them were devastating forest fires. They destroyed buildings and homes, changed lives. They destroyed natural resources. The Biscuit fire alone scorched nearly half a million acres, cost more than $150 million. It burned down over a dozen homes. You know, anytime our communities face the devastation of wildfire, it really does test the character of the people. For those

whose lives have been deeply affected and probably will be affected by this fire, we send our sympathies, and we wish God's blessings on their families.

The Federal Government can help. We will give grants, and the FEMA grants, all the SBA loans, the different things that happen when there's an emergency. I can assure you, Gordon and Greg will be all over us to make sure we appropriate the proper money to spend.

But the Government has got to do more than just spend money. I mean, we'll spend it, but we've got to effect wise policy, it seems like to me. I mean, how often— we write checks a lot on firefighting, and we'll continue to do that. But it seems like to me we ought to put a strategy in place to reduce the amount of money that we have to spend on emergency basis by managing our forests in a better, more commonsensical way.

The forest policy—the conditions of our forests didn't happen overnight. The experts who know something about forests will tell you that the condition, the overgrown and unhealthy condition, of a lot of our forest land happened over a century. It's taken a while for this situation to evolve. It may interest you to know that today there's 190 million acres of forests and woodlands around the country which are vulnerable to catastrophic fire because of brush and small trees that have been collecting for literally decades. A problem that has taken a long time to develop is going to take a long time to solve. So what we're going to talk about today is the beginnings of a solution. But we've got to get after it now. We have a problem in Oregon and around our country that we must start solving.

You see, the undergrowth issue, the problem of too much undergrowth, creates the conditions for unbelievably hot fires. These forest firefighters will tell you that these hot fires that literally explode the big trees can be somewhat mitigated by clearing out the undergrowth. And by the way, the undergrowth chokes off nutrients from older trees. It makes our forests more susceptible to disease. We got a problem. It's time to deal with the problem. And that's what we're going to talk about.

Before I talk about the solutions, I do want people to understand that if you are concerned about the endangered species, then you need to be concerned about catastrophic fire. Fires destroy the animals which, obviously, live amidst the raging fire. If you're concerned about old growth, large stands of timber, then you better be worried about the conditions that create devastating fires. The worst thing that can happen to old stands of timber is these fires. They destroy the big trees. They're so explosive in nature that hardly any tree can survive. We saw that with our own eyes, choppering in here. Thinning underbrush makes sense, makes sense to save our species. It makes sense—of animals. It makes sense to save the big stands of trees.

You know, what I'm telling you about a strategy to deal with our forests to make them healthy is not something that was invented in Washington, DC. It's the collective wisdom of scientists, wildlife biologists, forestry professionals, and as importantly, the men and women who risk their life on an annual basis to fight fires. That's who I've been listening to.

Our administration is taking their advice. Congress needs to take their advice. Congress needs to listen to the—[*applause*]. So having listened and realized that we've got a problem, I've proposed a Healthy Forest Initiative. And I proposed it right here in Oregon one year ago. At my direction, the Secretary of the Interior and the Secretary of Agriculture and the Chairman of the Council on Environmental Quality, Connaughton, who is here with us today, on my staff—these three—that's why they're here, by the way. I want you to look at them. They are responsible for putting this initiative into place.

Their job is to cut through bureaucratic redtape to complete urgently needed

thinning projects. That was the first task I gave them. We're going to focus on areas where thinning is the most critical, where the damage can be most severe by—caused by fires. We're working with the Western Governors Association to determine projects of the highest priority in each State. In other words, we're setting priorities, and we're getting after it.

We are speeding up the process of environmental assessments and consultations required by law. Look, we want people to have input. If somebody has got a different point of view, we need to hear it. This is America. We expect to hear people's different points of view in this country. But we want people to understand that we're talking about the health of our forests, and if there's a high priority, we need to get after it before the forests burn and people lose life.

We're expediting the administrative appeals process so that disputes over thinning projects are resolved more quickly. We want to hear people. We want them to have a point of view. We want to save our forests, too. That's what we want to do here in America. We want to deal with the problem. Nobody's to blame. The problem has existed for years. Now let us be the ones who start solving the problem. And that's what I'm going to ask Congress to do when they come back.

Our approach relies on the experience and judgment and hard work of local people. Metolius Conservation Area is such an example. Leslie was describing it to me. The Friends of the Metolius, a conservation group, came to the Forest Service with an interesting idea. What I'm about to tell you is called a collaborative effort—to do some commonsense things in our forests to protect them and protect the communities around the forests.

So these good folks came and said, "Look, why don't we set up some sample plots in the Deschutes Forest to be treated with thinning and burning and mowing and to leave some of the plots untreated, so people can see the difference between a treated plot and an untreated plot, to kind of break through the myths, the mythology, the propaganda of what it means to protect our forests?" And the Forest Service agreed, and they worked together, and they shared costs. And thousands have now come and have seen good forest management practices in place. They've seen what is possible to do. And I want to thank the folks for working hard in a collaborative way to share your wisdom and your hard work, to help educate our fellow citizens about the realities of what we're talking about when it comes to maintaining a healthy forest.

Bill Anthony is not with us today—I think he's fighting the fires—deserves a lot of credit for this program, as does Leslie. They're in the process, by the way, of treating 12,500 acres—additional 12,500 acres. I want to thank the Friends of the Metolius. I want to thank the local citizenry here for doing what is right. Ranger Bill says community participation has been critical to the success of the project, and that's the kind of initiatives we like and want. We want initiatives where the Federal Government works closely with the State government, with community groups, conservation groups, local people, in order to do what is right for our country and our States. You see, there's too much confrontation when it comes to environmental policy. There's too much zero-sum thinking. What we need is cooperation, not confrontation.

I appreciate the stewardship contracting programs that will be going on. I hope you do, as well. You see, the thinning projects that are going to go forward should help some of these local communities that hurt. And by the way, I fully understand Oregon's unemployment issue. It's the highest in the Nation. I'm sorry it's the way it is. There are some things we can do to help people. We want people working. We want people to have food on the table.

Stewardship contracting—what that means is, is that private organizations or businesses will be able to do the necessary thinning, and they'll be able to remove small trees and undergrowth, and they'll be able to keep part of what they remove as partial payment. That seems to make sense to me. First of all, somebody's working. It seems like the taxpayers come out okay. After all, if you're able to keep some of the thinning, which protects our forests, as part of the payment, it's a—takes a little load off the taxpayer. The local community's tax base will get better when somebody spends the money they make from thinning the projects, and the forests are more healthy. Stewardship contracting makes sense. It's an integral part of our plan.

I'll give you a quick report. The Healthy Forests Initiative is producing results. Last year, we treated 2¼ million acres of overgrown forests. By the end of the fiscal year in September, we will have treated more than 2.6 million acres of forest and rangeland. We're slowly but surely getting after it, as we say in Crawford, Texas. We're beginning to deal with the problem that we've—that will help make the country, by solving the problem, a better place.

This year alone, we'll spend more than $43 million of forest treatment projects here in the State of Oregon. And as we go forward with the Healthy Forests Initiative, if we can ever get it authorized by Congress, I look forward to working with the appropriators, working with Gordon and Greg, to get the projects funded. We just don't want the initiative authorized; we want the initiative funded so we can solve the problem.

But the initiative I've laid out is one step. Congress needs to act. People ought to understand up there in Washington that—or over there in Washington, way over there in Washington—[*laughter*]—that current law makes it too difficult to expedite the thinning of forests because it allows the litigation process to delay progress and projects for years and years. That's the

problem. And those delays, the endless litigation delays, endanger the health of our
forests and the safety of too many of our
communities.

So I've asked Congress to fix the problem. Gordon and Greg are working hard
to fix the problem. The law called the
"Healthy Forests Restoration Act" would
bring government and communities together to select high-priority projects relevant to local needs. In other words, it's
part of the prioritization of what I just described to you earlier. It would also direct
courts to consider the long-term threats to
forest health that could result if thinning
projects are delayed. In other words, it
says, "We have a national goal to protect
our—one of our finest assets, and that is
our forests. And therefore, you—Mr. Judge,
make sure you understand that a healthy
forest is a part of your consideration when
you're listening to these appeals."

The legislation makes forest health the
priority, a high priority, when courts are
forced to resolve disputes. And it places
reasonable time limits on litigation after the
public has had an opportunity to comment
and a decision has been made. Congress
must move forward with this bill. It's a
good, commonsense piece of legislation that
will make our forests more healthy, that
will protect old-growth stands, that will
make it more likely endangered species will
exist, that will protect our communities,
that will make it easier for people to enjoy
living on the edges of our national forests.

The House of Representatives passed the
bill—and I appreciate your good work,
Greg. The Agriculture Committee has
agreed on a bill. The Agriculture Committee agreed on a bill, and when the Senate returns, they need to pass the healthy
forests legislation and get it to my desk.

The administration is also working to
help communities of this region by implementing the 1994 Northwest Forest Plan.
This plan was designed to protect wildlife
and to support a viable woods-products industry in the Northwest. It was designed,

obviously, before I arrived in Washington.
It's a good plan. It makes a lot of sense.
It was a plan forged by conservationists,
industry professionals, government officials
who came together to decide on a reasonable target for sustainable timber harvesting
on a small portion of our forests. The plan
calls for harvesting of about a billion board
foot of timber per year. It will strengthen
our communities. It will help rural America. It will help our homebuilders. It makes
sense. It was a promise made to the people
of the Northwest. It's a promise I intend
to work with the Federal Government to
keep.

Good forest policy can be the difference
between lives surrounded by natural beauty
or natural disaster. And we're watching a
natural disaster unfold right here in this
part of the world. And we can do a better
job protecting our assets. We can do a better job protecting people in the communities. Now it's time for people who represent different parts of the country to
come together to see the devastation that
takes place out West on an annual basis
and allow these good people out West to
manage their assets in a way that we'll not
only be able to say we've done a job well-
done for future generations but we're protecting something that we hold dear, and
that is the forest lands of America.

Before I finish, I do want to talk about
another conservation issue that affects the
people of the west coast, and that's energy
reliability. First, I thought our Government
response to the power outage out East and
in the Midwest was a good response. You
know, after September the 11th, we came
together in a way to be able to better deal
with emergencies that affected America.
The Federal Government, the State government, the local governments all worked in
a very close way, and the communications
was good. The system survived. The system
responded well. We had a lot of good people who didn't panic and dealt with the
problem in a very professional way. And
I want to thank our citizens out East and

up in the Midwest for doing such a fine job of responding to a very difficult situation and being respectful for their neighbor.

And yesterday Secretary of Energy Abraham and the Canadian Minister of Natural Resources met in Detroit. It's the joint effort to find out what went wrong. We're going to try to find out as quickly as we can exactly what caused the rolling blackout. But this rolling blackout and the problem we've got here with hydropower, the problem in California recently should say loud and clear to members of the legislative branch of Government that we've got an energy issue that we need to solve in America.

I called together a—put the task force together and made 105 recommendations for our Government to look at about a comprehensive national energy plan, one that encourages conservation, one that encourages energy efficiency, one that realizes that we've got to be less dependent on foreign sources of energy. And part of that was to recognize that our infrastructure, the electricity infrastructure, needs to be modernized.

And we've taken some action without law passed by the legislative branch. For example, there's a bottleneck that plagued California for years. In other words, electricity wasn't able to move as freely from south to north, north to south, as we wanted. And we're now permitting lines so that that bottleneck can be removed. And the Department of Energy is working with the private sector to get the lines up and running so we can move more electricity.

And we've been dealing with the shortage of hydropower. As you know, you've got an issue in the Klamath Basin, and we've been trying to come up with reasonable policy so that people can farm the land and fish can live at the same time.

But Congress needs to act. I don't know if you know this or not, but for many years the reliability of electricity in America depended on companies observing voluntary

standards to prevent blackouts. I don't think those standards ought to be voluntary. I think they ought to be mandatory. And if there's not reliability backup for electricity, there ought to be a serious consequence for somebody who misuses the public trust. And Congress needs to have that in the law.

We ought to authorize the Federal Government to step in as last resort to put up new power lines where it best serves the national interest. We ought to make investment—new investment in a transmission of electricity easier to make. We've got some old laws that were passed a long time ago that make it harder for people to invest in new electricity lines, new transmission lines. That doesn't make any sense. If we've got a problem, let's deal with it.

The law that passed out of the House of Representatives deals with it. I'm confident—and the Senate passed a bill—in other words, out of the two bodies, they need to get together. I talked to Pete Domenici, the Senator from New Mexico. I talked to Billy Tauzin, the chairman from Louisiana. They both agreed on what I've just described to you as necessary in a new bill, so that we can say we solved the problem; we're modernizing our electricity system so the people of America don't have their lives disrupted like what happened during the rolling blackout that took place last week. So we're going to get us a good energy bill. We need an energy bill, an energy strategy, and we need the will to implement it.

Let me conclude by telling you that I'm incredibly proud of our country. You know, we've been through a lot. We've been through a recession. You're still in it here in Oregon. We had these people attack us because of what we stand for. We love freedom in America, and we're not going to change. We stood tall and strong. We're a determined country, to not only protect ourselves; we're determined as well to protect ourselves by spreading freedom throughout the world. We know that free societies will be peaceful societies. We believe in America that freedom is not America's gift to the world; it is God's gift to every single human being on the face of the Earth.

We've been through some tough times, and these tough times came to the right nation. Our values are strong. Our people are courageous and strong and compassionate. I love being the President of the greatest nation on the face of the Earth.

May God bless you all.

NOTE: The President spoke at 3:23 p.m. at the Deschutes County Fairgrounds. In his remarks, he referred to Gov. Ted Kulongoski of Oregon; Mayors Alan Unger of Redmond, Oran Teater of Bend, Richard Allen of Madras, Stephen Uffelman of Prineville, and David Elliott of Sisters, OR; Garland Brunoe, tribal council chairman, Confederated Tribes of Warm Springs; Bill Anthony, Sisters District Ranger, Deschutes National Forest; and Minister of Natural Resources Herb Dhaliwal of Canada.

Remarks at Ice Harbor Lock and Dam in Burbank, Washington
August 22, 2003

Thank you all very much. I appreciate you coming out to say hello. Thank you. Be seated, please. Thanks for coming out to say hello. It's a little different view from the views we have in Crawford. [*Laughter*] The temperature is a little cooler, too, I want you to know.

But thanks for coming. It's such an honor to be here at the Ice Harbor Lock and Dam. I found it interesting that another Texan came to dedicate the dam. Vice President Lyndon Johnson dedicated this unbelievable facility in 1962. He said it's "an asset of astounding importance to the region and to America." He was right in 1962, and when I tell you it's an asset of astounding importance to this region of America in 2003, I'm right as well.

We just had a great tour, seeing this facility and its technological wonders. This work has added to the strength of your State, and it's added to the prosperity of the people. It's really important that we remember that when we're talking about national assets. After all, people's money built this facility, and we want the facility to help the people. The facility has been a crucial part of the past in this region, and I'm here to tell you it's going to be a crucial part of the future as well.

I was pleased to see the incredible care that goes into protecting the salmon that journey up the river. It's an important message to send to people, it seems like to me, that a flourishing salmon population is a vital part of the vibrancy of this incredibly beautiful part of our country. I appreciate the commitment that we are making as a country and that you're making as a community for salmon restoration. What I saw was and what you know firsthand is that we can have good, clean hydroelectric power and salmon restoration going on at the same time. And that's what I want to spend some time talking about. We have a responsibility to work together to make sure the human condition is strong and to make sure that the salmon flourish. And we'll meet that challenge.

I thank Gale Norton for her leadership. She is the Secretary of the Department of the Interior. She is a lady from the West. She understands land management. She knows what I know, that the folks who live closest to the land are those that care most about the land. And we appreciate that attitude.

I'm traveling in some pretty darn good company too, when it comes to the congressional delegation. Old Doc Hastings has made a pretty good hand—[*applause*]. He informed me first thing, before he even said hello, that he was a grandfather again today. So congratulations, Doc. I wouldn't take too much credit for it, Doc, if I were you. [*Laughter*]

I appreciate so very much traveling with George Nethercutt as well. Both Doc and George are always telling me about how important eastern Washington is. Every time I talk to them, they're reminding me not only that the folks here are just fine, fine, down-to-earth, hard-working people, but our Nation is blessed to have the resources that are coming from this part of your beautiful State.

The western part of your State is beautiful as well, and it's well represented— parts of it are well represented by my close friend Jennifer Dunn. I'm glad you're here, Jennifer.

The Acting Secretary of the Army, Les Brownlee, is with us today. I appreciate you coming, Les. Thank you for being here. We've got a lot of folks from the Corps of Engineers that are with us, people who are making this dam work, and I want to thank them for their service to our country. I appreciate so very much the National Marine Fisheries Service, through the Commerce Department, the representatives that are here as well.

I thank all the mayors that have come out, the State and local officials. I like to tease the mayors and tell them they've got a pretty darn tough job. After all, if the pothole isn't filled, they're going to hear from somebody firsthand at the coffee shop. [*Laughter*] That doesn't happen to the President much. [*Laughter*] I thank the mayors for coming. Just keep the garbage picked up. [*Laughter*]

I appreciate so much the tribal chiefs that are here with us today, distinguished leaders that are here to make sure that the heritage of the salmon is protected and honored and revered, Chief Burke and Blackwolf, Sockzehigh, Seyler. I'm honored

you all are here, and thank you for coming as well, for taking time.

One of the things I've learned about Washington, DC, there's a lot of experts on the environment there. [*Laughter*] At least they think they are. They're constantly trying to tell people what to do. My judgment is, they—those who think they know what they're doing in Washington, DC, ought to come out and visit with the folks that are actually protecting the environment, people such as yourself. I have been to your State enough to know that the people of this great State are never very far away from some of nature's most beautiful sights. And the people who appreciate those beautiful sights the most are those who live close to the sights. They understand best of all what it means to be a good steward of land and water.

The Washington way of life depends and always will depend on the wise protection of the natural environment. It's been a part of your past; it's going to be an important part of the future of this State and our country, for that matter. And a vital part of the natural environment is the Pacific salmon.

Lewis and Clark, as Doc was—made sure to point it out, where Lewis and Clark stayed—where he thought they stayed. [*Laughter*] But he did say that they stayed in this part of the world a long time. I can see why. The weather's nice, and the scenery is beautiful. But think about what it was like when those rivers in 1805-time-frame were just full of salmon. It must have been an unbelievable sight for them, particularly if they were hungry. [*Laughter*]

Today, there are a lot fewer salmon in the waters. And the mission has got to be to fight the decline. The mission has got to be to make sure that we understand that without the salmon in the Columbia and Snake Rivers, that this would be a huge loss to this part of the world. That's part of what the focus of my short discussion is today, is to let you know that we understand in this administration that we want to work with the local folks to revitalize the salmon runs.

The good news is that salmon runs are up. And that's really positive. And we just need to make sure we keep that momentum. I want to talk about some ways we're going to do it. Gale mentioned one thing is that we can spend that money in Washington, and we're writing a pretty good-size check in '04. It helps keep the commitment about what I said when I ran for President. I said, look, we are concerned about the fish. We're also concerned about the citizens of Washington State who depend upon the dams for electricity and the water to water their land so we can have the crops necessary to eat in America.

But the economy of this part of the world has relied upon the steady supply of hydropower. And we've got an energy problem in America. We don't need to be breaching any dams that are producing electricity. And we won't. Part of a national energy policy has got to make sure that we increase supply and maintain supply. And I saw the six generators that are able to capture a steady flow of water that produces that power that enables people to live. We want the salmon to live; we want the quality of life in this part of the world to be strong as well.

You know something, I talk about people closest to the land care about the land more than most. Every day is Earth Day if you're a farmer. Farmers depend upon the quality of the land and the quality of the water. And I understand that. And I understand that this dam and the dams along this river have a got a lot to do with the ability for people to farm the land.

You know, one of the great things about our national security is that we don't have to worry about food from some other country. We produce enough to eat here in America, and that's good for our national security. I can't say the same for energy, by the way. We're reliant upon foreign sources of energy. That is a problem for national security. We're not reliant upon

foreign sources of food, and that's important. This dam helps us become—so that we don't get reliant upon foreign sources of food.

Our farmers depend upon the dams on this river. People who run the barges need the dams. The dams accommodate—in other words, commerce happens, people can make a living, people have food on the table so they can feed their families. At the same time, the salmon are getting more plentiful. And it's a positive story, and it's a story we've got to continue to make sure this stays positive.

We have shown the world that we can have good quality of life and, at the same time, save salmon. And that's exactly what this administration will continue to do. I understand we can't do it alone, but we can help. We can make a difference. As Gale mentioned, the budgets are increasing. We're helping on technology. I just saw some technology that enables the young salmon and steelhead to pass through the dam near the surface of the dam at lower speeds and lower pressures. That will help the young salmon runs. The technology is employed at the Lower Granite Dam. It will be installed soon here at Ice Harbor. In other words, the Federal Government is doing its part by gathering the technologies that will make the salmon runs stronger and better over time.

I bet in '62 there wasn't that much concern about salmon runs, when Vice President Lyndon Johnson was here. I haven't reviewed his entire speech; I don't know how much time he spent talking about technologies necessary to save salmon. But in 2003, we can say we're developing good, strong technologies to save salmon. We're getting better at it. And that's what—[*applause*].

And I appreciate so much the hard work of the Federal employees that are doing what we pay them to do. I also know my friend Donnie Evans, who is the Secretary of Commerce, has got conservation plans that are now being developed and implemented in Chelan and Douglas County public utility districts. It's a good, creative use of Federal money, it seems like to me, to create these conservation plans and habitat restoration programs, to be smart about how we develop the strategies necessary to encourage salmon runs to increase. The plan will minimize the impact of dams, improving fish-bypass systems and hatchery programs. And we'll continue to work to fund local habitat restoration programs. In other words, there's a lot going on. But the truth of the matter is, in order to make this strategy work, we're going to have to work with the local folks. That's the reality of the situation.

I know that—I saw some of the irrigation systems, spray systems—they look pretty darn modern to me. I suspect some of the oldtime farmers here will tell you that there's been a lot of technological advancement when it comes to conservation of water. The more water our farmers conserve by using efficient sprinkler systems, obviously the less operating costs they have. But also it helps the salmon. And so for the farmers who are here, I want to thank you for doing your part not only feeding America but being good stewards of the water you use.

There's a group called Fish First. I met a fellow named Gary Loomis. And I appreciate Gary coming today. Gary is a guy who cares about restoring salmon runs, salmon habitat. So he and a group of volunteers have come together to work on the salmon projects around the State of Washington. They're installing culverts to accommodate the fish. They're creating side channels and ponds. They're getting their money through private donations. There's a lot of people who care about salmon runs, and they ought to be helping by contributing money. And they're using volunteers and some public grants.

As I understand that Gary Loomis' group is going to add another 4,900 foot of stream channel, mainly through volunteer work.

And I appreciate what you're doing, Gary. I want to—why don't you stand up and give people a chance to look at you and let you know the—[applause]. I want to thank you for what you're doing. This will give me a chance to tell the people of the great State of Washington and Oregon that if you're interested in salmon runs, if you want to do your part about conserving this great legacy, volunteer with groups like Gary Loomis' group.

There's a lot of good conservation groups that have a good commonsense view about making sure that the quality of human life is strong and the quality of fish life is vibrant and healthy as well. Volunteer help makes a difference.

I appreciate the positive attitude that people have here in this part of the world, the can-do attitude: "Here is a problem; let's go solve it together." And that's what we're here to confirm. It makes a—it's a lot better than what happens a lot of times when it comes to conservation issues. And that is, people just file lawsuit after lawsuit after lawsuit, just kind of tie everything up in endless litigation, and nothing gets better.

We've got that issue, by the way, with our forests. I was in Oregon yesterday, saw the devastating forest fires that are taking place. It's just sad to see national assets just go up in tremendous flames because we have not done a good job of thinning out our forests and protecting our forests. And a lot of the reason why is because people just file lawsuits, and we get stuck in the court, and nothing happens. The forests don't benefit. People in the communities close to the forest are—have their lives endangered because of the kindling that has piled up. We need to cut through all this business and get solving the national problems.

And so the good news about what's happening here is it looks like you've been able to bypass all the endless litigation, come up with solutions to the problem so that the people can say, you know, "Job

well done." Generations—future generations can say these folks had a chance and
they responded.

And I want to thank you for what you
do to make sure that this part of the world
is as vibrant and healthy, the heritage of
the salmon remains strong. There's no
doubt in my mind you will accomplish the
objective, no doubt in my mind we will
help. We want to be helpers, not hinderers,
coming out of Washington, DC.

You know, the amazing thing about this
country is when we put our mind to something, we can do a lot. We can do a lot.
My mind is still focused on protecting
America, by the way. We're going to hunt
the terrorists down wherever they are and
bring them to justice. And we're making
progress. See, in America we know that
freedom—free countries will be peaceful
countries. We also know that freedom is
not America's gift to the world; it is the
Almighty's gift to every human being.

Abroad, this great Nation will lead the
world to more peaceful times. We'll promote freedom. We worry about the human
condition when people are enslaved by tyranny. And at home, we'll protect our assets.
We'll conserve our beautiful environment,
and at the same time, we'll work to make
sure that people can make a living, that
people can work hard, put money on the
table; they can do their duty as a mom
or a dad for—to feed their families.

Listen, America is a fabulous country,
fabulous not only because of the values we
hold dear but fabulous because of the nature of the people, who are the American
people.

Thank you for coming. May God bless
you.

NOTE: The President spoke at 10:17 a.m. In
his remarks, he referred to Gary Burke,
chairman, board of trustees, Confederated
Tribes of the Umatilla Indian Reservation;
Harold Blackwolf, Sr., chair, Fish and Wild-
life Committee, Confederated Tribes of the
Warm Springs Reservation of Oregon; Ross
Sockzehigh, tribal council chairman, Yakama
Nation; Warren Seyler, tribal business coun-
cil chairman, Spokane Tribe; and Gary
Loomis, president, Fish First.

Remarks Following a Meeting With Economic Leaders and an Exchange With Reporters in Seattle, Washington
August 22, 2003

The President. It's a pleasure to be here
in beautiful Seattle. I just met with members of the congressional delegation and
also members of the business community,
both large and small businesses, to talk
about the fact that this economy here in
Washington State is not as strong as it
should be.

I'm fully aware that the unemployment
numbers here are some of the highest in
the country, and that's of concern. This is
a resource-based State with a significant
high-tech component. Both of those sectors
have been hit very hard by the economic
downturn. And so we talked about ways
to stimulate growth.

The first thing I talked about was the
fact that the tax plan that the Congress
passed and I signed, the most recent tax
plan, is now kicking in. People are getting
their child tax credits, which will be positive. It will be positive for the people of
this State. People are getting more money
back, and the more money they have, the
more money they'll have to spend. And
that's good news.

I talked about trade policy which will
help the high-tech industry here in the

State of Washington. We talked about the Healthy Forests Initiative, which is a commonsense plan to make sure that we save our forests before they get destroyed by catastrophic fire.

Yesterday I choppered over the fire in Oregon and saw the effects of a backward forest policy, a policy that has allowed for undergrowth to develop and provide the kindling necessary for explosive fires. I saw some interesting signs—said, "Save our mature large trees." I agree. I also saw the fires destroy the mature stands of large trees. It's unbelievable how powerful these fires raged throughout. And we've got to do something about it. A healthy forests initiative will help protect the resources of a resource-based economy.

I talked today—we talked today about energy. The good folks in the State of Washington, or the capital—people who spend money on capital investment know that we need to have an energy policy. Today I talked about something that made eminent sense to me, and that is when you've got good, clean sources of energy like hydropower, you don't destroy those sources, particularly with the Nation short of energy. And so we had a very good discussion about ways to create the conditions of economic vitality and growth.

The Federal Government can help, and the State of Washington has got to also set the conditions necessary for people to want to be here. I mean, one of the things we can do at the Federal level is pass medical liability reform. It's a national issue. I mean, it makes sense for us to have medical liability reform. If the State of Washington needs to send a message that this would be a good place to do business, they may—ought to have the legislature pass liability reform or workers' compensation reform. There's a lot of things the State of Washington can do as well.

And we had a very vital discussion. And the reason why I wanted to have this discussion is I'm concerned about the size of the unemployment rate here in this important State.

I'll answer a couple of questions, then I've got to go to another event. Jennifer [Jennifer Loven, Associated Press].

Situation in the Middle East

Q. Thank you, sir. I want to ask you about the Middle East.

The President. Middle East, yes.

Q. Palestinians militants have promised more suicide bombings. Israel itself has talked about more pinpoint strikes on militant chiefs. What can you do to make sure that the progress in the recent months doesn't get destroyed?

The President. Yes, well, we'll just keep working the issue, of course, hard and reminding people of this important fact, that if people want there to be peace in the Middle East, if the Palestinians want to see their own state, they've got to dismantle the terrorist networks.

You just opened your question by saying that some in the Palestinian territories have announced there's going to be more suicide bombings. Suicide bombings are acts of terror. Suicide bombings kill innocent people. Children, women—they don't care; they're indiscriminate. They just kill for the sake of killing. Those people who conduct suicide bombings are not interested in the vision that I have outlined, and that is a Palestinian state living side by side with Israel in peace.

What the United States will continue to do is to remind those who love peace and yearn for freedom in that part of the world to join together and to battle those few who want to destroy the ambitions of many. I will continue to work with leaders in the neighborhood to encourage them to cut off the money and the aid and the help that goes to these terrorist organizations, all of which aim to destroy any hope for peace.

I am and will continue to work the issue. I think it's important for us to—for the United States to stay very much engaged, and I will.

Randy [Randy Mikkelsen, Reuters].

Iraq/War on Terror

Q. Mr. President, it seems like the conflict in Iraq is becoming more of a guerrilla war directed against the West or international institutions. How important is it that more countries contribute troops to Iraq? And are you willing to give more political authority to the United Nations to achieve that goal?

The President. Yes, well, look, that's a very interesting question. It's—the way I view this is that Iraq is turning out to be a continuing battle in the war on terror. You know, it's one thing to remove the Saddam Hussein regime from power in order to protect America and our friends and allies, which we did. And then there are—we found resistance from former Ba'athist officials. These people decided that, well, they'd rather fight than work for peaceful reconstruction in Iraq because they weren't going to be in power anymore.

I also believe there's a foreign element that is moving into Iraq, and these will be Al-Qaida-type fighters. They want to fight us there because they can't stand the thought of a free society in the Middle East. They hate freedom. They hate the thought of a democracy emerging. And therefore, they want to violently prevent that from happening. And it's hard to characterize what kind of movement it is since this is the—this is one of the major battles of the first war of the 21st century.

As I told the American people after 9/11, one, I would never forget 9/11 and the lessons learned about protecting the security of this country, but also that we were facing a different kind of war. And having said that, we do need and welcome more foreign troops into Iraq, and there will be more foreign troops into Iraq. And what that will do is that will enable many of those troops to guard the infrastructure. If you notice what's happening, of course, is as the life of the average Iraqi begins to improve, those who hate freedom destroy the infrastructures that we've been improving. It's part of their strategy. So we'll get more people guarding that.

And in the meantime—and that will help free up our hunter teams. We're getting better human intelligence. Every day that goes by, we're getting more solid evidence from Iraqi citizens about the whereabouts of certain former thugs—or current thugs of a former regime, is a better way to put it, like "Chemical Ali." And we're winning.

And it's—we've been there for 120 days since major operations, or something like that. We've haven't been there a long time. And these people—let me finish. Just getting warmed up. [*Laughter*] These people have been subjugated for years and years and years. Torture chambers were prevalent throughout the Iraqi society. Mass graves—discovered mass graves of innocent people whose lives were slaughtered because they didn't agree with Saddam Hussein. And you can imagine the psychology of a country that has been through a—life under Saddam. Slowly but surely, people are now beginning to develop the habits necessary for a free society to emerge.

But we're going to stay the course. Now, your other question was the United Nations. Well, I've always said the United Nations ought to have a vital role, and they were playing a vital role in Iraq, such a vital role that the killers decided to destroy the very people that were providing food for the hungry and medicine for the afflicted. Now, what kind of mindset is that? That's—it is that type of mentality that we must defeat if we expect the world to be secure and peaceful.

And so yes, there will be a vital role for the U.N. As a matter of fact, we're discussing regulation—I mean, resolutions now about how to encourage other nations to participate in the process.

And let me—one more. Ryan [Ryan Donmoyer, Bloomberg News].

Q. Thank you, sir.

The President. Fine, Ryan. That's a short question? If it is a short question, I can call on Bennett [Bennett Roth, Houston Chronicle]. If it's not a short question, he gets filibustered.

National Economy

Q. Sir, three tax cuts, two wars, and now a new military role in Liberia, and your administration is now projecting deficits up near a trillion dollars this year and next. Meanwhile, a major jobless recovery, as you've just mentioned here today in Washington, and Wall Street is becoming more and more nervous about the effect of these deficits in the long-term economy. Can this economy sustain long-term deficits?

The President. We'll have the deficit in half over a 5-year period of time if Congress holds the line on discretionary spending. And one of my jobs is to make sure they do. I proposed reasonable budgets on discretionary spending, and I expect Congress to join me on those budgets.

Let me remind the people that—to whom you're writing this erudite article what caused the deficit. It was caused by the lack of revenues coming into the Treasury because of a recession. Half of the deficit was because of the recession that took place in the first quarter—first three quarters of 2001.

And remember, the stock market started to decline in March of 2000. That caused a lack of revenue coming into the Treasury. Then the country went into recession. And recession by its very nature means less business activity, less money in circulation, less monies coming into the Treasury.

And then we were at war, and I decided to request from Congress enough money to fight and win the war. That's what the American people expect. They expect a Commander in Chief to support the troops. And that's what I did and will continue to do.

Part of the deficit is also caused by the fact that Congress passed the tax relief I asked for. But the reason I asked for the tax relief is to stimulate economic growth. And so the—those who are worried about the deficit must first worry—I hope would worry first about people being able to find work, like in Washington State. I am more concerned about somebody finding a job than I am about numbers on paper. But having said that, I want to repeat that we've got a plan to reduce the deficit in half in 5 years.

Final question, Bennett of the Houston Chronicle. I've known him for a long time. For those of you who don't know him, he's a fine lad. [*Laughter*]

Space Shuttle Columbia Accident Report

Q. And it's sort of a Texas-related question. Mr. President, next week there's going to be a report issued on the Space Shuttle *Columbia* that's expected to be highly critical of NASA. Do you support the resumption of manned space flights? Do you think the program should be better funded and restructured? Where do you see the future?

The President. Let me first—I've been a strong supporter of NASA. I want to look at the report before I comment. You may have seen the report; I haven't, in which case I want to look at it. I do believe that a space program is important for a country that is trying to stay on the leading edge of technological change. But let me look and first see what the report says, how critical it is, what it says, what it means. And I'll answer—try to answer that very question after I've had a chance to enrich my knowledge about a pending report.

Thank you all.

Birthday of Jennifer Loven

Q. It's her birthday.

The President. Today is your birthday?

Q. No. [*Laughter*]

Q. Yes, it is.

The President. You shouldn't be so shy in front of national cameras. [*Laughter*]

Q. I'd rather it not be a topic, thank you. [*Laughter*]

The President. Would you like for your compadres to break out in a "Happy Birthday" here on TV?

Q. They've already done that, thank you.

The President. They have? Should we have the business community sing? [*Laughter*] Happy birthday.

Thank you all.

NOTE: The President spoke at 12:50 p.m. at Boeing Field-King County International Airport. In his remarks, he referred to former President Saddam Hussein of Iraq; and former Iraqi Ba'ath Party official Ali Hassan al-Majid (known as "Chemical Ali"). A portion of these remarks could not be verified because the tape was incomplete.

Statement on the Designation of Hamas Leadership and European Funding Sources Under Executive Order 13224
August 22, 2003

At my direction, the Treasury Department has moved today to block and freeze the assets of six top Hamas leaders and five nongovernmental organizations that I am advised provide financial support to Hamas. By claiming responsibility for the despicable act of terror on August 19, Hamas has reaffirmed that it is a terrorist organization committed to violence against Israelis and to undermining progress toward peace between Israel and the Palestinian people.

I call upon all nations supportive of peace in the Middle East to recognize Hamas as a terrorist organization and to take all appropriate actions to deny it support.

The President's Radio Address
August 23, 2003

Good morning. Earlier this week, terrorists struck the United Nations headquarters in Baghdad. The U.N. personnel and Iraqi citizens killed in the bombings were engaged in a purely humanitarian mission. Men and women in the building were working on reconstruction, medical care for Iraqis, and the distribution of food. Among the dead was Sergio Vieira de Mello, the U.N. Representative for Iraq, a good man serving an important cause.

On the same day, a terrorist in Jerusalem murdered 20 innocent people riding a bus, including 5 Americans. The killer had concealed under his clothing a bomb filled with metal fragments, designed to kill and injure the greatest number of people possible. Among the 110 people hurt were 40 children.

These two bombings reveal once again the nature of the terrorists and why they must be defeated. In their malicious view of the world, no one is innocent. Relief workers and infants alike are targeted for murder. Terrorism may use religion as a disguise, but terrorism violates every religion and every standard of decency and morality.

The terrorists have declared war on every free nation and all our citizens. Their goals are clear: They want more governments to resemble the oppressive Taliban that once ruled Afghanistan. Terrorists commit atrocities because they want the civilized world to flinch and retreat so they can impose their totalitarian vision. There will be no flinching in this war on terror, and there will be no retreat.

From Afghanistan to Iraq to the Philippines and elsewhere, we are waging a campaign against the terrorists and their allies wherever they gather, wherever they plan, and wherever they act. This campaign requires sacrifice, determination, and resolve, and we will see it through. Iraq is an essential front in this war. Now we're fighting terrorists and remnants of that regime who have everything to lose from the advance of freedom in the heart of the Middle East.

In most of Iraq, there is steady movement toward reconstruction and a stable, self-governing society. This progress makes the remaining terrorists even more desperate and willing to lash out against symbols of order and hope like coalition forces and U.N. personnel. The world will not be intimidated. A violent few will not determine the future of Iraq, and there will be no return to the days of Saddam Hussein's torture chambers and mass graves.

Working with Iraqis, coalition forces are on the offensive against these killers. Aided by increasing flow of intelligence from ordinary Iraqis, we are stepping up raids, seizing enemy weapons, and capturing enemy leaders. The United States, the United Nations, and the civilized world will continue to stand with the people of Iraq as they reclaim their nation and their future.

We're determined as well not to let murderers decide the future of the Middle East. A Palestinian state will never be built on a foundation of violence. The hopes of that state and the security of Israel both depend on an unrelenting campaign against terror, waged by all parties in the region. In the Middle East, true peace has deadly enemies. Yet America will be a consistent friend of every leader who works for peace by actively opposing violence.

All nations of the world face a challenge and a choice. In continued acts of murder and destruction, terrorists are testing our will, hoping we will weaken and withdraw. Yet across the world, they are finding that our will cannot be shaken. Whatever the hardships, we will persevere. We will continue this war on terror until all the killers are brought to justice, and we will prevail.

Thank you for listening.

NOTE: The address was recorded at 10:30 a.m. on August 22 in Bend, OR, for broadcast at 10:06 a.m. on August 23. The transcript was made available by the Office of the Press Secretary on August 22 but was embargoed for release until the broadcast. The Office of the Press Secretary also released a Spanish language transcript of this address.

Statement on the Terrorist Bombings in Mumbai, India
August 25, 2003

I strongly condemn the bombings in Mumbai, India, which killed dozens of innocent people and injured many more. Acts of terror are intended to sow fear and chaos among free peoples. I hope that the perpetrators of these murders will be identified quickly and brought to justice.

On behalf of all Americans, I send condolences to all affected by today's tragedy and to the Government and people of India.

Statement on the Death of John J. Rhodes
August 25, 2003

John Rhodes was a statesman and a leader in the United States Congress. He was admired by Republicans and Democrats alike for his 30 years of tireless work for the people he represented and the country he loved. Laura joins me in sending our thoughts and prayers to his wife, Elizabeth, and the entire Rhodes family.

Remarks at a Bush-Cheney Luncheon in St. Paul, Minnesota
August 26, 2003

Thanks for the warm welcome. I appreciate such a huge response for our invitation to come for a little light meal. [*Laughter*] It's an honor to be back in the beautiful State of Minnesota and two such vibrant cities. The temperature differential is nice too, I might add. [*Laughter*]

I came up from Crawford today. What I really want to do is thank you for your support and your friendship and to let you know that today we're laying the groundwork for what is going to be a great national victory in November of 2004.

I appreciate the fact that you have contributed, but I want you to know I'm going to count on you to contribute more. I need you to tell your neighbors, and for those of you who go to coffee shops, you be telling them in the coffee shops that this President and this administration will continue to work for a positive and hopeful vision for every single American.

I'm loosening up, and I'm getting ready for the campaign. [*Laughter*] But there's going to be plenty of time for politics, because I've got a job to do. I'm focused on the people's business, and we have a lot on our agenda in Washington, DC. Until the political season starts for me, I will continue to work to earn the confidence of every American by keeping this Nation secure and strong and prosperous and free.

My big regret today is that the First Lady is not traveling with me. She's in Crawford with Barney. [*Laughter*] But I want you to know that it is a great comfort to live in the White House with Laura Bush. She is a great First Lady, a fabulous wife. I love her dearly, and she sends her best.

I want to thank Ben Whitney for his willingness to lead this campaign here in the State of Minnesota. I appreciate my friend Rudy Boschwitz for taking a leadership role for this event today and for the remaining events. I want to thank all the State cochairmen, starting with a fine man and a guy who is doing a good job as your Governor, Tim Pawlenty. Tim, thank you for coming today.

I'll never forget the rally that I attended here in 2002 for United States Senator Norm Coleman. I'm sorry Norm can't be here, but it's a joy to work with him in the United States Senate. He is doing a fine job on behalf of the citizens of Minnesota.

I thank Congressman Gil Gutknecht for coming today. I appreciate his hard work, and it's been a joy to work with him and others of the Minnesota delegation. I want to thank your State auditor for coming. I appreciate the leadership of the legislature for being here, the speaker of the house as well as the Minnesota minority leader in the State senate. I'm honored you all have taken time out of your day to come to say hello.

I appreciate my friend Mercer Reynolds, who is the national fundraising chairman for Bush-Cheney. He's from Cincinnati, Ohio. He's a businessperson. He's taking time out of his life to work hard to see that we raise the monies necessary to wage a viable and strong campaign.

I want to thank Rob Eibensteiner, who is the chairman of the Republican Party of Minnesota. I want to thank former Governor Al Quie for coming. But most of all, I want to thank you all for your loyal and strong support.

You know, in the last 2½ years, this Nation has acted decisively to confront great challenges. I came to the office of President of the United States to solve problems instead of passing them on to future Presidents and future generations. I came to seize opportunities instead of letting them slip away. We are meeting the tests of our time.

Terrorists declared war on the United States of America, and war is what they got. We have captured or killed many key leaders of the Al Qaida network, and the rest of them know we're on their trail. In Afghanistan and Iraq, we gave ultimatums to terror regimes. Those regimes chose defiance, and those regimes are no more. Fifty million people in those two countries once lived under tyranny, and now they live in freedom.

Two-and-a-half years ago, our military was not receiving the resources it needed, and morale was beginning to suffer. We increased the defense budget to prepare for the threats of a new era. And today, no one in the world can question the skill and the strength and the spirit of the United States military.

Two-and-a-half years ago, we inherited an economy in recession. And then our country was attacked, and scandals broke out in corporate America, and we were headed to war, which all affected the people's confidence. But we acted. We passed tough new laws to hold corporate criminals to account. And I have twice led the United States Congress to pass historic tax relief to get our economy moving again.

Here's what I believe, and here's what I know, that when Americans have more take-home pay to spend, to save, or invest, the whole economy grows and people are more likely to find a job. I also understand whose money we spend in Washington, DC. It is not the Government's money; it is the people's money that we spend in our Nation's Capital.

We're returning more money for people to help them raise their families. We're reducing taxes on dividends and capital gains to encourage investment. We're giving small businesses incentives that are needed to hire new people. With all these actions, we're laying the foundation for greater prosperity and more jobs across our country so that every single person has a chance to realize the American Dream.

Two-and-a-half years ago, there was a lot of talk about education reform, but there wasn't much action. So I called for and the Congress passed the No Child Left Behind Act. With a solid bipartisan majority, we delivered the most dramatic education reforms in a generation. We're bringing high standards and strong accountability measures to every public school in America. See, we believe that every child can learn the basics of reading and math. We believe every school must teach the basics of reading and math. This administration is challenging the soft bigotry of low expectations. The days of excuse-making are over. In return for Federal money, we expect results in every single classroom so that not one child in America is left behind.

We reorganized the Government, the largest reorganization since the Defense Department was reorganized in the late forties and early fifties. And we did so to create the Department of Homeland Security to safeguard our borders and ports and to better protect the American people.

We passed a trade promotion authority to open up new markets for Minnesota's farmers and ranchers and entrepreneurs and manufacturers. We passed budget agreements that is helping to maintain much needed spending discipline in Washington, DC. On issue after issue, this administration has acted on principle, has kept its word, and has made progress for the American people.

The United States Congress has shared in these great achievements. I particularly enjoy working with Speaker of the House Hastert and Majority Leader Frist. I'm proud of Norm Coleman and the members of the congressional delegation that you've sent to Washington from the State of Minnesota. I will continue to work with these leaders to change the tone in Washington, DC, to get rid of the needless partisan bickering and to focus on the people's business and to concentrate on results.

And that's the nature of the men and women I've asked to join my administration, results-oriented people. I have put together a fantastic administration on behalf of the American people. There has been no greater Vice President of the United States than Richard B. Cheney. Mother may disagree. [*Laughter*]

In 2½ years, we have come far; we've done a lot; we've taken on a lot of problems. But our work is only beginning. We have great goals worthy of this great Nation. First, America is committed to expanding the realm of freedom and peace for our own security and for the benefit of the world. And second, in our own country, we must work for a society of prosperity and compassion so that every citizen has a chance to work and succeed and realize the great promise of our country. It is clear that the future of freedom and peace depend on the actions of America. This Nation is freedom's home and freedom's defender. We welcome this charge of history, and we're keeping it.

Our war on terror continues. The enemies of freedom are not idle, and neither are we. This country will not rest; we will not tire; and we will not stop until this danger to civilization is removed.

Yet, our national interest involves more than eliminating aggressive threats to our security. Our greatest security comes from the advance of human liberty, because free nations do not support terror. Free nations do not attack their neighbors. Free nations do not threaten the world with weapons of mass terror. Americans believe that freedom is the deepest need and hope of every human heart. And I believe that freedom is the right of every person and the future of every nation.

America also understands that unprecedented influence brings tremendous responsibilities. We have duties in the world. When we see disease and starvation and hopeless poverty, we will not turn away. On the continent of Africa, this great Nation is committed to bringing the healing power of medicine to millions of men and women and children now suffering with AIDS. Our great country is leading the world in this incredibly important work of human rescue.

We face challenges at home as well. We've got big challenges here at home, and no doubt, our actions will prove that we're equal to those challenges. First, I'm concerned about people not being able to find a job. I want our people working. And therefore, we'll continue to work to create the environment necessary to have a strong entrepreneurial spirit, to make sure capital flows, to make sure the workforce expands so that anybody in the State of Minnesota or elsewhere who wants to work and can't find a job will be able to do so.

We have a chance to keep our commitment to America's seniors by strengthening and modernizing Medicare. A few weeks ago, the Congress took historic action to improve the lives of our older Americans. For the first time since the creation of Medicare, the House and the Senate have passed reforms to increase the choices for seniors and to provide coverage for prescription drugs.

The recess is almost over. It is now time for both Houses to come together to iron out their differences and to get a bill to my desk. The sooner they finish the job, the sooner America's seniors and those of us who will be seniors soon will have a modern Medicare plan. We owe it to our seniors.

For the sake of our health care system, we need to cut down on the frivolous lawsuits which increase the cost of medicine. People who have been harmed by a bad doctor deserve their day in court. Yet, the system should not reward lawyers who are fishing for rich settlements. Because frivolous lawsuits drive up the cost of health care, they affect the Federal budget.

Medical liability reform is a national issue that requires a national solution. I have proposed a plan—[*applause*]—I proposed a good plan to reform medical liability. The House of Representatives passed a good bill. It is stuck in the Senate. It is time for the United States Senate to realize that no one has ever been healed by a frivolous lawsuit.

I have a responsibility as President to make sure the judicial system runs well. And I have met that duty. I have nominated superb men and women for the Federal courts, people who will interpret the law, not legislate from the bench. Some Members of the Senate are trying to keep my nominees off the bench by blocking up-or-down votes. Every judicial nominee deserves a fair hearing and an up-or-down vote on the Senate floor. It is time for Members of the Senate to stop playing politics with American justice.

The Congress needs to complete work on a comprehensive energy plan. I came to your great State to lay out my vision for a comprehensive energy plan. And now it's time for the Congress to act. And the recent breakdown of the deliverability of electricity on the east coast should send a clear signal to the United States Congress

that we need a comprehensive energy plan, that we need to modernize our system, that we need mandatory reliability standards, and we need incentives to encourage investment. This country also must become less dependent on foreign sources of energy. For economic security and for national security, we must use our technology to explore in environmentally safe ways to increase the energy supply of the United States of America.

Our strong and prosperous Nation must also be a compassionate nation. I will continue to advance our agenda of compassionate conservatism by applying the best and most innovative ideas to helping our fellow citizens in need. There are still millions of men and women who want to end their dependence on the Government and become independent through hard work. We must work to build on the welfare reform successes of the immediate past to bring work into the lives of more of our citizens.

Congress should complete the "Citizen Service Act" so that more Americans will serve their communities and their country. And both Houses should reach agreement on my Faith-Based Initiative to support the armies of compassion, to support the Christians and Jewish people and Muslims, all who've heard the universal call to help a neighbor in need, to encourage the mentoring of children and caring for the homeless and offering hope to the addicted.

A compassionate society must also promote opportunity for all, including the independence and dignity that come from ownership. This administration will constantly strive to promote an ownership society in America. We want more citizens owning their own home. We want people to own and manage their own retirement accounts. We want people to have control over their own medical accounts. We want there to be more ownership of small businesses in America because we understand when America—an American owns something, he or she has a vital stake in the future of our country.

In a compassionate society, people respect one another and they take responsibility for the decisions they make. We're changing the culture of America from one that has said, "If it feels good, do it," and "If you've got a problem, blame somebody else," to a culture in which each of us understands that we're responsible for the decisions we make in life.

If you are fortunate enough to be a mother or father, you're responsible for loving your child with all your heart and all your soul. If you're concerned about the quality of the education in the community in which you live, you're responsible for doing something about it. If you're a CEO in corporate America, you're responsible for telling the truth to your employees and your shareholders. And in a responsibility society, each of us is responsible for loving our neighbor just like we'd like to be loved ourself.

We can see the culture of responsibility and the culture of service growing around us, particularly since 9/11, 2001. You know, I started what's called the USA Freedom Corps to encourage Americans to extend a compassionate hand to a neighbor in need, and the response has been significant. Our charities and our faith-based organizations are vibrant and strong all across America. And policemen and firefighters and people who wear our Nation's uniform are reminding us what it means to sacrifice for something greater than yourself. Once again, the children of America believe in heroes, because they see them every day. In these challenging times, the world has seen the resolve and the courage of America, and I've been privileged to see the compassion and the character of the American people.

All the tests of the last 2½ years have come to the right nation. We're a strong country, and we use our strength to defend the peace. We're an optimistic country, confident in ourselves and in ideals bigger than ourselves. Abroad, we seek to lift whole nations by spreading freedom. At home, we seek to lift up lives by spreading opportunity to every corner of our country. This is the work that history has set before us. We welcome it. And we know that for our country and for our cause, the best days lie ahead.

Thank you for coming, and may God bless.

NOTE: The President spoke at 12:12 p.m. at the St. Paul RiverCentre. In his remarks, he referred to Ben Whitney and Rudy Boschwitz, Minnesota State finance cochairmen, Bush-Cheney '04, Inc.; Patricia Awada, Minnesota State auditor; Steve Sviggum, speaker, Minnesota State House of Representatives; and Dick Day, minority leader, Minnesota State Senate.

Remarks at the American Legion National Convention in St. Louis, Missouri
August 26, 2003

The President. Thank you all. Thanks for that warm welcome. It is great to be here in St. Louis, Missouri, at the 85th annual convention of the American Legion. I wonder if I'm the only member here today from Post 77 in Houston, Texas.

Audience member. No. [*Laughter*]

The President. Seems like they'd have given you a better seat. [*Laughter*]

It is always an honor to be with people who have served America and who love America. When the American Legion held its first caucus in this city back in 1919, Legionnaires dedicated this organization to the service of God and country. Times change, but those are still the right priorities. On behalf of your fellow citizens, I thank the American Legion and the Ladies Auxiliary for your idealism and for your faithful service to God and country.

I'm honored to be traveling today with Secretary of Veterans Affairs Tony Principi. He served in Vietnam, and he serves his comrades in my Cabinet. He's a tireless advocate for our Nation's veterans. I want you to understand the facts of this good man's leadership. The budget for Veterans Affairs has gone up by $15 billion since I took office, a 30-percent increase. And my budget for fiscal year 2004 includes the largest discretionary increase for the Department of Veterans Affairs ever requested by a President. The Department, under Tony's lead, has made major progress in reducing the backlog of veterans' disability claims and the number of veterans waiting for health care. And we will continue to work to make sure those backlogs are eliminated.

I want to thank Ron Conley, the national commander of the American Legion, for his kind introduction and for his leadership of this distinguished group of citizens. I appreciate Senator Jim Talent and Congressman Todd Akin from the State of Missouri, who are here with us today. I thank Elsie Bailey, American Legion's lady auxiliary national president. I'm honored to be on the stage with Major General Patrick Brady, Medal of Honor recipient.

I know in the audience somewhere is my friend Arlene Howard. There she is. Arlene, thank you. I don't know if you remember the speech I gave in front of the Congress right after the attacks of September the 11th, but I held up the badge of one of the brave who were killed. It was the badge of Arlene's son. I'm honored you're here, Arlene. I appreciate you coming. I can't wait to give you a hug.

I want to thank the board of directors for the invitation. And I want to thank you all for being such great Americans. The American Legion is an effective and respected voice for the veteran, and you speak with authority. In the years following the First World War, leaders of this organization helped to establish the U.S. Veterans Bureau. Following World War II, you helped secure passage of the GI bill. You've supported the memorials to those who fought in World War II and Korea and Vietnam, so the sacrifices of those wars are always remembered.

For two generations, you have demanded a full accounting of Americans whose fate is undetermined. And my administration will not rest until that accounting is complete. And having fought under the American flag and seen it folded and given to families of your friends, you are committed, as am I, to protecting the dignity of the flag in the Constitution of the United States.

In the 20th century, the American flag and the American uniform stood for something unique in history. This Nation gained great power, and we used that power in the service of human freedom. Americans liberated continents and concentration camps. America's Armed Forces humbled tyrants and raised up and befriended nations that once fought against us. Our Nation led a great alliance against a Communist empire until that empire was gone and its captives were free. America's veterans have all been a part of this great story of perseverance and courage, and people and nations across the world are better off because of your service.

On Memorial Day last year, I visited the military cemetery at Normandy and saw the grave of one of the founders of the American Legion, Brigadier General Theodore Roosevelt, Jr. When Roosevelt landed with the first wave of his unit on D-day, he and his men found themselves in a different part of Utah Beach from the point they expected. Roosevelt quickly sized up the situation and called in a whole division to the new sector. Turning a challenge into an advantage, he declared, "We'll start the war from here."

Well, a great challenge came to America on September the 11th, 2001. Enemies who plotted for years in secret carried out missions of murder on our own soil. It was a day of suffering and sorrow. It was also a day of decision for our country. As a united and resolute people, America declared, "We'll start the war from here."

In this first war of the 21st century, America and all free nations are facing a new threat and fighting a new enemy, a global network of terror supported by outlaw regimes. We've seen the hand of the terrorist enemy in the attacks on our country. We've seen the deadly work of the terrorists in Bali, in Mombasa, in Riyadh, in Jakarta, in Casablanca. On a single day last week, we saw the true nature of the terrorists once again. In Baghdad, they attacked a symbol of the civilized world, the United Nations headquarters, and killed men and women who were there to bring humanitarian help to the Iraqi people. They killed a respected U.N. Special Representative, Sergio Vieira de Mello from Brazil. And on the same day in Jerusalem, a terrorist murdered 21 innocent people who were riding a bus, including little children and 5 Americans.

The terrorists' aim is to spread chaos and fear by killing on an ever-widening scale. They serve their cause by sacrificing the innocent. They celebrate the murder of women and children. They attacked the civilized world because they bear a deep hatred for the values of the civilized world. They hate freedom and religious tolerance and democracy and equality for women. They hate Christians and Jews and every Muslim who does not share their narrow and violent vision.

No nation can be neutral in the struggle between civilization and chaos. Every nation that stands on the side of freedom and the value of human life must condemn terrorism and act against the few who would destroy the hopes of the many.

Because America stands for freedom and tolerance and the rights of all, the terrorists have targeted our country. During the last few decades, the terrorists grew bolder, believing if they hit America hard, America would retreat and back down. Five years ago, one of the terrorists said that an attack could make America run in less than 24 hours. They're learning something different today. The terrorists have not seen America running; they've seen America marching. They've seen the armies of liberation. They have seen the armies of liberation marching into Kabul and to Baghdad. The terrorists have seen speeding tank convoys and roaring jets and Special Forces arriving in midnight raids. And sometimes justice has found them before they could see anything coming at all.

We've adopted a new strategy for a new kind of war. We will not wait for known enemies to strike us again. We will strike them in their camps or caves or wherever they hide before they hit more of our cities and kill more of our citizens. We will do everything in our power to deny terrorists weapons of mass destruction before they can commit murder on an unimaginable scale. The security of this Nation and our friends requires decisive action. And with a broad coalition, we're taking that action around the globe. We are on the offensive against terror, and we will stay on the offensive against terror.

In Afghanistan, we acted against the Taliban regime that harbored Al Qaida and ruled by terror. The Taliban felt pretty strong when they were whipping women in the streets and executing them in soccer fields. When our coalition moved in, the Taliban ran quickly for the caves. But the caves could not hide these killers from justice. We've sent a message that is understood throughout the world: If you harbor a terrorist, if you support a terrorist, if you feed a terrorist, you're just as guilty as the terrorists. And the Taliban found out what we meant.

Afghanistan today is a friend of the United States of America. Because we acted, that country is not a haven for terrorists and the people of America are safer from attack. That nation still faces challenges, and our coalition forces there still face dangers. Yet we're working every day to make sure that Afghanistan finds its future as a free and stable and peaceful nation.

America and the new Afghan Army are working together in a major operation called Warrior Sweep, which is hunting down terrorists one by one. NATO is now taking a leading role in keeping Afghanistan secure. New roads are being built, medical clinics are opening, and many young girls are going to school for the first time, thanks to our coalition and the United States of America.

The Al Qaida terrorists lost a base in Afghanistan, but they operate in many other places. We're on their trail, from Pakistan to the Philippines to the Horn of Africa. Earlier this month, we captured a major terrorist named Hambali. He's a known killer and was a close associate of September the 11th mastermind Khalid Sheikh Mohammed. Hambali was one of the world's most lethal terrorists and is suspected of planning the attack on Bali and other recent acts of terror. We're making steady progress. Nearly two-thirds of known senior Al Qaida leaders, operational managers, and key facilitators have either been captured or killed.

Now Al Qaida is wounded, yet not destroyed. It remains a grave danger to the American people. Terrorist networks are still finding recruits and still plotting attacks and still intending to strike our country. Yet our resolve is firm, and it is clear: No matter how long it takes, we will bring to justice those who plot against America.

We've also pursued the war on terror in Iraq. America and our coalition removed a regime that built, possessed, and used weapons of mass destruction, a regime that sponsored terror, and a regime that persecuted its people. Our military coalition destroyed the Iraqi regime while taking extraordinary measures to spare innocent life. The battle of Iraq was conducted with the skill and honor of a great military, the United States Armed Forces.

Because of our military, catastrophic weapons will no longer be in the hands of a reckless, unstable dictator. Because of our military, Middle Eastern countries no longer fear subversion and attack by Saddam Hussein. Because of our military, Iraq will no longer be a source of funding for suicide bombers in the Middle East. Because of our men and women in uniform, the torture chambers in Iraq are closed, the prison cells for children are empty, and the people who speak their minds need not fear execution.

In all the debates over Iraq, we must never forget the brutal nature of the regime of Saddam Hussein. Mass grave sites, literally thousands of people buried in mass grave sites, were recently discovered by our troops. They contain the remains not only of executed men and women but of executed children as well. Our people in uniform, joined by fine allies, ended this nightmare in Iraq, removed a threat to the world, and they have made our Nation proud.

The work of our coalition in Iraq goes on because that country is now a point of testing in the war on terror. The remnants of Saddam's regime are still dangerous, and terrorists are gathering in Iraq to undermine the advance of freedom. Al Qaida and the other global terror networks recognize that the defeat of Saddam Hussein's regime is a defeat for them. They know that a democratic Iraq in the heart of the Middle East would be a further defeat for their ideology of terror. They know that the spread of peace and hope in the Middle East would undermine the appeal of bitterness, resentment, and violence. And the more progress we make in Iraq, the more desperate the terrorists will become. Freedom is a threat to their way of life.

They have sabotaged water mains and oil pipelines and attacked local police. Last week, they killed aid workers bringing food and medicine to the country. The terrorists have killed innocent Iraqis and Americans and U.N. officials from many nations. They have declared war on the entire civilized world, and the civilized world will not be intimidated. Retreat in the face of terror would only invite further and bolder attacks. There will be no retreat.

We are on the offensive against the Saddam loyalists, the foreign fighters, and the criminal gangs that are attacking Iraqis and coalition forces. We're receiving more and more vital intelligence from Iraqi citizens, information that we're putting to good use. Our recent military operations have included almost 200 raids netting more than 1,100 detainees. Since the end of major combat operations, we have seized more than 8,200 tons of ammunition, thousands of AK–47s, and rocket-propelled grenades and other weapons.

And as we help the Iraqi people establish security, we are working through that famous deck of cards. So far, of the 55 most wanted Iraqi leaders, 42 have been captured or killed. The brutal, vicious sons of the dictator are gone. Recently, we captured the former Vice President of Iraq. He was one of Saddam Hussein's most feared enforcers. And recently, as well, we captured the man known as "Chemical Ali." He earned his nickname by ordering chemical weapon attacks on whole Iraqi villages, killing thousands of citizens. "Chemical Ali's" savage career is over. The search goes on for other former leaders of Iraq, and we will find them. After decades of smothering fear, the Iraqi people can be certain: The regime of Saddam Hussein is gone, and it is never coming back.

Ultimately, the security of Iraq will be won by the Iraqi people themselves. They must reject terror, and they must join in their own defense. And they're stepping forward. More than 38,000 Iraqis have been hired as police officers. Iraqi police and border guards and security forces are increasingly taking on critical duties. Over 1,400 Iraqi civil defense corps volunteers are being trained to work closely with coalition forces. Twelve thousand Iraqis will be trained in the next year for the country's new army.

At the same time, 31 countries have contributed 21,000 forces to build security in Iraq. I will continue to challenge other countries to join in this important mission.

In most of Iraq today, there's steady progress toward reconstruction and civil order. Iraq's Governing Council, representing the nation's diverse groups, is steadily assuming greater responsibility over the country. The coalition provisional authority led by Ambassador Paul Bremer is implementing a comprehensive plan to ensure a successful, democratic Iraq and a better future for the Iraqi people.

Building a free and peaceful Iraq will require a substantial commitment of time and resources, and it will yield a substantially safer and more secure America and the world. I'll work with the Congress to make sure we provide the resources to do the work of freedom and security.

Iraq's progress toward self-determination and democracy brings hope to other oppressed people in the region and throughout the world. It is the rise of democracy that tyrants fear and terrorists seek to undermine. The people who yearn for liberty and opportunity in countries like Iran and throughout the Middle East are watching, and they are praying for our success in Iraq.

More progress will come in Iraq, and it will require hard and sustained efforts. As many of you saw firsthand in Germany and Japan after World War II, the transition from dictatorship to democracy is a massive undertaking. It's not an easy task. In the aftermath of World War II, that task took years, not months, to complete. And yet the effort was repaid many times over as former enemies became friends and allies and partners in keeping the peace.

Likewise, the work we do today is essential to the peace of the world and for the security of our country. America is a nation that understands its responsibilities and keeps its word. And we will honor our word to the people of Iraq and those in the Middle East who yearn for freedom. Murderers will not determine the future of Iraq, and they will not determine the future of the Middle East.

In Jerusalem as in Baghdad, terrorists are trying to undermine the hopes of peace with acts of violence. Their desperation also grows as the parties move closer to a just settlement. But terrorists do not speak for the Palestinian people. They do not serve the Palestinian cause. And a Palestinian state will never be built on the foundation of violence.

Now is the time for every true friend of the Palestinian people, every leader in the Middle East, and the Palestinian people themselves to cut off all money and support for terrorists and actively fight terror on all fronts. Only then can Israel be secure and the flag rise over an independent Palestine. And to bring that day closer, America will be a consistent friend of all who work for peace.

For nearly 2 years, on many fronts, the United States and our friends have conducted a global campaign against terror. We met the enemy on desert sands and mountain passes, wherever they choose to gather and fight. We've had successes, yet our mission continues. The stakes could not be greater for the American people. All of us who have taken an oath to defend this Nation will do our duty.

Our military forces in the war on terror are showing the definition of "duty." In hostile conditions and remote parts of the Earth, brave Americans are sacrificing for freedom and the security of others. Some have been wounded, and some have been killed. The veterans in this hall understand the loss and sadness that have come to military families. This Nation is grateful to every man and woman who serves, and we honor the memory of all who have fallen.

We also remember what this fight is about. Our military is confronting terrorists in Iraq and Afghanistan and in other places so our people will not have to confront terrorist violence in New York or St. Louis or Los Angeles. Our Armed Forces are doing the work they are called to do. They're taking the fight to the enemy so that America and our friends can live in peace.

The war on terror is a test of our strength. It is a test of our perseverance, our patience, and our will. This Nation has been tested before. By the character of men and women like you, we've come through every trial. And so it is today. Our course is set. Our purpose is firm. No act of terrorists will weaken our resolve or alter their fate. Our only goal, our only option, is total victory in the war on terror. And this Nation will press on to victory.

Thank you for having me. May God bless you, and may God continue to bless America.

NOTE: The President spoke at 3 p.m. at the St. Louis Convention Center. In his remarks, he referred to Nurjaman Riduan Isamuddin (known as Hambali), Al Qaida's chief operational planner in Southeast Asia; Khalid Sheikh Mohammed, senior Al Qaida leader responsible for planning the September 11, 2001, terrorist attack, who was captured in Pakistan on March 1; former President Saddam Hussein and former Vice President Taha Yasin Ramadan of Iraq; former Iraqi Ba'ath Party official Ali Hassan al-Majid (known as "Chemical Ali"); and L. Paul Bremer III, Presidential Envoy to Iraq. The Office of the Press Secretary also released a Spanish language transcript of these remarks.

Statement on the Report of the Columbia Accident Investigation Board
August 26, 2003

Today the Columbia Accident Investigation Board released its report on the tragic accident that claimed the lives of seven brave astronauts. These men and women assumed great risk in service to all humanity. On behalf of a grateful Nation, I once again recognize their sacrifices and those of their loved ones. Their service will never be forgotten.

Our Nation also owes its appreciation to Admiral Harold Gehman, Jr. (retired) as well as the other 12 members of the Columbia Accident Investigation Board. As Board Chair, Admiral Gehman and his team have worked tirelessly over the past seven months conducting an exhaustive review of the circumstances surrounding this accident. The next steps for NASA under Sean O'Keefe's leadership must be determined after a thorough review of the entire report, including its recommendations.

Our journey into space will go on. The work of the crew of the *Columbia* and the heroic explorers who traveled before them will continue.

Remarks at a Dinner for Senator Christopher S. "Kit" Bond of Missouri in St. Louis
August 26, 2003

Thanks for the warm welcome. It's such an honor to be here in the great State of Missouri. I am here because I believe Kit Bond is the right man for the United States Senate.

And I want to thank you for his—for your strong support for this fine Senator. Looks like you've got a few friends here in Missouri, Senator. [*Laughter*] Actually, I wasn't his first choice to come tonight. [*Laughter*] Laura is stuck on the ranch. [*Laughter*] But she sends her very best to Kit and to Linda.

Just as a kind of step back, I am really fortunate that Laura Bush said yes when I asked her to marry me. She is a great First Lady and a fabulous wife. I appreciate—you know, Senator Bond and I both married above ourselves. [*Laughter*] And it's great to see Linda. She's done a lot for him. She shortened his speeches and shortened his waistline. [*Laughter*] He's getting in fighting form for the '04 elections.

I'm also honored to be here with former Senator Jack Danforth. What a distinguished citizen of your State he is. He's working hard to bring peace to the Sudan. It's about as tough as an assignment as somebody can be given. But because of his steady demeanor and patience and his faith in freedom and peace, I think we'll achieve peace in the Sudan, and Jack Danforth will deserve a lot of credit.

I'm also honored to be here with the junior Senator from the great State of Missouri, a man who's doing a fabulous job on your behalf, Senator Jim Talent.

Speaking about Missouri citizens doing a fine job, John Ashcroft is a very good Attorney General. I am proud of the job he is doing. You trained him well. [*Laughter*]

Also traveling with me today is another member of my Cabinet, the Secretary of Veterans Affairs, a friend of the veterans, Tony Principi. Thank you for coming, Mr. Secretary. He and I were at the American

Legion Convention today and had a chance to talk about our foreign policy. And I'll speak a little bit about that later on.

I appreciate Congressman Todd Akin and Congressman Kenny Hulshof as well from the mighty delegation from the State of Missouri. These are two strong allies and good friends, and I appreciate their service.

I know that Secretary of State Matt Blunt is with us, and his wife, Melanie. I know that Catherine Hanaway, the speaker of the house, is with us, and I know that State Senator Peter Kinder are here. And I appreciate the members of the State delegation from Missouri for coming as well.

Ann Wagner is the cochair of the Republican National Committee, and I'm really proud of her service to the Republican Party not only here in Missouri but across the Nation. Annie, thank you very much for your hard work.

And finally, I want to thank the State chairman for Bush-Cheney 2004. Everybody's got to have a good uncle— [*laughter*]—and I've got a great uncle.

The reason I'm here is because Kit Bond understands the challenges which face our Nation, and he's willing to join in constructive ways to do something about it. I think the best types of people who go to Washington are those who can recognize a problem and then have the courage and will to do something about it. And that's what I appreciate about Kit Bond. He and I share this value, that the future of freedom and peace depends upon the actions of America. We believe that this Nation is freedom's home and freedom's defender. We believe that everybody yearns for freedom and that every nation should be free.

This is—history has given this country a charge to keep, and we're keeping it. You know, this Nation was pretty secure for a while, secure that oceans could protect us. And then 9/11, 2001, came upon us. It was an historic moment because we realized that we weren't safe from an enemy which hates what we stand for. Be-

cause we love freedom and human dignity, because we love the fact that people can worship freely and speak freely, there's an enemy in the world which hates us. And since we're not going to change, in order to do our jobs, we must find them before they hurt America again.

Kit Bond understands that the best way to secure the homeland of America is to find the enemies of freedom one by one and bring them to justice. And I appreciate his support in making this world more free, making America more secure, and making the world more peaceful.

We're after Al Qaida. Slowly but surely, we're dismantling the terrorist network which has hijacked a great religion, which murders in the name of Islam. One by one, we're bringing them to justice. We've captured or killed over two-thirds of the Al Qaida operative network. Just a while ago, we got this guy Hambali, who we think was the instigator of the bombing in Bali. One by one, Al Qaida is meeting its demise. It doesn't matter where they hide, it doesn't matter where they cringe, the United States of America will find them and bring them to justice.

Part of the war on terror is to prevent hostile regimes from teaming up with terrorist networks. And that's why we went into Afghanistan. I sent a clear message: If you harbor a terrorist, if you feed a terrorist, you're just as guilty as the terrorist. And the Taliban in Afghanistan understand exactly what we mean.

And I appreciate Senator Bond's understanding of the need for the United States to uphold doctrine. When we say something in this country, we better do it, for the credibility of the world.

We've got a lot of work to do in Afghanistan, and we're doing it. We're training an Afghan army so they can best protect themselves. NATO is now involved in Afghanistan. And I want to thank our German friends for taking an active role in making Afghanistan more secure. We're building roads; we're opening up hospitals; and many young girls go to school for the first time, thanks to the United States of America.

We gave a clear ultimatum to Saddam Hussein that he must disarm. He chose defiance, and Saddam Hussein is no more. He will not be able to threaten anybody with weapons of mass destruction. He will not be able to provide money for suicide bombers that were killing Israelis. Saddam Hussein will no longer have torture chambers. He is a man who is not in power, thanks to the United States of America and our friends and allies.

And we've got a lot of work to do in Iraq. You see, terrorists can't stand the thought of a free society in the Middle East. People who hate freedom are revolted at the fact that there may be a society that honors human rights and dignity, that treats men and women equally. Terrorists can't stand the thought of success in Iraq.

We're at a crucial point in history in Iraq. And I look forward to working with Senator Bond and Senator Talent and Members of the House to provide the resources necessary to make sure that Iraq is not only secure but that Iraq is free and peaceful. A peaceful Iraq is in the long-term interest of the United States of America.

And we're making progress there. You see, if you've been tortured—and remember, this is a country where we discovered thousands of people who had been executed and placed in mass graves, men, women, and children executed by Saddam Hussein. It's a country which had been terrorized and brutalized. It's a country which couldn't comprehend freedom. So it's going to take awhile for people to develop the habits necessary for a free society to emerge. But I'm absolutely confident, when we stay the course, a strong ally of the United States and any country which loves freedom will emerge. And that will have a positive effect on Israel and a Palestinian state. It will have a positive effect in a region which is—harbored and educated and grew terrorists.

The long-term interests of the United States of America depend on this country doing what's right. And I'm proud to have Senators who understand that and are willing to stand with this administration to make sure we keep our word to the people of Iraq, that we hear the ambitions of those who love freedom in Iran, that we stand strong against the terrorists who would like to destroy the Middle East peace process. This country is leading the world to freedom and peace. It's inherent in our values. We understand that freedom is not America's gift to the world; freedom is God's gift to every individual in the world.

I appreciate Senator Bond's support of a policy which says that when this country sees hopelessness and despair around the world, we will not turn our back. I'm proud to be leading a nation which is leading the world in the fight against AIDS on the continent of Africa.

I recently traveled to Africa. I'll never forget going to Uganda, a country which is beginning to show what is possible in arresting that terrible pandemic. We went to a clinic, and we saw young mothers ravished by AIDS, the desperate look in their eyes. I could tell when they looked at the President of the United States, they saw hope. I remember seeing the children's choir—these are children of orphans—who sang hymns to us. It's a sad moment for me because I realized their moms and dads were gone. It was a joyous moment, though, to realize that people of faith had come to surround them with love. They too look at the United States for hope.

I want to thank Senator Bond for his support on the AIDS initiative. The United States is leading the world in an incredibly important work of human rescue.

I believe our foreign policy is compassionate when it needs to be compassionate and tough when it needs to be tough. But it's based upon a strong belief that freedom is universal and the strong knowledge that free societies will be peaceful societies.

When I came to Washington, DC, our military was underfunded, and morale was beginning to suffer. I proposed defense budgets to prepare our military for threats of a new era. Senator Bond was a strong supporter of those defense budgets, and no one in the world today can question the skill, the honor, the sacrifice, the utility of the United States military.

When we came into office, the country was in recession, and we started getting better. The economy was getting a little better; then the enemy hit us. And then we had some corporate scandals; we had some people in our society who forgot what it means to be a responsible citizen. They didn't tell the truth to their shareholders and their employees, and that affected the people's confidence. And then on your TV screens you saw the words "march to war," which is not a very conducive phrase for economic development. But we acted. We passed tough laws to hold corporate criminals to account, and I want to thank Senator Bond's support on that.

And in order to get our economy growing, I called upon the Congress. Senator Bond and Senator Talent and others were strong supporters of historic tax relief. We understand that when people have more money in their pocket, they will save, spend, invest. And when they do so, somebody is more likely to find a job.

I appreciate Senator Bond's willingness to join the administration and insisting that Congress hold the line on spending. We understand whose money we spend in Washington. It is not the Government's money; it is the people's money. And he is a good steward of the people's money.

When Congress returns, we'll be debating a crucial issue, and that is Medicare. For the first time since the creation of Medicare, we have a chance to reform the system that needs to be reformed. Inherent in both plans out of the House and the Senate is the idea that we will trust seniors

to make the choices that they need in order to develop their health care plans and health care needs. And inherent in both plans is the knowledge and understanding that we need to have prescription drug coverage for our seniors. I want to thank Senator Bond for his willingness to stand up and join us in modernizing Medicare. We owe our seniors a modern Medicare system.

There are a lot of issues that relate to health that will be before our Congress. A significant issue is the issue of frivolous lawsuits. Frivolous lawsuits drive up the cost of health care. Frivolous and junk lawsuits drive up the cost of Medicare, Medicaid, veterans health benefits. Medical liability reform, therefore, is a national issue which requires a national solution.

We got a good bill out of the House of Representatives. It is stuck in the United States Senate. Kit Bond is one of the Senators, if it does get unstuck, will be responsible for passing good medical liability reform out of the United States Senate.

This country needs an energy bill. We need to have a national energy strategy. The blackouts on the east coast should make it clear to the skeptics in Congress that we need to modernize the electricity grid. We need mandatory reliability law. We need to encourage more investment into the transmission of electricity. We need to conserve more. We need more efficiency. But for the sake of economic security and for the sake of energy security and national security, we need to become less dependent on foreign sources of energy.

I appreciate working with Senator Bond on commonsense environmental policy. We both disagree with the judge's decision about the waterflows into the Missouri River. And we both agree that we must do a better job of preserving one of the most important assets we have in America, which is our national forests. We need a commonsense, reasonable forest policy to prevent the raging forest fires from destroying this incredibly valuable asset.

I have an obligation to fill the judiciary with capable, honest, decent people. I have fulfilled that obligation. I have nominated superb women and men to the Federal bench, people who will interpret the law, not use the bench from which to legislate. And Senator Bond has been a strong supporter of my judicial nominees. But we have a problem in the United States Senate. There are some Senators who refuse to give my nominees an up-or-down vote. It is time for some of those Senators to stop playing politics with American justice.

I have an obligation to set great goals for this country. One of the goals I've set is to spread peace and freedom. Another great goal is to spread compassion throughout our land. I want our society to be an ownership society. See, I believe if you own something, you have a vital stake in the future. I believe if you own something in America, it helps with dignity and independence of life. We want more people owning their home. We have a minority homeownership gap in America. I look forward to working with Senator Bond to help narrow that gap.

We want people owning and managing their own health care plans. We want people owning and managing their own retirement plans. Kit Bond is a strong believer in the small-business owner of Missouri and America. We want more people owning their own small business. I look forward to working with Senator Bond to promote the ownership society of America.

Finally, I look forward to working with Senator Bond to get a faith-based initiative out of the United States Senate. I believe strongly that this Government should not fear faith but should welcome faith-based givers, neighborhood healers and helpers, when we see somebody who hurts. We all asked a question in Washington, DC: "Is the program effective that's helping save life? Is the Christian program or the Jewish program or the Muslim program effective at changing lives and saving lives?"

That's the question we ought to be asking in Washington. The truth of the matter is, the great strength of America lies in the hearts and souls of the American people. We have people who hurt in our country. We have children who need to be mentored. We've got people who are hopelessly addicted to drugs. We need to welcome the armies of compassion, no matter what their faith, into the compassionate delivery of help and succor to those of our citizens who hurt.

Kit Bond will be a valuable ally in the passage of a much needed faith-based initiative that allows for faith-based programs to access Federal money, all in the aim of loving a neighbor just like we'd like to be loved ourself.

You just heard some of the reasons you need to send him back up there. Perhaps the greatest reason is he believes like I do, that both of us are fortunate to represent great people, that we're fortunate to be in positions of responsibility to represent the greatest nation on the face of the Earth.

I want to thank you for helping this good man. May God bless you all, and may God continue to bless America.

NOTE: The President spoke at 6:40 p.m. at the Renaissance Grand Hotel. In his remarks, he referred to former Senator John C. Danforth, Special Envoy for Peace in the Sudan; Missouri Secretary of State Matt Blunt and his wife, Melanie; Catherine Hanaway, speaker, Missouri State House of Representatives; Missouri State Senator Peter Kinder; Ann Wagner, cochairman, Republican National Committee, and chairman, Missouri Republican Party; William H.T. "Bucky" Bush, Missouri State chairman, Bush-Cheney '04, Inc.; Nurjaman Riduan Isamuddin (known as Hambali), Al Qaida's chief operational planner in Southeast Asia; and former President Saddam Hussein of Iraq.

Letter to Congressional Leaders Transmitting an Alternative Plan for Pay Increases for Civilian Federal Employees
August 27, 2003

Dear Mr. Speaker: (*Dear Mr. President:*)

I am transmitting an alternative plan for across-the-board and locality pay increases payable to civilian Federal employees covered by the General Schedule (GS) and certain other pay systems in January 2004.

Under title 5, United States Code, civilian Federal employees covered by the GS and certain other pay systems would receive a two-part pay increase in January 2004: (1) a 2.7 percent across-the-board increase in scheduled rates of basic pay derived from Employment Cost Index data on changes in the wages and salaries of private industry workers, and (2) a locality pay increase based on Bureau of Labor Statistics' salary surveys of non-Federal employers in each locality pay area, which would cost about 10 percent of payroll for the calendar year. Including increases for blue-collar and other workers, the total Federal employee pay increase would cost about 13 percent of payroll in calendar year 2004. For Federal employees covered by the locality pay system, the overall average pay increase would be about 15.1 percent.

For each part of the two-part pay increase, title 5, United States Code, authorizes me to implement an alternative pay plan if I view the adjustment that would otherwise take effect as inappropriate due to "national emergency or serious economic conditions affecting the general welfare." For the reasons described below, I have determined that it would be appropriate to exercise my statutory alternative plan authority to limit the January 2004 GS pay increases.

A national emergency has existed since September 11, 2001, that now includes Operation Enduring Freedom in Afghanistan and Operation Iraqi Freedom. Full statutory civilian pay increases costing 13 percent of payroll in 2004 would interfere with our Nation's ability to pursue the war on terrorism. Such increases would cost about $13 billion in fiscal year 2004 alone—$11 billion more than the 2 percent overall Federal civilian pay increase I proposed in my 2004 Budget—and would build in later years.

Such cost increases would threaten our efforts against terrorism or force deep cuts in discretionary spending or Federal employment to stay within budget. Neither outcome is acceptable. Therefore, I have determined that a total pay increase of 2 percent would be appropriate for GS and certain other employees in January 2004.

A 2 percent pay increase should be complemented by $500 million dollars from the Human Capital Performance Fund, which I proposed in my FY 2004 Budget and which is now contained in H.R. 1588, the National Defense Authorization Act for Fiscal Year 2004. Favorable congressional action to establish full funding for this initiative would be a key step towards rewarding the highest performing and most valuable employees in agencies with rigorous and disciplined performance management systems. Providing higher pay for employees whose exceptional performance is critical to the achievement of the agency mission is preferable to spreading limited dollars across-the-board to all employees regardless of their individual performance or contribution.

I will allocate 1.5 percent of the 2 percent total increase to an across-the-board increase under section 5303 of title 5, United States Code, and use the remaining 0.5 percent of payroll to continue the implementation of the locality pay program under section 5304. Our national situation precludes granting larger pay increases to GS employees at this time.

Accordingly, I have determined that—

(1) Under the authority of section 5303(b) of title 5, United States Code, the pay rates for each statutory pay system will be increased by 1.5 percent, effective on the first day of the first applicable pay period beginning on or after January 1, 2004; and

(2) Under the authority of section 5304a of title 5, United States Code, locality-based comparability payments in the percentages set forth in the attached table will go into effect in January 2004.

Finally, the law requires that I include in this report an assessment of the impact of my decision on the Government's ability to recruit and retain well-qualified employees. I do not believe this decision will materially affect our ability to continue to attract and retain a quality Federal workforce. To the contrary, since any pay raise

above the 2 percent I have proposed would likely be unfunded, agencies would have to absorb the additional cost and could have to freeze hiring in order to pay the higher rates. Moreover, GS quit rates are at an all-time low of 1.7 percent per year, well below the overall average quit rate in private enterprise. Should the need arise, the Government has many compensation tools, such as recruitment bonuses, retention allowances, and special salary rates, to maintain the high-quality workforce that serves our Nation so very well.

Sincerely,

GEORGE W. BUSH

NOTE: Identical letters were sent to J. Dennis Hastert, Speaker of the House of Representatives, and Richard B. Cheney, President of the Senate.

Message on the 40th Anniversary of Dr. Martin Luther King, Jr.'s "I Have a Dream" Speech
August 28, 2003

I send greetings to those gathered to celebrate the 40th anniversary of Dr. Martin Luther King, Jr.'s historic "I Have a Dream" speech.

Through his leadership, courage, and determination, Dr. Martin Luther King, Jr. brought tremendous good to our country. His vision and words caused Americans to examine their hearts and live up to the ideals of our Constitution.

In his speech 40 years ago, Dr. King expressed his dream that people would be judged by the content of their character and not by the color of their skin. He viewed the summer of 1963 as a time for

America to renew its commitment to equality. Today, we have come a long way, but there is still work to do to realize Dr. King's dream. As we honor this important anniversary, I encourage all Americans to continue the march to equality and opportunity for all.

Laura joins me in sending our best wishes for a memorable celebration.

GEORGE W. BUSH

NOTE: An original was not available for verification of the content of this message.

Letter to Congressional Leaders Transmitting a Report on Federal Expenditures for Climate Change Programs and Activities
August 28, 2003

Dear Mr. Chairman:

Consistent with section 555(b) of the Consolidated Appropriations Resolution, 2003 (Public Law 108–7), I transmit herewith a report prepared by my Administration of Federal expenditures for climate change programs and activities. This report includes both domestic and international programs and activities related to climate change, and associated expenditures by line item as presented in the President's Budget Appendix amended to reflect enacted FY 2003 appropriations.

Sincerely,

GEORGE W. BUSH

NOTE: Identical letters were sent to Ted Stevens, chairman, Senate Committee on Appropriations; and C.W. Bill Young, chairman, House Committee on Appropriations. This letter was released by the Office of the Press Secretary on August 29.

Letter to Congressional Leaders Reporting on Blocking Property of the Former Iraqi Regime, Its Senior Officials and Their Family Members, and Taking Certain Other Actions
August 28, 2003

Dear Mr. Speaker: *(Dear Mr. President:)*

Consistent with section 204(b) of the International Emergency Economic Powers Act (IEEPA), 50 U.S.C. 1703(b), and section 301 of the National Emergencies Act, 50 U.S.C. 1631, I hereby report that I have exercised my authority to expand the scope of the national emergency declared in Executive Order 13303 of May 22, 2003, to address the unusual and extraordinary threat to the national security and foreign policy of the United States posed by obstacles to the orderly reconstruction of Iraq, the restoration and maintenance of peace and security in that country, and the development of political, administrative, and economic institutions in Iraq.

In United Nations Security Council Resolution (UNSCR) 1483 of May 22, 2003, the U.N. Security Council decided that U.N. member states shall freeze the assets of the former Iraqi regime, Saddam Hussein, and other senior officials of the former Iraqi regime, and their immediate family members and cause the transfer of those assets to the Development Fund for Iraq. The assets of the former Iraqi regime, Saddam Hussein, and other senior Iraqi officials have already been frozen pursuant to the Iraqi Sanctions Regulations, 31 C.F.R. part 575, which implemented the 1990 Executive Orders that imposed economic sanctions with respect to Iraq. The order that I have now issued broadens the scope of persons whose assets may be frozen under those orders by adding the immediate family members of former Iraqi senior officials whose assets may be frozen. This order also allows for the confiscating and vesting of some of those assets and provides for the transfer of all vested assets to the Development Fund for Iraq in a manner consistent with paragraph 23 of UNSCR 1483. The Development Fund for Iraq will be used by the Coalition Provisional Authority in a transparent manner to meet the humanitarian needs of the Iraqi people, for the economic reconstruction and repair of Iraq's infrastructure, for the continued disarmament of Iraq, for the costs of Iraqi civilian administration, and for other purposes benefiting the Iraqi people. By this order and related measures, the United States Government is implementing the requirements of paragraph 23 of UNSCR 1483.

Among other measures, unless licensed or otherwise authorized pursuant to this order, any attachment, judgment, decree, lien, execution, garnishment, or other judicial process with respect to assets blocked pursuant to this order is prohibited by section 1 of this order. I further note that Presidential Determination No. 2003–23 issued on May 7, 2003, made inapplicable with respect to Iraq section 620A of the Foreign Assistance Act of 1961, Public Law 87–195, as amended, and any other provision of law that applies to countries that have supported terrorism, including, but not limited to, 28 U.S.C. 1605(a)(7), 28 U.S.C. 1610, and section 201 of the Terrorism Risk Insurance Act.

I have ordered that all property and interests in property of the former Iraqi regime or its state bodies, corporations, or agencies, or of the following persons, that are in the United States, that hereafter come within the United States, or that are or hereafter come within the possession or control of United States persons, are blocked and may not be transferred, paid, exported, withdrawn, or otherwise dealt in:

(a) the persons listed in the Annex to this order; and

(b) persons determined by the Secretary of the Treasury, in consultation with the Secretary of State,

(i) to be senior officials of the former Iraqi regime or their immediate family members; or

(ii) to be owned or controlled by, or acting or purporting to act for or on behalf of, directly or indirectly, any of the persons listed in the Annex to this order or determined to be subject to this order.

I have authorized the Secretary of the Treasury, in consultation with the Secretary of State, to confiscate property that is blocked pursuant to this order and that he determines, in consultation with the Secretary of State, to belong to a person, organization, or country that has planned, authorized, aided, or engaged in armed hostilities against the United States. All right, title, and interest in any property so confiscated shall vest in the Department of the Treasury and shall promptly be transferred to the Development Fund for Iraq.

I have delegated to the Secretary of the Treasury, in consultation with the Secretary of State, the authority to take such actions as may be necessary to carry out the purposes of my order, including the promulgation of rules and regulations. I have also authorized the Secretary of the Treasury, in consultation with the Secretary of State, to employ all powers granted to me by IEEPA and by section 5 of the United Nations Participation Act, 22 U.S.C. 287c, to carry out the purposes of this order.

I am enclosing a copy of the executive order I have issued. The order is effective at 12:01 a.m. EDT on August 29, 2003.

Sincerely,

GEORGE W. BUSH

NOTE: Identical letters were sent to J. Dennis Hastert, Speaker of the House of Representatives, and Richard B. Cheney, President of the Senate. This letter was released by the Office of the Press Secretary on August 29. An original was not available for verification of the content of this letter. The Executive order of August 28 is listed in Appendix D at the end of this volume.

Statement on the Bombing in Najaf, Iraq
August 29, 2003

I strongly condemn the bombing today outside the Imam Ali mosque in Najaf, Iraq, that killed dozens of innocent Iraqis. This vicious act of terrorism was aimed at Ayatollah Mohammed Baqir al-Hakim, at one of Shi'a Islam's holiest sites, and at the hopes of the people of Iraq for freedom, peace, and reconciliation.

I extend my deepest condolences to the families of the victims and my hopes for a quick recovery for the injured. I have instructed American officials in Iraq to work closely with Iraqi security officials and the Governing Council to determine who committed this terrible attack and bring them to justice. I also extend my sym-pathies to all Iraqis and to Shi'a Muslims around the world.

Ayatollah Hakim had been jailed and tortured for his religious beliefs by the regime of Saddam Hussein, and he had spent many years in exile. He returned to his native land this year after its liberation. His murder today, along with the murder of many innocent men and women gathered for prayer, demonstrates the cruelty and desperation of the enemies of the Iraqi people.

The forces of terror must and will be defeated. The united efforts of Iraqis and the international community will succeed in achieving peace and freedom.

The President's Radio Address
August 30, 2003

Good morning. On this Labor Day weekend, Americans pay tribute to the spirit of hard work and enterprise that has always made this Nation strong. Every day, our workers go to factories and offices and farms and produce the world's finest goods and services. Their creativity and energy are the greatest advantage of the American economy.

Worker productivity accelerated last year at the fastest rate in more than a half century. This higher productivity means our workers receive higher wages, our Nation's exports get a competitive boost in world markets, and our economic recovery gains momentum at a crucial time.

The Jobs and Growth Act I signed in May ensures that workers enjoy more of the benefits of their work through more take-home pay. Tax relief was based on the conviction that workers are entitled to keep more of their hard-earned wages. That be-lief, after all, is why America celebrates Labor Day and not tax day.

For America's families, tax relief has come at just the right time. For a family of four with a household income of $40,000, tax relief passed over the last 2½ years means they get to keep nearly $2,000 more of their own money.

Millions of families this past month received checks for up to $400 per child because we increased the child tax credit. This tax relief, more than $13 billion worth, means that America's workers can save, invest, and make purchases they have been putting off. Many moms and dads are using their extra income to take care of back-to-school expenses.

As consumer spending rises, manufacturers are seeing more new orders for their goods. Low interest rates mean businesses have better balance sheets, and families have saved billions of dollars by refinancing their homes. These are the signs of a reviving economy.

Now we must build on this progress and make sure that the economy creates enough new jobs for American workers. Next week I will travel to Ohio, Missouri, and Indiana to talk about my agenda for job creation across America.

As part of this agenda, our Nation needs a comprehensive energy plan so that our businesses and homes can rely on a steady and affordable supply of energy. The recent blackout in the Northeast shows how important reliable energy is to the American economy and demonstrates the need to take action on good energy policy. So when Members of Congress return from the summer recess, I will again ask them to pass a sound energy bill as soon as possible.

America needs legal reform, because junk lawsuits can destroy a business, and they're making health care coverage less affordable for employers and workers. And Congress must restrain Government spending so that we can bring the deficit down by half within the next 5 years.

We must negotiate trade agreements with other nations. My administration will be vigilant in making sure our agreements are followed by all our trading partners. With free trade and a level playing field, American workers can successfully compete with any workers in the world.

This long weekend is a well-deserved reward for the millions of men and women who make this economy go. I wish all Americans a happy and restful Labor Day.

Thank you for listening.

NOTE: The address was recorded at 9:55 a.m. on August 29 at the Bush Ranch in Crawford, TX, for broadcast at 10:06 a.m. on August 30. The transcript was made available by the Office of the Press Secretary on August 29 but was embargoed for release until the broadcast. The Office of the Press Secretary also released a Spanish language transcript of this address.

Remarks on Labor Day in Richfield, Ohio
September 1, 2003

Thank you all. I don't know about you, but we needed a little rain in Crawford. [*Laughter*] Send it that way, if you don't mind. [*Laughter*] Thank you so much for coming out on Labor Day. I appreciate so many folks enduring the rain to say hello to the President. I am thrilled you are here, and I'm thrilled I'm here.

The working people of this country deserve a day off, and it looks like you're enjoying it. [*Laughter*] I want you to know that I know the strength of the American economy comes from hard-working men and women. This country prospers because of people who give their best effort every day to support their families, to go to work, to make America a better place. One man who traveled with me today, who understands this, and who loves his country, is Mr. Frank Hanley. I'm proud to be traveling with him, and I know you're proud to have him as your president.

You know, it's interesting that it was union leaders who first suggested a day to honor America's workers. And I'm glad we do. And I'm proud to be here in Ohio with Ohio families celebrating Labor Day. I'm grateful to the Operating Engineers for hosting us today. This union represents men and women of great skill and great professional pride.

I want you to think back to that fateful day, September the 11th, and what happened afterwards. It was then that the whole world saw the skill and commitment and incredible work of the Operating Engineers who manned the heavy equipment to clear Ground Zero. You overcame unimaginable challenges; you removed the rubble in record time. You are now working to make sure America is prepared for any emergency, and this Nation is grateful for your skill and your sacrifice.

We're also grateful to some other hardworking Americans who don't have the day off, the people of the United States military who are winning the war against terror. The war against terror goes on. It goes on because we love freedom, and we're not going to change, and our enemies hate freedom. It goes on because there are coldblooded killers who have hijacked a religion. It goes on because we refuse to relent. And the best way to protect our homeland, the best way to make sure that we listen to the lessons of September the 11th, 2001, the best way to do our solemn duty to the American people is to chase the killers down, one by one, and bring them to justice.

And so on this Labor Day, when many have the day off, we thank our men and women who wear our uniform. We thank them and their families. We thank their sacrifice, and we want all to know, you make our Nation proud.

I appreciate our Secretary of Labor, Elaine Chao, for her hard work and her outreach to labor leaders all across the country.

I want to thank Jim Gardner, the general vice president and business manager of Local 18 for—he's the host of this event. I want to thank Jim for setting up this beautiful site and for the weather. [*Laughter*]

I traveled today as well with Chuck Canterbury. He's the president of the Fraternal Order of Police. I appreciate you coming, Chuck. I want to thank those who wear our Nation's uniform when it comes to providing police protection and fire protection. We appreciate your service.

I like to remind people that a culture of responsibility is coming in America. One of the reasons why is that we see every day people who are willing to serve something greater than themself in life. Our children see heroes again, because they see police men and women and firefighters and emergency teams and military personnel who sacrifice for something greater than themselves in life. And for all the officers who are with us today, I thank you for your line of service for America.

I want to thank Governor Bob Taft for greeting me at the airport today. I appreciate so very much two United States— the two United States Senators from the State of Ohio who are with me today, and I suspect may be looking for a ride back to Washington—[*laughter*]—Senator George Voinovich and Senator Mike DeWine. Steve LaTourette and Ralph Regula, Members of the House of Representatives, are with us today as well, and I appreciate them coming. I mentioned Governor Taft, and Jennette Bradley, the Lieutenant Governor, is with us. Jim Trakas is with us, who is the Ohio State house majority leader. I want to thank all the local officials for coming out to say hello.

Today I want to talk about our economy. I want people to understand that when somebody wants to work and can't find a job, it says we've got a problem in America that we're going to deal with. We want everybody in this country working. We want people to be able to realize their personal dreams by finding a job. And we've got a lot of strengths in this economy. One of the greatest strengths, of course, is the workforce. We've got the best workers in the world. We're the most productive workers in the entire world. Productivity is up. What productivity means is that we've got a lot of hard work, and we're using new technologies to make people more effective when it comes to the job, and that's important.

You see, in 1979, it took more than 40 hours of labor to make a car, and now it takes 18 hours. We're productive. Our workers are really productive in America. Higher productivity not only means we can produce better products, but it means our people are better off. The more productive you are, the better off our workers are. You see, it's better to operate a backhoe than it is a shovel. That's what we mean by productivity. Higher productivity means that workers earn more, and it means it takes less time for workers to earn the money to buy the things they need.

In 1908, the average factory worker had to labor for more than 2 years to buy a Model T—more than 2 years of work to buy a car. Today, you can buy a family vehicle for about 7 months of salary. The higher the productivity rates, the better it is for American workers. We're a productive nation because of the good, hard-working Americans, and that's what we're here to celebrate today.

You know, I also want you to focus on what we have overcome. I mean, we're a strong nation. We've got great foundations for growth, and we've overcome a lot as a country over the last couple of years. In early 2000, the stock market started to decline. That affects you. It affects your savings. It affects your pension accounts. It was a forerunner of the recession that came. First quarter of 2001, we were in recession, but we acted to come out of that recession. We acted with tax relief, and it created big noise and big debate in Washington. But here's what I believe, and here's what I know: When you've got more money in your pocket, it means you're going to spend or save and invest. And when you spend and save or invest, somebody is going to produce a product for you to be able to spend your money on. When somebody produces a product, it's more likely somebody is going to be able to find a job. Tax relief was needed to stem the recession.

They tell me it was a shallow recession. It was a shallow recession because of the tax relief. Some say, "Well, maybe the re-cession should have been deeper." That bothers me when people say that. You see, a deeper recession would have meant more families would have been out of work. I'm interested in solving problems quickly. I want more people working.

No, we did the right thing with tax relief, and we were beginning to pull out when the terrorists hit us. And they struck us hard. Cost our American economy about $80 billion. The attack of September the 11th had a high price tag to it. That's the equivalent of wiping out about one-fifth of Ohio's economy. But we acted. Not only did we go on the offensive with a mighty and skilled military; we did some things to keep our people back at work.

And one of the things that the Operating Engineers know we did—and I want to thank Frank for working with us—is that we fought for terrorism reinsurance to make sure big construction projects stayed on schedule. We worked to preserve thousands of jobs for America's construction workers, because we want people working in America. We want people to put food on the table. We want moms and dads to be able to do their duty as a mom or a dad.

And so we began to recover from the terrorist attacks, and then we found out some of the citizens, some of the corporate CEOs, forgot what it means to be a responsible American. They forgot to do their duty. They didn't tell the truth to their shareholders and their employees. So we acted. We passed two new tough laws. And now the message is clear: If you don't tell the truth, there is going to be serious consequences. We expect the best out of corporate America.

Yet the economy was still bumping along. We hadn't recovered from all the challenges, and so we passed tax relief again. I called upon Congress to pass the jobs-and-growth package, and we lowered taxes once again to create jobs. When you reduce taxes, people have more money. And I'm going to remind you of what we did. If you're a mom or a dad, we increased the child credit to $1,000 per child, and we put the checks in the mail, $400 additional per child for American families, so you get to decide to do with—with the money. It's your choice. You see, after all, in Washington, we don't spend the Government's money; we spend your money.

We reduced the marriage penalty. What kind of Tax Code is it that discourages marriage? [*Laughter*] We want to encourage marriage. We gave incentives to small businesses so that they can hire more people. We reduced taxes on capital gains and dividends to protect your savings accounts. We want the pension plans strong. We want the 401(k)s doing well. We reduced all taxes. We thought it was fairer not to try to pick and choose winners. If you pay taxes, you deserve relief. Three million people are now off the tax rolls; 3.9 million households received tax relief.

No, we're making a difference. And the economy is beginning to grow, and that's what I'm interested in. I come with an optimistic message. I believe there are better days ahead for people who are working and looking for work. Economic output is rising faster than expected. Low interest rates mean that families can save billions by refinancing their homes. I bet some of you have refinanced your homes, put a little extra money into your pocket. Consumer spending is on the rise. Companies are seeing more orders, especially orders for heavy equipment.

No, things are getting better. But there are some things we've got to do to make sure the economy continues to grow. I want you to understand that I understand that Ohio manufacturers are hurting, that there's a problem with the manufacturing sector. And I understand for a full recovery, to make sure people can find work, that manufacturing must do better. And we've lost thousands of jobs in manufacturing, some of it because of productivity gains— in other words, people can have the same

output with fewer people—but some of it because production moved overseas.

So I told Secretary Don Evans of the Commerce Department, I want him to appoint an Assistant Secretary to focus on the needs of manufacturers, to make sure our manufacturing job base is strong and vibrant. In other words, any part of a good recovery for the State of Ohio and other manufacturing States has got to be for the manufacturing sector to come around. One way to make sure that we—the manufacturing sector does well is to send a message overseas, say, "Look, we expect there to be a fair playing field when it comes to trade." See, we in America believe we can compete with anybody just so long as the rules are fair, and we intend to keep the rules fair.

We have a responsibility that when somebody hurts, Government has got to move. And that's why we've signed extensions to the unemployment insurance, so people can get their feet back on the ground. Elaine's Department, the Department of Labor, passes out emergency grants for people who are hurting to cover health care costs and child care costs and other critical needs. And that's a useful role for the Government.

I proposed to Congress a new idea to help people get back to work, particularly those that are—have the hardest time finding work. We call them reemployment accounts. I proposed spending $3.6 billion to help a million Americans find work. We'd write—put some money aside for somebody to use for daycare or retraining, to be able to move. If they're able to find a job in a prescribed period of time, they'd be able to keep the difference between what we gave them to begin with and what was unspent, in other words, a reemployment bonus. It's a novel approach to help a million Americans who are having a tough time finding work to find work. Reemployment accounts make sense. Congress needs to act.

We've also got to make sure that our people get the right skills. Listen, technology changes. I understand that. You know that. We want our people to be trained, to keep up with new technology, just like they do right here. I want to thank the Operating Engineers. I want to thank Frank for his leadership. I want to thank the local leaders for their leadership and understanding that in order for a man or woman to stay up, there needs to be re-training opportunities. As our economy changes, people need to be retrained. The Operating Engineers do a great job right here of helping people. That's all the worker wants, is to be helped, be given the skills necessary to realize his or her dreams.

The high-growth job training initiative in this administration is aiming just to do that. It's a collaborative effort with community colleges to help team up people with the jobs that are needed, to make sure that the changes in our economy don't leave people behind. And education can help a lot, and we're going to continue to stay focused on education in this administration. We not only want our little ones to be able to read and write and add and subtract; we want to make sure the older ones have a chance to realize the opportunities of tomorrow as well. And we will.

And finally, I want to talk about another issue right quick—or two other issues right quick. One of them is, this country needs an energy policy. If you rely upon a manufacturing base for job employment, you need energy. We need a policy. I've been talking about this for a couple of years. Congress needs to get me an energy bill. You learned firsthand what it means to have a—what it means to modernize the electricity grid, if you know what I mean. [*Laughter*] The grid needs to be modernized.

First, we need to find out—and will find out—what went wrong, why you had your electricity shut down out here. But we ought to use this as an opportunity to modernize the system. They used to have—

in the law they had, you know, said these electricity deliverers could have voluntary reliability standards. We don't need voluntary reliability standards. We need mandatory reliability standards. We want to make sure there's incentives for people to put new poles in the ground and invest.

The energy sector has been hamstrung by old laws. We need new laws. And I've been calling on Congress to do this. And when they get back, they need to stop politicking and get a good energy plan, so that we can make sure the economy continues to grow.

I'll tell you what else we need to do. We need to use our technologies to be able to explore for energy in environmentally friendly ways. For the sake of national security, for the sake of economic security, we need to become less dependent on foreign sources of energy.

A sound energy policy makes sense. And so does good highway policy. We proposed some increases over the last 6 years. These highway bills come in 6-year increments. I proposed $30 billion more spending on highways over the next 6 than the last 6. We not only want to make sure our people can find jobs and work, like the people who are pushing these big equipment around, but we want people driving on better roads. We want to be able to deal with congestion so we can get our people moving around.

There's a lot we can do. We've done a lot to lay the foundation for economic growth. And there's a lot we can do when Congress gets back to make sure that this economic recovery continues so people can find work. On Labor Day, we're committed to helping those who have got a job keep a job and committed to those who are looking for work to find a job. That's the commitment of this Labor Day.

We're also committed to our freedom and to peace, and we will stay on the offensive to protect our freedom. And we will stay with the notion that the more free societies are, the more peaceful they become. See, we love freedom and we love peace in America, and we intend to make the world a more peaceful place. This country will lead the world to peace.

I really enjoy coming out and seeing people bring their kids out. I want to thank you for bringing them. It reminds me of one of the things that's happening in our country. It's a new spirit in America. There's a cultural change taking place, it seems like to me, and that is, we're getting away from the era that said, "If it feels good, just go ahead and do it," and "If you've got a problem, blame somebody else," to an era in which each of us understands we're responsible for the decisions we make in life.

If you're a mom or a dad, if you're lucky enough to be a parent, you're responsible for loving your child with all your heart and all your soul. That's your job. If you're worried about the quality of education in the neighborhood in which you live, then you're responsible for doing something about it. As I mentioned, if you happen to be a CEO in corporate America, you're responsible for telling the truth. You're responsible for treating your employees with respect. If you're an American in the responsibility era, you're responsible for loving a neighbor like you'd like to be loved yourself.

I want to thank those of you who reach out to somebody who hurts, somebody in need. You see, the great strength of the country is not our military might or economic prowess; the great strength of the country is the heart and soul of the American people. Millions of acts of kindness and decency go on on a daily basis. Millions of acts of decency and kindness help define the true worth and the true strength of this great American country.

And so on Labor Day, a day in which we honor the worker, let us honor those who work to make our society and country a more compassionate place by helping a neighbor in need, by doing your job as a citizen of the country, by being a patriotic person, which means more than just putting your hand over your heart. It means serving your country in ways large and small, all aimed at lifting up this Nation, all aimed at keeping us the greatest nation on the face of the Earth.

May God bless you all, and may God continue to bless America. Thank you all.

NOTE: The President spoke at 11:12 a.m. at the Richfield Training Center. In his remarks, he referred to Frank Hanley, general president, International Union of Operating Engineers; James H. Gardner, business manager, International Union of Operating Engineers Local 18; Chuck Canterbury, national president, Fraternal Order of Police; Gov. Bob Taft and Lt. Gov. Jennette Bradley of Ohio; and James Trakas, majority whip, Ohio State House of Representatives.

Message to the Senate Transmitting the Protocol to the Denmark-United States Treaty of Friendship, Commerce, and Navigation
September 2, 2003

To the Senate of the United States:

With a view to receiving the advice and consent of the Senate to ratification, I transmit herewith the Protocol to the Treaty of Friendship, Commerce, and Navigation Between the United States and Denmark of October 1, 1951, signed at Copenhagen on May 2, 2001. I transmit also, for the information of the Senate, the report of the Department of State with respect to this protocol.

The protocol will establish the legal basis by which the United States may issue treaty-investor (E–2) visas to qualified nationals of Denmark, by supplementing the U.S.-Denmark friendship, commerce, and navigation (FCN) treaty to allow for entry and sojourn of investors, a benefit provided in the large majority of U.S. FCN treaties. United States investors are already eligible for Danish visas that offer comparable benefits to those that would be accorded nationals of Denmark under E–2 visa status.

The United States has long championed the benefits of an open investment climate, both at home and abroad. It is the policy of the United States to welcome market-driven foreign investment and to permit capital to flow freely to seek its highest return. Denmark also provides an open investment climate. Visas for investors facilitate investment activity, and thus directly support U.S. policy objectives.

I recommend that the Senate consider this protocol as soon as possible, and give its advice and consent to ratification of the protocol at an early date.

GEORGE W. BUSH

The White House,
September 2, 2003.

Remarks at the Signing Ceremony for Legislation to Implement the Chile and Singapore Free Trade Agreements
September 3, 2003

Good afternoon. Thanks for coming. I'm honored to welcome you to the White House, and I'm pleased that you could join us today as the United States takes an important step to promote economic growth, to bring lower prices to American consumers, and to generate high-wage jobs for American workers.

With the agreements I sign today, America's economic relationships with Chile and Singapore will be based on free trade, and we will be bound even closer to two of our good friends. The benefits will flow to all our countries. And by these agreements, we are moving toward a great goal, a world that trades in freedom in the Western Hemisphere, in Asia, and beyond. I want to thank all those who worked so hard to complete these agreements. I commend the Members of the Congress for moving quickly to approve this implementing legislation.

I'm pleased to be joined by members of my Cabinet who have worked hard on these agreements and are working hard on future agreements to be passed. Secretary of State Powell is doing a fabulous job on behalf of the American people, Secretary Ann Veneman of the Department of Agriculture, Secretary Don Evans, Department of Commerce, and our Trade Representative, Bob Zoellick.

I also appreciate the Members of Congress who are up here with me today, Senators Hatch and Baucus; as well as Chairman Bill Thomas, David Dreier, and Phil Crane from the House of Representatives, good, strong Members of the Senate and the House who have worked closely with this administration to create an environment for economic growth and high-wage jobs through free trade.

I also welcome other Members of the Senate and the House who are with us today. Thank you all for coming. The stage just wasn't big enough for you. [*Laughter*]

I appreciate Ambassador Bianchi from Chile and also Ambassador Heng Chee Chan from Singapore. I appreciate you all coming. I want to thank the representatives of the business community who are here with us today.

We support free trade in America because it is vital to the creation of jobs. It's vital to the success of our economy. Exports accounted for roughly one quarter—one quarter—of our economy's growth in the 1990s.

Jobs and exporting plants pay wages that average up to 18 percent more than jobs in nonexporting plants. Over the past decade, NAFTA and the Uruguay Round have raised the standards of living of the average American family of four by up to $2,000 a year. Free trade is important for the American citizen. The continued advance of free trade is essential to this Nation's prosperity.

The United States also supports free trade because a world that trades in freedom will grow in prosperity and in security. For developing nations, free trade tied to economic reform has helped to lift hundreds of millions of people out of poverty. The growth of economic freedom and ownership in developing countries creates the habits of liberty and creates the pressure for democracy and political reform. Economic integration through trade can also foster political cooperation by promoting peace between nations. As free trade expands across the Earth, the realm of human freedom expands with it.

When Congress passed trade promotion authority last year, I promised to use that tool aggressively to open up new markets for American exporters and to help create high-paying jobs for American workers, and we moved. I want to thank Ambassador Zoellick and his team from all across our administration for getting to work right away, and we've seen results.

The free trade agreement with Chile is our first ever with a South American country. The agreement will benefit many American industries, including agriculture and construction equipment, autos and auto parts, computers, medical equipment, paper products, and financial services. American-made heavy machinery, such as a motor grader, costs $11,220 more in Chile be-cause of extra tariffs. If that machinery were made in Canada or the European Union, it would carry no tariff. Our trade agreement with Chile will eliminate these kinds of tariffs, and our manufacturers will be able to compete on a level playing field. And as we sell that heavy equipment into Chile, somebody is more likely to find work in America in a good, high-paying job.

The agreement with Chile also includes new protections for intellectual property, a secure legal framework for U.S. investors, and strong provisions for protecting labor and the environment. For decades, Chile has proven the power of open trade and sound policies. It has become one of the strongest economies in the developing world. By establishing free trade with the world's largest economy, Chile will have the opportunity to advance even further and to help make the entire region more prosperous.

The agreement between the United States and Singapore is also historic, the first between the United States and an Asia-Pacific country. Singapore is already America's 12th-largest trading partner and imports a full range of American products, from machine parts and computers to agricultural products. This agreement will increase access to Singapore's dynamic markets for America's exporters and service providers and investors. The agreement contains state-of-the-art protections for Internet commerce and intellectual property that will help drive growth and innovation in our technology sectors. There are also strong labor and environmental protections in our agreement with Singapore.

I signed this legislation today fully expecting to sign many more free trade agreements. We're now negotiating with Australia and Morocco, five nations in Central America, and the Southern African Customs Union. Soon we will begin negotiations with Bahrain and the Dominican Republic. We're working with 33 other nations in our hemisphere to create the Free

Trade Area of the Americas. We're encouraging the free flow of commerce and investment among our partners in APEC and ASEAN and hope to build on the success of our trade agreements with Jordan and Israel by establishing a U.S.-Middle East free trade area within a decade to create new opportunity and new hope in a region that needs both.

The greatest gains from world trade will come from completing the World Trade Organization's global negotiations. We made good progress since the negotiations started nearly 2 years ago, and WTO members can build on this progress next week in Cancun, Mexico. Completing the global negotiations by the 2005 deadline is essential, because opening global markets is a pathway to economic success for rich and poor nations alike. The spread of free trade reflects this Nation's convictions. We believe in the dignity of every human being. We believe in freedom.

Free trade also serves the interests of the United States. It serves in the interest of our workers. We will benefit from more trading partners around the world. We want our partners to grow in wealth. We want them to grow in freedom. Chile and Singapore are examples of economic liberty and demonstrate the great promise of trade. I'm honored to sign into law these two pieces of legislation implementing our free trade agreements with our friends Chile and Singapore.

NOTE: The President spoke at 2:25 p.m. in the East Room at the White House. In his remarks, he referred to Chile's Ambassador, Andres Bianchi; and Singapore's Ambassador, Heng Chee Chan. H.R. 2738, the United States-Chile Free Trade Agreement Implementation Act, approved September 3, was assigned Public Law No. 108–77. H.R. 2739, the United States-Singapore Free Trade Agreement Implementation Act, also approved September 3, was assigned Public Law No. 108–78. The Office of the Press Secretary also released a Spanish language transcript of these remarks.

Joint Statement Between the United States of America and the Kingdom of The Netherlands
September 3, 2003

President Bush and Prime Minister Balkenende today agreed that progress in fighting the global tragedy of HIV/AIDS requires more and better coordination among donor and recipient governments, international organizations, non-governmental organizations (NGOs), and the private sector.

The United States and the Netherlands therefore agree to cooperate on HIV/AIDS prevention, treatment, and care in countries in which both the United States and the Netherlands have significant activities, including countries that will receive special focus in the President's Emergency Plan for AIDS Relief. The plan will start in Rwanda and Ghana and may expand to Zambia, Ethiopia, and possibly Sudan once a peace agreement is signed.

The cooperation agreement will highlight political leadership and public-private partnerships, which are a focus of both the President's Emergency Plan for AIDS Relief and the Netherlands 2003 AIDS Action Plan.

This cooperation agreement is the first step of a joint initiative in which the United States and the Netherlands will seek to coordinate HIV/AIDS activities, strategies, and programs in African countries.

NOTE: An original was not available for verification of the content of this joint statement.

Remarks in Kansas City, Missouri
September 4, 2003

Thank you very much. Please be seated. I appreciate the warm welcome. It's nice to be back here in Kansas City. I feel comfortable here. After all, it's a place of good baseball, pretty good football, and really good barbecue.

I have come to this important city, right here in the heart of America, to speak about the future of our Nation's economy. I want to talk about jobs and job creation. Kansas City in many ways symbolizes the incredible energy and ingenuity and flexibility of our economy. It wasn't all that long ago that Kansas City was known for rail lines and stockyards. Now, the economy is a more modern economy because of the spirit of enterprise that exists here and because of the willingness for the people to work hard, because of the optimism of the people in this part of the world. And I share your optimism about the future of this Nation.

America's economy today is showing signs of promise. We're emerging from a period of national challenge and economic uncertainty. The hard work of our people and the good policies of our Government are paying off. Our economy is starting to grow again. Americans are feeling more confident. I am determined to work with the United States Congress to turn these hopeful signs into lasting growth and greater prosperity and more jobs.

I want to thank Terry Dunn for his kind introduction. I like a good, short introduction. [*Laughter*] I appreciate Pete Levi, the president of the Greater Chamber.

I flew from Washington here today with two fine Americans: Senator Jim Talent, who's doing a great job for the people of Missouri, and Congressman Sam Graves.

On the plane ride down, Sam told me that his mother was going to be here today. And I said, "I hope you're still listening to your mother." [*Laughter*] I'm still listening to mine—[*laughter*]—most of the time. [*Laughter*]

I want to thank Paul Rodriguez and CiCi Rojas from the Hispanic Chamber of Commerce for—[*applause*]. I also want to thank the board of directors and the members of the chamber for allowing me to come to discuss with you the future of this country.

Before I do so, though, I had the honor of meeting Tom Holcom. He's a Missouri native who was out there at Air Force One when—at the airport when we landed, to greet me at Air Force One. He started Angel Flight Central. He is a—it's a nonprofit organization that provides free air transportation to those in need due to a crisis.

The reason I bring this up is that I know the great strength of America is the heart and soul of the American people. And everywhere I go, I like to herald those quiet heroes who are making a difference in people's lives by volunteering time. I like to tell people that it's important for this Nation to usher in a period of personal responsibility. And part of a responsibility society is to love a neighbor just like you'd like to be loved yourself.

I want to thank Tom for using his time and talent to help somebody in need. I want to thank you all, if you're a member of the army of compassion in this United

States of America, for serving your community by helping somebody who hurts, by reaching out a hand to a neighbor in need. No, Government can help. We can pass out money. But Government cannot put hope in people's hearts or a sense of purpose in people's lives. That is done when a kind soul puts their arm around a brother and sister in need and says, "I love you. What can I do to help?"

Events of the last few years have revealed the amazing resilience of our Nation's economy. In our country's history, recessions have typically resulted from single, unexpected shocks such as spikes in energy prices or sudden shifts in markets. Since 2000, our economy has been dealt not just one shock, but three—a set of challenges with few parallels in American history.

First, the stock market began a steady decline in March 2000, as investors realized that the economy was not healthy. Businesses faced overcapacity during that period of time and cut their budgets for new investment in technology or equipment. And by early 2001, this economy was in recession.

And secondly, we were attacked on a fateful day, September the 11th, 2001. An enemy which hates America attacked us and killed a lot of our citizens. It brought our Nation great grief and shock, and it disrupted our economy. The stock market shut down for days. Commercial airlines were devastated. Travel and tourism industry has struggled since, and the costs of higher security are still being paid. The economic impact of those attacks is estimated at $80 billion in economic damage and lost output, which is nearly equivalent to wiping out the entire economy of Kansas for one year.

The economic impact of September the 11th continued because of the uncertainty from the war on terror—from operations in Afghanistan or war on terror in Iraq or relentless hunt for the killers. In times of conflict, decisionmakers are hesitant to make major purchases, businesses are hesi-

tant to hire new people. The march to war is not conducive for hopeful investment. Our military campaigns in the war on terror have cost our Treasury and our economy. Yet, they have prevented greater costs.

We will protect this Nation from further attack and, therefore, protecting our economy from major disruption. The safety of our people, the security of the American people is of paramount concern to me. With a broad coalition, we are taking and will continue to take action around the globe. We will remain on the offensive against terrorist killers. We will stay on the offensive, and this Nation will prevail. [*Applause*] Thank you.

As we fought this war, our Nation's economy was dealt a third major blow. We discovered corporate malfeasance in boardrooms across America. The scandals—corporate scandals—erased savings of Americans—of some Americans. It forced the layoffs of thousands, and it undermined the confidence of investors. But we took action. I signed tough new laws. In an era of personal responsibility, if you're a CEO in corporate America, we expect you to tell the truth to your shareholders and employees alike. And if you don't, there's going to be serious consequence.

In each case, this administration did not stand by and hope that the problem would solve itself. We acted with a strong belief in the spirit of the American people and in free markets. We acted to keep the entrepreneurial spirit of America alive and well. I based decisions on a fundamental principle: When our economy is struggling, the best thing that Government can do to stimulate growth is to let people keep more of their own money.

So I asked for and the Congress passed major reductions in Federal taxes. We lowered taxes of every American who pays taxes. We raised the child credit to $1,000 per child. We reduced the marriage penalty. Seems like to me the Tax Code ought to encourage marriage, not discourage marriage.

These actions have brought substantial savings to the taxpayers and have been critical in fighting the effects of recession. Under the tax relief we passed in 2001 and 2003, a married couple with two children and a household income of $40,000 have seen their Federal income tax bill fall this year from $1,978 to $45.

Thanks in part to the reductions we passed, real disposable personal income—that which is left in paychecks and other income after taxes are taken out—has increased at 3.4-percent rate in the first 2½ years of my administration. That's a faster increase than the pace set in the 1990s. People are keeping more of their own money.

That tax relief is taking pressure off of families and is adding momentum to economic growth. Tax relief came at the exact right time. I say that because during the first year of a typical recession, consumer spending rises only at 0.3 percent. That's a typical recession. In the most recent recession, thanks in part to the tax cuts, consumer spending rose by nearly 10 times that rate. When people have more money in their pocket, consumer spending will stay strong, and that spending has continued.

Throughout this recession, consumers have shown a belief in America's future by buying homes. In the typical recession, housing investment falls by 10 percent and doesn't recover for nearly 2 years. Thanks to tax relief and low interest rates, housing investment dropped by only one percent in this recession and then began to rise above prerecession levels within only one year.

This July, housing starts reached their highest level since 1986. Homeownership in America is now at 68 percent, one of the highest levels ever recorded. And many Americans have refinanced their homes, saving themselves billions of dollars. And that helps our economy grow as well.

As Americans grow more confident and make more purchases, small and large businesses around the country are seeing the benefits. Purchasing managers have reported rising new orders for both goods and services in each month since May. Orders for high-tech equipment have been declining—had been declining since 2000. They have risen steadily since April.

Investors are showing greater confidence in the stock market. Thanks to our efforts to reduce taxes on stock dividends, dozens of major companies have announced plans to either increase their existing dividend payout or pay dividends for the first time, which will put billions of dollars in cash into the pockets of American shareholders. And that is good for our economy.

For small businesses—and I know we've got some small-business owners here today—the outlook is improving. I found it interesting that Americans are starting sole proprietorships at a faster rate than they did in the 1990s. The tax relief we passed helps small businesses. Most small businesses are either sole proprietorships or Subchapter S corporations, which means they pay tax at the individual income tax level. And therefore, when you reduce individual income taxes, you're providing much needed capital for small businesses all across America.

Since small businesses create most of the new jobs in America, we recognized we needed to do more. And so, we gave further encouragement to small businesses by raising the annual expense deduction from $25,000 to $100,000. By helping small businesses, by creating the environment for capital accumulation and capital investment at the small-business level, not only are we sustaining the entrepreneurial spirit in America, but we're helping Americans find work.

The recession was hard on a lot of Americans. Over the past 2½ years, I've met with dozens of our fellow citizens, families who have struggled to meet emergency bills, seniors who saw their savings hurt by stock market declines, small-business owners who had to put in a lot of work just to keep their dream alive. These Americans were helped by tax relief. Had we not taken action, this economy would have been in a deeper recession. It would have been longer, and as many as 1.5 million Americans who went to work this morning would have been out of a job.

Instead, because we did act, the recession was one of the shallowest in modern economic history. Some critics, who opposed tax relief to start with, are still opposing it. They argue we should return to the way things were in 2001. What they're really saying is they want to raise taxes. Higher taxes will not create one job in America. Raising taxes would hurt economic growth. Tax relief is putting this Nation on the path to prosperity, and I intend to keep it on the path to prosperity.

I was told of a story of the Nebraska Furniture Mart. It's an interesting American story. It's a story of a family that started this company in Omaha, Nebraska, and they wanted to build a store right here in Kansas City, Kansas. It wasn't the best time to open up a store, but the people running the company thought it was a good risk, a good market. They planned on bringing—or hiring 550 new workers for their new store, because the tax relief we passed put more money in people's pockets, and the demand for the goods they sold in that store was greater than they expected. So Furniture Mart hired 1,000 people instead of 550.

Robert Batt and his family—they run the company—he said this; he said, "We just believe in America, and we do what we excel at, selling furniture. The customers are out there. We've never had a layoff in 67 years." Not only have they not had a layoff in 67 years, they had enough confidence and the policies of the administration were working such that they were able to provide work for 1,000 of our fellow citizens.

Even as this economy is looking up, it's hard to feel confidence if you're somebody looking for a job. People who have been hit hard in the manufacturing sector know what I'm talking about. Parts of this country are not doing as well as they should, regions like the Pacific Northwest and parts of the Midwest. Part of the current problem is that job creation lags behind improvements in the overall economy. Of course, it takes a while for job creation to catch up. Usually, when the economy comes out of a recession, jobs are the last thing to arrive. Employers tend to rely on overtime until they're sure it makes sense to hire another worker.

Yet, there's another basic reason for lagging employment, and that is increases in worker productivity. Over the long term, higher productivity lifts workers' wages and standards of living, and it helps the economy. We've got the most productive workers in the world right here in America. And that's good for the long-term economic prospects. You see, higher levels of productivity means that we'll see better paying jobs for the American worker. But there is a downside in the short term. When a business can produce more per employee—in other words, productivity has gone up per person—it does not hire new people right away to meet rising demand.

So therefore, the agenda that I've got and I'm going to describe to you, to build on what we have done already, has one thing in mind, and that is, our economy must grow faster than productivity increases to make sure that people can find a job. I'm interested in Americans going to work. That's what I'm interested in.

And we will continue to help individuals get through the tough times and to prepare for better times. My administration supported the extensions of the unemployment benefits so that people that have been laid off get the help they need. Our economy demands new and different skills. We are a changing economy. And therefore, we must constantly educate workers to be able to fill the jobs of the 21st century.

And so therefore, I went to Congress and asked for increased funding for Pell grants for higher education scholarships. Now, more than 1.9 million community college students receive those grants. Community colleges are great places for people to learn new skills so they can fill the new jobs of the 21st century. And that's why the Department of Labor has begun a high-tech job training initiative to create partnerships between employers—those people who know what kind of jobs are needed—community colleges, and career centers so that those looking for work can match education and the skills they learn with the jobs that actually exist.

And for those who are having the hardest time finding work, I proposed to the Congress a new idea called Reemployment Accounts. These accounts will provide a job-seeker with up to $3,000 to pay for training, daycare, transportation, relocation expenses, whatever it takes to find a new job. And if they find a job quicker than the allotted time for the $3,000, they get to keep the difference between what they've spent and the $3,000 as a reemployment bonus. These accounts, if Congress will act, will help more than 1 million of our fellow citizens receive the training necessary to become employable, to meet the—to be able to fill the new jobs of the 21st century.

What's interesting is, right now, is that as the economy is getting a little better, employers are now beginning to decide whether to hire more workers. Hiring is a big decision, especially big for a small company. After all, when you take on a new employee, you not only show confidence in the person; you've got to have confidence in your company's future. And there are six specific actions we can take to help build that confidence, so that people can find a job.

First, people are more likely to find work if health care costs are reasonable and predictable. Adding an employee often requires more than paying a wage. You know that. It means providing benefits such as health insurance. But company costs for health benefits have been rising nearly 10 percent a year since 2000. These increases cut the capacity to create jobs, and we've got to deal with them. We've got to take this issue straight on.

We can help small businesses by allowing them to join together to shop for health insurance, allowing them to pool their risks in what's called associated health care plans. It makes sense to give small businesses the same bargaining power that big companies enjoy, so they can reduce their health care costs. The House of Representatives has passed a good bill. It is time for the Senate to act. I thank Senator Talent for his support and leadership.

In order to address another cost of rising health care, we must fix the problem of frivolous lawsuits against our doctors and hospitals. Litigation or the fear of litigation is causing doctors to quit the practice of medicine. Medicine is becoming less accessible because of the frivolous lawsuits. And the doctors that continue to practice who fear a lawsuit will try to protect themselves from the lawsuit by overprescribing, by covering themselves, by practicing defensive medicine, which drives up the cost of health care for everybody. And it drives up the cost of health care to the Federal budget. Frivolous lawsuits increase the cost to the Federal budget because of increases in Medicaid costs and Medicare costs and veterans' costs. Therefore, medical liability reform is a national issue that requires a national solution.

I proposed to the United States Congress a reasonable reform for medical liability. Any patient that has been harmed should recover all economic damages. We should have a cap of $250,000 on noneconomic damages. If harm is caused by serious misconduct, we ought to have reasonable punitive damages. The House passed the bill; it is stuck in the Senate. It is time for the United States Senate to pass medical liability reform, for the sake of job creation in America.

Secondly, we ought to take action on a lawsuit culture that affects the workers in every business, not just the docs. Industry estimates show that litigation is a $200-billion-a-year burden on the U.S. economy. Obviously, when big money goes to trial lawyers, it doesn't go to workers. So I proposed—and the House has approved, and it's stuck in the Senate—an idea to help relieve the cost of lawsuits. And that is class action reform. We ought to make it easier to move class action and mass tort lawsuits into the Federal courts so that trial lawyers won't be able to shop around our country to find a favorable court.

And as we are reforming class action, it also makes sense to make sure that when a verdict is handed down, that the money actually goes to the people who have been harmed.

Thirdly, a growing economy depends on steady, affordable, reliable supplies of energy. And yet, as we've seen recently, businesses have had to cope with constant uncertainty, uncertainty because of shortages and energy price spikes or blackouts. It is hard to be able to plan for the future when you're worried about energy supply. And this is especially true for manufacturing companies, which use about a third of the Nation's energy.

And so we needed a comprehensive national energy plan, one that seeks to upgrade the electricity grid, that makes reliability standards by those who deliver electricity mandatory, not voluntary. We need to promote new technologies and alternative sources of energy. Someday we may just be growing our energy right here in the State of Missouri. But in the meantime, we've got to find more sources of energy here at home in an environmentally friendly way. I've been calling for Congress to pass a comprehensive energy plan for 2 years. For the sake of national security, for the sake of economic security, we need to be less reliant on foreign sources of energy.

People are more likely to find work if the resources of businesses are not spent complying with endless and unreasonable Government regulation from Washington, DC. We will meet our duty to enforce laws, whether it be environmental protection laws or worker safety laws. But we want to simplify regulations in this administration. And we're working hard to do so.

I'll just give you one example. We streamlined tax reporting requirements for small businesses, helping 2.6 million small businesses save what is estimated to be 61 million hours of unproductive work. By streamlining regulations, by making regulations more simple, the small businesses that were affected by this change have now got more money to invest in their businesses, which means it's more likely they will hire somebody. Easing the burden of excessive regulation on all businesses is important for job creation all across our country.

Fifth, people are more likely to find work if we continue to expand trading opportunities for our goods and services. My administration is opening up new markets around the world for products that carry the international mark of quality, a label that says, made or produced in America.

Yesterday I signed legislation creating free trade agreements with Singapore and Chile. These agreements will lower tariffs on American-made goods and make our goods more competitive abroad.

Let me give you an example of what I'm talking about. American-made heavy machinery, such as motor grader, costs $11,200 more when sold in Chile because of extra tariffs. If that machinery were made in Canada or the European Union, it would carry no tariff. Therefore, an American product, because of the tariffs that existed, were priced out of the reach of the buyer in Chile. Because of what the bill I signed—because of my desire to make sure the playing field is level around the world, manufacturers will be able to compete on a level playing field. And there's no doubt in my mind that when the playing field is level, American workers can compete with anybody in the world.

Finally, people are more likely to find work if businesses and their workers can be certain that the lower tax rates of the last years will stay in place. Today, you don't have that confidence they'll stay in place, and there's a good reason—because under the laws that were passed, tax relief is set to expire.

The death tax, which is being phased out and will disappear in 2010 but comes back to life because of a quirk in Senate rules, will be revived in 2011. That doesn't make any sense to say to the small-business owner or the farmer or the rancher, "We're going to phase out the death tax, which is a bad tax to begin with, and then let it pop back to life." But that's reality.

Or how about this: The capital gains tax reductions, a vital part of encouraging capital formation, will rise by a third in 2008. The incentives for small businesses will vanish in 2006. At midnight on December 31, 2004, the $1,000 child credit is set to fall back to $700 per child. The marriage penalty will take a bigger bite. That's the way the Congress did it.

What Congress needs to do is to get this message: When we threw out the old taxes, Americans didn't expect to see them sneaking in through the back door. For the sake of growth—for the sake of economic growth, for the sake of job creation, the United States Congress must make these tax cuts permanent.

I know there's talk about the deficit. The deficit is caused when less revenues come into the Treasury relative to expenditures. And when you have a recession, less revenues come into the Treasury. But also remember, that time we're at war. My attitude is, any time we put one of our soldiers in harm's way, we're going to spend what is ever necessary to make sure they have the best training, the best support, and the best possible equipment.

And the tax relief, which is stimulating economic growth, is a part of the deficit. It's about a quarter of the deficit. But this economy, as it grows, will yield more money to the Treasury. And I've laid out a 5-year plan to reduce the deficit in half. That assumes I have a willing partner in the Congress. Congress must hold the line on unnecessary spending.

I have proposed a 4-percent increase in discretionary spending for this year's budget. It's about equal to the increase of the average family budget. If it's good enough for American families, it ought to be good enough for the appetite of some of the Congressmen. They need to stick with that agreement. They need to understand that in order to cut the deficits in half, we must have spending discipline in Washington, DC. And I will insist upon spending discipline in Washington, DC.

There's a lot we can do now that the Congress is back in town. And I look forward to working with both Republicans and Democrats to set the framework for continued economic prosperity and growth.

I mentioned earlier, I'm optimistic about our future in this country. If you've seen what I've seen, you'd be optimistic too. I've seen the great spirit of the country. I know the attitude of the American people. I know the determination and will, the willingness to work hard, the willingness to place family above self, the willingness to serve something greater than yourself—that's the American spirit. And it is strong, and it is alive, and it is great.

I have confidence in the future of America. I have confidence in our economy, because I have great confidence in the creativity and the enterprise of the American people.

Thank you for coming. May God bless you, and may continue to bless America.

NOTE: The President spoke at 11:31 a.m. at the Kansas City Convention Center. In his remarks, he referred to Terrence P. Dunn, chairman of the board, and Peter S. Levi, president, Greater Kansas City Chamber of Commerce; Paul Rodriguez, chair-elect, and CiCi Rojas, president, Hispanic Chamber of Commerce of Greater Kansas City; and

Thomas H. Holcom, Jr., member, board of directors, Angel Flight Central, Inc.

Statement on the Withdrawal of the Nomination of Miguel A. Estrada To Be a United States Court of Appeals Circuit Judge
September 4, 2003

It is with regret that, at the request of Miguel Estrada, I have today withdrawn his nomination to the United States Court of Appeals for the DC Circuit. I understand and respect his decision and wish Mr. Estrada and his family the best.

Mr. Estrada received disgraceful treatment at the hands of 45 United States Senators during the more than 2 years his nomination was pending. Despite his superb qualifications and the wide bipartisan support for his nomination, these Democrat Senators repeatedly blocked an up-or-down vote that would have led to Mr. Estrada's confirmation. The treatment of this fine man is an unfortunate chapter in the Senate's history.

NOTE: The Office of the Press Secretary also released a Spanish language version of this statement.

Statement on Signing the Prison Rape Elimination Act of 2003
September 4, 2003

Today, I have signed into law S. 1435, the "Prison Rape Elimination Act of 2003." The Act provides for analysis of the incidence and effects of prison rape in Federal, State and local institutions, and for information, resources, recommendations and funding to protect individuals from prison rape. The Act also creates a National Prison Rape Reduction Commission.

Section 7(h) of the Act purports to grant to the Commission a right of access to any Federal department or agency information it considers necessary to carry out its duties, and section 7(k)(3) provides for release of information to the public. The executive branch shall construe sections 7(h) and 7(k)(3) in a manner consistent with the President's constitutional authority to withhold information when its disclosure could impair deliberative processes of the Executive or the performance of the Executive's constitutional duties and, to the extent possible, in a manner consistent with Federal statutes protecting sensitive information from disclosure.

GEORGE W. BUSH

The White House,
September 4, 2003.

NOTE: S. 1435, approved September 4, was assigned Public Law No. 108–79. An original was not available for verification of the content of this statement.

Remarks to Langham Company Employees in Indianapolis, Indiana
September 5, 2003

Thank you all. Thanks for coming. It's such an honor to be here with the Langham family and the employees of this incredibly vibrant company. I want to thank the CEO for such a fine introduction. I am honored that Cathy would invite me here and give me a chance to talk about some of the challenges which face our Nation, the challenge of making sure this Nation is secure and the challenge to make sure people can find work.

I know you all have been through some challenges here in the State of Indiana because of some recent flooding. Today I had the privilege of telling your Governor when I landed that I recently signed a disaster declaration that will provide Federal funds to help the folks who suffered as a result of the disaster that took place in many parts of your State.

There are a lot of Americans looking for work, and we need to do something about that in Washington, DC. We've taken steps to get our economy growing again, and there are some very hopeful signs that progress is being made. I'm optimistic about the future of this country. Yet today's unemployment report shows we've got more to do, and I'm not going to be satisfied until every American who's looking for a job can find a job.

I have laid out a comprehensive plan for job creation all across America. And for the sake of our fellow citizens, I look forward to working with the United States Congress to get this comprehensive plan passed. And one Member who will help get this plan passed, and a man who represents Indiana with such distinction and class, a man who is a person with whom my administration works closely, the chairman, Dick Lugar.

I want to thank John and Margaret Langham, as well as Cathy, for allowing my entourage to—[*laughter*]—which is quite large these days—[*laughter*]—to invade this beautiful facility. I want to thank the employees for welcoming us. I know it's not easy to have your day disrupted by a Presidential trip, but I'm honored to be here. [*Laughter*] And I want to thank you for your hard work.

One thing is for certain, that you've earned the respect of the Langham family. Walking in here, Cathy was telling me how proud she is of the 55 fellow workers, people who make this small business grow and become vibrant. So I want to congratulate you for your productivity and your hard work as well. You know, one of the great things about America is that we've got the best workforce in the world. We've got the finest workers and finest employees.

I also know that the attorney general of the great State of Indiana is with us today, Steve Carter, and I appreciate Steve being here. I want to thank Zionsville High School for being here today. I appreciate you all singing. I'm sorry I didn't get to hear you. I want to thank the Kobes for leading the Pledge. I appreciate Brenda Williams coming.

Today when I landed there at the airport, I also not only spoke to the Governor and the attorney general, but I spoke to a lady named Joyce Irwin. You probably don't know who Joyce is. She is—I will tell you, though. She is a soldier in the army of compassion. She's one of the thousands of people all across our country who have heard a call to love a neighbor just like you'd like to be loved yourself.

There's great talk about the might of America, and we're mighty. And I intend to keep it that way. We've got great military might, economic might. But the truth of the matter is, the great strength of America is the heart and soul of the American people. The great strength of our country is the fact that there are millions of our fellow citizens like Joyce Irwin who are willing to lend a hand to a neighbor in need. The great strength of America is the fact that on a daily basis, there are millions of acts of kindness and mercy that helps change America to a more hopeful place, one heart, one soul at a time.

Joyce Irwin is a volunteer. She's active with the Little Red Door Cancer Agency, the Fairbanks Hospital, the Meridian Street United Methodist Church. She helps round up donations of clothing to those who need to be clothed, food for those who need to be fed. But most important, she dedicates her time to those who need to be loved. My call to our fellow Americans is love your neighbor just like you'd like to be loved yourself. Thank you, Joyce.

I mentioned the fact that our Nation is facing big challenges. One of the big challenges, of course, is for me, my administration, and those of us who have been honored to serve the American people, to do our solemn duty and protect the security of the American people. We must never forget the lessons of September the 11th, 2001, a sobering reminder that oceans no longer can protect us from forces of evil who can't stand what America stands for. There are people in this world who hate the thought that we believe in free societies, we believe people should worship freely, speak their mind freely. And since we're not going to change, since we're not going to change our attitude about freedom, we've still got an issue with these terrorists.

And we're doing everything we can to protect the homeland. We've got better coordination amongst law enforcement agencies. We're monitoring our ports and points of entry in ways we never have before. We've got emergency preparedness teams in place. But the best way to secure the homeland, the best way to do our duty to provide security for the American people and future generations of American people, is to hunt the terrorists down, one by one, and bring them to justice.

Not only must we stay on the offensive against those who would do us harm, and not only we must—must we continue to disrupt terrorist training camps to deal with dictatorial regimes who would threaten us and/or arm terrorists to threaten us, but we also must continue to promote freedom. Free societies are likely to be peaceful societies. Free societies are societies which won't threaten their neighbors or use weapons of mass destruction. America believes that freedom is not America's gift to the world, that freedom is God's gift to every individual who lives in this world.

And at home, we must recognize that while the signs are pretty good about our economy, there's still people looking for work. And we've got to do something about that. I said I was optimistic about our economy, and I am, for good reason. We have been through a lot. And yet, we're still strong. Let me remind you of what we've been through.

The attacks on America cost us about $80 billion. That's a lot of money. The attacks hurt our economy at a time when we were beginning to recover from a recession. In March of 2000, the stock market started to decline. Investors began to realize, well maybe this economy wasn't quite as strong as it had been in the past. And we were in recession in the first quarters of 2001. We had negative growth. People were beginning to look for work. Things weren't good.

But the economy began to come back because we actually passed a really good tax bill out of the Congress. And then the enemy hit us, and it hurt. It hurt economically. It hurt the Nation's psyche to think that we were vulnerable to coldblooded killers that could come and in one day take the lives of thousands of innocent people.

But we began to recover. We took some actions in Washington. For example, we passed terrorism insurance plan to help encourage building of large construction projects, keep those hardhats working. We dealt with the airline industry for the short term. I mean, we took action, and we started getting better.

And then a third thing happened. We had some of our fellow citizens forget to—forgot what it means to be a responsible citizen. We had some corporate CEOs who didn't tell the truth to their employees and to their shareholders. And that affected the confidence of the people, affected the confidence of people that were thinking about investing. So we took action there, by the way. We passed tough laws. The message is clear: If you don't tell the truth, there's going to be serious consequences.

In spite of these challenges, the economy is growing. I think one of the main reasons it's growing is because of the tax cuts we passed. I believe that when somebody has more money in their pocket, they will demand an additional good or a service. And when they demand additional good or a service, in our society somebody will produce that good or a service. And when somebody produces that good or a service, it means somebody is likely to find work. The tax relief plan we passed that let you keep more of your own money came at the right time.

We cut rates on everybody who pays income taxes. We didn't try to pick or choose winners. We said, "If we're going to have tax relief, if you pay tax, you ought to get relief."

We increased the child credit from $600 per child to $1,000 per child. We want to help our moms and dads with the responsibility of raising their children. And by the way, because of the '03 bill, we put the check in the mail in July of this year.

We reduced the effects of the marriage penalty. It doesn't make any sense to penalize marriage in the Tax Code. We wanted to help those who own stock directly or indirectly. Many of you own stocks through your pension plans. Many of you own stocks and bonds directly. So we cut taxes on dividends and capital gains to encourage investment. And that particularly helps our seniors. Many of our seniors rely upon dividend income, and they're retirement age, and that helps our seniors realize—have good—be able to have more money in their pocket as they get in their retirement years.

And all in all, we began to affect people's pocketbooks in a positive way. If you're a family of four making $40,000, your tax bill went from $1,978 to $45, thanks to the tax bill we passed.

We always talk about numbers in Washington. And that's okay. It helps us try to understand where we're going. But what I like to do is try to relate what this tax plan means for our fellow citizens.

The Bakers are with us, Doug and Mindy. I had a chance, by the way, to visit with some of our fellow citizens earlier. And I got to listen to what this tax bill—these tax bills meant for them. And the Bakers are with us, Doug and Mindy. They've got three children, by the way, all of them 5 years or younger. Amazing thing is, is that Mindy Baker doesn't have gray hair yet. [*Laughter*] But they got their check in the mail for the increase in the child credit. It was $800. The reason they didn't get 1,200 is because the littlest one, Josiah, wasn't born in time.

But I want to tell you what they told me. They said, that tax relief means peace of mind—their words, not mine. He said, "I'm taking care of my family. We're now prepared to take care of unexpected things." The $800 mattered to the Baker family, just like it mattered to the Biby family—they're with us, the proud mom and dad of Jacob and James. They saved about $1,900 as a result of the tax relief. He told me, Kevin Biby told me, he said, "You know, I'm going to use that money to help repair my car." That means the guy who repairs the car, he's getting a little extra work. That means he's going to be able to have a little money in his pocket as well.

Sharon Okey is with us here. Sharon has got the toughest job in America; she's a single mom of five kids. She's got a college junior. She got that check in the mail for the child credit. She told me, she said, it helped Jennifer, her oldest, go to college. It mattered. It matters when people take that money, for example, and go buy school supplies. Somebody's got to produce the school supplies. Somebody's got to sell the school supplies. It affects economic vitality and growth when people are spending money. The more money people have in their pockets when times are slow, the more likely it is our economy is going to recover. And that's why I fought for and Congress passed tax relief on behalf of the working people of America.

Greg and Cathy Habegger are with us today—Habeggers are with us, and they've got Jack and Ben, so they got a check in the mail too, plus the rate reductions. They're saving about $1,700 a year. He said it helped pay for some paint and furniture for their house. Well, when they went out and bought the furniture, it means somebody who's making furniture has got more job security. And maybe if that furniture manufacturing company was full, maybe they're at capacity, that extra piece of furniture could cause somebody else to find work.

If you see what I'm saying—in other words, when we put money in circulation—by the way, it's your money, not the Government's money—when it's your—got your money to spend, and you're circulating it around, it has an effect on the economy.

So not only are we helping people do their jobs as moms and dads, and not only are we providing financial relief when times are tough so families can breathe a little easier, we're also helping somebody who's looking for work. Money in circulation through increased demand means somebody is going to likely find work when they produce the product to meet that demand.

And let me tell you what else the tax relief did. It helped the small businesses all across America, small businesses just like this. And that's important because small businesses create most of the new jobs in

America. If your small-business sector is vibrant and healthy, somebody is likely to find a job.

Now, what's interesting about tax relief that a lot of people didn't understand is that most small businesses are what they call sole proprietorships or Subchapter S corporations, just like this one. It's a Subchapter S corporation, which means that the business pays taxes at the individual income tax rates. So when you reduce individual income taxes, the sole proprietorship or the Subchapter S really receives tax relief. The tax cuts help small businesses because it gave them more money, more money in their coffers to expand their job base. You just heard Cathy say, as a result of the tax relief, she now feels comfortable about adding five new employees. Tax relief means new jobs for Americans.

Part of the plan to stimulate growth amongst the small businesses was to allow small businesses to deduct up to $100,000 of new equipment, investment in new equipment and technologies. It used to be only $25,000. So you see, when you increase the capacity for somebody to deduct more, you provide an incentive for people to make bigger purchases. And so the Langhams have told me that they're thinking about buying some new computer software that will make the employees of this company more productive, will make the company more competitive, and will also help somebody who is making the computer software. That's how the economy works.

When the Langhams spend money, not only does it help their own employees, not only will it help the five folks that they're fixing to hire, but it helps the people providing products for this company. Tax relief is stimulating growth and tax relief is stimulating job creation all across the country.

But as I mentioned to you, we've got more work to do, and I want to talk about some things that can be done. There are still people looking for work. The economy is growing. Homebuilding is strong. People are getting more confident. The purchases of factory orders for heavy machinery is good, and it's up. But people are still looking for work.

One of the reasons why is that when you're coming out of slow times, job creation is the last thing to arrive on the scene. A lot of employers are saying, "Well, I want to make sure the economy is as good as it sounds like before I put on a new worker."

Another reason why is because our workers are so productive. Productivity—we've got the highest productivity, the most productive workers, in the world. And when productivity goes up, it means that a worker can have more output per hour. And therefore, in order for job creation to grow, the economy must grow faster than productivity gains. In other words, if a worker can do more per hour, in order for a new worker to be hired, the demand must be increased by as much, if not greater than, productivity increases.

And so, we've got a short-term problem. Long term, it's good that we're more productive. It means higher wages for the American worker. It means we're more competitive overseas. Short term, this economy needs to crank up faster than productivity increases in order for somebody to find a job.

And so, that's what I want to talk to you about, how best to encourage continued growth, how to make sure this economy continues to grow. Well, first of all, we need to deal with our health care issue. We want to make sure health care is available and health care is affordable. One way to make sure health care is affordable for small businesses like the Langhams' is to allow for the creation of what we call association health plans, which will allow small businesses to come together to pool risk and to have bargaining power just like big businesses can.

Another way we can work on health care costs and to make sure health care is available for our citizens is to deal with this issue of medical liability. There's too many frivolous lawsuits which are driving up the cost of medicine. If you're a doctor and you're afraid you're going to get sued, you practice unnecessary medicine in order to cover yourself in a court of law. That drives up your cost of medicine. It drives up the Langhams' cost for health care. Preventative medicine, because of litigation, is running up your bill.

Now, I believe if you've been harmed by a doc, you ought to have your day in court, and you ought to recover full economic damages. And I think that's only fair in America. I do think there ought to be a cap at 250,000 on noneconomic damages. And I think there ought to be reasonable punitive damages. There ought to be reasonable punitive damages.

And because high cost of health care run up the cost of the Federal budget—you see, when health care goes up, Medicaid budgets go up, and Medicare budgets go up, and the Veterans Health Administration budgets go up. Because it affects our budget, I believe medical liability reform is a national issue which requires a national solution. The House of Representatives act. The Senate must pass good medical liability reform on behalf of economic vitality and on behalf of the workers all across the country.

Some other things we can do: We can get a class action reform out of the United States Senate. And one thing we can do is make sure these lawyers aren't able to shop all around the country for a favorable jury, by moving class action suits into the Federal court. And we need to reform the system so that when there is a verdict, the lawyers don't get the money, but the people who have been harmed get the money.

We need to continue to work for regulatory relief on small and large businesses, so that instead of filing needless paperwork, you're working to make your workforce more productive and to meet the needs of your customers.

We need to make sure we have an energy policy. If we want this economy to continue to grow—we're interested in economic growth. This is a State that relies upon the manufacturing sector a lot, in Indiana. You need to have reliable sources of energy if you want your economy to grow. We need an energy policy. I've been talking to Congress about this for 2 years. It doesn't make any sense to have haphazard policy.

We need energy policy to make sure our electricity grid is brought up to date and is more modern. We need energy policy that encourages alternative sources of energy, like those grown right here in the fields of Indiana, called corn, converted to ethanol. We need to make sure we develop environmentally friendly ways to explore for more energy. We need clean coal technology. We need, for the sake of national security and economic security, to be less dependent on foreign sources of energy.

I believe when you see the label "Made in the U.S.A.," it's the stamp of quality. And therefore, one way to encourage job growth is to open up markets and to level the playing field for U.S. products. Just give us a level playing field, and we can compete with anybody, anyplace, anytime.

And finally, in order for there to be economic vitality and job creation and growth, there needs to be certainty in the Tax Code. In other words, people who are making investments must understand what the rules are going to be. The problem is, is that all the tax relief I've discussed with you, because of quirks in the rules, start fading out in 2005. The child credit, at some point in time, will go back down. The marriage penalty will go up. In other words, what I described to you goes away. If Congress is really interested in job creation, they will make every one of the tax relief measures we passed permanent.

You will hear talk about the deficit. We have a deficit. We have a deficit in part because of the recession. When you have a recession, you get less money into your treasury. When the economy slows, there's less revenue coming to Washington, DC. About half of the deficit is caused by the recession that we're trying to get out of.

A quarter of the deficit is caused by the fact that we're spending money to defend America. My attitude is, anytime we put one of our troops in harm's way, they deserve the best pay, the best training, and the best possible equipment. This Nation will spend what it takes to win the war on terror and to protect the American people.

About a quarter of the deficit was caused by the tax relief. But the tax relief is helping us recover from the recession. It was needed. It was needed to make this economy grow. And as the economy grows, more revenues come into the Treasury. The best way to cut down the deficit—and I've got a plan to reduce it in half in 5 years—is for Congress to set priorities and not overspend.

Discretionary spending prior to my arrival was increasing at 8.7 percent. Working with fine Senators like Dick Lugar, we've got discretionary spending down during this budget cycle to 4 percent.

There is no question that we've been challenged. But those challenges came to the right people. I have been so proud of our country. We are a country that is determined and strong and tough when we need to be tough and compassionate when we need to be compassionate. We've overcome a lot. We've overcome war, attacks on our country, recessions, corporate scandals. And yet we're still strong. We're vibrant. We're a great nation. We're a great nation because of our ideals and our beliefs. We believe in human dignity. We believe everybody has worth. We believe in freedom and the promise of freedom.

Ours is a nation dedicated to a world of peace, and we will use our strength to achieve peace. And ours is a nation dedication to uplifting every citizen who lives in this country by giving every person a chance to realize the great promise, the American Dream.

Thank you all for coming. May God bless you, and may God bless America.

NOTE: The President spoke at 2:54 p.m. in the warehouse at the Langham Co. In his remarks, he referred to Gov. Frank O'Bannon of Indiana; and Cathy Langham, president, John Langham, vice president, finance and administration, and Margaret Langham, vice president, operations, Langham Co.

Remarks at a Bush-Cheney Reception in Indianapolis
September 5, 2003

Thank you very much. I appreciate it. Thanks. Thank you all. Please be seated. Thanks for the warm welcome. It's great to be back in the great State of Indiana. It's such a beautiful part of America. You know, Vice President Cheney and I did pretty well in the year 2000 in this State. [*Laughter*] The next time around we should do even better, riding on the coattails of my man Mitch.

I want to thank you all for coming tonight. It's a spectacular turnout. What we're doing is laying the groundwork for a strong foundation for what will become a great victory in November of 2004.

I'm going to count on you for energizing the grassroots, for putting up the signs and mailing out the mailers and making the phone calls, for going to the coffee shops and reminding your fellow citizens that ours is a vision that includes everybody. Ours is a hopeful and optimistic vision for everybody who lives in the United States of America.

The political season is coming pretty soon, and I'm loosening up. I'm getting ready, but right now I've got a job to do. And my job is to work on behalf of the people of America. I'm going to continue to work hard to earn the confidence of every American, keeping this Nation secure and strong and prosperous and free.

I appreciate so very much my friend Al Hubbard. I didn't realize he was so articulate. [*Laughter*] Maybe he wasn't. [*Laugh-ter*] But he's a great friend. I want to thank his leadership.

My regret tonight is that the First Lady is not traveling with me. I married above myself. Laura is a remarkable person. I love her dearly. She's doing a great job on behalf of the American people.

I want to thank Bob Graham for his work on this event. I, too, want to thank all the table captains and people who have worked hard to make this an enormous success. I appreciate my friend Mercer Reynolds from Cincinnati, Ohio, who is the national chairman of the Bush-Cheney campaign. He's a business guy who's taking time out of his life to help us collect enough money to wage a viable campaign in 2004.

I'm honored that members of the congressional delegation are with us. I'm particularly pleased that the chairman is with us, a fine American, a great friend, a person whose counsel and advice I take seriously, Senator Dick Lugar; a person with whom I've played golf and don't intend to play again since he took money from me— [*laughter*]—Congressman Dan Burton; and another star of the congressional delegation is with us, and that's Congressman Mike Pence.

I'm so pleased we've got State officials with us, Todd Rokita, who is the secretary of state—Mr. Secretary, I'm glad you're here—the State auditor, Connie Nass, is with us; the Republican house leader, Brian

Bosma, is with us today, as is State Representative Mike Murphy. I'm so honored you all are taking time out of your day to be here. All politics is local. You have to work to prepare the groundwork for a new Governor who's coming soon, Mitch Daniels.

Speaking about my man Mitch, I noticed a gracious move by David McIntosh in today's newspaper, a move of party unity, a move of serving something greater than himself. David, I appreciate your class act. I'm proud to call you friend, and I'm glad you're here tonight. Thank you for coming.

There are people who have worked in my administration who are here. But one of the more famous Indianapolis citizens is with us tonight, who is serving our country with distinction, a man who understands the Faith-Based Initiative about as well as anybody in the country, and that's my friend Stephen Goldsmith. Thank you for coming, Stephen.

Finally, I'd like to thank Jim Kittle, who is the chairman of the Indiana Republican Party. Get your uniform on, Jim. We're ready to roll. But I appreciate your service. Thank you all again for coming. It's a huge turnout.

In the last 2½ years, our Nation has acted decisively to confront great challenges. I came to this office to solve problems, not to pass them on to future Presidents and future generations. I came to seize opportunities instead of letting them slip away. I believe this administration is meeting the tests of our time.

Terrorists declared war on the United States of America, and war is what they got. We've captured or killed many leaders of the Al Qaida network, and the rest of them know we're on their trail. In Afghanistan, in Iraq, we gave ultimatums to terror regimes. Those regimes chose defiance, and those regimes are no more. Fifty million people—50 million people in those two countries once lived under tyranny, and now they live in freedom.

Two-and-a-half years ago, our military was not receiving the resources it needed, and morale was beginning to suffer. We increased the defense budget to prepare for the threats of a new era. And today, no one in the world can question the skill and the strength and the spirit of the United States military.

Two-and-a-half years ago, we inherited an economy in recession. And then the attacks came on our country, and we had scandals in corporate America, and war. All affected the people's confidence. But we acted. We passed tough new laws to hold corporate criminals to account. And to get the economy going again, I have twice led the United States Congress to pass historic tax relief for the American people.

Here is what I know, and here's what I believe, that when Americans have more take-home pay to spend, to save, or to invest, the whole economy grows, and people are more likely to find a job. We understand whose money we spend in Washington, DC. It is not the Government's money we spend; it's the people's money.

We're returning more money to people to help them raise their families. We're reducing taxes on dividends and capital gains to encourage investment. We're giving small businesses incentives to expand and to hire new people. With all these actions, we're laying the foundation for greater prosperity and more jobs across America so every single person in this country has a chance to realize the American Dream.

Two-and-a-half years ago, there was a lot of talk about education reform, but there wasn't much action. So I acted. I called for and Congress passed the No Child Left Behind Act. With a solid bipartisan majority, we delivered the most dramatic education reforms in a generation. We're bringing high standards, and in return for Federal money, strong accountability measures to every public school in America. We believe that every child can learn the basics of reading and math, and we believe every school must teach the basics. This administration is challenging the soft bigotry of low expectations. The days of excuse-making are over when it comes to education. We now expect results in every classroom so that not one child in America is left behind.

During these 2½ years, we reorganized our Government and created the Department of Homeland Security to better safeguard our borders and ports and to protect the American people. We passed trade promotion authority to open up new markets for Indiana's farmers and ranchers and entrepreneurs and manufacturers. We passed budget agreements to help maintain much needed spending discipline in Washington, DC. On issue after issue, this administration has acted on principle, has kept its word, and has made progress for the American people.

The U.S. Congress has shared in these great achievements. I've got a great working relationship with Speaker Hastert and Leader Frist, and I intend to keep it that way. I look forward to working with Members of Congress to change the tone in Washington, DC, to get rid of the needless partisan bickering, and to focus on results, so the people know we have done our job.

And those are the kind of people I've attracted to my administration. I've put together a fantastic administration to serve the American people, good, honorable, decent people. Our Nation has had no finer Vice President than Vice President Dick Cheney. Mother may have a different opinion. [*Laughter*]

In 2½ years—in 2½ years' time, we have come far, but our work is only beginning. I have set great goals worthy of a great nation. First, America is committed to expanding the realm of freedom and peace for our own security and for the benefit of the world. And second, in our own country, we must work for a society of prosperity and compassion so that every citizen—every single citizen—has a chance to work and to succeed and realize the great promise of our land.

It is clear that the future of freedom and peace depend on the actions of America. This Nation is freedom's home, and we are freedom's defender. We welcome this charge of history, and we are keeping it. Our war on terror continues. The enemies of freedom are not idle, and neither are we. This country will not rest. We will not tire. We will not stop until this danger to civilization is removed.

Yet our national interest involves more than eliminating aggressive threats to our safety. Our greatest security comes from the advance of human liberty, because free nations do not support terror. Free nations do not attack their neighbors. Free nations do not threaten the world with weapons of mass terror. Americans believe that freedom is the deepest need and hope of every human heart. And I believe that freedom is the right of every person. And I believe that freedom is the future of every nation.

America also understands that unprecedented influence brings tremendous responsibilities. We have duties in the world, and when we see disease and starvation and hopeless poverty, we will not turn away. On the continent of Africa, America is now committed to bringing the healing power of medicine to millions of men and women and children now suffering with AIDS. I've called upon a fine citizen of Indianapolis to lead an incredibly important mission of human rescue. I want to thank Randy Tobias for his willingness to serve in a great cause.

We face challenges at home as well, and our actions will prove that we're equal to those challenges. The economy is getting better. But so long as people who want to work are looking for a job, I will continue to work to make the conditions for capital investment for the entrepreneurial spirit to remain strong. I care when I hear that people are not working.

As well, we have a duty to make a commitment to America's seniors by strengthening and modernizing Medicare. A few weeks ago, the Congress took historic action to improve the lives of older Americans. For the first time since the creation of Medicare, the House and Senate passed reforms to increase choices for our seniors and to provide coverage for prescription drugs. Now that the Congress is back from their August break, it is time for the House and the Senate to iron out their differences and to get a bill to my desk. The sooner they get the job done, the sooner American seniors will get the health care they need.

And for the sake of our health care system, we need to cut down on the frivolous lawsuits which increase the cost of medicine. People who have been harmed by a bad doctor deserve their day in court, yet the system should not reward lawyers who are simply fishing for rich settlements. Because frivolous lawsuits drive up the cost of health care, they affect the Federal budget. And therefore, medical liability reform is a national issue which requires a national solution. I have proposed a good plan to the Congress. The House of Representatives responded with a good bill. The bill is now stuck in the United States Senate. Senators must realize that no one in America has ever been healed by a frivolous lawsuit.

I have a responsibility as your President to make sure the judicial system runs well, and I have met that duty. I have nominated superb men and women for the Federal courts, people who will interpret the law, not legislate from the bench. Some Members of the Senate are trying to keep my nominees off the bench by blocking up-or-down votes. Every judicial nominee deserves a fair hearing and an up-or-down vote on the floor of the United States Senate. It is time for some Members of the Senate to stop playing politics with American justice.

In order to make sure we have economic vitality, the Congress needs to complete work on a comprehensive energy plan. Our Nation must realize that our electricity grid needs to be modernized. I have proposed

a modernization plan to the Congress. We need to promote alternative sources of energy like ethanol. We need to use our technologies to be able to explore for energy here at home in environmentally friendly ways. We need clean coal technology. For the sake of economic security and for the sake of national security, this Nation must become less dependent on foreign sources of energy. Both the Senate and House have passed an energy bill. They need to get together and get a bill to my desk.

Our strong and prosperous Nation must also be a compassionate nation. I will continue to advance our agenda of compassionate conservatism. We will apply the best and most innovative ideas to the task of helping our fellow citizens in need.

There are still millions of men and women who want to end their dependence on Government and become independent through hard work. Congress must work with us to build on the success of welfare reform, to bring work and dignity into more of—in the lives of more of our fellow citizens.

Congress should complete the "Citizen Service Act" so that more Americans can serve their community and their country. And both Houses should reach agreement on my Faith-Based Initiative to support the armies of compassion that are mentoring our children, that are caring for the homeless, that are offering hope to the addicted. Our Nation should not fear faith. We should welcome faith into the lives and to help heal our fellow citizens who hurt.

A compassionate society must promote opportunity for all, including the independence and dignity that come from ownership. This administration will constantly strive to promote an ownership society in America. We want more people owning a home. We will continue to promote policies which will close the minority homeownership gap in America. We want people controlling their own health care plans. We want people in control of their own retirement accounts. And we want more people owning a small business, because we understand in this administration, when an American owns something, he or she has a piece of the future, a vital stake in the future of our country.

In a compassionate society, people respect one another and take responsibility for the decisions they make. The old culture of America is changing. The old culture used to say, "If it feels good, do it," and "If you've got a problem, blame somebody else." It's changing to a new day in which each of us understands that we're responsible for the decisions we make in life.

If you're fortunate enough to be a mom or a dad, you're responsible for loving your child with all your heart and all your soul. If you're worried about the quality of the education in the community in which you live, you're responsible for doing something about it. If you're a CEO in corporate America, you're responsible for telling the truth to your shareholders and your employees.

And in the new responsibility society, each of us is responsible for loving our neighbor just like we'd like to be loved ourself. The culture of service and the culture of responsibility is growing around us. I started what we call the USA Freedom Corps to encourage Americans to extend a compassionate hand to neighbors in need, and the response has been strong. People have heard the call to serve our country.

Our charities are strong. Our faith-based efforts are vibrant. People are being healed because fellow Americans are serving our Nation by loving somebody. Policemen and firefighters and people who wear our Nation's uniform are constantly reminding us what it means to sacrifice for something greater than yourself. Once again, the children of America believe in heroes, because they see them every day.

In these challenging times, the world is seeing the resolve and the courage of America, and I have been privileged to see the compassion and character of the American people. All the tests of the last 2½ years have come to the right nation. We're a strong country, and we use that strength to defend the peace. We're an optimistic country, confident in ourselves and in ideals bigger than ourselves. Abroad, we seek to lift whole nations by spreading freedom. At home, we seek to lift up lives by spreading opportunity to every corner of America. This is the work that history has set before us. We welcome it. And we know that for our country and for our cause, the best days lie ahead.

May God bless you all. Thank you all.

NOTE: The President spoke at 6:18 p.m. at the Murat Centre. In his remarks, he referred to Indiana gubernatorial candidate Mitchell Daniels, Jr.; Allan B. Hubbard, former chairman, Indiana State Republican Party; former Indiana gubernatorial candidate David McIntosh, who withdrew his candidacy September 4; Stephen Goldsmith, chair, board of directors, Corporation for National and Community Service; and Randall Tobias, nominee to be Global AIDS Coordinator.

The President's Radio Address
September 6, 2003

Good morning. This month, as students across the Nation are starting a new school year, parents, teachers, and principals are starting to notice a difference in America's schools. The No Child Left Behind Act that I signed into law last year is raising standards for student achievement, giving parents more information and more choices, requiring more accountability from schools, and funding education at record levels.

The premise of the No Child Left Behind Act is simple: All children can learn, and the only way to make sure our children are learning is to measure their progress with tests. So the No Child Left Behind Act requires regular testing in the basics of reading and math for every child in every school, starting in the third grade. And the law sets a clear goal for American education: Every child in every school must perform at grade level in reading and math, which are the keys to all learning.

To meet this goal, all 50 States and the District of Columbia and Puerto Rico have designed accountability plans that have been approved by the Department of Education and are now being put into effect in America's schools. School districts across America are now providing parents with lists of outside tutors who can give extra help at no cost to low-income children in underperforming schools. Those parents also have the option of transferring a son or a daughter out of a school that is not doing the job to a better public school or charter school. And soon every community in America will have report cards on every local public school, so citizens can measure progress and push for reform.

While we're demanding excellence from schools, we're also giving them extra resources to succeed. Since this new law went into effect, 40 States have received a total of nearly $1.3 billion in grant money to support scientifically based reading instruction in kindergarten through the third grade.

My budget for next year includes more than $1.1 billion for effective reading programs, 4 times the amount we were spending on these programs when I took office. And overall Federal spending for elementary and secondary education is higher than ever before. My budget for next year boosts education funding to $53.1 billion, an increase of nearly $11 billion since I took office.

Schools are getting the Federal resources and help they need to improve, and parents are getting the information and options they need to support reform. And we're just beginning. This new school year will be a year of challenges and hard work and great progress. And through it all we will keep in mind the focus of all our efforts, our children, who deserve an education worthy of this great Nation. Together we will make sure that every child learns and no child is left behind.

Thank you for listening.

NOTE: The address was recorded at 8:55 a.m. on September 5 in the Cabinet Room at the White House for broadcast at 10:06 a.m. on September 6. The transcript was made available by the Office of the Press Secretary on September 5 but was embargoed for release until the broadcast. The Office of the Press Secretary also released a Spanish language transcript of this address.

Address to the Nation on the War on Terror
September 7, 2003

Good evening. I have asked for this time to keep you informed of America's actions in the war on terror.

Nearly 2 years ago, following deadly attacks on our country, we began a systematic campaign against terrorism. These months have been a time of new responsibilities and sacrifice and national resolve and great progress.

America and a broad coalition acted first in Afghanistan, by destroying the training camps of terror and removing the regime that harbored Al Qaida. In a series of raids and actions around the world, nearly two-thirds of Al Qaida's known leaders have been captured or killed, and we continue on Al Qaida's trail. We have exposed terrorist front groups, seized terrorist accounts, taken new measures to protect our homeland, and uncovered sleeper cells inside the United States. And we acted in Iraq, where the former regime sponsored terror, possessed and used weapons of mass destruction, and for 12 years defied the clear demands of the United Nations Security Council. Our coalition enforced these international demands in one of the swiftest and most humane military campaigns in history.

For a generation, leading up to September the 11th, 2001, terrorists and their radical allies attacked innocent people in the Middle East and beyond, without facing a sustained and serious response. The terrorists became convinced that free nations were decadent and weak. And they grew bolder, believing that history was on their side. Since America put out the fires of September the 11th and mourned our dead and went to war, history has taken a different turn. We have carried the fight to the enemy. We are rolling back the terrorist threat to civilization, not on the fringes of its influence but at the heart of its power.

This work continues. In Iraq, we are helping the long-suffering people of that country to build a decent and democratic society at the center of the Middle East. Together we are transforming a place of torture chambers and mass graves into a nation of laws and free institutions. This undertaking is difficult and costly, yet worthy of our country and critical to our security.

The Middle East will either become a place of progress and peace, or it will be an exporter of violence and terror that takes more lives in America and in other free nations. The triumph of democracy and tolerance in Iraq, in Afghanistan, and beyond would be a grave setback for international terrorism. The terrorists thrive on the support of tyrants and the resentments of oppressed peoples. When tyrants fall and resentment gives way to hope, men and women in every culture reject the ideologies of terror and turn to the pursuits of peace. Everywhere that freedom takes hold, terror will retreat.

Our enemies understand this. They know that a free Iraq will be free of them—free of assassins and torturers and secret police. They know that as democracy rises in Iraq, all of their hateful ambitions will fall like the statues of the former dictator. And that is why, 5 months after we liberated Iraq, a collection of killers is desperately trying to undermine Iraq's progress and throw the country into chaos.

Some of the attackers are members of the old Saddam regime who fled the battlefield and now fight in the shadows. Some of the attackers are foreign terrorists who have come to Iraq to pursue their war on America and other free nations. We cannot be certain to what extent these groups work together. We do know they have a common goal—reclaiming Iraq for tyranny.

Most but not all of these killers operate in one area of the country. The attacks you have heard and read about in the last few weeks have occurred predominantly in the central region of Iraq, between Baghdad and Tikrit, Saddam Hussein's former stronghold. The north of Iraq is generally stable and is moving forward with reconstruction and self-government. The same trends are evident in the south, despite recent attacks by terrorist groups.

Though their attacks are localized, the terrorists and Saddam loyalists have done great harm. They have ambushed American and British service members, who stand for freedom and order. They have killed civilian aid workers of the United Nations, who represent the compassion and generosity of the world. They have bombed the Jordanian Embassy, the symbol of a peaceful

Arab country. And last week, they murdered a respected cleric and over a hundred Muslims at prayer, bombing a holy shrine and a symbol of Islam's peaceful teachings.

This violence is directed not only against our coalition but against anyone in Iraq who stands for decency and freedom and progress. There is more at work in these attacks than blind rage. The terrorists have a strategic goal. They want us to leave Iraq before our work is done. They want to shake the will of the civilized world. In the past, the terrorists have cited the examples of Beirut and Somalia, claiming that if you inflict harm on Americans, we will run from a challenge. In this, they are mistaken.

Two years ago, I told the Congress and the country that the war on terror would be a lengthy war, a different kind of war, fought on many fronts in many places. Iraq is now the central front. Enemies of freedom are making a desperate stand there, and there they must be defeated. This will take time and require sacrifice. Yet we will do what is necessary; we will spend what is necessary, to achieve this essential victory in the war on terror, to promote freedom, and to make our own Nation more secure.

America has done this kind of work before. Following World War II, we lifted up the defeated nations of Japan and Germany and stood with them as they built representative governments. We committed years and resources to this cause. And that effort has been repaid many times over in three generations of friendship and peace. America today accepts the challenge of helping Iraq in the same spirit, for their sake and our own.

Our strategy in Iraq has three objectives: destroying the terrorists; enlisting the support of other nations for a free Iraq; and helping Iraqis assume responsibility for their own defense and their own future.

First, we are taking direct action against the terrorists in the Iraqi theater, which is the surest way to prevent future attacks on coalition forces and the Iraqi people. We are staying on the offensive with a series of precise strikes against enemy targets increasingly guided by intelligence given to us by Iraqi citizens. Since the end of major combat operations, we have conducted raids seizing many caches of enemy weapons and massive amounts of ammunition, and we have captured or killed hundreds of Saddam loyalists and terrorists. So far, of the 55 most wanted former Iraqi leaders, 42 are dead or in custody. We are sending a clear message: Anyone who seeks to harm our soldiers can know that our soldiers are hunting for them.

Second, we are committed to expanding international cooperation in the reconstruction and security of Iraq, just as we are in Afghanistan. Our military commanders in Iraq advise me that the current number of American troops, nearly 130,000, is appropriate to their mission. They are joined by over 20,000 service members from 29 other countries. Two multinational divisions led by the British and the Poles are serving alongside our forces, and in order to share the burden more broadly, our commanders have requested a third multinational division to serve in Iraq.

Some countries have requested an explicit authorization of the United Nations Security Council before committing troops to Iraq. I have directed Secretary of State Colin Powell to introduce a new Security Council resolution which would authorize the creation of a multinational force in Iraq, to be led by America. I recognize that not all of our friends agreed with our decision to enforce the Security Council resolutions and remove Saddam Hussein from power. Yet we cannot let past differences interfere with present duties. Terrorists in Iraq have attacked representatives of the civilized world, and opposing them must be the cause of the civilized world. Members of the United Nations now have an opportunity and the responsibility to assume a broader role in assuring that Iraq becomes a free and democratic nation.

Third, we are encouraging the orderly transfer of sovereignty and authority to the Iraqi people. Our coalition came to Iraq as liberators, and we will depart as liberators. Right now, Iraq has its own Governing Council, comprised of 25 leaders representing Iraq's diverse people. The Governing Council recently appointed cabinet ministers to run Government departments. Already more than 90 percent of towns and cities have functioning local governments, which are restoring basic services. We're helping to train civil defense forces to keep order and an Iraqi police service to enforce the law, a facilities protection service, Iraqi border guards to help secure the borders, and a new Iraqi army. In all these roles, there are now some 60,000 Iraqi citizens under arms, defending the security of their own country, and we are accelerating the training of more.

Iraq is ready to take the next steps toward self-government. The Security Council resolution we introduce will encourage Iraq's Governing Council to submit a plan and a timetable for the drafting of a constitution and for free elections. From the outset, I have expressed confidence in the ability of the Iraqi people to govern themselves. Now they must rise to the responsibilities of a free people and secure the blessings of their own liberty.

Our strategy in Iraq will require new resources. We have conducted a thorough assessment of our military and reconstruction needs in Iraq and also in Afghanistan. I will soon submit to Congress a request for $87 billion. The request will cover ongoing military and intelligence operations in Iraq, Afghanistan, and elsewhere, which we expect will cost $66 billion over the next year. This budget request will also support our commitment to helping the Iraqi and Afghan people rebuild their own nations after decades of oppression and mismanagement. We will provide funds to help them improve security, and we will help them to restore basic services such as electricity and water and to build new schools, roads, and medical clinics. This effort is essential to the stability of those nations and, therefore, to our own security. Now and in the future, we will support our troops, and we will keep our word to the more than 50 million people of Afghanistan and Iraq.

Later this month, Secretary Powell will meet with representatives of many nations to discuss their financial contributions to the reconstruction of Afghanistan. Next month, he will hold a similar funding conference for the reconstruction of Iraq. Europe, Japan, and states in the Middle East all will benefit from the success of freedom in these two countries, and they should contribute to that success.

The people of Iraq are emerging from a long trial. For them, there will be no going back to the days of the dictator, to the miseries of humiliation he inflicted on that good country. For the Middle East and the world, there will be no going back to the days of fear when a brutal and aggressive tyrant possessed terrible weapons. And for America, there will be no going back to the era before September the 11th, 2001, to false comfort in a dangerous world. We have learned that terrorist attacks are not caused by the use of strength. They are invited by the perception of weakness. And the surest way to avoid attacks on our own people is to engage the enemy where he lives and plans. We are fighting that enemy in Iraq and Afghanistan today so that we do not meet him again on our own streets, in our own cities.

The heaviest burdens in our war on terror fall, as always, on the men and women of our Armed Forces and our intelligence services. They have removed gathering threats to America and our friends, and this Nation takes great pride in their incredible achievements. We are grateful for their skill and courage and for their acts of decency, which have shown America's character to the world. We honor the sacrifice of their families. And we mourn every American who has died so bravely, so far from home.

The Americans who assume great risk overseas understand the great cause they are in. Not long ago, I received a letter from a captain in the 3d Infantry Division in Baghdad. He wrote about his pride in serving a just cause and about the deep desire of Iraqis for liberty. "I see it," he said, "in the eyes of a hungry people every day here. They are starved for freedom and opportunity." And he concluded, "I just thought you'd like a note from the frontlines of freedom." That Army captain and all of our men and women serving in the war on terror are on the frontlines of freedom. And I want each of them to know, your country thanks you, and your country supports you.

Fellow citizens, we've been tested these past 24 months, and the dangers have not passed. Yet Americans are responding with courage and confidence. We accept the duties of our generation. We are active and resolute in our own defense. We are serving in freedom's cause, and that is the cause of all mankind.

Thank you, and may God continue to bless America.

NOTE: The President spoke at 8:31 p.m. in the Cabinet Room at the White House. In his remarks, he referred to former President Saddam Hussein of Iraq; and Ayatollah Mohammed Baqir al-Hakim, a Muslim cleric killed in a terrorist bombing in Najaf, Iraq, on August 29. The Office of the Press Secretary also released a Spanish language transcript of this address.

Remarks at Kirkpatrick Elementary School in Nashville, Tennessee
September 8, 2003

Thank you all very much. I am honored to be at a school which refuses to leave any child behind. A good school begins with a good principal, somebody who is willing to challenge the soft bigotry of low expectations. And that's what Kim Fowler has done, and we're honored to be here. And I want to thank you for putting up with this huge entourage that travels with me. [*Laughter*]

We're here because, as you may remember, the Federal Government passed an innovative law recently, and a lot of people are wondering what that law means. And we have used this school as an example of what is possible for parents and for educators to make sure that not a single child gets left behind.

Before I begin to talk about the school, I do want to say that I am most appreciative that the superintendent of schools from Nashville public schools is with us today. He's an innovator. He believes in

setting high expectations for every child. It's not my first time I have been in Pedro Garcia's presence.

I love the motto of the school district here: Whatever It Takes—whatever it takes to succeed. And Pedro, thank you for setting a good example. We appreciate what you're doing, and we appreciate what the Nashville schools are doing to take advantage of the No Child Left Behind Act.

When I was looking for somebody to be the head of the Department of Education, I wanted somebody who had been on the frontlines of education, perhaps a superintendent of schools. And I knew a man in Houston, when I was the Governor of Texas, who was setting high standards and using innovation when innovation was needed to make sure the children of Houston, Texas, learned. And that man is with us today, who is now the head of the Department of Education, the Secretary of

Education, Rod Paige. And thank you for coming.

He's not the only person in this audience who has been the Secretary of Education. Senator Lamar Alexander was the Secretary of Education and did a fine job. I'm so honored you're here, Senator. Thank you for coming.

And I'm honored also to have traveled down with Senator Bill Frist, the majority leader of the United States Senate. He's doing a fabulous job for the country. As well, we've got Congressman Zach Wamp and Congressman Lincoln Davis and Congresswoman Marsha Blackburn with us from the mighty Tennessee delegation. We're honored you all are here, and thank you for coming.

The mayor of Nashville, Tennessee, Bill Purcell, is here. And Mr. Mayor, thank you for coming. I'm honored you would take time out to greet us. It means a lot that you're here, and we appreciate you coming as well.

Finally, when I landed at the airport, I had the honor of meeting Brenda Wilson. The people of this good elementary school know who Brenda is; people around the city may not. She's a soldier in the army of compassion. She's a person who volunteers to make sure the children can learn. She represents the thousands of people in this city and in this State who say, "If I've got a problem with a public school, I'm going to be involved with it. Instead of hoping that some distant government insists upon excellence, I, Brenda Wilson, will dedicate myself by donating time to make sure children get the very best."

She volunteered from 1995 to 2002 in this school. She did such a good job that you've named her the coordinator of volunteer services. That means if a child is going hungry, somebody will help find the food. If a child needs clothing, somebody will help find the clothes. If a child needs extra tutorial help beyond that which I'm going to describe, Brenda's job is to find people to volunteer, and she herself volunteers.

You know, there's a lot of talk in our—across our country about how strong America is. And we're strong, and I intend to keep us that way. But the true strength is not our military strength or our military muscle. The true strength is the heart and soul of the American people, people who are willing to say, "How can I help somebody? What can I do to make my community a better place?" Brenda, thank you for being one of those soldiers in the army of compassion. I appreciate you being here. Thank you, Brenda.

So there's been a lot of talk about the No Child Left Behind Act. Let me describe the principles inherent in the act, what we're doing to make sure no child gets left behind, and why I'm here at this elementary school.

First, as I mentioned, this society of ours must challenge the soft bigotry of low expectations. I believe, Kim believes, I know the teachers at this good school believe that every child can learn. We believe in the potential of every single child and, therefore, must insist that every child learns. See, if you don't believe certain children can't learn, then the tendency is just to shuffle them through the system. If you don't believe every child has worth, then the system tends just to give up on the child and move them through. And then at the end of high school, people can't read, and we've created a social problem.

So the No Child Left Behind Act says that we're going to challenge the soft bigotry of low expectations. And I want to thank Kim for doing that, and I want to thank the teachers in this school and across this city who are willing to challenge the soft bigotry of low expectations. Teaching is a noble profession; it's an honorable profession. And we want to thank our teachers, not only at this school but across this city and this State for agreeing to teach.

So, in other words, the bill basically says, "We believe in high expectations, and we believe it so strongly, we want to measure to see if those expectations are being met."

It's one thing to say, "I believe in high expectations," but unless you measure, you don't know whether expectations are being achieved.

And so, for the first time, the Federal Government has said, "In return for Federal dollars, we're going to measure"—not we, the Federal Government, but the State and local authorities will measure. In return for the Federal Government writing checks to States and to children, we want to know.

The person who doesn't believe certain children can learn just don't—doesn't care about the measurement system. If you do care about each child, then you want to know whether or not expectations are being met.

There's a lot of talk—listen, I cut my teeth in accountability in the State of Texas. I've heard every excuse in the book why not to measure. "Oh, you're teaching to test," you'll hear. Well, if you're teaching a child to read, that child will pass the test. "We're testing too much." My attitude is, is that in order to know, in order to diagnose a problem, you have to measure it in the first place. You cannot solve a problem until you measure in the first place.

And so the Congress did the right thing in insisting that we hold people accountable for results, and now we measure. And for the schools that are doing great, there ought to be nothing but praise. And for the schools that need help in meeting high expectations, there needs to be extra resources. And that's what this bill did. The budget for next year boosts funding for elementary and secondary education to $53.1 billion. That's a 26-percent increase since I took office. In other words, we understand that resources need to flow to help solve the problem.

Of that money, a lot of it goes to Title I—Title I money to help certain children. That's to the tune of $12.3 billion. That's a 41-percent increase for Title I students. And that's where the money goes, to help the Title I students in this school on special needs.

Now, the other thing we've done, which I'm proud of, is to fund effective reading programs. If you can't read, you're not going to do math. And if you can't read, you can't be a scientist. If you can't read, you can't understand history. If you can't read, you're going nowhere, if the truth be known. And so we've spent money for reading programs, money that will fund curriculum that actually works. There's a science with reading; it's not an art. They know what it takes to teach a child how to read. I appreciate the fact that the Nashville school system and this school uses reading programs that will teach a child how to read, not that sound good or feel good but actually achieve the results necessary so no child is left behind.

And so, the resources were there for—not only to make sure that teacher training is available and methodologies that work. I know we've had a lot of teacher training programs all around the country. It's beginning to make a significant effect. We started with the early grades first. We've got money in place to fund the measurement systems, to make sure the measurement systems get up and running and operate well. And we've got money in place to help students that need extra work.

And that's why we're here, because there is a triggering event in the bill, and it says that if schools are not meeting expectations, then parents should be given different options. If students—if the school is not achieving that which is expected and there's a chance a child will be left behind, then one remedy is to give parents the choice to choose another public school or perhaps to send their—a child to a tutorial sessions like we just saw today.

We have come from a really interesting little laboratory of excellence that Kim set up where three different providers were tutoring children. It gave me a chance to see that this school and this school district has not only reached out to parents but has reached out to educational providers that say, "We want to enlist your services to make sure no child is left behind." We measure. We determine which children need help. Parents are then given the option to decide what kind of tutors is needed to meet that child's needs.

The school district and the school don't fear extra help. They welcome extra help. They have used the measuring system not to punish anybody but determine what else is needed to make sure the child gets extra help. We not only saw the children learning and practicing to read; we met their parents. They could provide the testimony a lot more eloquently than me. But when you hear a parent—a mom say to me, "My child was at a second-grade level; the measurement system saw that she needed help. Thankfully, the Federal Government passed a law which provides extra time on tasks for my child, and now she's reading at the fifth-grade level, and she's in the fourth grade," that's a good sign. It means this particular child will not be left behind. It means the system is working. We measure to determine who needs help, and we provide the help.

And so, one of the problems we face— obviously, not here, but one of the problems we face is whether or not other school districts are properly advertising that which is available for students that need help. We've come to Nashville because the superintendent of schools has decided to make it widely known that extra services for children are available; made it widely known that summer school, after-school programs, Saturday programs, tutorials provided by the school district and/or private enterprise, are all available for parents whose children qualify.

You see, if you measure and then don't provide extra help, the measurement system is empty. If you measure, determine who needs help, and then provide the extra help, we have done our duty as adults to provide the skills necessary for children to succeed in life. And that's what this school

is doing. The tutorials have got to make sure that the programs have got proven track records, that they relate to directly what is needed to meet the curriculum needs of a school.

One other thing that's interesting that we have discovered is that research shows that after-school tutoring programs can do a lot for student achievement. That makes sense. If you focus on a child, focus energies on an individual child and stay on it and stay on task and if you believe every child can learn, then we will succeed.

And so, what I want people to understand around the country is that leaders, education leaders and Governors must advertise to the parents that which is now available under the No Child Left Behind Act, just like they're doing here in Nashville, Tennessee.

Kim was telling me they sent out flyers to parents in her—the parents of the children who go to her school. They're aggressive in the outreach to make sure parents know that which is available. And that's what other States must now do; other States must seize the moment. Other States must not fear measurement but use the measuring tool as a way to determine who needs help. And the resources are there to provide that help. Other States must challenge the soft bigotry of low expectations. Other States must do their duty to their children.

Kim Fowler is—has got the right attitude. She is not intimidated by measurement. She's not afraid to be held to account. She looks at the tests as a way to help people. She knows that you don't teach self-esteem—there's not a course that says the self-esteem—you teach a child to read, and he or she earns self-esteem. And that's the right attitude.

I'm so thankful that we've got people like Kim all across America who have got the right attitude. And I'm so thankful that we've got teachers like the teachers here that work with Kim, to make sure that no child is left behind.

Lakeisha Begley is a fourth-grader here. She was way below grade level. The system kicked in. Barbara, her mama, said that, one, she was appreciative of the fact that she had a choice. See, she was notified—said, "Your daughter's not doing well"—and then was given an option, a range of options. The school and the district trust the parents to make the right choice. It's not one of these paternalistic things that, "This is what's going to happen." They say, "We've got a problem with your child. We're going to give you some options from which to choose." So she signed up for a private tutor.

Barbara said she's already seen the difference. The child is excited. The child can't wait to read. "From day one, Lakeisha learned better study skills," she said. She was thrilled about doing it and thrilled about learning. The program motivated her to learn more. And that's what we're here to talk about, how to make sure we can put programs in place that motivate our children who need help to learn more.

I'm excited to be here. I'm excited to be here because I believe that this country can solve any problem that we face. We face a problem, to make sure every child can read. The statistics are loud and clear, too many of our fourth-graders cannot read at grade level. The Federal Government decided to do its part by not only providing the resources but by insisting upon results.

We are challenging the soft bigotry of low expectations. We believe every child can learn. And I'm convinced when these programs are fully implemented, children will learn, and America will be better off.

Thank you for having me here today. May God bless you all.

NOTE: The President spoke at 2:40 p.m. in the auditorium. In his remarks, he referred to Kim Fowler, principal, Kirkpatrick Elementary School; Pedro E. Garcia, director of schools, Metropolitan Nashville Davidson County Board of Public Education; and Kirkpatrick student Lakeisha Begley, and her grandmother, Barbara Stegall. The Office of the Press Secretary also released a Spanish language transcript of these remarks.

Remarks at a Bush-Cheney Reception in Nashville
September 8, 2003

Thank you all very much. Thanks for coming. Lamar puts it a little less delicately: "Without Tennessee, there would be no Texas." [*Laughter*] Without Tennessee, there would be no President George W. Bush.

I want to thank you all for coming tonight. I really appreciate your support and your friendship and your prayers. Tonight is the beginning of what is going to be a successful campaign here. We're laying the groundwork not only for a victory here in Tennessee, but we're laying the groundwork for what is going to be a victory in November of 2004.

I appreciate your contributions, but I will remind you there are other contributions to make. Going to need you to put your signs in the yard, need you to put out the mailers. When you go to the coffee shop, make sure you talk it up. [*Laughter*] And remind them that this administration has a vision which is positive and hopeful and optimistic for every single American.

The political season will come in its own time. I'm loosening up. [*Laughter*] And I'm getting ready. But I've got a job to do, and right now I'm focused on the people's business. We will continue to work hard to earn the confidence of every American by keeping this Nation secure and strong and prosperous and free.

I have only one regret tonight, and that is that the First Lady didn't come with me. I am one lucky man that Laura Bush said yes. We're there on bended knee, I said, "Would you marry me?" She is a fabulous First Lady, a great wife.

I'm proud to have been introduced by a fabulous United States Senator, Senator Bill Frist. He is doing a great job, not only for Tennessee but for our Nation. He's a steady hand. He's a good man to deal with. He's got our country's interests at heart, and I'm proud, like you are, to call him friend.

I'm also proud to call Lamar Alexander friend. He too is doing a fabulous job in the United States Senate. We've got two Members from the House of Representatives with us tonight. One of the event's vice chairmen, Congresswoman Marsha Blackburn—I'm honored that Marsha is with us. I want to thank you for coming, Marsha. And Congressman Zach Wamp is with us as well.

I appreciate all those who put this event together. My great friend from Cincinnati, Ohio, who is our national finance chairman, Mercer Reynolds. I want to thank Mercer for being here. I want to thank Jim Haslam, our State finance chair, for his hard work. I want to thank all who put this event together. I particularly want to thank Beth Harwell, the State party chairman.

I want to thank Gracie Rosenberger for performing the anthem. You know, when you come to Nashville, you hope to see some of your favorite entertainers. Fortunately, some of them showed up tonight, starting with Michael W. Smith, my good friend, and Debbie. I'm also so pleased that Ricky Skaggs came tonight. He's a—that boy can sing. Steve Wariner is with us tonight. Brad Paisley flew in from California to be with us tonight. I want to thank them all for coming.

There's less road rage at NASCAR now because Darrell Waltrip is retired, but I'm

still glad to call him—I'm glad he's here. But most of all, I really want to thank you all for being here. It means an awful lot.

In the last 2½ years, our Nation has acted decisively to confront great challenges. I came to this office to solve problems instead of passing them on to future Presidents and future generations. I came to seize opportunities instead of letting them slip away. This administration is meeting the tests of our time.

Terrorists declared war on the United States of America, and war is what they got. We have captured or killed many key leaders of Al Qaida, and the rest of them know we're on their trail. In Afghanistan and in Iraq, we gave ultimatums to terror regimes. Those regimes chose defiance, and those regimes are no more. Fifty million people—50 million people in those two countries once lived under tyranny, and now they live in freedom.

Two-and-a-half years ago, our military was not receiving the resources it needed, and morale was beginning to suffer. So we increased the defense budget to prepare for the threats of a new era. And today, no one in the world can question the strength, the skill, and the spirit of the United States military.

Two-and-a-half years ago, we inherited an economy in recession. And then our country was attacked, and we began a march to war. And there were some corporate scandals, all of which affected the confidence of the American people. But we acted. We passed tough new laws to hold corporate criminals to account. And to get the economy going again, I have twice led the United States Congress to pass historic tax relief for the American people. Here is what I know, that when Americans have more take-home pay to spend, to save, or invest, the whole economy will grow, and people are more likely to find a job.

We also understand whose money we spend in Washington. We don't spend the Government's money; we spend the people's money. We are returning more money to the people to help them raise their families. We're reducing taxes on dividends and capital gains to encourage investment. We're giving small businesses incentives to expand and to hire new people. With all these actions, this administration is laying the foundation for greater prosperity and more jobs across America so every one of our citizens can realize the great promise of our country.

Two-and-a-half years ago, there was a lot of talk about education reform, but there wasn't much action. So I acted. I called for and the Congress passed the No Child Left Behind Act. With a solid bipartisan majority, we delivered the most dramatic education reforms in a generation. We're bringing high standards and strong accountability measures to every public school in America. You see, we believe that every child can learn the basics of reading and math, and we expect every school in America to teach the basics of reading and math. In return for Federal money, we now expect results.

I went to Kirkpatrick Elementary School today, and they're achieving results. They're using the accountability system to focus efforts on children who need help. I saw private tutoring lessons being—taking place because of the No Child Left Behind Act. The days of excuse-making are over. We expect every child to learn. We want to make sure in this country that not one single child is left behind.

The last 2½ years, we reorganized the Government and created the Department of Homeland Security to better guard our borders and our ports and to better protect the American people. We passed trade promotion authority to open up new markets for Tennessee's farmers and ranchers and entrepreneurs and manufacturers. We passed budget agreements to bring much needed spending discipline to Washington, DC. On issue after issue, this administration has acted on principle. We have kept our word, and we have made good progress on behalf of the American people.

And the United States Congress shares in these great achievements. I appreciate working with Bill Frist and Speaker Denny Hastert. We've got a great relationship. We will continue to work to change the tone of Washington, DC, to elevate the discourse, to focus on the people's business by focusing on results.

And those are the kind of people I have attracted to my administration. I have put together a fantastic team to serve the American people, good, honorable, decent Americans from all walks of life who are in Washington, DC, for one reason, to serve the country they love. Our Nation has had no finer Vice President than Vice President Dick Cheney. Mother may have a different opinion. [*Laughter*]

In 2½ years, we have come far, but our work is only beginning. I've set great goals worthy of a great nation. First, America is committed to expanding the realm of freedom and peace for our own security and for the benefit of the world. And second, in our own country, we must work for a society of prosperity and compassion so that every single citizen has a chance to work, to succeed and realize the American Dream. It is clear that the future of freedom and peace depend on the actions of America. This Nation is freedom's home and freedom's defender. We welcome this charge of history, and we are keeping it.

Our war on terror continues. The enemies of freedom are not idle, and neither is America. This country will not rest; we will not tire; we will not stop until this danger to civilization is removed.

Yet, our national interest involves more than eliminating aggressive threats to our security. Our greatest security comes from the advance of human liberty, because free nations do not support terror. Free nations do not attack their neighbors. Free nations do not threaten the world with weapons of mass destruction. Americans believe that freedom is the deepest need and hope of every human heart. And I believe that freedom is the right of every person and that freedom is the future of every nation.

This country also understands that unprecedented influence brings tremendous responsibilities. We have duties in the world. And when we see disease and starvation and hopeless poverty, we will not turn away. On the continent of Africa, America is now committed to bringing the healing power of medicine to millions of men and women and children now suffering with AIDS. This great land, this compassionate Nation, is leading the world in this incredibly important work of human rescue.

We also face challenges at home, and our actions will prove worthy of those challenges. So long as anybody is looking for a job and can't find work, I will continue to try and foster an environment that encourages the entrepreneurial spirit, that encourages job creation in the private sector so people can find work.

We have a duty to keep our commitment to America's seniors by strengthening and modernizing Medicare. Congress took historic action; both the House and the Senate took historic action to improve the lives of older Americans. For the first time since the creation of Medicare, the House and Senate has passed reforms to increase choices for seniors and to provide coverage for prescription drugs. It is now time for both bodies to iron out their differences, to keep our commitment to America's seniors today and seniors-to-be tomorrow and modernize the Medicare system.

For the sake of our health care system, we need to cut down on the frivolous lawsuits which increase the cost of medicine. People who have been harmed by a bad doctor deserve their day in court. Yet, the system should not reward lawyers who are fishing for rich settlements. Because frivolous lawsuits drive up the cost of health care, they affect the Federal budget. Therefore, medical liability reform is a national issue which requires a national solution. I have proposed medical liability reform. It

has passed the House. It is stuck in the Senate. Senator Frist is working hard to get that bill off the floor. Nobody has been healed by a frivolous lawsuit in America.

I have a responsibility as President to make sure the judicial system runs well, and I have met that duty. I have nominated superb men and women for the Federal courts, people who will interpret the law, not legislate from the bench. Some Members of the Senate are trying to keep my nominees off the bench by blocking up-or-down votes. Every judicial nominee deserves a fair hearing and an up-or-down vote on the floor of the Senate. It is time for some Members of the United States Senate to stop playing politics with American justice.

The Congress needs to complete work on a comprehensive energy plan. We need to modernize our electricity grid. We need to encourage more investment and to make sure reliability standards are mandatory, not voluntary. We need to explore for new sources of energy in environmentally friendly ways. We need to use technology to come up with alternative sources of energy. We need to encourage conservation. What we really need to do, for the sake of national security and economic security, is to become less dependent on foreign sources of energy.

Our strong and prosperous Nation must also be a compassionate nation. I will continue to advance our agenda of compassionate conservatism. We will apply the best and most innovative ideas to the task of helping our fellow citizens who hurt. There are still millions of men and women who want to end their dependence on Government and become independent through hard work. We must build on the success of welfare reform to bring work and dignity into the lives of more of our fellow citizens.

Congress should complete the "Citizen Service Act" so that more Americans can serve their communities and their country. And both Houses should reach agreement on my Faith-Based Initiative to encourage the armies of compassion to love those who hurt, to mentor our children, to care for the homeless, to offer hope to the addicted. This great Nation should not fear the works of faith. We should welcome faith into the community of help.

A compassionate society must promote opportunity for all, including the independence that come from ownership. This administration will constantly strive to promote an ownership society all throughout America. We want more people owning their home. I have put forth policies to decrease the minority homeownership gap in America. We want people owning and managing their own health care accounts. We want people owning and controlling their own retirement accounts. We want more people owning their own small business, because when a person owns something in America, he or she has a vital stake in the future of this country.

In a compassionate society, people respect one another and take responsibility for the decisions they make. We're changing the culture of this country from one that has said, "If it feels good, do it," and "If you've got a problem, blame somebody else," to a culture in which each of us understands we are responsible for the decisions we make in life.

If you are fortunate enough to be a mother or father, you're responsible for loving your child with all your heart and all your soul. If you're concerned about the quality of education in your community, you're responsible for doing something about it. If you're a CEO in corporate America, you're responsible for telling the truth to your shareholders and your employees. And in the new responsibility society, each of us is responsible for loving our neighbor just like we'd like to be loved ourselves.

We can see the culture of service and responsibility growing around us. I started the USA Freedom Corps to encourage Americans to extend a compassionate hand to a neighbor in need, and the response has been fantastic. Faith-based programs and charitable programs are strong and vibrant all across America. Policemen and firefighters and people who wear the Nation's uniform are reminding us what it means to sacrifice for something greater than yourself. Once again, the children of America believe in heroes, because they see them every day. In these challenging times, the world has seen the resolve and the courage of America. And I have been privileged to see the compassion and the character of the American people.

All the tests of the last 2½ years have come to the right Nation. We're a strong country, and we use our strength to defend the peace. We're an optimistic country, confident in ourselves and in ideals bigger than ourselves. Abroad, we seek to lift up whole nations by spreading freedom. At home, we seek to lift up lives by spreading opportunity to every corner of America. This is the work that history has set before us. We welcome it. And we know that for our country and for our cause, the best days lie ahead.

May God bless you all. Thank you very much.

NOTE: The President spoke at 6 p.m. at the Loews Vanderbilt Plaza Hotel. In his remarks, he referred to Debbie Smith, wife of entertainer Michael W. Smith; and Darrell Waltrip, retired NASCAR driver.

Remarks at a Bush-Cheney Luncheon in Jacksonville, Florida
September 9, 2003

Thank you all very much. Glad you're here. Thanks for coming. It's great to be in Florida. It's great to be with a great Governor. [*Laughter*] I'm not surprised he has been so successful; we both share the same political consultant—[*laughter*]—Mother. [*Laughter*]

Thanks for coming. This is a huge crowd, and it's a good sign. Today we're laying the groundwork for what is going to be a great national victory in November of 2004. Jeb is right; I'm going to need your help. I'm going to need your help in putting up the signs. I'm going to need your help when you go to those coffee shops to talk it up, put out the mailers. I want you to remind people that the vision I have for America is optimistic and hopeful for every single citizen who lives in this country.

The politics season—you know, there's a lot of talk about politics these days. And I'm loosening up. [*Laughter*] I'm getting ready. The truth of the matter is, the political season will come in its own time, because I've got a job to do. I've got to do the people's work, people's business. And there's a lot on the agenda. And I want you to know, as friends and supporters, I will continue to work hard to earn the confidence of all Americans by keeping this Nation strong and secure and prosperous and free.

I regret that Laura is not traveling with me today. She is a fabulous First Lady. I was a lucky man when she said, "Yes, I agree to marry you." I love her dearly, and I'm proud of the job she's doing on behalf of all Americans.

Just like I love my brother. He's a courageous man. He's a strong man. He stands on principle, and nothing can shake him.

I appreciate my friends Al Hoffman and Tom Petway and Johnny Rood and Zach Zachariah, and you all for making this a spectacular event. I want to thank my friend Mercer Reynolds from Cincinnati, Ohio, who is the national finance chairman. There's this fellow who has taken time out of his life to go help us raise the monies necessary to wage a viable campaign in 2004.

I appreciate the fact that we've got elected officials with us today. The Lieutenant Governor, Toni Jennings, is with us. The attorney general is with us, Charlie Crist. I appreciate the speaker, Johnnie Byrd, being here today. I want to thank Jim King, the senate president. I had a chance to ride in the limousine with the mayor of this great city, John Peyton. It didn't seem like traffic was a problem for—to me. [*Laughter*]

I want to thank Carole Jean Jordan, who is the chairwoman of the Republican Party, for being here.

You know, we're here at a—I appreciate so very much a really fine, strong man, a man of great character, Jack Del Rio, who is the head coach of the Jaguars, for joining us today. I'm real proud he came. And I'm honored that the quarterback and his wife, Mark Brunell, came with us. I want to tell you something about him. He didn't say to me, "Can you still run a fly pattern?" He didn't say, "How are you on the down and out?" He said, "Mr. President, my family prays for you." I'm proud that both have come.

Before I begin, I do want to make mention of former Congressman Charles Bennett, a man who served his country and this community, longstanding United States Congressman from this part of the country, who is an honest, honorable, decent man who loved America. Today I know that he's being buried, and our thoughts and prayers go to his family during this tough moment. And we thank Congressman Bennett for being such a great American.

In the last 2½ years, our Nation has acted decisively to confront great challenges. I came to this office to solve problems instead of passing them on to future Presidents and future generations. I came to seize opportunities instead of letting them slip away. This administration is meeting the tests of our time.

Terrorists declared war on the United States of America, and war is what they got. We have captured or killed many key leaders of Al Qaida. And I can assure you, we're on the trail of the rest of them.

In Afghanistan, in Iraq, we gave ultimatums to terror regimes. Those regimes chose defiance, and those regimes are no more. Fifty million people in those two countries once lived under tyranny, and today they live in freedom.

Two-and-a-half years ago, our military was not receiving the resources it needed, and morale was beginning to suffer. We increased the defense budget to prepare for the threats of a new era, and today no one in the world can question the skill and the strength and the spirit of the United States military.

Two-and-a-half years ago, we inherited an economy in recession. And then the attacks came on our country, and we had corporate scandals, and we began to march to war, which all affected the people's confidence. But we acted. We passed tough new laws to hold corporate criminals to account. And I twice led the United States Congress to historic tax relief to get our economy going again.

I understand this, that when Americans have more take-home pay to spend, to save, to invest, the whole economy grows, and someone is more likely to be able to find a job. I also understand whose money we spend in Washington, DC. It's not the Government's money; it's the people's money. So we're returning more money to Americans to help them raise their families. We're reducing taxes on dividends and capital gains to encourage investment. We're

giving small businesses incentives to expand so they can hire new people.

With all these actions, this administration has taken bold steps to lay the foundation for greater prosperity and for more jobs across America, so that every one of our citizens can realize the American Dream.

Two-and-a-half years ago, there was a lot of talk about education reform, but there wasn't much action. So I called for and the Congress passed the No Child Left Behind Act, and we passed it with a solid bipartisan majority. And by doing so, we delivered the most dramatic education reforms at the Federal level in a generation. We're bringing high standards, strong accountability measures to every public school in America.

We're bringing to the country what Governor Jeb Bush has brought to Florida, the belief that every single child can learn, the belief that every school must be challenged to make sure that they teach the basics of reading and math. Just like your Governor is doing here, we're doing nationwide. We are challenging the soft bigotry of low expectations. The days of excuse-making are over. In return for Federal money, we expect results in every classroom all across America, so that not one single child is left behind.

During that 2½-year period, we reorganized the Government and created the Department of Homeland Security to better safeguard our ports and borders and better protect the American people. We passed trade promotion authority to open up new markets for Florida's farmers and ranchers and manufacturers and entrepreneurs. We passed much needed budget agreements to bring spending discipline to Washington, DC. On issue after issue, this administration has acted on principle. We've kept our word, and we've made progress on behalf of the American people.

The United States Congress shares in these great achievements, and I want to thank the members of the Florida congressional delegation for working closely with the administration—some members of the Florida congressional delegation. [*Laughter*] I've got a great relationship with Leader Bill Frist and Speaker Denny Hastert. We're working hard to change the tone of Washington, DC, to end all the needless partisan bickering, to elevate the discourse, to focus on results so the people know that we're doing their business.

And those are the kind of people I've attracted to my administration. I have put together a great team of honorable, decent people to serve the American people. Our country has had no finer Vice President than Vice President Dick Cheney. Mother may have a second opinion. [*Laughter*]

In 2½ years—in 2½ years, we have done a lot, and we've come far. But our work is only beginning. I have set great goals worthy of a great nation. First, America is committed to expanding the realm of freedom and peace for our own security and for the benefit of the world. And second, in our own country, we must work for a society of prosperity and compassion, so that every citizen—every single citizen—has a chance to work and succeed and realize the great promise of our country.

It is clear that the future of freedom and peace depend on the actions of America. This Nation is freedom's home. This Nation is freedom's defender. We welcome this charge of history, and we are keeping it.

Our war on terror continues. The enemies of freedom are not idle, and neither are we. This country will not rest; we will not tire; we will not stop until this danger to civilization is removed. We are confronting that danger in Iraq, where Saddam Hussein's holdouts and foreign terrorists are desperately trying to throw Iraq into chaos by attacking coalition forces and aid workers and innocent Iraqis.

And there's a reason. They know that the advance of freedom in Iraq will be a major cause of defeat for terror. This collection of killers is trying to shape the will of the civilized world. They're challenging the resolve of the United States of America. This country will not be intimidated.

We are aggressively striking the terrorists in Iraq, defeating them there so we will not have to face them in our own country. We're calling on other nations to help Iraq build a free country which will make us all more secure. We're standing with the Iraqi people as they assume more of their own defense and move toward self-government. These aren't easy tasks, but they're essential tasks. And we will finish what we have begun. We will win this essential victory in the war on terror.

Our greatest security comes from the advance of human liberty, because free nations do not support terror. Free nations do not attack their neighbors. Free nations do not threaten the world with weapons of mass terror. Americans believe that freedom is the deepest need and the deepest hope of every human heart. And I believe that freedom is the right of every person and the future of every nation.

America also understands that unprecedented influence brings tremendous responsibilities. We have duties in the world. And when we see disease and starvation and hopeless poverty, we will not turn away. On the continent of Africa, America is now committed to bringing the healing power of medicine to millions of men and women and children now suffering with AIDS. This great land, this compassionate people, is leading the world in the incredibly important work of human rescue.

We've got challenges here at home, and there's no doubt our actions will prove that we're equal to those challenges. I'm going to continue to work to create an environment that is strong for the entrepreneur and creates the conditions for economic growth. Just so long as somebody is looking for a job who wants to work and can't find one, says to me we've got a problem. Economic vitality, to me, means Americans will be able to find a job.

We have a duty to keep our commitment to America's seniors by strengthening and modernizing Medicare. The United States Congress took historic action in both bodies to improve the lives of older Americans. For the first time since the creation of Medicare, the House and the Senate have passed reforms to increase choices for our seniors and to provide coverage for prescription drugs. They are now back from vacation. It is time for the House and the Senate to reconcile their differences, to keep our promises to not only the seniors of today but those of us who are fixing to be seniors tomorrow, and modernize the Medicare system.

For the sake of our health care system, we need to cut down on the frivolous lawsuits which increase the cost of medicine. And I appreciate the leadership of Governor Jeb Bush on this issue here in the State of Florida. Listen, people who have been harmed by a bad doc deserve their day in court, no question about it. Yet the system should not reward lawyers who are simply fishing for a rich settlement.

Because frivolous lawsuits drive up the cost of health care, they affect the Federal budget. And therefore, medical liability reform is a national issue that requires a national solution. I submitted a good plan to the Congress. The House of Representative acted; the Senate hasn't. Senators must understand that no one in America has ever been healed by a frivolous lawsuit. We need medical liability reform now.

I have a responsibility as President to make sure the judicial system runs well, and I have met that duty. I have named superb men and women for the Federal courts, people who will interpret the law, not legislate from the bench. Yet, some Members of the Senate are trying to keep my nominees off the bench by blocking up-or-down votes. Every judicial nominee deserves a fair hearing and an up-or-down vote on the Senate floor. It is time for some Members of the United States Senate

to stop playing politics with American justice.

This country needs a comprehensive energy plan. I have proposed a comprehensive energy plan, and the Congress needs to complete its work on a plan. Listen, we need to modernize the electricity grid. We need to encourage new investment into the electricity grids all across America, and we need to make sure that the reliability standards are mandatory, not voluntary. We need new sources of energy. We need to use our technology to find alternative sources of energy. We need to use our technologies to encourage conservation. We need to use our technologies so that we can explore for environmentally friendly ways for new energy. What this country needs for economic security and national security is to become less dependent on foreign sources of energy.

Our strong and prosperous Nation must also be a compassionate nation. I will continue to advance our agenda of compassionate conservatism. We will apply the best and most innovative ideas to the task of helping our fellow citizens who hurt.

There are still millions of men and women who want to end their dependence on the Government and become independent through hard work. We must build on the success of welfare reform to bring work and dignity into the lives of more of our fellow citizens. Congress should complete the "Citizen Service Act" so that more Americans will serve their communities and their country. And both Houses should reach agreement on my Faith-Based Initiative, which will support the armies of compassion that are mentoring our children, that are caring for the homeless, that are offering hope to the addicted. This Nation should not fear faith. We ought to welcome faith into the compassionate delivery of help to those who suffer.

A compassionate society must promote opportunity for all, including the dignity that comes from ownership. This administration will constantly strive to promote an ownership society all across America. We want more of our citizens owning their own home. Today in America, we have a minority homeownership gap. I have proposed plans to the United States Congress to reduce that gap, and they must act.

We want more people owning and controlling their own health care plans. We want Americans being able to own and control their own retirement accounts. We want more people owning their own small business, because I understand and this administration understands that when a person owns something, he or she has a vital stake in the future of the United States of America.

In a compassionate society, people respect one another and take responsibility for the decisions they make. The culture of this country is changing from one that has said, "If it feels good, do it," and "If you've got a problem, blame somebody else," to a new culture in which each of us understands that we are responsible for the decisions we make in life. If you are fortunate enough to be a mom or a dad, you're responsible for loving your child with all your heart and all your soul. If you're worried about the quality of the education in the community in which you live, you're responsible for doing something about it. If you're a CEO in corporate America, you are responsible for telling the truth to your employees and your shareholders. And in a responsibility society, each of us is responsible for loving our neighbor just like we'd like to be loved ourself.

The culture of service and responsibility is growing around us in America. I started what's called the USA Freedom Corps, an opportunity for people to serve in their communities. And the response has been strong. Our faith-based community is strong. Charitable programs are vibrant. Americans are hearing the call to serve something greater than themselves. After all, our policemen, firefighters, people who wear the Nation's uniform are reminding us on a daily basis what it means to sacrifice for something greater than yourself. Once again, the children of America believe in heroes, because they see them every day.

In these challenging times, the world has seen the resolve and the courage of America. And I have been privileged to see the compassion and the character of the American people. All the tests of the last 2½ years have come to the right Nation. We're a strong country, and we use that strength to defend the peace. We're an optimistic country, confident in ourselves and in ideals bigger than ourselves.

Abroad, we seek to lift whole Nations by spreading freedom. At home, we seek to lift up lives by spreading opportunity to every corner of our country. This is the work that history has set before us. We welcome it. And we know that for our country and our cause, the best days lie ahead.

May God bless you all, and may God continue to bless America. Thank you all.

NOTE: The President spoke at 12:21 p.m. in the Touchdown Club at Alltel Stadium. In his remarks, he referred to Gov. Jeb Bush and Lt. Gov. Toni Jennings of Florida; Charlie Crist, Florida State Attorney General; Johnnie Byrd, speaker, Florida State House of Representatives; James E. "Jim" King, Jr., president, Florida State Senate; Mayor John Peyton of Jacksonville, FL; Al Hoffman, finance chairman, Republican National Committee; Tom Petway III and Zach Zachariah, Florida State finance cochairmen, and Mercer Reynolds, national finance chairman, Bush-Cheney '04, Inc.; Carole Jean Jordan, chairwoman, and John Rood, finance vice chairman, Republican Party of Florida; Jack Del Rio, head coach, Jacksonville Jaguars football team, and Jaguars quarterback Mark Brunell and his wife, Stacy; and former President Saddam Hussein of Iraq.

Remarks at Hyde Park Elementary School in Jacksonville
September 9, 2003

Thanks for coming. Please be seated—unless you don't have a chair. [*Laughter*] Thanks for coming, and thanks for letting me come. We're thrilled to be at Hyde Park Elementary School. I'm here to talk about some recent reforms we've had in education, the Federal role in education. I want to describe to you the No Child Left Behind Act and the principles behind the No Child Left Behind Act, and why I believe the No Child Left Behind Act, in combination with the efforts of Governors like Jeb Bush and fantastic teachers who are in this room, are going to help America realize its full promise.

Before I begin—you may recall, I was a Governor as well, and I spent a lot of time on making sure the Texas schools were as good as they could possibly be. I learned some pretty interesting lessons as the Governor. And one lesson is that in order for schools to succeed, you'd better have you a good principal. Dr. Nancy Miller is a really good principal. She believes in the worth of each individual. She believes in high standards. She believes in empowering her teachers to do the right thing. She's constantly willing to challenge the status quo if the status quo is not good enough.

We're at Hyde Park Elementary School because it is one of the many successful schools in Jacksonville and across the State of Florida. And I want to thank Dr. Miller, and I want to thank the teachers of Hyde Park for not only listening to your hearts but using logic and sound thought to challenge mediocrity wherever you might find it. You know, one of the inherent principles in the No Child Left Behind Act is that we believe every child can learn, and we want to continue to raise the bar, continue to raise expectations so that every child does learn.

I appreciate so much Secretary Rod Paige for joining us. I like to remind people that he actually knows what he's talking about when it comes to public schools because he was the superintendent of public schools in Houston, Texas. It's a pretty tough assignment, I want you to know. It's not an easy school district to govern. But he did a heck of a good job. He too believes every child can learn. He believes in setting high standards. He believes in asking the question, "Are we meeting the standards?" And I'm honored that Rod has served our country so well. And I'm proud to have him on the stage with me today. Thank you, Rod.

And then there's Brother. [*Laughter*] We were educated by the same person—[*laughter*]—Mother. [*Laughter*] We both have a passion for making sure every child learns. That's how we were raised, to do the best we could do in the schoolrooms. The truth of the matter is, when you really think about it, education—true education begins at home. Every mom and dad is a teacher. We had a pretty darn good teacher, I want you to know.

I'm proud of my brother. He's willing to take risks on behalf of the children of the State of Florida. He's willing to stand up to the critics. He's willing to stand strong when it comes to insisting upon certain principles. We love him, and I'm proud that he has joined us here today as well.

I want to thank Jim Horne, the Florida commissioner of education. These commissioners of these States have got big jobs already, and then we've compounded their job. We've got a new Federal law that needs to be implemented, and we expect these commissioners to implement the law, and Jim is doing just that.

I'm honored that the mayor is here, Mayor Peyton. He's a—I know, I saw him sitting over there. [*Laughter*] He drove from the airport to the football stadium with us. And I told him, I said he's doing a pretty good job of handling the traffic. We didn't see a lot. [*Laughter*]

I know we've got State legislators here. My only admonition to the State legislators is to make sure that public education is the number one priority of the State of Florida, to do the best you can do about setting priorities.

I want to thank General John Fryer, the superintendent of schools here. I thought it was pretty interesting, when I was reading the background of the schools here. I see that you got you a general—[*laughter*]—running the school system. That's good. [*Laughter*] It's also good that somebody who served this country in one capacity is willing to serve again.

And one of the things that Laura and I are trying to do is encourage people to serve the public school system, particularly Laura. She's spending a lot of time heralding Troops to Teachers programs to encourage people who have served in one capacity to go ahead and get back in the classroom or to serve your community by teaching in the school system. We need more of our fellow Americans who are looking for something to do to get involved in public education. Teaching is a noble profession. Teaching is a chance to leave behind a really important legacy, and that is a saved life.

I want to thank Kim Barnes, who is the chairman—chairwoman of the Duval County School Board. That's probably the hardest job in America, is to be on the school board. [*Laughter*] It's difficult because a lot of pressures and a lot of people who have got opinions. And so I want to thank the school board members who are here with us today for serving this important community, for lending your time and talents to always, hopefully, raising the bar and always insisting on the best.

We've got some interesting—we had an interesting forum. I'm going to describe what we discussed a little earlier, but we've got Wandra Sanders here, who's a teacher at Hyde Park, a representative of—we had a chance to visit with Teresa Nelson, who's a parent, and a mom or a dad.

By the way, schools really do well when mothers and dads take an interest in the school. And for you parents who are here, I want to thank you very much for not only, obviously, loving your child but also working hard to make sure the school in your community, in your neighborhood, has not only the resources necessary to succeed but your time and talents to help these good, hard-working teachers and this good principal to achieve their objectives.

We've got some folks from around the country who are here, and I'm going to talk about why they're here a little bit. But I do want to recognize Eli Broad. He is the president of the Broad Foundation. He is from Los Angeles, California. He is an incredibly successful business person. He and his wife put together a little nest egg. And they asked a question, "What can we do to help the country?" And they have decided that they would lend their resources and talents to the improvement of public education all across America. And Eli, thank you so very much for your generosity.

Tom Luce is with us. He's from the great State of Texas. [*Laughter*] I've known Tom a long time. He runs what's called Just for the Kids. Just for the Kids is a program that said, how can we make the accountability systems all around America become an effective tool to make sure no child is left behind. Tom has been an agitator for change in our State of Texas ever since I've known him, and I'm proud he's here. Thank you for coming, Tom.

Bill Cox is with us today. Bill Cox is the managing director of School Evaluation Services for Standard & Poor's. Standard & Poor's is a part of this new initiative that I'm going to describe here in a little bit. And I want to thank Bill and people from Standard & Poor's who have joined us as well. I find it interesting that Standard & Poor's, which is mainly associated with stocks and bonds, is associated with the true wealth of our country, and that is the children of our country. And thank you for coming as well. I'm honored you're here.

Today when I landed at the Naval Air Station, I met a guy named Daniel Trifiletti. You don't know Daniel. I didn't know him until I got the chance to read his background. He's a high school student who is a mentor for kids in middle school. He's an amazing guy, when you think about it, that he is willing to take time to help somebody else.

I bring this up because there's a lot made about the might of the United States of America, and we're plenty mighty. We're strong militarily. And by the way, I intend to keep it that way, in order to make the world more peaceful. But that's not the true strength of the country. The true strength of the country is the heart and soul of our citizens. Really think about what makes America unique. It's the fact that we've got millions of people who are willing to dedicate their time to help somebody else. And I think it's a remarkable part of our country and the fabric of our country.

I also find it to be great that we have a high school student who is willing to be a soldier in the army of compassion, and that's Daniel. And so, Daniel, I want to thank you for coming. I want to thank you for setting the example. I want to thank you for serving meals at the local soup kitchen. I want to thank you for your participation in Habitat for Humanity. I want to thank you for lending your talents to help some kid achieve his or her dreams. Welcome, and thank you for being a leader.

I like to tell people that the No Child Left Behind Act was the most dramatic reforms in public education in a generation. And here's why I think it is: First, inherent in the law is the belief that every child can learn. That sounds simple, doesn't it?

Sometimes, if you think back to past practices in public schools, that necessarily wasn't the attitude. When you had a system that was just shuffling kids through, it said to me that some perhaps thought certain kids couldn't learn, and therefore, the best thing to do was just move them on.

If you believe every child can learn, if you're willing to challenge the soft bigotry of low expectations, then you want to know, is it true that each child is learning? That's what you want to find out. A system which measures progress for each child is a system in which the inherent philosophy is, I believe every child can learn.

If you don't want to know, then you probably don't believe they can learn. If you do want to know, then you have this sense of high expectations for each child. And so for the first time, the Federal Government said, "In return for money from the Federal Government, we are now going to ask the questions, can a child read and write? Can a child add and subtract?" For the first time, the Federal Government got involved in education in a different way. We expect results. If you believe every child can learn, then you shouldn't fear that question, or those questions. You shouldn't fear results.

People who believe that children can learn say, "I want to be measured to show you that I'm teaching every child. That's what I want to show you. I'm a teacher because I love children. I'm a teacher because I care about the future. I want to show you. I want to show you, the community and the taxpayers and the moms and dads, that I can teach and our children are learning."

And so we changed the attitude of the Federal Government toward just handing out money. You know, I've heard all the debates about accountability systems. I mean, you hear it's discriminatory to measure. It is discriminatory not to measure. It is pure discrimination—it is discrimination not to measure, because guess who gets shuffled through the system? Guess who just gets shoved through? It's generally children whose parents don't have money. It's generally minority kids. We're just going to move them through and hope they come out okay in the end. Well, they don't come out okay in the end. We must focus early to make sure every child can read and write and add and subtract. The measurement system is the way you save lives in America.

And so the Federal Government said not only in return for money, you'll measure, we said we're going to disaggregate results. That's a fancy word that says we want to know whether or not Hispanic students are learning, whether or not the African American students are learning. We want to know if every child is learning; that's what we want to know. We want to take a look at every single possible group of citizens to determine whether or not we are meeting the high standards that we believe so strongly in our hearts.

So we've got a new system. And we're putting money behind what we said we would do. The '04 request by the administration—that's me—[*laughter*]—is $53.1 billion for the Elementary and Secondary School Act, which, as you know, is where the majority of Federal money comes from. That's a significant increase since I became the President of the United States. The Title I portion of that title in the appropriations bill is $12.3 billion. That's up 41 percent since I became President of the United States. We're putting money into the system.

We've got a brand new reading initiative where we will have spent, since the No Child Left Behind Act was passed, $1.2 billion for reading instruction. By the way, we're trying to promote curriculum which actually works. We want to make sure, if we spend money on reading, that children learn to read. We want to make sure as we spend money on reading, teachers know how to teach that which works. Part of that money went to teacher training. Eight thousand Florida teachers have now been

retrained since the law came into being. They're retrained on curriculum which work. So the whole purpose is to take Federal money and focus it on Title I kids and on teachers and on reading curriculum. It's to make sure we meet the objective, make sure we meet the high standards that we believe are necessary.

The money also, by the way, goes to help children who could conceivably be left behind. I was in Nashville, Tennessee, yesterday at Kirkpatrick Elementary School. A part of the monies I just described to you are used for after-school tutoring programs. Those go to a low-performing—low-performing schools, low-income people. You don't get that money here at Hyde Park because you're not a low-performing school. But they still have after-school tutoring here. It's one of the reasons why I think the children are doing well and no child is being left behind here.

At Kirkpatrick School, a parent is notified because the school district's aggressive. They reach out to parents. They say, "These options are available for your parents. Here's a list of providers, a specialist in reading and math that are now available for your child so that your child, at no cost, can get after-school tutoring." In other words, the No Child Left Behind Act does hold people to account, but it says that there are—we want to help people out of mediocrity when we find it. And there's resources available providing incredibly important tutoring.

You know, one of the things I called for yesterday was to make sure Governors and superintendents make it very clear to parents that, where applicable, that there is money available for low-income tutoring, money available for special focus, money available to make sure that every child has an opportunity to succeed. As well, the system says that after a period of time, if schools don't improve, then a parent can send their child to another public school or a charter school. In other words, there's different options available to moms and dads. And that's positive, and that's helpful, and that's healthy.

In order for parents to be involved—and for that matter, citizens to be involved—they have to be able to make informed decisions. As Luce reminded me, he said, "Without data, without facts, without information, the discussions about public education mean that a person is just another opinion." In other words, what we're interested in doing is laying out the facts for people to see so people can make informed decisions.

And so therefore, I'm going to describe to you a really innovative plan that is being produced by Tom and Eli and Standard & Poor's in conjunction with the Department of Education. It's a $50-million plan, plus $5 million from the Federal Government, to create a data bank for every citizen in the country to access to determine how the schools are doing all around the country.

It's an interesting opportunity, when you think about it, certainly necessary for parents in order for them to make an informed opinion about their child. It will help principals determine whether or not the curriculum their particular school is using works. It should help teachers decide—know whether or not what they're doing is working or not working. It will make sure that best practices is—becomes a integral part of the dialog all throughout the school system.

You know, people say to me, "Well, we can't have a measuring system because it's going to be punitive." Quite the contrary. A measuring system is a useful tool. A measuring system will allow people to know where they stand relative to where they need to go. You cannot solve a problem until you first diagnose the problem. And that's exactly what the accountability system that States design, not the Federal Government, is intended to do.

You might hear us talk about,"Well, the Federal Government told us to design a accountability system, but we have to pay for it"—not true. The Federal Government said—in this case, we said, "You need to design a system to show us whether or not you're achieving objectives with all this money we're sending you. And, oh, by the way, here's a little extra money for you to design the systems so we can measure."

So this month, we're beginning a new public/private effort that will post information about test results and student achievement on the Internet so all parents, all teachers, can monitor progress of their local schools, their schools relative to other schools in the neighborhood, the schools relative to schools from county to county. The program will help States analyze the data, the test results, the financial data, and other school information required by the Federal act to be posted.

In other words, we're not only going to measure, but an effective measurement system is one that says, "Oh, by the way, here are the results for everybody to see, not just a few people, not just a planner here or maybe a measurement expert there." We want full disclosure. We have nothing to hide in America when it comes to results. As a matter of fact, since the measurement systems is a tool to achieve that which we believe, which is every child can learn, there needs to be full disclosure. It's an essential part of developing trust in the public school system. It's an essential part of making sure that the best practices are shared widely across any particular school district or any State. It is essential that parents have data at their disposal.

I can assure you that a parent who understands what's going on is going to be a less frustrated parent. The parent will be more comfortable when there's full disclosure about the results and the progress toward the standard of excellence that's being made.

I mention the fact that there's $50 million from the private sector being put up. That's where Eli came in. That's an incredibly generous contribution to make, when you think about it. I'll tell you why it's so generous, is because the access to the Internet will be at no cost. I mean, this is a man who said, "How can I help public schools?" He said, "I want to be an integral part of the accountability system nationwide." And initially, there will be 10 States up by the end of this January. By the end of '04, every State will be—have their results posted, school by school, district by district, county by county, all across the State.

If you're fixing to move from point X to Florida—of course, that seems like what's happening, at least according to the Governor, people are moving here and not moving out—you'll be able to get on the Internet, and you can determine whether the school in your particular neighborhood, how it's faring relative to other schools. If you're a teacher and you've got a cousin who is a teacher, and they're saying, "Well, our school system in Tampa is a little better than it is here in Jacksonville," you can get on the Internet to determine whether that's the case. [*Laughter*]

If you're a principal and you hear a school is using a reading curriculum that seems to make sense and you want to determine whether or not it's working, you can get on. And not only can you get on the system to determine how that school is doing, you can get on the system to determine whether or not the reading curriculum is working for Hispanic kids, African American kids, Anglo kids.

In other words, this is full disclosure of information, because we believe every child can learn. We know that by using information correctly, every child's problems can be addressed. And we know how essential it is that every child does learn in America. The truth of the matter is, we're talking about the future of this country right now.

I mean, I spent a lot of time on the security of our Nation, and I can assure you I will continue spending time on the security of our Nation. One aspect of that security is to deal with people who hate America. It's to go get them before they get us, and that's what we'll continue to do. But when you really think about it, when you put your mind to it, a second aspect of the security of America is to make sure every child is educated. Our country—I'm talking about every aspect of security, economic security, security of our families. A hopeful America is what I believe in and I know you believe in. A hopeful America is an America in which each child can read and write and add and subtract. A hopeful America is where children say, "You know, I'm going to get an education early, and I'm going to go to college." A hopeful America is where people can dream and realize their dreams because the education system is fulfilling its promise.

America's past has been defined by a public school system that has met the needs of a complex society. This No Child Left Behind Act and the good work of our principals and teachers and good cooperation and hard work of Governors like Jeb Bush will mean that the public school system in the future will meet the needs of a complex society. Working together, we'll make sure that we fulfill our promise to the future, and that is, no child will be left behind in America.

May God bless you all, and may God bless our country.

NOTE: The President spoke at 1:50 p.m. in the auditorium. In his remarks, he referred to Gov. Jeb Bush of Florida; Mayor John Peyton of Jacksonville, FL; Nancy Miller, principal, Hyde Park Elementary School; John C. Fryer, superintendent, Duval County Public Schools; and Kris Barnes, chairman, Duval County School Board. The Office of the Press Secretary also released a Spanish language transcript of these remarks.

Remarks at a Bush-Cheney Reception in Fort Lauderdale, Florida
September 9, 2003

Thanks for coming. Great to be back in beautiful Fort Lauderdale. I appreciate so many folks showing up tonight, and I'm honored to be introduced by a great Governor. I'm not surprised he's so successful. We both share the same political consultant—[*laughter*]—Mother. [*Laughter*]

This is a fantastic turnout, and I'm so honored you're here. What we're doing is laying the framework and the foundation for what will be a great victory in November of 2004. I appreciate your contributions, but Jeb is right. We're going to count on you to energize the grassroots, to make the phone calls, and to put up the signs. And when you go to the coffee shop, you tell them that this administration is committed to making sure that our country is positive and hopeful and optimistic for every single citizen who lives in America.

There's a lot of politics in the air, it seems like. And I'm loosening up, and I'm getting ready. The truth of the matter is, the political season will come in its own time. I've got a job to do. I've got a job to do on behalf of the American people, and there's a lot on the agenda. But I will assure you, my administration will continue to work hard to earn the confidence of all Americans by keeping this Nation secure and strong and prosperous and free.

I am sorry Laura didn't travel with me today, not as sorry as you, probably. [*Laughter*] But I am really proud of Laura. She's a fabulous wife, great mom, and a terrific First Lady for the United States of America.

I want to thank this cast of characters who is on the stage with me tonight: my great friend Al Hoffman, who is the honorary State finance chair; Tom Petway, who is the State finance cochair; Zach Zachariah, the State finance cochair; and my friend Jim Blosser, who is the event chair-

man tonight. I want to thank you guys for your hard work. Thank you all.

Also, I want to thank my friend Mercer Reynolds, the national finance chairman, from Cincinnati, Ohio, who is taking a lot of time off to make sure that this campaign is well-funded. I appreciate members of the statehouse who are here. Johnny Byrd, the speaker of the house, is with us today. Other members of the statehouse, State senators are with us. I want to thank you all for coming. Make sure you do what Brother says to do—[*laughter*]—most of the time. [*Laughter*] I'm honored that our attorney general, Charlie Crist, is with us today. I know we've got local officials with us. I particularly want to say thanks to the mayor, Jim Naugle of Fort Lauderdale, and Oliver Parker, mayor of Lauderdale-by-the-Sea.

But most of all, I want to thank you all for coming. This is a big turnout. It makes me feel pretty spunky to see this many people out there.

In the last 2½ years, our Nation has acted decisively to confront great challenges. I came to this office to solve problems and not pass them on to future Presidents and future generations. I came to seize opportunities instead of letting them slip away. This administration is meeting the tests of our time.

Terrorists, coldblooded killers, declared war on the United States of America, and war is what they got. We have captured or killed many key leaders of Al Qaida, and the rest of them know we're on their trail. In Afghanistan and Iraq, we gave ultimatums to terror regimes. Those regimes chose defiance, and those regimes are no more. Think about this: 50 million people who once lived under tyranny in those two countries now live in freedom, thanks to the United States of America and our friends and allies.

Two-and-a-half years ago, our military was not receiving the resources it needed, and morale was beginning to suffer. So we increased the defense budgets to prepare for the threats of a new era. And today, no one in the world can question the skill and the strength and the spirit of the United States military.

Two-and-a-half years ago, we inherited an economy in recession. And then the attacks came on our country, and we had scandals in corporate America, and war. All affected the people's confidence. But we acted. We passed tough new laws to hold corporate criminals to account. And to get the economy going again, I have twice led the United States Congress to pass historic tax relief.

I know that when Americans have more take-home pay to spend, to save, or to invest, the whole economy grows and people are more likely to find a job. I also know whose money we spend in Washington, DC. We do not spend the Government's money; we spend the people's money.

We're returning the money to the people so they can better raise their families. We're reducing taxes on dividends and capital gains to encourage investment. We're giving small businesses incentives to expand and, therefore, to hire new workers. With all these actions, we are laying the foundation for greater prosperity and more jobs so that everybody in America has a chance to realize the great promise of our country.

Two-and-a-half years ago, there was a lot of talk about education reform, but there wasn't much action. So I acted. I called upon the Congress to pass the No Child Left Behind Act. And with a solid bipartisan majority, we delivered the most dramatic education reforms in a generation. We bring high standards and strong accountability to every public school in America. We are challenging the soft bigotry of low expectations, because we believe every child can learn the basics of reading and math, and we insist that every school teach the basics of reading and math. In return

for Federal money, we're now asking schools to show us whether or not children are learning to read and write and add and subtract. We're providing extra resources to make sure that not one single child is left behind in America.

We reorganized our Government to create the Department of Homeland Security to better guard our ports and borders and to protect the American people. We passed trade promotion authority to open up new markets for Florida's ranchers and farmers and entrepreneurs and manufacturers. We passed budget agreements to—so that we have much needed spending discipline in Washington, DC. On issue after issue, this administration has acted on principle. We have kept our word, and we have made progress for the American people.

The Congress gets a lot of credit. I'm happy to work with Speaker Hastert and Senator Frist. We're working hard to change the tone in Washington, to get rid of all the needless politics, to elevate the discourse, to focus on results, so the people know we went to the Nation's Capital to serve our country.

And those are the kind of people who I've attracted to my administration. I have put together a fabulous team on behalf of the American people, good, honorable, hard-working, decent Americans. Our country has had no finer Vice President than Dick Cheney. Mother may have a second opinion. [*Laughter*]

In 2½ years—2½ years, we've done a lot. We have come far, but our work is only beginning. I have set great goals worthy of a great nation. First, America is committed to expanding the realm of freedom and peace, not only for our own security but for the benefit of the world. And second, in our own country, we must work for a society of prosperity and compassion so that every single citizen has a chance to work and to succeed and realize the American Dream. It is clear that the future of peace and freedom depend on the actions of America. This Nation is freedom's home. This Nation is freedom's defender. We welcome this charge of history, and we are keeping it.

Our war on terror continues. The enemies of freedom are not idle, and neither are we. This country will not rest. We will not tire. We will not stop until this danger to civilization is removed. We are confronting that danger in Iraq, where Saddam Hussein holdouts and foreign terrorists are desperately trying to throw Iraq into chaos by attacking coalition forces, aid workers, and innocent Iraqis. They know that the advance of freedom in Iraq would be a major defeat for their cause of terror. The collection of killers is trying to shake the will of the United States of America and the civilized world. This country will not be intimidated.

We are aggressively striking the terrorists in Iraq. By defeating them there, we will not have to face them on our own streets. We're calling other nations to help Iraq build a free country, which will make us all more secure. We're standing with the Iraqi people as they assume more of their own defense and move toward self-government. These are not easy tasks, but they are essential tasks. We will finish what we have begun, and we will win this essential victory in the war on terror.

Yet I understand that our greatest security comes from the advance of human liberty, because free nations do not support terror. Free nations do not attack their neighbors. And free nations do not threaten the world with weapons of mass terror. Americans believe that freedom is the deepest need and hope of every human heart, and I believe that freedom is the right of every person and the future of every nation, including nations like Cuba.

America also understands that unprecedented influence brings tremendous responsibilities. We have duties in the world. And when we see disease and starvation and hopeless poverty, we will not turn away. On the continent of Africa, this great, strong, compassionate Nation is now committed to bringing the healing power of medicine to millions of men and women and children now suffering with AIDS. This great land is leading the world in this incredibly important work of human rescue.

We face challenges at home as well. And our actions will prove that we are equal to those challenges. So long as anybody who wants to work cannot find a job, I will continue to work to create an environment that emphasizes job growth.

As well, we must keep our duty and commitment to America's seniors by strengthening and modernizing Medicare. Congress took historic action to improve the lives of older Americans. For the first time since the creation of Medicare, the House and the Senate have passed reforms to increase choices for our seniors and to provide coverage for prescription drugs. It is now time for the House and the Senate to iron out their differences, to modernize Medicare, not only for the seniors who are depending upon Medicare today but for those of us who will be depending upon Medicare tomorrow. We have an obligation to the future of this country.

For the sake of our health care system, we need to cut down on the frivolous lawsuits which increase the cost of medicine. I appreciate Jeb's leadership on this issue here in the State of Florida. Listen, people who have been harmed by a bad doctor of course deserve their day in court. The system should not reward lawyers who are simply fishing for rich settlements.

Because frivolous lawsuits drive up the cost of health care, they affect the Federal budget. Medical liability reform is a national issue that requires a national solution. I have put out a good reform plan for medical liability. The House acted. It is stuck in the Senate. Senators must understand, we need to change the system. No one has ever been healed in America because of a frivolous lawsuit.

I have a responsibility as President to make sure the judicial system runs well, and I have met that duty. I have nominated superb men and women to the Federal courts, people who will interpret the law, not legislate from the bench. Some Members of the United States Senate are trying to keep my nominees off the bench by blocking up-or-down votes. Every judicial nominee deserves a fair hearing and an up-or-down vote on the floor of the United States Senate. It is time for some Members of the United States Senate to stop playing politics with American justice.

Our Congress needs to complete work on a comprehensive energy plan. It should be clear to the Congress that we need to modernize our electricity grid. [*Laughter*] We have put forth a plan to do so. We must promote energy efficiency and more conservation. We must use our technologies to discover new sources of energy. We must use technology to find more energy here at home in environmentally friendly ways. For the sake of economic security and for the sake of national security, this Nation must become less dependent on foreign sources of energy.

Our strong and prosperous Nation must also be a compassionate nation. I will continue to advance our agenda of compassionate conservatism. We will apply the best and most innovative ideas to the task of helping our fellow citizens who hurt. There are still millions of men and women who want to end their dependence on Government and become independent through hard work. We must build on the success of welfare reform to bring work and, therefore, dignity into the lives of more of our fellow citizens.

Congress should complete the "Citizen Service Act" so that more Americans can serve their communities and their country. And the Congress should reach agreement on my Faith-Based Initiative to support the armies of compassion, Christian, Jew, Hindu, and Muslim, all of whom are serving our country by mentoring children, by caring for the homeless, and by offering hope to the addicted. Our Nation should not fear faith. We should welcome faith into the compassionate delivery of those who hurt.

A compassionate society must promote opportunity for all, including the independence and the dignity that come from ownership. This administration will constantly strive to promote an ownership society in America. We want more people owning their own home. We have a minority home-ownership gap in America, and I have submitted plans to the United States Congress to close that gap. We want more Americans owning and managing their own health care accounts. We want more Americans owning and managing their own retirement accounts. We want more Americans starting their own small business, because we understand in the Bush administration that when a person owns something, he or she has a vital stake in the future of our country.

In a compassionate society, people respect one another, and they take responsibility for the decisions they make. We're changing the culture of America from one that has said, "If it feels good, just go ahead and do it," and "If you've got a problem, blame somebody else," to a culture in which each of us understands that we are responsible for the decisions we make in life. If you're lucky enough to be a mom or a dad, you're responsible for loving your child with all your heart and all your soul. If you're concerned about the quality of the education in your community, you're responsible for doing something about it. If you're a CEO in corporate America, you are responsible for telling the truth to your shareholders and your employees. And in this new responsibility society, each of us is responsible for loving our neighbor just like we'd like to be loved ourself.

We can see the culture of service and the culture of responsibility growing around us here in America. It was right after 9/11/2001; I started what's called the USA Freedom Corps to encourage Americans to extend a compassionate hand to a neighbor in need. And the response has been great.

Our faith-based organizations are vibrant and strong. Our charities are doing well here in America. People understand the call to serve something greater than yourself in life, just like our policemen and firefighters and people who wear our Nation's uniform. Once again, the children of America believe in heroes, because they see them every day. And in these challenging times, the world has seen the resolve and the courage of America. And I've been privileged to see the compassion and the character of the American people.

All the tests of the last 2½ years have come to the right nation. We're a strong country, and we use our strength to defend the peace. We're an optimistic country, confident in ourselves and in ideals better than ourselves. Abroad, we seek to lift up whole nations by spreading freedom. At home, we seek to lift up lives by spreading opportunity to every corner of America. This is the work that history has set before us. We welcome it. And we know that for our country and for our cause, the best days lie ahead.

Thank you for coming. May God bless.

NOTE: The President spoke at 6:18 p.m. at the Hyatt Regency Pier Sixty-Six. In his remarks, he referred to Gov. Jeb Bush of Florida; and Charlie Crist, Florida State Attorney General.

Remarks Following Discussions With Prime Minister Sabah of Kuwait and an Exchange With Reporters
September 10, 2003

The President. A couple of questions. First, we'll have a couple of statements.

It's my honor and honor of senior members of my administration to welcome you, sir, to the Oval Office. Kuwait is a steady and strong friend of the United States. I thank you for your friendship.

This country led a vast coalition to make the world more secure and more peaceful, and Kuwait was steadfast in your support of our common desire to respect human life, to promote peace, and I want to thank you for that very much. We called upon you to make some difficult choices, and you made those choices, and the world is better off as a result of the decisions your Government made. So it's my honor to welcome you here, sir, today.

Prime Minister Sabah. I would like to take this opportunity to thank the President, and thank you, Mr. President, for this invitation and for asking us to come here. I believe that the discussions that I had with you were frank discussions, and they were discussions between friends, people who are friends and allies together.

I would like to assure you that this friendship and the alliance between our two countries and our two peoples will continue. And it will not be limited to the official Government levels, but it will be also, and continue to be, between the people. This relationship will continue to exist because we strongly believe that it's in the interest of the peoples in both countries as well as the region.

Once again, Mr. President, thank you, sir, for this invitation.

The President. Mr. Prime Minister.

Terry [Terence Hunt, Associated Press].

PLO Prime Minister-Designate Ahmed Korei

Q. Mr. President, what's your evaluation of the new Palestinian Prime Minister? Do you think he's someone that you'll be able to work with as well as you were able to work with Mr. Mahmoud Abbas?

The President. Well, time will tell. I still believe strongly that two states living side by side in peace is a hopeful vision for the future of the Middle East. The roadmap is still there. The fundamental question is whether or not people, peaceful people, will be on the road.

And one of the essential tenets of the roadmap is that people are responsible, parties need to be responsible for creating the conditions necessary for peace to prevail. Probably the most—the most important condition for peace to prevail is for all parties to fight off terror, to dismantle organizations whose intent is to destroy the vision of peace.

And the Prime Minister-designee—I understand he accepted the position minutes ago—the question is, will he be confirmed by his—Parliament? And his job is, if he's interested in a two-state solution, is to consolidate power within his administration, to get the security forces under control—all security forces—and then to unleash those security forces against killers. And we can make progress if that's the case.

But the Prime Minister and I discussed this subject. He made a very interesting point, that nations need to cut off funding to terrorist groups. And I appreciated that very much. In other words, that's part of the responsibility. Israel, of course, has got responsibility not only to protect her people but to create the conditions necessary for those in the Palestinian Authority who do believe in peace, who do believe in the vision, to prevail.

And so it's tough times there now, and we mourn the loss of innocent life. But the vision is still there, because I strongly believe it's in the interest of everybody that two states live side by side in peace.

Would you care to call on somebody from the press?

Kuwait

Q. Mr. President, what do you expect from Kuwait, to play a role in the future in peace and the future of Iraq? And how do you view this visit and Kuwait as an ally to the United States?

The President. Well, this is a very important visit, because it gives me a chance to publicly offer my sincere thanks to an important leader in the Oval Office. Secondly, we did discuss our mutual responsibilities to promote peace. I assured the Prime Minister that this country would stay in Iraq to fulfill our promise to Iraqi citizens who are desperate for peace and for the chance to succeed.

The Prime Minister said that he appreciated our commitment. He was glad to be reassured that we will finish the job and said he'd be willing to help. And I appreciate that.

Our friendship is one where we're able to have mutual but frank discussions, and we will continue our discussions over lunch. And I am grateful for his presence and his willingness to talk frankly about issues that relate to our future.

Steve [Steve Holland, Reuters].

New U.N. Resolution on Iraq

Q. Given the French and German opposition, how are you going to get a new U.N. resolution on Iraq? Are you willing to concede any control to the U.N.?

The President. Oh, I think that—we're hopeful we can get a good resolution. We're in consultations now. I think it's in everybody's interest that Iraq be free and be peaceful. And we will continue to work through issues. I don't think they're opposed to the resolution. I think you're putting words in their mouth that—they may want to fine-tune a resolution, and we're—listen, we're open for suggestions.

But what is necessary is, however, to trust the Iraqi people to—the Governing Council to come up with a timetable for elections. They're making good progress there now. They've got ministers in charge of key parts of the country. They are beginning to put in place the timetable necessary for the writing of a constitution. And there will be free elections. And that ought to be decided by the Governing Council. These are people who know full well how best to move Iraq forward.

And we'll work with all parties involved. My call, however, to nations is, is that let us not get caught up in past bickering. Let us move forward. A free Iraq is in everybody's interest. A peaceful Iraq is in the world's interest. And I'm confident we can work together to achieve that. The Secretary of State will be going around the world urging people to make serious contributions, and I will, once again, make that plea. We expect and hope that our friends contribute to the reconstruction of Iraq. It is in your interest that you do so.

Final question, Dick—Stretch [Richard Keil, Bloomberg News].

Funding for Iraq and Domestic Programs

Q. Mr. President, the $87 billion you say will be needed for peacekeeping in Iraq accounts for roughly a fifth of the domestic discretionary spending next year. Realistically, sir, how can you do that and hold the line on domestic programs without gutting those programs? Can you really have one——

The President. Of course, we can do— first of all, the $87 billion, it's important to spend that money. It's in our national interest that we spend it. A free and peaceful Iraq will save this country money in the long term. It's important to get it done now.

And yes, I also believe the 4-percent discretionary—increase in discretionary spending number I sent up to Congress makes sense. Somebody—I heard somebody say, "Well, what we need to do is have a tax increase to pay for this." That's an absurd notion. You don't raise taxes when an economy is recovering. Matter of fact, lower taxes will help enhance economic recovery. We want our people going back to work. We've got good momentum now in our economy. We don't want to destroy that momentum.

But the $87 billion is worth it. And I look forward to working with Congress to get that number completed and get the job done.

Thank you all.

NOTE: The President spoke at 11:58 a.m. in the Oval Office at the White House. A reporter referred to former Prime Minister Mahmoud Abbas (Abu Mazen) of the Palestinian Authority. Prime Minister Sabah spoke in Arabic, and his remarks were translated by an interpreter.

Remarks at the Federal Bureau of Investigation Academy in Quantico, Virginia
September 10, 2003

The President. Thanks a lot. Please be seated. Thanks for the warm welcome. I'm proud to visit the FBI Academy here at Quantico, where so much hard and essential work in the war on terror goes on.

The FBI Academy, new agents who risk their lives to keep America safe learn their craft. In forensics lab, experts examine vital evidence that leads to victory against terror. In the engineering research facility, special-

ists apply the latest technology to fight crime and terror. You do a terrific job for the American people, and I'm here to tell you our Nation is grateful.

Quantico is also known as the "crossroad of the Corps"——

Audience members. Hooah!

The President. ——since so many Marines pass through the Marine Corps University here. I'm sure it's just a coincidence that Quantico, population 561 fine souls, is said to have the highest number of barber shops—[*laughter*]—per capita than any town in the Nation. What strikes me, it looks like all those barbers specialize in one kind of haircut. [*Laughter*]

I appreciate the men and women who wear our Nation's uniform. The Marines make us proud. I appreciate the men and women from the Department of Homeland Security who are with us today. You've been given a great responsibility, and you're carrying it out with focus and professionalism.

I want to thank the DEA agents who are with us today. By working to keep drug money from financing terror, you're playing an important part of this war. I also thank the first-responders from the nearby communities who are with us today. You're the ones Americans count on in times of emergency, and you do not let us down.

The lives of every person here were changed by the events of September the 11th, 2001. You felt the anger and the sense of loss that day. You stood ready to serve your country in a time of need. And each of you now has a part in protecting America against the threats of a new era.

For 2 years, this Nation has been on the offensive against global terror networks, overseas and at home. We've taken unprecedented, effective measures to protect this homeland. Yet, our Nation has more to do. We will never be complacent. We will defend our people, and we will win this war.

I appreciate the Attorney General being here today. I picked a good man, who's doing a fine job on behalf of all Americans, when I picked John Ashcroft to be the Attorney General of the United States.

I appreciate my friend Tom Ridge. See, we were both Governors at one time, so I got to know him as the Governor of a relatively small State—[*laughter*]—Pennsylvania. He did a great job as Governor. He's been given an enormous task to reorganize our Government. I'm proud that he's taken on the Secretary of the Department of Homeland Security. I'm proud of the job he's doing on behalf of America.

I'm also honored to be up here with Bob Mueller, who is the head of the FBI. He was just recounting what it was like to go to the Marine Corps University— a couple of decades ago. [*Laughter*] A proud Marine then, he's now proud to run the FBI. He knows what I know: Our Nation is fortunate to have such fine men and women work for the Federal Bureau of Investigation.

I appreciate John Gordon being up here. He's the Homeland Security Adviser, works right there in the White House. I meet with him every single day. He's got good, sound judgment and good advice. I'm honored that Congresswoman Jo Ann Davis is with us today. Congresswoman, we're glad you're here. Thank you for coming today. I appreciate Dwight Adams, who is the Director of the FBI Laboratory. He just gave me a fine tour. It's pretty sophisticated facilities. I appreciate the chance to see it.

Tomorrow, America will mark a sad anniversary. The memories of September 11th will never leave us. We will not forget the burning towers and the last phone calls and the smoke over Arlington. We will not forget the rescuers who ran toward danger and the passengers who rushed the hijackers. We will not forget the men and women who went to work on a typical day and never came home. We will not forget the death of schoolchildren who were on a school trip.

And we will never forget the servants of evil who plotted the attacks. And we will never forget those who rejoiced at our grief and our mourning.

America honors and remembers the names of all victims. And tomorrow, some families will be thinking of one name in particular, a person they still love and deeply miss. The prayers of our whole Nation are with the families of the lost who feel a grief that does not end.

Tomorrow's anniversary is a time for remembrance. Yet history asked more than memory. The attacks on this Nation revealed the intentions of a determined and ruthless enemy that still plots against our people. The forces of global terror cannot be appeased, and they cannot be ignored. They must be hunted; they must be found; and they will be defeated. We will not wait for further attacks on innocent Americans. The best way to protect the American people is to stay on the offensive, to stay on the offensive at home and to stay on the offensive overseas.

And that is what this country is doing. We've undertaken a global campaign against terrorist networks. We're going after the terrorists wherever they hide and wherever they plan. We will keep them on the run. We'll bring them to justice. We have made clear the doctrine that says, "If you harbor a terrorist, if you feed a terrorist, if you hide a terrorist, you're just as guilty as the terrorists." We're holding regimes accountable for harboring and supporting terror.

We're determined to prevent terrorist networks from gaining weapons of mass destruction. We're committed to spreading democracy and tolerance and freedom in the Middle East, to replace the hatred and bitterness with progress and hope and peace.

These 24 months have been a time of progress against the enemy. Terrorists have lost their training camps in Afghanistan. They lost the protection of the Taliban. Al Qaida has lost nearly two-thirds of its known leaders. They've either been captured or they've been killed. Terror networks have lost access to some $200 million, which we have frozen or seized in more than 1,400 terrorist accounts around the world. The terrorists have lost a sponsor in Iraq. And no terrorist networks will ever gain weapons of mass destruction from Saddam Hussein's regime. That regime is no more.

Now we are engaged in other essential missions in the war on terrorism. We're helping the Afghan people to build free institutions after years of oppression. We're working with the Iraqi people to build a new home for freedom and democracy at the heart of the Middle East. The spread of freedom is one of the keys to the victory against terror. The Middle East will either be a place of increasing hope or a place of a bitterness and violence that exports terrorism—exports terrorism to America or other Nations. By removing the tyrants who support terror and by ending the hopelessness that feeds terror, we are helping the people of the Middle East, and we're strengthening the security of America.

The terrorists understand what is at stake. They understand that the advance of freedom will discredit their cause, and they know that the advance of freedom will isolate them from sources of support. That is why Saddam holdouts and foreign terrorists are desperately trying to throw Iraq into chaos by attacking our forces, by killing aid workers, by destroying innocent Iraqis. This collection of killers is desperately trying to shake the will of the civilized world, but America will not be intimidated.

We are following a clear strategy with three objectives: We're going to destroy the terrorists; we'll enlist the support for a free Iraq—international support for a free Iraq; and we'll quickly transfer authority to the Iraqi people. We're aggressively striking the terrorists in Iraq with great troops. We're using better intelligence, because we know when we defeat them there, we won't have to face them in our own country.

We're calling on other nations to help Iraqis build a free nation, which will make us all more secure. We're helping the Iraqi people assume more of their own defense and move toward self-government. I recognize these are not easy tasks, but they're essential tasks. And this country will do what is ever necessary to win this victory in the war on terror.

As we wage this war abroad, we must remember where it began, here on our homeland. In this new kind of war, the enemy's objective is to strike us on our own territory and make our people live in fear. This danger places all of you, every person here and the people you work with, on the frontlines of the war on terror.

Our methods for fighting this war at home are very different from those we use abroad. Yet our strategy is the same: We're on the offensive against terror; we're determined to stop the enemy before they can strike our people.

Every morning I am briefed from the latest information on the threats to our country, and those threats are real. The enemy is wounded but still resourceful and actively recruiting and still dangerous. We cannot afford a moment of complacency. Yet, as you know, we've taken extraordinary measures these past 2 years to protect America. And we're making progress. There are solid results that we can report to the American people.

We have shut down phony charities that serve as fronts for terrorists. We've thwarted terrorists in Buffalo and Seattle, in Portland, Detroit, North Carolina, and Tampa, Florida. More than 260 suspected terrorists have been charged in United States courts; more than 140 have already been convicted.

We're making progress because we have got skilled professionals on the job, and we've got a clear strategy. We reorganized our Government to enhance our strategy, and we set three national objectives for homeland security: One, to prevent attacks on America; to reduce our vulnerabilities; and to prepare for any attack that might come.

Under Director Mueller, the FBI is transforming itself to face the new threats of our time. Instead of just investigating past crimes, the agency is now dedicated to preventing future attacks. Since September the 11th, the share of FBI resources dedicating to fighting terror has more than doubled. The agency remains fully committed to its traditional law enforcement duties. Yet now the FBI is better at analyzing threats and sharing more infor-

mation with other agencies at every level of Government. The FBI, much to the chagrin of the enemy, is fully engaged on the war on terror. America is proud of your efforts.

To make our antiterror efforts more effective, we established the Terrorism Threat Integration Center to merge and analyze in a single place all the vital intelligence on global terror from across our Government. We're doing a better job of talking to each other. The left hand now knows what the right hand is doing. We're gathering intelligence and preparing the homeland and the people in charge of protecting the homeland with the best information we can possibly find.

We also have merged 22 Federal agencies into the Department of Homeland Security. Employees of DHS go to work every day with a single overriding responsibility, to make America more secure. Secretary Ridge and his team have done a fine job in getting the difficult work of organizing the Department, and we appreciate your service to America as well.

DHS has spearheaded a massive overhaul of security at America's airports. Some 48,000 professional screeners, employed and supervised by the Transportation Security Administration, are now on the job across America. With new equipment, we're now screening every bag that goes to every airplane. The cockpit doors of every large passenger airplane that flies in the United States have been hardened. Thousands of Federal air marshals are flying on commercial flights. We're determined to protect Americans who travel by plane and to prevent those planes from being used as weapons against the American people.

The Department of Homeland Security is focused on making the border more secure. Our Smart Border strategy uses technology and background checks to allow lawabiding travelers to cross the border, while officials concentrate on possible threats. We've improved the entry process. People coming into the United States will soon be met by a single uniformed officer, rather than the separate officials from Customs, Agricultural, and Immigration.

Working with the State Department, DHS is doing a better job of screening visa applicants and keeping track of short-term visitors while they're in our country. America will remain a welcoming society. We welcome families and tourists, students and business people from other countries. But our border must be closed to criminals and terrorists.

Since September the 11th, 2001, America has made the largest commitment to securing our seaports since World War II. In these 2 years, the Coast Guard, which is now part of the Department of Homeland Security, has conducted more than 124,000 port security patrols, more than 13,300 air patrols, and has boarded more than 92,000 vessels. DHS now requires electronic advance cargo manifests from ships 24 hours before containers are loaded onto ships, giving officials time to check for potential dangers. We're enforcing tough rules that require ports and vessels and facilities to upgrade their security. This Nation is determined to protect our ports from all the threats around the world.

We're determined as well to reduce the vulnerabilities of our Nation's infrastructure. The Department of Homeland Security is working closely with State and local governments to identify key vulnerabilities in our communications systems, our power grids, and our transportation networks, and we're taking action to protect them. DHS has established a National Cyber Security Division to examine cybersecurity incidents, to track attacks, and to coordinate nationwide responses. DHS is also helping the operators of chemical facilities improve security. We're working on Congress—with Congress on new legislation that establishes uniform standards for security of chemical sites.

Even with all these measures, there is no such thing as perfect security in a vast and free country. So all levels of government must be prepared to respond quickly and effectively to any emergency. In responding to most incidents, local officials such as firefighters will be the first on the scene. America's first-responders need to be well-equipped, and they need to be well-trained.

The Federal Government has a responsibility to help, and we're meeting that responsibility. We've committed nearly $8 billion over the past 2 years to better equip and train our State and local first-responders and hospitals and laboratories. I proposed more than 5 billion more for the coming fiscal year. We're spending this money wisely, I want you to know. We're targeting resources where they're needed, where they'll do the most good.

An effective response system requires effective communications. You know that. First-responders know what I'm talking about. So we're upgrading communication systems all across the country to make sure that people from all agencies, at all levels of government, can talk to one another in crisis.

We're making a special effort to prepare for the possibility of a biological or chemical attack. We've improved our ability to quickly detect such attacks if they occur. We've enlarged the strategic national stockpile of drugs and vaccines and medical supplies. We now have on hand, for instance, enough smallpox vaccine to immunize every American in the case of an emergency.

Earlier this year, I proposed Project Bio-Shield which will speed the development of new vaccines and treatments for biological agents that could be used in a terrorist attack. The Senate needs to act on this important measure. The House has acted, and I appreciate their action. For the sake of national security, the Senate needs to pass Project BioShield.

Since September the 11th, this Nation has been unrelenting in the work on protecting the homeland. And we'll stay that way. That's our duty. That's our job. We accept the responsibility.

Across our Government, there's a new spirit, sense of mission. In our country, Americans are volunteering to help, and I want to thank them for that. For example, they're volunteering their expertise in the Citizen Corps efforts to help local communities prepare for emergencies. And I appreciate the bipartisan efforts in Congress to prepare our country and to give law enforcement officials the tools they need.

Almost 2 years ago, I signed the USA Patriot Act. That essential law, supported by a large bipartisan majority in the Congress, tore down the walls that blocked America's intelligence and law enforcement officials from sharing intelligence. It enabled our team to talk to each other, to better prepare against an enemy which hates us because of what we love—freedom.

The Patriot Act imposed tough new penalties on terrorists and those who support them. But as the fight against terrorists progressed, we have found areas where more help is required. Under current Federal law, there are unreasonable obstacles to investigating and prosecuting terrorism, obstacles that don't exist when law enforcement officials are going after embezzlers or drug traffickers. For the sake of the American people, Congress should change the law and give law enforcement officials the same tools they have to fight terror that they have to fight other crime.

Here's some examples. Administrative subpoenas, which enable law enforcement officials to obtain certain records quickly, are critical to many investigations. They're used in a wide range of criminal and civil matters, including health care fraud and child abuse cases. Yet, incredibly enough, in terrorism cases, where speed is often of the essence, officials lack the authority to use administrative subpoenas. If we can use these subpoenas to catch crooked doctors, the Congress should allow law enforcement officials to use them in catching terrorists.

Today, people charged with certain crimes, including some drug offenses, are not eligible for bail. But terrorist-related crimes are not on that list. Suspected terrorists could be released, free to leave the country or worse, before the trial. This disparity in the law makes no sense. If dangerous drug dealers can be held without bail in this way, Congress should allow for the same treatment for accused terrorists.

Let me give you another example. Under existing law, the death penalty applies to many serious crimes that result in death, including sexual abuse and certain drug-related offenses. Some terrorist crimes that result in death do not qualify for capital punishment. Sabotaging a defense installation or a nuclear facility in a way that takes innocent life does not carry the Federal death penalty. This kind of technicality should never protect terrorists from the ultimate justice.

These and other measures have long been on the books for other crimes. They have been tested by time, affirmed by the court, and what we are proposing, they are fully consistent with the United States Constitution.

Members of the Congress agree that we need to close the loopholes—not every Member, but a lot of them agree with that. People in law enforcement are counting on Congress to follow through. We're asking a lot of these folks out here. You need to have every tool at your disposal to be able to do your job on behalf of the American people. The House and the Senate have a responsibility to act quickly on these matters. Untie the hands of our law enforcement officials so they can fight and win the war against terror.

Two years ago, this Nation saw the face of a new enemy. We discovered that there is no safety behind vast oceans. For our own safety, we resolve to take the battle to the enemy. America is making progress on every front—every front—in this war. For that progress, we know who to thank. We thank the men and women who wear our Nation's uniform. We thank their families. We thank our intelligence officers. We thank every branch of law enforcement. We thank our first-responders.

All of you may serve on different fronts, but you're serving in the same war. I don't know how long this war will go on, but I do know this: However long it takes, this Nation will prevail.

May God bless you all. Thank you all very much.

NOTE: The President spoke at 3:04 p.m. In his remarks, he referred to Dwight E. Adams, Assistant Director, Laboratory Division, Federal Bureau of Investigation; and former President Saddam Hussein of Iraq. The Office of the Press Secretary also released a Spanish language transcript of these remarks.

Statement on the Death of Edward Teller
September 10, 2003

Edward Teller was a tireless patriot and great American who devoted much of his life to making Americans more secure. During his life, Dr. Teller received honors including the National Medal of Science and, in July, the Presidential Medal of Freedom. His notable contributions to the security of our Nation will not be forgotten. Laura joins me in sending condolences to his family.

Message to the Congress on Continuation of the National Emergency With Respect to Certain Terrorist Attacks
September 10, 2003

To the Congress of the United States:

Section 202(d) of the National Emergencies Act, 50 U.S.C. 1622(d), provides for the automatic termination of a national emergency unless, prior to the anniversary date of its declaration, the President publishes in the *Federal Register* and transmits to the Congress a notice stating that the emergency is to continue in effect beyond the anniversary date. Consistent with this provision, I have sent to the *Federal Register* the enclosed notice, stating that the emergency declared with respect to the terrorist attacks on the United States of September 11, 2001, is to continue in effect for an additional year.

The terrorist threat that led to the declaration on September 14, 2001, of a national emergency continues. For this reason, I have determined that it is necessary to continue in effect after September 14, 2003, the national emergency with respect to the terrorist threat.

GEORGE W. BUSH

The White House,

September 10, 2003.

NOTE: The notice of September 10 is listed in Appendix D at the end of this volume.

Remarks on the Anniversary of September 11
September 11, 2003

Today our Nation remembers—we remember a sad and terrible day, September the 11th, 2001. We remember lives lost. We remember the heroic deeds. We remember the compassion and the decency of our fellow citizens on that terrible day.

Also, today is a day of prayer. We pray for the husbands and wives and moms and dads and sons and daughters and loved ones of those who still grieve and hurt. We pray for strength and wisdom. We thank God for the many blessings of this Nation, and we ask His blessings on those who especially hurt today.

Thank you.

NOTE: The President spoke at 8:03 a.m. to journalists at St. John's Episcopal Church. The Office of the Press Secretary also released a Spanish language transcript of these remarks.

Remarks on the Anniversary of September 11 and an Exchange With Reporters
September 11, 2003

The President. This morning, we had a chance to go to a church service to remember the victims and pray for their families, the victims of 9/11/2001. Today—this afternoon, Laura and I are here to thank the brave souls who got wounded in the war on terror, people who were willing to sacrifice in order to make sure that attacks such as September the 11th don't happen again.

I want to thank the staff of Walter Reed, the docs and the nurses and the caregivers, the people who look after the families, for enabling me to say to our fellow citizens that when somebody gets hurt, somebody who wears our uniform gets injured, they get the absolute best care as quickly as possible. I was able to pin the Purple Heart on a number of people upstairs. I was able to hug their parents and thank them. I'm just so grateful that our country has got people who are willing to serve in a cause greater than themselves.

I'll answer a couple of questions, and then I've got to go.

Usama bin Laden Tape

Q. Sir, does this new bin Laden tape concern you at all?

The President. First of all, they're analyzing it. Secondly, his tape reminds us that the war on terror goes on. As well, his rhetoric is trying to intimidate and, you know, create fear. And he's not going to intimidate America. We are at war because of what he and his fellow killers decided to do 2 years ago today. And we will stay at war until we have achieved our objective, the dismantlement of terrorist organizations.

And it just reminds us of the duty we have got to do. And I say "we," my administration and all who serve our country, our duty is to protect our fellow citizens from people like bin Laden.

War on Terror

Q. Mr. President, people are reminded of what happened 2 years ago—think about what's happened in the past 2 years. What can you say to them to make them feel like this won't happen again, that there won't be another——

The President. Yes. Well, I can just tell them—people that, first of all, we have—we're slowly but surely dismantling Al Qaida. We are not only destroying terrorist training camps, cutting off their money; we're either killing or capturing a lot of their leadership.

And as I told the American people right after September the 11th, 2001, this would be a different kind of war, and this would be a long war. And we're fighting this war on a lot of fronts, the major front of which is now in Iraq. And we're making steady progress toward achieving our objective, and we will continue to make progress. You can't negotiate with these people. You can't try to talk sense to these people. The only way to deal with them is to find them and bring them to justice, and that's what the United States—and a lot of other countries working with the United States—will continue to do.

U.N. Resolution on Iraq

Q. Sir, are we any closer to getting a U.N. resolution?

The President. Colin is going to be overseas starting tomorrow and over the weekend, and we'll see when he comes back.

But the key thing for the United Nations resolution is that it will hopefully encourage other nations to participate. And I think other nations have an obligation to participate. A free Iraq will be in their Nation's benefit. It will make the world more peaceful and more secure. And a free Iraq in the heart of the Middle East will make it more easy for us to not only secure America and other free nations but will make it easier for there to be peace in the long run.

And therefore, I would hope that nations would participate, and to the extent that some nations need an additional United Nations resolution, this could be helpful in encouraging international participation. But Colin is sitting down with other foreign ministers from the Perm 5 as well as Kofi Annan, starting tomorrow.

Okay, well, thank you all.

NOTE: The President spoke at 4:30 p.m. at the Walter Reed Army Medical Center. In his remarks, he referred to Usama bin Laden, leader of the Al Qaida terrorist organization; Secretary of State Colin L. Powell; and Secretary-General Kofi Annan of the United Nations. A tape was not available for verification of the content of these remarks.

Remarks to Military Personnel and Families at Fort Stewart, Georgia
September 12, 2003

The President. Thank you all very much. Thanks for the warm welcome. It's a fine day here in Georgia. Of course, the Governor told me every day is a fine day in Georgia.

Audience members. Hooah!

The President. It's a great day to visit the soldiers and the families of the 3d Infantry Division and to visit Fort Stewart. When I came here in February of 2001, it was my first—one of my first official

trips, my first visit to an Army post as Commander in Chief, and my first chance as President to say: Hooah!

Audience members. Hooah!

The President. Since we last met, soldiers of the 3d Infantry Division have fought in Afghanistan and have hunted terrorists in Pakistan; you've launched the coalition offensive into Iraq, defeated the enemy in Najaf; you took the Saddam Hussein International Airport and seized his palaces; and you led the fighting into Baghdad the day the statue of the dictator was pulled down.

Audience members. Hooah!

The President. Following that day of liberation, 3d ID soldiers have helped the Iraqi people to recover from years of oppression, to begin the work of building a free Iraq. Two months ago, the Sergeant Major of the Army, Jack Tilley, spoke to the 3d ID troops in Fallujah. He said this—he said, "Be proud of who you are. Stand up straight. You made history." As Commander in Chief, I second those words. You made history. You've made our Nation proud. And you have earned the Presidential Unit Citation.

After a long deployment, the 3d ID is now home. America is grateful for your devoted service in hard conditions. America is grateful to the men and women right here on this base who supported your mission.

And we're especially grateful to our military families. I know it has been a tough 9 months for Fort Stewart families. But you've been loyal and patient, and you've looked out for one another. I want to thank you for the support you've given to your loved ones. Thank you for the love of your country. Our Nation is grateful.

I want to thank General Blount for inviting me here today. I told him, I said he's a pretty eloquent speaker for a good warrior. [*Laughter*] I appreciate General Ellis, good to see him again today, the commander of U.S. Forces Command.

I'm honored to be traveling with two fine United States Senators, Senator Zell Miller and Senator Saxby Chambliss of the great State of Georgia, strong supporters of the United States military. As well, we traveled down with Jack Kingston and Max Burns, two fine Members of the House of Representatives. As well, they are strong supporters of the United States military.

Of course, I already mentioned the Governor once. He said, "Every day is a beautiful day in Georgia." I'm proud to be

with him. He's a good friend, solid American.

I also am pleased to be here with Brigadier General Joe Riojas, assistant division commander; Bob Caslen—Colonel Caslen, assistant division commander; Colonel Larry Burch; Colonel John Kidd; Sergeant Major Kellman; and Captain Vern Tubbs. I want to thank you all very much for bringing me here today. It's an honor to be here.

Two-and-a-half years ago—or 2 years ago, this Nation came under enemy attack. Two years ago yesterday we were attacked. On a single morning, we suffered the highest casualties on our own soil since the Civil War. America saw the face of a new adversary, an enemy that plots in secret, an enemy that rejects the rules of war, an enemy that rejoices in the murder of the innocent. We made a pledge that day, and we have kept it: We are bringing the guilty to justice; we are taking the fight to the enemy.

In this new kind of war, America has followed a new strategy. We are not waiting for further attacks on our citizens. We are striking our enemies before they can strike us again. As all of you know, wars are fought on the offensive. The war on terror will be won on the offensive, and America and our friends are staying on the offensive. We're rolling back the terrorist threat not on the fringes of its influence but at the heart of its power.

In Afghanistan, America and our broad coalition acted against a regime that harbored Al Qaida and ruled by terror. We've sent a message that is now understood throughout the world: If you harbor a terrorist, if you support a terrorist, if you feed a terrorist, you're just as guilty as the terrorists. And the Taliban found out what we meant. Thanks to our men and women in uniform, Afghanistan is no longer a haven for terror, and as a result, the people of America are safer from attack.

We are hunting the Al Qaida terrorists wherever they still hide, from Pakistan to the Philippines to the Horn of Africa. And we're making good progress. Nearly two-thirds of Al Qaida's known leaders have been captured or killed. The rest of them are dangerous, but the rest of them can be certain we're on their trail. Our resolve is firm. The resolve of this Nation is clear: No matter how long it takes, we will bring justice to those who plot against America.

And we have pursued the war on terror in Iraq. Our coalition enforced the demands of the U.N. Security Council in one of the swiftest and most humane military campaigns in history. Because of our military, catastrophic weapons will no longer be in the hands of a reckless dictator. Because of our military, Middle Eastern countries no longer fear subversion and attack by Saddam Hussein. Because of our military, the torture chambers in Iraq are closed, and people who speak their minds need not fear execution. Because of our military, the people of Iraq are free.

Now we're working with the Iraqi people to build a decent and democratic society, a country that is an example of peace, not an exporter of violence. This undertaking is difficult, and it is costly. Yet it is worthy of our country, and it is critical to our security. You've seen how Saddam holdouts and foreign terrorists are desperately, desperately trying to undermine Iraq's progress and to throw that country into chaos. You know, they understand that a free Iraq will be free of them, free of assassins and torturers and secret police. As democracy and freedom rise in Iraq, their ambitions will fall just like the statues of Saddam Hussein.

The terrorists have a strategic goal. They want America to leave Iraq before our work is done. You see, they believe their attacks on our people and on innocent people will shake the will of the United States and the civilized world. They believe America will run from a challenge. They don't know us very well.

Audience members. Hooah!

The President. They're mistaken. Iraq is now the central front in the war on terror.

This Nation will complete our work, and we will win this essential victory.

The people of our military have faced many hardships in Iraq, and you faced them with courage. You know the names of some who fought for our country and didn't come home, who died in the line of duty. You remember them as comrades and friends. This Nation will remember them for their unselfish courage, for their sacrifice in a time of danger to America. We honor their memory. We pray for God's comfort on their family and loved ones.

All who serve understand what this fight is about. Our military is confronting terrorists in Iraq and Afghanistan and in other places, so that our people will not have to confront terrorist violence in our own cities.

Our strategy in Iraq has three objectives. First, we are destroying the terrorists by swift and decisive action. We continue to launch raids against these enemies. We're rounding them up. We're seizing their weapons. And as for the leaders of the former regime, we're working our way through the famous deck of cards. The Iraqi people are helping with critical leads, and with each new capture the word gets out.

In a letter home this summer, an American soldier described the following scene in Baghdad after two of those cards were dealt with. He wrote: "The whole city was erupting in gunfire. There were tracer rounds flying through the air all over. Everyone was hyped to the max. Then we got the call over the radio. It was celebration fire because we caught Saddam's sons." Altogether, 42 of the 55 most wanted former Iraqi leaders have been captured or killed. It's a matter of time for the rest of them.

Our second objective is to bring in other nations to help Iraq build a free country; that'll make the world more secure. Already two multinational divisions—perhaps you saw brothers and sisters in combat when you were in Iraq—divisions led by the Brits and the Poles, they're sharing responsibilities with us. And we thank all the nations who have contributed.

It's time for others to join us. Tomorrow Secretary Powell will be in Geneva, consulting with friends and allies and the officials of the United Nations. He'll carry a message: No free nation can be neutral in the fight between civilization and chaos. Terrorists in Iraq have attacked representatives of the civilized world, and opposing them and defeating them must be the cause of the civilized world.

Our third goal is to encourage the orderly transfer of sovereignty and authority to the Iraqi people. We're helping to train Iraqi civil defense forces and police and border guards. In these and other roles, some 60,000 Iraqis are now helping to secure their country. Iraq's new Governing Council represents the nation's diverse groups. Ninety percent of the communities have local councils. In Baghdad, a new city council is at work, chosen by all the neighborhoods in the cities. In the months ahead, the Iraqis will be drafting a new constitution, and this will prepare the way for elections. With our help, and with the great strength of its own people, Iraq is getting rid of the days of dictatorship and terror and is moving toward a future of stability and freedom. And life is returning to normal for a lot of the citizens in Iraq.

The day the regime fell, only 30 percent of the hospitals in Iraq were functioning. Now almost every hospital in Iraq is open. America and our coalition have provided more than 22 million doses of vaccine to over 4 million children and a million pregnant women. We're refurbishing more than 1,000 schools in Iraq.

One school in Baghdad is called the Hiba School. It was founded by a woman named Sarahiah, for children with Down syndrome. The old regime gave the Hiba School no help. You see, Down syndrome children were viewed as hopeless and useless. By now a unit of American soldiers

has—but now a unit of American soldiers has taken the Hiba School under its wing. They've been collecting donations from home to pay for supplies and clothing for the children and salaries for the teachers. The effort has been led by Lieutenant Colonel Bowyer of the 1st Armored Division. He's got a special interest. You see, his own son, Samuel, has Down syndrome.

Sarahiah calls Colonel Bowyer "our first friend and our best friend." And in the Hiba School, the Iraqi children have put up a picture of Sam Bowyer on the wall to thank him—to thank his dad, to thank our country.

See, the Iraqi people are coming to know the kind of men and women we've sent to liberate their country. In your courage and in your compassion, the people of our Armed Forces represent the best of American character.

When I addressed the Nation a few nights ago from the White House, I read a letter I'd received from an Army captain serving in Baghdad. Some of you know him. You gave him a pretty good seat here today—Captain Vern Tubbs. He wrote about his pride in serving a just cause and about the deep desire for Iraqis for liberty. "I see it," he said, "in the eyes of a hungry people every day here. They're starved for freedom and opportunity." Captain Tubbs and all of you have helped put Iraq on the path to freedom and opportunity. And every man, woman, and child in Iraq can be certain of this: The old regime is gone, and the regime is never coming back.

As America carries out its strategy for security and reconstruction, we need the resources to do the job in Iraq. Soon I will send Congress a request for additional money we need to keep our commitments. In this time of challenge of America, as we ask so much of our military, we in Government have a solemn responsibility to give you every tool you need to achieve victory.

This base and all of you serving here are critical to the defense of the United

States. You've shown that, once again, by enduring a long deployment and performing brilliantly every day under difficult and dangerous circumstances, that you're worthy of the task, and you're worthy of our trust. Our whole Nation has been reminded that we can never take our military for granted. I will keep our military strong.

This was the message of another President, John F. Kennedy, when he visited Fort Stewart in 1962 and spoke to the troops on Donovan Field. President Kennedy said this: "Regardless of how persistent our diplomacy may be in activities stretching all around the globe, in the final analysis it rests upon the power of the United States, and that power rests upon the will and courage of our citizens and upon you in this field." Soldiers and families of Fort Stewart, those words are still true today. Peace and America's security depends on you.

In meeting the dangers of a new era, the world looks to America for leadership. And America counts on the men and women who have stepped forward as volunteers in the cause of freedom.

I want to thank you all for your good service. Thank you for the credit and honor you bring to our country every day. May God bless you. May God bless your families, and may God continue to bless America.

NOTE: The President spoke at 10:02 a.m. at Trent Field. In his remarks, he referred to Gov. Sonny Perdue of Georgia; Gen. Larry R. Ellis, USA, commanding general, U.S. Army Forces Command; Gen. Buford C. Blount III, USA, commanding general, Brig. Gen. Jose D. Riojas, USA, assistant division commander, Col. Robert L. Caslen, Jr., USA, assistant division commander, Col. Glenn L. Burch, USA, chief of staff, Col. John M. Kidd, USA, garrison commander, and Sgt. Maj. Julian A. Kellman, USA, division command sergeant major, 3d Infantry Division, Fort Stewart and Hunter Army Airfield; former President Saddam Hussein of Iraq; former President Hussein's sons, Uday and Qusay, who were killed July 22 by U.S. military forces in Mosul, Iraq; and Lt. Col. Richard Bowyer, USA, 1st Armored Division.

Remarks at a Luncheon for Gubernatorial Candidate Haley Barbour in Jackson, Mississippi
September 12, 2003

Thank you all. Please be seated. Thanks for coming. I'm glad to be back in Mississippi. I thank the warm welcome for a former Texas Governor who's proud to be on stage with the future Mississippi Governor. I'm here to remind the good people of this State—Republican, Democrat, or independent—if they're interested in good government, if they want somebody to call upon the best of Mississippi, if they're interested in every person being able to achieve their dreams in this State, they need to elect Haley Barbour as the Governor of Mississippi.

I like his slogan: Mississippi can do better. It says when he's your Governor, he'll have an optimistic outlook for all the people of this State. He believes in high standards and raising that bar. He believes in the vast human potential of Mississippi. There's no doubt in my mind that when you elect Haley Barbour as Governor of Mississippi, Mississippi will do better.

And I know him. This isn't just your typical hot air. [*Laughter*] I know him well. He recounted some of our history. We've been friends for a long time. So when I say, for example, he believes in personal responsibility, I know he believes that way. And when he says he's going to focus on education to make sure no child is left behind in Mississippi, I know he believes that.

Haley has served at the highest levels of Government, but let me assure you of one thing: Whether it was in my conversations with him in Washington, DC, or in Austin, Texas, he always talked about Yazoo City. [*Laughter*] It is safe to say he never forgot his roots. No, there's no doubt in my mind this good man can do the job. If the people of this State give him a chance, they're going to realize that he's going to call upon the best of Mississippi.

He and I share something else in common. We both married above ourselves. [*Laughter*] I'm proud to be on stage with Marsha, had a chance to say hello to Sterling and Reeves. My only advice to those boys was, listen to your mother. [*Laughter*] I'm still listening to mine.

Laura sends her love. She sends her love not only to Haley and Marsha; she sends her very best to many of our friends out here today. She is a fabulous wife, by the way, and a great First Lady for America.

Speaking about a guy who married well, Senator Lott is with us. [*Laughter*] Tricia and Trent are really good friends of Laura and mine. We both love our country, and we both love Scottish terriers. [*Laughter*] Let me tell you something about Trent: Mississippi is really, really lucky to have him as a United States Senator.

You've got some pretty good Congressmen, too. I'm proud to call Roger Wicker and Chip Pickering friends. These guys are doing a great job on behalf of this State. It's great to see Chip and his beautiful wife today. I do want you to do me a favor, if you don't mind, a little personal privilege from the President. I hope you give your dad my best, Judge Charles Pickering. I nominated him to a higher court because I believe in his character. I trust his judicial philosophy. He's a man who will interpret the law, not legislate from the bench. Some Senators are playing politics with American

justice. They did this man and this country a disservice. It is time for some on the Senate floor to stop playing politics with people like Charles Pickering's good name.

There's a lot of people here hoping Haley runs good at the top of the ticket, starting with the Lieutenant Governor, Amy Tuck. I'm proud to have welcomed her to the Oval Office the other day. It is—along with Travis Little—they were up there to, oh, get a picture or two taken. [*Laughter*] But it was good to talk to Amy again. I had the honor of welcoming her to the Republican Party. I appreciate the courage of your decision, Amy, and I appreciate your willingness to lead. Thank you for being here. Of course, I did meet Senator Little.

I also want to thank State auditor Phil Bryant for being here. I want to thank the—thank you, Phil. I appreciate Mike Retzer, my long-time friend, for working hard for the Bush-Cheney campaign. There is another election around the corner one of these days. We'll be back. [*Laughter*]

I also know you've got some candidates here running, and I always like to mention candidates who have decided to take on the task of a statewide race, because it's not an easy job. It's not easy to ask your family to run—have to ask your family to join you in running. But we've got Julio Del Castillo here, who's the candidate for secretary of state. We've got Scott Newton, the candidate for attorney general. We've got Max Phillips, the candidate for agriculture commissioner. And we've got Tate Reeves, the candidate for treasurer. Thank you all for running, I hope you help them.

It's good to see your former Governor, Kirk Fordice, here today. Kirk, good to see you, sir.

I want to thank Jim Herring, the chairman of the Mississippi Republican Party, for his hard work. And I want to thank all the folks involved with grassroots politics here in Mississippi. I want to thank Cindy Phillips, who is the national committeewoman, as well.

Finally, there is a special fellow here that my family has known for a long time. He's a really great American, great fellow from Mississippi. Laura and I occasionally slide across the street there in Washington, DC, to go to church at the little St. John's Church in Lafayette Square. One of our favorite things when we get to church is to shake hands and to say hello to one of the special Americans, and that's my friend Sonny Montgomery. It looks like they still remember you here, Sonny. [*Laughter*]

I first want to thank you for your generosity but remind you that there is more to do in the campaign for an important race like Governor. You've got to turn out the vote. You've got to go to your coffee shops and tell the people that may not be quite as interested in politics as you are that there's a lot at stake for Mississippi. When they're just about to sip that coffee, you tell them that Haley Barbour has got a clear vision for the future of this State. He's not going to win it on his looks alone. [*Laughter*] He's going to win it because he cares about people.

See, when he hears somebody is looking for a job, it bothers him. If somebody is looking for a job and can't find work, it means you've got a problem here in Mississippi. That's the way I feel about the Nation. He and I share a philosophy: The role of Government is not to create wealth; the role of Government is to create an environment in which entrepreneurship can flourish, in which small businesses can grow to be big businesses. And that's why, for example, in Washington, I worked with the Congress to pass tax relief. When the economy goes slow, if you let people have more of their own money, they're likely to demand a good or a service.

Haley understands that. He understands whose money we spend in Government. We're not spending the Government's money; we're spending the people's money. And you better have you a Governor who

understands that when he gets you elected to represent this great State.

This economy is beginning to pick up a little steam, but there are still some citizens who hurt. So long as they're hurting, we've got to keep creating an environment for economic growth. It will be important to have a Governor in Mississippi who understands that fiscal discipline is necessary at the State capital. If you're interested in job creation, Government has got to be fiscally disciplined. If you're interested in job creation, you've got to put policy in place that encourages small-business growth. After all, most small businesses—most new jobs are created by small businesses in America. Haley has got a plan. He's got good ideas. He comes with the right philosophy, and he's got a plan to create jobs here in Mississippi. For the people in Mississippi who are interested in job creation, the right man for the job is Haley Barbour.

By the way, one way to make sure this is a good State in which to create jobs is to have a Governor who's willing to take off the—take on the plaintiffs' attorneys and fight for real, meaningful litigation reform. You don't want it said that the fastest growth industry in your State is the plaintiffs' bar. That's not good for attracting industry and creating jobs. You don't want the greatest wealth accumulation in any State to be in the hands of plaintiffs' attorneys. You need to get you a Governor who understands that, who's tough enough to stand up to the special interests that oftentimes dominate State politics, is willing to look those in the eye who are trying to ruin the condition for job creation, who are running your doctors out of your State, look them in the eye and say, "I demand that we have reasonable tort reform in the State of Mississippi." And that man is Haley Barbour.

Last time I came to your beautiful State, I was here because I was worried about docs getting run out of Mississippi. I'll never forget meeting with the guy from the Delta. It was a fellow; he came down from the North. He heard a call. He's what you might call a faith-based doctor, practicing real medicine, but he was motivated by faith to help people who hurt, a fantastic person. The guy never grew up in Mississippi but heard there was a need for health care in this State, so he came here. He wanted to give of his time and talents so somebody might live a better life.

And he told me the stories about what it's like to live in a State where the system isn't fair anymore, where the lawyers have pushed too far. And he left your State of Mississippi because the premiums went up too high. You lost a good heart in your State because the system is awry. You need you a Governor who understands that health care must be accessible and affordable, a Governor that when he says he's going to get you medical liability reform, will get you real medical liability reform, not only for the sake of the docs but, more importantly, for the sake of the people who need good health care. Haley Barbour is that Governor.

In order for this State to reach its full potential, you need to have a Governor who understands the number one priority of any State is the education of the children of that State. Haley understands that. We passed good law in Washington, DC. It's an interesting change of attitude for the Nation's Capital. It used to be we just passed out money in Washington. And we're pretty good at that, by the way. But now we've said, if you're going to receive money for education purposes and elementary and secondary act money and Title I money within that title, is now we expect to see whether or not the children are learning to read and write and add and subtract.

See, the State of Mississippi needs a Governor, just like our country needed a President, that was willing to challenge the soft bigotry of low expectations. When you lower the bar, you get bad results. If you believe certain children can't learn, you'll have a system that just shuffles the kids

through. If you believe it's impossible to teach a certain type of child, guess what's going to happen? That type of child will never learn.

I believe every child can learn. I believe it's in the reach with every State and every school to teach the basics. And therefore, in return for Federal money, I expect the basics to be taught. And I want to thank Senator Lott and the Congressman here who stood with me on that important initiative. Now, in return for Federal money, States must show people whether or not our children are learning to read and write and add and subtract. If you believe they can learn, then you want to know. If you believe that the best can happen, then we want to see. We don't want somebody to theorize whether it's happening. We want concrete proof. And if it's not happening, we will use the measurement systems not as a way to punish the good teachers, but to correct the situation.

Haley Barbour agrees with that philosophy. He believes about raising the bar. He believes, support the teachers. But most of all, he knows that we must correct problems early, before they're too late, to make sure that not one single child gets left behind in the State of Mississippi.

I appreciate the fact that Haley understands that there are people who hurt in Mississippi; there are people who are lonely and addicted, people who are homeless, and people who are hungry. He also understands what I know, that the Government can hand out money, but it cannot put hope in people's hearts or a sense of purpose in people's lives. That's done when a loving soul puts their arm around somebody who hurts and says, "I love you. What can I do to help you?"

The true strength of this country is the hearts and souls of the American people. That's our strength. And the job of people in positions of responsibility is to rally that spirit. That's why the Faith-Based Initiative that I proposed in Washington is so vital.

It's an initiative that Haley fully understands. It's an initiative that he wants to get started here.

Listen, there are great programs that come out of Government, and sometimes they work, and sometimes they don't. But we ought to use all avenues, all our strengths, to achieve the common goal that everybody feels the great hope of America. When we find somebody who's lonely and addicted on drugs, we ought not to fear a faith-based program's involvement with that person. You see, sometimes it takes a change of heart to change a habit. And when we find effective programs based upon faith, Government at the Federal level and State level should not fear faith, we should welcome faith into the important delivery of human services to people who hurt.

I had a chance to talk to Haley on Air Force One coming down. He came over to Fort Stewart, and I thought it might be okay if I shared some thoughts on the war on terror. So I think I will. I was in Fort Stewart; it's the home of the 3d Infantry Division. They're the troops who took it up the west side, from the south of Iraq to free Baghdad. What an honor it is to stand up in front of fantastically brave troops and to thank them on behalf of a grateful nation.

It's important for me to continue to do this because this Nation still remains at war. It's a different kind of war. You saw how different it was on September the 11th, 2001. Instead of armies marching across plains or Air Forces bombing Pearl Harbor, we were attacked by coldblooded killers who took our own assets and flew them into the buildings without regard to the nature of the victim. These people didn't care if they were young kids, women, men—no such thing in their mind as innocent or guilt. They're interested in one thing, death.

On that day, this country decided that no matter how long it took, we would find those who would inflict harm upon America

and bring them to justice. I will never forget the lessons of September the 11th, 2001, so long as I am your President. I have a solemn duty to protect America, and we're making progress. We're slowly but surely bringing the Al Qaida killers to justice. I remind people that over two-thirds of the known operatives and leaders are either dead or captured. And I can assure you, we're after the rest of them. No matter how long it takes, no matter what the cost, we will bring those who harmed America and want to harm America to justice. We owe it to future generations of Americans. We owe it to the peace and security of the world to use our strength to find the killers.

Therapy will not work with these kind of people. Treaties make no sense. There's only one thing: Get them before they get us, to stay on the offensive.

Right after September the 11th, I laid out a new American doctrine that said, "If you harbor a terrorist, if you feed a terrorist, if you house a terrorist, you're just as guilty as the terrorists." And the Taliban found out what the United States of America meant. Not only were we able to destroy terrorist training camps and cut off support for these killers when we routed the Taliban out of Afghanistan, but we did something even—as important: Young girls now go to school for the first time, because the Taliban is no more. Girls go to school, thanks to the might of the United States of America.

And that's important, because we believe everybody matters. We believe every life is precious. We believe and know that freedom is not America's gift to the world; it is the Almighty's gift to every individual in the world. And we've brought freedom to the people of Iraq in a military operation that was one of the swiftest and most humane military operations in history. We rid the world of Saddam Hussein, and we freed millions of people in Iraq. There are no more torture chambers in Iraq. There will be no more mass graves in Iraq.

Schools are—the hospitals are now opened. Schools are flourishing. And one thing is for certain: Terrorist groups will no longer find support in Iraq, and terrorist groups will not ever be able to get weapons of mass destruction in Iraq because Saddam Hussein is no more.

But I understand this, that in order to make sure America is secure in the long run and the world is more peaceful, we must spread freedom. Free people don't attack their neighbors. Free people don't develop weapons of mass destruction. The truth of the matter is, the greatest security for America in the long term is the spread of liberty. And that's why it's so important in the heart of the Middle East that we establish a free society in Iraq. It is so important that we succeed. And that's why I went to the Nation the other night and asked for a significant amount of money from the United States Congress to fund the efforts necessary to make Iraq secure and free and peaceful. The money we spend today to achieve this incredibly important objective will be money that others don't have to spend in future years. We would rather win our war against terror in Iraq than to fight them here on the streets of America. And we must succeed in making sure that freedom takes hold in that important part of the world.

There is no doubt in my mind America will prevail. See, I understand the country pretty well. I know the people of America. We are resolved, and we are strong, and we're plenty tough when we have to be tough. The truth of the matter is, this is a country as well that's got a great heart, great generosity. Not only are we going to work hard here in Mississippi and other places to make sure promise is available and hope is available for everybody, ours is a nation that is willing to lead the world in the incredibly important work of human rescue. We're going to provide medicine to millions of men and women and children suffering from AIDS on the continent of Africa.

See, that's the spirit of the country. That's the country we are. We believe in freedom for everybody. We believe in hope. We believe in opportunity. And when we see suffering, we will not turn our back.

I believe that when you find somebody good and honorable, you give him a chance to represent you. In this State, you've found a man that's good and honorable. The guy has got the experience to do the job, a fellow that when he picks up the phone, the President might just go ahead and answer it. [*Laughter*] It's a man who will represent you with class. He'll call upon the best of this State. This is a man who is serving for the right reason: He believes in serving something greater than himself in life. And that man is your next Governor, Mr. Haley Barbour. Thank you for supporting him.

God bless, and God bless America.

NOTE: The President spoke at 1:33 p.m. at the Mississippi Coliseum. In his remarks, he referred to Marsha Barbour, wife of Haley Barbour, and their sons Sterling and Reeves; Tricia Lott, wife of Sen. Trent Lott; Leisha Pickering, wife of Rep. Charles W. "Chip" Pickering, Jr.; Mississippi State Senator Travis L. Little; former Rep. G.V. "Sonny" Montgomery of Mississippi; Judge Charles W. Pickering, Sr., whose nomination to be U.S. Circuit Judge for the Fifth Circuit failed on March 14, 2002, when the Senate Judiciary Committee refused to send it forward for a vote by the Senate; Mike Retzer, treasurer, Republican National Committee; and former President Saddam Hussein of Iraq.

Remarks at the Power Center in Houston, Texas
September 12, 2003

The President. Thank you all very much. Be seated. Kirbyjon can tell it. [*Laughter*] Heck, I might sound inarticulate compared to him. [*Laughter*]

Reverend Caldwell. No, no.

The President. Yes. Let's see how to start here. First, it's glad to be back—I'm glad to be back to Texas. It's good to see some of my buddies. I'm looking at a man right here on the front row I went to the seventh grade with in Houston, Texas. I see my friend "Big Tuna" I used to play basketball with at the Y. I never forget my friends, and I've got a lot of friends here in Texas, and I'm thrilled to be with you. Thank you all for coming tonight.

But thank you for coming to support this wonderful program. You'll hear me say this a couple of times in what's going to be a short address. Pastor Caldwell said, "Speak all you want, but don't exceed 7 minutes." [*Laughter*]

I think the fact that people are willing to contribute money to save lives is a powerful testimony to the strength of America. I think that when people are willing to support a social entrepreneur like Kirbyjon Caldwell and the others at the Windsor Village Church who have heard a call and are out to save any life they can find that needs to be saved—the fact that you support them speaks to your heart as well. And so today I first want to say thanks. Thanks for contributing hard-earned money to make Houston, Texas, the best place it can be.

And I'm proud to be up here with my friend. Sometimes it's not easy to be the friend of George W. Bush—I know that—[*laughter*]—if you know what I mean. [*Laughter*] But let me tell you something. It's good to have a friend that I can call before a debate and say, "Do you mind saying a prayer?" It's good to have a friend to go with you to Ground Zero. He's not

a political friend; he's a friend. He rises above that, that friendship. And it's good for this community to lift up a man like Kirbyjon Caldwell who acts for the best interests of all the citizens of this community. And I'm proud to call him friend.

And we both married above ourselves.

Reverend Caldwell. Amen.

The President. Yes, sir. Well, you don't need to "amen" it that loud, but—[*laughter*]. Laura sends her love to Kirbyjon and Suzette and to all our buddies here. She is a fantastic First Lady, by the way. I really lucked out. And she's doing great, she really is.

Suzette is a unique person. I just had had my picture taken with a group of Prayer Warriors organized by Suzette Caldwell. You know, it's a unique country, when you think about it, that people would pray for me. People I'll never know, people I'll never have a chance to say thank you to, pray for me. Suzette organized such a group, and I had a chance to say thank you to the group. But it shows the kind of person Suzette is. And I want to thank you for your friendship as well. I want to thank you for your prayers. I feel them, and it means a lot—it means a lot. And so, Suzette, I want to thank you for your friendship as well. It's great seeing your kids. They're little livewires, little—one of them is like a little Kirbyjon, you know—[*laughter*]—hard to control. [*Laughter*]

It's great to see Booker and Jean Caldwell as well. Kirbyjon and I both lucked out; we've got good, strong mothers. I hope you're still listening to yours, Kirbyjon. [*Laughter*] I'm listening to mine, I can assure you. [*Laughter*]

I'm traveling today with a great friend of Houston, Texas, a friend of mine, a man who has agreed to serve our community—communities all across the country as the Secretary of Education, Mr. Rod Paige. I like to remind people that when I was picking the Cabinet, I wanted for the education man, somebody that had actually been an educator. We had enough theory in Washington. We wanted somebody that had actually done the job. And as you know, he did a great job as the superintendent of the Houston Independent School District. What I love about Rod is, he is willing to challenge the soft bigotry of low expectations. He raises the bar, and he's not afraid to measure to determine whether or not we're meeting those standards.

We passed a really important piece of legislation called the No Child Left Behind Act. And the way you make sure no child is left behind is, you raise standards. You hold people accountable. You correct problems before—early, before they're too late. I am absolutely convinced that under Rod's leadership at the Department of Education, it is less likely a child is going to be left behind in America. And I want to thank you for your service.

I know some of my running buddies from the State government are here, Lieutenant Governor David Dewhurst and Railroad Commissioner Michael Williams. I want to thank you all for coming. I'm proud you're here. I know Congresswoman Sheila Jackson Lee is here, and I'm—there she is—and I'm honored that you're here. Thank you for coming, Congresswoman. I appreciate it. One thing about Sheila Jackson Lee is, when I see her, she's never afraid to offer up any advice. [*Laughter*] It's become a habit of ours, hasn't it? [*Laughter*]

I appreciate the fact that we've got two former Secretaries of Commerce here, one Houstonian, Bob Mosbacher, and new Texan, Bill Daley. And I want to thank them both for coming. I appreciate them being here. I appreciate my friend Oxford. He's actually making a pretty good hand. Thanks for putting on this event. Great to see you.

Genora Boykins, who's the chairperson of the CDC, I want to thank her for opening this event up. I thank my friend Jodi Jiles, who's the treasurer of the Community Development Corporation. I've known Jodi for a long time.

You know, I have had the chance to hear Kirbyjon preach, and he's a pretty darn good preacher. He reminds me of the preacher that got going one day, and about three-quarters of the way through the sermon, a guy was so moved on about pew three that he popped up and screamed, "Use me, Lord. Use me." The preacher plowed on through and finished up and didn't think anything of it until the next Sunday. About the same time in his sermon, this guy gets so moved—I'm sure some of you have been so moved by Kirbyjon that you think about popping up—this guy popped up again and he screamed, "Use me, Lord. Use me." After the service was over, the preacher sought the fellow out. He said, "Fine, I appreciate your willingness to help, and therefore, I suggest and would like for you to scrape and paint all the pews." The next Sunday the preacher is up there letting it go. The guy pops up and he says, "Use me, Lord. Use me, but in an advisory capacity." [*Laughter*]

I'm at the Power Center today because this place is full of doers, not advisers. This was once an empty Kmart building. It is now a building full of love. It was used to sell goods, and now it provides incredibly important services to help save lives.

I find it interesting that they named the center the Power Center. This—we're not talking about electricity in this power. We're talking about a higher power that caused this center to be. I find it also interesting that in the midst of this—or at least the last time I came, Suzette showed me the prayer facility right in the middle of the center. You had a bank. You've got a school, and you've got a women and children's clinic, the WIC program—it's a Government program. You've got some job training. You've got the Houston Community Center—Community College facility, I mean. But in the midst, there's a prayer center. People should realize that the reason why this program is successful is because the power in the Power Center comes from a higher calling, a higher source of power.

And the reason why I came to see the Power Center in the first place was two-fold: One, I felt I had an obligation as the Governor of the State to support programs that were changing people's lives in a positive way; and secondly, I had heard that beyond good intentions there were good results here and that the Power Center was a unique faith-based program. And it helped me develop a philosophy of government that I want to explain right quick to you.

And part of my reason I'm doing this is because I'm sending a message to the Congress at the same time. [*Laughter*] They might not be here, except for one very distinguished Congresswoman, but the TV cameras are here. It gives me a chance to speak directly to good social policy in America.

I saw people's lives changed because of faith. Right here at the Power Center is a good example. I saw the fact that with the proper application of the call to love a neighbor like you'd like—love yourself, with resources and social entrepreneurship, souls could change. And I recognized that, at the time in Texas and now nationally, that the absolute best way to make sure that the promise of America extends its reach into every neighborhood, the best way to help heal those who hurt is to bring all the resources of our country to bear. And the most powerful resource of all is the ability to transform lives through faith.

I don't talk about a particular faith. I believe the Lord can work through many faiths, whether it be the Christian faith, Jewish faith, Muslim faith, Hindu faith. When I speak of faith, I speak of all faiths, because there is a universal call, and that main universal call is to love your neighbor. It extends throughout all faith.

That's what the Power Center says to me. It's a living example of what is possible not only in Houston but in communities all around our country, because there are faith-based communities all around our country. There are churches on every corner. There are synagogues in every town. There are people of faith who have heard a call. It seems like to me, this society of ours must rally the people of faith. Amongst our plenty, there are people who hurt. There's addiction and loneliness, social problems that can only be cured by love.

I've been searching for that bill, by the way, ever since I've been in government, the bill that says you'll love somebody. Sheila Jackson will sponsor it, and I'll sign it. [*Laughter*] But there is no such bill. People don't get their inspiration to help a neighbor in need from government. They get their inspiration from a higher being. And yet, government has thwarted faith to be involved in our communities because of what they call the doctrine of separation of church and state. And that's a noble doctrine. The church should never be the state, and the state certainly should never be the church. But our Government must not fear the application of faith into solving social problems. We must not worry about people of faith receiving taxpayers' money to help people in need.

In my judgment, that doesn't obscure the line of church and state. It enhances the capacity of state to save lives by tapping into this fundamental powerful resource of ours, the heart and soul of the American people.

And yet in Washington, DC, there is an attitude that we should not welcome faith-based programs into the budgets of our Government. As a matter of fact, there are regulations that specifically prohibit faith-based programs from job training, for example, or Head Start or some housing programs. There is a fear that funding faith will somehow change the doctrine of church and state.

I completely disagree. The discrimination against faith-based programs at the Federal level prevents us from using all our resources to save lives. And for those who hurt, we need to use every resource we have. For those who are lonely, we need to use every resource. For those who are hungry, we need to use every resource. For those who look for housing, we need to use every resource. And so one of my missions is to work with people to end the discrimination in Washington, DC, against faith-based programs.

The other problem we have, besides just outright regulations saying that you cannot use money for housing or Head Start or job training programs, is the fact that oftentimes groups that try to access Federal money—by the way, and the purpose of the money is to save lives, in many cases—the groups that apply have to change their board of directors in order to access the money, or have to take the cross off the wall, in the case of the Christian faith-based program. But it's hard to be a faith-based program if you can't practice faith. If the effectiveness of the program is based upon faith, our Government must allow that program to practice its faith.

You see, up to now, the question has been, what is the process? My question is, what are the results? If we're saving lives, if the Salvation Army is doing what it does so very well, we ought to welcome programs that succeed. We ought to say, "You're welcome into the fabric, the social fabric, of America in changing lives."

So that's what we're off to do. And I have signed an Executive order—Presidents sign Executive orders. [*Laughter*] It says that we'll have a level playing field for faith-based programs when they apply for Federal money. I've got offices in each Cabinet set up to make sure that the faith-based programs have a friendly ear when they come to apply, that they're not facing the same old bureaucratic morass, that they get a welcoming ear. Rod has got one in his office. HUD has got one. Social—Cabi-

nets have got them in their offices because I want people who have got a good idea about how to change somebody's life to have a sympathetic ear in Washington, DC.

I want people to know that you ought to come. Not only are people allowed to come and make their case and to get help on grantmaking, but we also assure them that, in reverse, the Government is not going to force them to change their habits and change their ways and change their basic reason for existing.

And we're beginning to make some progress. Slowly but surely, we're changing the culture. We'll finalize new regulations later this month that will open up a lot of money available to faith-based programs. And that's important, because it means that we'll do a better job of encouraging the neighborhood healers to fulfill their mission.

Obviously, not all money will be Federal money. That would be bad for the fabric of America. That's why you're here, see. That's why I came. I want to encourage private foundations not to discriminate against faith-based programs. I want to encourage individuals to give. But what I'm also telling you is that the Federal Government needs to take an active role, in my judgment.

Let me tell you some of the kinds of things that are taking place, and hopefully this will stimulate other thought for others who may want to try to compete for taxpayers' money to help save lives. The Department of Health and Human Services recently awarded $7 million of grants to 15 faith-based groups who support abstinence education. One of the grants, for nearly $500,000, a new grant, went to A Woman's Concern. It's a group of faith-based health centers in the Boston area. It seems like it makes sense to me that when you're trying to help people make right choices, that you ask people of faith to be included in the process. This won't be a punitive—it wouldn't be punitive education. It would be education done out of the kindness of somebody's heart. Faith-based programs work.

We've got a—the Department of Labor has awarded $21 million to faith-based groups for job training. I asked Kirbyjon on the way in from Ellington Field, I said, "Are you able to access Federal money for your job training program?" He said, "I didn't know we were able to." Well, you will be able to. What's wrong with having faith-based programs? What's wrong with having a church be able to reach out to a prisoner, somebody who just got out of prison, somebody who's desperate for love? What's wrong with a church, a place of love, surrounding that soul and at the same time having a job training program to help them? I'll tell you what's wrong with it—nothing's wrong with it. And the Federal Government ought to welcome faith-based programs to help save lives.

In East Harlem, the Exodus Transitional Community is using grants from Labor and Justice to help released prisoners get a job. That's the kind of thing I'm talking about. Exodus helped 252 people last year. This year, with the new grant, they'll help 375. And that may not sound like a lot because there's a lot of prisoners. But think about if there was Exodus programs or Exodus-type programs all over. Instead of 375, we'll be talking about 375 times thousands. And then all of a sudden, souls who were once lost are then found. People who thought they didn't have hope can find hope.

HUD, the Department of Housing and Urban Development, is supporting faith-based groups like Uplift Fourth Ward. You may have heard about the program. The Rose of Sharon Missionary Baptist Church in Houston runs it. Uplift Fourth Ward, the folks in it—there you go. [*Laughter*] I'm glad you invited somebody, Kirbyjon—[*laughter*]—from Uplift Fourth Ward. It is a chance to rehabilitate historic buildings and provide safe and affordable housing to low-income seniors. Who says housing programs have to be done out of the old traditional construction company? Why can't

housing companies be started out of faith-based institutions?

There's program after program that have started—but we're just starting, is my point to you. Congress needs to hear the call. Congress needs to not thwart efforts. You see, my attitude is, if a faith-based program provides help to anybody in need regardless of their religion, we should not fear that program. My view is, is that the program ought to stand on its own. The money won't go for proselytizing. The money will go to the social service intended for that program.

I believe we ought to empower people to be able to make choices on where they receive their help. I can't think of anything more vital in America than to have a program aimed at changing drug addiction in America and a program that will allow faith-based programs to be an integral part of helping somebody kick alcohol and drugs. I say that because I know firsthand what it takes to quit drinking, and it takes something other than a textbook or a manual. If you change a person's heart, you can change their life.

Our society must not fear the use of faith to solve life's problems. We must welcome faith, and Congress must not block these important initiatives. There are lives to be saved. There are soldiers in the army of compassion ready to save them, and the Federal Government ought to be on the side of the soldiers in the armies of compassion.

We'll continue working on the Compassionate Capital Fund. I've asked for $100 million this year. It's a way to help startup social entrepreneurs learn how to apply for grants. It gives people ways to fulfill their mission, to realize their dreams. I believe we ought to have a national mentoring program, particularly for children whose mom and dad may be in a prison, for junior high students. I've asked for $450 million. I hope Congress funds it. I just told you about my view on drug rehabilitation. Look, when we find suffering in our society today, we can't turn away.

And just as an aside, we can't turn away overseas, either. I'm proud of the United States of America. This great Nation is going to spend $15 billion over the next 5 years in the important work of human rescue by providing medicine and help to millions and millions of men, women, and children suffering from AIDS on the continent of Africa.

I'm incredibly proud of our country. We're a really strong nation. We need to be strong. We're at a war with people who hate America, and I'll keep us strong militarily. We'll be strong to meet the challenges. We'll continue to push for freedom and peace overseas. The world is going to be peaceful, thanks to the United States of America. America will be more secure, thanks to the focus and strength of the American people.

But at home, we need to work to save lives as well. A secure America is a hopeful America. A secure America is an educated America. A secure America is a place where people realize the American Dream is meant for them as much as it is meant for me.

People say, "Well, your country's strong." I say, "Yes, we are, but you don't really understand the strength of America. It's the hearts and souls of our citizens." That's the true strength of this country. The Power Center tapped into that strength. Your contributions tonight recognize that strength and support it. And our Government must stand side by side with that strength as well.

I'm incredibly optimistic about our country and its future. I've seen firsthand the great character of the American people. And it's that character, it's that determination, it is that optimism that allows me to boldly predict: America will overcome any problem she faces, abroad and here at home.

Thank you all for coming. May God bless you, and may God bless our country.

NOTE: The President spoke at 5:49 p.m. In his remarks, he referred to Rev. Kirbyjon H. Caldwell, senior pastor, Windsor Village United Methodist Church, his wife Suzette, and his parents Booker and Jean Caldwell; Lt. Gov. David Dewhurst of Texas; Michael L. Williams, chair, Texas Railroad Commission; and Genora Boykins, chairperson of the board, and Jodi Jiles, treasurer, Pyramid Community Development Corp.

Statement on the Death of Johnny Cash
September 12, 2003

Johnny Cash was a music legend and American icon whose career spanned decades and genres. His resonant voice and human compassion reached the hearts and souls of generations, and he will be missed. Laura joins me in sending our thoughts and prayers to his family.

Letter to the Speaker of the House of Representatives Transmitting Amendments to the FY 2004 Budget
September 12, 2003

Dear Mr. Speaker:

I ask the Congress to consider the enclosed amendments to the FY 2004 Budget for the Departments of Agriculture, Homeland Security, and Housing and Urban Development, as well as the Corps of Engineers.

These amendments would not change the total pending Presidential Request for FY 2004. However, they would adjust upward the total discretionary budget authority requested by $0.9 billion, bringing the total discretionary funding agreed to by the Administration and the Congress to $785.6 billion. This increase in discretionary funding is fully offset by a corresponding decrease in mandatory funding. All other proposals are assumed to be funded within this constraint.

This transmittal also contains FY 2004 budget amendments for the Legislative Branch and FY 2003 supplemental proposals for the Judicial Branch. As a matter of comity, appropriations requests of the Legislative and Judicial Branches are commonly transmitted without change.

The details of these proposals are set forth in the enclosed letter from the Director of the Office of Management and Budget.

Sincerely,

GEORGE W. BUSH

NOTE: An original was not available for verification of the content of this letter.

The President's Radio Address
September 13, 2003

Good morning. Two years ago this week, America suffered a brutal attack. We will never forget the burning towers and the smoke over Arlington Cemetery and the passengers who rushed the hijackers. Yet history asks for more than memory. On September the 11th, 2001, we began a war on global terror that continues to this hour.

In the decades before that terrible day, the terrorists conducted a series of bolder and bolder attacks in the Middle East and beyond. They became convinced that free nations were decadent and weak and would never offer a sustained and serious response. They now know otherwise.

Together with a coalition of nations, we have struck back against terror worldwide, capturing and killing terrorists and breaking cells and freezing assets. In Afghanistan, we removed the Taliban regime that harbored Al Qaida. In Iraq, we defeated a regime that sponsored terror, possessed and used weapons of mass destruction, and defied the United Nations Security Council for 12 years. We have helped to liberate people from oppression and fear.

Today, with our help, the people of Iraq are working to create a free, functioning, and prosperous society. The terrorists know that if these efforts are successful, their ideology of hate will suffer a grave defeat. So they are attacking our forces, international aid workers, and innocent civilians. Their goal is to drive us out of Iraq before our work is done. They are mistaken, and they will fail. We will do what is necessary to win this victory in the war on terror.

We are following a clear strategy with three objectives: Destroy the terrorists; enlist international support for a free Iraq; and quickly transfer authority to the Iraqi people. Through a series of ongoing operations, our military is taking direct action against Saddam loyalists and foreign terrorists. One major effort underway right now, called Operation Longstreet, is seeking and finding our enemies wherever they hide and plot. Already, this operation has yielded hundreds of detainees and seized hundreds of weapons, and we will remain on the offensive against the terrorists.

We are expanding international cooperation in rebuilding Iraq. Today in Geneva, Secretary of State Powell is meeting with Secretary-General of the United Nations and representatives of the five permanent members of the Security Council. They are discussing ideas for a new resolution to encourage wider participation in this vital task.

And we're moving forward on a specific plan to return sovereignty and authority to the Iraqi people. We have created a Governing Council made up of Iraqi citizens. The Council has selected a committee that is developing a process through which Iraqis will draft a new constitution for their country. Day-to-day operations of many government tasks have been turned over to ministers appointed by the Governing Council. And when a constitution has been drafted and ratified by the Iraqi people, Iraq will enjoy free and fair elections, and the coalition will yield its remaining authority to a free and sovereign Iraqi Government.

We have a strategy in Iraq and a mission. We will fight and defeat the terrorists there so we don't have to face them in America. And we will help transform Iraq into a example of progress and democracy and freedom that can inspire change and hope throughout the Middle East.

Thank you for listening.

NOTE: The address was recorded at 1:20 p.m. on September 11 in the Cabinet Room at the White House for broadcast at 10:06 a.m. on September 13. In his remarks, the President referred to Secretary-General Kofi Annan of the United Nations. The transcript was made available by the Office of the Press Secretary on September 12 but was embargoed for release until the broadcast. The Office of the Press Secretary also released a Spanish language transcript of this address.

Statement on the Death of Frank O'Bannon
September 13, 2003

Frank O'Bannon was a dedicated public servant and a good and decent man. He led a distinguished career, including service in the Air Force, in the Indiana State senate, and as Lieutenant Governor. Since being sworn in as Governor of Indiana in 1997, he has served the people of his State with integrity and devotion. Laura joins me in sending our thoughts and prayers to his wife, Judy, and their family.

Remarks at the Detroit Edison Powerplant in Monroe, Michigan
September 15, 2003

Thank you all. Please be seated, unless you don't have a seat. [*Laughter*] Thanks for the warm welcome. I appreciate the chance to come to this vital facility to meet the workers who make it go, meet the planners who keep it modern, and meet some of the people who benefit from the electricity that's generated out of here.

I come knowing our Nation faces some great challenges. The biggest challenge we face is the security of our people. We've got to make sure that America is secure from the enemies which hate us. And we've got to make America secure by having an economy that grows so people can find work.

On the first front, to make sure America is secure, we're making good progress. The 2 years from September the 11th—we got hit. We got hit by people who cannot stand what America believes in. We love freedom, and we're not going to change. And they probably won't either. Therapy won't work with this bunch. [*Laughter*]

So we will bring people to justice. It doesn't matter how long it takes. America and many of our friends will find those who would harm the American people and bring them to justice. The only way to win the war on terror is to stay on the offensive. We can do a lot of things here at home. We can support our first-responders. We can make sure our law enforcement agencies talk to each other. We can make sure our ports are more secure, our borders are reasonable about understanding who is coming in and why they're coming in. But the best way to make sure the homeland is secure is to hunt these killers down one by one and bring them to justice, which the United States of America will do.

As part of making sure America is secure, I laid out a doctrine that said, "If you harbor a terrorist, if you feed a terrorist, if you hide a terrorist, you're just as guilty as the terrorists. To provide money to terrorists, you're guilty. And we will hold you account." And the Taliban found out what we meant.

We gave an ultimatum to Mr. Saddam Hussein. We said, "Get rid of your weapons." He ignored not only the United States but the civilized world. That regime is no more. And one thing is for certain: No terrorist organization will ever get a weapon of mass destruction from Mr. Saddam Hussein.

Our Nation is more secure. The world is becoming more free and, therefore, more peaceful. This Nation yearns for peace, but we understand the nature of the enemy. For those of you who have got relatives in the United States military, I want to thank you, for a grateful nation. And you thank them, on behalf of the Commander in Chief and the people of this country, for the sacrifices they are willing to make on behalf of the rest of us.

Economic security is on my mind. I'm sure the numbers are beginning to look better, but there's still people looking for work. My attitude is, so long as somebody is looking for work, then we've got to continue to try to create the conditions necessary for job growth. We want our people working. We want the moms and dads to be able to make a living, to be able to put food on the table for their children.

National security means economic security for every single citizen. And one of the lessons we learned a while ago was that a reliable, affordable electrical power is essential for economic growth in America. It's an essential part of an economic plan. If you're interested in creating jobs, you'd better have energy. You're not going to have an economy grow without reliable sources of energy.

Lights went out last month—you know that. [*Laughter*] It might have been good for candle sales, but it certainly wasn't good for—job growth. It recognizes that we've got an issue with our electricity grid, and we need to modernize it. We need to make sure it works in the future. The first thing we're going to do is find out what went wrong and address the problem. Secretary of Energy Spence Abraham, right here, from the State of Michigan, is leading that investigation. We want the facts. We'll put the spotlight of truth on the facts, and then we'll deal with it. But also, it's clear that the power grid needs an overhaul. It needs to be modernized. As we go into an exciting new period of American history, we want the most modern electricity grid for our people.

When I first got in in Washington, I put out a plan, a national energy strategy. I felt like we needed an energy strategy for the country. If energy is an issue, first of all you need a strategy and a plan. And we laid one out. And part of that plan modernizes—called for the modernization of the electricity grid. We need more investment. We need research and development to make sure we're—as we invest new technologies, they're the latest and best for the people of this country. We also want to make sure voluntary reliability standards for utilities are now mandatory reliability standards. When somebody says they're going to be reliable, we don't want it to be maybe reliable or perhaps reliable. We want mandatory reliability standards, so people can count on the deliver—to have their electricity delivered.

This is part of the plan I announced, as well as we've got to make sure that the energy we use, we have the best technologies to make sure we burn it as clean as we can. That's why I have a strong initiative for clean coal technology. We want to make sure we encourage conservation. But the truth of the matter is, we need to become less dependent on foreign sources of energy, For the sake of economic security.

We lead the world in new technologies when it comes to energy, and we not only can find new ways of producing energy and make sure we do so in an efficient way, we can make sure we do so in a clean way. You know right here what I'm talking about, at this plant. We lead the world in technologies to make the production of energy cleaner. And so therefore, I'm confident in predicting to the American people, not only can we promote job security and increase jobs, but we can do so in way that protects our environment. And I believe we have a duty to do so. I believe a responsible nation is one that protects the environment.

Yet the Government sometimes doesn't help. And that's what I'm here to discuss—[laughter]—those moments when the Government doesn't help, when the Government stands in the way. For example, powerplants are discouraged from doing routine maintenance because of Government regulations. And by "routine maintenance," I mean replacing wornout boiler tubes or boiler fans. And all that does is, it makes the plant less reliable, less efficient, and not as environmentally friendly as it should be. So I changed those regulations—my administration did. And I'm here to explain why we did, in a way that I hope the American people can understand.

Before I begin, I do want to thank Tony Earley for that introduction. I just had a great tour of your facility, Tony, by Paul—Paul Fessler. He said to make sure I didn't bring up the Michigan-Notre Dame game. [Laughter] So I won't bring it up. [Laughter]

I'm traveling today with Marianne Horinko, who is the Acting Administrator of the Environmental Protection Agency. She's a good, commonsense lady. She's smart. She's capable. She understands that we can grow our economy and protect the environment at the same time. It's not one or the other; it's both. When we talk about environmental policy in this Bush administration, we not only talk about clean air;

we talk about jobs. And I believe we can do both, and so does Marianne. I want to thank you for your service.

I thank Paul for the tour, and I was joined on the tour by Mike Smith, who is a senior union committeeman, Local 223. I appreciate Mike taking me around and introducing me to some of the fellow workers in the plants. At least the ones I met, morale seemed high. People enjoy working here. You're providing a service. For all the workers who work here, I want you to know you're providing an important service. You're creating the conditions so people can find a job. You're working hard to make sure somebody can turn on a light switch, and they can realize the comforts of modern life. Thanks for what you do.

I'm also traveling today with Members of the United States Congress, Congresswoman Candice Miller and Congressman Fred Upton. I want to thank you all for coming. I appreciate you being here. We've got the secretary of state, Terri Lynn Land, with us, the attorney general, Mike Cox, the speaker of the house, Rick Johnson, members of the—all working hard at the State level. I'm glad they are here too. And finally, Mayor Al is with us, the mayor of Monroe. Al Cappuccilli is here. Thank you, Mayor, for being with us. You must be filling the potholes—[*laughter*]—picking up the garbage—[*laughter*]—that's the way to go.

Today when I landed, I met Claire Jennings. Let me describe right quick—[*applause*]—it sounds like they know you, Claire. [*Laughter*] One of the things I try to do when I come to communities is to herald those folks who are volunteering their own time to make the world a better place. It's amazing the people I've been able to meet in our country. We've got all kinds of people from all walks of life taking time out to mentor a child or to take care of a—somebody who is lonely, to help heal a broken heart, surround somebody who hurts with love. It's really the strength of our country. I'm proud of

our military. I intend to keep our military strong. But the strength of the country is the heart and souls of our citizens. It's the willingness of people to lend a helping hand. What Claire has done is, she decided to enhance the wildlife growth around this plant. She decided to make this important facility a wildlife refuge as well.

And it worked. It's a beautiful setting. It's a wonderful—she's done a wonderful job, as have coworkers, in making sure the 800 acres here at the Monroe plant is spectacular to look at. And it will leave behind something like a legacy for future generations. So Claire, I want to thank you for setting a good example. I'm glad you brought your daughter too.

I said as plainly as I could that I believe we can grow our economy and protect the quality of our air at the same time. And we made progress doing just that. Let me give you a statistic or two. Our economy has grown 164 percent in three decades. That's pretty good growth. And yet, according to a report that the EPA is releasing today, air pollution from six major pollutants is down by 48 percent during that period of time. So you nearly double your economy, and yet pollution is down by nearly 50 percent.

That should say to people that we can grow our economy, that we can work to create the conditions for job growth, and that we can be good stewards of the air that we breathe. And this plant is a good example of that achievement. Since 1974, the power generated from here has increased by 22 percent. You've created more power so more people can live a decent life. And yet, the particulate matter emissions have fallen by 80—81 percent. You're good stewards of the quality of the air as well. You work hard in this plant to put energy on the grid, and at the same time, you're protecting the environment.

There's reason for this progress, and it's because our Nation made a commitment. Starting in the Clean Air Act of 1970, we set high goals. We said, "This is a national priority. Let's work together to achieve these priorities." And we are working together. This administration, my administration strongly supports the Clean Air Act, and I believe that by combining the ethic of good stewardship—in other words, convince people that it's an important goal—and the spirit of innovation, we will improve the quality of our air even further, and, at the same time, make sure people can find a job.

There is more to do, and so I want to talk about three ideas that—three commonsense steps that I put out to help us meet the new air quality standards and further improve quality of life. I hope you find that they make sense. They certainly do to me. They're commonsense ways to deal with our environment.

First, we're going after the pollution that comes from diesel vehicles. We worked with the energy companies and the agricultural concerns and the manufacturers; we worked with environment groups; we worked with union groups to come up with a commonsense policy. And we did. We developed one, and it's now being implemented. Oil companies will lower the sulphur in diesel fuel. We'll enforce new emission limits on diesel truck engines. And we're going to put forward new rules that will control pollution from off-road vehicles like heavy construction equipment. The stakeholders came; we developed good policy. Everybody is on board, and now we're headed toward a cleaner—cleaner quality air for all Americans.

Secondly, I proposed what's called Clear Skies legislation. Again, you heard the CEO talk about this legislation. Clear Skies legislation will help cut powerplant emissions without affecting job growth and/or jobs at this plant. We're interested in reducing the nitrogen oxide, sulphur dioxide in mercury, coming out of the powerplants around America. We've put forth a plan; we brought people in a room; we discussed it with them. The stakeholders agreed; union workers—union leaders have agreed; utilities have agreed; manufacturing companies have agreed to a plan that will reduce those three key pollutants by 70 percent over a reasonable period of time.

We've got an interesting approach. It's been tried in the past. It's a cap-and-trade system. We put mandatory caps on emissions. It's a little different look than maybe you're used to. Instead of the Government telling utilities where and how to cut pollution, we will work with them to create a cap, how much to cut and when we expect it cut by, but you figure out how. You're a lot better in figuring out the how than people in Washington, DC.

Each year, each facility will need a permit for each ton of pollution it emits. Companies that are able to reduce their pollution below the amount can sell the surplus to others that need more time to meet the national goal and the national standard. In other words, there's an incentive system built into it. The system makes it worthwhile for companies to invest earlier in controls and therefore pollute less. It ensures that high standards are met in a commonsense way that is cost-effective and saves jobs. And under the legislation, communities that have had trouble meeting air quality standards will finally have a clear and a more effective method to get them help.

I'm going to be talking about this tomorrow at the White House. I'll be doing it in Washington because I expect Congress to act. Instead of playing politics with environmental legislation, we need to come together and do what's right for American workers and American families. Clear Skies is good, sound legislation and needs to be passed.

Finally, I want to speak to one other matter. It's called New Source Review. We need to fix those and have—we're in the process of fixing what they call New Source Review regulations. After I explain it, I think it will make sense as to why we're doing it.

The old regulations, let me start off by telling you, undermined our goals for protecting the environment and growing the economy. The old regulations on the book made it difficult to either protect the economy or—protect the environment or grow the economy. Therefore, I wanted to get rid of them. I'm interested in job creation and clean air, and I believe we can do both.

One of the things we've got to do is encourage companies to invest in new technologies, convince utilities to modernize their equipment, so they can produce more energy and pollute less. In other words, as technologies come on, we want to encourage companies to make investment in those technologies. Yet old regulations, the ones we're changing, actually discourage companies from even making routine repairs and replacing old equipment. That's the reality. Regulations intended to enhance air quality made it really difficult for companies to do that which is necessary to not only produce more energy but to do it in a cleaner way.

Powerplants and companies wanted to make one change they could afford. The regulators could come in and order them to change everything, making every change a massive multiyear battle. That's the reality here at Monroe plant. The people who are trying to modernize this plant and do their job on behalf of the people of Michigan found out that the regulations were so complex that they could be interpreted any different way. And that's what happened. And when you have complex regulations that are open for interpretation, guess what happens? The lawyers come in. [*Laughter*] And then you have litigation, and then things grind to a standstill.

So a lot of planners and people who were charged with providing electricity and to protect the air decided not to do anything. They didn't want to have to fight through the bureaucracy or fight through the endless lawsuits. And when that happens, fewer powerplants are upgraded. They become old and tired, which means people start losing their jobs, which means our economy is not robust so people can find work if they're looking for work, which means some cases, energy costs are higher than they should be.

And so we decided to do something about it—I did. It's been in the process for a while, and I decided to move, particularly when I heard stories like this one here at Monroe. In 1999, Detroit Edison made a decision to upgrade the turbine steam generators here. That's a vital decision. For the men and women who work at that plant, you understand, when I say "vital decision," that it is a vital decision. The company wanted to give more efficient—wanted this plant to have new, efficient blades on the turbines, which will allow more electricity to be generated with the same amount of coal without causing emission increases. It seems like a common-sense policy. If I were running this plant, I would want to modernize it so we could produce more energy for the same amount of input and continue doing a good job of protecting the quality of the air. That's the kind of corporate behavior that I appreciate.

Yet when the company took the plan to the EPA, the first thing that happened is they had to wait a year for an answer. [*Laughter*] They said, "We've got a good way to do something, but please tell us if we can move forward." And the answer wasn't forthcoming. And when the answer did come back, it was so complicated, because the rules are so complicated, that Detroit Edison decided to delay part of the project until its experts could decipher the details of the ruling. On the one hand, the rules are so complex that the answer coming back was even more complex, evidently, because nothing happened for a while.

Now, finally, the project is going to be complete. Detroit Edison decided to move forward, 5 years after it decided to begin. That's inefficient. That doesn't make any sense. The quicker we put modern equipment into our powerplants, the quicker people are going to get more reliable electricity. If we're interested in job creation in America, we'd better have the most modern facilities to make sure that electricity is available so people can expand their job base. And yet the rules didn't let that happen. The rules created too many hurdles, and that hurts the working people.

And so, as I said, we decided to do something about it. We began to review the old rules and regulations. And we wanted to do so in a careful way. The EPA held five public meetings. More than 100 groups were represented, citizens and industry and local officials. There were thousands of comments. In other words, we said, "If you've got a problem with the change, please bring them forward. Or you support the change, bring them forward." We wanted to hear from people, and the EPA did a good job of collecting data.

In December, we issued the first set of rules to clarify and simplify regulations for manufacturers to do projects in an energy-efficient way and to promote policy that would discourage pollution. And now we've issued new rules that will allow utility companies like this one right here to make routine repairs and upgrades without enormous costs and endless disputes. We simplified the rules. We made them easy to understand. We trust the people in this plant to make the right decisions.

There is a lot of debate about New Source Review—the change of New Source Review. It makes sense to change these regulations. It makes sense for the workplace environment. It makes sense for the protection of our air. Not only do I believe that, but union leaders believe that. Manufacturers believe that. The utilities believe that. A bipartisan coalition in Congress believes it. We have done the right thing.

Monroe plant is a living example of why we acted. The people at this plant wanted to put the most modern equipment, use the most modern technology to make sure

the people of Michigan got energy at a reasonable and affordable price and at the same time protect the environment. Government policy prevented them from doing so. We have changed the Government policy for good of the people of this country.

I mentioned the challenges we face, but I'm an optimist, because I understand America. It's been my privilege to see the character of the American people. We are resolute. We're plenty tough when we have to be tough. We're also compassionate. Ours is a resourceful nation. We set goals, and we work together to achieve those goals. Ours is a nation that, when we hear that somebody is looking for work and can't find work, cares about that person.

I want to make sure this environment, economic environment of ours is as healthy as it can be. The American people have got to understand, a healthy economic environment means we'd better have energy. We'd better be producing that energy. There's electricity so people can expand their manufacturing facilities. If you've got an issue with the manufacturing base, you'd better make sure you've got a reliable supply of energy for the manufacturers, like they've got right here in Michigan.

We can overcome problems. We're smart and resourceful people. We're also a compassionate people, people who are willing to love a neighbor just like we love ourselves. That's what I love most about America. I love the fact that there are people who hurt—I love the fact that when somebody is hurting in your neighborhood, you're likely to walk across the street and say, "What can I do to help?" It's a fabulous country we have.

Oh yes, we've got problems, but there's no doubt in my mind, because of the character of the American people, we can overcome any problem that's in our way.

I want to thank you all for coming out today. May God bless you, and may God continue to bless America.

NOTE: The President spoke at 12:40 p.m. In his remarks, he referred to Anthony F. Earley, Jr., chairman and chief executive officer, DTE Energy; Paul Fessler, director, Monroe Power Plant; Mike Smith, chief steward, Utility Workers Union of America Local 223, Power Generation Division; Mayor Al Cappuccilli of Monroe, MI; and former President Saddam Hussein of Iraq.

Remarks at a Bush-Cheney Reception in Drexel Hill, Pennsylvania
September 15, 2003

The President. Thanks for your warm welcome. Thanks for coming out tonight. I'm honored so many showed up. Thanks for coming. Thanks for your friendship, and thanks for your strong support. I appreciate the generous contributions you have made. The truth of the matter is, what we're doing is we're laying the groundwork for what is going to be a great nationwide victory in November of 2004.

I'm going to count on you for more than just contributions. I need your help. I need you to put up the signs, to mail out the brochures. When you go to the coffee shop, you look them in the eye, and you tell them this administration has got a hopeful and optimistic vision for every single American.

There's a lot of talk in the air, a lot of political talk, and the truth of the matter is, I'm loosening up. [*Laughter*] I'm getting ready. But the political season will come in its own time. I've got a job to do. I'm focused on the people's business in Washington, DC. I've got a lot on the agenda, and I will continue to work hard to earn the confidence of all Americans by keeping this Nation secure and strong and prosperous and free.

Most of you probably wish you were at the fundraiser a month ago when Laura was the keynote speaker. [*Laughter*] If so, you've got great judgment. She's a fabulous First Lady.

Audience member. So was your Mom! [*Laughter*]

The President. I'm sorry she's not here tonight. And speaking about my mother, I'm still listening to her, by the way. [*Laughter*]

I want to thank my friend David for being a fine chairman. He's been a longtime friend. I've called upon him time and time again to help, and he's never let me down. David, thank you, and the great team you put together, for—[*applause*].

I've got two great campaign cochairmen for the State of Pennsylvania, two fine United States Senators, men with whom I work closely on key issues, Senator Santorum and Senator Specter. Thank you all for your—[*applause*]. Like me, Arlen married above himself. [*Laughter*] And I'm proud that Joan is with us today as well. Thank you for coming, Joan.

I'm also honored that members of the Pennsylvania congressional delegation are with us today, Congressman Gerlach, Congressman Weldon, Congressman Greenwood. Congressman Sherwood is with us. It's good that you brought your family, Don. From the great State of New Jersey, Congressman Jim Saxton is with us as well.

I'm also pleased that Attorney General Mike Fisher is with us today. General, thank you for coming. We've got another attorney general with us, from the State of Delaware, Jane Brady. Thank you for being here, Jane. I'm so pleased to be able to say hello to Bill Scranton. He's one of the great Pennsylvania political families. I'm honored you're here, Bill. Thank you for coming.

Finally, I have the pleasure of saying hello to a fantastic lady and her two children, Connie Katz. Connie is here. She is representing her husband, who is running a spirited campaign for the mayor of Philadelphia, Pennsylvania. And we're proud you're here.

I want to thank the grassroots activists who are here. I particularly want to thank Bob Asher, a national committeeman from Pennsylvania, and Alan Novak, who is the chairman. I thank my friend Mercer Reynolds, who is the national chairman of this campaign. He's from Cincinnati, Ohio, and he's taken a lot of time out of his life to help gather the resources necessary to wage a strong campaign in '04.

Finally, I want to thank Bill Kay, who is the owner of this establishment. I want to thank Bill and all the good folks who have worked hard to put on this event. Most of all, thank you all.

In the last 2½ years, our Nation has acted decisively to confront great challenges. I came to this office to solve problems, not to pass them on to future Presidents and future generations. I came to seize opportunities instead of letting them slip away. This administration is meeting the tests of our time.

Terrorists declared war on the United States of America, and war is what they got. We have captured or killed many key leaders of the Al Qaida network, and the rest of them know we're on their trail. In Afghanistan and in Iraq, we gave ultimatums to terror regimes. Those regimes chose defiance, and those regimes are no more. Fifty million people in those two countries once lived under tyranny, and now they live in freedom.

Two-and-a-half years ago, our military was not receiving the resources it needed, and morale was beginning to suffer. So we increased the defense budgets to prepare for the threats of a new era. And today, no one in the world can question the skill and the strength and the spirit of the United States military.

Two-and-a-half years ago, we inherited an economy in recession. And then the attacks came upon our country, as well as corporate scandals and the march to war, all of which affected the confidence of the American people. But we acted. We passed new laws to hold corporate criminals to account. And to get the economy going again, I have twice led the United States Congress to pass historic tax relief for the American people.

I believe and I know that when Americans have more take-home pay to spend, to save, or invest, the whole economy grows, and people are more likely to find a job. This administration also understands whose money we spend in Washington. It's not the Government's money. It's the people's money. We are passing more of the people's money so they can help raise their families. We're reducing the taxes on dividends and capital gains to encourage savings and investment. Small businesses now have new incentives to expand and to hire new people. With all these actions, we're laying the foundation for greater prosperity and more jobs, so that every single citizen of this country can realize the great promise of America.

Two-and-a-half years ago, there was a lot of talk about education reform, but there wasn't much action. So I acted. I called upon and Congress passed the No Child Left Behind Act. With a solid bipartisan majority, we delivered the most dramatic education reforms in a generation. We now bring high standards and strong accountability measures to every public school in America. We believe every child can learn the basics of reading and math, and we expect every school to teach the basics of reading and math. This administration is challenging the soft bigotry of low expectations. The days of excuse-making are over. We expect results in every single classroom, so that not one child is left behind.

We reorganized our Government and created the Department of Homeland Security to safeguard the borders and ports and to make America more secure. I picked a good man to run that Department. Tom Ridge is doing a great job. You trained him well. [*Laughter*]

We passed trade promotion authority to open up new markets for Pennsylvania's entrepreneurs and farmers and manufacturers. We passed much needed budget agreements to bring spending discipline to Washington, DC. On issue after issue, this administration has acted on principle, has kept its word, and has made progress for the American people.

The Congress gets a lot of credit. I appreciate working with Members of the Congress. Got a great relationship with the majority leader, Bill Frist, and Speaker Denny Hastert. We're going to continue to work together to try to change the tone of Washington, DC, to get rid of the needless bickering and endless politics and to focus on the people's business by focusing on results. Those are the kind of people I've asked to serve in my administration. I've put together a great team on behalf of America, good, honest, honorable citizens to serve the people of this country. Our country has had no finer Vice President than Dick Cheney. Mother may have a different opinion. [*Laughter*]

In 2½ years, we've done a lot. We have come far, but our work is only beginning. I have set great goals worthy of a great nation. First, America is committed to expanding the realm of freedom and peace, not only for our own security but for the benefit of the world. And second, in our own country, we must work for a society of prosperity and compassion, so that every citizen has a chance to work and to succeed and to realize the American Dream.

It's clear that the future of peace and freedom depend on the actions of America. This Nation is freedom's home. We are freedom's defender. We welcome this charge of history, and we are keeping it. Our war on terror continues. The enemies of freedom are not idle, and neither are we. This country will not rest; we will not

tire; we will not stop until this danger to civilization is removed.

We are confronting that danger in Iraq, where Saddam holdouts and foreign terrorists are desperately trying to throw that country into chaos by attacking coalition forces and aid workers and innocent Iraqis. They know that the advance of freedom in Iraq would be a major defeat for the cause of terror. This collection of killers is trying to shake the will of America and the civilized world. But America will not be intimidated.

We're aggressively striking the terrorists in Iraq, defeating them so we will not have to face them in our own country. We're calling on other nations to help to build a free Iraq, which will make them more secure. And we're standing with the Iraqi people as they assume more of their own defense and move toward self-government. These aren't easy tasks, but they're essential tasks. We will finish what we have begun. We will win this essential victory in the war on terror.

Our greatest security, however, comes from the advance of human liberty, because free nations don't support terror. Free nations don't attack their neighbors. Free nations do not develop weapons of mass terror to blackmail the world. Americans believe that freedom is the deepest need and hope of every human heart. And I believe that freedom is the right of every person, and I believe that freedom is the future of every nation.

America also understands that unprecedented influence brings tremendous responsibilities. We've duties in the world, and when we see disease and starvation and hopeless poverty, we will not turn away. On the continent of Africa, America is now committed to bringing the healing power of medicine to millions of men and women and children suffering with AIDS. This great, strong, compassionate Nation is leading the world in this important work of human rescue.

We face challenges here at home, and our actions will prove that we're equal to those challenges. So long as anybody who wants to work is looking for a job, means that I'll continue to work for an environment that encourages the entrepreneurial spirit to flourish, working hard to make sure the environment is such that jobs grow so people can find work.

We have a duty to keep our commitment to America's seniors by strengthening and modernizing Medicare. The Congress took historic action to improve the lives of older Americans. For the first time since the creation of Medicare, the House and the Senate have passed reforms to increase choices for our seniors and to provide coverage for prescription drugs. It is now time for both bodies to iron out their differences to get a good bill to my desk. It is time for the Congress to fulfill the promise of our seniors today and those of us who are going to be seniors tomorrow.

For the sake of our health care system, we need to cut down on the frivolous lawsuits which increase the cost of medicine. People who have been harmed by a bad doc deserve their day in court. Yet the system should not reward lawyers who are simply fishing for a rich settlement. Frivolous lawsuits drive up the cost of health care, and therefore, they affect the Federal budget. Medical liability reform is a national issue which requires a national solution.

I appreciate working with Congressman Greenwood. The House passed a good bill to reform the system. The bill is stuck in the United States Senate. Senators must realize that no one has ever been healed by a frivolous lawsuit in America. Not these people.

I have a responsibility as President to make sure the judicial system runs well, and I have met that duty. I have nominated superb men and women for our Federal courts, people who will interpret the law, not legislate from the bench. Members of— some Members of the United States Senate

are trying to keep my nominees off the bench by blocking up-or-down votes. Every judicial nominee deserves a fair hearing and an up-or-down vote on the Senate floor. It is time for some Members of the United States Senate to stop playing politics with American justice.

Congress needs to complete work on a comprehensive energy plan. The lessons of last summer ought to be an indication that we need to modernize our electricity grid. You all know it well here. I have submitted such a plan that will make the reliability standards mandatory, not voluntary, that will encourage new investment so we can say as we head into the 21st century, "We're doing everything we can to make sure power is available to the American citizens."

We need to use our technology to promote conservation. We need to be able to explore for energy in environmentally friendly ways. We need an energy plan. For the sake of economic security and for the sake of national security, this Nation needs to be less dependent on foreign sources of oil.

Our strong and prosperous Nation must also be a compassionate nation. I will continue to advance our agenda of compassionate conservatism, applying the best and most innovative ideas to the task of helping our fellow citizens who hurt. There are still millions of men and women who want to end their dependence on Government and become independent through hard work. Congress must build on the success of welfare reform to bring work and dignity into the lives of more of our fellow citizens. They should complete the "Citizen Service Act," so more Americans can serve their communities and their country. And both Houses should reach agreement on the Faith-Based Initiative, to support the armies of compassion that are mentoring our children and caring for the homeless and offering hope for the addicted. It's in our churches and synagogues and mosques, it's where we find Hindus and Jews and Christians and Muslims, that we find decency and compassion. This country should not fear faith in the important works of saving lives.

A compassionate society must promote opportunity for all, including the independence and dignity that come from ownership. This administration will constantly strive to promote an ownership society in America. We want more of our citizens owning their own home. We have a minority homeownership gap in America. I have submitted plans to the Congress to close that gap. We want more citizens owning and managing their own health care plans. We want our citizens owning and managing their own retirement accounts. We want more people owning their own business, because we understand that when a person owns something, he or she has a vital stake in the future of America.

In a compassionate society, people respect one another and take responsibility for the decisions they make. We're changing the culture of America from one that has said, "If it feels good, do it," and "If you've got a problem, blame somebody else," to a culture in which each of us understands we are responsible for the decisions we make in life. If you are fortunate enough to be a mom or a dad, you're responsible for loving your child with all your heart and all your soul. If you're worried about the quality of the education in the community in which you live, you're responsible for doing something about it. If you're a CEO in corporate America, you're responsible for telling the truth to your shareholders and your employees. And in a responsibility society, each of us is responsible for loving a neighbor just like we'd like to be loved ourselves.

We can see the culture of service and responsibility growing around us here in America. I started the USA Freedom Corps to encourage Americans to extend a compassionate hand to a neighbor in need. And

the response has been strong. Charities are strong. Our grassroots faith-based organizations are strong all across America. Policemen and firefighters and people who wear this Nation's uniform are reminding us what it means to sacrifice for something greater than yourself. Once again, the children of America believe in heroes, because they see them every day.

In these challenging times, the world has seen the resolve and the courage of America. And I've been privileged to see the compassion and the character of the American people. All the tests of the last 2½ years have come to the right nation. We're a strong country, and we use that strength to defend the peace. We're an optimistic country, confident in ourselves and in ideals bigger than ourselves.

Abroad, we seek to lift up whole nations by spreading freedom. At home, we seek to lift up lives by spreading opportunity to every corner of this country. This is the work that history has set before us, and we welcome it. And we know that for our country and for our cause, the best days lie ahead.

May God bless you all. Thank you all.

NOTE: The President spoke at 6:35 p.m. at Drexelbrook. In his remarks, he referred to David Girard-diCarlo, Pennsylvania State cochairman, Robert Asher, Pennsylvania finance cochairman, and Mercer Reynolds, national finance chairman, Bush-Cheney '04, Inc.; Joan Specter, wife of Senator Arlen Specter; Pennsylvania State Attorney General Mike Fisher; Connie Katz, wife of Philadelphia, PA, mayoral candidate Sam Katz, and their children, Philip and Lauren; Alan Novak, chairman, Pennsylvania Republican Party; L. William Kay II, managing partner, Drexelbrook Associates; and former President Saddam Hussein of Iraq.

Remarks on Proposed Clear Skies Legislation
September 16, 2003

Thank you all. Please be seated. Thanks for coming. The sky is clear—[*laughter*]—and we intend to keep it that way. I just met with a diverse group of our fellow citizens from the manufacturing sector, from organized labor, the environmental community. I met with Federal, State, and local officials. We had a good discussion about how to protect our environment and grow our economy. These groups don't always get along, but they agreed on this goal: The Nation must take the next bold step and continue to make our air cleaner with the Clear Skies legislation. And that's what we're here to talk about today.

The Clear Skies legislation will continue the great progress we have made against air pollution. Over the past three decades, we've reduced the Nation's air pollution by half. But there is more to do. Clear Skies legislation would further improve the health of our citizens, promote new technologies that would dramatically decrease emissions, help communities meet environmental standards, and help create new jobs for American workers. Congress must act on this initiative.

I appreciate members of my administration who are here to work on this initiative, Secretary Gale Norton of the Department of Interior and Marianne Horinko, who is the Acting Administrator of the EPA. Thank you both for coming.

I'm pleased to see that Senator Jim Inhofe of Oklahoma is here. He's the chairman of the Environment and Public Works Committee. I have spoken to the Senator right up there on the Truman Balcony about this issue. And he's committed to working with us to get a good piece of legislation moving. Mr. Senator, thank you for coming.

I also appreciate Senator Voinovich, who's the chairman of the Clean Air, Climate Change, and Nuclear Safety Sub-committee, for coming today, great State of Ohio. Thank you for coming, Senator.

I see my good friend Joe Barton from Texas who's here, the chairman. Mr. Chairman, we're glad you're here, the chairman of the Energy and Air Quality Subcommittee. I appreciate your interest in this topic. It's an important subject for America.

I want to thank Charlie Norwood, Congressman from Georgia, Fred Upton, Congressman from Michigan, John Sweeney, the Congressman from New York, John Shimkus, the Congressman from Illinois, and Wayne Gilchrest, the Congressman from Maryland. Thank you all for being here today.

We've got a nice diverse group of local officials who are with us today. Lieutenant Governor of Oklahoma Mary Fallin is here. Thank you, Governor. I'm glad you're here.

Jim Garner, who's the mayor of the village of Hempstead and, as importantly, is the president of the U.S. Conference of Mayors, thank you for coming, Mr. President. It's got a nice ring to it. [*Laughter*]

Mayor Bob Young of the city of Augusta is with us today. Bob, thank you for coming. State Senator Beverly Gard from Indiana is coming. She had an eloquent testimony about the need for us to make sure we have manufacturing jobs in America. Clear Skies is—addresses that issue. Thank you for coming, Senator.

Harry Alford, who is the president and CEO of the National Black Chamber of Commerce, is with us. Thank you, Harry. Bruce Davis, who is the president of Kanawha Manufacturing Company, is with us today. Steve Higdon, who is the president of the Greater Louisville Chamber of Commerce, is with us. He spoke eloquently about the need for legislation to make sure jobs in Louisville are saved.

Brian Houseal, who is the executive director of the Adirondack Council, for coming. I appreciate Brian being here. I was in the Adirondacks 2 years ago. Were you there, Sweeney? Yes, you were there. I think it was May, and it snowed. [*Laughter*] But it's such a beautiful part of our country. I want to thank you for your leadership on this issue.

Chuck MacFarlane, who is the president of Otter Tail Power Company. It is a small utility in the Dakotas, but it's an important part of making sure rural America has got a chance to succeed economically. And I say it's an important part—Otter Tail's viability is an important part, the capacity to bring electricity to our citizens is an important part of any economic plan.

Jerry Roberts is with us. I want to thank Jerry. He's from Monroe, the Monroe plant that we were at the other day. He's the treasurer of the Local 223, Utility Workers of America; it's an AFL–CIO affiliate. I want to thank you for coming.

See, what we're talking about is good for the working people of this country. What we're talking about makes sense for those who work for a living, and I'll explain why in a minute. I thank all the small-business leaders who are here and the community leaders. I want to thank you for your efforts, your deep concern about getting this legislation moving.

See, these people are here because they want a piece of legislation moving. They know we must get something done. And they're asking me what they could do in the room. And I said, "Well, I'm confident the chairmen are going to carry the load. We've just got to make sure that once these bills get moving, that the undecideds hear from us, that people understand the benefits as to why we need this legislation."

With the landmark Clean Air Act of 1970, our Nation set high goals for air quality. And this administration strongly supports those goals. I believe that by combining the ethic of good stewardship and the spirit of innovation, we will continue to improve the quality of our air and the health of our economy and improve the chance for people to have a good life here in America.

You know, a lot of times I talk about the fact that we can grow our economy and protect our environment. We've shown over the last decades that that is possible. Our economy has grown 164 percent in three decades. According to the EPA report released yesterday, air pollution from six major pollutants is down by 48 percent during that time. It's possible to grow the economy and protect the air. We're proving it here in America.

And so the question is, how do we not only continue that improvement but to do more in a way that makes sense? And that's what I want to discuss with you. I've got three ideas or three commonsense points that I want to talk about to improve the quality of our life here in America.

First, this administration is taking a strong stand when it comes to air pollution that comes from diesel vehicles. We made a bold step and a bold proposal. Before we made the proposal, we wisely sought advice from environmental groups, from agricultural concerns, from manufacturers, from energy companies, to develop a strategy that will reduce emissions from diesel use.

Oil companies will now lower the sulfur in diesel fuel. There will be tough new limits—emission limits on diesel truck engines. And we're putting forward sensible new rules that will control pollution from off-road vehicles like heavy construction equipment. We put together a good plan to deal with this important issue, a plan supported by a lot of interests.

Secondly, we're meeting new air quality standards by fixing some old regulations that weren't working very well. It's what they call New Source Review regulations. See, we want to encourage our companies to invest in new technologies and modernize equipment where possible, so that we can produce more electricity and pollute less. That's what we want to do. It makes sense, doesn't it, to have policy that says to a plant like the one we visited in Monroe yesterday, "We want to encourage you to get with the latest technology, so you can do your job of providing more electricity but do it in a way that protects the environment." Unfortunately, old regulations discourage companies from doing that. We had old regulations on the books that made it very difficult for utilities to make wise decisions.

As a matter of fact, it made it difficult for them to even have routine repairs or replace old equipment. You see, if powerplants or other companies wanted to make a change they could afford, under the old regulations, regulators would come in and order all kinds of changes. They would make it such that there would be a multiyear bureaucratic battle. See, the rules were so complex that they were open for interpretation.

Complex rules also opens decisions to litigation. You know, when something's really complex, it makes it easy for lawyers to sue and tie things up. Plant managers weren't able to put the latest technology in place to improve the quality of our air because of fear of bureaucratic battle and lawsuit. That didn't seem to make any sense to us in this administration, because we understand when plants become inefficient and old and stale and tired, the cost to the consumer goes up, reliability of energy supplies is decreased, jobs are lost. In fact, the spirit of the Clean Air Act is disregarded.

So we did something about it in this administration. We reviewed the old rules. We held public meetings. We had more than 100 groups participate in hearings. We considered thousands of comments. We had a good, healthy debate. And now we're taking action. We're replacing the old rules with simple, clear, easy-to-understand rules that will allow utility companies to make

routine repairs without enormous costs and enormous disruptions to their plants.

And the country is going to be better off for it. By changing the New Source Review regulations, Americans are going to have more reliable electricity at better cost, and the skies will be cleaner. And it was finally time to act, and this administration acted.

Third way to clean our air is through the Clear Skies proposal. This legislation sets mandatory limits on the pollution that contributes heavily to smog, to acid rain, and nitrogen deposits that damage our streams and our bays. Our goal over the next 15 years is to reduce sulfur dioxide emissions by 73 percent, nitrogen oxide emissions by 67 percent, and to have mandatory limits on mercury emissions, cutting those emissions by 69 percent. These standards will be set, and our powerplants will have the flexibility to meet the standards. That's an important part of this initiative.

Clear Skies will establish overall caps on emissions, and instead of Government telling utilities where and how to cut pollution, we will tell them how much to cut and when we expect progress to be made. Every year, each facility will need a permit of each ton of pollution it emits. Plants that can reduce their pollution below that amount are allowed to sell the surplus to other plants that need more time.

This is a system, cap-and-trade, with built-in incentives. It has worked in the past. It will make it financially worthwhile for companies to invest earlier in controls and therefore pollute less. And by taking this action—and I urge Congress to take the action—we'll have more affordable energy, more jobs, and cleaner skies. The people here today share a conviction that Clear Skies is a sound way to clean our air and keep the economy growing. And I'm sure when Congress looks at this initiative, they'll agree.

The Adirondack Council is here, and I want to thank you for coming. They support this approach. You see, they've seen cap-and-trade work. The forests in the Adirondacks were and are still threatened by acid rain. There was a severe problem. In 1990, the Congress set ambition goals for cutting, by half, pollution that leads to acid rain and created the cap-and-trade system I just described.

And the law—1990 law had an incredibly positive effect. The Adirondacks are on their way back. The damage from acid rain is being repaired, but there is more to do when it comes to acid rain. By placing stringent limits on the pollution that causes acid rain and harms our water, Clear Skies will help us to complete the job that was started in 1990. It's a good, sound piece of environmental legislation.

We've got State and local officials here. See, they support Clear Skies because they want their communities to be able to have clean air and good manufacturing jobs. Combined with the administration's rules on diesel emissions and Clear Skies, State and local leaders will have the ability to meet national standards without sacrificing good jobs—good manufacturing jobs.

See, there's now a tradeoff to be made. The rules are such that it's likely a lot of cities are going to lose the capacity to have good manufacturing jobs. A lot of inner-city people aren't going to be able to find work. The legislation on the books is counterproductive. We've got to change it with good, commonsense legislation. And that's what we're here to talk about.

This legislation has support from utility companies. Why? Because there will be certainty, and they'll be given the incentive and flexibility to invest in new technologies. And of course, the unions support it, because a reliable energy source is important for job creation. But think about all the jobs that will come as new technologies are installed in the plants.

No, there's a lot of benefit for this piece of legislation. I'm anxious to get it started in Congress. See, we've had to deal with some issues in this country. We've had to deal with the fact that too many of our citizens are looking for work. One way to make sure that the job supply is steady and growing in the long term is to have a realistic energy policy coupled with realistic environmental policy. It's a very important part of a growing job base. People need certainty when it comes to planning. People need to know the rules are going to encourage investment and change, not discourage it. People need to know there's going to be less lawsuits that prevent rational thought from going forward. People in this country must understand that we can have a pro-growth agenda, a pro-job agenda, and a pro-environment agenda at the same time, and Clear Skies legislation is just that.

I want to thank you for coming. I want to thank you for your interest. God bless you all.

NOTE: The President spoke at 2:38 p.m. in the East Garden at the White House. In his remarks, he referred to Mayor Bob Young of Augusta, GA; and Gerald Robertson, treasurer, Utility Workers Union of America Local 223.

Homeland Security Presidential Directive/HSPD–6—Directive on Integration and Use of Screening Information To Protect Against Terrorism
September 16, 2003

Subject: Integration and Use of Screening Information to Protect Against Terrorism

It is the policy of the United States to (1) develop, integrate, and maintain thorough, accurate, and current information about individuals known or appropriately suspected to be or have been engaged in conduct constituting, in preparation for, in aid of, or related to terrorism (Terrorist Information); and (2) use that information as appropriate and to the full extent permitted by law to support (a) Federal, State, local, territorial, tribal, foreign-government, and private-sector screening processes, and (b) diplomatic, military, intelligence, law enforcement, immigration, visa, and protective processes.

This directive shall be implemented in a manner consistent with the provisions of the Constitution and applicable laws, including those protecting the rights of all Americans.

To further strengthen the ability of the United States Government to protect the people, property, and territory of the United States against acts of terrorism, and to the full extent permitted by law and consistent with the policy set forth above:

(1) The Attorney General shall establish an organization to consolidate the Government's approach to terrorism screening and provide for the appropriate and lawful use of Terrorist Information in screening processes.

(2) The heads of executive departments and agencies shall, to the extent permitted by law, provide to the Terrorist Threat Integration Center (TTIC) on an ongoing basis all appropriate Terrorist Information in their possession, custody, or control. The Attorney General, in coordination with the Secretary of State, the Secretary of Home-

land Security, and the Director of Central Intelligence shall implement appropriate procedures and safeguards with respect to all such information about United States persons. The TTIC will provide the organization referenced in paragraph (1) with access to all appropriate information or intelligence in the TTIC's custody, possession, or control that the organization requires to perform its functions.

(3) The heads of executive departments and agencies shall conduct screening using such information at all appropriate opportunities, and shall report to the Attorney General not later than 90 days from the date of this directive, as to the opportunities at which such screening shall and shall not be conducted.

(4) The Secretary of Homeland Security shall develop guidelines to govern the use of such information to support State, local, territorial, and tribal screening processes, and private sector screening processes that have a substantial bearing on homeland security.

(5) The Secretary of State shall develop a proposal for my approval for enhancing cooperation with certain foreign governments, beginning with those countries for which the United States has waived visa requirements, to establish appropriate access to terrorism screening information of the participating governments.

This directive does not alter existing authorities or responsibilities of department and agency heads to carry out operational activities or provide or receive information. This directive is intended only to improve the internal management of the executive branch and is not intended to, and does not, create any right or benefit enforceable at law or in equity by any party against the United States, its departments, agencies, entities, officers, employees or agents, or any other person.

The Attorney General, in consultation with the Secretary of State, the Secretary of Homeland Security, and the Director of Central Intelligence, shall report to me through the Assistant to the President for Homeland Security not later than October 31, 2003, on progress made to implement this directive and shall thereafter report to me on such progress or any recommended changes from time to time as appropriate.

GEORGE W. BUSH

Remarks at the Rededication of the Rotunda at the National Archives
September 17, 2003

Speaker Hastert, Mr. Chief Justice, Justice Kennedy, Justice Thomas, Senator Frist and Senator Daschle, Representative Pelosi, Members of Congress, Governor Carlin, ladies and gentlemen: Laura and I are pleased to join with all of you for this morning's important ceremony. And all of us here today are honored to witness the unveiling of our Declaration of Independence, our original Constitution, and the Bill of Rights. Because of the careful, patient work carried out these last 2 years, all Americans and visitors from across the world can once again step forward and see our Nation's founding documents.

This new display is certainly preferable to the burlap sacks once used to carry the Declaration. Since the Declaration of Independence first left Philadelphia in a horse cart, the founding documents have been moved many times, including a secret trip to Fort Knox during World War II. For the last half-century, their home has been this Rotunda.

When President Harry Truman stood here 51 years ago, he rightly praised modern methods of document preservation. These methods served us well. In our day, preservation has become an even higher art, through the skill of conservators like those who accepted this very demanding assignment. The work of handling the fragile parchment and preparing it for these new encasements had to be difficult and must have been pretty nerve-wracking. I don't know how you practice for a job like that. [*Laughter*] But I do know there's little margin for error. And so, to all the professionals involved in this great task, we thank you for your work, and we thank you for the contribution to our country.

Many Americans have seen reproductions of the Declaration of Independence. A lot of us have seen reproductions of the Constitution. We know so well the first three words of our Constitution, "We the people." Yet, as familiar as these documents are, to see them in their originals is a moving experience. I hope a lot of our fellow citizens come to this Rotunda and see firsthand the work of our Founding Fathers.

Looking at the faded names of Hancock and Adams and Jefferson, Franklin, and others, you can better see the bravery behind the stirring words declaring independence. It was one thing to nod in agreement as the text was read and approved. It's quite another to take the quill and add your name, becoming at that instant the enemy of an empire. And each of the signers, as his pen moved across the page, had not only reached a great turning point in his own life but in the life of the world. The true revolution was not to defy one earthly power but to declare principles that stand above every earthly power, the equality of each person before God and the responsibility of government to secure the rights of all.

The courage of America's first leaders gave us the Declaration. Their patience and wisdom gave us the Constitution. They were patient through long and contentious and learned debates and discussions. They were wise in their understanding of human nature, with all its virtues and all the temptations. The supreme law of this land is the work of practical minds addressed to practical questions, like how to govern effectively and also limit the powers of government, how to represent the will of the people and to control the passions of temporary majorities. Framers devised answers that can now be found in constitutions across the world: Separate branches; enumerated powers; checks and balances; specific protections of the Bill of Rights.

Taken together, our founding documents set a standard that is the test and the burden of every generation. The text written by a slaveholder would become an unanswerable brief against slavery. The Constitution drafted and approved by men alone would, by its own logic, eventually assure the full participation of women. The ideals of our Founders were stronger than any flaws of the Founders. They rebuke our failures and guide our reforms. "These Charters of Freedom," said Martin Luther King, "are a promissory note, a pledge of justice to all who are denied it."

In the course of two centuries, the ideals of our founding documents have defined America's purposes in the world. Since July 4th, 1776, to this very day, Americans have seen freedom's power to overcome tyranny, to inspire hope even in times of great trial, to turn the creative gifts of men and women to the pursuits of peace. We have seen freedom's power in Europe and Asia and Africa and Latin America, and we will see freedom's power in the Middle East. Every person in every culture has the inalienable right to life, liberty, and the pursuit of happiness. America owns the Declaration of Independence and the Constitution, but the ideals they proclaim belong to all mankind.

This morning, exactly 216 years after the Constitutional Convention finished its business, the American people can take pride in the care we have given to preserving the work of the founding generation. Their words first guided a nation of scarcely 4 million souls. Yet even in their own day, the Founders knew they had put large events in motion, and free people everywhere remain in their debt.

In this Rotunda are the most cherished material possessions of a great and good nation. By this rededication, we show our deep respect for the first principles of our Republic and our lasting gratitude to those first citizens of the United States of America.

May God continue to bless our country. Thank you.

NOTE: The President spoke at 11 a.m. in the Rotunda for the Charters of Freedom at the National Archives and Records Administration. In his remarks, he referred to Archivist of the United States John Carlin.

Remarks Following a Meeting With the Congressional Conference Committee on Energy Legislation and an Exchange With Reporters
September 17, 2003

The President. I want to thank Members from both political parties for coming down here today to discuss the energy bill that's in conference. I really do appreciate the commitment of all the parties here at the table to work together to get an energy bill on behalf of the American people, a comprehensive energy plan that will address supply and conservation, help us modernize our electricity grid.

It's a compelling issue, and there was a good spirit here. Obviously, there's not 100-percent agreement, but there is agreement that we need to get something done. And I want to thank the Members. I want to thank the chairman and the ranking members for taking time to come.

And I'm pleased with the commitment by Senator Domenici and Congressman Tauzin to see if they can't get a bill down here by mid-October—I believe is what he told me—Billy—and to my desk. And we look forward to working with them. I think the American people are—know we need to have a national energy policy. And it's a chance to get it done, into law.

Thanks for coming. I'll answer a couple of questions. Terry [Terence Hunt, Associated Press], do you want to start?

U.N. Resolution on Iraq

Q. Mr. President, how is the administration recasting the proposed U.N. resolution on Iraq to meet the objections of some countries?

The President. We're still talking about it, Terry. I mean, we are—had some discussions this morning on it. The key is to make sure that the political situation in Iraq evolves in a way that will lead to a free and—a free society. The Iraqis need to develop a constitution and then have free elections. Then we can—and then we deal with the sovereignty issue. And so therefore, we're talking amongst ourselves.

King [John King, Cable News Network].

Saddam Hussein and the Attacks of September 11

Q. Mr. President, Dr. Rice and Secretary Rumsfeld both said yesterday that they have seen no evidence that Iraq had anything to do with September 11th. Yet, on "Meet the Press," Sunday, the Vice President said Iraq was a geographic base for the terrorists, and he also said, "I don't

know, or we don't know," when asked if there was any involvement. Your critics say that this is some effort—deliberate effort to blur the line and confuse people. How would you answer that?

The President. No, we've had no evidence that Saddam Hussein was involved with the September the 11th. What the Vice President said was, is that he has been involved with Al Qaida. And Al Zarqawi, Al Qaida operative, was in Baghdad. He's the guy that ordered the killing of a U.S. diplomat. He's a man who is still running loose, involved with the poisons network, involved with Ansar Al Islam. There's no question that Saddam Hussein had Al Qaida ties.

Caren [Caren Bohan], Reuters.

Energy Legislation

Q. Thank you, Mr. President.

The President. Step forth and speak.

Q. I know that the ANWR drilling provision is very important to you, but are you willing to sacrifice it to get a broader bill?

The President. One thing I've learned, Caren, is not to negotiate with myself, particularly in front of cameras. The conferees will work as hard as they can to come up with a good bill that can pass both bodies. And we look forward to working with them. I think it's very important for our country to recognize that we need to become less dependent on foreign sources of crude and, therefore, find ways to do that. We had a good discussion. That's certainly a contentious issue, and you'll find strong opinions around the table about this. And the job of the conferees is to work through these issues, and we look forward to helping them.

Yes, final question.

Funding for Domestic Priorities and Iraqi Reconstruction

Q. Mr. President, how do you respond——

The President. Identify yourself, please.

Q. Pam Fessler from NPR.

The President. Oh, Pam, of course—[*in-audible*]. How do I respond?

Q. How do you respond to criticism that you are asking for $20 billion in aid to reconstruct Iraq at a time when a lot of domestic work, such as the No Child Left Behind and the Help America Vote Act are not being fully funded?

The President. Well, I will start with—by responding this way: The No Child Left Behind funding is the largest increase in elementary and secondary school funding in a long time. And the Title I part of the Elementary and Secondary School Act funding is a large increase as well—historic increases.

Secondly, that it is vital that we succeed in Iraq, that a free Iraq will make America more secure. A free Iraq will change the dynamics of the Middle East, which will be important for peace. And I appreciate the support of Congress and the understanding of Congress that we will succeed in Iraq. And so the $20 billion is to help rehabilitate that country, so that the people of that country can live a free and hopeful life.

Listen, thank you all for coming.

NOTE: The President spoke at 4:48 p.m. in the Cabinet Room at the White House. In his remarks, he referred to former President Saddam Hussein of Iraq; senior Al Qaida associate Abu Musab Al Zarqawi; and USAID officer Laurence Foley, who was killed in Amman, Jordan, on October 28, 2002.

Letter to the Speaker of the House of Representatives Transmitting a Supplemental Appropriations Request for Ongoing Military and Intelligence Operations in Iraq, Afghanistan, and Elsewhere
September 17, 2003

Dear Mr. Speaker:

Two years ago, we responded to attacks on America by launching a global war against terrorism that has removed gathering threats to America and our allies and has liberated the Iraqi and Afghan people from oppression and fear.

America is making steady progress in the war on terror. Nearly two-thirds of al Qaeda's leadership has been captured or killed. In Afghanistan, we removed the Taliban from power and shut down terrorist training camps. In Iraq, we led a coalition that removed a dangerous tyrant who sponsored terror, possessed and used weapons of mass destruction, and for 12 years defied the clear demands of the United Nations Security Council.

Today, I am submitting a request for 2004 supplemental appropriations for ongoing military and intelligence operations in Iraq, Afghanistan, and elsewhere. Our men and women in uniform, alongside our coalition partners, are bringing peace and stability to Iraq and fighting the terrorist threat. In Afghanistan, our Armed Forces continue to track down terrorists and provide security as the Afghan people rebuild their nation. Our commitment to ongoing operations against terrorism is worthy of our country and critical to our security.

My request also supports the Coalition Provisional Authority's reconstruction operations in Iraq and supports reconstruction efforts in Afghanistan. These reconstruction funds are essential to secure the transition to self-government and to create conditions for economic growth and investment. By helping the Iraqi and Afghan people build free and democratic nations, America and our allies are bringing freedom and hope to a troubled region, and undermining a key base of operations for terrorists. The sooner we achieve these conditions, the sooner our troops will return home.

This request reflects urgent and essential requirements. I ask the Congress to appropriate the funds as requested, and promptly return the bill to me for signature. I hereby designate the specific proposals in the amounts requested herein as emergency requirements. I urge the Congress not to attach items that are not directly related to the emergency abroad.

The details of the request are set forth in the enclosed letter from the Director of the Office of Management and Budget.

Sincerely,

GEORGE W. BUSH

NOTE: An original was not available for verification of the content of this letter.

The President's News Conference With King Abdullah II of Jordan at Camp David, Maryland
September 18, 2003

President Bush. Thanks for coming. His Majesty and I will answer some questions after a couple of statements.

First, I'm so pleased to welcome my friend King Abdullah and Queen Rania to Camp David. I want to thank them so very much for rearranging their schedules to get up here ahead of Hurricane Isabel. Laura and I look forward to spending some quality time with two really fine people.

We're going to have some serious discussions today. Then we'll have a nice lunch, and then we'll batten down the hatches and spend a good evening with our friend. The King is a good friend, and I say with certainty he is a fine man. He's a reformer who's working to build a country that is tolerant and modern and prosperous. He cares deeply for the people of Jordan. I know firsthand. I have seen his passion for the people in that important country. He suffers when people suffer. He exults when people succeed. He's a leader who takes risk for peace. He's a peaceful man.

King Abdullah and I last met more than 3 months ago in Aqaba, Jordan. He hosted a very important meeting. It was a moment of great hope for the people of the Middle East. At that meeting, Prime Minister Abbas—former Prime Minister Abbas strongly condemned terror. Prime Minister Sharon committed Israel to supporting the emergence of a viable Palestinian state. The King affirmed the commitment of his country to help forge a lasting peace.

In the weeks that followed, there was good progress. Israel withdrew from Gaza City and Bethlehem and turned responsibility for security in—there over to the Palestinian Authority. Hundreds of prisoners were released. Checkpoints were removed. Some unauthorized outposts were taken down.

And on the Palestinian side, Prime Minister Abbas made a good-faith effort to meet the commitments made at Aqaba. Yet, at every turn, he was undercut by the old order. I remain committed, solidly committed, to the vision of two states living side by side in peace and security. Yet, that would only happen with new Palestinian leadership committed to fighting terror, not compromised by terror.

I look forward to discussing with His Majesty how we can encourage Palestinian reform, how we can work together to fight off the terrorists who want to destroy the hopes of many, and how we can move forward to peace, peace in a region that needs peace.

I appreciate the King's cooperation in the critical efforts to build a stable Iraq. The hearts of the American people go out to the people of Jordan for the ruthless attack on the Embassy in Baghdad. That attack just once again shows the nature of terror, indiscriminate killing of innocent people, all trying to intimidate and create fear.

I look forward to hearing His Majesty discuss his efforts to continue to work for long-lasting jobs for the Jordanian people, how we can work together to expand trade, what we can do together to enhance our friendship that has endured across the generations. Today, as the United States works to bring—helps to work to bring peace and hope to the Middle East, we can rely on Jordan as a vital partner. And that's why Laura and I are so honored to welcome you, sir, to Camp David, and thank you for coming.

King Abdullah. Thank you very much, Mr. President, for those very kind words of welcome. And I'm particularly delighted, myself and my wife, Rania, and our delegation, to really be able to visit with you again and discuss many of the issues that are facing both our countries.

I'm also particularly honored by the strong, genuine dedication that you have shown in trying to make our part of the world a better place. It took a lot of courage to come to the Middle East, to meet in Sharm el-Sheikh with Arab leaders, and then again to come to Aqaba and give hopes to the Israelis and Palestinians to move forward. And as you rightly said, we did see progress.

Unfortunately, there is a lull at the moment. But again, your dedication to really reach out to the overwhelming majority of Israelis and Palestinians that have been suffering for so many years and put your heart behind making their future far more hopeful. And this is what I believe this weekend is all about. The President has always been committed to solving the problems of the Middle East. And I've seen, from personal experience, his outward dedication to make a hope for Israelis and Palestinians—equally so, your dedication and your desire for

Iraqis to have a new dawn. And we're extremely appreciative of the time that you are spending with us over the weekend to see what we can do together to face the challenges ahead of us.

So a warm thanks from myself and my delegation for your dedication, your continued friendship, and really, your genuine desire to make life for all of us in the Middle East a much better place. Thank you very much.

President Bush. Thank you, sir. Thanks. Terry [Terence Hunt, Associated Press].

Reform of the Palestinian Authority

Q. Mr. President, you have refused to talk with Yasser Arafat. And Israel says that it's going to remove him. Yet, he is picking ministers for the new Prime Minister and is in virtual control of the Government. How are you going to deal with the Arafat situation in terms of Middle East peace? And is it possible to continue to go around him?

President Bush. Mr. Arafat has failed as a leader. And as I mentioned, Prime Minister Abbas was undermined at all turns by the old order—that meant Mr. Arafat. And the people of the Palestinian territory must understand if they want peace, they must have leadership who is absolutely 100 percent committed to fighting off terror. I believed Prime Minister Abbas when he told me at Sharm el-Sheikh, then at Aqaba, then in the Oval Office, he would do everything in his power to fight terror, that he would work to consolidate the security forces so that he could fight terror. And his efforts were undermined, and that's why we're now stalled. I'm still committed to peace, because I believe the vast majority of people want peace. I'm committed to the roadmap.

But I'll remind those who focus on the roadmap that the first thing the roadmap said was that there must be security in order for peace to advance, that there must be a collective effort to fight off terror. Mr. Arafat has failed in that efforts. And hopefully, at some point in time, a leadership of the Palestinian Authority will emerge which will then commit itself 100 percent to fighting off terror. And then we'll be able to consolidate the power necessary to fight off terror.

And when that happens, the world will come together to provide the conditions for hope. The world will come together to help an economy grow so that the Palestinian people can have a hopeful future. The first thing that must happen is an absolute condemnation and defeat of those forces who will kill innocent people in order to stop a peace process from going forward.

Your Majesty, do you want to call on somebody?

Terrorism and the Roadmap for Peace

Q. Your Majesty, the roadmap provides a monitoring system to ensure that Israelis and Palestinians are fulfilling their obligations, and the U.S. has its own envoy in the region to monitor the process. What about enforcing stricter monitoring mechanism involving the Quartet and the international community?

King Abdullah. Well, I think these are some of the issues that we can discuss. I think it's more important now to see how we can move the process back on track. I'm sure monitoring and other issues out there can be discussed at a later date. We're talking now about the principle of getting the movement forward again and Israelis and Palestinians engaging positively in the right direction.

President Bush. Let me remind—I gave a speech on June 24, 2002, which laid out a vision for how to achieve peace. And I said, "Everybody has got responsibilities." His Majesty has assumed his responsibility. He's a leader. He has stood up and said, "Look, we will work for a peaceful solution." Other leaders in the region must do the same. We must cut off money to terrorist organizations. We must work together. Israel has got responsibilities.

But let me remind you that it is very difficult to stay on a road to peace when there are terrorists bombing and killing people. And that's what must be stopped. In order for there to be a peace, we must stop terror, and it requires a collective effort. All people are responsible.

And the speech I gave on June 24th still stands as—at least the U.S. view—of how to achieve what we want, which is peace and a Palestinian state. I think a Palestinian state is one of the most hopeful things for a—for the Palestinian people and for the Israelis, for that matter.

But first things first, defeat those who want to stop this from happening. And make no mistake about it, the terrorists who are bombing and killing aren't interested in a peaceful Palestinian state. They don't share our mutual vision, a peaceful vision and a hopeful vision.

Steve [Steve Holland, Reuters].

European Support in Iraq

Q. Thank you. Do you think you can count on Europeans to provide financial contributions for Iraq? And what happens if they don't?

President Bush. Do I think that we can count on the Europeans to provide? Yes, I think we're getting help, and I would remind you that there is a—two multinational divisions led by—one led by Britain, one led by Poland—full of other European countries. And I—that's help. In terms of reconstruction, A, we're getting help, and—because Colin Powell will continue to ask for help.

One of the things I must do and will continue to do is make the case that a peaceful and secure Iraq is not only in the interests of the neighborhood—certainly in Jordan's interest that there be a nation that is peaceful and prosperous—but it's in Europe's interest as well, and the Americans' interest. You see, freedom in Iraq will change the nature of the neighborhood in a positive way. A free Iraq will mean this good man will have a partner in peace, somebody with whom he can work—to not only establish good trade but to work for additional peace. And it's in Europe's interest that that happen.

And so we will continue to make the case that reconstruction aid is necessary. And we'll also remind our European friends that we're making good progress there, that businesses are beginning to flourish; hospitals are open; pregnant women are receiving medicines; young children are getting vaccinated. I mean, there's case after case after case where life is improving for the average Iraqi citizen. And we would hope that they would participate in this momentum that is taking place on a daily basis.

It is—and I can't—we'll see. I will have a much better feel for attitude after next week. As you know, I'll be at the United Nations General Assembly. We'll be giving an address there Tuesday morning, and then we'll be meeting with a variety of world leaders. His Majesty and I, he will be giving me a report on what he knows. He's got pretty good antennae. He's well plugged-in, and he knows what's going on in the world, and he also is—he has got good friends in Europe and he will—part of our discussions will center on how best to broaden the coalition of participants.

Yes.

U.N. Resolution on Iraq/Hurricane Isabel

Q. Do you expect you'll have a U.N. resolution by the time you get to New York?

President Bush. Probably not. We're still working it. The question was, will we have a U.N. resolution by the time I get to New York? No, I don't think so, but it could be. We'll continue to work it, though. And the whole purpose, of course, is to make sure that the nations feel—if they need a U.N. resolution, they'll have one, in order to justify participation.

And the other thing, of course, is that the U.N. resolution must promote an orderly transfer of sovereignty to what will be a freely elected government based upon a constitution. So in other words, we must have—the constitution must be written, and there will be free elections, and then sovereignty will occur once the Iraqi people are able to express their opinions. And so we'll be working on that as well.

Listen, thank you all for coming. We appreciate you all as well adjusting your schedules. I know this was supposed to take place at a different time, but we wanted to get this over with, so that you didn't have to float down the hill, if you know what I mean.

And by the way, we're very well prepared for Hurricane Isabel. I met this morning by SVTS—that's video conferencing—with Tom Ridge and John Gordon of the NSC staff, fully briefed on the path of the storm. I'm assured that the Homeland Security Department is in close contact with the States' emergency preparedness offices. We've got prepositioned equipment in place. Proper warnings have gone out, and the communications systems are up and running, so that when the storm hits, the response for the citizens will be an effective response. And we'll—of course, I'll be monitoring the situation. I'll be in close contact with the emergency management people.

All right, get going before it starts raining. Thank you all very much.

NOTE: The President's news conference began at 10 a.m. In his remarks, he referred to former Prime Minister Mahmoud Abbas (Abu Mazen) and Chairman Yasser Arafat of the Palestinian Authority; and Prime Minister Ariel Sharon of Israel. A reporter referred to Prime Minister-designate Ahmed Korei of the Palestinian Authority.

Message to the Congress on Continuation of the National Emergency With Respect to Persons Who Commit, Threaten To Commit, or Support Terrorism
September 18, 2003

To the Congress of the United States:

Section 202(d) of the National Emergencies Act (50 U.S.C. 1622(d)) provides for the automatic termination of a national emergency unless, prior to the anniversary date of its declaration, the President publishes in the *Federal Register* and transmits to the Congress a notice stating that the emergency is to continue in effect beyond the anniversary date. Consistent with this provision, I have sent the enclosed notice, stating that the national emergency with respect to persons who commit, threaten to commit, or support terrorism is to continue in effect beyond September 23, 2003, to the *Federal Register* for publication. The most recent notice continuing this emergency was published in the *Federal Register* on September 20, 2002 (67 FR 59447).

The crisis constituted by the grave acts of terrorism and threats of terrorism committed by foreign terrorists, including the terrorist attacks in New York, Pennsylvania, and against the Pentagon committed on September 11, 2001, and the continuing and immediate threat of further attacks on United States nationals or the United States that led to the declaration of a national emergency on September 23, 2001, has not been resolved. These actions pose a continuing unusual and extraordinary threat to the national security, foreign policy, and economy of the United States. For these reasons, I have determined that it is necessary to continue the national emergency declared with respect to persons who commit, threaten to commit, or support terrorism and maintain in force the comprehensive sanctions to respond to this threat.

GEORGE W. BUSH

The White House,
September 18, 2003.

NOTE: An original was not available for verification of the content of this message. The notice of September 18 is listed in Appendix D at the end of this volume.

Letter to Congressional Leaders Reporting on Efforts in the Global War on Terrorism
September 19, 2003

Dear Mr. Speaker: (Dear Mr. President:)

On September 24, 2001, I reported the deployment of various combat-equipped and combat support forces to a number of locations in the Central and Pacific Command areas of operation. On October 9, 2001, I reported the beginning of combat action in Afghanistan against al-Qaida terrorists and their Taliban supporters. In my reports to the Congress of March 20 and September 20, 2002 and March 20, 2003, I provided supplemental information on the deployment of combat-equipped and combat support forces to a number of foreign nations in the Central and Pacific Command areas of operations and other areas. As a part of my efforts to keep the Congress informed, I am reporting further on United States efforts in the global war on terrorism.

Our efforts in Afghanistan continue to meet with success, but, as I have stated in my previous reports, the United States campaign against terrorism will be lengthy. To date, U.S. Armed Forces, with the assistance of numerous coalition partners, have executed a superb campaign to eliminate the primary source of support to the terrorists who viciously attacked our Nation on September 11, 2001. The heart of al-Qaida's training capability has been seriously degraded. The Taliban's ability to brutalize the Afghan people and to harbor and support terrorists has been virtually eliminated. Pockets of al-Qaida and Taliban forces remain a threat to United States and coalition forces and to the Afghan government. What is left of both the Taliban and the al-Qaida fighters is being pursued actively and engaged by United States and coalition forces.

Due to our success in Afghanistan, we have detained hundreds of al-Qaida and Taliban fighters who are believed to pose a continuing threat to the United States and its interests. The combat-equipped and combat support forces deployed to Naval Base, Guantanamo Bay, Cuba, in the Southern Command area of operations since January 2002 continue to conduct secure detention operations. We currently hold more than 650 enemy combatants at Guantanamo Bay.

In furtherance of our worldwide efforts against terrorists who pose a continuing and imminent threat to the United States, our friends and allies, and our forces abroad, we continue operations in other areas around the globe. We continue to work with the Government of the Philippines to protect United States and Philippine citizens and to defeat international terrorism in the Philippines.

We continue to conduct maritime interception operations on the high seas in the Central and European Command areas of responsibility and have expanded these efforts to the Pacific Command areas of responsibility to prevent the movement, arming, or financing of international terrorists who pose a continuing threat to the United States.

Combat-equipped and combat support forces also have been deployed to Georgia and Djibouti to assist in enhancing counterterrorism capabilities. The United States forces headquarters element in Djibouti provides command and control support as necessary for military operations against al-Qaida and other international terrorists in the Horn of Africa region, including Yemen. We continue to assess options for working with other nations to assist them in this respect.

I have taken these actions pursuant to my constitutional authority to conduct United States foreign relations and as Commander in Chief and Chief Executive. In addition, these actions are consistent with Public Law 107–40. As I stated in my previous reports, it is not possible to know at this time either the duration of combat operations or the scope and duration of the deployment of U.S. Armed Forces necessary to counter the terrorist threat to the United States. I will direct additional measures as necessary to exercise our right to self-defense and to protect United States citizens and interests. Such measures may include short notice deployments of special operations and other forces for sensitive operations in various locations throughout the world.

I am providing this report as part of my efforts to keep the Congress informed, consistent with the War Powers Resolution and Public Law 107–40. Officials of my Administration and I have been communicating regularly with the leadership and other Members of Congress, and we will continue to do so. I appreciate the continuing support of the Congress in our efforts to protect the security of the United States of America and its citizens, civilian and military, here and abroad.

Sincerely,

GEORGE W. BUSH

NOTE: Identical letters were sent to J. Dennis Hastert, Speaker of the House of Representatives, and Richard B. Cheney, President of the Senate.

Letter to Congressional Leaders Transmitting a Report on the Decision on Investments by Singapore Technologies Telemedia Pte. Ltd.
September 19, 2003

Dear Mr. Speaker: (Dear Mr. President:)

Attached is a classified report on my decision to take no action to suspend or prohibit the proposed 61.5 percent investment by Singapore Technologies Telemedia Pte. Ltd., a company indirectly owned by the Government of Singapore, in Global Crossing Ltd. I have taken this decision under the authority vested in me as President by section 721 of the Defense Production Act of 1950, also known as the "Exon-Florio"

provision, 50 U.S.C. App. 2170. This report, prepared by my Administration, is submitted consistent with subsection (g) of that provision.

Sincerely,

GEORGE W. BUSH

NOTE: Identical letters were sent to J. Dennis Hastert, Speaker of the House of Representatives, and Richard B. Cheney, President of the Senate.

The President's Radio Address
September 20, 2003

Good morning. Every day, millions of Americans put in long hours building businesses of their own. Their hard work strengthens the economy, creates most of the new jobs in America, and supplies the innovation that drives our future prosperity. As we mark National Small Business Week, our Nation honors the enterprise and hard work of small-business owners and employees.

Small businesses are a key to upward mobility, particularly for women and minorities. There are over 3 million minority-owned small businesses across America, and that number is rising. And women-owned businesses now employ more than 9 million Americans. For the sake of all small businesses and our entire economy, my administration is pursuing an aggressive pro-growth, pro-jobs agenda.

The tax relief I have signed since I took office will save 25 million small-business owners an average of more than $2,800 this year. Income tax relief is particularly helpful for business owners who pay their business taxes at their individual income tax rates. We have reduced the burden of unnecessary regulation on small businesses, and we have passed much needed incentives for investment and new equipment, which will help our small businesses grow and create high-paying jobs.

These policies are working. A recent survey of small businesses shows rising optimism among owners, evidence of improving sales, and more plans to invest and hire new workers. This is good news for our communities and good news for people looking for work. Still, there is more to be done. I have proposed a six-point plan to create jobs, strengthen small businesses, and build employer confidence.

First, people are more likely to find work if we can control health care costs. We can help by allowing small businesses to band together and pool their risks so they have the bargaining power of big companies. Also, I have proposed reasonable limits on the lawsuits that are raising health care costs for everyone.

Second, we need to address the broader problems of frivolous litigation. We need effective legal reforms that will make sure that settlement money from class actions and other litigation goes to those harmed and not to trial lawyers.

Third, we need a sound national energy policy. Growing businesses depend on affordable and reliable supplies of energy and a modern electrical grid so that we can avoid crippling blackouts. I submitted an energy bill to the Congress 2 years ago, and it's time for Congress to pass it so I can sign it into law.

Fourth, we must continue to reduce the burden of needless regulation on employers. My administration's policy is to make sure every proposed regulation does not place an undue burden on the small businesses of America.

Fifth, we are encouraging trade by opening markets for our goods and services.

When the rules are fair and enforced and the playing field is level, our workers, farmers, ranchers, and small-business owners can compete with anybody in the world.

Sixth, we need to make sure tax relief is permanent. Businesses and families need to have the confidence that all the benefits of tax relief will not disappear in coming years. And small-business owners, ranchers, farmers want the death tax buried for good.

Over the past 2 years, Americans have been tested at home and abroad, but our confidence and optimism have never wavered. We are defending the peace of the world. We are building the prosperity of our country. And we are turning loose the great energy and enterprise of one of the Nation's great strengths, the drive and determination of our entrepreneurs.

Thank you for listening.

NOTE: The address was recorded at 6:40 p.m. on September 17 in the Cabinet Room at the White House for broadcast at 10:06 a.m. on September 20. The transcript was made available by the Office of the Press Secretary on September 19 but was embargoed for release until the broadcast. The Office of the Press Secretary also released a Spanish language transcript of this address.

Remarks Following a Briefing on Hurricane Damage at the Virginia State Police Academy in Richmond, Virginia
September 22, 2003

If I may have your attention for a second, first, I want to thank Governor Warner for his hospitality and leading this important State through Hurricane Isabel. I also want to congratulate those of you who work with me at the Federal level. You're doing a fabulous job, and I'm proud of you. I know a lot of you have come from other parts of our country and your

families are at home, and I want to thank you for just taking a little extra effort to help a fellow citizen in need.

The response to this hurricane has been really great. The planning for it has been great. The response during the hurricane was great, and the response after the hurricane has been great. And I want to thank you all for working hard to make it happen.

You make me proud to be a fellow employee of the people at the Federal level.

We've got a lot of work to do. The Governor and I were discussing the needs here of the citizens of Virginia. We're going to keep working hard to get the electricity up and running. There are crews working 24/7 so that people can get the electricity they need. I was talking to Congressman Bobby Scott and Congressman Eric Cantor about the needs of their district. And they're, like the Governor, deeply concerned about the fact that too many of the citizens don't have electricity. A lot do now, but too many don't. But I want to thank the companies for bringing in extra workers. And I want to thank those workers, who are manning the chainsaws and getting the lines back up so people can have electricity.

In the meantime, we're working to make sure that we get water and ice to the people so that they can move on with their lives. I want to thank the local folks, State folks, and the county and city police, firefighters and emergency responders and the mayors for their hard work as well. The truth of the matter is, the frontline on any emergency is the local people. And you've done your State proud, and you've done your citizens proud.

I want to thank the people who are loving their neighbor just like they'd like to be loved themselves. There's a lot of neighborliness taking place in the State of Virginia and North Carolina and Maryland, where somebody hurts and somebody's lonely, somebody needs help is finding refuge and solace because a fellow citizen has taken it upon him or herself to help somebody in need.

You know, the true character of this country comes out during times of stress and emergency. And this country has responded once again. So on behalf of a grateful nation, I want to thank people at all levels of our Government for working extra hard to help our country when it needed help.

May God bless those who hurt. May God bless those who still mourn the loss of life. And may God continue to bless America. Thank you all very much.

NOTE: The President spoke at 2:54 p.m. In his remarks, he referred to Gov. Mark Warner of Virginia.

Remarks Following Discussions With Iraqi Ministers
September 22, 2003

President Bush. We're going to have a couple of statements here. First, it's my honor to welcome two Ministers from Iraq—free Iraq—the Minister of Public Works, the Minister of Electricity, people charged with improving the lives of the Iraqi citizens, people who the Governing Council has picked to lead these ministries.

And we've had a fascinating discussion. These two good souls have found that the system wasn't conducive for—the system they inherited was not conducive for taking care of the citizens. It was a—the infra- structure was old and tired; power was centralized. Really, they inherited a system of a corrupt tyrant.

And their job now is to improve life. I love their spirit. I love the fact that they are dedicated to doing their jobs. And I also appreciate the appraisal of what's going on in Iraq, the assessment that we're making good progress toward achieving our objective.

So thank you all for coming here to America. We're proud of you and proud of you being pioneers for a free people. And welcome.

If you'd like to say a few words, Madam Minister, we'd like to hear them.

Minister Nesreen Berwari. Well, on September 3d, the Governing Council formed an Iraqi Government. And this has been the most significant move after two steps before that. Forming the Government and Iraqis taking care of their own affairs has been received very well by the Iraqi people.

A sense of progress is being sensed in the streets of Iraq. More work is being done. And the work on restoring services to pre-war levels has been achieved. Now we're working on planning for the next year program. We have great plans to improve services. Our mission is to show a different governance. We want to tell the Iraqis that the change that has happened 4 months ago is for their own benefit, through improving the public service.

But also investing on Iraq that can become an asset to itself and to the rest of the world, an Iraq that can add values of peace and prosperity to itself, to the region, and to the rest of the world. A working Iraq is in the best interests of everybody, and you don't have to do a lot of investment, because Iraq is rich, rich with people, rich with oil, rich with water. We only needed help in the beginning, and we will do it ourself and contribute to the rest of the world.

Our visit this week is to seek support, continuous support from the U.S. Government who liberated us, and we're very thankful for that, and to pledge and show our commitment to the future partnership and cooperation.

Thank you.

President Bush. Mr. Minister, Minister of Electricity.

Minister Aiham Alsammarae. Thank you, Mr. President, for the opportunity. We are, since of course the war until now, we are working very hard to rebuild the electricity, which is destroyed by almost 30 years of

system, that you know how was a system of doing things—almost no technical background for it.

We lost a lot of power. We lost a lot of powerplants over the year. We don't have really, in the time when the war is over, more than 3,300 megawatt out of actually, before the war, almost 4,400. We are right now reaching that number back again. We have a plan to, by next June, to build another 2,000 to 3,000 megawatt. This is all—will make Iraq again having a lot of opportunities for work, because the employment will be high. When you have electricity, you have oil to produce. When you have electricity, you have a treatment for the water.

All that I like to talk about this more and more, but I like to tell you about what's happening in Iraq the last 5 months. The last 5 months, Iraqis, they have the freedom to talk. We have almost right now 86 newspaper, while before the war we have only 3 or 4 newspapers, all controlled by the Government. All the 86 newspapers are not controlled by anyone right now except the individuals who own them.

We have actually the people right now talking freely in the market. They go and get, for example, dishes. We know that every single Iraqis right now, he can go and buy anything he wants. This is the freedom which we missed before, and we got it over the last 5 months. If the Iraqi people and the American help us for the next year and a half, I almost guarantee—I guarantee it to the President but I almost guarantee it to the American people that we will have different Iraq, Iraq who is going to help the United States and the free world and also help the area around us, because we are going to build a democracy and Iraq will become example for all the Middle East areas and all the countries around us.

We need the help of the Americans right now to build Iraq so you have a secure country here, and you have a secure world, and we have a secure Iraq. And I appreciate it, and thank you very much.

President Bush. Thank you all.

NOTE: The President spoke at 4:26 p.m. in the Oval Office at the White House.

Statement on the Transition of the Secretary General of the North Atlantic Treaty Organization
September 22, 2003

I welcome today's decision by NATO to appoint Jaap de Hoop Scheffer, the Dutch Foreign Minister, as its next Secretary General, beginning in January 2004. Mr. de Hoop Scheffer is a leader deeply committed to freedom and to strong and effective transatlantic cooperation. I look forward to working with him.

I also commend Lord Robertson for his many achievements during his 4 years as Secretary General. Under his leadership, NATO welcomes seven new countries. He helped launch a new relationship between NATO and Russia. He spearheaded an ambitious agenda of transformation to make NATO forces lighter, faster, and better able to meet the challenges of the 21st century.

During his tenure, NATO mounted its first operation outside its traditional area, proving that our Alliance can address terrorist threats where they arise. He made NATO a vital partner in the war on terror and in the effort to rebuild the newly freed nations of Afghanistan and Iraq.

The American people will always remember Lord Robertson's leadership when after the September 11th attacks NATO invoked its solemn collective defense clause for the first time in its history. On behalf of all Americans, I extend best wishes to Lord Robertson as he prepares to depart his post as Secretary General of NATO and America's gratitude for a job well done.

Remarks Prior to Discussions With Secretary-General Kofi Annan of the United Nations in New York City
September 23, 2003

I appreciate being here with the Secretary-General. He's a leader and a friend. We look forward to working with the United Nations to achieve big objectives. The big objective, of course, is for there to be peace and freedom—peace in the Middle East, freedom for people who are oppressed.

I assured the Secretary-General our Nation will still continue to provide help for famine and disease. We're mostly going to talk about today the need for the United Nations and the free world to work against slavery in all forms, particularly the sex slavery that takes place all over the world—in our civilized world. The world must combine our resources and our will to stop this abhorrent practice.

Mr. Secretary, thank you, sir. It's great to be back.

NOTE: The President spoke at 9:50 a.m. at the United Nations Headquarters. A tape was not available for verification of the content of these remarks.

Address to the United Nations General Assembly in New York City
September 23, 2003

Mr. Secretary-General; Mr. President; distinguished delegates; ladies and gentlemen: Twenty-four months ago—and yesterday in the memory of America—the center of New York City became a battlefield and a graveyard and the symbol of an unfinished war. Since that day, terrorists have struck in Bali, Mombasa, in Casablanca, in Riyadh, in Jakarta, in Jerusalem, measuring the advance of their cause in the chaos and innocent suffering they leave behind.

Last month, terrorists brought their war to the United Nations itself. The U.N. headquarters in Baghdad stood for order and compassion, and for that reason, the terrorists decided it must be destroyed. Among the 22 people who were murdered was Sergio Vieira de Mello. Over the decades, this good and brave man from Brazil gave help to the afflicted in Bangladesh, Cypress, Mozambique, Lebanon, Cambodia, Central Africa, Kosovo, and East Timor, and was aiding the people of Iraq in their time of need. America joins you, his colleagues, in honoring the memory of Senor Vieira de Mello and the memory of all who died with him in the service to the United Nations.

By the victims they choose and by the means they use, the terrorists have clarified the struggle we are in. Those who target relief workers for death have set themselves against all humanity. Those who incite murder and celebrate suicide reveal their contempt for life itself. They have no place in any religious faith. They have no claim on the world's sympathy, and they should have no friend in this chamber.

Events during the past 2 years have set before us the clearest of divides, between those who seek order and those who spread chaos, between those who work for peaceful change and those who adopt the methods of gangsters, between those who honor the rights of man and those who deliberately take the lives of men and women and children without mercy or shame.

Between these alternatives, there is no neutral ground. All governments that support terror are complicit in a war against civilization. No government should ignore the threat of terror, because to look the other way gives terrorists the chance to regroup and recruit and prepare. And all nations that fight terror as if the lives of their own people depend on it will earn the favorable judgment of history.

The former regimes of Afghanistan and Iraq knew these alternatives and made their choices. The Taliban was a sponsor and servant of terrorism. When confronted, that regime chose defiance, and that regime is no more. Afghanistan's President, who is here today, now represents a free people who are building a decent and just society. They're building a nation fully joined in the war against terror.

The regime of Saddam Hussein cultivated ties to terror while it built weapons of mass destruction. It used those weapons in acts of mass murder and refused to account for them when confronted by the world. The Security Council was right to be alarmed. The Security Council was right to demand that Iraq destroy its illegal weapons and prove that it had done so. The Security Council was right to vow serious consequences if Iraq refused to comply. And because there were consequences, because a coalition of nations acted to defend the peace and the credibility of the United Nations, Iraq is free, and today we are joined by representatives of a liberated country.

Saddam Hussein's monuments have been removed, and not only his statues. The true monuments of his rule and his character—the torture chambers and the rape rooms and the prison cells for innocent children—are closed. And as we discover the killing fields and mass graves of Iraq, the true scale of Saddam's cruelty is being revealed.

The Iraqi people are meeting hardships and challenges, like every nation that has set out on the path of democracy. Yet their future promises lives of dignity and freedom, and that is a world away from the squalid, vicious tyranny they have known. Across Iraq, life is being improved by liberty. Across the Middle East, people are safer because an unstable aggressor has been removed from power. Across the world, nations are more secure because an ally of terror has fallen.

Our actions in Afghanistan and Iraq were supported by many governments, and America is grateful to each one. I also recognize that some of the sovereign nations of this Assembly disagreed with our actions. Yet there was and there remains unity among us on the fundamental principles and objectives of the United Nations. We are dedicated to the defense of our collective security and to the advance of human rights. These permanent commitments call us to great work in the world, work we must do together. So let us move forward.

First, we must stand with the people of Afghanistan and Iraq as they build free and stable countries. The terrorists and their allies fear and fight this progress above all, because free people embrace hope over resentment and choose peace over violence.

The United Nations has been a friend of the Afghan people, distributing food and medicine, helping refugees return home, advising on a new constitution, and helping to prepare the way for nationwide elections. NATO has taken over the U.N.-mandated security force in Kabul. American and coalition forces continue to track and defeat Al Qaida terrorists and remnants of the Taliban. Our efforts to rebuild that country go on. I have recently proposed to spend an additional $1.2 billion for the Afghan reconstruction effort, and I urge other nations to continue contributing to this important cause.

In the nation of Iraq, the United Nations is carrying out vital and effective work every day. By the end of 2004, more than 90 percent of Iraqi children under age 5 will have been immunized against preventable diseases such as polio, tuberculosis, and measles, thanks to the hard work and high ideals of UNICEF. Iraq's food distribution system is operational, delivering nearly a half-million tons of food per month, thanks to the skill and expertise of the World Food Program.

Our international coalition in Iraq is meeting it responsibilities. We are conducting precision raids against terrorists and holdouts of the former regime. These killers are at war with the Iraqi people. They have made Iraq the central front in the war on terror, and they will be defeated. Our coalition has made sure that Iraq's former dictator will never again use weapons of mass destruction. We are interviewing Iraqi citizens and analyzing records of the old regime to reveal the full extent of its weapons programs and its long campaign of deception. We're training Iraqi police and border guards and a new army, so the Iraqi people can assume full responsibility for their own security.

And at the same time, our coalition is helping to improve the daily lives of the Iraqi people. The old regime built palaces while letting schools decay, so we are rebuilding more than a thousand schools. The old regime starved hospitals of resources, so we have helped to supply and reopen hospitals across Iraq. The old regime built up armies and weapons while allowing the nation's infrastructure to crumble, so we are rehabilitating powerplants, water and sanitation facilities, bridges, and airports. I proposed to Congress that the United States provide additional funding for our work in Iraq, the greatest financial commitment of its kind since the Marshall plan. Having helped to liberate Iraq, we will honor our pledges to Iraq, and by helping the Iraqi people build a stable and peaceful country, we will make our own countries more secure.

The primary goal of our coalition in Iraq is self-government for the people of Iraq, reached by orderly and democratic process. This process must unfold according to the needs of Iraqis, neither hurried nor delayed by the wishes of other parties. And the United Nations can contribute greatly to the cause of Iraq self-government. America is working with friends and allies on a new Security Council resolution which will expand the U.N.'s role in Iraq. As in the aftermath of other conflicts, the United Nations should assist in developing a constitution, in training civil servants, and conducting free and fair elections.

Iraq now has a Governing Council, the first truly representative institution in that country. Iraq's new leaders are showing the openness and tolerance that democracy requires, and they're also showing courage. Yet every young democracy needs the help of friends. Now the nation of Iraq needs and deserves our aid, and all nations of good will should step forward and provide that support.

The success of a free Iraq will be watched and noted throughout the region. Millions will see that freedom, equality, and material progress are possible at the heart of the Middle East. Leaders in the region will face the clearest evidence that free institutions and open societies are the only path to long-term national success and dignity. And a transformed Middle East would benefit the entire world by undermining the ideologies that export violence to other lands.

Iraq as a dictatorship had great power to destabilize the Middle East. Iraq as a democracy will have great power to inspire the Middle East. The advance of democratic institutions in Iraq is setting an example that others, including the Palestinian people, would be wise to follow. The Palestinian cause is betrayed by leaders who cling to power by feeding old hatreds and destroying the good work of others. The

Palestinian people deserve their own state, and they will gain that state by embracing new leaders committed to reform, to fighting terror, and to building peace. All parties in the Middle East must meet their responsibilities and carry out the commitments they made at Aqaba. Israel must work to create the conditions that will allow a peaceful Palestinian state to emerge. And Arab nations must cut off funding and other support for terrorist organizations. America will work with every nation in the region that acts boldly for the sake of peace.

A second challenge we must confront together is the proliferation of weapons of mass destruction. Outlaw regimes that possess nuclear, chemical, and biological weapons and the means to deliver them would be able to use blackmail and create chaos in entire regions. These weapons could be used by terrorists to bring sudden disaster and suffering on a scale we can scarcely imagine. The deadly combination of outlaw regimes and terror networks and weapons of mass murder is a peril that cannot be ignored or wished away. If such a danger is allowed to fully materialize, all words, all protests, will come too late. Nations of the world must have the wisdom and the will to stop grave threats before they arrive.

One crucial step is to secure the most dangerous materials at their source. For more than a decade, the United States has worked with Russia and other states of the former Soviet Union to dismantle, destroy, or secure weapons and dangerous materials left over from another era. Last year in Canada, the G–8 nations agreed to provide up to $20 billion, half of it from the United States, to fight this proliferation risk over the next 10 years. Since then, six additional countries have joined the effort. More are needed, and I urge other nations to help us meet this danger.

We're also improving our capability to interdict lethal materials in transit. Through our Proliferation Security Initiative, 11 nations are preparing to search planes and ships, trains, and trucks carrying suspect cargo and to seize weapons or missile shipments that raise proliferation concerns. These nations have agreed on a set of interdiction principles consistent with legal—current legal authorities. And we're working to expand the Proliferation Security Initiative to other countries. We're determined to keep the world's most destructive weapons away from all our shores and out of the hands of our common enemies.

Because proliferators will use any route or channel that is open to them, we need the broadest possible cooperation to stop them. Today I ask the U.N. Security Council to adopt a new antiproliferation resolution. This resolution should call on all members of the U.N. to criminalize the proliferation of weapons—weapons of mass destruction, to enact strict export controls consistent with international standards, and to secure any and all sensitive materials within their own borders. The United States stands ready to help any nation draft these new laws and to assist in their enforcement.

A third challenge we share is a challenge to our conscience. We must act decisively to meet the humanitarian crises of our time. The United States has begun to carry out the Emergency Plan for AIDS Relief, aimed at preventing AIDS on a massive scale and treating millions who have the disease already. We have pledged $15 billion over 5 years to fight AIDS around the world.

My country is acting to save lives from famine as well, providing more than $1.4 billion in global emergency food aid. And I've asked our United States Congress for $200 million for a new famine fund, so we can act quickly when the first signs of famine appear. Every nation on every continent should generously add their resources to the fight against disease and desperate hunger.

There's another humanitarian crisis spreading, yet hidden from view. Each year, an estimated 800,000 to 900,000

human beings are bought, sold, or forced across the world's borders. Among them are hundreds of thousands of teenage girls and others as young as 5 who fall victim to the sex trade. This commerce in human life generates billions of dollars each year, much of which is used to finance organized crime.

There's a special evil in the abuse and exploitation of the most innocent and vulnerable. The victims of sex trade see little of life before they see the very worst of life, an underground of brutality and lonely fear. Those who create these victims and profit from their suffering must be severely punished. Those who patronize this industry debase themselves and deepen the misery of others. And governments that tolerate this trade are tolerating a form of slavery.

This problem has appeared in my own country, and we are working to stop it. The PROTECT Act, which I signed into law this year, makes it a crime for any person to enter the United States or for any citizen to travel abroad for the purpose of sex tourism involving children. The Department of Justice is actively investigating sex tour operators and patrons, who can face up to 30 years in prison. Under the Trafficking Victims Protection Act, the United States is using sanctions against governments to discourage human trafficking.

The victims of this industry also need help from members of the United Nations, and this begins with clear standards and the certainty of punishment under the laws of every country. Today, some nations make it a crime to sexually abuse children abroad. Such conduct should be a crime in all nations. Governments should inform travelers of the harm this industry does and the severe punishments that will fall on its patrons. The American Government is committing $50 million to support the good work of organizations that are rescuing women and children from exploitation and giving them shelter and medical treatment and the hope of a new life. I urge other governments to do their part.

We must show new energy in fighting back an old evil. Nearly two centuries after the abolition of the transatlantic slave trade and more than a century after slavery was officially ended in its last strongholds, the trade in human beings for any purpose must not be allowed to thrive in our time.

All the challenges I have spoken of this morning require urgent attention and moral clarity. Helping Afghanistan and Iraq to succeed as free nations in a transformed region, cutting off the avenues of proliferation, abolishing modern forms of slavery—these are the kind of great tasks for which the United Nations was founded. In each case, careful discussion is needed and also decisive action. Our good intentions will be credited only if we achieve good outcomes.

As an original signer of the U.N. Charter, the United States of America is committed to the United Nations. And we show that commitment by working to fulfill the U.N.'s stated purposes and giving meaning to its ideals. The founding documents of the United Nations and the founding docu-ments of America stand in the same tradition. Both assert that human beings should never be reduced to objects of power or commerce, because their dignity is inherent. Both require—both recognize a moral law that stands above men and nations, which must be defended and enforced by men and nations. And both point the way to peace, the peace that comes when all are free. We secure that peace with our courage, and we must show that courage together.

May God bless you all.

NOTE: The President spoke at 10:59 a.m. in the General Assembly Hall at the United Nations Headquarters. In his remarks, he referred to Secretary-General Kofi Annan, General Assembly President Julian Hunte, and Special Representative for Iraq Sergio Vieira de Mello of the United Nations; President Hamid Karzai of Afghanistan; and former President Saddam Hussein of Iraq. The Office of the Press Secretary also released a Spanish language transcript of these remarks.

Remarks Prior to Discussions With President Jose Maria Aznar of Spain in New York City
September 23, 2003

President Bush. It's my honor to visit again with my very close friend, a great friend of our country, Jose Maria Aznar. Jose Maria is a very strong leader who's got a vision that's based upon the principles of human dignity and freedom.

And we'll spend time talking about Iraq. We're both convinced and strongly believe that our goals in Iraq are the right goals, and we'll accomplished the goals.

He's a steadfast friend, and I'm so proud to be with you again.

[At this point, President Aznar spoke in Spanish, and no translation was provided.]

President Bush. Thank you, sir.

NOTE: The President spoke at 12:02 p.m. at the U.S. Mission to the United Nations. A tape was not available for verification of the content of these remarks.

Remarks at a Luncheon Hosted by Secretary-General Kofi Annan of the United Nations in New York City
September 23, 2003

Mr. Secretary-General; distinguished members of the United Nations community; excellencies; ladies and gentlemen: America is honored that you all are here. Since the founding of the U.N. more than 50 years ago, my country has been proud to host this organization. I'm pleased to join you in opening the 58th session of the U.N. General Assembly. Mr. Secretary-General, I am grateful for your leadership, and I'm proud to call you friend.

The United Nations has suffered great loss in the cause of peace. The terrorist attack against the U.N. headquarters in Baghdad took the lives of 22 servants of peace, including Sergio de Mello, a man who dedicated his life to promoting human rights throughout the world. The people of my country mourn with you. We share

your resolve to continue this important work. We gather in this city, at this Assembly, to meet urgent challenges of our time. We will work together to promote peace and human dignity.

Mr. Secretary-General, with admiration for you and with confidence in the future of this organization, I offer a toast to your leadership and to the United Nations.

NOTE: The President spoke at 1:45 p.m. at the United Nations Headquarters. In his remarks, he referred to U.N. Special Representative for Iraq Sergio Vieira de Mello. The transcript released by the Office of the Press Secretary also included the remarks of Secretary-General Annan. A tape was not available for verification of the content of these remarks.

Remarks at a United States Reception in New York City
September 23, 2003

The President. Thank you all very much. Please be seated. [*Laughter*]

Audience member. Not everyone has a seat.

The President. Unless you don't have a chair. [*Laughter*] For the sake of world harmony, I will give a short speech—[*laughter*]—and then we can all go to bed. [*Laughter*]

First, I want to thank the American Museum of Natural History for their wonderful hospitality. We've got trustees here and the leadership of this fantastic place. It's such a wonderful opportunity for Laura and me and our delegation to show off one of the really fantastic landmarks of New York City. So on behalf of our delegation, thanks for

your wonderful hospitality. It's a beautiful place to have a wonderful reception.

Laura and I and the Secretary are honored to welcome the Presidents and Prime Ministers and Foreign Ministers and U.N. Ambassadors and anybody else who managed to sneak in tonight. [*Laughter*] We're glad you're here. It's been a fantastic reception for us, and thank you for coming.

I really want to say quickly a word about Kofi Annan. I admire his decency and his vision and his compassion for our fellow human beings. He's a great leader of the United Nations, and we're proud to call him friend.

Somebody whispered in my ear that Mayor Bloomberg is here. He is the mayor of New York City. Michael is the mayor of a great city. On September the 11th, this Nation saw the remarkable spirit of the people who live in this city. We'll always remember how our fellow citizens who happen to be New Yorkers instantly rallied to help their neighbors in need. New York's famous skyline was wounded, but its spirit remained steadfast.

In pursuing the terrorists, we honor the memory of the fallen, and we defend civilization itself. I want all the world leaders to remember that. In working to alleviate poverty, disease, and human suffering, we spread hope to millions, and we undermine the ideologies of resentment and hate and terror. The United Nations plays a vital role in all these efforts, and all our nations have a duty to advance its founding principles of tolerance and freedom and human rights.

A wing of this building is named for Theodore Roosevelt. He was one of my predecessors. He was a warrior for peace who faced the world without illusions, and I want to quote what he said. He said, "If we are to be a really great people, we must strive in good faith to play a great part in the world. We cannot avoid meeting great issues. All that we can determine for ourselves is whether we shall meet them well or ill."

He was speaking for Americans, but his words are true of every people in the world today. We're meeting great issues of security and compassion, and we must and we will meet them well.

Welcome to New York. May God bless you all.

NOTE: The President spoke at 8:47 p.m. at the American Museum of Natural History. In his remarks, he referred to Secretary-General Kofi Annan of the United Nations.

Remarks Following Discussions With Chancellor Gerhard Schroeder of Germany and an Exchange With Reporters in New York City
September 24, 2003

President Bush. Listen, thank you all for coming. Gerhard and I just had a very good meeting. The first thing I told him, I said, "Look, we've had differences, and they're over, and we're going to work together." And I believe when Germany and America works together, we can accomplish a lot of positive things. We're both committed to freedom. We're both committed to peace. We're both committed to the prosperity of our people. And I reaffirmed to Gerhard that America and German relations are very important to this administration. I have said so repeatedly. I said so in the Bundestag, and I reiterated it today with the Chancellor.

We will work together in Afghanistan. I appreciate his efforts to help with a— help Iraq grow to be a peaceful and stable and democratic country. We talked about the Middle East. We talked about proliferation concerns. In short, we talked about the things we can do together to benefit mankind, and I'm really happy we had the meeting today.

Thank you, sir.

Chancellor Schroeder. I can only comment and very much confirm what the President has just said. We addressed a whole range of international topics, but we didn't just exclusively talk about international affairs. We also addressed the economic situation, because we feel that our problems, when it comes to that, are similar indeed. Both of our economies are by now so closely intertwined that it really makes sense to think about them conjointly.

I cannot conceal that I was very pleased indeed that the President did appreciate the contribution Germany is making within Afghanistan. We very much are trying to make this a sustainable contribution, and I think our people on the ground are doing a good job. And therefore, I have to say I'm proud of the work they're doing for us and for us together.

We then proceeded to actually talk about the situation in Iraq, and indeed, we very much feel that the differences that have been, have been left behind and put aside by now. We are both agreed that we want to look into the future together. And I would like to reiterate the fact that Germany has a very strong, in fact a vested interest, in a stable and very democratic Iraq and to development to that effect. It is very important not just for Iraq as such but for the whole of the region, for Germany and, therefore, also for Europe.

We certainly have emphasized the fact, and I have once more said this to the President myself, how very much we would like to come in and help with the resources that we do have. We could very much envisage that we will assist in providing training for security staff, be it police functions or be it some form of military function. We do have the capacities for that available in Germany, and we would very much like to put them to that purpose.

President Bush. Thank you, sir.

President's U.N. Address

Q. Mr. President, what about the response to your speech yesterday?

President Bush. I can only judge by your reaction to it. [*Laughter*]

NOTE: The President spoke at 9:35 a.m. at the Waldorf-Astoria Hotel. A tape was not available for verification of the content of these remarks.

Statement on Congressional Passage of the Department of Homeland Security Appropriations Act, 2004
September 24, 2003

To win the war on terrorism, we are staying on the offensive abroad and protecting Americans at home. I applaud Congress for passing the Department of Homeland Security appropriations bill. These funds will help make Americans and their families even safer through stronger border enforcement, improved transportation security, and continued support for police, firefighters, and emergency-response teams. I look forward to signing this legislation.

Statement on the Death of Hugh Gregg
September 24, 2003

Hugh Gregg left an indelible mark on the State he loved and on the lives of the people of New Hampshire. He served his country in time of war and served his State with distinction as Governor, statesman, and successful business leader. In all of his endeavors, he acted with integrity and honor. He will be missed. Laura joins me in sending our condolences to his wife, Catherine, his two sons, and his family during this difficult time.

Letter to the Speaker of the House of Representatives Transmitting a Fiscal Year 2004 Budget Amendment
September 24, 2003

Dear Mr. Speaker:

I ask the Congress to consider the enclosed FY 2004 budget amendment for International Assistance Programs. This amendment would not increase the budgetary resources proposed in my FY 2004 Budget.

The details of this request are set forth in the enclosed letter from the Director of the Office of Management and Budget. Sincerely,

GEORGE W. BUSH

NOTE: This letter was released by the Office of the Press Secretary on September 25.

Remarks Following a Meeting With the Congressional Conferees on Medicare Modernization and an Exchange With Reporters
September 25, 2003

The President. Listen, thank you all for coming. Today we met with the conferees on Medicare and had a good and frank discussion about the need to work together to get a Medicare bill that modernizes the system, that fulfills the promises to America's seniors, that uses the latest technology to improve the health care of our elderly.

And in my judgment, the sentiment was optimistic. I believe people know it's possible to get it done. And there's a lot of work to get done, but fortunately, we're surrounded here by conferees that are plenty capable, plenty smart, and care deeply about the future of the country.

And so I want to thank them for coming. I want to thank you for your commitment to our seniors, and I look forward to working with you to get a good bill out of both bodies and to my desk before you go home this fall.

I'd like to take a couple of questions. Terry [Terence Hunt, Associated Press].

Medicare Reform Legislation

Q. Mr. President, with huge Federal budget deficits, do you have any qualms about spending $400 billion on Medicare prescription drugs?

The President. First of all, no, I don't. I think it's the right thing to do. We have an obligation to our seniors. Secondly, we've proposed a plan that reduces the deficit in half by 5 years—within 5 years. I absolutely believe we're doing the right thing.

Iran/Meeting With President Vladimir Putin of Russia

Q. Sir, what did you think of the discovery of traces of weapons-grade uranium——

The President. Do what now?

Q. What did you think of the discovery of weapons-grade—traces of weapons-grade uranium in Iran? And will this be on your agenda with President Putin this weekend?

The President. It was on my agenda—it will be on my agenda with President Putin this weekend. It was on my agenda with many of the world leaders I met with in New York. It is very important for the world to come together to make it very clear to Iran that there will be universal condemnation if they continue with a nuclear weapons program. And I will tell you, the response was very positive. People understand the danger of the Iranians have a nuclear weapons program. But you bet; I'll talk to President Putin about it this weekend.

Saddam Hussein/Lessons of 9/11

Q. Sir, in February of 2001, your Secretary of State said that the sanctions against Iraq had prevented Saddam from developing any significant capability with respect to weapons of mass destruction. A year-and-a-half later, before the U.N., you called Saddam a grave and gathering danger. And I'm wondering, what changed in that time? Was it the nature of the threat? Did you get new intelligence? Or did 9/11 put a new—set a new playing field for those——

The President. Yes, the Secretary of State said the same thing as well, that Saddam was a threat. Nine-eleven changed my calculation. It made it really clear we have to deal with threats before they come on our shore. You know, for a long period

of time we thought oceans could protect us from danger, and we learned a tough lesson on September the 11th. It's really important for this Nation to continue to chase down and deal with threats before they materialize, and we learned that on September the 11th.

OPEC Production Cuts/National Economy

Q. Mr. President?
The President. Yes.
Q. OPEC yesterday announced an agreement to cut oil production by 3.5 percent.
The President. Yes.
Q. What is your reaction to that? What do you think of it? And what are the consequences for the U.S. economy?
The President. My reaction is, is that I would hope our friends in OPEC don't do things that would hurt our economy.

NOTE: The President spoke at 3:19 p.m. in the Cabinet Room at the White House. In his remarks, he referred to former President Saddam Hussein of Iraq. A tape was not available for verification of the content of these remarks.

Statement on the National Do-Not-Call Registry
September 25, 2003

Unwanted telemarketing calls are intrusive, annoying, and all too common. When Americans are sitting down to dinner or parents are reading to their children, the last thing they want is a call from a stranger with a sales pitch.

For that reason, I have strongly supported the actions of the Federal Trade Commission and the Federal Communications Commission to establish a National

Do-Not-Call Registry and protect consumers.

The millions of people who have signed up for the list have the right to reduce unwanted telephone solicitations. I commend Congress for its rapid action to support the Registry, and I look forward to signing this legislation.

Message on the Observance of Rosh Hashanah, 5764
September 26, 2003

I send greetings to those observing Rosh Hashanah.

For the Jewish community in the United States and around the world, this holiday marks the beginning of the New Year and the onset of the Days of Awe. Rosh Hashanah is a time to seek the mercy and forgiveness of the Almighty and your fellow man, to reflect on past actions, and to demonstrate renewed commitment to faith and family. May you find inspiration for the days ahead as you remember the devotion of Abraham and Isaac and their willingness to sacrifice everything to do right.

During this holy time, I encourage you to pray for peace and mutual understanding throughout the world. May we build a future of promise and compassion for all, and may the coming year be filled with hope and happiness.

Laura joins me in sending our best wishes for a blessed Rosh Hashanah.

GEORGE W. BUSH

NOTE: An original was not available for verification of the content of this message.

The President's Radio Address
September 27, 2003

Good morning. Earlier this week, I spoke to the United Nations, which has become, like our country, a target of terrorism. In the past month, terrorists have made two bombing attacks on the U.N. headquarters in Baghdad, killing Iraqi citizens, U.N. officials, and international aid workers. On Tuesday, I conveyed the sympathy of our country for the losses of the U.N. and the gratitude of our country for the relief efforts of the U.N. in Iraq. I also expressed America's determination to fight and win the war on terror for the safety of our own people and for the benefit of all mankind.

The world is safer today because, in Afghanistan, our broad coalition destroyed the training camps of terrorists and removed the brutal regime that sponsored terror. The world is safer today because we continue to hunt down Al Qaida and its terrorist allies and have captured or killed nearly two-thirds of Al Qaida's known leaders and key facilitators.

The world is safer today because, in Iraq, our coalition ended a regime that cultivated ties to terror while it built weapons of mass destruction. And for the safety of the people of Iraq and of all free nations, our forces are now conducting a systematic campaign to defeat holdouts of the old regime and other terrorists who have joined them.

In the struggle between terrorist killers and peaceful nations, there is no neutral ground. All nations must join in confronting this threat where it arises, before the terrorists can inflict even greater harm and suffering. And all nations should stand with the people of Afghanistan and Iraq as they build a future based on freedom and democracy.

Our coalition is helping the Iraqi people to build a secure, hopeful, and self-governing nation which will stand as an example of freedom to all the Middle East. We are rebuilding more than a thousand schools, supplying and reopening hospitals, rehabilitating powerplants, water and sanitation facilities, bridges, and airports. We are training Iraqi police, border guards, and a new army, so that the Iraqi people can assume full responsibility for their own security. Iraq now has its own Governing Council, has appointed interim government ministries, and is moving toward elections. Iraq's new leaders are showing the openness and tolerance that democracy requires, and also the courage. Yet every young democracy needs the help of friends. America is providing that help to Iraq, and all nations of good will should do their part as well.

Our goal is a free Iraq, where the Iraqi people are responsible for their own affairs. We want Iraq's governmental institutions to be strong and to stand the test of time, so I called on the United Nations to take up vital responsibilities in this effort. America is now working with friends and allies on a new Security Council resolution which will expand the U.N.'s role in Iraq. As in the aftermath of other conflicts, the United Nations should assist in developing a constitution, training civil servants, and conducting free and fair elections. Many U.N. members, from the Philippines to Poland and now Germany, have expressed their commitment to helping build a democratic and stable Iraq.

The stakes in Iraq are high, for the Middle East and beyond. If freedom and progress falter in the Middle East, that region will continue to export violence that takes lives in America and around the world. If democracy and tolerance and peace advance in that region, it will undermine the bitterness and resentment that feed terrorism. The terrorists understand this, so they have chosen to fight against order and liberty in Iraq. They must and they will be defeated. And I am confident that more nations will rally to the side of the Iraqi people and help them to build a free and peaceful nation.

Thank you for listening.

NOTE: The address was recorded at 11:35 a.m. on September 26 in the Cabinet Room at the White House for broadcast at 10:06 a.m. on September 27. The transcript was made available by the Office of the Press Secretary on September 26 but was embargoed for release until the broadcast. The Office of the Press Secretary also released a Spanish language transcript of this address.

The President's News Conference With President Vladimir Putin of Russia at Camp David, Maryland
September 27, 2003

President Bush. Thank you all for coming. I'm proud to welcome my friend Vladimir Putin to Camp David. President Putin has visited the White House; he's visited our ranch in Crawford; and now he visits Camp David. I'm honored to have him here, and I appreciate the great dialog we've had last night and today.

For decades, when the leaders of our two countries met, they talked mainly of missiles and warheads, because the only common ground we shared was the desire to avoid catastrophic conflict. In recent years, the United States and Russia have made great progress in building a new relationship. Today, our relationship is broad, and it is strong.

Russia and the United States are allies in the war on terror. Both of our nations have suffered at the hands of terrorists, and both of our Governments are taking actions to stop them. No cause justifies terror. Terrorists must be opposed wherever they spread chaos and destruction, including

Chechnya. A lasting solution to that conflict will require an end to terror, respect for human rights, and a political settlement that leads to free and fair elections.

President Putin and I talked about expanding our cooperation in Iraq and in Afghanistan. The President and I agree that America, Russia, and the entire world will benefit from the advance of stability and freedom in these nations, because free and stable nations do not breed ideologies of murder or threaten people of other lands. I was encouraged that it is clear that our Governments will continue to work together on this very important matter, a matter of freedom and peace.

The President and I also discussed ways to broaden Russian-American military cooperation. We're determined to improve our joint ability to fight terror, to keep peace in troubled regions, and stop the spread of weapons of mass destruction. We strongly urge North Korea to completely, verifiably, and irreversibly end its nuclear programs. We strongly urge Iran to comply fully with all of its obligations under the Nuclear Non-Proliferation Treaty. We're seeking to intensify our missile defense cooperation, because both of our countries are threatened by outlaw regimes that could be armed with deadly weapons.

We welcome the growing economic relationship between our two countries. We will continue to work together to expand cooperation in the energy sector. We recognize lower trade barriers and mutual investment will benefit both our nations. American and Russian officials are meeting more often and discussing broad range of issues.

Old suspicions are giving way to new understanding and respect. Our goal is to bring the U.S.-Russian relationship to a new level of partnership. I respect President Putin's vision for Russia, a country at peace within its borders, with its neighbors, and with the world, a country in which democracy and freedom and rule of law thrive. Because of the President's vision and his desires, I'm confident that we'll

have a strong relationship which will improve the lives of our fellow citizens as well as help make the world more peaceful.

Mr. President, welcome.

President Putin. Thank you very much. Good afternoon, ladies and gentlemen. First of all, I would like to cordially thank the President of the United States of America, Mr. Bush, for his invitation. Our host has created, beginning yesterday, a very relaxed and tranquil atmosphere conducive to having a calm and open, very frank talk on the major problems and on the broader picture of relations between Russia and the United States.

Our talks today have once again confirmed that our relations are based on a clear vision and a clear understanding of special responsibility of Russia and the United States for ensuring international security and strengthening strategic stability. We have convinced—we have proven once again that our partnership is not subject to political dealmaking.

Despite all the difficulties that we have to overcome, the spirit and the basic principles of our relationship have remained the same, mutual confidence, openness, predictability, and consideration, and respect of interests of each other. We value very much the level of relationship that we have reached with the United States.

According to already established tradition, President Bush and I have focused on specific issues. And fight against terrorism continues to be among priorities of our cooperation. I agree with the assessment that the President of the United States has just given. In this sphere, we act not only as strategic partners but as allies. Our agencies are conducting an open and professional dialog on the entire range of questions in this sphere, including attempts by terrorist organizations to commit new terrorists' acts and to gain access to weapons of mass destruction.

We have also discussed today about the implementation of provisions of the Treaty on Strategic Offensive Reductions. After the ratification of the treaty, its implementation, in our assessment, is going successfully. We intend to take this work under our control in the future as well.

Russia and the United States intend to pursue close cooperation for strengthening international regimes and nonproliferation mechanisms. We discussed in detail the situation around nuclear programs of Iran and North Korea. In our—it is our conviction that we shall now give a clear but respectful signal to Iran about the necessity to continue and expand its cooperation with IAEA.

As to the North Korean nuclear problem, I believe that the primary—the priority now is to unblock the conflict situation around the Korean Peninsula to create a favorable climate, favorable atmosphere for a constructive dialog. And Russia believes that ensuring nuclear nonproliferation regime should be accompanied by extending to North Korea guarantees in this sphere of security. We intend to continue our joint work with the United States in resolving this issue.

I would like to stress separately the situation around Iraq. Our countries, just like the entire international community, have a common task, to ensure the speediest possible settlement and normalization of the situation in Iraq. We want to see Iraq a free, democratic, and united state. We believe that in solving the very difficult problems that the people of Iraq are facing today, an important role shall be played by the provisional Governing Council of Iraq, along with the Special Representative of the Secretary-General of the United Nations.

We also talked about the situation in the Middle East. And we believe that there is no reasonable alternative to consistent implementation of the roadmap.

Significant attention during the negotiation was paid to Russian-American cooperation in trade and economic sphere. I would like to remind you that in the first 6 months of 2003, the volume of Russian-American mutual trade has increased more than by one-third. It's a good platform for future progress.

There is also good grounds for future cooperation in energy sphere. We are also improving cooperation in the sphere of information and communication technologies and in the exploration of space.

And in conclusion, I would like to draw the primary result of our negotiations. We have succeeded in reaching substantial progress on the way of forming the relations of real and mutually respectful partnership between Russia and the United States. I would like to thank President Bush for his constructive approach and for his interest in the discussion of all the questions, of all the issues that we have touched upon. This was a very useful meeting.

President Bush. Thanks. We'll take a couple of questions here, two per side.

Iran and the IAEA/Russian Stance on Iraq

Press Secretary Scott McClellan. Jennifer [Jennifer Loven, Associated Press], with the AP.

Q. Yes, sir. You mentioned that you talked about Iran. Did you receive any specific commitments from President Putin that Russia would stop selling nuclear technology to Iran?

And to Mr. Putin, did you—are you ready to make any commitments now to contribute either troops or resources in Iraq? And if not, what will help you to get there?

President Bush. We share a goal, and that is to make sure Iran doesn't have a nuclear weapon or a nuclear weapons program. We also understand that we need to work together to convince Iran to abandon any ambition she may have, ambitions toward the development of a nuclear weapon. What's important is we understand it's in our national interest that Iran doesn't develop a nuclear weapon.

So the most important thing that came out of these meetings was a reaffirmation of our desire to work together to convince Iran to abandon her ambitions, as well as to work with other nations so that there is a common voice on this issue. You heard the President say that the IAEA process must go forward. We firmly agree. I found this part of our discussions to be very satisfactory, from the U.S. point of view.

President Putin. We indeed paid much attention to this issue. I would like to reiterate that Russia has no desire and no plans to contribute in any way to the creation of weapons of mass destructions, either in Iran or in any other spot, region in the world. I would like to reiterate that we comply firmly with the provisions of the Non-Proliferation Treaty, because this course is in our national interest.

As to the joint work, we are ready to proceed. As to our possible participation in the normalization of the—in the settlement in Iraq, in the normalization of life in Iraq, Russia is interested in seeing it occurring as soon as possible.

At the same time, we understand that this is a very complicated process that should be based on a solid legal and administrative base and should go ahead stage by stage. The degree and the extent and level of Russia's participation in the restoration of Iraq will be determined after we know the parameters of the resolution—of the new resolution on Iraq.

Russia-U.S. Relations/U.S. Visa Policy

Q. First question, addressed to both Presidents. There is an opinion that Russian-American relations have, nevertheless, a declarative character. Have you given any specific instructions to your Governments the—as you discussed it in your communique?

President Bush. Yes. Da.

Q. And the second question——

President Bush. No, we only got one question, please. You've already asked two, one to me and one to him. Now you want to ask four, two to me and—no, forget it.

Q. Two parts——

President Bush. Oh, two parts of the same question?

Q. Because my colleague asked two questions, on Iraq and Iran—[*laughter*]—[*inaudible*].

President Bush. Yes, okay. [*Laughter*] I knew she set a bad precedent. [*Laughter*]

Q. So the next question is for you, Mr. President Bush. Sir, the question is, as you know, as you probably do know, Mr. President, that visa practices implemented by your embassies abroad, including by your Embassy in Russia, with respect to those people who would like to travel to the United States, and that does not add sympathies to—does not add sympathies. And do you know that even journalists who came here to cover your visit had to undergo a special interview at the Embassy in Moscow? And do you expect any changes to take place in these practices?

And as a followup question, does my question—will my——

President Bush. No wonder you got interviewed. [*Laughter*]

Q. And as a followup question, can I be assured that my question will not lead to a denial of visa for me, personally? [*Laughter*]

President Bush. That's right. No. *Nyet.* [*Laughter*] No, the President raised the issue of visas. He expressed concern that our visa policy was cumbersome and didn't expedite the travel of legitimate journalists and business people and artists and educators. Our intention is not to slow down visits. Our intention is to make sure that visitors who come are reasonable people. What is happening is, is that policy—visa policy changed after September the 11th, 2001, and we're trying to make it as modern and as efficient as possible. And we've got some work to do.

And it was so long that you asked your first question, I'll try to remember what it was. Oh, yes. Yes, we've got a checklist of things we need to work through. In other words, we understand that it's one thing to set a strategic vision for our relationship, but there must be practical consequences of the relationship. We're tasking different agencies and agencies' heads with discussions and action plans that we will be able to monitor.

President Putin. Regarding declarative character of the relations between Russia and the United States, where do, as we say in Russia, legs grow; where do such questions come from? This happens because people expect from us constantly some kind of revolutions. Now, just positive development in the relationship is no longer sufficient for them. I would like to point your attention that due to rapprochement between Russia and the United States, we manage to establish and to create in the world an atmosphere and trust—of trust and strategic stability.

This had very practical results, including in such sensitive areas as combating terrorism. I have never said this in public. I'm going to do it today. When counterterrorist operation began in Afghanistan, we were approached by people through several channels—we were approached by people who intended to fight against Americans in Afghanistan. And if by that time President Bush and I had not formed appropriate relationship, as we have—so no one knows what turn would the developments in Afghanistan had taken. You know what was the Russia's position, and it helped to a great extent to achieve further results that we have achieved in Afghanistan and was for a very good purpose.

I have just said that in only 6 first months of this year, the volume of our mutual trade has increased by more than one-third. We are talking about Russia's balanced policy in the world energy sphere. We conduct a very high-level energy dialog with the United States, including at the very top level. And it's difficult to say what prices would be now—how high prices for fuel in international energy markets would be now, if we had not had such dialog.

We continue to pursue cooperation in such sensitive areas as space. And it is indeed so that upon the results of today's meeting, we have compiled a checklist of different issues on which we have given instructions to specific agencies in our Government. That is why our cooperation is not declarative but extremely concrete and pragmatic.

President Bush. The next questioner will ask one question, in defiance to the precedent-setting by the AP reporter.

Press Secretary McClellan. Caren [Caren Bohan], with Reuters.

Support for Iraqi Reconstruction

Q. Mr. President, are you disappointed that more countries have not come forward with pledges of aid for Iraq's reconstruction?

President Bush. I am pleased with the amount of cooperation we're receiving, a coalition of nations inside of Iraq working hard to bring security to that country as well as to help rebuild a country. I recognize that some countries are inhibited from participation because of the lack of a U.N. resolution. We are working to get a satisfactory resolution out of the U.N. We spent some time discussing that today.

As well there will be donor conference—a donor conference that we will be attending and look forward to getting more participants. It is in the national interest of free nations that Iraq be free and peaceful. And one of the things that interested me about Vladimir's comments was that he recognizes that we cannot allow power vacuums to exist into which rogue nations will enhance their capacity to hurt free nations.

So our message is twofold: On the one hand, it's in the interest of nations to work for a secure and peaceful Iraq; and secondly, it's in our moral interest to help the Iraqi people get back on their feet after living under such tyranny. Remember, we discovered torture chambers, rape rooms, and mass graves where children and women as well as men had been brutalized and buried.

Russia-U.S. Relations

Q. The question is for both Presidents. Now we can state that despite differences over Iraq, these differences have not led to the worsening of relations either between you, personally, or between our two countries. How can it be explained? Due to what reasons did it actually happen?

President Bush. Trust. Listen, I—Vladimir and I had some very frank discussions about Iraq. I understood his position. He understood mine. But because we've got a trustworthy relationship, we're able to move beyond any disagreement over a single issue. Plus, I like him. He's a good fellow to spend quality time with.

President Putin. Thank you, George, for your warm words. I would like to confirm everything that has been said by the President and to send him a response.

I would like to add just one thing. There are two reasons why such problems between our states and between us, personally, have not emerged. We had differences over Iraq in terms of practical ways how to resolve this problem, but we had understanding on the essence of this problem. And the second and the most important point, fundamental interests of our two countries are much more solid, are much stronger than the developments that you have just mentioned. And in our actions, we wish to be guided by these strategic interests of our two countries without excessive emotions or ambitions.

Thank you.

President Bush. Good job. Thank you.

NOTE: The President's news conference began at 11:04 a.m. In his remarks, President Putin referred to Ramiro Armando de Oliveira Lopes da Silva, acting U.N. Special Representative for Iraq. President Putin spoke in Russian, and his remarks were translated by an interpreter.

Joint Statement Between the United States of America and the Russian Federation
September 27, 2003

President George W. Bush and President Vladimir V. Putin held productive discussions at Camp David, Maryland, on September 26 and 27, 2003. Building on the Joint Declaration on the New Strategic Relationship of May 24, 2002, and other joint documents, they focused on practical ways to broaden and deepen cooperation and partnership between the United States and Russia, overcoming obstacles and fulfilling their shared vision of a new strategic relationship to deal with the challenges and opportunities of the 21st Century.

The Presidents discussed a broad range of bilateral and international issues, including counter-terrorism; preventing proliferation of weapons of mass destruction; the situations in the Middle East, Iraq, Iran, and North Korea; strengthening the NATO-Russia relationship; progress in creating conditions to expand economic and commercial relations; cooperation in high technology, housing, and health; and people-to-people contacts, as well as other questions of mutual interest.

The Presidents agreed on next steps in a number of areas to strengthen the existing U.S.-Russia partnership. They issued specific instructions to their respective governments identifying tasks to be undertaken by the appropriate agencies and specifying timelines for doing so, and they underscored their shared intention to monitor fulfillment of these tasks. In particular, they identified key areas where progress might be made in the near term, including, among other issues:

- implementing effectively the Strategic Offensive Reductions Treaty (Treaty of Moscow), and continuing efforts to increase transparency and build confidence on strategic issues;
- building cooperation between the American and Russian military establishments, as critical to joint efforts in areas such as counter-terrorism, missile defense, and peacekeeping;
- strengthening commercial and economic relations through further cooperation in enhancing global energy security, eliminating barriers to trade and investment, promoting high-tech-nology cooperation, and protecting intellectual property rights;
- strengthening consultation and cooperation in dealing with regional problems; and
- deepening cooperation in the battle against HIV/AIDs, which will benefit the United States and Russia, and contribute to the global effort against this modern plague.

The Presidents agreed to remain in close contact to ensure progress across the broad agenda that they have defined.

NOTE: An original was not available for verification of the content of this joint statement.

Remarks Honoring the 2003 Stanley Cup Champion New Jersey Devils
September 29, 2003

Thank you all for being here. Please be seated. It's my honor to welcome to the Rose Garden the Stanley Cup champs. Congratulations. It's a—I had the honor of meeting your captain. I saw a quote; he said, "It's an awesome experience," talked about winning, what it's like to win as a team. And I want to congratulate the team that is with us today.

I want to thank Peter Simon, who is the chairman. I appreciate Lou Lamoriello, who is the general manager and the president and CEO of the New Jersey Devils. I want to congratulate Pat Burns, the Jack Adams Award winner, which I guess means he's a really good coach. Gary Bettman, the commissioner, is with us. Mr. Commissioner, good to see you.

They tell me this cup is 110 years old. That makes it older than the Oval Office. [*Laughter*] I see it's got all the names of the players who have won it, and now your names are on it. It's a fantastic legacy to athleticism and desire and drive, a couple of cuts here and there—[*laughter*]—maybe a missed tooth or two. [*Laughter*]

The concept of a team is just really important. I have a chance to welcome champs to the White House on a regular basis, and it seems to be a common ingredient, where people are willing to put something above individual achievement, called the team. They kind of work together for something bigger than self-glory. It's the common ingredient of all the champs that come here, and it's been the common ingredient of this team, led by a very capable captain and great players.

One of the things that's interesting about the Stanley Cup is that each player gets to spend time with it. It must be pretty neat. The cup has traveled throughout North America and Europe. It's been to some famous sites recently. It was at the McDonald's drive-through in New Glasgow, Nova Scotia. [*Laughter*] It must have been a pretty interesting moment for that burger-flipper. [*Laughter*] Fill her up. [*Laughter*] It showed up at the Bob Evans restaurant in Brunswick, Ohio. It went to Filthy McNasty's Bar and Grill in Toronto. [*Laughter*] I don't know who took it there, but—[*laughter*]—I bet you're pretty happy the cup can't talk—[*laughter*]—if you know what I mean.

Most important, though, these players took it to hospitals and schools, to senior centers, and to a home for neglected and abused children. They took it to fire and police crews that are working long hours to keep their communities safe. They took it to the people in our Armed Forces. In other words, this cup helped inspire people, helped lift up lives.

When I met Scott Stevens, he wasn't out there as a great hockey player. He was out there at the airport in Newark because he works for the Boys and Girls Clubs of Newark, participates in after-school programs to help kids make healthy choices in their life. He was involved with the Hockey Fights Cancer campaign.

What I'm telling you about is that champs are people who serve their community—off the ice, in this case. Champs are people who not only serve something great-

er than themself, called their team, but their community. Champs are people who understand that when you're the champion, somebody looks at you. They wonder, "What is it like to be a champ?" So when you make right choices, set out the right examples, hug somebody who hurts, you're really helping our country. And if you're from Canada or other countries, you're helping your country too. I'm most appreciative—the thing I'm most appreciative about, I love your athletic skill, but I love the fact that you're compassionate people as well.

So it's my honor to welcome you to the Rose Garden as the great champs of the National Hockey League. Congratulations. Welcome.

NOTE: The President spoke at 2:04 p.m. in the Rose Garden at the White House. In his remarks, he referred to Peter Simon, chairman, Louis A. Lamoriello, chief executive officer, president, and general manager, Pat Burns, head coach, and Scott Stevens, captain, New Jersey Devils; and Gary B. Bettman, commissioner, National Hockey League. Following his remarks, the President was presented with a New Jersey Devils jersey.

Remarks on Signing Legislation To Ratify the Authority of the Federal Trade Commission To Establish a Do-Not-Call Registry
September 29, 2003

Good afternoon. Thank you all for coming, and welcome back to the White House.

This summer, the Federal Trade Commission, ably headed by Tim Muris, and the Federal Communications Commission, ably headed by Michael Powell, joined to create a national Do-Not-Call Registry. The registry allows Americans to shield their home and cell phone numbers from most unwanted telemarketing calls. By signing up over the phone or online, people can pro-

tect their privacy and their family time from intrusive, annoying, unwelcome commercial solicitations.

The Do-Not-Call Registry is a practical solution to address a growing concern. I'm honored that Senator Stevens is with us, the chairman; Congressman Billy Tauzin, the chairman, is with us; Ed Markey, ranking member; Fred Upton. I appreciate you all coming.

The reason they're here is they acted to a response from the judiciary. They acted as well because the American people clearly like the idea of a Do-Not-Call Registry. After all, since the first signup day 3 months ago, Americans have entered over 50 million telephone numbers in the Do-Not-Call Registry.

While many good people work in the telemarketing industry, the public is understandably losing patience with these unwanted phone calls, unwanted intrusions. And given a choice, Americans prefer not to receive random sales pitches at all hours of the day. And the American people should be free to restrict these calls.

Last week, a Federal judge objected to the Do-Not-Call Registry on the grounds that Congress had not authorized its creation. So the House and the Senate author-ized its creation. You acted swiftly, and I want to congratulate you very much. It's a really good action. The Senate voted 95–0; the House 412–8. This affirmed the decision by the FTC, and it's affirmed the wishes of the American people.

The Do-Not-Call Registry is still being challenged in court. Yet, the conclusion of the American people and the legislative branch and the executive branch is beyond question. So today I'm pleased to sign this important piece of legislation into law. Want to come and join us?

NOTE: The President spoke at 3:40 p.m. in the Roosevelt Room at the White House. H.R. 3161, approved September 29, was assigned Public Law No. 108–82. The Office of the Press Secretary also released a Spanish language transcript of these remarks.

Statement on the Death of Althea Gibson
September 29, 2003

Althea Gibson rose above segregation and discrimination to become a world-class tennis player. In 1957 and 1958, she won both Wimbledon and the United States Open, displaying her remarkable spirit, determination, and skill. In breaking the racial barrier in championship tennis, she furthered America's progress in recognizing individuals for their character and abilities, not their skin color. Laura and I send our prayers and condolences to the family and friends of Althea Gibson.

Message to the Congress Reporting on the Memorandum of Understanding Between the Secretaries of State and Homeland Security Concerning Implementation of Section 428 of the Homeland Security Act of 2002
September 29, 2003

Message to the Congress of the United States:

Consistent with section 428(e)(8)(A) of the Homeland Security Act of 2002 (Public Law 107–296) (the "Act"), I am pleased to report that the Secretary of State and the Secretary of Homeland Security have completed a Memorandum of Understanding concerning implementation of section 428 of the Act. The Memorandum of Understanding will allow the Departments of State and Homeland Security to work cooperatively to create and maintain an effective, efficient visa process that secures

America's borders from external threats and ensures that our borders remain open to legitimate travel to the United States.

GEORGE W. BUSH

The White House,

September 29, 2003.

NOTE: The related notice of September 29 is listed in Appendix D at the end of this volume.

Remarks at a Bush-Cheney Luncheon in Chicago, Illinois
September 30, 2003

Thank you all very much. Thanks for coming. Please be seated. Thanks for the warm welcome. I always love coming to the great city of Chicago. It's really one of the great cities in our country. I was here last summer, and I'm really happy the baseball season is still going on. It's exciting for the citizens of this city to know that the Cubs are still alive and kicking. I wish you all the best.

Thanks for your help. And what we're doing today is laying the groundwork, putting down the foundation for what is going to be a great national victory in November of 2004. I appreciate your generosity. I want to thank you for your hard work. I thank you for your contributions, but I'm going to call on you to do more. I'm going to ask you to go to your coffee shops, drug stores, community centers and remind the people that this administration has got a message that is positive and hopeful and optimistic for every single American.

I'm getting ready, and I'm loosening up. But there's a time for politics. This political season will come in its own time. Right now I'm focused on doing the people's business. I've got a job to do, and there's a lot on the agenda. I will continue to work hard to earn the confidence of every American by keeping this Nation strong and secure, prosperous, and free.

I want to thank Pat Ryan and all those who worked hard to put this event on. It is a fantastic turnout, and I understand how much' work goes into a successful lunch

like today, and I really thank you a lot. I appreciate your leadership, Pat.

I'm also honored to be introduced by the great Speaker of the House, Denny Hastert. He's truly one of the greats. I really do enjoy working with Denny. He's a no-nonsense kind of fellow. He looks you in the eye and tells you what he believes. And that's refreshing in Washington, DC, by the way. He cares a lot about the people of his district, the people of this State, and he loves his country. And like me, he married above himself. [*Laughter*] And I'm glad Jean is here with us today as well.

Speaking about wives, I notice Laura was doing a little diplomacy today. [*Laughter*] I'm really proud of her. She is a fabulous woman, a great mom, a great wife, and a terrific First Lady for the people of this country.

I'm honored as well that members of the Illinois congressional delegation are here. I want to thank them for their hard work on behalf of this State and for helping out at this fundraiser today. Mark Kirk; Phil Crane—Congressman Crane is with us. Judy Biggert is with us. Dan Manzullo is with us. John Shimkus is with us. I appreciate you all coming, and I'm honored to call you friend.

We had a member—a meeting of the former Governors club behind the stage here. And I'm a member. It was good to see two other members. That would be Jim Edgar and Jim Thompson, and I'm honored they're here. I'm proud to call them friend.

I want to thank Bob Kjellander, who is the national committeeman from this State, and Mary Jo Arndt, who is the national committeewoman. I want to thank all the grassroots activists. I'm glad to know Mary Jo brought her family with her. [*Laughter*] I want to thank my friend Mercer Reynolds, who is a Cincinnati businessman who is my national finance chairman. But most of all, I want to thank you all for coming.

The last 2½ years, our Nation has acted decisively to confront great challenges. I came to this office to solve problems and not pass them on to future Presidents and future generations. I came to seize opportunities and not let them slip away. This administration is meeting the tests of our time.

Terrorists declared war on the United States of America, and war is what they got. We've captured or killed many of the key leaders of the Al Qaida network that orchestrated the attacks on America on September the 11th, 2001. And the rest of them know we're on their trail. In Afghanistan and Iraq, we gave ultimatums to terror regimes. Those ultimatums chose to—those regimes chose defiance, and those regimes are no more. Fifty-million people in those two countries once lived under tyranny, and now they live in freedom.

Two-and-a-half years ago, our military was not receiving the resources it needed, and morale was beginning to suffer. So we increased the defense budget to prepare for the threats of a new era. And today, no one in the world can question the skill and the strength and the spirit of the United States military.

Two-and-a-half years ago, we inherited an economy in recession. And then our country was attacked, and we began a march to war. We found out some of our corporate citizens forgot to tell the truth—all of which affected the confidence of our country. But we acted. We passed tough laws to hold corporate criminals to account. And to get the economy going, we have twice led the United States Congress to pass historic tax relief for the American people.

Here's what the Speaker and I know: We know that when Americans have more take-home pay to spend, save, or invest, the whole economy grows, and people are more likely to find a job. We understand whose money we spend in Washington, DC. We do not spend the Government's money. We spend the people's money. And so we're returning more money to American families to help them meet their needs. We're reducing the taxes on dividends and capital gains to encourage investment. We give small businesses incentives to expand and hire new people. With all these actions, we're laying the foundations for greater prosperity and economic vitality and more jobs across America, so that every single one of our citizens is able to realize the great promise of America.

Two-and-a-half years ago, there was a lot of talk about education reform, but there wasn't much action. So I acted. I called for and Congress passed the No Child Left Behind Act. With a solid bipartisan majority, we delivered the most dramatic education reforms in a generation. We're bringing high standards and strong accountability to every public school in America. See, we believe every child can learn the basics of reading and math. That's what we believe. And we expect every school to teach the basics of reading and math.

We are challenging the soft bigotry of low expectations. In return for Federal money, we expect results. The days of excuse-making are over. We want every child to learn to read and write and add and subtract, so that not one single child is left behind in America.

We reorganized the Government and created the Department of Homeland Security to safeguard our borders and ports and to make the American people more secure. We passed trade promotion authority to open up new markets for Illinois' ranchers and farmers and manufacturers and entrepreneurs. We passed budget agreements—and Mr. Speaker, thank you for working on those—to bring much needed spending discipline to Washington, DC. On issue after issue, this administration has acted on principle. We have kept our word, and we have made progress for the American people.

We have done a lot, and the Congress deserves a lot of the credit. We have set out goals. We have met those goals, thanks in large part to the leadership of Speaker Denny Hastert. He and Senator Bill Frist are great leaders of the United States Congress. They work closely with the administration. They've got one thing in mind. They want to work with us to get rid of this needless partisan bickering that dominates the Washington, DC, landscape and the zero-sum politics of Washington. And we can do that by not only working to change the tone in Washington but by focusing on results, by saying, "Here's what we're going to do," and then go out and do it. Speaker Hastert, you are a great leader of the House of Representatives of the United States.

I've asked good people to join my administration, people who are as well working to change the tone in Washington, good, solid citizens who are there to serve something greater than themselves, good people like Don Rumsfeld, who was educated right here in this part of the—of our country. Now, I've got a strong team, solid Americans from all walks of life. Our country has had no finer Vice President than Dick Cheney. Mother may have a different opinion. [*Laughter*]

Now, we've done a lot in 2½ years. We've come far, but our work is only beginning. I have set great goals worthy of a great nation. First, America is committed to expanding the realm of freedom and peace for our own security and for the benefit of the world. And second, in our own country, we must work for a society of prosperity and compassion, so that every citizen has a chance to work and to succeed

and to realize the American Dream. It is clear that the future of freedom and peace depend on the actions of America. This Nation is freedom's home, and we are freedom's defender. We welcome this charge of history, and we are keeping it.

Our war on terror continues. The enemies of freedom, those who hate America, are not idle, and neither are we. This country will not rest. We will not tire, and we will not stop until this danger to civilization is removed.

We're confronting that danger in Iraq, where Saddam holdouts and foreign terrorists are desperately trying to throw Iraq into chaos by attacking coalition forces and aid workers and innocent Iraqis. They know that the advance of freedom in Iraq would be a major defeat in the cause of terror. This collection of killers is trying to shake the will of America and the civilized world. But America will not be intimidated.

Aggressively striking the terrorists in Iraq, we're defeating them there so we don't have to face them in our own country. We call on other nations to help build a free Iraq. We stand with the Iraqi people as they assume more of their own defense and move towards self-government. These aren't easy tasks, but they are essential tasks. We will finish what we have begun, and we will win this essential victory in the war on terror.

Yet our greatest security comes from the advance of human liberty, because free nations do not support terror. Free nations do not attack their neighbors. Free nations do not threaten the world with weapons of mass terror. Americans believe that freedom is the deepest need and hope of every human heart. And I believe that freedom is the right of every person and that freedom is the future of every nation.

America also understands that unprecedented influence brings tremendous responsibilities. We have duties in the world. And when we see disease and starvation and hopeless poverty, we will not turn away. On the continent of Africa, America is now committed to bringing the healing power, the healing power of medicine, to millions of men and women and children now suffering with AIDS. This great land, this great strong and compassionate Nation, is leading the world in this incredibly important work of human rescue.

We face challenges at home as well. The Speaker knows that, and I know it. And our actions will prove equal to those tasks. So long as anybody in America who wants to work is looking for a job, I will work hard to make the conditions for economic growth positive and strong. I want our people working in America.

We have other duties as well. We have a duty to keep our commitment to America's seniors by strengthening and modernizing Medicare. Congress took historic action to improve the lives of older Americans. For the first time since the creation of Medicare, the House and the Senate have passed reforms to increase the choices for our seniors and to provide coverage for prescription drugs. The next step is for both Houses to reconcile their differences, to iron out the details, and get a bill to my desk. The sooner they finish the job, the sooner we can say we have done our duty to America's seniors.

And for the sake of our health care system, we need to cut down on the frivolous lawsuits which increase the cost of medicine. People who have been harmed by a bad doc deserve their day in court. Yet the system should not reward lawyers who are simply fishing for rich settlements. Frivolous lawsuits drive up the cost of health care, and therefore, they affect the Federal budget. Medical liability reform is a national issue which requires a national solution. And so I proposed a good bill, and I worked with the Speaker on it. We passed a good bill out of the House of Representatives, but the bill is stuck in the Senate. And the Senate must act on behalf of the American people. Those Senators must understand that no one has ever been healed by a frivolous lawsuit.

I have a responsibility to make sure the judicial system runs well, and I have met that duty. I've nominated superb men and women for our Federal courts, people who interpret the law, not legislate from the bench. Some Members of the Senate are trying to keep my nominees off the bench by blocking up-or-down votes. Every judicial nominee deserves a fair hearing and an up-or-down vote on the Senate floor. It is time for some of the Members of the United States Senate to stop playing politics with American justice.

Congress needs to complete work on a comprehensive energy plan. The Speaker knows this, and Mr. Speaker, I appreciate your leadership on this issue. As we learned a while ago, we need to modernize our electricity grid. [*Laughter*] We need to bring it up to the standards of the 21st century. We need to make sure that the delivery of electricity is not a voluntary act. It's a—requires mandatory reliability standards. We need to make sure we do a better job of using our technologies to conserve more energy. We need to develop alternative sources to foreign oil. We need clean coal technology. One of the things we need to do is, for economic security and national security, to become less dependent on foreign sources of energy.

Our strong and prosperous Nation must also be a compassionate nation. I will continue to advance our agenda of compassionate conservatism, applying the most innovative ideas to the task of helping our fellow citizens in need. There are millions of men and women who want to end their dependence on government, become independent through hard work. We must build on the success of welfare reform to bring work and dignity into the lives of more of our fellow citizens.

Congress should complete the "Citizen Service Act," so more Americans can serve their communities and their country. And both Houses should finally reach agreement on my Faith-Based Initiative to support the armies of compassion which exist all around our country, that are mentoring our children, that are caring for the homeless, that offer hope to addicted. This great Nation should not fear faith, should not fear those who rely upon faith as their motivation to provide help to those who hurt. We need to welcome faith in our society.

A compassionate society must promote opportunity for all, including the independence and dignity that come from ownership. See, this administration will constantly strive to promote an ownership society in America. We want more people owning their own home. We want people owning and managing their health care accounts. We want people owning and managing their own retirement accounts. We want more people owning a small business, because we understand that when a person owns something, he or she has a vital stake in the future of our country.

In a compassionate society, people respect one another and take responsibility for the decisions they make. We're changing the culture of America from one that has said, "If it feels good, just go ahead and do it," and "If you've got a problem, blame somebody else," to a culture in which each of us understands we are responsible for the decisions we make in life. If you are fortunate enough to be a mom or a dad, you're responsible for loving your child. If you're concerned about the quality of the education in the community in which you live, you're responsible for doing something about it. If you're a CEO in corporate America, you're responsible for telling the truth to your shareholders and your employees. And in the new responsibility society, each of us is responsible for loving our neighbor just like we'd like to be loved ourselves.

We can see the culture of service and responsibility growing around us here in America. You know, I started what's called the USA Freedom Corps to encourage Americans to extend a compassionate hand to a neighbor in need, and the response has been really strong. People want to serve. People want to be involved in their community. Our faith-based and charities are strong, providing the much needed healing to those who need help.

Policemen and firefighters and people who wear our Nation's uniform are reminding us what it means to sacrifice for something greater than yourself. Once again, the children of America believe in heroes, because they see them every day. In these challenging times, the world has seen the resolve and the courage of America. And I've been privileged to see the compassion and the character of the American people.

All the tests of the last 2½ years have come to the right Nation. We're a strong country, and we use that strength to defend the peace. We're an optimistic country, confident in ourselves and in ideals bigger than ourselves. Abroad, we seek to lift whole nations by spreading freedom. At home, we seek to lift up lives by spreading opportunity to every corner of America. This is the work that history has set before us, and we welcome it. And we know that for our country and for our cause, the best days lie ahead.

May God bless you all.

NOTE: The President spoke at 12:30 p.m. at the Sheraton Chicago Hotel and Towers. In his remarks, he referred to Patrick G. Ryan, luncheon chairman; Jean Hastert, wife of Speaker of the House of Representatives J. Dennis Hastert; former Gov. Jim Edgar and former Gov. James R. Thompson of Illinois; Robert Kjellander, Illinois national committeeman, and Mary Jo Arndt, Illinois national committeewoman, Republican National Committee; Mercer Reynolds, national finance chairman, Bush-Cheney '04, Inc.; and former President Saddam Hussein of Iraq.

Remarks Following a Meeting With Business Leaders and an Exchange With Reporters in Chicago
September 30, 2003

The President. Mr. Mayor, thank you. I want to thank the business leaders here from the Chicago area for sharing with me their concerns about our economy. I think it's safe to say most people share the sense of optimism I do but recognize there's still work to be done, particularly when it comes to job creation.

We talked about good legal policy. We talked about the need for an energy plan. We talked about fair trade for American manufacturers. We talked about the need for China to make sure that China's got a monetary policy which is fair. And I assured the leaders here that I would work to—I'd represent the manufacturing sector and the—all sectors of our economy when it comes to world trade.

The thing I'm concerned about is people being able to find a job. We put the conditions in place for good job creation, but I recognize there's still people who want to work that can't find a job. And we're dedicated to hearing the voices of those folks and working hard to expand our economy.

And so I want to thank you all for taking time. Mr. Mayor, I wish the Cubs all the best. [*Laughter*] I made a significant contribution to the Cubs, as you might recall——

Participant. Sammy.

The President. ——when I was a—yes, Sammy Sosa. I'll take great delight when they win.

Participant. Thank you for Sammy.

The President. Thanks for coming.

Let me answer a couple of questions. Then we've got to go to Cincinnati. Deb [Deb Riechmann, Associated Press].

Justice Department Investigation of Classified Information Leak

Q. Do you think that the Justice Department can conduct an impartial investigation, considering the political ramifications of the CIA leak, and why wouldn't a special counsel be better?

The President. Yes. Let me just say something about leaks in Washington. There are too many leaks of classified information in Washington. There's leaks at the executive branch; there's leaks in the legislative branch. There's just too many leaks. And if there is a leak out of my administration, I want to know who it is. And if the person has violated law, the person will be taken care of.

And so I welcome the investigation. I'm absolutely confident that the Justice Department will do a very good job. There's a special division of career Justice Department officials who are tasked with doing this kind of work. They have done this kind of work before in Washington this year. I have told our administration—people in my administration to be fully cooperative.

I want to know the truth. If anybody has got any information, inside our administration or outside our administration, it would be helpful if they came forward with the information so we can find out whether or not these allegations are true and get on about the business.

Yes, let's see, Kemper [Bob Kemper, Chicago Tribune]. He's from Chicago. Where are you? Are you a Cubs or White Sox fan? [*Laughter*] Wait a minute. That doesn't seem fair, does it? [*Laughter*]

Q. Yesterday we were told that Karl Rove had no role in it.

The President. Yes.

Q. Have you talked to Karl, and do you have confidence in him——

The President. Listen, I know of nobody—I don't know of anybody in my administration who leaked classified information. If somebody did leak classified information, I'd like to know it, and we'll take the appropriate action. And this investigation is a good thing.

And again I repeat, you know, Washington is a town where there's all kinds of allegations. You've heard much of the allegations. And if people have got solid information, please come forward with it. And that would be people inside the information who are the so-called anonymous sources, or people outside the information—outside the administration. And we can clarify this thing very quickly if people who have got solid evidence would come forward and speak out. And I would hope they would. And then we'll get to the bottom of this and move on.

But I want to tell you something, leaks of classified information are a bad thing. And we've had them—there's too much leaking in Washington. That's just the way it is. And we've had leaks out of the administrative branch, had leaks out of the legislative branch, and out of the executive branch and the legislative branch, and I've spoken out consistently against them, and I want to know who the leakers are.

Thank you.

NOTE: The President spoke at 2:10 p.m. at the University of Chicago. In his remarks, he referred to Mayor Richard M. Daley of Chicago, IL; and Chicago Cubs baseball player Sammy Sosa. The Office of the Press Secretary also released a Spanish language transcript of these remarks. A tape was not available for verification of the content of these remarks.

Statement on Signing the Legislative Branch Appropriations Act, 2004
September 30, 2003

Today I have signed into law H.R. 2657, the "Legislative Branch Appropriations Act, 2004" for the fiscal year ending September 30, 2004, and making emergency supplemental appropriations for fiscal year 2003.

Section 103 of the Act establishes in the House of Representatives an Office of Interparliamentary Affairs. To ensure consistency with the President's constitutional authority to conduct the Nation's foreign affairs, the executive branch shall construe section 103 as assigning the Office functions limited to protocol and travel support for the House of Representatives.

Several provisions of the Act make specified changes in statements of managers of the House-Senate conference committees that accompanied various bills reported

from conference that ultimately became laws. As with other committee materials, statements of managers accompanying a conference report do not have the force of law. Accordingly, although changes to these statements are directed by the terms of the statute, the statements themselves are not legally binding.

GEORGE W. BUSH

The White House,
September 30, 2003.

NOTE: H.R. 2657, approved September 30, was assigned Public Law No. 108–83. An original was not available for verification of the content of this statement.

Letter to the Speaker of the House of Representatives on Reallocation of Funds Previously Transferred From the Emergency Response Fund
September 30, 2003

Dear Mr. Speaker:

In order to continue responses necessary as a result of the September 11th terrorist attacks, I am notifying the Congress of my intent to reallocate funds previously transferred from the Emergency Response Fund (ERF).

At this time, $290 million of ERF funds will be transferred to the Department of State to accelerate a variety of initiatives already underway in Afghanistan.

The details of this action are set forth in the enclosed letter from the Director of the Office of Management and Budget.

Sincerely,

GEORGE W. BUSH

Letter to the Speaker of the House of Representatives on Providing Funds for the Department of Homeland Security's Counterterrorism Fund
September 30, 2003

Dear Mr. Speaker:

In accordance with provisions of the Consolidated Appropriations Act, 2001 (Public Law 106–554), and the Consolidated Appropriations Resolution, 2003 (Public Law 108–7), I hereby request and make available $38,100,000 for the Department of Homeland Security's Counterterrorism Fund. Of these funds, I hereby designate $28,748,918 as an emergency requirement pursuant to Public Law 106–554.

These funds would allow the Department of Homeland Security to continue to improve the security at our Nation's ports by deploying radiation monitoring devices nationwide and strengthening the system that is used to identify potential threats posed by international cargo shipments and international passengers.

The details of this action are set forth in the enclosed letter from the Director of the Office of Management and Budget.

Sincerely,

GEORGE W. BUSH

Statement on Signing the Department of Defense Appropriations Act, 2004
September 30, 2003

Today, I have signed into law H.R. 2658, the "Department of Defense Appropriations Act, 2004."

Sections 8007 and 8103 of the Act prohibit the use of funds to initiate a special access program or to initiate a new start program, unless the congressional defense committees receive advance notice. The Supreme Court of the United States has stated that the President's authority to classify and control access to information bearing on the national security flows from the Constitution and does not depend upon a legislative grant of authority. Although the advance notice contemplated by sections 8007 and 8103 can be provided in most situations as a matter of comity, situations may arise, especially in wartime, in which the President must act promptly under his constitutional grants of executive power and authority as Commander in Chief of the Armed Forces while protecting certain extraordinarily sensitive national security information. The executive branch shall construe sections 8007 and 8103 in a manner consistent with the constitutional authority of the President.

Section 8065 of the Act provides that, notwithstanding any other provision of law, no funds available to the Department of Defense for fiscal year 2004 may be used to transfer defense articles or services, other than intelligence services, to another nation or an international organization for international peacekeeping, peace enforcement, or humanitarian assistance operations, until 15 days after the executive branch notifies six committees of the Congress of the planned transfer. To the extent that protection of the U.S. Armed Forces deployed for international peacekeeping, peace enforcement, or humanitarian assistance operations might require action of a kind covered by section 8065 sooner than 15 days after notification, the executive branch shall construe section 8065 in a manner consistent with the President's constitutional authority as Commander in Chief of the Armed Forces.

A proviso in the Act's appropriation for "Operation and Maintenance, Defense-Wide" prohibits implementation of and purports to prohibit planning for consolidation of certain offices within the Department of Defense. Also, sections 8010(b), 8041(b), and 8115 purport to specify the content of a portion of a future budget request to the Congress for the Department of Defense. The executive branch shall construe these provisions relating to planning and making of budget recommendations in a manner consistent with the President's constitutional authority to require the opinions of the heads of departments and to recommend for congressional consideration such measures as the President shall judge necessary and expedient.

Section 8005 of the Act relating to requests to congressional committees for reprogramming of funds shall be construed as calling solely for notification, as any other construction would be inconsistent with the principles enunciated by the Supreme Court in *INS* v. *Chadha.*

A proviso within the appropriation for "Operation and Maintenance, Air Force" earmarks an amount of funds for a grant to a college for the purpose of funding minority aviation training, and section 8089 of the Act provides that, in implementing a healthcare interagency partnership under that section, Native Hawaiians shall have the status of Native Americans who are eligible for healthcare services. The executive branch shall implement the proviso and section 8089 in a manner consistent with the requirement to afford equal protection of the laws under the Due Process Clause of the Fifth Amendment to the Constitution.

Sections 8082, 8091, 8117, and 8131 of the Act make clear that the classified annex accompanies but is not incorporated as a part of the Act, and therefore the classified annex does not meet the bicameralism and presentment requirements specified by the Constitution for the making of a law. Accordingly, the executive branch shall construe the classified annex references in sections 8082, 8091, 8117, and 8131 as advisory in effect. My Administration continues to discourage any efforts to enact secret law as part of defense funding legislation and encourages instead appropriate use of classified annexes to committee reports and joint statements of managers that accompany the final legislation.

GEORGE W. BUSH

The White House,
September 30, 2003.

NOTE: H.R. 2658, approved September 30, was assigned Public Law No. 108–87. This statement was released by the Office of the Press Secretary on October 1.

Remarks Prior to Discussions With Prime Minister Mir Zafarullah Khan Jamali of Pakistan
October 1, 2003

President Bush. Listen, Mr. Prime Minister, thank you. It's my honor to welcome you to the Oval Office. I look forward to our discussions. We will have discussions here in the Oval Office. Then we'll go to have lunch. And over lunch we'll discuss a wide range of issues: Our mutual desire to fight terror; our keen desire to bring stability and peace throughout the world; look forward to discussions about our bilateral relations in regards to commerce and opportunities to enhance the livelihood of our fellow citizens.

There's a lot of Pakistani Americans who are pleased you are here today, sir. And on their behalf, I welcome you to the Oval Office. And it gives me a chance to say publicly how much we appreciate the friendship of Pakistan.

Prime Minister Jamali. Thank you, Mr. President.

President Bush. You're welcome.

Prime Minister Jamali. Well, I can see you're pleased. I'm sure that the Pakistan community is pleased that I'm here. And Pakistan is helping as a partner—is a partner as far as the fight against terrorism is concerned, as far as our bilateral relations are concerned. We want a long, lasting friendship with the United States, and that is why I'm here, to bring a message of the new democratic setup which I set in Pakistan the last 10 months. And in short, we intend getting that through—of course, with a pat on the back as far as President Bush is concerned. [*Laughter*] Will that be all right?

Thank you very much.

President Bush. Thank you, sir. Glad you're here.

NOTE: The President spoke at 11:41 a.m. in the Oval Office at the White House. A tape was not available for verification of the content of these remarks.

Remarks on Signing the Department of Homeland Security Appropriations Act, 2004
October 1, 2003

Thank you for the warm welcome. Please be seated, unless you don't have a seat. [*Laughter*] I'm proud to be with the men and women of the newest agency of our Government. And today I'm honored to sign the first appropriations bill for this Department.

Many of you have served your country for years, in agencies with proud histories and honored traditions. Some of you are new to the Federal service. All of us share a great responsibility. Our job is to secure the American homeland, to protect the American people. And we're meeting that duty together.

On September the 11th, 2001, enemies of freedom made our country a battleground. Their method is the mass murder of the innocent, and their goal is to make all Americans live in fear. Yet our Nation refuses to live in fear. And the best way to overcome fear and to frustrate the plans of our enemies is to be prepared and resolute at home and to take the offensive abroad.

The danger to America gives all of you an essential role in the war on terror. You've done fine work under difficult and urgent circumstances, and on behalf of a grateful nation, I thank you all for what you do for the security and safety of our fellow citizens.

I appreciate Tom Ridge agreeing to lead this important Department. I'm honored to call him friend, and I'm proud of the job he is doing. I appreciate General John Gordon, who is the Homeland Security Adviser in the White House. I want to thank the very capable Department of Homeland Security leadership who are with us today.

I'm also honored to share this bill signing with Members of the United States Senate and the United States House of Representative who did an excellent job of getting this bill through. I appreciate so very much the Senator from Mississippi, Thad Cochran, the chairman of the Senate Appropriations Subcommittee on Homeland Security. I'm also honored that three Members of the House are up here to join in the bill signing ceremony, starting with the chairman of the House Appropriations Committee, Bill Young of Florida; Hal Rogers of Kentucky, the chairman of the House Appropriations Subcommittee on Homeland Security; Congressman Martin Sabo from Minnesota, the ranking member of the House Appropriations Subcommittee on Homeland Security. I want to thank you all for a job well done.

I'm also so pleased that Members in the Senate and the House of both political parties are with us today. The stage wasn't big enough to hold you. Thank you for coming. Thanks for your hard work, and thanks for working together to do what's right for America.

This time 2 years ago, America was still in the midst of a national emergency. Smoke was rising from Ground Zero; recovery teams were carefully sifting through debris; and chaplains were comforting families and blessing the dead. Our Nation does not live in the past; yet we do not forget the past and the grief of that time. We do not forget the men and women and children who were lost that day. We do not forget the enemies who rejoiced as America suffered or those who seek to inflict more pain and grief on our country.

September the 11th, America accepted a great mission, and that mission continues to this hour. We will do everything in our power to prevent another attack on the American people. And wherever America's enemies plot and plan, we'll find them, and we will bring them to justice.

The war on terror has set urgent priorities for America abroad. We are not waiting while dangers gather. Along with fine allies, we are waging a global campaign against terrorist networks, disrupting their operations, cutting off their funding, and we are hunting down their leaders one by one. We're enforcing a clear doctrine: If you harbor a terrorist, if you feed a terrorist, if you support a terrorist, you're just as guilty as the terrorists, and you can expect to share their fate.

We're determined to prevent terror networks from gaining weapons of mass destruction. We're committed to spreading democracy and tolerance. As we hunt down the terrorists, we're committed to spending—spreading freedom in all parts of the world, including the Middle East. By removing the tyrants in Iraq and Afghanistan who supported terror and by ending the hopelessness that feeds terror, we're helping the people of that region, and we're strengthening the security of America.

The war on terror has also set urgent priorities here at home. Oceans no longer protect us from danger. And we're taking unprecedented measures to prevent terrorist attacks, reduce our vulnerabilities, and to prepare for any emergency. That's what you're doing. Each of you plays a vital role in this strategy to better secure America. Agencies that once worked separately to safeguard our country are now working together in a single Department, and that's good for America. You have the authority to quickly put the right people in place as we respond to danger. You've got good leadership. Every member of this Department has an important calling, and you need to know, when you come to work every day, your fellow citizens are counting on you.

Those in Customs and Immigration are performing essential work in controlling our borders and, at the same time, in reducing the backlog of immigrant applicants as we move toward a standard of 6-month processing time for all applications. At the Transportation Security Administration and the Coast Guard, you protect the vast road, rail, and sea and air networks that are critical to the American economy. DHS scientists and engineers work to detect deadly chemical, biological, and nuclear weapons. DHS experts help the public and private sectors to identify and address vulnerabilities in our power grids, chemical plants, communications systems, and transportation networks. At FEMA, you joined forces with State and local authorities to respond quickly and effectively to any emergency.

All of you have been given a hard job, and you're rising to the challenge. The American people understand the importance of your work, and so does the United States Congress. The Homeland Security bill I will sign today commits $31 billion to securing our Nation, over $14 billion more than pre-September 11th levels. The bill increases funding for the key responsibilities at the Department of Homeland Security and supports important new initiatives across the Department.

We're providing $5.6 billion over the next decade to fund Project BioShield. Under this program, DHS will work with the Department of Health and Human Services to accelerate the development and procurement of advanced vaccines and treatments to protect Americans against biological or chemical or radiological threats.

We're providing $4 billion in grants for our Nation's first-responders. We're focusing $725 million on major urban areas where it is most needed. We're also providing $40 million for Citizen Corps Councils through which volunteers work with first-responders to prepare their communities for emergencies. We're ensuring that America's firefighters and police officers and emergency medical personnel have the best possible training and equipment and help they need to do their job.

We're better securing our borders and transportation systems while facilitating the flow of legitimate commerce. Our Container Security Initiative will allow for the screening of high-risk cargo at the world's largest ports and intercept dangerous materials before they reach our shores, supporting the efforts to strengthen our air cargo security system for passenger aircraft, to expand research on cargo screening technologies. We're making sure the Coast Guard has the resources to deploy additional maritime safety and security teams and patrol boats and sea marshals to protect our ports and waterways.

More than $900 million in this bill will go to science and technology projects, including a major effort to anticipate and counter the use of biological weapons. With more than $800 million, we will assess the vulnerabilities in our critical infrastructures; we'll take action to protect them.

We're doing a lot here. And we're expecting a lot of you. When the terrorist enemies came into our country and took thousands of innocent lives, we made a decision in this country: We will not wait for enemies to strike again. We'll take action to stop them. We're not going to stand by while terrorists and their state sponsors plot, plan, and grow in strength. By the actions that we continue to take abroad, we are going to remove grave threats to America and the world. History has given us that charge, and that is a charge we will keep.

We have been charged to protect our homeland as well. And that's why we're taking actions to strengthen our defenses and to make our Nation more secure. This bill is a major step forward in our ongoing effort, and I'm pleased to sign into law the Department of Homeland Security Appropriations Act of 2004.

May God bless you all.

NOTE: The President spoke at 2:07 p.m. at the Department of Homeland Security. H.R. 2555, approved October 1, was assigned Public Law No. 108–90. The Office of the Press Secretary also released a Spanish language transcript of these remarks.

Statement on Signing the Department of Homeland Security Appropriations Act, 2004
October 1, 2003

Today, I have signed into law H.R. 2555, the "Department of Homeland Security Appropriations Act, 2004." This is the first regular appropriations act for the Department of Homeland Security.

The executive branch shall construe as calling solely for notification the provisions of the Act that purport to require congressional committee approval for the execution of a law. Any other construction would be inconsistent with the principles enunciated by the Supreme Court of the United States in 1983 in *INS* v. *Chadha*. Such provisions include the purported approval requirements in the appropriations for expenses for the development of the United States Visitor and Immigrant Status Indicator Technology project; customs and border protection automated systems; immigration and customs enforcement automated systems; operations, maintenance, and pro-

curement of marine vessels, aircraft, and other related equipment of the air and marine program; expenses of the United States Secret Service; and also in sections 504, 511, and 516. To the extent that section 519 of the Act purports to allow an agent of the legislative branch to prevent implementation of the law unless the legislative agent reports to the Congress that the executive branch has met certain conditions, the executive branch shall construe such section as advisory, in accordance with the *Chadha* principles.

GEORGE W. BUSH

The White House,
October 1, 2003.

NOTE: H.R. 2555, approved October 1, was assigned Public Law No. 108–90.

Interview With African Journalists
October 2, 2003

The President. Listen, thanks. Just a couple of thoughts and then I'll answer your questions.

I'm really looking forward to welcoming President Kibaki here to Washington for a state dinner. It's quite a dramatic event. I think the President will really enjoy the ceremony we have. My first hope is that the weather accommodates the arrival, because it is impressive. And it's a way for us to send a strong message, not only to the President but to the people of Kenya, that one, we respect the friendship, two, we like the cooperation that we have, particularly on counterterrorism, three, we respect democracy in our country, and we like leaders who uphold the democratic traditions. The President has done that. It was a good, clean election. He won overwhelmingly. He is following through on some of his campaign pledges, which is an important part of democracy. One of the campaign pledges, as you know, is he's interested in fighting corruption, and he's taking action.

Our visit is a chance to signal clearly that our strategy on the continent of Africa to work with nations to help solve regional disputes and, particularly in this case, the Sudan, where the Kenyan Government has been most helpful and very constructive. So this is an important visit for us. It comes on the heels of my trip to the continent. It was an impressive trip for me. I remember it and will remember it for a long time.

There are issues on the continent that are important for America, and there are opportunities on the continent that are important for the people on the continent and the world. And Kenya is a key player and a leader in east Africa. So that's why he's coming, and I look forward to it. It's going to be a grand day.

Let me answer a couple of questions. We'll go around and save Charlie until the last here.

Martin.

Arrest of Kenyan Journalists

Q. Mr. President, it's a pleasure to be here. Overall——

The President. Please don't take it personally, Charlie. [*Laughter*]

Q. Overall, how does Kenya rank on your scorecard, since a new government took over in January? And in that light, how do you—what would you say about recent events where three journalists were arrested and intimidated into talking about, you know, where they got a source. Kenya has a leak issue of its own. [*Laughter*] That kind of seemed to——

The President. Yes. I'm against leaks, Martin. [*Laughter*] And I would suggest all governments get to the bottom of every leak of classified information. [*Laughter*] And by the way, if you know anything, Martin, would you please bring it forward and help solve the problem? [*Laughter*]

Q. In this particular case, it's actually the method with which they went around dealing with it. That kind of, like, sent a chilling message.

The President. No, I understand. First, the fact that Kenya is coming—the President is coming for a state dinner, as I say, is a sign of our respect for the President and for the importance of Kenya and meeting common goals and common objectives.

Our country believes in a free press, a free, unfettered press. And we believe that part of having a society which is able to battle corruption is a society in which the press flourishes. And I must say, I don't know all the particulars, so it's hard for me to comment about this particular incident, but I will make the case that a free press is essential to a democratic and free and honest government. The press, you know, has got the capability, a very powerful capability of holding people to account, and I respect that element in the press.

So, again, I don't know the particulars, but the President will hear me talk about all aspects of democracy.

Kevin.

Travel to Kenya/Terrorism

Q. Yes. Mr. President, thank you very much for inviting me. I appreciate it very much.

You mentioned in your opening remarks about Kenya's cooperation with the United States on counterterrorism matters. You're no doubt well aware too that Kenya has been harmed, economically harmed by the many travel advisories, both by the United States and Britain, that have been issued, no doubt for warranted reasons. But at the same time, is there a way that the United States can be helpful to Kenya in this respect?

The President. Well, first of all, a lot of Americans love to travel to Kenya. It is a spectacular destination spot. We have an obligation as a government to call it as we see it, though, when it comes to security matters. It's very important for us as a government to maintain our credibility with the American people and to say—you know, to make assessments. And we have made the assessment that at the moment, Kenya is a place where our citizens should be wary of traveling. And the bombing of Mombasa is clearly an example of what we're talking about.

However, we also believe it's important to work with Kenya to relieve the situation. It's not only for our own national interests; it's for Kenya's interest that we mutually deal with terrorists. That's why we put forth the $100 million on the East African Counterterrorism Initiative. Kenya will be a key player in that. Kenya has been very cooperative on intel; we're sharing intelligence.

The intent of the terrorists, of course, is to spread fear. That's one of their weapons, in that they're willing to kill innocent people, in that they're willing to murder anybody who is convenient to murder. They then are able to spread fear, and one of the consequences of terrorist activity is to create an environment of fear. We're working with Kenya to relieve the environment.

And you know, we had a restriction on our families at the Embassy; that has been changed. So in other words, things are improving. And at some point in time, hopefully soon, we'll be able to make a declaration about Kenya. But we will do so, you know, by keeping, kind of, the real situation in mind. And I do want to emphasize, though, that obviously we don't believe that the situation is permanent. Otherwise, we wouldn't be dealing with the President like we are, in kind of a very public way. And we believe that together we can change circumstances. We have seen circumstances change from lack of security to security, a place where it was hard to travel to a place where it's easy to recommend travel. And I believe that can happen here in Kenya.

But I understand fully the concerns of people who make a living as a result of U.S. citizens and citizens from Great Britain traveling.

Q. Right, right. And if I may, I mean, the Government—the Kenyan Government obviously looks to the United States to be supportive and helpful. And the advisories have had the opposite effect. I recognize that you're trying to do what you can——

The President. No, actually, I'm sure the President will bring this up. I hope he does bring this up, because we will be able to explore ways to work to create the conditions so that the advisories can come off.

And we just want—but we err on the side of caution when it comes to issuing advisories. You know, we'd all like to—we certainly don't want to damage our friend, unnecessarily damage our friend. On the other hand, we have an obligation to be frank and honest with the American people. So we'll work through it.

Q. Thank you.

The President. Thank you, Kevin.

Esther.

Global HIV/AIDS Initiative

Q. Thank you, Mr. President, for this opportunity to talk to you this morning. Looking back, Mr. President, you've talked about your trip in Africa. And I'm wondering whether there's anything that you look back and say the U.S. did not involve itself with Africa and which you would like to do now, when you're in the office?

The President. Well, I felt like we needed to expand the AIDS initiative. But I felt that way before I went. And so when I went, I was, one, delivering the message that we will help. We will help to the tune of $15 billion over 5 years. There's been, you know, debate about whether or not I meant $15 billion over 5. I do mean it. But some have suggested, well, maybe the best way to spend that money is divide $15 billion by 5, and it will be $3 billion a year. We think there's a better way to do it, and we're working with Congress to get the appropriations out as we speak.

The judgment from the administration's perspective and listening to the experts is it's best to ramp up, start slower and end up with more in the end, in order to make sure the dollars are spent efficiently and that help is delivered in a way that saves lives. And that's what we're working through with the Congress right now, through the appropriations process. But my message was, is that we're very sincere about this program and that the United States must expand its efforts.

I also was really, as best as I could, calibrating the delivery systems in some of the countries we went to. In other words, it's one thing to provide the aid and the money and the medicines. The other question is, can they actually get to the people that need help? The vibrancy of the faith-based programs or the charities or the NGOs—

how strong are they in these receptive countries? How receptive is the Government to receive the help? Will the Government be counterproductive to our efforts?

And you know, look, admittedly, I didn't go to every single country that's going to receive help from this emergency AIDS initiative. But it gave me a sense to then be able to listen to others who had been to the countries and to calibrate and to get a sense of what the infrastructures look like. Kenya is a part of this initiative. And I look forward to talking to the President about this initiative. It is a vital initiative.

Slavery in West Africa

Q. Mr. President, I'm wondering about the 58th session of the U.N. General Assembly, where you talked about illegal trade of human trafficking, which is rampant in west Africa, like Togo, Benin, and Burkina Faso. And I'm wondering what the U.S. Government is doing in collaboration with the African governments to eradicate this problem, which also comes about because of poverty, some parents willing to give out their children to go and work as sex slaves or do cheap labor, because they have no money.

The President. Well, no, I appreciate that. It's hard to believe a parent would be willing to send their daughter into sex slavery, willingly. But in—yes, I mean, as a dad, it's just hard for me to fathom.

Q. They probably won't know what happens to their children, but they give them for money.

The President. Well, yes, they're not specifically—that's what I thought. I mean, I doubt that they would—you know, I don't know. Look, first, it's to improve the economic of the continent by trade. AGOA is a real opportunity, and we're sincere about AGOA. And we believe in AGOA, and we're leading the way on AGOA. And that will help, hopefully, alleviate the poverty that sends people into such desperate straits that they're willing to sell their child—in essence, is what you're saying.

Secondly, in terms of the role of the United States in terms of sex slavery, it is very essential for the United States to start with the big megaphone, which is what I did. And I called upon the Security Council, kind of the collection of nations, to speak with one voice. And then we can start working bilaterally. It's not just in western Africa where there's an issue. There's an issue in parts of Europe. There's an issue in parts of the Far East. And I intend to bring this issue up as I meet with leaders, particularly in affected areas.

I've met with—gosh, I don't know how many leaders of African nations I have met with. I would say a lot.

African Affairs Senior Director Jendayi Frazer. Over 26.

The President. My only point is, is that I'm constantly meeting with leaders, which will give me an opportunity to bring this issue up. In order to solve the problem, it's not only the need to address poverty; it's also the need for governments to deal with those who are the slave traders or the slave masters, however you want to call them. We've dealt with this issue once in our civilized history. Unfortunately, as I mentioned, we need to deal with it again.

So this is an effort where it's going to take a collective effort around the world. The United States alone cannot change. We can do our part about sending signals. We can do our part about helping alleviate poverty. We can do our part about—and by the way, we've got a program, one of the most active programs—we're the active nation in the world when it comes to helping alleviate hunger, for example. Maybe that's part of the root cause of—I know it's part of the root cause of desperation as well as disease. But we also pass laws and hold people to account. In other words, it's one thing to call for action, but then we must do it ourselves. And we've got the laws on the books to do so and will.

Charlie, it's about time. [*Laughter*]

Situation in Zimbabwe

Q. Yes, sir. On your trip to Africa, after your meeting with President Mbeki in South Africa, we felt that your attitude or stance was that you would let President Mbeki and the regional leaders in southern Africa take the lead on Zimbabwe.

The President. Zimbabwe, yes.

Q. Yes. Zimbabwe, if anything, has gotten worse. Are you satisfied with the kind of pressures that Mbeki has—President Mbeki has placed or the countries of the neighborhood has placed on Zimbabwe, some additional pressures?

The President. Let me review the history of this. I did speak very clearly to President Mbeki about Zimbabwe. I said, "You and the neighborhood must deal with this man. You're sending a bad signal to the world." Along with Prime Minister Blair, we've been the two most outspoken leaders on this issue. And then our Secretary of State has followed up consistently.

I know there was an impression at the press conference, where I publicly said, "Mr. Mbeki assures me he'll deal with this issue," in essence is what I said. But no, our Government has not changed our opinion about the need for the region to deal with Zimbabwe and the leadership there. In order for there to be a country, a prosperous country, it is—this is a country which was a food exporter, in a region that needs food. It's a country where the economy has fallen apart as the result of bad governance.

And we're constantly making the point to leadership that comes in. I made the point in New York to the leader of Mozambique, who is in the neighborhood.

Q. Oops, my tape—don't worry.

The President. I'm just getting—cranking up, Charlie. [*Laughter*]

Q. I will remember. [*Laughter*]

The President. No, you won't remember. It's impossible to remember eloquence. [*Laughter*] You must capture it. [*Laughter*]

No, nobody should read any—look, we are pressing the issue regularly.

Q. Are you satisfied, though, with what Mr. Mbeki and the other people are doing?

The President. The only time that this Government and I, personally, will be satisfied is when there is an honest government, reformed government, in Zimbabwe. That's our goal. That's the definition of satisfaction. And that hasn't happened yet. Therefore, we're not satisfied.

Q. With Mr. Mugabe or Mr. Mbeki?

The President. With the process. Well, certainly not with Mr. Mugabe. And when President Mbeki says they are working on it, to achieve this goal, I take him for his word. And I am going to remind all parties that the goal is a reformed and fair government. And that hasn't been achieved yet. And we'll continue to press the issue, both privately and publicly, which I just did.

Q. Mr. President, can I ask about——

The President. Not yet. [*Laughter*] We're having an orderly discussion. It reminds me of an American press conference. When I ask the journalists, please ask one question, and they ask four or five at the same time in the same breath. It's hard to believe—there's a tremendous lack of discipline in the U.S. press corps. [*Laughter*] Like the other day, I was embarrassed when the AP—a fantastic organization, a wonderful reporter—was able to ask four questions in one breath—[*laughter*]—setting a terrible precedent for the Russian press that followed up.

Q. I have four today, sir. [*Laughter*]

The President. I'm sure you do. You've already asked one: "How's the knee?"

Q. Three, then. [*Laughter*]

African Growth and Opportunity Act/ Millennium Challenge Accounts

Q. Mr. President, you mentioned AGOA and how it's anticipated that it will help alleviate poverty in Africa. However, most countries in Africa are still struggling just to begin to export products and don't seem to have the capacity to fully exploit what AGOA promises. And that seems to be an ongoing issue. If it's textiles, there's no capacity to reach the maximum quotas reserved for Africa. And by extension——

The President. So far.

Q. Right. And AGOA seems to be Africa's stepping stone to globalization. Now, just recently, the World Trade Organization meeting collapsed, and that seemed to symbolize a growing frustration among most developing countries, and particularly in Africa, that globalization and AGOA in the same—is not really fair. It's not a level playing field. Does this whole process need to be rethought to try to give them a little more capacity, to probably go in and try and build structures so that they can compete?

The President. Yes, listen, here—we've got a full-scale strategy on dealing with economic opportunity. First, let me talk about the Millennium Challenge Account, which is a central part of the strategy, which basically says we're willing to add aid if countries develop the habits necessary to be able to develop a just and honorable society: transparency, anti-corruption, focus on the people, a market orientation to their economy.

Secondly, AGOA creates opportunity. It's up to the nations to seize the opportunity. Our aid will help. We're more than willing to work with nations to help develop an entrepreneurial class that is able to seize the moment. And AGOA treats African nations fairly when it comes to our markets. And so our strategy is to help African nations develop the infrastructure necessary to achieve the markets.

And it starts with good governance, in our judgment. That's the best thing we can affect—and fight corruption, going to insist upon transparency, insist upon education practices that will help, and we provide help for this. On a wide range of areas, we help nations help themselves develop the economy necessary to take advantage of trade.

I believe that trade is the only way to help nations grow out of poverty. And so we've been open with our markets. The bilateral relationship between the United States and the continent of Africa is a strong relationship. I was sorry to see that there was a setback at the World Trade Organization, because I think that global trade will benefit the African Continent as well. It's important to open up markets, and that will provide opportunity for the African business sector.

And there's been good progress in many countries, by the way, as a result of AGOA. The amount of trade that is coming to the United States from the continent is dramatic. I can't cite the statistic exactly right this second. If I'm not mistaken, the trade from Kenya to the United States is upward of $400 million.

Q. Yes, it's up substantially.

The President. That's substantial. Martin, that's good progress. I think expectations ought to be realistic that market-oriented economies aren't going to happen instantly. It takes—there's a process that will help, but the fact that trade is up $400 million in Kenya is very positive. It means there's more activity, more jobs, more hope, more opportunity, all of which can be fostered by good, honest government, by the way, or it can be squandered by corrupt government. And that's one of the reasons why the Millennium Challenge Account is part of our strategy on the continent, is to promote the habits of good and honest, decent government.

Kevin.

Kenya's Role in Africa

Q. Yes, thank you, Mr. President. You mentioned Sudan at the outset and the importance of Kenya and moving negotiations forward. Kenya has often seen itself as an island of stability surrounded by countries that have had serious conflicts and continue to have. Is the United States going to be discussing that with Mr. Kibaki and perhaps offering some specific assistance as Kenya

tries to bring peace to Somalia, Sudan, and the Great Lakes region?

The President. Yes, interesting. Absolutely, we'll be talking about this, because I view that the best role the United States can play is be supportive of regional leaders and/or the capacity, for example, of African peacekeeping forces to carry the task of dealing with civil dispute. And Kenya is playing a vital role in the Sudan, along with former Senator Jack Danforth. They work closely together. It's a vital role to play.

And we will be encouraging President Kibaki to continue on being a regional leader. We will discuss it. If he has got suggestions about how our State Department and AID programs can help him do a better job as a regional leader, we're interested in listening.

We also believe that we ought to continue training forces such as ECOWAS, as an example, to be prepared to take on peacekeeping missions on the continent.

Liberia is another—am I answering your question, Charlie? [*Laughter*]

Q. No, I've got it in my head here. [*Laughter*]

The President. I'll save it. That way I won't force you to have to think of another question. [*Laughter*] You might have to slip into the baseball playoffs. [*Laughter*]

Anyway, yes, we will talk about that. It's a key role. You see, I believe that Africa is plenty capable—African nations are plenty capable of dealing with dispute. I believe there are very capable leaders on the continent who are good, strong leaders. And the role of the United States is not to supplant them as problemsolvers, but to help them solve problems. And one of the reasons why I think AGOA is such a strong statement by the United States is it says we have faith in the capacity of the people to take advantage of this opportunity.

I talked about the potential of the African Continent. It's way beyond—oftentimes people talk about the potential of Africa as resource potential. I view it as people potential. And so this country takes a supportive role in dealing with the leadership and recognizing that there àre some strong leaders that are capable of handling the problems, as opposed to supplanting them.

Q. Thank you.

The President. Esther.

Developing Civil Society in Africa

Q. Mr. President, I'm wondering, as Africa joins the rest of the world in fighting terrorism, whether there are any plans to involve not only the governments but also the civil society and religious leaders who reach the common man?

The President. Yes. You know, the answer is, of course. And let me put it this way to you—and I say this a lot, Esther, as I explain to the American people why we make the decisions we make. Free societies are societies which will not support terror. Free societies are societies which aren't at war with their neighbors. I mean, freedom has the capacity to change the behavior of the people.

So, you bet. I mean, a free society is a society which, in itself, recognizes the value of civil society. Free societies are societies in which the civil society is the strength of the society. And to the extent that there are religious leaders preaching hatred that go beyond the scope of free speech and free religion, we try to work with leaders to work with their religious counterparts not to preach hatred and violence. But the United States is committed to the overall spread of free, honest, open government. That's the heart of the Millennium Challenge Account.

The Millennium Challenge Account—again, this is—I'm trying to share with you as much of my philosophy about dealing with the continent as anything else. I believe—obviously, I believe that people are plenty capable of developing honest government and transparent government and focusing resources where they need to be focused. That's why we have laid out the initiative. That's why we've created this en-

tirely new approach to foreign aid on the continent and elsewhere, by the way.

It essentially says I believe in the inherent goodness of men and women and their capacity to govern themselves. And therefore, we want to work with governments that make that choice. I recognize not everybody is going to make that choice, and I recognize sometimes the path of least resistance is corruption. And it's very tempting to take—you know, the head of a government to be corrupt, as Kenya has learned. And you've got a leader now who is willing to stand up and fight corruption. You've got an anti-corruption czar in Kenya, which is a positive development. Now the person must do their work. You've got anti-corruption legislation, which is positive development.

And so one of the key messages from this visit is, "Mr. Kibaki, you're proving our point. You're leading. You're showing what is possible." And to the extent that we work with civil—that in itself spurs a civil society which is vibrant and strong. A civil society—kind of the underpinnings of a free society as opposed to a centralized government. And the habits of freedom change the attitudes of people.

Now, look, I readily concede there must be economic vitality and growth along with that in order to alleviate poverty. And part of the central component of our AIDS initiative is recognizing that a pandemic that sweeps through a continent will destroy the hopes of people. It's incredibly debilitating to the spirit when kids grow up as orphans after their parents have died a tough death. And this pandemic is wiping out a generation.

And that's why I feel so passionate about leading the world. Not just the United States but the world must step up and help in a way that actually works, in a way that changes the attitudes toward AIDS and save lives.

Charles.

Liberia

Q. Yes.

The President. They ever call you "Charles"?

Q. I had a schoolteacher once call me Charles. [*Laughter*]

The President. I'll join the crowd. Charles, what's on your mind?

Q. I'm open to learning. [*Laughter*] I do, indeed, have a Liberia question.

The President. Thank you, sir. I was hoping you would bring it up. This isn't the first time you've asked me about Liberia.

Q. No, nor the last.

The President. Nor the last, yes, I was about to say. [*Laughter*]

Q. There was gunplay in Monrovia, I guess, yesterday.

The President. There was.

Q. There's deep suspicion of this process in the sense that—among Liberians—that these rebel groups aren't much better than Charles Taylor. And without getting some significant control of the country, independent, if you will, anything free and fair seems remote. And there's puzzlement—which is my question to you, at the—well, what one Liberian characterized as the aloofness of this administration toward the Liberian situation in terms of concrete people on the ground. There's puzzlement over this. How do you respond?

The President. Yes, I respond this way, Charles.

Q. Go ahead.

The President. Got the tape cranked up, will you?

Q. Yes, I want to get——

The President. Once again, this will be a—[*laughter*].

Q. Yes.

The President. I made it very clear from the beginning, our strategy in Liberia. Now, remember, I have just told you that I believe on the continent of Africa is—African nations are plenty capable of dealing with issues such—of civil unrest, like in Liberia.

And I believe it's very important for our Government to be consistent in our message, that we will help, we will help train troops. And I said from day one, Charlie, that we would provide help to ECOWAS— by the way, a group of folks we helped train in the past—and we would provide enough presence to enable ECOWAS to come in and do their job. And we moved a Marine group of troops in, secured the port. Remember the first issue was the port? Would the United States act to secure the airport and port? Yes, we did. Would we create the conditions necessary for ECOWAS to move in, and then eventually blue-helmet the operation, which happened yesterday, and that encouraged others to participate along with the United Nations? You bet we did.

Now, we've kept a presence there. We've kept a presence there to help ECOWAS. So we've done everything we said we would do. And the strategy has worked. I recognize there was sporadic fire, or however you want to describe it, yesterday. And I suspect that that may happen on an infrequent basis.

But the process is working. The United Nations will move in. They will help supervise the elections. Hopefully, they will be free and fair. This is a good role for the United Nations. And in the meantime, more troops will be coming in. We worked collaboratively with the United Nations to help sign up nations to blue-helmet—to be blue-helmeted. And so I'm pleased with the progress we have made in Liberia. We have kept our word. We have done exactly what we said we would do.

Q. Just not exactly what you were asked to do.

The President. Well, sometimes, Charlie, we don't do exactly what everybody asks us to do. We get a lot of requests. And in this case, it fit—the strategy was a part of a larger strategy on the continent to help people help, in this case, the regional situation to resolve it.

ECOWAS has done a very good job. President Obasanjo gets a lot of credit for responding and moving Nigerian troops in and providing the command structure along with our help. I think the situation has turned out a lot better than people assumed it was going to, and there's progress still to be done. And the United Nations is now in charge of the process, but we're keeping people there to help with our Nigerian friends.

Q. Thank you, Mr. President.

The President. Thank you all, yes. I guess it's over. [*Laughter*]

NOTE: The interview began at 9:30 a.m. in the Roosevelt Room at the White House and was made available by the Office of the Press Secretary on October 2 but was embargoed for release until 8 p.m. In his remarks, the President referred to President Mwai Kibaki of Kenya; President Thabo Mbeki of South Africa; President Robert Mugabe of Zimbabwe; Prime Minister Tony Blair of the United Kingdom; Secretary of State Colin L. Powell; President Joaquim Alberto Chissano of Mozambique; former Senator John C. Danforth, Special Envoy for Peace in the Sudan; and President Olusegun Obasanjo of Nigeria. A reporter referred to former President Charles Taylor of Liberia. Participating in the interview were Martin Mbugua, correspondent, Daily Nation; Kevin Kelley, correspondent, The EastAfrican; Charlie Cobb, senior writer and diplomatic correspondent, allafrica.com; and Esther Githui, international broadcaster, Voice of America Swahili Services. A tape was not available for verification of the content of this interview.

Remarks at a Reception Celebrating Hispanic Heritage Month
October 2, 2003

Thank you very much. *Sientese. Sientese, Embajador.* Thank you for coming. *Bienvenidos. Mi casa es su casa.* I want to thank you all for coming to celebrate Hispanic Heritage Month.

You know, this Nation is blessed by the talents and the hard work of Hispanic Americans, and we're really blessed by the values of *familia y fe* that strengthen our Nation on a daily basis. It is fitting we honor Hispanic Americans in our country. It's part of our country—an incredibly important part of our country. I also think it's fitting that the way to honor Hispanic Americans is to revel in the vitality of the Hispanic culture that was displayed today, the music that honors the roots, the rhythm, the life of the Latino.

I appreciate my Ambassador to Mexico, Tony Garza. He's been a long-time friend. He was the secretary of state in the State of Texas. It gave him a chance to learn diplomacy. [*Laughter*] He's a great man and a great friend.

I have asked people from Hispanic heritage to join my administration: Hans Hertell, who is the Ambassador to the Dominican Republic, is with us. Hans brought his family with him. [*Laughter*]

I've got a Cabinet Secretary *de Cuba*, who is Mel Martinez. I don't know if you know Mel's story. This speaks volumes about our Nation and about Mel's upbringing. In the early sixties, Cuban parents were worried about their sons growing, their daughters growing up in tyranny. They were afraid about what it would be like for a child to grow up in a world in which terror reigned and there was no freedom. And so Mel's parents put him on an airplane destined for the United States of America.

Imagine the choice of a parent—I would daresay there's really only one country, though, that a parent would be feeling comfortable of sending their child to, and that's America, because of what we stand for. Mel is Pedro Pan. He is now in the Cabinet of the President of the United States, which speaks volumes about you, Mel, and volumes about our country as well.

Hector Barreto is with us today, runs the SBA. Where are you, Hector? *Donde esta?* Thank you, Hector. Everybody needs to have a good *abogado.* [*Laughter*] I've got a really good one. [*Laughter*] Al Gonzales is my lawyer and close friend. Eduardo Aguirre is the Director of Citizenship and Immigration Services. Welcome, Eduardo. Gaddi Vasquez—*donde esta,* Gaddi? Where is he? Peace Corps, running the Peace Corps. He's out recruiting new members. [*Laughter*] *Adonde?* Oh, yes, there he is. Gaddi got here a little late. [*Laughter*] I want to thank these folks for serving our administration so well.

We've got ambassadors from around the world here with us today. I am honored that *Embajador* Jose—Juan Jose Bremer *de Mexico esta aqui.* Good to see you, Jose. Hugo Guiliani *de el* Dominican Republic. *Senor Embajador.* Luis Alberto Moreno Mejia *de Colombia. Embajador* Rene Leon from El Salvador, good to see you, sir. Francisco Javier Ruperez *de Espana.* Murilo Gabrielli, who is the Deputy Chief of Mission from Brazil, thank you for coming, Murilo.

I'm so honored that Members of the United States Congress are here with us today. The Senator from the great State of Texas—I emphasize "the great State of Texas"—John Cornyn. The chairwoman of the Congressional Hispanic Conference, Ileana Ros-Lehtinen from Florida. Mario Diaz-Balart from Florida is with us. Devin Nunes from California—*donde esta* Devin? It's an old trick here in Washington, get your name on the roster, but don't show up. [*Laughter*] At least you get mentioned. [*Laughter*] Bob Beauprez of Colorado is with us. Jon Porter is with us, from the

great State of Nevada. Thank you, Jon. Jerry Weller is with us. From Arizona, Rick Renzi is with us. And finally, from New Mexico, Steve Pearce. Thank you for coming. I want to thank you all for being here. It's a good sign that Members of the Congress take an interest in the Hispanic Heritage Month. And I appreciate you coming.

I also want to thank Brian Sandoval, who is the attorney general from the State of Nevada. It's awfully kind for him to come all the way over here. Brian, thank you, sir.

I am so pleased that my friend Emilio Estefan is here. Emilio helps put this event on. Emilio puts this event on—or helps us put this event on every year. And it's awfully kind of you to do this. It's good to see you.

I am also honored that Lisa Guerrero is with us. Lisa, thank you very much for serving as the emcee. I appreciate you being on TV on Monday nights too. [*Laughter*]

Carlos Ponce—thank you for coming, Carlos. I appreciate you, Carlos. It's good to see you again. It's good to see you on Monday night as well.

I'm so honored that Father Cutie is here. Thank you very much for leading us in the blessing.

Bacilos, thank you, guys, for being the young stars. The Ambassador turned to me and said, "These are the young dudes, the young stars of the music scene." [*Laughter*] I can see why. Congratulations. Thank you for your leadership.

Alexandre, thank you very much. Fantastic. You know, Alexandre, I love your spirit. It's clear to see your heart and soul, and thank you very much. You were good *tambien, mi amigo de Puerto Rico.* What a voice. Thank you very much.

I am—let me see. I'm probably going to leave somebody out here as we get moving through here. Victor, thank you. Awesome job. I appreciate you coming.

Obviously, the person who invited the guest list here knows I love baseball. We've got a lot of the baseball stars here. I do love baseball. One of my favorite baseball players of all time is a person who's going to be in the Hall of Fame, and that's Rafael Palmeiro of the Texas Rangers. I want to thank you for coming. And Lynne is here. Thank you for coming, Lynne.

I'm glad you brought your manager with you. He's not exactly a Latino ballplayer, but he's a fine guy, and that's Buck Showalter. Thank you for coming, Buck, and thank you for bringing your family. It's good to see you all.

Magglio Ordonez of the Chicago White Sox is with us. Where are you, Magglio? Yes, thank you, buddy. Congratulations. Great season, yes. We're watching you. We've got the dish upstairs. [*Laughter*] Bartolo Colon—*donde esta* Bartolo? I can see why you can throw it hard. [*Laughter*] *Fuerte.*

Carlos Beltran of the Kansas City Royals—Carlos, good job. *Donde esta* Jose Lima? There he is—Jose. Yes. You're back. [*Laughter*] Congratulations on having a great year. Tino Martinez, Saint Louis Cardinals; Nelson Figueroa of the Pirates. Where's Nelson? Yes, thank you, Nelson. Are you sure you're old enough to qualify? [*Laughter*] Vladimir Guerrero—yes, Vladimir. Glad you're here, Vladimir. Thanks for coming.

I also know your general manager really well. He's a really good guy, isn't he? Omar Minaya, *mi amigo.* Thank you for coming, Omar. And congratulations. I knew you'd make it all along. You're probably wondering why I didn't make you general manager of the Rangers, but nevertheless—[*laughter*]—Omar is the general manager of the Montreal Expos. He really does a great job, and I've known Omar a long time. He's a great baseball guy. More important, he's a good person. I'm really proud to have you here.

Just to show you that we're multisport people here, it is my honor to welcome Carlos Arroyo. Carlos, I want to thank you

very much for coming. He's the basketball player for the Utah Jazz. Carlos.

Katie, thank you very much for leading us in the anthem. You've got a beautiful voice. You've got a lot of poise and a lot of talent, and we're honored that you're here with us today. Thanks for coming. We're really glad you're here. And thanks for bringing your little brother. I hope he's nice to you all the time. [*Laughter*]

The contributions of the Hispanic community have made this country stronger and better. Today we honor the contributions with the entertainment we had here in the East Room. I don't know if you know this, but this is a common occurrence for the Bush administration, to honor men and women of Hispanic descent, to honor their presence and listen to their talents. But this has happened throughout the years in the White House.

There's been some interesting moments here. Pablo Casals was a Spanish-born cellist. He lived in Puerto Rico. He performed for two Presidents—catch this—the first was Theodore Roosevelt in 1904 and the second was John Kennedy in 1961—57 years in between his first and second visit. Nevertheless, he graced this room and this house.

We've also had Jose Limon. He's a modern dancer—Edward Villella to my family's friend Gloria Estefan. You should have brought her. [*Laughter*]

One Hispanic entertainer we remember in a special way today is the Queen of Salsa, Celia Cruz. She was an unforgettable performer who fled Cuba in 1960. She became a U.S. citizen and spent the rest of her life sharing the rhythms of her homeland with people all around the world. Celia Cruz passed away 3 months ago. We miss her, and we honor today to welcome her husband, Pedro. *Bienvenidos.*

We are not only blessed with the culture of the Hispanic in America; we're also blessed by the fact that our country is strengthened because of the spirit of hard work and enterprise. It's part of the Latino culture. We see the spirit in thousands of small businesses and the careers of business people all across our country. One of the most vibrant parts of our economy is the small-business sector, and one of the vibrant parts of the small-business sector is the Latinos who own small businesses, really one of the great success stories of America.

Tell you a story about Lou Sobh, who is with us today. In 1960, he left Mexico, no money, and he couldn't speak the language. He came to America. He didn't—he couldn't speak the language at all, so he worked, and he taught himself English. He ended up becoming a janitor in a department store, a hard worker. He had a dream, and he was working toward his dream. He served in the United States Army. He got out of the Army, and he had a dream to open up his own car dealership. Today, he owns 14—not one car dealership but 14 car dealerships. He employs 800 people. He's got three car franchises in Mexico. He's living proof of the American Dream—an incredibly important part of our Nation, the Latino spirit of hard work and drive and enterprise. And Lou, I want to congratulate you for being a success and setting an example. Thank you for coming, sir.

Today, as we celebrate Hispanic Heritage Month, we also must take pride in the generations of Hispanic Americans who have served in America's Armed Forces, served to protect and defend a nation they love. Forty-two Hispanic Americans—42—*cuarenta y dos*—have earned the highest military decoration, the Medal of Honor. That's a lot. Today, men and women of Hispanic heritage continue to serve and sacrifice in the defense of freedom. They have our respect, and they have our gratitude.

Earlier this year, at the National Naval Medical Center, I had an amazing experience. Eduardo was there. I had the chance and privilege of meeting a patriot, Master Gunnery Sergeant Guadalupe Denogean.

Sergeant Denogean is an immigrant from Mexico. He has served in the Marine Corps for 25 years. Last spring, he was wounded in combat in Basra, Iraq, and he was sent back for treatment. They asked Sergeant Denogean, did he have any requests? He said he had two. He wanted a promotion for the corporal who helped rescue him, and the second request is he wanted to be an American citizen.

I was there the day Sergeant Denogean took his oath of citizenship. Eduardo administered the oath. In a hospital where he was recovering, this son of Mexico raised his right hand and pledged to support and defend the Constitution of the United States of America. What made that moment amazing to me is that he had kept that oath for decades before he took it. I'm proud of the sergeant. I'm proud to call him citizen. I'm proud to call him fellow citizen to America.

Through the lives of people like Sergeant Denogean and Lou and Celia Cruz, it is clear that the American Dream belongs to *todos*. It's for everybody, not just a few. And that's the greatness of our country. It's the spirit of America. And it's important that this generation and future generations keep that dream alive.

We've got to make sure that hard work is a place that is respected and rewarded. We must make sure that our entrepreneurs, entrepreneurs from all walks of life have the opportunity to dream and work hard and realize their ambitions. We must make sure that the dream of homeownership is available for every citizen in our country. We must make sure that every child gets educated, that the public schools educate every single child, those whose parents may speak English, those whose parents may not yet speak English. Education belongs to everybody. High standards belongs to everybody. We must challenge the soft bigotry of low expectations in American public schools.

We're proud of our country. We're a strong country. We're militarily strong, and

I'll keep us that way. But our wealth isn't really found in our military or our pocketbooks. The true strength of America is found in the character of the American people, in the courage of the people, the creativity of our people, and in the compassion of our people.

As Governor, and now as President, I've seen the character of America and the character of millions of Hispanic Americans who make our Nation a better place. The warmth and the vitality of the Hispanic culture, the energy and faith of Hispanic men and women are great gifts to America.

I want to thank you all for coming to celebrate those gifts. *Que Dios los bendiga a todos, y que Dios bendiga a los Estados Unidos.* Thank you for coming.

NOTE: The President spoke at 3:35 p.m. in the East Room at the White House. In his remarks, he referred to Secretary Murilo Gabrielli, head of the Cultural and Public Affairs section, Brazilian Embassy in Washington, DC; Lisa Guerrero, FOX Sports broadcast journalist; Carlos Ponce, actor and television personality; Father Alberto Cutie, Telemundo network talk show host; Latin music group *Bacilos*; Brazilian musician Alexandre Pires; Lynne Palmeiro, wife of baseball player Rafael Palmeiro; Edward Villella, founding artistic director and chief executive officer, Miami City Ballet; and entertainer Gloria Estefan. The Office of the Press Secretary also released a Spanish language transcript of these remarks.

Statement on House of Representatives Passage of Legislation Banning Partial-Birth Abortion
October 2, 2003

I applaud the House for passing the ban on partial-birth abortion so soon after the congressional conferees completed their work. Today's action is an important step that will help us continue to build a culture of life in America. I look forward to the Senate passing this legislation so that I can sign this very important bill into law.

Remarks Following a Meeting With Former New York City Police Commissioner Bernard B. Kerik and an Exchange With Reporters
October 3, 2003

The President. Thank you all for coming. I'll make a couple of statements. I'm going to ask Bernie Kerik to make a statement, and I'll answer two questions before I go to Milwaukee.

First, I want to welcome Bernie Kerik to the South Lawn and to the Oval Office. We just had a fascinating discussion about what he did in Iraq, what he saw in Iraq. He can speak for himself. But let me characterize it this way, that he went to help the Iraqis organize a police force. He showed up at times of chaos and confusion. Because of his leadership, his knowledge, and his experience, he was able to stand up a police force in Baghdad in a very quick period of time. I think he told me he opened up 37 different precinct stations——

Mr. Kerik. Thirty-five.

The President. ——35 different precinct stations. They activated and trained 35,000

Iraqi police force. And that's important because the ultimate solution to the security issues in Iraq is for the Iraqi citizens to manage their own affairs.

Bernie went there and made a big difference. And for that our Nation is very grateful. We appreciate it a lot.

Mr. Kerik. Thank you.

The President. We're going to start training police officers in Jordan soon. As well, tomorrow, 750 new Iraqi army soldiers will graduate from training. Part of our strategy is to enable the Iraqis to protect themselves. Mr. Kerik can speak to this, but in a very short period of time, we're making great progress. Iraq is becoming more secure, and that is good. It is good for our overall mission because a free and peaceful Iraq will mean that America is more secure.

I'll make one other comment, then Bernie will say a few words.

Mr. David Kay reported to the Nation. I want to thank him for his good work. He is a thoughtful man. He and his team have worked under very difficult circumstances. They have done a lot of work in 3 months, and he reported on an interim basis.

The report states that Saddam Hussein's regime had a clandestine network of biological laboratories, a live strain of deadly agent botulinum, sophisticated concealment efforts, and advanced design work on prohibited longer range missiles. The report summarized the regime's efforts in this way, and I quote from the report: "Iraq's WMD programs spanned more than two decades, involved thousands of people, billions of dollars, and was elaborately shielded by security and deception operations that continued even beyond the end of Operation Iraqi Freedom."

That is what the report said. Specifically, Dr. Kay's team discovered what the report calls, and I quote, "dozens of WMD-related program activities and significant amounts of equipment that Iraq concealed from the United Nations during the inspections that began in late 2002."

In addition to these extensive concealment efforts, Dr. Kay found systematic destruction of evidence of these illegal activities. This interim progress report is not final. Extensive work remains to be done on his biological, chemical, and nuclear weapons programs. But these findings already make clear that Saddam Hussein actively deceived the international community, that Saddam Hussein was in clear violation of United Nations Security Council Resolution 1441, and that Saddam Hussein was a danger to the world.

The Commissioner will say a few words.

Mr. Kerik. Thank you. I just—first, I want to take this opportunity to thank the President for giving me the honor and allowing me to go to Iraq—to go to Iraq and help the Iraqi people, give the Iraq people back their country.

And we did so—and we did so quite quickly, and that continues on a daily basis. Four months ago—4½ months ago, when I arrived in Iraq, there were no police—very few, if any. There were no police stations. There were no cars. There was no electricity. They didn't have telephones, communications, radios. They basically had nothing. They had no equipment. They had no weapons, except for those they had ordered kept on the side. In the last 4 months, we brought back more than 40,000 police, 450 cars in Baghdad, stood up 35 police stations in Baghdad.

And I know I constantly hear as I come back—I listen to the press, and I listen to some of the public, some of the criticism. And they talk about, "It's taking too long." Well, try to stand up 35 police stations in New York City. It would take you about 11 years, depending on who is in the city council. It takes a while. You only have 24 hours in a day. But they have made tremendous progress. The police are working; they're working in conjunction with the military. They are arresting the Fedayeen Saddam and the Ba'athists.

And I read some of the articles about this, about Dr. Kay's report today. In my opinion, there was one weapon of mass destruction in Iraq, and it was Saddam Hussein. I visited the mass graves. I watched the videos of the Mukhabarat, the intelligence services, interrogate, torture, abuse, and execute people day after day. I watched them tie grenades to the necks of people or stuff grenades in the pockets of people as they interviewed them and then detonate those grenades and watch the people disappear. I watched a video of Saddam sitting in an office and allowing two Doberman Pinschers to eat alive a general, a military general because he did not trust his loyalty. There was one weapon of mass destruction. He's no longer in power, and I think that's what counts today.

I understand, probably more than anyone, what a threat Iraq was and the people that threatened Iraq was. I was beneath the towers on September 11th when they fell. And I—again, I just—I want to thank the President for the honor in allowing me to go there, because I lost 23 people. I wear this memorial band for the 23 I lost. They were defending the freedom of our country. I got to go on their behalf to Iraq, to bring freedom to Iraq and take one less threat away from us in this country. So, Mr. President, thank you.

The President. Good job, Bernie.

Mr. Kerik. Thank you, sir.

The President. I'll answer a couple of questions.

Iraqi Weapons of Mass Destruction

Q. Mr. President, are you still confident that you'll—that weapons of mass destruction will be found in Iraq? And how long do you think that that search will go on? Is that an open-ended search until something is found?

The President. That's a question you need to ask David Kay. He'll be interviewing with the press today—his opinion. I can only report to what his interim report says.

Q. Well——

The President. Let me—let me finish, please.

Q. Yes.

The President. His interim report said that Iraq's weapons of mass destruction program spanned more than two decades. That's what he said. See, he's over there under difficult circumstances and reports back. He says that the WMD program involved thousands of people, billions of dollars, and was elaborately shielded by security and deception operations that continued even beyond the end of Operation Iraqi Freedom. In other words, he's saying Saddam Hussein was a threat, a serious danger.

Decision on War in Iraq

Q. There's a poll out in which a lot of people today are wondering whether the war was really worth the cost.

The President. Yes.

Q. How do you respond to that, sir?

The President. Yes, I don't make decisions based upon polls. I make decisions based upon what I think is important for the security of the American people. And I'm not going to forget the lessons of 9/11, September 2001. I'm not going to forget what Mr. Kerik described, the bombing that killed innocent life. This administration will deal with gathering dangers where we find them. The interim report of Mr. Kay showed that Saddam defied 1441 and was a danger. We gave him ample time to deal with his weapons of mass destruction. He refused. So he's no longer in power, and the world is better off for it.

I can't think of any people who think that the world would be a safe place with Saddam Hussein in power. Sometimes the American people like the decisions I make; sometimes they don't. But they need to know I'll make tough decisions based upon what I think is right, given the intelligence that I know, in order to do my job, which is secure this country and to bring peace.

Thank you all.

Q. But isn't the issue that you overstated the threat in the view of critics——

The President. Bernie, you're a good man.

NOTE: The President spoke at 8:44 a.m. on the South Lawn at the White House. In his remarks, he referred to David Kay, CIA Special Advisor for Strategy Regarding Iraqi Weapons of Mass Destruction Programs; and former President Saddam Hussein of Iraq.

Remarks at the Midwest Airlines Center in Milwaukee, Wisconsin
October 3, 2003

Thanks for coming. Thanks for the warm welcome. It's nice to be back in Milwaukee. Today I'm going to talk about some of the challenges which face our country and why I believe our country can overcome any challenge we face.

One of the reasons I'm optimistic about the future of our economy is because of the entrepreneurial spirit of America, the entrepreneurial spirit that is strong in Milwaukee and in the great State of Wisconsin, the fact that there are people who are risktakers and job creators and people who, like me, see a better future for those who are looking for work. I'm here to herald the small businesses which are the strength of the economy of the United States of America.

I want to thank Tim for inviting a few of his friends here today. [*Laughter*] Thanks for coming out. Thanks for your leadership, Tim. I appreciate your willingness to give me a chance to talk about our country.

I traveled today with a man who you trained well, a person who serves in my Cabinet in one of the most difficult jobs of all, Secretary of Health and Human Services. He represents our country with class and distinction, and that is Tommy Thompson. Where's Tommy? There you go. [*Applause*] Let us not get carried away. [*Laughter*] You know him well. He's a good guy.

Today I also had the privilege of flying from Washington to Milwaukee with three members of the congressional delegation from the great State of Wisconsin, Jim Sensenbrenner, Tom Petri, and Paul Ryan. These are fine—[*applause*]. We had a great visit on the plane. There is no air raids on Air Force One, by the way. [*Laughter*] And it's a chance for us to talk about issues of concern. And one thing is clear: The three love the State of Wisconsin, and they represent you well. And I'm proud to call them friends, and I enjoy working with them. I enjoy working with them to try to change the tone in Washington, to elevate the discourse, to get rid of needless politics and partisan bickering and focus on the people's business. They understand what I'm talking about, and they're good, strong leaders.

I want to thank the members of the statehouse who have come today: Jack Voight, who is the State treasurer; Mary Panzer, who is the State senate majority leader; Steve Foti is the State assembly majority leader. I want to thank you all for coming as well. A lot of local officials here, starting with Scott Walker of—the county executive. The sheriff is here, David Clarke. I want to thank everybody else for coming too.

Today when I landed, I met a fellow named Roy Bubeck. You don't know Bubeck at all, and I didn't either—maybe some of you do. The reason I herald him is because he is a soldier in the army of compassion. He's one of these kind citizens who has decided to make a difference in other people's lives. A lot of times we talk about the strength of America, and people automatically think about maybe the size of our wallet or the strength of our military. No, the strength of our country is the fact that we've got fantastic citizens who hurt when somebody hurts, who worry when somebody needs help.

Roy runs Badger Mutual Insurance Company. He understands that he employs a lot of really decent folks who care about the community in which they live. And he's assumed his responsibility as a CEO in this way: He offers paid leave to employees to go out and help in a neighborhood. He's encouraged people in his company to mentor a child. He's encouraged people to go tutor, so that if a child is having trouble learning to read, he or she can succeed in life. What I'm telling you is, he is encouraging people of compassion by providing leave for those folks from their business.

No, the strength of this country is the fact that when communities all across America, when we find somebody who hurts, there is some good soul willing to stand up and say, "I love you." America's greatness is the heart and soul of the American people.

And I want to thank Roy for his leadership and encourage others who are CEOs in corporate America to encourage those who've heard the call to love a neighbor like you'd like to be loved yourself to do so by good corporate policy.

I said we had faced some challenges. I want to review some of the challenges we faced. If we can summarize the obstacles we overcome, you'll see why I'm such an optimistic person, because we have overcome a lot as a nation.

First of all, the market—stock market began a decline in March of 2000. That affected a lot of citizens, because we are slowly but surely becoming an ownership society in America. More and more people are owning equities or bonds as a result of 401(k)s or pension plans. A stock market

decline affects people. They affect their pocketbooks. They affect their—obviously, their wealth, and the market began a decline. In early 2001, we had a recession, three quarters of negative growth. In other words, our economy was not doing very well.

We acted, and Congress—with the Congress, we acted by passing tax relief. And by far, the vast majority of economic historians would say that as a result of the tax relief, the recession was shallow, because we started coming out after three quarters.

Some have said, "Well, maybe the recession should have run its course. Maybe it should have been deep, and you shouldn't have had the tax relief." My concern is about the people who are looking for work. You see, I'm not worried about the numbers. What I am worried about is the lives affected by recession. Shallow recession was good because fewer people were laid off, fewer people hurt, fewer people were worried about their future.

Things started getting going okay, though. And then we were attacked on September the 11th, 2001, and that hurt us. It hurt the economy, but it hurt our psyche as well. See, for—we grew up in a time when we thought oceans could protect us, that there may have been threats overseas, but we could pick or choose which threats to deal with because we were invulnerable here in America. And that changed on that fateful day. All of a sudden, it became apparent to all of us that an enemy could hurt us at home, an enemy that hates what we stand for.

Our security became threatened. We had a new responsibility in Washington, DC, and at the State level and at the local level to do everything we can to secure the homeland. We have a new charge to keep. September the 11th not only affected us in the pocketbook; it changed the strategic vision of our country, that we just couldn't see threats gathering overseas and ignore them, that we had to deal with them before they came to hit us.

The realities of September the 11th changed the way America must view threats. I vowed on September the 11th—after September the 11th, that I would do everything in my power, with a great country, to hunt down those who killed Americans, plotted against Americans, and bring them to justice. And that's exactly what we are doing.

Thanks to a lot of brave Americans and coalition friends, we're dismantling Al Qaida, person by person. Doesn't matter how long it takes, we will complete the job for the security of our country. I also put a doctrine out after September the 11th, 2001, that said, "If you harbor a terrorist, if you house a terrorist, if you feed a terrorist, you are just as guilty as the terrorists," and we upheld that doctrine.

We upheld that doctrine in Afghanistan. The Taliban was a regime which allowed for the Al Qaida to train. It gave them safe haven. At the same time, by the way, they were one of the most barbaric regimes in the history of mankind. The United States led a coalition to not only uphold that doctrine but to free the people of Afghanistan. We believe strongly in this country that freedom is not America's gift to the world. We believe strongly that freedom is God's gift to every individual in the world.

Thanks to the United States and our coalition, the Afghan people are free from the Taliban, America is more secure, and young girls—many young girls for the first time now go to school. We not only acted to make our country more secure, to do our duty to deal with threats or the potential threats, but at the same time we freed people.

We took action in Iraq as well. I made it clear that we wanted to work with the international community; we want to enforce the United Nations resolutions that time and time again had called for Mr. Saddam Hussein to disclose and destroy weapons of mass destruction. He ignored the world. He chose defiance. He is no

more, and the world is a better place because of it.

Yesterday, Dr. David Kay and his team reported to the Congress about 3 months of investigations into the regime of Saddam Hussein and his weapons programs. It's an interim report. By the way, it was completed under incredibly difficult circumstances.

Let me tell you what the report said. It states that Saddam Hussein's regime had a clandestine network of biological laboratories; they had a live strain of deadly agent called botulinum; that he had sophisticated concealment efforts—in other words, he's hiding his programs—that he had advanced design work done on prohibited long-range missiles.

The report summarized the regime's efforts this way, and I quote Dr. Kay, his report: "Iraq's WMD programs spanned more than two decades, involved thousands of people, billions of dollars, and it was elaborately shielded by security and deception operations that continued even beyond the end of Operation Iraqi Freedom." That's what this man stated in his report. That's what the report said.

Specifically, Dr. Kay's team discovered what the report calls, and I quote, "dozens of WMD related program activities and significant amounts of equipment that Iraq concealed from the United Nations during the inspections that began in late 2002." In addition to these extensive concealment efforts, Dr. Kay found systematic destruction of evidence of the illegal activities.

This interim progress report is not final. Extensive work remains to be done on his biological, chemical, and nuclear programs. But these findings already make clear that Saddam Hussein actively deceived the international community, was in clear violation of United Nations Security Council Resolution 1441, and was a danger to the world. The world is a better place when we got rid of Saddam Hussein.

We have more work to do in Iraq. A free Iraq, a peaceful Iraq will help change an area of the world that needs peace and freedom. A peaceful Iraq and a free Iraq is part of our campaign to rid the world of terror. And that's why the thugs in Iraq still resist us, because they can't stand the thought of free societies. They understand what freedom means. See, free nations are peaceful nations. Free nations don't attack each other. Free nations don't develop weapons of mass destruction. There will be a free and peaceful Iraq. What's taking place in Iraq is the evolution of a society to be democratic in nation—nature, a society in which the people are better off.

I met with Bernie Kerik this morning in the Oval Office. He was a former police commissioner in New York City. He was charged with going to Baghdad to help the Iraqis develop a police force. When he got there, there was no police force. The place was in shambles. And in a very quick period of time—remember, we've been there for about 4 months-plus—he helped develop a police force. Over 37,000 Iraqis now are patrolling the streets of Baghdad to make it a safer place.

The reason I bring this up is, we'll work hard to bring the thugs and terrorists to justice in Baghdad. We would rather fight them there than our own streets. But eventually, Iraq will be safe and secure because the Iraqi people have made the decision to live a peaceful and free life. And it's happening. It's happening every day. We will stay the course. We will not be intimidated by thugs who are trying to create fear and the conditions for us to remove. A free Iraq is essential to making sure that America and the future generations of America are able to live in peace and freedom.

No, the attacks of September the 11th and the march to war leading up to the Iraqi excursion affected the psychology of the country. We had a recession, and we had the attacks, the national emergency, plus the march to war. But we're a strong country. We're a resilient country because

the entrepreneurial spirit is strong, and things seem to be okay.

We also had another hurdle to cross, and that is we had some corporate CEOs that forgot their responsibility to our society. They didn't tell the truth. They didn't tell the truth to their employees and their shareholders. They failed to uphold the high standards expected in America. And therefore, they're going to pay the price. We expect people in positions of responsibility to behave responsibly and to tell the truth.

We passed tough laws. I want to thank the Congress for working on those laws. And we're holding people to account. By far, the vast majority of people in corporate America are honest, decent folks. But we need to send a signal that we expect honesty throughout our country.

And then the country wasn't—Government wasn't—the economy wasn't growing like we wanted, and so I called Congress back into action one more time on tax relief, historic tax relief. We passed tax relief. It's based upon this theory: When somebody has more money in their pocket, they're more likely to demand a good or a service. And in our society, when you demand a good or a service, somebody is going to produce the good or a service. And when somebody meets that demand with production, it means somebody is more likely to be able to find a job. The tax relief we passed, letting people keep more of their own money, is an essential ingredient to making sure people can find work in America.

So we expanded the child credit from $600 to $1,000 per child and worked with Congress to get that extra $400 per child paid out to families this summer. The check was in the mail, and it actually got to you, I hope.

We reduced the effects of the marriage penalty. What kind of Tax Code is it that discourages marriage? It's a Tax Code that needed to be changed. We cut the taxes on dividends and capital gains to help encourage investment and savings. This action particularly helped many seniors, because a lot of seniors rely upon investment income to live on. And as a positive effect, it also helped with capital formation.

We reduced the taxes on everybody who pays taxes. We didn't pick or choose. Everybody who pays taxes will get a reduction.

This is an important part of the tax relief plan, what I just described, the reduction of taxes on everybody who pays, because it has a incredibly positive effect on small businesses. Cutting the individual tax rates has got an effect on small businesses, because most small businesses are Subchapter S corporations or sole proprietorships, which means they pay tax at the individual tax rate.

It's very important for our countrymen to understand that part of the tax relief plan. Two-thirds of those who pay the top rate in our Tax Code, individual Tax Code, are small-business owners. Seventy percent of new jobs in America are created by small businesses. It seems to make sense, if you're trying to create new jobs, to allow small businesses to keep more of their own money. If 70 percent of the new jobs in America are created by small business, and by reducing all tax rates puts money into small-business' pockets, it seems to make sense that people ought to be supporting the tax cuts all across America.

The tax relief plan meant more capital in the pockets of the small-business owners, which means somebody is more likely to find a job, and that's what we're here talking about. We care about our fellow citizens. We want to make sure somebody who is hurting has a chance to succeed in life by working. We also encouraged investment to small businesses by increasing the annual expense deduction of investments from $25,000 to $100,000. See, that encourages people to buy a piece of equipment, for example.

Today I met with three businessowners here from the Milwaukee area. I met with Al Hentzen. Al has got a—what he calls a general industrial business. It provides paints and coatings for industry. He's been in business 80 years. He explained to me that the tax relief plan that we passed encouraged him and helped him add 12 new employees this year. Now, you see, there's a lot of Als all across America. If the plan helped Al, there's no telling how many other people made the same decision Al did. You add 12 here; you add 12 there; you add 50 here; and all of a sudden, people are finding work. Small businesses create 70 percent of the new jobs. The tax plan we passed encouraged Al, Al Hentzen, to add 12 new employees this year, and he's optimistic about adding more next year.

Al Hentzen says, "We're not putting tax relief back into our pockets." This is what the leader of this small business or medium-size business says: "It goes right back into the company, whether in new people or in machinery." And you see, when Al and his company decides to buy a machine, somebody has got to make the machine. And that means somebody in the machine-making company is more likely to find a job as well. When Al makes a decision, he increases demand for a product. That demand for that product will be met in our marketplace. The more demand there is for a product, the more likely one of our citizens is going to find work.

I talked to John Stollenwerk today. He runs Allen-Edmonds. I happen to have one of his products on my feet. [Laughter] You probably think this is a gross pander— [laughter]—but I wear John Stollenwerk's products nearly every day, except when I'm running. [Laughter] He makes a great product, one of the world's finest shoes.

He bought the company 20 years ago. He made the conscious decision to fix it up to make the right decisions so he could keep people working here in Wisconsin. He says, "Not only am I successful because of the products we make, but I'm successful because of the people that work with him." I appreciate that attitude. See, there's a company CEO that focuses on his employees and understands that without good employees, he's not going anywhere.

He bought a million dollars' worth of equipment because of the incentives we put into the tax package. That's a million dollars of purchases in the marketplace. Somebody is meeting the demand for that million dollars' worth of equipment. He says, "I will take the money and invest it." This is the money that he has saved from the tax relief plan. He's a Subchapter S corporation. They pay taxes at the individual rates. When we cut the individual rates, he ends up with more cashflow, plus the incentives on the investment side. He says, "I will take that money and invest it and spend it, and I will do it more efficiently than the Federal Government could."

Big John Weise is with us today. I say "Big John" because he's a big guy. [*Laughter*] His business is called F. Barkow, Inc. He helps get glass windows safely to factories and construction sites. This company has been doing this for 125 years. They have gone from horse-drawn carriages to now make products for trucks to move glass.

He told me that as a result of the tax plan passed by the Congress, now in effect, that he is going to purchase a turret press to replace the one that his company has had in place since 1971. Somebody is going to make that turret press for him. There's somebody who's getting a job because John has decided to make an additional purchase because of the tax relief plan.

As well the new turret press—a 1971 press may be a good press, but it's not going to be as good as one manufactured 34 years later or 33 years later. See, technology is changing. When he gets the new press, it's going to make him more productive. And as a more productive company, it means he can compete better. So not only is the decision he made good for the turret manufacturer, it's good to making sure his company can stay competitive, so

he can compete. We have a competitive marketplace.

New investment helps our owners and our companies compete. That's what we want. We want open competition. It's good for consumers. It's good for America that we compete. This tax relief helped him a lot, and it helped him make a lot of good decisions. He wants a new forklift, two new welding machines, a metal cutter. In other words, the tax relief increased demand. It's helping him make his company more productive. But the people who are making the products for John's company are also likely to find work.

No, the tax relief we passed was necessary for economic vitality. If you're interested in job creation, you need to support this tax relief that we passed. You wonder why I say, "Support it," because I'm going to tell you a little later on, it's fixing to go away unless we do something about it. But in the meantime, I do want to share with you the fact that there is some positive signs that we're growing. Inflation is low. After-tax incomes are rising. Homeownership is near record highs.

That's great, by the way. We want people owning things in our society. You know, America is better off when we're an ownership society. If you own something, you have a stake in the future of our country. We want people from all walks of life owning a home. We have a minority homeownership gap in America, and we've got to do something about it. And I've submitted a good, solid plan to the United States Congress, and I hope they act on it. We want more people owning things in America. Productivity is high. In other words, our workers are incredibly efficient. We've got the best workers in the world, and our productivity is high.

Today there was a report on unemployment which shows that we added 57,000 new jobs in America. It's the first time that's happened in 7 months. Things are getting better. But there's still work to do. A lot of Wisconsin manufacturers hurt. It's tough sledding, tough times, and I understand that. We've got manufacturers in a lot of parts of our country that are lagging the rest of economic vitality. It's a slow sector. And what I'm about to describe to you is what more we can do to not only help our small businesses but help our manufacturing sectors to create the conditions so the manufacturing sector can compete and survive and succeed.

First, Washington must put good forth—good policies forth that will help small businesses deal with health care costs. Health care costs are on the rise. It affects a lot of small businesses. It makes it tougher to cashflow and to be positive and optimistic. One of the things I think we need to do, and I think it would make a big difference, is to allow small businesses to band together and to pool their risks, called associated health care plans, so that they can have the same purchasing power as big companies have. One way to help small businesses control costs is for Congress to pass the associated health care plans. I strongly support them. I think they're necessary.

And as well in order to help control costs, we need medical liability reform. I have analyzed, or had analyzed for me, what all these lawsuits—[laughter]—I delegate. [Laughter] Let me start over. [Laughter] People on my staff—[laughter]—looked at the cost of preventative medicine. [Laughter] You see, there's a lot of lawsuits flying around which caused some docs to quit practicing medicine, which makes medicine less available, and some docs to practice preventative medicine so that if and when they get sued, they can say they did everything possible in order to protect themselves from lawsuit. That drives up the cost of medicine. It costs our Federal Government billions of dollars. The practice of practicing preventative medicine costs the Government billions, which drives up the cost of Medicaid and Medicare and veterans health costs.

Therefore, I've concluded that medical liability is a national problem that requires a national solution. I've submitted a good plan to the Congress. I want to thank the three Members here who supported medical liability reform in the House. It is stuck in the Senate. These Senators must understand—that are holding up this bill—that medical liability reform is necessary. It's good for our small-business sector, which will be good for job creation. It is good for American consumers. No one's ever been healed by a frivolous lawsuit.

We need to do something about class-action lawsuits as well. We've got a system today where people are able to shop a class-action lawsuit for a sympathetic jury in the State courts, even though this is Federal in nature. In other words, they cross jurisdictional boundaries. They're shopping it, who can find the best jury. And then the lawyers get all the money, and the people damaged don't. It's a system that needs reform. There's a good bill that has passed the House of Representatives. It is stuck in the Senate. It's action that would allow class action and mass tort actions to be tried in the Federal courts. And the other reform is to let the people who have been harmed to get the money and not the lawyers. We need class-action reform, for the sake of job creation. We need tort reform at the State level, for the sake of job creation as well.

We need a national energy policy. The manufacturing sector needs a reliable supply of energy. The uncertainty that comes with an antiquated electricity grid is difficult on the manufacturing sector. The manufacturing sector consumes a lot of energy, and therefore this Nation needs a national energy plan. We need to use our technologies to conserve better. We need to use our technologies to help develop new sources of energy. I mean, I'd like to be growing our way out of an energy crisis. We need ethanol. We need biofuels. But we also need to make sure we emphasize clean coal technology. We've got a lot of coal. We've got technological know-how. We've got to make sure that the Congress passes a national energy strategy that utilizes the resources at hand. What I'm telling you is, for the sake of economic security and for the sake of national security, we need a national energy strategy so we become less dependent on foreign sources of energy.

Fourthly, we need less regulation on small businesses. And regulation ties up all kinds of time that could be used for productive uses for meeting demand. We're working on it at the Federal level. I've streamlined tax reporting requirements recently for America's small businesses. The way we calculate it is, is this year, 2.6 million small-business owners will save 61 million hours as a result of tax simplification. That's 61 million more hours that will go to help the company compete. Some regulations are necessary; over-regulating is not necessary. And it puts enormous strain, particularly on the small-business sector in America.

Fifth, we've got to have free trade policy that includes fair trade. See, I believe if you're good at something, you ought to promote it. I want Wisconsin's farmers selling their product overseas. Allen-Edmonds sells 25 percent of their goods overseas. We need to be knocking down trade barriers so we can sell our products to other people. We also have got to make sure other people treat us fairly. Our manufacturing sector needs to be fair—treated fairly.

So we've been talking to countries about currency policy to make sure that the currency policies of a government don't disadvantage America. Fair trade means currency policies is fair. The manufacturing sector is concerned about the playing field being level. This administration will work to level that playing field. We can compete with anybody. We just expect the rules to treat us fairly.

Finally, this tax relief plan I described to you needs to be permanent. You say, "Why isn't it permanent?" Well, that's

Washington. [*Laughter*] You see, in order to get it out of one of the bodies there, they had to make the tax relief temporary. We got rid of the death tax, it looked like, which is important for small-business owners and Wisconsin's farmers and because we—see, we don't believe it's fair to tax a person's assets twice. If you're working all your life to build up your small business and you want to leave it to whoever you want to leave it to, they shouldn't—that asset shouldn't be taxed twice, shouldn't tax your income when you're making money, and shouldn't tax it when you pass it on to your son, daughter, whoever you want to pass it on to. It doesn't make—we're working with the Congress to get rid of it. It's nearly got rid of, but because of a quirk in the rules in the Senate, it will come back in 2011. It's kind of hard to plan, isn't it? [*Laughter*] You kind of phase it out, and it pops back up.

The child credit, which has gone from $600 to $1,000, falls back to $700 in 2005. The Government giveth—[*laughter*]—and Government taketh away. Marriage penalty begins to scale back up. A family of four making $40,000 income will go up $922 in the year 2005.

My point to the Congress is that people who invest capital in the small-business sector need certainty in the Tax Code. People who are planning for the future need to know what the rules are going to be in the future. And the idea of passing tax relief which is here one day and gone tomorrow is not good for economic recovery. For the sake of job creation, we need to put certainty in the Tax Code. All the tax relief we passed must be permanent.

You will hear all kinds of reasons to raise taxes. One of them will be the deficit. Yes, we have a deficit. Half the deficit is caused by the fact that our country went into recession. When you go into recession, there's less revenues coming into the Treasury.

About a quarter of our deficit was caused by the fact that we're at war. And when we put our troops into harm's way, when we ask a lot of our young men and women to sacrifice for our freedom and our security, they must have the best pay, the best equipment, and the best possible training. We will spend what it takes to support our troops, and we will spend what it takes to defend the homeland.

About a quarter of the deficit came because we passed back taxes to the people, actually passed back your own money. And that was necessary to get the economy going. If half the deficit was caused because we lost revenues, it seems to make sense that we want to crank up the economy so we get those revenues back, the revenues come back in the Treasury. No, one quarter of the deficit was caused by the tax relief necessary to stimulate economic growth, the tax relief that also was necessary to make sure the recession was not so deep, that it didn't hurt people.

So we have a deficit. The best way to solve the deficit—and I have submitted a budget to the Congress which will cut the deficit in half for 5 years—is to keep in place the economic vitality package and to hold the line on unnecessary spending in Washington, DC, is to bring much needed fiscal discipline to our Nation's Capital.

Now, we've been tested. This country has been tested. Two-and-a-half years, a lot of circumstances has tested our resolve and our character, and we met that test. This is a strong nation.

We're not going to be intimidated by thugs and killers. They don't understand our Nation. Those who attacked us thought we'd fold tent and kind of file a lawsuit. [*Laughter*] They just don't understand the resolve. They don't understand the courage of our military. They don't understand our will to do our duty, which is to protect the American people.

We're a strong nation. The entrepreneurial spirit in this country is really strong. We've got people who put that sign out there, say, "The American Dream is meant for you, that if you want to own your own business, get after it." Government's role is not to create wealth but the conditions in which the entrepreneurial spirit can flourish.

You're welcome to the American Dream, no matter who you are or where you're from. The entrepreneurial spirit is strong, and that's what's going to lead this recovery. The people are going to be able to find work because the small-business owners of America are risktakers, bold thinkers, and love their country, and are willing to expand the job base.

No, the spirit of America is strong. There are thousands of our citizens who, when they see somebody who hurts, are loving them, like I said earlier. There are people, when they see the hunger—hungry, provide the food, when they know somebody is homeless, provide the shelter. There are people who are helping little children understand what is necessary to learn to read. There are drug addicts who suffer. Yet there are great faith-based programs in America who are helping to heal hearts first and then change habits. The faith of this country—[*applause*]. We're a strong country because of our values. We believe in justice, we believe in human dignity, and we believe in freedom. And it is such an honor to represent this great land.

May God bless you all, and may God bless America. Thank you all.

NOTE: The President spoke at 10:29 a.m. In his remarks, he referred to former President Saddam Hussein of Iraq; David Kay, CIA Special Advisor for Strategy Regarding Iraqi Weapons of Mass Destruction Programs; Albert Hentzen, president and chief executive officer, Hentzen Coatings, Inc.; John Stollenwerk, president and chief executive officer, Allen-Edmonds Shoe Corp.; and John R. Weise, president, F. Barkow, Inc.

Remarks at a Bush-Cheney Luncheon in Milwaukee
October 3, 2003

Thanks for coming. Thanks for that rousing Wisconsin welcome. It's such an honor to be back here. It's a great State, full of a lot of really neat people, and I want to thank you for your friendship. And I want to thank you for your contributions and help and prayers. With your help, Vice President Cheney and I came pretty darn close of carrying this State in 2000. There's no doubt in my mind, in 2004 we're going to win the State of Wisconsin. And that victory in Wisconsin is going to be part of a great nationwide victory in November of 2004.

I want to thank you for your help in getting there. I appreciate the fact that you've contributed your money, and now I need you to contribute your time. When you put up those signs at the right time, knock on the doors, when you go to your coffee shops—if you live in a community with a coffee shop—you tell them that this administration is working for everybody. We believe in a hopeful, positive, optimistic vision for every single person who is fortunate enough to live in this country. You tell them that this is an administration focused on the people's business.

You know, I'm loosening up for this campaign. I'm kind of getting ready. [*Laughter*] But the political season will come in its own time. I've got a job to do. I've been entrusted to lead this great Nation, and I will do so. We've got a lot on our agenda in Washington, DC. And what I'm going to do until the political season comes, I will work hard to earn the confidence of every American by keeping this Nation strong and secure and prosperous and free.

Rick, I want to thank you for your leadership and thank you for your kind introduction. I've known Rick for a while. When he says we're going to win, I believe him. And I want to appreciate him energizing the grassroots, and I want to thank all of you grassroots participants for getting ready to go.

I traveled today with a really good, fine friend, a man I'd say you trained well, a person who is making an enormous contribution to my Cabinet and to our country, a person who has got a huge job running the Department of Health and Human Services, and that's Tommy Thompson.

I heard Tommy whispering to somebody; he said, "You know, the campaign made a mistake in sending George W. They should have sent Laura." [*Laughter*] Speaking about Laura, she just got back from a sensitive diplomatic mission. [*Laughter*] You probably saw the picture in the newspaper. [*Laughter*] But I'm proud that she represented our country, because she does it with such class. She is a fabulous First Lady.

She sends her best and sorry she can't be here. Right after here, I'm going to fly back to Washington, and she's organizing a National Book Festival. She loves books. She loves the idea of people teaching kids how to read books, and she's going to herald some of our great authors. She's making an enormous contribution. I'm lucky she said yes when I said, "Will you marry me?" [*Laughter*]

I want to thank the Members of the Congress flying with us today—who flew with us today, and one who met us here today. The chairman, Jim Sensenbrenner, is with us, and it's been a joy to work with Jim. He's a good, strong patriot. Tom Petri is with us today, good, honorable, decent guy. Tom, I want to thank you for your friendship, and I appreciate you coming today. A young star—we've got some young stars from the State of Wisconsin, people who are making a big difference in the Halls of Congress, and they've done so in a quick period of time. That would be Paul Ryan, the Congressman from this part of the world, and Congressman Mark Green.

I want to thank people from the statehouse who have joined us today. John Gard, who is the speaker of the assembly. Mary Panzer, who is the senate majority leader, is with us today. Mary, thank you for coming. Jack Voight, your State treasurer is with us. Jack, thank you for being here. Scott McCallum, the former Governor, is with us. Scott, I'm honored that you're here. Thank you for coming. And Scott Walker, local man, is with us today. I appreciate you, Scott. Thanks for the good work you're doing.

My friend Mercer Reynolds from Cincinnati, Ohio, who is the national finance chair of the Bush-Cheney 2004 campaign, he's taking time out of his business to travel the country with us and organize this very important fundraising effort we're doing nationwide. Mercer, I want to thank you for coming. Glad you're here.

I appreciate my longtime friend Jim Klauser for taking on the State campaign chairman role for the State of Wisconsin. San Orr is the State finance chairman. Jon Hammes is the State finance cochair. San Orr is the cochair as well. We've got cochairmen here. I'm thankful for your hard work. Thanks for making this event go so well. Mary Buestrin is the national committeewoman from this State. I appreciate all of you all, again, for coming.

I particularly want to say something about the Arrowhead High School Choir. I am glad you're here. Thanks for coming.

In the last 2½ years, this Nation has acted decisively to confront great challenges. I came to this office to solve problems, not to pass them on to future presidents and future generations. I came to seize opportunities and not let them slip away. This administration is meeting the tests of our time.

Terrorists declared war on the United States of America, and war is what they got. We've captured or killed many of the key leaders of Al Qaida, and the rest of them know we're on their trail. In Afghanistan and Iraq, we gave ultimatums to terror regimes. Those regimes chose defiance, and those regimes are no more. Fifty million people—50 million people in those two countries once lived under tyranny, and today, they live in freedom.

Two-and-a-half years ago, our military was not receiving the resources it needed, and morale was beginning to suffer. So we acted. We increased the defense budget to prepare for the threats of a new era, and no one today in the world can question the skill and the strength and the spirit of the United States military.

Two-and-a-half years ago, we inherited an economy in recession. And then we had the attacks on our country, coupled with the march to war, and corporate scandals. All of those events affected the confidence of the American people. But we acted. We passed tough laws to hold corporate criminals to account. And to get the economy going, I have twice led the United States Congress to pass historic tax relief for the American people.

We believe and know that when people have more money in their pocket, more money to spend, to save, or invest, the whole economy grows, and someone is more likely to find a job. We also understand whose money we're spending in Washington, DC. We're not spending the Government's money. We spend the people's money. And we're sending more of the people's money back to them so they can help raise their families. We reduced the taxes on dividends and capital gains to encourage investment. We're giving small businesses incentives to expand their businesses and hire new people.

With all these actions, by being proactive, we're laying the foundation for greater prosperity and more jobs, so that each and every single purpose—person in this country has a chance to realize the American Dream.

Two-and-a-half years ago, there was a lot of talk about education reform in Washington, DC, but there just wasn't much action. So I acted. I called for and Congress passed the No Child Left Behind Act. With a solid, bipartisan majority, we delivered the most dramatic education reforms in a generation. Finally we are bringing high standards and accountability to public schools. We said, in return for the receipt of Federal money, "Please show us whether or not a child is learning to read and write and add and subtract." We're challenging the soft bigotry of low expectations. We believe in raising the bar. We believe in high standards. We believe every child can learn. And for the first time in Federal history, we're insisting that every child learns. We don't want one single child left behind in America.

We reorganized our Government and created the Department of Homeland Security to better safeguard our borders and ports and to protect the American people. We passed trade promotion authority to open up new markets for Wisconsin's entrepreneurs and manufacturers and farmers. We passed, with the Congress, much needed spending discipline. We passed budget agreements to help hold the line on spending.

On issue after issue, this administration has acted on principle. We have kept our word, and we have made progress for the American people. And the Congress gets a lot of credit. I've got a great relationship with Speaker Denny Hastert. He's a good, solid man. I've got a great relationship with Senator Bill Frist, the majority leader. We're working together; we're working together to get results for the American people. We're working hard to change the tone in Washington, DC. It needs a—it needs a tonal change. There's too much partisan bickering. There's too much zero-sum politics. We need to focus on results, not politics. And those are the kind of people I've surrounded myself with in Washington.

I've put together a fantastic administration for the American people. We've got a great National Security staff, a great economic team. We've got people who have come to Washington to serve the people, not petty partisan politics. Richard B. Cheney is the greatest Vice President our country has ever had. Mother's got a second opinion. [*Laughter*]

In 2½ years, if you think about it—and you tell them at the coffee shops—in 2½ years, this administration has come far. We've done a lot. We've tackled a lot of tough problems. But our work is only beginning. My job is to set great goals worthy of a great nation.

First, America is committed to expanding the realm of peace and freedom for our own security and for the benefit of the world. And second, in our own country, we must work for a society of prosperity and compassion, so that every citizen has a chance to work and to succeed and to realize the great promise of our land. It is clear that the future of freedom and peace depend on the actions of America. This Nation is freedom's home, and we are freedom's defender. We welcome this charge of history, and we are keeping it.

The war on terror continues. There's still people out there that hate America, cold-blooded killers who hate what we stand for. These people are not idle, and neither are we. This country will not rest; we will not tire; we will not stop until this danger to civilization is removed.

We continue to confront that danger in Iraq, for Saddam holdouts and foreign terrorists are desperately trying to throw Iraq into chaos by attacking coalition forces, aid workers, innocent Iraqis. See, they know that the advance of freedom in Iraq will be a major defeat in the cause of terror. This collection of killers is trying to shake our will. They're trying to frighten the civilized world. They don't understand this country. They don't understand this administration. We will not be intimidated.

We are aggressively striking the terrorists in Iraq, defeating them there so we will not have to face them in our own country. We'll call on other nations to continue to help us in Iraq. See, by making Iraq a free country, it'll make the world more secure. We'll stand with the Iraqi people as they assume more of their own defense and move toward self-government. These aren't easy tasks. I know that. But they're essential tasks. We will finish what we have begun, and we will win this essential victory in the war on terror.

Our greatest security comes from the advance of human liberty, because free nations don't support terror. Free nations do not attack their neighbors. Free nations do not threaten the world with weapons of mass terror. Americans believe that freedom is the deepest need and hope of every human heart. And I believe that freedom is the right of every person, and I believe that freedom is the future of every nation.

America also understands that unprecedented influence brings tremendous responsibilities. We have duties in the world. And when we see disease and starvation and hopeless poverty, we will not turn away. On the continent of Africa, this great Nation is committed to bringing the healing power of medicines to millions of men and women and children now suffering with AIDS. I want to thank Tommy for his good work. He's a part of our great land's leadership. We're leading the world in providing this incredibly important work of human rescue.

We face challenges here at home as well, but we'll be equal to those challenges. First of all, any time anybody who is looking for work and can't find a job is still looking, I think we've got a problem. I will continue to work to create an environment in which the entrepreneurial spirit flourishes, in which small businesses can grow, so that people in America can find work.

I just had a great session with small-business owners here in Milwaukee. The optimism is high. The spirit is strong. We will continue to create the conditions for increased employment in America, so everybody can find a job.

We also need to keep our commitment to America's seniors by strengthening and modernizing Medicare. A few weeks ago, earlier in the summer, Congress took historic action to improve the lives of older Americans. For the first time since the creation of Medicare, the House and the Senate have passed reforms to increase the choices available for America's seniors and to provide coverage for prescription drugs. Tommy's working this issue on the Hill. He's working with the House and the Senate so they can iron out their differences and get a good bill to my desk. We have a duty to America's seniors. We have a duty to those of us who are going to be seniors to make sure that we have a modern Medicare system.

And for the sake of our health care system, we need to cut down on the frivolous lawsuits which increases the cost of medicine. People who have been harmed by a bad doc deserve their day in court, no doubt about it. Yet, the system should not reward lawyers who are simply fishing for a rich settlement. Because of frivolous lawsuits, docs practice defensive medicine, which drives up the cost of health care. And they therefore affect—frivolous lawsuits affect the Federal budget. Medical liability reform is a national issue which requires a national solution. The House of Representatives passed a good bill to reform the system. It is stuck in the United States Senate. The Senators must understand that no one has been healed by a frivolous lawsuit in America.

I have a responsibility as the President to make sure the judicial system runs well. And I have met that duty. I have nominated superb men and women for the Federal benches, people who will interpret the law, not legislate from the bench. Yet some Members of the United States Senate—you might know some of them—[laughter]—are trying to keep my nominees off the bench by blocking up-or-down votes. Every judicial nominee deserves a fair hearing and an up-or-down vote on the Senate floor. It is time for some Members to stop playing politics with American justice.

The Congress needs to complete work on a comprehensive energy plan. Wisconsin is a State—it is a manufacturing State. Manufacturers need reliable sources of energy. The manufacturing sector lags in America. And one way to help us was good trade policy that levels the playing field, good tax policy that encourages investment, less regulations.

But as well we need to have an energy plan. I submitted one 2 years ago. This summer, we had a problem with our electricity grid. You might remember that. It should be a wake-up call to the Congress that we need to modernize our ability to move electricity around America. We need to make sure that reliability standards for electricity are mandatory, not voluntary. We need to encourage more investment into modernizing the grid. We need to use our technological capacities to increase conservation, to find new sources of energy. But we need to use the old sources of energy in an environmentally friendly way to make sure we're less dependent on foreign sources of crude. The Congress needs to get an energy bill to my desk. For the sake of national security and for the sake of economic security, they need to get a bill to my desk soon.

Our strong and prosperous Nation must also be a compassionate nation. I will continue to advance our agenda of compassionate conservatism, which means we'll apply the best and most innovative ideas to the task of helping our fellow citizens in need. There's still millions of men and women who want to end their dependence on Government and become independent through hard work. We must build on the success of welfare reform, to bring work and dignity into the lives of more of our fellow citizens.

Congress should complete the "Citizen Service Act," to encourage more Americans to serve in their communities. And Congress should finally pass my Faith-Based Initiative, to help empower the armies of compassion which exist all across America. The soldiers in that army mentor children; they care for the homeless; they offer hope to the addicted. One of the great strengths of America is the faith of the American people. People of all faiths, Hindu, Muslim, Christian, and Jew, should be welcomed by our Government to help people who hurt, to help save lives. This Government should not fear faith. We should welcome faith.

A compassionate society must promote opportunity for all, including the independence and dignity that come from ownership. This administration will constantly strive to promote an ownership society in America. We want more people owning their own home. We want people to own and manage their own retirement accounts. We want people to own and manage their own health accounts. And we want more people owning a small business. You see, we understand in this administration that when somebody owns something, he or she has a vital stake in the future of our country.

In a compassionate society, people respect one another, and they take responsibility for the decisions they make. The culture of America is changing from one that has said, "If it feels good, just go ahead and do it," and "If you've got a problem, blame somebody else," to a new culture in which each of us understands that we are responsible for the decisions we make in life.

If you're fortunate enough to be a mom or a dad, you're responsible for loving your child. If you're worried about the quality of the education in which you live, you're responsible for doing something about it. If you're a CEO in corporate America, you're responsible for telling the truth to your shareholders and your employees.

And in a responsibility society, each of us are responsible for loving a neighbor just like we'd like to be loved ourself. We can see the culture of service and responsibility growing around us here in America. I started what's called the USA Freedom Corps to encourage Americans to extend a compassionate hand to a neighbor in need. The response has been very strong. Go to the web page and take a look at it, if you're interested in serving your community by helping somebody who hurts.

Our faith-based charities are strong in America. People have heard the call, just like policemen and firefighters and people who wear our Nation's uniform are reminding us what it means to sacrifice for something greater than ourselves. Once again, the children of America believe in heroes, because they see them every day. In these challenging times, the world has seen the resolve and courage of America, and I have been fortunate enough to see the compassion and the character of the American people.

All the tests of the last 2½ years have come to the right nation. We are a strong country, and we use our strength to defend the peace. We're an optimistic country, confident in ourselves and in ideals bigger than ourselves. Abroad, we seek to lift up whole nations by spreading freedom. At home, we seek to lift up lives by spreading opportunity to every corner of America. This is the work that history has set before us. We welcome it, and we know that for our country and for our cause, the best days lie ahead.

May God bless you. Thank you all.

NOTE: The President spoke at noon at the Italian Community Center. In his remarks, he referred to Rick Graber, chairman, Republican Party of Wisconsin; and Milwaukee County Executive Scott Walker.

The President's Radio Address
October 4, 2003

Good morning. This weekend in Iraq, 750 Iraqi citizens completed their military training and became the first battalion of the new Iraqi Army. For decades, Iraq's army served the interests of a dictator. Today, a new army is serving the Iraqi people. And less than a year from now, Iraq will have a 40,000-member military force, trained and dedicated to protecting their fellow citizens.

Our coalition is helping to train and equip Iraq's new army so that Iraqis can take over border protection and other security duties as soon as possible. Soldiers in the new battalion join more than 80,000 other Iraqis who are defending their country's security. Iraq now has a Civil Defense Corps of nearly 2,500, a border guard force of 4,700, and a facility protection service of over 12,000. And more than half of the Iraqis under arms are police officers, instructed by professionals like New York City's outstanding former police chief, Bernard Kerik. Iraq's neighbor, Jordan, has announced that it will help Iraq train additional police officers.

For three decades, the police in Iraq were the feared enforcers of a dictatorship. Now Iraq's new police are enforcing the just laws of an emerging democracy. Already the Iraqi police are assuming greater responsibility and greater risks. This week, Iraqi officers aided a series of joint raids by American troops, leading to the arrest of more than 50 suspected criminals and terrorists. We're on the offensive against the desperate holdouts and Saddam loyalists who oppose progress in Iraq. The free nation we are helping to build will be free of them.

The United States is standing with the Iraqi people as they move toward self-government. My wartime funding request to Congress includes more than $5 billion to help the people of Iraq take responsibility for their own security. These funds will be used to prepare the Iraqi Army, to train public safety and emergency personnel, and to establish a fair and effective judicial system.

Greater security is essential to Iraq's future. A secure Iraq will protect the nation's schools and the hospitals that are opening and the roads that are being built and the water and power facilities we are repairing. Across Iraq, our coalition is turning over responsibility to the future leaders of that country. Those leaders include women. Just this weekend, a conference is being held at the University of Babylon to affirm the vital role of women in the Iraqi society.

The transition to self-government is a complicated process, because it takes time to build trust and hope after decades of oppression and fear. Yet we are making steady progress, and we will keep our promise to fully return Iraq's Government to Iraq's people as soon as possible.

The men and women of our coalition have shown bravery and skill and compassion in Iraq. And they know their mission. They know that we are fighting terrorists in Iraq so that we will not have to face them and fight them in the streets of our own cities. Our forces know that a secure and sovereign Iraq will be a setback for terrorists and an inspiration to all who dream of freedom in the Middle East. And the world can be certain, this essential mission in the war on terror will be completed.

Thank you for listening.

NOTE: The address was recorded at 11:27 a.m. on October 2 in the Cabinet Room at the White House for broadcast at 10:06 a.m. on October 4. The transcript was made available by the Office of the Press Secretary on October 3 but was embargoed for release until the broadcast. In his remarks, the President referred to former President Saddam Hussein of Iraq. The Office of the Press Secretary also released a Spanish language transcript of this address.

Statement on the Terrorist Attack in Haifa, Israel
October 4, 2003

I condemn unequivocally the vicious act of terrorism committed today in Haifa, Israel.

This murderous action, aimed at families gathered to enjoy a Sabbath lunch, killed and injured dozens of men, women, and children.

This despicable attack underscores once again the responsibility of Palestinian authorities to fight terror, which remains the foremost obstacle to achieving the vision of two states living side by side in peace and security. The new Palestinian Cabinet must dedicate itself to dismantling the infrastructure of terror and preventing the kind of murderous actions that we witnessed today.

The American people join me in expressing condolences to Prime Minister Sharon and all the people of Israel and in reiterating our common dedication to the cause of fighting terrorism.

Message on the Observance of Yom Kippur, 5764
October 5, 2003

*In all thy ways acknowledge Him, and
He shall direct thy paths.*

PROVERBS 3:6

Yom Kippur is a time for people of the Jewish faith to draw near to God and seek His forgiveness through repentance and prayer. For Jews in the United States and around the world, this day marks the end of the High Holy Days and the sealing of God's judgment in the books of life. May you find hope and comfort in remembering the lessons of Jonah, the power of prayer, and the mercy of the Almighty.

Faith plays an important role in the lives of many Americans, offering strength and guidance for the challenges of each new day. As you renew your commitment to your faith and family on this holy day, may your actions reflect a compassionate spirit, and may you be inscribed and sealed for a good year and long life.

Laura joins me in sending our best wishes for a blessed Yom Kippur.

GEORGE W. BUSH

NOTE: An original was not available for verification of the content of this message.

Remarks at a Welcoming Ceremony for President Mwai Kibaki of Kenya
October 6, 2003

President Bush. Mr. President, Madam First Lady, members of the Kenyan delegation, on behalf of the American people, Laura and I are pleased to welcome you to the United States. This is the first state visit by the leader of an African country during my administration and the first visit of President Kibaki since his historic election last year.

Under President Kibaki's leadership, Kenya is pursuing important reforms and making the difficult and necessary and rewarding transition to permanent, multiparty democracy. Mr. President, your courage serves the Kenyan people well, and you honor the American people with your visit.

Kenya is a nation of rich traditions and ancient history. The Great Rift Valley, which runs through Eastern Kenya from Lake Rudolf to Lake Victoria, is known as the "cradle of civilization." The story of Kenya is inseparable from the story of mankind. And out of this proud past, Kenya is building a modern, prosperous, and

peaceful future. In building that future, Kenya will have a partner in the United States.

Our countries face common challenges, and we meet them with shared values. Both our nations are threatened by terrorists, and both have suffered. In one savage act 5 years ago in Nairobi, members of the Al Qaida network murdered more than 200 Kenyans and Americans. Our countries grieved together then and after September the 11th and after the attack last November in Mombasa.

Yet we have done more than grieve. We are working together to defeat the terrorists, to cut off their funding, to deny them sanctuary, and to bring them to justice. There can be no compromise with this evil, and the Government of Kenya is a vital ally in the ongoing war against terror.

We're also working together to create a better world, to end long-simmering conflicts, and to alleviate the suffering caused by poverty and hunger and disease. Our goal is to end the hopelessness that feeds terror and to help spread the blessings of liberty that are the birthright of every man, woman, and child on this Earth.

The partnership between our nations is sustained by the friendship between our people. Some 7,000 Americans live in Kenya. Thousands of our citizens love to travel to Kenya. One of the Peace Corps' largest programs is in Kenya, helping to encourage private enterprise, to fight AIDS, and to improve the nation's schools.

Every year, thousands of Kenyans come to study at American universities, more than from any other African country, including two of the President's children. And the United States is enriched by the many Americans who trace their ancestry to Kenya, many of whom live right here in Washington. Kenya and the United States have been friends since the days of Jomo Kenyatta and John F. Kennedy.

Mr. President, I'm proud to join you in carrying our friendship forward in this new century. Welcome to the White House, and welcome to the United States of America.

President Kibaki. Mr. President, thank you for your kind remarks. I wish to thank you for—Mr. President, the Government, and the people of the United States, for the warm welcome and hospitality extended to me and my delegation since our arrival. I feel privileged to have been accorded such a great honor and look forward to successful deliberations on matters of mutual interest to our two nations.

Mr. President, Kenya values the warm and cordial friendship that exists between the two nations. Following our successful democratic elections last December, my

Government is determined to uphold democratic values, human rights, good governance, and the rule of law, and to empower our people.

We thank the Government and the people of the United States for supporting Kenya to achieve democratic change. Mr. President, we are committed to deepening our ties with the United States.

I commend you for your various initiatives for supporting development in Africa and, in particular, the recent announcement of 15 billion U.S. dollars' assistance in the fight against HIV/AIDS, tuberculosis, malaria, of which Kenya is a beneficiary.

We equally welcome your personal efforts in promoting trade and investment opportunities through AGOA. Your recent announcement of the Millennium Change Account Initiative will help promote sustainable development in Africa.

Mr. President, our two nations have been victims of international terrorism. Kenya stands with the United States and the international community in fight against this global menace, in our conviction that no just cause can be served by taking away innocent lives.

Finally, Mr. President, I look forward to fruitful discussions on the various issues affecting our two nations, the Horn of Africa, and the international community.

NOTE: The President spoke at 9:21 a.m. on the South Grounds at the White House, where President Kibaki was accorded a formal welcome with full military honors. In his remarks, President Bush referred to Lucy Kibaki, wife of President Kibaki.

The President's News Conference With President Mwai Kibaki of Kenya
October 6, 2003

President Bush. It's my honor to welcome President Kibaki to the White House. Thank you, sir, for coming.

President Kibaki. Thank you.

President Bush. Today we affirm the growing strategic relationship between the United States and the African Continent. And we continue the longstanding partnership between the United States and Kenya.

President Kibaki's election last December showed Kenyans and Africans and people throughout the world the power of the ballot and the benefits of peaceful, democratic change. The President won a mandate for reform, and he is moving ahead with an ambitious agenda, redrafting Kenya's constitution, liberalizing its economy, fighting corruption, and investing in education and health care. With these steps, Kenya will attract investment, strengthen its role in the world, and improve the lives of its people. Success will take time, and progress may sometimes seem uneven. Yet, the benefits of democracy and freedom and investment in people are certain, and they are lasting.

Today the President and I discussed our alliance in the war on terror. In Nairobi and Mombasa and beyond, terrorists have made Kenya a battleground. The President affirmed the fact that the Kenyan people refuse to live in fear. Kenyan security forces have disrupted terror operations and have arrested suspected terrorists. Earlier this year, I announced a $100 million counterterrorism initiative to provide east Africa with training, equipment, and assistance to strengthen the security of those nations in east Africa. Kenya is our key partner in this initiative, and its Government clearly has the will to fight terror, and my Government will continue to give them the help they need to do so.

The President and I also discussed efforts to achieve peace in Sudan, an effort in which Kenya plays the leading role. Two able envoys, General Sumbeiywo and Senator John Danforth, have helped bring Africa's longest running civil war to—very close to a peaceful end. America will stay engaged in this effort.

I appreciate your efforts, Mr. President. Yet, only the north and south can arrive at a just and comprehensive peace, and I urge them to do so quickly.

In Somalia, we will continue to work with Kenya to bring unity and reconciliation to a badly divided land. The establishment of an effective representative government in Somalia will help stabilize the region and dispel the hopelessness that feeds terror.

President Kibaki and I share a deep commitment to waging a broad, effective effort against the AIDS virus, which afflicts nearly 30 million people on the African Continent. In Kenya alone, some one million children have been orphaned due to AIDS. I fully support the President's declaration of total war—his words—on this disease, and I'm proud to stand with him. The United States is Kenya's largest bilateral donor in the fight against AIDS. Our support will grow under my Emergency Plan for AIDS Relief, which is a firm commitment to spend $15 billion over 5 years to turning the tide against this disease.

Mr. President, America also stands with you in your work of modernizing the Kenyan economy, rewarding the enterprise of your people. Trade and growth are the only sure ways to lift people and nations out of poverty. I'm committed to keeping America's markets open to African goods and to increasing commercial ties with African nations. Kenya is one of America's most important economic partners in Africa. American investment in Kenya totals more than $285 million, and trade between our two countries tops $400 million per year.

These numbers have grown in recent years under the African Growth and Opportunity Act, AGOA. And they have the potential to grow even more as reforms in your country take hold, Mr. President. Kenya and the United States are old friends working together to face new challenges. Our relationship is strong, and it's growing stronger, and I'm grateful for the leadership and vision of the President.

Welcome.

President Kibaki. Thank you. It is my pleasure to be here with you, Mr. President.

This morning we had a fruitful meeting with my good friend, President Bush. Our discussions centered on bilateral, regional, and international issues of mutual interest to our two nations. I was encouraged by a keen interest and concern that President Bush has shown on issues affecting Kenya and Africa, in particular, the establishment of the Millennium Challenge Account and the 15 billion U.S. dollars' HIV/AIDS program bears testimony to this particular commitment.

We reaffirmed our mutual desire to further deepen our cooperation for the benefit of our two countries. President Bush welcomed the efforts made by Kenya in consolidating democracy, particularly after the successful general elections of December, the year 2002. We share the common desire to promote and entrench democracy in Africa and the need to support Kenya as a model of democracy.

I briefed President Bush on the priorities of my Government; that includes economic revival, education, health, and security. I am pleased by the willingness of the Bush administration to support our efforts to promote and sustain our economic recovery. President Bush shared my concern over the devastating effects of the HIV/AIDS pandemic and other infectious diseases, especially in Africa. I briefed the President on the vigorous campaign my Government is conducting against the HIV/AIDS pandemic. I am confident that these efforts

are benefiting substantially from the support of the U.S. Government.

We discussed at length the issue of terrorism. Kenya, like United States, has in the past suffered at the hands of terrorism. The attacks have strengthened our resolve to intensify and enhance our cooperation with the United States and the international community in the fight against terrorism.

I have requested the U.S. Government to support Kenya, to strengthen its security as an essential element in the fight against terrorism. This assistance will also enhance Kenya's role as a peacemaker in the Horn of Africa. President Bush expressed his appreciation for the leadership that Kenya has taken in the peace process in Sudan and IGAD. We note with satisfaction the historic signing of an agreement on the 25th of September, 2003, in Naivasha, Kenya, to address the transitional security arrangements for the parties to the conflict.

On Somalia, I emphasized that in order to maintain the democratic gains and to sustain the war against terrorism, it is essential that Somalia stabilizes. In this respect, it is important that the U.S. to— for the U.S. to increase its involvement in the search for peace in Somalia. It is pertinent that all parties involved in the peace process remain engaged. I requested the U.S. Government to assist in this regard, and I thank you very much indeed.

President Bush. Thank you, Mr. President.

The President has kindly agreed to take a couple of questions, and so have I. We'll start with the American side and then alternate back and forth.

First, Associated Press, Terry Hunt, Mr. President.

Israeli Air Strike in Syria/Palestinian Authority Responsibilities

Q. Thank you, Mr. President. Mr. President, do you think that Israel's air strike in Syria was justified? And do you think that you can work with the Palestinian Prime Minister, who says he would not use force under any circumstances against Palestinian militants?

President Bush. Terry, I talked to Prime Minister Sharon yesterday. I expressed our Nation's condolences at the needless murder of innocent people by the latest suicider. That murder came on a weekend of a high holy holiday.

Secondly, I made it very clear to the Prime Minister, like I have consistently done, that Israel has got a right to defend herself, that Israel must not feel constrained in terms of defending the homeland. However, I said that it's very important that any action Israel take should avoid escalation and creating higher tensions.

The speech I gave June 24, 2002, should explain to the world and to the American people the policy of this Government. We have not changed. Parties need to assume responsibility for their actions. In order for there to be a Palestinian state, the Palestinian Authority must fight terror and must use whatever means is necessary to fight terror. In order for this roadmap, which is a—as a way to get to a peaceful settlement, people have got to assume responsibility. All parties must assume responsibility. The Palestinian Authority must defeat the terrorists who are trying to stop the establishment of a Palestinian state, a peaceful state, in order for there to be peace.

Mr. President, want to call on somebody?

President Kibaki. Well, we hardly have anything to add to that particular statement, because it's fully adequate.

President Bush. You're welcome to call on somebody from your press corps, Mr. President.

April [April Ryan, American Urban Radio Networks], you're not in his press corps. You're trying to play like you're in his press corps. [*Laughter*]

Q. They put me over here.

President Bush. I know, but this is subversion, and this isn't—[*laughter*].

Leadership in Kenya

Q. I'd like to ask the President of Kenya a question. My name is Esther Githui; I work for the Voice of America. Mr. President, there has been very good will for you and Kenyans after you took over the Government. But I'm wondering why you have repeatedly asserted that you're in charge of Kenya. Is there any doubt that you are the President of Kenya?

President Kibaki. No, there is no doubt at all. There is no—no one has any doubt, certainly not in Kenya. Look by the way they voted. And look by the way they support the present Government. So I don't see anybody who has any doubt—well, anybody who has any doubt, he can ask us. [*Laughter*] You know, I mean—[*inaudible*]—you know, truly.

President Bush. Steve Holland [Reuters].

Iraq Stabilization Group

Q. Thank you, Mr. President. What is the purpose of the Iraq Stabilization Group? And is this an acknowledgment that the effort to stabilize Iraq is flagging? Does it diminish the authority of Secretary Rumsfeld?

President Bush. Yes. You know, it's common for the National Security Council to coordinate efforts, interagency efforts. And Condi Rice, the National Security Adviser, is doing just that. And this group formed within the National Security Council is aimed at the coordination of interagency efforts as well as providing a support group to the Department of Defense and Jerry Bremer. That's the purpose.

And listen, we're making good progress in Iraq. Sometimes it's hard to tell it when you listen to the filter. We're making good progress. I had a—Bernie Kerik came in the other day, and he described to me what it was like to set up a police force in Baghdad right after our successful efforts there. I was really impressed. I was impressed by the—his work. I was impressed by the spirit of the Iraqi citizens desirous to start taking care of business on their own.

And the truth of the matter is, in order for us to succeed in Iraq—and that is to provide the security necessary for a peaceful country to evolve—the Iraqis must take responsibility, and they are. The situation is improving on a daily basis inside Iraq. People are freer. The security situation is getting better. The infrastructure is getting better. The schools are opening. The hospitals are being modernized. And I really appreciate the effort of the Americans who are there and our coalition partners who are there who are working under very difficult circumstances.

Condi's job and Condi's team is going to make sure that the efforts continue to be coordinated so that we continue to make progress.

Mr. President.

President Kibaki. Well, we first of all want to congratulate America for the effort they are making. You know, it is important for all of us to think of the present and the future, because what has passed, has passed. And I think we can gain plenty by focusing on the present.

President Bush. April, are you going to try again to look like you're in the—be careful. [*Laughter*] Mr. President, call on who you—[*laughter*].

President Kibaki. Yes, yes.

President Bush. I exposed you. [*Laughter*]

Q. [*Inaudible*]

President Bush. That's right. [*Laughter*]

Kenya-U.S. Relations/African Debt Relief

Q. My name is Martin Mbugua, for the East African Standard, and I have a question for each President.

President Bush. Yes.

President Kibaki. Yes.

Q. Your Excellency, a lot of people see your trip to the United States as yet another begging trip. How different is this trip for those people who are seeing it as another lineup for aid?

And Mr. President, a lot of times people have talked about the debt that saddles a lot of African countries. You can give a lot of aid, but it's likely to do nothing if the country is sending all the money out. Are you looking to use your influence at the G–8 and the Bretton Woods institution to probably try and ease that, perhaps even forgive the debt for progressive countries?

President Bush. Thank you.

President Kibaki. Well, first for us, I don't think that we are in any way one of those countries which gain nothing or add nothing. But we definitely do gain by talking to friends like America and seeking help. Now, if you are seeking for help, you cannot adequately say publicly whether it is adequate or whether it is not. [*Laughter*]

So really, if you are asking for help, you really don't ask—you don't say how much. And so, really the question isn't—should not be asked of me.

President Bush. Let me tell you, in many ways, we're the country asking for help. We asked the President in Kenya for help in fighting terror, and the response has been strong. And we appreciate that response. We support HIPC. We'll continue to support HIPC. We also support trade with Kenya.

And the President, in talking about what he would like to see in our relationship, brought up international financial institutions, what can be done with the World Bank and/or the International Monetary Fund. And the President understands, like I understand, that it's the choice of the Kenyans to make. And that's why his anticorruption policy is so important, because as that policy takes root, as he deals with judges and/or whoever, Government officials that do not honor the integrity of the system, the international financial institutions will take notice and be more likely to become involved with Kenya.

And so we talked a lot about a lot of things, debt, IMF, trade, all aimed at lifting lives and helping Kenya realize her potential. I've long believed that African nations are plenty capable of making the right decisions and managing their own affairs. Our foreign policy recognizes that, and we will work with governments in particular that have developed the habits necessary for strong democracies and market economies to grow. This is such a leader. So our relationship is a complementary relationship, and it is important that it be strong like it is today.

April, you're really beginning to bother the President. [*Laughter*]

President Kibaki. No, no. [*Laughter*]

President Bush. Okay, I am anxious to hear what you've got to say. Go ahead. Let her rip.

Q. [*Inaudible*]

President Bush. No, not you.

Q. Thank you so much.

President Bush. Yes, April.

Justice Department Investigation of Classified Information Leak

Q. Mr. President, on another issue, the CIA leak-gate. What is your confidence level in the results of the DOJ investigation about any of your staffers not being found guilty or being found guilty? And what do you say to critics of the administration who say that this administration retaliates against naysayers?

President Bush. No, first of all, I'm glad you brought that question up. This is a very serious matter, and our administration takes it seriously. As members of the press corps here know, I have at times complained about leaks of security information, whether the leaks be in the legislative branch or in the executive branch. And I take those leaks very seriously.

And therefore, we will cooperate fully with the Justice Department. I've got all the confidence in the world the Justice Department will do a good, thorough job. And that's exactly what I want them to do, is a good, thorough job. I'd like to know who leaked, and if anybody has got any information inside our Government or outside our Government who leaked, you ought to take it to the Justice Department so we can find out the leaker.

I have told my staff I want full cooperation with the Justice Department. And when they ask for information, we expect the information to be delivered on a timely basis. I expect it to be delivered on a timely basis. I want there to be full participation, because, April, I am most interested in finding out the truth.

And you know, there's a lot of leaking in Washington, DC. It's a town famous for it. And if this helps stop leaks of—this investigation in finding the truth—it will not only hold someone to account who should not have leaked—and this is a serious charge, by the way. We're talking about a criminal action, but also hopefully will help set a clear signal we expect other leaks to stop as well. And so I look forward to finding the truth.

Q. What about retaliation? People are saying that it's retaliation——

President Bush. I don't know who leaked the information, for starters. So it's hard for me to answer that question until I find out the truth. You hear all kinds of rumors. And the best way to clarify the issue is to—full participation with the Justice Department.

These are professionals who are—professional prosecutors who are leading this investigation, and we look forward to—look, I want to know. I want to know, and the best way to do this is for there to be a good, thorough investigation, which apparently is going to happen soon. And all I can tell you is, inside the White House, we've said, "Gather all the information that's requested and get it ready to be analyzed by the Justice Department."

Listen, thank you all very much. Mr. President, I'm glad you're here.

President Kibaki. Very good.

President Bush. Appreciate it.

President Kibaki. Thank you very much.

President Bush. Thank you, sir. Very good job.

NOTE: The President's news conference began at 11:38 a.m. in the East Room at the

White House. In his remarks, he referred to Lt. Gen. Lazarus Sumbeiywo, Kenya's envoy to the Sudan; former Senator John C. Danforth, Special Envoy for Peace in the Sudan; Prime Minister Ariel Sharon of Israel; L. Paul Bremer III, Presidential Envoy to Iraq; and Bernard B. Kerik, former commissioner, New York City Police Department. A reporter referred to Prime-Minister-designate Ahmed Korei of the Palestinian Authority.

Remarks at a State Dinner Honoring President Mwai Kibaki of Kenya
October 6, 2003

[The President's remarks are joined in progress.]

It is a real honor for us to welcome you. Our two nations are old friends and natural partners. We both emerged from a colonial past to become free nations. We stood together during the cold war, opposing imperial communism. Today, we stand together against the forces of terror and in the defense of human dignity.

We both understand the danger and cost of terrorism. It has brought damage to both our economies and grief to both our nations. With us tonight are two women who suffered terribly on August 7, 1998. Susan Hirsch lost her husband, Abdulrahman Mohamed Abdulla, a Kenyan citizen, in the attack on the U.S. Embassy in Dar es Salaam, Tanzania. And Susan Bartley lost her husband, Julian, our U.S. Consul General, and her son, Jay, when the terrorists struck our Embassy in Nairobi. Both of you are honored guests here tonight, and we honor as well the memory of your loved ones.

America and Kenya are committed to the war on terror, and we seek a just and peaceful world beyond the war on terror. Kenya is finding what America has found, that democracy and liberty and free markets are honorable and just and indispensable to real progress. The challenges of freedom are real; yet the benefits of freedom are great and everlasting.

There is a Swahili proverb which says, "Forever persist; a rope can cut stone." Kenya and its leaders have been persistent and courageous in the cause of freedom. You're resolved in the fight against terror. Kenya is an example to all of Africa and a respected partner of America.

For all these reasons, Mr. President, I'm pleased to offer a toast to the enduring friendship between Kenya and the United States of America.

NOTE: The President spoke at 8:36 p.m. in the State Dining Room at the White House. The transcript issued by the Office of the Press Secretary did not include the complete opening portion of President Bush's remarks but did include the remarks of President Kibaki.

Remarks Following a Cabinet Meeting and an Exchange With Reporters
October 7, 2003

The President. Thank you all for coming. I met with my Cabinet. We talked about national security matters and economic security matters. We're making good progress on the economy. Looks like we're growing, and that's important. Last month we—people are finding work, but we're not satisfied with the progress that is being made. We talked about ways to continue the economic vitality of our country. The tax cuts need to be made permanent so there's certainty in the Tax Code. We need an energy plan so that our businesses and employers, both large and small, know there's a reliable source of energy available.

We talked about trade and this administration's commitment to free and fair trade, that administrative officials will continue to press certain countries to open up their markets to U.S. product. We talked about the need to have associated health care plans so that our small businesses have affordable health care. And finally, we talked about the need for legal reform. There's just too many lawsuits, junk lawsuits which drive up the cost of health care.

And in a lot of these matters, the Congress needs to join with this administration to pass good law so that the American people can find work. We're an optimistic administration because good things are beginning to happen in our country. We will not rest until everybody who is looking for work can find a job.

I want to thank the members of the Cabinet for serving our Nation with such class and distinction. And I'll be glad to answer some questions, starting with the AP man [Scott Lindlaw, Associated Press].

California Gubernatorial Election

Q. Thank you, Mr. President. Back in August, you said you thought Arnold Schwarzenegger would make a good Governor. We've learned some new things about him. There's an election today. Do you still feel that way?

The President. I feel like the California people are going to make a wise decision, that they—they are now in charge of the process. And it looks like there's a pretty active turnout in absentee ballots, and people are taking it seriously, and I have no idea how the election is going to turn out.

Q. Is he the kind of guy you could work with?

The President. If he's the Governor, I'll work with him, absolutely. He's obviously waged a spirited campaign. He's captured a lot of people's imagination. I haven't been paying that close attention to it, because I've got a job to do here in Washington. But the process is about over. The people of California are going to speak, and I look forward to seeing what the results are. I may not stay up for it—[laughter]—all night long. I'll be reading your stories first thing in the morning.

Dana [Dana Bash, Cable News Network].

Disclosure of CIA Employee's Identity

Q. Mr. President, beyond the actual leak of classified information, there are reports that someone in the administration was trying to—after it was already out—actively spread the story, even calling Ambassador Wilson's wife "fair game." Are you asking your staff if anyone did that? Would it be wrong or even a fireable offense if that happened?

The President. Well, the investigators will ask our staff about what people did or did not do. This is a town of—where a lot of people leak. And I've constantly expressed my displeasure with leaks, particularly leaks of classified information. And I want to know; I want to know the truth. I want to see to it that the truth prevail, and I hope we can get this investigation done in a thorough way, as quickly as possible.

But the Justice Department will conduct this investigation. The professionals in the Justice Department will be involved in ferreting out the truth. These are citizens who will—were here before this administration arrived and will be here after this administration leaves. And they'll come to the bottom of this, and we'll find out the truth. And that will be—that's a good thing for this administration.

Stretch [Richard Keil, Bloomberg News].

National Economy

Q. Mr. President, a survey of economists that we published yesterday found that—it was between 40 and 50 of them—and they think that the growth rate over the next year may only be in the low 3-percent range, and that's below the 4-percent range that you and your economic advisers have said will be needed to create the kind of jobs that will really keep the growth going. Does that concern you? Do you think those predictions are accurate?

The President. Well, one thing is certain, that the growth rate is going to be positive, as opposed to the negative growth rate we inherited. In other words, we came into office and dealt with a recession, then dealt with attacks, then dealt with corporate scandals, dealt with the march to war, all of which affected the confidence of the people. And we put forth a very aggressive tax plan, because we believe that that is the best way to help this country grow out of recession.

I've just outlined other things that need to happen in order to make sure that the people are able to find work. Dick, I am not very good about guessing about the economy. There's all kinds of experts; you'll probably find all kinds of opinions. But I do know that the actions we have taken were necessary actions and that are good—they were good actions for economic vitality and growth.

The Congress needs to work with us for an energy plan. They need to work with us for good liability reform. We will continue to press to open up foreign markets. I'm a free trader, but I'm also a fair trader. And I believe our manufacturing sector, for example, must be treated fairly in foreign markets.

We need an energy plan. We've debated an energy plan for too long. This administration has put forth a very good energy plan. And Congress needs to quit debating the idea, get the differences reconciled, and get a bill to my desk. I'm confident Senator Domenici and Representative Tauzin want to do just that. So there are other things to do to get this economy moving, and we'll see what—see what happens.

I will tell you I'm optimistic, and I'm optimistic because things are improving. But there's a lot more to do.

Randy [Randall Mikkelsen, Reuters].

Disclosure of CIA Employee's Identity/ Israeli Foreign Policy

Q. Mr. President, how confident are you the investigation will find the leaker in the CIA case? And what do you make of Sharon's comment that Israel will strike its enemies at any place, any time?

The President. This is the dual question. [*Laughter*] I'm trying to figure out if I want to answer either of them, since you violated a major rule. [*Laughter*] At least it's not a cell phone. [*Laughter*]

Randy, you tell me, how many sources have you had that's leaked information that you've exposed or have been exposed? Probably none. I mean this town is a—is a town full of people who like to leak information. And I don't know if we're going to find out the senior administration official. Now, this is a large administration, and there's a lot of senior officials. I don't have any idea. I'd like to. I want to know the truth. That's why I've instructed this staff of mine to cooperate fully with the investigators—full disclosure. Everything we know, the investigators will find out. I have no idea whether we'll find out who the leaker is, partially because, in all due respect to your profession, you do a very good job of protecting the leakers. But we'll find out.

In terms of Prime Minister Sharon, I have constantly said Israel should defend herself. But I've also told—as I mentioned to you at the press availability yesterday—that it's important for the Prime Minister to avoid escalation, that the decisions he makes to defend her people are valid decisions. We would be doing the same thing. This country will defend our people.

But we are also mindful when we make decisions, as the Prime Minister should be, that the—that he fully understand the consequences of any decision and that while he defends his people that there is not—that he doesn't create the conditions necessary for—that would cause the escalation—the violence to escalate.

Q. Did the strike on Syria—did the strike on Syria cause an escalation?

The President. The Prime Minister must defend his country. It's essential. This is a country which recently was attacked by a suicider that killed innocent children and women, people that were celebrating in a restaurant. And he must do what is necessary to protect himself. At the same time, as I said yesterday and will continue to say to Ariel Sharon, "Avoid escalating violence."

Listen, thank you all. Anybody else did not get a question in this vaunted press corps?

American League Championship Series

Q. Red Sox—Red Sox or Yankees?

The President. Listen, I'm excited about the playoffs. I tuned in after the state dinner that was somewhat covered in the press yesterday. [*Laughter*] But it was—you know, it's good for baseball. My team, of course, was eliminated in June. [*Laughter*] Thank you all.

NOTE: The President spoke at 11:42 a.m. in the Cabinet Room at the White House. In his remarks, he referred to Prime Minister Ariel Sharon of Israel. A reporter referred to former Ambassador Joseph C. Wilson IV.

Statement on Senator Don Nickles' Decision Not To Seek Reelection
October 7, 2003

For more than two decades, Don Nickles has served the people of Oklahoma and America as a distinguished United States Senator. As a longtime member of the Senate leadership and most recently as chairman of the Senate Budget Committee, he has led efforts to keep Government spending in check and to keep more money in the pockets of American taxpayers. He has left his mark on virtually every major issue

that has moved through the Senate. Senator Nickles is a friend and trusted adviser, and I look forward to working with him for the remainder of his time in the Senate and in the future.

Laura and I extend our thanks and best wishes to Don, Linda, and their four children, Don, Jenny, Kim, and Robyn, for their commitment to public service, and we wish them all the best.

Statement on the Decision by the Court of Appeals for the Tenth Circuit on the Do-Not-Call Registry
October 7, 2003

Today's decision by the U.S. Court of Appeals for the Tenth Circuit to allow the FTC to enforce the Do-Not-Call Registry is a victory for Americans who want to re-

duce the nuisance of unwanted telephone solicitations. The American people have the right to limit annoying telemarketing calls, and I am pleased that both the Federal

Trade Commission and the Federal Communications Commission will now be able to ensure that Americans have that choice while the courts continue to consider the issues.

Remarks on Domestic Violence Prevention
October 8, 2003

President Bush. Thank you all for coming, and welcome to the White House. In a few moments, I will sign a proclamation naming October National Domestic Violence Awareness Month. I do so to focus attention on this urgent and very important issue. I will announce two initiatives we are launching to combat domestic violence in our country.

A home, a family, should be a place of support, should be a peaceful place, not a place of cruelty and brutality. Domestic violence betrays the most basic duties of life. It violates the law. It's wrong. It is a crime that must be confronted by individuals, by communities, and by government.

All of you here today have taken up the vital cause—the really important cause—of defending the vulnerable from domestic violence. Too often its victims suffer in secret and in silence. You make it easier for them to step out of the shadows and get the help and love they need. Your compassion is saving lives. Your country is grateful. Thank you for what you do.

I appreciate Tommy Thompson being here. He's the Secretary of Health and Human Services. Many of the initiatives on family violence come from his Department. As Governor of Wisconsin, he made a name for dealing with domestic violence, and he's carried his passion, as have I, to Washington, DC, to help.

I appreciate Jack Potter, who is the Postmaster General. There's a reason he is here. It has something to do with a stamp that I'll be describing here. [*Laughter*]

I appreciate very much Diane Stuart, the Director of the Office of Violence Against Women, from the Department of Justice. Thank you for coming. Thank you for being a leader.

We've got a special Senator here with us today, a person who flew all the way back from his home State of Colorado. He's here because he sponsored the legislation creating the Stop Family Violence stamp. I'm honored that you've come back, Senator Campbell. Ben Nighthorse Campbell is a compassionate, decent human being, and I'm proud to call him friend. Thanks for coming.

I want to thank Sheryl Cates, who is the executive director of the National Domestic Violence Hotline and the Texas Council on Family Violence. She's on the stage with me. The hotline received its one millionth call in August. That's a lot of calls, but it's a lot of help as well. And I want to thank Sheryl for being here, my fellow Texan. [*Laughter*] Lynn Rosenthal is the executive director of the National Network to End Domestic Violence. Lynn is with us as well here. Thank you for coming. And Rita Smith, the executive director of the National Coalition Against Domestic Violence, is on the stage as well. These three women are leaders in the attempt to make somebody's life better, and I really appreciate you all coming.

As well we've got Monique Blais who's with us today. Monique brought her mother, Marci, to the White House. [*Laughter*] The reason Monique is here is that she designed the artwork for the Stop Family Violence stamp. And I really appreciate your talents, and when people see the stamp, they'll—when I say "talent," they'll know what I mean when I say "talent," because it's really a great piece of work. We want to thank you for coming. And I want to thank you all for being here.

Domestic violence cuts across every line of geography and income. Abuse is found in every community in our country—every community—and it must be fought in every community. Hundreds of thousands of incidents of domestic violence are reported every year. The sad news is, many go unreported. About a third of women murdered each year in America are killed by this type of violence, and nearly half the households where domestic violence occurs also has a child under 12 years old. There's more than one victim.

Women and children are facing dangers in this country, and they need strong allies. That's what we're here to talk about. I'm not only here to thank you for being strong allies, I'm asking others around our country to work with the people here. There's plenty of opportunities for our fellow citizens to step forth and be a partner in helping save and heal lives.

Fortunately, there are people, victims who can find help. That's the good news about America. The bad news is, there's too much domestic violence. The good news is, people can find help. Faith-based and community groups provide refuge and counseling and good legal advice. And a lot of time, an abused woman needs good, solid legal advice.

Industry groups are recycling old cell phones. It's an interesting contribution, isn't it? They're saying, "Here's an opportunity for you to be able to call to get help."

Lifetime television—I know some folks representing Lifetime television are here—is promoting domestic violence awareness in its programming and public service campaigns, and we thank you for that. Part of making sure that we help save lives is to educate people about the opportunities available.

Business Strengthening America is a private organization of business leaders who are responding to a call I gave them earlier, after September the 11th. I said, "Why don't you become an active participant, as responsible business leaders, in helping meet our society's needs?" They've joined forces with the Corporate Alliance to End Partner Violence. Those two groups are working to raise awareness of the issues in the workplace, and as importantly, they're encouraging employees to become volunteers in the efforts to help those who have been abused.

I want to thank the responsible corporate leaders in America for hearing the call that in a responsible society, you've got to behave responsibly yourself and encourage others to follow their heart.

The fight against domestic violence is a national movement. I urge people to join the movement. Part of an awareness month is not only making people aware but a call to service. Today all of us up here are calling people to service, to serve your community and your country. If you want to love your neighbor like you'd like to be loved yourself, there's ample opportunity to do so in the fight against domestic violence.

Our Government is engaged in the fight, as it should be. Government has got a duty to treat domestic violence as a serious crime. It's part of our duty. If you treat something as a serious crime, then there must be serious consequences. Otherwise, it's not very serious. Last year, Federal prosecutors for violence against women crimes increased—Federal prosecutions increased by 35 percent. Our prosecutors are doing their job. They're finding the abusers, and they're throwing the book at them. And that's important.

People who commit crimes must understand with certainty, there is a consequence. One way to change behavior is to make it clear to people in our society, if you break the law, if you beat up a woman, if you abuse your wife, you will be held to account. There must be certainty in the law, and we must have prosecutors who understand that we expect them to be tough. And they are.

The administration has also increased funding for Justice Department's Violence Against Women's programs by $100 million this year. We're now spending money at the highest levels in our Nation's history, and it's money well spent. Programs which help local communities combat domestic violence and sexual assault and stalking and helps the victims of those crimes are now funded at $390 million a year. And I want to thank Ben and the Members of the Congress for working to see that our appropriations request was met.

I'm going to talk about two other measures that I think will help in the fight against domestic violence. First, I've directed $20 million in 2004 to help communities create family justice centers, where victims of domestic violence can find the services they need in one place, one central location. Too often, the services designed to help victims are uncoordinated and scattered throughout communities.

Imagine what it would be like if you were an abused person trying to find help, and you went from one place to another. With laws and police and all the rules and regulations of a free society, it must be confusing and disheartening. The victim has been so traumatized, and then she has to tell her story over and over again, which repeats the trauma. There's a better way to do this. There's a better way to help people who need help in our society.

San Diego figured it out. They've got a city attorney named Casey Gwinn—who's right there—who recognized that there's a more compassionate way to help people who have been abused. And so he did something about it. He created what's called the San Diego Family Justice Center. It's a full-service center for domestic violence victims, where police officers and prosecutors and probation officers and civil attorneys and counselors and doctors and victims advocates and chaplains all come

together to help somebody. The runaround is over in San Diego. There's a central location where somebody who desperately needs help can find compassion and help. Victims can pick up food vouchers. They can get help with transportation. They can file for a temporary restraining order against their abusers. They can sign up for supervised visitation programs to keep their children safe. They can get their cell phone there. They can find help.

The San Diego Family Justice Center opened a year ago. It has already served thousands of victims. They tell me the story of Caitlin Effgen, who is a brave woman who lives in San Diego. It's probably, unfortunately, a typical story I'm about to tell you. What's atypical is that she found help in a brand new way of helping victims of domestic violence. Her boyfriend started hitting her. She tried to break up with him, and he began to stalk her. In other words, he was not only abusing her one way, he decided to abuse her another as well. And she went to the authorities and got a restraining order, which, as the experts will tell you, sometimes it works and sometimes it didn't, because in her case, the boyfriend continued to harass her, just wouldn't leave her alone. You can imagine the fear she felt. He pled guilty to charges, but he still stalked and haunted her mind.

And then she discovered the center. They helped her get counseling. They got another restraining order. A victims advocate joined her and her dad in court. In other words, she got all the help she needed. I can imagine the relief that she must have felt when somebody who heard the call to love a neighbor did just that. The guy ended up in—behind bars, which was the right thing to do, and I congratulate the San Diego law enforcement officers. But more important, she got to remember what life was like without her misery. Those are her words, not mine. She found compassion.

The funding I've set aside will help begin a national movement toward more of these centers. Twelve will be funded through this initiative. When they work, there's another 12 and maybe even more. Maybe we can escalate the request. But the point is, we have found what can work in order to provide efficient help, to channel the compassion so somebody can get their life back together. So I want to thank you for coming, Casey. Good job. You're doing your duty as a public servant.

The second initiative will expand the good work of community and faith-based groups as they provide counseling and mentoring and other services to children who have witnessed domestic violence. The children who witness domestic violence are prone to depression and anxiety. That's natural. You could imagine what it would be like for a little child to witness such an act. They need help and love. We have a moral obligation in our society to help relieve the suffering and to show that there is a better life.

I like to remind people, you know, that— I wish Government could make people love one another. I would sign the piece of legislation. [Laughter] But I know that there are loving people who are willing to love. It's a—by the way, a lot of times it's from a higher law; it's not the law of government. And so what we want to do is spend $5 billion—$5 million this year on initiatives—[laughter]—a million here, a million there. [Laughter] Let's start small—what do you think—[laughter]—to start an initiative called Safe and Bright Futures for Children. That's what we want to start. The Department of Health and Human Services will provide funding to community and faith-based groups to help children escape the cycle of violence, to get counseling, to get mentoring, to become involved in healthy activities like sports or scouting or community services.

The money will support programs at sites all across America. We believe it will be— make a difference in lives. One such program is run by the Reverend Cheryle Albert, who is with us today. She works with

Safe Haven Interfaith Partnership Against Domestic Violence in Boston, Massachusetts. Probably rooting for the Red Sox, aren't you? [Laughter] She teaches congregations about domestic violence. She helps train them to help troubled families through crisis intervention and counseling. Here's what she says: "The power behind domestic violence is that it's a secret. We work with the faith community because we feel it's the best way to break the silence."

When men and women face violence and injustice, it is important for our Government to understand that oftentimes they turn to their churches or synagogues or mosques for help, as they should. These are places of love. They exist because of love. They are wise to do so, and our Government should not fear the faith-based programs which help save lives. Matter of fact, we ought to welcome the faith-based programs into helping people who suffer.

Oftentimes, it requires faith to help heal a heart and to help bring a bright future into some child's life. This initiative welcomes the faith-based programs all across our society. This initiative takes taxpayers' money to encourage faith-based programs to become important partners in the fight against domestic violence.

I am not the least bit hesitant to encourage our Government to use Federal tax money to rally the armies of compassion which exist in every society in America. We must not fear faith in America. We must welcome faith in America to help solve our problems.

Now, to the stamp. And the stamp will be placed out in the hall; you can see it on the way out. The Safe and Bright Futures program will be supported by the sales of the stamp. There have been three such stamps. This is the third where the revenues collected from the sales of the stamps, designed by one of our Nation's budding artists—[laughter]—will be—will use that money. And as I understand it, the stamp is for sale today? That's why the head of the Post Office is here. [*Laughter*]

Audience member. Buy them.

President Bush. Buy them? Well, and so anybody who wants to support effective programs in our fight against domestic violence ought to buy the stamp. The money goes to these programs, and it's a great way for people to use the mail and to express their desires to make their communities a better place.

I want to thank you all for coming today. I want to thank you for your commitment. For those who are involved with saving lives, it's a hard job. It's got to be hard to provide a shoulder onto which someone can cry or a sympathetic ear for some child who wonders what their future is like. That can only be accomplished, however, when loving Americans hear the call. If any American is interested in serving, one good way to do so is to become involved in these programs that are saving lives as a result of the brutal crime of domestic violence.

The strength of our country is not our military. It's not our wallet. The strength of our country is the heart and soul of the American people. And today I'm honored to be in the presence of Americans who serve your country and your community by helping people who have been hurt.

May God bless your work. May God bless those who are victims of domestic violence. And may God continue to bless our country. Thank you.

NOTE: The President spoke at 3:13 p.m. in the East Room at the White House. The National Domestic Violence Awareness Month proclamation of October 8 is listed in Appendix D at the end of this volume.

Remarks at the Republican National Committee Presidential Gala
October 8, 2003

Thank you all for coming. Go ahead and be seated, unless you don't have a seat. [*Laughter*] I'm honored you all are here. I appreciate your warm welcome. I thank you for your strong support and friendship. I thank you for your contributions. I thank you for your grassroots work. I thank you for your prayers. There's a lot of happy folks here tonight. There's some Cubs fans. There's some Red Sox fans, and there are some happy people from California.

I am so glad that Laura came with me tonight. As you know, she's back home from an official trip. She went to Russia to help them with literacy. She went to France. [*Laughter*] You may have seen the picture in the newspaper. [*Laughter*] Last time I was in France, I got a nice welcome but nothing like that. [*Laughter*] Laura is a great First Lady. I'm really proud of her.

I want to thank my friend Ed Gillespie for leading our great party. He could be doing a lot of other things. There's no doubt we picked the right man to lead us into this election year. I appreciate the fact that Cathy, his fine wife, is supporting Ed in this really important mission.

I not only want to thank Ed, I want to thank all of the RNC members who are here, all the county officials, all the grassroots activists. We're going to win in 2004. I appreciate your support. I appreciate the friendship of all those on the stage here tonight who helped set a record. It's important to be well funded as you go into a campaign, and you've made it possible.

I want to thank my friend Al Hoffman and his wife, Dawn, for their longtime friendship. I want to thank Ann Wagner, our party cochairman. I want to thank the gala cochairmen, Brad Freeman and David

Girard-diCarlo and Carl Linder. I want to thank all those who worked hard to make this event go so successfully.

I appreciate Monsignor Marc Filacchione who is here, the chaplain from the New York City Fire Department. I want to thank Lieutenant Kim Royster from New York—from the New York City Police Department. I'm really thankful you brought your Governor with you, a great Governor in George Pataki.

I want to thank the Wright Touch Orchestra, Jonathan Yeaworth, and Michael Israel, as well as Michael Feinstein for providing entertainment here tonight.

I know we've got Members of the United States Congress with us. I had a meeting right before I came here with Speaker Denny Hastert. He told me that he wasn't able to make it. He said he's heard me speak before. [Laughter] But he is a great Speaker. He is a great leader for the United States Congress.

I appreciate Tom DeLay and Roy Blunt and all the House Members who are here. I also know that Bill Frist, the Senate majority leader, is here as well. What a class act he is.

I've got two goals in '04. One is slightly selfish. [Laughter] And the other is to make sure that Denny Hastert remains the Speaker of the House and Bill Frist the leader of the Senate.

It is in our Nation's interest that Hastert remain the Speaker and Bill Frist the majority leader. These are strong leaders. They have led the Congress in a lot of important matters. We've achieved a lot of results together, results that are good for Republicans and Democrats and Independents, results that are good for all Americans.

You know, I wasn't sure what to expect when I became your President. I was certain there would be some challenges. I wasn't exactly sure what to expect, but I knew there was going to be some problems to solve. And therefore, I knew I needed to surround myself with really strong, competent, capable people. I've assembled a

great administration of Americans from all walks of life who have put their country above self.

This country is blessed to have a great Vice President in Dick Cheney. I listen to a great national security team and a great domestic policy team. Some of my members—some of the members of my Cabinet are here tonight. The Secretary of Interior, Gale Norton, is with us. The Secretary of Agriculture, Ann Veneman, is with us. The Secretary of Commerce, Don Evans, is with us. The Secretary of Labor, Elaine Chao, is with us. And the Secretary of Energy, Spence Abraham, is with us. Thank you all for coming, and thank you for a job well done.

I knew we would face challenges, and I was right. We're at war. We face an enemy that cannot stand what America stands for. We love freedom. We love the right for people to worship freely, to speak freely. And we're not going to change, and neither will they. We got attacked on September the 11th, and this Nation must never forget the lessons of September the 11th.

We must never forget the lives lost. We must never forget the fact that oceans no longer protect us from an enemy which hates us. We must never forget the nature of our enemy. These people are nothing but coldblooded killers. They've hijacked a great religion and kill innocent men, women, and children. They know no law. They know no rules. We must remember that the best way to deal with this enemy is to stay on the offensive. We must not tire. We must not weary. We must not be afraid.

This administration is leading the world to make the world more secure. We have a solemn duty, not only to our homeland but to help others who embrace freedom. History has called us into action, and we will not let history down. We must remember that one of the lessons of September the 11th is these killers will try to find safe harbor. And that's why I laid out a new doctrine for American foreign policy. It said, "If you harbor a terrorist, if you feed a terrorist, if you hide a terrorist, you're just as guilty as the terrorists."

It's important, as you begin to make the case for this administration, that not only do we lay out doctrine, but more importantly, we enforce doctrine. And the Taliban found out what we meant. Because of the bravery of our troops in Afghanistan, America is more secure, the world is more peaceful, and the people of that country are now free.

One of the important lessons of September the 11th, 2001, is that our country must deal with gathering threats before they materialize, before they come back to haunt us. And that's what we did in Iraq. We saw a gathering threat, a man who had possessed and used weapons of mass destruction on his own people, a man who sponsored terror, a man who is a danger in the region in which he lived.

But it wasn't just us who recognized a threat. Free nations recognized the threat. The United Nations passed resolution after resolution after resolution calling upon Mr. Saddam Hussein to disclose his weapons and to disarm. And finally, in Security Council Resolution 1441, led by the United States, he was told that he had one final chance to disarm—disclose what he had and disarm, or there would be serious consequences. The world spoke. He chose defiance, and Saddam Hussein is no more.

The lessons of September the 11th are lessons we must not forget. I was not about to leave the security of the American people in the hands of a madman. I was not going to stand by and wait and trust the sanity and restraint of Mr. Saddam Hussein.

So our coalition acted, and we acted in one of the swiftest and most humane military campaigns in history. Iraq is free. America is more secure. Since the liberation of Iraq, our investigators have found evidence of a clandestine network of biological laboratories, advanced design work

on prohibited long-range missiles, an elaborate campaign to hide these illegal programs.

There's a lot more to investigate. Yet it is now undeniable—undeniable—that Saddam Hussein was in clear violation of United Nations Security Council Resolution 1441. It is undeniable that Saddam Hussein was a deceiver and a danger. The Security Council was right to demand that Saddam disarm. And America was right to enforce that demand.

Thanks to our brave troops and a coalition of nations, America is now more secure, the world is more peaceful, and Iraq is free. Iraq is free of a brutal dictator. Iraq is free of the man who caused there to be mass graves. Iraq is free of rape rooms and torture chambers. Iraq is free of a brutal thug. America did the right thing.

One of the problems we faced when we came was that morale in our military was beginning to suffer. So this administration worked with the Congress to pass new budgets for our defense, budgets that would meet the threats of a new era. And today, nobody in this world can question the skill and the spirit and the strength of the United States military. In order to win this war on terror, our military must be strong. I will keep the United States military strong.

We faced another problem. You might remember that in March of 2000, the stock market began to decline, and right about the time we got sworn in, the country was headed into a recession. That's a problem. That's a challenge, mainly a challenge for people who want to work. It's a challenge for those who have got to put bread on the table for their families.

And just as the economy was kind of getting better, thanks to a historic tax cut, the enemy hit us. September the 11th hurt, but we're dealing with that. I said then that it didn't matter how long it's going to take, those who inflicted harm on America would be brought to justice, and that's precisely what we're doing.

The battles in Afghanistan and Iraq affected consumer confidence. Corporate scandals affected consumer confidence. But we acted. We weren't timid. We did what we thought was right. We not only passed one tax relief package for the American people, we passed two, because we know when you have more money in your pocket, it's your choice to save or to spend or invest. More money means more growth, and more growth means more jobs.

There's more to do. We need to make sure we open up markets for America's entrepreneurs and farmers and ranchers. And while we open up markets, this administration will make sure that trade is not only free but it is fair.

We need an energy plan. We need reliable sources of energy. For the sake of national security and economic security, we need to be less reliant on foreign sources of energy.

We need tort reform, and we've got to make sure that there's certainty in the Tax Code. This tax relief we passed, because of a quirk in the rules, will go away. For the sake of economic vitality, for the sake of job creation, the Congress must make the tax relief permanent.

This administration has got a strong agenda to keep this Nation secure and prosperous. And we lead. We're willing to stake out the high ground and lead. My job as your President is to set great goals worthy of a great nation.

First, this country is committed to expanding the realm of freedom and peace, not only for our own security but for the benefit of the world. It is essential that this Nation not grow weary in the war on terror. It's essential that we remain determined and strong. You see, the enemies want to create a sense of fear and intrepidation. They don't understand America like I know America. This Nation will not be intimidated. We will continue our

war on terror until this threat to civilization is removed.

But the war on terror is more than just chasing down the killers or holding tyrants to account. The war on terror—our security comes in the war on terror from the spread of human liberty. See, free nations do not develop weapons of mass destruction. Free nations do not intimidate their neighbors. Free nations are peaceful nations. And so one of the missions of this administration is to spread freedom. I understand that freedom is the deepest need and hope of every heart. And I believe that freedom is the right of every person and the future of every nation. And that's exactly what we're now doing in Iraq. We believe that freedom is not America's gift to the world, we believe that freedom is God's gift to each and every individual.

And so we're working in Iraq, working with other nations to make sure that Iraq is free and peaceful. Terrorists don't like that. Freedom is a threat. Freedom contradicts their way of life. A free Iraq in the middle of the Middle East will change the world. This is historic times. This Nation will stay the course until Iraq is free and peaceful and prosperous.

And in our own country, we must work for a society of prosperity and compassion—and compassion—so that every single citizen has a chance to work and succeed and realize the great promise of this country. That starts with making sure that everybody can find work. This administration understands the role of Government is not to create wealth but an environment in which the entrepreneur can flourish, in which small businesses grow to be big businesses. We will stay with our progrowth policy until our fellow citizens can find a job.

We understand that a compassionate and hopeful tomorrow requires that every child be educated. We have led on this issue. We called for Congress to pass historic education reforms, and they responded. And now, in return for record amounts of

Federal money, we expect every public school in America to teach the basics.

And we say, "You must measure to show us whether or not a child can read or write and add and subtract. And if they can't, there will be extra resources to help that child." But at some point in time, if a child is trapped in a school which will not teach and will not change, we believe the parent ought to have different options to liberate that child. No child should be left behind in America.

A hopeful tomorrow—make sure America keeps its promises. We have led on the issue of Medicare. The House passed a bill. The Senate passed a bill. They're working out differences to give seniors more choices, more options, just like the Members of Congress have, and at the same time, prescription drug coverage. Congress needs to come together and get a good Medicare bill to my desk.

There are a lot of ways to make sure America remains hopeful, a prosperous economy, good health care, a great education system. But we must remember that in our society, there are some who seem hopelessly lost, some who hurt, some who are lonely. Government can pass out money, but it cannot put hope in a person's heart or a sense of purpose in a person's life. And that's why the job of the President is to capture the great spirit of our country, to call people to service.

I recognize that our strength is not in our armies or in our pocketbooks. Our strength is in the hearts and souls of American citizens, people from all faiths, all walks of life, whether they be Christian, Jew, or Muslim, or Hindu, people have heard the universal call to love a neighbor just like they'd like to be called themselves. No, that's our strength.

In order to make sure this country meets the great goal of hope and respect and decency, the President must be willing to rely upon the strength of the country. And that's why I put forth a Faith-Based Initiative, recognizing that in our houses of worship of all faiths, we find love and compassion and decency.

There are some whose problems can only be solved when a brother or sister puts their arm around you and says, "I love you. What can I do to help you? I want to mentor you. I want to teach you how to read. I'll provide food if you're hungry, shelter if you need a place to stay." No, the strength of this country is the heart and soul of the American people, the decency, the compassion, the soldiers in the armies of compassion.

There's no question in my mind that America will be a hopeful place. And there's no question in my mind that with your help, in November of 2004 we will win a great victory and will continue to work to keep America strong and secure and prosperous and free.

Thank you all for coming. May God bless. God bless you all.

NOTE: The President spoke at 7:53 p.m. at the Washington Hilton Hotel. In his remarks, he referred to Ed Gillespie, chairman, Ann Wagner, cochairman, and Al Hoffman, finance chairman, Republican National Committee; and former President Saddam Hussein of Iraq.

Remarks at Pease Air National Guard Base in Portsmouth, New Hampshire
October 9, 2003

Thanks for coming. Thanks for such a warm welcome. I'm pleased to be back in the great State of New Hampshire again. And I'm honored to be with the Army and

Air National Guard, and with reservists from every branch of our military. You are demonstrating that duty and public service are alive and well in New Hampshire. You stand ready to defend your fellow citizens, and you need to know your fellow citizens are grateful.

All of you are balancing jobs and your lives and public service. You care about your communities, and you care about your country. Today I'm going to talk about two great priorities for our country. We'll promote economic growth and create jobs for America, and we'll wage the war on terror until it is won.

I want to thank Major General Blair for the introduction and for putting up with my entourage. [*Laughter*] I want to thank his commander in chief, the Governor of the great State of New Hampshire, for joining us today, Governor Benson, and first lady Denise. I want to thank Major General Joseph Simeone, Brigadier General John Weeden, Brigadier General Benton Smith, Colonel Protzmann—Carolyn Protzmann, Lt. Colonel Robert Monahan, and Lt. Colonel Leroy Dunkelberger, State Command Sergeant Michael Rice, Command Chief Master Sergeant Ronald Nadeau. And thank you all. Thank you for coming to say hello. I'm honored that you are here.

This State is fortunate to have an excellent Governor. You're fortunate to have an excellent congressional delegation as well. I'm proud to be here today with two fine United States Senators, my friend Judd Gregg—and his wife, Cathy—and my friend John Sununu. Thank you, Senators, for being here. These Senators are strong supporters of your mission. They appreciate what you do. They vote for strong defense budgets because they know what I know, that any time we put our troops into harm's way, you must have the best training, the best equipment, the best possible pay. Congressman Charlie Bass and Congressman Jeb Bradley, who are with us today, understand that as well. Thank the Congressmen

for coming with me today. Thank you all for being here.

My friend Ruth Griffin is here from the Executive Council of New Hampshire. Maureen Barrows is here as well. I appreciate the local officials who have come—State and local officials—to greet me and to be here with you today.

I know that the New Hampshire Wildcat hockey players are here. I'd like to give you some advice, but I don't know how to ice skate. [*Laughter*]

Today when I landed, I met a lady named Cathy Rice. It's important for me to herald the armies of the soldiers of compassion, people I meet when I land in respective cities. It's important because it helps our country understand our true strength is not our military might or the size of our wallet. The true strength of America is the hearts and souls of fellow citizens who are willing to help people who need help.

You see, Cathy Rice supports—provides support services to hundreds of New Hampshire National Guard families. She helps find babysitters and prepares meals and assists with paying bills, helps families when there's a deployment. She knows people stay behind; they worry about their loved ones. She helps fill that void with love and compassion and care. She offers support to the New Hampshire Army National Guard Family Volunteer Program. It's an important service. It's an important part of completing the mission. She does so because she cares about a fellow citizen.

I'm proud of Cathy. I'm proud of her heart. I want to thank her for her service and encourage each and every one of you to love a neighbor just like you'd like to be loved yourself. America's strength is the heart and soul of our citizens.

New Hampshire has had citizen soldiers since before America was a country. Militia and volunteers and guardsmen have served from the Revolution to the Civil War to World War II to Desert Storm. Honor and service and courage are great New Hampshire traditions, and you're upholding those traditions. We live in an era of new threats, and the citizens of New Hampshire are stepping forward to meet those dangers.

Citizen soldiers have performed mid-air refueling missions for coalition forces in Iraq. You're training members of the Afghan National Army. You're guarding suspected terrorists at Guantanamo Bay, preparing for homeland security missions. Citizen soldiers are serving on every front on the war on terror, and you're making your State and your country proud.

Serving your country can bring sacrifice and uncertainty and separation. Your lives can be changed in a moment, with a sudden call to duty. I want to thank you for your willingness to heed that important call. And I want to thank your families. I want to thank your sons and daughters, your husbands and wives, who share in your sacrifice, who are willing to sacrifice for our country, and who stand behind you.

You're serving at a time of testing for this Nation. And we're meeting the tests of history. We're defeating the enemies of freedom. We're confronting the challenge to build prosperity for our country. Every test of America has revealed the character of America. And after the last 2 years, no one in the world, friend or foe, can doubt the will and the character and the strength of the American people.

When you become the President, you cannot predict all the challenges that will come. But you do know the principles that you bring to the office, and they should not change with time or with polls. I took this office to make a difference, not to mark time. I came to this office to confront problems directly and forcefully, not to pass them on to other Presidents and other generations. The challenges we face today cannot be met with timid actions or bitter words. Our challenges will be overcome with optimism and resolve and confidence in the ideals of America.

Because we believe in our free enterprise system, we can be confident in our economy's future. Our economy has been through a lot. When I took office, the stock market had been declining for 9 months, and our economy was headed into recession. And just as we started to recover, the attacks of September the 11th struck another blow to our economy. And then investor confidence was shaken by scandals—scandals in corporate America, dishonest behavior we cannot and we will not tolerate in our country. And then we faced the uncertainty that preceded the battles of Afghanistan and Iraq.

No, we've been through a lot. But we acted. We led. We acted to overcome these challenges and acted on principle. Government doesn't create wealth. The role of Government is to create the kind of conditions where risktakers and entrepreneurs can invest and grow and hire new workers. We acted to create the conditions for job growth so people can find work. When Americans have more take-home pay, more money in their pocket to spend or save or invest, the whole economy grows, and people are more likely to find a job. So I twice led the United States Congress to pass historic tax relief for the American people.

We wanted tax relief to be broad and fair as possible, so we reduced taxes on everyone who pays income taxes. We have a Tax Code that penalizes marriage. That doesn't make sense. [*Laughter*] So we reduced the marriage penalty. It costs a lot to raise children—we understand that in Washington, DC—and it costs a lot to pay for their education. So we increased the child credit to $1,000 per child. And when we said, "The check was in the mail," we meant it.

We recognize that it's counterproductive to discourage investment, especially during an economic recovery. So we quadrupled the expense deduction for small-business investment and cut tax rates on dividends and capital gains.

It is unfair to tax the estates of people—people leave behind after a lifetime of saving or building a small business or running a farm. When you leave this world, the IRS shouldn't follow you. [Laughter] So we're phasing out the Federal death tax.

I proposed and signed these measures to help individuals and help families, but I did so as well to help small businesses. See, most small-business owners pay taxes under the individual tax rates, and therefore, when we cut all rates, small businesses benefit. We help mom-and-pops and start-ups and small businesses by allowing higher expense deductions.

The reason I did so is because I understand small businesses create most of the new jobs in America. If we're worried about job creation, if we want there to be jobs for America, we must encourage small businesses. See, small businesses are the first to—usually the first to take risk, the first to hire new people. By helping small businesses, we help the entire economy.

These actions are helping people across this State. We've cut taxes on 112,000 small-business owners in New Hampshire. We've reduced the marriage penalty for 192,000 couples. We've increased the child credit for 124,000 families. See, I know this: I know that New Hampshire citizens can spend their money better than the people in Washington, DC.

We're following a clear and consistent economic strategy, and I'm confident about our future. Last month this economy exceeded expectations and added net new jobs. Inflation is low. After-tax incomes are rising. Homeownership is at record highs. And productivity is high, and it is rising as well. Factory orders, particularly for high-tech equipment, have risen over the last several months. Our strategy has set the stage for sustained growth. By reducing taxes, we kept a promise, and we did the right thing at the right time for the American economy.

We're moving forward, but we are not satisfied. We can't be satisfied so long as we have fellow citizens who are looking for work. I understand that here in New Hampshire, one out of every five jobs have been lost in the manufacturing sector. That's an issue we must deal with. We must act boldly from this point forward to create jobs for America. So I want Congress to join me in a six-point plan to encourage job creation.

First, we must help small businesses grow and hire by controlling the high cost of health care. I have laid out a plan to do so.

We must confront the junk lawsuits that are harming a lot of good and honest businesses. I have laid out a plan to do so.

We must have a sound national energy policy. We must keep the lights on and make America less dependent on foreign sources of energy.

We must continue to cut useless Government regulations that choke job creation. We must work for a free trade policy that opens up markets and levels the playing field for American workers and manufacturing companies.

And we need to make sure the tax relief we passed doesn't disappear in future years. Now, you're wondering why I would say that. Well, because of a quirk in the legislation, the tax cuts that we passed are scheduled to go away unless we act. See, the child credit goes away in a couple of years. In other words, you get the $1,000 now; it's going down to $700 in a couple years—unless the Congress acts. The death penalty which is scheduled to go away comes back unless the Congress acts.

You see, when we passed tax relief, I know most Americans did not expect to see higher taxes come back through the back door. I also understand for job creation, it's important to have certainty in the Tax Code. People have got to be able to plan. And so if Congress is really interested in job creation, they will make the tax cuts we passed permanent.

And as we overcome our challenges to the economy, we're answering great threats to our security. September the 11th, 2001, moved our country to grief and moved our country to action. We made a pledge that day, and we have kept it: We will bring the guilty to justice; we will take the fight to the enemy.

We now see our enemy clearly. The terrorists plot in secret. They target the innocent. They defile a great religion. They hate everything this Nation stands for. These committed killers will not be stopped by negotiations; they won't respond to reason. The terrorists who threaten America cannot be appeased. They must be found. They must be fought, and they must be defeated.

This is a new kind of war, and we must adjust. It's a new kind of war, and America is following a new strategy. We're not waiting for further attacks. We're striking our enemies before they can strike us again. We've taken unprecedented steps to protect our homeland. And for those of you who are here who are on the frontlines of homeland protection, thank you. Thank you for what you're doing.

Yet wars are won on the offensive, and our friends and America are staying on the offensive. We're finding them. We're on the hunt. We're rolling back the terrorist threats, not on the fringes of its influence but at the heart of its power. We're making good progress. We're hunting the Al Qaida terrorists wherever they hide, from Pakistan to the Philippines to the Horn of Africa to Iraq. Nearly two-thirds of Al Qaida's known leaders have been captured or killed. Our resolve is firm; our resolve is clear: No matter how long it takes, all who plot against America will face the justice of America.

We have sent a message understood throughout the world, "If you harbor a terrorist, if you support a terrorist, if you feed a terrorist, you are just as guilty as the terrorists." And the Taliban found out what we meant. Thanks to our great military, Afghanistan is no longer a safe haven for terror, the Afghan people are free, and the

people of America are more secure from attack.

And we have fought the war on terror in Iraq. The regime of Saddam Hussein possessed and used weapons of mass destruction, sponsored terrorist groups, and inflicted terror on its own people. Nearly every nation recognized and denounced this threat for over a decade. Last year, the U.N. Security Council—in Resolution 1441—demanded that Saddam Hussein disarm, prove his disarmament to the world, or face serious consequences. The choice was up to the dictator, and he chose poorly.

I acted because I was not about to leave the security of the American people in the hands of a madman. I was not about to stand by and wait and trust in the sanity and restraint of Saddam Hussein. So our coalition acted, in one of the swiftest and most humane military campaigns in history. And 6 months ago today, the statue of the dictator was pulled down.

Since the liberation of Iraq, our investigators have found evidence of a clandestine network of biological laboratories. They found advanced design work on prohibited longer range missiles. They found an elaborate campaign to hide these illegal programs. There's still much to investigate, yet it is now undeniable that Saddam Hussein was in clear violation of United Nations Security Council Resolution 1441. It is undeniable that Saddam Hussein was a deceiver and a danger. The Security Council was right to demand that Saddam Hussein disarm, and we were right to enforce that demand.

Who can possibly think that the world would be better off with Saddam Hussein still in power? Surely not the dissidents who would be in his prisons or end up in mass graves. Surely not the men and women who would fill Saddam's torture chambers or the women in his rape rooms. Surely not the victims he murdered with poison gas. Surely not anyone who cares about human rights and democracy and stability in the Middle East. There is only one decent and humane reaction to the fall of Saddam Hussein: Good riddance!

Now our country is approaching a choice. After all the action we have taken, after all the progress we have made against terror, there is a temptation to think the danger has passed. The danger hasn't passed. Since September the 11th, the terrorists have taken lives. Since the attacks on our Nation that fateful day, the terrorists have attacked in Casablanca, Mombasa, Jerusalem, Amman, Riyadh, Baghdad, Karachi, New Delhi, Bali, and Jakarta. The terrorists continue to plot and plan against our country and our people.

America must not forget the lessons of September the 11th. America cannot retreat from our responsibilities and hope for the best. Our security will not be gained by timid measures. Our security requires constant vigilance and decisive action. I believe America has only one option: We must fight this war until the work is done.

We're fighting on many fronts, and Iraq is now the central front. Saddam holdouts and foreign terrorists are trying desperately to undermine Iraq's progress and to throw that country into chaos. The terrorists in Iraq believe that their attacks on innocent people will weaken our resolve. That's what they believe. They believe that America will run from a challenge. They're mistaken. Americans are not the running kind.

The United States did not run from Germany and Japan following World War II. We helped those nations to become strong and decent democratic societies that no longer waged war on America. And that's our mission in Iraq today. We're rebuilding schools—a lot of kids are going back to schools—reopening hospitals. Thousands of children are now being immunized. Water and electricity are being returned to the Iraqi people. Life is getting better.

It's a lot better than you probably think. Just ask people who have been there. They're stunned when they come back—when they go to Iraq, and the stories they tell are much different from the perceptions that you're being told life is like.

You see, we're providing this help not only because we've got good hearts but because our vision is clear. A stable and democratic and hopeful Iraq will no longer be a breeding ground for terror, tyranny, and aggression. Free nations are peaceful nations. Our work in Iraq is essential to our own security, and no band of murderers or gangsters will stop that work or shake the will of America.

Nearly every day in Iraq we're launching swift, precision raids against the enemies of peace and progress. Helped by intelligence from Iraqis, we're rounding up the enemy. We're taking their weapons. We're working our way through the famous deck of cards. We've already captured or killed 43 of the 55 most wanted former Iraqi leaders, and the other 12 have a lot to worry about. [Laughter] Anyone who seeks to harm our soldiers can know that our soldiers are hunting for them.

Our military is serving with great courage. Some of our best have fallen. We mourn every loss. We honor every name. We grieve with every family. And we will always be grateful that liberty has found such brave defenders.

In defending liberty, we are joined by more than 30 nations now contributing military forces in Iraq. Great Britain and Poland are leading two multinational divisions. And in this cause, with fine allies, we've got the Iraqis as well. They care about the security of their country. They want to be free. They love freedom just like we love freedom. Last week, the first battalion of the New Iraqi Army completed its training. Within a year, Iraq will have a 40,000-member military force. Tens of thousands of Iraqi citizens are also guarding their own borders, defending vital facilities, and policing their own streets. Six months ago, the Iraqi people welcomed their liberation. Today, many Iraqis are armed and trained to defend their liberty.

Our goal in Iraq is to leave behind a stable, self-governing society which will no longer be a threat to the Middle East or to the United States. We're following an orderly plan to reach this goal. Iraq now has a Governing Council, which has appointed interim Government ministers. Once a constitution has been written, Iraq will move toward national elections. We want this process to go as quickly as possible, yet it must be done right. The free institutions of Iraq must stand the test of time. And a democratic Iraq will stand as an example to all the Middle East. We believe, and the Iraqi people will show, that liberty is the hope and the right of every land.

Our work in Iraq has been long. It's hard, and it's not finished. We will stay the course. We will complete our job. And beyond Iraq, the war on terror continues. There will be no quick victory in this war. We will persevere, and victory is certain.

I am confident of victory because I know the character of our military, shown in people like Master Sergeant Jack Negrotti of Plaistow, New Hampshire. Jake is a member of the New Hampshire Air National Guard who's volunteered for overseas deployments 3 times since September the 11th. He served in Pakistan, Afghanistan, and Iraq. Right now Jake is an airport manager at Baghdad Airport, helping make sure our military and humanitarian operations move ahead.

People like Jake Negrotti are showing what it means to be a patriot and a citizen. We're honored to have Jake's wife, Donna, and his children, Alicia and Christopher, with us here today. Next time you talk to Jake, Donna, you tell him his President appreciates his service, and his country is grateful.

The war on terror has brought hardship and loss to our country, beginning with the grief of September the 11th. Let us also remember that the first victory in this war came on that same day, on a hijacked plane bound for the Nation's Capital. Those men and women on Flight 93 took action, served their country, knowing they would die. They found incredible courage in their final moments to save the lives of others. In those moments and many times since, terrorists have learned that Americans are courageous and will not be intimidated. We will fight them with everything we have.

Few are called to show the kind of valor seen on Flight 93 or on the field of battle. Yet all of us do share a calling, to be strong in adversity and to be unafraid in danger. We Americans have come through so much together, and we have much yet to do. If we're patient, united, determined, our Nation will prosper, and our Nation will win.

May God bless you all. Thank you all very much.

NOTE: The President spoke at 9:50 a.m. In his remarks, he referred to Maj. Gen. John E. Blair, adjutant general, Maj. Gen. Joseph K. Simeone, deputy adjutant general, Brig. Gen. John J. Weeden, assistant adjutant general, and Command Sgt. Maj. Michael Rice, New Hampshire National Guard; Gov. Craig Benson of New Hampshire and his wife, Denise; Brig. Gen. Benton "Chick" M. Smith, assistant adjutant general, headquarters, New Hampshire Air National Guard; Col. Carolyn J. Protzmann, vice wing commander, Lt. Col. Robert T. Monahan, operations group commander, Col. Leroy Dunkelberger II, mission support group commander, and Wing Command Chief Master Sgt. Ronald H. Nadeau, 157th Air Refueling Wing, New Hampshire Air National Guard; Ruth L. Griffin, councilor, New Hampshire Executive Council; Maureen Barrows, chair, Rockingham County Board of Commissioners; and former President Saddam Hussein of Iraq.

Remarks to the Greater Manchester Chamber of Commerce in Manchester, New Hampshire
October 9, 2003

Thanks for the warm welcome. It's good to be back in New Hampshire again. I've spent some quality time here. [*Laughter*] It's good to see many of our friends. It seems like Manchester is a popular destination place these days—[*laughter*]—not just because the leaves are changing. [*Laughter*] This city was the scene of my first great victory in 2000, the perfect flip at the Presidential Pancake Flip-off. [*Laughter*] I would suggest some of our other fellow Americans practice. [*Laughter*]

I want to thank the Chamber and the Business Industry Association for inviting me here today to talk about two great priorities of our country, to create jobs for America and to win the war on terror.

I wish Laura was with me today. She sends her best wishes. You might remember that she has recently been on a diplomatic mission. She went to Russia, and she was in France. Perhaps you saw the picture—[*laughter*]—of her in France. [*Laughter*] Last time I was in France, I got a nice welcome but nothing like that. [*Laughter*] She's such a great representative for our country. I'm really proud to call her wife. I love her dearly.

I want to thank Raymond for his kind introduction. I appreciate Harold Turner as well for letting me come. Thank you all for coming. I traveled from Pease Air Force Base with your fine Governor and First Lady, Denise. Craig, I'm proud to call you friend. Thank you for serving your great State. I'm also here with my buddy Judd Gregg and his wife, Kathy. Don't mess with Kathy. [*Laughter*]

I'm also honored to be here with a fine United States Senator, John Sununu. I appreciate you coming, John. Congressmen Charlie Bass and Jeb Bradley flew down from Washington with me today. I know the mayor of Manchester and the mayor of Nashua are here with us today. I'm honored you are here. Members of the executive council are here; State representatives are here; State senators are here. The attorney general is here. There are a lot of people here that I need to thank. I appreciate you coming and giving me a chance to visit with you.

When I landed today in Manchester, I met a fellow named Robert Perkins. He is one of the thousands of citizens who volunteer in your State. I like to point out people like Robert Perkins, because it gives me a chance to remind our fellow citizens that our true strength is not our military might. Our true strength is not the size of our wallet. The strength of this country is the heart and soul of fellow citizens who are willing to love a neighbor just like they'd like to be loved themselves.

Robert Perkins volunteers at the Boys and Girls Club here in Manchester. He helped create the chapter in 1995. He has dedicated 5 to 10 hours each week over the past 5 years. My call to our citizens is, in order to make America as hopeful and promising a place as possible, help somebody who hurts. Put your arm around somebody in need. And for those of you who already do so, like Robert Perkins, thank you for being patriots.

Since I was last here, New Hampshire lost one of its finest citizens, Governor Hugh Gregg. He loved his country, and he served it well. He loved this State, and he believed in the common sense and wisdom of its people. This tradition continues in his good family. We honor Hugh Gregg's memory, and my family was proud to be his friend.

I began my visit this morning at Pease, with the New Hampshire Army and Air Guardsmen and reservists from every branch of our military. New Hampshire guardsmen have served on every front of the war on terror, from Afghanistan to Iraq to protecting our homeland to guarding the detainees at Guantanamo Bay. I went to tell them how much I appreciated the fact that they are showing what it means to be patriots and citizens. I told them that our country is grateful for their service.

America is being tested. We're being tested abroad, and we are being tested here at home. And we're meeting the tests of history. We're defeating the enemies of freedom. And at the same time, we're confronting challenges to build the prosperity of our Nation. Every test of America has revealed the character of America. After 2 years, no one in the world, friend or foe, can doubt the strength or the will of the American people.

When you become the President, you can't predict all the challenges that will come. But you do know the principles you bring to office, and they should not change. They shouldn't change with time, and they shouldn't change with polls. I took this office to make a difference, not to mark time. I came to this office to confront problems directly and forcefully, not to pass them on to future Presidents and future generations.

The challenges we face today cannot be met with timid actions or bitter words. Our challenges will be overcome with optimism and resolve and confidence in the ideals of our country.

Because we believe in our free enterprise system, we can be confident in our economy's future. Our economy has been through a lot, been through some tough times. When I took office, the stock market had been declining for 9 months, and the economy was headed into a recession. And just as we started to recover, the enemy attacked us on September the 11th, and that struck a blow to our economy. And then investor confidence was shaken by scandals in corporate America—dishonest behavior we cannot and we will not tolerate in our America. And then we faced the

uncertainty that preceded the battles of Afghanistan and Iraq.

We have acted to overcome all these challenges, and I've acted on principle. See, Government doesn't create wealth. The role of Government is to create the conditions where risktakers and entrepreneurs can invest and grow and therefore hire new workers. I've acted to create the conditions for job growth. See, I understand that when Americans have more take-home pay to spend, to save, or invest, the whole economy grows, and someone is more likely to find a job.

And so I twice led the United States Congress to pass historic tax relief for the American people. We wanted tax relief to be as broad and as fair as possible, so we reduced taxes on everyone who pays taxes. I don't think it makes sense to penalize marriage in the Tax Code. We want to reward and honor marriage. And so we reduced the marriage penalty. We understand it takes a lot of—to raise a family and to educate a child, so we increased the child credit to $1,000. This summer I said the check would be in the mail, and it was.

It's counterproductive to discourage investment, especially during an economic recovery. So we quadrupled the expense deduction for small business investment and cut tax rates on dividends and capital gains. It is unfair to tax the estates people leave behind after a lifetime of saving and building up their business or running the family farm. When you leave the world, the IRS shouldn't follow you. So we're phasing out the Federal death tax.

I proposed and signed these measures to help individuals and families, but I also know the effect it would have on small businesses. See, most small businesses in America pay taxes under the individual income tax rates. Most small businesses are sole proprietorships or Subchapter S corporations, and so when you cut all taxes, you benefit the small-business owner in America. And when you couple that with the higher expense deductions, we've really put the wind under the sails of small businesses. And that's important, because small businesses create most new jobs in our country. They're usually the first to take risks and the first to hire new people. The tax relief plan we passed helps small businesses, which helps economic growth, which means it's more likely somebody is going to find a job.

The actions we're taking are helping people. We've cut the taxes on 112,000 small-business owners in New Hampshire. We've reduced the marriage penalty for 192,000 couples. We've increased the child tax credit for 124,000 families. I understand this, that New Hampshire citizens can better spend their own money than the people in Washington.

We're following a clear and consistent economic strategy, and I'm confident about the future of this country. Last month, the economy exceeded expectations and added net new jobs. Inflation is low. After-tax incomes are rising. Homeownership is at record levels. Productivity is high, and it is rising. Factory orders, particularly for high-tech equipment, have risen over the last several months. Our strategy has set the stage for sustained growth. By reducing taxes, we kept a promise, and we did the right thing at the right time for the American economy.

Just as our economy is coming around, some are saying now is the time to raise taxes. To be fair, they think any time is a good time to raise taxes. [Laughter] At least they're consistent. But I strongly disagree. A nation cannot tax its way to growth or job creation. Tax relief has put this Nation on the right path, and I intend to keep this Nation on the path to prosperity.

We are moving forward, but we cannot be satisfied. We can't be satisfied, so long as we have fellow citizens who are looking for work. Here in New Hampshire, one out of every five jobs that have been lost are manufacturing jobs. And that's a problem. I believe we must act boldly to stem the tide of job loss. So I'm asking Congress to join me in carrying out a six-point plan for jobs for America.

Businesses are more likely to hire people if the health care for workers is affordable. We need to allow association health care plans, where small businesses can pool risk and gain the same bargaining power as big businesses. And in order to control health care costs, we need effective legal reform, medical liability reform at the Federal level.

Defensive medicine against frivolous lawsuits runs up the Federal budgets. It increases the cost of Medicare and Medicaid and veteran health benefits. Medical liability reform is a national problem that requires a national solution. The House has passed a good bill. It is stuck in the Senate. Senators must understand no one has been healed by a frivolous lawsuit in America.

Unfair lawsuits are also harming a lot of good and honest employers. There are too many large settlements that leave plaintiffs with a small sum and lawyers with a fortune. Class actions and mass tort suits that reach across State lines should be tried in a Federal court so lawyers cannot shop around looking for a favorable judge. And most of the money in a judgment or settlement should go to those who have actually been harmed, not the lawyer. A good bill has passed the House. It is stuck in the Senate. We need class action tort reform out of the United States Senate.

Our economy will grow stronger and create more jobs if we have a sound national energy policy. The manufacturing sector of New Hampshire and around our country need reliable sources of energy. We need better infrastructure. We need to modernize the delivery of electricity and natural gas so cities and businesses and employers are not left in the dark.

We'll continue to give low-income people help with their fuel bills this winter. We must use our technology to develop plain and efficient energy sources so we can sustain economic growth and protect the environment. We need more energy production close to home. For the sake of national security and for the sake of economic security, America must be less dependent on foreign sources of energy. We passed a good bill out of the House and the Senate. They must come together and get a bill to my desk before they go home for Christmas.

Most people will find jobs when employers don't have to waste time and resources complying with needless Government regulations. For the sake of American workers, we're cutting unnecessary rules and making some of the rules still on the books simpler to understand. This administration understands that small-business owners should spend more time building companies and pleasing customers and less time filling out the endless forms the Federal Government requires.

To create jobs, we are pursuing free trade agreements that will open up markets for New Hampshire products. Last month, I signed trade agreements with Singapore and Chile, and we are working toward other free trade agreements across the globe. Expanded trade will help New Hampshire companies like Len-Tex and Warwick Mills and Tender to sell more goods, which will mean more jobs and better jobs for New Hampshire workers. I will insist that for free—not only will we have free trade but that there be a level playing field, that the people with whom we trade treat America fairly. I firmly believe that when the rules are fair, American workers and entrepreneurs can compete with anybody, anyplace, and anytime.

There is one more thing we need to do. We need to make sure that all the tax relief we have passed doesn't disappear in future years. See, there's a quirk in the legislation. The tax cuts that we passed are scheduled to go away unless we act. The child credit will drop in several years. The death tax that we put to extinction will pop back up 10 years after enactment. In other words, there's uncertainty in the Tax Code. See, Americans hear about tax relief. They don't expect to see higher taxes sneak

through the back door. For the sake of job creation, for the sake of people looking for work, the United States Congress should make every one of the tax cuts we passed permanent.

We have a responsibility to set good policies in Washington, and we are. Yet the real strength is found in the creativity and the entrepreneurial spirit of the American people. The entrepreneurial spirit is strong in this country. It's one of the great aspects of our national character. And that's why I'm so confident about the future of our economy.

Brain Stowell is here. He's a second-generation entrepreneur based in Claremont, New Hampshire. I met Brian backstage. His family owned a cabinetmaking company called Crown Point Cabinetry, which started by his dad, Norm, in a garage, 25 years ago. Brian said, "If you talk about me, make sure you talk about my dad, Norm."

Now that business employs 90 people. From the garage to now being an employer of 90 people, that's what America is all about. This year, four—this week, Brian added four new workers. Most new jobs in America are created by small-business owners. In the next 2½ years, he plans on adding 25 workers. Folks working now not only know they'll have a job, but they're about to be joined by other working with them.

He says the tax cuts helped a lot. That's his words, not mine. Because of tax relief, he's putting more than $800,000 of his company's money at work in new equipment. See, he's made a decision. Tax relief, it creates demand. In a market-oriented economy, when there's more demand, somebody meets that demand with a service or a product. And when somebody meets that demand with a service or a product, somebody is more likely to find work.

He's going to buy a new router, made in North Carolina. There's a router-worker who's going to be a—benefit from his decision caused by tax relief. He's going to buy a sander made in Minnesota, spray booths made just outside of Boston, Massachusetts, a forklift made in Iowa, more than a dozen other pieces of equipment, nearly all of them made here in America. The tax relief encouraged Brian to make an investment. And when he makes an investment, not only will it help his company be more productive, the people who are making the equipment for Brian to purchase are more likely to find work and keep work.

He's an optimist. He's an optimist because he believes in the people in this country. Here's what he said. He said, "After September the 11th, everybody collectively held their breath, but our confidence has grown. We've turned a corner." Confidence like that is well-founded. We live in a country that rewards big dreams and honest effort. My job is to keep the entrepreneurial spirit alive and well through good policy in Washington, DC.

As we overcome challenges to our economy, we are also answering great threats to our security. September the 11th, 2001, moved our country to grief and moved our country to action. We made a pledge that day, and we have kept it. We're bringing the guilty to justice. We're taking the fight to the enemy. And we now see that enemy very clearly. The terrorists plot in secret. They kill the innocent. They defile a great religion. And they hate everything America stands for. These committed killers will not be stopped by negotiations. They won't respond to therapy or to reason. The terrorists who threaten America cannot be appeased. They must be found; they must be fought; and they must be defeated.

We are in a different kind of war than we're used to. We're in a new war, and it requires a new strategy. We're not waiting for further attacks. We're striking our enemies before they can strike us again. We've taken unprecedented steps to protect our homeland, yet wars are won on the offensive. And America and our friends are staying on the offensive.

We are rolling back the terrorist threat, not on the fringes of its influence but at the heart of its power. We're making good progress. We're hunting the Al Qaida terrorists and their allies wherever they hide, from Pakistan to the Philippines to the Horn of Africa to Iraq. Nearly two-thirds of Al Qaida's known leaders have been captured or killed. Our resolve is firm and clear: No matter how long it takes, all who plot against America will face the justice of America.

We have sent a message understood throughout the world, "If you harbor a terrorist, if you support a terrorist, if you feed a terrorist, you're just as guilty as the terrorists." And the Taliban found out what we meant. Thanks to our great military, Afghanistan is no longer a safe haven for terror. Afghanistan is free. Many young girls now go to the school for the first time in Afghanistan, and the people of America are safer from attack.

And we fought the war on terror in Iraq. The regime of Saddam Hussein possessed and used weapons of mass destruction. He sponsored terrorist groups, inflicted incredible terror on his own people. Nearly every nation, every nation, recognized and denounced this threat for over 10 years. The U.N. Security Council, in Resolution 1441, demanded that Saddam Hussein disarm, to prove his disarmament to the world or face serious consequences. The choice was up to the dictator. He chose poorly.

I acted because I was not about to leave the security of the American people in the hands of a madman. I was not about to stand by and wait and trust in the sanity and restraint of Saddam Hussein. So in one of the swiftest and most humane military campaigns in history, we removed the threat. Six months ago today, the statue of the dictator was pulled down.

Since the liberation of Iraq, our investigators have found evidence of a clandestine network of biological laboratories, advance design work on prohibited longer range missiles, an elaborate campaign to hide illegal weapons programs. There's still much to investigate. Yet it is undeniable—undeniable—that Saddam Hussein was in clear violation of the United Nations Security Council Resolution 1441. It's undeniable that Saddam Hussein was a deceiver and a danger. The Security Council was right to demand that Saddam disarm, and we were right to enforce that demand.

Who can possibly think that the world would be better off with Saddam Hussein still in power? Surely not the dissidents who would be in his prisons or end up in his mass graves. Surely not the men and women who would fill Saddam's torture chambers or rape rooms. Surely not the families of victims he murdered with poison gas. Surely not anyone who cares about human rights and democracy and stability in the Middle East. There's only one decent and humane reaction to the fall of Saddam Hussein: Good riddance!

Our country faces a choice. After all the action we have taken, after all the progress we have made against terror, there is a temptation to think that danger has passed. The danger hasn't passed. Since September the 11th, since that fateful day here in America, the terrorists have taken lives in Casablanca, Mombasa, Jerusalem, Amman, Riyadh, Baghdad, Karachi, New Delhi, Bali, and Jakarta. The terrorists continue to plot. They continue to plan against our country and our people. America must never forget the lessons of September the 11th.

America cannot retreat from our responsibilities and hope for the best. Our security will not be gained by timid measures. Our security requires constant vigilance and decisive action. I believe America has only one option. We must fight this war until our work is done.

We're fighting the war on terror on many fronts, and Iraq is now the central front. Saddam holdouts and foreign terrorists are trying desperately—desperately—to undermine Iraq's progress and throw the country into chaos. Terrorists in Iraq believe their attacks on innocent people will weaken our resolve. That's what they believe. They believe we'll run from a challenge. They're mistaken. Americans are not the running kind.

The United States did not run from Germany and Japan following World War II. We helped those nations to become strong and decent and democratic societies that no longer wage war against America. And this is our mission in Iraq. We're rebuilding schools. We're rebuilding hospitals. Thousands of young kids have received immunizations recently. We're returning electricity and water to the good people of that country.

We have pride in this help not only because our hearts are good, because our vision is clear. A stable and democratic and hopeful Iraq will no longer be a breeding ground for terror and tyranny and aggression. Free nations are peaceful nations. Our work in Iraq is essential to our own security. And no band of murderers and gangsters will stop that work or shake the will of America.

Nearly every day, we're launching swift precision raids against the enemies of peace. Helped by intelligence from the Iraqis, we're rounding up the enemy and taking their weapons. We're working our way through the famous deck of cards. We've already captured or killed 43 of the 55 most wanted former Iraqi leaders. The other 12 have a lot to worry about. Anyone who seeks to harm our soldiers can know that our soldiers are hunting for them. Our military is serving with great courage. Some of the best have fallen. We mourn every loss. We honor every name. We grieve with every family. And we'll always be grateful that liberty has found such brave defenders.

In defending liberty, we are joined by more than 30 nations now contributing military forces in Iraq. Great Britain and Poland are leading two multinational divisions. And in this cause with fine allies must be included the good people of Iraq. They want a peaceful country. They want security for their families.

Last week, the first battalion of the new Iraqi army completed its training. Within a year, Iraq will have 40,000 members in their military force. Tens of thousands of Iraqi citizens are guarding their own borders and defending vital facilities and policing their own streets. We're making good progress in Iraq. Six months ago, the Iraqi people welcomed their liberation—6 short months ago. And today, many Iraqis are armed and trained to defend their own liberty.

Our goal in Iraq is to leave behind a stable and self-governing society which will no longer be a threat to the Middle East or to the United States of America. We're following an orderly plan to reach this goal. Iraq now has a Governing Council which has appointed interim government ministers. Once a constitution has been written, Iraq will move toward national elections. We want this process to go as quickly as possible. Yet, it must be done right.

The free institutions of Iraq must stand the test of time. And a democratic Iraq will stand as an example to all the Middle East. I believe, and the Iraqi people will show, that liberty is the hope and the right of every land. I do not believe freedom is America's gift to the world. Freedom is God's gift to every individual in the world.

Our work in Iraq has been long and hard, and it is not finished. We will stay the course. We will complete the task. And beyond Iraq, the war on terror continues. There will be no quick victory in the war on terror, but if we persevere, victory is certain.

I'm confident of victory because I know the character of our country and our military, shown in the conduct of young men like Army Sergeant Matthew DeWitt of Hillsboro, New Hampshire. While serving in Iraq, Sergeant DeWitt stepped forward to volunteer on a dangerous mission to root out Saddam loyalists. In the fighting, he was seriously wounded. He's now receiving care at the Walter Reed Army Medical Center in Washington, DC. I was honored to visit him. He was awarded the Purple Heart. He doesn't consider himself a hero. He just says, "I was just doing my job." Yet it is great people like this 26-year-old from New Hampshire who protect us. We count on them, and we're proud of them.

The war on terror has brought hardship and loss to our country, beginning with the grief of September the 11th. Let us also remember that the first victory in this war on terror came that same day on a hijacked plane bound for the Nation's Capital. Those men and women on Flight 93, knowing they would die, found the courage to use their final moments to save the lives of others. In those moments and many times since, terrorists have learned about the courage of America and that we will not be intimidated. We will fight them with everything we have.

Few of us are called to show the kind of valor seen on Flight 93 or on the field of battle. Yet all of us share a calling to be strong in adversity and unafraid of danger. We Americans have come through so much together, yet there is a lot to do. And if we're patient and united and determined, this Nation will not only prosper; this Nation will be secure as we prevail in the war against terror.

Thank you for letting me come today, and may God bless you.

NOTE: The President spoke at 12:03 p.m. at the New Hampshire Holiday Inn-Center of New Hampshire. In his remarks, he referred to Raymond E. Pinard, chairman of the board, Greater Manchester Chamber of Commerce; Harold Turner, Jr., chairman, board of directors, Business and Industry Association; Gov. Craig Benson of New Hampshire and his wife, Denise; Mayor Robert A. Baines of Manchester, NH; Mayor Bernard A. Streeter of Nashua, NH; New Hampshire State Attorney General Peter W. Heed; and former President Saddam Hussein of Iraq.

Remarks at a Reception for Gubernatorial Candidate Ernie Fletcher in Lexington, Kentucky
October 9, 2003

Thanks for coming. It's great to be back in this beautiful State. It's good to see a lot of friends. I know something about the culture of Kentucky. I know the priorities of this State. I promise you I'll keep my speech short so you can get to the football game. [*Laughter*] All I can say is, thank goodness it wasn't basketball season, because nobody would be here. [*Laughter*]

I appreciate the warm welcome to this former Governor, and I'm proud to be here with the next Governor, Ernie Fletcher. For me, politics will come in time. I've got a job to do, and it's my honor to lead this country. But politics is upon the people of Kentucky, and I'm here because I want to make it as clear as I possibly can: In the interests of every person who lives in this State, whether they're Republican, Democrat, or independent, the best man to be the Governor of Kentucky is Ernie Fletcher.

I know him well. I've worked with him as a United States Congressman. The first thing I found out about Ernie is he loves his family, and he loves this State. I finally had to tell him to quit saying the word "Kentucky" every time he lobbied me on an issue. [*Laughter*] He cares a lot about people. He believes in personal responsibility, the dignity that comes from hard work, and the importance of a good education for every child. There's no question in my mind this man has the right values to lead this great State.

And I appreciate the fact that Ernie picked a good man named Steve Pence to be the Lieutenant Governor of this State. I picked him first. [*Laughter*] He was the U.S. Attorney for Western District of Kentucky, appointed by President George W. Bush. I looked at a lot of candidates. This man was the best candidate for the job. I'm proud that he served as U.S. Attorney.

I'm proud that he served as a lieutenant colonel in the Army Reserves. And I'm proud to be standing on this stage with the next Lieutenant Governor of the State of Kentucky.

Ernie and I both married above ourselves. [*Laughter*] I'm proud to be with Glenna and the Fletcher family. I want to thank you for your sacrifice and service. Glenna, you'll make a great first lady for this State, just like Laura has made a great First Lady for our country. I'm really proud of Laura. She recently went on a high-level diplomatic mission. She went to Russia to help promote a book festival with Lyudmila Putin—by the way, came back right after that in Russia and hosted a national book festival. She loves books. She loves reading. She wants every child to read in America.

And then she—before she went to Russia, she stopped off in France. [*Laughter*] Now, you may have seen the picture. I went to France. [*Laughter*] I had a nice reception, but I wasn't treated like that. [*Laughter*] No, she's great. I'm proud of her. I can't tell you how thankful I am that when I got on bended knee and said, "Will you marry me," she said yes. [*Laughter*] She sends her love and her best to all her friends here in the great Commonwealth of Kentucky.

I also thank Ruth Ann Pence and the Pence family for working hard to get the next Lieutenant Governor in office. It's a sacrifice for families when somebody makes the decision to run. It's a team effort, and I thank the families for what you're doing.

In our midst is a man who you must send back as the United States Senator from this great State, and that is Mr. Jim Bunning. He's strong. He's capable. He's the absolute right man for the job.

Speaking about Senators, Mitch's wife is in my Cabinet. That would be Mitch McConnell, and I'm speaking about Elaine Chao. She's done a fabulous job as the Secretary of Labor. Hi, Elaine. Need a ride back? [*Laughter*] Not much air rage on Air Force One, by the way. [*Laughter*]

Two Members of the United States Congress are with us today. A great Member, a fellow I remember campaigning with for my dad at his house, a person who has done a really good job for Kentucky—he is a person who is a leader in the House of Representatives, and that's Congressman Hal Rogers. As well we've got another fine Member from the House of Representatives with us, a good stalwart, a good ally, and that's Congressman Ron Lewis. I know the current Congressman, soon to be Governor, is really appreciative of the Members of the Congress for coming tonight. You know him as well as anybody.

I appreciate the members of the statehouse who are here. It's in your interest you're here, because you're going to be working with a fine man as Governor. We've got the senator, Dan Kelly, who's the majority leader. You're fixing to have a great Governor to work with, Senator. You've got State Representative Jeff Hoover, minority leader of the statehouse. And I want to thank the other members of the senate and the house who are here tonight as well. Help is on the way.

I know there's a lot of other candidates running for statewide office, too numerous to name, but I wish you all the best. I thank your families for making the sacrifice. I also want to thank all the grassroots activists who are here, people who are putting up the signs and dialing the phones and licking the envelopes. You can't win a race unless you energize the grassroots.

And we've got some fantastic leaders of the Republican Party who are with us tonight. Ellen Williams, my good friend, is the chairwoman of the Republican Party of the State of Kentucky. My friend Cathy Bailey, the national committeewoman and the State finance chair, by the way, for the Bush-Cheney 2004 campaign, is with us tonight.

But my message to the grassroots folks is it's one thing to come to a fundraiser—and that's important, don't get me wrong—but you need to go to your coffee shops. You need to go to community centers and your houses of worship, and you need to say to people who haven't made up their mind, "You've got a good man in Ernie Fletcher." You need to spread the word. You need to energize those folks. Find those folks that say, "My vote doesn't matter," and look them in the eye and says, "It does matter to have the right kind of Governor in the statehouse."

I appreciate Ernie's priorities. The number one priority of any Governor ought to be the education of the children of the State in which he's the Governor. That ought to be the priority. It's Ernie's priority. See, if you can't get education right, there's a dismal future for the State. It's essential that you have a Governor who stands tall for every child. And that starts with having a Governor who understands the dire need to challenge the soft bigotry of low expectations. You've got to have a Governor that believes that every child can learn and is willing to raise the standards, a Governor who believes in the worth and potential of every single child in his State. And that's Ernie Fletcher.

You see, if you do not believe that every child can learn, then you're willing to accept a system which simply shuffles children through the schools. And that's unsatisfactory. It should be unsatisfactory to everybody who lives in the State of Kentucky. It's important to know whether or not the children are learning to read and write and add and subtract. It's important to hold public schools accountable. That way, Governor Fletcher can praise the teachers and principals and parents in succeeding schools. And that way, Governor Fletcher can take the accountability measures and say, "We're not doing it right here." For the sake of Kentucky, put a Governor in who's willing to work hard to make sure not one single child is left behind.

Ernie talked about health care. Health care is an issue. It makes sense to have somebody who knows something about health care as the Governor. He does. I've worked with him closely on key issues. We worked on the Medicare bill together. See, we want to make sure the Medicare system is modern, so seniors have got choices. I'm not only talking about the seniors today; I'm talking about those of us who are fixing to be seniors. You've got to have a system that works. Let's make sure we have prescription drugs available for our seniors. Ernie has been a leader on this issue. He knows what he's talking about.

And he and I know this, that for the sake of affordable and available health care, we need to have medical liability reform. For the sake of the working people of this State, you better have you a Governor who is strong enough to stand up to the trial lawyers, somebody who is going to remind the people of this State that nobody has ever been healed by a frivolous or junk lawsuit.

And that's soon-to-be Governor Ernie Fletcher. We spent a lot of time in Washington talking about jobs. See, he and I understand this, that things might look okay, but so long as anybody is looking for work and can't find a job, it means we still have a problem. We've got to work to create the conditions for job growth. The role of our governments is not to create wealth—Ernie knows that—the role is to create the environment in which small businesses can flourish to be big businesses, in which the entrepreneurial spirit is strong.

We had a problem at the national level. When we came in—Vice President Cheney and I came in—the country was headed into a recession in the first quarter of 2001. We were in recession. The economy started coming around, and then the enemy hit us, and that hurt. And then we found out some of our citizens forgot to tell the truth.

We had some corporate scandals. And by the way, there's no excuse for that. They will be held to account. We expect corporate CEOs to be responsible citizens in America.

We vigorously waged the war on terror, and the battles of Afghanistan and Iraq affected the confidence of the American people. We had an issue with our economy. I went to the Congress. I said, "The best way to get the economy growing again, the best way to make sure people can find a job is to return the people's money." I proposed historic tax relief. We increased the child credit from $600 to $1,000. We reduced the marriage penalty. The code ought to encourage marriage, not discourage marriage.

We cut the taxes on everybody who pays taxes. We thought the fairest way to deal with tax relief was not to play favorites but to say, "If you pay tax, you get tax relief." We provided incentives for small businesses to expand, because Ernie and I understand that most new jobs in America are created by small businesses. No, we acted. I called upon Congress; this good man supported me. The tax relief came at the right time for American history.

Now, I've watched him carefully. He understands what I know: When we're spending money at the Government level, we're not spending the Government's money; we're spending the people's money. And you'd better have a Governor who understands that in your statehouse.

There's another thing we're working on in Washington to make sure our businesses flourish, and that's a reliable source of energy. I look forward to working with Ernie on clean coal technology. I want to use the resources at hand. You've got some great resources here in Kentucky. We've got to use them. We've got to make sure we use our technology so that the air is cleaner. But we need an energy policy for the sake of economic vitality. And for the sake of national security, we need to be less dependent on foreign sources of energy.

We've been working on a jobs plan at the national level, Ernie's working on a jobs plan here in Kentucky. He knows what he's doing. He's got the right philosophy. If anybody out there is listening and is worried about their job, I'd strongly suggest that you make Ernie Fletcher your Governor. He knows what he's talking about when it comes to job creation for the people of the Commonwealth of Kentucky.

Another thing I'm looking forward to working with Ernie on is homeland security. There's a lot responsibility at the State level when it comes to protecting the homeland. Make sure you've got a Governor who is well organized, who can make sure that there's a response mechanism in case the worst might happen, somebody who supports the first-responders, the fire and the policemen and the emergency service squads all over your State. I'm confident Ernie can do the job. I've worked with him on matters of homeland security.

The truth of the matter is, the best way to secure the homeland is never to forget the lessons of September the 11th, 2001, and chase the enemy down, one by one, and bring them to justice.

One of the big problems we had when we got to Washington was morale in the United States military was beginning to suffer. When we showed up, there was an issue in the military. So I proposed strong defense budgets to meet the threats of a new era. Congressman Fletcher was a strong supporter of those defense budgets. And today, thanks to his support and the good work of others here in this audience, no one—no one in the world—can doubt the strength and the spirit and the sacrifice and the class and the technological ability of the United States military.

Thank goodness we did strengthen our military, because we're still at war. I knew, after September the 11th, one of the hardest things for me to do would be to convince the people that there was a new kind

of war, and they had to be diligent and patient in order to do our duty, in order to answer history and secure our homeland. Ernie Fletcher got that right off the bat.

It's important that our country not forget the lessons of September the 11th. The first lesson is the nature of the enemy. These people are nothing but coldblooded killers. They've hijacked a great religion. They'll kill innocent women and children and men. They care not who they kill. They try to create fear and intimidation. Therapy won't work with these people. Negotiation won't work with these people. The only way to secure America is to stay on the offensive, and this country will stay on the offensive.

We're making good progress against Al Qaida. I vowed that we would bring those killers to justice, and we're making good progress. We're teaming up with other nations and, slowly but surely, bringing them to justice. About two-thirds of the Al Qaida leadership have either been killed or captured. And we're after the rest of them. I know we've got a family here who grieved because of the bombing in Bali. The man who ordered that bombing, masterminded the bombing, is now in custody. He's no longer a threat. May God rest your daughter. We have a duty, no matter whether the citizen lives here in America or elsewhere, to be tough and strong and vigilant, to use our resources and capabilities to bring killers to justice.

I also laid out another initiative that's an important lesson of September the 11th. It's important for those who harbor a terrorist and feed a terrorist and hide a terrorist to understand they're just as guilty as the terrorists. And the Taliban in Afghanistan found out exactly what we meant. Because of the bravery of the United States military and our friends and coalitions, the Taliban is no more. The people of Afghanistan are free. Many young girls go to school for the first time, thanks to the United States of America.

There's another lesson involved with September the 11th, and that is, when we see a gathering threat, we must deal with it. You see, in the past, oceans protected us, or so we thought. We felt—thought we were invulnerable to attack. So if we saw a gathering threat overseas, we might decide to deal with it, or might not. September the 11th changed that calculation. The enemy can strike anytime, anywhere in America with ruthless fashion. They know no rules. They know no bounds of decency. They kill in the name of great religion. And therefore, this Nation must deal with gathering threats when we find them.

And Saddam Hussein was a gathering threat. He possessed and he used weapons of mass destruction. He was a brutal tyrant and dictator to his own people. We discovered mass graves of men, women, and children. He had rape rooms and torture rooms. Words cannot describe the tyranny of this brutal man. I was not about to leave the security of the United States to the desires and hopes of this madman.

But we weren't alone. The world called for Mr. Saddam Hussein to disarm, to prove he had disarmed, not once but time after time. The world clearly saw the threat of Mr. Saddam Hussein. Last year, you might remember, we passed Security Council Resolution 1441. The United Nations said, "Mr. Saddam Hussein, you must declare your weapons. You must disarm for the sake of peace, or there will be serious consequences. Your choice." He made a bad choice. Saddam Hussein is no more.

Recently, there was a report about Mr. Saddam Hussein's weapons programs. If you read the report, it is absolutely clear that he was in defiance of Security Council Resolution 1441, that he was not only a danger but a deceiver. The United Nations was right to demand Saddam Hussein be disarmed, and the United States and our coalition was right to remove him from power.

And we have more work to do in Iraq. See, we're at an historic moment. A free Iraq, a peaceful Iraq in the heart of the land of terror will change the world and make America and our friends more secure. A peaceful Iraq in the heart of the Middle East will change the habits of countries that have spawned terrorists. It's essential we succeed for the long term. It's essential we succeed for our children and our grandchildren in developing a peaceful, democratic country. And make no mistake about it, we will succeed.

We're making great progress. I don't care what you read about. Just ask anybody who's been there. They will tell you that the schools are opening, the children are getting immunized, the electricity is up, water is purified and moving. We're making great progress in helping this nation establish itself. The Iraqis want a secure country. They're moms and dads just like you all are. They want to live in a peaceful, hopeful place. The marketplaces are burgeoning. The entrepreneurial spirit is growing. And they'll start taking over their own security. By the end of next year, we'll have 40,000 militia trained so they can deal with the thugs and the criminals and the Ba'athists who long for Saddam Hussein.

I talked to Bernie Kerik, the police chief of New York City, who was the commissioner there during 9/11. He went over there in the midst of chaos and set up a 37,000-person police force in Baghdad. No, it's different. We're making progress. This country is growing. I readily concede it's still hard work. There's thugs and killers who can't stand the thought of freedom. Freedom makes them nervous. And so, they're going to try to intimidate. See, you've got to understand, their goal is to try to frighten the United States of America. They want us to leave early. They want to inflict damage so that we run. They don't understand our country. We don't run from a challenge. We understand the stakes. We will stay the course, not only for our own security but for the peace of the world.

I've received great support from the United States Congress on this initiative. Ernie Fletcher understands the stakes. He understands the historic nature of what we are doing. He understands this war on terror. It will be good to have him as your Governor. He has got a vision.

I also know what he knows, that the true strength of this country is not our military might, however, or it's not the size of our wallets. That's not the true strength of America. The true strength of this country is the heart of the American people. We're a compassionate, decent nation. It's very important that you have a Governor who knows that Government can hand out money, but it cannot put hope in a person's heart or a sense of purpose in a person's life. That comes when loving citizens put their arm around somebody who hurts and says, "I love you. What can I do to help you? How can I make a difference in your life?" You need to have a Governor who knows that amidst the plenty of this great State, there are people who hurt. There are people who cry for help. There's homeless people. There's battered women. There's addicted people. And the best way to solve that is to rally the armies of compassion. Whether it be at the Federal level or at the State level, elected officials should never fear rallying faith, no matter what the religion, to help people in need.

No, the greatest strength of this country is the fact that there are thousands and thousands of people who have heard the universal call, whether they be Christian or Jewish or Muslim, to love a neighbor just like you'd like to be loved yourself. Problems will be solved one person at a time, one person—one conscience at a time, when our country gathers up the true strength, those who have heard the call, and help them provide the services that will save lives.

Ernie Fletcher understands that the people are the strength of this State. There's no doubt in my mind he'll make a great Governor. And it's my high honor to come and stand by his side and urge the good people of this State to vote him into office.

May God bless you all, and may God bless America.

NOTE: The President spoke at 6:11 p.m. in Heritage Hall at the Lexington Convention Center. In his remarks, he referred to Glenna A. Fletcher, wife of candidate Ernie Fletcher; Lyudmila Putina, wife of President Vladimir Putina of Russia; Ruth Ann Pence, wife of candidate Steve Pence; former President Saddam Hussein of Iraq; and Bernard B. Kerik, former commissioner, New York City Police Department.

Remarks on Cuba
October 10, 2003

Hola. Sientese. Thank you for coming. Welcome to the Rose Garden. It's my honor to host you for an important policy announcement.

I'm proud to be joined by our great Secretary of State Colin Powell and a son of Cuba, a graduate of the Pedro Pan program, Mel Martinez. I'm also pleased to be joined with other members who will

be—of my administration who will be charged with implementing policy. From the Department of Homeland Security, Under Secretary Asa Hutchinson is with us today. From the Treasury Department, Rick Newcomb, Director of the Office of Foreign Asset Control, is with us today. Rick, thank you for coming. Assistant Secretary for the Western Hemisphere Roger

Noriegais with us today. *Y por fin,* from my staff, Envoy Otto Reich.

As well we're honored to have distinguished Members of the Congress with us, starting with the very capable and able Senator from the State of Virginia, George Allen—*bienvenidos, Jorge—[laughter]*—from the State of Florida, Congressman Lincoln Diaz-Balart; *y su hermano,* Congressman Mario Diaz-Balart; Ileana Ros-Lehtinen; and Porter Goss. Thank you for coming. I'm honored you all are here.

The Secretary mentioned to me that Bob Dole is with us. Bob Dole is not with us.

One hundred and thirty-five years ago today, the struggle for Cuban freedom began at a sugar mill near Manzanillo. Carlos Manuel Cespedes, known as the Father of the Homeland, led an uprising against colonial rule. Today, the struggle for freedom continues—it hasn't ended—in cities and towns of that beautiful island, in Castro's prisons, and in the heart of every Cuban patriot. It is carried on by brave dissidents like Oscar Elias Biscet, Marta Beatriz Roque, Leonardo Bruzon Avila.

Last year in Miami, I offered Cuba's Government a way forward, a way forward toward democracy and hope and better relations with the United States. I pledged to work with our Congress to ease bans on trade and travel between our two countries if and only if the Cuban Government held free and fair elections, allowed the Cuban people to organize, assemble, and to speak freely, and eased the stranglehold on private enterprise.

Since I made that offer, we have seen how the Castro regime answers diplomatic initiatives. The dictator has responded with defiance and contempt and a new round of brutal oppression that outraged the world's conscience.

In April, 75 peaceful members of Cuban opposition were given harsh prison sentences, some as long as 20 years. Their crimes were to publish newspapers, to organize petition drives, to meet to discuss the future of their country. Cuba's political

prisoners are subjected to beatings and solitary confinement and the denial of medical treatment. Elections in Cuba are still a sham. Opposition groups still organize and meet at their own peril. Private economic activity is still strangled. Non-government trade unions are still oppressed and suppressed. Property rights are still ignored. And most goods and services produced in Cuba are still reserved for the political elites.

Clearly, the Castro regime will not change by its own choice, but Cuba must change. So today I'm announcing several new initiatives intended to hasten the arrival of a new, free, democratic Cuba.

First, we are strengthening enforcement of those travel restrictions to Cuba that are already in place. U.S. law forbids Americans to travel to Cuba for pleasure. That law is on the books, and it must be enforced. We allow travel for limited reasons, including a visit to a family, to bring humanitarian aid, or to conduct research. Those exceptions are too often used as cover for illegal business travel and tourism or to skirt the restrictions on carrying cash into Cuba. We're cracking down on this deception.

I've instructed the Department of Homeland Security to increase inspections of travelers and shipments to and from Cuba. We will enforce the law. We will also target those who travel to Cuba illegally through third countries, and those who sail to Cuba on private vessels in violation of the embargo.

You see, our country must understand the consequences of illegal travel. All Americans need to know that foreign-owned resorts in Cuba must pay wages—must pay the wages of their Cuban workers to the Government. A good soul in America who wants to be a tourist goes to a foreign-owned resort, pays the hotel bill; that money goes to the Government. The Government, in turn, pays the workers a pittance in worthless pesos and keeps the hard currency to prop up the dictator and his cronies. Illegal tourism perpetuates the misery of the Cuban people. And that is why I've charged the Department of Homeland Security to stop that kind of illegal trafficking of money.

By cracking down on the illegal travel, we will also serve another important goal. A rapidly growing part of Cuba's tourism industry is the illicit sex trade, a modern form of slavery which is encouraged by the Cuban Government. This cruel exploitation of innocent women and children must be exposed and must be ended.

Second, we are working to ensure that Cubans fleeing the dictatorship do not risk their lives at sea. My administration is improving the method through which we identify refugees and redoubling our efforts to process Cubans who seek to leave. We will better inform Cubans of the many routes to safe and legal entry into the United States through a public outreach campaign in southern Florida and inside Cuba itself. We will increase the number of new Cuban immigrants we welcome every year. We are free to do so, and we will, for the good of those who seek freedom. Our goal is to help more Cubans safely complete their journey to a free land.

Third, our Government will establish a Commission for the Assistance to a Free Cuba, to plan for the happy day when Castro's regime is no more and democracy comes to the island. This commission will be cochaired by the Secretary of State, Colin Powell, and the Secretary of Housing and Urban Development, Mel Martinez. They will draw upon experts within our Government to plan for Cuba's transition from Stalinist rule to a free and open society, to identify ways to hasten the arrival of that day.

The transition to freedom will present many challenges to the Cuban people and to America, and we will be prepared. America is not alone in calling for freedom inside of Cuba. Countries around the globe and the United Nations Human Rights Commission increasingly recognize the op-

pressive nature of the Castro regime and have denounced its recent crackdowns. We will continue to build a strong international coalition to advance the cause of freedom inside of Cuba.

In addition to the measures I've announced today, we continue to break the information embargo that the Cuban Government has imposed on its people for a half a century. Repressive governments fear the truth, and so we're increasing the amount and expanding the distribution of printed material to Cuba, of Internet-based information inside of Cuba, and of AM–FM and shortwave radios for Cubans.

Radio and TV Marti are bringing the message of freedom to the Cuban people. This administration fully recognizes the need to enhance the effectiveness of Radio and TV Marti. Earlier this year, we launched a new satellite service to expand our reach to Cuba. On May 20th, we staged the historic flight of Commando Solo, an airborne transmission system that broke through Castro's jamming efforts. Tyrants hate the truth. They jam messages. And on that day, I had the honor of speaking to the Cuban people in the native language.

It's only the beginning of a more robust effort to break through to the Cuban people. This country loves freedom, and we know that the enemy of every tyrant is the truth. We're determined to bring the truth to the people who suffer under Fidel Castro.

Cuba has a proud history of fighting for freedom, and that fight goes on. In all that lies ahead, the Cuban people have a constant friend in the United States of America. No tyrant can stand forever against the power of liberty, because the hope of freedom is found in every heart. So today we are confident that no matter what the dictator intends or plans, *Cuba sera pronto libre.*

De nuevo, Cuba libre. Thank you all.

NOTE: The President spoke at 11:03 a.m. in the Rose Garden at the White House. In his remarks, he referred to former Senator Bob Dole; and President Fidel Castro of Cuba.

The Office of the Press Secretary also released a Spanish language transcript of these remarks.

Memorandum on the Proposed Protocol Amending the Agreement for Cooperation Between the Government of the United States of America and the Government of the Republic of Indonesia Concerning Peaceful Uses of Nuclear Energy
October 10, 2003

Memorandum for the Secretary of State, the Secretary of Energy

Subject: Proposed Protocol Amending the Agreement for Cooperation Between the Government of the United States of America and the Government of the Republic of Indonesia Concerning Peaceful Uses of Nuclear Energy

I have considered the proposed Protocol Amending the Agreement for Cooperation Between the Government of the United States of America and the Government of the Republic of Indonesia Concerning Peaceful Uses of Nuclear Energy, signed at Washington on June 30, 1980, along with the views, recommendations, and statements of the interested agencies.

I have determined that the performance of the Protocol will promote, and will not constitute an unreasonable risk to, the common defense and security. Consistent with section 123 b. of the Atomic Energy Act of 1954, as amended (42 U.S.C. 2153(b)), I hereby approve the proposed Protocol and authorize you to arrange for its execution.

GEORGE W. BUSH

NOTE: An original was not available for verification of the content of this memorandum.

The President's Radio Address
October 11, 2003

Good morning. Six months ago this week, the statue of Saddam Hussein came down in the center of Baghdad, and Iraq began the transition from tyranny to self-government. The goal of our coalition is to help the Iraqi people build a stable, just, and prosperous country that poses no threat to America or the world. To reach that goal, we are following a clear strategy.

First, coalition forces in Iraq are actively pursuing the terrorists and Saddam holdouts who desperately oppose freedom for the Iraqi people. Secondly, we are committed to expanding international cooperation in the reconstruction and security of Iraq. And third, we are working closely with Iraqi leaders as they prepare to draft a constitution, establish institutions of a civil society, and move toward free elections.

As part of this strategy, we're helping Iraqis to rebuild their economy after a long era of corruption and misrule. For three decades, Iraq's economy served the interest only of its dictator and his regime. Saddam Hussein built palaces and monuments to himself while Iraq's infrastructure crumbled. He built up a massive war machine while neglecting the basic needs of his own people.

Now that the dictator is gone, we and our coalition partners are helping Iraqis to lay the foundations of a free economy. This coming week, the Iraqi economy will reach an important milestone with the introduction of a new currency. The new Iraqi dinar notes will bear the images of Iraq's proud heritage and not the face of a hated dictator. For more than a decade, different areas of Iraq have used two different versions of the dinar, and many of those notes were counterfeit, diminishing the value of those that were genuine. The new dinar will be used throughout Iraq, thereby unifying the economy and the country. The new currency will have special features that will make it difficult to counterfeit. Following World War II, it took 3 years to institute a new currency in West Germany. In Iraq, it has taken only 6 months, and the new currency symbolizes Iraq's reviving economy.

Iraq has a strong entrepreneurial tradition, and since the liberation of that country, thousands of new businesses have been launched. Busy markets are operating in villages across the country. Store shelves are filled with goods from clothing and linens to air conditioners and satellite dishes. Free commerce is returning to the ancient region that invented banking.

With our assistance, Iraqis are building the roads and ports and railways necessary for commerce. We have helped to establish an independent Iraqi central bank. Working with the Iraqi Governing Council, we are establishing a new system that allows foreign investors to confidently invest capital in Iraq's future. And we have helped re-store Iraq's oil production capacity to nearly 2 million barrels a day, the benefits of which are flowing directly to the Iraqi people.

Iraq is making progress. As the mayor of Kirkuk, Abdul Rahman Mustafa, recently said, "Our economic potential has barely been tapped." We must help Iraq to meet that potential. The request I have made to Congress for Iraqi reconstruction includes support for important health and training projects. Under our strategy, Iraq will have employment centers to help people find jobs. We intend to establish computer training and English language instruction and vocational programs to help Iraqis participate fully in the global economy. I urge Congress to pass my budget request soon so this vital work can proceed.

Americans are providing this help not only because our hearts are good but because our vision is clear. A stable, democratic, and prosperous Iraq will no longer be a breeding ground for terror, tyranny, and aggression, and a free Iraq will be an example of freedom's power throughout the Middle East. Free nations are peaceful nations. By promoting freedom and hope in other lands, we remove direct threats to the American people. Our actions in Iraq will increase our safety for years to come.

Thank you for listening.

NOTE: The address was recorded at 9:01 a.m. on October 10 in the Cabinet Room at the White House for broadcast at 10:06 a.m. on October 11. The transcript was made available by the Office of the Press Secretary on October 10 but was embargoed for release until the broadcast. In his remarks, the President referred to former President Saddam Hussein of Iraq. The Office of the Press Secretary also released a Spanish language transcript of this address.

Statement on Shirin Ebadi Receiving the Nobel Peace Prize
October 11, 2003

The United States congratulates Shirin Ebadi on receiving the Nobel Peace Prize—a first for an Iranian and for a Muslim woman. The prize recognizes her lifetime of championing human rights and democracy. I strongly support the Iranian people's aspirations for freedom and their desire for democracy. The future of Iran must be decided by the people of Iran. Americans look forward to the day when a free Iran stands as an example of tolerance, prosperity, and democracy in the Middle East and around the world.

Remarks at a Columbus Day Celebration
October 13, 2003

Thank you all. Please be seated. *Grazie,* Antonio. [*Laughter*] Thank you all for coming. I'm honored to join you in observing Columbus Day and to celebrate Columbus Day in the District named after Christopher Columbus.

The journey of the explorer from Genoa is one of the great stories of daring and discovery. And the journey of millions of immigrants from Italy is also a story of discovery and bravery, and that journey has enriched our country. That's really what we're celebrating today. America is a stronger and finer nation because of the influence of Italian Americans.

The veterans of America are better off as a result of the influence of Tony Principi, the Secretary—[*applause*]. He's really done a good job, and I'm proud of his commitment and service to our country as a Cabinet Secretary. I value his advice. I love his spirit. I'm also happy to report that, like me, he married well. [*Laughter*] And Liz is with us today, as is Captain Tony Principi, a captain in our Air Force who is celebrating his 30th birthday today. So happy birthday.

Members of my team are here. I want to thank them for coming—Roy Bernardi, who is the Assistant Secretary for Community Planning and Development at HUD, and I'm glad Alice is with you. Thanks for coming, Roy. You're doing a great job—former mayor of Syracuse, I want you to know. Pat Harrison is with us, Assistant Secretary of State for Education and Cultural Affairs. Dana Gioia, who is the Chairman of the National Endowment of Arts and is doing a great job. Thank you for coming, Dana. I appreciate it.

As you know, one of the things our Nation is doing right now is we're leading the fight against AIDS, particularly on the continent of Africa. One of the generals in the fight against AIDS is Tony Fauci from the National Institutes of Health. Thank you for coming. That would be Dr. Tony Fauci, a great man.

We've got Members of Congress with us today. First of all, the Senator from the great State of Wyoming, Mike Enzi. Thank you for coming, Senator. And Ginny Brown-Waite, from the—Congresswoman from Florida. Ginny Brown, thank you for coming, and I'm glad you brought Harvey along too. Thanks for coming, Harvey.

Stefano Stefanini, Deputy Chief of Mission from the Embassy of Italy, thank you for coming, sir. Give my best to my friend Silvio Berlusconi, who I'm close to, and I value his leadership and friendship, always such a joy to see him. So please pass on my very best.

Frank Guarini is here, who is the Chairman of the National Italian American Foundation, former Member from the great State of New Jersey. Frank, thank you for coming. Phil Piccigallo is with us, the national executive director of the Order of Sons of Italy is with us. Thank you for coming, Phil. Frank Caperino, the National President of UNICO National, is with us today. And thank you all for coming. Thanks for being here.

For nearly 70 years, our country has celebrated in honor of Columbus. And on this day, we celebrate the contributions of Italian Americans. You're among the many millions who claim Italian heritage, and you can claim that heritage with pride. And I know you do. [Laughter] I know you do.

Every aspect of our culture, whether it be art or music to law and politics, owes something to the influence of Italian Americans. You can take special pride in the deep tradition of service to this country. People of Italian descent oftentimes hear the call to serve something greater than themselves. Twenty-four Italian Americans have won the Congressional Medal of Honor. That's high service to something greater than yourself.

One of them was Marine Gunnery Sergeant John Basilone. You may have heard of this brave man. He died in the battle of Iwo Jima. He won both the Medal of Honor and the Navy Cross. It speaks to his valor and his service, but he wasn't alone. There's thousands who have sacrificed and served a country they love. Sure, they love their heritage, but most of all they love America and what America stands for.

Rocky Versace is an Italian American. He won the Medal of Honor in Vietnam because of the defiance he showed after being taken captive by the Viet Cong. I met his family last summer when I awarded him the Medal of Honor posthumously. Rocky set an example of bravery and dedication that changed the lives of his fellow soldiers but most of all honored the country he loves. He was of Italian descent, proud of his heritage, but most of all, he loved America. He loved what we stood for and was willing to sacrifice for it.

And that's what's happening today. People are willing to sacrifice for the country they love. They remember the lessons of September the 11th, 2001. And so do I. It's something we should never forget, especially the lessons of those who sacrificed, for lives lost.

Peter Ganci, you may have heard of Peter. He was the fire chief of New York City. He died at the World Trade Center when he went into the—into the destruction to save men and women. Fifty people—50 of his men were rescued before the second tower fell. The chief was in there urging them to flee for their safety. He ordered all out of the area. He refused to go. And his statement was, "I'm not leaving my men." One brave guy who embodies the best of the sons and daughters of Italy.

The faith of the Italian-American community in God is an important part of our Nation's fabric. The faith in family, the love of life, and the commitment to our country are great gifts. Italian Americans share those gifts generously. And that is why we celebrate Columbus Day.

And for the contribution the Italian Americans have made to America, I say: Thank you; we are grateful. But most of all, I ask God's blessings, not only of those of Italian descent but I ask God's blessings for all of us who are fortunate enough to live in the United States of America.

May God bless you all.

NOTE: The President spoke at 10:32 a.m. in Room 450 in the Dwight D. Eisenhower Executive Office Building. In his remarks, he referred to Elizabeth Ann Principi, wife of Secretary of Veterans Affairs Anthony J. Principi, and their son, Capt. Anthony Principi, Jr., USAF; Alice Bernardi, wife of Assistant Secretary of Housing and Urban

Development for Community Planning and Development Roy A. Bernardi; Anthony S. Fauci, Director, National Institute of Allergy and Infectious Diseases, National Institutes of Health; Harvey Waite, husband of Representative Virginia Brown-Waite; and Prime Minister Silvio Berlusconi of Italy.

Remarks Honoring the 2003 National Basketball Association Champion San Antonio Spurs
October 14, 2003

The President. Thank you all for coming. Thank you. Please be seated. Welcome. To all you San Antonio Spurs fans, we're glad you're here in the Rose Garden. I'm particularly glad the San Antonio Spurs are here today. We want to congratulate you on a fantastic championship run.

I first want to welcome my friend Peter Holt, who turned out to be a pretty darn good owner. [*Laughter*] It's more than I can say for the former Ranger ownership. [*Laughter*] But congratulations, Peter, to you and your organization. I want to thank R.C. Buford, who is the general manager, and Gregg Popovich, who is the manager of—the coach of the club. And I want to welcome the players and your wives and friends and family here. After this is over, I'd like to invite you in the Oval Office and let you see where the decisions are made that affect the peace and freedom of this world.

I want to welcome some huge San Antonio Spurs fans: Senator John Cornyn from San Antonio; Lamar Smith and Henry Bonilla as well from San Antonio. You got to know that during the playoffs, these guys were touting the Spurs. They were giving a pretty hefty line to anybody who dared bet against the Spurs, and you didn't let them down. So welcome. I'm glad you're here.

Danny Ferry is here. Where is Danny Ferry?

Audience member. He's there.

The President. Yes, there he is. He and I share an interesting relationship. As you may know, his father, Bob, won the NBA Championship ring. And so Danny and Bob Ferry are only the second father/son combination to ever win a championship ring— [*laughter*]—if you get my drift. [*Laughter*] We're members of the famous fathers club. [*Laughter*] And anyway, I want to welcome you here. You'll see where the—only the second son of a President office is in a minute. [*Laughter*]

I also—one of the things that happens when a championship team comes here, it gives me a chance to talk about the development of a culture, a winning culture inside an organization. I like to call it a culture of service, people being willing to serve something greater than themself, in this case, a team.

I was struck by Tim Duncan's comments after the sixth game when they were talking about the fantastic individual effort he had. And a reporter said, "What about that effort?" He said, "It's cool," but then immediately went on to talk about the accomplishments of his teammates, recognizing that you can't win a championship unless you're able to rely upon others and lift others up and participate with others and work hard with others. And it's a phenomenal tribute to the San Antonio Spurs that they've got such great individual players who are willing to work as a team. And it's a wonderful example for our country—it really is.

The other thing that struck me about this organization that is so powerful is that there is a culture of service when it comes to utilizing their positions as champs to make somebody else's life better. Gregg Popovich won a Point of Light for his drug—anti-drug programs in the early nineties. What a class act that must be for players to work for a coach who then takes time out of his private life to set a good example for the children of the community in which he lives and to work to rally the armies of compassion to make somebody else's life better, in this case to help a community fight off the scourge of drugs.

Or David Robinson, who is now heavily involved in education in the San Antonio community. He's not only a great husband but a great role model for others to see. I know many of you all do the same thing in your communities, that you care deeply about the lives of your fellow citizens, and I want to congratulate you. I think you're champs because you understand that serving something greater than yourself is the

road to championships. And that's what you're here to do, is to receive the accolades from our country for serving as not only great athletes but as great role models for children who look up to you.

So welcome to the Rose Garden. Congratulations on such a great, successful season. And may God continue to bless you, and may God continue to bless the United States of America. Thank you for coming.

NOTE: The President spoke at 10:56 a.m. in the Rose Garden at the White House. In his remarks, he referred to Peter Holt, chairman and chief executive officer, R.C. Buford, general manager, Gregg Popovich, head coach, Danny Ferry, director of basketball operations, Tim Duncan, center, and David Robinson, retired center, San Antonio Spurs; and Representatives Lamar Smith and Henry Bonilla of Texas.

Letter to Congressional Leaders Transmitting a Report on Iraq
October 14, 2003

Dear Mr. Speaker: (Dear Mr. President:)

Consistent with the Authorization for Use of Military Force Against Iraq Resolution of 2002 (Public Law 107–243), the Authorization for the Use of Force Against Iraq Resolution (Public Law 102–1), and in order to keep the Congress fully informed, I am providing a report prepared by my Administration. This report includes matters relating to post-liberation Iraq

under section 7 of the Iraq Liberation Act of 1998 (Public Law 105–338).

Sincerely,

GEORGE W. BUSH

NOTE: Identical letters were sent to J. Dennis Hastert, Speaker of the House of Representatives, and Richard B. Cheney, President of the Senate. This letter was released by the Office of the Press Secretary on October 15.

Remarks Following a Roundtable Discussion in Dinuba, California
October 15, 2003

Como esta? [*Applause*] Me, too. [*Laughter*] Thanks for coming. It's an honor to

be here. Fred, thank you very much for your hospitality on this beautiful day. It's been my honor to come to a place that's the embodiment of the American Dream. See, what we believe is, we believe people in this country ought to be able to work hard and dream big and realize their dreams. And the Ruiz family has done that.

It started with Grandma Rosie's pots and pans and the first batch of enchiladas. Fred was just telling me they produce 3 million burritos a day. For a man who likes burritos, I'm in heaven. [*Laughter*] I also like to thank the hospitality Louis Ruiz has shown me, the patriarch of this great family, the initial dreamer along with his son to build and create but, most importantly, to provide jobs for over 1,200 people—a chance for 1,200 people to realize their dreams. That's what America is all about. We're here to herald the greatness of America, the American spirit, the strength of our country.

I also had the honor of meeting Kim Ruiz Beck, who is the vice chairman of Ruiz Foods. I met the entire Ruiz family. They've got a big family. [*Laughter*] My only advice to the kids that were there was, "Listen to your mother. I'm listening to mine." And she's given me plenty of advice, I want you to know. [*Laughter*]

I appreciate the president of this company, John Signorino. I want to thank my friend Mel Martinez, who you've just met. Mel is the Secretary of Housing and Urban Development. He's in my Cabinet. He's got a lot to do about the housing initiative I'm going to talk about in a minute.

Mel is a fellow who was raised in Cuba. His mother and dad didn't like the idea of their son being raised in a totalitarian state where there was no freedom, where there's still no freedom. So you know what they did? When he was 15 years old they put him on an airplane to America. They found a program where a loving family would be welcoming young Mel with open arms. He fled tyranny because his parents love freedom, and now he's in the Cabinet of the President of the United States. And I'm proud of my friend.

Congressman Devin Nunes is with us today. Congressman, thank you for coming. George Radanovich as well is a Member of the United States Congress. Thank you for coming, Jorge. *Bienvenidos.*

I had the honor of driving from the airport to this facility with the mayor of Fresno, Alan Autry. He's a good man. He cares deeply about the people of Fresno. He's doing a great job. I'm proud to call him friend. I want to thank Mike Smith, who is the mayor of Dinuba.

We just had what we call a roundtable discussion—it happened to be at a square table—[*laughter*]—about homeownership, the idea of people owning a home is part of the American Dream. Farid Assemi is a homebuilder here, was here, and Cara Pierce is the director of Housing and Consumer Credit, and the Azel family were all sharing with me their stories and what they're doing to help people own a home. I want to thank them for coming.

When I landed at your airport, I met a fellow named Denny Klaseus. Denny brought some of his family with him. [*Laughter*] You know, there's a lot—the reason I bring up Denny is there's a lot of talk about our country's military might, and we're strong, and I'm going to keep us strong. And there is talk about the economy and the wealth of the country, and we'll do everything we can to make sure the economy grows. But the true strength of the country is the heart and souls of our American citizens. That's our strength. It's the thing that makes this country incredibly strong. I bring up Denny because he is what we call a soldier in the army of compassion.

Out of the First Church of the Nazarene, he has become a volunteer, see. He has heard the call, the universal call of all religions to love a neighbor just like you'd like to be loved yourself. He helps each month to organize and pick up food donations. He knows when somebody is hungry and hurts, there needs to be love to help that person. Denny sets a great example.

The Ruiz Company sets a good example by encouraging people like Denny to volunteer. My call to our fellow Americans is, love a neighbor. When you find somebody who hurts, put your arm around them. Mentor a child. Go see shut-ins. Tell somebody you love them on a daily basis. America can and will change, one heart, one soul, one conscience at a time, thanks to the soldiers in the armies of compassion. And Denny, thank you for being here.

Tomorrow I get to meet the Governor-elect. I'm looking forward to it. I'm going to share with him my optimism about the future of this country. I can't wait to talk to him about why I believe that America is on the right path, is on the path to making sure this Nation is secure and the world is more free and peaceful. We're on the right path to make sure our fellow citizens can find a job.

I'm optimistic, and I have reason to be optimistic. Our country has overcome a lot during the last couple of years. I want to remind you right quick what we have overcome, particularly as it relates to our economy.

First of all, the stock market started to decline in March of 2000. And then, just as we were going into office, the country went into a recession. That means there was negative growth. It means people were being laid off. Things weren't good in our economy. And then, just as things began to get better, the enemy hit us, on September the 11th, 2001, and that hurt us. It hurt the economy. It hurt the psyche of the American people. But we're a tough people. We're a determined people. And we began to get—it began to get right, and all of a sudden we found out that some of the leaders in corporate America forgot what it means to be a responsible citizen. They didn't tell the truth, and that hurt us. It shook the confidence. And then we had the march to war, both in Afghanistan and Iraq. All of these provided great challenges to our economy.

But we acted in Washington, DC. We passed tough laws—tough, new laws that says to the corporate criminal, "You'll be brought to justice for not telling the truth to your employee or your shareholders."

We also passed taxes. See, I believe that if somebody has more money in their pocket, that person is going to demand an additional good or a service. And when that person demands a good or a service in our marketplace, somebody will produce the good or a service. And when somebody produces that good or a service, somebody is more likely to find work. The best way to get out of a recession and to encourage job creation is to let the people keep more of their own money. And that's what we did.

I took the message to the people, and the Congress heard the message, and we passed historic tax relief. We said, "Everybody who pays taxes ought to get tax relief. If you're going to have tax relief, let's just treat everybody the same. If you pay taxes, you get tax relief. We're not going to try to pick or choose winners."

We said we want to encourage marriage in the Tax Code, not discourage marriage. So we've reduced the penalty on marriage. We understand how tough it is to raise a child in our society, and so we increased the child credit from $600 a child to $1,000 a child and put the check in the mail last summer.

We wanted to make sure that people had incentives to invest, so we reduced the tax on capital gains and dividends. And we want people, whether you're a farmer or a rancher or a small-business owner, to be able to pass your assets on from one generation to the next without the Government stepping in the way again. And so we got rid of the death tax.

But inherent in that tax—I want you all to understand that one of the things I kept in my mind the entire time that we were proposing this policy was the importance of the small-business owner in America. Most new jobs in America are created by small businesses. Most small businesses pay taxes at the individual income tax rates. And so when you hear me talking about cutting individual taxes, I want you to remember that it benefits a lot of small-business owners. If you're interested in creating jobs, you want to provide incentives for expansion to those who create jobs. And that's the small-business owner right here in the United States of America.

We also raised the expensing allowed for small businesses on purchases from $25,000 to $100,000 to encourage people to be purchasing things in our society. And it's making a difference. These policies are making a difference.

We are overcoming the challenges we have faced. Our economy is growing. Last month, we had an increase in net new jobs. The after-tax incomes of people are going up. The productivity of the American worker is strong. We've got the best workers in the world. The entrepreneurial spirit is vibrant. And low interest rates have encouraged a housing boom here in America, and that's good—that's good.

Low interest rates mean that people, for example, have got the capacity to refinance their home. And probably some of you all have done that. That's helped our economy. The Azels, who I met with today, Kelly and Dan—by the way, he's got a scratch handicap. [*Laughter*]. I told him I needed a lesson or two. He said that they were able to take their first home—they're newly wed, and the first thing they do is they buy a home, thanks to low interest rates. It's a fantastic way to start off your marriage. They then were able to refinance, which meant they could do some remodeling on their home. They paid off the loan on their car.

Low interest rates has helped the American citizens. It's helped them buy a home. It's helped them refinance if they own a home. It's put more money in circulation, which is good for job creation. Low interest rates makes it easier to buy a home. And homeownership is at near-record highs, and

that's good because we need to be an ownership society in America. We want people owning their own home. If you own your own home, you have a vital stake in the future of this country.

And even though homeownership is at near-record highs, we've got too many of our fellow citizens who happen to be minorities who don't own a home. Seventy-five percent of the Anglos in America own a home. The minority homeownership in America is below 50 percent. And it seems like to me we've got to do something about it. If it's good for America that people own a home, we want people from all walks of life owning their own home.

And so I let out a goal. I said over the next decade, we want there to be 5.5 million new minority homeowners. That's why Mel is here. He helped set the goal. He is going to help implement the Federal policy I'm about to describe to you about how to meet that goal. Last year, we did a pretty good job. There's now 809,000 new minority homeowners in America. And that's positive for the country. It's good for the economy. It's also good for the spirit of our country that more people are owning a home.

But here are some of the things that we intend to do, and we discussed today earlier. Sometimes people have trouble finding the downpayment for a home. It makes them nervous when they hear the downpayment. We need to have a downpayment fund to help people with downpayments if they qualify. The Congress—the House passed my request for $200 million a year. It's stuck in the Senate. The Senate needs to act. If they're interested in closing the minority homeownership gap, they need to act on the downpayment fund.

A lot of times, there are people—think about buying a home, and they don't like the complexity. They don't understand what it means and how to buy a home. It's obviously a big deal when somebody purchases a home, but it's confusing. People get nervous about it. And so we need more counseling and more education to make sure our fellow citizens know what it means to buy a home and can get comfortable with the idea of buying a home. And so we've doubled the amount of money available for community-based programs, faith-based programs to be able to brief their parishioners and/or their fellow citizens about the opportunities and the hope and what it takes to be able to purchase a home.

And finally, one other thing we're doing—amongst many, by the way—is simplifying the process to buy a home. A lot of people thinking about buying a home and all of a sudden they take a look at the fine print, and it kind of makes you nervous when you see a thick pile of paper with fine print. You're not exactly sure what you're buying into. So not only do we need to have counseling and education, but we've got to make sure the forms are more simple so that people know what they're doing. No, we're going to close this gap for the good of America.

I've also put out a six-point plan I want to share with you right quick that the Congress must pass in order to make sure the momentum of our economy continues. First and foremost, we've got to do a better job of controlling the high cost of health care. Small businesses need to be able to come together and form what's called associated health care plans to reduce the cost of health care. This country and this State must fight off the junk lawsuits that are making it awfully difficult for people to expand their businesses and hire people.

We need a national energy policy. If you're interested in growing the economy, people have got to make sure they've got a reliable source of energy. We need to encourage more conservation, more environmentally friendly ways of using the energy we have in hand. But one thing is for certain: For the sake of economic security and national security, we need to be less reliant on foreign sources of oil.

We need to cut out useless regulations and redtape that oftentimes come from Washington, and probably Sacramento, for that matter. We need to make sure that our trade policy, our trade policy opens up markets and creates a level playing field. I want to be selling U.S. farm products all over the world.

And finally, in order to make sure this economy continues to grow, there needs to be certainty in the Tax Code. All the tax relief I described to you goes away because of a quirk in the rules in the United States Senate. In other words, the Senate giveth on the one hand, and they taketh away with the other. In order to make sure our economy grows, all the tax relief I described needs to be made permanent by the United States Congress.

We're overcoming the challenges to our economy. And I also want you to know we're answering the great threats to our security. September the 11th, 2001, moved this country from grief to action. We made a pledge that day, and we have kept that pledge, that we will bring the guilty to justice, and we will take the fight to the enemy.

And we now see the nature of the enemy very clearly. These people are terrorists, coldblooded killers. They plot in secret. They target the innocent. They defile a great religion, and they hate everything America stands for. They're not going to be stopped by negotiations. They won't be appeased. Therapy is not going to work on them. [*Laughter*] They must be fought. They must be found, and they must be defeated. We are in a new kind of war, and it requires a new kind of strategy. We will not wait for further attacks. We will not hope for the best. We will strike our enemies before they can strike us again.

We've taken unprecedented steps to protect this homeland. We have a solemn duty to do so. Yet wars are won on the offensive, and America and our friends will stay on the offensive. We're hunting down the Al Qaida wherever they hide, whether it be from Pakistan or Iraq or the Philippines or the Horn of Africa. And we're making good progress. Nearly two-thirds of Al Qaida's known leaders have been captured or killed.

The resolve of this Nation is firm, and it is clear. No matter how long it takes, all who plot against America will face the justice of America. This administration has also sent a message that has been heard around the world: "If you harbor a terrorist, if you support a terrorist, if you feed a terrorist, you're just as guilty as the terrorists." And the Taliban in Afghanistan found out what we meant. Thanks to our great military, Afghanistan is no longer a haven for terror; America is safer from attack; and the long-suffering people of that country are now free. You need to remember, thanks to our Nation and a coalition of nations, many young girls now go to school for the first time in Afghanistan.

And we fought the war on terror in Iraq. The regime of Saddam Hussein possessed and used weapons of mass destruction. The regime of Saddam Hussein sponsored terrorist groups. The regime of Saddam Hussein inflicted terror on its own people. Nearly every nation recognized and denounced this threat for over a decade. And finally the United Nations Security Council, in Resolution 1441, demanded that Saddam Hussein disarm, prove his disarmament to the world, or face serious consequences. The choice was up to the dictator, and he chose poorly.

I acted because I was not about to leave the security of the American people in the hands of a mad man. I was not about to stand by and wait and trust in the sanity and restraint of Saddam Hussein. So we acted, in one of the swiftest and most humane military campaigns in history.

Since the liberation of Iraq, our investigators have found evidence of a clandestine network of biological laboratories, advanced design work on prohibited longer range missiles, an elaborate campaign to hide illegal programs. We've still got more

to investigate. Yet it is undeniable that Saddam Hussein was in clear violation of United Nations Security Resolution 1441, which said he must disarm, prove his disarmament, or face serious consequences. It is undeniable that Saddam Hussein was a deceiver and a danger. The United Nations Security Council was right to demand that Saddam disarm, and we were right to enforce that demand.

Who can possibly think the world would be better off with Saddam Hussein still in power? Surely not the dissidents who would be in his prisons or end up in the mass graves. Surely not the men and women who would fill Saddam's torture chambers or rape rooms. Surely not the families of victims he murdered with poison gas. Surely not anyone who cares about human rights and democracy and stability in the Middle East. There's only one decent and humane reaction to the fall of Saddam Hussein: Good riddance!

Our country now is approaching a choice. After all the action we have taken, after all the progress we have made against terror, there is a temptation to think the danger has passed. The danger hadn't passed. Since September the 11th, 2001, the terrorists have taken lives in Casablanca, Mombasa, Jerusalem, Amman, Riyadh, Baghdad, Karachi, New Delhi, Bali, Jakarta. Today an American died as a result of a terrorist attack in Gaza. No, they continue to plot. They continue to plan against our country and our people. America must not forget the lessons of September the 11th.

America cannot retreat from our responsibilities and hope for the best. Our security will not be gained by timid measures. Our security requires constant vigilance and decisive action. I believe America has only one option: We must, and we will, fight the war on terror until our work is done.

We're fighting on many fronts, and Iraq is now the central front. Saddam holdouts and foreign terrorists are desperately trying to undermine Iraq's progress. See, they hate freedom. They can't stand the thought of a peaceful and hopeful society. They want to throw the country into chaos. The terrorists believe their attacks on innocent people will weaken our resolve. They don't understand our country. See, they believe we'll run from a challenge. This country will not be intimidated by a group of cold-blooded killers. This country will stay the course.

We're making good progress in Iraq. We're after the killers. We've got better intelligence now. The Iraqi citizens are coming forward to help us secure their own country. We've got great strike teams of brave soldiers who are moving on a moment's notice to bring people to justice. And at the same time, we're making the country more secure. We're opening up hospitals and schools and roads. We're bringing electricity to the people who suffered under the hands of a tyrant, who spent his money on weapons and palaces and not on the people. Slowly but surely, this country is emerging as a peaceful and democratic and hopeful place. And that's in our national interest. A peaceful and hopeful Iraq will make America more secure, because there will be freedom in the heart of a part of the world that needs freedom. Free countries don't attack their neighbors. Free countries are peaceful countries.

But we also believe something else about freedom and liberty. We don't believe that freedom is America's gift to the world. We believe freedom is the God Almighty's gift to each and every person in the world.

No, we're making progress, and we'll do the job the right way. We'll make sure that Iraq has got a constitution and free elections. We'll make sure the job gets done the right way, so that the Iraqi people will show the Middle East and the world that liberty is the hope and the right of every land. The work in Iraq and the work on the war against terror has been tough, and it's been hard, but we're doing our duty to future generations of Americans. We're doing our duty to make sure that we spread freedom and peace and, at the same time, make America more secure.

This country has overcome a lot. We've overcome attacks and recessions and corporate scandals. We've overcome tyrants, people who have harbored terrorists. But there's no doubt in my mind that because of who we are and who we—what we stand for, this Nation can not only overcome challenges, but we'll do our duty to make sure America is as hopeful and secure for every person who is fortunate enough to live in this land.

May God bless you all, and may God continue to bless America.

Thank you all very much.

NOTE: The President spoke at 11:30 a.m. at the Ruiz Foods plant. In his remarks, he referred to Fred Ruiz, cofounder and chairman, Kim Ruiz Beck, vice chairman, and John Signorino, president, Ruiz Foods, Inc.; Fred Ruiz' parents, Rosie and Louis; Governor-elect Arnold Schwarzenegger of California; and former President Saddam Hussein of Iraq.

Remarks at a Bush-Cheney Reception in Fresno, California
October 15, 2003

Thanks for the warm welcome. It's great to be back in California. It's great to be back in Fresno. I was trying to figure out, since I've been running for President, this is either my third or fourth time here. And every time I come, I'm better off for it. [*Laughter*] It kind of reminds me of where

I was raised—good people, except you've got water and trees. [*Laughter*]

I know there's been some interesting changes here in the State of California. [*Laughter*] And tomorrow I have the honor of congratulating the Governor-elect in Riverside. And today I want to thank you all for your contributions and for your support. See, what we're doing is, we're laying the groundwork for what is going to be a great national victory in 2004.

I want you to know that your contributions are important, but so is your grassroots support. And by that I mean, when you go to the coffee shop—and I know there's a lot of farmers here who go to the coffee shops—[*laughter*]—tell everybody, or when you go to your community centers or your places of worship, you tell them that this administration is dedicating its efforts to making sure our country is hopeful for every citizen, that our message is optimistic, because we believe in the future of this country. That's what I'm counting on you to do.

And I'll do my part, but the political season is going to come in its own time. I'm warming up, and I'm getting ready, but I've got a job to do. I've got a job to do for our country, and there's a lot on the agenda. And I'm going to continue to work hard to earn the confidence of every American, regardless of their political party or where they're from, by keeping this Nation strong and secure and prosperous and free.

I bring greetings from First Lady Laura Bush. She is—[*applause*]—you got the B team. [*Laughter*] She has been in the Dominican Republic recently, meeting with the First Ladies of the different countries in our hemisphere. I'll be meeting her tomorrow in Riverside as we take off to Tokyo, and I'll be getting some advice from her about diplomacy. [*Laughter*] You may remember the picture of her trip to France. [*Laughter*] I went to France. [*Laughter*] And they were kind to me, but they—I wasn't treated that way by Jacques Chirac. [*Laughter*] But she is great. I am a lucky man that she agreed to marry me, and she's a fabulous First Lady.

I appreciate my friend Brad Freeman, who is the State finance chairman. I appreciate my friend Mercer Reynolds from Cincinnati, Ohio, who is the national finance chairman. These are two very capable, able business people who are taking time out of their lives to make sure this campaign is well funded.

I want to thank Members of the Congress who are here. George Radanovich is with us today. He is a good friend and a fine Congressman, as is Devin Nunes, and I appreciate Devin being here as well.

I had the honor of traveling from the airport out to Ruiz Foods, by the way, which was a fantastic experience, going out there. I love the story of America. I love the fact that people started with nothing and have built a fantastic food processing business. The Ruizes are here with us today. They were great hosts. They now process 3 million burritos a day. Are you having burritos for lunch?

But on the way out to the facility, Alan Autry was traveling with me, the great mayor of Fresno, California. And I appreciate him being here today, and I thank him for his friendship. Chuck Poochigian is here, the State senator, who's been a longtime friend of mine. And it's great to see his wife, Debbie. Bob Waterston is the supervisor of the Fresno County Board of Supervisors—all politics is local politics, and thank you for coming, Bob. My friend Bill Jones is here. He's a Fresno lad who has made a name for himself here in the great State of California. It's great to see you again, Bill. Thank you for coming.

Gerry Parsky is with us today; he's the State campaign chairman. Rosario Marin is with us today, the former Treasurer of the State—of the country. I want to thank all the cohosts for working so hard to make this event a recordbreaking event.

I appreciate Lance Corporal Nolan Cochran, who gave the Pledge of Allegiance. He's a brave young guy. He served his country with distinction. I had the honor of meeting him at the Bethesda Naval Hospital as he came back from the battlefields. And I was pleased to see his mom and dad. I'm glad to know his spirits are high and that he understands that he was making our country more secure in his sacrifice.

And finally, I want to thank JoAnna Dias, who sang the national anthem.

In the last 2½ years, our Nation has acted decisively to confront great challenges. I came to this office to solve problems, not to pass them on to future Presidents and future generations. I came to seize opportunities and not let them slip away. This administration is meeting the tests of our time.

Terrorists declared war on the United States of America, and war is what they got. We've captured or killed many of the key leaders of the Al Qaida network, and the rest of them know that we're on their trail. In Afghanistan and Iraq, we gave ultimatums to terror regimes. Those regimes chose defiance, and those regimes are no more. Fifty million people in those two countries once lived under tyranny, and now they live in freedom.

Two-and-a-half years ago, our military was not receiving the resources it needed, and morale was beginning to suffer. And so we increased the defense budgets to prepare for the threats of a new era. And today, no one in the world can question the skill and the strength and the spirit of the United States military.

Two-and-a-half years ago, we inherited an economy in recession. And then the attacks came on our country, and we had a march to war to defend ourselves, and we had scandals in corporate America, all of which affected the people's confidence. But this administration acted. We passed two tough new laws to hold corporate criminals to account. And to get the economy going again, I have twice led the United States Congress to pass historic tax relief for the American people.

Here's what I know. I know that when people have more take-home pay, more money in their pocket to save or to spend or invest, the whole economy will grow and someone is more likely to find a job. I also know this: I understand whose money we spend in Washington. We don't spend the people's money—I mean, we don't spend the Government's money; we spend the people's money. [Laughter] So we're returning more money to families. We've increased the child credit. And we said, "The check was in the mail," and it was in the mail. We reduced the taxes on dividends and capital gains to encourage investment. We gave small businesses incentives to expand and to hire new people.

With all these actions, by the fact—because we led, we are laying the foundation for greater prosperity and more jobs so that every single person in this country has a chance to realize the American Dream.

Two-and-a-half years ago, there was a lot of talk about education reform, but there wasn't much action. So I acted. I called for and the Congress passed the No Child Left Behind Act. With a solid bipartisan majority, we delivered the most dramatic education reforms in a generation. We insisted on high standards for every public school because we believe every child can learn.

Because we believe every child can learn, we're now saying that in return for Federal money, you must measure to determine whether every child is learning. We're challenging the soft bigotry of low expectations. We believe every child can learn the basics of reading and math. And we expect every public school in America to teach reading and math so that not one single child is left behind.

We reorganized our Government, the largest reorganization of any time in our Government's history since the Defense Department was reorganized. We created the Department of Homeland Security to better safeguard America.

We passed trade promotion authority to open up new markets for California farmers and ranchers and entrepreneurs. Listen, I understand free trade, and the cornerstone of free trade is not only for us to open up our markets but to make sure the playing field is level. We're really good at growing things in California. I want California farmers selling their crops overseas.

We passed budget agreements in Washington that is helping to maintain spending discipline. On issue after issue, this administration has acted on principle; we have kept our word; and we have made progress for the American people.

The Congress deserves credit. We've got a great Speaker in Denny Hastert and a great majority leader in Bill Frist. I appreciate the Congressmen who are here with us today. See, we're working to change the tone in Washington. There's too much politics in the Nation's Capital, too much zero-sum activity. And the best way to do that is to focus on the people's business and to focus on results. And those are the kind of people I've attracted to my administration. I think you can judge a President by the kind of people that he brings to Washington to serve the people, and I have put together a great team to serve the American people. We've had no finer Vice President than Dick Cheney. Mother may have a second opinion. [*Laughter*]

In 2½ years—in 2½ years—we have done a lot, and we have come far, but our work is only beginning. I have great goals worthy of a great nation.

First, America is committed to expanding the realm of freedom and peace for our own security and for the benefit of the world. And second, in our own country we must work for a society of prosperity and compassion, so that every citizen has a chance to work and succeed and to realize the promise of our country. It is clear that the future of freedom and peace depend on the actions of America. This Nation is

freedom's home and freedom's defender. We welcome this charge of history, and we are keeping it.

Our war on terror continues. The enemies of freedom are not idle, and neither are we. This country will not rest. We will not tire. We will not stop until this danger to civilization is removed. And we are confronting that danger in Iraq, where Saddam holdouts and foreign terrorists are desperately trying to throw Iraq into chaos by attacking coalition forces, by attacking international aid workers, and by killing innocent Iraqis. They know that the advance of freedom will be a major defeat in the cause of terror.

This collection of killers is trying to shake the will of the United States. They're trying to frighten us. They do not understand our country. We will not be frightened. We will stay on the offensive. We're aggressively striking the terrorists in Iraq, defeating them there so we will not have to face them in our own country.

We're calling other nations to help Iraq to build a free country. A free and peaceful Iraq will make the world more secure. And we'll stand with the Iraqi people, the long-suffering Iraqi people—they are people who put up with torture chambers and rape rooms and mass graves. We will help them assume more of their own defense and move as rapidly as possible toward self-government. These tasks are not easy, but they are essential tasks. And we will finish what we have begun. We will win this essential victory in the war on terror.

But I understand this: Our greatest security comes from the advance of human liberty, because free nations do not support terror. Free nations do not attack their neighbors. Free nations do not threaten the world with weapons of mass terror. Americans believe that freedom is the deepest need and hope of every human heart. And I believe that freedom is the right of every person. And I believe that freedom is the future of every nation.

America also understands that unprecedented influence brings tremendous responsibilities. We have duties in this world, and when we see disease and starvation and hopeless poverty, we will not turn away. On the continent of Africa, this great Nation, this strong Nation, is committed to bringing the healing power, the healing power of medicine to millions of men and women and children now suffering with AIDS. I am incredibly proud of the fact that this great land is leading the world in the important work of human rescue.

We've got challenges here at home, and our actions will prove equal to those challenges. So long as somebody in our economy—in our country is looking for a job, I will continue to try to create the conditions for job growth, to foster the entrepreneurial spirit, to make it easier for the small businesses who hire most new workers to be able to grow and to expand. I want everybody in this country finding a job.

And we have a duty to keep our commitment to our seniors by strengthening and modernizing Medicare. A few weeks ago, the Congress finally passed some Medicare reform. The House passed a version, and the Senate passed a version. For the first time since the creation of Medicare, both Houses have passed reforms to increase the choices for seniors and to provide a much needed prescription drug benefit. It is time for both bodies to reconcile their differences and to do their duty, not only for today's seniors but for those of us who will be seniors, to modernize the Medicare system.

For the sake of our health care system, we need to cut down on the frivolous lawsuits which increase the cost of medicine. People who have been harmed by a bad doc deserve their day in court. Yet, the system should not reward lawyers who are simply fishing for a rich settlement. Frivolous lawsuits drive up the cost of health care and, therefore, affect the Federal budget: Medicare goes up; Medicaid goes up; veteran health care costs go up because of the frivolous lawsuits. Medical liability reform is a national issue which requires a national solution.

And so I proposed a good, strong piece of legislation. The House passed it. It is stuck in the Senate. The Senate must act on behalf of the American people, and they must hear loud and clear that no one has ever been healed by a frivolous lawsuit.

I have a responsibility as President to make sure the judicial system runs well, and I have met that duty. I have nominated superb men and women for the Federal courts, people who will interpret the law, not legislate from the bench. Some Members of the Senate are trying to keep my nominees off the bench by blocking up-or-down votes. Every judicial nominee deserves a fair hearing and an up-or-down vote on the Senate floor. It is time for some of the Members of the United States Senate to stop playing politics with American justice.

Congress needs to complete work on a comprehensive energy plan. This Nation must promote energy efficiency and conservation and develop cleaner technology to help us explore for energy in environmentally sensitive ways. But for the sake of economic security and for the sake of national security, we need to be less dependent on foreign sources of energy.

Our strong and prosperous Nation must also be a compassionate nation. I will continue to advance our agenda of compassionate conservatism by applying the best and most innovative ideas to the task of helping our fellow citizens in need. There are still millions of men and women who want to end their dependence on the Government and become independent through hard work. We must build on the successes of the welfare reform to bring work and dignity into the lives of more of our fellow citizens. Congress should complete the "Citizen Service Act" so more Americans can serve their communities and their country.

And both Houses should reach agreement on my Faith-Based Initiative, so we can support the armies of compassion that are mentoring children, that are caring for the homeless and offering hope to the addicted. Our Government must not fear the influence of faith in our communities. We must welcome faith programs to help solve the intractable problems of our society.

A compassionate society promotes opportunity for all, including the independence and dignity that come from ownership. This administration will constantly strive to promote an ownership society in America. We want more people owning their homes. Today I discussed the minority homeownership gap. I described a plan that we put before Congress to close that gap. We want more people to own and manage their own health care plans. We want people to own and manage their own retirement accounts. We want more people owning their own small business in America, because we understand that when a person owns something, he or she will have a vital stake in the future of this country.

In a compassionate society, people respect one another, and they take responsibility for the decisions they make. We're changing the culture of this country from one that has said, "If it feels good, do it," and "If you've got a problem, blame somebody else," to one in which each of us understands that we are responsible for the decisions we make. If you are fortunate enough to be a mother or father, you're responsible for loving your child with all your heart. If you're concerned about the quality of the education in the community in which you live, you're responsible for doing something about it. If you're a CEO in America, you have a responsibility to tell the truth to your shareholders and your employees. And in this new responsibility society, each of us is responsible for loving our neighbor just like we'd like to be loved ourselves.

We see the culture of service and responsibility growing around us. Right after September the 11th, I started the USA Freedom Corps to encourage Americans to extend a compassionate hand to a neighbor in need, and the response has been strong. Our charities are strong. Our faith-based organizations are vibrant. Police and firefighters and people who wear our Nation's uniform are reminding us what it means to sacrifice for something greater than yourself. Once again, the children of America believe in heroes, because they see them every day.

In these challenging times, the world has seen the resolve and the courage of America. And I have been privileged to see the compassion and the character of the American people. All the tests of the last 2½ years have come to the right nation. We're a strong country, and we use that strength to defend the peace. We're an optimistic country, confident in ourselves and in ideals bigger than ourselves. Abroad, we seek to lift whole nations by spreading freedom. At home, we seek to lift up lives by spreading opportunity to every corner of America. This is the work that history has set before us. We welcome it. And we know that for our country and for our cause, the best days lie ahead.

Thank you for coming. God bless. Thank you all.

NOTE: The President spoke at 1:09 p.m. in Exhibit Hall South at the Fresno Convention Center. In his remarks, he referred to Governor-elect Arnold Schwarzenegger of California; President Jacques Chirac of France; Brad Freeman, California State finance chairman, and Mercer Reynolds, national finance chairman, Bush-Cheney '04, Inc.; Bill Jones, former California secretary of state; Gerald L. Parsky, chairman, Team California, California Republican Party Board of Directors; former U.S. Treasurer Rosario Marin; and former President Saddam Hussein of Iraq.

Statement on Japan's Announcement of Reconstruction Aid to Iraq
October 15, 2003

I welcome Japan's announcement that it will provide $1.5 billion toward immediate reconstruction needs in Iraq. I applaud this bold step, which will help mobilize international support for efforts to build a stable, peaceful, and democratic Iraq. Japan recognizes that this effort is critical to security and peace not only in Iraq and the Middle East but also for Japan and throughout the world. Japan's own history shows the power of international coopera-

tion to help a great people build democracy and prosperity and become a beacon of freedom that inspires all nations.

I also commend Japan's announcement that it is working on a larger aid package in preparation for the October 23–24 Madrid Donor's Conference. We look forward to working with Japan and other countries to make the Madrid Conference a success for the people of Iraq.

Statement on the Terrorist Attack on Americans in the Gaza Strip
October 15, 2003

I condemn in the strongest terms the vicious act of terrorism directed against Americans in Gaza today. We are working closely with the appropriate officials to bring the terrorists to justice.

Palestinian authorities should have acted long ago to fight terror in all its forms. The failure to create effective Palestinian security forces dedicated to fighting terror continues to cost lives. There must be an empowered Prime Minister who controls all Palestinian security forces, reforms that continue to be blocked by Yasser Arafat. The failure to undertake these reforms and dismantle the terrorist organizations constitutes the greatest obstacle to achieving the Palestinian people's dream of statehood.

The Americans who were attacked today were pursuing a vision for a better future for the Palestinian people. The U.S. Embassy officials traveling in Gaza were there to interview young Palestinian candidates seeking Fulbright scholarships to study in the United States. This is another example of how the terrorists are enemies of progress and opportunity for the Palestinian people.

On behalf of the American people, I send my heartfelt condolences to the families of the brave Americans who were killed and injured serving our country and its ideals.

Remarks at a Bush-Cheney Reception in Riverside, California
October 15, 2003

Thanks for the warm welcome. It's nice to be back in Riverside, California. I appreciate your hospitality. I appreciate your

friendship, and thank you for your strong support. I'm proud to have it.

I understand there's been a couple of changes here in California since I was last time here. And tomorrow at the Mission Inn, I have the opportunity to congratulate the Governor-elect of the great State of California, and I'm looking forward to it.

I'll tell you what we're doing here tonight. We're laying the foundation for what is going to be a great national victory in 2004. And I appreciate you being on the team and want to tell you that I'm going to continue to count on your support when you go to your houses of worship or your community centers or your coffee shops, and you tell the people who haven't made up their mind yet that this administration will continue to work for what's right and best for every single American.

The political season is going to come in its own time. I am kind of loosening up—[*laughter*]—and getting ready. But I've got a job to do. I'm focused on the people's business, and there's a lot on the agenda in Washington, DC. I will continue to work hard to earn the confidence of all Americans by keeping this Nation strong and secure and prosperous and free.

My one regret is that Laura isn't with me tonight. That's your regret too, I know. [*Laughter*] You kind of got the short straw. [*Laughter*] She was in the Dominican Republic today and is flying out. Tomorrow we'll meet at March Air Force Base, and then we're on a very exciting journey to Asia. I'm proud that she's going to be on my side. I'm going to get a few pointers from her about diplomacy. [*Laughter*] You might remember that she recently took a trip to France. [*Laughter*] You probably saw the picture of her visit there. [*Laughter*] I went to France. [*Laughter*] The people were nice to me, but I certainly wasn't treated that well by Jacques Chirac. [*Laughter*] Laura is great. I'm really lucky that she's my wife. She's a great First Lady for our country.

I appreciate very much two Members of the United States Congress coming today. I know they flew out for this event. They're leaving in the morning for votes tomorrow, and that's Congressman Ken Calvert from

this district—I appreciate you, Ken—and Congresswoman Mary Bono from the great State of California. Thank you, Mary.

I want to thank my friend Jim Brulte for being here today. I told him if he gets any skinnier, he's going to end up in a Subway ad. [*Laughter*] But I appreciate his leadership. He's a great minority leader of the State senate, the cochairman of this event. I also thank State Senator Dennis Hollingsworth who is here. I appreciate you coming, Senator. Jim Battin is here, another State senator. I appreciate you coming, Jim. Thank you. Ray Haynes, another State senator, is here. Pretty soon we're going to get the whole State senate here. [*Laughter*] Bonnie Garcia is a State assemblywoman. Russ Bogh is here with us. Thank you, Russ, for coming. I'm honored you're here. Bob Dutton, John Benoit, members of the statehouse. I want to thank all the local officials who are here, the supervisors and the mayors and—so honored you all are here. I appreciate the folks who have worked so hard to make this such a successful event.

I particularly want to thank my friend Brad Freeman and Gerry Parsky—my friends Brad Freeman and Gerry Parsky, who have been the leaders in this State for my campaign. As well I want to thank my friend Mercer Reynolds from Cincinnati, Ohio, who is the Bush-Cheney national finance chairman. He's taken a lot of time out of his life to make sure this campaign of ours is well-funded. It seems like he's doing a pretty darn good job.

But most of all, thanks to you all again for being here.

You know, in the last 2½ years, our Nation has acted decisively to confront great challenges. I came to this office to solve problems, not to pass them on to future Presidents and future generations. I came to seize opportunities instead of letting them slip away. This administration is meeting the tests of our time.

Terrorists declared war on the United States of America, and war is what they got. We have captured or killed many key leaders of the Al Qaida network, and the rest of them know we're on their trail. In Afghanistan and in Iraq, we gave ultimatums to terror regimes. Those regimes chose defiance, and those regimes are no more. Fifty million people in those two countries once lived under tyranny, and today they live in freedom.

Two-and-a-half years ago, our military was not receiving the resources it needed, and morale was beginning to suffer. And so we increased the defense budget to prepare for the threats of a new era. And today, no one in the world can question the skill and the strength and the spirit of the United States military.

Two-and-a-half years ago, we inherited an economy in recession. And then our country was attacked, and we had scandals in corporate America, and our Nation marched to war, all of which affected the people's confidence. But we acted. We passed tough new laws to hold corporate criminals to account. And to get the economy going again, I have twice led the United States Congress to pass historic tax relief for the American people.

Here is what we believe and what I know, that when Americans have more take-home pay to spend, to save, or invest, the whole economy grows, and people are more likely to find a job. We also know whose money we spend in Washington. It is not the Government's money; it is the people's money.

With all these actions, we are laying the foundation for greater prosperity and more jobs across our country, so that every single person in America has a chance to realize the American Dream. We're returning more money to people. We're helping them raise their families. We've reduced capital gains taxes and dividends. We're helping small businesses. When I hear that someone is looking for a job who wants to work and can't find that job, we will continue to work to create an environment that is

strong for the entrepreneur. We want the people of America working.

Two-and-a-half years ago, there was a lot of talk about education reform, but there wasn't much action. So I acted. I called for and the Congress passed the No Child Left Behind Act. With a solid bipartisan majority, we delivered the most dramatic education reforms in a generation. See, we're bringing high standards to public schools all across America. And we're going to have strong accountability measures to make sure that those standards are met. In return for Federal money, we're now saying to the public schools, "Show us whether our children can read and write and add and subtract. We believe they can. You show us if you're teaching them how to do so." You see, we're challenging the soft bigotry of low expectations. We believe every child can learn. We expect every school to teach so that not one single child is left behind.

We reorganized the Government and created the Department of Homeland Security to better safeguard our borders and better safeguard the American people. We passed trade promotion authority to open up markets for California's farmers and ranchers and entrepreneurs. We passed budget agreements that is helping to maintain much needed spending discipline in Washington, DC. On issue after issue, this administration has acted on principle. We have kept our word, and we have made progress for the American people.

And the Congress deserves a lot of credit for the success we've had. It's a great pleasure to work with Speaker Denny Hastert and majority leader Bill Frist. We're working hard to try to change the tone in Washington, DC, by focusing on results, not politics. We want to do what's right for the American people. By the way, those are the kind of people I've called to service in my administration. I have put together a superb team of Americans from all walks of life to serve in the administration. Our Nation has had no finer Vice President than

Dick Cheney. Mother may have a second opinion. [*Laughter*]

In 2½ years, we have done a lot. We have come far, but our work is only beginning. I have set great goals worthy of a great nation. First, America is committed to expanding the realm of freedom and peace for our own security and for the benefit of the world. And second, in our country, we must work for a society of prosperity and compassion, so that every citizen has a chance to work and succeed and realize the great promise of our country.

It is clear that the future of freedom and peace depend on the actions of America. This Nation is freedom's home and freedom's defender. We welcome this charge of history, and we are keeping it. Our war on terror continues. The enemies of freedom are not idle, and neither are we. This country will not rest; we will not tire; and we will not stop until this danger to civilization is removed.

We are confronting that danger in Iraq, where Saddam holdouts and foreign terrorists are desperately trying to throw Iraq into chaos by attacking coalition forces and aid workers and innocent Iraqis. They know that the advance of freedom in Iraq will be a major defeat for the cause of terror. This collection of killers is trying to shake the will of the United States of America. We will not be intimidated.

We are aggressively striking at terrorists in Iraq, defeating them there so we will not have to face them in our own cities. We're calling other nations to help Iraq to build a free country, which will make all of us more secure. And we're standing with the Iraqi people as they assume more of their own defense and move toward self-government. These aren't easy tasks, but they are essential tasks. We will finish what we have begun, and we will win this essential victory in the war on terror.

Our greatest security comes from the advance of human liberty, because free nations do not support terror. Free nations do not attack their neighbors. Free nations do not threaten the world with weapons of mass terror. Americans believe that freedom is the deepest need and hope of every heart. And I believe that freedom is the right of every person. And I believe that freedom is the future of every nation.

America also understands that unprecedented influence brings tremendous responsibilities. We have duties in this world, and when we see disease and starvation and hopeless poverty, we will not turn away. On the continent of Africa, America is now committed to bringing the healing power of medicine to millions of men and women and children suffering with AIDS. This great Nation is taking the lead. We're leading the world in this incredibly important work of human rescue.

We face challenges here at home as well. I talked about our need to make sure we continue to create the conditions for economic growth and vitality, so people can find work. As well we have a duty to keep our commitment to America's seniors by strengthening and modernizing Medicare. Congress took historic action. For the first time since the creation of Medicare, the House and the Senate passed reforms to increase choices for our seniors and to provide coverage of prescription drugs. The next step is for both Houses to iron out their differences and to get the bill to my desk. The sooner that Congress finishes the job, the sooner American seniors will get the health care they deserve.

And for the sake of our health care system, we need to cut down on the frivolous lawsuits which increase the cost of medicine. People who have been harmed by a bad doc deserve their day in court. Yet the system should not reward lawyers who are simply fishing for a rich settlement. Because frivolous lawsuits drive up the cost of health care, they affect the Federal budget. Medical liability reform is a national issue which requires a national solution. The House of Representatives passed a good bill to reform the system. The bill is stuck in the Senate. The Senate must act, and those Senators holding up the bill must understand that no one has ever been healed by a frivolous lawsuit in America.

I have a duty as President to make sure the judicial system runs well, and I have met that duty. I have nominated superb men and women for our Federal courts, people who will interpret the law, not legislate from the bench. Some Members of the Senate are trying to keep my nominees off the bench by blocking up-or-down votes. Every judicial nominee deserves a fair hearing and an up-or-down vote on the floor of the Senate. It is time for some Members of the United States Senate to stop playing politics with American justice.

This country needs a comprehensive energy plan, and the Congress needs to act. This Nation must promote energy efficiency and conservation. We must use technologies to help us find energy in an environmentally sensitive way. But for the sake of economic security and for the sake of national security, we must become less dependent on foreign sources of energy.

A strong and prosperous nation must also be a compassionate nation. I will continue to advance our agenda of compassionate conservatism by applying the best and most innovative ideas to the task of helping our fellow citizens in need. Congress should complete the "Citizen Service Act," so more Americans can serve their communities and their countries.

Both Houses should reach agreement on the Faith-Based Initiative to support the armies of compassion that are mentoring children and caring for the homeless and offering hope to the addicted. This Nation is a great nation because we believe in worshiping freely. This Nation should not fear faith and providing the compassionate help to people who hurt. We should welcome help from the Christian community and the Jewish community and the Muslim community, the Hindu community, to help people find help they need. Love comes from houses of worship. This Government ought to welcome the Faith-Based Initiative.

A compassionate society must promote opportunity for all, including the independence and dignity that come from ownership. This administration will constantly strive to promote an ownership society in America. We want more people to own their homes. We have a minority home-ownership gap in America, and today in Fresno, I discussed ways to narrow that gap.

We want people to own and manage their own health care plan. We want more people to own and manage their own retirement accounts. We want more people to own their own small business. You see, this administration understands that when a person owns something, he or she has a vital stake in the future of our country.

In a compassionate society, people respect one another and take responsibility for the decisions they make. We're changing the culture of America from one that has said, "If it feels good, just go ahead and do it," and "If you've got a problem, blame somebody else," to a culture in which each of us understands we're responsible for the decisions we make in life.

If you are fortunate enough to be a mom or a dad, you're responsible for loving your child with all your heart. If you're worried about the quality of education in the community in which you live, you're responsible for doing something about it. If you're a CEO in corporate America, you're responsible for telling the truth to your employees and your shareholders. And in the new responsibility society, each of us is responsible for loving our neighbor just like we'd like to be loved ourselves.

We see the culture of service and responsibility growing around us here in our country. I started what we call the USA Freedom Corps to encourage Americans to extend a compassionate hand to a neighbor in need, and the response has been strong, just like the response has been strong for charities all across our country and just like the response has been strong in our faith-based institutions. Policemen and firefighters and people who wear our Nation's uniform are reminding us what it means to sacrifice for something greater than yourself. Once again, the children of America believe in heroes, because they see them every day.

In these challenging times, the world has seen the resolve and the courage of America. And I have been privileged to see the compassion and the character of the American people. All the tests of the last 2½ years have come to the right nation. We're a strong country, and we use that strength to defend the peace. We're an optimistic country, confident in ourselves and in ideals bigger than ourselves.

Abroad, we seek to lift whole nations by spreading freedom. At home, we seek to lift up lives by spreading opportunity to every corner of America. This is the work that history has set before us. We welcome it. And we know that for our country and for our cause, the best days lie ahead.

May God bless you all. Thank you very much.

NOTE: The President spoke at 6:05 p.m. at the Riverside Convention Center. In his remarks, he referred to Governor-elect Arnold Schwarzenegger of California; President Jacques Chirac of France; Ray Haynes and Russ Bogh, California State assemblymen; Brad Freeman, California State finance chairman, Bush-Cheney '04, Inc.; Gerald L. Parsky, chairman, Team California, California Republican Party Board of Directors; and former President Saddam Hussein of Iraq.

Interview With Asian Print Journalists
October 14, 2003

The President. I'll make an opening statement. We'll go around and see how many times we can make it around.

First, I'm really looking forward to this trip. It is a long trip, and it is an important trip. It is a chance for me to say thanks to a lot of nations for cooperating with America, for being friends with America, for working with America to achieve common objectives. It's a chance to strengthen alliances, longstanding alliances. Alliances are important, an important part of our foreign policy. Together we can accomplish a lot of important objectives—no more important objective than continuing to fight terror.

It's going to be an important part of my discussions with each leader, to renew our efforts to find those who would kill innocent people and bring them to justice, disrupt cells, cut off financing, prevent the catastrophes that have taken place, that have taken innocent life, from happening again. That's really our call. And I go with a strong determination to continue to work with the leaders and to fight terror. And it's very important for them to look at me and listen to me, because my determination is just as strong today as it was on September the 12th, 2001.

Secondly, I'm looking forward to talking about economic matters. I will tell our friends that things are looking up for the U.S. economy but that there's more work to be done. And one of the key components of economic growth in America and job creation here, as well as job creation with our friends, is a trade policy that opens markets and at the same time recognizes that what we call a level playing field is prevalent, that trade must be free and it must, at the same time, be a fair policy, that people on both sides of any trade equation ought to be treated fairly.

I'll bring up the WTO, of course. It's a missed opportunity. I'll talk about free trade agreements with friends. We've just completed one with Singapore. There will be other trade agreements that we'll discuss. But a key component of—a key part of this trip is going to be the discussion about mutually beneficial economic policy.

And finally, an important part of the trip is for me to talk about the values of freedom and democracy and to herald the moderate Islamic movements in certain countries as their being a very important part of a hopeful society, that those movements are willing to participate in the democratic traditions of their respective countries. And one of the things that we stand for in this country is democracy, and I will remind people about those values. It's those shared values with some of our friends that have caused us to take very decisive action in the world, not only for world security but for freedom. It's an important shared value, and I look forward to speaking to the legislative bodies, the parliaments, and express my deep appreciation as well as our mutual shared goals of freedom and peace and opportunity.

So listen, thanks for coming. I'll be glad to answer some questions. We'll start with Paul John.

Australia-U.S. Relations

Q. Looking at the alliance between Australia and the United States, Mr. President, how important is Australia to America as an ally? And given the war on terrorism, do you think that this alliance, that this relationship is likely to become more important in the future?

The President. I would put—I would say that the alliance between America and Australia is a critical alliance. And the reason I say so is that Australia has got a keen understanding of the relationship between good, strong, decisive action and security and a relationship between freedom and peace.

And it's a very important connection and very important mutual understanding that helps us—"us" being all of us—take the action necessary to make the world more peaceful. So I call it a critical alliance.

I found that John Howard was a visionary person, who was able to see kind of beyond the immediate noise inherent in a democracy, and could see the future and realize that sometimes difficult decisions will yield short-term issues but long-term success. And I appreciate that vision. And it says to me that many in Australia share that as well. He's got good standing with the people. And therefore, when I go to Australia, I'll be speaking to a country which does understand the consequences of sacrificing for something greater than themselves.

And yes, the alliance in this relationship is going to be critical in the future because the war on terror goes on. See, John Howard understands that. And it's important to have friends and allies who understand that the war on terror is a long-term issue that requires decisive action and close cooperation. And so I go to Australia with a great deal of gratitude and respect. I look forward to speaking at the Parliament. I look forward, of course, having—breaking bread with my friend. He's a good guy. He's a very strong leader.

Australia's Role in the War on Terror

Q. Of course, we've just commemorated the 12-month anniversary of the Bali bombing.

The President. Yes.

Q. How concerned are you about terrorism in Southeast Asia, about the links that have been established there? And what role do you think that Australia should be playing in this? To what extent do you see a leadership role for Australia in combating regional terrorism?

The President. Well, there's no question that Southeast Asia has seen its share of violence from terrorist activities. That's why one of the key agenda items on my trip is to discuss terror and to remind people that we're dealing with coldblooded killers, people who just take innocent life in order to create and instill a sense of fear. They want people to be afraid, and they want governments to take action.

The great thing about the Australians is they're not afraid. Howard knows that— Prime Minister Howard knows that one of the tactics of the terrorists is to create the conditions so that people say, "Well, let's withdraw and let them have their way." And therefore, the relationship in Southeast Asia is an important relationship because— starting first and foremost with the strength of John Howard and the Australian people. The Australians know firsthand what it means to be attacked without impunity or without care. And I remind our people in our country that, yes, September the 11th was devastating here, but there have been other victims, including the victims in Bali.

And John has played a very important role. And there's a lot of things that we must continue to do together, and that's part of the purpose of my trip. First of all, we've got to identify who these people are, which requires good, smart intelligence-gathering, and the Australians are good at that. Secondly, it means that we've got to work to cut off funding. When we find cells in respective countries that are utilizing the international finance system to move money, we've got to collectively cut off money. John Howard knows that. And then we've got to have the capacity to move and work with other governments to bring these killers to justice. And the Australians are very good at that as well.

And so there's a major role to be played in this war on terror. It starts with the mentality, though, Paul John, it starts with a recognition about what is possible and what is needed. And the Prime Minister has shown that, as has the Parliament. And that's one of the key things I'm going to talk about when I go to Australia.

Yes, sir. Rikard.

Indonesia

Q. Yes. Indonesia is a moderate country, but the campaign against terrorism has invited much controversy between a small minority of militant groups and the more dominant militant groups—moderate groups.

The President. Moderate groups, yes.

Q. The problem is that the militants have big opportunities to voice its interest, ideology, and values, harming the process of— [*inaudible*]—and democratization in Indonesia. So what should be done?

The President. Well, I think it's very important for Indonesia to understand that— first of all, to herald the nature of its moderate Islamic population, to make it clear to the world that, by far, the vast majority of the Muslims in that country value democracy and want to have a peaceful life. At the same time, it's very important not to allow a few killers to define Indonesia. And therefore, there needs to be a focused, concerted effort to bring people to justice.

Now, one of the things I will thank the people from Thailand for is we brought Hambali to justice. He's the guy that masterminded the Bali bombing. And by the way, Paul John, I was over in—gosh, I can't even remember where it was. It was recently, where I met a mother and dad whose—oh, this was in Kentucky, Lexington, Kentucky, when I was there to help this fellow running for Governor. And a mom and dad came up to me and said, "We lost a twin daughter in the Bali bombing." This bombing struck a lot. It really hurt Australia. It hurts your own country.

And my point is, I'm going to continue to talk with Madam Megawati about this, that it is—we cannot allow Indonesia to be defined by the hatred of a few, and that it's very important that we combine efforts, not just the United States with Indonesia but all assets, to help Ms. Megawati bring the rest of the cells to justice and prevent this from happening. It's unfortunate that a country have an attack. It should be viewed as an opportunity for people of good will to come together and prevent this from happening.

There is a—Indonesia is a very important country. It's important because of its strategic location. It's important because of the nature of its population. It's important that this country succeed, and we look forward to working with Indonesia.

Reform of the Palestinian Authority

Q. Last September, in the U.N. General Assembly, President Megawati stated that terrorism issues cannot be solved without removing their roots in the Middle East conflict. As long as countries, great countries maintain injustice—unjust and a one-sided policy toward Middle East, the conflict will continue and the campaign against terrorism will suffer.

The President. First of all—I'll be glad to talk about my Middle East policy. I have with Ms. Megawati. And I made it very clear to her that the roadmap to peace still exists. The problem is, we need people who are willing to uphold their responsibilities. I gave a speech here in the Rose Garden on June 24, 2002, which laid out a vision for a Palestinian state living side by side with Israel. But I also said that the Palestinians must do everything in their power to fight off terror, to prevent the few that want to kill to stop the peace process from going forward from doing so.

And we had an opportunity to move the process forward when Mr. Abu Mazen stepped up and was willing to say publicly and clearly that the Palestinians wanted to dismantle the terrorist groups that were destroying innocent life, and that provided a hopeful moment. It allowed me to continue to articulate the policy that all parties are responsible. Israel is responsible for helping a peaceful Palestinian country emerge and create the conditions necessary for a peace to move forward. The Arab nations are responsible to not support these terrorist groups.

And unfortunately, the Prime Minister, who I stood by—next to in Aqaba, Jordan, no longer is in power because he was shoved aside by the old guard, which has failed the Palestinian people. This old guard has been in power for quite a period of time, and life is worse, not better. And therefore I will continue to remind Prime Minister Megawati that we do have a vision for two states living side by side in peace.

I was the first President, American President, ever to articulate that vision. But in order to do so, there are certain prerequisites. And one of the prerequisites is there be a universal condemnation and fighting of terror. And that applies not only to the Middle East; that applies elsewhere, because Indonesia, unfortunately, has seen—as has America and Australia and Thailand and the Philippines—a few people, a few killers—they don't have an ideology except for one, destruction to create fear. They've hijacked a great religion. They kill innocent life in the name of a great religion in order to have their way, in order to create conditions of fear.

And that we must fight them—we must fight them. There's no negotiations with these people. There's no, "We'll sit down at a peace table." You cannot deal with these killers that way. So I will continue to explain and articulate our Middle East policy but at the same time make it very clear that there's only one way to deal with the few who want to destroy the hopes of the many, and that is to bring them to justice.

And we are. We're making good progress. The world has significantly changed. If you think about what cooperation was like prior to September the 11th, 2001, compared to today, it's a different world. And so part of my trip is to continue to emphasize the mutual need, in order to enhance democracy and to support those peaceful people that live within Indonesia or in any other country to support them, to support their hopes and aspirations by defeating those who would like to—who run absolutely contrary to what moderate, peaceful people believe.

Roger.

Q. Roger.

The President. I'm just trying to be international in my flavor. [*Laughter*]

Upcoming APEC Summit Discussions

Q. Mr. President, are you concerned at the way American jobs are being sucked away to Asia, particularly China, but also Malaysia, Indonesia, Thailand? Are you going to be speaking to your APEC colleagues to try to help you do something about this?

The President. Well, I'm going to say that where there is trade imbalances, countries need to be mindful that we expect there to be fair trade. And I fully understand a competitive world is one that I think is positive, so long as the competition is fair. And we'll talk about currency with the Chinese and with my friend Prime Minister Koizumi. I will remind them that this Nation has a strong dollar policy, and we expect the markets to reflect the true value of currency, that the way that currencies ought to be valued is based upon economic activity, fiscal policy, monetary policy of the respective governments, the potential for growth, the potential for long-term viability of the economies. That's how our respective currencies ought to be valued.

Yes, we'll bring that up. And I am—my main focus here in America is there to be significant job creation. It looks like we're getting some positive results. Part of making sure that the job creation—momentum of the job creation is viable is to make sure—is to talk to our trading partners about fair trade. And there are some trade imbalances that I will be discussing.

Singapore-U.S. Relations

Q. Singapore supported you in the war in Iraq and in general, and you've signed a free trade agreement with Singapore recently.

The President. I did.

Q. But in the past, there have been tiffs over social and political issues. How do you characterize U.S.-Singapore relations now?

The President. Well, I would say they're very positive. I mean, I've had—first of all, we do free trade agreements with countries with whom we'd like to trade. I guess that's fairly logical. And these are countries we respect. And we respect Singapore people. We respect the Government, and we respect the fact that they want to trade with us. And the cooperation in the war on terror has been excellent with Singapore.

As you know, one of the interesting opportunities is to create a new—the use of technology to better have a handle on what's leaving ports, what's in containers, what's on ships, and have basically a port inspection process prior to a cargo leaving a particular port of exit. And Singapore has been in the lead on this, helping to establish kind of a virtual customs inspection process, so we're able to better track that which is being shipped and have a better handle about that which is coming into our respective countries. It makes eminent sense that we have full transparency from the point a cargo ship leaves until when it arrives in our ports. Singapore has been in the lead on this, and for that, I appreciate Prime Minister Goh's leadership.

On a personal basis, he has got a very good handle about—and a good feel for the neighborhood. And I value his advice. He is, as we say here in America, plugged in to the political currents and is a very savvy man. And I really have enjoyed my relationship with him. I'm looking forward to going to Singapore.

Q. Do you—I'm sorry.

The President. Go ahead.

Q. I was going to say——

The President. This is a followup on a followup. [*Laughter*]

Q. You stressed the war on terror——

The President. Our press corps does the same thing—if we don't stay with, they —[*laughter*]. I'm used to it. I'm well trained by them. [*Laughter*]

Addressing the U.S. Image in Southeast Asia

Q. You stressed dealing with moderate Muslims in Indonesia and other places, but there seems to have been a rising tide of anti-American sentiment in parts of Southeast Asia. Are you going to try and stem it?

The President. Sure, that's part of the purpose, is to make sure that the people who are suspicious of our country understand our motives are pure. We believe in freedom for all people. We believe in peace. We don't believe a few killers ought to determine the fate and the future of a lot of people. We believe in education. We believe in health. One of the things about this Nation is that we're strong militarily, but we're also very compassionate. We're helping lead the fight against international AIDS. Part of the trip is to say as clearly as possible, is that this country is a—is full of decent and caring people who care about the future of the people in these nations.

On the other hand, people have just got to understand that we've got to fight those who are willing to kill. As you can tell from my language, terrorists who take innocent life must be treated as coldblooded killers, because that's what they are.

And we will continue to work with our friends who understand that, to bring people to justice, so we don't go to funerals and lay wreaths, so we don't commemorate anniversaries of the brutal slaughter of innocent people in the name of a religion or in the name of—with any attempt to instill fear. That's all they're trying to do. They want us to crumple and go away, so they can then spread their false ideology based upon hate. And America's ideology is based upon compassion and decency and justice. And I look forward to making that case.

Pichai.

War on Terror in Southeast Asia

Q. Mr. President, you mentioned progress against terror. I just want your assessment. Has the threat of the network in Southeast Asia diminished as a result of the policies so far?

The President. Yes, it has. When Hambali is gone, thanks to the Thai officials, a major operator in the war on terror—one of Khalid Sheikh Mohammed's close buddies, the organizer of the attack that killed a lot of people—he has been brought to justice. And that is a major blow for the Al-Qaida-affiliated networks.

There's more to do. This is a—let me just remind everybody that, at least from our perspective, from the perspective of the Government of the United States, the war on terror is going to last a while. I don't know how long it is, but it's—it is very important that free nations understand that this is a long-term effort and that we just can't relent and can't yield.

And I knew one of the hardest tasks I would have is explaining that this is a different kind of war to our own people. Wars—we used to think about flotillas and bombing runs and whatever. And for the war on terror, although there has been some traditional battle moments, military moments—like parts of the battle for Baghdad, which is a part of the war on terror—most of the war on terror will be fought by the use of intelligence, highly trained teams that have got the capacity to move quickly, and the willingness and will of collective governments to stay on the hunt. And in—we're making good progress. But there's more to do.

Trade Negotiations

Q. All right. Could I just have a question on trade?

The President. Sure.

Q. The WTO failed——

The President. Wait, wait, wait. The meetings in Cancun did not go well, but I wouldn't condemn the WTO round to failure yet.

Q. Okay, but there's—there's a theory——

The President. Sometimes I have a bad habit of correcting the interlocutors—[*laughter*]—because sometimes they're not always correct. [*Laughter*]

Q. So what's the future, then? You feel that there's still an opportunity——

The President. I do. I do feel we can get the Doha round up and running. Now, the meetings were disbanded in Cancun. The sense I get is a lot of countries feel this was a missed opportunity and that our Ambassador, Zoellick, believes there is a framework to get the process restarted and moved forward, that there was substantial progress made, and that we're interested in getting the process up and running again. In other words, the United States has not quit on the process, is the best way to say it. And I look forward to talking to the Prime Minister about a free trade agreement. As you know, discussions are going on—with a bilateral free trade——

Q. That's right, yes.

The President. ——with Thailand. And we'll continue our discussions.

Q. Any announcement expected in——

The President. Well, you know the problem is, if I were to make the announcement now to you in order to help you with your editors, it would take away kind of the—yes, it would take away the excitement. I don't know. We'll see. We'll see. [*Laughter*]

Yes, Mercedes.

Mindanao/Philippines-U.S. Relations

Q. Thank you, sir. There is this 30-year-old, low-intensity war in Mindanao. And the United States, through your administration, has now a role in the peace process. Would you like to address that?

The President. Have not had a role? Or have had a role?

Q. They have a role now.

The President. Yes, a role in the peace——

Q. Right.

The President. Well, that's right. I made a statement when President Arroyo was here, urging the parties to come together and that we would—as a matter of fact, there was some progress. I'm not exactly sure where we are in the discussions, but shortly after her visit, the parties came to the table, which is a very positive development.

Let me speak to a broader issue, if you don't mind, in the Philippines. First of all, I respect President Arroyo. I respect her will. I respect her desire to deal with the Abu Sayyaf, for example. She's been very strong, and there's been progress made in dealing with the leaders of this group. There is still more to be done.

She knows, for example, very well that when U.S. citizens, or any citizen for that matter, gets kidnaped, killed, it defines the Philippines in a negative way. It doesn't really talk to the true character and the nature of the Philippines. The Philippines are loving, decent, kind people. And her country—these terrorists, again, want to create a different atmosphere, a different environment. And Gloria Arroyo knows that, and that's why she's been very strong. And that's why we've been in—got a very cooperative relationship. A training mission and now a comprehensive security review is ongoing, which I will discuss with President Arroyo.

So in the larger context, the President's strategy of dealing firmly with those who would kill, kidnap, maim, is a very good strategy, one that we support strongly, and are willing to cooperate to the extent that she asks for help.

In terms of bringing long-simmering disputes to peaceful conclusion, my judgment is the stronger a leader acts against terror, the more likely those people are going to be willing to want to sit down and conclude—make arrangements, make accord. And I believe that's one of the reasons why President Arroyo has been able to make some progress on long-simmering disputes.

Cancun WTO Meeting/Philippines-U.S.
Free Trade Agreement

Q. I have a question that relates to the Philippines and the WTO.

The President. Sure.

Q. In Cancun, the Philippines left the U.S. to join the G–21 countries.

The President. Yes.

Q. It appears that it displeased your administration.

The President. It displeased us? Well, I'm not—do I look displeased? I'm a friendly guy.

Q. Well, does that—does that put into a risk——

The President. No, not at all.

Q. ——the bilateral and trade agreement?

The President. No, it doesn't. Not at all. I mean, it's very important for me to explain to the leaders that we are interested in moving the process forward, that WTO negotiations are complicated and complex matters, that we believe that it is in the Philippines' interest, in Thailand's interest, or any other country's interest that the Doha round succeed, that we want to work through the difficult issues.

And I think a lot of countries, Mercedes, now believe that this was a missed opportunity, that it was an opportunity to make progress. And the fact that it didn't, that we didn't make progress, may actually serve as an impetus to get people back together. Let's don't miss this opportunity again. Let's move on. So the purpose of my trip is to say that we want Doha to succeed.

I'm also saying as clearly as possible that we will negotiate bilateral agreements with countries. Our strategy is to have a—is to have free trade worldwide, free trade regionally through the Free Trade of the Americas and free trade on a bilateral basis. And when Congress gave me what's called trade promotion authority, I then had the capacity to negotiate—our people to negotiate free trade agreements and then bring that to Congress in an up-or-down vote, which makes it more likely nations will want to negotiate with us. Singapore was one of the first—and Chile—were two countries that said, "Okay, fine, now the President's got it. We can negotiate a treaty. We know it won't be amended on the floor of the Congress, and therefore, we can negotiate in good faith. And the President will submit it for up-or-down votes."

This has given me the opportunity to be—to move forward on trade on a bilateral basis. And so we've got a two—a three-pronged strategy when it comes to trade. And we do hope that the WTO goes forward. But that won't prevent us from doing—negotiating bilaterally with nations.

Yes, sir. Yes, sir. One in English?

Q. Yes.

The President. Okay. My Japanese is a little limited. [*Laughter*]

Q. If you speak—if you speak Japanese?

The President. No, I don't speak Japanese. [*Laughter*] Some accuse me of not speaking English. [*Laughter*]

Japan's Reconstruction Aid to Iraq

Q. So before you come visit to Japan, we Japanese would like to hear your views on a couple things, first of all, your evaluation about Japan's contribution to reconstruction of Iraq.

The President. Yes, well, I talked to my friend Prime Minister Koizumi. And he is my friend, let me emphasize that. We've got a great relationship. And he told me that he would try to work with the leaders to come up with a reconstruction package for Iraq, and I believe he will. And I look forward to talking to him about it. And he's a fellow, when he says something, at least to me, he means it. And that's why I'm optimistic that Japan will be an active participant in the reconstruction of Iraq.

They certainly were an active participant in the reconstruction of Afghanistan. And for that we are grateful. Japan played a key role in the early stages of the postwar in Afghanistan environment—*loya jirga* got started, but also Japan took a lead in terms of the reconstruction effort.

North Korea

Q. One about North Korea.

The President. Yes.

Q. Well, how do you place the—North Korea's abduction of Japanese people in the six-party——

The President. Well, the key notion on the six-party framework is to make sure that the stated objective of the five countries involved with the six-party—with North Korea in the six-party discussions is achieved. The key objective, the most important objective is for there to be a Korean Peninsula that is free of nuclear weapons. That's the primary focus of our discussions, and we're making progress, because now there are five nations other than the United States—or four nations other than the United States sitting down the North Koreans, making the very same point.

And I will talk to the Prime Minister about how to—you know, what we need to do to keep the process alive and strong and to keep the coalition of the peaceful united so that we have one message and one voice.

In terms of the relationship between North Korea and Japan, that is for Prime Minister Koizumi to manage. Obviously, if you have abductees, it is a very serious issue. And it speaks to the nature of the North Korean Government and hence another reason for us to work for a nuclear-weapons-free Korean Peninsula.

Monetary Policy

Q. Given the recent depreciation of the dollar vis-a-vis the yen, what do you think of the dollar's devaluation?

The President. I think I'm for a strong policy. We have a strong dollar policy in this administration. Currencies ought to be valued based upon the respective strengths of the economies, based upon the policies of the governments. We have had a very progrowth policy in this administration. I've

worked with Congress to enact historic tax relief in order to give our people more of their own money back and let them spend it and drive demand for goods and service. And it's beginning to pay off. The economy is improving. And markets ought to be evaluating our respective currencies.

Q. So what is your view on Japan's——

The President. Well, that's my view, that markets ought to be determining respective to currencies.

North Korea

Q. Well, come back to the North Koreans——

The President. Sure. This is the multiple——

Q. I'm sorry.

The President. No, you're doing a fine job, Toshio, that's good. Short questions, short answers. [*Laughter*]

Q. I appreciate it.

The President. You're setting a new standard for the followup. Keep that in mind. [*Laughter*]

Q. Do you think the North Koreans' nuclear problem should be brought to the U.N. Security Council?

The President. No, I think——

Q. If yes, why? When?

The President. I appreciate that. That's part my discussions with Prime Minister Koizumi. First things first is that we've got to make sure our strategy of the five of us moves forward. I'm looking forward to discussing this with Mr. Hu Jintao. He has been a important part of these discussions, and I will visit the strategy with—about the mutual desire to move forward with Prime Minister Koizumi.

Yes, Mercedes.

Designation of the Philippines as a Major Non-NATO Ally

Q. Anything on the designation of the Philippines as a major NATO——

The President. Yes, we'll be discussing that. Short question, short answers.

Burma

Q. Yes, you mentioned democracy, a take on Burma. How do you see things going there now in recent developments?

The President. It's—pleased about Burma. I think the fact that Burma continues to—that there is an historic figure in Burma that needs to be treated with respect, and the wishes of the people need to be honored. And we will continue to speak out, and I will talk to the Prime Minister about that, as I have in the past.

He is concerned, as you know, about narcotics and the flow of narcotics. I believe free societies and the ability to control narcotics and terrorism go hand in hand. We will continue to press for freedom in Burma. Aung San Suu Kyi is a great figure. She is a heroic woman. And this country honors her, and we'll continue to press for her freedom. I did so at the United Nations. I will continue to do so on a bilateral basis.

The Presidency

Q. How does it feel to be the most powerful man in the world?

The President. Humbling.

Q. Humbling?

The President. Yes. And it also means there's tremendous responsibilities with that. Very interesting question; the fundamental question is what you do with power. And I believe it's very important for the President to work with others to lead for a more peaceful and free world. And part of that use of power now—we must use our power to fight terror.

And at the same time, we must use our power and wealth to help improve the lives of those who suffer. It's humbling to think about that. It is also an awesome responsibility which I take seriously. And part of the trip, I hope you can get from the tenor of these discussions, part of the trip is to say very clearly to our friends and allies, "We want to work together to achieve common objectives." I'm very serious about it.

Indonesia

Q. Yes. Can I just ask, Indonesia is one of the victims of terrorist attack, but, however——

The President. Which the innocent is? Yes, always.

Q. Indonesia also victimized by—[*inaudible*]—from several countries——

The President. The——

Q. Victimized, yes.

The President. In other words, people come from other countries to your country to create terrorist acts?

Q. Yes.

The President. Yes. That's why it's important that we cooperate closely to watch these terrorists, to track terrorists, to make sure we know who's coming in and out of our countries, to share intelligence, to get inside these networks as best we can, to use all means available to understand them, to watch their movements, and when they move, bring them to justice, arrest them, get them off the streets.

And you're right, countries are—if a country is viewed as a safe haven, terrorists will tend to flock to that country. And that's why the strong action of governments sends a clear sign: Not welcome here. And that's why arrests and strong action are necessary to prevent people from feeling comfortable about migration.

And that's why the decisions by Prime Minister Megawati to arrest people is a very important signal to people. And I continue to talk to her and work with her on this. I appreciate very much the efforts made by the Indonesian Government to bring terrorists to justice.

Australia's Role in the War on Terror/ Australia-U.S. Free Trade Agreement

Q. How confident can we be that we will see an Australia-America FTA and with the negotiations finalized by the end of this year, which is the deadline you said you wanted? And secondly, does the United States actually see Australia as its deputy sheriff in Southeast Asia?

The President. No. We don't see it as a deputy sheriff. We see it as a sheriff. [*Laughter*] There's a difference. I see you're playing off the Crawford visit to the ranch, the sheriff thing. [*Laughter*] Anyway, no, equal partners and friends and allies—there's nothing deputy about this relationship.

I'm optimistic on free trade agreement, and I'll talk to John about that. We did set a deadline. Deadlines are important. Sometimes you get things done, and we'll work toward that deadline. And part of our discussions will be the free trade agreement. It's in our Nation's interest to do so. We've got some heavy lift in certain areas that we're just going to have to work through them. And I know our negotiators and our people are talking in the spirit of trying to complete the agreement.

Okay, looking forward to it. Anybody gets to go with us?

Q. Thank you, Mr. President.

NOTE: The interview began at 9:40 a.m. in the Roosevelt Room at the White House, and the transcript was released by the Office of the Press Secretary on October 16. In his remarks, the President referred to Prime Minister John Howard of Australia; Nurjaman Riduan Isamuddin (known as Hambali), Al Qaida's chief operational planner in Southeast Asia; President Sukarnoputri Megawati of Indonesia; former Prime Minister Mahmoud Abbas (Abu Mazen) of the Palestinian Authority; Prime Minister Junichiro Koizumi of Japan; Prime Minister Goh Chok Tong of Singapore; Khalid Sheikh Mohammed, senior Al Qaida leader responsible for planning the September 11, 2001, terrorist attack, who was captured in Pakistan on March 1; Prime Minister Thaksin Chinnawat of Thailand; President Gloria Macapagal-Arroyo of the Philippines; President Hu Jintao of China; and Aung San Suu Kyi, leader of the National League for Democracy of Burma. Participants in the interview were: Toshio Mizushima, bureau chief of the Americas, Yomiuri Shimbun; Mercedes Tira Andrei, Washington correspondent, BusinessWorld; Pichai Chuensuksawadi, editor-in-chief, Bangkok Post; Roger Mitton, Washington correspondent, The Straits Times; Rikard Bagun, deputy chief editor, Kompas; and Paul John Kelly, editor-at-large, The Australian. A tape was not available for verification of the content of this interview.

Remarks in San Bernardino, California
October 16, 2003

Thank you all. Please be seated, Colonel. Thanks for coming. Thanks for the warm welcome. It's great to be in the Inland Empire with the 38th Governor of the great State of California.

We did have a good visit, and during that visit I was able to reflect upon how much we have in common. We both married well. [*Laughter*] Some accuse us both of not being able to speak the language. [*Laughter*] We both have big biceps. [*Laughter*] Well, two out of three isn't bad. [*Laughter*] We both love our country. Arnold Schwarzenegger is going to be a fine and strong leader for California. I'm proud to call him friend.

Mark, I want to thank you and the Inland Empire Economic Partnership for hosting this event. I appreciate it very much. And thank you all for coming. I appreciate Teri Ooms as well, as the president and CEO of the partnership.

I want to thank those from the military who are here, particularly James Rubeor, who is the colonel at March Air Force Base. I appreciate you coming, Colonel. I presume you left somebody behind to make sure Air Force One is fueled up. [*Laughter*]

We're leaving—I say we—Laura is coming from Washington this morning. I'm sorry she's not here. You drew the short straw when you got me. [*Laughter*] But she is—we're fixing to go overseas to represent our great country. I'm looking forward to the trip to remind the world about the challenges we face. I'm really here today to talk about the challenges we face at home as well.

I want to thank the local officials who have so kindly come. Most of all, I want to thank our citizens who are here, because I am talking about two of the great priorities for our country. One is to create jobs for America, and to win the war on terror—the two challenges we're faced with.

This country is being tested. We're being tested abroad, and we're being tested here at home. And we're meeting the tests of history. We're defeating the enemies of freedom, and we're confronting the challenges to build prosperity for our country. That's what we're doing. Every test of America has revealed the character of America. And over the last 2 years, no one in the world, friend or foe, can doubt the will and the strength of the American people.

When you become President, you cannot predict all the challenges that will come. But you do know the principles that you bring to office, principles that should not change with time or with polls. I took this office to make a difference, not to mark time. I came to this office to confront problems directly and forcefully, not to pass them on to future Presidents or future generations.

The challenges we face today cannot be met with timid, timid actions or bitter, bitter words. Our challenges will be overcome with optimism and resolve and confidence in the ideals of America. Because we believe in our free enterprise system, we can be confident in our economy's future.

Our economy has been through a lot. When I took office, the stock market had been declining for 9 months, and the economy was headed into a recession. And just as we started to recover, the killers came and attacked America on September the 11th, and that struck a blow to our economy. And then investor confidence was shaken by scandals in corporate America, dishonest behavior we cannot and will not tolerate in our country. And then we faced the uncertainty that preceded the battles of Afghanistan and Iraq.

The country has been hit hard during these times, and so has the great State of California. Declines in investment have hurt the tech sector. You lost manufacturing jobs. Farmers are wondering whether they'll be able to sell their products overseas. Unemployment in this important State is too high.

But we acted. I acted to overcome these challenges to this State and our country, and I acted on principle. Government does not create wealth. The role of Government is to create the conditions where risktakers and entrepreneurs can invest and grow and hire new workers.

We know how to create jobs for America. It starts when Americans have more take-home pay to spend, to save, or invest, which causes the economy to grow, and therefore, someone is more likely to find a job. So I twice led the Congress to pass historic tax relief for the American people. We wanted tax relief to be as broad and as fair as possible, so we reduced taxes on everyone who pays taxes. It doesn't make sense to penalize marriage in the Tax Code, so we reduced the marriage penalty. It costs a lot to raise children, and so we increased the child credit from $600 per child to $1,000 per child. And we put the checks in the mail directly to moms and dads.

It's counterproductive to discourage investment, especially during an economic recovery, so we quadrupled the expense deduction for small-business investment and cut taxes on dividends and capital gains. It is unfair to tax the estates people leave behind after a lifetime of saving money and building a business or running a farm. When you leave this world, the IRS should not follow you. [*Laughter*] So we're phasing out the Federal death tax.

I proposed and signed these measures to help individuals and families. But they also help the small businesses of America. See, most small-business owners pay taxes under the individual tax rate because they're Subchapter S's or sole proprietorships. And therefore, small business has benefited from the tax cuts. Millions of mom-and-pop companies are also benefiting from the higher expense deductions. And this is important because small businesses create most new jobs for our country, and they're usually the first to take risks. They're usually the first to hire people. By helping small businesses, we help our entire economy.

We are following a clear and consistent economic strategy, and I'm confident about our future. Last month, this economy exceeded expectations and added new jobs. Inflation is low. After-tax incomes are rising. Homeownership is at record highs. Productivity is high. Factory orders, particularly for high-tech equipment, have risen over the last several months. Our strategy has set the stage for sustained growth. By reducing taxes we kept a promise, and we did the right thing at the right time for the American economy.

Now our country is approaching a choice. Just as our economy is coming around, some in Washington are saying now is the time to raise taxes. To be fair, they think any time is a good time to raise taxes. [*Laughter*] At least they're consistent. [*Laughter*] I strongly disagree. A nation cannot tax its way to growth or job creation. Tax relief put this Nation on the right path, and I intend to keep America on the path to prosperity.

We're moving forward, but we're not satisfied. We cannot be satisfied so long as we have fellow citizens looking for work. We must continue to act boldly. So I'm asking Congress to join me in carrying out a six-part plan for job creation for America.

Businesses are more likely to hire people if health care for workers is affordable. One way to help our small-business owners is to allow association health care plans, where small businesses can pool risk and gain the same bargaining power as big businesses.

And to help control costs for small businesses, large businesses, and Government, we need effective legal reform to stop the frivolous lawsuits against doctors. We need more than tort reform just for medical liability. Unfair lawsuits harm a lot of good and small businesses. There are too many large settlements that leave the plaintiffs with a small sum and the lawyers with the fortune. Class action and mass tort cases that reach across State lines should be tried in the Federal court, so the lawyers cannot shop around looking for a favorable judge. We got a good bill out of the House. It's stuck in the Senate. The Senate must act. Job creation will occur when we've got legal reforms.

Our economy will grow stronger and create more jobs if we have a sound national energy policy. When we—we had a wake-up call this summer. We need to modernize our electricity grids. [*Laughter*] We need to make sure that we encourage investments so that the capacity to move electricity or natural gas is capable to sustain growth in the 21st century. We need to use our technology to develop clean and efficient energy sources, so that we can sustain economic growth and protect the environment. But one thing is for certain: For the sake of national security and for the sake of economic security, America must be less dependent on foreign sources of energy.

More people will find jobs when employers do not have to waste time and resources complying with needless Government regulations. For the sake of American workers, at the Federal level we're cutting unnecessary rules and making rules simpler to understand. Small-business owners should spend more time building companies and pleasing customers and less time filling out needless forms.

To create jobs in this country, we need to pursue free trade agreements that will open up foreign markets for American products. Expanded trade will help businesses large and small—businesses such as UVP, Inc., and Maney Aircraft based right out of here—will help them to sell more good and locally made products overseas. Free trade must be two ways. We're good at what we do. We ought to be allowed to sell what we do in other people's countries. Farmers ought to have markets opened up to them. California's ranchers and farmers are really good at what they do. We need a level playing field when it comes to trade, and a level playing field will help us create jobs here in America.

There's one more thing we need to do. We need to make sure that all the tax relief we passed does not disappear in future years. Employers need certainty in the Tax Code. Because of a quirk in the legislation, the tax cuts are scheduled to go away unless we act. When we passed tax relief, Americans did not expect to see higher taxes sneak through the back door. If Congress is interested in job creation, they will make every one of the tax cuts permanent.

We have a responsibility to set good policies in Washington. Governor Schwarzenegger has a responsibility to set good policy in Sacramento. Yet the true strength of this country is found in the creativity and the entrepreneurial spirit of America. And that is one reason and that is the main reason I am so confident about the future of our economy.

As we overcome challenges to our economy, we are answering great threats to our security. September the 11th, 2001, moved our country to grief and moved our country to action. We made a pledge that day, and we have kept it. We are bringing the guilty to justice. We're taking the fight to the enemy.

And now we see that enemy clearly. The terrorists plot in secret and target the innocent. They defile a great religion, and they hate everything this Nation stands for. These committed killers will not be stopped by negotiations. They will not respond to reason. The terrorists who threaten America cannot be appeased. They must be found. They must be fought, and they will be defeated.

In this new kind of war, America is following a new strategy. We are not waiting for further attacks. We are striking our enemies before they can strike us again. We have taken unprecedented steps to protect the homeland. Yet wars are won on the offensive, and America and our friends are staying on the offensive. We're rolling back the terrorist threat, not on the fringes of its influence but at the heart of its power.

We have sent a message understood throughout the world: "If you harbor a terrorist, if you support a terrorist, if you feed a terrorist, you're just as guilty as the terrorist." And the Taliban found out what we meant. Thanks to a great military, Afghanistan is no longer a haven for terror. The Afghan people are free, and the people of America are safer from attack.

And we fought the war on terror in Iraq. The regime of Saddam Hussein possessed and used weapons of mass destruction, sponsored terrorist groups, and inflicted terror on its own people. Nearly every nation recognized and denounced this threat for over a decade. Finally, the U.N. Security Council in Resolution 1441 demanded that Saddam Hussein disarm, prove his disarmament to the world, or face serious consequences. The choice was up to the dictator, and he chose poorly. [Laughter]

I acted because I was not about to leave the security of the American people in the hands of a madman. I was not about to stand by and wait and trust in the sanity and restraint of Saddam Hussein, so our coalition acted in one of the swiftest and most humane military campaigns in history. And nearly 6 months ago, the statue of the dictator was pulled down.

Since the liberation of Iraq, our investigators have found evidence of a clandestine network of biological laboratories, advanced design work on prohibited longer range missiles, and an elaborate campaign to hide illegal programs. There's still much to investigate, yet it is now undeniable that Saddam Hussein was in clear violation of United Nations Security Council Resolution 1441. It is undeniable that Saddam Hussein was a deceiver and a danger. The Security Council was right to demand that Saddam Hussein disarm, and America was right to enforce that demand.

Who can possibly think that the world would be better off with Saddam Hussein still in power? Surely not the dissidents who would be in his prisons or end up in his mass graves. Surely not the men and women who would fill Saddam's torture chamber or rape rooms. Surely not the families of victims he murdered with poison gas. Surely not anyone who cares about human rights and democracy and stability in the Middle East. There is only one decent and humane reaction to the fall of Saddam Hussein: Good riddance!

Now our country is approaching a choice. After all the action we have taken, after all the progress we have made against terror, there is a temptation to think that danger has passed. But the danger has not passed. Since September the 11th, the terrorists have taken lives in Casablanca, Mombasa, Jerusalem, Amman, Riyadh, Baghdad, Karachi, New Delhi, Bali, Jakarta. And most recently, American lives were lost by terrorist attack in the Gaza.

The terrorists continue to plot. They continue to plan against our country and our people. America must never forget the lessons of September the 11th. America cannot retreat from our responsibilities and hope for the best. Our security will not be gained by timid measures. Our security requires constant vigilance and decisive ac-

tion. I believe America has only one option: We will fight this war against terror until it is won.

We are fighting on many fronts. Iraq is now the central front. Saddam holdouts and foreign terrorists are trying desperately to undermine Iraq's progress and throw the country into chaos. The terrorists in Iraq believe their attacks on innocent people will weaken our resolve. They believe we will run from a challenge. They're mistaken. Americans are not the running kind.

The United States did not run from Germany and Japan following World War II. We helped those nations to become strong and decent and democratic societies that no longer waged war against America, that became our friends. That's our mission in Iraq today. We're rebuilding schools. We're repairing hospitals, restoring water and electricity, so the Iraqi people can live a normal life.

Americans are providing this help not only because our hearts are good but because our vision is clear: A stable and democratic and hopeful Iraq will no longer be a breeding ground for terror, for tyranny and aggression. Free nations are peaceful nations. Our work in Iraq is essential to our own security. And no band of murderers and gangsters will stop that work or shake the will of America.

Nearly every day in Iraq, we're launching swift precision raids against the terrorists. Helped by intelligence from Iraqis, we're rounding up the enemy, and we're taking their weapons, and we're working our way through the famous deck of cards. [*Laughter*] We've already captured or killed 43 of the 55 most wanted former Iraqi leaders. And the other 12 have got a lot to worry about. [*Laughter*] Anyone who seeks to harm our soldiers can know that our soldiers are hunting for them.

Our military is serving with courage, and some of the best have fallen. We mourn every loss. We honor every name. We grieve with every family, and we'll always be grateful that liberty has found such brave defenders.

In defending liberty, we are joined by more than 30 nations now contributing military forces in Iraq. Great Britain and Poland are leading two multinational divisions. We're in that cause with fine allies, and we thank them. And that includes the good people of Iraq. Last week, the first battalion of the new Iraqi army completed its training. Within the year, Iraq will have a 40,000-member military force. Tens of thousands of Iraqi citizens are guarding their own borders. They're defending vital facilities, and they're policing their own streets. Normal Iraqis want Iraq to be secure and peaceful.

Our goal in Iraq is to leave behind a stable, self-governing society which will no longer be a threat to the Middle East or to the United States. We're following an orderly plan to reach this goal. Iraq now has a Governing Council, which appointed interim Government ministers. Once a constitution has been written, Iraq will move toward national elections. We want the process to go as quickly as possible, yet it must be done right. The free institutions of Iraq must stand the test of time.

Today I want to thank the United Nations Security Council for unanimously passing a resolution supporting our efforts to build a peaceful and free Iraq. A democratic Iraq will stand as an example to all the Middle East. We believe and the Iraqi people will show that liberty is the hope and the right of every land.

Our work in Iraq has been long, and it's hard. It is not finished. Since September the 11th, nearly 10,000 California National Guard soldiers and airmen have been mobilized for this effort; 1,600 are currently in the Middle East. They're playing a vital role for the defense of this Nation. Our country is grateful to those who serve and their families who support them.

Americans have sacrificed in the cause of freedom and security, and that cause goes on. Beyond Iraq, the war on terror

continues. There will be no quick victory in this war. But if we persevere, our victory is certain.

I'm confident of that victory because I know the character of our military, shown in the conduct of young men like Joseph Robsky. He's a career soldier. He served with the Marines in Bosnia and saw the dangers of unexploded bombs, became an explosive ordnance disposal specialist with the Army's 759th Ordnance Company, based in California at Fort Irwin. Along with his unit, he was sent to Iraq. And on September the 10th of this year, he was killed disarming a bomb. Hear the words of his mother, Bonnie: "My son always said he had a job to do. He said the terrorist has to be stopped."

Staff Sergeant Joe Robsky's devotion to his Nation will not be forgotten. We'll always remember the words, "Terrorism must be stopped."

This war on terror has brought hardship and loss to our country, beginning with the grief of September the 11th. Let us also remember that the first victory in this war came on that same day, on a hijacked plane bound for the Nation's Capital. Somehow the brave men and women on Flight 93, knowing they would die, found the courage to use their final moments to save the lives of others. In those moments and many times since, terrorists have learned about America. They won't—we won't be intimidated. We'll fight them with everything we got. Few are called to show the kind of valor seen on Flight 93 or on the field of battle. Yet all of us do share a calling: Be strong in adversity and unafraid in danger.

We Americans have come through so much. We have much yet to do. If we're patient, united, and determined, our Nation will prosper, and our Nation will prevail.

May God bless you. Thank you all.

NOTE: The President spoke at 9:38 a.m. at the Radisson Hotel and Convention Center. In his remarks, he referred to Col. James T.

Rubeor, USAFR, commander, 452d Air Mobility Wing, March Air Reserve Base; Governor-elect Arnold Schwarzenegger of California; Mark Ostoich, chairman of the board, Inland Empire Economic Partnership; and former President Saddam Hussein of Iraq.

Statement on the United Nations Security Council Resolution on Iraq
October 16, 2003

I welcome today's unanimous passage of United Nations Security Council Resolution 1511. The world has an opportunity—and a responsibility—to help the Iraqi people build a nation that is stable, secure, and free. This resolution will help marshal even more international support for the development of a new, democratic Iraq. I look forward to continuing to work with the United Nations to aid the transition in Iraq to self-government and help the Iraqi people rebuild their nation.

Message on the Observance of the 25th Anniversary of the Pontificate of His Holiness John Paul II
October 16, 2003

I send greetings to those gathered to celebrate the 25th Anniversary of the Pontificate of His Holiness John Paul II.

As a priest, chaplain, professor, Auxiliary Bishop, Archbishop, Cardinal, and Pope, His Holiness has spent a lifetime sharing God's teachings and ministering to those in need. He has put hope in people's hearts and inspired acts of goodness and compassion. For the past 25 years, His Holiness has led worldwide efforts to develop a new culture of life that values and protects the lives of innocent children waiting to be born. He has also brought the love of the Almighty to people of all ages, particularly those who suffer or live in poverty, or who are weak and vulnerable. Pope John Paul II has shown the world not only the splendor of truth, but also the power of truth to overcome evil and to redirect the course of history.

The United States and the world are better because of his dedication to sharing his wisdom, guidance, and faith. Laura joins me in sending our best wishes on this special occasion.

GEORGE W. BUSH

NOTE: An original was not available for verification of the content of this message.

Letter to the Speaker of the House of Representatives Transmitting Fiscal Year 2004 Budget Amendments
October 16, 2003

Dear Mr. Speaker:

I ask the Congress to consider the enclosed FY 2004 budget amendments for the Departments of Agriculture and the Interior to reimburse emergency expenses to suppress forest fires in FY 2003.

These amendments would adjust upward the total discretionary budget authority requested by $0.4 billion, bringing the total discretionary funding agreed to by my Administration and the Congress to $786.0 billion. While this request increases total discretionary spending beyond the previously agreed upon level, my Administration and congressional leadership determined earlier this year that emergency funding could be added when mutually agreed upon in advance. This request is consistent with that agreement.

The requests in this transmittal are for the purpose of fulfilling known and urgent requirements that cannot reasonably be met through the use of existing agency funds. I hereby designate the specific proposals in the amounts requested herein as emergency requirements.

The details of these requests are set forth in the enclosed letter from the Director of the Office of Management and Budget.

Sincerely,

GEORGE W. BUSH

NOTE: This letter was released by the Office of the Press Secretary on October 17.

Message to the Congress on Continuation of the National Emergency With Respect to Significant Narcotics Traffickers Centered in Colombia
October 16, 2003

To the Congress of the United States:

Section 202(d) of the National Emergencies Act, 50 U.S.C. 1622(d) provides for the automatic termination of a national emergency unless, prior to the anniversary date of its declaration, the President publishes in the *Federal Register* and transmits to the Congress a notice stating that the emergency is to continue in effect beyond the anniversary date. Consistent with this provision, I have sent the enclosed notice, stating that the emergency declared with respect to significant narcotics traffickers centered in Colombia is to continue in effect beyond October 21, 2003, to the *Federal Register* for publication. The most recent notice continuing this emergency was published in the *Federal Register* on October 18, 2002.

The circumstances that led to the declaration on October 21, 1995, of a national emergency have not been resolved. The actions of significant narcotics traffickers centered in Colombia continue to pose an unusual and extraordinary threat to the national security, foreign policy, and economy of the United States and to cause unparalleled violence, corruption, and harm in the United States and abroad. For these reasons, I have determined that it is necessary to maintain economic pressure on significant narcotics traffickers centered in Colombia by blocking their property or interests in property that are in the United States or within the possession or control of United States persons and by depriving them of access to the United States market and financial system.

GEORGE W. BUSH

The White House,

October 16, 2003.

NOTE: This message was released by the Office of the Press Secretary on October 17. The notice of October 16 is listed in Appendix D at the end of this volume.

Statement on Congressional Passage of the Supplemental Funding Request To Support the War on Terror
October 17, 2003

I applaud the House and Senate for passing my supplemental funding request to support our mission and our troops deployed in Afghanistan, Iraq, and elsewhere. These funds will provide the resources necessary to make Iraq more secure and support its transition to self-government, which is critical to winning the war on terror. They will also continue our efforts to help build an Afghanistan that is prosperous, democratic, and at peace, and that contributes to regional stability.

I commend the House for wisely rejecting a proposal to convert part of the reconstruction funds to loans. It is unfortunate that a closely divided Senate voted to partially substitute loans for grants. Loans are the wrong approach—they would slow the reconstruction of Iraq, delay the democratic process, and send the wrong message to both the region and the world. The loan provision must be removed in conference.

I thank Chairmen Stevens and Young for their efforts and urge the conference committee to work to resolve their differences, fully fund my request, and send me legislation I can sign quickly.

Interview With Taro Kimura of Japan's FUJI TV
October 14, 2003

The President. Glad you're here. Ready to go.

Japan's Reconstruction Aid for Iraq

Mr. Kimura. Thank you very much, Mr. President, for this interview. I'm sure Prime Minister Koizumi is looking forward to have you over there. Actually, he is preparing a package for Iraqi reconstruction which includes $5 billion aid for the next 4 years and sending a couple of hundred Japanese self-defense forces over there for the humanitarian operation. Do you think Japan fulfilled her responsibility with this package?

The President. Yes. I'm very pleased. Prime Minister Koizumi and I are good friends. I admire him a lot, and I spoke to him about Japan helping in Iraq, just like Japan helped in Afghanistan. And he assured me he would work hard to develop a good package. It sounds like he has done so, and I'm grateful and thankful.

We've got great relations between America and Japan. We will keep them that way. And part of good relations is we see problems, and we work together, and see opportunities. And a free Iraq is a—a peaceful Iraq is a wonderful opportunity for Japan and the United States to work together to achieve because a free and peaceful Iraq will change the world in a positive way.

North Korea/Japanese Abductees

Mr. Kimura. Another subject, Mr. President, that the Prime Minister will bring up is the North Korean problem.

The President. Yes, yes.

Mr. Kimura. And he is working very hard to resolve the issue of abductees, Japanese.

The President. Yes.

Mr. Kimura. What could your administration do to help him realizing the reunification of the abductees' status?

The President. Well, that's a very interesting question. The primary objective of the five countries who are now engaged with North Korea is to get rid of nuclear weapons on the Korean Peninsula. That's our primary objective, and that ought to be our focus.

A major issue with the Prime Minister, of course, is the abductees. I've always said that the fact that North Korea kidnaped or abducted these people talks to the nature of the administration in North Korea. And of course, we will send strong signals that we object to that kind of behavior, that that is not a civil behavior.

But the first objective is for all of us to work together for the sake of peace and security, particularly in your part of the world, to get rid of any nuclear weapons and/or ambitions for nuclear weapons.

Mr. Kimura. For example, do you think it's possible that your administration demand North Korea to include this abduction program in whatever the comprehensive package——

The President. Well, I think it's very important. I'll talk to the Prime Minister about this, of course. I know this is a very sensitive subject, and I've spoken out about this terrible practice, a terrible part of history, that the North Koreans abducted. But the first thing we got to do is focus on our overall objective, and that is to make sure that the peninsula is nuclear weapons-free. And that's in Japan's interest, of course. And right now that's where our focus is.

Mr. Kimura. I understand—or I read Bob Woodward's book. And you've said you loathe Kim Chong-il. Do you still feel that same way?

The President. When I know a leader starves his people, allows his people to starve, and know there's detention camps and it's not a free society—it's a very, closed totalitarian society—he and I don't agree, obviously, on freedom and peace. And I hope that Kim Chong-il realizes that when five nations speak, we're very serious, and that it's in his country's interest to get rid of nuclear weapons and/or programs to develop nuclear weapons. Because the five countries that are now speaking in one voice are saying as clearly as possible to Mr. Kim Chong-il, "You need to change for your good and for the good of the country."

Monetary Policy

Mr. Kimura. There is speculation in Tokyo that you will speak to Mr. Koizumi to let dollar-yen rate float and not let the Japanese financial institute to intervene in the market. Is this the case?

The President. Well, I will talk to him about, one, our Government's strong dollar policy. And I will remind him that our position when it comes to currency exchanges is that the market ought to decide the relative values of currencies based upon the fiscal policy of each government, the monetary policy of each government, the future economic picture of each country. And that's what I will remind him. This will not be the first time that we have discussed dollar policy and/or trade matters.

Mr. Kimura. Lastly, I remember you've enjoyed yakitori when you were in Tokyo, the barbecued chicken.

The President. Yes, I did. [*Laughter*]

Mr. Kimura. And I wonder whether you will bear tasting sushi this time. I know you're not really particularly in favor of the raw fish.

The President. Well, I'm a beef man. You know I like good beef. Japan's got some of the greatest beef in the world. And— but I'm also, hopefully, a good enough guest not to demand a particular menu from my host. The Prime Minister and I have eaten a lot of meals together. And I'm confident that he will put together a good meal for both the First Lady, Laura, and me. And I really am looking forward to seeing him. He is—he is a great friend. He is an interesting man. I really enjoyed being around him. You know, one of the— he came to my ranch. And he and I sat down apart from the house in a beautiful part of the ranch and had a very long discussion just on a personal basis. And it

meant a lot to me. He's a leader of a great country and a great friend of the United States. And I'm grateful for our relationship.

Mr. Kimura. Thank you very much, Mr. President.

The President. Yes, sir, you're welcome.

NOTE: The interview was taped at 3:10 p.m. in the Library at the White House, and the transcript was released by the Office of the Press Secretary on October 18. In his remarks, the President referred to Prime Minister Junichiro Koizumi of Japan; and Chairman Kim Chong-il of North Korea. A tape was not available for verification of the content of this interview.

Interview With Antonio Baltazar V. Nebrida, Jr., of the Philippines' NBN TV–4
October 14, 2003

The Philippines' Role in the War on Terror

Mr. Nebrida. Mr. President, the Philippines has taken a position behind just about every initiative that the United States Government has taken against the global fight against terrorism. As a partner in this endeavor, what do you see the Philippines doing further?

The President. First of all, Gloria Arroyo, the President, has been very strong, and I appreciate that. And I appreciate my friendship with her. Secondly, the Philippines has recognized that there is a problem in parts of the country and have asked for some help, some training. And we're more than happy to provide it, because there's no question in my mind the will of the Government is to bring people to justice, and the Government has. In other words, there's a recognition of the problem and a willingness to deal with it.

I think that our relationship is such— it's a very close, longstanding relationship— is such that we will see opportunities to

work together, and we will work in concert. I would never ask the Philippines to do something that the Government was comfortable doing, but our relationship is good.

And one key thing that people need to understand is that the war on terror goes on, and therefore, it's important to have leaders who understand that. And the President understands that, and I appreciate her courage.

Upcoming Elections in the Philippines

Mr. Nebrida. Continuing with the program, the Philippines is coming into a very critical phase. We're getting our national and local elections in 2004. Are there apprehensions over the exercise itself, or the outcome of the election?

The President. Well, first of all, there's no apprehension over the outcome of the election. The people—we trust the people in America. We've got our own elections, by the way, coming up in 2004. I would hope that the Philippines would continue to serve as a good example of democracy in the region, in other words, that there be an inclusiveness and, of course, that the elections be carried off in a peaceful way. It will be a very important election for others to watch, and watch the example of the Philippines' elections. And the people will make the right decision. I know my friend is running again, and she's got a strong agenda to run on.

Filipino Americans

Mr. Nebrida. All right. Close historic links between the United States and the Philippines are seen in the very large and significant Filipino community in the United States.

The President. Yes.

Mr. Nebrida. How do you see the contribution of that particular community in nation-building here in the United States?

The President. Well, first of all, there's roughly 2 million Philippine Americans, which is a wonderful contribution to our country. These people are great people. And I know; I work with them right here in the White House. We've got some great Philippine Americans here that are proud of their country but most of all love America, because we stand for freedom and justice and opportunity. And the Philippine community has provided great contributions in business and arts and civic participation. And I'm really proud that there are that many Philippine Americans who are citizens of our great land.

Upcoming APEC Summit

Mr. Nebrida. You're heading for Thailand. The Philippines—our President is also heading for the APEC meeting there. You will be meeting each other. There are apprehensions over the emergence of bilateral agreements, trade agreements, and regional trading blocs. Is APEC still a relevant organization as far as the United States sees its allies and its partners?

The President. Yes, that's a very good question. It needs to be relevant, because APEC has—that room will fill up with leaders that can do a lot to shape a more peaceful world and a more prosperous world. Trade is a central element of our foreign policy, and many of our trading partners, like the Philippines, will be in that room. And we've got to talk about free trade and open trade. We cannot—you know, we must advance the agenda of the WTO.

There is a great opportunity to discuss ways to enhance prosperity. And I might remind everybody that this war on terror continues. There's a lot of wonderful leaders that will be in the room who have dedicated themselves to the proposition that we must deal with terror now or be dealing with it in more violent forms later. And President Arroyo is such a leader. So I'm looking forward to having a very frank discussion and a good discussion with APEC. I think APEC is relevant, and I think this meeting will help make it more relevant.

Mr. Nebrida. Mr. President, thank you so much.

The President. Thank you, sir.

Mr. Nebrida. Thank you for this opportunity to be with you, and it's indeed an honor and privilege.

The President. My honor, too. You're welcome. Thank you, sir.

NOTE: The interview was taped at 3:17 p.m. in the Library at the White House, and the transcript was released by the Office of the Press Secretary on October 18. In his remarks, the President referred to President Gloria Macapagal-Arroyo of the Philippines. A tape was not available for verification of the content of this interview.

Interview With Thepchai Yong of Thailand's Nation TV
October 14, 2003

Thailand-U.S. Relations

Mr. Yong. Mr. President, I understand that during your visit to Bangkok you'll be announcing that your administration will designate Thailand as a major non-NATO ally. What does it mean to Thailand and to Thai-American relations?

The President. First of all, you're a pretty darn good reporter. Secondly, it's probably best that I not reveal what the Prime Minister and I are going to talk about until after we talk about it.

However, having said that, Thailand and the United States are very close friends. The level of cooperation has been really strong, particularly in matters of common interests. We have a common interest to make sure our countries are secure from terrorism. As you know, the Thai Government very capably—I emphasize "capably"—brought to justice Mr. Hambali, the planner of the Bali bombings in Indonesia, the killer of hundreds of innocent lives. And I really—and it was a piece of really good work. My only point is that we value our relationship and friendship on this key matter.

Of course, I'll be talking economics as well. Our non-NATO ally status is something I want to speak to privately first with the Prime Minister and not on your TV screen, if you don't mind, but it's a very good question. [*Laughter*]

President's Upcoming Visit to Thailand/ Demonstrations

Mr. Yong. Some of the public opinion in Thailand, like in your country, doesn't always support what the Government does.

The President. Yes.

Mr. Yong. You may admire Thaksin, the Prime Minister, for being supportive of the antiterror campaign. But there are people in Thailand who are not happy with that, against the war in Iraq and, again, your

policy of preemption. And there are people who plan to stage a demonstration to demand that you be arrested during your visit in Bangkok. How do you respond to these critics?

The President. [*Laughter*] Well, I'm—first of all, a society which allows for people to express themselves is the kind of society I admire. I don't expect everybody to agree with my policies, and I appreciate the fact that they are able to express themselves. I'm not so sure I agree with their desire to have me arrested.

Look, some people disagree with my decision to take action against a thug who had been torturing his own people. We've discovered mass graves with hundreds of people that had been buried there, but it's also a man who used chemical weapons. And the United Nations—I didn't act alone. The critics must understand that I was acting in concert with the U.N., who for 10 years—which for years had said, "Disarm." And finally, I went to the U.N. and said, "Wait a minute. This is time to—let's take care of this man one way or the other, and give him a chance to disarm." And he didn't. So I said, "There ought to be serious consequences for not disarming," and we acted.

I'm going to tell you something, people have got to understand I'm not going to forget the lessons of September the 11th, 2001. These are coldblooded killers that received their support from different governments, and this Nation will act to protect our people, and just like I hope the people of Thailand would expect the Prime Minister to act to protect the people in Thailand.

Prime Minister Thaksin Chinnawat of Thailand

Mr. Yong. There is an increased recognition among South Asian countries that

Prime Minister Thaksin of Thailand is gradually emerging as a new regional leader. You have met him. You have talked to him. You see him being different from the other ASEAN leaders?

The President. Well, I certainly don't want to compare him to other leaders. I think that would be unfair. But I do see him as a very strong leader and a very capable leader. He's got a good grasp of the issues. He understands how economies work. He is not afraid to make tough decisions. He stands his ground in the face of criticism. And so I think he is a very interesting, dynamic leader.

Iraq

Mr. Yong. I think there are people in Thailand who doubt whether we made the right decision to send Thai troops to help in the reconstruction of Iraq.

The President. Yes.

Mr. Yong. With mounting casualties on the part of the American troops, there are people who doubt that it's worth the risk or not.

The President. Yes, well, I think—of course, in a free society, there are doubters. But people ought to understand that a free and peaceful Iraq is necessary for world security. A peaceful society in the midst of a part of the world that's been troubled is going to, for the long run, help—will help change the world in a positive way. And therefore, the idea of helping to rebuild a country ought to be something the Thai people accept.

You've got to understand, the people in Iraq lived under incredible tyranny and torture and rape rooms, the kinds of things the people in Thailand reject. These people were—the tyrant brutalized them and at the same time built up weapons and didn't spend the money on social services. And so not only are we making the world more secure and peaceful; we're actually making life better for people who had been brutalized by this man. And surely the people who respect human rights and decency understand the need to help.

Now, our troops are—we're in the process of hunting down these killers. And the more progress there is in Iraq, the more the terrorists get angry, because they can't stand freedom. So I look forward to making the case of the United States about why it was important to Thailand to contribute. It's important for humanitarian reasons, at the very minimum. But for the long term, it's important for peace and security.

Mr. Yong. Thank you very much for your time.

The President. I'm really looking forward to coming to your beautiful country.

NOTE: The interview was taped at 3:23 p.m. in the Library at the White House, and the transcript was released by the Office of the Press Secretary on October 18. In his remarks, the President referred to Nurjaman Riduan Isamuddin (known as Hambali), Al Qaida's chief operational planner in Southeast Asia; and former President Saddam Hussein of Iraq. A tape was not available for verification of the content of this interview.

Interview With Malcolm Brown of Singapore's Channel NewsAsia
October 14, 2003

Singapore's Role in the War on Terror

Mr. Brown. Talking about your trip specifically to Singapore, how happy are you with the measures that Singapore has taken, specifically regarding terrorism? And what are your concerns about the residual threat in the region?

The President. First, I'm very happy with the Government of Singapore's response to terrorism. They are strong, and they are resolute. They understand the task at hand, and they understand the dangers. Prime Minister Goh and I have had some great conversations about the region. He is a very knowledgeable man. He keeps me abreast of his views of different players in the region and what's going on.

Of course we're concerned about terrorism in the region, because, after all, there's been attacks in the region. I remind our own citizens here that we're still focused on September the 11th as kind of the defining terrorist moment, but there have been a lot of attacks. And the Bali bombing is a classic example of the terrorist activities, and that happens to come in Southeast Asia. The Prime Minister and the Government are concerned, obviously, about those kind of attacks. We'll have a good discussion about it. He's got a lot to offer, a lot of advice to offer, a lot of wisdom, and I listen to it.

Role of APEC Partners in Iraq

Mr. Brown. Mr. President, have your APEC partners done enough to help the United States in Iraq?

The President. In Iraq? Well, we can always use more. And as a matter of fact, the Japanese are going to make an announcement. We're out there working hard to convince others to participate in the reconstruction effort in Iraq. It's in their interests that Iraq be free and peaceful. And the reason it is, is because the region needs democracy. The region needs an example of what can happen in a peaceful society. The region needs something alternative to a type of society which breeds terrorism. I firmly believe that Iraq will emerge to be that example and that leader.

North Korea and Iraq

Mr. Brown. Clearly, the region is also concerned about North Korea.

The President. Yes.

Mr. Brown. You've described Saddam Hussein as a madman and a danger, and he was deposed by force. You've also said that you loathe Kim Chong-il, and he has a known nuclear program. Why this disparity?

The President. Because, first of all, remember in Iraq, we spent 11 years' or so worth of resolutions and discussions and diplomacy trying to convince Saddam Hussein to disarm. He chose not to. I believe we can solve the issue on the North Korean—with the North Korean issue on the Korean Peninsula peacefully.

As a matter of fact, we're making great strides toward that. You might remember, up until recent history, the whole issue is the United States and North Korea. And the Government signed an agreement with North Korea, and they didn't tell the truth. So I've decided to come with a new strategy, and that is, rather than just the United States being the interlocutor with North Korea, we convince others in the neighborhood, like the Chinese and the Russians and the Japanese and the South Koreans. And we're moving along. This will be a major part of our discussions in APEC, to keep this group together, to speak with one voice, and that is, to Kim Chong-il, "Get rid of your nuclear ambitions. No nuclear weapons on the Korean Peninsula." It's in all our interests we do so.

And we're making progress. Now he's hearing at least five voices, not just one. And I believe this can be solved peacefully. Force is the last resort for the United States, not the first resort. It's the last option, and I'm very hopeful that we can make good progress on this issue.

China's Space Program

Mr. Brown. On China, how do you see their space program? Is it a threat to the U.S.?

The President. No, it's an interesting development. I don't necessarily see it as a threat. I think it's a country that's now beginning to emerge as a sophisticated country, and it's got great potential. And I think it's interesting. I hope that they are able to make discoveries in space, like we did, that will—the technology that will come out of that will help mankind. No, I don't view it as a threat.

New Zealand-U.S. Relations

Mr. Brown. Finally, on a regional trade issue, with New Zealand, you'll meet Prime Minister Helen Clark on the sidelines, I understand, at APEC. Why does Australia have negotiations on a FTA [free trade agreement], and New Zealand doesn't? Is it to do with their nuclear policy?

The President. No, not really. I mean, we haven't gotten started with New Zealand. The nuclear policy, obviously, makes it difficult for us to have a military alliance, but we're friends with the New Zealands. We respect the New Zealand people. But Australia is farther along the road when it comes to trade discussions. Prime Minister Howard and I discussed trade at my ranch in Crawford. We hope to get it done by the end of this year. The people of New Zealand shouldn't read anything into it other than, we just haven't gotten started. And I respect the people of New Zealand. I respect that great country.

Mr. Brown. I'm going to have to call it a day. That's all.

The President. I think you did a fine job.

NOTE: The interview was taped at 3:30 p.m. in the Library at the White House, and the transcript was released by the Office of the Press Secretary on October 18. In his remarks, the President referred to Prime Minister Goh Chok Tong of Singapore; former President Saddam Hussein of Iraq; Chairman Kim Chong-il of North Korea; and Prime Minister John Howard of Australia. Mr. Brown referred to Prime Minister Helen Clark of New Zealand. A tape was not available for verification of the content of this interview.

Interview With Rosianna Silalahi of Indonesia's SCTV
October 14, 2003

Indonesia's Role in the War on Terror

Ms. Silalahi. Mr. President, thank you for your time. What specifically do you want to do by Megawati—President Megawati—in fighting terrorism? What—[*inaudible*]—some assistance to your country?

The President. First of all, President Megawati has responded to the war on terror, and I appreciate that. She's responded in a way that I think the people of her country ought to be proud—your country ought to be proud. Terrorism is such—it's such a stain. It's a horrible thing that people have to live with. The terrorists want to create fear. That's what they want to do. They want to kill innocent life to create fear.

And the Bali bombing was a terrible moment for Indonesia and obviously those who lost life. But President Megawati refuses to stand in fear of the terrorists. What I want her to do is to continue to work closely with the United States and others, to share intelligence, find money as it floats around, and to bring people to justice.

Information Sharing on Hambali

Ms. Silalahi. How do you expect President Megawati or Indonesia to cooperate with the United States if we don't have a chance to question Hambali one on one?

Overleaf: Visiting the Santa Monica Mountains National Recreation Area in Thousand Oaks, CA, August 15.

Above: Arriving at Andrews Air Force Base, MD, en route to Baghdad, Iraq, to spend Thanksgiving with U.S. troops, November 26.

Left: Calling world leaders, from the Oval Office, concerning the capture of Saddam Hussein, December 14.

Above right: Greeting U.S. troops during Thanksgiving dinner at the Bob Hope Dining Facility in Baghdad, Iraq, November 27.

Right: Meeting with Iraqi women leaders in the Oval Office, November 17.

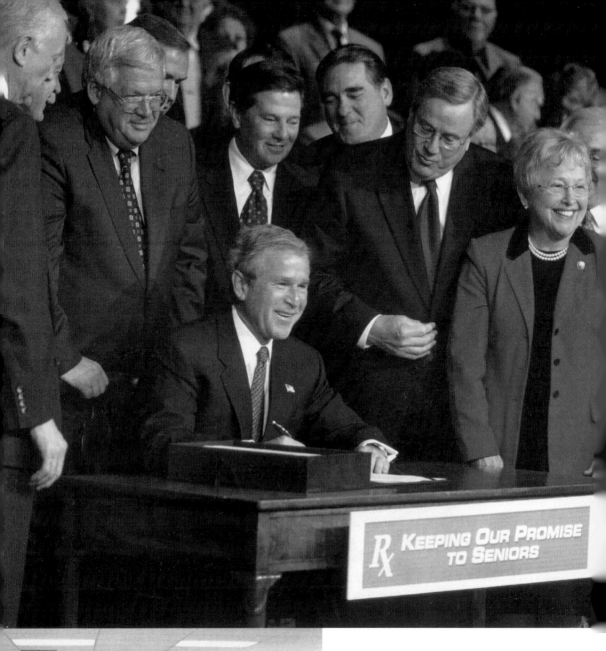

Above: Signing the Medicare Prescription Drug, Improvement, and Modernization Act of 2003, at DAR Constitution Hall in Washington, DC, December 8.

Left: Touring the Department of the Treasury's Financial Management Service regional center in Philadelphia, PA, July 24

Right: Touring Highland Park Elementary School in Landover, MD, July 7.

Above left: Greeting President Mwai Kibaki of Kenya and his wife, Lucy Kibaki, during an arrival ceremony on the South Lawn, October 6.

Left: Relaxing at Buckingham Palace prior to departing for a dinner at Winfield House in London, England, November 20.

Below left: Walking with Prime Minister John Howard of Australia at the Australian War Memorial in Canberra, October 23.

Above right: Standing with Queen Elizabeth II and Prince Phillip during a welcoming ceremony at Buckingham Palace in London, England, November 19.

Right: Touring The AIDS Support Organisation Service Centre in Entebbe, Uganda, July 11.

Overleaf: In front of the White House Christmas Tree in the Blue Room, December 7.

The President. I think the thing on Hambali is—first of all, the good news is he's not a problem anymore. He's not a threat. And as I explained to the President that we will share any information with her. But right now, the key is to find out as much as we possibly can, and when we get information, we will share it with her.

Ms. Silalahi. Well, the problem is that Indonesia needs a chance that—the Indonesian police to question Hambali directly, not just to share information.

The President. Yes.

Ms. Silalahi. When are you going to give us this chance?

The President. Right now, we're going to get as much information as we possibly can.

Ms. Silalahi. So there's no way that Indonesia will have their chance to question Hambali?

The President. I wouldn't say, "No way." You said, "No way." I didn't say, "No way." I said, "Right now, we're going to get as much information as we can to make sure America is secure and Indonesia's secure. And any information we get, we'll be glad to share with the President." I've explained this to her, and she understands.

Situation in the Middle East/Terrorism

Ms. Silalahi. Sir, Indonesia is a moderate and—[*inaudible*]—Muslim society. But the way U.S. handle terrorism issues and by the U.S. foreign policy in the Middle East is distancing society. Aren't you concerned that this moderate society could be militant eventually?

The President. Well, first of all, terrorism—the Bali bombers decided to kill innocent people based upon their own ideology of hatred. And our foreign policy in the Middle East is based on the same principles that I just discussed with you on the war on terror. In order for there to be a peaceful Palestinian state, people have got to fight terror. A few people are trying to destroy the hopes of a lot of people in the Palestinian territory.

And so I gave a speech—first of all, I'm the first President ever to articulate a Palestinian state and to support a Palestinian state. But to get there, it's very important for people to assume responsibilities, and one of the key responsibilities is for the Palestinian leadership to stand up and fight terror. And we've got a good man getting ready to do that. As you know, we had the meeting in Aqaba, Jordan, and we were making progress. And then he got eased out, pushed aside by the old guard, which has failed the Palestinian people. And so they're not assuming their responsibilities.

But I wouldn't—I think you can make all kinds of excuses for terror, but terrorists are interested in one thing, creating fear in free societies. That's what they want to do. The only way to deal with them is to bring them to justice. And you can do that and protect your civil liberties.

Indonesia-U.S. Relations

Ms. Silalahi. How do you propose to change anti-American sentiment in Indonesia?

The President. Explain what we're all about, explain that we're a compassionate country, that we love freedom and human rights and human dignity, that we care when people suffer. We've got a great—very compassionate foreign policy. One of the things I hope to do is, when I go to your country, explain that just like I'm explaining to you now.

And one of the big scourges of the world is AIDS, and the United States of America is leading the fight against AIDS, particularly on the continent of Africa. We believe in decency and human rights. We've always been a leader on human rights. And we speak out for human rights, because we believe in the dignity of each person.

Situation in Papua and Aceh

Ms. Silalahi. Speaking about human rights, Papua and Aceh are struggling to be independent because the human rights has become a critical issue. What is your standpoint about this?

The President. Our standpoint is that we don't think that—in Aceh, for example, that the issue should be solved and can be solved militarily. It ought to be solved through peaceful negotiations.

Ms. Silalahi. And how about Papua?

The President. Same, peaceful negotiations.

Ms. Silalahi. How about American citizens that got killed in Papua?

The President. We're not happy about that, of course, and I appreciate the Government's full cooperation with our Federal Bureau of Investigation that is now seeking out the evidence to determine who the killers were.

Ms. Silalahi. Does it change your military policy towards Indonesia?

The President. No, as a matter of fact, we're going to discuss mil-to-mil relations between Indonesia. And for a while, the Congress put restrictions on it. But now the Congress has changed their attitude, and I think we can go forward with a pack-

age of mil-to-mil cooperation because of the cooperation of the Government on the killings of two U.S. citizens.

Ms. Silalahi. Thank you, Mr. President. So many questions, but——

The President. So little time?

Ms. Silalahi. So little time.

The President. Well, give your mother my best.

Ms. Silalahi. I thank you very much.

NOTE: The interview was taped at 3:37 p.m. in the Library at the White House, and the transcript was released by the Office of the Press Secretary on October 18. In his remarks, the President referred to President Megawati Sukarnoputri of Indonesia; Nurjaman Riduan Isamuddin (known as Hambali), Al Qaida's chief operational planner in Southeast Asia; former Prime Minister Mahmoud Abbas (Abu Mazen) of the Palestinian Authority; and Edwin Burgon and Rick Spier, American citizens killed in an ambush in Indonesia's Papua province on August 31, 2002. A tape was not available for verification of the content of this interview.

Interview With Laurence Oakes of Australia's Channel 9 TV
October 14, 2003

President's Upcoming Visit to Australia

Mr. Oakes. Mr. President, thanks for speaking to us. What's the main purpose of your trip to Australia? Are you hoping for greater Australian contribution to the stabilization and rebuilding of Iraq?

The President. No, the main purpose is to thank the people of Australia and thank my friend John Howard for being strong in the face of terror and being understanding that we have a historic opportunity to bring peace and freedom to parts of the world that need peace and freedom. It really is the main purpose. Australia is a great country. I would define our relationship as a unique relationship. And I'm

looking forward to it. I've been there. They tell me it's kind of like Texas, which is another reason I want to go.

Mr. Oakes. I think that's right. But not everyone agrees—in Australia, agrees with you on the war. Some members of the opposition are talking about possibly protesting when you address the Parliament by wearing white armbands or turning their backs. Would that concern you?

The President. Not at all. No, it means that democracy is alive and well. It's a— I don't expect everybody to agree with us, but one thing is for certain, the Prime Minister was strong. And the Australian military performed brilliantly; I mean brilliantly. And I've talked to a lot of our generals and commanders about how the Australians participated, and they were just—A-plus was the rating. And I think a lot of people would like to hear that from the American President, and I'm going to tell them. And if somebody feels like they want to express discontent, that's okay. That's democracy.

Iraq

Mr. Oakes. Well, what about the suggestion from your critics that while you won the war, the peace is being bungled?

The President. They're wrong. We're making great progress in Iraq. We've got a pretty steep hill to climb. After all, one, we're facing a bunch of terrorists who can't stand freedom. These thugs were in power for a while, and now they're not going to be in power anymore, and they don't like it. And they're willing to kill innocent people. Their terrorist activities—we'd rather fight them there than here.

And secondly, that life is pretty darn good compared to what it was under Saddam Hussein. People aren't going to be tortured. They're not going to be raped. They're not going to mutilated. There are not going to be mass graves. And plus, that the infrastructure is improving. I talked to our Secretary of Commerce today. His exact—he's in Baghdad. He said, "Look," he said, "Mr. President," he said, "You're not going to believe the world here is a lot different than some in America think it is. There's a burgeoning marketplace." He met with women businessowners. I mean, there's excitement there about a free society emerging, and it's in our interests that this society be free.

Australian Detainees in Guantanamo Bay

Mr. Oakes. Sir, there are two Australian citizens being held in Guantanamo Bay.

The President. Yes.

Mr. Oakes. What's going to happen to them? And what do you say to people in Australia who think they should be either charged or released?

The President. Well, we would be glad to work with the Government on the issue. And if John wants to discuss it, I'm more than happy to discuss it. We're working with a variety of countries that have got people in Guantanamo Bay. These are people picked up on the battlefield. We're trying to learn more about them to make sure we fully understand——

Mr. Oakes. Are they being tortured?

The President. No, of course. We don't torture people in America. And people who make that claim just don't know anything about our country.

Australia-U.S. Free Trade Agreement

Mr. Oakes. Another issue between the two countries is the—possibly the free trade agreement.

The President. Yes, sir.

Mr. Oakes. Do you think you will get it, and will you be using this to push it along?

The President. Yes. I told John that we'd like to get a free trade agreement done by the end of this year, and I think it's a good opportunity to say that again. And he and I won't sit down and negotiate the fine points. That's what we've got fine staffs to do, but at our level we can encourage the negotiators to move along. Let's get it done. Let's resolve our differences. Australia is an important friend, an important economy, and I think trade is in our national interests.

War on Terror

Mr. Oakes. Australians have spent this week at memorial services for the victims of the Bali bombing. Can you hold out any hope for them that this—that the war on terrorism is actually getting somewhere?

The President. Yes, Hambali is no longer a problem. He's the guy that organized the Bali bombing. He won't be bombing anybody anymore. That's a positive step.

First of all, I understand what it means to be in a country that grieves over the senseless death of innocent life. And the Australians suffered a mighty blow. And the—matter of fact, the other day I was in Kentucky, you know, politics for a guy running for Governor. And a mother—a fine looking couple walked up, a mom and dad, said, "You've got to know, our daughter died in Bali," and tears in his eyes. And I gave him a big hug. And he said, "Mr. President, whatever you do, don't stop, so it doesn't happen again."

The best way to deal with terror is to be on the offensive and to find these people and bring them to justice. That's why Australia is such an important partner, equal partner, in the war on terror. John Howard gets it. He understands. The Prime Minister knows that we've got to be tough and at the same time create the conditions where there's an alternative to terrorism, and that's freedom and peace.

Mr. Oakes. One final question.

The President. Sure.

Australian, British, and U.S. Leaders' Popularity

Mr. Oakes. You're in trouble politically, if you believe the polls.

The President. Why do you say that?

Mr. Oakes. The polls show you dropping in popularity.

The President. Well, actually, there's a poll that showed me going up yesterday. Not to be on the defensive, but go ahead. [*Laughter*]

Mr. Oakes. Well, I was going to ask why you think you and Tony Blair seem to have lost support, but John Howard hasn't?

The President. Well, it must be his charisma. [*Laughter*] I don't know. Actually, I'm in pretty good shape politically. I really am. I didn't mean to sound defensive.

Mr. Oakes. No, sir.

The President. I am. Politicians, by the way, who pay attention to the polls are doomed to be kind of chasing—trying to chase opinion. What you need to do is lead, set the tone. And I've taken some tough decisions. And I will look forward to making the case that the decisions I have taken will make America more secure, make the world more peaceful, and make this country more prosperous. And so I'm upbeat about it. And as to why Howard is maintaining his popularity and—he married well, and he's smart.

Mr. Oakes. Sir, thank you. And I look forward to seeing you in Australia.

The President. Yes, sir. Looking forward to it. Thanks.

NOTE: The interview was taped at 3:44 p.m. in the Library at the White House, and the transcript was released by the Office of the Press Secretary on October 18. In his remarks, the President referred to Prime Minister John Howard of Australia; former President Saddam Hussein of Iraq; Secretary of Commerce Donald L. Evans; Nurjaman Riduan Isamuddin (known as Hambali), Al Qaida's chief operational planner in Southeast Asia; and Kentucky gubernatorial candidate Ernie Fletcher. Mr. Oakes referred to Prime Minister Tony Blair of the United Kingdom. A tape was not available for verification of the content of this interview.

The President's Radio Address
October 18, 2003

Good morning. During the decades of Saddam Hussein's oppression and misrule, all Iraqis suffered, including children.

While Saddam built palaces and monuments to himself, Iraqi schools crumbled. While Saddam supported a massive war machine, Iraqi schoolchildren went without textbooks, and sometimes teachers went unpaid. Saddam used schools for his own purposes: to indoctrinate the youth of Iraq and to teach hatred.

Under Saddam, adult illiteracy was 61 percent, and for women it was a staggering 77 percent. Iraq is a nation with a proud tradition of learning, and that tradition was betrayed by Saddam Hussein.

As part of our coalition's efforts to build a stable and secure Iraq, we are working to rebuild Iraq's schools, to get the teachers back to work, and to make sure Iraqi children have the supplies they need.

Six months ago, nearly all of Iraq's schools were closed, and many primary schools lacked electrical wiring and plumbing and windows. Today, all 22 universities and 43 technical institutes and colleges are open, as are nearly all primary and secondary schools in the country. Earlier this year, we said we would rehabilitate 1,000 schools by the time school started. This month, just days before the first day of class, our coalition and our Iraqi partners had refurbished over 1,500 schools.

Under Saddam, textbooks were so rare, six students had to share each one. So we're working with UNESCO to print 5 million revised and modern textbooks free of Ba'athist propaganda and to distribute them to Iraqi students. By the end of the school year, there will be enough textbooks for each Iraqi student. And for the first time in years, they will get to read the work of great Iraqi writers and poets—much of it banned by Saddam's regime.

We have assembled more than a million school supply kits, including pencils and calculators and note pads for Iraqi schoolchildren. We have distributed tens of thousands of student desks and teacher chairs and chalkboards. And to assure the health of students, we have delivered over 22 million vaccinations for Iraqi children.

In many cases, American soldiers have intervened personally to make sure Iraqi schools get the supplies they need. Army First Lieutenant Kyle Barden of Charlotte, North Carolina, wanted supplies for the 11 schools in Laylan, Iraq. In response to Kyle's request for help, North Carolina schoolchildren, doctors, businesses, and others have donated thousands of dollars to buy notebooks and pencils and colored pens.

Army Major Gregg Softy of the First Armored Division sent an e-mail to friends about Iraq schools. The response was overwhelming. Hundreds of packages were shipped, and a web site was established to encourage other Americans to contribute.

All of our efforts to improve Iraqi education ultimately serve the cause of security and peace. We want young Iraqis to learn skills and to grow and hope, instead of being fed a steady diet of propaganda and hatred. We're making progress, but there is still much work to do. The request I made to Congress for Iraqi reconstruction includes funds for additional health and training projects. I urge Congress to pass my budget request soon, so this vital work can proceed.

Our efforts will help Iraq reclaim its proud heritage of learning and bring it into the family of nations. An elderly man in Umm Qasr recently tried an Internet connection for the first time. He was stunned by the speed with which he could read newspapers from across the world. He said, "Our society has been cut off from the world, and now we are reconnected." As Iraq rejoins the world, it will demonstrate the power of freedom and hope to overcome hatred and resentment. And this transformation will make our Nation more secure.

Thank you for listening.

NOTE: The address was recorded at 8:25 a.m. on October 16 in Riverside, CA, for broadcast at 10:06 a.m. on October 18. The transcript was made available by the Office of the Press Secretary on October 17 but was embargoed for release until the broadcast. The Office of the Press Secretary also released a Spanish language transcript of this address.

Remarks Following Discussions With President Gloria Macapagal-Arroyo of the Philippines and an Exchange With Reporters in Manila, Philippines
October 18, 2003

President Macapagal-Arroyo. I'd like to thank President Bush for coming to the Philippines on this state visit. It affirms the warm and deep relations between our two countries. It's another building block in the revitalized and maturing alliance, rooted in shared histories and shared values, a common interest in global peace and prosperity, as well as a real commitment of combating terrorism and advancing freedom.

I'd like to take this opportunity to thank the United States for its support for the Philippines as a nonpermanent member of the Security Council for the term 2004 to 2005 and also for designating the Philippines as a major non-NATO ally.

I also welcome the Joint Defense Assessment named by our respective defense agencies. It recognizes that the world today requires a new perspective on political and economic security. The assessment recognizes the determination of the Philippines to take greater responsibility for its own political and economic security, even as it acknowledges that strong relations with the U.S. will contribute greatly to peace and prosperity, stability and security, especially from terrorism. Indeed, we must close ranks and stand firm against terrorist threats, however grave, however armed, and from whatever quarter.

When those violence happened in May 2001, the Philippines chose to fight terrorism, compensating for such modest means that it commands with an unshakable resolve to defeat it once and for all.

I thank President Bush for continued security assistance which enhances the means to defeat terrorism. I also appreciate the help of President Bush for increased economic assistance to alleviate poverty and other socio-economic ills from which terrorism draws its strength. I take pride in the robust economic ties that bind the Philippines and the United States.

This past week, in preparation for this visit, we witnessed the launching in the Philippines of Convergys, the largest customer care service company in the world, which is hiring 3,000 workers in its first year of operation. We also witnessed the launching of a new $50 million investment of Ford to launch the Philippines as an export hub for the world. We received $33 million of new USAID money for educational assistance in the conflict-affected areas, and we celebrated the electrification of 1,650 barangays with a contribution of one million pesos per barangay from Mirant, CalEnergy, and San Roque, all in preparation for your visit, Mr. President.

I look forward to the rest of my talks with President Bush and the officials of his administration. Once again, thank you, Mr. President, and thanks to Mrs. Bush for making this state visit to the Philippines.

President Bush. Madam President, thanks. It's been a—this is going to be a great trip, thanks to your wonderful hospitality. I want to thank you and your Government for such wonderful arrangements. And I want to thank the people of Manila for being so friendly to Laura and me as we drove through the streets. There was an outpouring of enthusiasm and waving that really made us feel great, and we want to thank your country very much.

I'm here to continue our important discussions. And I want to remind the people of this country what a great leader you've been when it comes to fighting terror. You've been strong and stalwart, and that's what's needed. The terrorists want to frighten people into inaction. They want to create fear and, therefore, have their way. And you have been strong, and I appreciate that very much. We want to continue to help you.

And I also want to thank you for your vision of understanding that freedom is important. It's a human right, and where there's human suffering and tyranny, that—at the same time, terrorist links—the free world must work to change conditions, hopefully in peaceful ways. But sometimes tyranny is so stubborn and ignores the reality that we have to take tough decisions. And Mr. President, you understand that, and I want to thank you very much for that.

I also want to continue to work on close ties, particularly when it comes to trade and jobs. We want the people of the Philippines working, and we want the people of America working. And by having good free trade and fair trade, we can help both countries.

And finally, I want to thank you very much for working together on matters of education. We've got a great education initiative, and you recognize, like I recognize, that education is the best way to fight poverty. And therefore, education is also a great way to enhance democracy.

Thank you for your leadership. Thanks for your hospitality. I'm looking forward to the rest of the day in this beautiful country.

President Macapagal-Arroyo. Thank you.

President Bush. If it's all right, we've got, obviously, some anxiety built up in our press corps there—[*laughter*].

Q. Mr. President——

President Bush. Yes. Speaking about anxiety, yes—[*laughter*]—the dean of the traveling crowd here.

Terrorist Threat in the Philippines

Q. How serious do you think the terrorism threat is here in the Philippines? And what specifically can you do to help President Arroyo deal with it?

President Bush. Well, I think the Abu Sayyaf is serious. It's serious because there are no rules when it comes to a crowd like the Abu Sayyaf. They kidnap. They kill. They maim. And there's only one way to deal with them, and that's to find them and to bring them to justice, which is precisely what the Arroyo Government has been doing.

I was briefed before you all came in about the progress made against the Abu Sayyaf group. Not only has the leadership been slowly but surely brought to justice, but many members of the Abu Sayyaf have been brought to justice.

The best thing we can continue to do within our respective constitutions and/or budgets is to work in a close, cooperative way, starting with intelligence sharing and then providing the assets and the capacity and training to move quickly when a particular target is found. The cooperation between the United States and the Philippines is strong. The success against this particular group is a model for the region, as far as I'm concerned, and I want to thank the President for that.

President Macapagal-Arroyo. Thank you.

APEC Summit Agenda

Q. Mr. President, you're trying to put security on the agenda at APEC. Do you think some leaders of this region, some countries are not doing enough to crack down on terrorism?

President Bush. No, I think security is on the agenda. What I'm trying to do and will do is to remind people that the war on terror goes on. See, the easiest thing to do is to think the war on terror is over with. It's certainly the most comfortable approach. And I just will remind people that, in view of the United States, that the United States is still threatened and our friends are threatened, and therefore, we must continue to cooperate and work. And the good news is that I don't have to convince Madam President of that. She understands that as well as anybody in the region.

We'll also, of course, talk about jobs. And I want our people working, and I know the President wants the people of the Philippines working. And trade is important. It's an important way to lift lives on both sides of the Pacific. But it's also important to have free—fair trade. In other words, we want the trade to be—markets to be equally open. And that's an important conversation that I will have with the members of APEC.

And the other thing, of course, is a chance to renew friendships and to be able to kind of continue discussions that I had been having in the past. The President and I, gosh, we've talked a lot. We've met a lot, and we've talked a lot. These meetings are important ways to keep our friendships going and to keep our common interests alive.

Q. Mr. President——

President Bush. Stretch [Richard Keil, Bloomberg News]. We call him Stretch. [*Laughter*]

President Macapagal-Arroyo. I can see why. [*Laughter*]

U.N. Security Council Resolution on Iraq

Q. You got a resolution through the U.N. this week, but some of the countries that opposed the war, going back to last year, France, Germany, Russia, still haven't come forward with any contributions. Do you think this—and some members of your administration cautioned us against assuming there will be any major inflow of contributions, troops, and money, as a result of this. Do you think that's a realistic outlook on things?

President Bush. Well, first, let me thank those countries for their vote at the U.N. That was a very important vote. And as a matter of fact, the first thing that the President and I discussed, and the first thing that Prime Minister Koizumi and I discussed was the vote at the U.N. It's important for these countries around the world to see the U.N. act the way the U.N. acted in a 15 to nothing U.N. Security Council resolution vote. It was a strong vote.

And as to whether or not they'll participate, time will tell. But I—take, for example, Germany. Germany is participating in the aftermath of certain battles in the war on terror. And that is in Afghanistan; they're making a very serious, important contribution. And for that we are very grateful. And there will be other ways for nations to contribute in the overall war on terror.

And I'm pleased with the progress we are making in Iraq. The President and I discussed that progress, and it's measurable progress. For example, we had a goal of 1,000 schools to open after the end of the conflict, and it wasn't 1,000 schools that were refurbished and opened, but it was 1,500—1,500 schools. And the electricity is coming on, and the water is more pure. And I can cite a series of examples where life is improving for the Iraqi citizen.

It is still a dangerous place because there are still haters and thugs and terrorists who are willing to take innocent life. And the reason why is, is because they want America to leave. They want to create the conditions of fear, and therefore, we'll say, "Well, we've had enough." But we're not leaving. See, we're not leaving until we complete the task.

And I am pleased with progress. And one of the President's ministers was there, talking about education matters and the need for us to continue to work together to improve the lives of the Iraqi citizens, and we will. It's in our interest that Iraq be free and peaceful. It will help change the world.

And I want to thank the President for her strong support. There are Philippine citizens there today.

All right, thank you all.

NOTE: President Macapagal-Arroyo spoke at approximately 2:30 p.m. at Malacanang Palace. In his remarks, President Bush referred to Prime Minister Junichiro Koizumi of Japan. Portions of these remarks could not be verified because the tape was incomplete.

Remarks to a Joint Session of the Philippine Congress in Quezon City, Philippines
October 18, 2003

Thank you all very much. Thank you. Mr. President, Mr. Speaker, Members of the Congress, distinguished guests, I thank you for your gracious welcome to the Republic of the Philippines. I also want to thank the citizens of Manila who lined the streets today for their warm and gracious welcome to Laura and me. It warmed our hearts. And I want to thank you for inviting me to be the first American President since Dwight Eisenhower to address this body.

Earlier this year, Laura and I hosted President and Attorney Arroyo at the White House, the first state visit from an Asian country during my administration. Today we are honored to visit America's oldest ally in Asia and one of America's most valued friends in the world.

The great patriot Jose Rizal said that nations win their freedom by deserving it, by loving what is just, what is good, what is great to the point of dying for it. In the 107 years since that good man's heroic death, Filipinos have fought for justice; you have sacrificed for democracy; you have earned your freedom.

America is proud of its part in the great story of the Filipino people. Together our soldiers liberated the Philippines from colonial rule. Together we rescued the islands from invasion and occupation. The names of Bataan, Corregidor, Leyte, Luzon evoke the memories of shared struggle and shared

loss and shared victory. Veterans of those battles are here today. I salute your courage and your service. Along the way and through the years, Americans have gained an abiding respect for the character of your nation and for the decency and courage of the Filipino people.

The Pacific is wide, but it does not divide us. Over 2 million American citizens trace their ancestry to these islands. The commerce between us is vibrant and growing. We work together each day in law enforcement and economic development and government reform. Our young people study at each other's universities. Many Filipinos teach in American public schools. And just this week, our two Governments launched a 6-year effort to extend greater educational opportunities to children in some of the poorest regions of this country. We understand—we both know that education helps defeat poverty.

The United States and the Philippines are warm friends. We cherish that friendship, and we will keep it strong. Our countries are joined by more than a market, even more than an alliance. This friendship is rooted in the deepest convictions we hold. We believe in free enterprise, disciplined by humanity and compassion. We believe in the importance of religious faith, protected by religious liberty. We believe in the rule of law, made legitimate by the will of the people. And we believe that democracy is the only form of government fully compatible with human dignity.

These ideals speak to men and women in every culture; yet they are under attack in many cultures in many parts of the world. A new totalitarian threat has risen against civilization. Like other militarists and fascists before them, the terrorists and their allies seek to control every mind and soul. They seek to spread chaos and fear, intimidate whole societies, and silence all opposition. They seek weapons of mass destruction to complete their hatred and genocide. The terrorists will continue their missions of murder and suicide until they're stopped, and we will stop them.

Every nation in Asia and across the world now faces a choice. Nations that choose to support terror are complicit in a war against civilization. Nations that try to ignore terror and hope it will only strike others are deluding themselves, undermining our common defense, and inviting a future of catastrophic violence. Nations that choose to fight terror are defending their own safety and the safety of free people everywhere.

The Philippines and the United States have seen the enemy on our own soil. Americans witnessed the murder of thousands on a single day. Filipinos have known bombings and kidnaping and brutal murders of the innocent. We've endured the violence and grief of terror. We know the enemy wants to spread fear and chaos. Our two nations have made our choice. We will defend ourselves, our civilization, and the peace of the world. We will not be intimidated by the terrorists.

We're on the offensive against the terrorists, draining their funds, disrupting their plans, and bringing them to justice, one person at a time. Here in the Philippines, one face of the enemy is the Abu Sayyaf group. These killers torture and behead their victims while acting or claiming to act in the name of God. But murder has no home in any religious faith. And these terrorists must find no home in the Philippines.

My Government and your Government pursue a common objective: We will bring Abu Sayyaf to justice. And we will continue to work together, along with our friends in Southeast Asia, to dismantle Jemaah Islamiyah, the terrorist network, as well as other groups that traffic in violence and chaos. As we fight the terrorists, we're also determined to end conflicts that spread hopelessness and feed terror.

The United States supports President Arroyo's campaign to establish a lasting peace with the Moro Islamic Liberation Front. Shortly before his death, Ustaz Hashim Salamat wrote a letter to me professing his rejection of terrorism. Only that commitment to peace can bring a better future to the people in Mindanao.

I call on all the members of the MILF to reject terror and to move forward with political negotiations. When a lasting peace is established, the United States is prepared to provide development assistance to Mindanao.

Yet there can be no compromise with terror. Philippine security forces have the right and the duty to protect local communities and to defeat terrorism in every form. In the war on terror, U.S.-Philippines military alliance is a rock of stability in the Pacific.

And this afternoon, President Arroyo and I agreed to update our defense cooperation. We completed the comprehensive review of Philippine security requirements announced last May. Today President Arroyo and her Government committed to a 5-year plan to modernize and reform your military. I commend the President and your military leadership for taking this bold action. My country will provide technical assistance and field expertise and funding.

But success requires more than American assistance. The Members of this body must invest in the Philippine military to ensure that your forces have the resources needed to win the war on terror and to protect the Philippine people.

Free nations have faced a great challenge all around the world and a great challenge in Iraq. Saddam Hussein pursued weapons of mass destruction, sponsored terrorism, oppressed his people, and for 12 years defied the demands of the United Nations. Finally, the U.N. Security Council in Resolution 1441 demanded that Saddam disarm, prove his disarmament to the world, or face serious consequences. Saddam Hussein chose defiance, and President Arroyo was one of the first world leaders to recognize the need for action. The Philippines joined the United States in supporting and enforcing the serious consequences. You rose to the moment, and the American people respect your courageous and principled stand.

Since the liberation of Iraq, we have discovered Saddam's clandestine network of laboratories suitable for biological and chemical weapons research, his design work on prohibited long-range missiles, his elaborate campaign to hide his illegal weapons programs. We've shut down terror camps, denied terrorists a sanctuary. By our actions, our coalition removed a grave and gathering danger. We also ended one of the cruelest regimes in our time. Saddam's rape rooms and torture chambers and children's prisons are closed forever. His mass graves will claim no victims. The world was right to confront the regime of Saddam Hussein, and we were right to end the regime of Saddam Hussein.

Now that the dictator is gone, Americans and Filipinos and many others share a common vision for that country. Coalition forces, including Filipino peacekeepers and medical workers, are working for the rise of freedom and self-government in Iraq. We're helping to build a free Iraq, because the long-suffering Iraqi people deserve lives of opportunity and dignity. And we're helping to build a free Iraq, because free nations do not threaten others or breed the ideologies of murder. By working for democracy, we serve the cause of peace.

Democracy always has skeptics. Some say the culture of the Middle East will not sustain the institutions of democracy. The same doubts were once expressed about the culture of Asia. These doubts were proven wrong nearly six decades ago when the Republic of the Philippines became the first democratic nation in Asia. Since then, liberty has reached nearly every shore of the western Pacific. In this region of the world and in every other, let no one doubt the power of democracy, because freedom is the desire of every human heart.

Sustaining liberty is not always easy. The world saw this last July here in the Philippines. And all free nations rejoiced when the mutiny against this Government failed. People of this land fought too hard, too long to surrender your freedom to the conspiracy of a few.

All of you in this chamber are the protectors of Philippine democracy, charged with upholding the legacy of Rizal and Quezon. Members of the Philippine Armed Forces are commissioned to fight for freedom, not to contend for power. I'm certain that in the coming election, this nation will show its deep commitment to democracy and continue to inspire people throughout Asia.

In this city, on a January morning in 1995, Pope John Paul II addressed millions of the faithful. He spoke of the goodness of the Filipino people and the strength of your democracy and the example this nation has set for others. He said, "May your light spread out from Manila to the farthest corners of the world, like the great light which shone in the night at Bethlehem." Ladies and gentlemen, the world needs the Philippines to continue as a light to all of Asia and beyond.

There is so much to be proud of in your beloved country, your commitments to democracy and peace and your willingness to oppose terrorism and tyranny. The United States and the Philippines have a proud history. And we face the future bound by the strongest ties two nations can share.

We stand for liberty, and we stand together.

May God bless. Thank you all very much.

NOTE: The President spoke at 4:50 p.m. in the Session Hall at the Philippine House of Representatives. In his remarks, he referred to Franklin M. Drilon, President, Senate of the Philippines; Jose de Venecia, Jr., Speaker of the Philippine House of Representatives; President Gloria Macapagal-Arroyo of the Philippines, and her husband, Jose Miguel Arroyo; Ustaz Salamat Hashim, former leader of the Moro Islamic Liberation Front; and former President Saddam Hussein of Iraq. A portion of these remarks could not be verified because the tape was incomplete.

Joint Statement Between the United States of America and the Republic of the Philippines
October 18, 2003

President Gloria Macapagal-Arroyo warmly welcomed President George W. Bush to Malacanang today for the first State visit of an American President to Manila in over 30 years. As the two Presidents highlighted during President Macapagal-Arroyo's State visit to the United States last May, the ties between the Philippine and American peoples are deeply rooted in shared history and values, as well as in a shared commitment to global peace, security and prosperity.

President Macapagal-Arroyo expressed her appreciation for the support extended by President Bush to the Veteran Equity bills pending in both houses of the U.S. Congress, designed to enhance benefits for Filipino veterans of World War II residing in the United States. Both Presidents noted that the American and Filipino fighting men of World War II remain a strong bond between the peoples of both nations. President Bush announced the doubling of U.S. funding for medical equipment at the Veterans Medical Center in Quezon City. President Bush highlighted his respect for the impressive contributions of Filipino-Americans to American social, cultural and economic life.

The two Presidents focused their discussion on the security challenges facing the United States and the Philippines, agreeing that the U.S.-Philippine partnership has taken on new vitality and importance in the context of the global war on terrorism. Presidents Macapagal-Arroyo and Bush reviewed recent successes in the war on terrorism, noting with satisfaction that a number of terrorist killers have been brought to justice. They agreed that while progress had been made in attacking terrorist organizations both globally and regionally, much work remains to be done.

President Bush praised President Macapagal-Arroyo's courage and strength in confronting terrorism in the Philippines and in Southeast Asia. He expressed particular appreciation for Philippine initiatives to improve and expand international counterterrorism cooperation and thanked President Macapagal-Arroyo for her leadership working with key ASEAN partners to address the terrorist threat on a regional basis. The two leaders agreed that such cooperation, particularly in the area of information sharing, is an essential component of the war on terrorism.

In recognition of the strength and vitality of the alliance, as well as its vital role in promoting regional security and combating global terrorism, President Bush informed President Macapagal-Arroyo that he had designated the Philippines as a Major Non-NATO Ally (MNNA). President Macapagal-

Arroyo thanked President Bush for this honor and expressed hope that this move would facilitate the modernization of the Philippine Armed Forces and the strengthening of our defense partnership.

In keeping with their May 19 pledge to conduct a comprehensive security assessment, the two Presidents also reviewed and endorsed the findings of the 2003 Joint Defense Assessment (JDA) of the Armed Forces of the Philippines' capabilities and requirements. The purpose of the JDA is to assist the government of the Philippines in developing a defense program that will improve the ability of the Philippine military to respond to threats to Philippine security.

President Arroyo noted the determination of her government to move forward on an ambitious program of military reform, including increased allocation of resources to Philippine national defense. President Bush committed to assist the Philippines in this effort.

The two Presidents agreed that their respective defense establishments would embark on a multi-year plan to implement the key recommendations of the Joint Defense Assessment. They agreed to direct their defense establishments to finalize details of the plan and begin its implementation.

President Macapagal-Arroyo welcomed substantial new U.S. programs of law enforcement training, equipment, and expertise in support of her efforts to strengthen the rule of law and to reform and strengthen the Philippines National Police and other law enforcement agencies.

President Bush commended President Macapagal-Arroyo for her steadfast leadership in pursuing economic reforms in the Philippines and welcomed her pledge to maintain resolve in pursuing reforms in revenue collection, energy privatization and intellectual property rights protection.

President Bush praised President Macapagal-Arroyo's determination to alleviate poverty and other socio-economic grievances that are too often exploited by terrorist organizations to recruit followers. President Arroyo welcomed the new, six year U.S. initiative to strengthen education in the poorest areas of the Philippines, particularly Mindanao, as supportive of her efforts. This new program complements the Philippine government's efforts to uplift the communities in the Autonomous Region of Muslim Mindanao (ARMM) and expand their access to education and training.

The two Presidents discussed the Philippine government's efforts to establish a durable, effective peace with the Moro Islamic Liberation Front (MILF). They expressed appreciation for Malaysia's role in facilitating the negotiating process. President Bush emphasized U.S. willingness to provide diplomatic and financial assistance in support of peace but emphasized that the MILF must first fully renounce terror and demonstrate its commitment to peaceful political negotiations.

Presidents Bush and Macapagal-Arroyo discussed the situation in Iraq. The two leaders reiterated their shared commitment to a free Iraq at peace with its neighbors and expressed unwavering determination to continue the important work of helping the Iraqi people build a stable, just and prosperous country that poses no threat to the world. President Bush thanked President Macapagal-Arroyo for the contributions made by the Philippines to security and reconstruction in Iraq. The two Presidents affirmed the vital role of the United Nations in postwar Iraq and stressed the need for more countries to contribute peacekeeping and humanitarian contingents to Iraq as that country prepares for sovereignty under a democratic regime.

The two leaders welcomed the six party talks in Beijing and reiterated their intention to work with other members of the Asia Pacific region to ensure the complete, verifiable and irreversible elimination of North Korea's nuclear weapons program.

President Bush congratulated the Philippines on its nomination by Asian countries to join the United Nations Security Council and expressed confidence that the Philippines would contribute to global peace and security.

President Bush and President Macapagal-Arroyo concluded the visit by celebrating the impressive gains made in Philippine-U.S. relations under their administrations, expressing confidence that today's State visit marks another concrete step forward in the development of a modern, mature relationship between friends and equals.

NOTE: An original was not available for verification of the content of this joint statement.

Remarks at a State Dinner Hosted by President Gloria Macapagal-Arroyo in Manila
October 18, 2003

The President. Thank you very much, Madam President and Attorney Arroyo, for your gracious hospitality. Laura and I are really grateful for your warm words of welcome. We also appreciate the distinction you have bestowed upon us this evening, the Order of the Sikatuna and the Order of Gabriela Silang. We are honored to accept them on behalf of the American people.

I represent the oldest democracy in the Americas. And I'm proud to pay tribute to the oldest democracy in Asia. The friendship between our countries is strong and warm and enduring, and we reaffirm that partnership here tonight.

Today I was the first United States President since Dwight Eisenhower to address a Joint Session of your Congress. In 1960, President Eisenhower expressed America's firm support for a fledgling democracy. Two generations later, I am pleased to show my country's support for the great democracy you have become.

The Philippines and the United States are linked by shared values, by shared history, and by a shared commitment to the defense of liberty. Only a few miles from this palace are the graves of 17,000 Americans who fought for freedom in the Pacific. Their lasting legacy and the legacy of the Filipinos who fought with them is a free and democratic Philippine nation.

Today, free nations are tested once again. Once again, we face determined enemies of freedom, the terrorists and their allies. Once again, we are depending on one another in an hour of need. Once again, we are relying on the strength of the great alliance between our two countries. Once again, we will prevail.

Madam President, I thank you for your friendship and counsel, for your courage and perseverance. And I offer this toast to you, to the great nation of the Philippines, and to the lasting friendship between our two peoples.

[At this point, the President offered a toast.]

The President. Thank you.

NOTE: The President spoke at 6:45 p.m. at Malacanang Palace. In his remarks, he referred to President Gloria Macapagal-Arroyo of the Philippines, and her husband, Jose Miguel Arroyo.

Remarks Following Discussions With Prime Minister Thaksin Chinnawat of Thailand and an Exchange With Reporters in Bangkok, Thailand
October 19, 2003

President Bush. Mr. Prime Minister, thank you very much for your grand hospitality. Our entire delegation is honored that you have worked so hard to make our stay comfortable and meaningful.

We just had a very good bilateral with our very close friend. I want to thank the Prime Minister for his strong support in the war on terror and remind our fellow citizens that because of his Government and his good work, Mr. Hambali, one of the masterminds of the Bali bombing, has been brought to justice. Mr. Prime Minister, the world is safer because of that. And I want to thank you, and I want to thank you for your support in Iraq.

I told the Prime Minister that this country is willing to grant major non-NATO ally status to Thailand, which is a very important recognition of your friendship and your strong support. As well we discussed the fact that we want to move forward the free trade agreement. We have the intention to begin negotiations on our free trade agreement, which is a very important step in our bilateral relations. And I want to thank you for that.

We also talked about a wide range of issues, including Burma and our deep desire for freedom to take place in Burma. We care deeply about Aung San Suu Kyi and the status of Aung San Suu Kyi, and we would like to see her free. I appreciate the sympathetic hearing I got from the Prime Minister. We share the same goal; the Government assured us of that, and I thank him for that.

All in all, it was very constructive visit, perhaps made more constructive by the fact that the Prime Minister went to university at Sam Houston State in Huntsville, Texas—[*laughter*]—and therefore, we speak the same language. [*Laughter*]

Thank you, sir, for your hospitality.

I thought I'd take a couple of questions.

North Korea

Q. Mr. President, would you be willing to offer North Korea some kind of non-invasion or non-aggression agreement or pact, maybe something short of a treaty, if it would get out of the nuclear weapons business?

President Bush. Well, that's exactly what I'm going to talk to the leader of China about here in a couple of hours, how to move the process forward. I've said as plainly as I can say that we have no intention of invading North Korea. And I've also said as plainly as I can say that we expect North Korea to get rid of her nuclear weapons ambitions. And the progress we're making on this issue is that we've convinced other nations to say the same thing, including China and Japan and South Korea and Russia—and Thailand. The Foreign Minister recently has had a trip there, and briefed us on his discussions with the North Korean Government.

We would like to see the Korean Peninsula without any nuclear weapons. And we will also be willing to discuss with the Chinese and our other partners how to move the process forward. That's precisely what I'm going to do.

Holland [Steve Holland, Reuters].

Usama bin Laden Tape/War on Terror

Q. Sir, bin Laden is threatening new attacks. How serious a threat is this, and will this discourage other countries from stepping forward in Iraq?

President Bush. I think that the bin Laden tape should say to everybody the war on terror goes on, that there's still a danger for free nations and that free nations need to work together more than ever to share intelligence, cut off money, and bring these potential killers or killers to justice. And we've got to find them. And that's one of the discussion points that the Prime Minister and I just had. It's something I'll discuss with other leaders here at APEC. This is still a dangerous world, and that tape just points out exactly what I meant.

David.

North Korea

Q. Mr. President——

Q. Mr. President——

Q. Which one?

President Bush. Neither. [*Laughter*] Both. [*Laughter*] The prettier one first. [*Laughter*]

Q. I'll let you go——

Q. I won't go there, Mr. President. If I could just follow up on your answer on North Korea. You've often said in recent days that you had made the decision on Iraq because you could not leave the security of the American people in the hands of a madman——

President Bush. Yes.

Q. You are now in a position where the CIA says, has long said that North Korea has maybe two weapons. There are some arguments they may now have four or six, while this slow diplomacy has gone on. Would you say that Kim Chong-il now poses as urgent and immediate a threat today as Saddam Hussein did a year ago?

President Bush. I would say that the situation is different between North Korea and Iraq, and that it's this, David, that we tried diplomacy for 12 long years in Iraq, and many Security Council resolutions for Iraq, and the world spoke clearly about Iraq. And Saddam Hussein ignored the world. And therefore, we put a coalition together to deal with Saddam Hussein.

We're making progress on the diplomatic front. I'd like to resolve all issues in a peaceful way, without using our military, and I think we have an opportunity to do so——

Q. Even if they're still building weapons while you do it?

President Bush. Well, we'll find out if they are or not. We—the key thing we're going to do is now, for the first time, have started to speak with not one voice but five voices to convince Mr. Kim Chong-il that he ought to change his way.

And today is—we're furthering the process with my discussions with Mr. Hu Jintao on this very subject. China is now very much engaged in the process. And as you very well know as a student of this issue, that hasn't been the case up until recently. As a matter of fact, the bilateral approach to dealing with North Korea didn't work. We signed an agreement with North Korea prior to our arrival in Washington, DC, and the North Koreans cheated. And so we're trying another approach. And I'm hopeful this will work, and we're making good progress on this approach.

Yes.

Q. Sir, can I just follow on one aspect of that, which is you're making very clear again today that you have no intention of invading North Korea, and you want them to know that. But in your mind, is there a distinction between saying that publicly and putting that down on paper in a non-aggression pact? Is that something you are unwilling to do?

President Bush. I'm going to look at all options. But you know, first of all, it is very important for us to work with our partners on this issue. That's the difference. And the difference is that we've now got four other voices besides ourselves who say the same message to Mr. Kim Chong-il, and that is, "Disarm." And we want to explore these options with our—with China and Japan, South Korea, and Russia. And that's what I intend to do.

Q. [*Inaudible*]—that's an important idea, you may——

President Bush. First of all, what's important is that the burden is on North Korea, not on America. North Korea must get rid of her nuclear ambitions. She must get rid of her weapons program. That's exactly the point we're trying to make—in a verifiable way, I might add. And we are—we think there's an opportunity to move the process forward, and we're going to discuss it with our partners.

We will not have a treaty, if that's what you're asking. That's off the table. Perhaps there are other ways we can look at—to say exactly what I said publicly on paper, with our partners' consent.

NOTE: The President spoke at 11:21 a.m. at the Grand Hyatt Erawan Bangkok. In his remarks, he referred to Nurjaman Riduan

Isamuddin (known as Hambali), Al Qaida's chief operational planner in Southeast Asia; Aung San Suu Kyi, leader of the National League for Democracy of Burma; President Hu Jintao of China; Minister of Foreign Affairs Surakiat Sathianthai of Thailand; Usama bin Laden, leader of the Al Qaida terrorist organization; former President Saddam Hussein of Iraq; and Chairman Kim Chong-il of North Korea. The President also referred to reporters David Gregory, NBC News, and David Sanger, New York Times. A tape was not available for verification of the content of these remarks.

Remarks at the Royal Thai Army Headquarters in Bangkok
October 19, 2003

Thank you very much, Mr. Minister. Thank you very much. Thank you very much. General Thammarak, commanders of the Royal Thai Armed Forces, members of the Royal Thai Army, veterans, members of the United States military, distinguished guests and citizens of Thailand, Mrs. Bush and I appreciate your kind welcome to the Royal Thai Army Headquarters. We are honored to be here.

We're honored to be in the Kingdom of Thailand. Today I'm pleased to convey the respect of the American Armed Forces and the good wishes of the American people. I'm grateful to His Majesty the King and Her Majesty the Queen for inviting us to this ancient and beautiful land.

Earlier today I met with Prime Minister Thaksin, and I was proud to reaffirm the great friendship between our nations. We share a belief in democracy and human rights and ethnic and religious tolerance. We also share a willingness to defend those values in times of danger. Our alliance of conviction is also an alliance of courage.

The Thai people have proven your commitment to freedom many times. With us

today are members of the Free Thai Movement, who showed such fierce courage during World War II. Other veterans have served in Korea and Vietnam, where the Americans and Thais fought and died together, and during the cold war, when our partnership was so vital to the stability of Asia. All the veterans hold an honored place in a great alliance, and I salute your service.

Today, our nations are challenged once again. We're threatened by ruthless enemies unlike others we have faced. Terrorist groups hide in many countries. They emerge to kill the innocent. They seek weapons to kill on a massive scale. One terrorist camp in the mountains of central Asia can bring horror to innocent people living far away, whether they're in Bali, in Riyadh, or in New York City. One murderous dictator pursuing weapons of mass destruction and cultivating ties to terror could threaten the lives of millions.

We must fight terrorism on many fronts. We must stay on the offensive until the terrorist threat is fully and finally defeated. To win the war on terror, we must hunt a scattered and resourceful enemy in dark corners around the world. We must break up their cells, shut off their sources of money. We must oppose the propaganda of hatred that feeds their cause. In the nations where resentment and terrorism have taken root, we must encourage the alternative of progress and tolerance and freedom that leads to peace.

Nations that choose to fight terror are defending their own safety and securing the peace of all mankind. The United States of America has made its choice. The Kingdom of Thailand has made its choice. We will meet this danger and overcome this evil. Whatever is asked of us, no matter how long it takes, we will push on until our work is done.

Three months after my country was attacked on September the 11th, 2001, Prime Minister Thaksin came to America and offered Thailand's help in the war on terror. Since then, Thailand has committed military forces outside Southeast Asia for the first time in more than 50 years. Some of you have just returned from Afghanistan, where you gave many months of service. Thai engineers rebuilt Afghanistan's national airfield and helped restore much of that country's infrastructure. And the Afghan people and the American people are grateful for your service. The Thai task force is a vital part of the multinational division in Karbala, Iraq, once again helping a shattered country rebuild after years of oppression.

Inside your own country, you are pursuing dangerous terrorists and finding them, and America thanks you for ending the lethal career of the terrorist Hambali, who is suspected of planning the attack on Bali and other acts of terror. Thailand pledged to fight the war on terror, and that pledge is being honored in full.

Thailand is also a force of good throughout Southeast Asia. When East Timor was torn by violence, Thai forces joined with Americans and Australians to bring stability, and they helped establish the world's newest nation. This important work has brought dignity to the people of East Timor and greater security to this region.

Together, our two nations are fighting the drug trade by sharing intelligence that helps Thai law enforcement officials interdict shipments and catch drug traffickers. We're fighting the trafficking in human beings to abolish a modern form of slavery.

America supports your country's humane efforts to find, defuse, and dispose of landmines. And having cooperated for decades to fight hepatitis and malaria, we're now working together to turn the tide against AIDS.

America and Thailand understand that trade and growth are the only sure ways to spread prosperity and lift people and nations out of poverty. And this morning I'm pleased to announce that the United States and Thailand are planning to launch negotiations toward a free trade agreement. This region and our world must one day trade in freedom.

In all our common efforts, we are confident of the outcome. We're confident in the power of freedom to overcome hatred and uplift whole nations. We're confident in the strength of our alliance, and I have acted to designate Thailand a major non-NATO ally of the United States. And we're confident in the character of those who defend us. American and Thai forces serve together and train together and study at military academies in each other's countries. We have come to know and respect one another.

America remembers and honors a young man named Kemaphoom Chanawongse, known to his family and friends as Ahn. He was born in Bangkok, the grandson of a Royal Thai Air Force veteran. He moved to America when he was 9 years old, fulfilled his great ambition to become a United States Marine. Ahn was part of the force that defeated the army of Saddam Hussein. He was killed in action near An Nasariyah. This son of Thailand, this American patriot, was buried among America's greatest military heroes at Arlington National Cemetery. This brave marine brought honor to the Nation he served and honor to the nation of his birth.

Thailand and the United States lie thousands of miles apart. Yet in the ideals we serve, we will always be close. America is grateful for your friendship. We respect the skill and valor of the Royal Thai military, and we're proud to stand by your side in the cause of peace. May God bless you.

NOTE: The President spoke at 12:40 p.m. In his remarks, he referred to Gen. (Ret.) Thammarak Isarangkun an Ayuttha, Thailand's Minister of Defense; King Phumiphon Adunyadet, Queen Sirikit, and Prime Minister Thaksin Chinnawat of Thailand; Nurjaman Riduan Isamuddin (known as Hambali), Al Qaida's chief operational planner in Southeast Asia; and former President Saddam Hussein of Iraq.

Remarks Following Discussions With President Hu Jintao of China in Bangkok
October 19, 2003

President Bush. President Hu and I have had a very constructive dialog. We talked about a lot of important issues. We talked about the issue of trade. We talked about the need to make sure that trade is open and that both countries benefit from trade. I congratulated China on its recent space launch. I thanked the President for his work on the recent Security Council resolution for Iraq. We talked about our mutual desire to wage and win the fight against terror. We spent time, of course, talking about North Korea. We have a mutual goal, and that is that the Peninsula be free of nuclear weapons.

I want to thank the President for leading the Beijing talks. We talked about how to advance the Beijing talks. We talked about how to advance them to achieving a mutual goal, which is a weapons-free Peninsula as well as addressing the security concerns of North Korea within the context of the six-party talks.

So we've had a very constructive dialog, and I want to thank the President.

President Hu. I just had a friendly meeting with President Bush. This is our second meeting in this year. I think that in itself shows the very sound momentum of the development of our bilateral relations.

We discussed the questions such as the economy and trade, the terror question, counterterrorism, Iraq, and North Korean nuclear issue. We both agreed that the economic cooperation and trade between our two countries have benefited our two peoples tremendously, and we stated our readiness to resolve whatever questions that might emerge in our economic exchanges and trade through dialog.

President Bush restated his Government's position of adhering to the "one China" policy, the three China-U.S. joint communiques, and his opposition to Taiwan independence. And we both stated our desire to further intensify our cooperation against the terrorism.

About the North Korean nuclear issue, I said to the President that China will continue to strengthen our communication and consultations with various parties concerned, and we will continue to work to promote the Beijing six-party talks process, so as to strive for a peaceful resolution of this issue.

I'm ready to work together with the President to promote further development of our constructive and cooperative relationship.

President Bush. Thank you, sir.

NOTE: The President spoke at 4:52 p.m. at the Grand Hyatt Erawan Bangkok. A tape was not available for verification of the content of these remarks.

Letter to President Hu Jintao on China's First Human Space Mission
October 19, 2003

Dear Mr. President:

On behalf of the American people, I congratulate you and the Chinese people on the successful completion of China's first human space mission. I was pleased to learn that Lieutenant Colonel Yang Liwei returned safely to earth. This mission was an historic triumph for the Chinese people and a milestone in the continued exploration of space.

The United States of America warmly welcomes the People's Republic of China's achievement in becoming only the third country to launch an astronaut into space, and wishes you continued success in this endeavor.

Sincerely,

GEORGE W. BUSH

NOTE: An original was not available for verification of the content of this letter.

Remarks at a State Dinner Hosted by King Phumiphon Adunyadet and Queen Sirikit of Thailand in Bangkok
October 19, 2003

Thank you, Your Majesty, for your warm and gracious welcome. Thanks also to Her Majesty the Queen for hosting this event. I thank as well the Grand Chamberlain who earlier today led us on a tour of the magnificent Temple of the Emerald Buddha. Laura and I have been seeing the famous hospitality of the Thai people, and we are most grateful.

The United States of America deeply values our alliance with the Kingdom of Thailand. Your Majesty, the world has changed greatly since your reign began 57 years ago. Yet thanks to your enlightened leadership and steady hand, the friendship between our two nations has remained constant.

Over the decades, we worked together to build the foundations of liberty in this region, rule of law, respect for human rights, free enterprise, and peace. Today, we continue to strive toward the same goals in the face of different challenges. Nations are working together in Afghanistan and Iraq. Royal Thai troops have served well in both places, helping Afghans and Iraqis make the transition from tyranny to self-government.

The emergence of these free nations is a setback for terrorism and radicalism. By sharing the duties of our coalition, Thailand is contributing to peace and stability in those two countries and increasing the security of all free nations.

Thailand has played a vital role in East Timor, helping create a new nation to bring dignity to nearly a million people and to stabilize an entire region. You are fully joined in the fight against the drug trade and against HIV/AIDS and other diseases.

Thailand is a principled, generous nation, rising to meet the challenges of our time. Thailand's positive influence in the world is inspired by the fine example of service that Your Majesty and Her Majesty the Queen set for your people. It's also vivid in the great, humane traditions of this land. America is honored to have your friendship.

So I offer a toast to Your Majesties, to the royal family, and to your great nation.

NOTE: The President spoke at 7:40 p.m. in the Chakri Throne Room at the Grand Palace. A tape was not available for verification of the content of these remarks.

Remarks Prior to Discussions With President Roh Moo-hyun of South Korea in Bangkok
October 20, 2003

President Bush. Thank you all for coming. It's my honor to have breakfast with a friend of the United States and a friend of mine, President Roh. We've got a very important and close relationship with South Korea. We share common goals. We want the world to be more free and peaceful. And that's why I'm so grateful for South Korea's support in places like Iraq.

We also share a goal to enhance the prosperity of our respective peoples. We will discuss ways to make sure our trade between our countries is free and fair. We have a common goal to make sure that the Korean Peninsula is nuclear-weapons-free. We're making good progress on peacefully solving the issue with North Korea. And during this breakfast, I will share ideas and listen to ideas from President Roh as to how to move the process forward.

These are important consultations with a close friend, and I want to thank the President for coming to have breakfast.

President Roh. It is my pleasure to meet with President Bush—[*inaudible*]—and it is to my greater pleasure to meet with him—[*inaudible*]. Korea and the United States have been promoting the friendship between each other based on mutual trust, and we have been addressing the problem in this period of cooperation and friendship.

The United States is currently making various efforts to promote global peace, and it has succeeded in winning the U.N. resolution regarding Iraq. And I would like to congratulate this meaningful progress.

I appreciate that the United States has been making efforts to make progress in the areas related to North Korea, and this issue is very critical for—[*inaudible*]—and the further progress of Korea. And in this regard, the six-party talks—[*inaudible*]—progress. And I would like to thank United States for helping us to achieve this important milestone. And I am thankful for Mr. Bush for making more efforts to continue to resume the six-party talks in the near future.

During today's breakfast with President Bush, I hope to have a meaningful dialog on how to resolve the North Korea nuclear issue and how to realign the—[*inaudible*]—alliance.

At the same time, I would like to commend the United States' effort in bringing peace and democracy in Iraq, and I would like to discuss with him how to reconstruct the economy there, and I would like to discuss with him how Korea can cooperate in this regard. And I would have a meaningful discussion on these points.

And in this meeting, I hope to have a serious discussion in accordance with the goals of the APEC in the areas of how to promote trade and mutual investment and how to promote regional security. And I am sure that we will—[*inaudible*].

Thank you.

President Bush. Thank you very much, Mr. President. Thank you.

NOTE: The President spoke at 8:30 a.m. at the Grand Hyatt Erawan Bangkok. A tape was not available for verification of the content of these remarks.

Joint Statement Between the United States of America and the Republic of Korea
October 20, 2003

On October 20, 2003, President George W. Bush of the United States of America and President Roh Moo-hyun of the Republic of Korea held a summit meeting in Bangkok, Thailand. At the meeting, the two Presidents noted with satisfaction that there has been smooth progress in building a comprehensive and dynamic alliance relationship between the two countries as declared in the Joint Statement adopted on May 14. In addition, the two Presidents had a broad and sincere exchange of views on various issues between the two countries, including North Korea's nuclear issue, Iraq reconstruction, and the issue of upgrading the U.S.-ROK alliance.

Regarding the U.S. request for the dispatch of additional troops to Iraq, President Roh explained that as a result of conducting a comprehensive review of the overall situation, including the importance of the U.S.-ROK alliance and national interest, the ROK government has decided to dispatch additional troops to Iraq so as to provide assistance for a prompt establishment of peace and reconstruction in Iraq. President Roh stated that the size, type and form of the troops as well as the timing of the dispatch will be decided by taking into account public opinion, the result of the survey teams and the characteristics and capability of the Korean military forces. President Bush expressed respect and gratitude to President Roh for making the principled determination to dispatch troops. President Bush also stated that the ROK's dispatch

of troops to Iraq will not only further strengthen the U.S.-ROK alliance and contribute to the reconstruction and stabilization of Iraq, but also will serve as an opportunity to increase the ROK's prestige in the international community.

President Bush and President Roh reconfirmed the principles agreed upon in their summit meeting in May, that they will not tolerate nuclear weapons in North Korea and that they are committed to a peaceful resolution of the issue. The leaders noted the importance of the Six Party talks for achieving the goal of the complete, verifiable and irreversible elimination of North Korea's nuclear weapons programs. The two Presidents shared the view that it is desirable to hold the next round of the talks at an early date and to make concrete progress. President Bush reiterated that the U.S. has no intention of invading North Korea and that the U.S. expects North Korea to end its nuclear weapons ambitions. President Bush explained how security assurances might be provided within the multilateral context, conditioned on North Korea's progress in nuclear dismantlement. President Roh expressed appreciation for President Bush's efforts toward resolving the issue. The two Presidents agreed to study ways and means to seek progress in the next round of the talks. The two Presidents also urged North Korea to respond positively to the other parties' diplomatic efforts and to refrain from any action which would exacerbate the situation.

President Bush and President Roh noted that the strong alliance between the ROK and the U.S. and the presence of US Forces Korea have made great contributions to peace and stability on the Korean peninsula as well as in Northeast Asia. The two Presidents agreed to pursue the relocation of USFK bases in careful consideration of the security environment on the Korean peninsula.

NOTE: An original was not available for verification of the content of this joint statement.

Joint Statement Between the United States of America and the Republic of Singapore
October 21, 2003

Prime Minister Goh Chok Tong and President George W. Bush held discussions on a broad range of issues during President Bush's first official visit to Singapore. This visit builds upon the strong and multi-faceted U.S.-Singapore partnership, which saw the signing of the U.S.-Singapore Free Trade Agreement earlier this year, and on a history of cooperation, congruent interests, and shared perspectives.

President Bush and Prime Minister Goh reviewed recent developments in Southeast Asia and regional efforts in the war against terrorism. They welcomed the recent arrest of Riduan Isamuddin (also known as Hambali) and the conviction of key perpetrators of the Bali bombings. They recognized that much headway had been made in disrupting terrorist networks, but agreed that more needed to be done and that the campaign against terrorism required a sustained long-term effort. The two leaders pledged to continue to work closely, both bilaterally and through multilateral institutions such as ASEAN, APEC, and the UN, to defeat terrorism.

The Prime Minister and the President also discussed the situation in Iraq. They expressed hope for Iraq's early reintegration into the global community. They welcomed the positive steps taken by the Coalition Provisional Authority and the Iraqi Governing Council, in particular the new investment laws passed to restore international investor confidence in the country. President Bush expressed gratitude for Singapore's contribution toward Iraq's reconstruction and commended the Singapore police training contingent's efforts to help train the Iraqi police to protect critical installations.

The President and the Prime Minister reaffirmed the need for a strong U.S. security presence in Asia, which continues to be vital for the peace and stability of the region. President Bush recognized the important role played by Singapore as a major security cooperation partner and expressed appreciation for Singapore's support for the U.S. as reflected in the 1990 Memorandum of Understanding between the U.S. and Singapore. Both leaders expressed concern over the emergence of new threats to global peace and stability such as terrorism and proliferation of weapons of mass destruction and agreed that such threats required even closer cooperation between the U.S. and Singapore.

To this end, Prime Minister Goh and President Bush agreed that the United States and Singapore would enter into negotiations for a Framework Agreement for the Promotion of a Strategic Cooperation Partnership in Defense and Security. This strategic framework agreement will expand upon the scope of current bilateral cooperation in areas of defense and security such as counterterrorism, counterproliferation of weapons of mass destruction, joint military exercises and training, policy dialogues, and defense technology. Both leaders expressed the desire to see this Framework Agreement implemented as soon as possible.

President Bush and Prime Minister Goh emphasized the value of collaborative efforts to respond to new health threats, including emerging diseases and use of biological agents by terrorists. In this regard, both leaders were pleased to endorse the Memorandum of Understanding (MOU) on collaboration recently concluded between the United States Department of Health and Human Services and the Singapore Ministry of Health. The MOU will establish the Regional Emerging Diseases Intervention (REDI) Center. Based in Singapore's newly opened Biopolis, the REDI Center will facilitate the exchange of information and expertise on surveillance; prevention and control of, and research on, communicable and non-communicable diseases; and on bioterrorism concerns. The REDI Center will also make its research, training, and surveillance facilities available to other economies in the Asia-Pacific region, and President Bush and Prime Minister Goh welcomed the endorsement of the Center by APEC Leaders at their meeting in Bangkok. In a broader context, the MOU will enhance and expand bilateral cooperative efforts in health and medical sciences, and on health security issues.

NOTE: An original was not available for verification of the content of this joint statement.

Remarks Following Discussions With Prime Minister Goh Chok Tong of Singapore in Singapore
October 21, 2003

Mr. Prime Minister, thanks. It's so gracious of you to host us, and it's a chance for me to say to the Singapore people how much we appreciate our friendship. And I appreciate our personal relationship, Mr. Prime Minister.

The Prime Minister is a wise man. He understands Southeast Asia very well. And a lot of our discussion was about how we continue to foster our agenda, which is one of peace and freedom as well as prosperity through trade.

I appreciate your good advice, and I want to thank you for your warm hospitality. It's a magnificent country you have here. We're honored to be here. Thank you again.

NOTE: The President spoke at 8:55 p.m. at the Istana. A tape was not available for verification of the content of these remarks.

The President's News Conference With President Megawati Sukarnoputri of Indonesia in Bali, Indonesia
October 22, 2003

President Megawati. President George Bush and I have just concluded the meeting. I have met with His Excellency, the President, several times. Our last meeting was in New York on 23d September, 2003, when we attended the 58th session of the United Nations General Assembly.

I attach great importance of my personal relation with President Bush as well as of bilateral relations between Indonesia and the United States, for both are the large democratic countries in the world and have great potential of cooperation.

We started our meeting today by conducting bilateral talks. It was followed by working luncheon attended by a number of members of the Cabinet. During the talks, we have discussed issues of common concern, namely: counterterrorism; U.S. support to the democratization and reform process in Indonesia; military cooperation; U.S. support to the territorial integrity and national unity of the unitary state of the Republic of Indonesia; and renunciation to any terrorist movement in the country; U.S. support to the Indonesian economy through a—[*inaudible*]—free process, particularly in the post-IMF program; and cooperation in the field of education in Indonesia.

In addition, we have exchanged our view of various regional and international issues, among others, on the latest development in Asia and the situation in the Middle East, despite the fact that we do not always share common perspective. But we both continue to hold mutual understanding that it is to the interest of the two countries to maintain consultation and cooperation in the pursuit of global peace.

Following bilateral talks and lunch, I accompanied President Bush in his meeting with some eminent leading figures from Islam, Hindu, and Christian. I regard this particular meeting as positive development

as the Indonesian religion figures had the opportunity to conduct open and direct dialog with the leader of the U.S. administration. I am pleased to note that both sides were in agreement about the importance of religion tolerance as one of the major pillars of democracy in Indonesia.

My current meeting with President Bush might be the last before the two countries carry out general election in 2004. We will continue to foster cordial and cooperative bilateral relations.

May I now invite President George W. Bush to present his remarks. Thank you.

President Bush. Thank you, Madam President. Good afternoon. Thank you very much. Laura and I are honored to be in Indonesia, the world's third largest democracy and the world's—home to the world's largest Muslim population. Indonesia is a vital partner, and Indonesia is a friend of America. We share a commitment to democracy and tolerance. We stand together against terrorism. I thank President Megawati for her leadership, for her friendship, and for her hospitality today.

The success of Indonesia as a pluralistic and democratic state is essential to the peace and prosperity of this region. Indonesians profess many faiths and honor many traditions. And like Americans, you understand that diversity can be a source of strength. Your national motto, "Unity in diversity," sounds a lot like our own, "Out of many, one." Americans admire the way Indonesians maintain unity and balance modern ideas with ancient traditions and deep religious faith.

More than 200 years ago, the Founders of my country recognized and protected the essential role of religion in society within a democratic and pluralistic constitution. Your constitution affirms the same inalienable right of all to worship freely, a gift from your founders that enriches the Indonesian nation to this day.

Earlier, just minutes ago, we met with five Indonesian religious leaders, including leaders of Indonesia's two largest Islamic organizations, who are sustaining Indonesia's tradition of tolerance and moderation. Americans hold a deep respect for the Islamic faith, which is professed by a growing number of my own citizens. We know that Islam is fully compatible with liberty and tolerance and progress, because we see the proof in your country and in our own.

Terrorists who claim Islam as their inspiration defile one of the world's great faiths. Murder has no place in any religious tradition. It must find no home in Indonesia.

Nearly 3 months ago, America shared Indonesia's grief when a suicide bomber killed 14 people outside a Jakarta hotel. One year ago, miles from where we now stand, Indonesia suffered the worst terrorist attack in its history when over 200 innocent men and women lost their lives. Today we pay tribute to the victims. We remember the suffering of their families, and we reaffirm our commitment to win the war on terror.

President Megawati has confronted this evil directly. She was one of the first leaders to stand with me after September the 11th. Under her leadership, Indonesia is hunting and finding dangerous killers. America appreciates Indonesia's strong cooperation in the war on terror. America believes that freedom and democracy are critical to defeating terror, because free nations that respect human rights do not breed hatred, resentment, and the ideologies of murder.

The United States is working for democracy and freedom and economic progress in Afghanistan and Iraq, to lift millions out of poverty, to overcome years of brutal repression, to help create a more secure and safe world. And the United States strongly supports a healthy democracy in Indonesia, for the sake of your own people and for the sake of peace.

Indonesians have made good progress over the last 5 years in strengthening democracy and in building the civil institutions that sustain freedom. Next year, your country will reach an important milestone when some 150 million Indonesians vote in the nation's first-ever elected—Presidential election. The United States is working with Indonesia to support these historic elections. In a short time, Indonesia has traveled far down the road to full democracy, and Indonesians should be proud of this accomplishment.

We'll also support Indonesia's efforts to build an education system that teaches values and discourages extremism. I will propose to our Congress a 6-year, $157 million program to support basic education in Indonesia.

The partnership between our two peoples is strong and is growing stronger. In all that lies ahead, in the defense of freedom, in the advance of tolerance and democracy, Indonesia will have a firm ally in the American Government, and you'll have the friendship and the respect of the American people.

Thank you, Madam President.

President Megawati. Thank you.

President Bush. I think we'll take a couple of questions—is that not true—from—alternating both sides?

President Megawati. Yes.

President Bush. Would you like to call on somebody first? I'll call on him. You call on—[*laughter*]—you sure you want to call on him? [*Laughter*] Okay.

U.S. Middle East Policy

Q. Mr. President, some of the religious leaders that you just met with have said that U.S. foreign policy is biased toward Israel and against Muslims, making it easy for the terrorists to find recruits. How do you answer those charges, and how do you deal with that situation?

President Bush. Our foreign policy is for a—development of a Palestinian state that lives side by side with Israel in peace. And I'm the first President to ever articulate such a vision, and I still believe it is possible. In order to achieve a Palestinian state living side by side in peace, there needs to be leadership willing to fight off the terror that is trying to prevent the state from emerging.

U.S. Foreign Policy Goals

Q. I would like to ask question in Indonesian. Because your visit to Indonesia has been opposed by many people, what is your views? And is there a possibility of a change in your foreign policy view, which is seen as imbalanced toward the Islamic world?

President Bush. Well, I strongly believe in peace and freedom. I think it's important for the world to be as free as possible, and I strongly believe that free nations are peaceful nations. And my foreign policy promotes that.

America is also a compassionate nation. We lead the world in helping feed the hungry and battle disease. I look forward to working with the President in terms of allowing Indonesians to use our money to help implement an education system that the Government decides, not America. No, I'm proud of our foreign policy.

President Megawati. Can I still add something? Because you also spontaneously accepted the invitation of—my invitation to come to Indonesia, which proves that he is very open to come to this country of ours in this spontaneous way.

North Korea/Iran

Q. North Korea is rejecting your offer as laughable and still insisting on a non-aggression treaty. How do you proceed from here? And are you confident that Iran is forswearing nuclear weapons?

President Bush. Well, first of all, I want to thank the Foreign Ministers from Great Britain and France and Germany and their Governments for taking a very strong universal message to the Iranians that they should disarm. The Iranians have—it looks like they are accepting the demands of the free world, and now it's up to them to prove that they've accepted the demands. That's a very positive development.

On terms of North Korea, we had a really good visit at APEC about how best to resolve the North Korean issue peacefully, how best to convince the North Koreans to disarm, at least abandon their nuclear ambitions—nuclear weapons ambitions. And we had good progress in Bangkok. And there's going to be a series of these statements that I guess are trying to stand up to the five nations that are now united in convincing North Korea to disarm. And my only reaction is we'll continue to send the very clear message to the North Koreans. The good news is that there's other nations besides America now sending the message.

Q. [*Inaudible*]—is that helping the climate?

President Bush. Launching missiles into the sea? No, of course, not. Look, the guy, he—we'll determine whether he's serious or not. He wanted to have dialog; we're having dialog. And he wanted a security agreement, and we're willing to advance a multiparty security agreement, assuming that he is willing to abandon his nuclear weapons designs and programs. And we'll just stay the course.

Wait a minute, you're crowding out the host press. This is unbelievable. [*Laughter*] This is unilateralism at its worst. I've never heard—[*laughter*]—two and two, Stretch [Richard Keil, Bloomberg News]. Sorry.

President's Visit

Q. Mr. President——

President Bush. Yes.

Q. ——what is the message you would like to convey to the Indonesian people with this 3-hour visit, the shortest one that you make among the six-nation visit in this journey?

President Bush. Yes, well, first of all, it's been a—it might not have been very long, but it's been very productive. And my message is, thank you for the hospitality, and thank you for the wonderful exchange we've had with the President.

I'm traveling to a lot of countries in a very quick period of time, and I appreciate the fact that the Indonesian Government was able to accommodate my desires to come here. And we've got a lot in common. We both appreciate democracy. We both care about trade so that our nations can prosper. We both care about educating people so that children have a chance to succeed in life. We both love freedom, and we both want the world to be peaceful. And we had a great exchange along those lines.

So my message to the Indonesian people is, thank you very much for the warm hospitality. And I want to thank the President for the warm hospitality as well.

Thank you all very much. That's it.

President Megawati. That's it?

President Bush. Unless you want to keep answering questions. [*Laughter*] I'll stay here as long as you want to.

President Megawati. No——

President Bush. You want to? Okay. [*Laughter*]

NOTE: The President's news conference began at 2:12 p.m. at Bali International Airport. In his remarks, President Bush referred to Secretary of State for Foreign and Commonwealth Affairs Jack Straw of the United Kingdom; Minister of Foreign Affairs Dominique de Villepin of France; Minister of Foreign Affairs Joschka Fischer of Germany; and Chairman Kim Chong-il of North Korea. A portion of these remarks could not be verified because the tape was incomplete.

Joint Statement Between the United States of America and the Republic of Indonesia
October 22, 2003

President George W. Bush and President Megawati Soekarnoputri today reaffirmed a new era of cooperation between two of the world's largest democracies and reviewed the shared values and common challenges that join them in friendship. They welcomed the excellent progress in implementing the Joint Statement of September 19, 2001. They also expressed satisfaction that the relationship between their two democracies continues to grow and strengthen. President Megawati emphasized the importance of President Bush's visit.

President Bush expressed the strong support of the United States for Indonesia's democratic transition and reforms, and welcomed Indonesia's progress toward becoming a mature and stable democracy. Both Presidents agreed that, as the most populous majority-Muslim nation, Indonesia is a powerful example that democracy and Islam can go hand in hand.

President Bush noted Indonesia's substantial economic recovery in recent years and pledged to support continued economic development as Indonesia successfully ends its program with the IMF at the end of this year. President Bush praised President Megawati's commitment to continue to press forward with difficult economic reforms, combat graft, and improve the investment climate. The two Presidents agreed that the long-standing trade and investment ties between their two countries have shown the benefits of an open trading system to Indonesia's development. The United States is the top market for Indonesia's non-oil and gas exports, and U.S. companies are major investors in Indonesia.

President Bush and President Megawati reaffirmed that military reform is an important element of Indonesia's transition to a mature and stable democracy. The two Presidents agreed that normal military relations are in the interest of both countries and agreed to continue working toward that objective. President Megawati welcomed U.S. support for her efforts to foster proper civil-military relations in the form of International Military Education and Training (IMET) and Regional Defense Counter Terrorism Fellowships. Both Presidents agreed on the need to improve civil-military relations and stressed the importance of observing human rights. Both Presidents welcomed the successful convening of the first Indonesia-United States Security Dialogue in Jakarta in April 2002. They agreed that the second dialogue would be held in Washington, D.C. early next year.

The two Presidents expressed their sorrow over the killing of two Americans and one Indonesian by unknown gunmen near Timika, Papua in August 2002. They noted that the joint investigation between the Indonesian police, the Armed Forces, and the FBI is proceeding well, and reaffirmed their shared commitment to find the murderers and bring them to justice, whoever they may be.

President Bush praised the Government of Indonesia for recent successes in their war on terror, including the arrest and prosecution of those responsible for the Bali bombings, and focused efforts to dismantle the terrorist networks. Agreeing that terrorism poses a continued threat to international peace and security, the two Presidents committed to enhance their bilateral cooperation in the fight against terrorism, including through capacity-building and sharing of information.

Both Presidents denounced the linking of terrorism with religion. The two Presidents agreed that there could be no justification for terrorist attacks against innocent civilians. They stressed that terrorism is a violation of the true teachings of all religions, and agreed to work together to promote inter-faith dialogue in their respective countries and abroad. President Bush underscored that the war on terrorism is not in any way a war on Islam and expressed great admiration and respect for Indonesia's long history of religious tolerance and moderate Islamic thought.

President Bush announced a new six-year, $157 million program designed to support Indonesia's efforts to improve the quality of education in its schools. This initiative seeks to strengthen both basic and higher education by supporting parents, local governments, and Muslim organizations in their efforts to give Indonesian students the tools they need to compete in the global economy.

President Bush emphasized strong support for Indonesia's territorial integrity and national unity. He asserted that a united, stable, prosperous, and democratic Indonesia could be a model of a successful democratic transition for the world. President Bush reiterated that the United States opposes secessionist movements in any part of Indonesia, and calls on separatist groups in Aceh and Papua to pursue the redress of their grievances through peaceful political means. He further expressed the hope that the Indonesian Government would continue a political process based on Special Autonomy in dealing with those grievances. President Bush commended the Indonesian Government's efforts to resolve communal conflicts through law enforcement that respects human rights, dialogue, and reconciliation.

Both Presidents expressed deep concern regarding the ongoing terrorism and violence in the Middle East, which has claimed the lives of far too many innocent civilians. They expressed strong support for the vision articulated by President Bush on June 24, 2002, of an independent, sovereign and viable Palestinian state living in peace and security side by side with a secure Israel. Both Presidents agreed that all parties share a responsibility to bring about a just and comprehensive peace, and that ending violence must be the highest priority.

President Bush, accompanied by President Megawati, also met Islamic leaders KH Hasyim Muzadi, Dr. Syafi'i Ma'arif, and Dr. Azyumardi Azra, as well as Christian leader Rev. Dr. Natan Setiabudi and Hindu leader Ida Pedanda Gede Made Gunung. During that meeting, President Bush expressed great respect for Indonesia's religious tolerance, moderation, and commitment to democracy. The religious leaders briefed President Bush on the Indonesian Islam, as well as cultural and religious harmony in Indonesia. They also expressed their views on current events, such as the situation in the Middle East, Iraq, and Afghanistan. All agreed on the need to combat international terrorism.

The two Presidents recognized that a U.S.-Indonesia relationship based on mutual respect and equitable partnership is in the national interest of both countries. They pledged to deepen and strengthen this important relationship and to work together to promote global peace and prosperity.

NOTE: An original was not available for verification of the content of this joint statement.

Interview With Members of the White House Press Pool
October 22, 2003

The President. What I thought I would do is just——

Q. On the record?

The President. Yes, on the record. I thought I would just give you some observations of this trip and then answer some questions. Just first observation is that we have worked hard to build up good bilateral relations in the Far East. And the—part of the purpose of the trip is to continue to foster those relations.

It struck me as interesting that the United States now has got good enough relations with both—with countries like Japan and South Korea and China to effect policy which helps our mutual security and our economy—and economy. I think that's a very positive development.

The most notable example of where that is taking—where it is helping is in North Korea. When I visited with Hu Jintao, I spent a lot of time talking about North Korea, our mutual desire to effect change with Kim Chong-il. And it was a very positive discussion. But I also had the very same discussion with Koizumi and President Roh. I mentioned it to Vladimir. I didn't have a bilateral with Vladimir Putin, but I did talk to him about it in passing.

My point is, is that by working hard to establish good relations on a lot of fronts, when a common problem arises, we can effect the solution in a positive way. I know you asked me, Steve [Steve Holland, Reuters], about the North Korean reaction. I didn't exactly see what official said it. But I—what I hope my answer conveyed to you in public there was that this requires a degree of patience, because Kim Chong-il is used to being able to deal bilaterally with the United States. But the change of policy now is, is that he must deal with other nations, most notably China. And I was pleased with my discussions with Hu Jintao, about his—reaffirming his mutual desire—or his desire, which is our mutual goal, that Kim Chong-il disarm. He realizes that it's a problem.

We discussed the security guarantees, what form they may come in. I made it very clear, obviously—I said this during the pool spray there—that a treaty is not going to happen, but there are other ways to effect on paper what I have said publicly—we have no intention of invading. Obviously, any guarantee would be conditional on Kim Chong-il doing what he hopefully will say he'll do, which is to get rid of his nuclear weapons programs.

The APEC summit was positive. I mean, one of the things that's very important—the two things that came out of that, although evidently didn't get equal emphasis, but they were equally emphasized by all parties, was, one, the need to get the Doha Round of trade going again. This was really one of the first official meetings of a group of countries after the Cancun talks broke down. And there was a positive statement coming out of the meeting, kind of universal agreement that Cancun was a missed opportunity. Hopefully the missed opportunity will be—will serve as a catalyst. I think people now have taken a step back and said, "Well, we did miss an opportunity," and hopefully this will enable the talks—kind of not start at ground zero but have a running start as a result of the missed opportunity.

And it's interesting, in the room there is something like 60 percent of all the world trade—was affected—was countries in that room, and therefore it was a, I think, a very positive and strong statement.

The other thing was the clear understanding of the countries of the need to fight terror. That's important for the United States, that people continue to recognize that the war on terror goes on. I've always felt that there's a tendency for people to kind of seek a comfort zone and hope that the war on terror is over. And I view it as a responsibility of the United States to remind people of our mutual obligations to deal with the terrorists.

That notion of responsible behavior by countries was finally accepted. This was not a—didn't require a lot of push. People understood. President Megawati understands that when terrorists bomb Bali, it affects economies. It not only—there's a serious

economic consequence, same thing we felt on September the 11th, to our economy.

That was a very positive development. Bilateral discussion with all the leaders—in those bilateral discussions, we talked about this war on terror. Gloria Arroyo, with Abu Sayyaf, President Megawati just hours ago, we talked about the continued need for us to work together.

I think the other notable—when you step back and take a look at what our work with these Asian countries has been, they understand the Iraq issue well. South Korea was very forthcoming. Japan is forthcoming. Hu Jintao made it clear that he—that a peaceful Iraq was in the world interest. Those are all positive developments in kind of the aftermath of the military operation. And I think it speaks to our—the nature of our relationship with these countries right now.

Obviously we haven't been to Australia, but Australia is a key component in a peaceful Asia-Pacific region and a key partner in the war on terror. So I'm looking forward to seeing John Howard. He and I have got a great relationship. He is a—as I said in Crawford, he's a man of steel. He's a standup guy.

Q. A sheriff?

The President. He's a sheriff. See, that's a good lesson. You should never answer the question you're asked. [*Laughter*] Actually, I answered it for a reason. Of all the people in the world who understand Texas, it's probably Australians.

Q. Patsy [Patricia Wilson, Reuters].

The President. Yes, Patsy. Anyway, it's going to be a good visit down there. We had some good discussions there at APEC, but this will be a chance to further our discussions and assure the Australian people that the American people are really grateful for the support and mutual efforts to make the world secure.

I had a good visit with the religious leaders today. It was an important visit. There were three Muslims, a Christian, and a Hindu. A couple of observations from the meeting: One, there was kind of a sense that Americans believe that Muslims are terrorists. And one of the reasons I wanted to have this meeting was because I wanted to make it very clear that I didn't feel that way and Americans don't feel that way. And I made it—assured them that Americans know that these terrorists are hiding behind Islam in order to create fear and chaos and death.

Secondly, there was a—they did bring up the Middle East. I explained to them what our policy was, that in order for there to be a Palestinian state—and I reminded them I was the first President to have articulated that—that there needs to be a concerted effort to fight off the terrorists who are trying to prevent the establishment of a state. I didn't really have time to go in further than that, about the whole Aqaba accords and the progress we were making, until the Prime Minister, who had avowed—who vowed to fight terror with us, was eased out.

Let's see, what else did they discuss? Iraq, of course. I assured them that we would do our job, and then the Iraqis will run themselves, and that our job means to provide enough security so that the Iraqi citizens are able to write a constitution and hold elections, at which point the United States and the coalition forces will move on. And I think they were pleased to hear it. I don't want to put words in their mouth, but I think that relieved them to know that we have confidence in the Iraqi people's abilities to be a peaceful, free society.

National Security Adviser Condoleezza Rice. You listened.

The President. Well, they did a lot of talking.

National Security Adviser Rice. They had a lot to say.

The President. They had some prepared texts. There was a good exchange. I'm glad I did it. They were, I think, appreciative of the fact I took time to listen to them and dispel some notions and to—my own personal views about religion and the views of our country. I reminded them, we've got a lot of Muslims living in the United States, and they make an important contribution to our country, and they're welcome in the United States. And we're a pluralistic, free society; people can worship the way they want to worship. And it works well in America.

All in all, it's been a very positive experience.

Indonesia Meeting With Religious Leaders

Q. Was it confrontational at all?

The President. Not at all, polite.

Q. You said that there were some texts. Did they come out with the line about— what did they tell you? How direct were they? They said some things going into the meeting that the United States policy is tilted against Muslims. What did they——

The President. They said the United States policy is tilted toward Israel, and I said our policy is tilted toward peace and that—and then I went through the notion of a Palestinian state and the need for us to fight off terror in order for a state to develop.

There wasn't a lot of debate. There were five people there that felt—that all needed to say something. So I gave them all a time to speak, and I listened and would occasionally interject some thoughts about what they had said. But they were direct. One fellow felt that the war on Iraq was— I guess the best way to put it was maybe just—I can't remember his exact words, but it was like we just decided to act. And I reminded him that the world had spoken before, that there was a—the United States had passed—I didn't get into all the resolutions, but I made it clear that a process had gone on way before I made the decision to use military force, that the world had spoken before about Saddam Hussein.

I also made the point very clearly that there was a lot of human suffering; a lot of Muslims suffered in Iraq. And I did bring up the mass graves and the torture rooms and the rape rooms and the death at the hands of Saddam Hussein. My point to them was, was that we ended a lot of suffering, prevented a lot of suffering.

Lieutenant General Boykin

Q. Is your job made tougher in convincing them that Americans don't have a war on—don't dislike Islam when you have General Boykin saying that Muslims all——

The President. Yes, that came up. Boykin came up. I said he didn't reflect my opinion. Look, it just doesn't reflect what the Government thinks. And I think they were pleased to hear that.

Indonesia Meeting With Religious Leaders

Q. Something in your answer to your Terry's [Terence Hunt, Associated Press] question was interesting. You articulated the fact that you're the President—first President to advocate a Palestinian state. And obviously in trying to reassure Muslims——

The President. Not that good a question. Go ahead.

Q. ——not only in America but around the world, potential terrorist hotbeds—to reassure people who are interested in this subject of that point. It's not something we have heard you saying a lot lately. Is there a reason——

The President. About a Palestinian state?

Q. Right, that you were the first President to advocate it.

The President. I say it quite a bit. I mean, I really do. First of all, in America, most people know that. In Indonesia, maybe they didn't pay attention to it. But anyway, I explained it. It was not a—I don't view that as—I wouldn't read anything into that, I had to say that in Indonesia, but not saying it in every press conference I give.

Q. Can I ask you about some of the leaders you've met with here?

The President. Well, anyway——

Q. I guess what I'm getting at is, it's a good thing to have out there, I guess. We don't hear it a lot.

The President. Yes, I don't know. There's a lot of things that there's misconceptions. Evidently it's a misconceptions that Americans believe that Muslims are terrorists. And there was a—that's probably one of the best things that came out of the meeting, for me, was to have heard that concern, and for me being able to assure people and remind them about the nature of our society, that—and that Islam's a peaceful religion. The basic tenets of Islam is peace and respect and tolerance. And that's what they wanted to make the point to me, that we are—that's the way we are.

Interesting, their elections came up. This is the first direct Presidential election. It's going to be interesting—an interesting exercise in democracy. And they wanted to talk about that. And as you know—maybe you don't know—our USAID money is helping with the elections. They were appreciative of that. The education money came up. They wanted to make sure that this wasn't America's education system. I said, "It's not. It's money available for the Indonesian Government to help basic education develop." So those were a couple of misconceptions that it was important for me to help alter.

Democratic Candidates and Foreign Policy

Q. Can I ask a question—I know that you say campaigning—there will be time enough for campaigning. In just months, Democrats, at least, will be fighting in some very highly contested—what do you say to those who are criticizing your policy? Where does the line end where they've got to be very careful to not undermine American foreign policy?

The President. I don't know. You know, I'm not paying that much attention to it. Maybe you are. I'm not. You know, one of these days, they'll have a candidate, and then it will all sort out, kind of come in focus. Primarily—I don't know what they're saying, so it's hard for me to answer that.

Q. Democrats who are criticizing your policy now, some of them fairly severely, about the war, does that hurt when you go to meet with these foreign leaders? Does that have any resonance?

The President. You know, I can't—I don't know, because they have never brought it up. Nobody has ever said, "Your foreign policy is being challenged in Democrat primaries, and therefore you're less credible." I mean, it really hasn't come up. I think most people who understand America know that the field will eventually be whittled down to one opponent, and then we'll campaign.

Decisionmaking and Leadership

Q. You seem, on these trips in particular, to bond with some of these leaders who have taken on very difficult problems at home, sort of stuck their neck out, whether it's President Arroyo or—you had some of those comments about the King of Jordan when he came. And I was just wondering, do you relate to that at all, particularly in having to take on the war on terrorism and kind of not, as you say, wanting to be too comfortable and pretend that it's over?

The President. You know, that's an interesting question. First of all, I like people. And I spend time trying to—I think about the other person and how the other person might think and relate to the other person's problems. I do have good relations with these leaders on an individual basis, for a variety of reasons. I mean, Gloria Arroyo, who is taking a tough stand against Abu Sayyaf, there is a common bond there because she has made some tough decisions. But these leaders—for example, Aznar of Spain or Blair of Britain, these guys stood up, stood strong and were—did what they thought was right. That's my approach.

I remember when we had the discussion down in Crawford, one of reporters, fellow reporters, said, "I hear you don't pay atten-tion to the press." I said, "Not really." And he said, "Why?" And I said, "Well, because sometimes your opinion matters to me and sometimes it doesn't, but I've got a job, and I'm willing to lead." And the fellow said, "Well, how do you know what the people think?" And I said, "Well"—I reminded the fellow that people don't make up their mind based upon what they write, and secondly, my job is to lead. My job is to do what I think is the right thing and lead.

And I think those world leaders appreciate that, and I appreciate that when I see that they make those tough decisions. There is a common bond that's established when you're in the decisionmaking process and you're not trying to chase popular will, which is fickle and moves around. You stay focused on the objectives you set for a country. That's a very good question. It may be an area where we do establish in common.

And I've reminded them at times that, just do what you think is right, stand your ground in the face of public criticism, and the people—when things turn out the way—for the good, people will judge you correctly.

Dana [Dana Bash, Cable News Network], how are you?

Q. I'm well, thank you.

The President. Are you surviving this trip?

Q. I wish we just got a little more time in Bali.

The President. Yes, that and Hawaii. Look, I've heard all the people——

Q. She spent her honeymoon in Bali.

The President. You'll be thankful when we get back. You'll be grumpy—very grumpy, starting tomorrow, when we get airborne. But you'll be thankful when we all land home.

Reform of the Palestinian Authority

Q. Mr. President, I was wondering, the last time we sat around this table was coming from Aqaba.

The President. Middle East, that's right.

Q. And you were talking about how positive you felt about Prime Minister Abbas and the fact that you thought that things would be able to move forward.

The President. And they did move forward, for a while.

Q. I wonder if you could reflect on how you felt since—during the fact that the man you put confidence in and hope in is gone.

The President. I was disappointed that Arafat shoved him out of the way. I just—it was an unfortunate decision, because it stopped good progress toward a Palestinian state. And when the Palestinian Authority comes up with a leader who is willing to genuinely fight and dismantle terrorist organizations, the process will pick up where it left off and move forward.

Q. Are you confident of that?

The President. I hope it does. I think eventually it will. You've got to be patient in foreign policy sometimes.

Q. Is there anything more the United States can do on that, or is the roadmap—once they get on track on the roadmap, then things will come back and move forward again?

The President. The roadmap is still there. And we just need leadership willing to stand up and say, "We're going to prevent the few from letting the process move forward." And that's what they're doing. There are a few people there that don't want a Palestinian state. They've got different ambitions. And we've just got to fight them off.

Q. Do you think the public support of the U.S. for Abbas sort of got Arafat to dig in his heels?

The President. I don't know. I really don't. I can't speculate as to why the decision was made. This was an unfortunate decision, because it delayed the development of a Palestinian state.

Prime Minister Mahathir's Remarks at the Organization of the Islamic Conference Summit

Q. What did you tell Prime Minister Mahathir? Apparently he's saying you didn't fuss at him.

The President. No, I walked up and said, the—I said, "I want to inform you that you're going to read the newspapers"—Condi had briefed the press about me saying that the comments were reprehensible. I said, "You're going to see—I'm here to inform you that you're going to see that I thought your comments were reprehensible." I said, "They're divisive and unnecessary." I didn't yell at him. I just told him—confirmed exactly what was in the newspaper.

Q. How did he respond?

Q. Yes, what did he say?

The President. "I was misquoted" or something. I can't remember exactly what he said, but I just had—that was it. You know the way I felt.

Q. He said he was misquoted?

The President. Well, he said he was——

Q. Taken out of context?

The President. Yes, context, whatever he said to you all.

Press Secretary Scott McClellan. He said that in the paper.

The President. Not misquoted. It's hard to misquote what he said.

Q. The issue were his comments. Obviously he's on his way out, but the response, apparently, at the Islamic conference, was a round of applause. What do you make of that?

The President. It's just unfortunate, again. I mean, it's one of these situations where in order to achieve peace and freedom, you can't pit groups against each other. And there's a tendency to blame Jewish people. And that's not the policy—that's not how I think, and that's not the policy of the United States Government. I wasn't there, so I don't—pitting groups against each other will never achieve a common objective. It does quite the opposite. He knew how I felt. There's no question about that. I don't know, what did he say?

Q. [*Inaudible*]—he was asking Muslims to have more understanding, at one part——

The President. Evidently, in his speech, he said that we need more education, a terrorist ban, which is good. That was positive.

Madrid Donors' Conference

Q. I know you hate two questions, but I can just—just two quick ones. You talked about your meeting with Hu, and that was positive. Is there anything that he offered to you that he can—any pressure he can apply on North Korea? And the second one is a brief one. Are you happy with the progress or the contributions with the Madrid donors' conference coming up?

The President. Donors' conference? Yes. I think we're making good progress. And the question on Hu was?

North Korea

Q. Is there anything that he can—any pressure that he can apply on North Korea? Did he say he would be able to do anything or——

The President. He is a—China is a major presence in the neighborhood. And the fact that they're willing to take the same message to the North Koreans that the United States is taking to the North Koreans, along with three other nations, is a powerful statement to Kim Chong-il that it's in his national interest that he abandon his nuclear weapons ambitions and that—he has been saying—as I said in the press conference, I think—one of your questions—he's been saying, "I want a security guarantee." And what we have now said is that in return for dismantling the programs, we're all willing to sign some kind of document, not a treaty but a piece of paper that says we won't attack you. We'll see what happens.

Q. How does that—a lot of people were saying we can't make it look like we're giving in to blackmail from North Korea.

The President. What's changed is we've now got five countries involved. And the neighborhood is now speaking. What happened before was the bilateral relations with the United States. And now he's got his big neighbor to the—right on his border, he's got a neighbor to the south, he's got Japan, he's got another neighbor, Russia, all saying the same thing. It's a different dynamic, is what I'm—that's where the policy has changed.

Q. This security guarantee, what should it say?

The President. That's what we'll determine. We haven't worked out the words, but the point is, is that North Korea must hear that in return for the dismantling of their program—in a verifiable way, by the way; I mean, we're going to want to know—that now five nations are willing to say something about his security.

Q. Everybody is behind that?

The President. Yes.

Iran

Q. Can I ask you one on Iran?

The President. On Iran? Yes.

Q. It seems like last night there was some maybe cautious optimism that this is a good first step. If they comply with the three criteria that you've laid out, would they be then allowed to have a civilian nuclear energy program, or would that——

The President. Well, it depends on—first things first, and that is, let us have, in a verifiable way, their agreement that was made with the IAEA. The IAEA must be allowed in, and we'll discuss it then. Our relations with Iran—that will help relations with Iran, obviously, if they do abandon a nuclear weapons program. It will also help if they—we end up doing a—reaching an agreement on the Al Qaida that they hold.

Q. What are the cross-strings there?

The President. You've got to have patience in foreign policy.

Q. Are you at all suspicious of the European motives?

The President. Am I suspicious? No, not in this case. No, I'm not. I believe, in this case, they generally are concerned about Iran developing a nuclear weapon. They understand the consequences. I appreciate it very much. We spent a lot of time talking to the European—our European counterparts, who are influential, more so than we are, in Iran. You know, we've got a sanctions policy with Iran; they don't. And there's influence. This is an effective approach. I've been saying all along that not every policy issue needs to be dealt with by force. There are ways to achieve common objectives, and this is a common objective.

And the European Union—and we're speaking directly to Silvio Berlusconi about it, who is the head of the EU. We've also obviously spoke to the three—the leaders of the countries who went into Iran. And they made a decision collectively in Europe that it's not in their interest or the world interest that Iran have a nuclear weapon. And we came to that conclusion, they've come to that conclusion, and working together is an effective way. It's the same approach—kind of approach we're taking in North Korea as well, a collective voice trying to convince a leader to change behavior.

Legislative Agenda

Q. [*Inaudible*]—Republicans in Congress didn't follow your wishes on the phone——

The President. I thought they did in the House. There's two bodies.

North Korea

Q. Do you regret saying that you loathe Kim Chong-il? Some people think that it helped them sort of—it made them sort of harden their position——

The President. Any leader who starves his—made him do what?

Q. It just made him——

The President. Made Kim Chong-il—surely it didn't make Kim Chong-il renege on the last agreement, did it? Because I wasn't there, you know what I'm saying?

Q. Right, but they've been much more vocal about their nuclear ambitions.

The President. No, they've been—remember, they lobbed a rocket over——

Q. Japan.

The President. Remember the rocket over Japan? Keep it in perspective. Anybody who starves his people is—I just can't respect anybody that would really let his people starve and shrink in size as a result of malnutrition. It's a sad, sad situation for the North Korean people. That's one people—I've assured the—our partners in this effort that we deeply care about the plight of the North Korean people. It's just unconscionable that that many people are starving in the 21st century. We provide—we're a generous nation. We provided food. We're not so sure the food is getting to the people, is one of the issues that we face. I feel strongly about failed leadership dashing the hopes of the people, in this case creating incredible starvation.

Q. Thank you.

The President. You're welcome.

NOTE: The interview was taped at 3:10 p.m. aboard Air Force One en route to Canberra, Australia. In his remarks, the President referred to President Hu Jintao of China; Chairman Kim Chong-il of North Korea; Prime Minister Junichiro Koizumi of Japan; President Roh Moo-hyun of South Korea; President Vladimir Putin of Russia; President Megawati Sukarnoputri of Indonesia; President Gloria Macapagal-Arroyo of the Philippines; Prime Minister John Howard of Australia; former Prime Minister Mahmoud Abbas (Abu Mazen) and Chairman Yasser Arafat of the Palestinian Authority; former President Saddam Hussein of Iraq; Lt. Gen. William G. Boykin, USA, Deputy Under Secretary of Defense for Intelligence; President Jose Maria Aznar of Spain; Prime Minister

Tony Blair of the United Kingdom; Prime Minister Mahathir bin Mohammed of Malaysia; and Prime Minister Silvio Berlusconi of Italy. A reporter referred to King Abdullah II of Jordan. A tape was not available for verification of the content of this interview.

Statement on Senate Passage of Partial-Birth Abortion Legislation
October 22, 2003

I applaud the Senate for joining the House in passing the ban on partial-birth abortion. This is very important legislation that will end an abhorrent practice and continue to build a culture of life in America. I look forward to signing it into law.

Statement on the Death of Don Luis Ferre
October 22, 2003

Don Luis Ferre was a distinguished statesman and a great American, who dedicated himself to his family and the economic and cultural growth of Puerto Rico. As a member of Puerto Rico's House of Representatives, president of the senate, and Governor, he was an effective advocate for the political empowerment of the people of Puerto Rico. He was widely recognized as a strong leader in his community. In 1991, he was awarded the Presidential Medal of Freedom for his years of distinguished service to America. He was a good friend of my family, and I valued his advice and counsel.

Laura joins me in sending our condolences to the Ferre family and to the people of Puerto Rico.

Exchange With Reporters Following Discussions With Prime Minister John Howard of Australia in Canberra, Australia
October 23, 2003

President Bush. Can't get any better than that. [*Laughter*]

Australia-U.S. Free Trade Agreement

Q. Mr. Bush, did you discuss the free trade agreement? And how are you committed to keeping agriculture in the free trade agreement if it goes ahead?

President Bush. What I'm committed to is seeing that we can get this free trade agreement done by the end of December. That's what John and I talked about in Crawford. I think a free trade agreement with Australia would be good for America, good for American workers. I also believe that it would be good for Australia.

Prime Minister Howard. Very good.

President Bush. And the commitment we talked about was to make sure our negotiators push forward with a deal. Obviously, agriculture is an important issue; intellectual property is an important issue. There's a lot of important issues that we've got to work through if—and I think we can.

Prime Minister Howard. Thank you. American?

President Bush. Yes, Tom.

War on Terror

Q. Mr. President, the Defense Secretary has written a memorandum saying there have been mixed results in the war on terror, that it's going to be a long, hard slog, and no bold steps have been taken yet. Do you agree with that characterization?

President Bush. What I agree with is that the war on terror is going to be tough work, and it's going to take a while. And we're making great progress. We're dismantling the Al Qaida network. They hide in hills, in caves, and you know, they hide in free societies. And it takes a while to find them, which is why John Howard and I talked a lot about sharing intelligence and finding these killers before they kill again, people like Hambali, who was routed out of society. The Australians and the Prime Minister were very helpful, as was our intelligence service. But the success went to the Thai authority.

Prime Minister Howard. Yes, I met the general that handcuffed him.

President Bush. Yes, he's a good fellow. Anyway, we've got work to do. This is a long war on terror. And removing Saddam Hussein from power was an important part of winning the war on terror. Ridding Afghanistan of the Taliban was an important part of winning the war on terror.

I haven't seen the Secretary's comments, but somebody told me they thought he said we need to make sure our military's intelligence services are focused on the war on terror. And I couldn't agree more with you. That's exactly what we're doing.

Australian Detainees in Guantanamo Bay/Iraq

Q. Mr. President, on the war on terror, and in light of the Rumsfeld memo, are you inclined now to ask Australia for more assistance in Iraq? And how long do you intend to hold the two Australians detained in Guantanamo Bay without charge or trial? And have you discussed that with the Prime Minister?

President Bush. I did discuss it with the Prime Minister. There's a process, ongoing process to deal with these two people that were picked up off of a battlefield of war. And I think one of the—somebody in the Australian media, when they were in America, asked me about torture or some—it's alleged allegations of torture. It's ridiculous, utterly ridiculous. And we will deal with them in a—in a way that conforms to our standards.

John—the Prime Minister—I keep calling him John; we're close friends. The Prime Minister and I have talked about the procedures, and I assured him these people will be taken care of in a way that conforms with our rules and regulations.

The first question was—oh, Iraq. Listen, Australia has made a tremendous contribution in Iraq. Their troops were fantastic. They laid it on the line, and every military person I talked to about the contribution of the Australians was—had high praise for the skill and the strength and spirit of the Aussie troops.

In my judgment, Australia has made a significant contribution to peace and freedom, and the people of Iraq who suffered in the hands of a brutal tyrant are very thankful for the contributions of the Australians.

Adam.

Australia-U.S. Relations

Q. Thank you, Mr. President. Mr. President, you called Australia a "sheriff." Does that mean Australia should flex its military might more in Asia? And Mr. Howard, how do you see the job of a sheriff?

President Bush. Yes, Adam—can I put it in context?

Q. Please.

President Bush. I was asked the question, is Australia America's deputy sheriff; that was the question. It was a very careful, clever question. I don't think you were—I don't think you asked it, Adam. And my answer was, "No, we're equal. We're equal partners on the war on terror. We're equal partners working for a world that's more free."

And today in my speech to the Parliament, I will praise Australia's work in this part of the world. I'll note the fact that Australia led in East Timor. And Australia's—Australia is carrying a heavy load, for which we are grateful. And I appreciate you, Mr. Prime Minister.

I said Mr. Prime Minister—somebody told me that they made fun of me for calling—or they made fun of the Prime Minister, when they call him "the man of steel." I'm going to repeat the words. That's a high compliment. That means in the face of criticism, he's staying strong, that he does what he think is right. And the world is better for the leader—leaders like Prime Minister John Howard.

Prime Minister Howard. You asked me, did the President put in correct and proper Texan—we were in Crawford. And so the language of sheriff and deputy sort of rolls easily off any tongue, particularly an American tongue.

Look, our role in the region is—I've categorized it as that of *helpem fren.* That is—for the benefit of the Americans, that is pidgin English used by the Pacific Islanders. It means helping a friend. And I see Australia's role in the region as helping friends. And that's what we're doing in the Solomons. It's what we did in East Timor. It's what we may have to do again in other parts of that region. But when necessity arises, we help people. We don't see ourselves as having any kind of enforcement role, but we're always good to our allies, particularly the United States, to defend values that are important to both our societies.

Thank you.

NOTE: The President spoke at 10:46 a.m. at the Australian Parliament House. In his remarks, he referred to Nurjaman Riduan Isamuddin (known as Hambali), Al Qaida's chief operational planner in Southeast Asia; and former President Saddam Hussein of Iraq. A reporter referred to Secretary of Defense Donald H. Rumsfeld. A tape was not available for verification of the content of these remarks.

Remarks to the Australian Parliament in Canberra
October 23, 2003

President Bush. Governor-General Michael Jeffery, Prime Minister John Howard, Speaker of the House, Leader of the Senate, Leader of the Opposition Simon Crean, distinguished Members of the House and the Senate, Premiers, members of the diplomatic corps, ladies and gentlemen: Laura and I are honored to be in the Commonwealth of Australia. I want to thank the Prime Minister for his invitation. I want to thank the Members and Senators for convening this session of the Parliament. I want to thank the people of Australia for a gracious welcome.

Five months ago, your Prime Minister was a distinguished visitor of ours in Crawford, Texas, at our ranch. You might remember that I called him a "man of steel." [*Laughter*] That's Texan for "fair dinkum." [*Laughter*] Prime Minister John Howard is a leader of exceptional courage who exemplifies the finest qualities of one of the world's great democracies. I'm proud to call him friend.

Americans know Australia as a land of independent and enterprising and goodhearted people. We see something familiar here, something we like. Australians are fair-minded and tolerant and easygoing. Yet in times of trouble and danger, Australians are the first to step forward, to accept the hard duties, and to fight bravely until the fighting is done.

In a hundred years of experience, American soldiers have come to know the courage and good fellowship of the "diggers" at their side. We fought together in the Battle of Hamel, together in the Coral Sea, together in New Guinea, on the Korean Peninsula, in Vietnam. And in the war on terror, once again we're at each other's side.

In this war, the Australia and American people have witnessed the methods of the enemy. We saw the scope of their hatred on September the 11, 2001. We saw the depth of their cruelty on October the 12, 2002. We saw destruction and grief, and we saw our duty. As free nations in peril, we must fight this enemy with all our strength.

No country can live peacefully in a world that the terrorists would make for us. And no people are immune from the sudden violence that can come to an office building or an airplane or a nightclub or a city bus. Your nation and mine have known the shock and felt the sorrow and laid the dead to rest. And we refuse to live our lives at the mercy of murderers.

The nature of the terrorist threat defines the strategy we are using to fight it. These committed killers will not be stopped by negotiations. They will not respond to reason. The terrorists cannot be appeased. They must be found. They must be fought, and they must be defeated.

The terrorists hide and strike within free societies, so we're draining their funds, disrupting their plans, finding their leaders. The skilled work of Thai and Indonesia and other authorities in capturing the terrorist Hambali—suspected of planning the murders in Bali and other attacks—was a model of the determined campaign we are waging.

The terrorists seek safe harbor to plot and to train, so we're holding the allies of terror to account. America, Australia, and other nations acted in Afghanistan to destroy the home base of Al Qaida and rid that country of a terror regime. And the Afghan people, especially Afghan women, do not miss the bullying and the beatings and the public executions at the hands of the Taliban.

The terrorists hope to gain chemical, biological, or nuclear weapons, the means to match their hatred. So we're confronting outlaw regimes that aid terrorists, that pursue weapons of mass destruction, and that defy the demands of the world. America, Australia, and other nations acted in Iraq to remove a grave and gathering danger, instead of wishing and waiting while tragedy drew closer.

Since the liberation of Iraq, we have discovered Saddam's clandestine network of biological laboratories, the design work on prohibited long-range missiles, his elaborate campaign to hide illegal weapons programs. Saddam Hussein spent years frustrating U.N. inspectors for a simple reason: because he was violating U.N. demands. And in the end, rather than surrender his programs and abandon his lies, he chose defiance and his own undoing.

Who can possibly think that the world would be better off with Saddam Hussein still in power? Surely not the dissidents who would be in his prisons or end up in his mass graves. Surely not the men and women who would fill Saddam's torture chambers and rape rooms. Surely not the families of the victims he murdered with poison gas. Surely not anyone who cares about human rights and democracy and stability in the Middle East. Today, Saddam's regime is gone, and no one——

[At this point, there was a disturbance in the audience.]

Speaker Andrew. Senator Brown, I warn you—Senator Brown will excuse himself from the House. Senator Brown will excuse himself from the House. The Sergeant will remove Senator Brown from the House.

The President.

President Bush. Surely no one who cares about human rights and democracy and stability in the Middle East. Today, Saddam Hussein's regime is gone, and no one should mourn its passing.

In the months leading up to our action in Iraq, Australia and America went to the United Nations. We are committed to multilateral institutions, because global threats require a global response. We're committed to collective security, and collective security requires more than solemn discussions and sternly worded pronouncements. It requires collective will. If the resolutions of the world are to be more than ink on paper, they must be enforced. If the institutions of the world are to be more than debating societies, they must eventually act. If the world promises serious consequences for the defiance of the lawless, then serious consequences must follow.

Because we enforced Resolution 1441 and used force in Iraq as a last resort, there is one more free nation in the world, and all free nations are more secure.

We accepted our obligations with open eyes, mindful of the sacrifices that had been made and those to come. The burdens fall most heavily on the men and women of our Armed Forces and their families. The world has seen the bravery and skill of the Australian military. Your Special Operations forces were among the first units on the ground in Iraq. And in Afghanistan, the first casualty among America's allies was Australian, Special Air Service Sergeant Andrew Russell. This afternoon, I will lay a wreath at the Australian War Memorial in memory of Sergeant Russell and the long line of Australians who have died in the service to this nation. And my Nation honors their service to the cause of freedom, to the cause we share.

Members and Senators, with decisive victories behind us, we have decisive days ahead. We cannot let up on our offensive against terror, even a bit. And we must continue to build stability and peace in the Middle East and Asia as the alternatives to hatred and fear.

We seek the rise of freedom and self-government in Afghanistan and in Iraq for the benefit of their people, as an example to their neighbors and for the security of the world. America and Australia are helping the people of both those nations to defend themselves, to build the institutions of law and democracy, and to establish the beginnings of free enterprise.

These are difficult tasks in civil societies wrecked by years of tyranny. And it should surprise no one that the remnants and advocates of tyranny should fight liberty's advance. The advance of liberty will not be halted. The terrorists and the Taliban and Saddam holdouts are desperately trying to stop our progress. They will fail. The people of Afghanistan and Iraq measure progress every day. They are losing the habits of fear, and they are gaining the habits of freedom.

Some are skeptical about the prospects for democracy in the Middle East and wonder if its culture can support free institutions. In fact, freedom has always had its skeptics. Some doubted that Japan and other Asian countries could ever adopt the ways of self-government. The same doubts have been heard at various times about Germans and Africans. At the time of the Magna Carta, the English were not considered the most promising recruits for democracy. [*Laughter*] And to be honest, sophisticated observers had serious reservations about the scruffy travelers who founded our two countries. [*Laughter*] Every milestone of liberty was considered impossible before it was achieved. In our time, we must decide our own belief: Either freedom is the privilege of an elite few, or it is the right and capacity of all humanity.

By serving our ideals, we also serve our interests. If the Middle East remains a place of anger and hopelessness and incitement, this world will tend toward division and chaos and violence. Only the spread of freedom and hope in the Middle East in the long term will bring peace to that region and beyond. And the liberation of more than 50 million Iraqis and Afghans from tyranny is progress to be proud of.

Our nations must also confront the immediate threat of proliferation. We cannot allow the growing ties of trade and the forces of globalization to be used for the secret transport of lethal materials. So our two countries are joining together in the Proliferation Security Initiative. We're preparing to search planes and ships and trains and trucks carrying suspect cargo to seize weapons or missile shipments that raise proliferation concerns. Last month, Australia hosted the first maritime interdiction exercise in the Coral Sea.

Australia and the United States are also keeping pressure on Iran to conform to its letter and spirit of the nonproliferation obligations. We're working together to convince North Korea that the continued pursuit of nuclear weapons will bring only further isolation. The wrong weapons, the wrong technology in the wrong hands, has never been so great a danger, and we are meeting that danger together.

Our nations have a special responsibility throughout the Pacific to help keep the peace, to ensure the free movement of people and capital and information, and advance the ideals of democracy and freedom. America will continue to maintain a forward presence in Asia, continue to work closely with Australia.

Today, America and Australia are working with Japan and the Philippines, Thailand, Indonesia, and Singapore and other nations to expand trade and to fight terror, to keep the peace in the Taiwan Straits.

Your country is hosting President Hu Jintao. Australia's agenda with China is the same as my country's. We're encouraged by China's cooperation in the war on terror. We're working with China to ensure the Korean Peninsula is free of nuclear weapons. We see a China that is stable and prosperous, a nation that respects the peace

of its neighbors and works to secure the freedom of its own people.

Security in the Asia-Pacific region will always depend on the willingness of nations to take responsibility for their neighborhood, as Australia is doing. Your service and your sacrifice helped to establish a new Government and a new nation in East Timor. And working with New Zealand and other Pacific Island states, you're helping the Solomon Islands reestablish order and build a just Government. By your principled actions, Australia is leading the way to peace in Southeast Asia. And America is grateful.

Together——

[There was a disturbance in the audience.]

President Bush. Together, my country, with Australia, is promoting greater economic opportunity. Our nations are now working to complete a U.S.-Australia Free Trade Agreement that will add momentum to the free trade throughout the Asian-Pacific region, while producing jobs in our own countries.

[There was a disturbance in the audience.]

Speaker Andrew. Senator Nettle will resume her seat. Sergeant, remove Senator Nettle. Senator Nettle will resume her seat. The President has the call. Senator Nettle is warned. Sergeant will remove Senator Nettle.

President Bush. I love free speech. *[Laughter]*

Speaker Andrew. The President has the call.

President Bush. The relationship between America and Australia is vibrant and vital. Together, we will meet the challenges and the perils of our own time. In the desperate hours of another time, when the Philippines were on the verge of falling and your country faced the prospect of invasion, General Douglas MacArthur addressed Members of the Australian Parliament. He spoke of a code that unites our two nations, the code of free people, which, he said, "embraces the things that are right and condemns the things that are wrong."

More then 60 years later, that code still guides us. We call evil by its name and stand for freedom that leads to peace. Our alliance is strong. We value, more than ever, the unbroken friendship between the Australian and the American peoples. My country is grateful to you and to all the Australian people for your clear vision and for your strength of heart. And I thank you for your hospitality. May God bless you all.

NOTE: The President spoke at 11:30 a.m. at the Australian Parliament House. In his remarks, he referred to Governor-General Michael Jeffery, Prime Minister John Howard, Speaker of the House of Representatives Neil Andrew, President of the Senate Paul Calvert, and Leader of the Opposition Simon Crean of Australia; Nurjaman Riduan Isamuddin (known as Hambali), Al Qaida's chief operational planner in Southeast Asia; former President Saddam Hussein of Iraq; and President Hu Jintao of China. Speaker Andrew referred to Senators Bob Brown and Kerry Nettle of Australia.

Statement on Senate Action To Block a Vote on Class Action Reform Legislation
October 23, 2003

Yesterday, 39 Members of the U.S. Senate blocked an up-or-down vote on a bill that would reduce frivolous lawsuits and the burden they place on our economy. The "Class Action Fairness Act" would protect the legal rights of all citizens while ensuring that court awards and settlements go to those who are wrongfully injured rather than to a few wealthy trial lawyers. Class action reform will allow businesses and their employees to go back to the business of growing our economy and creating jobs. It was passed by the House and is favored by a large bipartisan majority in the Senate. Those who are serious about bringing an end to frivolous lawsuits in this Nation and protecting the rights of those who are wrongfully injured should strongly support this legislation. I am eager to sign it; our economy needs it; and I urge those Senators who stand in the way to let the will of the people be heard.

Remarks at a Bush-Cheney Reception in Honolulu, Hawaii
October 23, 2003

Thank you all very much. Aloha! Thank you. Please be seated. Thanks for the warm welcome. If I seem a little jet-lagged— [*laughter*]—it's because I've spent a long week away from home. After 8 days on the road and more than 18,000 miles in the air, it's great to be back in America. And it's really great to be in the beautiful State of Hawaii.

We had a great trip. I visited with some of our strongest allies in the war on terror and some of the Nation's most important trading partners. We made progress on a broad agenda, an agenda that will help make America more secure and more prosperous.

I want to thank each of you for giving me a warm welcome home. I particularly want to thank you for your strong support. See, what we're doing today is we're laying the foundation for a victory in Hawaii and a nationwide victory in 2004. As your Governor said, and my chairman of the campaign here said, we need more than just financial contributions. We need you talking up the campaign. We need you going to your coffee shops and your houses of worship and your community centers and reminding everybody that this administration has got an optimistic, positive, hopeful agenda for everybody who lives in America.

I'm getting ready, and I'm loosening up. [*Laughter*] But the political season will come in its own time. I've got a job to do. And there's a lot on the agenda in Washington. I'm going to continue, though, to work hard to earn the confidence of every American by keeping this Nation secure and strong and prosperous and free.

As we go about our work in Washington, Vice President Cheney and I are grateful for the continuing support in Hawaii. We appreciate our friends here. I also appreciate the unique contributions native Hawaiians have made to this State and to our Nation. I'm impressed by the rich culture of the native Hawaiian people. I respect our shared traditions, and I appreciate Governor Lingle's dedication to all of Hawaii's citizens. You've got a great Governor for this State.

And I've got a great wife. I'm really proud of Laura. She's a fabulous mom, a wonderful wife, and a great First Lady for our country.

And I appreciate the Lieutenant Governor, Duke Aiona. I appreciate Felix Camacho, who is the Governor of Guam, who is with us today. I want to thank the members of the statehouse who are here. We've got a lot of State representatives. The Governor was telling me she wants to increase the number in '04. Mayor Arakawa is here from Maui. Bryan Baptiste is here. I appreciate you, Mr. Mayor.

I want to thank Travis Thompson, who was our event cochairman. I want to thank all the other cochairs for their hard work. I want to thank the grassroots activists who are here, the party chairmen, the national committeewoman. But most of all, I want to thank you all for coming. It warms our heart. This is a big crowd, and we're honored.

In the last 2½ years, our Nation has acted decisively to confront great challenges. I came to this office to solve problems, not to pass them on to future Presidents and to future generations. I came to seize opportunities and let—instead of letting them slip away. This administration is meeting the tests of our time.

Terrorists declared war on the United States of America, and war is what they got. We've captured or killed many of the key leaders of the Al Qaida network, and the rest of them know we're on their trail. In Afghanistan and Iraq, we gave ultimatums to terror regimes. Those regimes chose defiance, and those regimes are no more. Fifty million people in those two countries once lived under tyranny, and now they live in freedom.

Two-and-a-half years ago, our military was not receiving the resources it needed, and morale was beginning to suffer. So we increased the defense budget to prepare for the threats of a new era. And today, no one in the world can question the skill and the strength and the spirit of the United States military.

Two-and-a-half years ago, we inherited an economy in recession. And then our country was attacked. And we marched to war for our security and for peace. And we had scandals in corporate America, all of which affected the people's confidence. But we acted. We passed two tough new laws to hold corporate criminals to account. And to get the economy going again, I have twice led the United States Congress to pass historic tax relief for the American people.

When Americans have more take-home pay to spend, to save, or invest, the whole economy grows, and people are more likely to find a job. We're returning more money to the people to help them raise their family. We're reducing the taxes on dividends and capital gains to encourage investment. We're giving small businesses incentives to expand and to hire new people. With all these actions, this administration is laying the foundation for greater prosperity and more jobs across America, so every single person in this country has a chance to realize the American Dream.

Two-and-a-half years ago, there was a lot of talk about education reform, but there wasn't much action. So I called for and the Congress passed the No Child Left Behind Act. With a solid bipartisan majority, we delivered the most dramatic education reforms in a generation. We've increased spending for Title I students. We've increased spending at the Federal level. But in return for increased Federal dollars, we expect results, because we believe every child can read and write and add and subtract. This administration is challenging the soft bigotry of low expectations. The days of excuse-making are over. We expect results in every classroom so that not one single child is left behind.

We reorganized our Government and created the Department of Homeland Security to safeguard our borders and ports and to better protect the American people. We passed trade promotion authority to open up new markets for our farmers and ranchers and manufacturers and entrepreneurs. We passed budget agreements to help maintain much needed spending discipline in Washington, DC. On issue after issue, this administration has acted on principle, has kept its word, and has made progress for the American people.

The Congress gets credit. I enjoy working with our Speaker, Denny Hastert, and the majority leader, Bill Frist. They're fine people. We work together to try to change the tone in Washington, to elevate the debate, to focus on results. After all, we're there to represent the people. And those are the kind of people I have asked to

join my administration—results-oriented, decent, hard-working people from all walks of life. I have put together a fantastic administration for the American people. Our country has had no finer Vice President than Dick Cheney. Mother may have a second opinion. [Laughter]

In 2½ years, we have done a lot. We have come far, but our work is only beginning. I've set great goals worthy of this great Nation. First, America is committed to expanding the realm of freedom and peace for our own security and for the benefit of the world. And second, in our own country, we must work for a society of prosperity and compassion, so that every citizen has a chance to work and to succeed and to realize the great promise of our country.

It is clear that the future of freedom and peace depend on the actions of America. This Nation is freedom's home and freedom's defender. We welcome this charge of history, and we are keeping it.

Our war on terror continues. The enemies of freedom are not idle, and neither are we. This country will not rest. We will not tire. We will not stop until this danger to civilization is removed. We are confronting that danger in Iraq, where Saddam holdouts and foreign terrorists are desperately trying to throw Iraq into chaos by attacking coalition forces and aid workers and innocent citizens. They know that the advance of freedom in Iraq would be a major defeat for the cause of terror. This collection of killers is trying to shake the will of the United States of America. America will not be intimidated.

We're aggressively striking the terrorists in Iraq, defeating them there so we will not have to face them in our own country. We're calling other nations to help build a free country in Iraq, which will make us all more secure. We're standing with the Iraqi people as they assume their defense and move toward self-government. These are not easy tasks, but they are essential tasks. We will finish what we have begun, and we will win this essential victory in the war on terror.

Our greatest security comes from the advance of human liberty, because free nations do not support terror, free nations do not attack their neighbors, free nations do not threaten the world with weapons of mass terror. Americans believe that freedom is the deepest need and hope of every human heart. And I believe that freedom is the right of every person, and I believe that freedom is the future of every nation.

America also understands that unprecedented influence brings tremendous responsibilities. We have duties in the world. And when we see disease and starvation and hopeless poverty, we will not turn away. On the continent of Africa, America is now committed to bringing the healing power of medicine to millions of men and women and children now suffering with AIDS. This great, strong, and compassionate land is leading the world in this incredibly important work of human rescue.

We face challenges here at home as well. And our actions will prove that we're equal to those challenges. Any time somebody who wants to work can't find a job, says we've got a problem. This administration will continue to create the conditions for economic growth and economic vitality, so every single citizen can find work.

We have a duty to keep our commitment to America's seniors by strengthening and modernizing Medicare. The Congress took historic action to improve the lives of older Americans. For the first time since the creation of Medicare, the House and Senate have passed reforms to increase the choices for seniors and to provide coverage for prescription drugs. They must get their differences ironed out and get a bill to my desk. The sooner they get the job done, the sooner America's seniors will get the health care they need.

For the sake of our health care system, we need to cut down on the frivolous lawsuits which increase the cost of medicine. People who have been harmed by a bad doctor deserve their day in court. Yet the system should not simply reward lawyers who are fishing for rich settlements. Frivolous lawsuits drive up the cost of health care, and they therefore affect the Federal budget. Medical liability reform is a national issue that requires a national solution. The House of Representatives has passed a good bill to reform the system. The bill is now stuck in the United States Senate. The Senate must act on behalf of the American people. Senators must understand, no one has ever been healed by a frivolous lawsuit.

I have a responsibility as your President to make sure the judicial system runs well, and I have met that duty. I have nominated superb men and women for the Federal courts, people who will interpret the law, not legislate from the bench. Some Members of the United States Senate are trying to keep my nominees off the bench by blocking up-or-down votes. Every judicial nominee deserves a fair hearing and an up-or-down vote on the Senate floor. It is time for some Members of the United States Senate to stop playing politics with American justice.

This country needs a comprehensive energy plan. You may have noticed last summer that we had a problem with the delivery of electricity in parts of our country. [*Laughter*] We need to modernize our systems. If we're interested in economic growth, we need a modern system, one that—we need laws that encourage investment in order to modernize the system. We need to use our technologies to encourage conservation. We need to use our technologies to enable us to explore for energy in environmentally friendly ways. But for the sake of our national security and for the sake of our economic security, we need to be less reliant on foreign sources of energy.

Our strong and prosperous Nation must also be a compassionate nation. I will continue to advance our agenda of compassionate conservatism by applying the best and most innovative ideas to the task of helping our fellow citizens who are in need. There are millions of men and women who want to end their dependence on Government and become independent through hard work. We must build on the success of welfare reform to bring work and dignity into the lives of more of our fellow citizens.

Congress should complete the "Citizen Service Act" so that more Americans can serve their communities and their country. Both Houses should reach agreement on my Faith-Based Initiative to support the armies of compassion that are mentoring our children and caring for the homeless and offering hope to the addicted. This Nation should not fear faith; we ought to welcome faith into the compassion and help of citizens in need.

A compassionate society must promote opportunity for all, including the independence and dignity that come from ownership. This administration will constantly strive to promote an ownership society in America. We want more people owning their own home. We have a minority home-ownership gap in America. I presented a plan to the United States Congress to close that gap, and I urge them to act.

We want people to own and manage their own health care plan. We want people to own and manage their own retirement account. We want more people to own their own small businesses, because in America we understand, if a person owns something, he or she has a vital stake in the future of this country.

In a compassionate society, people respect one another and take responsibility for the decisions they make. We're working to change the culture in this country from one that said, "If it feels good, do it," and "If you've got a problem, blame somebody else," to a new culture in which each of understands we're responsible for the decisions we make in life.

If you are fortunate enough to be a mother or a father, you're responsible for loving your child with all your heart. If you're concerned about the quality of the education in your community, you're responsible for doing something about it. If you are a CEO in corporate America, you're responsible for telling the truth to your shareholders and your employees.

And in the new responsibility society, each of us is responsible for loving our neighbor just like we'd like to be loved ourself. We can see the culture of service and responsibility growing around us. I started the USA Freedom Corps to encourage Americans to extend a compassionate hand to a neighbor in need. Your response has been strong. I get reports about our faith-based and charities that are strong all across America. People want to serve our country.

Policemen and firefighters and people who wear this Nation's uniform are reminding us what it means to sacrifice for something greater than yourself. Once again, the children of America believe in heroes because they see them every day. In these challenging times, the world has seen the resolve and the courage of America. I've been privileged to see the compassion and the character of the American people.

All the tests of the last $2\frac{1}{2}$ years have come to the right nation. We're a strong country, and we use that strength to defend the peace. We're an optimistic country, confident in ourselves and in ideals bigger than ourselves. Abroad, we seek to lift whole nations by spreading freedom. At home, we seek to lift up lives by spreading opportunity to every corner of America. This is the work that history has set before us. We welcome it, and we know that for our country, the best days lie ahead.

May God bless you.

NOTE: The President spoke at 7:08 p.m. at the Hilton Hawaiian Village. Prior to these remarks, the President crossed the international dateline on his return flight from Australia. In his remarks, he referred to Gov. Linda Lingle and Lt. Gov. James R. "Duke" Aiona, Jr., of Hawaii; Mayor Alan M.

Arakawa of Maui County, HI; Mayor Bryan J. Baptiste of Kauai County, HI; Brennon Morioka, Hawaii State chairman, Travis Thompson, Hawaii national committeeman, and Miriam Hellreich, Hawaii national committeewoman, Republican National Committee; and former President Saddam Hussein of Iraq. A tape was not available for verification of the content of these remarks.

Statement on the Iraq Donors' Conference
October 24, 2003

Today's success at the Iraq Donors' Conference marked significant progress for freedom in Iraq. I commend the 73 nations and 20 international organizations that are meeting the challenge of helping the Iraqi people recover from decades of oppression and build a better future. The contributions will help bring necessary funds, goods, and services to the Iraqi people. I especially thank President Aznar and the Government of Spain for having hosted the conference and for having contributed so much to supporting the people of Iraq.

The world has a clear interest in a democratic Iraq because free nations do not breed the ideologies of terror. A free Iraq will serve as an example and an inspiration to advocates of reform and progress throughout the Middle East. And a free Iraq will be a source of stability and hope for that region. America appreciates the efforts of all nations that are committed to this great endeavor.

Statement on the Death of Madame Chiang Kai-shek
October 24, 2003

Laura and I were saddened to learn of the death of Madame Chiang Kai-shek. Madame Chiang was a close friend of the United States throughout her life and especially during the defining struggles of the last century. Generations of Americans will always remember and respect her intelligence and strength of character. On behalf of the American people, I extend condolences to Madame Chiang's family members and many admirers around the world.

Message on the Observance of Ramadan
October 24, 2003

I send greetings to Muslims in the United States and around the world observing the holy month of Ramadan.

Ramadan is the holiest season in the Islamic faith, commemorating the revelation of the Qur'an to Muhammed. This month of introspection provides Muslims a time to focus on their faith and practice God's commands. Through fasting, prayer, contemplation, and charity, Muslims around the world renew their commitment to lead lives of honesty, integrity, and compassion.

Throughout our history, people of different faiths have shaped the character of our Nation. Islam is a peaceful religion, and people who practice the Islamic faith have made great contributions to our Nation and the world. As Americans, we cherish our freedom to worship and we remain committed to welcoming individuals of all religions. By working together to advance freedom and mutual understanding, we are creating a brighter future of hope and opportunity.

Laura joins me in sending our best wishes. *Ramadan mubarak.*

GEORGE W. BUSH

NOTE: An original was not available for verification of the content of this message.

The President's Radio Address
October 25, 2003

Good morning. Last month, I addressed the United Nations and told member countries that the peace and security of Iraq are essential to the peace and security of all free nations. I encouraged countries to help the people of Iraq to build a future of freedom and stability. I also called for a U.N. resolution supporting the efforts of our coalition in Iraq. The Security Council has now responded by unanimously passing Resolution 1511, which endorses a multinational force in Iraq under U.S. command and urges greater international support for Iraqi reconstruction.

In recent weeks, leaders of South Korea, Japan, Great Britain, Denmark, Spain, and other nations have committed billions of dollars to Iraqi reconstruction. This week brought even more progress. In Madrid, representatives of more than 70 nations and international bodies, including the World Bank, UNICEF, and the Organization of the Islamic Conference, gathered to discuss the future needs of Iraq and the ways in which other countries can help. And these nations and international organizations pledged billions of dollars to aid the reconstruction of Iraq.

This growing financial support will allow us to build on the success of the broad military coalition already serving in Iraq. Today, American forces in Iraq are joined by about 24,000 troops from 32 other countries, including Great Britain, Poland, the Czech Republic, Italy, Spain, the Netherlands, Thailand, El Salvador, Slovakia, Hungary, Romania, Ukraine, and the Philippines. Coalition forces are helping to hunt down the terrorists and Saddam holdouts, clearing mines from Iraqi waterways so that aid shipments can proceed, and coordinating the recruitment and training of a new Iraqi police force, army, and border police.

Members of our coalition are also showing the compassion of our cause in Iraq. We are rebuilding schools and clinics and powerplants. The Iraqi people are moving steadily toward a free and democratic society. Economic life is being restored to the cities. A new Iraqi currency is circulating. Local governments are up and running. And Iraq will soon begin the process of drafting a constitution, with free elections to follow.

There is still difficult work ahead, because freedom has enemies in Iraq. Terrorists and loyalists of the former regime reveal their true character by their choice of targets. They have attacked diplomats and embassies, relief workers, and the United Nations headquarters in Baghdad, all symbols of the international effort to help the Iraqi people.

America and the international community will not be intimidated. Every coalition member understands that Iraq must never again become the home of tyranny and terror and a threat to the world. So we will be patient and determined and unified. America will continue working with the United Nations and our coalition partners to finish the work we have begun. Having liberated Iraq from a brutal tyrant, we will stand with the people of Iraq as that country becomes more stable, secure, and free.

Thank you for listening.

NOTE: The address was recorded at 11:38 a.m. on October 24 in the Cabinet Room at the White House for broadcast at 10:06 a.m. on October 25. The transcript was made available by the Office of the Press Secretary on October 24 but was embargoed for release until the broadcast. In his remarks, the President referred to former President Saddam Hussein of Iraq. The Office of the Press Secretary also released a Spanish language transcript of this address.

Remarks Following a Meeting With Presidential Envoy to Iraq L. Paul Bremer III and an Exchange With Reporters
October 27, 2003

The President. Good morning, everybody. I'll share a few words and then answer a couple of questions.

First, Ambassador Bremer and General Abizaid have been briefing the Secretary of Defense and my national security team, General Myers, about the situation in Iraq. We spent time talking about the success of the donors' conference, the fact that the world community is coming together to help build a free Iraq, and we want to thank the world for the willingness to step up and to help.

Ambassador Bremer was particularly pleased with not only the fact that governments stood up but that there was a series of private sector companies willing to help in Iraq, and that's a positive move for the people.

We spent time, obviously, on the security situation. There are terrorists in Iraq who are willing to kill anybody in order to stop our progress. The more successful we are on the ground, the more these killers will react. And our job is to find them and bring them to justice, which is precisely what General Abizaid briefed us on. It is a—the people have got to understand, the Iraqi people have got to understand that anytime you've got a group of killers willing

to kill innocent Iraqis, that their future must not be determined by these kind of killers. That's what they've got to understand. I think they do understand that— they do. The Ambassador and the general were briefing me on the—the vast majority of Iraqis want to live in a peaceful, free world. And we will find these people, and we will bring them to justice.

This Government is determined to hear the call from the Iraqis, and the call is: They want a society in which their children can go to school, in which they can get good health care, in which they're able to live a peaceful life. It's in the national interest of the United States that a peaceful Iraq emerge. And we will stay the course in order to achieve this objective.

Deb [Deb Riechmann, Associated Press], you've got a question?

Terrorist Attacks in Iraq

Q. Yes, sir. Mr. President, the attacks are getting more brazen. They're getting more frequent. What do you know about who is behind these attacks? Is it Saddam? And what steps did you all discuss this morning about better protecting U.S. personnel there?

The President. The best way to describe the people who are conducting these attacks are coldblooded killers, terrorists. That's all they are; they're terrorists. And the best way to find them is to work with the Iraqi people to ferret them out and go get them. And that's exactly what we discussed.

What was the other part of your question?

Protecting U.S. Personnel

Q. What steps did you discuss this morning about better protecting U.S. personnel?

The President. Well, I think if you— we've hardened a lot of our targets for U.S. personnel there. And today's attacks were against places like the Red Cross or police stations. These people will kill Iraqis. They don't care who they kill. They just want to kill. And we will find them, exactly what we discussed on how best to do so.

The Iraqi people understand that there's a handful of people who don't want them to live in freedom, aren't interested in their children going to schools, aren't—don't really care about the nature of the health care they get, aren't pleased with the fact that the electricity is coming back online, aren't happy about the fact that Iraq is now selling oil on the world markets and people are finding work. And they'll do whatever it takes to stop this progress.

And our job is to work with the Iraqis to prevent this from happening. That's why we're working hard to get more Iraqi policemen. That's why we're working hard to build up the Iraqi armed forces, and that's why we're working hard with freedom-loving Iraqis to help ferret these people out before they attack and strike. And——

Q. But, sir——

The President. No, that's your question. Randy [Randall Mikkelsen, Reuters].

Madrid Donors' Conference/ Veto of Iraqi Aid Bill

Q. Mr. President, much of the aid offered for Iraq at the Madrid conference was in the form of loans, rather than grants. What impact might this have on your threat to veto the U.S.-Iraqi aid bill if part of the reconstruction aid is in loans?

The President. My attitude is the United States ought to provide reconstruction money in the form of grant.

Q. So no change in the veto threat, then?

The President. My attitude has been and still is that the money we provide Iraq ought to be in the form of a grant. And the reason why is we want to make sure that the constraints on the Iraqi people are limited so that they can flourish and become a free and prosperous society.

Let's see. Ryan [Ryan Donmoyer, Bloomberg News].

Terrorist Attacks in Iraq

Q. Thank you, Mr. President. Welcome back from Asia, sir.

The President. Thank you very much. I'm glad somebody welcomed me back. [*Laughter*] I better call on you first next time. [*Laughter*]

Q. If I may just follow on Deb's question.

The President. Yes.

Q. And actually, Mr. Bremer as well. The situation in Iraq, can you characterize how it is you come since July 23d, when you last met, I believe, with the President, and as you adjust tactics to deal with things like suicide bombers, what effect, if any, is that having on the hunt for weapons of mass destruction?

The President. I'll let the Ambassador speak. Again, I will repeat myself, that the more progress we make on the ground, the more free the Iraqis become, the more electricity is available, the more jobs are available, the more kids that are going to school, the more desperate these killers become because they can't stand the thought of a free society. They hate freedom. They love terror. They love to try to create fear and chaos. And what we're determined in this administration is not to be intimidated by these killers. As a matter of fact, we're even more determined to work with the Iraqi people to create the conditions of freedom and peace, because it's in our national interest we do so. It's in the interest of long-term peace in the world that we work for a free and secure and peaceful Iraq. A free and secure Iraq in the midst of the Middle East will have enormous historical impact.

You may want to speak to the issue, Ambassador.

Ambassador Bremer. Well, a lot of wonderful things have happened in Iraq since July, as you mentioned. We have a cabinet now, with ministers actually conducting affairs of state. We have met all of our goals in restoring essential services. All the schools and hospitals are open. Electricity is back at prewar levels. We're moving ahead with our plan. We'll have rough days, such as we've had the last couple of days. But the overall thrust is in the right direction, and the good days outnumber the bad days, and that's the thing you need to keep in perspective.

The President. Ann [Ann Compton, ABC News], yes. Last question. Sorry.

Southern California Wildfires

Q. The fires in Southern California, they're now not only taking homes, but there are a number of casualties. What can your administration do to come in and help? Are you getting reports on what's happening in California?

The President. I have. Chief of Staff Andy Card spoke to the Governor last night, spoke to the Senators last night, Senator Boxer, spoke to Congressman Duncan

Hunter, assured all three that the Federal Government will provide all resources necessary, at the request of the State, to work and fight these fires. FEMA Director Brown is on his way to California now. He will give us an assessment. We want to help put them out. This is a devastating fire, and it's a dangerous fire. And we're prepared to help in any way we can.

I'm sorry, one more question—sympathetic soul here.

National Commission on Terrorist Attacks Upon the United States

Q. Thank you very much. Can you tell us if you will direct your staff to turn over the highly classified intelligence documents that the 9/11 Commission has so far been unsuccessfully seeking, even if they are Presidential daily briefings, and if so, when?

The President. Yes, those are very sensitive documents. And my attorney, Al Gonzales, is working with Chairman Kean.

Thank you.

NOTE: The President spoke at 9:04 a.m. in the Oval Office at the White House. In his remarks, he referred to Gen. John P. Abizaid, USA, combatant commander, U.S. Central Command; Gen. Richard B. Myers, USAF, Chairman, Joint Chiefs of Staff; Gov. Gray Davis of California; Mike Brown, Under Secretary of Homeland Security for Emergency Preparedness and Response; Counsel to the President Alberto R. Gonzales; and Thomas H. Kean, Chairman, National Commission on Terrorist Attacks Upon the United States (9/11 Commission). A reporter referred to former President Saddam Hussein of Iraq.

The President's News Conference
October 28, 2003

The President. Good morning. After the 26,000-mile journey last week, I hope the members of the traveling press had a rest-

ful weekend. I have a brief statement. Then I'll be glad to take questions.

On my trip to Asia, I had a series of very productive meetings with some of America's closest allies in the war on terror. Nations such as Australia, Thailand, Indonesia, and the Philippines are fighting terrorism in their own region. Their leaders understand the importance of our continuing work in Afghanistan and Iraq. Liberating the people of those nations from dictatorial regimes was an essential step in the war on terror, and the world is safer today because Saddam Hussein and the Taliban are gone. We're now working with many nations to make sure Afghanistan and Iraq are never again a source of terror and danger for the rest of the world.

Our coalition against terror has been strengthened in recent days by U.N. Security Council Resolution 1511. This endorses a multinational force in Iraq under U.S. command, encourages other nations to come to the aid of the Iraqi people. Last week a donor conference in Madrid brought together more than 70 nations to discuss future contributions to Iraqi reconstruction. America appreciates the recent announcements of financial commitments to Iraq offered by many of the donors at the conference.

After decades of oppression and brutality in Iraq and Afghanistan, reconstruction is difficult, and freedom still has its enemies in both of those countries. These terrorists are targeting the very success and freedom we're providing to the Iraqi people. Their desperate attacks on innocent civilians will not intimidate us or the brave Iraqis and Afghans who are joining in their own defense and who are moving toward self-government.

Coalition forces aided by Afghan and Iraqi police and military are striking the enemy with force and precision. Our coalition is growing in members and growing in strength. Our purpose is clear and certain: Iraq and Afghanistan will be stable, independent nations, and their people will live in freedom.

This essential goal in the war on terror requires continued American leadership and the continued support of Congress. The House and the Senate are now considering my supplemental request for operations in Iraq and Afghanistan. Most of this money is for the safety and success of our military, for their pay, for their weapons, ammunition, body armor, vehicles, fuel, and for every other resource they need to carry out their mission. Part of the money is for reconstruction, from the training of Afghan and Iraqi police and military personnel to the building of schools and clinics. These funding requests are just as critical to the overall success in Iraq.

I commend the House and the Senate for approving the supplemental request. I urged both Houses of Congress to reach agreement soon on a final bill so these vital funds can go quickly to where they are needed.

I also asked Congress to move forward on elements of my agenda for growth and jobs. After the shocks of the stock market decline, recession, terrorist attack, and corporate scandals, our economy is showing signs of broad and gathering strength. America is starting to add new jobs. Retail sales are strong. Business profits are increasing. The stock market has been advancing. The housing construction is surging, and manufacturing production is rising. All of this can—all of us can be optimistic about the future of the economy, but we cannot be complacent. I will not be satisfied until every American who is looking for work can find a job.

So I proposed additional measures to keep the economy on the path to greater job creation: taking action to control the rising cost of health care; protecting businesses from junk lawsuits; by cutting needless and costly Government regulations; by making permanent the tax cuts that have helped our economy.

One action Congress should take immediately is to pass a comprehensive energy bill, which I proposed more than 2 years ago. Our entire economy depends on steady, affordable supplies of energy. We must encourage conservation, promote efficient technology, modernize our electricity grid, and increase energy production here at home.

In the closing months of this year, Congress should also complete the vital work of strengthening and modernizing Medicare. The best way to provide our seniors with modern medicine, including prescription drug coverage and better preventative care, is to give them more choices under Medicare. When seniors have options, health plans will compete for their business by offering better coverage at affordable price. American seniors are counting on these reforms. I look forward to signing them into law.

Finally, the United States Senate must step up to serious constitutional responsibilities. I've nominated many distinguished and highly qualified Americans to fill vacancies on the Federal district and circuit courts. Because of a small group of Senators is willfully obstructing the process, some of these nominees have been denied up-or-down votes for months, even years. More than one-third of my nominees for the circuit courts are still awaiting a vote. The needless delays in the system are harming the administration of justice, and they are deeply unfair to the nominees themselves. The Senate Judiciary Committee should give a prompt and fair hearing to every single nominee and send every nomination to the Senate floor for an up-or-down vote.

Finally, of course, we are monitoring the fires in California. FEMA Director Brown is in the State. I express my deep concerns and sympathies for those whose lives have been hurt badly by these fires. The Federal Government is working closely with the State government to provide resources necessary to help the brave firefighters do their duty.

With that, I'll be glad to answer some questions, starting with Terry Hunt [Terence Hunt, Associated Press].

Terrorist Attacks in Iraq

Q. Thank you, Mr. President. Mr. President, you just spoke about the suicide bombers in Iraq as being desperate. But as yesterday's attacks show, they're also increasingly successful and seem to be trying to send a warning to institutions like the police and the Red Cross not to cooperate with the United States. Has the United States been able to identify who's behind this surge of attacks, where they come from, and how to stop them?

The President. Yes. I think it's a very interesting point you make in your question, "They're trying to send a warning." Basically, what they're trying to do is cause people to run. They want to kill and create chaos. That's the nature of a terrorist. That's what terrorists do. They commit suicide acts against innocent people and then expect people to say, "Well, gosh, we better not try to fight you anymore."

We're trying to determine the nature of who these people were. But I will tell you, I would assume that they're either, or, and probably both Ba'athists and foreign terrorists. The Ba'athists try to create chaos and fear because they realize that a free Iraq will deny them the excessive privileges they had under Saddam Hussein. The foreign terrorists are trying to create conditions of fear and retreat because they fear a free and peaceful state in the midst of a part of the world where terror has found recruits, that freedom is exactly what terrorists fear the most.

And so I—as I said yesterday, we will not be—I said today again, they're not going to intimidate America, and they're not going to intimidate the brave Iraqis who are actively participating in securing the freedom of their country.

Steve [Steve Holland, Reuters].

Syria and Iran

Q. Mr. President, if there are foreign terrorists involved, why aren't Syria and Iran being held accountable?

The President. Yes. Well, we're working closely with those countries to let them know that we expect them to enforce borders, prevent people from coming across borders if, in fact, we catch them doing that. The coalition forces have stepped up border patrol efforts. There are now more Iraqis patrolling the border. We are mindful of the fact that some might want to come into Iraq to attack and to create conditions of fear and chaos, and that's why General Abizaid, in his briefing to me yesterday, talked about the additional troops we have on the borders. And that is why it is important that we step up training for Iraqis, border patrol agents, so they can enforce their own borders.

John [John King, Cable News Network].

National Commission on Terrorist Attacks Upon the United States

Q. Mr. President, thank you. As you know, the Chairman of the Commission investigating the September 11th attacks wants documents from the White House and said this week that he might have to use subpoena power. You have said there's some national security concerns about turning over some of those documents to people outside of the executive branch. Will you turn them over, or can you at least outline for the American people what you think is a reasonable compromise so that the Commission learns what it needs to know and you protect national security, if you think it's that important?

The President. Yes. It is important for me to protect national security. You're talking about the Presidential daily brief. It's important for the writers of the Presidential daily brief to feel comfortable that the documents will never be politicized and/or unnecessarily exposed for public purview. I— and so therefore, the kind of the first statements out of this administration were very protective of the Presidential prerogatives of the past and to protect the right for other Presidents, future Presidents, to have a good Presidential daily brief.

Now, having said that, I am—we want to work with Chairman Kean and Vice Chairman Hamilton. And I believe we can reach a proper accord to protect the integrity of the daily brief process and, at the same time, allow them a chance to take a look and see what was in the—certain— the daily briefs that they would like to see.

Q. Do you need to bring them here so that the Chairman and Vice Chairman can see them——

The President. Well, we're working out— we're working out the procedures. My only point is, I do want to be helpful to Chairman Kean and Lee Hamilton. These are men of integrity. They're people who understand the process. They know the importance of the Presidential daily brief. They know the importance of the daily brief to future Presidents. And therefore, I think they will be mindful of the need to gather evidence and, at the same time, protect the capacity for Presidents to get unfettered, real, good intelligence.

Norah [Norah O'Donnell, NBC News].

Remarks on Iraq Aboard the U.S.S. Abraham Lincoln

Q. Mr. President, if I may take you back to May 1st when you stood on the U.S.S. *Lincoln* under a huge banner that said, "Mission Accomplished." At that time you declared major combat operations were over, but since that time there have been over 1,000 wounded, many of them amputees who are recovering at Walter Reed, 217 killed in action since that date. Will you acknowledge now that you were premature in making those remarks?

The President. Norah, I think you ought to look at my speech. I said, "Iraq's a dangerous place, and we've got hard work to do. There's still more to be done." And we had just come off a very successful military operation. I was there to thank the troops.

The "Mission Accomplished" sign, of course, was put up by the members of the U.S.S. *Abraham Lincoln,* saying that their mission was accomplished. I know it was attributed somehow to some ingenious advance man from my staff—they weren't that ingenious, by the way.

But my statement was a clear statement, basically recognizing that this phase of the war for Iraq was over and there was a lot of dangerous work. And it's proved to be right. It is dangerous in Iraq. It's dangerous in Iraq because there are people who can't stand the thought of a free and peaceful Iraq. It is dangerous in Iraq because there are some who believe that we're soft, that the will of the United States can be shaken by suiciders and—suiciders who are willing to drive up to a Red Cross center, a center of international help and aid and comfort, and just kill.

It's the same mentality, by the way, that attacked us on September the 11th, 2001: "We'll just destroy innocent life and watch the great United States and their friends and allies crater in the face of hardship." It's the exact same mentality. And Iraq is a part of the war on terror. I said it's a central front, a new front in the war on terror, and that's exactly what it is. And that's why it's important for us to be tough and strong and diligent.

Our strategy in Iraq is to have our strike forces ready and capable to move quickly as we gather actionable intelligence. That's how you deal with terrorists. Remember, these are people that are willing to hide in societies and kill randomly. And therefore, the best way to deal with them is to harden targets, harden assets as best as you can. That means blockades and inspection spots. And as you noticed yesterday, one fellow tried to—was done in as he tried to conduct a suicide mission. In other words, an Iraqi policeman did their job but as well—that we've got to make sure that

not only do we harden targets but that we get actionable intelligence to intercept the missions before they begin. That means more Iraqis involved in the intelligence-gathering systems in their country so that they are active participants in securing the country from further harm.

Remember, the action in Iraq was—to get rid of Saddam Hussein was widely supported by the Iraqi people. And the actions that we're taking to improve their country are supported by the Iraqi people. And it's going to be very important for the Iraqi people to play an active role in fighting off the few who are trying to destroy the hopes of the many. You've heard me say that before. That's just kind of the motto of the terrorists. It's the way they operate.

Plante [Bill Plante, CBS News].

U.S. Strategy in Iraq

Q. Mr. President, in—thank you. In recent weeks, you and your White House team have made a concerted effort to put a positive spin on progress in Iraq. At the same time, there's been a much more somber assessment in private, as with Secretary Rumsfeld's memo. And there are people out there who don't believe that the administration is leveling with them about the difficulty and scope of the problem in Iraq.

The President. Yes, I can't put it any more plainly: Iraq is a dangerous place. That's leveling. It is a dangerous place. What I was saying is, there's more than just terrorist attacks that are taking place in Iraq. There's schools opening. There are hospitals opening. The electricity—the capacity to deliver electricity to the Iraqi people is back up to prewar levels. We're nearly 2 million barrels of oil a day being produced for the Iraqi people. I was just saying we've got to look at the whole picture, that what the terrorists would like is for people to focus only on the conditions which create fear, and that is the death and the toll being taken.

No, Iraq is a dangerous place, Bill. And I can't put it any more bluntly than that.

I know it's a dangerous place. And I also know our strategy to rout them out—which is to encourage better intelligence and get more Iraqis involved and have our strike teams ready to move—is the right strategy. People are constantly taking a look at the enemy.

In other words, one of the hallmarks of this operation in Iraq as well as Afghanistan was the flexibility we've given our commanders. You might remember the "stuck in the desert" scenario that—during the dust storms, that we're advancing to Baghdad and all of a sudden there was—we got stuck. But remember that at that period of time, it also became apparent that Tommy Franks had the flexibility necessary to adjust based upon, in this case, weather conditions and what he found.

And that's exactly what's taking place on a regular basis inside of Iraq. The strategy remains the same. The tactics to respond to more suiciders driving cars will alter on the ground—more checkpoints, whatever they decide—how to harden targets will change. And so we're constantly looking at the enemy and adjusting. And Iraq's dangerous, and it's dangerous because terrorists want us to leave. And we're not leaving.

Let's see, Terry [Terry Moran, ABC News], then you, Stretch [Richard Keil, Bloomberg News].

Reform of the Palestinian Authority/Israeli Security Fence

Q. Thank you, sir. Mr. President, your policies on the Middle East seem so far to have produced pretty meager results as the violence between Israelis and Palestinians——

The President. Major or meager?

Q. Meager.

The President. Oh, okay.

Q. Meager.

The President. Meager.

Q. ——as the violence between Israelis and Palestinians continues. And as you heard last week from Muslim leaders in Indonesia, your policies are seen as biased towards Israel, and I'd like to ask you about that. The Government of Israel continues to build settlements in occupied territories, and it continues to build the security fence, which Palestinians see as stealing their land. You've criticized these moves mildly a couple of times, but you've never taken any concrete action to back up your words on that. Will you?

The President. My policy in the Middle East is pretty clear. We are for a two-state solution. We want there to be a Palestinian state living side by side with Israel. Now, in order to achieve a two-state solution, there needs to be a focused effort by all concerned parties to fight off terror. There are terrorists in the Middle East willing to kill to make sure that a Palestinian state doesn't emerge. It's essential that there be a focused effort to fight off terror.

Abu Mazen came here at the White House—you were here. You witnessed the press conference. He pledged a focused and concerted effort to fight terror so that we could have a Palestinian state emerge. And he asked for help, which we were willing to provide. Unfortunately, he is no longer in power. He was eased out of power. And I do not see the same commitment to fight terror from the old guard. And therefore, it's going to be very hard to move the peace process forward until there's a focused effort by all parties to assume their responsibilities.

You asked about the fence. I have said the fence is a problem to the extent that the fence is a opportunity to make it difficult for a Palestinian state to emerge. There is a difference between security and land acquisition, and we have made our views clear on that issue.

I've also spoken to Prime Minister Sharon in the past about settlement activities. And the reason why—that we have expressed concern about settlement activities is because we want the conditions for a Palestinian state on the ground to be positive, that when the Palestinians finally get people that are willing to fight off terror, the ground must be right so that a state can emerge, a peaceful state.

This administration is prepared to help the Palestinians develop an economy. We're prepared to help the long-suffering Palestinian people. But the long-suffering Palestinian people need leadership that is willing to do what is necessary to enable a Palestinian state to come forth.

Stretch.

Iraqi Support for U.S. Efforts

Q. Thank you, Mr. President. Senior U.S. intelligence officials on the ground in Iraq have estimated that we have, at most, 6 months to restore order there and quell the violence, or else we risk losing the support of the Iraqi populace, which you've said many times we need to make this mission work. Do you share that sense of pessimism? And if not, why not? And in addition, are you considering the possibility of possibly adding more U.S. troops to the forces already on the ground there to help restore order?

The President. That's a decision by John Abizaid. He makes that—General Abizaid makes the decision as to whether or not he needs more troops. I've constantly asked the Secretary of Defense, as well as when I was visiting with General Abizaid, does he have what it takes to do his mission? He told me he does.

Secondly, I believe the Iraqi people are appreciative of the reconstruction efforts. The small-business owners, who are all of a sudden beginning to realize there's a market developing, appreciate that. The mothers who send their children to the over 1,500 schools we've refurbished appreciate that. There are going to be new textbooks coming which no longer glorify the tyrant Saddam Hussein but glorify basic education or at least promote basic education. They will be there. I think the people of Iraq appreciate what is taking place inside the country.

And what we, of course, are going to do is implement the strategy, which is encourage Iraqis to help deal with the security issues. And that's what's taking place. We're getting better intelligence, more actionable intelligence, and the Iraqi citizens themselves are willing to fight off these terrorists. If you look at some of the brave actions by the Iraqi police, people who've died for the future of their country, you know what I'm talking about. There are people willing to sacrifice for the future of their country, the Iraqi citizen—the Iraqi citizens willing to sacrifice for the future of their country.

Rosen [James Rosen, FOX News].

Flexibility in Foreign Policy

Q. Thank you, sir. Perhaps the clearest, strongest message you have ever sent from any podium has been what you like to call the Bush doctrine, that is to say, if you feed a terrorist, if you clothe a terrorist, if you harbor a terrorist, you are a terrorist. And I'd like to follow up on the Middle East. You have noted that Yasser Arafat is compromised by terror. Condi Rice has said he "cavorts with terror." You've both noted that he is an obstacle to peace. He has, in political terms, choked off your last two Palestinian interlocutors. What is it that prevents you from concluding that he is, in fact, under your own definition of what a terrorist is, a terrorist and should be dealt with in the same way that you've dealt with Saddam Hussein and Charles Taylor?

The President. Yes. Well, not every action requires military action, Jim. We—as you noticed, for example in North Korea, we've chosen to put together a multinational strategy to deal with Mr. Kim Chong-il. Not every action requires military action. As a matter of fact, military action is the very last resort for us. And a reminder: When you mentioned Saddam Hussein, I just wanted to remind you that the Saddam Hussein military action took place after innumerable United Nations Security Council resolutions were passed, not one, two, or three but a lot. And so this Nation is very reluctant to use military force. We try to enforce doctrine peacefully or through alliances or multinational forums, and we will continue to do so.

Yes, Elisabeth [Elisabeth Bumiller, New York Times].

Iraq Stabilization Group

Q. Thank you, Mr. President. You recently put Condoleezza Rice, your National Security Adviser, in charge of the management of the administration's Iraq policy. What has effectively changed since she's been in charge? And the second question, can you promise a year from now that you will have reduced the number of troops in Iraq?

The President. The second question is a trick question, so I won't answer it. The first question was Condoleezza Rice. Her job is to coordinate interagency. She's doing a fine job of coordinating interagency. She's doing what—the role of the National Security Adviser is to not only provide good advice to the President, which she does on a regular basis—I value her judgment and her intelligence—but her job is also to deal interagency and to help unstick things that may get stuck, is the best way to put it. She's an unsticker. And—is she listening? Okay, well, she's doing a fine job.

Dana [Dana Milbank, Washington Post].

Disclosure of CIA Employee's Identity

Q. Thank you, Mr. President. You have said that you were eager to find out whether somebody in the White House leaked the identity of an undercover CIA agent. Many experts in such investigations say you could find out if there was a leaker in the White House within hours if you asked all staff members to sign affidavits denying involvement. Why not take that step?

The President. Yes. Well, the best person to do that, Dana, so that the—or the best group of people to do that so that you believe the answer is the professionals at the Justice Department, and they're moving forward with the investigation. It's a criminal investigation. It is an important investigation. I'd like to know if somebody in my White House did leak sensitive information. As you know, I've been outspoken on leaks. And whether they happened in the White House or happened in the administration or happened on Capitol Hill, it is a—they can be very damaging. And so this investigation is ongoing and—by professionals who do this for a living, and I hope they—I'd like to know.

Judy [Judy Keen, USA Today].

Partial-Birth Abortion Legislation/Theresa M. "Terri" Schiavo Case

Q. Sir, in your last campaign, you said that the American public was not ready for a complete ban on abortion. You're about to sign legislation that will ban a certain abortion procedure known as partial-birth. Do you believe that the climate has changed since the last campaign and all abortions should be banned? And do you believe your brother made the correct decision in Florida when he intervened in the case of a woman who had been ordered by the courts to be taken off life support?

The President. Yes, I believe my brother made the right decision. Yes, I'll sign the ban on partial-birth abortion. And no, I don't think the culture has changed to the extent that the American people or the Congress would totally ban abortions.

Let's see. Who's—Mark Smith [Associated Press Radio], a radio man.

Iraqi Aid Legislation

Q. Thank you very much, sir, for including our radio folks here.

The President. A face for radio. [*Laughter*]

Q. I wish I could say that was the first time you told me that, sir. [*Laughter*]

The President. The first time I did it to a national audience, though. [*Laughter*]

Q. Actually it was my wife the last time. [*Laughter*]

Your package of reconstruction aid, sir, that the Congress, as you point out, is considering—that's an emergency package, meaning it's not budgeted for. Put another way, that means the American taxpayer and future generations of American taxpayers are saddled with that. Why should they be saddled with that? I know you don't want the Iraqis to be saddled with large amounts of debt, but why should future generations of Americans have that——

The President. Well, first of all, it's a one-time expenditure, as you know, and secondly, because a secure—a peaceful and free Iraq is essential to the security, future security of America.

First step was to remove Saddam Hussein because he was a threat, a gathering threat, as I think I put it. And secondly is to make sure that in the aftermath of removing Saddam Hussein, that we have a free and peaceful country in the midst of a very troubled region. It's an historic opportunity. And I will continue to make that case to the American people. It's a chance to secure—have a more secure future for our children. It's essential we get it right.

You know, I was struck by the fact when I was in Japan recently that my relations with Prime Minister Koizumi are very close and personal. And I was thinking about what would happen if, in a post-World War II era, we hadn't won the peace as well as the war. I mean, would I have had the same relationship with Mr. Koizumi? Would I be able to work closely on crucial relations? I doubt it. I doubt it.

In other words, we've got very close alliances now as a result of not only winning a war but doing the right things in the postwar period. And I believe a free and peaceful Iraq will help effect change in that neighborhood. And that's why I've asked the American people to foot the tab for $20 billion of reconstruction. Others are stepping up as well: $13 billion out of the Madrid Conference, which may be just only a beginning.

And by the way, in the Madrid Conference, most of the money came from the World Bank and the IMF, which are lending institutions, as you know. The Iraqi oil revenues, excess Iraqi oil revenues, coupled with private investment, should make up the difference to fund the estimates of what the World Bank thought was necessary to help that country.

Q. Another radio? Another radio, Mr. President?

The President. Excuse me—particularly since you interrupted me, no.

And that's what the World Bank estimated it would cost, and it looks like we'll be able to help the Iraqis get on their feet and have a viable marketplace.

Bill Douglas [William Douglas, Newsday].

Reform of the Palestinian Authority/Iraq

Q. Speaking of—in speaking on Abu Mazen, do you feel this administration did everything it could to help him out with his situation?

The President. Yes, I do.

Q. And secondly, on Iraq, do you feel that the attacks that have happened recently will discourage some countries to contribute troops or manpower?

The President. Good question. I hope not. That's what the terrorists want. They want countries to say, "Oh, gosh, well, we better not send anybody there because somebody might get hurt." That's precisely what they're trying to do. And that's why it's important for this Nation and our other coalition partners to stand our ground, to improve our intelligence, to move quickly when we find good intelligence, and to bring people to justice.

The terrorists rely on the death of innocent people to create the conditions of fear that, therefore, will cause people to lose their will. That's their strategy, and it's a pretty clear strategy to me. And this country will stay the course. We'll do our job, and it's to our interest that we do our job. It's in our interest we do our job for a free world. A free Iraq is essential to creating conditions of peace. See, that's what this is all about. This is, how do we achieve a peaceful tomorrow? How do we do our duty for our children and our grandchildren?

We must never forget the lessons of September the 11th. The terrorists will strike, and they will kill innocent life—not only in front of a Red Cross headquarters. They will strike and kill in America too. We are at war. I said right after September the 11th, this would be a different kind of war; sometimes you'd see action, and sometimes you wouldn't. It's a different kind of war than what we're used to. And Iraq is a front on the war on terror, and we will win this particular battle in the war on terror.

And it's dangerous, and it's tough. And at the same time that we're confronting the danger, we're also helping rebuild a society. We put in a new currency, in place. For the financial types who are here, you'll understand how difficult that assignment is. And yet it seems to be going well. It's an achievement that is a very important achievement for the future of Iraq. A stable currency, a new currency, a currency without the picture of the dictator or the tyrant or the torturer, however you want to define him, is important for the future. And that's taking place. There's a market developing. There are women-owned small businesses now beginning to flourish in Iraq. And there's positive things happening in the midst of the danger.

And I hope that countries, when they take a look at the situation there, understand the nature of the terrorists and the strategy of the terrorists, and don't back off.

Tom Hamburger [Wall Street Journal], you got a question? If not, make one up.

Meeting With Religious Leaders in Indonesia/Lieutenant General Boykin

Q. Mr. President, tonight you're meeting with Muslim leaders——

The President. Yes.

Q. ——at an Iftaar dinner, and I wondered if you could tell us your reaction when you encountered Muslim leaders in Indonesia. Were you surprised at the hostility they expressed towards the United States and towards your policies, both in the Middle East—and also, I understand that some of them brought up specific comments made by General Boykin——

The President. Yes, they did.

Q. ——and I wondered if you would address those comments and whether you think that General Boykin ought to be disciplined or resign.

The President. Sure, I appreciate that. First, the characterization of hostility, that just wasn't the case. It was not a hostile meeting, nor did I sense hostility. Quite the contrary, I—the five leaders I met with were appreciative for a chance to express their views. But it was a very positive meeting, very hopeful.

Two things that came out of there that I think will interest you: One was that—the question was, "Why do Americans think Muslims are terrorists?" That was the universal question from the three Muslim leaders. And my answer was, "That's not what Americans think. Americans think terrorists are evil people who have hijacked a great religion." That's why Mr. Boykin's comments were—General Boykin's comments don't reflect the administration's comments. And by the way, there's an IG investigation going on inside the Defense Department now about that. He doesn't reflect my point of view or the view of this administration.

Our war is not against the Muslim faith. As a matter of fact, as you mentioned, tonight we're celebrating the Iftaar dinner with Muslim leaders. But we welcome Muslims in our country. In America, we love the fact that we are a society in which people can pray openly or not pray at all, for that matter. And I made that point to the Muslim leaders.

Secondly, the question was about the Middle Eastern policy. "Why is your policy so slanted toward Israel," was the question. And I informed them I was the first President ever to have advocated a Palestinian state. I did so at the United Nations. I also informed them that in order for a Palestinian state to go forward, as I told Terry, there must be a focused, concerted effort to destroy the terrorist networks who are trying to prevent a Palestinian state from emerging—which requires good, strong, capable leadership, is what it requires.

And so those were the two main points that were brought up. There was concern about General Boykin. It seemed like to me that we've got a challenge to make sure that people in countries like Indonesia understand the nature of the American people, that how we think is going to be an important part of good diplomacy in the long run, that we've got to fight off the imagery of a society which condemns entire swaths of people because of the acts of a few, which is not the way we are.

And I was pleased to get the opportunity to make that case to the leaders that were there. It was a very cordial and good discussion, and I'm going to drop them a note thanking them for showing up and giving me a chance to talk about the America I know and love.

Bill [Bill Sammons, Washington Times].

Aid Package for Iraq

Q. Thank you, Mr. President. After more than a year of being accused by your critics of waging war for oil, is it frustrating to now hear some of those same critics demand that you essentially take that oil in the form of loans instead of grants for reconstruction?

The President. Well, that's exactly the point I made to the Members of Congress who have come here to the White House to talk about loans or grants. I said, "Let's don't burden Iraq with loans. The only thing they'll be able to repay their loans with is oil." And hopefully, we'll get a good

solution out of the Congress on this issue. We're making progress. We're working hard with the Members to make the case that it's very important for us not to saddle Iraq with a bunch of debt early in its—in the emergence of a market-oriented economy, an economy that has been wrecked by Mr. Saddam Hussein. I mean, he just destroyed their economy and destroyed their infrastructure, destroyed their education system, destroyed their medical system, all to keep himself in power. He was the ultimate——

Q. [*Inaudible*]—on the part of your critics?

The President. No, that's my answer there.

Hillman [G. Robert Hillman, Dallas Morning News].

Foreign Policy and Domestic Politics

Q. Thank you, Mr. President. You have repeatedly urged Americans to have patience when they view postwar operations in Iraq. But isn't there a limit to American patience, particularly in an election year, when your foreign policies——

The President. Interesting question.

Q. ——will be the center of debate?

The President. Well, I think the American people are patient during an election year, because they tend to be able to differentiate between politics and reality. As a matter of fact, the American people are—the electorate is a heck of a lot smarter than most politicians.

And the only thing I know to do is just keep telling people what I think is right for the country and stand my—stand on what I believe, and that's what I'm going to do. And there's no question politics can—will create—get a lot of noise and a lot of balloon drops and a lot of hot air. I'll probably be right in the mix of it, by the way. But I will defend my record at the appropriate time and look forward to it. I'll say that the world is more peaceful and more free under my leadership and America is more secure. And that will be the—that will be how I'll begin describing our foreign policy.

Ed [Ed Chen, Los Angeles Times], and then Bob [Bob Deans, Cox Newspapers], and then I'm going to go eat lunch.

Q. Are we invited? [Laughter]

The President. It depends on your question.

Q. Fair enough. Mr. President, you talked about politics. For weeks, if not months now, when questions have been posed to members of your team, those questions have been dismissed as politics, and a time will come later to address those questions. You, indeed, have said that yourself. How can the public differentiate between reality and politics when you and your campaign have raised over $80 million and you're saying that the season has not started?

The President. Yes. You're not invited to lunch. [Laughter]

Look, we are—we're arming, raising money to wage a campaign. And there will be an appropriate time for me to engage politically; that is, in the public forum. Right now, I'm—yes, no question, I'm going out to our friends and supporters and saying, "Would you mind contributing to the campaign for the year '04?" To me, that's—and that's a part of politics, no question about it. And as you know, these are open forums; you're able to come and listen to what I have to say.

To me, there's a difference between that and actually engaging potential opponents in a public discourse in a debate, and there will be ample time for that. There will be ample time to differentiate views and to defend records in the face of political criticism. And I know that the campaign has started for some, in terms of the public debate from a political perspective. It just hasn't for me yet.

And we'll continue to lay the groundwork for the campaign. I mean, there's organizing efforts going on in States right now. There are people being put in place that are going to work hard to turn out the vote. I mean, after all, the election is nearly a year away. There will be—we're preparing different strategies in order to run a viable campaign.

But I'm focused on security of the American people, working with Congress to get a Medicare bill and an energy bill, and will continue to use the platform I have to urge passage of those two pieces of legislation. As a matter of fact, tomorrow I'll be giving a speech on Medicare, and the next day I'll be talking about energy and will continue to talk about job creation. But in terms of the balloon drops and all that business, it's going to take—it will be a little while for me to be catching the confetti, as they say.

Bob, last question.

Iraqi Weapons Program

Q. Thank you, sir. Mr. President——

The President. Fine-looking vest, fine-looking vest.

Q. Thank you, sir. [Laughter] It's inspired by some of the attire from your APEC colleagues last week. [Laughter]

The President. Yes. [Laughter]

Q. Sir, David Kay's interim report cited substantial evidence of a secretive weapons program. But the absence of any substantial stores of chemical or biological weapons there have caused some people, even who supported the war, to feel somehow betrayed. Can you explain to those Americans, sir, whether you were surprised those weapons haven't turned up, why they haven't turned up, and whether you feel that your administration's credibility has been affected in any way by that?

The President. David Kay's report said that Saddam Hussein was in material breach of 1441, which would have been casus belli. In other words, he had a weapons program. He's disguised a weapons program. He had ambitions. And I felt the report was a very interesting first report—because he's still looking for—to find the truth.

And the American people know that Saddam Hussein was a gathering danger, as I said. And he was a gathering danger, and the world is safer as a result for us removing him from power—"us" being more than the United States, of course—Britain and other countries who were willing to participate, Poland, Australia, all willing to join up to remove this danger.

And the intelligence that said he had a weapons system was intelligence that had been used by a multinational agency, the U.N., to pass resolutions. It had been used by my predecessor to conduct bombing raids. It was intelligence gathered from a variety of sources that clearly said Saddam Hussein was a threat.

And given the attacks of September the 11th, it was—we needed to enforce U.N. resolution for the security of the world. And we did. We took action based upon good, solid intelligence. It was the right thing to do to make America more secure and the world more peaceful.

And David Kay continues to ferret out the truth. This is a man—Saddam Hussein is a man who hid programs and weapons for years. He's a master at hiding things. And so David Kay will continue his search, but one of the things that he first found was that there is clear violation of the U.N. Security Council Resolution 1441. Material breach, they call it in the diplomatic circles. Casus belli, it means a—that would have been a cause for war. In other words, he said it's dangerous.

And we were right to enforce U.N. resolutions as well. It's important for the U.N. to be a credible organization. You're not credible if you issue resolutions and then nothing happens. Credibility comes when you say something is going to happen and then it does happen. And in order to keep the peace, it's important for there to be credibility in this world, credibility on the side of freedom and hope.

Thank you all very much.

NOTE: The President's news conference began at 11:15 a.m. in the Rose Garden at the White House. In his remarks, he referred to former President Saddam Hussein of Iraq; Mike Brown, Under Secretary of Homeland Security for Emergency Preparedness and Response; Gen. John P. Abizaid, USA, combatant commander, and Gen. Tommy R. Franks, USA (Ret.), former combatant commander, U.S. Central Command; Thomas H. Kean, Chairman, and Lee H. Hamilton, Vice Chairman, National Commission on Terrorist Attacks Upon the United States (9/11 Commission); former Prime Minister Mahmoud Abbas (Abu Mazen) of the Palestinian Authority; Prime Minister Ariel Sharon of Israel; Chairman Kim Chong-il of North Korea; Prime Minister Junichiro Koizumi of Japan; Lt. Gen. William G. Boykin, USA, Deputy Under Secretary of Defense for Intelligence; and David Kay, CIA Special Advisor for Strategy Regarding Iraqi Weapons of Mass Destruction Programs. The President also referred to Gov. Jeb Bush's order on October 21 for doctors to resume tube feeding of Theresa M. "Terri" Schiavo, a brain-damaged Florida patient. Reporters referred to Chairman Yasser Arafat of the Palestinian Authority; and former President Charles Taylor of Liberia.

Remarks at the Iftaar Dinner
October 28, 2003

Good evening. *Ramadan Kareem.* Welcome to the White House. I'm pleased to host all of you, our distinguished guests, during this blessed month of Ramadan.

For Muslims in America and around the world, this holy time is set aside for prayer and fasting. It is also a good time for people of all faiths to reflect on the values we hold common—love of family, gratitude to God, and a commitment to religious freedom. America is a land of many faiths, and we honor and welcome and value the Muslim faith.

I appreciate Secretary Powell being here today, the great Secretary of State of America. There are members of my administration scattered amongst you, and I appreciate them coming. I particularly want to thank the Secretary of Energy, Spence Abraham, for being here as well.

I appreciate Your Highness Sheik Hamdan bin Zayid, the Deputy Prime Minister and Minister of State for Foreign Affairs for the United Arab Emirates, for coming. I want to thank all the Ambassadors who are here and representatives of the members of the Organization of the Islamic Conference. We're honored you're here tonight. I want to thank the American Muslim leaders who are here with us today. I appreciate my friends coming. I particularly want to thank Imam Faizul Khan, who will lead us in prayer.

According to the teachings of Islam, Ramadan commemorates the revelation of God's word in the Holy Koran to the Prophet Mohammed. In this season, Muslims come together to remember their dependence on God and to show charity to their neighbors. Fasting during Ramadan helps Muslims focus on God's greatness, to grow in virtue, and cultivate compassion toward those who live in poverty and hunger.

The charity, discipline, and sacrifice practiced during Ramadan in America makes America a better, more compassionate country. The family gatherings that break the fast at the end of each day enrich our communities. And the heartfelt prayers offered at this time of year are a blessing in many lives, and they're a blessing to our Nation.

As we gather during this season, we are mindful of the struggles of the men and women around the world who long for the same peace and tolerance we enjoy here in America. Brave American and coalition troops are laboring every day to defend our liberty and to spread freedom and peace, particularly to the people of Iraq and Afghanistan.

The citizens of those countries have survived decades of tyranny and fear. Now, new leaders are emerging. They're emerging in Iraq in the form of medical workers and teachers and citizens of all backgrounds who are coming together to guide their country's future. They're moving toward self-government and practicing their faith as they see fit.

We will continue to support the people of Iraq and Afghanistan as they build a more hopeful future. And we will not allow criminals or terrorists to stop the advance of freedom. Terrorists who use religion to justify the taking of innocent life have no home in any faith.

As we defend liberty and justice abroad, we must always honor those values here at home. America rejects all forms of ethnic and religious bigotry. We welcome the values of every responsible citizen, no matter the land of their birth. And we will always protect the most basic human freedom, the freedom to worship God without fear.

Islam is a religion that brings hope and comfort to good people across America and around the world. Tonight we honor the contributions of Muslims and the tradition of Islam by hosting this Iftaar dinner at the White House.

I wish you all a very blessed Ramadan, and may God bless.

NOTE: The President spoke at 5:50 p.m. on the State Floor at the White House. In his remarks, he referred to Imam Faizul Khan, Islamic Center of the Washington Area.

Statement on Senate Confirmation of Michael O. Leavitt as Administrator of the Environmental Protection Agency
October 28, 2003

I am pleased the Senate acted today to confirm Governor Mike Leavitt as my new Administrator of the Environmental Protection Agency. Governor Leavitt is an exceptional leader who shares my commitment to reaching out across partisan lines to get things done. I know he will work closely with me to build upon my administration's initiatives to make our air and water cleaner, protect the land, and use technology to improve our environment while our economy grows and creates jobs. I thank Chairman Inhofe and Senator Reid for their leadership in ensuring Governor Leavitt's confirmation.

Statement on Signing the Check Clearing for the 21st Century Act
October 28, 2003

Today I have signed into law H.R. 1474, the "Check Clearing for the 21st Century Act." This Act is intended to update and modernize the Nation's check payment and collection systems. Section 16(b) of the Act purports to require executive branch officials to submit to the Congress recommendations for legislative action. The executive branch shall construe section 16(b) in a manner consistent with the President's authority under the Recommendations Clause of the Constitution to submit for the consideration of the Congress such measures as the President shall judge necessary or expedient.

GEORGE W. BUSH

The White House,
October 28, 2003.

NOTE: H.R. 1474, approved October 28, was assigned Public Law No. 108–100.

Message to the Senate Transmitting the Protocol Amending the Sri Lanka-United States Taxation Convention
October 28, 2003

To the Senate of the United States:

I transmit herewith, for Senate advice and consent to ratification, the Protocol Amending the Convention Between the Government of the United States of America and the Government of the Democratic Socialist Republic of Sri Lanka for the Avoidance of Double Taxation and the Prevention of Fiscal Evasion with Respect to Taxes on Income signed at Colombo on March 14, 1985, together with an exchange of notes, signed at Washington on September 20, 2002 (the "Protocol"). I also transmit, for the information of the Senate, the report of the Department of State concerning the Protocol.

The Protocol would amend the Convention to make it similar to tax treaties between the United States and other developing nations. The Convention would provide maximum rates of tax to be applied to various types of income and protection from double taxation of income. The Convention, as amended by the Protocol, also provides for resolution of disputes and sets forth rules making its benefits unavailable to residents that are engaged in treaty shopping.

I recommend that the Senate give early and favorable consideration to this Protocol in conjunction with the Convention, and that the Senate give its advice and consent to ratification.

GEORGE W. BUSH

The White House,
October 28, 2003.

Remarks on Medicare Reform Legislation
October 29, 2003

The President. Thank you all for coming. Good morning. Welcome to the White House. I'm glad you're here. We're meeting at an historic time, and the reason why is, after years of debate and deadlock, the Congress is on the verge of Medicare reform. And that's important. Prescription drug coverage for our seniors is within reach. Expanded coverage for preventive medicine and therapy is within our reach. More health care choices for seniors are within our reach.

Though a few difficult issues remain, the Congress has made tremendous progress. And now is the time to finish the work. The Congress needs to finalize legislation that brings our seniors the best of modern medicine. I want to sign the legislation into law before the year is out.

And the point person for this administration in working with the Congress to move the legislation along is Tommy Thompson, our Secretary. He has done a fabulous job. If he looks tired, it's because he's showing up early—[*laughter*]—and going to bed late, working for the seniors of America.

I want to thank Tom Scully, who is the Administrator—Scully is the Administrator of the Centers for Medicare and Medicaid Services. I appreciate you coming.

We've got other members of my administration who are concerned about the health of all Americans, including our seniors: Rich Carmona, the Surgeon General— thank you, General; the head of the Centers for Disease Control and Prevention, Julie Gerberding. Thank you, Julie, for being here. It's good to see you. The Director of the National Institutes of Health, Elias Zerhouni—Dr. Zerhouni is with us.

We've got a lot of other important people here, too, too many to name. But I have just come from a roundtable discussion with some seniors and some people involved in the process, a corporate executive who is from Caterpillar, who assures me that corporations have no intention of—if there's a Medicare reform bill signed by me, corporations have no intention to what they call dump retirees into a system they don't want to be dumped into. And I appreciate that commitment by Rich Lavin. Thank you for bringing that up.

I want to thank Jim Parkel from Fairfield, Connecticut, who is the president of the AARP, for being here. I appreciate my friend Jim "Buddha" Martin for being here today. He's very much concerned about the health of our citizens. And thank you all for coming. This is an important moment, as I said.

You see, the stories we heard remind Tommy and me that seniors depend upon Medicare and that the Medicare program is a basic trust that must be upheld throughout the generations. What we're talking about is trust, can people trust their Government to bring a modern system of health to our seniors. We made a commitment at the Federal level to provide good health care for seniors, and we must uphold that commitment. That's what we're here to discuss today, how best to do that.

Each of the seniors that we talked about—talked to understands that the system needs improvement, that Medicare needs to be modernized. I'm determined to meet this responsibility.

And let me share some of the stories we heard right quick. Neil LaGrow is with us. Neil, thank you. He takes 10 medications, about $525 a month he spends. He pays for it all. Because of these costs, he continues to work, although I must say he didn't complain about it. [*Laughter*] He likes to work. We need our seniors working, by the way, in terms of making contributions to our society. I'm not talking about being on the factory floor for 8 hours, but I am talking about passing on values from one generation to the next or helping in different community activities as you see fit. It's a really important contribution to our country. Neil does that. If he gets some help with his prescription drug costs, it's going to make his retirement a little easier. [*Laughter*] Isn't that right?

Mr. LaGrow. That's very right.

The President. Seniors should be able to plan their retirement better. The best way to do so is to make sure that they can afford the medicines necessary to keep them healthy. That's what we're talking about in this bill.

Joan Fogg is with us, from Richmond. She and her husband, Walter, are on Medicare, and they pay a goodly portion for drugs right out of their own pocket. "When we think we're getting down on money, we go ahead and cut the medication in half." That's what she said. "That's not the way it should be, but we deal with it. We have to." Joan is right, that's not the way it should be. That's why we want to modernize the system. That's why we want to work better for all seniors.

Most American seniors and people with disabilities are grateful for the current Medicare system. Yet they understand the system has problems. Our job is to address those problems. We should carefully correct the problems. That's what we're elected to do. Medicare was created at a time when medicine consisted mostly of house calls and surgery and long hospital stays. Now modern medicine includes preventative care, outpatient procedures, and at-home care. Life is changing. Medicare is not.

Many invasive surgeries are now unnecessary because of miraculous new prescription drugs. Most Americans have coverage for this new medicine. Three-quarters of seniors have some kind of drug coverage. But seniors relying exclusively on Medicare do not have coverage for most prescription drugs and many forms of preventative care. This is not good. It's not cost-effective medicine.

Medicare today will pay for extended hospital stays for ulcer surgery, at a cost of about $28,000 per patient, and that's important coverage. Yet Medicare will not pay for the drugs that eliminate the cause of ulcers, drugs that cost about $500 a year. So we're going to be talking about cost savings; there's an example of cost savings.

Medicare will pay many of the costs to treat a stroke, including bills from hospital and rehab center, doctors, home health aides, and outpatient care. Those costs can run more than $100,000, and this is essential coverage. Yet Medicare does not cover the blood-thinning drugs that could prevent strokes, drugs that cost less than $1,000 a year.

The Medicare system has many strengths. Yet it is often slow to respond to dramatic changes in medicine. It took more than a decade and an act of Congress to get Medicare to cover preventative breast cancer screenings. It took 10 years and then an act of Congress to change the system. That's not a good system. Our seniors should not have to wait for an act of Congress for improvements in their health care.

The best way to provide our seniors with modern medicine, including prescription drug coverage and better preventative care, is to give them better choices under Medicare. If seniors have choices, health plans will compete for their business by offering better coverage at more affordable prices.

The choices we support include the choice of making no change at all. I understand some seniors don't want to change, and that's perfectly sensible. If you're a senior who wants to stay in the current Medicare system, you'll have that option, and you'll gain a prescription drug benefit. That's what the reform does.

If you're a senior who wants enhanced benefits, such as coverage for extended hospital stays or protection against high out-of-pocket expenses, you'll have that choice. If you liked managed care plans, that option will be there. If you're a low-income senior, you will receive extra help each month and more generous coverage, so you can afford a Medicare option that includes prescription drug benefits.

We're applying a basic principle: Seniors should be able to choose the kind of coverage that works best for them, instead of having that choice made by the Government. Every Member of Congress gets to choose a health coverage plan that makes the most sense for them. So does every Federal employee. If this kind of coverage is good enough for the United States Congress, it's good enough for America's seniors.

For seniors without any drug coverage now, these reforms will make a big difference in their lives. In return for a monthly premium of about $35, or a dollar a day, those seniors now without coverage would see their drug bills cut roughly in half. A senior who has no drug coverage now and monthly drug costs of $200 a month would save more than $1,700 on drug costs each year. A senior with monthly drug costs of $800 would save nearly $5,900 on drug costs each year. Those are important savings, help change people's lives in a positive way.

I'm optimistic the House and the Senate negotiators will produce a bill that brings real savings to millions of seniors and real reform to Medicare. Once the legislation is passed, it will take some time to put into place. During this period, we'll provide all seniors with a Medicare-approved drug discount card that saves between 10 to 25 percent off the cost of their medicines. So they'll have a start to see savings immediately.

Low-income beneficiaries will receive a $600 subsidy along with their discount card to help them purchase their prescription medicines. The legislation Congress passes must make sure that the prescription drug coverage provided to many retirees by their employers is not undermined. That's what Rick and I just discussed. Medicare legislation should encourage employers to continue benefits, while also extending drug coverage to the millions of Medicare beneficiaries who now lack it.

These steps will strengthen Medicare, not only for today's seniors but for tomorrow's retirees. Many workers are counting on Medicare to provide good health care coverage in their retirement. That's what people are counting on. These reforms will give our workers confidence that Medicare will serve them with the very best of modern medicine.

The budget I submitted earlier this year commits an additional $400 billion over 10 years to implement this vision of a stronger Medicare system. We're keeping our commitments to the seniors of today. We must pursue these reforms so that our Medicare system can serve future generations of Americans.

The time to improve our Medicare system has come. Now is the time. I urge America's seniors to speak up, to call and write your representatives to urge them to work out a final bill. Speak up for prescription drug coverage. Speak up for health care choices. Speak up for a modern Medicare system that puts patients and doctors in charge.

I urge the Congress to act quickly, to act this year, not to push this responsibility to the future. We have the opportunity— we have the obligation to give seniors more choices and better benefits. We have come far, and now is the time to finish the job.

Thank you for coming. Appreciate it. Good to see you all. Thank you all.

NOTE: The President spoke at 11:06 a.m. in Room 450 in the Dwight D. Eisenhower Executive Office Building. In his remarks, he referred to Richard P. Lavin, vice president, Human Services Division, Caterpillar Inc.; and Jim Martin, president, 60 Plus Association. The Office of the Press Secretary also released a Spanish language transcript of these remarks.

Message to the Congress on Continuation of the National Emergency With Respect to Sudan
October 29, 2003

To the Congress of the United States:

Section 202(d) of the National Emergencies Act (50 U.S.C. 1622(d)) provides for the automatic termination of a national emergency unless, prior to the anniversary date of its declaration, the President publishes in the *Federal Register* and transmits to the Congress a notice stating the emergency is to continue in effect beyond the anniversary date. Consistent with this provision, I have sent the enclosed notice, stating the Sudan emergency is to continue in effect beyond November 3, 2003, to the *Federal Register* for publication. The most recent notice continuing this emergency was published in the *Federal Register* on October 31, 2002 (67 *Fed. Reg.* 66525).

The crisis between the United States and Sudan constituted by the actions and policies of the Government of Sudan that led to the declaration of a national emergency on November 3, 1997, has not been resolved. These actions and policies are hostile to U.S. interests and pose a continuing unusual and extraordinary threat to the national security and foreign policy of the United States. Therefore, I have determined it is necessary to continue the national emergency declared with respect to Sudan and maintain in force the comprehensive sanctions against Sudan to respond to this threat.

GEORGE W. BUSH

The White House,
October 29, 2003.

NOTE: The notice of October 29 is listed in Appendix D at the end of this volume.

Message to the Congress on Continuation of the National Emergency Regarding Weapons of Mass Destruction
October 29, 2003

To the Congress of the United States:

Section 202(d) of the National Emergencies Act (50 U.S.C. 1622(d)) provides for the automatic termination of a national emergency unless, prior to the anniversary date of its declaration, the President publishes in the *Federal Register* and transmits to the Congress a notice stating that the emergency is to continue in effect beyond the anniversary date. Consistent with this provision, I have sent to the *Federal Register* for publication the enclosed notice, stating that the emergency posed by the proliferation of weapons of mass destruction and their delivery systems declared by Executive Order 12938 on November 14, 1994, as amended, is to continue in effect beyond November 14, 2003. The most recent notice continuing this emergency was signed on November 6, 2002, and published in the *Federal Register* on November 12, 2002 (67 *Fed. Reg.* 68493).

Because the proliferation of weapons of mass destruction and the means of delivering them continues to pose an unusual and extraordinary threat to the national security, foreign policy, and economy of the United States, I have determined the national emergency previously declared must continue in effect beyond November 14, 2003.

GEORGE W. BUSH

The White House,
October 29, 2003.

NOTE: The notice of October 29 is listed in Appendix D at the end of this volume.

Remarks at the Dedication of the Oak Cliff Bible Fellowship Youth Education Center in Dallas, Texas
October 29, 2003

The President. Thank you all.

Audience members. USA! USA! USA!

The President. Thank you all.

Audience members. USA! USA! USA!

The President. Zip it. [*Laughter*] Thank you all for coming. It's great to be home. I'm glad to be with people who are transforming a community one heart and one soul at a time. That's what's taking place here, and that's why I'm here.

I want to thank you all for supporting Project Turn Around. I want to thank you for supporting with your resources, with your time, and with your prayers. I want to thank my friend Tony Evans for his leadership. He's what I like to call a social entrepreneur. We've got business entrepreneurs, and this country has got social entrepreneurs—those are people who use their wits and their talents as change agents, as positive change agents.

You can hear Tony on 500 radio stations. You can read 20 of his books. You can listen to his powerful sermons on Sunday. He is a busy man, and one of the advantages of being President is he'll take my phone call. [*Laughter*] And I'm glad he does. I appreciate his advice, and he's got good, sound advice. I appreciate his friendship; he is a loyal friend. And I appreciate his prayers. The greatest gift American people can give a President and his family is prayer, and I want to thank you for that.

Tony and I married well. [*Laughter*] I'm so honored to be with Lois Evans. Thank you very much for your hospitality. And the Evans family, Chrystal and Priscilla as well as Anthony, Jr. Anthony, Jr., was telling me—actually, he's a modest guy, so his dad was telling me—[*laughter*]—that he just got back from cutting a record with Michael W. Smith. I think that's what he said, kind of like that. Well, he was with Michael W. Smith. [*Laughter*] We'll see if the record happens or not. [*Laughter*]

Some of my greatest memories was living in Austin, Texas, and showing up for work at the Capitol. Two members of the legislative branch are here, people who I remember fondly, people who I miss. Senator Royce West and Representative Helen Giddings are with us.

I want you to know that I'm aware that Reverend E.K. Bailey passed, and I send our deepest sympathies to his family and to his congregation. He was a great leader here in the great State of Texas.

I bring up a preacher because I want to thank all the preachers who are here, the pastors, those who shepherd. One pastor who is not here is my friend Jack Graham from Prestonwood Baptist. I bring that up because social entrepreneurs find out ways to leverage resources in a proper way. And what Tony Evans has done with Pastor Jack Graham is to start an urban-suburban partnership. It's an opportunity for suburban churches to participate in salvaging lives and making lives better in neighborhoods where most members of the congregation will never go. It's a chance for urban and suburban churches to work on racial reconciliation. Social entrepreneurs think about ways to make societies a better place. And I want to thank Tony, and I appreciate Jack for having a vision about how to—about how to make America a better place, one neighborhood at a time.

A President must set great goals worthy of a great nation. We're a great nation. Therefore, a President must set big goals. I set a goal for this country to make the world more peaceful by spreading freedom. Freedom is not America's gift to the world; freedom is God's gift to each and every individual in the world.

I set a great goal here at home. I want the American Dream, the great hope of our country, to extend in every neighborhood in our country. I want every single person in this land to feel welcome and wanted and hopeful. It's a great domestic goal. And of course, when you think about setting goals, you've got to think about the tactics and strategies to achieve a goal. It's one thing to set a goal; it's another thing to actually meet the goal.

And one of the reasons I'm so thrilled to be here with Tony Evans is because he helped me understand how to best meet that goal. He probably didn't realize it at the time, but there's something about "mysterious ways." [*Laughter*] We were together in Greenville, Texas, in 1996. It's an unusual place for, you know, a Governor and a famous pastor to meet. But we were there because we were worried about racial reconciliation as a result of some fires that had destroyed church.

And I'll never forget his speech. It's stuck with me to this day. As a matter of fact, what I'm telling you is it's helped formulate policy, first at State level, now the Federal level, because he got up and he said, in speaking about programs meant to help people, welfare programs—he said, you know, get rid of your welfare programs; think differently. He said the best welfare programs are on every corner in America. They're open 24 hours a day. They've got a workforce that is guided by an ancient guidebook whose tenets have stood the test of time. They've got a motto over the door that says, "Love your neighbor like you would like to be loved yourself."

Tony went on to explain why faith-based programs, programs that emanate out of faith institutions work so well. He told the story; maybe he has told it to you. If he has, I've got to repeat it because the TV cameras are here. [*Laughter*] He said he's reminded of the time when a fellow had a house and he got a crack on the wall. And he went and got a painter or a plasterer, and a fellow came and covered it up. And 2 weeks later, the crack reappeared. And so he said, "Well, I better get another painter." And he did. And he repainted the crack. But it reappeared again. He finally got a wise painter who said, "Sir, you'll never fix the crack until you fix the foundation." Project Turn Around fixes the foundation.

That's what we're here to herald, programs such as Project Turn Around. It's got such a wonderful sense of mission. It says, "to rebuild lives from the inside out." It's a powerful statement, isn't it? Really think about it—"to rebuild lives;" that's a hopeful goal for our country. We want people to realize the great potential of America. Some lives have to be rebuilt. And it didn't say "from the outside in;" it said "from the inside out." It's a faith-based initiative built from the inside out, not from the outside in.

Listen to what you do through this ministry. There's a thousand volunteers who provide shelter and food and clothing. There's marriage counseling. It's vital that we have strong families in America. And they provide marriage counseling. Job training—somebody walks in this building, and they want to work. They just—there's human dignity that comes from work, and they can find a chance to train for jobs right here in Project Turn Around. Advice on starting a small business—that warms my heart. If you own something, you have a vital stake in the future of our country. There's nothing better than somebody realizing their dreams by starting and owning their own business. It's uniquely—not "uniquely," it's inherently American that people are able to do that right here. Who would think that in a church you would have a program to teach you how to start your own business? Social entrepreneurs think that way.

Project Turn Around is a complete program. A woman can find help during a crisis pregnancy. There's a tenderness and a practicality to Project Turn Around. This program is a beacon for Dallas. And this program is a model for the Nation.

We just came from the dedication of the Education and Youth Center. If you haven't been there yet, you need to go take a look. It's impressive. The brick and mortar is impressive. The architectural design is fantastic. What's more fantastic is what's going to take place inside the building.

I'm appreciative of the idea of the Fellowship Christian Academy taking root and taking wing here. This is a program which challenges the soft bigotry of low expectations. It raises standards. It believes every child can learn. See, that's important in education. We must challenge the mediocrity of a system. We must not let people just get shuffled through because their skin happens to be black. You know, people can't quit on a child. No child should be left behind. This school and this building understands that.

But the building across the street not only houses the school, it also houses a mentoring program that gathers children from 60 schools. Five thousand children a week are mentored. That's powerful; that is a powerful program.

One of my passions—and I spoke to the Congress about this at my State of the Union—was to help the children whose mom or dad may be in prison. My hope is that—and I know that Tony understands this—the mentoring program for that child, those children are necessary for the country to be hopeful for every single citizen. What this program understands—and what I hope other programs around the Nation understand—is that by mentoring a child, you shape the character of a child. And it's a high calling in life, because that influence reaches to eternity.

As I said, Government can hand out money—and we will, and that's an important aspect—but it cannot put hope in people's hearts. See, that's the disconnect. It can't put hope in people's lives. We must understand that amidst our plenty, there are people who hurt, deeply hurt. And the deepest needs are oftentimes found in the human heart. In order to help that need, people need to know they're valued and wanted. People need to know a higher power that is bigger than their problems.

What the faith-based programs say, time after time after time, is that miracles are possible when somebody puts their arm around a neighbor and says, "God loves you. I love you. And you can count on us both." Faith-based programs work. They are able to address the deepest needs of our heart.

And so when I heard Tony speak at Greenville, I began to act. It touched my heart, what he had to say. I wanted everybody to realize the vast potential then of the State of Texas, now all across America. So I started to work on and think about faith-based programs. They're effective. They're so effective that it points to a new role for government, a new political philosophy.

But first, let me say Government has no business funding religious worship or teaching. They don't want the church to be the state, and we don't want the state to be the church. However, our Government should support the good work of religious people who are changing America.

What does that mean from a practical sense, from where I sit? What does that mean? It means this, that when Government gives contracts to provide social services, religious groups should have an equal chance to compete. That's what that means. And when we make decisions on public funding, we should not focus on the religion you practice but on the results you deliver.

This has not been the attitude of government; let's be frank about it. The attitude

of government, particularly in Washington, has said religious groups need not apply. That's the way it has been. We're missing an opportunity to help change lives and to meet a major goal in our country, which is everyone should realize the great vast potential of America.

If you're allowed to apply for grants on that rare occasion, some are asked to change their board of directors, to remove the cross from the wall, to change the very things that make the faith-based program effective. And I'll give you an example of what I'm talking about. There's the Orange County Rescue Mission in Tustin, California. It's a fantastic initiative. They applied for funding from the Housing and Urban Development. We call it HUD. HUD said fine, but it had a few conditions to meet. In other words, there was access, perhaps, to Federal money, but let me tell you the conditions. The Rescue Mission had to form a secular nonprofit. They had to ban all religious activities from their facility. They had to rename their chapel and auditorium.

It's hard to be a faith-based program when you're forbidden from practicing your faith. It's hard to change hearts when you can't use the power you've got to change the hearts. Government action like this is pure discrimination. And when Government discriminates against religious groups, it is not the groups who suffer. The real loss is felt by the hungry who do not get fed, by the addicts who don't get help and treatment, by the children who drift toward self-destruction. For the sake of so many people in need, this country must support the armies of compassion.

I asked Congress to join me and pass what I called the Faith-Based Initiative, which would help change the culture of Washington and the behavior of bureaucracies. They have stalled. So I just signed an Executive order. The Executive order says that the Federal Government will have a level playing field when religious groups apply for Federal money. There will not be discrimination. That's what it says, pure and simple. Every bureaucrat in Washington who might be tempted to fall back to the old ways now knows exactly where I stand.

And we've set up faith-based offices. We're trying to change the culture, see. We're trying to change an attitude. So we set up faith-based offices in several important Cabinet departments. And that's important. This is important for people who are charged with good policy to have a faith-based office that will work directly with the social entrepreneurs of America, the Tony Evanses of the world, so they get a sympathetic ear and get help, not a cold shoulder.

And there's some changes. Slowly but surely, the culture is changing. Just last month, the Department of Health and Human Services finalized regulations that helped open up three programs to greater competition—in other words, began to level the playing field. Programs in which religious faith-based programs—by the way, I'm talking about Christians and Jewish people and Muslims, Hindus, people of all faiths. See, we've all heard that call to love a neighbor.

The Substance Abuse and Mental Health Services Administration, now opening up for grants. The Temporary Assistance for Needy Families, TANF, is now opening up for grants. The Community Service Block Grant Program is opening up for grants from faith-based institutions. These are billions of dollars of money now available for new social spending.

Let me tell you, by new social spending I mean spending dollars in a new way, in a way that's effective, in a way that will help change lives in a positive and constructive way. See, we want everybody in this country, every person—we want the addict; we want the single lonely mom; we want the child, the dyslexic child—all to feel a part of the future of this country.

Last month, HUD finalized new regulations that apply to aid programs covering $7.6 billion so that now religious groups that build housing will no longer face discrimination when they seek HUD funds. That's important. We want churches in the middle of neighborhoods that may need new housing to be able to have a chance to access some money to provide new housing. We have a minority homeownership gap in America that needs to be closed. We've got a program in front of Congress to help people with the downpayment. HUD has got a program to help people understand the fine print. We're trying to simplify contracts. But in order to help close the homeownership gap, it seems to make sense to allow inner-city churches to become active builders of homes, affordable homes, so people can find housing in the neighborhoods in which they worship.

Remember, I told you about the program in Orange County, the Orange County Rescue Mission. It has now reapplied for a contract for HUD. It doesn't have to force to—be forced to abide by those rules, those rules that make people nervous. Listen, nobody wants to apply for Federal grants if you think you have to change your mission. Nobody in their right mind is going to say, "Look, let me—let me access some of your money, but I've got to change the way I think." It defeats the purpose.

We're making changes of the culture in Washington, DC. It takes awhile, but we're working on it. And the fact that I can come here—[*applause*]—and the fact that I can come here and herald this program as a successful program helps change the culture. There's nothing like success to change cultures.

We've got some other projects here in Dallas. The Builders of Hope in West Dallas is a faith-based group building new homes for low-income families, which HUD is supporting. HHS is supporting the Faith Walk Center in Dallas, a program which fights drug abuse amongst young people. You've got to understand that sometimes, and a lot of times, the best way to help the addict, a person who is stuck on drugs and alcohol, is to change their heart. See, if you change their heart, then they change their behavior. I know.

We've got initiatives I've been talking to Tony about—he knows about this—called the Compassion Capital Fund. Sometimes entrepreneurs need startup capital, whether it be a business or the social entrepreneur needs startup capital. I don't think Evans needs startup capital. [*Laughter*] I think we're beyond the startup capital phase here at this fantastic, fantastic church. But it gives programs startup money and expansion money directly to the social entrepreneurs, and that's important. I'm calling on Congress to increase the budget to $100 million this year; they need to triple the amount of money available for this program.

And so what I'm telling you is, is that the best way to meet a national goal is to rally the strength of America. The strength of America is the people of America. And the people of America, a lot of people in America understand there's a higher authority than their Government and respond to that higher authority. All the levels of government—and I can only speak for the Federal Government, but I might be able to affect the State government and local government by just speaking—[*laughter*]—but all levels of government, the Federal Government, the State of Texas and all States, the city of Dallas and all cities, ought not to fear programs based upon faith. All levels of government must understand the power of faith programs to make the communities and States and country

in which we live a better place. It's the reality. This is living proof of it right here at Project Turn Around.

I love our country. I love what we stand for. We're a strong nation. And in this world today, we need to be strong. We need to defend ourselves, and we will. And we need to promote the peace, and we will. And when we see suffering around the world, this country should not turn its back. We're strong, but we're incredibly compassionate as a nation. This proud country, America, is leading the world in incredibly important work, like the work of human rescue for those who are dying from AIDS on the continent of Africa.

And we need to be strong at home too, strong of heart and strong of soul. Project Turn Around and other successful programs around our country show the strength, show the strength that bends down to help the child and the stranger and the outcast.

I want to thank you all so very much for your welcome. I want to thank you for your compassion and your care. I want to thank you for laying those strong foundations which help those who hurt, because by laying that strong foundation, you're changing America one heart, one soul, one conscience at a time.

God bless your work, and may God bless America.

NOTE: The President spoke at 6:18 p.m. In his remarks, he referred to Anthony T. Evans, senior pastor, Oak Cliff Bible Fellowship; and entertainer Michael W. Smith.

Remarks at a Bush-Cheney Luncheon in Columbus, Ohio
October 30, 2003

Thanks for coming. Thanks for the warm welcome. It is great to be back in Columbus. I feel comfortable coming here. I like good football. I like to be around good

people. And my grandfather was raised here. I don't know if you know that, but Prescott S. Bush was raised in Columbus, Ohio, and the last time I came to Ohio,

I said I was proud of the fact that my paternal grandfather was raised here. And my mother got me on the phone. She said, "You forgot about your maternal grandfather, Marvin; he grew up in Dayton." So, Mother, if you're paying attention—[*applause*]. I'm proud to be in Ohio, because my two grandfathers grew up in Ohio.

I'm proud of my family roots here. I am proud of what you all did in the year 2000. And I want to thank you for coming. Today we're laying the foundation for what is going to be an Ohio victory and a national victory in the fall of 2004. And I'm getting ready. I'm loosening up. [*Laughter*] But the political season will come in its own time. I have got a job to do. I've got a job to do for all Americans, and that is to keep this Nation secure and strong and prosperous and free.

My one regret about this event today is that Laura isn't traveling with me. She is a fabulous First Lady. She's doing a great job. She is working her way down to Crawford, where we'll spend the night tonight. She is stopping off in Tyler, Texas, to do a little political work herself. And then we're going to spend some time on the weekend, although I'm going to take off on Saturday. We've got some Governors' races coming up. But we're looking forward to getting some quality time together after spending a lot of quality time together on the airplane when we traveled throughout the Far East on a very successful trip. I want you to know our alliances with our friends are strong, and the world is more peaceful for it.

Speaking about a man who married well, so did your Governor. And I'm honored the first lady of Ohio is with us. Hope Taft, thank you for coming. And I'm proud to call Governor Taft my friend. I want to thank you for your service to your great State and appreciate your leadership.

We've got other officials here. The Lieutenant Governor, Jennette Bradley, is with us. Ken Blackwell is with us. Joe Deters is with us. Jim Petro, the attorney general,

Betty Montgomery, the State auditor—all friends and all great leaders for the State of Ohio. Thank you all for coming.

I'm honored that members of the statehouse are here, particularly the speaker of the house, Larry Householder. Sorry he didn't bring all his kids with him. [*Laughter*] Maybe the person serving the meals isn't sorry he brought all his kids with him. I think he said he's got six or seven kids, which is pretty darn good, Speaker. And I want to thank the president of the senate, Senator Doug White, for being here as well. I thank the legislators for coming. I'm proud to have your support, and I'm counting on your support as we get in this election cycle.

I selected a man from Ohio, from Cincinnati, Ohio, to be the national finance chairman of this campaign, and he's doing a terrific job. His name is Mercer Reynolds. I'm proud to call him friend. I'm proud he has taken on such a vital role for the Bush-Cheney 2004 campaign. I also want to thank Tim Timken and Bill DeWitt and Jo Ann Davidson for their hard work all across the State of Ohio. I want to thank the cochairmen of this event for making this an incredibly successful event. I want to thank the grassroots activists who are with us today: the party chairman, Bob Bennett; Michael Colley, who is the national committeeman; Martha Moore, the national committeewoman.

I'm honored you all are here. I'm going to need you and count on you to energize the grassroots here in the State of Ohio, to man the phones and put up the signs and mail the letters. I want you to remind people that when you do so, this administration has got a hopeful, optimistic vision for every single American.

In the last 2½ years, our Nation has acted decisively to confront great challenges. I came to this office to solve problems instead of passing them on to future Presidents and future generations. I came to seize opportunities and not let them slip away. This administration is meeting the tests of our time.

Terrorists declared war on the United States of America, and war is what they got. We've captured or killed many key leaders of the Al Qaida network, and the rest of them know we're on their trail. In Afghanistan and in Iraq, we gave ultimatums to terror regimes. Those regimes chose defiance, and those regimes are no more. Fifty million people in those two countries once lived under tyranny, and today they live in freedom.

Two-and-a-half years ago, our military was not receiving the resources it needed and morale was beginning to suffer, so we increased the defense budget to prepare for the threats of a new era. And today, no one in the world can question the skill and the strength and the spirit of the United States military.

Two-and-a-half years ago, we inherited an economy in recession, and then our country was attacked, and we had some scandals in corporate America, and we marched to war, all of which affected the confidence of the American people. But we acted. We took the lead. We passed tough new laws to hold corporate criminals to account. And to get the economy going again, I have twice led the United States Congress to pass historic tax relief for the American people.

I know that when Americans have more take-home pay to spend, to save, or invest, the whole economy grows, and people are more likely to find a job. So we returned more money to the people to help them raise their families. We reduced taxes on dividends and capital gains to encourage investment. We gave small businesses incentives to expand and to hire new people. With all these actions, we're laying the foundations for greater prosperity and more jobs across America so that every one of our citizens has a chance to realize the American Dream.

Two-and-a-half years ago, there was a lot of talk about education reform, and there wasn't much action. So I acted. I called for and the Congress passed the No Child Left Behind Act. With a solid bipartisan majority, we delivered the most dramatic education reforms in a generation. I believe that every child can learn. And this country ought to expect every child to learn. In return for Federal money, we have begun to ask the question, are you teaching our children? Are you holding up high standards? Are you willing to challenge the soft bigotry of low expectations? The days of excuse-making are over in public education. We expect results in every classroom so that not one single child is left behind.

We reorganized our Government and created the Department of Homeland Security to better safeguard our ports and borders and to protect the American people. We passed trade promotion authority to open up new markets for Ohio's manufacturers and farmers and ranchers. We passed budget agreements that is helping to maintain much needed spending discipline in Washington, DC. On issue after issue, this administration has acted on principle. We have kept our word, and we have made progress for the American people.

The United States Congress shares in the achievements. I thank the Speaker, Denny Hastert, and I thank Majority Leader Bill Frist for their hard work. We're working to try to change the tone in Washington. There's too much politics in the Nation's Capital, too much zero-sum attitude. We've got to lift the rhetoric and focus on results. And that's what we're working to do in the Nation's Capital, results for all the people.

And those are the kind of people I've asked to serve in my administration. When you're sitting around your coffee shops and community centers, you're talking up the campaign—which I hope you do—remind the people that I put together a great team on behalf of the American people—people from all walks of life, people who have come to our Nation's Capital to serve their country, people like Dick Cheney, our country's greatest Vice President we've ever had. Mother may have a different opinion. [*Laughter*]

In 2½ years, we have done a lot, if you think about it. We have come far, but our work is only beginning. I have set great goals worthy of a great nation. First, America is committed to expanding the realm of freedom and peace for our own security and for the benefit of the world. And second, in our own country, we must work for a society of prosperity and compassion so that every single citizen has a chance to work and to succeed and to realize the great promise of America. It is clear that the future of freedom and peace depend on the actions of America. This Nation is freedom's home and freedom's defender. We welcome this charge of history, and we are keeping it.

Our war on terror continues. The enemies of freedom are not idle, and neither are we. This country will not rest; we will not tire; we will not stop until this danger to civilization is removed.

We are confronting that danger in Iraq, where Saddam Hussein holdouts and foreign terrorists are desperately trying to throw Iraq into chaos by attacking coalition forces and aid workers and innocent Iraqis. They know that the advance of freedom in Iraq would be a major defeat for the cause of terror. This collection of killers is trying to shake the will of the United States of America. And we will not be intimidated.

We are aggressively striking the terrorists in Iraq. We will defeat them there so that we do not have to face them in our own country. We continue to call on other nations to help build a free country in Iraq. After all, it will make the world more secure when this happens. We're standing with the Iraq people as they assume more of their own defense and move toward self-government. And these aren't easy tasks, but they're essential tasks. They're essential for the future of our children and grandchildren. We will finish what we have

begun in Iraq, and we will win this essential victory in the war on terror.

Our greatest security comes from the advance of human liberty, because free nations don't support terror. Free nations do not attack their neighbors. Free nations do not threaten the world with weapons of mass terror. Americans believe that freedom is the deepest need and hope of every human heart. And I believe that freedom is the right of every person. And I believe that freedom is the future of every nation.

This country also understands that unprecedented influence brings tremendous responsibilities. And we have duties in this world. When we see disease and starvation and hopeless poverty, America will not turn away. This great, mighty Nation is leading the world in confronting a terrible disease on the continent of Africa. This Nation is bringing the healing power of medicine to millions of men and women and children now suffering with AIDS. This great land is leading the world in this incredibly important work of human rescue.

We face challenges here at home as well. I'm about to go to a business here in Ohio to talk about the economy. My attitude is that anybody—if anybody who wants to work in Ohio or in America is looking for a job and can't find a job, it says we've got a problem. I'll continue to work to create the conditions in which small businesses can grow to be big businesses, the conditions necessary for the entrepreneurial spirit to flourish. We want everybody working in America. We're making progress, but we will not stop until there are jobs aplenty for those who are looking for work.

We have a duty to keep our commitment to America's seniors by strengthening and modernizing Medicare. Congress is taking historic action to improve the lives of our older citizens. For the first time—hear this—for the first time since the creation of Medicare, the House and the Senate have passed reforms to increase the choices for our seniors and to provide coverage for prescription drugs. The House and the Senate must iron out their differences. They must come together and get a bill to my desk soon. We have a promise to keep to our seniors, and we must modernize the Medicare system for those of us who are fixing to become seniors.

For the sake of our health care system, we need to cut down on the frivolous lawsuits which increase the cost of medicine. People who have been harmed by a bad doctor deserve their day in court. Yet the system should not reward lawyers who are simply fishing for rich settlements. Frivolous lawsuits drive up the cost of health care, and they therefore affect the Federal budget. Medical liability reform is a national issue which requires a national solution. I proposed a good bill to solve the medical liability issue all across America. It was passed by the House. It is stuck in the Senate. Your two Senators are good votes on this issue. Some Senators need to hear loud and clear that not one single person has ever been healed by a frivolous lawsuit. We need medical liability reform now.

I have a responsibility as the President to make sure the judicial system runs well, and I have met that duty. I have nominated superb men and women for the Federal bench, people who will interpret the law, not legislate from the bench. Some of the Members of the United States Senate are trying to keep my nominees off the bench by blocking up-or-down votes. Every judicial nominee deserves a fair hearing and an up-or-down vote on the Senate floor. It is time for some Members of the United States Senate to stop playing politics with American justice.

This Congress needs to complete work on a comprehensive energy plan. If you're worried about manufacturing jobs in Ohio, you need an energy plan. It's hard to hire people if you can't find energy. I proposed a bill 2 years ago to the Congress, a bill which encourages us to use, in environmentally friendly ways, the resources at our disposal. We need clean coal technology in America. We need more natural gas. We need to encourage alternative sources of energy. We need to encourage conservation. We need to make sure the electricity system is reliable. As the people of northern Ohio found out, it's not that reliable at times. [*Laughter*] We need to modernize the system. We need an energy bill. For the sake of economic security and for the sake of national security, the Congress needs to complete the energy bill and get it to my desk.

A strong and prosperous nation must also be a compassionate nation. I will continue to advance our agenda of compassionate conservatism, which means we must apply the best and most innovative ideas to help our fellow citizens who are in need. There are a lot of men and women who want to end their dependence on government. They want to find work. They want to become independent through hard work, so we must build on the success of the welfare reform to bring work and dignity into the lives of more of our citizens. Congress should complete the "Citizen Service Act" so more Americans can serve their communities and their country.

Both Houses should reach agreement on my Faith-Based Initiative to help support the armies of compassion, which exists right here in Columbus, Ohio—they exist in every city in Ohio—the armies of compassion who are mentoring our children, caring for the homeless, who offer hope to the addicted. People of all faiths—Christians, Jewish, Muslims, Hindus—have heard a universal call to love a neighbor just like they'd like to be loved themselves. This Nation should not fear faith. We should welcome programs based upon faith to answer the deepest needs of the human heart which exist in our society.

A compassionate society must promote opportunity for all, including the dignity and the pride that comes from ownership. This administration will constantly strive to promote an ownership society in America.

We want more people owning their home. We have a minority homeownership gap in America. I presented a plan to Congress to close that gap. The more people that own their home, the better off America will be. We want people owning and managing their own health care plans and their own retirement accounts. We want more people owning their own business because we understand that when a person owns something, he or she has a vital stake in the future of our country.

A compassionate society is one in which people respect one another and take responsibility for the decisions they make. The culture of America is changing from one that has said, "If it feels good, do it," and "You got a problem, blame somebody else," to a culture in which each of us understands we are responsible for the decisions we make in life.

If you are fortunate enough to be a mom or a dad, you are responsible for loving your child with all your heart. If you're worried about the quality of the education in the community in which you live, you're responsible for doing something about it. If you're a CEO in corporate America, you're responsible for telling the truth to your shareholders and your employees.

And in a responsibility society, each of us is responsible for loving our neighbor just like we would like to be loved ourself. The culture of service and responsibility is growing here in America. I started what's called the USA Freedom Corps. If you're interested, you can go on the web page and look it up. It's a chance to—for people to serve their country, to serve their community, to help a neighbor who's in need. And the response has been great. It really

has been. People want to serve. People want to—want to help their country by helping somebody who might be struggling.

Policemen and firefighters and people who wear this Nation's uniform remind us what it means to sacrifice for something greater than yourself. Once again, the children of America believe in heroes, because they see them every day.

In these challenging times, the world has seen the resolve and the courage of America. And I've been privileged to see the compassion and the character of the American people. All the tests of the last 2½ years have come to the right nation. We're a strong country, and we use our strength to defend the peace. We're an optimistic country, confident in ourselves and in ideals bigger than ourselves.

Abroad, we seek to lift whole nations by spreading freedom. At home, we seek to lift up lives by spreading opportunity to every corner of America. This is the work that history has set before us. We welcome it. And we know that for our country, the best days lie ahead.

May God bless.

NOTE: The President spoke at 12:14 p.m. at the Hyatt Regency Columbus. In his remarks, he referred to Gov. Bob Taft, Secretary of State J. Kenneth Blackwell, and Treasurer of State Joseph T. Deters of Ohio; Jo Ann Davidson, chairperson for the Ohio Valley region, Bush-Cheney '04, Inc.; Robert T. Bennett, chairman, Ohio Republican Party; Michael F. Colley, Ohio national committeeman, and Martha C. Moore, Ohio national committeewoman, Republican National Committee; and former President Saddam Hussein of Iraq.

Remarks at the Central Aluminum Company in Columbus
October 30, 2003

Thanks for coming. I'm honored to be here in Columbus, Ohio. I appreciate so very much the warm hospitality. I like to come to good football country. I like to be with good, hard-working people, like the people here who are sharing the stage with me. I like to be with entrepreneurs. I like to be in the State where both my grandfathers were raised. My dad's dad was raised right here in Columbus. My mother's dad was raised in Dayton. So I feel quite at home here in the great State of Ohio.

I appreciate the good folks at Central Aluminum for letting me come and interrupt the work day. I've got some important things to talk about. The first thing I want to remind people of is, we're a great country because we've got great workers in America. The most productive workforce in the world is right here in America. Because of the spirit—the entrepreneurial spirit and the work ethic of America, our economy is strong, and it's getting stronger.

The figures for the third quarter—the economic figures for the third quarter show that the economy grew at an annual rate of 7.2 percent. That's the fastest growth we've had in nearly 20 years. Exports are expanding. Investment is rising. Housing construction is growing. The tax relief we passed is working. We left more money in the hands of the American people, and the American people are moving this economy forward.

We cannot expect economic growth numbers like this every quarter. Yet, by continuing a progrowth agenda, we will sustain growth and job creation in this country. We're on the right track, but we've got work to do, and I want to talk today about the need for this Nation to develop a comprehensive energy plan to make sure our fellow citizens can find work.

I appreciate Gale Roshon for opening up the plant. Thank you, sir. I want to thank John Wright. And I want to thank Bill, who showed me how the machine works. [*Laughter*] I'm honored that the State officials are with us today. Your fine Governor, Bob Taft, and the Lieutenant Governor have joined us, for which I'm grateful. The secretary of state and State auditor are with us. We've got local officials. We've got a lot of people who just came to say hello to the President, and I'm grateful. Thank you for coming.

This Nation has been through a lot in the last 2½ years. We have been challenged. And I've set some big goals for our country; one, we believe in freedom and peace. That's what we believe. And I also accept the responsibility of making sure this Nation is secure. This Nation must never forget the lessons of September the 11th in 2001. We must stay on the offensive against terrorists who would do harm to the American people.

We can't forget the lessons of September the 11th. We must understand there are people who hate what we stand for. And so we must find them and bring them to justice. We must defeat them where they hide so we don't have to face them in our own cities. I'm confident in the justice of our cause. I'm confident in the character and resolve of the American people. I'm confident in the skill and the honor of the American military.

And likewise, I am confident in the entrepreneurial spirit of this country, and I'm confident in our workforce. And the reason I'm confident is because I know what we've been through. We've been through a lot. The country was in recession when we first showed up in Washington, DC. And then the terrorists attacked us, and it hurt our economy. We went through a lot when the terrorists attacked. Not only do we have to reorder our thinking about how to make America secure, we had to remember the lessons when it came to protecting our country. But it also hurt our—the attacks hurt our country, hurt our economy. It set us back, and we began to recover from the attacks, in and out of recession. And then unfortunately we had some corporate citizens who forgot to tell the truth. They forgot what it meant to be a responsible citizen and didn't tell the truth to their shareholders and employees.

And then, as you know, we took decisive action to uphold doctrine. One doctrine was, "If you harbor a terrorist, you're just as guilty as the terrorists." And we went into Afghanistan and freed the people of Afghanistan from the clutches of a barbaric regime—at the same time made our country more secure.

We upheld the demands of the world by removing Saddam Hussein from power, not only for the benefit of the Iraqi people who suffered under this brutal tyrant but for the benefit of the security of the American people and peace in the world. And as we did so, it shook the confidence of the people. It's not a very—it doesn't inspire a lot of confidence when people turn on the TV and say, "march to war." In other words, it creates uncertainty and doubt.

And yet we've overcome all this. We sent a clear signal to the people that forgot to be responsible citizens that if you don't tell the truth, there is going to be serious consequences. And the American people are beginning to see what I meant about serious consequences for those who betrayed the trust. We're obviously doing everything we can to make the country more secure.

We also acted when it came to putting a little wind behind the sails of the entrepreneurs by letting people keep more of their own money. The tax cuts were an important part of our economic recovery. I believe that when people have more money in their pocket, they—you know, they're obviously—they're going to demand an additional good or a service. And in our society, when they demand a good or

a service, somebody will produce a good or a service. And when somebody produces that good or a service, it is more likely somebody is going to find a job.

I'm concerned about the stories I read, where people want to find work and can't find work. It means we've got a problem. If there's one person looking for work and can't find work, it says we have a problem. We've got to continue to create the conditions for economic growth. And the tax cut, the two tax cuts were an integral part of creating the conditions for growth.

And so we advocated and the Congress passed broad tax relief. I believe that if you're going to have tax relief you want it to be fair, and everybody who pays taxes ought to get tax relief. The Government should not try to pick and choose winners when it comes to tax relief.

We also understand that the Tax Code should not discourage marriage. So we provided relief—so we reduced the penalty on the marriage penalty. I understand it's hard to raise children, so we raised the child credit from $600 to $1,000 per child. We said the check was going to be in the mail. If you happen to be a mom or a dad raising children, it actually turned out to be in the mail, which was positive for our economy.

We wanted to encourage investment, not discourage investment, in order to enhance the economic recovery, so we cut taxes on dividends and capital gains, and we quadrupled the expense deduction for small-business investment. And that's important. In other words, this tax relief plan not only helped families and individuals, but it also helps small businesses. You say, "Well, why would you want to help small business?" Well, small businesses like this business create the most new jobs. If you're interested in job creation, you've got to focus your plan on small businesses.

So not only do we encourage small businesses to invest, we also, by cutting the taxes on the individuals, allow small businesses to keep more money, because most small businesses are Subchapter S or sole proprietorships, which means they pay tax at the individual income tax rates. Cutting individual income taxes provides capital for small businesses. Small businesses create more jobs, most new jobs in America. The tax cut was good for small businesses. The tax cut was good for job creation.

Not only were the third-quarter growth figures encouraging, there's some—also other encouraging signs. Housing starts are strong, and that's important, particularly if you're making aluminum siding—[laughter]—if you know what I mean. [Laughter] After-tax incomes are rising. Inflation is low. Productivity is high. Businesses are now receiving strong orders. Things are improving.

And we've got a choice to make. Just as the economy is coming around, some over in Washington say now is the time to raise taxes. To be fair, they think anytime is a good time to raise taxes. [Laughter] At least they're consistent. [Laughter] I strongly disagree. Tax relief put this Nation on the right path, and I intend to keep America on the path to prosperity.

There is still more to do to make sure our fellow citizens can find a job. And so I presented a six-point plan that Congress must act on. I'm going to talk about five parts of it, and then I'm going to spend a little time on the energy part of it.

Small businesses must have affordable health care for their employees. That's why we need association health care plans, so small businesses can pool risk just like big businesses do. Small businesses must be allowed to come together in order to pool risk to provide their employees with reasonably priced health care. And we need to have medical liability reform so that the frivolous lawsuits do not drive up the cost of health care.

Congress must act on medical liability reform. They ought to act to limit the junk lawsuits that harm good businesses. We need to cut useless regulations. We must work to open up markets for Ohio's manu-

facturers and Ohio's farmers. I want the markets to be open, and I want the playing field to be level, so that we have access.

The tax relief we passed is scheduled to go away. There is a—I'm not sure how to describe it—it's like the Congress giveth, and the Congress taketh away. [Laughter] But there is a quirk in the rules which says that a lot of the tax relief had to expire after 10 years. And in the recent tax package, they accelerated some of the expiration dates, which means the child credit will go down, the marriage penalty will go up, individual rates will change. For the sake of job creation, there needs to be certainty in the Tax Code. Entrepreneurs and small-business owners don't need to be trying to constantly guess where the taxes are going to be. People need to plan, and they need to plan for more than—on a more than a one-year horizon. If Congress is truly interested in job creation, they will make all the tax cuts we passed permanent.

To keep this economy moving, to sustain growth far in the future so people can work, we need a sound national energy policy. Every person who owns a home, every person who works on an assembly line, every person who drives a truck or runs a small business depends on reliable, affordable energy. That's what we depend upon. Our economic security and our national security requires secure sources of energy. We must become less reliant on foreign sources of energy.

I've come to Central Aluminum because this company and these employees rely upon reliable sources of energy. The company spends about 30 percent more on natural gas this year than it did last year. That's a cost that makes it hard to expand the workforce, when money goes into a 30-percent increase in your energy bill. By not having enough energy at home, our manufacturing sector is not doing as well as it should be. When the gas prices go up, the manufacturing sector hurts here in Ohio and around the country.

Congress needs to pass a sound energy plan to help deal with the issues that confront this good company, Central Aluminum. First, we need more energy production close to home. We need to produce in our own country, and we need to encourage exploration in our own hemisphere so we're less dependent from other parts of the world. Our Nation and our hemisphere have got natural gas, the energy used right here in this plant. But this resource has been hampered by restrictions on exploration.

Congress should allow reasonable exploration and responsible exploration to bring more natural gas to the market, which will lower the costs of the product. Congress should promote research into the next generation of nuclear plants and encourage investment in existing nuclear plants to expand a clean and unlimited source of energy.

Congress should encourage clean coal technology so that we can use our Nation's most plentiful energy resource in an environmentally responsible way. In other words, the energy bill ought to encourage the use of resources close to home. When you increase supply, it takes pressure off price. We need a commonsense, reasonable energy policy. I call upon Congress to pass that commonsense, reasonable energy policy.

Part of the energy bill I submitted—and by the way, we submitted a package to Congress 2 years ago and are kind of grinding through all the details now—but part of that package says America needs a better infrastructure as well. We need better pipelines, gas terminals, and powerlines so that the flow of energy is reliable.

You might remember what happened last summer. I certainly do. The rolling blackout affected this State of Ohio. That ought to be a signal that we need to modernize the electricity grid. The bill we're trying to get out of Congress understands that. The current grid is old, and it's inefficient in places. Incredibly enough, Federal law discourages new investment in the infrastructure. You got old laws on the books that need to be changed. We're heading into a new era. We've got to think new. We've got to be ready for the 21st century. By keeping investors from entering the electricity and the natural gas business, it stifles the capacity to provide more electricity and more natural gas. And remember, when you increase the supply of a product, it takes pressure off a price, which means people are more likely to be able to find a job.

We need to encourage new investment in a modern electric grid, ending old rules. We need mandatory—not voluntary—reliability standards for our power companies. We now need to make sure that the placement of new powerlines, which oftentimes get bogged down because local authorities block transmission lines, that the Federal energy officials have the authority to site new powerlines. That's what we need to do. We need to modernize our grid so the lights don't go off in people's homes, so that business owners are able to plan for a stable and expanding workforce. We need to wake up and realize we're heading into the 21st century, and we need a 21st century energy policy, is what we need to do.

And a 21st century energy policy says this country must develop and deploy the latest technology to provide a new generation, a different kind of energy, new sources of energy, cleaner and more efficient energy sources. A lot of companies in Columbus are doing some groundbreaking research on what I'm talking about. For example, we ought to expand tax credits for renewable energy sources like wind and solar power. We ought to see if we can't use technology to diversify our energy supply in a smart way. Congress should fund research in a new hydrogen fuel technology that I called for in my State of the Union. We ought to make sure that we use ethanol from corn and biodiesel made from soybeans. It seems to me to make sense that we ought to use our technology and know-how to grow our way out of dependence on foreign sources of energy.

In other words, we need a comprehensive plan. We need to encourage production, and we need to encourage conservation. We need to use the energy resources we've got at hand in an environmentally friendly way. And we need to advance new kinds of energy. But we've got to get after it. And that's my message to the United States Congress: Resolve your differences; understand that if you're interested in people finding a job, we need an energy policy. That's why I'm here. I want these people working. I want their friends to be able to find jobs. Get the bill done.

Now, we've overcome a lot in this country, and there's still more to do. We're making tremendous progress. But we can't rest. We can't rest. We're making great progress in helping people find a job. But as I said, so long as one person is looking for work, this administration will continue to figure out ways to encourage economic growth by empowering the entrepreneurs of America and the small businesses to do smart things to create a condition for economic growth. We'll continue to stay on the offensive when it comes to keeping the Nation secure.

As well I will continue to speak to the great character of the American people and to call people to action in order to help people understand that the American Dream is meant for them. Listen, there are people amidst our plenty who hurt, people who wonder whether or not America is meant for them. And I understand those challenges, but I also understand the strength of the country. It lies in the hearts and souls of our fellow citizens. I'm prob-

ably looking at people who are doing what I'm about to say—ask you to do, but there are thousands of people in our country who love a neighbor just like they'd like to be loved themselves, who are mentoring a child, who are helping feed the hungry, who are providing shelter for the homeless.

See, our society is changing and will continue to change one heart and one soul at a time, because our fellow citizens have heard the call to love a neighbor. And my call to you all is if you see somebody who hurts, help him. Remember that Government can hand out money—we do a pretty good job of it at times—but what we can't do is put hope in a person's heart or a sense of purpose in people's lives. That's done when a fellow citizen puts their arm around somebody who hurts and says, "I love you. What can I do to help you?"

Now, this is a fabulous country. We've met the challenges that have been put to us. There will be other challenges to come. I stand confident before you, knowing that we can meet any challenge because of the greatness of the people who live in America.

Thanks for coming by today. May God bless you all, and may God continue to bless America. Thank you all.

NOTE: The President spoke at 1:54 p.m. in the plant. In his remarks, he referred to Gale Roshon, owner, John Wright, general manager, and Bill Haines, press operator, Central Aluminum Co.; Gov. Bob Taft, Lt. Gov. Jennette Bradley, Secretary of State J. Kenneth Blackwell, and State Auditor Betty Montgomery of Ohio; and former President Saddam Hussein of Iraq. The Office of the Press Secretary also released a Spanish language transcript of these remarks.

Statement on Senate Passage of Healthy Forests Restoration Legislation
October 30, 2003

I commend the Senate for passing the "Healthy Forests Restoration Act." The bipartisan support for this commonsense legislation demonstrates that we are united in our goal of returning our Nation's forests to health by eliminating unnatural overgrowth and promoting early community involvement in forest management planning.

Restoring forest health is important to the safety of our communities and to the protection of wildlife, endangered species, water supplies, and forest resources. I urge the House and Senate to quickly resolve the differences in their bills so that I can sign this important legislation and we can fully implement my Healthy Forests Initiative.

Statement on Senate Action To Block a Vote on the Nomination of Judge Charles W. Pickering, Sr., To Be a United States Court of Appeals Circuit Judge
October 30, 2003

Today a minority of Senators once again blocked an outstanding judicial nominee from receiving an up-or-down vote in the United States Senate. The nomination of Judge Charles Pickering has been languishing in the Senate for over 2 years. He is a good, fair-minded man, and the treatment he has received by a handful of Senators is a disgrace. Judge Pickering was previously confirmed by the Senate and has led a distinguished career, including as a Federal district court judge for over a decade. He has wide bipartisan support from those who know him best.

More than one-third of my nominees for the courts of appeals are still awaiting a vote. The continued obstruction by a willful minority of the Senate is bad for our country, harmful for the provision of justice for all Americans, and damaging to the smooth functioning of our judicial system. It hurts America, and it is wrong.

One year ago today, I proposed a commonsense plan to return fairness and dignity to the judicial confirmation process. This plan, which would apply no matter who is President or which party controls the Senate, included specific proposals to fix the underlying problems that have long undermined the confirmation process. One year later, certain Senators are continuing their obstructionist tactics and are continuing to filibuster fine men and women who would make outstanding appeals court judges.

I again urge the Senate to put aside partisan politics and work to find a solution that will repair the process and ensure that all judicial nominees are treated fairly and that all Americans experience timely justice in our Federal courts. As I have said before, let each Senator vote how he or she thinks best, but give the nominees a vote.

Remarks at a Bush-Cheney Reception in San Antonio, Texas
October 30, 2003

The President. Thanks for the warm welcome. It is really good to be home, and it's good to be with so many friends. It seems like old home week here. [*Laughter*] I want to thank you all very much for your friendship and your strong support. I want to thank you for your prayers. I want to thank you for being my friend before I became the President—[*laughter*]—and my friend after I become the President—[*laughter*]—in 2009. No, no, we—[*applause*].

This is a fantastic event tonight. It not only lifts my spirits to be with a lot of people with whom I've served in the past and a lot of friends, but we're laying the foundation for what is going to be a great national victory in 2004. I'm loosening up—[*laughter*]—and I'm getting ready. But politics will come in its own time, because I've got a job to do.

Audience member. And you're doing a great one.

The President. Well, thank you very much. [*Laughter*] I'm focused on the people's business. I'm doing what's right for this country. I will continue to work to make sure this country is strong and secure, prosperous, and free.

I have a regret, and that is that the First Lady is not with me tonight. She's in Tyler. We're going to meet up in Crawford. She is a fabulous wife, a fabulous mother, and a great First Lady for America.

I want to thank the Loefflers for their friendship and their hard work. It's a fantastically successful event. As I look around, I see folks who hold high office. The chief justice of the supreme court is here, Tom Phillips; the attorney general is here, Greg Abbott; the secretary of agriculture is here, Susan Combs; Albert Hawkins, the commissioner of health and human services; Diane Rath, the workforce commissioner. I see Wentworth is here, the State senator; State

Representative Jones and Edmund Kuempel and Ken Mercer. Thank you all for coming. It's great to see you again. I miss my buddies in the statehouse. I've got such fond memories of working with people here in the great State of Texas. It was a fantastic experience.

I also want to thank my friend Mercer Reynolds from Cincinnati, Ohio, who is the national finance chairman for Bush-Cheney. He's doing a great job of——

Audience member. Go Mercer!

The President. ——laying the groundwork. Mercer brought his cousin. [*Laughter*] Most of all, I want to thank you all. Thanks a lot for coming.

In the last 2½ years, our Nation has acted decisively to confront great challenges. I came to this office to solve problems instead of passing them on to future Presidents and future generations. I came to seize opportunities instead of letting them slip away. This administration is meeting the tests of our time.

Terrorists declared war on the United States of America, and war is what they got. We've captured or killed many of the key leaders of the Al Qaida network, and the rest of them know we're on their trail. In Afghanistan and in Iraq, we gave ultimatums to terror regimes. Those regimes chose defiance. Those regimes are no more. Fifty million people in those two countries once lived under tyranny, and today they live in freedom.

Two-and-a-half years ago, our military was not receiving the resources it needed, and morale was beginning to suffer. So we increased the defense budgets to meet the threats of a new era. And today, no one in the world can question the skill and the strength and the spirit of the United States military.

Two-and-a-half years ago, we inherited an economy in recession. And then our country was attacked. And then we had some scandals in corporate America, and war. All those affected the people's confidence, but I acted. We passed tough new laws in Washington, DC, to hold the corporate criminals to account.

And to get the economy going again, I have twice led the United States Congress to pass historic tax relief for the American people. When Americans have more take-home pay to spend, to save, or invest, the whole economy grows, and people are more likely to find a job. So we're returning more money to the people to help them raise their families. We're reducing taxes on dividends and capital gains to encourage investment. We're giving small businesses incentives to hire new people. With all these actions, this administration has laid the foundation for greater prosperity and more jobs across America so that every single one of our citizens can realize the American Dream.

Two-and-a-half years ago, there was a lot of talk about education reform, but there wasn't much action. So I acted. I called for and the Congress passed the No Child Left Behind Act. With a solid bipartisan majority, we delivered the most dramatic education reforms at the Federal level in a generation. In return for Federal money, we expect public schools to teach children how to read and write and add and subtract, because we believe every child can learn to read and write and add and subtract. This administration is challenging the soft bigotry of low expectations. The days of excuse-making are over. We expect results in every single classroom so that not one single child in America is left behind.

We reorganized our Government and created the Department of Homeland Security to better safeguard our borders and ports and to protect the American people. We passed trade promotion authority to open up new markets for Texas farmers and ranchers and entrepreneurs. We passed much needed budget agreements to bring spending discipline to Washington, DC. On

issue after issue, this administration has acted on principle, kept its word, and made progress for the American people.

The Congress gets credit for these achievements. I've got a great relationship with Speaker Denny Hastert and Majority Leader Bill Frist. We're working hard to focus on results and to get rid of the needless politics that dominates the Nation's Capital. We're doing the work for the people. And those are the kind of people I've asked to join this administration. I put together a fantastic, diverse group of people to serve the American people. We've had no finer Vice President than Dick Cheney. Mother may have a second opinion. [*Laughter*]

In 2½ years, we have done a lot. We have come far, but our work is only beginning. I've set great goals worthy of a great nation. First, America is committed to expanding the realm of freedom and peace for our own security and for the benefit of the world. And second, in our own country, we must work for a society of prosperity and compassion so that every single citizen, every citizen, has a chance to work and to succeed and realize the great promise of our land.

It is clear that the future of freedom and peace depend on the actions of America. This Nation is freedom's home. We are freedom's defender. We welcome this charge of history, and we are keeping it.

The war on terror continues. The enemies of freedom are not idle, and neither are we. This country will not rest. We will not tire. We will not stop until this danger to civilization is removed.

We are confronting that danger in Iraq, where Saddam Hussein holdouts and foreign terrorists are desperately trying to throw Iraq into chaos by attacking coalition forces and international aid workers and innocent Iraqis. They know that the advance of freedom in Iraq would be a major defeat in the cause of terror. This collection of killers is trying to shake the will of America and the civilized world, and this country will not be intimidated.

We are aggressively striking the terrorists in Iraq, defeating them there so we will not have to face them in our own country. We're calling other nations to help Iraq to build a free country, which will make the world more secure. We're standing with the Iraqi people as they assume more of their own defense and move toward self-government. These aren't easy tasks, but they're essential tasks. We will finish what we have begun, and we will win this essential victory in the war on terror.

Our greatest security comes from the advance of human liberty, because free nations do not support terror, free nations do not attack their neighbors, free nations do not threaten the world with weapons of mass terror. Americans believe that freedom is the deepest need and hope of every human heart. And I believe that freedom is the right of every person, and I believe that freedom is the future of every nation.

America also understands that unprecedented influence brings tremendous responsibilities. We have duties in the world, and when we see disease and starvation and hopeless poverty, we will not turn away. This great, strong Nation is leading the world. On the continent of Africa, America is now committed to bringing the healing power of medicine to millions of men and women and children now suffering with AIDS. This great land is doing incredibly important work of human rescue.

We've got challenges here at home as well, and our actions will prove that we're equal to the challenges. We had some good news today on the economy. But let me tell you this, so long as anybody who wants to work can't find a job, means that I must continue to create the conditions for economic vitality and growth, to make sure the great entrepreneurial spirit of America is alive and well in every corner of this country.

We have a duty to keep our commitment to America's seniors by strengthening and modernizing Medicare. Congress has taken historic action to improve the lives of older Americans. For the first time since the creation of Medicare, the House and Senate passed reforms to increase the choices for seniors and provide coverage for prescription drugs. The next step is for both Houses to reconcile their differences and get a bill to my desk soon. We owe it to America's seniors, and we owe a modern Medicare system to those of us who are going to be America's seniors.

For the sake of our health care system, we need to cut down on the frivolous lawsuits which increase the cost of medicine. I appreciate the reforms that Governor Perry and the legislature did here in Texas. We recognize that people who have been harmed by a bad doc deserve their day in court, yet the system should not reward lawyers who are simply fishing for a rich settlement. Because frivolous lawsuits drive up the cost of health care, they affect the Federal budget. Medical liability reform is a national issue which requires a national solution. We proposed good law to the House and Senate. The House of Representatives passed a good bill. The bill is stuck in the United States Senate. I'm proud to report, our two United States Senators, the Senators from Texas, are on the right side of the issue. Those who have held up this important piece of legislation in the United States Senate must recognize that not one single person has ever been healed by a frivolous lawsuit.

I have a responsibility as the President to make sure the judicial system runs well, and I have met that duty. I have nominated superb men and women for the Federal courts, people who will interpret the law, not legislate from the bench. Some Members are trying to keep my nominees, people like Priscilla Owen, off the bench by blocking up-or-down votes. Every judicial nominee deserves a fair hearing and an up-or-down vote on the Senate floor. It is time for some of the Members of the United

States Senate to stop playing politics with American justice.

The Congress needs to complete work on a comprehensive energy plan. Two years ago, I submitted a plan to the United States Congress, a plan that will promote energy efficiency and conservation, that will develop new technologies, but will encourage exploration in an environmentally friendly way in our own country. For the sake of economic security and for the sake of national security, the Congress must act so we become less dependent on foreign sources of energy.

Our strong and prosperous Nation must be a compassionate nation. I will continue to advance our agenda of compassionate conservatism, which means we will apply the best and most innovative ideas to the task of helping our fellow citizens in need. There are still millions of men and women who want to end their dependence on the Government and become independent through hard work. We must build on the success of welfare reform to bring work and dignity into the lives of more of our fellow citizens.

Congress should complete the "Citizen Service Act" so more Americans can serve their community and their country. And both Houses should reach agreement on my Faith-Based Initiative to support the armies of compassion that are mentoring children, that are caring for the homeless, that are offering hope to the addicted. People from all faiths—Christian, Jewish, Muslim, Hindu—have heard a universal call. We must welcome that call. In order to heal the broken heart, this country must not fear faith. We must welcome faith in the essential delivery of need for people who hurt.

A compassionate society must promote opportunity for all, including the independence and dignity that come from ownership. This administration will constantly strive to promote an ownership society in America. We want more people owning their own home. This Nation has a minority homeownership gap. I presented a plan to the United States Congress to close that gap. America must act. The Congress must act. We want more people to own and manage their own health care accounts. We want more people to own and manage their own retirement accounts. We want more people owning their own small business. We understand in this administration that when a person owns something, he or she has a vital stake in the future of our country.

In a compassionate society, people respect one another and take responsibility for the decisions they make. The culture of America is changing from one that has said, "If it feels good, do it," and "If you've got a problem, blame somebody else," to a culture in which each of us understands we are responsible for the decisions we make.

If you're fortunate enough to be a mom or a dad, you're responsible for loving your child with all your heart. If you're worried about the quality of the education in the community in which you live, you're responsible for doing something about it. If you're a CEO in corporate America, you're responsible for telling the truth to your shareholders and your employees.

And in the new responsibility society, each of us is responsible for loving our neighbor just like we'd like to be loved ourself. The culture of service and responsibility is strong here in America. I started what's called the USA Freedom Corps to encourage Americans to extend a compassionate hand to a neighbor in need, and the response has been great. Faith-based charities and charitable programs are strong and vibrant. And that's important, really important, to make sure the future of this country is alive and well for every citizen.

Policemen and firefighters and people who wear our Nation's uniform are reminding us what it means to sacrifice for something greater than yourself. Once again, the children of America believe in heroes, because they see them every day.

In these challenging times, the world has seen the resolve and the courage of America. I've been privileged to see the compassion and the character of the American people. All the tests of the last 2½ years have come to the right nation.

We are a strong country, and we use that strength to defend the peace. We're an optimistic country, confident in ourselves and in ideals bigger than ourselves. Abroad, we seek to lift whole nations by spreading freedom. At home, we seek to lift up lives by spreading opportunity across our land. This is the work that history has set before us. We welcome it and know that for our country, the best days lie ahead.

God bless. Thank you all. Thank you all very much.

NOTE: The President spoke at 6:48 p.m. at the Marriott Rivercenter. In his remarks, he referred to Tom and Nancy Loeffler, event cohosts; Thomas R. Phillips, chief justice, Texas Supreme Court; State Attorney General Greg Abbott, Agriculture Commissioner Susan Combs, and Health and Human Services Commissioner Albert Hawkins of Texas; Diane D. Rath, chair and commissioner, Texas Workforce Commission; State Senator Jeff Wentworth and State Representatives Elizabeth Ames Jones, Edmund Kuempel, and Ken Mercer of Texas; Gov. Rick Perry of Texas; and Priscilla Owen, nominee to be U.S. Circuit Judge for the Fifth Circuit.

The President's Radio Address
November 1, 2003

Good morning. This week, terrorists launched a series of attacks in Iraq. Their targets included police stations in Baghdad and Fallujah, the headquarters of the International Red Cross, and living quarters for the Coalition Provisional Authority in Baghdad. The majority of their victims were Iraqis working to rebuild and restore order to their country and citizens of other nations engaged in purely humanitarian missions.

Some of the killers behind these attacks are loyalists of the Saddam regime who seek to regain power and who resent Iraq's new freedoms. Others are foreigners who have traveled to Iraq to spread fear and chaos and prevent the emergence of a successful democracy in the heart of the Middle East. They may have different long-term goals, but they share a near-term strategy to intimidate Iraqis from building a free government and to cause America and our allies to flee our responsibilities. They know that a free Iraq will be free

of them and free of the fear in which the ideologies of terror thrive.

During the last few decades, the terrorists grew to believe that if they hit America hard, as in Lebanon and Somalia, America would retreat and back down. Five years ago, one of the terrorists said that an attack could make America run in less than 24 hours. They have learned the wrong lesson. The United States will complete our work in Iraq. Leaving Iraq prematurely would only embolden the terrorists and increase the danger to America. We are determined to stay, to fight, and to win.

The terrorists and the Ba'athists loyal to the old regime will fail because America and our allies have a strategy, and our strategy is working. First, we are taking this fight to the enemy, mounting raids, seizing weapons and funds, and bringing killers to justice. One example is Operation Ivy Focus, a series of aggressive raids by the Army's 4th Infantry Division that in a little over a month has yielded the capture of more than 100 former regime members. In other operations, our soldiers have also seized hundreds of weapons, thousands of rounds of ammunition and explosives, and hundreds of thousands of dollars suspected of being used to finance terror operations.

Second, we are training an ever-increasing number of Iraqis to defend their nation. Today, more than 90,000 Iraqis are serving as police officers, border guards, and civil defense personnel. These Iraqi forces are also supplying troops in the field with better intelligence, allowing for greater precision in targeting the enemies of freedom. And we are accelerating our efforts to train and field a new Iraqi army and more Iraqi civil defense forces.

Third, we are implementing a specific plan to transfer sovereignty and authority to the Iraqi people. The Governing Council, made up of Iraqi citizens, has appointed ministers who are responsible for the day-to-day operations of the Iraqi Government. The Council has also selected a committee that is developing a process through which Iraqis will draft a new constitution for their country. When a constitution has been ratified by the Iraqi people, Iraq will enjoy free and fair elections.

All these efforts are closely linked. As security improves, life will increasingly re-turn to normal in Iraq, and more and more Iraqis will step forward to play a direct role in the rebirth of their country. And as the political process moves forward and more and more Iraqis come to feel they have a stake in their country's future, they will help to secure a better life for themselves and their children.

The terrorists and the Ba'athists hope to weaken our will. Our will cannot be shaken. We're being tested, and America and our allies will not fail. We will honor the sacrifice of the fallen by ensuring that the cause for which they fought and died is completed, and we will make America safer by helping to transform Iraq from an exporter of violence and terror into a center of progress and peace.

Thank you for listening.

NOTE: The address was recorded at 9:37 a.m. on October 31 at the Bush Ranch in Crawford, TX, for broadcast at 10:06 a.m. on November 1. The transcript was made available by the Office of the Press Secretary on October 31 but was embargoed for release until the broadcast. In his remarks, the President referred to former President Saddam Hussein of Iraq. The Office of the Press Secretary also released a Spanish language transcript of this address.

Remarks in Southaven, Mississippi
November 1, 2003

Thank you all. Thanks for coming. I'm honored to be here. I'm honored to be here with the next Governor of the State of Mississippi, Haley Barbour. It is great to be in northern Mississippi. I'm proud to be here with a lot of friends.

You know, I woke up in Crawford this morning. I said to First Lady Bush, I said, "I don't know if I'm going to be able to find the energy to be able to make it through a long day." You know, I'm kind of getting up in years and—[*laughter*]—and here I come to northern Mississippi, where thousands of our fellow citizens are here. You've energized me. I'm thrilled to be here. Thanks for coming.

I appreciate you coming. I appreciate you coming. Haley and I married above ourselves. I'm thrilled that the next first lady of Mississippi is with us today, and that's Marsha. And Laura sends her love.

I'm sorry she's not with me. She's been a fabulous First Lady for our country.

I've known Haley for quite a while. He used to run in high circles. I guess in this part of the world, you say he used to pick high cotton. [*Laughter*] But one thing about him, no matter how high the circle he ran in, he always loved to talk about Mississippi. He's proud of this State, and that's the kind of Governor you need, somebody who will relate to people from all walks of life. One of the things about his campaign that I like a lot is, Haley is proud to be a Republican, but he also wants to be the Governor of Democrats and independents. He's reaching out. He understands his job is to represent everybody when he gets to be the Governor in three days.

I like the fact that he's an optimist. He's got a positive view for the great State of Mississippi. He believes in the great potential of the great State of Mississippi. That's the kind of Governor you want, somebody who sees a positive future for every single citizen. That Governor is Haley Barbour.

I like the fact that Haley Barbour is a man of good values. He honors his family. He treasures his relationship with the Almighty. He believes in hard work. He believes everybody has worth. It's these kind of values that are necessary to have in your statehouse here in Mississippi. I'm proud to stand with this man. Haley Barbour is the right man to lead the State of Mississippi.

And in order to have this good man lead the State of Mississippi, he needs your help. We're coming down to voting time here in Mississippi. It's time to make sure that people get the message that you've got a good man in Haley Barbour. That means you need to go out and find your neighbors, Republicans, Democrats, independents, people who don't care about political parties at all, to get to the polls. Remind them they have a duty as a citizen of this free country to vote. And once you get them headed to the polls, make sure

they do what's in the best interests of the State of Mississippi and vote for Haley Barbour.

I'm so thankful that we've got a great United States Senator with us today, a man who is a leader on the floor of the United States Senate, a strong ally of mine, a great friend of the people of Mississippi, and that's Senator Thad Cochran. As well another fine Representative for the State of Mississippi in Washington, DC, a man who's done a great job in the United States Congress, friend and ally, and that would be Congressman Roger Wicker.

I had the honor of welcoming some Mississippi citizens to Washington a while ago, and one of the citizens that came was a courageous politician, a leader who didn't do the politically expedient thing but decided that she would find a home in a different political party, somebody who stood by her convictions, somebody who said, "Principle matters a lot to me," and that's the next Lieutenant Governor of the State of Mississippi, Amy Tuck.

I know we've got a lot of other statewide candidates here. When you get in that booth for Haley and Amy, make sure you remember Phil Bryant, Julio Del Castillo, Scott Newton, Max Phillips, Tate Reeves, all fine candidates running for statewide office.

Not only should people vote for Haley because he's so pretty to look at—[*laughter*]—well—[*laughter*]—he's got the right issues. He knows what he's talking about when it comes to the issues. He knows when people in Mississippi are looking for work, you better have a progrowth policy for the State of Mississippi.

We share the same philosophy. First of all, we're concerned about people looking for work, and secondly, we know that in order to get an economy growing, you've got to do two things: You must have fiscal discipline in the statehouses around the country. Haley Barbour knows how to manage a budget. Haley Barbour will be wise with the taxpayers' money in the State of Mississippi.

I know where Haley stands because when I stood up in front of the Congress and the country and advocated a progrowth policy for our economy, he was strong by my side. I said this, I said, "If people have more money in their pockets, they're more likely to demand a good or a service. And when somebody demands a good or a service in our economy, somebody will produce a good or a service. And when somebody produces the good or a service, it means somebody is more likely to find a job." The tax cuts we passed came at the right time.

Haley Barbour also understands that in order for your economy to grow, you better make sure you've got a legal system that is fair, a legal system that isn't dominated by the plaintiff's bar, a legal system that doesn't have so many frivolous lawsuits that it makes it hard for people to find a job. You better have you a Governor who's willing to stand up to the trial attorneys and have medical liability reform, so that people can get good health care in the State of Mississippi.

I appreciate the fact that Haley Barbour has set as a priority the education of every child in the State of Mississippi. I used to like to say when I was in Texas, education is to a State what national defense is to the Federal Government, the number one priority. Haley Barbour understands that every child must be educated in the State of Mississippi. He stands strong with the teachers of Mississippi. He stands on the side of the parents of Mississippi. He wants to challenge the soft bigotry of low expectations by raising the bar for every single child.

Finally, I appreciate the fact that Haley Barbour not only has supported me on this issue I'm about to talk about but is willing to do—have his own version of a faith-based initiative here in the State of Mississippi. And he understands what I know, that some of the problems in our society

are problems of the heart, that while Government can hand out money, Government cannot put hope in a person's heart or a sense of purpose—[applause]. No, the great strength of America lies in the hearts and souls of our fellow citizens. And you need a Governor who is willing to rally the armies of compassion.

We should never have the state fund the church, or the church try to be the state. But what we should have is States and the Federal Government willing to empower those who have heard the universal call to love a neighbor just like we'd like to be loved ourselves. We need mentors for our children. We need people to help the homeless. We need to help the addicted. And faith-based programs work.

It's also been helpful to have a friend like Haley who supported me and others in Washington, DC, to make sure that Mississippi judges get a fair hearing. I've named some good people to serve on the Federal bench, people who will use the bench to interpret the law and not try to write law. I want to thank Senator Cochran and Senator Lott and, of course, Haley for standing strong with a nominee I named from Mississippi, Charles Pickering. I stand strong with Judge Pickering, and it's time for some Members of the United States Senate to stop playing politics with American justice.

I look forward to working with Haley to make sure that the State of Mississippi has got what's needed to protect the homeland. You've got valuable ports that need to—we need to work on to make sure that nobody comes and harms any of our fellow citizens. I look forward to working with him to make sure that the resources we're spending out of Washington for those on the frontline of homeland security are well-coordinated and well-spent. I look forward to making sure our police forces and firefighters and emergency-response teams are well-coordinated between the Federal Government and the State government and the local governments. Haley would be a good leader when it comes to working on homeland security matters.

But I want to remind you that the best way to protect the homeland is to hunt down the enemy, one by one, and bring them to justice. The terrorists declared war on the United States of America, and war is what they got. This country will not rest; we will not tire; we will do what it takes to remove this danger from civilization and make America secure.

For those of you who have got relatives in the United States military, I want to thank you. And you make sure you send word to them that their Commander in Chief is incredibly proud of the sacrifices they're making on behalf of our Nation.

And I also want you to know that I understand that the best way to secure America is to advance human liberty. Free nations do not attack their neighbors. Free nations do not develop weapons of mass terror. The United States of America strongly believes that freedom is the right of every single person, that freedom is not America's gift to the world, that freedom is the Almighty's gift to every person who lives in this world. With the advance of human freedom, the world will be more peaceful, and America will be more secure.

We've overcome a lot of challenges in the last 2½ years, and there will be other challenges. And in my judgment, the best way for Mississippi to deal with the challenges you face is to make sure you put a Governor in place who's optimistic and hopeful, somebody who can unite this State to get people pulling in the same direction, somebody who firmly believes in his heart of hearts that Mississippi "can do better." And that person and that leader is the next Governor of the State of Mississippi, Haley Barbour.

NOTE: The President spoke at 10:08 a.m. at the DeSoto Civic Center. In his remarks, he referred to gubernatorial candidate Haley Barbour and his wife, Marsha; Amy Tuck, incumbent candidate for Lieutenant Governor; Phil Bryant, incumbent candidate for State auditor of public accounts; Julio Del Castillo, candidate for Mississippi secretary of state; Scott Newton, candidate for State attorney general; Max Phillips, candidate for State commissioner of agriculture and commerce; Tate Reeves, candidate for State treasurer; and Charles W. Pickering, Sr., nominee to be U.S. Circuit Judge for the Fifth Circuit.

Remarks in Paducah, Kentucky
November 1, 2003

The President. Thank you all.

Audience members. Four more years! Four more years! Four more years!

The President. Thank you all very much. It's actually 3 more days—[*laughter*]—3 more days until Ernie Fletcher becomes the Governor of Kentucky. Thanks for coming. I appreciate you taking some time out of your Saturday afternoon to say hello. I'm honored so many people in western Kentucky came out. It's good to be back in Paducah. It's not my first time here.

The first time here, I was knocking on doors asking for the vote, for me. [*Laughter*] This time I'm back, knocking on doors, asking the vote for Ernie Fletcher.

And the reason why, there's no doubt in my mind he is the best candidate for the job. I like the fact that he was a fighter pilot. [*Laughter*] That says something about him, doesn't it? I like the fact that he was a physician. He's a healer. I like the fact that he's an engineer. I like the fact that he's been an effective United States Congressman. I know, I work with him closely.

You should like the fact that when he becomes the Governor and he calls up to Washington, the President will answer the phone. I appreciate the fact that, like me, he married well. [*Laughter*] Laura sends her love to the people of western Kentucky. You drew the short straw; you got me. But I can't wait for Glenna to become the first lady of Kentucky. She'll bring a lot of class to the Governor's mansion. Glenna, Glenna Fletcher is a good soul.

I like and support Ernie Fletcher because he's a man of integrity. He understands that when you assume an oath of office, you have an obligation to bring honor to the office that you assume. If you're interested in having somebody set a good example at your State capitol, if you want somebody who will send the right signal to the youth of Kentucky, the right man is Ernie Fletcher.

I'm here to embrace his candidacy, but most importantly, I'm here to ask you to go out and turn out the vote. When you guys are driving your cycles, make sure when you see another cycler that you get them to go vote. When you farmers are going to your coffee shops, make sure you tell your people that work the land with you to get out the vote.

See, we have an obligation in the free society to vote. I urge all people in this great State to vote. And when you're on the phones urging them to vote, make sure you tell them what's in their interest, and what's in their interest is to have Ernie Fletcher as the Governor of the State of Kentucky.

I appreciate the fact that when Ernie wins, he's going to be the Governor of everybody. He's not going to say, "I'm the Governor of this particular political party or that political party." He's going to be the Governor of every single citizen. So when you're out canvassing for the vote, when you're knocking on doors, you'll find some disgruntled Democrats. Make sure

you encourage them to vote. You'll find discerning independents. Make sure you encourage them to vote. I'm here to ask you to do your duty as a citizen to vote and to do extra work to make sure you turn out to vote for this good man, Ernie Fletcher.

And don't forget to put in a good word for Steve Pence. [*Laughter*] See, he's running for the Lieutenant Governor. He's from western Kentucky; he knows how you think. It makes sense to put him in as Lieutenant Governor. See, Ernie picked him, but I picked him first. [*Laughter*] I don't know if you recall, but I named him the U.S. Attorney for western Kentucky. I did because he's a man of integrity; he's a good, honest man, the kind of fellow that when he holds office you can say, "I'm proud of the way he's conducting himself in office."

I also want to thank very much the United States Senators who have joined us, strong allies, good people, people who will make you proud here in the great State of Kentucky, starting with Mitch McConnell. I appreciate you coming, Mitch. Speaking of somebody who married well—[*laughter*]—he married so well, I picked his wife to be in my Cabinet—[*laughter*]—the Secretary of Labor, Elaine Chao, doing a great job. I appreciate you, Elaine.

When I was a kid, I always hoped to have a Jim Bunning baseball card. [*Laughter*] Now, I get to call him Senator, and so do you. It's vital you send this good man back to the United States Senate in 2004.

Kentucky has sent some fine folks up to Washington in the United States Congress, the House of Representatives. Two of them are here with us, besides Ernie, and that's Congressman Ed Whitfield and Congressman Ron Lewis. [*Applause*] Thank you all for coming. Hi, Ed. I'll try it again. And Congressman Ron Lewis, good to see you, Ron. Thanks for coming.

As well we've got some other good folks who have decided to run for office. Trey

Grayson is running for secretary of state. Jack Wood is trying to become the attorney general; he's running hard. Linda Greenwell is running for State auditor.

In order to be a good Governor, you'd better be running on a good platform, so you've got to run for a reason. You've got to give people a reason to vote for you. Ernie Fletcher has done that. He mentioned jobs. Let me tell you something: We both share the same passion for our fellow citizen who is looking for work. So long as one person is looking for work, so long as one person who wants to work can't find a job, it says we've got an issue here in America.

I put forth a strong, progrowth package; that means a package that encourages economic growth so people can find work. Ernie Fletcher supported that plan. We need a pretty good dose of medicine for our economy. Remember, when I first came into office, we were in recession. That's three quarters of negative growth. We were going backwards, and then the enemy hit us. And then we had some of our corporate citizens who forgot to tell the truth. By the way, if you notice, some of those who forgot to tell the truth are now paying the price for not telling the truth.

All of that affected the confidence of the American people, so we acted. We acted on this theory—and this is important to have a Governor who understands how it works—when a person has got more money in their pocket, they're going to demand a good or a service. And when they demand a good or a service, somebody is going to produce that good or a service. And when somebody produces that good or a service, somebody is more likely to find a job. The tax cuts we passed came at the right time, and they're helping this economy.

In order to make sure your economy grows, you better make sure you've got a Governor who's not going to play politics with the people's money, somebody to

bring some fiscal discipline to the statehouse. So it's not only a combination of progrowth policies, but you better watch how the money is spent. Ernie Fletcher is a fiscal watchdog. He understands whose money we spend in government. We're not spending the government's money. We're spending the people's money, and you better have a Governor who knows that.

In order to make sure that Kentucky is a good place for people to do business so people can find work, you need a Governor who's willing to stand up to the plaintiff's attorneys. You see, what you don't want is a State dominated by plaintiff's attorneys so you've got a bunch of frivolous and junk lawsuits that on the one hand deny a person a chance to get their day in court, and on the other hand make it awfully costly for the State of Kentucky. You need medical liability reform. You need a Governor who's willing to stand up and be tough.

When I was the Governor of Texas, I used to tell our people that education is to a State what national defense is to the Federal Government, the top priority. One of the reasons I'm proud to stand by Ernie is because he understands that we must educate every single child in the State of Kentucky. He'll stand with the teachers. He'll stand with the parents. He will challenge what I call the soft bigotry of low expectations. See, when you lower the bar, when you have low expectations, you're going to get lousy results. You must have a Governor who's willing to raise the bar, to set high standards, to have high hopes for every single child. You must make sure you've got a Governor who insists that the curriculum used in public schools works, not based upon some fancy theory but actually works. You've got to make sure every child can read. You need to use phonics in the classroom. Ernie Fletcher understands that.

And finally, there are a lot of people who hurt around our country. You must have a Governor who understands that government can hand out money—and we do a pretty good job of it sometimes—but what government cannot do is put hope in a person's heart or a sense of purpose in people's lives. That's done when a fellow citizen surrounds a soul with love. It's done when people who have heard the universal call to love a neighbor just like you'd like to be loved yourself step forward and say, "I want to be a part of the fabric of change in a society. I want to help feed the hungry, house the homeless. I want to be there to help the drug addict understand that if you change your heart, you can change your behavior." It is essential.

I have put forth a Faith-Based Initiative, and I'm talking about all faiths, all faiths. And I put out a Faith-Based Initiative because I want the great strength of the country, the heart and soul of the American people, to rally to the cause of those who hurt. It's important to have a Governor who does not fear faith but welcomes faith and to—providing help for those who hurt, and that Governor is going to be Ernie Fletcher.

I look forward to working with Ernie Fletcher to make sure that the homeland security initiative is done well here in Kentucky. We want to make sure that there's good coordination between the Federal, the State, and the local authorities, to make sure your good police folks and firefighters and emergency-response teams have a coordinated strategy to be able to deal with a situation if it were to occur. The thing I appreciate about Ernie Fletcher is he understands what I know, that the best way to secure the homeland is to hunt the killers down, one by one, and bring them to justice, what America will do.

We must never forget the lessons of September the 11th, 2001. We must understand that we can't sit back and hope for the best, that when we see danger we must respond. We must respond in a way that is responsible. We are responsible for the security of the people of this country. We must use every power we have to make sure that another attack does not occur. The lessons of September the 11th, 2001, are indelibly etched in my mind. I will not forget the responsibility that we have to the people, and neither will Ernie.

For those of you with loved ones in the United States military, you get a hold of them either by e-mail or phone or letter, and you tell them their Commander in Chief is incredibly proud of the sacrifices they are making for this country.

But I also want you to know that we'll stay on the offensive, but we'll also stay on the offensive for the spread of freedom. The greatest security America can gain is from the advance of human liberty. Free nations do not attack their neighbors. Free nations do not develop weapons of mass terror to threaten or blackmail the world. No, the greatest security for America will come when America continues to lead the world toward a free society. We understand—we understand—that freedom is not America's gift to the world; freedom is God Almighty's gift to each and every person that lives in the world.

In this war on terror, I've had no stronger supporter than Ernie Fletcher. I'm proud to stand with this man. There's no doubt in my mind he'll make a great Governor. There's no doubt in my mind he'll be a Governor for every single person that lives in this vital and important State. There's no doubt in my mind he's got a vision that's clear and hopeful, a vision that will provide the best opportunity, so that everybody who lives here can say, "I've been given my chance to succeed. I've been given a good education. The environment for finding a job is strong. I can raise my family in peace and security." There's no doubt in my mind that the right person to lead this great State into the 21st century is Ernie Fletcher.

Thank you all for coming. May God bless. God bless you all. Work hard. Thank you all.

NOTE: The President spoke at 12:44 p.m. at Barkley Regional Airport. In his remarks, he referred to Glenna A. Fletcher, wife of gubernatorial candidate Ernie Fletcher.

Remarks in London, Kentucky
November 1, 2003

The President. Thank you all for coming. Thank you for being here. I'm honored to be here. Thanks for so many people showing up today. It's a beautiful day to talk about the next Governor of the State of Kentucky.

My only regret is I wasn't here a month ago for the fried chicken festival. [*Laughter*] I appreciate so many folks showing up. It's a good sign, Ernie. It's a good sign people care about their government. It's a good sign that people know they have got a responsibility to vote. I'm here to say as clearly I can, the right person to become the next Governor of the State of Kentucky is Ernie Fletcher.

I want to thank you all for bringing your families. I also want to thank the Bush Volunteer Fire Department for coming. That's a heck of a name you chose. [*Laughter*] I'm proud to share it with you, and thanks for what you do.

I can say without any uncertainty at all that Ernie is the right man to be the Governor. Listen to this: He's a fighter pilot. That says something. And he's a healer. He's a doctor. He's an engineer. He did a fine job in the United States Congress. He's had good experience. He married well—[*laughter*]—just like me. I appreciate Glenna. I appreciate the sacrifices she's making for the people of this great State.

The people of this State must be assured that when they elect somebody to high office, that person will uphold the dignity of that office. You want your kids looking at somebody who—for whom you can be proud. Ernie Fletcher values his faith. He values his family. He understands the responsibilities that you must assume when you get elected to high office. The right man for the job is Ernie Fletcher.

It's one thing to be listening to the speeches; it's another thing to be doing the work. I'm asking you to go out and turn out the vote. I'm asking you to go to your coffee shops, your farm implement dealers, your community centers, your houses of worship, and remind people they have a duty to vote. In this free land you have a duty to exercise your responsibility. And you might also remind them when they're heading to the polls, he's the right man for the job.

And don't overlook those disgruntled Democrats, either. [*Laughter*] They want good, clean government in Frankfort. There's plenty of independents you can encourage to go vote. This is voter turnout time now. The good people of this part of the State understand what I'm talking about. You go find your neighbors and get them to the polls, and you'll be proud of the job he does on behalf of everybody in this State.

Make sure that you also get them to vote for the Lieutenant Governor. [*Laughter*] It's kind of natural, isn't it? I'm proud of the fact that Ernie picked Steve Pence. He's a good, solid man. See, I picked him first. I don't know if you know this or not, but I named him to be the U.S. Attorney for western Kentucky. I looked long and hard to get the right person to do this important job. Steve Pence was the man. He's not only the man to be the U.S. Attorney; he's the man to become your Lieutenant Governor.

Laura sends her love to the people of eastern Kentucky. She's a fabulous First

Lady. I'm really proud of her. You drew the short straw. You got me. [*Laughter*]

I'm so proud to be on the same platform with two great United States Senators. First, Senator Mitch McConnell—he represents Kentucky really well. He also married well. [*Laughter*] He married so well, I put Elaine, his wife, into the Cabinet. [*Laughter*] I'm proud of the job she's doing for the working people of this country. I'm also proud to be here with Jim and Mary Bunning, two great citizens of this State. It is really important you send him back to the United States Senate in '04.

The truth of the matter is, I'm here because a great friend of my family's said, "Listen, if you want to help Ernie, you make sure you come to London." He said, "If you really want to do some good for this good man, you make sure you come to the heart of my district." I think you know who I'm talking about.

Audience members. [*Applause*]

The President. Yes. A great American, a great friend, a wonderful Congressman from this part of the world, one of the real powers in the Halls of Congress, a man who thinks constantly about the people in this district, and that would be Hal Rogers. It's been a real pleasure to get to know Cynthia as well. I like a man who married a younger woman. [*Laughter*]

I'm also proud to be here with the former Governor, Governor Louie Nunn. I appreciate Governor Nunn being here today as well. Thank you, Louie. Adam Koenig is with us. He's running for the State treasurer, and he wants your vote. You talk about a man who picked a good name running for the commissioner of agriculture—[*laughter*]—Richie Farmer is throwing his hat in the ring, and he wants your help.

I'm proud to be here with my friend David Williams, the president of the State senate. Ellen Williams runs the party here, and Mike Duncan is the national committeeman. And all of you all involved in the grassroots—that means fixing to turn out the vote; that's what that means to me—thanks for coming. It's been a real joy to be here.

I also want to thank Rebecca Lynn Howard for singing so beautifully for you all.

What's important for a Governor candidate is to have a good agenda, a good platform; you've got to run for a reason. And Ernie is running for the right reason. First of all, he and I share a concern: Anytime any of our citizens who wants to work and can't find a job, it says we've got a problem, and you better get you a Governor here in Kentucky who understands what it means to create the environment so jobs can grow.

You know, when I came into office, the country was in a recession. And then the enemy hit us. And then we found out some of our citizens forgot what it means to be responsible. They didn't tell the truth to their shareholders and their employees. By the way, some of them are finding out what it means to be held accountable.

So I went to the Congress and said, "We've got to be concerned about the fact that people aren't working." But I went with this principle—and Ernie understands this; that's why I'm bringing it up; it's important you have a Governor who understands how to create that environment for job growth and job creation. When a person has more money in his or her pocket, he or she is likely to demand a good or a service. And when you demand a good or a service, somebody is going to produce that good or a service. And when somebody produces that good or a service, somebody is more likely to find a job. The tax relief that Ernie supported strongly came at the right time for the American economy and the American people. When you have more money in your pockets, somebody is more likely to find a job.

In order to make sure that you've got an economy that's strong here in Kentucky, you better make sure you've got a Governor who is wise with the people's money. And that starts with understanding this principle: In government, we don't spend the government's money; that's your money. We spend the people's money. And Ernie is not going to play politics with your money. He's going to set priorities. He's going to be wise about how to spend the taxpayers' money.

In order to make sure you've got an economy that grows, you better have a legal system that is fair and balanced. Junk lawsuits make it hard to have a State that creates jobs. You need a Governor who's willing to stand up to the plaintiff's bar, somebody who will stand strong and say, "If you need your day in court, you'll have a day in court, but frivolous and junk lawsuits make it hard for people to find work." And frivolous and junk lawsuits make it hard for people to get good, affordable health care. You need medical liability reform in this State.

I used to say in Texas that education is to a State what national defense is to the Federal Government. The top priority of any State is to make sure every child gets a good education. And that's Ernie Fletcher's top priority. Ernie is going to stand with the teachers. Ernie is going to stand with the parents. Most importantly, Ernie is going to stand with the children. He'll challenge what I call the soft bigotry of low expectations. He believes every child can learn. He'll raise the standards and insist that our children learn to read and write and add and subtract. You need a Governor who will make sure no child is left behind in the State of Kentucky.

He's right on a lot of the issues. He's running on a good, solid platform. This is a platform, by the way, that's good for Republicans and Democrats and independents. This is a Kentucky platform.

One of the things I like most about his platform is his understanding of the role of faith in our society. The state should never fund the church, and the church should never try to be the state. But in order to heal broken hearts, in order to address some of the deepest needs of our fellow citizens, whether they be the homeless or the addict or the child who needs special love, we must welcome faith in our society. We must rally the armies of compassion.

I look forward to working with Ernie to make sure the Federal efforts and the State efforts and the local efforts here in Kentucky are well-coordinated when it comes to protecting the homeland. I look forward to working with him to make sure that our first-responders, the brave police and firefighters and emergency management teams, get resources necessary to do the job you expect them to do.

But I also want you to know, and he understands this, that the best way to protect the homeland is to chase the killers down, one at a time, and bring them to justice. We must never forget the lessons of September the 11th, 2001. We must understand we have a duty and responsibility to provide security for the people of this country. Therapy is not going to work with that bunch. [*Laughter*] We must be smart. We must be tough. We will not tire. We will not rest until this danger to civilization is removed.

When I came into office, morale in the U.S. military was beginning to suffer, so we increased the defense budget. Ernie Fletcher stood right by my side, making sure our troops, our brave troops, got the best training, the best pay, and the best possible equipment.

But I want you to know, the best way to safeguard America is to work to spread freedom, is to make sure that freedom can take hold around the world. See, free societies don't attack their neighbors. Free societies do not develop weapons of mass terror to blackmail or threaten the world. We understand this—it's very important—that freedom is not America's gift to the world; freedom is the Lord Almighty's gift to each person in the world.

I'm proud that Ernie stood strong on these tough issues. I'm proud I could count on him. And you can count on him when he's your Governor. He's a good, honest man. He's a decent man. He's an honorable man. And I'm here to ask you to turn out the vote here, in this important part of the State, and send this man to the statehouse, who will do you a great job.

Thanks for coming. May God bless, and may God bless America.

NOTE: The President spoke at 5 p.m. at London-Corbin Airport. In his remarks, he referred to Glenna A. Fletcher, wife of gubernatorial candidate Ernie Fletcher; Cynthia Rogers, wife of Representative Harold "Hal" Rogers; Secretary of Labor Elaine L. Chao; and country music entertainer Rebecca Lynn Howard.

Remarks in Gulfport, Mississippi
November 1, 2003

The President. Thank you all very much. Thanks for coming. I'm proud to be here in southern Mississippi. Thanks for your time. It's a beautiful night to be with the next Governor of the State of Mississippi.

I'm here to say it as plainly as I can say it. The right man to be the Governor of Mississippi is Haley Barbour. We've known each other a long time. Even when he was in high cotton—[*laughter*]—running with the big shots—[*laughter*]—he always talked about Mississippi. He loves this State, and he loves the people of Mississippi. I think he's going to be a great Governor because he's going to be the Governor of everybody. He's not going to be the Governor of one political party or another. He's going to represent every single person who's fortunate enough to live in the great State of Mississippi.

He's going to be a fine Governor because he's an optimist. He's got a clear and optimistic and positive vision for this great State. He believes in the potential of the State because he believes in the people of Mississippi. Haley Barbour is a family man, a man of faith. There is no doubt in my mind he is going to be a great Governor of this big State.

Plus, he married well. [*Laughter*] Marsha is going to be a great first lady. And speaking about great First Ladies, I'm sorry Laura is not with me today. I know it;

you got the short straw. [*Laughter*] But after I shake enough hands, I'm going to head back to Crawford, and I'm going to tell her that there's no doubt in my mind that the people of this great State support Haley Barbour to be the next Governor.

And the definition of support means not only coming out to a big rally like this; it means doing your duty to vote. In our free society, you have a duty and an obligation to go to the polls. I'm asking you to ask your friends and neighbors to go to the polls as well. Don't be afraid to talk to that disenchanted Democrat—[*laughter*]—or the discerning independent. They want good government too. And Haley Barbour is going to give them good government. Turn out that vote. Work hard to get this man into office.

I'm proud to be onstage as well with your Lieutenant Governor, Amy Tuck. She's a woman of conscience. She made a tough decision. She decided she wanted to be a principled politician. [*Laughter*] That's what you need. That's what you want in your statehouse. You want a principled Governor, and you want a principled Lieutenant Governor, and you'll have a principled Lieutenant Governor in Amy Tuck.

I appreciate so very much Tricia Lott being here. She's a great friend of mine and Laura's. She married well—[*laughter*]—Senator Lott, who does a fantastic job for the people of Mississippi. He came out to the airport. He said, "Look, I've heard you speak before." [*Laughter*] He's heading north—[*laughter*]—to rally the vote for Haley. I said, "You've got an excused absence just so long as you send your wife." [*Laughter*]

I appreciate so very much Congressman Chip Pickering and his wife, Leisha, for being here as well. Chip's one of the rising stars in the United States House of Representatives, a good, honorable, decent family man who cares deeply about the people of this State.

I'm also honored to here with Margaret Ann Pickering. She is the wife of Charles Pickering, Judge Pickering. You may have— [*applause*]. My job as the President is to find good, honorable citizens to serve on the high courts. When I picked Charles Pickering to serve in the high court, I picked a smart, intelligent, perfectly capable judge. It is time for some of the Members of the United States Senate to stop playing politics with American justice.

I want to thank Scott Newton, who's running for the attorney general. I appreciate you coming, Scott. Don't forget him when you get in the booth.

I want to thank the mayors who are here and the local officials. I particularly want to thank the Lynyrd Skynyrd band.

But most of all, I want to thank you all. It's got to make a candidate that's coming down the stretch feel great to see so many people. They've been working hard and knocking on doors and making the phone calls, and here you all show up and give them extra energy, and I want to thank you for coming.

It's important to have the right platform when you're running for Governor. You've got to believe in something. You can't get by just on your pretty looks. [*Laughter*] Well, in Haley's case—[*laughter*]. You've got to stand for something, and I appreciate what he stands for.

First of all, he shares the same concerns I have. When we hear that a fellow citizen is looking for work and can't find a job, that says we've got a problem. We want all our people working. We want people to be able to put bread on the table for their families. We want people to realize their ambitions. It's important to have a Governor who understands the role of government is to create an environment for small businesses to grow to be big business, to create an environment which is pro-growth and pro-jobs. Haley Barbour understands that.

You know, we face an issue in Washington, and that is the country was in recession just about the time we arrived. Then the enemy hit us. That hurt our economy. We had some of our citizens forget to tell the truth. They forgot what it means to be a responsible citizen, so they kind of— they fudged the books a little bit. They're weren't open and honest with their employees and shareholders. They now know what it means to be held accountable.

War, a national emergency, and a recession all affected our economy. That's why I went to the United States Congress, not once but twice, and said, "Let's let the people keep more of their own money. If you're interested in job creation, if you want economic growth, have tax cuts for the American people."

And the economy is beginning to recover, thanks to the hard work of the American people. You need to have you a Governor in the great State of Mississippi who understands what it means to create an environment for job growth, who hurts when he hears people are working, and that man is Haley Barbour.

It's also important, if you want to have a good economic environment so people can find work, that you have a Governor who will manage the budget well. And that starts with having somebody who understands whose money government spends. We don't spend the government's money in Washington or here in Mississippi, see. We're spending the people's money. And Haley Barbour understands that. He'll be a good steward of the people's money. He will set priorities for the people of Mississippi. He won't play politics with the people's money.

In order to make sure people can find work, you better have a legal environment that is reasonable. People need to be able to have their day in court. The problem is, frivolous and junk lawsuits clog up the dockets. They make it hard for employers to hire people who are looking for work. You need a Governor who is strong enough to stand up to the personal injury trial lawyers, a Governor who is tough enough to insist upon medical liability reform for the people of Mississippi.

I used to say, when I was the Governor of Texas, education is to a State what national defense is to the Federal Government. It's the top priority. That's the way it ought to be here in Mississippi. You'll have you a Governor, Haley Barbour, who will set education as the top priority for this State, and that's the way it should be.

Haley will stand with the hard-working teachers all across the State of Mississippi. Haley will stand with the parents of the schoolchildren all across the State of Mississippi. Haley will stand with the schoolchildren by challenging the soft bigotry of low expectations, by raising the bar, by insisting upon standards and insisting upon curriculum that will teach our children how to read and write and add and subtract.

No, Haley's got a good, strong platform. And he understands what I understand, that amidst our plenty there are broken hearts, there are people who hurt, there are people who are addicted or homeless, there are people who need to be fed. He also understands that government can hand out money—sometimes we do a pretty good job of it—but what government cannot do is put hope in people's hearts or a sense of purpose in people's lives. That is done when somebody who has heard the universal call to love a neighbor just like you'd like to be loved yourself puts their arm around somebody who needs love.

Government should never sponsor religion, and religion should never try to be the state. But it's essential to make sure America is hopeful, that government not fear the role of faith in the lives of providing compassionate help for people who hurt. I look forward to working with Governor Haley Barbour to make sure the Faith-Based Initiative, which will come out of Washington, DC, is implemented in such a way that people have got hope for the future.

I look forward to working with Haley Barbour to make sure that the homeland security initiative is well implemented, to make sure there's good coordination between the Federal Government and the State government and the local governments, to make sure our first-responders, the brave police and firefighters and emergency squads, have got the help necessary to do their job here in Mississippi.

But he and I understand this: The best way to secure the homeland is to chase the killers down and bring them to justice, which is exactly what America will do. We must never forget the lessons of September the 11th, 2001. America cannot afford to sit back and hope for the best. In order to make America secure, we must stay on the offensive. This country will not tire; we will not rest until the danger to civilization is removed.

A lot of people support the military here in this part of our country, and I want to thank you for that. A lot of you have got relatives who wear the Nation's uniform. When you e-mail them or write them a letter or talk to them on the phone, you tell them the Commander in Chief is incredibly proud of the sacrifice and service they're giving to this Nation.

We'll stay on the offensive. We'll do what it takes to keep this country secure. But I want you to know, I fully understand the best way for long-term security is for this Nation to work to spread freedom around the world. See, free nations don't attack their neighbors. Free nations don't develop weapons of mass terror to blackmail or threaten the world. That's why we will succeed in Iraq. A free Iraq, a free and peaceful Iraq, is in this national—is in our national interests. It's in the interests of our children and our grandchildren. Can you imagine what will take place, the change that will take place when democracy flourishes in the midst of a part of the world that has been an area of hate and violence?

I also understand this, that freedom is not America's gift to the world, freedom is the Almighty's gift to every person who lives in this world.

I want to thank you all for taking time out of your Saturday evenings to come out here. You're showing a strong commitment to your State, and I'm proud for that. You're showing a strong commitment of what it means to be a citizen living in a democracy. I'm going to ask you to take it a little extra farther.

Audience members. [*Inaudible*]

The President. Thank you. [*Laughter*] If you love me so much, make sure you turn out to vote. [*Laughter*] Make sure you go to the polls. Make sure you put this good man in office. Mississippi can do better, and Haley Barbour will lead Mississippi to that day.

Thanks for coming. May God bless. Thank you all.

NOTE: The President spoke at 6:28 p.m. at Jones Park. In his remarks, he referred to gubernatorial candidate Haley Barbour and his wife, Marsha; Amy Tuck, incumbent candidate for Mississippi Lieutenant Governor; Representative Charles W. "Chip" Pickering, Jr., of Mississippi; Charles W. Pickering, Sr., nominee to be U.S. Circuit Judge for the Fifth Circuit; and rock music group Lynyrd Skynyrd.

Remarks at CraneWorks in Birmingham, Alabama
November 3, 2003

Thanks for the warm welcome. It's great to be back in the great State of Alabama. I'm honored you all came out. Today I'm going to talk about a couple things on my mind. One is our economy. I want to make sure people are working here in Alabama and all across America. I'm going to talk about how to make America a more secure place.

Before I do, I want to thank the CraneWorks boys for hosting us, the brothers, the Upton boys—[*laughter*]—entrepreneurs, job creators, dreamers, people who have created something out of nothing. I want to thank the employees as well for being such hard-working, good folks here at CraneWorks. I'm honored to be in your place of business. I'm honored here—in a company that is creating jobs, new jobs,

to be talking about how best we can continue to create new jobs all across America. This economy of ours is growing. The entrepreneurial spirit is strong. But there's more work to do, and that's what I want to talk to you all today about. Before I do so, I do want to thank David and Steve for hosting us.

I want to thank Rom Reddy as well. Rom is a local entrepreneur. He started Nexcel Synthetics. I'm going to talk a little bit about his business, but I know he's got some employees here as well, hard-working people who have helped take this startup company from nothing to something in a quick period of time. The chief executive officer has got a bright and enthused future about this little company. He's talking about creating more jobs, but he also said,

"When you get up there, make sure you recognize the people that work with me in my company, because I wouldn't be having, or we wouldn't be having the success we're having without the good, hard-working people that are working with Rom." So wherever you are, thank you for coming.

I'm traveling in some pretty fancy company today, at least from the airport to here. Your Governor, Bob Riley, is here today, and I want to thank my friend for serving the State of Alabama. I appreciate you being here, Governor.

Two really fine United States Senators are here with us, strong allies, good friends, and that's Richard Shelby and Jeff Sessions. I appreciate you all coming. The mighty Alabama congressional delegation is strong and active. Spencer Bachus and Robert Aderholt and Jo Bonner and Mike Rogers and Terry Everett are all with us today. Congresspeople, thanks for coming. Attorney general from the State of Alabama is with us, Bill Pryor. I'm honored that Judge Pryor is here.

Today, when I landed out there, I met a fellow named Jason Nabors. You probably never heard of Jason. He is a soldier in the army of compassion here in Birmingham, Alabama. The reason I like to bring up people who are volunteering in their community is, oftentimes people look at America and say, "Well, that's a mighty country," because we've got a strong military; it's a mighty country because our wallets are heavier than other people around the world. No, we're a mighty country because the people who live here in this country are decent, caring, compassionate people who have heard the call to love a neighbor just like you'd like to be loved yourself.

Jason Nabors works at a local law firm, and by the way, his law firm encourages the lawyers in that firm to find a way to contribute to the Birmingham community by helping somebody who hurts. He's involved with First Look. It is a nonprofit organization that is created to increase the number of youngsters and young adults in the service to the people of Alabama by encouraging them to follow their hearts, by mentoring a child, by helping somebody who may be addicted, by feeding the hungry and housing the homeless.

I see we've got Scouts with us today. There's nothing better than being a Boy Scout leader and sending good signals and examples to the youth of America. For all of you who take time out of your busy lives to help somebody in need, I want to thank you from the bottom of my heart. You are the strength of our country.

When we talk about our economy and the future of our country, it's important to remember what we have been through. See, we've been through a lot here in America. The stock market started to decline about 9 months before Dick Cheney and I showed up in Washington, and then the country was in a recession. That means three quarters of negative growth. That means we were headed backwards. That means people were not finding work. That means we had trouble on the homefront of many homes across the country, because people weren't able to do their job of providing food for their families; they were looking for work.

And then we began to recover somewhat, and the enemy hit us on September the 11th, 2001, and that hurt. It hurt us economically. Frankly, it hurt us psychologically, because most of us grew up in a period where we thought oceans would protect us from harm. We saw a problem overseas, we could deal with it if we felt it was necessary for our security, but we at home were secure. We were protected. It was a big blow to us. It hurt a lot. We responded. We dedicated ourselves to the security of this country. We understood the challenge. America is a tough, resolved nation when we're challenged.

And then we began to recover from that, and our confidence was shaken by the fact that some of our chief executive officers forgot what it meant to be responsible citizens. They didn't tell the truth. They didn't tell the truth to their employees. They didn't tell the truth to their shareholders. They betrayed the trust. We passed laws, by the way, that are sending a clear signal: If you betray the trust, there will be a consequence; we will hold you responsible for not telling the truth. But the fact that some in corporate America betrayed the trust affected our confidence.

And then, as you well know, we marched to war in Afghanistan and Iraq for the security of our country and for the peace of the world, all of which affected our confidence. It affected the economy. I mean, Alabama has been hit hard by—in the manufacturing sector, the textile sector. These are challenges, but we met the challenges with action. We took tough action in order to move this economy forward.

First of all, as I mentioned, we passed new laws that say if you're going to cheat, we will hold you to account. And if you noticed, some of those who behaved irresponsibly are now being held to account. Secondly, we acted on principle. We said the best way to get this economy going and the best way to help people find work is to let people keep more of their own money. We understand how the economy works. If a person has more of his or her own money, they're likely to demand a good or a service, and when somebody demands a good or a service, in this economy, somebody is going to produce the good or a service. And when somebody produces a good or a service, somebody is more likely to find a job.

And so therefore, I went to the Congress, not once but twice, and said, "In order for people to be able to find work here in the country, let's pass meaningful, real tax relief." And I want to thank the two Senators and the Members of Congress who are here today for joining me in passing tax relief so people can find work. We wanted tax relief to be as broad and as fair as possible, so we reduced taxes on everybody who pays taxes. We thought that was a fair principle. Government shouldn't try to pick or choose winners and losers on who gets tax relief. If you're going to reduce taxes, reduce them on everybody, which is precisely what we did. We felt like the marriage penalty sent the wrong signal. See, we want people to be married. We think marriage is good. We think it's a part of a—[*applause*]—but the Tax Code penalized marriage. And so we've reduced the marriage penalty.

We understand that it's—when the economy is slow and people are worried about the future, that it takes a lot to raise a child. And so we increased the child credit from $600 per child to $1,000 per child. This summer, I remember going to Pennsylvania where they were cutting the checks, and I said, "The check's in the mail." Fortunately, it turned out to be in the mail. [*Laughter*] People got money back, money in their pocket. If you had a child, you got $400 per child. That meant you're in a position to demand the additional good or a service, which meant somebody was more likely to find work here.

We also wanted to encourage investment. If you're interested in job creation, then you must be interested in encouraging investment. When people invest in plant equipment, for example, it means somebody is going to have to produce the plant—produce the equipment. And so we encouraged investment by quadrupling the expense deduction for small business investment. I'm going to talk a little bit about that in a second. But we also cut taxes on dividends and capital gains to encourage investment. More investment means more jobs.

We also believe that if you're a small business or a farmer or a rancher, you ought to be able to leave your assets to whomever you choose without the Government getting in the way again, so we're phasing out the Federal death tax. We don't believe the IRS should follow you into your grave. [*Laughter*]

We passed these measures to help individuals, but the measures we passed also are incredibly important to the small-business sector of America. The small-business sector of our country is vital for job creation. See, most new jobs in America are created by small businesses. Most small businesses pay a tax at the individual income tax level.

See, if you're a Subchapter S, or a limited liability corporation, just like the two small businesses I've spoken of today, then when we cut individual taxes, it's really a cut in taxes for small businesses. It means small-business owners have got more money to invest, and when they invest, it means somebody is more likely to find a job. It is essential for those politicians in Washington to know that individual income tax relief is incredibly important for job creation, not only because it stimulates demand but because it provides a vital boost in the arm for the small-business sector here in America. The Uptons bought nine cranes last year in order to rent them out. And they told me that one of the reasons why is because of the tax relief. It provided an incentive for them to purchase additional equipment.

Now, that means a couple of things: Somebody has got to make the equipment, which means somebody is working; somebody has got to maintain the equipment, go rent the equipment; it means people here at CraneWorks are more likely to keep a job; but in the Uptons' case, or this case, you've actually added 15 jobs this year. Now, that's a lot for a startup company, but it's a really a lot when you think about the 15 jobs here and the 15 jobs there and this small business in another State. It's the compound effect of the hiring decisions of millions of small businesses that paint a good perspective for people to be able to find work. If you're interested in job creation in America, you've got to understand the role small businesses play in the creation of new jobs in this economy. CraneWorks is such an example.

Steve Upton says about investing, "You go out there; you take your risks"—these are his words, not mine—"you put people to work; you get aggressive; and you get business." That's the entrepreneurial spirit. That's what America is all about. That just goes with having a vision for a better tomorrow. That vision was cleared up somewhat by the tax plan we passed, and I appreciate the Congressmen understanding and the Senators understanding the vital role that small business plays.

Now look, CraneWorks isn't going to succeed because of Government policy. It's up to the Uptons to figure out how to build a strategy that works. It's up to the Uptons to figure out a marketing plan. It's up to them to make wise investment decisions. It's up to them to treat their employees with dignity. But all Government is doing is trying to put a little wind at their sails, and it seems to be working.

I appreciate Rom Reddy. He's an entrepreneur. He said the tax relief helped him gain confidence in making investments—as he said, leveraged up the opportunity to make investments, so he bought $6 million in new equipment so he could get in the artificial turf business. And somebody had to make the equipment when he purchased it. Somebody had to sell the equipment. In other words, it's part of economic activity, when people make rational decisions in the marketplace. Tax relief encouraged rational decisions to be made in the marketplace.

Rom's company has gone from zero sales, zero turf sales, to 17 million in a quick period of time. He's added 60 new jobs in one year. Sixty people are now working. The tax relief helped him to have the confidence necessary to move forward. By the way, a lot of his sales are going in Europe and China. See, I'm going to talk a little bit about what it means to open up markets, but I just want you to know that his business is going to be more successful because he's developing a product that he's confident he can sell in other markets, which is good for job creation, and it's good for the 60 he's got working for him and the some he intends to add. Tax relief puts money into the pockets of those who are hiring new people.

We've got a consistent and effective strategy, and we're making progress. Remember, this last week, a surprising announcement—at least, it confounded some of the experts—that our third quarter economic growth was vibrant. And that's good. Inflation is down, and that's good. After-tax incomes are up. People are keeping more of their own money, and that's really important for economic growth.

We've got the best workforce in the world here in America, incredibly high productivity gains, which is vital for competition and job creation in the long run. By reducing taxes, this administration kept a promise. We did the right thing at the right time for the American economy.

And our country is approaching a choice now. Just as our economy is gaining some momentum, some in our Nation's Capital, some in Washington, are saying now is the right time to raise taxes. To be fair, they think any time's a good time to raise taxes. [*Laughter*] They're consistent. [*Laughter*] So am I. I strongly disagree. Raising taxes now will wreck economic recovery and will punish hard-working Americans and endanger thousands of jobs.

There's some other things we can do to make sure that the momentum in our economy continues, and I want to talk about them right quick. It's what we call the six-point plan. I've laid it out for Congress to consider. First, in order to make sure our small-business sector is strong and vibrant and make sure they continue to create new jobs, we must allow small businesses to form what we call associated health plans. That will allow small businesses to pool risk so that they can better control the cost of health care.

We also must have medical liability reform. I'm worried about the—what I call frivolous lawsuits that make it hard for docs to practice medicine and run up the cost of medicine. It makes medicine less affordable and less available. And by the way, frivolous lawsuits increase the cost of the Federal budget to Medicaid and Medicare and veterans health benefits. You need your day in court when you run into a bad doc, but we've got to control these frivolous lawsuits because they're making health care too costly. Since it affects the Federal budget, medical liability reform is a national issue that requires a national solution. The Senate needs to pass that bill.

And the Senate needs to get out for the junk lawsuits that make it hard to do business. It's important that we have a judicial system that's fair and balanced. Class action lawsuits oftentimes are not fair and balanced. After all, the money goes to the lawyers and not to the people who got hurt. We need a system that's fair and balanced, and the Senate needs to act on that.

We've got to cut useless government regulations. We need to do it at the Federal level. Riley needs to do it here at the State level. We need to make sure our entrepreneurs are focused on job creation, not filling out needless paperwork.

But I believe if you're good at something, you ought to promote it. We're great farmers. We're really good ranchers. We're great entrepreneurs. We ought to be opening up markets for U.S. products. If you're interested in job creation, companies ought to be encouraged to sell overseas. If you're good at something, let's promote it. I'm concerned, like you are, that trade is not on a level playing field, so this administration is spending a lot of time to make sure that trade is a two-way street, that it's fair, that it's open.

But I want you to know that 220 foreign companies from 30 nations have located right here in Alabama, in factories and offices, which means jobs for Alabama citizens. Trade, if it's done right, can help create new jobs, and that's what this administration is committed to doing.

We also ought to make sure that tax relief is permanent. It's hard for me to explain the rules in Washington. Let me put it to you this way: the Congress giveth and the Congress taketh away—not because of these Members, by the way. But much of the tax relief we passed is scheduled to go away, and that's a problem if you're a small-business owner.

The Upton boys need to have certainty in the Tax Code, so when they plan in the future, they know what the rules are going to be. If you're raising a family, you don't want the child credit to go back down again. If you're married, you don't want the marriage penalty to raise. And yet, because of the quirk in the law, the taxes we passed will steadily increase over time. And we've got to make the tax relief permanent. For the sake of job creation, the Congress must make the tax relief permanent.

And finally, we need a national energy policy. If you're in the manufacturing sector, you rely upon energy. And the thought of energy supplies being disrupted because of shortages makes it hard for people to plan and be aggressive about the future. We had a wake-up call this summer. It became quite evident that some of the electricity grid needs to be modernized so that people can know the lights are going to be on in their houses, so businessowners can plan for the future.

We submitted a plan to Congress about 2 years ago that had some key principles. One, we need to modernize the electricity grid. We need to encourage more investment. Those providing electricity must do so on a—must have reliability standards not on a voluntary basis, on a mandatory basis. We're going to make it mandatory that you make sure you've got backup systems available for the people, so if the electricity goes out here, you can crank it back up there. But the system needs to be modernized. It's antiquated in some parts.

Secondly, we need to use our technologies to encourage conservation. That's very important. Conservation is a vital part of the future of our country. We also use our technologies to find different sources of energy. I think it would be great if we were able to grow our way out of an energy crisis, have the farmers produce product that'll be converted into fuel. That makes sense.

But we've also got to find more energy and use the energy we've got at home. We need clean coal technology. We need to use our technologies to explore in environmentally friendly ways. Let me tell you what I'm telling you, for the sake of national security and for the sake of economic security, we need to be less reliant on foreign sources of energy.

The House passed a bill. The Senate passed a bill. They're now reconciling their differences. They need to get the job done. They need to get an energy bill to my desk. They need to make sure that this country is planning for the future with good, sound energy policy.

We've overcome a lot in this country. The economy took some serious shocks. But you know, the entrepreneurial spirit is strong, and the workforce is vibrant. We handled a lot; we've overcome it. And now we're growing. And the six-point plan I laid out is a plan that says to the Congress, "Let's get together to make sure the economic momentum continues." We want people working. We're saddened by the fact that somebody might be looking for work and can't find a job. There's more jobs to be created here in America. We've laid the foundation for growth. They need to get these other six things done so we can continue the momentum.

I'm optimistic about our future because I'm optimistic when I meet people like Rom and the Upton boys. They love their country. They love the people working with them. The entrepreneurial spirit in their heart is strong. They take risk. They're willing to make calculated risk in order to not only expand their businesses but to make employment possible for people here in the great State of Alabama.

As we overcome the challenges to the economy, we're also answering the challenges to the national security. September the 11th, 2001, moved the country to grief. It also moved us to action. We must never forget the lessons of September the 11th, 2001. We must never forget that tragic day.

I made a pledge that day, and we've kept it. We will bring the guilty to justice. We will secure America. We put together a Homeland Security Department to do the best we possibly can in coordinating Federal efforts and State efforts and local efforts to protect people. We're doing everything we can to get resources to the—those on the frontline of national, State, and local emergency. That would be your firefighters and your police officers and your emergency-management teams. But the best way to secure the homeland is to hunt the enemy down one at a time and bring them to justice, which is what America is going to do.

America cannot retreat from our responsibilities. We can't hope for the best. See, that's what September the 11th taught us, that we must be diligent and active. We can't hope terrorists will change their attitudes. I like to remind people that therapy is not going to work with this bunch. [*Laughter*] And that's why we've got some really incredibly brave people on the hunt. We will win the war on terror; there's no doubt in my mind. We will not rest; we will not tire until the danger to America and civilization is removed.

We have got a great United States military, and some of the best have fallen in service to our fellow Americans. We mourn every loss. We honor every name. We grieve with every family. And we will always be grateful that liberty has found such brave defenders.

We have put the best on the job of securing America and defending the peace. Five hundred soldiers in the 877th Engi-

neer Battalion, the Alabama National Guard, are deployed. They're fixing roads so life will be better. They're rebuilding orphanages. They're repairing schools. These proud sons and daughters of Alabama were responsible for demolishing the final hideout of the thugs, the sons of Saddam Hussein.

We're grateful for them, and I'm grateful to their families for making the sacrifice. You see, freedom's home is America. We're freedom's defender. We understand that the advance of human liberty is in our national interests. We remember the lessons of September the 11th, but we also remember that free nations do not attack their neighbors, free nations do not develop weapons of mass terror to blackmail or hold hostage the world. We also know that America—that freedom is not America's gift to the world; that's what we know; freedom is the Almighty's gift to everybody who lives in this world.

The terrorists and the killers and those who harbor terrorists cannot stand the thought of a free society in their midst. That's why the mission in Iraq is vital. A free Iraq will be a peaceful Iraq, and a free and peaceful Iraq are important for the national security of America. A free and peaceful Iraq will make it more likely that our children and grandchildren will be able to grow up without the horrors of September the 11th. We'll defeat the terrorists there so we don't have to face them on our own streets.

The enemy in Iraq believes America will run. That's why they're willing to kill innocent civilians, relief workers, coalition troops. America will never run. America will do what is necessary to make our country more secure.

We've come through a lot in this country, and yet, there is a lot more to do. By being patient and united and determined, by remembering the values that make us a strong and unique nation, this country will prosper, and our Nation will prevail.

I want to thank you all for coming. May God bless you all, and may God continue to bless America.

NOTE: The President spoke at 10:35 a.m. in the equipment warehouse. In his remarks, he referred to David and Steve Upton, own-ers, CraneWorks; Rom L. Reddy, founder, chairman of the board, and chief executive officer, Nexcel Synthetics, LLC; and Uday and Qusay Hussein, sons of former President Saddam Hussein of Iraq, who were killed July 22 by U.S. military forces in Mosul, Iraq.

Remarks at a Bush-Cheney Luncheon in Birmingham, Alabama
November 3, 2003

The President. Thank you all very much. Thanks for coming. I told Shelby I wanted a short introduction. [*Laughter*] He delivered. [*Laughter*] Thanks for coming. I'm thrilled to be back in the great State of Alabama. I do have a lot of friends here, and I appreciate your friendship, and I appreciate your support. What we're doing here is laying the foundation for what is going to be a great national victory in 2004.

And I'm getting ready for it. [*Laughter*] I'm loosening up. [*Laughter*] But I want you to know that politics will come in its own time. As my strong supporters, you've got to know that I know I've got a job to do. And so when you start laying the grassroots organization and you go to your coffee shops and your houses of worship and your farm implementation dealership, you tell them the President is doing the job. He's doing the job for every single American. I will keep America strong and secure and prosperous and free.

My regret is that Laura didn't come. A lot of people are——

Audience member. [*Inaudible*]

The President. Yes, I'm sure it is. [*Laughter*] She said, "Mine, too." [*Laughter*] She understands you drew the short straw. [*Laughter*] For the people in Mobile who are here, thank you for coming up. But you drew the long straw, and Laura had a fabulous visit down to Mobile, Alabama. But she sends her best. I've got to tell you, I'm really proud of her. She is a fabulous wife, a great mother, and a wonderful First Lady.

I want to thank Richard and Annette for their friendship. Shelby is a good man, and he told me, he said, "I'm going to make sure this fundraiser is successful." I know here we're talking about our election campaign, but it's very important you send Senator Shelby back to the United States Senate. And I also like your other Senator a lot, Senator Jeff Sessions. He's doing a fabulous job for Alabama.

I'm proud to be here with my friend the Governor of Alabama, Bob Riley. I appreciate Governor Riley coming. I'm also honored to be with many members of the Alabama congressional delegation: Jo Bonner and Terry Everett and Mike Rogers and Robert Aderholt and Spencer Bachus. I want to thank all of them for coming.

And I want you all to know who came up here with Robert's mother, that I know where Winston County, Alabama, is— [*laughter*]—mobile homes and Republicans. [*Laughter*]

I appreciate so very much Attorney General Bill Pryor. I want to thank my friend Mercer Reynolds from Cincinnati, Ohio, who is the national finance chairman for Bush-Cheney. He's an entrepreneur, like many of you all are. He is taking time out of his life to help us gather the resources necessary to run a vibrant campaign, and I appreciate his help. And I want to thank Mike Thompson. Mike is our State finance chairman here in Alabama, and obviously he has done, along with many others, a fabulous job of organizing this fundraiser.

I want to thank Marty Connors and Edgar Welden and Bettye Fine Collins, all of whom are very much involved in grassroots politics here in Alabama. I'm going to be counting on you. I'm going to be counting on you to put up the signs and to send out the letters and counting on you to get this grassroots organization alive and well here. We can't win this without your help.

I want to thank you for—all of you who are involved in grassroots politics. I want to thank the local officials and the State officials who are here. I want to thank the mayors who are here.

I had the honor of meeting Johnny Spann, whose son, Mike, was one of the first casualties in the war on terror in Afghanistan. Our prayers are with the Spann family. I want to thank Johnny for his spirit and his strength, and I want to thank Mike for giving his life for a cause greater than himself.

And finally, I want to thank Dr. Charles Durham, the pastor of the First Presbyterian Church of Tuscaloosa. I'm not surprised that Shelby made sure that the pastor here was from Tuscaloosa. [*Laughter*]

Most of all, I want to thank you all for coming.

In the last 2½ years, our Nation has acted decisively to confront great challenges. I came to this office to solve problems, instead of passing them on to future Presidents and future generations. I came to seize opportunities instead of letting them slip away. My administration is meeting the tests of our time.

Terrorists declared war on the United States of America, and war is what they got. We've captured or killed many of the key leaders of Al Qaida network, and the rest of them know we're on their trail. In Afghanistan and in Iraq, we gave ultimatums to terror regimes. Those regimes

chose defiance, and those regimes are no more. Fifty million people in those two countries once lived under tyranny, and today, they live in freedom.

Two-and-a-half years ago, our military was not receiving the resources it needed, and morale was beginning to suffer. So we increased the defense budgets to prepare for the threats of a new era, and today, no one in the world can question the skill and the strength and the spirit of the United States military.

Two-and-a-half years ago, we inherited an economy in recession. And then our country was attacked. And we had scandals in corporate America, and we marched to war, all of which affected the people's confidence. But we acted. We passed tough new laws to hold corporate criminals to account. And to get the economy going again, I have twice led the United States Congress to pass historic tax relief for the American people.

We know that when Americans have more take-home pay to spend, to save, or invest, the whole economy grows, and people are more likely to find a job. So we're passing money back to the people to help them raise their families. We're reducing taxes on dividends and capital gains to encourage investment. We're giving small businesses incentives to expand and to hire new people. With all these actions, we're laying the foundation for greater economic prosperity and jobs across America so every single person in this country can realize the American Dream.

Two-and-a-half years ago, there was a lot of talk about education reform, but there wasn't much action. So I called for and the Congress passed the No Child Left Behind Act. With a solid bipartisan majority, we delivered the most dramatic education reforms in a generation. We insist upon high standards and accountability in every public school in America because we believe every child can learn. We are challenging the soft bigotry of low expectations. In return for increased Federal money, we expect results. We want to see results. The days of excuse-making are over. We expect results because we don't want one single child in America left behind.

We've reorganized our Government and created the Department of Homeland Security to better safeguard our borders and ports and to better protect the American people. We passed trade promotion authority to open new markets for Alabama's farmers and entrepreneurs and manufacturers. We passed budget agreements to help maintain a much needed spending discipline in Washington, DC. On issue after issue, this administration has acted on principle, has kept its word, and has made progress for the American people.

And the Congress has shared in these great achievements. I've got a great relationship with Denny Hastert, the Speaker of the House, and Bill Frist, the majority leader, as I do with the Alabama Senators and congressional delegation. They deserve a lot of credit. We're working hard to change the tone in Washington. And the truth of the matter is, there's just too much needless politics up there. We're focusing on the people's business, focusing on results.

And those are the kind of people I've attracted to my administration. I've put together a superb team on behalf of the American people, starting with a Birmingham soul, Condi Rice, who is doing a fabulous job. Our country has had no finer Vice President than Dick Cheney. Mother may have a different opinion. [*Laughter*]

We've done a lot in 2½ years. We've come far. But our work is only beginning. I have set great goals worthy of a great nation. First, America is committed to expanding the realm of freedom and peace for our own security and for the benefit of the world. And second, in our own country, we must work for a society of prosperity and compassion so that every citizen has a chance to work and succeed and to realize the great promise—the great promise—of America.

It is clear that the future of freedom and peace depend on the actions of America. This Nation is freedom's home and freedom's defender. We welcome this charge of history, and we are keeping it.

Our war on terror continues. And the enemies of freedom are not idle, and neither are we. This country will not rest; we will not tire; we will not stop until this danger to civilization is removed. We are confronting that danger in Iraq, where Saddam holdouts and foreign terrorists are desperately trying to throw Iraq into chaos by attacking our forces and aid workers and innocent Iraqi citizens. They know that the advance of freedom in Iraq will be a major defeat for the cause of terror. This collection of killers is trying to shake the will of America. We will not be intimidated.

We are aggressively striking the terrorists in Iraq, defeating them there so we will not have to face them in our own country. We're calling other nations to help Iraq to build a free country, which will make us all more secure. We're standing with the Iraqi people as they assume more of their own defense and move toward self-government. These are not easy tasks, but they're essential tasks for the security of the United States and for the peace of the world. We will finish what we have begun, and we will win this essential victory in the war on terror.

Our greatest security comes from the advance of human liberty, because free nations do not support terror, free nations do not attack their neighbors, free nations do not develop weapons of mass terror. Americans believe that freedom is the deepest need and hope of every human heart. And I believe that freedom is the right of every person, and I believe that freedom is the future of every nation.

America also understands that unprecedented influence brings tremendous responsibilities. We have duties in this world, and when we see disease and starvation and hopeless poverty, we will not turn away. On the continent of Africa, America is now committed to bringing the healing power, the healing power of medicine to millions of men and women and children now suffering with AIDS. This great land is leading the world in this incredibly important work of human rescue.

We face challenges here at home as well, and our actions will prove that we're equal to those challenges. I just spent some time at CraneWorks, a successful small business here in Alabama. I went there to deliver this message as clearly as I could: So long as anybody in our country is looking for work and can't find a job, I know we have a problem. My job as the President is to continue to create an environment for small businesses to grow to be big businesses, an environment that rewards the entrepreneurial spirit.

We have a duty to keep our commitments to America's seniors by strengthening and modernizing Medicare. The Congress has taken historic action. The House acted and the Senate acted to improve the lives of older Americans. For the first time since the creation of Medicare, the Congress is passing reforms to increase choices for our seniors and to provide coverage for prescription drugs. Those two bodies need to iron out their differences and to modernize the Medicare system. We owe it to our seniors and we owe it to those of us who are going to be seniors to have a modern Medicare system.

For the sake of our health care system, we need to cut down on the frivolous lawsuits which increase the cost of medicine. People who have been harmed by a bad doc deserve their day in court. Yet the system should not reward lawyers who are simply fishing for a rich settlement. Frivolous lawsuits drive up the cost of health care, and they therefore affect the Federal budget. Medical liability reform is a national issue which requires a national solution. The House of Representatives passed a good bill. It is stuck in the United States

Senate. Senators must realize that no one has ever been healed by a frivolous lawsuit.

I have a responsibility as the President to make sure the judicial system runs well, and I have met that duty. I have nominated superb men and women to the Federal courts, people who will interpret the law, not legislate from the bench. I have nominated really good, honest people like Bill Pryor. Bill Pryor will make a fantastic judge on the court of appeals. Because of a small group of Senators who are willfully obstructing the process, some of my nominees, like Bill, have had to wait months, in some cases, even years, for an up-or-down vote. But needless to say, delays in the system are harming the administration of justice. They are deeply unfair to the nominees themselves. It is time for some Members of the United States Senate to stop playing politics with American justice.

The Congress needs to complete work on a comprehensive energy plan. Our Nation must promote energy efficiency. We must work to increase conservation. We must develop cleaner technology to explore for supplies of energy at home in environmentally friendly ways. But for the sake of our economic security and for the sake of our national security, we must become less dependent on foreign sources of energy.

Our strong and prosperous Nation must also be a compassionate nation. I will continue to advance our agenda of compassionate conservatism, which means we'll apply the most innovative and effective ideas to the task of helping our fellow citizens in need. There are still millions of men and women who want to end their dependence on Government and become independent through hard work. We must build on the success of welfare reform to bring work and dignity into the lives of more of our citizens.

Congress should complete the "Citizen Service Act" so that more Americans can serve their communities and their country. Both Houses should reach agreement on my Faith-Based Initiative to support the armies of compassion that are mentoring children and caring for the homeless and offering hope to the addicted. This Nation of ours—[*applause*]—Government should welcome the great work that comes out of our Christian houses and Jewish temples and Muslim institutions. We must not fear faith in our society. We must welcome faith and welcome the armies of compassion who are healing hearts and helping change America one soul at a time.

A compassionate society must provide— promote opportunity for all, and that includes the independence and dignity that come from ownership. This administration will constantly promote an ownership society in America. We want more people owning their home. We've got homeownership—a minority homeownership gap in America. I've submitted a plan to Congress to close that gap.

We want more people owning their own health care plans and managing their own health care plans. We want people to manage and own their own retirement accounts. We want more people owning their own small business. We understand that when a person owns something, he or she has a vital stake in the future of America.

In a compassionate society, people respect one another, respect their points of view, and they take responsibility for the decisions they make. The culture of America is changing from one that has said, "If it feels good, do it," and "If you've got a problem, blame somebody else," to a new culture in which each of us understands we are responsible for the decisions we make in life. If you are fortunate enough to be a mom or a dad, you're responsible for loving your child with all your heart. If you are concerned about the quality of the education in the community in which you live, you're responsible for doing something about it. If you're a CEO in corporate America, you're responsible for telling the truth to your shareholders and your employees.

And in this new responsibility society, each of us is responsible for loving our neighbor just like we'd like to be loved ourselves. We can see the culture of service and responsibility growing around us. I started what's called the USA Freedom Corps. If you're interested, you can go right on the computer and look it up. It's a chance to encourage people to extend a compassionate hand to a neighbor in need, and the response has been strong. America is a giving country. The heart and soul of the American people is really the strength of our country.

Policemen and firefighters and people who wear our Nation's uniform are reminding us what it means to sacrifice for something greater than yourself. Once again, the children of America believe in heroes because they see them every day.

In these challenging times, the world has seen the resolve and the courage of America. And I have been privileged to see the compassion and the character of the American people. All the tests of the last 2½ years have come to the right Nation. We're a strong country, and we use that strength to defend the peace. We're an optimistic country, confident in ourselves and in ideals bigger than ourselves. Abroad, we seek to lift whole nations by spreading freedom. At home, we seek to lift up lives by spreading opportunity to every corner of America. This is the work that history has set before us. We welcome it, and we know that for our country, the best days lie ahead.

God bless. Thank you all.

NOTE: The President spoke at noon at the Sheraton Birmingham Hotel. In his remarks, he referred to Senator Richard Shelby of Alabama and his wife, Annette; Mercer Reynolds, national finance chairman, and Mike Thompson, Alabama State finance chairman, Bush-Cheney '04, Inc.; Marty Connors, chairman, Alabama Republican Party; W. Edgar Welden, Sr., Alabama national committeeman, and Bettye Fine Collins, Alabama national committeewoman, Republican

National Committee; and former President
Saddam Hussein of Iraq.

Statement on Senate Passage of the "Emergency Supplemental Appropriations Act for Defense and for the Reconstruction of Iraq and Afghanistan, 2004"
November 3, 2003

I commend Congress for providing vital funds to support our mission and our troops deployed in Afghanistan, Iraq, and elsewhere. These resources, coupled with the growing assistance of international donors, will provide essential support to make Iraq more secure and to help the Iraqi people transition to self-government. The funds will also enable us to continue our efforts to help Afghanistan become a peaceful, democratic, and prosperous nation that contributes to regional stability.

Our country is being tested. Those who seek to kill coalition forces and innocent Iraqis want America and its coalition partners to run so the terrorists can reclaim control. The strong bipartisan show of support for this bill underscores that America and the world are united to prevail in the central front in the war on terror by helping build a peaceful, democratic, and prosperous Iraq.

I thank Chairmen Stevens and Young for their efforts and look forward to signing this bill.

Remarks on the California Wildfires and an Exchange With Reporters in Harbison Canyon, California
November 4, 2003

The President. A lot of people in this neighborhood lost all their possessions, but the spirit is strong. America has got some wonderful citizenry who just refuse to be defeated. I met some families here that are obviously crushed by the material loss, and they look forward to rebuilding—rebuilding their lives. And the role of government, the Federal Government and the State government and the local government, is helping as best as we can.

You know, the worst of nature can bring out the best in our fellow human beings. And to a person, they were thankful for the fact that neighbors do care about neighbors and people are helping people here.

It's just tough for a lot of folks who live in this part of the world.

I want to thank the supervisor and firefighters for welcoming us here.

Let me answer a few questions, and we'll keep going.

Q. What do you say to these people——

The President. Hold it one second, please. We've got an order——

Q. I'm sorry.

Iraq/California Wildfires

Q. Thanks, Mr. President. I've got a couple questions. One, what's your evaluation, your assessment of this scene you've seen here? And two, to more and more Americans, the situation in Iraq is looking like a hot war. Are we back to major combat operations?

The President. No, we're back to finding these terrorists and bringing them to justice. And we will continue to find the terrorists and bring them to justice. These people want to—"these people" being the terrorists and those who would kill innocent life—want us to retreat. They want us to leave, because they know that a free and peaceful Iraq in their midst will damage their cause. And we will stay the course. We will do our job.

First question?

Q. What's your—what do you see when you look at this scene here?

The President. I see more tragedy and heartache. I see the loss of a lot of material possessions. However, I see a strong spirit which exists here. I see people who are resolved to rebuild their lives. Amidst their tears, they do see hope, and that is a great tribute to the people in this part of California. This State has been devastated: Over 3,300 homes have been destroyed; 4,000-some-odd structures have been destroyed; hundreds of thousands of acres have been burned. And yet the spirit is strong. People are resolved to move on with their life, and we want to help them. That's why I'm here with Federal agencies, with the Governor and Governor-elect, as well as local officials, all of whom are determined to provide the resources necessary to help.

Iraq

Q. Mr. President, again on Iraq, sir. Are you moving to a process of Iraqification, trying to use Iraqi——

The President. What was the word?

Q. Iraqification—to accelerate the transition to the Iraqi people, instead of bringing in more international aid. Are you having trouble getting a broader——

The President. Randy, [Randall Mikkelsen, Reuters] we'll do both. We'll bring in aid from those countries that want to help. We had a very successful donors' conference. We just passed the supple-

mental yesterday. As you know, I look forward to signing it. I believe I'm going to sign it tomorrow. And it is a commitment by our Government and our country to help the Iraqis rebuild their society. And that rebuilding is part of the development of a peaceful and free Iraq. And a peaceful and free Iraq is essential to the security of the United States. This will help change the world in a positive way, so that years from now, people will sit back and say, "Thank goodness America stayed the course and did what was necessary to win this battle in the war on terror."

Q. You seem to be accelerating the process of turning it over to Iraqis. Is that correct?

The President. As you know, from the moment of liberating the country from Saddam Hussein, we have now stood up over 70,000 Iraqi citizens to be police, border patrol, and beginnings of the military, so that Iraqis will be able to run their own country. That has been our mission all along, to develop the conditions such that a free Iraq will emerge, run by the Iraqi citizens.

You remember early on, I kept saying I've got great confidence in the capacity of the Iraq people to run their own country. And it is to this Nation's advantage that there be a peaceful and free Iraq. It's in our security interests. And it will help promote world peace for Iraq to emerge as a free and peaceful country.

Edward [Ed Chen, Los Angeles Times].

California Wildfires

Q. Mr. President, clearly the residents here appreciate your coming and your seeing the devastation here. Do you bring additional help, beyond what has been announced, sir?

The President. No, what I do is I answer questions, Ed, as to whether or not the help that is available is being delivered. Hopefully, I get the truth. I mean, if there is a frustration at the Federal level, I need to know about it. I haven't heard that yet.

I've been—frankly, Mike Brown and FEMA have been getting high marks. But I want to see, as best as the President can possibly see, the truth.

First of all, I've seen the truth of the devastation of a fire. That's evident. Now I want to know whether or not the help that is available is being expedited and made available. So far the marks appear to be good. But if we're slow and if we're not doing what we need to be doing, we'll adjust and respond.

Former President Saddam Hussein's Role in Iraq

Q. You said that Saddam Hussein is no longer a menace, but there's reports that he may be behind these attacks. So how can we be sure that he is, in fact, no longer a menace?

The President. Well, he's no longer running a country. He's no longer got rape rooms, no longer raping young girls, having young girls raped because their families don't agree with them. He's no longer torturing people. He's no longer developing mass graves. Remember, we discovered thousands and thousands and thousands of men, women, and children in mass graves in Iraq. He's no longer running the—no longer threatening people, and he is no longer in power. We'll get him. We'll find him.

Q. He's not behind these attacks, though?

The President. Oh, I'm sure he's trying to stir up trouble. As I've said, Saddam loyalists, those are the people, the torturers and murders and thugs that used to benefit from Saddam Hussein's regime are the ones—some of the ones creating the havoc, trying to create the conditions so that we leave, testing our will. And I'm sure that— I don't know, look, I can't tell you what he's doing. All I can tell you is, he's not running Iraq. And all I can tell you as well, there's a lot of—some people who are upset by the fact that he's no longer in power.

Loss of Life in Iraq

Q. Mr. President, as you know, Sunday was the deadliest day in Iraq since the end of major combat. What was your reaction to the downing of the Chinook and the 16 soldiers who were killed on board? And also, should Americans be prepared for more such deadly days ahead?

The President. I am saddened any time that there's a loss of life. I'm saddened, because I know a family hurts. And there's a deep pain in somebody's heart. But I do want to remind the loved ones that their sons and daughters—or the sons in this case—died for a cause greater than themselves and a noble cause, which is the security of the United States. A free and secure Iraq is in our national security interests. We are at war.

And it's essential that the people of America not forget the lessons of September the 11th, 2001. We are vulnerable to attack. There are people that hate us, and there are people who are willing to take thousands of lives in acts of tremendous violence. And the United States must understand that and adjust to the new realities. And part of that reality is defeating terrorism and defeating the terrorists.

And that's precisely what the loved ones who died on that day were doing. They were making America more secure. And I want to thank their families for the ultimate sacrifice.

Yes, ma'am. You've been very patient, unlike some of the others in the press corps——

Q. Well, they took all my questions.

The President. ——that's the case.

California Wildfires

Q. No, I'm kidding. You've had a chance to talk to a few of the families here. You know, I live here so I've seen the destruction, as I'm seeing it firsthand here for the first time. How do you continue to get these—give these folks hope? I mean, sometimes we're giving up.

The President. That's a really good question. The best thing I can do is to listen and hug and empathize as best as I can empathize. It's very difficult for me to put myself in their position, because it's their home and their possessions. As the lady just said, she said, "All my pictures are gone. All my memories have been destroyed in one act of nature." And it is a sad moment for me to hear that.

On the other hand, best as I possibly can, I try to encourage her and lift up her spirit by reminding her that some of the most precious things are still there, her husband, her daughter, who is, by the way, serving in the United States military. This was the lady up here with whom hopefully she'll be reunited soon and can hug and kiss and love.

But it's a very sad moment to listen to the stories of those who are obviously devastated by what has taken place. And all our jobs, for those of us who are still standing, have got our lives intact, is to comfort and provide comfort and help.

I met a lady at the airport when I landed at Miramar. She's a Red Cross volunteer. She spent 100 hours this week helping people who hurt. And I suspect the citizens here who are—at the darkest moments will find light when a fellow citizen loves them. And the response, as I understand, in this neighborhood had been terrific, where people have come together and they want to help their—help their fellow citizens.

Okay, listen, thank you all.

NOTE: The President spoke at 9:37 a.m. In his remarks, he referred to Governor Gray Davis and Governor-elect Arnold Schwarzenegger of California; Dianne Jacob, supervisor, second district, County of San Diego; former President Saddam Hussein of Iraq; Mike Brown, Under Secretary for Emergency Preparedness and Response, Department of Homeland Security; and Red Cross volunteer Suellen Mayberry. A tape was not available for verification of the content of these remarks.

Remarks to Off-Duty Firefighters and Volunteers in El Cajon, California
November 4, 2003

The President. Thank you all. Thanks for such a warm greeting. I want to say a couple of things. First, I want to say it's a great pleasure to be in the presence of people who have dedicated their lives to saving life, people who have heard a call, and the call is to serve something greater than yourself.

And I saw firsthand the—Governor Davis and Governor-elect Schwarzenegger and I saw firsthand what it means for people to draw a line in the sand and say, "This fire is not getting any farther." We saw devastation on one side—and for those victims, we send our prayers and our love—but we saw what heroic efforts meant, for people who said, "We're not going to yield." And

we're here, first and foremost, to thank you all for setting such a great example and for serving your community and for saving lives. There's no better calling, is there? God bless you for that. Thank you.

I want to thank all the State officials who are working hard. See, one of the things I'm looking for is to make sure that there's good cooperation between the Federal Government and the State government and the local firefighters. I want to make sure FEMA is doing its job. Sometimes the President gets the Cook's tour, if you know what I mean. [*Laughter*] I'm interested in hearing the truth, and I believe I've been told the truth and that there has been good coordination. And if we need to learn any lessons, we'll learn the lessons.

But I want to thank you all for not only fighting the fires, but I want to thank those who are now responsible for helping rebuild lives, for the quick response—to answer people's questions and to make those State and Federal loans and grants available quickly to the communities that have been hurt. I want to thank all the local officials who are here, the mayors and the supervisors, the fire chiefs, everybody who is serving their community. Thanks for coming. Thanks for giving us a chance to praise your efforts.

As well I want to thank the leaders of the tribal nations who are here, the Members of the United States Congress. I suspected that they might be here because they want a nice ride back to Washington. [*Laughter*] But then I realized that they care deeply about the people whose lives have been upset. After all, Duncan Hunter—Congressman Hunter lost his own home in the fire.

He reflected the spirit, by the way, of the people who we've met. He said, "Don't worry about me. I'm going to rebuild. You don't have to worry about me, Mr. President. I'm going to rally. I'm going to pick up my life and move it on." And those are the citizens I met today, up in this valley where this fire just came roaring through like a chimney. All their possessions were gone, but to the person, their spirit was strong and able. They said, "God is on my side," one family said. I said, "We heard."

I want to thank Bill Clayton. Mike Simpson——

Audience member. Woo-hoo!

The President. Yes. Mike, I'm glad your sister came. [*Laughter*] I want to thank Chief Jeff Bowman, Bill McCammon, Chief Bill McCammon, and Chief Ernie Mitchell for the briefing we had today, to see the scope and the size of this massive amount of destruction that took place. I think when people realize the scope of the fires, the

historic nature of these fires, they'll realize what a superhuman effort you all put in to save lives. This is, to me, an ultimate act of sacrifice.

I do want to pay tribute and homage to Steve Rucker. Steve's fire chief said he wasn't sent there; he asked to go. And that's the spirit of a lot of the people here we're looking at. You weren't sent there; you asked to go. You've heard a call, and you've responded, and you put your life at risk. To Steve's family, we send our deepest condolences and prayers to his comrades. We thank you for honoring his fallen memory. May God bless him, and may God bless his loved ones as well.

When I landed at Miramar—and by the way, the fire was right up there to the runway—I met a lady named Sue Mayberry. She's a Red Cross volunteer. This week, she volunteered 100 hours of her time to help people who hurt. She set up an emergency shelter at a high school or a school in Ramona. And then the fires came roaring toward Ramona. So she and others moved 550 families safely to Julian.

The reason I bring up Sue is there are a lot of people who are deeply concerned about the 27,000 displaced persons. There are people in your communities, when they hear that over 3,300 homes have been destroyed, they want to do something about it. They want to help a neighbor in need.

And so for all the great citizens of this wonderful State who have heard the call to love a neighbor just like you would like to be loved yourself, who, when they see somebody who hurts, are willing to put their arm around a neighbor in need, I want to thank you from the bottom of our collective hearts.

There are a lot of citizens who wonder what tomorrow is going to be like. And when a citizen provides a ray of hope, just a little bit of love, it brightens that person's future. It's amazing what nature has—we've seen the worst of nature. But when you go to these communities and you realize what's taken place, you see the absolute best of mankind.

For Californians who want to help, please do. Please know that some of your citizens hurt. Please help them any way you can. The Federal Government's response is needed and necessary. I brought officials with me just to make sure it's active and vibrant. The State's response is needed and necessary. But the truth of the matter is, the best response is the response you hear from the citizens whose lives have been affected, the response—the refusal to give up, the notion that tomorrow can be a better day, the refusal to be defeated. And after all, that is the spirit of America, isn't it? It's a fabulous country because of the people who make up this country. And it's my honor to represent this country.

May God bless you all, and may God bless California, and may God bless America. Thank you all very much.

NOTE: The President spoke at 11:09 a.m. at Gillespie Field. In his remarks, he referred to Governor Gray Davis and Governor-elect Arnold Schwarzenegger of California; Bill Clayton, division chief, California Department of Forestry; Mike Simpson, captain, San Diego County Rural Fire District; Jeff Bowman, fire chief, San Diego Fire-Rescue Department; William J. McCammon, chief, Alameda County Fire Department; Ernest Mitchell, chief, Pasadena Fire Department; and Steven L. Rucker, engineer, Novato Fire Protection District, who died on October 29 in San Diego County.

Remarks on Signing the Partial-Birth Abortion Ban Act of 2003
November 5, 2003

The President. Thank you very much. Good afternoon. I'm pleased that all of you have joined us as the Partial-Birth Abortion Ban Act of 2003 becomes the law of the land. For years, a terrible form of violence has been directed against children who are inches from birth, while the law looked the other way. Today, at last, the American people and our Government have confronted the violence and come to the defense of the innocent child.

I want to thank you all for coming. Many of you have worked long and hard to see this bill come to fruition, and we thank you for your efforts.

Audience member. Thank you, Mr. President.

The President. I see some members of my Cabinet have come. I appreciate the good work of the Attorney General, John Ashcroft. Secretary of the Department of Health and Human Services Tommy Thompson is here. Thank you, Tommy.

There are a lot of Members of the Senate and House here today. I want to thank you all for passing this important legislation. I'm glad you're here. The primary Senate sponsor is with us, Senator Rick Santorum. Senator Orrin Hatch and Senator Mike DeWine helped as well in the Senate. Thank you all very much. Steve Chabot was the primary House sponsor, and Steve is with us. Thanks for coming, Steve. I'm thankful that our Speaker is with us today. Mr. Speaker, I appreciate you coming. The majority leader, Tom DeLay, as well—thank you for coming, Tom. I'd like to mention three other Members of the House. Henry Hyde is with us today. Mr. Chairman, we appreciate you coming. Jim Oberstar is with us. Jim, thank you for being here, sir. I appreciate you coming. Bart Stupak from Michigan is with us as well. Thanks for coming, Bart, glad you're here.

I appreciate His Eminence, Cardinal Egan, who's with us today. Thank you very much, sir.

In passing this legislation, Members of the House and Senate made a studied decision based upon compelling evidence. The best case against partial-birth abortion is a simple description of what happens and to whom it happens. It involves the partial delivery of a live boy or girl and a sudden, violent end of that life. Our Nation owes its children a different and better welcome. The bill I am about to sign protecting innocent new life from this practice reflects the compassion and humanity of America.

In the course of the congressional debate, the facts became clear. Each year, thousands of partial-birth abortions are committed. As Dr. C. Everett Koop, the pediatrician and former Surgeon General, has pointed out, the majority of partial-birth abortions are not required by medical emergency. As Congress has found, the practice is widely regarded within the medical profession as unnecessary, not only cruel to the child but harmful to the mother and a violation of medical ethics.

The facts about partial-birth abortion are troubling and tragic, and no lawyer's brief can make them seem otherwise. By acting to prevent this practice, the elected branches of our Government have affirmed a basic standard of humanity, the duty of the strong to protect the weak. The wide agreement amongst men and women on this issue, regardless of political party, shows that bitterness in political debate can be overcome by compassion and the power of conscience. And the executive branch will vigorously defend this law against any who would try to overturn it in the courts.

America stands for liberty, for the pursuit of happiness, and for the unalienable right of life. And the most basic duty of Government is to defend the life of the innocent. Every person, however frail or vulnerable, has a place and a purpose in this world. Every person has a special dignity. This right to life cannot be granted or denied by Government, because it does not come from Government. It comes from the Creator of life.

In the debate about the rights of the unborn, we are asked to broaden the circle of our moral concern. We're asked to live out our calling as Americans. We're asked to honor our own standards, announced on the day of our founding in the Declaration of Independence. We're asked by our convictions and tradition and compassion to build a culture of life and make this a more just and welcoming society. And today we welcome vulnerable children into the care and protection of Americans.

The late Pennsylvania Governor Robert Casey once said that when we look to the unborn child, the real issue is not when life begins but when love begins. This is the generous and merciful spirit of our country at its best. This spirit is reflected in the Partial-Birth Abortion Ban Act of 2003, which I am now honored to sign into law.

God bless.

[*At this point, the President signed the bill.*]

The President. Thank you all.

NOTE: The President spoke at 1:40 p.m. at the Ronald Reagan Building and International Trade Center. In his remarks, he referred to Edward Cardinal Egan, Archdiocese of New York. S. 3, approved November 5, was assigned Public Law No. 108–105. The Office of the Press Secretary also released a Spanish language transcript of these remarks.

Message to the Senate Transmitting the Convention on International Interest in Mobile Equipment and the Protocol on Matters Specific to Aircraft Equipment
November 5, 2003

To the Senate of the United States:

I transmit herewith, for Senate advice and consent to ratification, the Convention on International Interest in Mobile Equipment and the Protocol on Matters Specific to Aircraft Equipment, concluded at Cape Town, South Africa, on November 16, 2001. The report of the Department of State and a chapter-by-chapter analysis are enclosed for the information of the Senate in connection with its consideration.

The essential features of the Convention and Aircraft Protocol are the establishment of an international legal framework for the creation, priority, and enforcement of security and leasing interests in mobile equipment, specifically high-value aircraft equipment (airframes, engines, and helicopters), and the creation of a worldwide International Registry where interests covered by the Convention can be registered. The Convention adopts "asset-based financing" rules, already in place in the United States, enhancing the availability of capital market financing for air carriers at lower cost. The Convention's and Protocol's finance provisions are consistent with the Uniform Commercial Code with regard to secured financing in the United States.

This new international system can significantly reduce the risk of financing, thereby increasing the availability and reducing the costs of aviation credit. As a result, air commerce and air transportation can become safer and environmentally cleaner through the acquisition of modern equipment facilitated by these instruments. The new international system should increase aerospace sales and employment, and thereby stimulate the U.S. economy.

Negotiation of the Convention and Protocol has involved close coordination between the key Federal agencies concerned with air transportation and export, including the Departments of State, Commerce, and Transportation, as well as the EXIM bank, and U.S. interests from manufacturing, finance, and export sectors.

Ratification is in the best interests of the United States. I therefore urge the Senate to give early and favorable consideration to the Cape Town Convention and Aircraft Protocol, and that the Senate promptly give its advice and consent to ratification, subject to the seven declarations set out in the accompanying report of the Department of State.

GEORGE W. BUSH

The White House,
November 5, 2003.

Remarks on the 20th Anniversary of the National Endowment for Democracy
November 6, 2003

Thank you all very much. Please be seated. Thanks for the warm welcome. Thanks for inviting me to join you in this 20th anniversary of the National Endowment for Democracy. Staff and directors of this organization have seen a lot of history over the last two decades. You've been a part of that history. By speaking for and standing for freedom, you've lifted the hopes of people around the world, and you've brought great credit to America.

I appreciate Vin for the short introduction. I'm a man who likes short introductions, and he didn't let me down. But more importantly, I appreciate the invitation. I appreciate the Members of Congress who are here, Senators from both political parties, Members of the House of Representatives from both political parties. I appreciate the ambassadors who are here. I appreciate the guests who have come. I appreciate the bipartisan spirit, the nonpartisan spirit of the National Endowment for Democracy. I'm glad that Republicans and Democrats and independents are working together to advance human liberty.

The roots of our democracy can be traced to England and to its Parliament, and so can the roots of this organization. In June of 1982, President Ronald Reagan spoke at Westminster Palace and declared the turning point had arrived in history. He argued that Soviet communism had failed precisely because it did not respect its own people, their creativity, their genius, and their rights. President Reagan said that the day of Soviet tyranny was passing, that freedom had a momentum which would not be halted. He gave this organization its mandate: to add to the momentum of freedom across the world. Your mandate was important 20 years ago. It is equally important today.

A number of critics were dismissive of that speech by the President. According to one editorial of the time, "It seems hard to be a sophisticated European and also an admirer of Ronald Reagan." [*Laughter*] Some observers on both sides of the Atlantic pronounced the speech simplistic and naive and even dangerous. In fact, Ronald Reagan's words were courageous and optimistic and entirely correct.

The great democratic movement President Reagan described was already well underway. In the early 1970s, there were about 40 democracies in the world. By the middle of that decade, Portugal and Spain and Greece held free elections. Soon there were new democracies in Latin America, and free institutions were spreading in Korea, in Taiwan, and in East Asia. This very week in 1989, there were protests in East Berlin and in Leipzig. By the end of that year, every communist dictatorship in Central Europe° had collapsed. Within another year, the South African Government released Nelson Mandela. Four years later, he was elected President of his country, ascending, like Walesa and Havel, from prisoner of state to head of state.

As the 20th century ended, there were around 120 democracies in the world, and I can assure you, more are on the way. Ronald Reagan would be pleased, and he would not be surprised.

We've witnessed, in little over a generation, the swiftest advance of freedom in the 2,500-year story of democracy. Historians in the future will offer their own explanations for why this happened. Yet we already know some of the reasons they will cite. It is no accident that the rise of so many democracies took place in a time when the world's most influential nation was itself a democracy.

The United States made military and moral commitments in Europe and Asia which protected free nations from aggression and created the conditions in which new democracies could flourish. As we provided security for whole nations, we also provided inspiration for oppressed peoples. In prison camps, in banned union meetings, in clandestine churches, men and women knew that the whole world was not sharing their own nightmare. They knew of at least one place, a bright and hopeful land where freedom was valued and secure, and they prayed that America would not forget them or forget the mission to promote liberty around the world.

Historians will note that in many nations, the advance of markets and free enterprise

---

° White House correction.

helped to create a middle class that was confident enough to demand their own rights. They will point to the role of technology in frustrating censorship and central control and marvel at the power of instant communications to spread the truth, the news, and courage across borders.

Historians in the future will reflect on an extraordinary, undeniable fact: Over time, free nations grow stronger, and dictatorships grow weaker. In the middle of the 20th century, some imagined that the central planning and social regimentation were a shortcut to national strength. In fact, the prosperity and social vitality and technological progress of a people are directly determined by the extent of their liberty. Freedom honors and unleashes human creativity, and creativity determines the strength and wealth of nations. Liberty is both the plan of heaven for humanity and the best hope for progress here on Earth.

The progress of liberty is a powerful trend. Yet, we also know that liberty, if not defended, can be lost. The success of freedom is not determined by some dialectic of history. By definition, the success of freedom rests upon the choices and the courage of free peoples and upon their willingness to sacrifice. In the trenches of World War I, through a two-front war in the 1940s, the difficult battles of Korea and Vietnam, and in missions of rescue and liberation on nearly every continent, Americans have amply displayed our willingness to sacrifice for liberty.

The sacrifices of Americans have not always been recognized or appreciated, yet they have been worthwhile. Because we and our allies were steadfast, Germany and Japan are democratic nations that no longer threaten the world. A global nuclear standoff with the Soviet Union ended peacefully, as did the Soviet Union. The nations of Europe are moving towards unity, not dividing into armed camps and descending into genocide. Every nation has learned or should have learned an important lesson: Freedom is worth fighting for, dying for,

and standing for, and the advance of freedom leads to peace.

And now we must apply that lesson in our own time. We've reached another great turning point, and the resolve we show will shape the next stage of the world democratic movement.

Our commitment to democracy is tested in countries like Cuba and Burma and North Korea and Zimbabwe, outposts of oppression in our world. The people in these nations live in captivity and fear and silence. Yet, these regimes cannot hold back freedom forever, and one day, from prison camps and prison cells and from exile, the leaders of new democracies will arrive. Communism and militarism and rule by the capricious and corrupt are the relics of a passing era. And we will stand with these oppressed peoples until the day of liberation and freedom finally arrives.

Our commitment to democracy is tested in China. That nation now has a sliver, a fragment of liberty. Yet, China's people will eventually want their liberty pure and whole. China has discovered that economic freedom leads to national wealth. China's leaders will also discover that freedom is indivisible, that social and religious freedom is also essential to national greatness and national dignity. Eventually, men and women who are allowed to control their own wealth will insist on controlling their own lives and their own country.

Our commitment to democracy is also tested in the Middle East, which is my focus today and must be a focus of American policy for decades to come. In many nations of the Middle East, countries of great strategic importance, democracy has not yet taken root. And the questions arise: Are the peoples of the Middle East somehow beyond the reach of liberty? Are millions of men and women and children condemned by history or culture to live in despotism? Are they alone never to know freedom and never even to have a choice in the matter? I for one do not believe it. I believe every person has the ability and the right to be free.

Some skeptics of democracy assert that the traditions of Islam are inhospitable to the representative government. This "cultural condescension," as Ronald Reagan termed it, has a long history. After the Japanese surrender in 1945, a so-called Japan expert asserted that democracy in that former empire would, quote, "never work." Another observer declared the prospects for democracy in post-Hitler Germany are, and I quote, "most uncertain at best." He made that claim in 1957. Seventy-four years ago, the Sunday London Times declared nine-tenths of the population of India to be, quote, "illiterates not caring a fig for politics." Yet when Indian democracy was imperiled in the 1970s, the Indian people showed their commitment to liberty in a national referendum that saved their form of government.

Time after time, observers have questioned whether this country or that people or this group are ready for democracy, as if freedom were a prize you win for meeting our own Western standards of progress. In fact, the daily work of democracy itself is the path of progress. It teaches cooperation, the free exchange of ideas, and the peaceful resolution of differences. As men and women are showing from Bangladesh to Botswana to Mongolia, it is the practice of democracy that makes a nation ready for democracy, and every nation can start on this path.

It should be clear to all that Islam, the faith of one-fifth of humanity, is consistent with democratic rule. Democratic progress is found in many predominantly Muslim countries, in Turkey and Indonesia and Senegal and Albania, in Niger and Sierra Leone. Muslim men and women are good citizens of India and South Africa, of the nations of Western Europe, and of the United States of America.

More than half of all Muslims in the world live in freedom under democratically constituted governments. They succeed in democratic societies, not in spite of their faith but because of it. A religion that demands individual moral accountability and encourages the encounter of the individual with God is fully compatible with the rights and responsibilities of self-government.

Yet there's a great challenge today in the Middle East. In the words of a recent report by Arab scholars, the global wave of democracy has, and I quote, "barely reached the Arab states." They continue: "This freedom deficit undermines human development and is one of the most painful manifestations of lagging political development." The freedom deficit they describe has terrible consequences for the people of the Middle East and for the world. In many Middle Eastern countries, poverty is deep, and it is spreading. Women lack rights and are denied schooling. Whole societies remain stagnant while the world moves ahead. These are not the failures of a culture or a religion. These are the failures of political and economic doctrines.

As the colonial era passed away, the Middle East saw the establishment of many military dictatorships. Some rulers adopted the dogmas of socialism, seized total control of political parties and the media and universities. They allied themselves with the Soviet bloc and with international terrorism. Dictators in Iraq and Syria promised the restoration of national honor, a return to ancient glories. They've left instead a legacy of torture, oppression, misery, and ruin.

Other men and groups of men have gained influence in the Middle East and beyond through an ideology of theocratic terror. Behind their language of religion is the ambition for absolute political power. Ruling cabals like the Taliban show their version of religious piety in public whippings of women, ruthless suppression of any difference or dissent, and support for terrorists who arm and train to murder the innocent. The Taliban promised religious purity and national pride. Instead, by systematically destroying a proud and working society, they left behind suffering and starvation.

Many Middle Eastern governments now understand that military dictatorship and theocratic rule are a straight, smooth highway to nowhere. But some governments still cling to the old habits of central control. There are governments that still fear and repress independent thought and creativity and private enterprise, the human qualities that make for a strong and successful societies. Even when these nations have vast natural resources, they do not respect or develop their greatest resources, the talent and energy of men and women working and living in freedom.

Instead of dwelling on past wrongs and blaming others, governments in the Middle East need to confront real problems and serve the true interests of their nations. The good and capable people of the Middle East all deserve responsible leadership. For too long, many people in that region have been victims and subjects. They deserve to be active citizens.

Governments across the Middle East and north Africa are beginning to see the need for change. Morocco has a diverse new Parliament. King Mohamed has urged it to extend the rights to women. Here is how His Majesty explained his reforms to Parliament: "How can society achieve progress while women, who represent half the nation, see their rights violated and suffer as a result of injustice, violence, and marginalization, notwithstanding the dignity and justice granted to them by our glorious religion?" The King of Morocco is correct: The future of Muslim nations will be better for all with the full participation of women.

In Bahrain last year, citizens elected their own Parliament for the first time in nearly three decades. Oman has extended the vote to all adult citizens. Qatar has a new constitution. Yemen has a multiparty political system. Kuwait has a directly elected national assembly, and Jordan held historic elections this summer. Recent surveys in

Arab nations reveal broad support for political pluralism, the rule of law, and free speech. These are the stirrings of Middle Eastern democracy, and they carry the promise of greater change to come.

As changes come to the Middle Eastern region, those with power should ask themselves: Will they be remembered for resisting reform or for leading it? In Iran, the demand for democracy is strong and broad, as we saw last month when thousands gathered to welcome home Shirin Ebadi, the winner of the Nobel Peace Prize. The regime in Tehran must heed the democratic demands of the Iranian people or lose its last claim to legitimacy.

For the Palestinian people, the only path to independence and dignity and progress is the path of democracy. And the Palestinian leaders who block and undermine democratic reform and feed hatred and encourage violence are not leaders at all. They're the main obstacles to peace and to the success of the Palestinian people.

The Saudi Government is taking first steps toward reform, including a plan for gradual introduction of elections. By giving the Saudi people a greater role in their own society, the Saudi Government can demonstrate true leadership in the region.

The great and proud nation of Egypt has shown the way toward peace in the Middle East and now should show the way toward democracy in the Middle East. Champions of democracy in the region understand that democracy is not perfect. It is not the path to utopia, but it's the only path to national success and dignity.

As we watch and encourage reforms in the region, we are mindful that modernization is not the same as Westernization. Representative governments in the Middle East will reflect their own cultures. They will not and should not look like us. Democratic nations may be constitutional monarchies, federal republics, or parliamentary systems. And working democracies always need time to develop, as did our own.

We've taken a 200-year journey toward inclusion and justice, and this makes us patient and understanding as other nations are at different stages of this journey.

There are, however, essential principles common to every successful society in every culture. Successful societies limit the power of the state and the power of the military, so that governments respond to the will of the people and not the will of the elite. Successful societies protect freedom with the consistent and impartial rule of law, instead of selectively applying the law to punish political opponents. Successful societies allow room for healthy civic institutions, for political parties and labor unions and independent newspapers and broadcast media. Successful societies guarantee religious liberty, the right to serve and honor God without fear of persecution. Successful societies privatize their economies and secure the rights of property. They prohibit and punish official corruption and invest in the health and education of their people. They recognize the rights of women. And instead of directing hatred and resentment against others, successful societies appeal to the hopes of their own people.

These vital principles are being applied in the nations of Afghanistan and Iraq. With the steady leadership of President Karzai, the people of Afghanistan are building a modern and peaceful Government. Next month, 500 delegates will convene a national assembly in Kabul to approve a new Afghan constitution. The proposed draft would establish a bicameral Parliament, set national elections next year, and recognize Afghanistan's Muslim identity while protecting the rights of all citizens. Afghanistan faces continuing economic and security challenges. It will face those challenges as a free and stable democracy.

In Iraq, the Coalition Provisional Authority and the Iraqi Governing Council are also working together to build a democracy, and after three decades of tyranny, this work is not easy. The former dictator ruled by terror and treachery and left deeply ingrained habits of fear and distrust. Remnants of his regime, joined by foreign terrorists, continue their battle against order and against civilization. Our coalition is responding to recent attacks with precision raids, guided by intelligence provided by the Iraqis themselves. And we're working closely with Iraqi citizens as they prepare a constitution, as they move toward free elections and take increasing responsibility for their own affairs. As in the defense of Greece in 1947 and later in the Berlin airlift, the strength and will of free peoples are now being tested before a watching world. And we will meet this test.

Securing democracy in Iraq is the work of many hands. American and coalition forces are sacrificing for the peace of Iraq and for the security of free nations. Aid workers from many countries are facing danger to help the Iraqi people. The National Endowment for Democracy is promoting women's rights and training Iraqi journalists and teaching the skills of political participation. Iraqis themselves, police and border guards and local officials, are joining in the work, and they are sharing in the sacrifice.

This is a massive and difficult undertaking. It is worth our effort. It is worth our sacrifice, because we know the stakes. The failure of Iraqi democracy would embolden terrorists around the world, increase dangers to the American people, and extinguish the hopes of millions in the region. Iraqi democracy will succeed, and that success will send forth the news, from Damascus to Tehran, that freedom can be the future of every nation. The establishment of a free Iraq at the heart of the Middle East will be a watershed event in the global democratic revolution.

Sixty years of Western nations excusing and accommodating the lack of freedom in the Middle East did nothing to make us safe, because in the long run, stability cannot be purchased at the expense of liberty. As long as the Middle East remains a place where freedom does not flourish, it will remain a place of stagnation, resentment, and violence ready for export. And with the spread of weapons that can bring catastrophic harm to our country and to our friends, it would be reckless to accept the status quo.

Therefore, the United States has adopted a new policy, a forward strategy of freedom in the Middle East. This strategy requires the same persistence and energy and idealism we have shown before, and it will yield the same results. As in Europe, as in Asia, as in every region of the world, the advance of freedom leads to peace.

The advance of freedom is the calling of our time. It is the calling of our country. From the Fourteen Points to the four freedoms to the speech at Westminster, America has put our power at the service of principle. We believe that liberty is the design of nature. We believe that liberty is the direction of history. We believe that human fulfillment and excellence come in the responsible exercise of liberty. And we believe that freedom, the freedom we prize, is not for us alone; it is the right and the capacity of all mankind.

Working for the spread of freedom can be hard. Yet, America has accomplished hard tasks before. Our Nation is strong. We're strong of heart, and we're not alone. Freedom is finding allies in every country. Freedom finds allies in every culture. And as we meet the terror and violence of the world, we can be certain the Author of freedom is not indifferent to the fate of freedom.

With all the tests and all the challenges of our age, this is, above all, the age of liberty. Each of you at this endowment is fully engaged in the great cause of liberty, and I thank you. May God bless your work, and may God continue to bless America.

NOTE: The President spoke at 11:05 a.m. in the Hall of Flags at the U.S. Chamber of Commerce. In his remarks, he referred to Vin Weber, chairman, National Endowment for Democracy; former President Lech Walesa of Poland; former President Vaclav Havel of the Czech Republic; King Mohamed VI of Morocco; President Hamid Karzai of Afghanistan; and former President Saddam Hussein of Iraq. The Office of the Press Secretary also released a Spanish language transcript of these remarks.

Remarks on Signing the Emergency Supplemental Appropriations Act for Defense and for the Reconstruction of Iraq and Afghanistan, 2004
November 6, 2003

Thank you all for coming. Good afternoon, and welcome to the White House. On September the 11th, 2001, America grieved for our losses, and we made a commitment. We determined to conduct the war against terror on the offensive. We determined to confront and undermine threats abroad before they arrive in our own cities.

We're waging this war in relentless pursuit of the Al Qaida network. We're waging this war in Afghanistan against Taliban remnants and Al Qaida killers. We're waging this war in Iraq against Saddam loyalists and foreign terrorists who seek the return of tyranny and terror. We're pursuing long-term victory in this war by promoting democracy in the Middle East so that the nations of that region no longer breed hatred and terror.

Today the United States is making a critical financial commitment to this global strategy to defeat terror. We're supporting our service men and women in the field of battle. We're supporting reconstruction and the emergence of democratic institutions in a vital area of the world.

The American people accept these responsibilities now, in our time, so that we will not face far greater dangers in the future. With this act of Congress, no enemy or friend can doubt that America has the resources and the will to see this war through to victory.

I want to thank our Secretary of State, Colin Powell, and Secretary of Defense, Don Rumsfeld, for their extraordinary leadership during these tough times. I appreciate Deputy Secretary Rich Armitage, Deputy Secretary Paul Wolfowitz for joining us today as well. Thank you all for coming.

Josh Bolten, a member of my Cabinet, the Director of the Office of Management and Budget—the keeper of the money—is with us. Andrew Natsios, the Administrator of the USAID, is with us today. Andrew, thank you for coming. There he is, right there.

I appreciate the leadership of the Congress being here today. Speaker Denny Hastert and Leader Bill Frist are with us. Thank you all for coming. Thank you for your strong leadership.

I also want to pay a particular mention to Chairman Ted Stevens and Chairman Bill Young for doing a fabulous job on a very tough issue. Thank you very much.

There are a lot of Members of the Senate and House with us. Thank you all for coming, for making a good, courageous vote. I particularly want to pay homage to Mitch McConnell of Kentucky for his leadership on the floor, Jerry Lewis from California, and Norm Dicks from Washington for supporting your chairman and getting this bill out.

I want to thank the military and civilian staff members of the Coalition Provisional Authority who are with us. Thank you for serving our country. We appreciate the sacrifices you are making.

Today, in Iraq and Afghanistan, the world sees a test of will and a clash of strategies. The strategy of our enemies, whether Al Qaida, Ba'athist, Taliban, or others, is to intimidate newly free men and women who are trying to establish democracy and to cause America and our allies to flee our responsibilities. Their goal is to halt and reverse all progress toward freedom in the Middle East, to reinstate permanently the rule of fear and oppression.

The strategy of America and our allies is equally clear. We are employing targeted and decisive force against the killers. We're training and equipping Iraqis and Afghans to defend their own nations. We're helping the Iraqi and Afghan people build just and democratic governments. And we will meet our duties until the job is done.

The terrorists and their supporters have had many setbacks in the last 2 years. They have lost many leaders, many training camps, and two countries, and we will not relent until they are fully and finally defeated.

The legislation I'm about to sign commits $87 billion to America's global offensive against terror. More than $65 billion of these new funds will pay for ongoing military operations. We're supporting such basic military necessities as air, rail, and sea transportation for American and coalition troops to the theaters of action.

We will purchase ammunition for our weapons and fuel and spare parts for airplanes and helicopters and vehicles. We will replace equipment lost or damaged in combat. We'll acquire vital new equipment, such as armored humvees and body armor and communications gear. Our service men and women are carrying out their missions with skill and honor, and they deserve the finest equipment and best weapons we can provide.

This legislation contains needed funds to pay our soldiers, sailors, airmen, and marines, including the additional pay our forces receive for hazardous duty. We will also cover the salaries of National Guard and Reserve troops who have left jobs and homes and families in an hour of national need. The American Government will keep its responsibilities to all who risk their lives for America.

This legislation also includes nearly $20 billion to help build stable democratic societies in Iraq and Afghanistan. We will help train and equip the growing number of Iraqis and Afghans who are fighting and dying to defend and secure their rights. We'll help to upgrade hospitals and schools and repair infrastructure and improve basic services, including water, electricity, and sanitation.

Our investment in the future of Afghanistan and Iraq is the greatest commitment of its kind since the Marshall plan. By this action, we show the generous spirit of our country, and we serve the interest of our country, because our security is at stake. The Middle East region will either become a place of progress and peace, or it will remain a source of violence and terror. And we're determined to see the triumph of progress and the triumph of peace in that region. We will do all in our power to ensure that freedom finds a lasting home in Afghanistan and in Iraq.

We know this will require patience and sacrifice. I just had the honor of meeting PFC Phillip Ramsey and SPC Alex Leonard, two brave Americans who were wounded in action. We thank you for your service.

Recent attacks have shown once again the cruelty of the enemy. They don't care whose lives they take, men, women, or children. They're coldblooded. They're heartless. We're engaged in a massive and dif-

ficult undertaking, but America has done this kind of hard work before.

After World War II, we made long-term commitments to the transformation of Germany and Japan so that those nations would not be sources of war but our partners in peace. That investment in peace has been repaid many times over. Now our generation will show the same perseverance and the same vision in the cause of peace.

I appreciate the solid bipartisan support for this bill in the House and the Senate. I also appreciate that reconstruction funds for Iraq have been provided in the form of grants so that this struggling nation is not burdened with new debt at a moment of new hope.

The establishment of a free Iraq and a free Afghanistan will be watershed events in the history of the Middle East, watershed events in the global democratic revolution that has already transformed Europe and Latin America and much of Africa and Asia. The resources we commit today will further advance the cause of freedom, thereby serving the cause of peace and enhancing the security of the American people.

Now I'm pleased to sign into law the Iraq and Afghanistan supplemental appropriations bill.

NOTE: The President spoke at 1:12 p.m. in the East Room at the White House. In his remarks, he referred to former President Saddam Hussein of Iraq. H.R. 3289, approved November 6, was assigned Public Law No. 108–106.

Statement on Signing the Emergency Supplemental Appropriations Act for Defense and for the Reconstruction of Iraq and Afghanistan, 2004
November 6, 2003

Today, I have signed into law H.R. 3289, the "Emergency Supplemental Appropria-

tions Act for Defense and for the Reconstruction of Iraq and Afghanistan, 2004."

The Act supports our mission and our troops deployed in Iraq, Afghanistan, and elsewhere, which will better secure the safety of America and the world.

Sections 1108 and 1113 of the Act prohibit the use of appropriated funds for certain activities unless the congressional defense committees receive advance notice. Although such advance notice can be provided in most situations as a matter of comity, situations may arise in which the President must act promptly pursuant to his constitutional responsibilities while protecting certain extraordinarily sensitive national security information. The executive branch shall construe these sections in a manner consistent with the constitutional authority of the President to classify and control access to information bearing on the national security.

The Act incorrectly refers to the Coalition Provisional Authority (CPA) as if it were established pursuant to U.N. Security Council resolutions. The executive branch shall construe the provision to refer to the CPA as established under the laws of war for the occupation of Iraq.

Section 2203(b)(2)(C) requires executive agency heads to furnish certain reports to the chairman and ranking minority member of "[e]ach committee that the head of the executive agency determines has legislative jurisdiction for the operations of such department or agency to which the information related." The executive branch shall, as a matter of comity and for the very narrow purpose of determining to whom an agency will submit the report under this provision, determine the legislative jurisdiction of congressional committees.

Section 2215(b)(4) of the Act calls for a report on "the progress being made toward indicting and trying leaders of the former Iraqi regime for" specified crimes.

The executive branch shall construe the provision as calling for a report on the activities of the relevant systems of justice, and not on whether any given individual has committed any of the enumerated crimes, which is a matter to be determined by an appropriate tribunal according to applicable law.

Title III of the Act creates an Inspector General (IG) of the CPA. Title III shall be construed in a manner consistent with the President's constitutional authorities to conduct the Nation's foreign affairs, to supervise the unitary executive branch, and as Commander in Chief of the Armed Forces. The CPA IG shall refrain from initiating, carrying out, or completing an audit or investigation, or from issuing a subpoena, which requires access to sensitive operation plans, intelligence matters, counterintelligence matters, ongoing criminal investigations by other administrative units of the Department of Defense related to national security, or other matters the disclosure of which would constitute a serious threat to national security. The Secretary of Defense may make exceptions to the foregoing direction in the public interest.

Provisions of the Act that require disclosure of information, including section 3001(h)(4)(B) of the Act, shall be construed in a manner consistent with the President's constitutional authority to withhold information that could impair foreign relations, national security, the deliberative processes of the Executive, or the performance of the Executive's constitutional duties.

GEORGE W. BUSH

The White House,
November 6, 2003.

NOTE: H.R. 3289, approved November 6, was assigned Public Law No. 108–106.

Remarks on Presenting the National Medals of Science and Technology
November 6, 2003

Thank you all very much. Please be seated. Welcome to the White House. I'm pleased to be in such distinguished company here in the East Room. I want to congratulate our honorees, and I want to welcome your families and friends.

Each year, our Nation honors outstanding work in science and technology. These honorees have given exceptional service in their fields and bring great credit to themselves and credit to our country. Today we express America's pride in their achievement and our respect for these national laureates of science and technology.

I want to thank Sam Bodman, who is the Deputy Secretary of the Department of Commerce, for joining us. I thank Phil Bond, who is the Under Secretary of Technology for the Department of Commerce. I want to thank the Director of the Office of Science and Technology Policy for the President, Dr. John Marburger, for being here. Arden Bement is the Director of the National Institute of Standards and Technology; thank you, sir. Rita Colwell is the Director of the National Science Foundation. John Bordogna is the Deputy Director of the National Science Foundation. Thank you all for coming.

I want to thank the panelists who selected this outstanding group of laureates for their hard work. We've got two Members of the United States Senate with us today, members from the mighty Delaware delegation. [*Laughter*] Joe Biden and Tom Carper, welcome. Thank you all for coming, appreciate you being here.

We've got students from Benjamin Banneker High School with us today. I found it very interesting and wise that the students met one-on-one with each of the laureates to help develop their interest in science. Thank you for not only being scholars and pioneers but teachers as well.

The National Medal of Science honors pioneering scientific research that has enhanced our basic understanding of life and the world around us. The National Medal of Technology recognizes the achievements of men and women who embody the spirit of American innovation and have enhanced the Nation's global competitiveness. Both these medals are authorized by acts of Congress. They're the highest honors the President can bestow for attainment in science and technology.

The men and women we honor today probably didn't begin their careers with the expectation of receiving such honors. Most great achievers in the fields of science and technology have a sense of calling. They're drawn to the work by their curiosity and by their talent. They carry out their work with patient effort and the openness to truth that leads to discovery. The highest reward for their work is the good they do and the knowledge they leave behind.

The medals we confer today are a way of expressing our own gratitude to some of the most gifted and visionary men and women in America. The men and women are helping to enhance the Nation's health and economic prosperity. They've made their contributions to progress in a variety of fields, from physics to genetics to mathematical theory to engineering to the development of semiconductors. Some of them have made achievements beyond their own fields of endeavor, thereby showing the great potential of interdisciplinary research. Each of these recipients has set a standard of excellence. Each is widely admired by peers and sets a fine example for the next generation of scientists, mathematicians, and engineers. And all of them represent the finest qualities of their professions and the finest qualities of our country.

This great Nation provides opportunities and institutions that make achievement possible. We've got a vibrant free enterprise system. We've got the world's finest universities and generous support for scientific and technological endeavor. Yet, all the great achievements we honor today are the sum of individual effort. And when we speak of American creativity and American ingenuity, we're speaking of men and women like our national laureates of science and technology. They have freely accepted the toil of overcoming challenges.

They have put their considerable gifts to good purpose. Their fellow Americans are grateful to them. All humanity is in your debt.

And now I ask the military aide to read the citations. It's my honor to present the medals to the national laureates of science and technology.

NOTE: The President spoke at 3:04 p.m. in the East Room at the White House. Following his remarks, the President presented the medals.

Message to the Congress on Reimbursement for District of Columbia Public Safety Expenses Related to Security Events and Responses to Terrorist Threats
November 6, 2003

To the Congress of the United States:

Consistent with Division C, District of Columbia Appropriations Act of Public Law 108–7, the Consolidated Appropriations Resolution, 2003, I am notifying the Congress of the proposed use of $10,623,873 provided in Division C under the heading "Federal Payment for Emergency Planning and Security Costs in the District of Columbia." This will reimburse the District

for the costs of public safety expenses related to security events and responses to terrorist threats.

The details of this action are set forth in the enclosed letter from the Director of the Office of Management and Budget.

GEORGE W. BUSH

The White House,
November 6, 2003.

Remarks at a Bush-Cheney Luncheon in Winston-Salem, North Carolina
November 7, 2003

Thanks for your warm welcome. Thank you for coming. I appreciate you. Thanks. Thank you all. Please be seated. Listen, it is great to be back in Winston-Salem. It's a incredibly beautiful part of our country, but more beautiful are the people who live here. And I want to thank you for your friendship. I want to thank you for your support. I want to thank you for coming today. What we're doing is laying the

foundation for what will be a great national victory in November of 2004.

We had a good run in 2000, thanks to you all. And the Vice President and I expressed our deepest appreciation for the hard work you all put in in the year 2000. We'll do even better in 2004 here in North Carolina. I want to thank you for—[*applause*]. I'm loosening up. [*Laughter*] I'm getting ready, but I've got a job to do.

I've got to work on the people's business in Washington, DC. We've got a lot on the agenda, and so when you go to your coffee shops, your houses of worship, or your community centers, please tell them, Republican, Democrat, or independent alike, that the President is focused on the people's business and he will keep this Nation secure and strong and prosperous and free.

I regret that Laura isn't with me today. You drew the short straw. [*Laughter*] She's a fabulous wife, a great mother, a wonderful First Lady. I'm really proud of the job she has done. She sends our very best to our friends here in North Carolina—her very best to our friends here in North Carolina. We've got a great friend in the Culbertsons. I'm so proud to know the Culbertsons. I want to thank them for their friendship and their leadership.

I appreciate so very much traveling today with Congressman Richard Burr. He flew down on Air Force One. There isn't much air rage on Air Force One. [*Laughter*] He is going to make a great United States Senator for North Carolina. It's good to see Brooke Burr. I appreciate so very much that David Burr was here, his dad, who gave the invocation.

I'm sorry that Senator Elizabeth Dole is not here, who, by the way, is doing a really good job for the people of North Carolina. I appreciate the Senator whose place she took, a man who stood strong, a man who stood on principle, Jesse Helms. Speaking about former Senators, I know Jim Broyhill is here. I appreciate you coming, Senator. I will pass your best on to your good friend my—I will pass your best on to your good friend number 41—[*laughter*]—if you know who I'm talking about there—[*laughter*]—who, by the way, is going to jump out of an airplane on his 80th birthday. I know it—[*laughter*]—Mother had the same reaction. [*Laughter*]

I want to thank very much my friend the mayor of Charlotte, Pat McCrory, who is here with us today. Mayor, thank you

for coming. Good to see you. I know there's a lot of statehouse folks here and local government officials. I want to thank you all for being here. I appreciate your service to your great State and to your communities.

I've asked a North Carolina graduate to serve as the national finance chairman for the Bush-Cheney campaign of '04. Mercer Reynolds is doing a fantastic job of working hard on our behalf, and I want to thank Mercer for his dedication and his friendship. I also want to appreciate—appreciate Dr. Aldona Wos, the State chairman for Bush-Cheney. Thank you very much for your hard work.

We've got a lot of grassroots activists who are here, people who are actually going to get on the phone and put up the signs and lick the envelopes, all necessary to make sure that we run a vibrant campaign. I want to thank Ferrell Blount for his leadership here in North Carolina. I want to thank all the grassroots activists for what you're fixing to do when we're coming down the stretch in 2004.

Chief Linda Davis is here. I'm honored the chief is with us. I appreciate the fine job she is doing. It's not the first time I have seen the chief. I know you're proud of the job she does here in Winston-Salem. I want to thank her for coming.

But most of all, thank you all once again. It's a great turnout. It makes a fellow feel good to see so many people supporting him.

The last 2½ years, our Nation has acted decisively to confront great challenges. I came to this office to solve problems instead of passing them on to future Presidents and future generations. I came to seize opportunities instead of letting them slip away. My administration is meeting the tests of our time.

Terrorists declared war on the United States of America, and war is what they got. We've captured or killed many of the key leaders of the Al Qaida network, and the rest of them know we're on their trail.

In Afghanistan and in Iraq, we gave ultimatums to terror regimes. Those regimes chose defiance, and those regimes are no more. Fifty million people—50 million people in those countries once lived under tyranny, and today, they live in freedom.

Two-and-a-half years ago, our military was not receiving the resources it needed, and morale was beginning to suffer. So we increased the defense budgets to prepare for the threats of a new era. And today, no one in the world can doubt or question the skill or the strength or the spirit of the United States military.

Two-and-a-half years ago, we inherited an economy in recession, and then our Nation was attacked. And then we had some scandals in corporate America, and then we marched to war, war in Afghanistan and Iraq, all of which affected the people's confidence. That's tough hurdles to cross, when it came to our economy. Yet, this administration acted. We passed tough new laws to hold corporate criminals to account. And to get the economy going again, I have twice led the United States Congress to pass historic tax relief for the American people.

I know that when Americans have more take-home pay to spend, to save, or invest, the whole economy grows and people are more likely to find a job. So we're returning more money to the people to help them raise their families. We're reducing taxes on dividends and capital gains to encourage investment. We're giving small businesses incentives so they can hire new people. With all these actions, this administration has laid the foundation for greater prosperity and more jobs across America so every single citizen can realize the American Dream.

Two-and-a-half years ago, there was a lot of talk about education reform, but there wasn't much action. So I acted; I called for and Congress passed the No Child Left Behind Act. With a solid bipartisan majority, we delivered the most dramatic education reforms in a generation. We believe every child can learn to read and write and add and subtract. We expect every child to learn to read and write and add and subtract. This administration is challenging the soft bigotry of low expectations.

We dramatically increased Title I funding. For the first time, the Federal Government is now asking the question, "Are you succeeding?" We're asking the question of every single public school: whether or not we're meeting the high standards that we expect. The days of excuse-making are over. This country will stay focused on the basics to make sure every child learns to read and write and add and subtract so not one single child is left behind.

We reorganized the Government and created the Department of Homeland Security to better safeguard our ports and borders and to better protect the American people. We passed trade promotion authority to open up markets for North Carolina's farmers, ranchers, and entrepreneurs. But I understand that trade is a two-way street, that if we have trade with other neighbors and countries, we expect there to be fair trade coming the other way. We passed much needed budget agreements to help maintain spending discipline in Washington, DC.

On issue after issue, this administration has acted on principle, has kept its word, and has made progress for the American people. A lot of the credit goes to the Congress, people like Congressman Burr, people with whom we've—people like Speaker Denny Hastert, Majority Leader Bill Frist.

We're working hard to focus the town on results, not on senseless politics. There's too much politics in Washington, DC. The leadership in the administration—we're trying to set a better standard. See, the people want us there to do the business. People there want us to do what's right for the country. That's what we're working hard to do, to change that culture in Washington.

And those are the kind of people I've asked to serve in our Government. I put together a fantastic team of people from all walks of life to serve the American people. Our country has had no finer Vice President than Dick Cheney. Mother may have a second opinion. [*Laughter*]

In 2½ years, we've done a lot. We have come far, but our work is only beginning. I've set great goals worthy of a great nation. First, America is committed to expanding the realm of freedom and peace for our own security and for the benefit of the world. And second, in our own country, we must work for a society of prosperity and compassion so that every citizen, every single citizen has a chance to work and to succeed and to realize the great promise of America.

It is clear that the future of freedom and peace depend on the actions of America. This Nation is freedom's home and freedom's defender. We welcome this charge of history, and we are keeping it. The war on terror continues. The enemies of freedom aren't idle, and neither are we. This country will not rest; we will not tire; we will not stop until this danger to civilization is removed.

We are confronting that danger in Iraq, where Saddam holdouts and foreign terrorists are desperately trying to throw that country into chaos by attacking coalition forces, by attacking the people who are there to provide aid to the long-suffering Iraqi citizens, and by attacking Iraqi citizens themselves. See, they know that the advance of freedom in Iraq would be a major defeat in the cause of terror. This collection of killers is trying to shake the will of America and the civilized world, and this country will not be intimidated.

Impressively striking the terrorists in Iraq, defeating them there so we will not have to face them in our own country, we're calling on other nations to help. But you see, a free Iraq, a peaceful Iraq, a peaceful Iraq in the heart of the Middle East will make the entire world more secure.

We're standing with the Iraqi people, the very capable, competent Iraqi people, as they assume more of their own defense and as they move toward self-government. These are not easy tasks, but they are essential tasks. And we will finish what we have begun. We will win this essential victory in the war on terror.

Our greatest security comes from the advance of human liberty, because free nations do not support terror, free nations do not attack their neighbors, free nations do not threaten the world with weapons of mass terror. Americans believe that freedom is the deepest need and hope of every human heart. And I believe that freedom is the right of every person, and I believe that freedom is the future of every nation.

America also understands that unprecedented influence brings tremendous responsibilities. We have duties in this world. And when we see disease and starvation and hopeless poverty, we will not turn away. On the continent of Africa, America is now committed to bringing the healing power, the healing power of medicine to millions of men and women and children now suffering with AIDS. This great, powerful, strong, compassionate land is leading the world in this incredibly important work of human rescue.

We face challenges here at home as well, and our actions will prove equal to those challenges. So long as any of our citizens who want to work can't find a job, it says to me we've got a problem. I will continue to try to create an environment of job creation and job growth by enhancing the entrepreneurial spirit of America. We've had some good news recently about our economy. But we won't rest until everybody who wants to work can find a job.

I'm going to talk today at one of your fine community colleges about the need for us to make sure there is adequate worker training programs to train—to help train the good citizens of North Carolina for the jobs which actually exist in the State of North Carolina.

We have a duty to keep our commitment to America's seniors by strengthening and modernizing Medicare. A few weeks ago, Congress took historic action to improve the lives of older Americans. For the first time since the creation of Medicare, the House and the Senate have passed reforms, reforms which will increase the choices for our seniors, reforms which will provide coverage for prescription drugs.

The next step is for both Houses to reconcile their differences and to get a good bill to my desk. We must handle our responsibilities in Washington by making sure the Medicare system is vibrant and viable and real, not only for seniors today but for those of us who are fixing to be seniors tomorrow.

For the sake of our health care system, we need to cut down on the frivolous lawsuits which increase the cost of medicine. People who have been harmed by a bad doctor deserve their day in court. Yet the system should not reward lawyers who are simply fishing for a rich settlement. Frivolous lawsuits drive up the cost of health care, and they therefore affect the Federal budget. Medical liability reform is a national issue which requires a national solution. I put forth a good piece of legislation which passed the House of Representatives. It is stuck in the United States Senate. It is time for some of the Senators to understand that no one has ever been healed by a frivolous lawsuit. We need medical liability reform—today.

I have a responsibility as the President to make sure the judicial system runs well, and I have met that duty. I have nominated superb men and women to serve on the Federal courts, people who will interpret the law, not legislate from the bench. Here in Carolina, I nominated Judge Terry Boyle for the Fourth Circuit Court of Appeals. I nominated this good man, this man of integrity, more than 2 years ago. We're still waiting for his vote in the United States Senate because a small group of Senators is willfully obstructing the process. Too many nominees like Judge Boyle are being denied an up-or-down vote. These needless delays in the system are harming the administration of justice. They're deeply unfair to the nominees and their families themselves. It is time for some of the Members of the United States Senate to stop playing politics with American justice.

The Congress needs to complete work on a comprehensive energy plan. Our Nation must promote better energy efficiency, better conservation. We must develop clean technology to help us explore in environmentally friendly ways. But for the sake of economic security, for the sake of national security, this Nation must become less dependent on foreign sources of energy.

A prosperous nation must also be a compassionate nation. I will continue to advance our agenda of compassionate conservatism, which says we will apply the most innovative ideas, the most effective ideas to the task of helping our fellow citizens who hurt.

There are still millions of men and women who want to end their dependence on Government and become independent through hard work. We must build on the success of the welfare reform by bringing work and dignity into the lives of more of our fellow citizens. Congress should complete the "Citizen Service Act" so more Americans can serve their communities and their country.

And both Houses should reach agreement on my Faith-Based Initiative to support the armies of compassion that are mentoring our children, caring for the homeless, and offering hope to the addicted. Oftentimes, many of the problems that our citizens face are problems of the heart. And Government can hand out money, but it can't put hope in people's hearts or sense of purpose in people's lives. That's done when people from any faith put their arms around a brother and sister in need and says, "I love you." Our Government should not fear the work of our faith-based programs. We ought to welcome faith-based programs and the healing of citizens who hurt.

A compassionate society must promote opportunity for all, including the independence and dignity that come from ownership. This administration will constantly strive to promote an ownership society in America. We want more people owning their own home. Today in America, we have a minority homeownership gap. I've submitted a plan to the United States Congress to close that gap. We want more people owning and managing their own retirement accounts. We want them owning and managing their own health care accounts. We want more people owning their own small business in America. We understand that when a person owns something, he or she has a vital stake in the future of our country.

In a compassionate society, people respect each other and people take responsibility for the decisions they make. The culture of America is changing from one that has said, "If it feels good, do it," and "You got a problem, blame somebody else," to a culture in which each of us understands we are responsible for the decisions we make in life.

If you're fortunate enough to be a mom or a dad, you're responsible for loving your child with all your heart. If you're worried about the quality of the education in Winston-Salem, North Carolina, you're responsible for doing something about it. If you're a CEO in corporate America, you're responsible for telling the truth to your shareholders and your employees.

And in the new responsibility society, each of us is responsible for loving our neighbor just like we would like to be loved ourself. The culture of service and the culture of responsibility is growing around us here in America. I started what's called the USA Freedom Corps in order to encourage Americans to extend a compassionate hand to a citizen in need, and the response has been fantastic. People from all walks of life are willing to help, willing to stand up, willing to make a difference in their communities. Our faith-based programs are strong and vibrant and growing. The social entrepreneurship in American is an integral part of the fabric of our society.

You've got policemen and firefighters and people who wear our Nation's uniform remind us what it means to sacrifice for something greater than yourself. Once again, the children of America believe in heroes, because they see them every day. In these challenging times, the world has seen the resolve and the courage of America. And I have been privileged to see the compassion and the character of the American people.

All the tests of the last 2½ years have come to the right nation. We're a strong country, and we use that strength to defend the peace. We're an optimistic country, confident in ourselves and in ideals bigger than ourselves. Abroad, we seek to lift whole nations by spreading freedom. At home, we seek to lift up lives by spreading opportunity to every corner of America. This is the work that history has set before us. We welcome it, and we know that for our country, the best days lie ahead.

May God bless you all.

NOTE: The President spoke at noon in the M.C. Benton, Jr. Convention and Civic Center. In his remarks, he referred to Jim Culbertson, North Carolina State finance chair, Bush-Cheney '04, Inc., and his wife, Germaine; Brooke Burr, wife of Representative Richard Burr; Ferrell Blount, chairman, North Carolina Republican Party; and Linda Davis, chief, Winston-Salem Police Department.

Remarks in a Discussion With Students and Faculty at Forsyth Technical Community College in Winston-Salem
November 7, 2003

The President. Yes, Gary. First, I want to thank you very much for being a host. It's not easy to host the President and his entourage. [*Laughter*] But we have an interesting opportunity to have a discussion for the country. It's a discussion about the importance of education and jobs. It's a discussion about the importance of making sure the education system is flexible enough to help train people for jobs which exist today and will exist tomorrow. So I really want to thank you for hosting this. This is an important dialog.

The economy has obviously taken its toll on parts of North Carolina: The manufacturing sector has been hit; the textile industry has been hit; people have lost work. And yet in other sectors of the economy, here in North Carolina, are growing. And we've got to make sure we're able to match the skills and talent and drive of North Carolina citizens with the jobs of the future. And a great place to do that is at the community colleges here in North Carolina and all around the country. And that's really what we're here to herald.

So I want to thank you for giving me the chance to visit. I look forward to hearing our panelists. I want to thank you all for taking time out of your day to come and help educate the country about this fantastic program and effort you've got right here. So, Dr. Green, you're a good man for hosting us, and I appreciate it.

[*The discussion continued.*]

The President. That's what I was going to ask. It's very important for this type of education to be demand-driven.

Lucas Shallua. That is correct.

The President. I remember the old days in Texas. There would be job training programs; they really didn't care whether the jobs actually existed. All they want to do is make sure you're trained. [*Laughter*] So you end up with, like, 1,500 hairdressers for 25 jobs.

And so my question to you is—first of all, let me make it clear. On the grant, what we're talking about is a $754,000 grant to Forsyth Tech. The Congressman gets a lot of credit for arranging this because we were very aware that certain sectors of the country were losing jobs, see. The job mix is shifting. The economy, as it grows, sometimes there's a different shift in the type of jobs available. You hear a lot of talk about productivity increases; you mentioned productivity increases. A lot of the manufacturing sector is seeing job loss because the worker is more productive. In other words, an hour of a person's time yields more product, and unless demand outstrips productivity, it's a pressure on the job base.

But productivity increases, by the way, are going to mean higher paying jobs. It's important for our economy to have productivity increases, because in the long run, it makes a lot of sense. In the short run, it creates some dislocation for workers. We're going to hear from some in a minute. And the job grant program recognized that this part of the world had had some job losses and yet there were some wonderful workers and wonderful people who were anxious to be able to employ their skills in a field that was actually growing.

And so my question to you is, is that as you—and the doc here—as you have a curriculum change, explain to people how it is demand-driven, the curriculum change—in other words, a curriculum that's actually relevant to the job base here in the local communities.

[*The discussion continued.*]

The President. First of all, I thank you for the credit, but you get the credit, see. You're the person that made the decision that you want to do something with your life. I can't make that decision for you. That's your call to make, and you get the credit. And for that, I really—I appreciate that a lot.

Let me say something about one of the interesting innovations, and it's an important innovation, is these one-stop centers that the community college system is plugged into. A one-stop center is a place where a person such as Scott can go and say, "I've got this interest. What's available?" You called it up on the web, or you used the high-tech world to help bring information to your screen. And the one-stop centers are really kind of a innovative idea to allow for people to not only find what may be available. In other words, they have a look to judge demand for jobs themselves. They say, "Oh look, these people are looking for work here; this industry is looking for work here." But it also helps people find job training programs. It's very important for the community colleges to be plugged into these one-stop centers because they become the bridge to the job, become the—help create the skill set necessary for someone to access a job. And as well one-stop centers have got, like, resume help.

And so for those out there who are interested in doing what Scott and the others up here have done, I suggest you go to your regional one-stop centers. You'll find a lot of help. The job of the people there is to help you find—match your interests or your inclinations with jobs that actually exist.

I appreciate you bringing it up, Scott. You made the decision. You made the decision to go back to school, which isn't easy, particularly for an old guy like you, and—[*laughter*].

Scott Hiner. Well, there is a lot of government help out there. You just have to go find it——

The President. Yes.

Mr. Hiner. ——and like I said, I really appreciate it being out there.

The President. Well, I appreciate you saying that. We—as the economy changes, as technology changes, the slowest part of change is the workforce. And we've just got to understand that we've got to make sure our workers—who are the most productive in the world, the hardest working people in the world, the finest people in the world—have the skills necessary to move on with their lives, and I appreciate the example you've set.

[*The discussion continued.*]

The President. Yes. So if somebody is listening right now and they say "biotechnology field," how would you describe that? Give somebody a sense for what it means. I'm sure there's a lot of people frightened—"biotechnology" is a long word. It sounds—[*laughter*]. They may say, "Well, I don't know if I'm smart enough to be in biotechnology," or "It sounds too sophisticated, to be in biotechnology." It didn't frighten you. Why?

Sandra Moser. Because I was thinking pharmaceuticals and things like that, and they're going to teach me. You know, they're going to teach me what I need to know. They're not going to let me out of there until I know it. [*Laughter*]

Gary Green. That's right.

The President. And how is your education being paid?

Ms. Moser. Through the TAA.

The President. Yes, good. Good. TAA is a program like the Pell grant program. The good doctor here mentioned Pell grants. People ought to take a look at Pell grants. Many of the community college students in our country have their education funded by Pell grants. We've dramatically increased the funding of Pell grants. It's up to about $12.7 billion now on an annual basis, which means people can be able to find a grant. These are grants, not loans, by the way.

That's why they're called Pell grants. Otherwise, you know, it's Pell loans. [*Laughter*]

But the budget is up quite dramatically over the last couple years, by 45 percent. The reason I say that is, it's important for people to know, as both our friends here have mentioned, that there is a way to make sure that you get your—your education is funded if you work hard, if you look hard. There's money available, and that's important for people to know.

Thank you. Good job.

[*The discussion continued.*]

Jan Robertson. When you go, like, into a doctor's office or something, you get to dictate what the doctor says and put it on the computer, and then you get to put it in the file for the patient, whatever, so they can understand them, because—have you ever seen them write? Do you understand—[*laughter*].

The President. Yes, I have. Some people say my writing is worse than the doctor's. [*Laughter*] But I won't take it personally.

Ms. Robertson. So they need a little help.

The President. Tell us why are you—what were you doing before you came here?

Ms. Robertson. I was in a textile plant, and it went overseas. And I wanted to get—to better myself, so I went to the medical field.

The President. You're a mother?

Ms. Robertson. Yes.

The President. How old is your child?

Ms. Robertson. Five.

The President. Single mom?

Ms. Robertson. Yes.

The President. You've got the toughest job in America.

Ms. Robertson. Yes.

The President. Yes, you do. That's good. And so have you started class here?

Ms. Robertson. Yes, this fall.

The President. You making all A's?

Ms. Robertson. Not quite, but I'm getting there. [*Laughter*]

The President. People are listening. [*Laughter*] And so you're studying medical transcription.

Ms. Robertson. Yes.

The President. And are you good on the computer?

Ms. Robertson. I'm getting better.

The President. That's good. So that's part of the curriculum.

Ms. Robertson. Yes.

The President. And so what has happened here is that they've come and they've helped this education institution develop a curriculum that is actually practical, so you believe that once you finish the curriculum you'll be able to walk right out and sign up for work.

Ms. Robertson. Yes, and also it helps you where you can do it at your own—at your home.

The President. Oh, good, so you can do your first job, the most important job, which is to be a mother——

Ms. Robertson. Yes.

The President. ——and then be a student.

Thanks. Congratulations. How is your kid doing, learning to read?

Ms. Robertson. Oh, yes.

The President. That's the most important thing you can do right now, is teach your child. Get them to read more than they watch TV. Sorry to all the TV cameras out there. [*Laughter*]

[*The discussion continued.*]

The President. Well, I appreciate you bringing that up. We had a recent report out which—this is the beginning of good news for jobseekers—over the last 3 months, the economy, the entrepreneurs, the private sector, and others, have driven the job base up by 285,000 jobs, new jobs, which is good. So in other words, things are beginning to brighten up for people looking for work, which is positive. And therefore, we must make sure that people are trained for jobs that exist.

[*The discussion continued.*]

The President. And by the way, as these jobs get more sophisticated, in other words, the training level is higher, no question about it. But the pay is better. And that's what productivity increases do in a society. As our society, particularly North Carolina economy, shifts from textiles to biotechnology, the pay gets better. And all we've got to do is bridge from the textile sector to the biotechnology sector with smart education practices. And that's what we're here talking about.

It requires—a smart education system requires a community college which is flexible in their curriculum. If they're rigid, this good man here wouldn't be designing a curriculum. If they were rigid, they wouldn't be listening to the employers of the community say, "Listen, this is what we need. We need this kind of person or that kind of person."

And the reason I'm here is because this is a model for others to follow. In other parts of the country there's also workers being displaced. And yet, there's great hope and opportunity because there's wonderful job opportunity, so long as the training facilities are modern and active and not rigid.

And I want to thank you for understanding that, and I want to thank you for listening to people that are looking for workers. But they're not looking for just the average worker, they're looking for a trained worker. And so therefore, job training programs are essential. Government spends about $15 billion a year on job training programs.

I've got to tell you, though, we need a little help from the Congress—Congressman—to make sure that there's some flexibility, not on how much money we spend but how we spend it. Because these job training programs—he listed about three of them already, and for every job training program there's kind of a Government prescription with it, which means that the more prescriptive programs are, the less flexible they are. And the less flexible job training money is, it makes it very difficult

to be able to meet the needs of the local community.

And therefore, I'm trying to work with Congress, Doc, to make sure that these monies coming out of Washington are able to have enough—have as few strings attached as possible, so that the States and the local community colleges can apply that money to meet the needs of the local employers. And then we'll be able to say for certain that the job training initiatives are meeting the needs.

Yes, but thanks for—thanks for being an entrepreneur.

[The discussion continued.]

The President. The job of the Government is to make sure that the entrepreneurial spirit of America is strong, to make sure that people feel comfortable in taking risk, that they're willing to start a small business and grow it to a big business. And one of the interesting aspects of making sure the entrepreneurial spirit is strong is tax policy. And there's been a lot of talk—you've heard, I'm sure, the talk about the tax relief. Hopefully, you've seen some of it in your pockets, like increasing that child credit for your 5-year-old. But what's interesting is that most small businesses are sole proprietorships or Subchapter S corporations. That's when they're startups. I'm sure you've seen that here in North Carolina. And as a result, when you—these are companies that pay tax at the individual income tax rate, so that when you cut taxes on the individual, you're also providing capital infusion into small businesses.

And one of the very important things for our Government to do is to also understand there needs to be certainty in the Tax Code. If you're a planner, an entrepreneur, in any field, you've got to know that the tax policy today is likely to be the tax policy tomorrow, because uncertainty creates—difficult to plan, and therefore, makes it difficult for people to hire.

And so one of the things I'm going to ask Congress to do is make sure all this tax relief we pass is permanent. See, it goes away. She, unfortunately, is going to have to pay—receive less money in her child credit if they don't make the tax relief permanent. The small-business owner, if they don't make the tax relief permanent, will have to pay a inheritance tax or death tax on the business they've created, which I don't think is fair. I think you should only be taxed once, not twice. The marriage penalty relief is—it's going to go away. And it's important that there be certainty in order to make sure this economy continues to grow.

I want to thank you for bringing up the entrepreneurial spirit. That's the thing that makes America such a wonderful place, the kind of place where people, if you have a dream, are able to realize your dream. That applies not only to the business owner, the person coming to the Research Triangle, the person who thinks they've got a better idea than their neighbor and is willing to put a little something out there, time and capital, on the line. It also applies to our workers, people who have got their own dreams, their own set of dreams, the dream of making sure the child grows up in a wonderful little comfortable, peaceful household. And our job in the Government is to help people realize their dreams. That's really what it is. We can't make people dream, but we can help people once they start to dream.

And I thank you all for the compliments on the Government. But the compliments really belong here. See, you're doing what needs to be done. And that's why I've got such wonderful optimism about our country. I'm very optimistic about the fact that we'll keep the peace. I'm very optimistic about the fact that people will find work, because there's a wonderful spirit here in America.

I met this guy right there. See him? Put your hand up. He's a volunteer firefighter. Well, not you, Burr. [*Laughter*] He's a volunteer firefighter. He came out to the airport to say hello. It's an interesting concept, isn't it, volunteer firefighters, people volunteering to put their lives on the line in order to save lives.

I recently went out to California. I explained it to him when I was at the airport. A lot of people on the frontlines in the fire out there were volunteers. The reason I bring that up is, it should remind us that the strength of the country is not our military, is not our pocketbooks; it's the heart and soul of people. The entrepreneurial spirit is the strength of the country. The willingness for people to volunteer in a fire department is the strength of the country. And once you realize how strong this country is in spirit, you can't help but be optimistic about the future.

Thank you for having me here, Doc. Listen, I want to thank you all for sharing your stories. It's not easy to stand up in front of all these cameras. I know. [*Laughter*] Although the cameramen are fine people. But it's—you were able to help us make a point, that people who have lost work should have hope, that with a little initiative, a little ingenuity, a little drive, there's help for you. The economy's growing, new jobs are being created. And we—there's an opportunity, and I hope you seize it. I hope you seize it, because there's a wonderful, wonderful future ahead for people who may at this moment think their days are—the future is a little dark. And we've got three citizens right up here who are willing to see the—can see that bright light. So thanks for coming.

Thank you all for coming.

NOTE: The discussion began at 1:05 p.m. Participants in the discussion included: Gary M. Green, president, Lucas D. Shallua, biotechnology program coordinator, and Scott Hiner, Sandra Moser, and Jan Robertson, students, Forsyth Technical Community College; Richard Dean, president, Wake Forest University Health Sciences; and William Dean, president, Idealliance. In his remarks, the President also referred to Representative Richard Burr of North Carolina; and Brian

Koontz, fire chief, County Line Volunteer
Fire Department.

Statement on House of Representatives Action on the Defense
Authorization Conference Report
November 7, 2003

I commend the House for passing the
Defense Authorization conference report
and showing strong bipartisan support for
America's national security, our troops, and
their families. This bill includes my request
for a third straight pay raise, more resources for equipment and training, and
quality of life improvements so that our
military continues to be the finest fighting
force in the world.

The legislation also makes good progress
toward transforming and modernizing our
military so that it is best prepared to protect Americans.

Finally, I am pleased that the House has
resolved the issue of concurrent receipt for
military retirees in a fair and responsible
manner.

The President's Radio Address
November 8, 2003

Good morning. This week, we heard
some good news about the effects of tax
relief on the American economy. The Department of Labor reported that our economy added 126,000 new jobs in October.
And over the past 3 months, there were
286,000 new jobs. The unemployment rate
fell to 6 percent. The 4-week average for
jobless claims has declined in 6 of the past
7 weeks, and manufacturers reported that
orders and shipments are both rising.

This news comes one week after we
heard that economic output rose at a 7.2
percent annual rate in the third quarter,
the fastest pace of growth in nearly 20
years. America's economy is getting stronger every day. American companies are investing. Americans are buying homes at a
record pace, and homeownership is near
record levels. Stock market values have
risen, adding about $2 trillion in wealth

for investors since the beginning of the
year.

We can all be encouraged, but we cannot
be satisfied. These are early signs of
progress. Now we must turn this progress
into broad and lasting gains for all Americans. Our improving economy is also a
changing economy, and some workers need
help preparing for new jobs and new industries.

In Winston-Salem, North Carolina,
where I traveled this week, manufacturing
jobs have been declining for decades. The
textile industry and furniture makers and
farmers are hurting. In Winston-Salem, I
also saw a good program at a community
college that is training unemployed workers
for new jobs in industries which are growing, such as biotechnology. Local businesses, along with the Department of

Labor, are supporting this job training program. We must give more workers the opportunity to learn new skills so they can get ahead and provide for their families.

My administration is investing more than $15 billion each year in job training and employment services. Americans can go to more than 1,900 one-stop career centers around the country, where, in a single location, they can check job listings, get help with a job application, and sign up for job training programs.

We're also helping more students attend community colleges, where so many people find new skills. We boosted our request for Pell grants, which help adults of all ages pay for college, by 45 percent since I took office. And I've asked Congress to establish personal reemployment accounts for out-of-work Americans to help them in their job search. These accounts would give up to $3,000 to unemployed workers to get training, to find child care, or to relocate to a city where there is a job.

The most important thing we can do to help those looking for work is to make sure our current economic growth results in more new jobs. I have proposed a six-point economic plan to encourage companies to expand and hire workers. We must bring health care costs under control, reform our civil courts to end the junk lawsuits hurting

small businesses, cut needless regulations so that small-business owners can focus on pleasing their customers instead of pleasing bureaucrats. We must pass a national energy policy to ensure an affordable and reliable supply of energy to our economy, promote free trade agreements that bring good jobs to America, and make tax relief permanent, so the gains we have seen do not disappear when tax relief is scheduled to go away.

The tax relief of the past 2 years was based on a principle that when Americans keep more of their own earnings, they spend more and invest more and move the economy forward. We're now seeing that happen. Our economy is on a rising road, and now we must take the remaining steps to ensure that our economy becomes a lasting expansion and our prosperity extends to every corner of America.

Thank you for listening.

NOTE: The address was recorded at 9:20 a.m. on November 7 in the Cabinet Room at the White House for broadcast at 10:06 a.m. on November 8. The transcript was made available by the Office of the Press Secretary on November 7 but was embargoed for release until the broadcast. The Office of the Press Secretary also released a Spanish language transcript of this address.

Remarks at a Bush-Cheney Luncheon in Little Rock, Arkansas
November 10, 2003

Thank you all. Thank you all very much. Thanks for coming. Thank you. Please be seated, thanks. Thanks for coming. Thanks for the warm welcome. I appreciate your fine words, Skinny. [*Laughter*] I got off the airplane, I wasn't sure who I was looking at. [*Laughter*]

So we get in the limousine, and we're driving here from the airport, and the Governor says, "Do you still follow college

football?" [*Laughter*] I wasn't exactly sure what he was driving at. I said, "Yeah, I pay attention to it." He said, "Were you paying attention to it a couple of weeks ago?" I said, "Yes, I sure was, Governor. Congratulations to the Hawgs."

Thank you all for coming today. What we're doing today is we're laying the foundation for what is going to be a victory in Arkansas in '04 and a nationwide victory in '04.

I want to thank you for your hard work and for your strong support. I want to thank you for what you did in 2000. I remember—[*applause*]—yes. I remember coming as the last stop we made prior to getting back to Texas after a long, long campaign. And we went to northwest Arkansas, and the crowds were huge. I remember flying over and seeing the line of red lights, all trying to get into the event. It was really a—put the wind at my back coming off of a tough campaign, the people of Arkansas did. I want thank you for support then. I want to thank you for the support that you've shown today. I want to thank you for what you're fixing to do, which is to man the grassroots and to get on the phones and get the signs out and to turn out the vote. When you're out working the vote right now, you tell them the President is focused on keeping America strong and secure and prosperous and free.

The political season will come in its own time. I'm loosening up—[*laughter*]—and I'm getting ready. But I got a job to do, and I'll keep working on the people's business, doing what's right for America. I've got a job to do for everybody who lives in this country.

My regret today is that the First Lady isn't traveling with me. You drew the short straw. [*Laughter*] But I'm proud of Laura. She's a great wife, a great mother, and is a fantastic First Lady for America. She sends her very best to all her friends here in Arkansas.

Speaking about our friends, I'm proud to call your Governor friend and Janet Huckabee friend. Mike is doing a great job for the people of Arkansans. He's a strong leader. I appreciate his friendship, and I appreciate his leadership. I also want to thank your Lieutenant Governor, Win Rockefeller, and Lisenne for being here today. It's good to see you again, Governor. I appreciate your friendship.

You got a fine Congressman named Boozman representing you in Washington, DC. John, you're doing a great job. I'm proud to call you ally and friend. I want thank all the State and local officials who are here. I see former—some former Congressmen. Jay Dickey and John Paul, it's good to see you.

I appreciate the grassroots folks who are here, the people who are making this party work. I want to thank Warren Stephens and French Hill, who are the State finance cochairmen, for taking on the task of seeing to it that my campaign and the campaign of Vice President Cheney's is well-organized and well-funded. I appreciate all the folks who have made this event such a great success. Most of all, I thank you all for coming.

In the last 2½ years, our Nation has acted decisively to confront great challenges. I came to this office to solve problems instead of passing them on to future Presidents and future generations. I came to seize opportunities instead of letting them slip away. My administration is meeting the tests of our time.

Terrorists declared war on the United States of America, and war is what they got. We've captured or killed many of the key leaders of the Al Qaida network, and the rest of them know we're on their trail. In Afghanistan and in Iraq, we gave ultimatums to terror regimes. Those regimes chose defiance, and those regimes are no more. Fifty million people in those two countries once lived under tyranny, and today, they live in freedom.

Two-and-a-half years ago, our military was not receiving the resources it needed, and morale was beginning to suffer. So we increased the defense budgets to prepare for the threats of a new era. And today, no one in the world can question the skill and the strength and the spirit of the United States military.

Two-and-a-half years ago, we inherited an economy in recession. And then our Nation was attacked, and we had some scandals in corporate America, and we went to war to make America more secure, all of which affected the people's confidence. But we acted. We passed tough new laws to hold corporate criminals to account. And to get the economy going again, I have twice led the United States Congress to pass historic tax relief for the American people.

I know that when Americans have more take-home pay to spend, to save, or invest, the whole economy grows and people are more likely to find a job. So we're returning more money to the people to help them raise their families. We're reducing taxes on dividends and capital gains to encourage investment. We're giving small businesses incentives so they can hire new people. With all these actions, we have laid the foundation for greater prosperity and more jobs across America so every single person in this country can realize the great American Dream.

Two-and-a-half years ago, there was a lot of talk about education reform, but there wasn't much action. So I acted. I called for and the Congress passed the No Child Left Behind Act. With a solid bipartisan majority, we delivered the most dramatic education reforms in a generation.

I appreciate your Governor leading on this issue. I appreciate the fine reading initiative you got here in this State. You see, we believe that every child in every public school can learn to read and write and add and subtract. We are challenging the soft bigotry of low expectations.

We've increased the Federal budget to help Title I students, to help make sure every child can read. But we expect results. The days of excuse-making are over. We want results in every single classroom so that not one single child is left behind.

We reorganized our Government and created the Department of Homeland Security to better safeguard our borders and

ports and to protect the American people. We passed trade promotion authority to open up new markets for Arkansas' farmers and ranchers and entrepreneurs. We passed budget agreements that are helping to maintain spending discipline in Washington, DC. On issue after issue, this administration has acted on principle, has kept its word, and has made progress for the American people.

And the United States Congress has shared in these substantial achievements. I want to thank John. I also want to thank Speaker Hastert and Leader Frist. They're good friends. We're working hard to change the tone in Washington, DC. There's a lot of needless politics in the Nation's Capital. We're focused on the people's business. You sent us to Washington to work on behalf of the people, not special interests, not lobbyists, but the people. And that's what we're doing.

I've surrounded myself with people in my administration who are focused on results. I have put together a fine team of public servants to represent America. There is no finer Vice President in our Nation's history than Dick Cheney. Mother may have a second opinion. [*Laughter*]

In 2½ years, we have come far, but our work is only beginning. I've set great goals worthy of a great nation. First, America is committed to expanding the realm of freedom and peace for our own security and for the benefit of the world. And second, in our own country, we must work for a society of prosperity and compassion so that every single citizen has a chance to work and to succeed and to realize the promise of America. It should become clear—it should be clear—that the future of freedom and peace depend on the actions of America. This Nation is freedom's home and freedom's defender. We welcome this charge of history, and we are keeping it.

The war on terror continues. The enemies of freedom are not idle, and neither are we. This country will not rest; we will not tire; we will not stop until this danger to civilization is removed.

We are confronting that danger in Iraq, where Saddam holdouts and foreign terrorists are desperately trying to throw Iraq into chaos by attacking coalition forces and aid workers and innocent Iraqis. They know that the advance of freedom in Iraq would be a major defeat for the cause of terror. This collection of killers is trying to shake the will of America and the civilized world. America will not be intimidated.

We're aggressively striking the terrorists in Iraq, defeating them there so we will not have to face them in our own country. We're calling on other nations to help Iraq to become a free country, which will make the world more secure. We're standing with the Iraqi people as they assume more of their own defense and move toward self-government. These are not easy tasks, but they are essential tasks. We will finish what we have begun, and we will win this essential victory in the war on terror.

Our greatest security comes from the advance of human liberty, because free nations do not support terror. Free nations do not attack their neighbors. Free nations do not threaten the world with weapons of mass terror. Americans believe that freedom is the deepest hope and need of every human heart. And I believe that freedom is the right of every person, and I believe that freedom is the future of every nation.

America also understands that unprecedented influence brings tremendous responsibilities. We have duties in this world, and when we see disease and starvation and hopeless poverty, we will not turn away. On the continent of Africa, America is now committed to bringing the healing power of medicine to millions of men and women and children now suffering with AIDS. This great, powerful Nation is a compassionate nation, and we are leading the world in this incredibly important work of human rescue.

We face challenges here at home, and our actions will prove worthy of the challenges. So long as any of our citizens who want to work can't find a job, we must work to make sure the entrepreneurial spirit, the environment for job growth is strong. The numbers look good. I'm encouraged by what I see, but too many of our fellow citizens aren't working.

I've laid out a six-point plan to the United States Congress to make sure job creation remains strong and vibrant. I will stay focused on our economy until the American people are able to put food on the table and take care of their family responsibilities by finding a job.

We have a duty to keep our commitment to America's seniors by strengthening and modernizing Medicare. Congress has taken historic action to improve the lives of older Americans. For the first time since the creation of Medicare, the House and the Senate have passed reforms to increase choices for seniors and provide coverage for prescription drugs. It is time for the House and the Senate to reconcile their differences and to get a bill to my desk. We owe it to our seniors to have a modern health care system available for them, and we owe it to those of us who are going to be seniors to make sure the Medicare system is modern.

And for the sake of our health care system, we need to cut down on the frivolous lawsuits which increase the cost of medicine. People who have been harmed by a bad doctor deserve their day in court. Yet the system should not reward lawyers who are simply fishing for a rich settlement. Because frivolous lawsuits drive up the cost of health care, they affect the Federal budget. Therefore, medical liability reform is a national issue that requires a national solution. I submitted a good bill to reform the medical liability system of our country to the House—to the Congress. The House of Representatives has acted. It is stuck in the United States Senate. It is time for some Senators to understand that no one in this country has ever been healed by a frivolous lawsuit. We need medical liability reform.

I have a responsibility as the President to make sure the judicial system runs well, and I have met that duty. I've nominated superb men and women to the Federal courts, people who will interpret the law, not legislate from the bench. Yet some Members of the United States Senate—you might even know some—[laughter]—are trying to keep my nominees off the bench by filibusters, by blocking up-or-down votes. Every judicial nominee deserves a fair hearing and an up-or-down vote on the Senate floor. Is it time for Members of the Senate to stop playing politics with American justice.

Congress needs to complete work on a comprehensive energy plan. We must promote energy efficiency and conservation. We must use technologies to be able to use the resources at hand. But for the sake of economic security and for the sake of national security, this Nation must become less reliant on foreign sources of energy.

A strong and prosperous nation must also be a compassionate nation. I will continue to advance our agenda of compassionate conservatism, which means we will apply the best and most effective and most innovative ideas to the task of helping our fellow citizens in need. Still, millions of men and women who want to end their dependence on Government and become independent through hard work must build on the success of welfare reform to bring work and dignity into the lives of more of our fellow citizens. Congress should complete the "Citizen Service Act" so more Americans can serve their communities and their country. And both Houses should reach agreement on my Faith-Based Initiative to support the armies of compassion that are mentoring our children, caring for the homeless, and offering hope to the addicted. Our Government should not fear faith. We should welcome faith and the healing power of faith into the lives of more of our citizens.

A compassionate society must promote opportunity for all, including the independence and dignity that come from ownership. This administration will constantly strive to promote an ownership society in America. We want more people owning their own home. Today in America, we have a minority homeownership gap. I've submitted plans to the United States Congress to close that gap. We want more people owning and managing their own retirement accounts, owning and managing their own health care plans. And we want more people owning their own small business. We understand that when a person owns something, he or she has a vital stake in the future of America.

In a compassionate society, people respect one another and take responsibility for the decisions they make. The culture of America is changing from one that has said, "If it feels good, do it. If you've got a problem, blame somebody else," to a new culture in which each of us understands we are responsible for the decisions we make.

If you're fortunate enough to be a mom or a dad, you're responsible for loving your child with all your heart. If you're worried about the quality of the education in Little Rock, Arkansas, or anywhere in Arkansas, you're responsible for doing something about it. If you're a CEO in corporate America, you're responsible for telling the truth to your shareholders and your employees.

And in the new responsibility society, each of us is responsible for loving a neighbor just like we'd like to be loved ourselves. The culture of service, the culture of responsibility is growing here in America. You know, I started what's called the USA Freedom Corps to encourage Americans to extend a compassionate hand to neighbors in need, and the response has been great. People want to serve. People want to help their communities. Policemen and firefighters and people who wear our Nation's uniform are reminding us what it means to sacrifice for something greater than yourself. Once again, the children of America believe in heroes, because they see them every day.

In these challenging times, the world has seen the resolve and the courage of America. And I've been privileged to see the compassion and the character of the American people. All the tests of the last 2½ years have come to the right nation. We're a strong country, and we use that strength to defend the peace. We're an optimistic country, confident in ourselves and in ideals bigger than ourselves. Abroad, we seek to lift up whole nations by spreading freedom. At home, we seek to lift up lives by spread-ing opportunity to every corner of America. This is the work that history has set before us. We welcome it. And we know that for our country, the best days lie ahead.

May God bless you all. Thank you all.

NOTE: The President spoke at 11:55 a.m. at the Statehouse Convention Center. In his remarks, he referred to Gov. Mike Huckabee of Arkansas and his wife, Janet; Lt. Gov. Win Rockefeller of Arkansas and his wife, Lisenne; Representative John Boozman and former Representatives Jay Dickey and John Paul Hammerschmidt of Arkansas; and former President Saddam Hussein of Iraq.

Remarks in a Discussion With Employers and Employees at BMW Manufacturing Corporation in Greer, South Carolina
November 10, 2003

The President. Well, Carl, thanks. Yes, I'm delighted to be here. I appreciate so very much you all letting me come by to say a few words. We're going to have kind of a discussion about jobs. When I hear somebody in our country wants to work and can't find a job, it says to me we've got a problem, we've got to keep working to make sure people are able to work. So we're here to really talk about jobs.

Before we do, I do want to say something, though, about this company. I understand 26 of your employees, your fellow employees, are in Iraq. I know a lot of you have got relatives who serve in the United States military. I want to thank you. I want you to tell them thank you on behalf of a grateful nation for working to see to it that this Nation is secure. You've got to understand that free nations are peaceful nations. The more freedom there is in the world, the more secure America becomes. We must never forget the lessons of September the 11th, 2001. And I want you to pass on to your fellow employees and loved ones, this Commander in Chief is grateful for the sacrifice and service.

Before we get kind of this discussion going on, I want to say a couple of things. I want to thank the Governor for being here. Governor Sanford is here. Senator Lindsey Graham is with us. Congressmen DeMint, Brown, Wilson, and Barrett are with us as well. Speaker Wilkins. When the President shows up, you know, all kinds of people show up. [*Laughter*] But I'm glad to be in their company. They're good folks. They're friends.

The other thing is, is that we come in a time of pretty upbeat assessment about our economy. More than pretty upbeat—third quarter growth was strong. Last week we saw the unemployment numbers drop. The private sector is growing. Entrepreneurship is vibrant. And about—over 280,000 new jobs were created over the last 3 months, and that's positive. That's really good, particularly if you're somebody looking for work.

But we're here to talk about policies to make it even better. That's what we want. We're not satisfied. And we're not satisfied because I do understand some are struggling.

But with that, Carl, I want to thank you for your hospitality. I look forward to hearing from our fellow citizens about what's on your mind and really am grateful so many of you all showed up and gave me a chance to come and to say hello.

[*The discussion continued.*]

The President. Well, I appreciate it. First of all, it says to me that our workers are the best in the world. People are really productive. You know, you hear this—a lot of talk about trade. You're living the trade world. And if we do a good job about making sure trade is free and fair, people are going to find work here in America. That's what this is all about. In other words, we welcome people coming here. We welcome their money. I know the workers welcome the chance to work. And we're good about it. We're good at workers. And that's what this plant shows.

And so I appreciate very much, most importantly, the—I appreciate the deployment of capital from overseas to America. But most importantly, I appreciate the hardworking Americans who are making it an attractive place for people to invest right here in South Carolina. We're the most productive workforce in the world right now by far. Our productivity per worker is way out of sight. And we've just got to keep it that way because, you see, high productivity, it creates a short-term problem, unemployment. If one worker can put out more goods, unless the economy grows, it's going to be hard to hire new people. But in the long run, high productivity means better pay, better living.

And so what you've just told me is, this workforce is doing its job. And there's no doubt in my mind this workforce can compete with anybody in the world. And my job is to make sure that we have a level playing field, see that we've got fair trade—free and fair trade. We want free trade because we want you to be able to sell what you make here out of the State of South Carolina overseas. That's what we want. Because if you're not selling those cars overseas, then it's—some of you may not be working, and we want you working.

But I appreciate that, Carl. Thanks.

Carl Flescher, Jr. Steve, I wonder if you might want to tell the President a little bit about your company.

Stephen Thies. Sure, Carl. Mr. President, Spartanburg Steel and Spartanburg Stainless are two privately held manufacturing companies here. We call ourselves "SSP"; it's a little easier to say than the full name. Spartanburg Steel began production here in 1962, so it's an old company. But we make metal stampings—today, we make metal stampings in welded assemblies for BMW, principally for the X5 sport activity vehicle, which is produced here at the plant. You can see some of our parts are surrounding us here today. You see some metal parts around the room, around the stage. A number of these assemblies are made at our company. Spartanburg Steel has grown nicely because of its relationship with BMW. That growth is helping our owners, our associates, and our suppliers as well.

Now, we have a second company here in Spartanburg as well. It's called Spartanburg Stainless Products, also "SSP," okay? And Spartanburg Stainless makes metal stampings and assemblies, but we also make beer kegs. We're the only American beer keg manufacturer in North America. [*Laughter*]

The President. I quit drinking in '86. [*Laughter*] But I bet some of the people out here use the product. [*Laughter*] I'm not going to point out which ones. [*Laughter*]

Mr. Thies. Well, we did notice a dip in demand at a point in time—[*laughter*]—but probably no relationship. [*Laughter*]

The President. Pretty observant fellow, aren't you? [*Laughter*]

[*The discussion continued.*]

The President. Yes. Let me amplify on that real quick. Sorry to interrupt. Tax policy—good tax policy is important for economic growth. And if you—and I just want to make sure everybody understands what he's talking about there. First of all, I hope you saw the tax relief. Particularly if you're a mom or a dad, you did, because we increased the child credit. We reduced rates. I'm going to tell you why, just so that you understand the logic. If you have more money in your pocket, you're going to demand an additional good or a service. And when you demand an additional good or a service, somebody is going to produce the good or a service. And when somebody produces it, it means somebody is more likely to, first, keep a job, and if there's enough demand out there, somebody is—it means the job base will expand.

What he's talking about was incentives we provided to encourage businesses to invest. And when a business invests in, say, a piece of equipment, somebody has to make the equipment. That in itself encourages economic vitality and growth. The tax relief we passed came at the right time. What we now need to do is make it permanent. Interestingly enough, because of a quirk in the rules in the United States Senate, the tax relief we passed begins to go away in '05. In order to make sure that people can plan for capital investment and you can plan your lives, the Congress needs to make the tax relief permanent.

[*The discussion continued.*]

The President. Good. Well, I presume your company wouldn't be doing well if it hadn't been for somebody willing to invest here in South Carolina and the BMW plant. What people have got to understand is that when BMW builds cars, there's a spinoff effect. Businesses in the area benefit as well. The more work you all do

at BMW, the more likely somebody is going to be doing work in an associated supplier. Economic vitality depends upon the money circulating in our economy. And not only does tax policy help, but good trade policy helps, being willing to welcome foreign investment into the State of South Carolina.

What I'm more interested in is, are you working? I don't really care who owns the plant. What I want to know is, are they paying you when they say they're going to pay you? Is your job—is your check showing up?

[*The discussion continued.*]

The President. Yes, I appreciate that. These stories are stories of an economy that's changing. We went through—we've been through a tough time. There's no doubt about it. We've been through a recession. The enemy hit us on September the 11th. It affected not only our psychology but it affected the economy. It just did. It's just a reality.

Unfortunately, we had some corporate citizens who didn't tell the truth. They forgot what it means to be a responsible citizen. They kind of fudged the numbers. They're going to be held to account, by the way. That's how you need to treat people who—[*applause*].

We marched to war. I don't if you remember, on your TV screens last summer it—a year ago, summer—it said, "March to War." You turn on the TV, and there it says, "March to War." That's not a very conducive environment in which people are willing to take risk. It's not a positive thought. It's a—necessary, in my judgment, obviously, to make America secure, but it's not positive. I know it's not.

So we've overcome a lot. Plus, the economy is restructuring. And so the fundamental question is, what do you do about it? One, you encourage growth, the creation of new jobs. Most new jobs in America are created by small businesses. And so we had a small-business focus. But the other thing we've got to understand is that as the society becomes more productive and the nature of the jobs change, we've got to make sure there's worker training programs. We've got over 1,700 one-stop sites for workers to go to. These guys did their own one-stop shopping. But not everybody may have the same ability to do that. And you can get on a computer and find out the jobs available in your neighborhood.

And as importantly, the job training programs available—I mean, somebody listening out there today who is wondering whether or not they can find work, there are ample opportunities to find job training programs that will help train you for jobs which actually exist. And that's a very important concept. There's a little bit of a change—it used to be that Government would judge you on just, did you have job training programs. And therefore, they have 1,000 hairdressers for 50 jobs, which didn't make sense. What you're trying to do now is match demand for jobs with jobs—with the people.

There's a lot of Pell grant money available, and that's important for people to know, so they can go to a community college. And then there's monies available for community colleges—I know the Governor is working on this—to make sure the community colleges become laboratories for educating workforce for the jobs which exist. There are jobs available.

And so the fundamental question is, how do we help people find those jobs? And one thing we've got to do is focus on—you know, technology roars through the economy and society, and labor is left behind. And so we've got to make sure labor stays caught up. As society changes, as the economy changes, we've got to have programs that actually make sense and programs that focus—the job training programs—on making sure that the workforce, the most productive in the world, has got the skills necessary to meet the jobs of the future.

I want to thank you two guys for taking the initiative. We can have every job training program in the world sitting out there, but it also requires people willing to take the initiative and be responsible citizens. I appreciate the example you set. I'm glad BMW is vibrant and doing well. I'm glad you're selling products overseas as well as here at home, so Spartanburg has had the opportunity to hire these two guys. This is a success story. And I want to thank you very much for being a part of it. I appreciate you.

[The discussion continued.]

The President. Good job. Remember, I talked about job training. A good company is one that works hard to train the workforce. A good company is a company which says, "How do we keep our workers on the front edge of change?" It sounds like BMW does that, and I appreciate you then passing on the skills you learned. And a good company also provides good health care, good retirement, and obviously, the added benefit of letting people travel to see a different part of the world, which is a pretty interesting concept when you think about it, yes.

Well, thank you for sharing your story with us.

[The discussion continued.]

The President. Well, I appreciate that story. Look, I know there's a lot of textile workers here in this State who are worried about their future. Some have lost their job, and obviously we care about that a lot. And in the Government we'll try to do everything we can to make sure that the rules are fair.

But Henry's story is an interesting story, and the wife's story is an interesting story, about somebody who said, "Wait a minute, there's a better job." And it does take—and it's hard to leave work; I understand that. It's unsettling. But you've just got to know—and I want to emphasize again what Henry said—there are programs to help people transition from one kind of job to a job which has got more security and a better paying job—and a better paying job.

And that's what's happening in the workforce, the jobs are better paying. There's health care jobs; there's jobs in the manufacturing sector. And a productive workforce means that people are going to be able to make more money over the long term. That's what that means. And we've just got to make sure that we help people get there.

And part of the reason I've come to talk with people who've been through this before is, I want people who are listening to know that there is hope, that they're going to have to have a little drive, but there's plenty of help for people who are trying to transition from an industry that may not be on firm footing to other jobs that will be long-lasting jobs. It's important for people here in South Carolina to know that. And I want to thank you, Henry, for sharing your story, and tell your wife congratulations on being—where is she? Yes, I'll tell her. I'll tell her myself. [*Laughter*] Thank you for doing what you did. It's a great example to set. And congratulations.

[*The discussion continued.*]

The President. Yes, Barry, before you begin, tell them what you told me about Texas. Remember, you were going to——

Barry Bell. Well, actually, I was supposed to be going to Texas this week for a hunting trip. But I sort of backed out of that, and I'm here with you now. [*Laughter*]

The President. That's right, yes. I knew he was my kind of guy when he said he wanted to go on a hunting trip. I don't know if I would have canceled if I'd have been him, but thank you. [*Laughter*]

[*The discussion continued.*]

The President. I appreciate the story. Let me pick up on one thing. Again, obviously it's a good company, which is one that

keeps your people on the cutting edge of change by having training.

I also want to pick up on what he just said. It's a little off the subject, but a responsible citizen is somebody who loves their child with all their heart, a citizen who says, "I want to put my family"—is a citizen I'd love to have working for me—a citizen who said, "I want my family first, I weep when I think about the thought of missing my child's baseball games," the kind of guy I want working for me, the kind of guy I want working with me. I appreciate that.

[*The discussion continued.*]

The President. Well, I appreciate that. It's like, I was in North Carolina the other day, and the hospital people are looking for work, so they went to this junior college, a community college, and helped the people design a curriculum that would then enable people to come out of the course with the skills necessary to be hired. And that's what we've got to do. We've got to make sure that we tailor curriculum for the jobs which will exist, because there's a lot of fine people in our country, hardworking, decent, honorable people, that all they want is a chance. And when the economy races by them, all they're asking for is, "Give me some skills so I can go out and be a productive employee." And sometimes you find it inside your company. Sometimes it requires a community college to have the program necessary. All the time it requires a citizen initiative; that's what it requires.

You did mention Government. Just remember, the role of the Government is to see to it that this economy gets going by having good policy. The tax policy is good policy. The health care policy for small business is important. We've got one other thing—education policy is important, obviously.

There's one other thing I want to mention right quick, because it's now up in Congress. Manufacturing companies need energy. Like, you're not going to be working long if you don't have energy to run this plant. It's a practical matter. And we've got an energy bill that we're trying to get out, an energy bill which says we'll work on conservation, an energy bill that says our electricity system needs to be modern. You may remember what happened last summer. I mean, there was a pretty clear signal that parts of the electricity grid need to be modernized; they're old and ancient and tired. The utilities—we're working on voluntary reliability standards; I think they ought to be mandatory reliability standards. That means if you're responsible for moving electricity, it must be mandatory that you've got reliability in your system.

So we've got an energy bill up there. Let me just make this very clear to you. We can find energy at home, and we need to do that. We can do it in environmentally friendly ways by using technology. We need to have clean coal technology. We need to be finding natural gas in our own hemisphere. For the sake of your economic security and your job security and for the sake of national security, this country must become less dependent on foreign sources of energy.

Listen, I'm honored you all came out to say hello. I appreciate you giving me a chance to—Carl and you all—to come and talk about jobs and what's happening in the economy and how we can continue to create an environment for job creation. I'm excited about the future because I know the nature of America. We've overcome a lot in this country. We really have. But I'm not surprised, because I know the nature of the citizens who live in this country. People are tough when they need to be tough and compassionate when they need to be compassionate, people who work hard. As I said, and I meant it, the best workforce in the world is right here in America, right here in front of me.

There's going to be other challenges in front of America. But there's no doubt in my mind we will meet every challenge because of the nature of this country. This country is freedom's home. This country is freedom's defender. And this country believes the American Dream ought to be available to everybody. And we need to create that environment so people can realize that dream.

I am so proud to be with you all. I want to thank you for your hospitality. May God bless you and your families, and may God continue to bless our great country. Thank you very much.

NOTE: The President spoke at 4:10 p.m. Participants in the discussion included: Barry Bell, production section leader, Carl Flescher, Jr., vice president for corporate communications, and Archie "Lane" Gist and Henry Campbell, production associates, BMW Manufacturing Corp.; Brian Ludwiczak, maintenance supervisor, and Fred Wilson, quality manager, Spartanburg Steel Products; and Stephen Thies, president and chief executive officer, Spartanburg Steel Products and Spartanburg Stainless Products. In his remarks, the President also referred to Gov. Mark Sanford of South Carolina; and David H. Wilkins, speaker, South Carolina State House of Representatives.

Statement on Signing the Department of the Interior and Related Agencies Appropriations Act, 2004
November 10, 2003

Today, I have signed into law H.R. 2691, the Department of the Interior and Related Agencies Appropriations Act, 2004.

Under the appropriations heading "Construction" for the Bureau of Indian Affairs, the Act refers to one subsection of title 25 of the United States Code that do not exist (25 U.S.C. 2505(f)) and one provision in title 25 that exists (25 U.S.C. 2005(a)) but which, as is plain from the text of the Act, is not the provision to which the Act was intended to refer. The Director of the Office of Management and Budget shall submit immediately on my behalf for the consideration of the Congress legislation to correct these errors in the Act. If corrective legislation is not enacted before execution of the provisions under the appropriations heading becomes necessary, the Attorney General shall provide a legal opinion to the Secretary of the Interior on how to faithfully execute the appropriations heading in light of the errors it contains.

The executive branch shall construe sections 101 and 325 of the Act, which purport to require the executive branch to submit to the Congress in certain circumstances a request for a supplemental appropriation or for enactment of other legislation, in a manner consistent with the President's constitutional authority to submit for the consideration of the Congress such measures as the President judges necessary and expedient.

Many provisions in the Act purport to require the consent or approval of committees of the Congress before executive branch execution of aspects of the Act or purport to preclude executive branch execution of a provision of the Act upon the written disapproval of such committees. The executive branch shall construe such provisions to require only notification to the Congress, because any other construction would contravene the constitutional principles set forth by the United States Supreme Court in 1983 in its decision in *INS v. Chadha.*

GEORGE W. BUSH

The White House,
November 10, 2003.

NOTE: H.R. 2691, approved November 10, was assigned Public Law No. 108–108.

Remarks at a Bush-Cheney Reception in Greenville, South Carolina
November 10, 2003

Thank you all for coming. I'm honored to be here. Please be seated.

Mr. Speaker, thank you for those warm remarks. South Carolina will always have a big part of my political career. I'm proud of all the people here. I want to thank you for your friendship. I remember 2000 very well. Today we're laying the foundation for what will be a South Carolina and a national victory in 2004.

I'm proud to have your support. I'm loosening up. [*Laughter*] I'm getting ready. But politics will come in its own time. See, I've got a job to do. And when you go to your coffee shops and your farm implementation dealers or your places of worship, you tell them that George W. Bush is working hard for everybody, working hard to make sure this country remains strong and secure and prosperous and free.

I appreciate my friend David Wilkins. He's the kind of friend that is with you when times are good and when times are bad. Mr. Speaker, I appreciate your leadership on this event—made an enormous difference tonight for this very successful fundraiser. I also want to thank your dear wife, Susan. You and I both married very well.

Speaking about marrying well, I am sorry that Laura is not here, and I'm sure you are as well. [*Laughter*] You drew the short straw. [*Laughter*] She is a fabulous wife, a great mother, and she's doing a wonderful job as our country's First Lady.

I'm honored that the Governor is here, Governor Mark Sanford. I appreciate his leadership and his friendship, and I also appreciate the great service that Jenny, the wonderful first lady of South Carolina, is providing to your State. Thank you for coming, Governor.

I see you don't really care who you sit next to. [*Laughter*] You've chosen to sit next to the Senator from the great State of South Carolina, Senator Lindsey Graham, strong ally and good friend. I appreciate you coming.

South Carolina has sent some fantastic people to Congress, good allies, good friends. Henry Brown and Joe Wilson and Gresham Barrett and Jim DeMint are people you can be proud of that represent you. I know this is DeMint's district. He's doing a fine job as a United States Congressman. But I'm proud of all of them that are representing your great State there in Washington.

I know the Lieutenant Governor is with us today, Lieutenant Governor Bauer. I know the attorney general is with us, Henry McMaster. I know there's other State officials who are here. I want to thank you all for coming tonight.

Some of my club members are with us. I'm a member of the ex-Governors club,

and so is Beasley, Campbell, and Edwards. I appreciate all three of those distinguished South Carolinian citizens for joining us tonight.

Speaking about ex-members, Charlie Condon, who is a former attorney general of this great State, is with us, and a friend of mine as well. I appreciate Charlie coming.

Most of all, I'm glad you're here. I want to thank you for working hard to get this event on. My friend Mercer Reynolds is the national finance chairman for Bush-Cheney '04. He's a fellow from Cincinnati, Ohio. He was educated up the road in Chapel Hill. He still came anyway. [*Laughter*]

I appreciate Dr. Eddie Floyd and John Rainey and Barry Wynn, all of them personal friends. All of them have worked hard to make this a tremendously successful event.

I want to thank the grassroots activists who are here, the people who are going to put up the signs and mail the mailers and get on the telephone to turn out the vote. I cannot win without your help. I want to thank you for what you've done in the past. I want to thank you for what you're fixing to do when we come down the pike next year. I appreciate Sarah Reese. I appreciate Todd Graham leading the pledge. And I want to thank the Governor's School Choir for joining us as well.

In the last 2½ years, this Nation has acted decisively to confront great challenges. I came to this office to solve problems, not to pass them on to future Presidents and future generations. I came to seize opportunities instead of letting them slip away. My administration is meeting the tests of our time.

Terrorists declared war on the United States of America, and war is what they got. We've captured or killed many key leaders of the Al Qaida network, and the rest of them know we're on their trail. In Afghanistan and in Iraq, we gave ultimatums to terror regimes. Those regimes chose defiance, and those regimes are no more. Fifty million people in those two countries once lived under tyranny, and today, they live in freedom.

Two-and-a-half years ago, our military was not receiving the resources it needed, and morale was beginning to suffer. So we increased the defense budgets to prepare for the threats of a new era, and today, no one can question the skill, the strength, and the spirit of the United States military.

Two-and-a-half years ago, we inherited an economy in recession. And then our country was attacked, and we had scandals in corporate America, and we marched to war for our own security and for the peace of the world, all of which affected the people's confidence. But I acted. We passed tough new laws to hold corporate criminals to account. And to get the economy going again, I have twice led the United States Congress to pass historic tax relief for the American people. I understand that when Americans have more take-home pay to spend, to save, or invest, the whole economy grows and people are more likely to find a job. So we're returning more money to the people to help them raise their families, reducing taxes on dividends and capital gains to encourage investment. We're providing small businesses with incentives so they can hire new people.

With all these actions, this administration has laid the foundation for greater prosperity and more jobs across America so every single person in this country has a chance to realize the American Dream.

Two-and-a-half years ago, there was a lot of talk about education reform, but there wasn't much action. So I called for and Congress passed the No Child Left Behind Act. With a solid bipartisan majority, we delivered the most dramatic education reforms in a generation. We believe every child can learn to read and write and add and subtract. We are challenging the soft bigotry of low expectations. We've increased Federal funding, but in return for additional Federal dollars, we expect results in every classroom so that not one single child is left behind.

We created the Department of Homeland Security to better safeguard our ports and borders and better protect the American people. We passed trade promotion authority to open up new markets for South Carolina entrepreneurs and manufacturers and farmers. We passed budget agreements to help maintain spending discipline in Washington, DC.

On issue after issue, this administration has acted on principle, has kept its word, and has made progress for the American people. And the Congress gets a lot of credit for the success we have had. I've enjoyed my work with the South Carolina delegation. I enjoy working with Speaker Denny Hastert, Majority Leader Bill Frist, two fine Americans.

We're working hard to change the tone in Washington, DC. There's too much needless politics in the Nation's Capital. We're doing the people's business by focusing on results, and we're achieving good results for the people. Those are the kind of people I've attracted in my administration. I want people who are results-oriented people, can-do people, people from all walks of life. I have put together a fantastic administration for the American people. Our country has had no finer Vice President than Dick Cheney. Mother may have a second opinion. [*Laughter*]

We've done a lot in 2½ years. We've come far, but our work is only beginning. I've set great goals worthy of a great nation. First, America is committed to expanding the realm of freedom and peace for our own security and for the benefit of the world. And second, in our own country, we must work for a society of prosperity and compassion so that every citizen has a chance to work and to succeed and to realize the promise of our country.

It is clear that the future of freedom and peace depend on the actions of America. This Nation is freedom's home and freedom's defender. We welcome this charge of history, and we are keeping it. The war on terror continues. The enemies of freedom are not idle, and neither are we. This country will not rest; we will not tire; we will not stop until this danger to civilization is removed.

We are confronting that danger in Iraq, where Saddam holdouts and foreign terrorists are desperately trying to throw Iraq into chaos by attacking coalition forces and aid workers and innocent Iraqis. They know that the advance of freedom in Iraq would be a major defeat for the cause of terror. This collection of killers is trying to shake the will of the United States and the civilized world. America will not be intimidated.

We are aggressively striking the terrorists in Iraq, defeating them there so we do not have to face them in our own country. We're calling on other nations to help Iraq to build a free country, which will make us all more secure. We're standing with the Iraqi people as they assume more of their own defense and move toward self-government. These aren't easy tasks, but they're essential tasks. We will finish what we have begun, and we will win this essential victory in the war on terror.

Yet, our greatest security comes from the advance of human liberty, because free nations do not support terror, free nations do not attack their neighbors, free nations do not threaten the world with weapons of mass terror. Americans believe that freedom is the deepest need and hope of every human heart. And I believe that freedom is the right of every person, and I believe that freedom is the future of every nation.

America also understands that unprecedented influence brings tremendous responsibilities. We have duties in this world. And when we see disease and starvation and hopeless poverty, we will not turn away. On the continent of Africa, America is now committed to bringing the healing power of medicine to millions of men and women and children suffering with AIDS. This great, strong, compassionate land is leading the world in this incredibly important work of human rescue.

We've got challenges here at home as well. We will prove equal to those challenges. Anytime one of our citizens who wants to work can't find a job, it says to me that we must continue to strive to enhance the entrepreneurial spirit of America. We've had some good numbers recently. We're making progress. But enough of our—not enough of our citizens are working.

I spent some quality time today at the BMW plant talking about jobs and job creation and job training. So long as people are looking for work, this President and this administration will work for a progrowth policy so our people can find work.

We have a duty to keep our commitment to America's seniors by strengthening and modernizing Medicare. The Congress has taken historic action to improve the lives of older citizens. For the first time since the creation of Medicare, the House and the Senate have passed reforms to increase the choices for our seniors and to provide coverage for prescription drugs. It is now time for the House and the Senate to iron out their differences and to get a good bill on my desk so we keep the promise to America's seniors to have a modern health care system.

For the sake of health care, we also need to cut down on the frivolous lawsuits which increase the cost of medicine. People who have been harmed by a bad doc deserve their day in court. Yet the system should not reward lawyers who are simply fishing for a rich settlement. Frivolous lawsuits drive up the cost of health care, and they therefore affect the Federal budget. Medical liability reform is a national issue which requires a national solution. The House of Representatives passed a good bill. The bill is stuck in the Senate. Some Senators must recognize that no one has ever been healed by a frivolous lawsuit. We need medical liability reform.

I have a responsibility as President to make sure the judicial system runs well, and I have met that duty. I have nominated superb men and women to the Federal courts, people who will interpret the law, not legislate from the bench. Some members of the Senate are trying to keep my nominees off the bench by blocking up-or-down votes. Every judicial nominee deserves a fair hearing and an up-or-down vote on the Senate floor. It is time for Members of this U.S. Senate to stop playing politics with American justice.

The Congress needs to complete work on a comprehensive energy plan. This Nation must promote energy efficiency and conservation, no doubt about it. But we must use our technologies to be able to use the resources we have at hand in environmentally friendly ways. We need clean coal technology. We need more natural gas exploration. We need safe nuclear energy. For the sake of economic security and for the sake of national security, we must become less reliant on foreign sources of energy.

Our prosperous and compassionate—prosperous and strong Nation must be a compassionate nation. I will continue to advance our agenda of compassionate conservatism, which says we'll apply the most innovative and effective ways and ideas to help our fellow citizens who hurt. There are still millions of men and women who want to end their dependence on Government and become independent through hard work. We must build on the success of welfare reform to bring work and dignity into the lives of more of our fellow citizens.

Congress should complete the "Citizen Service Act" so that more Americans can serve their communities and their country. Both Houses should reach agreement on my Faith-Based Initiative to support the armies of compassion that are mentoring our children and caring for the homeless and offering hope to the addicted. People of all faiths in America hear a universal call. People of all faiths can do things Gov-

ernment cannot do, which is to heal broken hearts. Our Government must not fear the influence of faith in helping people who hurt in our society.

A compassionate society must promote opportunity for all, including the independence and dignity that come from ownership. This administration will constantly strive to promote an ownership society in America. We want more people to own their own home. Today in America, we have a homeownership gap, a minority homeownership gap. I proposed plans to the United States Congress to close that gap. We want more people to own and manage their own retirement accounts. We want people to own and manage their own health care plans. We want more people owning their own small business. This administration understands that when a person owns something, he or she has a vital stake in the future of America.

In a compassionate society, people respect one another and take responsibility for the decisions they make. The culture of America is changing from one that has said, "If it feels good, do it," and "If you've got a problem, blame somebody else," to a culture in which each of us understands we are responsible for the decisions we make in life.

If you're fortunate enough to be a mother or a father, you are responsible for loving your child with all your heart. If you're concerned about the quality of the education in the community in which you live, you're responsible for doing something about it. If you're a CEO in corporate America, you're responsible for telling the truth to your shareholders and your employees. And in the responsibility society, each of us is responsible for loving a neighbor just like we would like to be loved ourself.

The culture of service and responsibility is growing here in America. I started what's called the USA Freedom Corps to encourage Americans to extend a compassionate hand to a neighbor in need, and the response has been strong. People are signing up to help. Faith-based programs and charities are vibrant here in America. Firemen and policemen and people who wear our Nation's uniform are reminding us what it means to sacrifice for something greater than yourself. Our children again believe in heroes, because they see them every day.

In these changing times, the world has seen the resolve and the courage of America. And I've been privileged to see the compassion and the character of the American people. All the tests of the last 2 ½ years have come to the right nation. We're a strong country, and we use that strength to defend the peace. We're an optimistic country, confident in ourselves and in ideals bigger than ourselves. Abroad, we seek to lift whole nations by spreading freedom.

At home, we seek to lift up lives by spreading opportunity to every corner of America. This is the work that history has set before us. We welcome it, and we know that for our country, the best days lie ahead.

May God bless you all. Thank you very much for coming.

NOTE: The President spoke at 6:12 p.m. at the Palmetto Expo Center. In his remarks, he referred to David H. Wilkins, speaker, South Carolina State House of Representatives, and his wife, Margaret Susan; Lt. Gov. R. Andre Bauer and former Governors David M. Beasley, Carroll A. Campbell, and James B. Edwards of South Carolina; Eddie Floyd, John Rainey, and Barry Wynn, South Carolina State finance cochairmen, Bush-Cheney '04, Inc.; opera singer Sarah Reese; and former President Saddam Hussein of Iraq.

Remarks at a Veterans Day Ceremony in Arlington, Virginia
November 11, 2003

Thank you all very much. Thank you for the warm welcome. Thank you, Secretary Principi, for doing a really fine job to represent our Nation's veterans. Members of the Cabinet, Members of the Congress, members of our military, veterans, Commander Berger, representatives of veterans organizations, and fellow Americans: Laura and I are proud to join all of you and citizens across our country as we honor the service of America's veterans.

We observe Veterans Day on an anniversary—not of a great battle or of the beginning of a war but of a day when war ended and our Nation was again at peace. Ever since the armistice of November the 11th, 1918, this has been a day to remember our debt to all who have worn the uniform of the United States.

Our veterans have borne the costs of America's wars and have stood watch over America's peace. And today, every veteran can be certain: The Nation you served and the people you defended are grateful.

Our Nation knows this national cemetery as the final resting place of those lost to the violence of war. Yet, most of the markers here stand over the graves of Americans who lived beyond their years of military service. On the hills of Arlington and in the daily lives of our country, veterans have a special place. We honor them all for their service in uniform. And we honor America's veterans for the full lives of their service they continue to lead.

Today, more than 25 million Americans wear the proud title of veteran or retired military. Their ranks include young men and women who gave good years to our all-volunteer military and recently returned to civilian life. Our veterans include more than 11 million men and women from the conflicts of Korea and Vietnam who earned this Nation's gratitude and respect. More than 4 million living Americans served in World War II, under the command of Eisenhower and Bradley and Nimitz. And on Veterans Day 2003, it is still possible to thank, in person, almost 200 Americans who were in uniform when the guns of World War I went silent 85 years from today. All the men who served when Woodrow Wilson was the Commander in Chief are now more than 100 years old, and they can know that America is still proud of them.

Every veteran has his or her own story of entering military service. Many enlisted on Monday morning, December 8th, 1941, or at the beginning of other conflicts. For some, military life began with the initiation at an academy. For others, it began with a letter from the United States Government. Yet when their service is complete, veterans of every era, every background, and every branch have certain things in common. And those shared commitments and experience formed bonds that last a lifetime.

Every veteran has lived by a strict code of discipline. Every veteran understands the meaning of personal accountability and loyalty and shared sacrifice. From the moment you repeated the oath to the day of your honorable discharge, your time belonged to America; your country came before all else. And whether you served abroad or at home, you have shared in the responsibility of maintaining the finest fighting force in the world.

Veterans who took the oath and served in battle have known the hardships and the fears and the tragic losses of war. These memories follow them through life and are sometimes hard to bear. Yet our war veterans, wherever they fought, can know this: In the harshest hours of conflict, they serve just and honorable purposes.

Americans are a peaceful people, and this Nation has always gone to war reluctantly and always for a noble cause. America's war veterans have fought for the security of this Nation, for the safety of our friends, and for the peace of the world. They humbled tyrants and defended the innocent and liberated the oppressed. And across the Earth, you will find entire nations that once lived in fear, where men and women still tell of the day when Americans came and set them free.

America's mission in the world continues, and we count on the same kind of people to carry it out. Today, in assignments around the world, more than 1.4 million Americans are on active duty, earning the title of veteran by serving in the cause of freedom. In 2 years and 2 months since our country was attacked, the men and women of our Armed Forces have engaged the terrorist enemy on many fronts. They've confronted grave dangers to defend the safety of the American people. They have liberated two nations, Afghanistan and Iraq, delivering more than 50 million people from the hands of dictators. Those who serve and fight today are adding great achievements of their own to America's history. America is grateful for their daring, grateful for their honor, and grateful for their sacrifice.

On this Veterans Day, with our Nation at war, Americans are deeply aware of the current military struggle and of recent sacrifice. Young Americans have died in liberating Iraq and Afghanistan. They've died in securing freedom in those countries. The loss is terrible. It is borne especially by the families left behind. But in their hurt and in their loneliness, I want these families to know your loved ones served in a good and just cause. They died in distant lands to fight terror, to advance freedom, and to protect America. They did not live to be called veterans, but this Nation will never forget their lives of service and all they did for us.

At this hour, many thousands are following their duty at great risk. One young man serving in Iraq recently said this: "We in the military signed up and pledged to protect this great country of ours from enemies foreign and domestic." "We're fighting," he said, "so that the next generation might never have to experience anything like September the 11th, 2001."

Today and every day, the prayers of the American people are with those who wear our country's uniform. They serve a great cause, and they follow a great tradition, handed down to them by America's veterans. Our veterans from every era are the finest of citizens. We owe them the life we know today. They command the respect of the American people, and they have our lasting gratitude.

Thank you for coming today. May God bless America, and may God bless all who defend it.

NOTE: The President spoke at 11:38 a.m. at Arlington National Cemetery. In his remarks, he referred to David Berger, national commander, Army and Navy Union of the United States of America.

Remarks at the Heritage Foundation President's Club Luncheon
November 11, 2003

Ed, thank you very much. It's an honor to be here. I appreciate your invitation. I want to thank you for your decades of leadership in the conservative movement. Presidents come and go, except here at the Heritage Foundation. [*Laughter*] I appreciate being with your good bride, Linda, the trustees of the Heritage, the longtime Heritage supporters, and the Ronald Reagan Fellow at Heritage, a man who is a fine leader, a fine Attorney General, Ed Meese.

It's appropriate that we gather in the building named for Ronald Reagan. The Heritage Foundation emerged as an important voice in Washington during the Reagan years. The American people gave Ronald Reagan his mandate for leadership. Yet it was the Heritage Foundation, with a book by that title, from which he drew ideas and inspiration. Ever since, in the councils of Washington, Heritage has been an advocate for free enterprise, traditional values, and the advance of liberty around the world. My administration has benefited from your good work, and so has our country. Thank you for what you do.

We meet on Veterans Day, and I know there are many veterans in this room. On behalf of the Nation, I thank you for your service to our country. The title of "veteran" is a term of great respect in America. All who served, whether for a few years or for many, have put the Nation's needs above their own. All stood ready if the order came to risk everything for their country's cause. Our wars have taken from us some of our finest citizens and every hour of the lifetimes they had hoped to live. And the courage of our military has given us every hour we live in freedom.

In every generation, members of the Armed Forces have been loyal to one another and faithful to the ideals of America. After the Second World War, returning veterans often said they had just been doing their jobs, or didn't talk about their service at all. Yet they knew the stakes of the fight they had been in and the magnitude of what they had achieved. Long after putting away his uniform, one American expressed his pride in having served in World War II. He said, "I feel like I played my part in turning this from a century of darkness into a century of light." This is true of all who have served and sacrificed in the struggles of the 20th century. They maintained the greatest fighting force in the world. They kept our country free, and we're grateful to them all.

We come to this Veterans Day in a time of war. And today's military is acting in the finest traditions of the veterans who came before them. They've given all that we've asked of them. They are showing bravery in the face of ruthless enemies and compassion to people in great need. Our men and women in uniform are warriors, and they are liberators, strong and kind and decent. By their courage, they keep us safe; by their honor, they make us proud.

When we lose such Americans in battle, we lose our best. And the time—this time of brave achievement is also a time of sacrifice. Not far from this place, at Army and Navy medical centers, young servicemembers are recovering from injuries of war. Not far from here, at Arlington National Cemetery, as in hometowns across America, we have laid to rest young men and women who died in distant lands. For their families, this is a terrible sorrow, and we pray for their comfort. For the Nation, there is a feeling of loss, and we remember and we honor every name.

Our people in uniform know the cost and risk of war. They also know what is at stake in this war. Army Command Sergeant Major Ioakimo Falaniko recently lost his son, Private Jonathan Falaniko, in an attack near Baghdad. Father and son both served in Iraq in the same unit, the 1st Armored Division's Engineer Brigade. At his son's memorial service, Command Sergeant Major Falaniko said this: "What our country brings to Iraq is a chance for freedom and democracy. We're making a difference every day. My son died for a good cause. He answered the Nation's call."

Our mission in Iraq and Afghanistan is clear to our servicemembers and clear to our enemies. Our men and women are fighting to secure the freedom of more than 50 million people who recently lived under two of the cruelest dictatorships on Earth. Our men and women are fighting to help democracy and peace and justice rise in a troubled and violent region. Our men and women are fighting terrorist enemies thousands of miles away in the heart and center of their power so that we do not face those enemies in the heart of America. Our men and women are fighting for the security of America and for the advance of freedom, and that is a cause worth fighting for.

The work we are in is not easy, yet it is essential. The failure of democracy in Afghanistan and Iraq would condemn every advocate of freedom in those two countries to prison or death and would extinguish the democratic hopes of millions in the Middle East. The failure of democracies in those two countries would provide new bases for the terrorist network and embolden terrorists and their allies around the world. The failure of democracy in those two countries would convince terrorists that America backs down under attack, and more attacks on America would surely follow.

The terrorists cite the examples of Beirut and Somalia as evidence that America can be made to run. Five years ago, one of the terrorists said that an attack could make America retreat in less than 24 hours. The terrorists are mistaken.

The United States will complete our work in Iraq and in Afghanistan. Democracy in those two countries will succeed, and that success will be a great milestone in the history of liberty. A democratic revolution that has reached across the globe will finally take root in the Middle East. The stagnation and isolation and anger of that region will give way to progress and opportunity. America and the world will be safer from catastrophic violence because terror is not the tool of the free.

The United States has made an unbreakable commitment to the success of freedom in Afghanistan and Iraq. We have a strategy to see that commitment through. In Afghanistan, we're helping to build a free and stable democracy as we continue to track down and destroy Taliban and Al Qaida forces. Following years of cruel oppression, the Afghan people are living with hope, and they're making steady progress.

In Iraq, the terrorists have chosen to make a stand and to test our resolve. Their violence is concentrated in a relatively small area of that country. Yet the terrorists are dangerous. For the sake of Iraq's future, for the sake of America's security, these killers must be defeated.

After the swift advance of our coalition to Baghdad and the removal of Saddam Hussein from power, some remnants of the regime fled from the battlefield. Over time, Ba'ath Party and Fedayeen fighters and other Saddam loyalists have organized to attack our forces, to terrorize international aid workers, and to murder innocent Iraqis. These bitter holdouts would rather see Iraqis dead than see them free.

Foreign jihadists have arrived across Iraq's borders in small groups with the goal of installing a Taliban-like regime. Also present in the country are some terrorists from Ansar Islam and from Al Qaida, who are always eager to join in the killing and who seek revenge after their defeat in Afghanistan. Saddam loyalists and foreign terrorists may have different long-term goals, but they share a near-term strategy: to terrorize Iraqis and to intimidate America and our allies.

Recent reporting suggests that despite their differences, these killers are working together to spread chaos and terror and fear. Since the fall of Saddam Hussein, 93 percent of terror attacks have occurred in Baghdad and five of Iraq's 18 provinces. The violence is focused in 200 square miles known as the Ba'athist Triangle, the home area of Saddam Hussein and most of his associates. Here, the enemy is waging the battle, and it is here that the enemy will be defeated.

In the last few months, the adversary has changed its composition and method, and our coalition is adapting accordingly. We're employing the latest battlefield technology to locate mortar positions and roadside bombs. Our forces are moving against specific targets based on intelligence gathered from Iraqis. We're conducting hundreds of daily patrols. Last month alone, we made 1,500 raids against terrorists. The recent operations have resulted in the capture or death of more than 1,000 killers, the seizure of 4,500 mortar rounds; 1,600 rocket-propelled grenades have been seized, thousands of other weapons and military equipment. Our coalition is on the offensive in Iraq, and we will stay on the offensive.

The long-term security of Iraq will be assured by the Iraqis themselves. One hundred and eighteen thousand Iraqis are now serving as police officers and border guards, civil defense personnel, and in the facilities protection service. Iraq's security forces join in operations with our troops, and they patrol towns and cities independently. Some 700 troops are now serving in the new Iraqi army. Thousands more are being trained, and we expect to see 35,000 Iraqi troops in the field by the end of next year. Increasingly, the Iraqi people are assuming the responsibilities and the risks of protecting their own country. And their willingness to accept these duties is one of the surest signs that the Iraqis want freedom and that the Iraqis are headed toward self-government.

Under our strategy, increasing authority is being transferred to the Iraqi people. The Iraqi Governing Council has appointed ministers who are responsible for the day-to-day operations of the Iraqi government. The Council has also begun the process that will lead to a new constitution. No friend or enemy should doubt Iraq liberty will find a lasting home.

Iraqis are a proud people, and they want their national independence. And they can see the difference between those who are attacking their country and those who are helping to build it. Our coalition is training new police; the terrorists are trying to kill them. We're protecting pipelines and powerplants for the good of the Iraqi people; the terrorists are trying to blow them up.

We're turning authority over to Iraqi leaders; the terrorists are trying to assassinate them. We're offering aid and self-rule and hope for the future; the terrorists offer nothing but oppression and death. The vast majority of Iraqis know exactly what is going on in their country today. Having seen the worst of tyranny, the Iraqi people will reject the return of tyranny.

After decades of a dictator's sustained assault on Iraq's society and dignity and spirit, a Jeffersonian democracy will not spring up in a matter of months. We know that our Ba'athist and terrorist enemies are ruthless and cunning. We also know that the lives of Iraqis have improved greatly in 7 short months. Yet, we know the remaining tasks are difficult.

We also know a few things about our own country. America gained its own independence and helped free much of the world by taking on difficult tasks. We're a confident people, and we have a reason to be confident. Our Armed Forces are skilled and powerful and humane. They're the best in the world. I will keep them that way.

We've got good friends and allies serving with us in Iraq. There are 32 countries standing beside our troops. Our commanders have the capabilities they have requested, and they're meeting a changing enemy with flexible tactics. The Congress has provided the resources we need to support our military and to improve the daily lives of newly liberated people. Other nations and organizations have stepped up to provide more than $18 billion to the emerging democracies of Afghanistan and Iraq. The peoples of those two countries are sacrificing for their own liberty. And the United States once again is fighting in the cause of our Nation, the great cause of liberty. And we know that the cause of liberty will prevail.

Much is asked of us, and we have answered this kind of challenge before. In the summer of 1948, the Soviet Union imposed a sudden and total blockade on the city of Berlin in order to force the allies out. More than 2 million people would soon be without food or fuel or medicine. The entire world watched and wondered if free peoples would back down, wondered whether free people would abandon their commitments. It was at the outset of the cold war, and the will and the resolve of America were being measured.

In an urgent meeting, all the alternatives were discussed, including retreat. When the moment of decision came, President Harry Truman said this: "We stay in Berlin, period. We stay in Berlin, come what may." By the determination of President Truman, America and our allies launched the Berlin airlift and overcame more than 10 months of siege. That resolve and the daring of our military saved a city and held back the Communist threat in Europe.

Nearly four decades later, Ronald Reagan came to West Berlin with the same kind of resolve, and vision beyond the cold war. When he called on the Soviets to tear down that wall, he was asserting a confident new doctrine. He believed that communism can not only be contained but transcended, that no human barrier could hold back the spread of human liberty. The triumph of that vision eventually turned enemies into friends, healed a divided continent, and brought security and peace to Europe and America.

Two years into the war on terror, the will and resolve of America are being tested in Afghanistan and in Iraq. Again the world is watching. Again we will be steadfast. We will finish the mission we have begun, period.

We are not only containing the terrorist threat, we are turning it back. We believe that freedom is the right of every person. We believe that freedom is the hope of every culture. We believe that freedom is the future of every nation in the Middle East. And we know as Americans that the advance of freedom is the surest path to peace.

May God bless you all.

NOTE: The President spoke at 1:16 p.m. at the Ronald Reagan Building and International Trade Center. In his remarks, he referred to Edwin J. Feulner, president, The Heritage Foundation, and his wife, Linda Leventhal; former Attorney General Edwin Meese III; and former President Saddam Hussein of Iraq.

Remarks on Presenting the Presidential Medal of Freedom To Secretary General Lord Robertson of the North Atlantic Treaty Organization
November 12, 2003

Good morning. I'm proud to welcome members of the diplomatic corps and my administration, and of course Lord Robertson, the Secretary General of NATO, to the White House. I've been honored to host Lord Robertson here at the White House many times over the past 3 years. I'm grateful that he's come once more before he leaves his post.

The Presidential Medal of Freedom is our Nation's highest civil award, given to individuals of exceptional merit and integrity. For Lord Robertson, it is a fitting tribute to his long and distinguished career of service to his nation, to our alliance, and to the world.

NATO is the most successful alliance in history, and Lord Robertson has led NATO during some of the most challenging years of its history. Not long ago, some questioned whether NATO could or should survive the end of the cold war. Then the Alliance proved its enduring worth by stopping ethnic cleansing in Bosnia and keeping the peace in Kosovo. Some wonder whether NATO could adopt to the new threats of the 21st century. Today, NATO forces are fighting terror in Afghanistan and supporting a multinational division in Iraq.

Today in Iraq, a member of NATO, Italy, lost some proud sons in the service of freedom and peace. The United States sends our deepest condolences to the families who died—of the soldiers and policemen who died. We appreciate their sacrifices. I appreciate the steadfast leadership of Prime Minister Berlusconi, who refuses to yield in the face of terror.

Lord Robertson is a patient leader. He's a determined leader, and over the past 4 years his skills and talents have made many achievements possible. Lord Robertson oversaw the largest expansion in NATO's history, a major milestone in the fulfillment of our shared vision of a Europe whole, free, and at peace. He helped open a new chapter in NATO's relationship with Russia through the creation of the Russian-NATO Council. He ensured that NATO would honor its commitment to come to the defense of fellow NATO member Turkey. And he pursued an ambitious agenda of transformation to make NATO forces lighter, faster, and better able to respond to complex and ever-changing threats.

America owes a special debt to Lord Robertson. When our Nation was attacked on September the 11th, 2001, Lord Robertson led NATO to invoke, for the first time in its history, Article V, which states that an attack against one NATO Ally is an attack against all. Americans will never forget that vital support from our closest allies on one of the darkest days of our history.

Our alliance continues to face and to meet the threats to peace and prosperity and freedom. Lord Robertson's leadership has been crucial to meeting these challenges. His tenure at the helm of this institution shows the power of collective defense when free nations act to serve great causes and free nations act to produce results. Lord Robertson's efforts and vision leave behind a legacy of effective multilateralism that will benefit this Alliance for years to come.

When NATO was founded over half a century ago, President Harry Truman said this: "By this treaty, we are not only seeking to establish freedom, freedom from aggression and from the use of force in the North Atlantic community, but we're also actively striving to promote and preserve peace throughout the world." We honor Lord Robertson here today for his dedication to the high ideals of the NATO Alliance, the promise of peace throughout the world.

I'm going to ask the military aide now to read the honor. It is my honor to welcome this good man, to present the Medal of Freedom to the Right Honorable Lord Robertson of Port Ellen.

NOTE: The President spoke at 11:54 a.m. in the Roosevelt Room at the White House. In his remarks, he referred to Prime Minister Silvio Berlusconi of Italy. The transcript released by the Office of the Press Secretary also included the remarks of Secretary General Lord Robertson.

Message to the Congress on Continuation of the National Emergency With Respect to Iran
November 12, 2003

To the Congress of the United States:

Section 202(d) of the National Emergencies Act (50 U.S.C. 1622(d)) provides for the automatic termination of a national emergency unless, prior to the anniversary date of its declaration, the President publishes in the *Federal Register* and transmits to the Congress a notice stating that the emergency is to continue in effect beyond the anniversary date. Consistent with this provision, I have sent the enclosed notice, stating that the Iran emergency declared by Executive Order 12170 on November 14, 1979, is to continue in effect beyond November 14, 2003, to the *Federal Register* for publication. The most recent notice continuing this emergency was published in the *Federal Register* on November 13, 2002 (67 *Fed. Reg.* 68929).

Our relations with Iran have not yet returned to normal, and the process of implementing the January 19, 1981, agreements with Iran is still underway. For these reasons, I have determined that it is necessary to continue the national emergency declared on November 14, 1979, with respect to Iran, beyond November 14, 2003.

GEORGE W. BUSH

The White House,
November 12, 2003.

NOTE: The notice of November 12 is listed in Appendix D at the end of this volume.

Remarks Following a Meeting With Judicial Nominees and an Exchange With Reporters
November 13, 2003

The President. I have the job of nominating people to serve on the Federal benches. I have handled my duty in the right way by picking superb men and women to serve our country as Federal judges, people of integrity and honor, people of high intelligence, three of whom are with me today. Carolyn Kuhl, Janice Brown, Priscilla Owen really represent the best of America—superb, superb women.

And yet, these three women are being denied a chance to serve on the bench because of ugly politics in the United States Senate. These folks deserve an up-or-down vote on the Senate floor. If they get an up-or-down vote on the Senate floor, they will be confirmed because the majority of justices believe they should serve. And yet a few Senators are playing politics. And it's wrong, and it's shameful, and it's hurting the system.

I have told these three ladies I will stand with them until the bitter end because they're the absolute right pick for their respective positions. And the Senators who are playing politics with their nominations are acting shamefully. And I want to thank you all for being such stalwarts for justice and fairness and decency, and I appreciate you standing here.

Carolyn Kuhl. Thank you, Mr. President.

The President. Let me answer a couple quick—please.

Iraq

Q. Mr. President, could you tell us your ideas about how you would like to see—speed up the transfer of power in Iraq? Are you interested in setting up, for example, an interim government before a constitution is written?

The President. What I'm interested in doing is working with Ambassador Bremer and the Governing Council to work on a plan that will encourage the Iraqis to assume more responsibility. Ambassador Bremer sat right here yesterday and talked to me about the Iraqis' desire to be more involved in the governance of their country. And that's a positive development because actually that's what we want. We want the Iraqis to be more involved in the governance of their country. And so Ambassador Bremer, with my instructions, is going back to talk to the Governing Council to develop a strategy. And he'll report back after he's consulted with the very people that we want to assume more responsibility.

Yes.

Steel Tariffs

Q. Mr. President——

The President. You're in there, Stretch [David Gregory, NBC News].

Q. What's your timetable for deciding on whether to lift the steel sanctions? And how far do you think the U.S. industry has gone now in restructuring toward——

The President. Well, that's exactly what I'm reviewing now. Part of the—the decision was based upon the International Trade Commission's finding that our industry had been harmed, and therefore, I imposed some tariffs in order to allow for a restructuring of the industry. I'm in the process of reviewing the extent to which the industry has been restructured. I'm going to make a decision within a reasonable period of time.

Q. Mr. President?

The President. Yes, Stretch.

Q. Thank you, sir.

The President. Excuse me, I couldn't tell if you wanted to ask a question or not today. [*Laughter*]

Iraq

Q. How worried——

The President. Is this about the judges?

Q. Yes, right.

The President. Okay.

Q. I would—if I had time, I would. What are you prepared to do about the fact and how worried are you about the fact that ordinary Iraqis appear to be more irritated with the presence of U.S. troops and more supportive of Iraqi insurgents?

The President. Well, first of all, the goal of the terrorists, whether they be Ba'athists or mujahideen fighters or Al-Qaida-type fighters, is to create terror and fear amongst average Iraqis, is to create the conditions where people are just so fearful for their lives that they cannot think positively about freedom. That's their goal.

Our goal, of course, is to continue to work with those Iraqi citizens who understand that freedom is a precious commodity, those who understand that there is a hopeful life possible in a part of the world where a lot of hope has been diminished in the past. And that's the struggle— that's the struggle. And we're going to prevail because, well, one, we got a good strategy to deal with these killers. Two, I believe by far the vast majority of Iraqis do understand the stakes and do want their children to grow up in a peaceful environment and do want their children going to a school and do want to be able to live a free life that is prosperous. That's what I believe. And I—recently, I was told by— for example, Bremer was telling me about a survey done by an American firm in Baghdad, for example, and it said that by far the vast majority of people understand that if America were to leave and the terrorists were to prevail in their desire to drive us out, the country would fall into chaos. And no one wants that, and so I'm confident we'll prevail in the long run. And I'm confident we're doing good work right now.

Yes.

Q. Mr. President, are you——

Judicial Nominations

The President. Do you have a followup on the judges?

Q. Yes, well, the Democrats say they have confirmed 98 percent of your judges——

The President. Yes.

Q. ——and by focusing on the few that they are opposing, that you're picking essentially an unfair fight.

The President. Well, our circuits—circuit courts remain, in some cases, dangerously vacant. And here are three cases where people are being treated unfairly. My question is, why won't they give these three ladies an up-or-down vote? Where's the justice? These are eminently qualified people. These are three women who are—represent the best of American jurisprudence. And why won't they let them come to the floor? If they're so fair, bring them up to a vote—today. Let these three nominees get onto the floor of the United States Senate for an up-or-down vote, and then I will listen to whether or not they're fair or not.

Yes, last question, then I've got to go.

President's Upcoming Visit to the United Kingdom

Q. Are you concerned, Mr. President, that the massive amount of protesters that are going to be in London next week will undercut your message of unity in Iraq?

The President. I am so pleased to be going to a country which says that people are allowed to express their mind. That's fantastic. You know, freedom is a beautiful thing. And the fact that people are willing to come out and express themselves says I'm going to a great country.

And secondly, I don't expect everybody in the world to agree with the positions I've taken. But certainly, those should agree with the goals of the United States, which is peace and freedom. You see, we believe that freedom is not America's gift to the world. We believe freedom is the Almighty's gift to everybody in the world. We believe free societies are peaceful societies. We believe in human justice and human dignity and human rights. We cry when we hear stories about people being tortured, women being raped in rape rooms. We weep when we discover mass graves of innocent Iraqis. We understand that tyranny is not the form of government that will bring hope and justice. And therefore, we're not only willing to defend our own security; we're also willing to defend the rights of others.

Thank you.

NOTE: The President spoke at 8:30 a.m. in the Oval Office at the White House, following a meeting with Carolyn B. Kuhl, nominee to be U.S. Circuit Judge for the Ninth Circuit; Janice Brown, nominee to be U.S. Circuit Judge for the District of Columbia Circuit; and Priscilla Owen, nominee to be U.S. Circuit Judge for the Fifth Circuit. In his remarks, he referred to L. Paul Bremer III, Presidential Envoy to Iraq.

Remarks at a Bush-Cheney Luncheon in Orlando, Florida
November 13, 2003

The President. Thank you all. Thanks for coming. Thanks, Jeb—I mean, Governor. [*Laughter*] It's hard to get used to it. [*Laughter*] The thing I love about Jeb is he's a modest fellow. When the Florida Marlins won, he was trying to take credit for their success. [*Laughter*] I told him he doesn't have any idea what it takes to run a championship baseball team. [*Laughter*] He reminded me I don't either. [*Laughter*]

Love being back in Florida with our friends. Thank you all for coming. I appreciate your support a lot. It means a lot to me. Listen, the political season is going to come in its own time. I'm loosening up, and I'm getting ready. But I've got a job to do for everybody who lives in this country. And I'm going to continue doing that job. And as you work the phones and go to the coffee shops and houses of worship, I want you to remind the people that I'm going to work hard to keep America strong, to keep America secure. I'll work hard to make sure we're prosperous and free.

I regret one thing about this event, and that is Laura is not with me.

Audience members. Oh-h-h.

The President. I know it. I know it. [*Laughter*] You drew the short straw.

[*Laughter*] She is a fabulous sister-in-law. She's a great wife, a wonderful mother, and she's doing a heck of a good job as the First Lady of this country. I'm really proud of her. She sends her very best to all our friends here in central Florida.

I'm proud of my brother. I tell you, he is a—he has been a superb Governor. He is a principled man, principled man. When he says something, you can book it. He is a man of his word. He is a courageous person, and he's got his priorities absolutely right. He loves his faith. He loves his family, and he loves his Florida.

I want to thank the other cast of characters who have joined me on this stage. That would be Tom Petway, Zach Zachariah, and David Brown, all of whom are working hard to make sure that this campaign is well-financed. I want to thank you for your hard work. I appreciate your efforts.

Mel Martinez is here today. He serves in my Cabinet. Where are you? There he is. Mel. He's done a superb job in my Government. You'll hear me talk a little bit about the homeownership gap a little later on. He's the leader in making sure that we promote ownership here in America. He is a—I love his story—it's the story of America, as far as I am concerned. As you know, Mel was a part of what they call Pedro Pan—Peter Pan. It's a program that—where Cuban moms and dads had the courage to send their children—I think Mel was 13 at the time—to send this teenager to America so that they could grow up in freedom. It speaks a lot about the mom and dad. It speaks a lot about the compassion of the American families who received the Mel Martinezes of the world. As well it speaks a lot about Mel and the other men and women who came from Cuba to flee to freedom. And Mel—it touches my heart to know that this man, who could have been living in repression and tyranny, is now in the Cabinet of the President of the United States.

I want to thank Congresswoman Katherine Harris and Congressman Tom Feeney for joining us today. Thank you all for coming. I appreciate my friend Bill McCollum, former Congressman from this part of the world, for being here. Thank you for coming, Bill.

I know we've got members of the statehouse here. You're probably standing by, waiting for your orders from Governor Bush on what to do next. [*Laughter*] Oh, yes, that's not the way it works. [*Laughter*]

The Lieutenant Governor, Toni Jennings, is here, and I want to thank Toni for coming. Charlie Crist is here. I appreciate Charlie for being here, the attorney general. We call him "General" now. [*Laughter*] Tom Gallagher is here. I appreciate both the statewide holders. I know State Senator Dan Webster is with us today. I want to thank you for coming, Dan.

I know my friend Rich Crotty is here, one of the cochairmen of the event. But most of all, I want to thank you all for coming.

Audience members. [*Inaudible*]

The President. Well, Crotty—[*laughter*]—a couple of distant cousins leading the charge there. [*Laughter*] Finally, my friend Mercer Reynolds is with us, who is the national finance chairman for Bush-Cheney '04. He's from Cincinnati, Ohio. He's an entrepreneur and a business guy who has taken time out of his life to work hard, to encourage you all to participate. It looks like he as well as the Floridian leadership did a fabulous job. I'm proud you're here, and I thank you for coming.

Over the last 3 years, our Nation has acted decisively to confront great challenges. I came to this office to solve problems and not pass them on to future Presidents and future generations. I came to seize opportunities instead of letting them slip away. My administration is meeting the tests of our time.

Terrorists declared war on the United States of America, and war is what they got. We've captured or killed many of the key leaders of the Al Qaida network, and the rest of them know we're on their trail. In Afghanistan and in Iraq, we gave ultimatums to terror regimes. Those regimes chose defiance, and those regimes are no more. Fifty million people in those two countries once lived under tyranny, and today, they live in freedom.

Three years ago, our military was not receiving the resources it needed and morale was beginning to suffer, so we increased the defense budgets to prepare for the threats of a new era. And today, no one in the world can question the skill and the strength and the spirit of the United States military.

Three years ago, the economy was in trouble, and then recession was beginning. Then the attacks happened on our country. That affected economic growth. We had some scandals in corporate America. We marched to war in order to make America more secure and the world more peaceful. That all affected the way our people felt about the future, but we acted. We acted. We passed tough new laws to hold corporate criminals to account, and in order to get this economy going again, I have twice led the United States Congress to pass historic tax relief for the American people.

I know that when Americans have more take-home pay to spend, to save, or invest, the whole economy grows, and people are more likely to find a job. We're returning more money to the people to help them raise their families, reducing taxes on dividends and capital gains to encourage investment. We're giving small businesses incentives to expand and to hire new people. With all these actions, we're laying the foundation for greater prosperity and more jobs across America, so every single citizen has a chance to realize the American Dream.

Today, the American economy is strong, and it is getting stronger. Third quarter growth in our economy was at the fastest pace in nearly 20 years. That's a good sign. People are finding more new jobs are being created. That's a good sign. Productivity is high. Business investment is rising. The housing construction is strong. The tax relief we passed is working. We left more money in the hands of the American people, and our economy is growing stronger.

Three years ago, there was a lot of talk about education reform, but the truth of the matter is, in Washington, there was not much action. So I acted. I called for and the Congress passed the No Child Left Behind Act. With a solid bipartisan majority, we delivered the most dramatic education reforms in a generation.

See, we believe in high standards. We're going to challenge the soft bigotry of low expectations. We believe every child can learn to read and write and add and subtract, and we expect every child to learn to read and write and add and subtract. We've increased the education budgets for Title I students. But for the first time, now the Federal Government is saying, "Show us some results." For the first time, we're saying the days of excuse-making are over. We expect results in every classroom so not one single child is left behind.

We reorganized our Government and created the Department of Homeland Security to better safeguard our ports and borders and better secure the American people. We passed trade promotion authority to open up markets for Florida's farmers and ranchers and entrepreneurs. We passed budget agreements to maintain much needed spending discipline in Washington, DC. On issue after issue, this administration has acted on principle, has kept its word, and has made progress for the American people.

The Congress gets a lot of credit for the progress we've made. I want to thank the Speaker, Denny Hastert, and Majority Leader Bill Frist for providing strong leadership. I want to thank the Members who are here. And you've got a great delegation from Florida with whom I've been able to work. I want to thank them for their hard work. See, what we're trying to do is to change the tone in Washington, DC. We're trying to get rid of all the needless politics and focus on the people's business, focus on results, and not the ugly process that sometimes takes on. We're making good progress. We really are.

And one of the reasons why this administration has been successful is because I've called upon people from all walks of life, people like Mel Martinez, to join our Government. I have put together a fantastic administration for the American people. Our country has had no finer Vice President than Dick Cheney.

Audience member. [*Inaudible*]

The President. Okay, I agree. Mother may have a second opinion. [*Laughter*]

In 3 years, we've come far, we've done a lot. But our work is only beginning. I've set great goals worthy of a great nation. First, America is committed to expanding the realm of freedom and peace for our own security and for the benefit of the world. And second, in our own country, we must work for a society of prosperity and compassion so that every citizen has a chance to work and to succeed and realize the great promise of America.

It is clear that the future of freedom and peace depend on the actions of America. This Nation is freedom's home and freedom's defender. We welcome this charge of history, and we are keeping it. The war on terror continues. The enemies of freedom are not idle, and neither are we. This country will not rest; we will not tire; we will not stop until this danger to civilization is removed.

We are confronting that danger in Iraq, the latest front in the war on terror. We're confronting that danger where Saddam holdouts and foreign terrorists are desperately trying to throw Iraq into chaos by attacking coalition forces and international aid workers and innocent Iraqi citizens. They know that the advance of freedom in Iraq would be a major defeat for the cause of terror. This collection of killers is trying to shake the will of America. America will not be intimidated.

We're aggressively striking the terrorists in Iraq, defeating them there so we will not have to face them in our own country. We're calling for other nations to help. You see, a free Iraq will make the whole world more secure. We're standing with the Iraqi people as they assume more of their own defense and as they move toward self-government.

These are not easy tasks, but they are essential tasks. We will finish what we have begun, and we will win this essential victory in the war on terror. Our greatest security comes from the advance of human liberty, because free nations do not support terror, free nations do not attack their neighbors, free nations do not threaten the world with weapons of mass terror.

Americans believe that freedom is the deepest need and hope of every human heart. I believe that freedom is the future of every nation. And I know that freedom is not America's gift to the world; freedom is God's gift to every man and women who lives in the world.

We understand that unprecedented influence brings tremendous responsibilities. We have duties in this world, and when we see disease and starvation and hopeless poverty, we will not turn away. On the continent of Africa, America is leading the world. We are committed to bringing the healing power, the healing power of medicine to millions of men and women and children suffering with AIDS. This mighty, strong, powerful Nation is a compassionate nation. And I'm proud to say, we're doing everything we can in the important work of human rescue.

We've got challenges here at home, and we'll be equal to the challenges. We'll continue to push a progrowth environment. I want people working. We'll continue to work on our economy until everybody who wants to work and is not working today can find a job.

We have a duty to keep our commitment to America's seniors by strengthening and modernizing Medicare. After years of debate and delay and deadlock, the Congress is nearing final passage of the biggest improvements in senior health care in nearly 40 years. We're on the verge of giving our seniors prescription drug coverage, expanded coverage for preventive medicine and therapies, more health care choices. Members of Congress have supported these Medicare reforms with their words. Now it is time to support these reforms with their votes. The House and the Senate must quickly reconcile their differences and send me a bill. We need to give our seniors a modern Medicare system before the year is out.

And for the sake of our health care system, we need to cut down on the frivolous lawsuits which increase the cost of medicine. I appreciate Jeb's leadership on this important issue, and it's an important issue. If you've been harmed by a bad doctor, you deserve your day in court. Systems shouldn't reward lawyers who are simply fishing for a rich settlement. Jeb's taken on this issue, and so have I. And the reason I have is because frivolous lawsuits drive up the cost of health care, and they therefore affect the Federal budget. Medical liability reform is a national issue that requires a national solution.

I put out a good proposal. It was passed by the House of Representatives. It is stuck in the United States Senate. It is important for those Senators who are preventing this bill from going forward to understand that nobody has ever been healed by a frivolous lawsuit.

I have a responsibility as the President to make sure the judicial system runs well, and I met that duty. I've nominated superb men and women for the Federal courts, people who will interpret the law, not legislate from the bench. Today I met with three superb women in the Oval Office before I got on the airplane to come to Florida, three fantastic nominees, people who will represent their judiciary with class and distinction and integrity. Yet, their nominations are being held up. They can't get a vote on the floor. I call upon the Florida Senators to let these three women get a vote on the floor of the United States Senate. Every nominee deserves a fair hearing and an up-or-down vote. It's time for Members of the United States Senate to stop playing politics with American justice.

This country needs a comprehensive energy plan. We must promote energy efficiency and conservation and develop clean technologies to help us explore in environmentally sensible ways for energy. For the sake of economic security and for the sake of national security, this Nation must become less dependent on foreign sources of energy. They passed a bill out of the House. They passed a bill out of the Senate. They need to reconcile their differences and get the energy plan to my desk before they go home this Christmas.

A strong and prosperous nation must also be a compassionate nation. I'm going to continue to advance our agenda of compassionate conservatism, which means we will apply the most effective, innovative techniques and ideas to help fellow citizens who hurt. There's still a lot of people in our country, millions of men and women who want to end their dependence on Government and become independent through hard work. We've got a bill on the success of welfare reform to bring work and dignity into the lives of more of our citizens.

Congress needs to complete the "Citizen Service Act" so that more Americans can serve their communities and their country. Both Houses should reach agreement on my Faith-Based Initiative to support the armies of compassion, the soldiers of which are mentoring children, caring for the homeless, offering hope to the addicted. Government can hand out money, but it cannot put hope in people's hearts. This country is strong because we're a country of all faiths, we welcome all faiths. And our Government should not fear the positive influence of faith when it comes to the help of healing broken hearts.

A compassionate society must promote opportunity for all, including the independence and dignity that come from owning something, from ownership. This administration will constantly strive to promote an ownership society in America. We want more people owning their own home. There is a minority homeownership gap in America that must be closed. Mel and I have developed a plan to close that gap. I've submitted elements of the plan to the United States Congress.

We want more people owning and managing their own health care plans. We want more people owning and managing their own retirement accounts. We want more people owning their own small business. This administration understands that when a person owns something, he or she has a vital stake in the future of our country.

A compassionate society—in a compassionate society, people respect one another, and they take responsibility for the decisions they make in life. The culture of America is changing from one that has said, "If it feels good, do it," and "If you've got a problem, blame somebody else," to a culture in which each of us understands we're responsible for the decisions we make in life. If you're fortunate enough to be a mom or a dad, you're responsible for loving your child with all your heart. If you're worried about the quality of the education in the community in which you live, you're responsible for doing something about it. If you're a CEO in corporate America, you're responsible for telling the truth to your shareholders and your employees. And in a responsibility society, each of us is responsible for loving our neighbor just like we'd like to be loved ourself.

I said the culture is changing, and the culture of service is growing. I started what's called the USA Freedom Corps to give Americans a chance to participate in making their communities and cities and neighborhoods better, and the response has been fantastic. Our charities are strong. Neighborhood healers are active all across America. Our policemen and firefighters and people who wear our Nation's uniform remind us on a daily basis what it means to sacrifice for something greater than yourself. Once again, the children of Amer-

ica believe in heroes, because they see them every day.

In these challenging times, the world has seen the resolve and the courage of the American people. I've been privileged to see the compassion and character of the American people. All the tests of the last years have come to the right Nation. We're a strong country, and we use our strength to defend the peace. We're an optimistic country, confident in ourselves and in ideals bigger than ourselves.

Abroad, we seek to lift whole nations by spreading freedom. At home, we seek to lift up lives by spreading opportunity to every corner of America. This is the work that history has set before us. We welcome it, and we know that for our country, the best days lie ahead.

May God bless you all.

NOTE: The President spoke at 12:09 p.m. at Disney's Grand Floridian Resort and Spa. In his remarks, he referred to Gov. Jeb Bush of Florida; Tom Petway III and Zach Zachariah, Florida State finance cochairmen, Bush-Cheney '04, Inc.; and Tom Gallagher, chief financial officer, Florida Department of Financial Services.

Remarks at the Engelwood Neighborhood Center in Orlando
November 13, 2003

Thanks for coming. Thanks for the warm welcome. I want to thank the Engelwood Neighborhood Center for hosting us. [*Applause*] You're awfully kind to have us. Behave yourself. [*Laughter*] I wish I had time for a workout. I saw your facilities. [*Laughter*] One good way to help people maintain their health is to encourage people to exercise. And I want to thank those of you who are encouraging people of all ages to get a little exercise on a daily basis. The best way to make sure your health is strong is to prevent disease in the first place.

Nothing like going out for a good stroll to keep yourself healthy.

I also want to thank our friends in my administration and the seniors who are participating in the discussions in Denver, Philadelphia, Phoenix, Cleveland, and Dallas. I notice that Surgeon General Carmona is hosting an event on the SMU campus. That kind of warms my heart, because First Lady Laura Bush went to SMU. I don't know if they still remember her there—[*laughter*]—but I certainly remember her here. [*Laughter*] And she sends her very best.

I want to thank you all for being here at what I would call an historic time when it comes to the health of our seniors, because I believe, with hard work and the right focus and with your help, we can reform Medicare. We can reform Medicare for the benefit of people who are on Medicare, and we can reform Medicare for those of us who are soon to be on Medicare. We have an obligation in this country. After years of debate and deadlock and delay, both Houses of Congress are nearing final passage of the biggest improvements in senior health care in 40 years. We're on the verge of giving seniors prescription drug coverage, expanded coverage for preventative maintenance medicine and therapy, and more health care choices.

Members of Congress say they support these Medicare reforms. Now it's time for a final vote. Members of Congress must resolve their remaining differences. The House and the Senate must resolve their differences and get a bill to me. For the sake of America's seniors, I call on the United States Congress to get the job done.

I appreciate Josefina's service to our Nation. As you know, she's the Assistant Secretary for Aging, U.S. Department of Health. Her boss, Tommy Thompson, a former Governor of Wisconsin, Cabinet Secretary, is now—has been on the Hill today working out the differences between the House and the Senate. He is intricately involved in making sure we get us a good Medicare bill.

I want to thank my brother, the Governor of this great State, who cares. He's got the right priorities. I know his priorities because we were both raised by the same mother. [*Laughter*] By the way, she wants there to be a modern Medicare system. [*Laughter*] But Jeb prioritizes his faith and his family and the people of Florida. He cares deeply about the people here. I'm proud of his leadership. They may say I'm

not very objective, but he's a great Governor.

I'm honored that five distinguished Members of the United States House of Representatives have joined us here for this discussion. They are people who are going to help make the decision. I view them as allies in this important issue as well as allies in helping us keep the peace around the world. They are Congressman Ric Keller, Congressman John Mica, Congressman Adam Putnam, Congressman Katherine Harris, and Congressman—Congresswoman Katherine Harris, and Congressman Tom Feeney. I'm honored you all are here.

I appreciate so very much your interest in this issue. I want to thank you for working with us. It's a tough issue. It's a tough issue because it's a complex issue, but modernizing Medicare is the right thing to do. We must not miss this opportunity. I ask the Members to go back and take—share the passion that not only I share—have but the others in the audience have about those of us in Washington doing our duty, doing what we're called to do, and that is to tackle tough issues and lead.

I want to thank Rhonda Medows, who is the secretary of the Agency of Health Care Administration. Rhonda, thank you for coming. I want to thank Terry White for being here. It's good to see you again, Terry. He's the secretary of the Florida Department of Elder Affairs. They know what I'm talking about, for the need for us to have a modern Medicare system. You know more than they know, because you live on Medicare; you understand the system needs to be changed and modernized.

I want to thank the mayor of Orlando, Buddy Dyer, for coming. Mr. Mayor, I'm honored you're here. Thank you for taking time. I appreciate Rich Crotty, who is the chairman of Orange County, for being here as well. Thank you, Rich, for coming. I appreciate the interest of Federal, State, and local officials in this very important subject.

I want to thank—I just came from what they call a roundtable discussion. Generally we have roundtable discussions sitting at square tables. [*Laughter*] You know how Government works. [*Laughter*] Jeb and I met with Estelle Baker and Loretta De Maintenon; the MacDonalds, Marge and Mac; and Beverly and Dick Allred. The reason we did is because we want to hear firsthand their stories. I'll share some of their stories with you. But you know, there's nobody—the best people to share with us the need to modernize Medicare are those who rely on Medicare. And they're able to tell the good news about Medicare and the bad news about Medicare, what works in Medicare and what doesn't work in Medicare. Both of us like to listen to people who have had firsthand experiences, and I want to thank the meeting participants for sharing their stories with us.

Today when I landed—at your fantastic airport, by the way—I met Tillie—[*applause*]. Crotty, that's a good sign when people clap when I mention the airport. [*Laughter*] I met a very interesting woman named Tillie Walther. Tillie is here. Tillie is a volunteer for the Retired and Senior Volunteer Program. It's called RSVP. She dedicates a lot of time to help other people.

The reason I bring up Tillie is that when people focus on America, they think about our great military might, and I'll keep our military mighty. They think about our pocketbooks; we're working hard to make sure they're full. The truth of the matter is, the great strength of our country is the heart and souls of our citizens, people who are willing to take time out of their day to make somebody else's life better. And Tillie is such a person. She's leading by example. I love her spirit. I love the example she sets. My call to people here and around our country is to love your neighbor just like you'd like to be loved yourself. Find a way to help somebody in need. Find a way to help somebody who hurts, and the country will be better off. Thank you, Tillie.

Thanks for coming. I'm really, really honored you're here.

Many seniors depend upon Medicare. That's what we're here to talk about. And the Medicare program is a basic trust that must be upheld throughout the generations. Our Government has made a commitment to our seniors—the Federal Government has made a commitment to our seniors through the Medicare program. We made a commitment to provide good health care for seniors, and we must uphold that commitment.

Each of the seniors that I talked to today understands that Medicare needs to be modernized. It needs to be changed. It needs to be brought into the 21st century. They all want the Medicare system that allows them to pick the health care coverage that best meets their needs. And I want to share with you some of the thoughts that we had.

Marge and Mac MacDonald, they take seven different medications at a cost of about $300 a month, and they have no prescription drug coverage. That is not exactly how the planners of Medicare envisioned a senior spending their years of retirement. That's expensive. It's costly. Marge says she's frustrated that Washington has not delivered a prescription drug benefit under Medicare. She says, "I'm tired of the talk." This is her words, not mine. "I'm tired of the talk. Sooner or later, somebody needs to do something. What is the point of retiring at all if you're going to worry about whether you have the money you need to survive?" Marge is right. We've had plenty of talk in Washington. We've debated this issue for a long time. Now is the time for action.

Estelle Baker—I mentioned Estelle earlier—she, in addition to her Medicare benefits, she has drug coverage through a supplemental insurance policy. Perhaps some of you all have the same type of arrangement. She said it's time for all seniors to have that kind of coverage. She said, "Seniors should have the same kind of safety net—some kind of safety net, and it should be done as soon as possible." In other words, that—what you're hearing from people is that when people retire, they don't want to have to worry. They've been worrying, probably raising their kids and worrying about their jobs and worrying about this and worrying about that. We don't want our seniors worrying about a health care system that is not meeting their needs.

Every senior I've talked to is grateful about the Medicare system, and it's done a lot. In many ways, it's fulfilled the promise, up until recent history, and therefore the system needs to be undated. That's what we're here to discuss. That's what Congress must hear. They must hear your voice that the system needs to be updated, that while the system has worked, we can do a better job.

Remember, Medicare was created at a time when medicine consisted mostly of house calls and surgery and long hospital stays. That was the nature of medicine when Medicare was created, and therefore the Medicare system responded to that. Now modern medicine includes preventative care, outpatient procedures, at-home care, and miraculous new prescription drugs. Medicine has changed; Medicare hasn't.

Three-quarters of seniors have some kind of drug coverage, and that's positive news. Yet seniors relying exclusively on Medicare do not have coverage for prescription drugs—for most prescription drugs and for many forms of preventative care. That needs to be fixed. This is not good medicine. It's not cost-effective. Medicare needs to change.

For example, Medicare will pay—I want you to hear this example. Medicare will pay for extended hospital stays for ulcer surgery, at the cost of about $28,000 per patient. That's important coverage, particularly if you have an ulcer. Yet, Medicare will not pay for the drugs that eliminate the cause of most ulcers, drugs that cost about $500 a year—willing to pay the $28,000 for the hospital stay but not the $500 to try to keep the person out of the hospital in the first place. To me, that says we've got a system that needs to updated and modernized. It's not enough for Medicare to pay to treat our seniors after they get sick. Medicare should be covering the medications that will be keeping our seniors from getting sick in the first place.

The best way to provide our seniors with modern medicine, including prescription drug coverage and better preventative care, is to give them better choices under Medicare. If seniors have choices, health care plans will compete for their business by offering better coverage at affordable prices. That's a fact. With greater choice, we can give American seniors the very best of modern medicine.

It's very important for people on Medicare to know that one of the choices that I strongly support and Members of Congress support is allowing people to remain in traditional Medicare programs. We fully understand that some seniors simply do not want to change, and that's understandable. In any system, modernization must say to the seniors, "If you're happy where you are, you stay there." If you're a senior who wants to stay in Medicare and you're concerned about prescription drugs, you should be able to get a Medicare-approved prescription drug coverage. That's what the bill says. And that's what we want to happen: There's no reason for you to leave Medicare and that the Medicare system needs to be modernized to include prescription drugs.

If you're a senior who wants enhanced benefits, something a little different, something better, something that meets your particular needs, such as a new Medicare-approved private plan that includes a drug benefit along with other options, coverage for extended hospital stays or protection against high out-of-pocket expenses, you should have that choice as well. In other words, there are—a variety of choices ought to be available for seniors. If you like managed care plans, if you're happy with that, that option ought to be available. And if you're a low-income senior without much savings, you will receive extra help each month and more generous coverage so you can afford a Medicare option that includes prescription drug benefits.

That's the reform in front of Congress. It's moving forward. We've just got to make sure it moves forward to completion. That's what we're here to discuss today. In Medicare reform, we're applying this basic principle: Seniors should get to choose the kind of coverage that works best for them, instead of having that choice made solely by the Government. You see, every Member of Congress gets to choose a health care plan that makes the most sense for them, and the same for Federal employees. If choice is good for Members of the Congress, then choice is good for America's seniors.

For seniors without any drug coverage now, the reforms will make a big difference in their lives. In return for a monthly premium of about $35, or $1 a day, most seniors now without coverage will see their drug bills cut roughly in half. A senior who has no drug coverage now and a monthly drug cost of $200 would save more than $1,700 on drug costs each year. A senior with monthly drug costs of $800 would save nearly $5,900 on drug costs each year.

Putting improvements into place are going to take some time, and so we need to give seniors some immediate savings. We'll provide all seniors with a Medicare-approved drug discount card that would save between 10 to 25 percent off the cost of their medicines. So in other words, when the bill—as the bill—when it passes, and I'm an optimist—particularly with your help, I will even be more optimistic—that in the time the bill transitions between the old system and the new system, there will be a Medicare-approved drug discount card for you. Low-income beneficiaries will receive an annual $600 subsidy, along with

their discount card, to help them purchase their prescription medicines.

And the legislation that Congress passes must make sure that the prescription drug coverage provided to many retirees by their employers is not undermined. We don't want the system to undermine some of the really good plans that you may have received as a result of your previous employer. Medicare legislation should encourage employers to continue the benefits, while also extending drug coverage to the millions of Medicare beneficiaries who now lack it.

Congress should also make sure that Medicare rests on solid accounting. The current Medicare system accounting does not always give a clear indication of its long-term financial health. I support the Medicare system that alerts future Congresses and Presidents when Medicare's costs are rising faster than expected, so they can address the problem. The accounting safeguard that we're working on in the bill will help Medicare stand on a strong financial foundation. We owe that to the taxpayers of our country.

The important thing we're talking about here is, not only will the steps we're taking strengthen Medicare for today's seniors but also for tomorrow's retirees. It seems to be a popular thought with the baby boomers. Many workers are counting on Medicare to provide good health care coverage in their retirement. These reforms will give our workers confidence that Medicare will serve them with the very best of modern medicine, and that's important for people to know. The budget I submitted earlier this year commits an additional $400 billion over 10 years to implement this vision of a stronger Medicare system. This is enough to meet our commitments to the seniors today and to future generations of Americans.

I urge the seniors and all Americans to speak up and to call or write your Representatives or Senators and urge them to get a final bill that meets the goal I just outlined. You need to speak up for prescription drug coverage. You need to speak up for health care choices. You need to speak up for a modern Medicare system that puts patients and doctors in charge. For years, our seniors have been calling for a prescription drug benefit. For years, American seniors have been calling for more choices in their health care coverage, and now we'll see who is really listening in Washington, DC.

The choice is simple: Either we will have more debate, more delay, and more deadlock, or we'll make real progress. I made my choice. I want real progress, and I urge the Congress to take the path of progress and give our seniors a modern Medicare system. We've come far. Let's finish the job.

Thank you for coming. God bless.

NOTE: The President spoke at 2:07 p.m. In his remarks, he referred to Surgeon General Richard Carmona; Josefina Carbonell, Assistant Secretary for Aging, Department of Health and Human Services; Gov. Jeb Bush of Florida; and Rich T. Crotty, chairman, Orange County Governing Board. The Office of the Press Secretary also released a Spanish language transcript of these remarks.

Remarks Prior to Discussions With President Carlo Azeglio Ciampi of Italy and an Exchange With Reporters
November 14, 2003

President Bush. Thank you all for coming. Mr. President, it is my honor to welcome you to the Oval Office. You come at a difficult period for your country. You come at a time when your nation grieves for the brave sons who lost their life. I send our Nation's gratitude and prayers to the loved ones who are grieving today in Italy.

I want to thank you for the friendship between our two nations. I want to thank you for your strong leadership in standing up to the terrorists who are trying to create fear and chaos. And I want to thank you for your understanding that a free and peaceful Iraq will help make the entire world more peaceful.

And so it is my privilege and honor to welcome a close friend to the Oval Office. Welcome.

President Ciampi. Today I come to the United States as President of the Italian Republic and as a staunch advocate of European integration. I will go to Arlington Cemetery this afternoon. No Italian, no European can ever forget how much democratic Europe owes to the young Americans who gave their lives for our freedom. On Sunday I will go to Ground Zero to honor the victims of terrorism.

President Bush. Thank you.

President Ciampi. I want to thank President Bush for his words, for expressing solidarity in connection with the horrible attack against Italian forces in Iraq. Italy went to Iraq not to take part in a war but to contribute to rebuild a country. This is the identity of the Italian Republic, to build peace, to solve post-conflict situations. We have done it in the past, and we do it in many parts of the world today.

With President Bush, we agreed on the goal to accelerate full implementation of United Nations Resolution 1511. We support the idea of drawing a roadmap for the Iraqi political process in order to establish a full-fledged Government.

The ideals of democracy and freedom have their roots and their strongest foundation in Europe and North America. As it happens, even among friends, there have been problems between us on specific aspects of transatlantic cooperation. We are committed, especially us Italians, to put them fully behind us, for they do not dent and cannot dent the—[*inaudible*]—solidarity between Europe and the United States. Upholding Atlantic cohesion is a duty and a necessity.

I already mentioned to President Bush, and we will continue to do so during the working lunch, about the rationale of what the European Union wants to do to become more united and speak with a single voice. We are progressing in bringing about and completing a constitutional treaty which will enable the European Union to function better and, again, to speak with a single voice.

A united, stronger—with a new configuration of Europe, it will be a stronger Europe with 25 member states and over 450 million citizens and will reinforce and extend a vast area of security and peace. And they will become a better partner also for the United States.

I intend to continue my conversation with President Bush so that we can work together, United States, Italy, Europe, to reinforce pressures to bring about a solution to the conflict of Israel and Palestinian problems, so that we can arrive to a right and just solution. And this will help us to fight, better, terrorism. And we have to fight terrorists—terrorism in a better way so that the Islamic world will know that we view them as a civilization both near and friendly to ours.

In conclusion, I think that we should reinforce our action to increase the actions also within the international institutions, such as the United Nations, to whose establishment the United States has made a fundamental contribution. Italy will continue to fight, with determination, terrorists.

President Bush. Thank you. Listen, we'll have a couple of questions here. We'll alternate between the American press and the Italian press. We expect there to be some order here during the question-and-answer period. In order to set the example, Jennifer [Jennifer Loven, Associated Press], would you like to begin in a calm and rational way?

Coalition Goals and Tactics in Iraq

Q. I would. With the speeding up of the transfer of power in Iraq, do you envision that meaning a quicker reduction of U.S. forces there?

President Bush. Well, we are—I instructed Ambassador Bremer to take—to go back to Iraq with the instructions that we will work with the Governing Council to speed up the political process in a rational way. That's what he's going to do, on the belief that we've made a lot of progress on the ground, that the Governing Council is better prepared to take more responsibility.

In terms of security, we will do whatever it takes to help Iraq develop into a free and peaceful country. That is our goal. And we will stay there until the job is done, and then we'll leave. And the enemy has changed tactics on the ground, and so we're changing our response, and that's what you're beginning to see now. The discussions with General Abizaid and the discussions with Bremer and all the different pieces of evidence to that effect are really saying that as the enemy changes, so will we. And we'll bring them to justice, and Iraq will be more secure, and Iraq is going to be free. And that's in the Nation's interest that it be so.

Would you like to call on an Italian member of the press? There is traveling press from Italy, isn't there? Would anybody care to ask a question?

It's the old double-question trick.

Q. It's a question to both you, President Bush, and President Ciampi. Italy is going through very difficult times, as it is the case for other countries who are present in Iraq. And so the question is, will the presence of U.S. and Italian troops in Iraq change their strategy in order to respond to the deterioration of the situation?

President Bush. That's a very good question. I'll go first, if you don't mind. The answer to your question is yes. It's very important that our commanders on the ground be given flexibility to be able to adjust tactics to an enemy that is changing its tactics. First of all, the enemy wants to create the condition of fear. They want people to fear them. They will lose that aspect of the battle because our will will remain strong.

And secondly, we must use more Iraqis to gather intelligence and to be on the frontline of securing their own country. And that's exactly what we're doing.

And third, when we find actionable intelligence, we will strike fast to bring killers to justice. And that's what we're doing as well.

President Ciampi. I only want to add a few words, and this concerns exclusively tactical maneuvers that have to be decided by the commanders who are on the field, onsite. Our military forces received specific and very clear instructions when they went to Iraq. The implementation of these instructions stem from the assessment of their commanders on the field.

President Bush. Yes, very good. Steve [Steve Holland, Reuters]. Yes, sorry.

Q. Can you envision pulling U.S. troops out of Iraq before Saddam Hussein is found?

President Bush. Look, we will stay until the job is done, and the job is for Iraq to be free and peaceful. A free and peaceful Iraq will have historic consequences. And we'll find Saddam Hussein. The goal is for a free and peaceful Iraq, and by being strong and determined, we will achieve that objective.

Final question here. I promised the President I would buy him lunch, and if we keep answering questions, we won't be able to eat lunch.

President Ciampi. I have nothing else to add.

President Bush. Okay.

Sir, please.

Humanitarian Aid Workers in Iraq

Q. I have a question to President Bush. Given the difficult security situation in the country and given the fact that the Red Cross left the country, what can be done to ensure and guarantee the protection of the return of the Red Cross and also of other humanitarian organizations?

President Bush. Yes, that's an excellent question. Thank you for asking that. First, there are Red Cross workers still there. The headquarters left Baghdad, but many workers are still there. Secondly, there are—besides the Red Cross, there are other organizations still in place that are delivering the humanitarian help that is needed to help Iraq rebuild herself.

It is very important for the leaders of the NGOs to recognize that if they don't go into Baghdad, they're doing exactly what the terrorists want them to do. The situation on the ground for the Iraqi citizens, the humanitarian situation, is improving, and the main reason why is because there are ministries up and running, staffed by very capable Iraqi citizens.

We will stay the course, and as more and more Iraqis realize freedom is precious and freedom is a beautiful way of life, they will assume more and more responsibilities, not only for security but for humanitarian reasons as well.

Finally, I want to thank the Italian people once again for working toward a world that is more humane and more decent and more peaceful. The Iraqi people deserve to live a life of freedom. The Iraqi people deserve to have their children go to schools. The Iraqi people deserve to be free of torture chambers and mass graves. And the work we are doing together is humane and compassionate and necessary for peace, and I thank the people of Italy.

Thank you all.

President Ciampi. I just want to add that the Italian Red Cross is still in Iraq, and they're still carrying out their duties, and they're giving assistance to the people who is really in need of assistance.

President Bush. All right. We've got to go eat. I hope you do too.

NOTE: The President spoke at 11:55 a.m. in the Oval Office at the White House. In his remarks, he referred to L. Paul Bremer III, Presidential Envoy to Iraq; and Gen. John P. Abizaid, USA, combatant commander, U.S. Central Command. President Ciampi spoke in Italian, and his remarks were translated by an interpreter.

Interview With British Journalists
November 14, 2003

The Oval Office

The President. I wanted to show you this shrine to democracy here, kind of give you a sense of who I am.

Laura designed that—that would be my wife. I wanted people to, when they walk in here, to have a sense of optimism. I wanted people to say, "The person whose office is in here, or who works in here, is an optimistic person." And I thought she did a fabulous job capturing my sense about our future.

Well, as you can see, it's got sun rays.

Q. Has it worked? Have people coming in——

The President. See, that's what you're supposed to tell me. [*Laughter*]

Q. Can we—[*inaudible*]—the enemy to you? [*Laughter*]

The President. I don't ask everybody that comes in to work. I just want you to know why we do what we do with the rug. This looks like Texas; it's a Texas star. These are paintings of Texas. This is a guy named Onderdonk, a great Texas painter. That's what our ranch looks like. That's west Texas, where—far west Texas. Where I was raised, it's flatter than that. Laura's mother was raised in that country. It's a really special part of the room.

Q. Is that actually the ranch?

The President. No, it's not. It looks like it—two other Texas paintings. Obviously, I love Texas. It's very important for a President to know who he is before you take this job, a lot of pressure here, a lot of decisionmaking. If you try to figure out who you are on the job——

Q. It's too late.

The President. ——you're not doing a very good job. Exactly. Before I get to there—well, Washington, George Washington, of course. It's kind of hard to envision Rutherford B. Hayes above the mantel, isn't it?

Anyway, Lincoln is this country's greatest President, so I put him on the wall. I think he was the greatest President, because the job of President is to unite the country to achieve big objectives. It's hard to achieve big things if you're not united. We're achieving freedom and peace, so we'll spend a little time talking about it—Iraq.

At home, a compassionate America is a big objective. In order to do that, a President must call upon people to serve their neighbors in need. I understand the limits of government when it comes to compassion. The truth of the matter is, the great strength of our country is the heart and souls of our citizens, incredibly passionate people here. My job is to call them to, as I like to put it, to love their neighbor like they would like to be loved themselves, which leads to this painting here.

It's called "A Charge To Keep." It's based upon a Methodist hymn. As you know, there was a renegade Englishman named John Wesley, and we are Methodists—at least, I am Methodist, and my wife is a Methodist. And we sang this hymn at my first inaugural church service as Governor. And my friend O'Neill, who is not a Methodist—he introduced Laura and me in their backyard in Midland—he said, "I've got a painting based upon that hymn, and would you like to hang it in the Governor's office?" I said, "I don't think it's going to fit." It turned out to be perfect.

The hymn talks about serving something greater than yourself in life. Personally, it speaks to my spirituality. But my job as the President is not to promote a religion. My job is to capture what I call the spirit of America, to call upon people to serve, and that painting reminds me of that.

Q. What painting is it again?

The President. Pardon me?

Q. What's it called?

The President. "A Charge To Keep I Have."

Q. Is that possible——

The President. I think it is, yes. This, by the way—now we're going to get to the—this is the beginning. I hope you're recording all this.

Q. Can we go again? [*Laughter*]

The Resolute Desk/Churchill Bust

The President. This desk was given to America by Queen Victoria. By the way, I would like to talk about two things here in the Oval Office, two articles, one the desk and one a bust, that should describe how I value the relationship with our close and unique friend, which is why I'm so grateful that I've been invited to go. You're about to get the preamble to the discussions.

This desk is called the H.M.S. *Resolute* Desk. The timber is from the H.M.S. *Resolute,* which was rescued in the Arctic, and Queen Victoria, out of gratitude for the relationship, made this desk from the timber. It's a beautiful desk. Not every President has used this.

It has some interesting features. Roosevelt put the door on the desk to cover up his infirmities. He didn't want people to know he was in a wheelchair. John-John Ken put his head out of the desk, probably the most famous Oval Office photo. His dad was looking out at the South Lawn there. Reagan put the bottom on the desk so his knees wouldn't hit. So it's been an interesting history. I love it.

Q. What are you going to do to it?

The President. I don't know. Good question. I'm just going to treat it like a treasure, which is what it is.

Q. Does this mean we're forgiven for burning down the White House? [*Laughter*]

The President. Well, that's another part of the White House. This was built after that tragic occurrence. As a matter of fact, there's a painting hanging in there that we love to show people, where Dolly Madison cut out the picture of George Washington, rolled it up, and ran with it before the White House burned, thanks to a savage attack. [*Laughter*]

Q. It was all a mistake.

The President. Of course it was.

Q. Identification problem.

The President. Yes, exactly. Weren't sure where they were. This is, of course, Churchill. Tony Blair knew that I was an admirer of Churchill, and he arranged for this bust to be loaned here. I am an admirer. I thought Churchill was a clear thinker. I thought he was a—the kind of guy that stood tough when you needed to stand tough. He represented values that both countries hold dear, the value of freedom, the belief in democracy, human dignity of every person. I admired his wit. I wish I could be as witty as he was, because he had a fantastic mind and a charming guy.

And there's some interesting political lessons there. Sometimes you're up. Sometimes you're down. But you've got to do what you think is right. And that's the lesson of Winston Churchill, who was a strong leader.

So anyway, he sits here, along with Lincoln and Ike.

All right. So welcome to the Oval Office.

Q. Thank you very much.

President's Upcoming Visit to the United Kingdom

The President. The President must understand in this office that the person is never bigger than the office. If you think you're bigger than the office, you'll fail as President. The Presidency is bigger than the person. It will last—stay here a lot longer than any individual. That's an important lesson here that Presidents must understand. Come on in.

Just a couple of comments, then we'll answer questions for a while. I am looking forward to the trip. It's going to be a really interesting and fun experience for Laura and me. Obviously, staying at Buckingham Palace is going to be an historic moment. I never dreamt when I was living in Midland, Texas, that I would be staying in Buckingham Palace. Buckingham Palace has got a resonance to it here in America which is pretty grand and pretty magnificent. I've been looking forward to it.

I'm really looking forward to spending time with my friend—and I emphasize "my friend"—Tony Blair. He's a smart, capable, trustworthy friend, and we've got a lot to talk about. We'll talk about Iraq. We'll talk about trade. We'll talk about commerce. We'll talk about issues that we can work together on to help human suffering.

I'll be doing different events. I'll be giving a speech there that I'm working on now, that will confirm my understanding of the importance of this relationship. But I'll talk about other ambitions that we can work on together to promote freedom and peace and a compassion agenda that I think our countries are uniquely suited to work on.

So I'm looking forward to it. It's going to be an exciting trip for us, and I really thank Her Majesty for opening the invitation. I've got my tails all set out and ready to go. [*Laughter*] Had to rent them, but—[*laughter*]—just don't tell anybody.

Q. It gets a bit noisy in the palace when the morning papers arrive, so you'll need to——

The President. They do? Yes. I guess I'll have to go to bed early and wake up early. Anyway, let's go around while we've got time.

President's Upcoming Meeting With Families of Fallen British Soldiers

Q. May I just begin by asking what you hope to take away from the visit? And in particular, can I ask you what message you will have for families of the British servicemen who have been killed in Iraq?

The President. Sure.

Q. Because I gather you'll get to meet.

The President. I am going to meet some. Look, there's two messages. One, the prayers of the American people and the prayers of the President are with them as they suffer. I believe in prayer. I believe that there is a comforting and healing Almighty, and I'll ask that their souls be comforted.

Secondly, that I will tell them that their loved one did not die vain. The actions we have taken will make the world more secure and the world more peaceful in the long run, that a free Iraq, free of weapons of mass destruction, free of tyranny, is not only good for the long-suffering Iraqi people, which in itself is important, but is going to be good for the long-term for countries which love freedom. Can you imagine the historic change, the landmark moment that is taking place now, where we've got a free—a country which is emerging to be free and peaceful in the midst of a part of the world where violence and tyranny and terror have reigned?

And I view this as an historic moment, and I will share with them, just like I share with our own families here, a deep grief, my sorrow for the sacrifice, but the fact that what is taking place today is a noble cause.

Prime Minister Tony Blair

Q. Mr. President, to focus it back on Mr. Blair and Britain, here is a guy who has lost two Ministers, who has lost a large part of the Parliamentary party, and who—it could be said, polls—has lost the faith of a large part of the country over Iraq. He's still, as you saw the other night in the Lord Mayor's banquet speech, 100 million percent there, and this against the great tide of popular opinion. What have you got on him? What's the relationship? And what's the——

The President. Well, that's just Tony——

Q. And what's the payoff? [*Laughter*]

The President. Freedom and peace. Tony Blair is making decisions for the right reasons. He is a—in my relationship with him, he is the least political person I've dealt with. And I say that out of respect. He makes decisions based upon what he thinks is right.

He's plenty independent. If he thinks—if he thought the policy that we have both worked on was wrong, he'd tell me. He believes it's in his country's interest that we work for a free and peaceful Iraq. He, as much as any world leader, saw the consequences of September the 11th, 2001. Obviously, there are more—those consequences and that moment has directly affected my foreign policy. See, it changed the nature of the Presidency. It changed the security arrangements of the United States of America. I vowed to the American people I would never forget the lessons of September the 11th, 2001, and that is we are no longer protected by oceans. We're vulnerable to attack by terrorists.

Tony Blair understands the devastation that terror can bring to a country in a civilized world. He knows the tactics of the terrorists are to create fear and chaos. He knows what they want is for the civilized world to retreat so that their tyranny and their bloodshed and their unbelievable barbaric form of government, like the Taliban, will take hold. And he refuses to allow his country to be terrorized, and he refuses to allow peoples to become subjugated to that kind of ideologies. And I respect him greatly for that.

And I admire him as a strong leader. He tells you what he thinks, and he does what he says he's going to do. And that's about as high a compliment as I can pay a fellow leader.

President's Popularity/Decisionmaking

Q. Mr. President, you're going to find, I think, quite a large number of people on the streets demonstrating during your visit for a variety of reasons, which highlights a rather striking contrast between—you're still a pretty popular President at home, but you're not a very popular President in various states around the world.

The President. Yes.

Q. Does that—how do you account for the lack of popularity around the world? And does it matter to you?

The President. Well, first of all, I—it's kind of—all I can tell you is I went to the Philippines. There was thousands and thousands and thousands of people out there, and they were waving with all five fingers. [*Laughter*]

No, look, I frankly haven't paid that much attention to what you just described. But first, I admire a country which welcomes people to express their opinion. I'm proud of Great Britain's tradition of free speech. I remember going to Hyde Park and seeing Speaker's Corner—what do they call it, Speaker's Corner?

Q. Yes.

The President. People up there expressing their opinion. And it's kind of—it's a longstanding tradition. People speak their mind.

Q. Mr. President——

The President. Let me finish here.

Q. Sure.

The President. And I fully understand not everybody is going to agree with the decisions I've made. I don't expect everybody to agree. And I make decisions based upon—in the foreign policy arena, made decisions based upon a couple of principles. One, how best to secure America? That's my biggest responsibility. See, I was there right after September the 11th. I saw the smoke. I saw the devastation. I heard the grief. I hugged the firefighters whose—the families of the firefighters who rushed in to save. I saw the heroism. And I vowed right then and there that I would use everything in my power to prevent America from being attacked again.

But there's a greater ambition as well, because I understand that free societies are societies which do not breed terror. And I gave a speech the other day, and in that speech I said the are certain folks who I think don't believe that freedom can take hold in parts of our world. And I reminded them about some of the statements about the post-World War II Japan, that there were some skeptics who said that, well, Japan couldn't possibly be a free society or a democratic society.

I thought about that when I was eating dinner with Koizumi, Prime Minister Koizumi—he's a good friend—thinking about what would happen if we had not done a good job with the peace after World War II. Would America and Japan be able to work together, for example, on the North Korean issue, had it not been done right?

My point to you is that free societies and democratic societies are transforming societies. And we have a chance to transform by working together, transform in a positive way whole societies and whole regions of the world.

And finally—and people don't—I can understand people not liking war, if that's what they're there to protest. I don't like war. War is the last choice a President should make, not the first. And it was the last choice, after endless years of diplomacy

took place—resolution after resolution after resolution after resolution that was put forth in the U.N. condemning the—and warning the world, frankly, of the dangers of Saddam Hussein and condemning his programs and insisting that he disarm. And finally, in 1141, as you know, by unanimous vote, the world said—at least the U.N. Security Council said, "Disarm or there will be serious consequences."

And he didn't disarm. He had no intention of disarming. And so then the fundamental question came down to a couple of things, one, the definition of serious consequence. Serious consequence is not another resolution or another debate inside the U.N. And I understand people loathe war. So do I. And yet, we are war. That's what September the 11th taught us. It's a different kind of war. And I intend to, so long as I'm the President, wage that war vigorously to protect the American people.

And there's all kinds of ways to wage it. And the best way to win, in the long run, though, is the spread of freedom. And that's what's happening. But sure, I can understand people not agreeing with the decision I made.

Q. But it is striking, isn't it, that opinion poll after opinion poll——

The President. I don't know. I don't read them.

Q. ——huge solidarity after 9/11——

The President. I just don't pay attention to the polls. If I were trying to be President paying attention on the polls, I'd be running around in circles. It's a great—that's one of the reasons I've got Winston Churchill's bust here is, at least from my reading of the history, he pretty much said what he thought, did what he thought was right, and led. He was courageous in his leadership.

And you know the interesting thing about Presidents and Prime Ministers is you're never going to be around to judge history, judge the true merit of the history, of the decisions you make. Short-term history is—

it's hard to call it unobjective. It's very subjective, I guess, is the best way to put it. After all, the person who has written the history hasn't had a chance to see the full effects of the decisionmaking.

And in my case, most of the short-term historians probably aren't that thrilled with me being President in the first place, which might color the short-term history. [*Laughter*] But my only point is, I think a President must not try to write the legacy of every moment. The President just does what he thinks is right and try to explain as clearly as I can—part of the purpose of my visit to your great country is to use the opportunities I've had to speak directly, like I'm doing right now, to people about why I made the decisions I made.

Go ahead, go ahead.

Iraq

Q. On Iraq, you mentioned you're having intensive consultations these days——

The President. Constantly.

Q. Yes.

The President. With Blair, by the way.

Q. Indeed.

The President. Weekly.

Q. Seeming to point to the need to hand over—or a desire to hand over power faster to the Iraqis? Where is this going?

The President. Yes. Well, we—Jerry Bremer is here in town today. I think he just had a press availability. And we discussed all options and just to make sure we understand where we are relative to the situation on the ground.

We want the Iraqis to understand that we believe they're plenty capable of running their own country. See, we're of the school of thought, this administration—and Tony is the same way, if I could put words in his mouth—that believe the Iraqi people are plenty capable of running a peaceful country.

And therefore, the sooner the people— the more the people realize that, I think the more comfortable they'll be with their future. And the sooner that sovereignty is

handed over in a way commensurate with a—with a stable country, the better off it is. That's been our position all along. So we're constantly reviewing the progress.

There's been—obviously, it's tough. We lost Italian police today. These killers are— they're hardnosed people. They'll kill because they want to intimidate. They want us to leave. That's their goal.

They've got different ambitions. Some would like to see a Taliban-type government, that would be the mujahideen-type people. Some want to revenge the loss— the defeat in Afghanistan. They would be your Al-Qaida-types. And the Ba'athists, of course, want to get back in power. They represent roughly 18 percent of the people, and they've had 100 percent of the power, and they like that. And obviously, in a free society, that's not going to be the case, power sharing as opposed to not power sharing.

And so there are elements of the Ba'athists and Saddam holdouts that are desperately trying—and I use the word "desperate" because they see the progress being made. And there is progress being made. And I certainly don't want to underestimate the security situation. I know how tough it is. I know how tough it is firsthand.

And yet, on the humanitarian side, in 7 months we've got a new currency moving through the system, which is pretty remarkable when you think about it. The oil revenues, which belong to the Iraqi people, are now up to 2.1 million barrels. Prior to going in, I think if you were to review some of the writings and speculation, they would have said, "Well, that's what's going to take place if the oil reserves are destroyed. How is the coalition going to handle that?"

You might remember there was talk about sectarian violence, that all we would do is create a vacuum and longstanding bitterness and hatred would take hold, and Shi'ites and Sunnis and Kurds would all be after each other. That hasn't happened.

Electricity is up to prewar levels, although it has dipped this month because of maintenance. My only point to you is that these killers are beginning to see a society begin to emerge, a peaceful society, which is a major defeat for terror. And you bet we're consulting on a regular basis to determine how best to deal with the tactics on the ground. The enemy is changing tactics, and we'll change tactics with them.

But I do—I talk to Tony a lot. He's got good wisdom on this subject. Our intelligence services are very close. Our militaries are talking to each other. You've got this—Government officials there amongst the CPA, and our relationship is good there. And it's very important for us to continue to discuss these issues closely. And then, of course, I stay in touch with Bremer. And—sorry.

Q. Well——

The President. Are you trying to dominate? You're doing a fine job. [*Laughter*] No, go ahead.

Q. No, go——

The President. We'll make it around. I promise you. I'll wait. Nice try. I call down to these characters all the time for hogging the mike, as we say. He's one of the worst of them.

Blair/Bush Relationship

Q. Regarding the nature of the pressure that Prime Minister Blair is under, is that putting pressure on the decisionmaking, your own relationship——

The President. Not as far as I can tell.

Q. Or pressure for change or change of tactic or anything?

The President. Never once has he said to me, ever, "Gosh, I'm feeling terrible pressure." Our discussions go as you would hope leaders of two allies would go: What can we do to help each other? What can we do to succeed? I have never heard him complain about the polls or wring his hands. I'm telling you, the relationship is a very good relationship because I admire

him, and I admire somebody who stands tough. And I admire somebody who has got a vision which is a vision that is peaceful, and somebody who shares that same deep feeling that freedom is an incredibly important part of changing the world. Free societies do not attack each other. And Tony Blair doesn't hold an elitist view that says only certain people should be free or can be free or capable of freedom. And I admire that in him.

And so to answer your question, you say he's—look, it may be hard for you to believe, and these guys will tell you, I—and ladies will tell you, excuse me, guys and ladies—that my style of leadership is to lay out an agenda based upon principle and lead. And I don't pay that much attention to what is written about me or polls. And I think they will verify that what I've just told you is true. And it's not to say I don't respect the press. I do respect the press. But sometimes it's hard to be an optimistic leader. A leader must project an optimistic view. It's hard to be optimistic if you read a bunch of stuff about yourself, if you know what I mean.

I don't know how much time Tony looks at polls or anything. I'm just telling you from my perspective, my relationship, he is the kind of person with whom I like to consult, a person I'm proud to call friend, because he's willing to make the tough decision and stand by it. And he makes a tough decision based upon what he thinks is right.

Flexibility in Foreign Policy

Q. Mr. President, we've heard—or heard from the administration emanating the phrase, "No war in '04."

The President. Who said that?

Q. Behind the scenes.

The President. Oh, yes. Is that you, Lindlaw [Scott Lindlaw, Associated Press]? [*Laughter*]

Q. Well, there you go. It's now in the lexicon.

The President. We're at war. We are at war, see? I don't mean to anticipate your question, but I'm just going to tell you, we're at war now. We're at war with terror. But go ahead.

Q. My point is——

The President. And Iraq is just one of the—is a front in the war on terror.

Q. That's where I'm going. I'm going to Syria, and I'm going to Iran. These are countries which, by the criteria of Iraq, you could argue, have the same application.

The President. Not really, because re- member, the—first of all, not every situa- tion needs to be resolved through military action, and I would cite you North Korea and Iran. Secondly, the case in Iraq was unique, is unique, because the world, for over a decade, had spoken. The diplomatic route was tried. No one can argue with that. We tried, I think it was 12 resolutions, if I'm not mistaken, culminating in 1441 which said, "Disarm, or you face serious consequences." I remember going to the U.N. to give that speech. And basically I was looking forward to giving that speech because I wanted the U.N. to understand that they are a vital institution, but their vitality depended upon their willingness to have some meaning to their words.

And we're at war. Okay? The war on terror goes on. And the war on terror is going to take a while. America is vulnerable to attack. So is your country, by the way. And the only way to win this war is to do everything you can to protect your homeland but to stay on the offensive, which is what we're going to do.

And having said that, not every situation requires a military response. As a matter of fact, I would hope very few situations would require a military response. Let me talk about Iran. The Iranians must hear from a unified world that it is unacceptable for them to develop a nuclear weapon. And I want to thank—I thanked Tony the other day on our videoconference we had, for he and his Foreign Minister Straw and the French Foreign Minister and the German

Foreign Minister, delivering a message on behalf of all of us that a nuclear weapon is unacceptable. The IAEA, an international organization, as you know, based out of the United Nations, is now very much involved in this issue. The United States position is, is that we appreciate their focus, and we expect there to be a transparent regime inside of Iran. They admitted they had— were enriching, that they hadn't disclosed their enrichment under the Nuclear Non- Proliferation Treaty. They had made that admission, which says that we need to be on guard.

My point to you in regards to your ques- tion on war is that there is a way to deal with this issue in an international forum, which we are now doing. There's bilateral pressure; there's trilateral pressure; and there is multilateral pressure, I guess is the best way to put it. And that's the best way to deal with it.

Let me talk about North Korea, if you don't mind, right quick, to show you, at least, how I think on foreign policy issues. North Korea is a—had a bilateral relation with the United States, and the leader would insist that the United States come to the table and provide different aid, and he, the leader, would not—"he," Kim Chong-il, would not develop a nuclear weapon. And so our country agreed to that. It turns out he was developing highly en- riched uranium suitable for a nuclear weap- on. The thought of Kim Chong-il having a nuclear weapon is very dangerous and/ or the capacity to export a nuclear weapon into the hands of terrorists.

By the way, terrorist networks who are willing to kill with car bombs are also will- ing to kill on a massive scale. The idea of weapons of mass destruction in the hands of terrorist organizations is a dan- gerous, dangerous thought for the 21st cen- tury. And we've got to deal with it.

So I looked at the history and realized that the bilateral relations with Kim Chong- il hadn't worked. There's a real politic here, when somebody says they're going to do something and they don't do it. That should be a warning signal, and it was. So I went and worked with the Chinese and convinced the Chinese through a variety of means of argument that they need to be involved, and they now are involved. They're hosting these talks. So you've got the Chinese, and you've got the Americans, and of course, South Korea and Japan and now Russia are all involved. So you've got five countries saying the same message to Kim Chong-il: We expect you not to develop a nuclear weapons program.

And my point to you is, is that there are ways to rally constituencies and nations toward a common objective, which is precisely what we're doing. That is exactly what the U.N. tried to do and others tried to do, and the U.N., as far as Iraq went. It's just at the end, some countries decided that serious consequences meant something other than—something different than what I thought serious consequences meant, I guess is the best way to put it.

Steel Tariffs

Q. Can I ask a question about trade?
The President. Please, yes. Let me guess. [*Laughter*]
Q. You had a ruling on Monday——
The President. We did.
Q. ——which was not favorable to the U.S. decision last year. Are you going to lift the tax?
The President. Well, let me kind of review the bidding right quick on this issue. The International Trade Commission ruled that imports were harming the industry. Therefore, I felt obligated to take a look at that ruling and make a decision based upon that ruling, which as you know, I did. And we're now in the process of looking at a lot of things. One, of course, is whether or not the respite given helped the industry to restructure and to the extent at which it did restructure.
Somebody went off.
Q. Not me.

The President. I would hate for this profundity to be lost. [*Laughter*] To answer—a very short answer—I am listening, looking, and we'll decide at an appropriate time. I haven't made up my mind yet.

Iraq and Afghanistan/Democracy in the Middle East

Q. Just one last question on Iraq and Afghanistan.
The President. Sure.
Q. Is it really—it's inconceivable that you could consider pulling out——
The President. It is inconceivable.
Q. However, bin Laden is at large, and Saddam Hussein. How close are you to finding these people?
The President. No, first of all, I wouldn't—I think that your—let me answer your question this way. We will find them. Okay? Yes, we're not pulling out until the job is done. Period.
Q. And that includes finding those two?
The President. Yes, that's part of it. But even bigger is a free and democratic society. That is the mission. And again, I'd repeat—I know I'm sounding like a broken record to you. I just want you to get a sense for how strongly I feel for the mission we are on.

I gave a speech the other—I think I might have—or mentioned it to you. I gave a speech about democracy in the Middle East. I believe a—first of all, I believe that the Middle Eastern countries are plenty capable of being democratic countries. Their democracy won't be Western. We don't expect them to look like America. We expect the governments to be modern, however, and that includes, well, women's rights and including women into the future of their societies.

So the mission in Iraq is a free and peaceful and stable country. It will be a—this is a transforming mission. It is a milestone, as I said it, a milestone in the history of liberty. And Tony Blair understands that. He looks—and I would hope—what they would say this of me: I look beyond the signs and the moment to be able to see out, out in years, out in history.

It's an exciting time to be leaders of our two countries. It is exciting in the sense that, working together, we can transform society in a positive way. And I say, "working together," I mean with everybody. There's some unbelievable devastation besides terror going on in the world. And I look forward to reminding the British people that our country proudly is leading the world when it comes to the battle of AIDS. I put forth an initiative of $15 billion, $10 billion new money on top of $5 billion we're already spending over a 5-year period of time, to help get antiretroviral drugs into the hands of the healers and helpers that are in these ravished countries. Can you imagine living in a world—we are living in a world, you don't need to imagine it, it's happening—in a world in which the pandemic of AIDS is wiping out an entire generation on a continent? And we must do something about it. And it's sad, and yet, we have an opportunity to lead.

And I look forward to talking to my good friend about how we can work together. And it's not only the United States working with Britain; it's the United States working with Europe, whole, free, and at peace—whole, free, and at peace. Today I was able to present the Medal of Freedom, which is the highest civil award that I give, to Lord George Robertson. I don't know if you all were in there and saw it or not. Were you there?

Q. On TV.

The President. Yes, I'm sorry. Well, you know, security risk. [*Laughter*]

Anyway, it was a—but the reason I bring that up is that during my tenure here as President, we worked with George and Tony Blair and other countries to expand NATO and the most significant expansion ever, except for the initial thrust. And we expanded to the Baltics. And by the way, we not only expanded to the Baltics, but at the same—in the same period of time,

got rid of the ABM Treaty, which I felt codified hatred and distrust.

And yet, relations are good. And we're moving forward. NATO is an incredibly important institution, and NATO is an instrument for freedom.

Yes, one last.

Q. One last question. Can I ask a question about European defense?

The President. Yes. Anyway, what I was going to say is, is that the relations with Europe are vital and important. We've got good relations. Obviously, there was some disgruntlement about the decision made on Iraq, but I would remind you that Germany has troops in Afghanistan supporting that mission there, for which we're very grateful. And they're doing a darn good job.

Yes, last question. Yes, okay, last two questions, then I've got to go. I'm heading toward television. I'm trying to beam my way into Great Britain.

Q. David Frost will wait. [*Laughter*]

The President. That's easy for you to say. He gets to ask the questions, not you. Go ahead. [*Laughter*]

European Defense Force

Q. There was a fuss from American officials after Tony Blair met with Jacques Chirac and Gerhard Schroeder in Berlin and appeared to take forward the European initiative on defense. I wanted to ask you what your administration was worried about—whether you could trust Tony Blair to keep the thing—Atlantic alliance——

The President. Let me make sure you understand our position. What we believe, that Europe needs to take more of a defense posture and should act independently of NATO if NATO chooses not to take on the mission. We also believe that the European Defense Force—we agree with Tony Blair that it should not undermine the vitality of the NATO mission. And I trust Tony Blair to make the right decision there.

I don't know what chirping you're hearing about it, but at least in the President's chair, I'm confident that when he says—this is the man, remember, he has told me things and has stuck to his word. And therefore, I say with confidence that when he says to me that NATO is a vital relationship and the European Defense Force will not undermine NATO's capacities and/or ability to move when it needs to move, I believe him.

Last question.

President's Upcoming Visit to the United Kingdom

Q. Yes, if I may, I gather your program includes a visit to the northeast of England——

The President. It does.

Q. ——which is Jordyland. And I was wondering how your Jordy was, and how you might all understand each other?

The President. My Jordy is probably just about as bad as my English. [*Laughter*] And I hope they understand Texan. You know what I'm saying?

Q. Yes, exactly.

The President. We may be talking above each other. I can't wait to go to his constituency. It's going to be—it will be good to get out into the countryside. I like—it's hard for a President to get out to the countryside. I travel in somewhat of a bubble.

Q. You'll need your phrase book.

The President. What?

Q. You'll need your phrase book while you're out there.

The President. Yes. They'll need theirs too, I'm afraid. [*Laughter*] But I'm looking forward to it. This is going to be an historic trip, and it's going to be one that will be in my memory for a long time. I'm really looking forward to it.

I appreciate you all giving me a chance to visit with you. Thanks for coming by.

NOTE: The interview was taped at 2:08 p.m. on November 12 in the Oval Office at the White House. The transcript was made available by the Office of the Press Secretary on November 12 but was embargoed for release until noon, November 14. In his remarks, the President referred to Joseph I. O'Neill III, managing partner, O'Neill Properties, Ltd.; Queen Elizabeth II and Secretary of State for Foreign and Commonwealth Affairs Jack Straw of the United Kingdom; Prime Minister Junichiro Koizumi of Japan; former President Saddam Hussein of Iraq; L. Paul Bremer III, Presidential Envoy to Iraq; Minister of Foreign Affairs Dominique de Villepin of France; Minister of Foreign Affairs Joschka Fischer of Germany; Chairman Kim Chong-il of North Korea; and Secretary General Lord Robertson of NATO. Journalists referred to Lord Mayor Robert Finch of London, United Kingdom; Usama bin Laden, leader of the Al Qaida terrorist organization; television journalist Sir David Frost of the BBC; President Jacques Chirac of France; and Chancellor Gerhard Schroeder of Germany. Participants in the interview were: Andrew Gowers, Financial Times; Martin Newland, Daily Telegraph; and Paul Potts, Press Association. A tape was not available for verification of the content of this interview.

Remarks on Signing the National Employer Support of the Guard and Reserve Week Proclamation
November 14, 2003

Thank you all for coming. Thanks for the warm welcome. Welcome to the people's house.

In a few moments, I will sign a proclamation in honor of employers across America who have shown their support for our

National Guardsmen and reservists. In times of need, our Nation counts on the guard and reserve members to fulfill their commitments of service. We value their courage, and we honor their sacrifice. They are defending their Nation in the war on terror, and they're serving in a just cause.

Our guardsmen and reservists depend on the understanding of their employers. Across America, where units have been activated, employers at offices and factories and schools, hospitals, and other workplaces have been understanding and really supportive. They've given priority to the needs of our Nation. Employers have shown great consideration for their workers who have been called to duty and great support for the Nation's defense. These companies have the gratitude of our Nation. They have the gratitude of the Commander in Chief.

I appreciate members of my team who are here today. Secretary Elaine Chao of the Department of Labor and Secretary Tony Principi of the Department of Veterans Affairs, thank you both for coming. I appreciate Deputy Secretary Paul Wolfowitz at the Department of Defense for being here as well. Under Secretary David Chu; thank you for coming, David. I appreciate Acting Secretary of the Army Les Brownlee for being here. I see that General Pete Pace is here, Vice Chairman of the Joint Chiefs of Staff. I appreciate Assistant Secretary Thomas Hall, Assistant Secretary for Reserve Affairs, for coming; thank you, sir. I appreciate David Janes, the Acting National Chairman of the Employer Support of the Guard and Reserve group. Thank you for coming.

Most of all, I thank you all for being here, particularly those who wear our Nation's uniform.

American citizen soldiers have served in every conflict since the Revolutionary War. Some of the most legendary names in American military history are associated with Guard and Reserve units. The famed "Keystone Division," as the Pennsylvania National Guard was long known, once marched under the command of Omar Bradley. The "Rainbow Division," which drew soldiers from Guard units in 26 States and from the District of Columbia, was led in World War I by a young brigadier general named Douglas MacArthur. In 1905, 21-year-old Harry S. Truman joined the Missouri National Guard. Our 33d President learned much from his experiences in the Guard, and so did the 43d President.

But most of all, I remember the high caliber of the people with whom I served. Today, more than 1.2 million men and women serve in the Guard and the Reserve. That's almost half of America's total military strength. These men and women face the difficult challenge of balancing military duty with civilian employment. They know that the call to active duty can come at any time.

And they're always ready. Guardsmen and reservists are now serving around the world, in places like Afghanistan and in Iraq. They serve here at home as well, in the war on terror. They're meeting the terrorist enemy abroad so our fellow citizens do not have to face the enemy at home.

They are part of our efforts to employ targeted and decisive force against cold-blooded terrorist killers. They're helping to train and equip Iraqis and Afghans to defend their own nations. They're helping the Iraqi and Afghan people build just and free and democratic governments. They're helping to defend the American homeland.

Our guardsmen and reservists are showing great skill and courage, and America honors their unselfish dedication to duty. Our guardsmen and reservists rely on the support and patience of their families, their wives and husbands and daughters and sons who must bear the prolonged absence of a loved one. They rely on their civilian employers to put the national interest above the corporate or self interests. Employers of guard and reserve members make possible the contributions of our citizen soldiers. By supporting the mobilization of patriots, employers are demonstrating their own patriotism.

With us today are representatives of companies that have given outstanding support to the Guard and to the Reserve. Central Atlantic Toyota Distribution Center, D.H. Griffin Wrecking Company, Miller Brewing, Pacific Gas and Electric Corporation, Tyson Foods are all winners of this year's Secretary of Defense Employers Support Freedom Award.

These companies do all their utmost to support and encourage service in America's National Guard and Reserve. They provide pay, health care benefits, and job security to the men and women who are called to active duty. They recognize that their workers are fighting to keep America free.

Other companies are making equally important contributions. Albertson's, Clear Channel Airports, Home Depot, and Verizon all provide outstanding support to their employees during mobilizations. All of us appreciate the generosity and the public spirit shown by these outstanding companies and many others like them around our country.

Members of the guard and reserve are with us today. We're proud of your service. We thank you for your sacrifice. The war on terror has drawn on many of America's strengths, and one of the greatest strengths is the citizen-soldier, like Specialist James Dexter of the Illinois National Guard. At home, Specialist Dexter is a volunteer firefighter. In Iraq, he is serving as a military police officer. On three separate occasions in a single month, Specialist Dexter rushed to the scene of traffic accidents, twice saving the lives of American soldiers and Iraqi citizens and once putting out a dangerous fire. He was awarded the Bronze Star. He has earned the gratitude of our country for his service.

America needs the Guard and Reserves more today than we have had in decades. We're at war. Yet we're fortunate that so many of our citizens have heeded the call to serve a cause greater than themselves. And we are fortunate that our Guard and Reserve units have received such support from America's business community. As a sign of America's gratitude, I'm pleased to invite representatives from the nine companies here today to join me in signing a proclamation designating National Employer Support of the Guard and Reserve Week.

May God bless you all, and may God continue to bless our great country.

NOTE: The President spoke at 2:16 p.m. in the East Room at the White House. In his remarks, he referred to Rear Adm. David Janes, USN (Ret.), National Chair, National Committee for Employer Support of the Guard and Reserve. The Office of the Press Secretary also released a Spanish language transcript of these remarks. The proclamation of November 14 is listed in Appendix D at the end of this volume.

Statement on Senate Action To Block Votes on Judicial Nominations
November 14, 2003

Today's partisan action to block up-or-down votes on Justice Priscilla Owen, Judge Carolyn Kuhl, and Justice Janice Rogers Brown is inconsistent with the Senate's constitutional responsibility and is just plain wrong. Once again, a partisan minority of Senators has thwarted the will of the majority and stood in the way of voting on superb judicial nominees.

These obstructionist tactics are shameful, unfair, and have become all too common. At a time when the American people have important issues backlogged in the courts, partisan Senators are playing politics with the judicial process at the expense of timely justice for the American people.

I commend Senate Republicans, especially Leader Frist, Chairman Hatch, and Senator Santorum, for their leadership and commitment to the Constitution and basic fairness. During their 40-hour debate, these Senators have focused on the damaging vacancies that exist on the Federal courts of appeals, the highly qualified individuals I have nominated to serve, and the Senate's obligation to vote on every judicial nominee.

No matter who is President or which party controls the Senate, the American people deserve a well-functioning, independent judiciary and a commitment by all Senators to live up to their constitutional obligation.

Statement on Congressional Action on Comprehensive Energy Legislation
November 14, 2003

I applaud the House and Senate for reaching agreement on a comprehensive energy bill. America will be safer and stronger with a national energy policy that will help keep the lights on, the furnaces lit, and the factories running. A good energy bill is part of my six-point economic plan to create the conditions for job creation and a sustained recovery. By making America less reliant on foreign sources of energy, we also will make our Nation more secure. I commend the Congress for its hard work on this important issue.

Memorandum on Return of Activated Military Members to Federal Civilian Employment
November 14, 2003

Memorandum for the Heads of Executive Departments and Agencies

Subject: Return of Activated Military Members to Federal Civilian Employment

As we welcome home returning Federal civil servants who were called to active duty in the continuing Global War on Terrorism, we recognize the contributions they have made in the defense of freedom. Whether they served with the Reserve Forces or the Air and Army National Guard, each of them has my personal gratitude and the respect and admiration of a grateful Nation.

The Federal Government will continue to be the model for employer support to the Guard and Reserve. We are the guarantors of the rights of returning service members under the Uniformed Services Employment and Reemployment Rights Act, and I am personally committed to providing each of them with our full support, recognition, and assistance. Accordingly, I hereby direct you to grant Federal employees under your authority who are returning from active duty 5 days of uncharged leave from their civilian duties, consistent with the provisions of Federal law.

We also are grateful for the extra efforts of the many Federal civilian employees who, in the absence of their fellow acti-vated workers, have contributed to the War on Terror, and I urge you to recognize these Federal employees by appropriate means.

GEORGE W. BUSH

Letter to Congressional Leaders Reporting on the Deployment of United States Military Personnel as Part of the Kosovo International Security Force
November 14, 2003

Dear Mr. Speaker: *(Dear Mr. President:)*

In my report to the Congress of May 14, 2003, I provided information regarding the continued deployment of combat-equipped U.S. military personnel as the U.S. contribution to the NATO-led inter-national security force in Kosovo (KFOR) and to other countries in the region in sup-port of that force. I am providing this sup-plemental report prepared by my Adminis-tration, consistent with the War Powers Resolution (Public Law 93–148), to help ensure that the Congress is kept fully in-formed on continued U.S. contributions in support of peacekeeping efforts in Kosovo.

As noted in previous reports, the U.N. Security Council authorized member states to establish KFOR in U.N. Security Coun-cil Resolution 1244 of June 10, 1999. The mission of KFOR is to provide an inter-national security presence in order to deter renewed hostilities; verify and, if necessary, enforce the terms of the Military Technical Agreement (MTA) between NATO and the Federal Republic of Yugoslavia (FRY) (which is now the Union of Serbia and Montenegro); enforce the terms of the Un-dertaking on Demilitarization and Trans-formation of the former Kosovo Liberation Army; provide day-to-day operational direc-tion to the Kosovo Protection Corps; and maintain a safe and secure environment to facilitate the work of the U.N. Interim Ad-ministration Mission in Kosovo (UNMIK).

Currently, there are 17 NATO nations contributing to KFOR. The U.S. contribu-tion to KFOR in Kosovo is about 2,100 U.S. military personnel, or approximately 11 percent of KFOR's total strength. Addi-tionally, U.S. military personnel occasionally operate from Macedonia, Albania, and Greece in support of KFOR operations. Seventeen non-NATO contributing coun-tries also participate with NATO forces in providing military personnel and other sup-port personnel to KFOR.

The U.S. forces are assigned to a sector principally centered around Gnjilane in the eastern region of Kosovo. For U.S. KFOR forces, as for KFOR generally, maintaining a safe and secure environment remains the primary military task.

The KFOR forces operate under NATO command and control and rules of engage-ment. The KFOR coordinates with and supports UNMIK at most levels, provides a security presence in towns, villages, and the countryside, and organizes checkpoints and patrols in key areas to provide security, protect minorities, resolve disputes, and help instill in the community a feeling of confidence.

The UNMIK continues to transfer non-reserved competencies under the Constitu-tional Framework document to the Kosovar Provisional Institutions of Self-Government (PISG). The PISG includes the President, Prime Minister and Kosovo Assembly, and has been in place since March 2002. Mu-nicipal elections were successfully held for a second time in October 2002.

NATO continues formally to review KFOR's mission at 6-month intervals. These reviews provide a basis for assessing current force levels, future requirements, force structure, force reductions, and the eventual withdrawal of KFOR. NATO has adopted the Joint Operations Area plan to regionalize and rationalize its force structure in the Balkans. KFOR has transferred full responsibility for public safety and policing to UNMIK international and local police forces throughout Kosovo except in the area of Mitrovica, where the responsibility is shared due to security concerns. The UNMIK international police and local police forces have also begun to assume responsibility for guarding patrimonial sites and established border-crossing checkpoints.

The continued deployment of U.S. forces has been undertaken pursuant to my constitutional authority to conduct U.S. foreign relations and as Commander in Chief and Chief Executive. I appreciate the continued support of the Congress in these actions.

Sincerely,

GEORGE W. BUSH

NOTE: Identical letters were sent to J. Dennis Hastert, Speaker of the House of Representatives, and Ted Stevens, President pro tempore of the Senate.

The President's Radio Address
November 15, 2003

Good morning. This week I traveled to Florida to visit with seniors about an important goal for my administration and this Nation. After years of debate and deadlock, the Congress is finishing work on the biggest improvements in senior health care coverage in nearly 40 years.

Some important details of the Medicare legislation have to be worked out, but leaders in both the House and the Senate have already agreed to four clear-cut improvements to Medicare.

First, within 6 months of Medicare reform law, all seniors would be eligible for a Medicare-approved drug discount card. This card would give seniors an immediate 10- to 25-percent savings on the cost of their medicines. For seniors with typical drug costs of $1,285 a year, the card would deliver annual savings of up to $300. And for low-income seniors, the discount card would include a $600 annual credit toward drug costs.

Second, beginning in 2006, we would establish Medicare prescription drug coverage for all seniors who want it, at a monthly premium of about $35. For most seniors without coverage today, the new coverage would cut their annual drug bills roughly in half.

Third, seniors with the greatest need will get the most help. Low-income seniors would pay a reduced premium or no premium at all for the new drug coverage. And low-income seniors would also have lower copayments for their medicines.

Fourth, our seniors would enjoy more choices in their health coverage, including the same kind of choices that Members of Congress and other Federal employees enjoy. If seniors have more choices, health plans will compete for their business by offering better coverage at affordable prices.

The choices we support include the choice of remaining in the traditional Medicare program. Some seniors don't want change, and if you're a senior who wants to stay in the current Medicare system, you will have that option. And with that option, you will also be able to get Medicare-approved prescription drug coverage.

Some seniors may choose a new Medicare-approved private plan that includes a drug benefit, along with other options. Such options could include coverage for extended hospital stays or protection against high out-of-pocket medical expenses. Others may prefer managed care plans. Under the approach I support, seniors would have these options as well.

American seniors are calling for these improvements. Among the seniors I met in Florida was Marge MacDonald. Marge and her husband Mac do not have prescription drug coverage, and they are frustrated. Here is what Marge says: "I'm tired of the talk. Sooner or later, somebody needs to do something." Marge is right. The time for delay and deadlock has passed. Now is the time for action.

I ask seniors and all Americans to speak up, to call and write your Representatives and Senators and urge them to work out a final bill. Congress has an historic opportunity to give all our seniors prescription drug coverage, health care choices, and a healthier, more secure retirement. We must make these improvements this year, during this session of Congress. And with your help, we will get the job done.

Thank you for listening.

NOTE: The address was recorded at 10:35 a.m. on November 14 in the Cabinet Room at the White House for broadcast at 10:06 a.m. on November 15. The transcript was made available by the Office of the Press Secretary on November 14 but was embargoed for release until the broadcast. The Office of the Press Secretary also released a Spanish language transcript of this address.

Statement on the Announcement of a Transition Plan by the Iraqi Governing Council
November 15, 2003

I welcome the announcement by the Iraqi Governing Council of a political timetable as called for by the United Nations in U.N. Resolution 1511. This statement is an important step toward realizing the vision of Iraq as a democratic, pluralistic country at peace with its neighbors.

The plan outlined by the Governing Council meets a key mutual objective of the coalition and the Iraqi people: the restoration of sovereignty to a body chosen by the citizens of Iraq and based in a legal framework. It also commits Iraq to a process for drafting a permanent, democratic constitution that protects the rights of all citizens.

The U.S. stands ready to help the Governing Council and all Iraqis translate this new timeline into political reality. The American people are committed to the future of an Iraq that is democratic and prosperous.

Statement on Terrorist Attacks in Istanbul, Turkey
November 15, 2003

I condemn in the strongest possible terms the terrorist attacks today in Istanbul, where Turkey's diverse religious communities of Muslim, Jewish, and Christian believers have flourished together for centuries. The focus of these attacks on Turkey's Jewish community, in Istanbul's synagogues where men, women, and children gathered to worship God, remind us that our enemy in the war against terror is without conscience or faith. Turkey has suffered terrible losses from terrorism for decades, and the United States stands resolutely with Turkey in the global war on terrorism. On behalf of the American people, I express our condolences to the families of the victims, to Turkey's Jewish community, and to all the people of the Turkish Republic.

Statement on the Announcement of a Bipartisan Agreement on Medicare Legislation
November 15, 2003

The bipartisan Medicare agreement announced today by leaders in Congress represents a significant achievement in our Nation's efforts to provide affordable prescription drug coverage for our seniors. Seniors have waited a long time for help in paying for prescription drugs, and I am pleased that we are now on the verge of providing them with the help they need and the health care choices they deserve. This bipartisan agreement is the most significant improvement in senior health care coverage in nearly 40 years. I applaud the hard work and the leadership from both sides of the aisle, and I urge the Congress to pass this legislation soon so I can sign it into law.

Remarks on Arrival From Camp David, Maryland, and an Exchange With Reporters
November 16, 2003

The President. Thank you. Today I spent some time in prayer for our service men and women who are in harm's way. I prayed for their families. I prayed for those who are still in harm's way, whether it be American troops or coalition troops.

The sacrifice that our folks are making in Iraq will serve our Nation's interests in the short term and long term. It's best to defeat the terrorists in Iraq so we don't have to defeat them here. As well a free and stable Iraq, in the heart of a part of the world where there is frustration and anger, where the recruiters of hatred are able to find terrorists—a free Iraq will be a transforming event. And I appreciate the families who are making the sacrifices along with our troops.

As well in Iraq, it was a tough week, but we made progress toward a sovereign and free Iraq. The Iraqi Governing Council has laid out a timetable for the transfer of sovereignty. We're pleased with that timetable. We think it makes sense. On the one hand, the politics is moving on; on the other hand, we're going to stay tough and deal with the terrorists.

I also talked to Prime Minister Erdogan over the weekend, expressed our deep condolences for the senseless death caused by bombings in Turkey. He assured me that he would fight the terrorists and bring the terrorists to justice. I told him we would help, and we're grateful. But it's just a reminder that the war on terror takes place on different fronts.

At home, I am pleased with the progress made on the energy bill and on Medicare. I want to thank the leaders in the House and the Senate for coming together on two important pieces of legislation. On Medicare, it looks like there's agreement in principle to provide our seniors with a modern Medicare plan, and that's very positive news. I urge the Members of the House and the Senate to take a look at it, vote it, and get it to my desk as soon as possible. And I'm pleased that we're finally developing a national energy plan. So we're making good progress on the domestic front here at home.

Let me answer a couple of questions.

Saddam Hussein Audiotape

Q. Can you comment on the latest tape, reportedly from Saddam Hussein, that's being aired now?

The President. I haven't seen the specifics. I suspect it's the same old stuff. You know, it's propaganda. We're not leaving until the job is done, pure and simple. A free and peaceful Iraq will be a historic event. And I'm sure he would like to see us leave, if, in fact, it's his voice. And I know that elements of the Ba'athist Party, those who used to torture, maim, and kill in order to stay in power, would like to see us leave. We will do our job.

Randy [Randall Mikkelsen, Reuters].

Helicopter Crash in Iraq

Q. Mr. President, what information do you have about the chopper crash——

The President. No more than you have, but it's sad. It's a sad day when we lose life. It doesn't matter whether it's in a chopper crash or an IED, the loss of life is sad.

Iraqi Transition Plan

Q. What plans do you have for security after the new transition plan is implemented, after the Iraqi sovereignty is granted? How do you ensure——

The President. Well, it depends on what's taking place on the ground. Somebody told me, they said, "Well, this means there's going to be less troops." Politics is going to go forward. The political process will move on. And we'll adjust our troop level according to the security situation in Iraq.

Yes. Who are you with, first of all? I haven't seen——

Q. Fox News Channel.

The President. Very good. Welcome.

Protests During President's Upcoming Visit to the United Kingdom

Q. Are you concerned at all about the protests that you're going to be facing in London when you go?

The President. No, I'm not concerned at all. I'm glad to be going to a free country where people are allowed to protest. Not the least bit.

Yes, who are you with?

Q. I'm with CNN.

The President. Good.

Iraq

Q. Do you see the use of surface-to-air missiles as an escalation in the conflict in Iraq?

The President. It's symptomatic of the fact that there was a lot of weapons lying around. And we've just got to bring these killers to justice, which we will. The military is adjusting. You've been reading about the fact that they're adjusting their strategy and their plans. That's exactly what the Commander in Chief expects, flexibility on the ground to change response to a change of tactics with the enemy.

Hillman [G. Robert Hillman, Dallas Morning News].

President's Upcoming Visit to the United Kingdom

Q. Yes, are you concerned at all with your visit to London, that it comes at a kind of uncomfortable time in some respects for Prime Minister Blair——

The President. No, I'm not concerned about my trip to London. I'm really looking forward to it. It's the second "are you concerned" question about my trip to England. I'm really looking forward to it. It's going to be a fantastic experience. I know you—do you have something else on the "concerned" question there? I cut you off. I beg your pardon.

Q. No, there have just been, you know, immense speculation that this is coming at an awkward political time for you and the Prime Minister, for that matter.

The President. Awkward political time for me?

Q. [*Inaudible*]—the situation in Iraq.

The President. No, I'm looking forward to the trip. I'm honored to have been invited. I look forward to my consultations with Tony Blair. We visit all the time via telephone or via secure video link. I'm looking forward to sitting down with him in person. It's going to be a great trip.

I guess—everywhere—every time I go somewhere, there is immense speculation. I'm not suggesting you're the speculators, but I remember before I went to the Far East, there was some speculation about this and speculation about that. No, I'm looking forward to it. It's going to be a great trip.

Yes, sir.

Steel Tariffs

Q. Mr. President, are you any closer to a decision on steel?

The President. Than I was Friday?

Q. Yes.

The President. Well, if there is a date at which I'm going to make it, I guess I'm 2 days closer. But no, I'm thinking about it. I've got some considerations. People are presenting reports to me, which I will look at, and let you know at the appropriate time, when I make up my mind.

Yes, sir. Who——

Q. NBC News.

The President. Very good.

Medicare Reform Legislation

Q. Okay, thank you. Mr. President, what do you think the chances are of getting the Medicare bill passed?

The President. The what? Medicare? You know, that's a good question. I think it's good. I think—I'm pleased we've come this far. And I think there's going to be immense pressure on Members of both the House and the Senate to support this bill. It is a good piece of legislation. It is a complex piece of legislation. After all, we're changing a Medicare system that has been stuck in the past for a long period of time.

I'm beginning to get a sense of the supporters for this piece of legislation. And there's some mighty active groups of people who are interested in good health care for our seniors that are getting mobilized, and so I think we've got a good chance of passing it. I know I will be actively pushing the bill, because it conforms to the principles I laid out of prescription drugs for our seniors, choice for seniors, accountability for the Medicare plan. There's a lot of good features in this bill. I look forward to working to see its passage.

Listen, you all have a wonderful Sunday. Thank you very much.

NOTE: The President spoke at 12:51 p.m. on the South Lawn at the White House. In his remarks, he referred to Prime Minister Recep Tayyip Erdogan of Turkey; former President Saddam Hussein of Iraq; and Prime Minister Tony Blair of the United Kingdom.

Interview With Sir David Frost of BBC Television
November 12, 2003

President's Upcoming Visit to the United Kingdom

Mr. Frost. Mr. President, a lot of people say this might be your first trip to London, but it's not.

The President. No, it's not. I've been there a couple of times. I remember, Laura and I went to see "Cats" in London. Gosh, I remember going to some nice pubs when I was a drinking man in London. It's a great city, and I'm looking forward to going.

Mr. Frost. We're looking forward to seeing you there, too. In fact, of course, you're famous for the fact that normally social—dressing up socially is not your favorite thing, and you once said that marvelous quote, "Read my lips: No new tuxes."

The President. That's right. [*Laughter*]

Mr. Frost. Are you going to take a new tux this time?

The President. I'm going to take a tux, and I'm going to take tails. And don't tell anybody, but I had to rent them. [*Laughter*] I'm sure you won't tell anybody.

Mr. Frost. This is entirely between us.

The President. I'm looking forward to—it's a huge honor to be invited by Her Majesty to stay in Buckingham Palace. It's hard to imagine me even considering staying in Buckingham Palace when I was living in Midland, Texas. It's just one of those things. And Buckingham Palace has got a tremendous mystique to it, and so Laura and I are really looking forward to coming.

President's Agenda in the United Kingdom

Mr. Frost. And you pinch yourself about those things too. What would you like to see come out of this trip in terms of—in addition to the fun part?

The President. Well, I've got some business to do with Tony Blair. We've got a lot of things to discuss. We're going to talk about how to continue to spread freedom and peace. We'll talk about how to work the compassion agenda on the AIDS Initiative, for example. We're going to spend some time talking about that.

I value his advice, and I—every time I visit with him, whether it be on the phone or on video or in person, I come away with a—some interesting ideas about how to advance a positive agenda.

Secondly, I look forward to speaking to the people of your great country. I'm going to have a chance to give a speech to talk about the importance of our relationship, the unique relationship between America and Great Britain. And I'll have a chance to answer some questions, I'm sure, from what we call the Fourth Estate here, the mighty media. I look forward to it.

Protests/War on Terror

Mr. Frost. And Tony Blair on Monday night—and he would probably have told you—is expecting there to be quite a lot of protesters about the war. What would be your message to those protesters?

The President. Well, freedom is a beautiful thing, I would first say, and aren't you lucky to be in a country that encourages people to speak their mind. And I value going to a country where people are free to say anything they want to say. Secondly, I would say that I understand you don't like war, and neither do I. But I would hope you understand that I have learned the lessons of September the 11th, 2001, and that terrorists declared war on the United States of America and war on people that love freedom, and I intend to lead our Nation, along with others like our close friends in Great Britain, to win this war on terror, that war is my last choice, not my first choice, but I have an obligation as the President to keep our country secure.

Blair-Bush Relationship

Mr. Frost. And at the same time, you'll be working with Tony Blair, and what is the key to your working together so well? I mean, it's like you have a special relationship. Is partially the bond, the bond that you're both men of strong faith?

The President. I think so. Tony is a man of strong faith. You know, the key to my relationship with Tony is he tells the truth, and he tells you what he thinks, and when he says he's going to do something, he's going to do it. I trust him, therefore. I've seen him, under some tough—tough circumstances, stand strong, and I appreciate that in a person.

The other thing I admire about Tony Blair is that he's got a vision beyond the current. In other words, he can see a world that is peaceful, and he agrees with me that the spread of democracy and freedom in parts of the world where there's violence and hatred will help change the world, that there are reformers in the Middle East that long for democracy, that long to live in a free world. And Tony Blair, like me, agrees—kind of rejects the elitist point of view that only a certain type of person can adapt the habits of freedom and democracy. And he knows that freedom in the Middle East will help change that world in dramatic fashion. So it's an historic moment which he has been willing to seize, and I'm honored to be working with him to seize the moment.

Public Opinion/Lessons of September 11

Mr. Frost. And in terms of as you look at the world, Mr. President, at the moment and you see the protesters in Australia or wherever they are and you see that poll that came out, an EU poll the other day that shows that the United States was second among the most dangerous countries in terms of war in the world—level, for God's sake, with North Korea and Iran—when you see things like that, do you think the world is out of step with America, or America is out of step with the world?

The President. Well, first of all, you've got to know, I don't pay attention to the polls. I just don't. I've got a job to do for the American people. It's a job that was changed on September the 11th, 2001, and I refuse to—I refuse to forget—I'll never forget the lessons, is a better way to put it, of what happened to this country. And there are terrorists who are willing to kill innocent life in order to create fear and chaos. There are terrorists who want the free world to retreat from duties so that they can impose Taliban-type governments and enslave people. There are people like Saddam Hussein, who tortured and maimed and killed and, at the same time, threatened and created the conditions of instability. And I know some people don't understand the need to deal with that, but I feel firmly we must deal with those issues.

Mr. Frost. But do you need to woo people more in the rest of the world?

The President. We wooed—we did a pretty good job of wooing them at the United Nations. After all, remember, 1441 was a unanimous vote that said, after a decade of sending messages to Mr. Saddam Hussein for him to disarm, 1441 said, "Disarm or there will be serious consequences." And that was a unanimous vote. In other words, the world, at least the Security Council, came together and sent a clear signal. Obviously, there was a disagreement about the definition of "serious consequence." But I can assure you, "serious consequence" isn't more resolutions or more debate. "Serious consequence" was with dealing with Mr. Saddam Hussein today, before it became too late.

And I understand people don't agree with that position. But nevertheless, I'm convinced that the decisions we made—and there's a lot of countries that made that decision with us—that decision will make the world more peaceful and more free. That decision is in the long-term interests of people who love freedom.

1551

France and Germany

Mr. Frost. And will you ever be able to forgive Jacques Chirac and Chancellor Schroeder for their actions of that time in undermining the second resolution?

The President. Of course. It's like, I can understand why people express their disagreement with the policy. I understand not everybody is going to agree with every decision that I make or others make. But I've had meetings with Gerhard Schroeder and Jacques Chirac since then. They've been very cordial meetings. Gerhard Schroeder has now committed German troops to Afghanistan, which is a very important mission, to help stabilize that good country as it not only enacts a constitution but heads toward elections. And I appreciate the contribution of the German Government toward Afghanistan. I'm proud to say that it is a vital contribution, and I appreciate their willingness to work with us.

Again, we're not going to agree on every issue, but a Europe which works closely with America and an America which works closely with Europe means the world will be better off.

EU-U.S. Relations

Mr. Frost. The difference really is, between Tony Blair and them, is that Tony Blair sees Europe as a partner of the United States, and they perhaps see Europe as a rival of the United States.

The President. I don't think Germany sees that, for starters. In my conversations with Gerhard Schroeder, they never yielded that impression. I think Germany understands it's important for the bilateral relationship between America and Germany to be strong. It's in our economic interests that it's strong. It's in the interest of peace that it be strong.

I understand there was kind of this notion of multipolarity, which means that somehow the values of America need to be offset. But we're for peace; we're for freedom. This country is leading the world

when it comes to fighting AIDS. And I can assure you, having studied this issue a lot, and I understand the pandemic of AIDS on the continent of Africa, we'll be better off—the people of Africa will be better off if Europe and the United States work together to fight the pandemic of AIDS. My only point is, there's a lot we can do working together.

European Defense Force

Mr. Frost. And what about the—I gather that you have some misgivings about the proposed European army, the danger that it might be a threat to NATO.

The President. Yes, here's the thing, first of all, I believe that the European defense force ought to take on more responsibility on those missions which NATO turns down. I think it's good for the United States' interests. I think it's good for NATO's interests, so long as the defense force doesn't undermine the vitality of NATO. And Tony Blair tells me that the discussions he's having with other European countries will in no way undermine NATO, and I take his word for it. He's been a man who's been true to his word on a lot of issues, and I believe he'll be true to his word on this issue.

Iraqi Weapons of Mass Destruction

Mr. Frost. Tell me about—in terms of Iraq, tell me about weapons of mass destruction. The fact that we didn't find them, and so on, has been much discussed. But do you think that you were the victim of a failure of intelligence in a way?

The President. Not at all.

Mr. Frost. No?

The President. No, not at all. I think our intelligence was sound. I know the British intelligence was sound. It's the same intelligence that caused the United Nations to pass resolution after resolution after resolution. It's the same intelligence that was used by my predecessor to bomb Iraq. I'm very confident we got good intelligence. And not only that, Mr. David Kay, who went over to kind of lead the effort to find the weapons or the intent of weapons, came back with a report that clearly stated that Mr. Saddam Hussein would—had been in material breach of Resolution 1441. In other words, had the inspectors found what Kay found, they would have reported back to the United Nations that he was in breach, that he was in violation of exactly what the United Nations expected him not to do.

We'll find the truth. But this guy for many years had been hiding weapons, deceiving weapons. He had dual-use programs that could have been sped up. Nobody could say that Saddam Hussein wasn't a danger. Not only was he a danger to the free world—and that's what the world said; the world said it consistently—he was a danger to his own people as well. Remember, we discovered mass graves with hundreds of thousands of men and women and children clutching their little toys, as a result of this person's brutality.

Go ahead. Sorry.

Mr. Frost. But in terms of—did you feel, in terms of if there wasn't a failure of intelligence, that there was a sort of exaggeration in what was predicted? I mean, did you ever believe that stuff, for instance? Did you ever believe that stuff about him having weapons of mass destruction that could be unleashed in 45 minutes, or did you never really believe that?

The President. I believe he was a dangerous man.

Mr. Frost. But you didn't believe that.

The President. Well, I believed a lot of things. But I know he was a dangerous man. And I know that for the sake of security, he needed to be dealt with. After all—again I repeat this because it's a very important point that people in your country must remember, and that is, the world had spoken, universally spoken, about this man's danger for 12 long years. And in order for—at the very minimum, in order for a multinational organization to be valid and effective, something has to happen other

than resolutions. And when an organization says, "If you don't disarm"—in other words, in order to say, "They don't disarm," intelligence convinced a lot of nations, including France, that he had weapons. In other words, he had to disarm something. "Dismantle your programs. If you don't do that, there will be a serious consequence."

And the fundamental question is, what is a "serious consequence"? It's not another resolution. It's not more empty debate. A "serious consequence," in this case, was removing Saddam Hussein so that his weapons programs would not be activated. And David Kay found evidence of weapons programs. He found some biological weapons—evidence of biological weapons. And it doesn't take much time——

Mr. Frost. But we really need the big discovery, don't we?

The President. Well, that's pretty big, what I just told you. Now remember, for a long period of time, it was assumed that he didn't have a nuclear weapons program. And yet, after 1991, the world had to—changed its attitude about this man's nuclear weapons program and admitted that it was very advanced. A nuclear weapon in the hands of somebody like Saddam Hussein, particularly given the lessons of September the 11th, 2001, would be a horrendous development. And we had to deal with him. And we did—in a way, by the way, that was a compassionate way. We spared innocent life. We targeted the guilty, and we moved hard and fast. And very little of Iraq was touched in toppling Saddam Hussein.

Planning for Iraq After Combat Operations

Mr. Frost. Did we, in fact—people have said, Mr. President, as you know, that the same meticulous planning that went into winning the war didn't go into winning the peace, and we were a bit unprepared for some of the surprises, the unpleasant surprises, you know, the terrorists and all of that that came along. Is that a fair comment?

The President. No—[laughter]—it's not a fair comment. We look at all contingencies and are dealing with the contingencies. Look, let me—if I could step back and maybe think out loud here about some of the stories or some of the speculation that was going on before we went into Iraq: One, the oil revenues would be blown up; the oil fields would be destroyed. They weren't. As a matter of fact, oil production is up to 2.1 million or 2.2 million barrels a day, to the benefit of the Iraqi people. That's a very important point.

Remember, there was speculation about sectarian violence, that the long-suppressed Kurds or Shi'a may take out their anxieties and their frustrations on the Sunnis. That didn't happen. There was talk about mass starvation; it didn't happen. Refugee flows that would be unmanageable—that never happened. And so a lot of the contingency that we had planned for didn't happen. What has happened is that in a relatively small part of the country, there are Ba'athist——

Mr. Frost. You call it now the Ba'athist Triangle.

The President. ——Sunni Triangle, they are attacking. And they're attacking not only coalition forces; they're attacking innocent Iraqis, because what they're trying to do is stop the spread of progress.

Mr. Frost. It's almost a guerrilla war there, really.

The President. Well, I would call it a desperate attempt by people who were totally in control of government, through tyrannical means, to regain power. This is nothing more than a power grab.

Now, there are some foreign fighters, mujahideen types or Al Qaida or Al Qaida affiliates involved as well. They've got a different mission. They want to install a Taliban-type Government in Iraq, or they want to seek revenge for getting whipped in Afghanistan. But nevertheless, they all have now found common ground for a brief period of time. And what we will do is, we will use Iraqi intelligence; we will use Iraqi security forces—we're up to about 118,000 Iraqi folks in one type of uniform or another securing the country—to be a integral part of chasing these killers down and to bring them to justice before they kill innocent life.

Mr. Frost. But it must have taken us a bit by surprise, or otherwise we'd have prepared for it, the level of this—the combination of the, what, 700, perhaps, foreign terrorists who came into Iraq, and so on. That was——

The President. I don't think so. I think a lot the people who came in initially wish they hadn't come in initially, or they're not wishing at all right now. But no, we understood it was going to be tough. We've been there for 7 months, David, which seems like a long time, particularly giving the news cycles the way they are. I'm certainly not complaining about the news cycles, but nevertheless, there's a certain sense of impatience that has now crept into the world. And my job is to enable our operators and military to make adjustments necessary to succeed. We've got the same strategy, which is a peaceful Iraq. The tactics shift, depending upon the decisions of the enemy. We're making progress.

That's not to say it's not tough. Of course, it's tough. What they want to do is, they want to shake the will of the free world. And the good news about having a partner like Tony Blair is, he won't be shaken. And neither will I, and neither will Jose Maria Aznar. I heard Berlusconi stand up with a strong statement after the Italian police had been murdered. And we, of course, send our sympathies and prayers to the Italian people. But Berlusconi said, "They're not going to run us out."

And that's what these terrorists need to hear. And more importantly, or as importantly, the Iraqi citizens need to hear that. They need to know that we won't leave the country prematurely. They need to know two things: We're not going to cut and run; and two, we believe they have the capacity to run their own country.

Timetable for Iraq

Mr. Frost. The cut-and-run thing, obviously, is absolutely vital. And you've said you're not going to cut and run. You'll be there as long as it takes. Tony Blair, in his speech on Monday night, said, "We're not going to retreat one inch." I mean, we're there for how long it takes to produce a successful Iraqi democracy, are we?

The President. Yes, absolutely.

Mr. Frost. Whether that's years and years or what?

The President. Well, we don't think it will be years and years, because, first of all, we think the Iraqi people are plenty capable of running their own country, and we think they want to run their own country. And just today I had discussions with Jerry Bremer, our Ambassador in Baghdad, who flew back to discuss ways——

Mr. Frost. Oh, yes——

The President. Well, just to discuss ways to do—to assure the Iraqi people that we have confidence in their capability. See, some in the world, some in the world don't believe that Iraq can run itself. They believe that, "Might as well let them have a military dictatorship or a tyrant. That's the only way they can be governed."

I disagree, and Tony Blair disagrees with that. We believe that democracy will take hold in Iraq, and we believe a free and democratic Iraq will help change the Middle East. There are hundreds of reformers that are desperate for freedom. Freedom—freedom is not America's gift to the world or Great Britain's gift to the world. Freedom is the Almighty's gift to everybody who lives in the world.

Role of Saddam Hussein

Mr. Frost. Is there any likelihood that Saddam himself could be behind this violence?

The President. Saddam Hussein is a violent man. Listen, he tortured and maimed and killed. He had rape rooms, and people disappeared because they spoke out against him. We've discovered mass graves. He's a brutal, brutal tyrant—brutal tyrant. We did the Iraqi people a great favor by removing him. So I wouldn't be surprised that any kind of violence is promoted by him, but I don't know. I don't know. All I know is, we're after him.

Role of World Opinion in Regime Change

Mr. Frost. That's one of the interesting things. I mean, nobody has time for a moment for Saddam Hussein. Some people are worried in England and around the world by the idea of regime change, because they say, "Once we've done regime change, Britain and America with Saddam Hussein, what can we say if India wants to do regime change with Pakistan, or Pakistan wants to do regime change with India?"

The President. Well, see, I can understand their concerns, except they forgot the history. This issue has been discussed in the United Nations for over a decade. And the United Nations, as a multilateral international body, passed resolution after resolution after resolution calling for Saddam Hussein to disarm. In other words, the diplomatic process went forward. There was plenty of diplomacy. And to the critics, I would say that there will be diplomacy when it comes to India and Pakistan. The world will speak out clearly.

The problem is, is that when the world speaks out clearly and then nothing happens, all we've got is empty words. It's tyrants that take advantage of that. Tyrants—if tyrants don't fear—feel like they can torture and kill with impunity, feel like they can blackmail the world, and all the world does is put out empty words, it makes multilateralism extremely ineffective.

If I could take a second to remind your viewers that, obviously, not every situation needs to be solved militarily. Military option is the last option, as far as I'm concerned. And I would refer people to North Korea, where we've got a multilateral attempt to convince Kim Chong-il to get rid of his nuclear ambitions. We understand, just like Saddam Hussein, that he has been torturous to his people—people in North Korea are starving to death—and that weapons of mass destruction in his hands given his history, just like weapons of mass destruction in Saddam's hands given his history, is a very dangerous element. It's a dangerous—it inhibits the capacity for peace and freedom to spread.

But what I've done is, I've convinced China and South Korea and Japan and Russia to speak with one voice to the North Koreans, and say, "Get rid of your nuclear ambitions." We're also, at the same time, working on a counterproliferation regime that will stop his ability to ship weapons of mass destruction or a nuclear warhead to a terrorist group. In other words, we're working together in a multilateral, multinational fashion to bring peace and stability to the world.

War on Terror

Mr. Frost. Someone who knows how passionate you are about this war on terror and Iraq and so on said, "I know George Bush, and I think, in terms of his legacy, he'd rather—I'll tell you how strongly he feels. He said he'd rather be defeated by the voters than by the terrorists." Is that true?

The President. I'd rather not be defeated by either. [*Laughter*] And we will not be defeated by the terrorists. I say that confidently, because the allies in the war on terror are strong and steadfast, and there's no stronger and steadfast ally in the war on terror than Tony Blair. He understands the stakes. He knows that freedom is being challenged. He understands as well that the spread of freedom and democracy, in the long run, will defeat terror. And that's why the battle—the stakes are so high in Iraq right now. By the way, Iraq is a front in the war on terror. And it's important for people to understand that, because the war takes place elsewhere.

Reform of the Palestinian Authority

Mr. Frost. And in—one of the reasons that people say, in the Arab world—obviously there was your landmark speech last week—but in the Arab world, that you won't really be able to address the balance against America until the United States is seen not to tilt towards Israel in the Middle East. What do you think about that?

The President. I think about that: I think it's an excuse, because America—I am the first President ever to go to the United Nations——

Mr. Frost. And say, two——

The President. Two states side by side in peace.

Mr. Frost. ——two states.

The President. No President has ever said that. And I said it, and I said it with conviction, because I believe it is in Israel's interest that there be a peaceful Palestinian state, and I know it's in the Palestinians' interest. However, to achieve a peaceful Palestinian state, the emergence of a peaceful Palestinian state, a state where people are willing to risk capital, a place where people are willing to develop an economy, there must be a focused effort to defeat terror. And there hasn't been with the current Palestinian leadership.

I went in and embraced, in Aqaba, Jordan, Abu Mazen. And the reason I did so, David, is because he came to the Oval Office and he said, "I will join you in the fight against terror. We're not going to allow the few to destroy the hopes of the many." As well, I could sense in his talk, in his feeling, that he has—he's got great trust in the Palestinian people. In other words, given the chance, the Palestinian people will develop the habits of democracy, and out of that will come a great state, a peaceful state. And I trusted him, and we were working with him. We were making good progress. And I was working with Ariel Sharon. I gave a speech on June

24th, 2002, which says, "All of us have responsibilities, and you, Israel, have a responsibility."

Prime Minister Ariel Sharon of Israel

Mr. Frost. Do you think Ariel Sharon could ever emerge as a man of peace?

The President. Yes, I do. I believe he wants peace for his people. I truly do. I mean, he's a man who has presided over suiciders, where he has to go to the funerals of women and children because some cold-blooded killer is trying to destroy the hopes of all the people in the region. And it's—yes, I believe so. And I believe he believes in a Palestinian state. I've asked him in the Oval Office, I said, "Listen, am I out there by myself on a Palestinian state, or will you support it?" He said he will. But both of us understand, as do a lot of other people, that for a state to emerge, there must be a focused effort to get after the Hamas killers, for example, who want to destroy the hopes of the people that believe in a Palestinian state. And there hasn't been that effort.

Anyway, let me finish my Abu Mazen story, if you don't mind. I embraced the guy, and I believe that he is a—I believe he's a partner with whom we can work, and he's shoved out. Progress is being made, and he is shoved aside by the old guard. And that's unacceptable behavior. It's just unacceptable.

British Detainees at Guantanamo Bay

Mr. Frost. Guantanamo. You're going to get asked about, obviously, in England, what's going to happen to our British detainees. Tony Blair was talking about it in the House of Commons this week and saying, hopefully they'd be tried before a proper court or repatriated to be tried in the U.K. Will you have any good news for us on that? For him on that?

The President. You mean right here, sitting right here, me and you, talking—the good news is, one, they'll be treated fairly, like they are. And two, I'm working closely with Tony to come up with a solution that he's comfortable with. And I emphasize, a solution that he's comfortable with. These prisoners are being treated—these were illegal non-combatants picked up off of a battlefield. And they're being well-treated, and they will go through a military tribunal at some point in time, which is—a military tribunal, which is in international accord—or in line with international accords.

Mr. Frost. As we approach the end of this interview, Mr. President—I could carry on for hours, actually, but I know you've got a lot to do, more than the rest of us. As we approach the end of this interview, what would you say is the most important lesson you've learned in life in the Presidency?

The President. The most important lesson in life in the Presidency is to have a clear vision of where you want to lead, and lead. I've got a clear vision: It's a world that is more free and therefore more peaceful; a world based upon human rights, human dignity, and justice; a world that does not discriminate between one group of people or—a vision that does not discriminate between one group of people or another, because I believe all people have the desire to be free. And I'm willing to lead there.

And the people of this country will make their—you asked about politics—they'll make the decision as to whether or not they—I've have been honest with them and open with them and whether or not they like my leadership style. A lot of it will have to do with the economy, of course, whether I get another 4 years. But I think it's important to know where you want to lead, and lead.

Bush Team for a Second Term

Mr. Frost. Would you hope to present to the country the same team, Dick Cheney and Donald Rumsfeld and Colin Powell and Condi Rice, for the second term?

The President. It's been a fabulous team, and Cheney for certain. And I haven't—

obviously, I'm not going to talk to my Cabinet ministers until after the election. But I'm proud of this team. I put together one of the finest teams, one of the finest administrations any President has ever assembled. These are good, honest, decent, hard-working, experienced people who give me good, unvarnished advice and, when I make a decision, say, "Yes, sir, Mr. President, we'll go execute it."

Mr. Frost. Well, thank you for your decision to do this interview.

The President. Thank you, sir. I enjoyed seeing you.

NOTE: The interview was taped at 3:08 p.m. on November 12 in the Map Room at the White House for later broadcast on BBC One's "Breakfast With Frost." The transcript was released by the Office of the Press Secretary on November 17. In his remarks, the President referred to Queen Elizabeth II and Prime Minister Tony Blair of the United Kingdom; former President Saddam Hussein of Iraq; Chancellor Gerhard Schroeder of Germany; President Jacques Chirac of France; former President William J. Clinton; David Kay, CIA Special Advisor for Strategy Regarding Iraqi Weapons of Mass Destruction Programs; President Jose Maria Aznar of Spain; Prime Minister Silvio Berlusconi of Italy; L. Paul Bremer III, Presidential Envoy to Iraq; Chairman Kim Chong-il of North Korea; and former Prime Minister Mahmoud Abbas (Abu Mazen) of the Palestinian Authority. Portions of this interview could not be verified because the tape was incomplete.

Interview With Trevor Kavanagh of The Sun
November 17, 2003

The Oval Office

The President. Have you ever been in the Oval Office before?

Mr. Kavanagh. Once, just once.

The President. Okay. The rug was designed by my wife. Every President gets to design his own rug. You probably didn't know that.

Mr. Kavanagh. Fabulous.

The President. I wanted mine—mine was designed by my wife, Laura. And I wanted people to have a sense of optimism when they came in here, that this is a guy who kind of sees a better world, not a worse world. Sometimes the Oval can be foreboding, and I wanted it to be cheery. So I hope you felt that.

This is called "A Charge To Keep." It's based upon a Methodist hymn. One of America's great imports from England was John Wesley. And it talks about serving something greater than yourself, which speaks to my own personal faith. As a President, it speaks to my need to capture the spirit of America and call on people to serve. You've probably followed some of my domestic policy, but one of the things that's important is to call on people to serve their communities by helping neighbors who hurt. The de Tocquevillean view of America at that point was just kind of a civic fabric of loving organizations; part of my vision, as well, is to energize them.

The painting's of Texas. That's kind of what my ranch looks like, by a guy named Onderdonk. He's a Texas landscape artist. The bluebonnets are not quite that big. Blair and I—well, he's been there, and he would recognize kind of the look, if he were here. This is west Texas, where my wife's family was raised. We were both raised in west Texas, but this is farther west than where I was raised. It's called El Paso. But it's a famous Texas artist and historian who painted that.

More Texas. The reason I have Texas up there is it's where I'm from. And in this job if you can't figure out who you are—you better know who you are because of the pressures and the decisionmaking process and all the noise of politics and all that.

Really quickly, this is a desk given to us by Queen Victoria. A famous desk called the U.S.S. *Resolute*, and it's wood from the *Resolute*. The door was put on by Roosevelt to cover his infirmities. Out of the door poked John Kennedy's son——

Mr. Kavanagh. Oh, yes, I remember.

The President. I chose to use this. Ronald Reagan put the bottom on to make the desk high so it won't bump your knees. I love the desk. I love its history. It does speak to the great relationship between America and Great Britain; I'm sitting at a desk given to our country by Queen Victoria.

And finally, the Churchill bust is on loan from the Brits. Tony Blair knew I was a great admirer of Churchill, so here he sits, along with Lincoln and Eisenhower.

That's it. Welcome.

Mr. Kavanagh. Fantastic. Thank you very much, Mr. President. Where would you like me?

The President. Sit right here. Take Vice President Cheney's seat.

Mr. Kavanagh. I'm more than a little impressed by being here and by sitting in this seat.

The President. Well, you know, this is a shrine to democracy, and we treat it as such. And it's an honor to serve here.

Mr. Kavanagh. Well, I would like to thank you on behalf of our readers for giving them and me the time to talk to you.

The President. Well, I'm glad you're here, thanks.

World After Afghanistan and Iraq

Mr. Kavanagh. We're a very pro-American newspaper, and our readers were shocked and deeply moved by September the 11th. And they supported what hap-

pened subsequently in Afghanistan and a little more reluctantly in Iraq, but in fact, the majority of our readers were behind the action.

I think what they would like to know—we've talked with them in a way which is quite interesting. We actually spent a weekend with about 2,000 of our readers.

The President. Really? [*Laughter*] Good marketing tool. [*Laughter*] That's interesting.

Mr. Kavanagh. Yes. And the one question they wanted to ask you is, is the world a safer place after the conflict than it was before?

The President. Yes, much safer. It's safer for a couple of reasons. One, the free world has recognized the threat. In order to make the world safe, you've got to actually see reality. And the reality is that there are cold-blooded killers who were trying to intimidate, create fear, create hostility, and to shape the will of the civilized world.

And a lot of countries have seen the threat for what it is. So, therefore, step one is recognizing the problem. Tony Blair recognizes the problem. Jose Maria Aznar recognizes the problem. Silvio Berlusconi recognizes the problem. Clearly, the United States recognizes the problem. After all, the clearest indication that we were at war and that the stakes had changed dramatically was September the 11th. After all, we were a country which was able to sit back in our—kind of in our geographical posture and pick and choose where a threat might emerge and say we may have to deal with that or we may not deal with it. We were pretty confident that we were protected ourselves by oceans. That changed. And one of my vows to the American people is I won't forget the lessons of September the 11th, 2001.

Secondly, the world is safer because the actions we have taken will ultimately strengthen multinational institutions. Take the theater in Iraq. The United Nations had recognized that Saddam Hussein was a threat. They recognized it in not one resolution but multiple resolutions and yet didn't do anything about it. And therefore, the resolutions became weak, became just words.

And as a result of enforcing 1441, which said that you disarm or there will be serious consequences, now when multinational institutions speak, hopefully people will take them seriously. And in order to win the war on terror, there needs to be alliance and cooperation because these are killers that are capable of hiding in societies. They're patient. They're lethal. They pop up and will destroy. And by the way, they don't care who they destroy. There are no rules for these people. They will kill children just as soon as they'll kill somebody in a military uniform.

Thirdly, the world is safer because there is a—and by the way, multinational forum doesn't necessarily mean U.N. It can also mean collaborations, like the collaboration that's now taking place with North Korea in dealing with Kim Chong-il, who is a threat to peace. And now it's not just the United States dealing with Kim Chong-il; it's the United States, China, South Korea, Japan, and Russia in a collaborative effort. Or the fine work—the initial fine work done by the foreign ministers of Great Britain, France, and Germany in telling Iran to get rid of its nuclear ambitions. I say "initial fine work" because the Iranians, in the past, have had clandestine operations. And therefore, in order to make sure that the words that have been issued to them are true, there must be transparency.

Fourthly, we dealt Al Qaida. We are tough on Al Qaida. Now, you know, there are key figures still looming in caves and remote regions of the world, but we're dismantling them. If you were to look at Al Qaida as a business organization, middle management is no longer. That's not to say that they're not grooming junior executives to take over certain roles. But we're tough, and we're on their trail, and we're still hunting them down. Make no mistake

about it. And as a result of dismantling Al Qaida, the world is safer.

We've also dealt with the tyrants in Afghanistan, which is an incredibly dangerous regime, dangerous not only to the free world because they provided housing, training, money, safe haven, but also they were just tortuous and barbaric to their own people. And in Iraq, Saddam Hussein was clearly a threat to peace. And we can argue about the definition of "serious consequence," and I respect the debate, but no one can justify this man's behavior to his people. We've discovered mass graves with over 300,000 people there, rape rooms, and torture rooms. He is paying suiciders to go kill innocent Israelis. He had a weapons program as discovered—I promise you this is going to be a short answer, eventually. I saw you looking at the clock; your glance can't escape me. [*Laughter*]

This is an important question. It is the question.

Mr. Kavanagh. Of course, absolutely.

The President. David Kay discovered a weapons program that was in material breach of 1441. In other words, it was in violation of precisely what the United Nations had asked him not to do. Saddam Hussein, in 1991, it was assumed that he—his nuclear weapons program would be active in the out-years, and in fact, the inspectors discovered he's got nuclear ambitions, not only real and active but his program was a lot farther along than we thought. And had he ever developed a nuclear weapon, had he been allowed to have a nuclear weapon, he would have been the ultimate source of international blackmail.

And so the removal of Saddam Hussein makes the world safer. And as importantly, the removal of Saddam Hussein gives the Iraqis a chance to live in freedom, which is the ultimate—freedom is the ultimate route to security. I strongly believe that free nations are peaceful nations. Free nations are not terrorist havens, do not become terrorist havens. Free nations won't create conditions of strife and resentment that breeds anxiety and terror.

And therefore, the world is becoming safer, is safer, and will be even more safe when Iraq becomes free. And Iraq will be free, and it'll be peaceful. And we need peace and freedom in that part of the world.

Now, there's an interesting debate going on as to whether or not people like the Iraqis will ever adapt the habits of freedom. There's kind of an elitism that takes place in our country, in your country, and elsewhere, feels, well, "Certain people can't be free. They can't adapt the habits of democracy." I strongly disagree. I strongly disagree.

And so, yes, the world is safer, and the world is more peaceful.

Future U.S. Activity in Iraq

Mr. Kavanagh. Okay. That answer will resonate with our readers. Nonetheless, there is concern about the events, particularly in the last week or so, when things have escalated. I think this causes concern everywhere. Are we going to increase military presence there? Are we going to pull out? There's a fear that——

The President. You don't have to worry about us pulling out.

Mr. Kavanagh. There's a famous T-shirt slogan which shows the American flag and the words, "These colors don't run." Do you stand by that?

The President. Yes, absolutely. Absolutely. Our will is being tested. See, the tactics of the terrorists is to kill as many innocent people as possible and, therefore, try to shape the will of the Iraqis. As progress is made—and we're making interesting progress, and I'll cite some examples in a minute that I think are fascinating. But as the Iraqis begin to say, "Wait a minute. Life can be better," and their instincts kick in about what it means to live in a free society, the terrorists want to shake that. They want to scare them. They want the police not to become police. And

we've got over 118,000 people now, Iraqi citizens, in uniform beginning to conduct operations for their own security.

They, of course, want to kill our own soldiers and, therefore, try to shake the will of the American people and the President and the command structure. They killed those Italians. And they were hoping that Berlusconi would say, "Oh, my goodness, this is too big a fight. We'll leave." We're not leaving. We're staying there to get the job done. Of course we mourn the death of any citizen. But I recognize that it is— I still remember the death, what happened to us on September the 11th as well. I was there at Ground Zero right after the attacks, and I remember this kind of haze and the smells and the death and destruction. I'll always remember that, of course. And as I've told you, I vowed not to forget the lessons.

Mr. Kavanagh. That changed everything?

The President. Absolutely. Look, what changed for me was sitting on Air Force One and getting the reports that we were under attack. And I made up my mind then, right then, that we didn't need a bunch of legal briefs. I didn't need a bunch of—you know, let's kind of hold hands and hope to get the right answer. We were at war, and we were going to win the war. And I still feel that same exact determination today that I did then.

Mr. Kavanagh. So you'll stay in Iraq even——

The President. We will do our job.

Mr. Kavanagh. ——after there's an interim council, a Government which is——

The President. Yes. There's a lot of talk right now about the political process, as there should be. And we are interested in the Iraqis assuming more responsibility on the political side and on the security side. And a political process in which the Iraqis assume more responsibility will make the security side come together quicker as well in our judgment.

And therefore, Bremer came here, he took instructions back from me to talk to the Governing Council to find out what is feasible when it comes to the passing of more power to the Governing Council. That's where we are right there.

On the security side, absolutely we're there. The goal is for Iraq to be peaceful and free. I understand the consequences of a free and peaceful Iraq in the midst of the Middle East. We can have the debate all day long as to whether the Middle East will ever adapt the habits of democracy and freedom. I think they will, obviously, and I'm confident they will. I like to tell people in this country, freedom is not America's gift to the world; freedom is not Great Britain's gift to the world; freedom is the Almighty's gift to everybody in the world.

Freedom for Iraq

Mr. Kavanagh. And this is what you'll tell the demonstrators? Or this is what you would tell the demonstrators if you had 5 minutes with them?

The President. Of course I would, absolutely. I will say, "You may disagree with our tactics. Nobody likes war. War is my last choice." If the demonstrators are there as anti-war protestors, they may be there for other reasons as well—global trade—and I'd be glad to talk to them about that as well. But in terms of war, I can understand why people are anxious about war. I can understand why citizens in Great Britain, protestor or not, wonders about why a President would commit to war, because nobody likes war.

On the other hand, I would tell them, the skeptics and the critics, that I have a job to protect the security of the United States of America and that Saddam Hussein was a security risk, as witnessed by the international community speaking loudly on that subject 12 different times. But I would tell those who doubt our policy that we share a common goal, which is peace, and that free societies are peaceful societies. They may say, "Well, you can't possibly expect a country like Iraq to be free," and

then we'd have an interesting philosophical debate because I believe freedom exists in the heart of every single human being. It may take longer for people to accept freedom, if they've been tortured and brutalized like Saddam Hussein did.

Secondly, I would tell the skeptics that not only is the world more secure as a result of the decisions we made, the Iraqi people now have a chance to live in a society which is hopeful and optimistic, a society in which you're able to speak your mind, a society in which you don't have to pay homage to a brutal tyrant and his two brutal sons, which is precisely how they had to live in the past.

Threats to World Peace

Mr. Kavanagh. So how do you respond to those people who were polled by the Europe Commission and found that America was—alongside Iran, North Korea—is the second most powerful threat to world peace?

The President. You just have to tell them, "Watch what happens." The world is going to be more peaceful, and the free world will be more secure as a result of the decisions we've taken.

United Kingdom's Contribution in Iraq

Mr. Kavanagh. Can I ask you about the special relationship, the role the British soldiers play in Iraq and are still playing?

The President. Sure.

Mr. Kavanagh. Would you like to tell me about you feel about our contribution?

The President. Yes, I'll tell you about your troops. They are well trained. They are well motivated, and they're really good at what they do. And our soldiers and our generals and our commanders really appreciate being side-by-side with the Brits. They trust them, and that's important.

Secondly, in Basra, the Brits have brought an interesting strategy in dealing in Basra because you have dealt in Northern Ireland. In other words, it was kind of a transfer of experience that has been incredibly useful and important. I am really proud of our—not only our alliance because it's close now, and I intend to keep it that way.

I've got a great personal relationship with Tony Blair. Let me tell you something about him just real quick, because it relates also to the trust of the troops. He's a man who comes in here, and he says he's going to do something, and as I said—as they say in Texas, you can book him when he says he's going to do something; you can take it to the bank. Because every time he has said something, he has done it, and I appreciate that a lot. It's not always the way it is in politics, whether it be domestic or international politics. Sometimes they'll come and look you in the eye and say, "Oh, don't worry, Mr. President, we're with you and behind you," and it turns out they're way behind you. You can't find them when the heat gets on. But that's not the way Tony Blair is, and that's not the way the Brits' command structure is, and that's not the way the soldiers in the field have been. They've been tough and capable and decent people—that's the other thing about militaries. Both our militaries are full of compassionate people, because not only are we chasing down people and bringing them to justice, as we say, but there are schools being built, orphanages being opened, hospitals being supplied, thanks to compassionate British troops and American troops as well, and other troops. It speaks to the honor of our respective militaries. These are honorable people.

President's Upcoming Meeting With Families of Fallen British Soldiers

Mr. Kavanagh. You're going to speak to some of the families of those who have already died in Iraq and also September the 11th.

The President. Yes.

Mr. Kavanagh. You're going to see them, I guess, on Downing Street.

The President. Well, I'm not sure exactly where, but you bet. I am going to see them.

Mr. Kavanagh. What are you going to say to them?

The President. Well, I'm going to first of all ask for God's blessings, because I understand how bad they hurt. I can't imagine what it would be like, if I were a mother or a dad, to have lost a child. I'm a proud dad. It's got to shatter a person's heart to lose a loved one, and I will do the best I can to provide some comfort. I have done this here in America as well. It's part of my duty as the leader of this country to comfort those who have sacrificed.

I'll also explain to them as best as I can that the sacrifices that their loved one has made is for a noble cause, and that's peace and freedom. I strongly believe that what we're doing today will make it easier for this person's grandchild to grow up in a free world and a peaceful world.

I'll tell you an interesting story, kind of dawned on me a while ago. I was talking to Prime Minister Koizumi of Japan in Tokyo. We were having dinner, actually. And I kind of reflected on what it would be like—during our dinner, I reflected on what it would be like if America and the Allies hadn't done a good job in post-World War II. Would I be sitting with a Prime Minister of Japan, with whom I've got great relations, talking about how to deal with Kim Chong-il and North Korea? It's an interesting thought.

Mr. Kavanagh. Very interesting.

The President. Beyond that is whether or not somebody 50 years from now is going to be sitting with a leader from Iraq or any other country in that region saying, "Thank goodness George W. and Tony Blair held the line, because I'm now able to deal with terrorist threats or potential terrorist threats with an ally. I'm able to help bring more peace to the world."

Presidents and Prime Ministers should never worry about their short-term history, how they're viewed in short-term history. There's no such thing as short-term history, except for the musings of somebody who's not very objective to begin with, because if you set big goals and work on big items, the President or the Prime Minister won't be around to see the effects of those policies. And therefore, I don't worry about the short-term history. I think in terms of long-term history. I know what we're doing now is going to have an effect, a positive effect on this world.

France, Germany, and NATO

Mr. Kavanagh. Can I just backtrack a little?

The President. Sure.

Mr. Kavanagh. You were talking earlier about the contributions countries like Britain and Italy have made, and others.

The President. Spain, Poland, a lot of people.

Mr. Kavanagh. You didn't mention France and Germany in that. You seem very critical of France.

The President. Look, my attitude is the past is there. It's past, and now let's go on. I'll tell you one example of why that attitude is important, and that is Germany's contribution in Afghanistan. And it's a positive contribution, more than positive; it's incredibly helpful. They've got a number of troops there. It's the first deployment of German troops, as I understand, outside of their soil since World War II. It's a positive—yes, I think that's right. Check the facts. But anyway, it's helpful, really helpful.

Mr. Kavanagh. And NATO?

The President. Yes, NATO is important.

Mr. Kavanagh. But France is a semidetached member of NATO——

The President. Well, it's a historic role——

Mr. Kavanagh. They won't be a rival——

The President. I certainly hope not. See, there's no need to rival the United States and our friends. Our goals are peace.

Mr. Kavanagh. But France wants to counter.

The President. You mean multipolarity? Well, I think we need to work against multipolarity, and the reason why I know we need to work against multipolarity is a Europe working with American can do a lot together. A united Europe working with America can do a lot together. We can promote peace. We can fight off terror, which is necessary, and there needs to be full cooperation in order to defeat the terrorists. We can work on issues like global AIDS.

I'm real proud of our country's contribution to global AIDS, just to give you a sense of my feeling on this. We are a fortunate country. We're prosperous—and by the way, we're becoming more prosperous, which is good news.

Global AIDS Initiative

Mr. Kavanagh. I'd like to ask you about that.

The President. Okay. But I believe we owe a lot to the world's peace, and we owe a lot to those who suffer, because of our fortune, because of our wealth. I'm proud of the fact that Congress has supported my initiative to provide a large sum of money. And as importantly, I'm proud of our NGOs and faith-based organizations that are willing to help provide the infrastructure so that we can get help to beat this pandemic. We're a prosperous country, and yet in our world an entire generation is about to be wiped out. And I feel strongly about America's need to be involved and Europe's need to be involved in this issue together, just like I feel strongly we need to provide food for the hungry, just like I feel strongly that when we see tyranny, that we need to work for freedom.

Every situation, of course, doesn't require military action. I just repeat—I want your readers to know, the military is my last choice, not my first choice. See, I understand the consequences of war. I understand the risks of war. I understand first-hand, particularly when I go and hug the moms and dads and brothers and sisters and sons and daughters of those who died.

I also see the consequences of not acting, of hoping for the best in the face of these tyrannical killers. So therefore, our foreign policy will be active. We'll work closely with our friends and allies, and we're going to stay on the offensive against the terrorists.

National Economy/Steel Tariffs

Mr. Kavanagh. Let me just ask you one quick question on the economy.

The President. Yes.

Mr. Kavanagh. It's going great guns. You're revising figures upwards. You introduced tax cuts. You promised tax cuts; you introduced them. Is this a message to the rest of the world too?

The President. Well, I think people ought to look at progrowth policies and how to stimulate the entrepreneurial spirit. To me, one of the unique qualities of our country is the individualism of our country and the willingness of people to take risks to better themselves. Most new jobs in America are created by small businesses, and that's an exciting aspect of our economy, because it not only is good economics to have the job-hiring dispersed throughout society, it also is such a hopeful part of our economy, when you think about somebody in America can start their own business and grow it and then actually own something. They become the owner of this piece of property.

Our tax policy was very effective at stimulating small-business growth, because most small businesses pay tax at the individual income tax level. When you hear "small business" or "small corporation," you think "corporate tax." But in America most small businesses are sole proprietorships or Subchapter S's, so that when we cut all rates, not trying to select rate cuts but all rates,

it really affected capital formation in the small business.

This economy and this country, more importantly, is tough and resilient. We've been through a lot. When I showed up here, we were in recession. I guess we were headed into recession. But the first—I show up—Dick Cheney and I are here; we get sworn in in late January; and the first quarter of '01 is recession or the beginnings of a recession. And then the attacks hurt us, and we had corporate scandals. But I think the world is beginning to see America will deal with corporate scandals in a tough way. It doesn't matter whether you're—we will hold people to account. I believe, in criminal matters, that there has to be consequences for bad behavior, and clear consequences, and that's how you deter bad behavior. And our SEC and our prosecutors are moving quickly.

The war affected people, but we're overcoming that. It's not only good tax policy, but we've got to work on making sure Congress doesn't overspend, and that's tough. But I'm holding the line. We've done pretty good on our budget agreements so far. We need better legal policy. I've been pushing tort reform at the national level on class action suits, all of which make it easier for people to kind of calculate risk when it comes to employing capital, which is the essence of promoting the entrepreneurial spirit.

Trade is a very important element. I'll be dealing—real quickly—I'm going to take a good look at the steel issue. The International Trade Commission made a ruling. It said our industry was being harmed by imports. I felt I had an obligation to take that report seriously, which I did. I imposed tariffs to see whether or not—to give the breathing room for the industry to restructure. I'm not analyzing the extent to which they restructured. Having said that, I am a fierce free trader. I believe in free trade. I know free trade is important between America and Great Britain, and I will continue to resist any protectionist tendencies here. In order for us to be free traders, however, we've got to enforce the rules of free trade, and I was doing so through the International Trade Commission's report.

Sorry I cut you off.

Mr. Kavanagh. Not at all.

The President. First Lady Bush is standing out there. We're getting ready to award the National Humanities Award here.

Mr. Kavanagh. Many thanks.

The President. See you over there.

NOTE: The interview began at 9:31 a.m. on November 14 in the Oval Office at the White House. The transcript was made available by the Office of the Press Secretary on November 14 but was embargoed for release until 8 a.m., November 17. In his remarks, the President referred to Prime Minister Tony Blair of the United Kingdom; President Jose Maria Aznar of Spain; Prime Minister Silvio Berlusconi of Italy; Chairman Kim Chong-il of North Korea; Prime Minister Junichiro Koizumi of Japan; former President Saddam Hussein of Iraq; L. Paul Bremer III, Presidential Envoy to Iraq; and David Kay, CIA Special Advisor for Strategy Regarding Iraqi Weapons of Mass Destruction Programs. A tape was not available for verification of the content of this interview.

Remarks Following Discussions With Members of the Governing Council of Iraq and Members of the Baghdad Advisory Council and an Exchange With Reporters
November 17, 2003

The President. It's been my honor to host one of the most extraordinary meetings I've had as the President of the United States. I'm seated here with five courageous, brave Iraqi women who believe in the people of Iraq, believe in the future of Iraq, who love their freedoms, who look forward to working to see that their nation is a free and peaceful country.

The stories of these five courageous leaders is a story of human tragedy on the one hand and human hope on the other. And I am so honored that they're here. Two members of the Governing Council are with us. I'll ask each member to say a couple of words, and then I'll be glad to answer a couple of questions.

Would you like to start? The leader of the delegation. And by the way, there is an extensive group of Iraqi women in the room next door that I will go talk to here in a minute with these—along with these other five leaders here.

Raja Habib al-Khuzai. I lead the delegation of the 17 women, Iraqi women, and we represent Iraq. And all of us are different ethnic and religious groups, but we are from Iraq. And we are all Iraqis, and Iraq is just one nation. And we are looking forward to see the new, democratic Iraq, and everyone will live in peace. We don't like wars anymore, and we suffered a lot.

Songul Chapouk. Yes. I'm also from the Governing Council. I'm also leading these women. And I am from the Turkoman community, and it's a pleasure for me to be in America. And I work for my people. I'd like to see Iraq have a new Government, and I'd like to see my people—more security. And I'd like to say that my people in Iraq, all of them, Kurdish, Turkoman, Arab, they're all working together. And the Sunni Triangle, there is no Sunni Triangle; they're all Iraqi.

We all like Iraq. We all like America, and we don't want them let—we don't want them to leave us. We need them because we have open borders and we don't have army and we don't have trained policemen, so we need them at this time. And we ask them to not leave us, please, at this time, because this is a very, very difficult condition for us. Our children like you, our children want you to stay, and all Iraqi people like your forces.

Thank you very much.

The President. I assured these five women that America wasn't leaving. When they hear me say, "We're staying," that means we're staying. And that's precisely what the terrorists want to do, is to try to drive us out of Iraq before these leaders and other leaders are able to put their Government together and live in peace. And we will succeed—we will succeed.

Let me answer a couple of questions. Hunt [Terence Hunt, Associated Press].

Iraqi Transition/U.S. Cooperation

Q. Sir, I'd like to pick up there on what you just said about "America isn't leaving" and what this woman said about they want us to stay. Is it fair to think of this provisional Government that's going to be established as any part of an exit strategy? Or——

The President. No. The politics will go forward. The political process is moving on. The Iraqi people are plenty capable of governing themselves. We're in the process now of working with the Governing Council to put in place the necessary laws so that people feel comfortable about the evolution of the Government. The Governing Council itself is going to be making these decisions, and it's full of capable people.

On the other hand, we will continue to work with the Iraqi people to secure its country. We fully recognize that Iraq has become a new front on the war on terror and that there are disgruntled Ba'athists as well as Fedayeen fighters and mujahideen types and Al Qaida types that want to test the will of the civilized world there. And we will work with Iraqis to bring people to justice. We talked about the high price the Iraqi citizens are paying. There's a lot of brave and courageous Iraqi soldiers and police who are chasing down these terrorists, and they're paying a price for it.

And the reason I bring that up is, the Iraqi people want to be free. And we will continue to work with them to develop a free society. And a free Iraq is not only in the interests of these five courageous women; a free Iraq is in our interests. A free Iraq in a part of the world that is troublesome and dangerous will set such a good example. We're talking about an historic opportunity to change parts of the world, and Iraq will be the leader of that change.

It's important for American citizens to know that what is taking place in Iraq will be in the long-term security interests for their children and their grandchildren. And I want to thank these five pioneers for freedom who are sitting here with me today.

Last question, Steve [Steve Holland, Reuters].

Al Qaida and Terrorist Attacks

Q. Al Qaida appears to be taking responsibility for bombings in Istanbul, Riyadh, Baghdad. Are we seeing a reconstitution of Al Qaida?

The President. We're seeing the nature of Al Qaida. They'll kill innocent people anywhere, anytime. That's just the way they are. They have no regard for human life. They claim they're religious people, but they're not. Religious people do not murder innocent citizens. Religious people don't just indiscriminately bomb.

The bombing in Istanbul, I was told today, may have taken more Muslim lives than any other religion. They just kill, and they're trying to create fear and chaos.

I had a good talk with Prime Minister Erdogan, who assured me that, one, he understood his responsibilities to protect people from all religions within his country and, two, that he would chase these killers down and bring them to justice. There's only one way to deal with Al Qaida: find them and bring them to justice. And that's exactly what the United States and a lot of other nations, including a free Iraq, will do. We do this in the name of humanity. We do this in the name of freedom, and we do it in the name of peace.

Thank you all very much.

NOTE: The President spoke at 1:57 p.m. in the Oval Office at the White House. In his remarks, he referred to Prime Minister Recep Tayyip Erdogan of Turkey.

Remarks Honoring NCAA Spring Championship Teams
November 17, 2003

Please be seated. Thanks for coming. Let's see, I forgot who said, "This is the people's house, and we're just letting you live here." You're right. Welcome to the people's house. I'm glad to be just living here for a while.

I'm also really glad to honor some of our country's really fine individuals to the White House, all of whom worked to make their team successful. It is—we call this championship day, where champions come, people who put their talents to good use, and people who have got a lot of talents to continue to put to use to make sure our country is as hopeful and compassionate as possible. So welcome to the White House. We're really thrilled you're here.

We've got some pretty interesting characters with us today. [*Laughter*] Every person has got to have a good lawyer, particularly in America. And I got a good one, and that's Judge Al Gonzales, who is the White House legal counsel, who graduated from Rice University. Judge, thank you for coming.

We have got Members from the United States Congress with us today. From the great State of Texas, Chris Bell and John Culberson. Thank you all for coming, Chris and John. I'm glad you're here. I suspect I know why you're here. Rush Holt from the State of New Jersey is with us. Rush, thank you for coming. Mark Kennedy is with us. Mark, good to see you, sir, glad

you're back. Cliff Stearns—hi, Cliff, how are you?

We've got the university leaders with us. Chancellor Nancy Cantor from the University of Illinois is with us. Chancellor, we're honored you are here. Jim Barker, the president of Clemson University; Malcolm Gillis, from Houston, Texas, Rice University. Thank you all for coming, and thank you for bringing the people from your universities here to the White House. We're glad you're here.

First, I want to honor an individual. I said this, that we're going to honor teams, but we're going to first start off with an individual here on Champions Day. The man I'm about to introduce has been winning college football games since Harry Truman was in the White House. [*Laughter*] His teams have picked up 409 victories in the course of his career, and that's John Gagliardi. The reason why his teams play so well is because not only is he a good coach, he's first and foremost a very decent person who honors values, who believes in the potential of every individual, who leads through example.

Coach Gagliardi, we're honored that you're here. We appreciate so very much Peggy and Jim being with you. Coach Gagliardi told me Jim—or Jim told me he's the offensive coordinator. He said, "I kind of like"—I said, "I kind of like a guy who follows in his father's footsteps." [*Laughter*] But it's such an honor to welcome this fine human being with us today. Coach

Gagliardi, congratulations, and thank you very much for being here, sir.

Every team here did really well. But only one team was undefeated, and that was the Mighty Illini tennis team. They were 32–0. Coach Tiley, I don't know if it was the scheduling that did it. [*Laughter*] You had a lot of really good players; I know that. I'm so glad you're here. I appreciate the fine tennis players being here. I want to congratulate you on your undefeated season. I want to congratulate you on being national champs in men's tennis.

The Lady Gators are with us from Florida. If you've got any complaints, Lady Gators, about this day, just go ahead and write the Governor. [*Laughter*] This is the fourth team from your distinguished university to make it to the White House. I appreciate Coach Thornqvist. I'm honored that the Lady Gators are with us today. And I want to congratulate you as well for being the national champs, representing your school.

The Clemson golf team started the year at number one—this will be your Clemson men's golf team—and they ended the year at number one. That's called a wire-to-wire, start to finish. I appreciate very much Larry Penley; he's been the coach. He's been there for only two decades. He's taken a while to get it right. No. [*Laughter*] I want to congratulate Coach Penley and the mighty Clemson golf team. I know the people down there in South Carolina are really proud of you.

Last year I had the honor of hosting the Princeton women's lacrosse team, and so I just kind of said, "You think you'll be back next year?" They said, yeah, they thought they'd be back next year. I like people who do what they say they're going to do. [*Laughter*] I want to congratulate the Princeton women's and Coach Sailer for winning your sport back-to-back. These are great athletes and great scholars with us. And I'm real proud that you're here. So I asked them once again, "Are you going to be back next year?" They said, "How

about you?" No. They said—[*laughter*]. I appreciate—[*laughter*]—never mind. [*Laughter*]

The USC women's golf team is with us. Mikaela Parmlid was the national champ last year, the individual championship. The thing I like about her, she was more interested in helping her team win. And thanks to Andrea Gaston, the Lady Trojans, they beat a difficult field and are national champs from USC. I bet there are some men's football players that'd like to be here as well from your university. [*Laughter*]

The mighty Virginia Cavalier lacrosse team is here. This is—I didn't know much about lacrosse. I kind of saw it in the periphery for a while. Then I watched—I happened to be working out upstairs and watched the finals. Whew, it's a tough game, and banging each other over the heads with sticks, and—[*laughter*]—but I'm proud of Coach Starsia and the Cavaliers for winning this important championship, a 9–7 championship game. It was a classic of conditioning and toughness and desire. And I'm proud to say that you won it.

We've also got the UCLA softball team here with us, ladies' softball team. I can remember when I was the Governor of Texas, I used to work out in the weight room. And I can remember the Texas girls telling me, they said, "Don't worry, Governor, we'll be the national champs." They forgot about Coach Enquist's team. The UCLA Bruins are a great ladies' softball team. It's a tough field, and they had great pitching—a very competitive team. And I want to congratulate you all for being here. I asked if there are any that are going to be on the Olympic team. I think three or four hands went up who will be representing the United States in Olympic softball. I pity the teams they play. [*Laughter*]

Finally, the mighty Rice Owls are here with us. I grew up in Houston. I can remember going over to the ballpark over there on the campus to watch the Rice teams of old play. Coach Graham and the

Owls not only represented a fine university well, they represented a great baseball State. They—I told Coach Graham, I said, "It's great to be with people who go to a fine school and at the same time beat a really tough, tough field in baseball." And so I want to congratulate the mighty Owls for coming. I know a lot of folks in Houston are really proud of your accomplishments. So are a lot of people in Texas.

So this is championship—we're honored to have the teams with us—championship day. The thing—the lesson I love about team sports and about champions is that champions work hard. They live a good, clean life in order to succeed. But they all serve something greater than themself in life. And that's an important example for our country. It's important for people to recognize that serving something greater than yourself in life makes you a whole person, helps you understand the significance of life.

My call to these champs is to remember that now that you're a champion, a lot of people, particularly young kids, are looking at you, wondering what it's like to be a champ, wondering what it's like to serve the school or the region or the State so very well. It means you've got a little extra task at hand, means you got to understand that you're an example for somebody and you can actually affect somebody's life in a positive way by how you handle the responsibilities of being a champion.

Again, congratulations for working hard, for winning. Congratulations for what you have done. Congratulations for what you're going to do with your life. May God bless you all, may God bless your universities, and may God continue to bless our great country.

NOTE: The President spoke at 2:40 p.m. in the East Room at the White House. In his remarks, he referred to Malcolm Gillis, president, and Wayne Graham, head baseball coach, Rice University; John Gagliardi, head football coach, St. John's University, his wife, Peggy, and their son, Jim, offensive coordinator, St. John's University football team; Craig Tiley, men's tennis head coach, University of Illinois at Urbana-Champaign; Gov. Jeb Bush of Florida; Roland Thornqvist, women's tennis head coach, University of Florida; Larry Penley, men's golf head coach, Clemson University; Chris Sailer, women's lacrosse head coach, Princeton University; Andrea Gaston, head coach, and Mikaela Parmlid, former player, women's golf, University of Southern California; Dom Starsia, men's lacrosse head coach, University of Virginia; and Sue Enquist, head softball coach, University of California-Los Angeles.

Remarks Following a Meeting With Congressional Leaders
November 17, 2003

I just had the honor of meeting with the Medicare Conference Working Group. I first thanked them for their extraordinary leadership on developing a fine piece of legislation for Medicare. There are Republican leaders at this table; there are Democrat leaders at this table. These are Americans who understand we have an obligation to our seniors to modernize and strengthen the Medicare system.

The bill that will be offered to the House and the Senate modernizes and strengthens Medicare. There's 400 billion additional dollars available for our seniors in this bill. There's prescription drug coverage in the bill for our seniors. This vote will demonstrate whether the Members of the House and the Senate will help keep our commitment to America's seniors. I look forward to working with the Members around the table to secure passage of this very important and historic piece of legislation. I urge members of both political parties to study the legislation, to remember the promise we have made to America's seniors, and to vote yes for this legislation.

Thank you.

NOTE: The President spoke at 4:20 p.m. in the Cabinet Room at the White House. A tape was not available for verification of the content of these remarks.

Message to the Senate Transmitting the Council of Europe Convention on Cybercrime
November 17, 2003

To the Senate of the United States:

With a view to receiving the advice and consent of the Senate to ratification, I transmit herewith the Council of Europe Convention on Cybercrime (the "Cybercrime Convention" or the "Convention"), which was signed by the United States on November 23, 2001. In addition, for the information of the Senate, I transmit the report of the Department of State with respect to the Convention and the Convention's official Explanatory Report.

The United States, in its capacity as an observer at the Council of Europe, participated actively in the elaboration of the Convention, which is the only multilateral treaty to address the problems of computer-related crime and electronic evidence gathering. An overview of the Convention's provisions is provided in the report of the Department of State. The report also sets forth proposed reservations and declarations that would be deposited by the United States with its instrument of ratification. With these reservations and declarations, the Convention would not require implementing legislation for the United States.

The Convention promises to be an effective tool in the global effort to combat computer-related crime. It requires Parties to criminalize, if they have not already done so, certain conduct that is committed through, against, or related to computer systems. Such substantive crimes include offenses against the "confidentiality, integrity and availability" of computer data and systems, as well as using computer systems to engage in conduct that would be criminal if committed outside the cyber-realm, i.e., forgery, fraud, child pornography, and certain copyright-related offenses. The Convention also requires Parties to have the ability to investigate computer-related crime effectively and to obtain electronic evidence in all types of criminal investigations and proceedings.

By providing for broad international cooperation in the form of extradition and mutual legal assistance, the Cybercrime Convention would remove or minimize legal obstacles to international cooperation that delay or endanger U.S. investigations and prosecutions of computer-related crime. As such, it would help deny "safe havens" to criminals, including terrorists, who can cause damage to U.S. interests from abroad using computer systems. At the same time, the Convention contains safeguards that protect civil liberties and other legitimate interests.

I recommend that the Senate give early and favorable consideration to the Cybercrime Convention, and that it give its advice and consent to ratification, subject to the reservations, declarations, and understanding described in the accompanying report of the Department of State.

GEORGE W. BUSH

The White House,
November 17, 2003.

Statement on the Massachusetts Supreme Judicial Court Decision on the State's Ban of Same Sex Marriages
November 18, 2003

Marriage is a sacred institution between a man and a woman. Today's decision of the Massachusetts Supreme Judicial Court violates this important principle. I will work with congressional leaders and others to do what is legally necessary to defend the sanctity of marriage.

Statement on House of Representatives Action on Comprehensive Energy Legislation
November 18, 2003

I am pleased with the strong bipartisan support for a national energy policy that will use technology, conservation, renewables, and increased production of energy at home. For the past 2 years, the passage of a comprehensive national energy policy has been a top priority for my administration, and I commend the House for its vote today and urge the Senate to act expeditiously as well. America will be more prosperous and more secure when we are less dependent on foreign sources of energy. Reliable and affordable energy is critical to our economic security, our national security, and our homeland security.

NOTE: The Office of the Press Secretary also released a Spanish language version of this statement.

Statement on Signing the Animal Drug User Fee Act of 2003
November 18, 2003

Today, I have signed into law S. 313, the "Animal Drug User Fee Act of 2003." The Act is designed to expedite the animal drug development process, while continuing to ensure the safety and effectiveness of animal drugs.

Section 4(a) of the Act purports to require the Secretary of Health and Human Services to submit legislative recommendations to the Congress and to establish procedures by which the Secretary must formulate such recommendations. The legislative power does not extend to requiring the Executive submit legislative recommendations to the Congress nor to specifying procedures by which the Executive must formulate any legislative recommendations that the Executive makes. The executive branch shall execute section 4(a) in a manner consistent with the Constitution's exclusive commitments to the President of the authority to submit for the consideration of the Congress such measures as he judges necessary and expedient and the authority to supervise the unitary executive branch.

GEORGE W. BUSH

The White House,
November 18, 2003.

NOTE: S. 313, approved November 18, was assigned Public Law No. 108–130.

Message to the Congress Transmitting the National Money Laundering Strategy
November 18, 2003

To the Congress of the United States:

Consistent with section 2(a) of the Money Laundering and Financial Crimes Strategy Act of 1998 (Public Law 105–310; 31 U.S.C. 5341(a)(2)), enclosed is the 2003 National Money Laundering Strategy, prepared by my Administration.

GEORGE W. BUSH

The White House,
November 18, 2003.

Remarks at Whitehall Palace in London, United Kingdom
November 19, 2003

Thank you very much. Secretary Straw and Secretary Hoon, Admiral Cobbold and Dr. Chipman, distinguished guests: I want to thank you for your very kind welcome that you've given to me and to Laura. I also thank the groups hosting this event, the Royal United Services Institute and the International Institute for Strategic Studies. We're honored to be in the United Kingdom, and we bring the good wishes of the American people.

It was pointed out to me that the last noted American to visit London stayed in a glass box dangling over the Thames. [*Laughter*] A few might have been happy to provide similar arrangements for me. [*Laughter*] I thank Her Majesty the Queen for interceding. [*Laughter*] We're honored to be staying at her house.

Americans traveling to England always observe more similarities to our country than differences. I've been here only a short time, but I've noticed that the tradition of free speech, exercised with enthusiasm—[*laughter*]—is alive and well here in London. We have that at home too. They now have that right in Baghdad as well.

The people of Great Britain also might see some familiar traits in Americans. We're sometimes faulted for a naive faith that liberty can change the world. If that's an error, it began with reading too much John Locke and Adam Smith. Americans have, on occasion, been called moralists who often speak in terms of right and wrong. That zeal has been inspired by examples on this island, by the tireless compassion of Lord Shaftesbury, the righteous courage of Wilberforce, and the firm determination of the Royal Navy over the decades to fight and end the trade in slaves.

It's rightly said that Americans are a religious people. That's in part because the "Good News" was translated by Tyndale, preached by Wesley, lived out in the example of William Booth. At times, Americans are even said to have a puritan streak. And where might that have come from? [*Laughter*] Well, we can start with the Puritans.

To this fine heritage, Americans have added a few traits of our own, the good influence of our immigrants, the spirit of the frontier. Yet, there remains a bit of England in every American. So much of our national character comes from you, and we're glad for it.

The fellowship of generations is the cause of common beliefs. We believe in open societies ordered by moral conviction. We believe in private markets humanized by compassionate government. We believe in economies that reward effort, communities that protect the weak, and the duty of nations to respect the dignity and the rights of all. And whether one learns these ideals in County Durham or in west Texas, they instill mutual respect, and they inspire common purpose.

More than an alliance of security and commerce, the British and American peoples have an alliance of values. And today, this old and tested alliance is very strong.

The deepest beliefs of our nations set the direction of our foreign policy. We value our own civil rights, so we stand for the human rights of others. We affirm the God-given dignity of every person, so we are moved to action by poverty and oppression and famine and disease. The United States and Great Britain share a mission in the world beyond the balance of power or the simple pursuit of interest. We seek the advance of freedom and the peace that freedom brings. Together, our nations are standing and sacrificing for this high goal in a distant land at this very hour, and America honors the idealism and the bravery of the sons and daughters of Britain.

The last President to stay at Buckingham Palace was an idealist, without question. At a dinner hosted by King George V in 1918, Woodrow Wilson made a pledge. With typical American understatement—[*laughter*]—he vowed that right and justice would

become the predominant and controlling force in the world.

President Wilson had come to Europe with his Fourteen Points for peace. Many complimented him on his vision, yet some were dubious. Take, for example, the Prime Minister of France. He complained that God himself had only Ten Commandments. [*Laughter*] Sounds familiar. [*Laughter*]

At Wilson's high point of idealism, however, Europe was one short generation from Munich and Auschwitz and the Blitz. Looking back, we see the reasons why. The League of Nations, lacking both credibility and will, collapsed at the first challenge of the dictators. Free nations failed to recognize, much less confront, the aggressive evil in plain sight. And so dictators went about their business, feeding resentments and anti-Semitism, bringing death to innocent people in this city and across the world, and filling the last century with violence and genocide.

Through World War and cold war, we learned that idealism, if it is to do any good in this world, requires common purpose and national strength, moral courage, and patience in difficult tasks. And now our generation has need of these qualities.

On September the 11th, 2001, terrorists left their mark of murder on my country and took the lives of 67 British citizens. With the passing of months and years, it is the natural human desire to resume a quiet life and to put that day behind us, as if waking from a dark dream. The hope that danger has passed is comforting, is understanding, and it is false. The attacks that followed on Bali, Jakarta, Casablanca, Bombay, Mombasa, Najaf, Jerusalem, Riyadh, Baghdad, and Istanbul were not dreams. They're part of a global campaign by terrorist networks to intimidate and demoralize all who oppose them.

These terrorists target the innocent, and they kill by the thousands. And they would, if they gain the weapons they seek, kill by the millions and not be finished. The greatest threat of our age is nuclear, chemical, or biological weapons in the hands of terrorists and the dictators who aid them. The evil is in plain sight. The danger only increases with denial. Great responsibilities fall once again to the great democracies. We will face these threats with open eyes, and we will defeat them.

The peace and security of free nations now rests on three pillars. First, international organizations must be equal to the challenges facing our world, from lifting up failing states to opposing proliferation. Like 11 Presidents before me, I believe in the international institutions and alliances that America helped to form and helps to lead. The United States and Great Britain have labored hard to help make the United Nations what it is supposed to be, an effective instrument of our collective security. In recent months, we've sought and gained three additional resolutions on Iraq, Resolutions 1441, 1483, and 1511, precisely because the global danger of terror demands a global response. The United Nations has no more compelling advocate than your Prime Minister, who at every turn has championed its ideals and appealed to its authority. He understands as well that the credibility of the U.N. depends on a willingness to keep its word and to act when action is required.

America and Great Britain have done and will do all in their power to prevent the United Nations from solemnly choosing its own irrelevance and inviting the fate of the League of Nations. It's not enough to meet the dangers of the world with resolutions. We must meet those dangers with resolve.

In this century, as in the last, nations can accomplish more together than apart. For 54 years, America has stood with our partners in NATO, the most effective multilateral institution in history. We're committed to this great democratic Alliance, and we believe it must have the will and the capacity to act beyond Europe where threats emerge. My Nation welcomes the growing unity of Europe, and the world needs America and the European Union to work in common purpose for the advance of security and justice. America is cooperating with four other nations to meet the dangers posed by North Korea. America believes the IAEA must be true to its purpose and hold Iran to its obligations.

Our first choice and our constant practice is to work with other responsible governments. We understand as well that the success of multilateralism is not measured by adherence to forms alone, the tidiness of the process, but by the results we achieve to keep our nations secure.

The second pillar of peace and security in our world is the willingness of free nations, when the last resort arrives, to restrain ° aggression and evil by force. There are principled objections to the use of force in every generation, and I credit the good motives behind these views. Those in authority, however, are not judged only by good motivations. The people have given us the duty to defend them, and that duty sometimes requires the violent restraint of violent men. In some cases, the measured use of force is all that protects us from a chaotic world ruled by force.

Most in the peaceful West have no living memory of that kind of world. Yet in some countries, the memories are recent. The victims of ethnic cleansing in the Balkans, those who survived the rapists and the death squads, have few qualms when NATO applied force to help end those crimes. The women of Afghanistan, imprisoned in their homes and beaten in the streets and executed in public spectacles, did not reproach us for routing the Taliban. The inhabitants of Iraq's Ba'athist hell, with its lavish palaces and its torture chambers, with its massive statues and its mass graves, do not miss their fugitive dictator. They rejoiced at his fall.

In all these cases, military action was preceded by diplomatic initiatives and negotiations and ultimatums and final chances

---

° White House correction.

until the final moment. In Iraq, year after year, the dictator was given the chance to account for his weapons programs and end the nightmare for his people. Now the resolutions he defied have been enforced.

And who will say that Iraq was better off when Saddam Hussein was strutting and killing or that the world was safer when he held power? Who doubts that Afghanistan is a more just society and less dangerous without Mullah Omar playing host to terrorists from around the world? And Europe too is plainly better off with Milosevic answering for his crimes instead of committing more.

It's been said that those who live near a police station find it hard to believe in the triumph of violence. In the same way, free peoples might be tempted to take for granted the orderly societies we have come to know. Europe's peaceful unity is one of the great achievements of the last half-century. And because European countries now resolve differences through negotiation and consensus, there's sometimes an assumption that the entire world functions in the same way. But let us never forget how Europe's unity was achieved: by Allied armies of liberation and NATO armies of defense. And let us never forget, beyond Europe's borders, in a world where oppression and violence are very real, liberation is still a moral goal, and freedom and security still need defenders.

The third pillar of security is our commitment to the global expansion of democracy and the hope and progress it brings as the alternative to instability and hatred and terror. We cannot rely exclusively on military power to assure our long-term security. Lasting peace is gained as justice and democracy advance.

In democratic and successful societies, men and women do not swear allegiance to malcontents and murderers; they turn their hearts and labor to building better lives. And democratic governments do not shelter terrorist camps or attack their peaceful neighbors; they honor the aspira-

tions and dignity of their own people. In our conflict with terror and tyranny, we have an unmatched advantage, a power that cannot be resisted, and that is the appeal of freedom to all mankind.

As global powers, both our nations serve the cause of freedom in many ways, in many places. By promoting development and fighting famine and AIDS and other diseases, we're fulfilling our moral duties as well as encouraging stability and building a firmer basis for democratic institutions. By working for justice in Burma, in the Sudan, and in Zimbabwe, we give hope to suffering people and improve the chances for stability and progress. By extending the reach of trade, we foster prosperity and the habits of liberty. And by advancing freedom in the greater Middle East, we help end a cycle of dictatorship and radicalism that brings millions of people to misery and brings danger to our own people.

The stakes in that region could not be higher. If the Middle East remains a place where freedom does not flourish, it will remain a place of stagnation and anger and violence for export. And as we saw in the ruins of two towers, no distance on the map will protect our lives and way of life. If the greater Middle East joins the democratic revolution that has reached much of the world, the lives of millions in that region will be bettered, and a trend of conflict and fear will be ended at its source.

The movement of history will not come about quickly. Because of our own democratic development—the fact that it was gradual and, at times, turbulent—we must be patient with others. And the Middle East countries have some distance to travel.

Arab scholars speak of a freedom deficit that has separated whole nations from the progress of our time. The essentials of social and material progress—limited government, equal justice under law, religious and economic liberty, political participation, free press, and respect for the rights of women—have been scarce across the region. Yet that has begun to change. In an arc of reform from Morocco to Jordan to Qatar, we are seeing elections and new protections for women and the stirrings of political pluralism. Many governments are realizing that theocracy and dictatorship do not lead to national greatness; they end in national ruin. They are finding, as others will find, that national progress and dignity are achieved when governments are just and people are free.

The democratic progress we've seen in the Middle East was not imposed from abroad, and neither will the greater progress we hope to see. Freedom, by definition, must be chosen and defended by those who choose it. Our part, as free nations, is to ally ourselves with reform, wherever it occurs.

Perhaps the most helpful change we can make is to—change in our own thinking. In the West, there's been a certain skepticism about the capacity or even the desire of Middle Eastern peoples for self-government. We're told that Islam is somehow inconsistent with a democratic culture. Yet more than half of the world's Muslims are today contributing citizens in democratic societies. It is suggested that the poor, in their daily struggles, care little for self-government. Yet the poor especially need the power of democracy to defend themselves against corrupt elites.

Peoples of the Middle East share a high civilization, a religion of personal responsibility, and a need for freedom as deep as our own. It is not realism to suppose that one-fifth of humanity is unsuited to liberty. It is pessimism and condescension, and we should have none of it.

We must shake off decades of failed policy in the Middle East. Your nation and mine, in the past, have been willing to make a bargain, to tolerate oppression for the sake of stability. Longstanding ties often led us to overlook the faults of local elites. Yet this bargain did not bring stability or make us safe. It merely bought time while problems festered and ideologies of violence took hold.

As recent history has shown, we cannot turn a blind eye to oppression just because the oppression is not in our own backyard. No longer should we think tyranny is benign because it is temporarily convenient. Tyranny is never benign to its victims, and our great democracies should oppose tyranny wherever it is found.

Now we're pursuing a different course, a forward strategy of freedom in the Middle East. We will consistently challenge the enemies of reform and confront the allies of terror. We will expect a higher standard from our friends in the region, and we will meet our responsibilities in Afghanistan and in Iraq by finishing the work of democracy we have begun.

There were good-faith disagreements in your country and mine over the course and timing of military action in Iraq. Whatever has come before, we now have only two options: to keep our word or to break our word. The failure of democracy in Iraq would throw its people back into misery and turn that country over to terrorists who wish to destroy us. Yet democracy will succeed in Iraq, because our will is firm, our word is good, and the Iraqi people will not surrender their freedom.

Since the liberation of Iraq, we have seen changes that could hardly have been imagined a year ago. A new Iraqi police force protects the people instead of bullying them. More than 150 Iraqi newspapers are now in circulation, printing what they choose, not what they're ordered. Schools are open with textbooks free of propaganda. Hospitals are functioning and are well supplied. Iraq has a new currency, the first battalion of a new army, representative local governments, and a Governing Council with an aggressive timetable for national sovereignty. This is substantial progress, and much of it has proceeded faster than similar efforts in Germany and Japan after World War II.

Yet the violence we are seeing in Iraq today is serious, and it comes from Ba'athist holdouts and jihadists from other countries and terrorists drawn to the prospect of innocent bloodshed. It is the nature of terrorism, in the cruelty of a few, to try to bring grief in the loss to many.

The Armed Forces of both our countries have taken losses, felt deeply by our citizens. Some families now live with a burden of great sorrow. We cannot take the pain away, but these families can know they are not alone. We pray for their strength. We pray for their comfort, and we will never forget the courage of the ones they loved.

The terrorists have a purpose, a strategy to their cruelty. They view the rise of democracy in Iraq as a powerful threat to their ambitions. In this, they are correct. They believe their acts of terror against our coalition, against international aid workers, and against innocent Iraqis will make us recoil and retreat. In this, they are mistaken.

We did not charge hundreds of miles into the heart of Iraq and pay a bitter cost of casualties and liberate 25 million people only to retreat before a band of thugs and assassins. We will help the Iraqi people establish a peaceful and democratic country in the heart of the Middle East. And by doing so, we will defend our people from danger.

The forward strategy of freedom must also apply to the Arab-Israeli conflict. It's a difficult period in a part of the world that has known many. Yet, our commitment remains firm. We seek justice and dignity. We seek a viable independent state for the Palestinian people, who have been betrayed by others for too long. We seek security and recognition for the state of Israel, which has lived in a shadow of random death for too long. These are worthy goals in themselves, and by reaching them we will also remove an occasion and excuse for hatred and violence in the broader Middle East.

Achieving peace in the Holy Land is not just a matter of the shape of a border. As we work on the details of peace, we must look to the heart of the matter, which is the need for a viable Palestinian democracy. Peace will not be achieved by Palestinian rulers who intimidate opposition, who tolerate and profit from corruption, and maintain their ties to terrorist groups. These are the methods of the old elites, who time and again had put their own self-interest above the interest of the people they claim to serve. The long-suffering Palestinian people deserve better. They deserve true leaders capable of creating and governing a Palestinian state.

Even after the setbacks and frustrations of recent months, good will and hard effort can bring about a Palestinian state and a secure Israel. Those who would lead a new Palestine should adopt peaceful means to achieve the rights of their people and create the reformed institutions of a stable democracy.

Israel should freeze settlement construction, dismantle unauthorized outposts, end the daily humiliation of the Palestinian people, and not prejudice final negotiations with the placements of walls and fences.

Arab states should end incitement in their own media, cut off public and private funding for terrorism, and establish normal relations with Israel.

Leaders in Europe should withdraw all favor and support from any Palestinian ruler who fails his people and betrays their cause. And Europe's leaders and all leaders should strongly oppose anti-Semitism, which poisons public debates over the future of the Middle East.

Ladies and gentlemen, we have great objectives before us that make our Atlantic alliance as vital as it has ever been: We will encourage the strength and effectiveness of international institutions; we will use force when necessary in the defense of freedom; and we will raise up an ideal of democracy in every part of the world. On these three pillars we will build the peace and security of all free nations in a time of danger.

So much good has come from our alliance of conviction and might. So much now depends on the strength of this alliance as we go forward. America has always found strong partners in London, leaders of good judgment and blunt counsel and backbone when times are tough. And I have found all those qualities in your current Prime Minister, who has my respect and my deepest thanks.

The ties between our nations, however, are deeper than the relationship between leaders. These ties endure because they are formed by the experience and responsibilities and adversity we have shared. And in the memory of our peoples, there will always be one experience, one central event when the seal was fixed on the friendship between Britain and the United States. The arrival in Great Britain of more than 1.5 million American soldiers and airmen in the 1940s was a turning point in the Second World War. For many Britons, it was a first close look at Americans, other than in the movies. Some of you here today may still remember the "friendly invasion."

"Our lads," they took some getting used to. There was even a saying about what many of them were up to—in addition to being "overpaid and over here." [*Laughter*] At a reunion in north London some years ago, an American pilot who had settled in England after his military service said, "Well, I'm still over here and probably overpaid. So two out of three isn't bad." [*Laughter*]

In that time of war, the English people did get used to the Americans. They wel-comed soldiers and fliers into their villages and homes and took to calling them "our boys." About 70,000 of those boys did their part to affirm our special relationship. They returned home with English brides.

Americans gained a certain image of Britain as well. We saw an island threatened on every side, a leader who did not waver, and a country of the firmest character. And that has not changed. The British people are the sort of partners you want when serious work needs doing. The men and women of this Kingdom are kind and steadfast and generous and brave. And America is fortunate to call this country our closest friend in the world.

May God bless you all.

NOTE: The President spoke at 1:24 p.m. in the Royal Banqueting House. In his remarks, he referred to Secretary of State for Foreign and Commonwealth Affairs Jack Straw, Secretary of State for Defense Geoffrey Hoon, Queen Elizabeth II, and Prime Minister Tony Blair of the United Kingdom; Rear Adm. Richard Cobbold, director, Royal United Services Institute for Defence and Security Studies; John Chipman, director, International Institute for Strategic Studies; American magician David Blaine, who spent 44 days in isolation suspended above the River Thames; former President Saddam Hussein of Iraq; Mullah Omar, head of the deposed Taliban regime in Afghanistan; and former President Slobodan Milosevic of the Federal Republic of Yugoslavia (Serbia and Montenegro). The Office of the Press Secretary also released a Spanish language transcript of these remarks.

Remarks at a Dinner Hosted by Queen Elizabeth II in London
November 19, 2003

Your Majesty, Your Royal Highness, and distinguished guests: Laura and I are deeply honored to accept Your Majesty's gracious hospitality and to be welcomed into your home. Through the last century and into our own, Americans have appreciated the friendship of your people. And we are grateful for your personal commitment across five decades to the health and vitality of the alliance between our nations.

Of course, things didn't start out too well. [*Laughter*] Yet, even at America's founding, our nations shared a basic belief in human liberty. That conviction more than anything else led to our reconciliation. And in time, our shared commitment to freedom became the basis of a great Atlantic alliance that defeated tyranny in Europe and saved the liberty of the world.

The story of liberty, the story of the Magna Carta and the Declaration of Independence, continues in our time. The power of freedom has touched Asia and Latin America and Africa and beyond. And now our two countries are carrying out a mission of freedom and democracy in Afghanistan and Iraq. Once again, America and Britain are joined in the defense of our common values. Once again, American and British servicemembers are sacrificing in a necessary and noble cause. Once again, we are acting to secure the peace of the world.

The bonds between our countries were formed in hard experience. We passed through great adversity together. We have risen through great challenges together. The mutual respect and fellowship between our countries is deep and strong and permanent.

Let us raise our glasses to our common ideals, to our enduring friendships, to the preservation of our liberties, and to Her Majesty, the Queen of the United Kingdom of Great Britain and Northern Ireland.

NOTE: The President spoke at 8:49 p.m. in the Ballroom at Buckingham Palace. In his remarks, he referred to Prince Philip, Duke of Edinburgh. The transcript released by the Office of the Press Secretary also included the remarks of Queen Elizabeth II. A tape was not available for verification of the content of these remarks.

The President's News Conference With Prime Minister Tony Blair of the United Kingdom in London
November 20, 2003

Prime Minister Blair. Good afternoon, everyone. First of all, can I extend the warmest possible welcome to the President of the United States and to the First Lady to Downing Street and say how delighted I am to see them both here.

And as you would expect, I think, I would like to say some words about the latest terrorist outrage that has occurred today in Turkey. First of all, I would wish to express my deepest sympathy and condolences to the families of the victims. Some will be British; many will be Turkish citizens. I would like to express my condolences also to the Government and to the people of Turkey.

Once again we're reminded of the evil these terrorists pose to innocent people everywhere and to our way of life. Once again we must affirm that in the face of this terrorism there must be no holding back, no compromise, no hesitation in confronting this menace, in attacking it wherever and whenever we can, and in defeating it utterly.

It should not lessen, incidentally, in any way at all our commitment to Iraq. On the contrary, it shows how important it is to carry on until terrorism is defeated there as well, because it is in a free, democratic, and stable Iraq that not just the violence but the wretched and backward philosophy of these terrorists will be defeated and destroyed.

Yesterday, as some of you will have heard, the President of the United States delivered a powerful, telling speech extolling the virtues of freedom, justice, democracy, and the rule of law, not just for some people but for all the peoples of our world. Today the fanatics of terror showed themselves to be callous, brutal murderers of the innocent, and the contrast could not be more stark.

There may be some who think that Britain would gain from standing back from this struggle, even some who believe that we and the United States and our allies have somehow brought this upon ourselves. Let us be very clear: America did not attack Al Qaida on September the 11th; Al Qaida attacked America and, in doing so, attacked not just America but the way of life of all people who believe in tolerance and freedom, justice and peace.

Say we issue for you, in the light of this latest outrage, a short summary on the casualties and cost of terrorism. It's quite interesting to see just how many countries have been affected, what the cost of terrorism is, how many thousands of people have died over this past period of time—many of the victims, incidentally, Muslim people, not least the civilians murdered in Iraq.

So this is a time to show strength, determination, and complete resolve. This terrorism is the 21st century threat. It is a war that strikes at the heart of all that we hold dear, and there is only one response that is possible or rational: to meet their will to inflict terror with a greater will to defeat it; to confront their philosophy of hate with our own of tolerance and freedom; and to challenge their desire to frighten us, divide us, unnerve us, with an unshakable unity of purpose; to stand side by side with the United States of America and with our other allies in the world to rid our world of this evil once and for all.

In the course of the discussions that President Bush and myself had yesterday and today, we also, of course, discussed many other issues, and let me just run through a few of those with you. There will be two communiques put out afterwards, one on Iraq, one on the other issues we discussed, and I can just simply list them for you.

Obviously, we discussed the situation in relation to the WTO and world trade and the issues to do with steel, with which we're familiar. We agreed a special joint task force on the issue of HIV/AIDS in relation to global health, a preoccupation of both our Governments. We, of course, discussed the issues to do with weapons of mass destruction and the threat that it poses; the Middle East and the Middle East peace process. And since we have the successive G–8 chairmanships in the next couple of years, we also discussed how we might use those to make progress on all these issues, including some of the challenging and difficult issues to do with climate change, world trade, and poverty.

So, once again, Mr. President, welcome here. It's a very, very great pleasure and honor to have you here in our country, and we're delighted to see you. Thank you for that magnificent speech yesterday. And it's my pleasure to ask you to address this simple gathering.

President Bush. Thank you, Mr. Prime Minister. It's my honor to be standing by the side of a friend. And Laura and I were so honored to be invited by Her Majesty the Queen to come to the United Kingdom for this state visit. It's been a fantastic experience for us.

I also want to express my deep sympathy for the loss of life in Turkey. The nature of the terrorist enemy is evident once again. We see their contempt—their utter contempt—for innocent life. They hate freedom. They hate free nations. Today, once again, we saw their ambitions of murder. The cruelty is part of their strategy. The terrorists hope to intimidate. They hope to demoralize. They particularly want to intimidate and demoralize free nations. They're not going to succeed.

Great Britain, America, and other free nations are united today in our grief and united in our determination to fight and defeat this evil wherever it is found. Britain and America have shared the suffering caused by terrorism before. On September the 11th, 2001, no country except America lost more lives than Britain. Since that day, no ally has accomplished more or sacrificed more in our common struggle to end terror, and we are grateful.

Our shared work of democracy in Afghanistan and Iraq is essential to the defeat of global terrorism. The spread of freedom and the hope it brings is the surest way in the long term to combat despair and anger and resentment that feeds terror. The advance of freedom and hope in the greater Middle East will better the lives of millions of that region and increase the security of our own people.

I've just come from a meeting with families of British servicemen who were killed in Iraq. These brave men died for the security of this country and in the cause of human freedom. Our nations honor their sacrifice. I pray for the comfort of the families.

Our mission in Iraq is noble and it is necessary. No act of thugs or killers will change our resolve or alter their fate. A free Iraq will be free of them. We will finish the job we have begun.

Together, Great Britain and the United States met the defining challenges of the last century. Together, we're meeting new challenges, challenges that have come to our generation. In all that lies ahead in the defense of freedom and the advance of democracy, our two nations will continue to stand together.

I'm honored to be here, Mr. Prime Minister. I thank you for your leadership and your friendship.

Prime Minister Blair. We'll take three questions from British journalists, three questions from U.S. journalists. Andy, you start us off.

Timetable for Iraq

Q. Andy Marr from the BBC. Could I ask both leaders about the agenda on Iraq? You are both engaged in an unpredictable and dangerous war, as we've seen today. And yet, you say you want to bring the troops home starting from next year. Now, how is that possible when the security situation is still so unresolved? You haven't got Saddam Hussein. Aren't you stuck in Iraq, with your enemies holding the exit door?

President Bush. I said that we're going to bring our troops home starting next year? What I've said is that we'll match the security needs with the number of troops necessary to secure Iraq. And we're relying upon our commanders on the ground to make those decisions.

Q. So you'll keep a certain number of troops in Iraq for a longer time?

President Bush. We could have less troops in Iraq; we could have the same number of troops in Iraq; we could have more troops in Iraq, what is ever necessary to secure Iraq.

Prime Minister Blair. Let me make it absolutely clear for our position as well. We stay until the job gets done. And what this latest terrorist outrage shows us is that this is a war; its main battleground is Iraq. We have got to make sure we defeat these terrorists, the former Saddam people in Iraq, and we must do that because that is an essential part of defeating this fanaticism and extremism that is killing innocent people all over our world today.

And I can assure you of one thing, that when something like this happens today, our response is not to flinch or give way or concede one inch. We stand absolutely firm until this job is done—done in Iraq, done elsewhere in the world.

President Bush. Andy, if I may have a followup to—it's kind of a new thing, a followup to the answer. One thing that's happening that you need to know that will help us make the necessary calculations for troop levels is that there's a lot of Iraqis beginning to be trained to deal with the issue on the ground. There's Iraqis being trained for an army. There's Iraqis being trained for an intelligence service. There's Iraqis being trained for additional police work. There are Iraqis being trained for asset protection. There are Iraqis being trained for border guards. There's over 130,000 Iraqis now who have been trained, who are working for their own security. So part of the answer to your question is how fast the new brigades of Iraqi army are stood up, how effective they are.

We believe that the Iraqi citizens want to be free. We know that they're willing to work for their own freedom. And the more people working for their own freedom, the more we can put that into our calculations as to troop levels.

Thank you for letting me butt in there, again.

Tom.

Terrorist Attacks/Transition Plan for Iraq

Q. Tom Raum from the Associated Press. For both of you, Mr. President, Mr. Prime Minister, do the attacks today, do you view them as a direct attack on the alliance? And does the fact that these attacks are coming sort of with an increasing intensity and randomness, does that make it less likely that you'll be able to turn over sovereignty to an Iraqi council by June?

President Bush. Well, first of all, in Iraq, we're working on two tracks. We're working on a political track, and we believe that the timetable that the Governing Council has set for itself is an accurate timetable. And we'll work with the Governing Council to turn over sovereignty.

It's their decision, and we agreed with their decision, based upon the conditions on the ground. And some of those conditions were the fact that there wasn't the sectarian violence that was predicted. Iraq remained intact. There wasn't the mass of refugee flows that had been predicted.

There wasn't starvation that had been predicted. In other words, the conditions on the ground were such that the Governing Council felt like they could move forward in a constructive way, and we supported that.

Secondly, these terrorist attacks are attacks on freedom, and they attack when they can. And our job is to secure our homelands and chase down these killers and bring them to justice. And we're making good progress with Al Qaida. And if you were to view Al Qaida's organization structure as kind of a board of directors and then there would be the operating management, we are dismantling the operating management, one person at a time. We're on an international manhunt.

That's why relations and cooperation between our intelligence services are essential to secure the people of our respective countries. And I will tell you, the Prime Minister's cooperation has just been unbelievably good, as has the intelligence service of Great Britain, a fine group of people, by the way, people who are dedicating their lives to the security of the people of this great country. And the more we share intelligence with other nations, the more likely it is that we'll be able to rout out these terrorists.

That's why the phone call I had with Prime Minister Erdogan was an important phone call, when I assured him we're willing to work with the Turkish Government, as are the Brits willing to work with the Turkish Government, to share information and to find these killers so they don't kill again.

I don't know the nature of the casualties today, but I do know the nature of the casualties in the recent attack in Istanbul. More Muslims died in that attack. These are Al Qaida killers killing Muslims, and they need to be stopped, and we will stop them.

Prime Minister Blair. See, here's where we got to—we've got to see what this struggle is about, because you can see it clearer and clearer day-by-day. This is a struggle between fanaticism and extremism on the one hand and people who believe in freedom and in tolerance on the other. And these attacks have been building for years. They came to their height, okay, on September the 11th, but that actually wasn't the first attack that Al Qaida was perpetrating against America and other countries. And you look round the world today, and I tell you, in virtually every place there is trouble and difficulty, these terrorists and fanatics are making it worse, whether it's Kashmir, whether it's Palestine, whether it's Chechnya, wherever it is. And they're prepared to kill anyone. They're prepared to shed any amount of bloodshed, because they know how important this battle is.

And here's why Iraq is important in this; because in the end, their case, which is based on dividing people—the Arab world and the Western world, the Muslim world and the Christian world and other religions—their case is that we are in Iraq to suppress Muslims, steal their oil, to spoil the country. Now, we know you know that all those things are lies. They know, therefore, that if we manage to get Iraq on its feet as a stable, prosperous, democratic country, the blow we strike is not just one for the Iraqi people; it is the end of that propaganda. And that's why they're fighting us.

And when you say, is this attack today directed at our alliance? It's directed at anybody who stands in the way of this fanaticism. And that's why our response has got to be to say to them, as clearly as we possibly can, "You are not going to defeat us because our will to defend what we believe in is actually, in the end, stronger, better, more determined than your will to inflict damage on innocent people."

And that's what this whole thing is about. That's why when I hear people talking about the alliance between our two countries, this is not an alliance that's based on simply Britain and America and the ties that go back in history and all the rest

of it. This is a real living alliance about the struggle going on today, in the early 21st century. And if we don't win this struggle, it's not just Britain and America that's going to suffer. People everywhere are going to suffer, and that's why it's important.

If they think that when they go and kill people by these terrorist attacks, they are going to somehow weaken us or make us think, "Well, let's shuffle to the back of the queue and hide away from this," they are wrong. That is not the tradition of my country, and it's not the tradition of the British people or the American people.

Adam [Adam Boulton, Sky News].

British Detainees at Guantanamo Bay

Q. What do you say to those people, both those who support what your two Governments have done since September 11th and those who oppose it, that in fact the treatment of the captives in Guantanamo Bay actually belies all your talk of freedom, justice, and tolerance? And on a specific point, in view of the comments from the Secretary of State and from Charles Kennedy and Michael Howard, is there on the minority of British nationals held captive an explicit offer from the United States to repatriate them? And if that depends on a request from you, Prime Minister, are you prepared to make it now?

Prime Minister Blair. First of all, let me just deal with the very specific issue of the British nationals over in Guantanamo Bay. We are in discussion about this. I've already said in the House of Commons it will be resolved in one of two ways. Either they will be tried by the military commission out there, or alternatively, they'll be brought back here. Now, we're in discussion at the moment——

Q. How——

Prime Minister Blair. It will be resolved at some point or other. It's not going to be resolved today, but it will be resolved at some point soon.

Let me just say this to you, however, about Guantanamo Bay. Indeed, the people that are there—again, let's just remember, this arose out of the battle in Afghanistan, that arose out of September the 11th and the attack there. And the very fact that we are in discussion about making sure there are fair procedures for trial—or alternatively, it's up to us, as the President very fairly has said, these people come back here—is an indication that we actually treat people differently. So even though this arose out of this appalling, brutal attack on America on September the 11th, nonetheless, we make sure that justice is done for people.

President Bush. These are—justice is being done. These are illegal noncombatants picked up off of a battlefield, and they are being treated in a humane fashion. And we are sorting through them on a case-by-case basis. There is a court procedure in place that will allow them to be tried in fair fashion. As to the issue of the British citizens, we're working with the British Government.

Randy [Randall Mikkelsen, Reuters].

Trade Policy/The Doha Round

Q. Mr. President and Mr. Blair, how accurate would it be to conclude that the new China trade quotas, along with a weakening dollar and your disagreement with the WTO on steel, altogether constitute a reelection strategy of boosting U.S. exports at the expense of free trade principles?

And Mr. Blair, I'd like to know how these policies are affecting Europe and the U.K.

Prime Minister Blair. Mr. President, you should answer that one first. [*Laughter*]

President Bush. My administration is committed to free trade—the first administration in a long time to achieve trade promotion authority from the Congress. And we're using that to promote free trade agreements on a bilateral basis, on a hemispheric basis. And we're strongly advocating a successful round for the—the Doha round of the WTO.

Secondly, free trade agreements require people honoring the agreements. And there are market disruptions involved with certain Chinese textiles; we're addressing those disruptions. And we look forward to visiting with our Chinese counterparts on this particular matter. And as I have been saying publicly, that free trade also requires a level playing field for trade.

In terms of the steel issue, it's an issue that the Prime Minister has brought up not once, not twice, but three times. It's on his mind. It's also on my mind. And I'm reviewing the findings about the restructuring of our steel industry, which is—the ITC ruling basically said that the industry needs some breathing time to restructure. I'm looking at the findings right now and will make a timely decision.

But I will reiterate, we believe strongly in free trade. We just want to make sure that free trade is also trade in which all parties are treated fairly.

Prime Minister Blair. Obviously, we've stated opposition. I know the President is well aware of it, and as you just heard, the administration will make its decision in the coming period of time.

The other thing I would draw your attention to is the joint belief in the importance of the WTO doing well and getting the deadlock that there was at Cancun resolved. That's immensely important.

And never forget, incidentally—I said this in the House of Commons yesterday—whatever the disagreements on trade between Europe and America—and ever since I've been Prime Minister there have been such disagreements on particular issues—trade between Europe and America is vast. In fact, I think it is right to say it has doubled since 1989. It amounts to a huge amount of money and jobs both ways every single year. So that's not to say we don't have to resolve these issues, and I hope we can resolve them soon, but I don't think we should forget the bigger picture, either.

Nick.

London Demonstrations/War on Terror

Q. Nick Robinson, ITV News. What do you say to people who today conclude that British people have died and been maimed as a result of you appearing here today, shoulder-to-shoulder with a controversial American President?

And Mr. President, if I could ask you, with thousands on the street—with thousands marching on the streets today here in London, a free nation, what is your conclusion as to why apparently so many free citizens fear you and even hate you?

President Bush. I'd say freedom is beautiful. It's a fantastic thing to come to a country where people are able to express their views.

Q. Why do they hate you, Mr. President? Why do they hate you in such numbers?

President Bush. I don't know that they do. All I know is that it's—that people in Baghdad, for example, weren't allowed to do this up until recent history. They're not spending a lot of time in North Korea protesting the current leadership. Freedom is a wonderful thing, and I respect that. I fully understand people don't agree with war. But I hope they agree with peace and freedom and liberty. I hope they care deeply about the fact that when we find suffering and torture and mass graves, we weep for the citizens that are being brutalized by tyrants.

And finally, the Prime Minister and I have a solemn duty to protect our people, and that's exactly what I intend to do as the President of the United States, protect the people of my country.

Prime Minister Blair. To answer your first question and your other, indeed, people have the right to protest and to demonstrate in our countries, and I think that's part of our democracy. And all I say to people is—and this is the importance, I think, of the speech the President made

yesterday—listen to our case as well. I mean, we listen. That's what a democratic exchange should be about, but listen to the case that we are making.

Because there is something truly bizarre about a situation where we have driven the Taliban out of Government in Afghanistan, who used to stop women going about the street as they wished, who used to prevent girls going to school, who brutalized and terrorized their population, there's something bizarre about having got rid of Saddam in Iraq from the Government of Iraq, when we've already discovered just so far the remains of 400,000 people in mass graves—there is something bizarre about these situations happening and people saying that they disagree, when the effect of us not doing this would be that the Taliban was still in Afghanistan and Saddam was still in charge of Iraq. And I think people have got to accept that that is the consequence of the position therein.

Now, as for your first point, just let me say this. What has caused the terrorist attack today in Turkey is not the President of the United States, is not the alliance between America and Britain. What is responsible for that terrorist attack is terrorism, are the terrorists. And our response has got to be to unify in that situation, to put the responsibility squarely on those who are killing and murdering innocent people, and to say, "We are going to defeat you, and we're not going to back down or flinch at all from this struggle." For all the reasons I've given you earlier, this is what this struggle is about.

And when you look—as you can see from the list of the people from 60 different nationalities who have died in terrorist attacks, thousands of people from every religion, every part of the world, you aren't going to stop these people by trying to compromise with them, by hesitating in the face of this menace. It's defeat them or be defeated by them. That's what we're going to do.

Religion/Shared Values

Q. Thank you, Mr. President, Mr. Prime Minister. Mr. President, when you talk about peace in the Middle East, you've often said that freedom is granted by the Almighty. Some people who share your beliefs don't believe that Muslims worship the same Almighty. I wondered about your views on that.

And Mr. Prime Minister, as a man also of faith, I'd like to get your reaction to that.

President Bush. I do say that freedom is the Almighty's gift to every person. I also condition it by saying freedom is not America's gift to the world. It's much greater than that, of course. And I believe we worship the same God.

Prime Minister Blair. And I believe that if people are given the chance to have freedom, whatever part of the world they're in, whatever religion they practice, whatever faith they have, if they're given the chance to have freedom, they welcome it. And I think it is the most appalling delusion that actually affects some people even within our own societies that somehow, though we in our countries love freedom and would defend freedom, somehow other people in other parts of the world don't like it.

And the reason why they like freedom is because then, if you've got freedom and democracy and the rule of law, you can raise your family, you can earn a decent standard of living, you can go about your daily business without fear of the secret police or terrorism. And in those types of societies, the terrorists who thrive on hatred and fanaticism, they get no breathing ground, they get no breathing space.

And the really important thing—and I just wanted to say this about the President's speech yesterday, because I hope—people sometimes say to me, "Well, you've got a Republican President, a center-left Government here in Britain, how can you two guys work together?" On this issue, I believe people from whatever side of the political spectrum they're on can respond to the call, that in the end, the best security we can have is not just through our armed forces and intelligence services, magnificent though they are, but actually through our values, through the spread of those values of freedom and justice and tolerance throughout the world.

And the case the President made yesterday, I think, is a really powerful call, not just to people in our own countries but to people right throughout the world, that these are basic human values. They're not the—in the ownership exclusively of America or Britain or the West or any particular religion; they're human values. And actually, every time you give people the chance to have those values, they opt for them. Of course they do, because they're the values that sustain the human spirit.

NOTE: The President's news conference began at 12:15 p.m. at the Foreign and Commonwealth Offices, 10 Downing Street. In his remarks, the President referred to Queen Elizabeth II of the United Kingdom; and Prime Minister Recep Tayyip Erdogan of Turkey. Prime Minister Blair referred to former President Saddam Hussein of Iraq. A reporter referred to Charles Kennedy, leader of the Liberal Democrats party of the United Kingdom; and Michael Howard, leader of the Conservative Party of the United Kingdom.

Effective Multilateralism To Build a Better World: Joint Statement by President George W. Bush and Prime Minister Tony Blair
November 20, 2003

President George W. Bush and Prime Minister Tony Blair reaffirm the unique alliance of values and common purpose that binds the United States and the United Kingdom. We confront great challenges: global terrorism, the spread of weapons of mass destruction, poverty and disease, and hostile dictators who oppress their own people and threaten peace. We, and our allies among the world's democracies, have a special responsibility to take action and mobilize international institutions to meet these challenges and build a more secure, just, and prosperous world.

We applaud the achievements of the Transatlantic Alliance, the foundation of our security, under whose aegis Europe whole, free, and at peace is becoming reality. We welcome NATO's major and growing role in Afghanistan, and its support for the Polish-led multinational division in Iraq. We welcome NATO's new cooperation with Russia, Ukraine, and other members of the Partnership for Peace. We reaffirm our support for a European Security and Defense Policy (ESDP) of the European Union that improves Europe's capabilities to act, and develops in a way that is fully coordinated, compatible, and transparent with NATO. We seek a dynamic, mutually-reinforcing relationship between NATO and the EU, without duplication and divisiveness, and grounded in the essential NATO-EU agreements which underpin it. With new members and new capabilities, NATO will be a cornerstone of world security in the 21st century.

We urge all nations to join together in common purpose, to put aside temporary disagreements, and to recognize our responsibility to work for the common good in the world. Our tasks are great, but so are our capabilities, when we work together.

Effective multilateralism, and neither unilateralism nor international paralysis, will guide our approach. We must:

- Launch efforts to promote freedom in the nations of the greater Middle East. We have a vision of this region moving toward peace through freedom. We cannot sacrifice our commitment to democracy to purchase security, for in that case we shall have neither. We applaud those in the region striving to advance human rights and economic freedom, fight corruption, and advance equal justice under law. The leaders of the Transatlantic community and the G8 must find new ways to cooperate with the people and states of the region to promote democratic development, economic freedom, and security, over the years that true transformation will take. We will work in partnership with those leaders in the region who are promoting political and economic reform and development.

We reaffirm our commitment to the vision of peace between two states—Israel and Palestine—living side by side in peace and security. The Roadmap to peace remains the way to achieve this vision, and we call on all parties to fulfill their obligations under its terms, taking effective action to stop all terrorism, and refraining from steps that would prevent or prejudge the terms of a final settlement. To this end, we will remain actively involved with the leaders of the region and work closely with the international community.

- Continue the fight against international terrorism. What we have begun we will

finish. Terrorists must know no sanctuary, neither in the mountains of Afghanistan or Iraq, nor hidden in the
cities of Europe or America, nor disguised as freedom fighters or charities.
We will continue to enhance our joint,
bilateral work, internationally and
through strengthened domestic cooperation.

- Strengthen global efforts against
proliferators of weapons of mass destruction. We must increase international capacity and will to deal effectively with this threat. We will intensify
efforts to counter both Iran's and also
North Korea's dangerous nuclear programs; and also strengthen the basis
for multilateral counter-proliferation
and non-proliferation actions, including
through the Proliferation Security Initiative and through our upcoming G8
Presidencies.
- Promote global health. Fighting the
global HIV/AIDS pandemic requires
sustained international effort, coordination, and resources. The U.S. and UK
will work together to strengthen efforts
in prevention, treatment, care, and
support, beginning in five African
countries. To further this collaborative
effort, we will establish a Special Joint
Task Force on HIV/AIDS. This Task
Force will focus our national efforts,
and enlist the efforts of others, aimed
at the struggle against HIV/AIDS. We
will pursue a comprehensive approach
to expanding the delivery of HIV/
AIDS prevention, care and treatment,
including greater access to safe and effective medicines, better health system
delivery, and building a skilled force
of health workers. We share a commitment to rapidly increasing the availability of HIV treatment in the most
affected countries, to reducing HIV infection rates, and to developing programs to provide care and support for
those infected with, and affected by,

HIV/AIDS, including orphans and vulnerable children. We call on others to
join us to fulfill the G8 goal of eradication of polio by 2005.
- Support development in Africa. We reaffirm our support for Africa and for
NEPAD, through the G8 Africa Action
Plan. We have agreed to work to support the development of effective African mechanisms to prevent conflict
and run peacekeeping operations; continue to work for a return to democrat-
ically-accountable government and the
rule of law in Zimbabwe; and support
the building of peace in Liberia and
Sierra Leone. We will deliver on the
commitments we made at Monterrey
and in the Africa Action Plan to improve the effectiveness of our development assistance. We welcome the
launch of the Africa Partnership
Forum, expanding the international
support for Africa's development.
Building Africa's foundation for success is our shared goal, and we commit
to support the Forum's efforts in the
region. We will work through bilateral
and multilateral channels to improve
trade opportunities in Africa.
- Advance an open trade regime. We are
committed to an open, fair, and multilateral world trading system. Recognizing that WTO Ministerial in Cancun
was a missed opportunity, we reaffirm
our commitment to a successful conclusion of the WTO's Doha Development Agenda. We will work with our
international partners to achieve a successful conclusion to the Round that
will benefit both developed and developing countries. We call for a resumption of the negotiations, and encourage
all parties to make serious and substantial contributions to these important
negotiations.
- Increase technological cooperation on
cleaner energy. We will bring together
our scientific and technological

strengths to accelerate development of practical and efficient technologies for the use and production of clean energy. To help improve human health by reducing pollution, and address the challenge of climate change by mitigating greenhouse gases, we have established a joint team to implement the energy, science and technology commitments from Evian through both of our G8 Presidencies.

- Deepen defense cooperation. We will work to remove barriers to increased defense industrial cooperation, interoperability, and information exchange. Our goals include achieving fair and consistent reciprocal access to each other's equipment markets, maximizing information sharing, and extending joint working and training opportunities. We will create a closer and more open relationship by the removal of outdated barriers between our armed forces and officials. We consider it a high priority to implement a licensing exemption that will facilitate defense trade between our countries. We reaffirm our strong commitment to proceed with the Joint Strike Fighter project.

- Promote innovative education initiatives. We are committed to increasing the number and quality of U.S.-UK school partnerships. To this end, we are inaugurating a new annual prize— the Transatlantic Education Prize—to reward schools for particularly creative and innovative partnerships. The first prizes will be awarded early next year and will include reciprocal visits for head teachers and principals.

NOTE: An original was not available for verification of the content of this joint statement.

Declaration on Iraq by President George W. Bush and Prime Minister Tony Blair
November 20, 2003

For the first time in decades, the Iraqi people are enjoying the taste of freedom. Iraqis are starting to rebuild their country and can look to a brighter future. They are free of Saddam Hussein and his vicious regime; they can speak freely; practice their religion; and start to come to terms with the nightmare of the last 35 years, in which hundreds of thousands of Iraqis were murdered by their own government.

But Iraq is still threatened by followers of the former regime, and by outside terrorists who are helping them. The struggle is difficult. Yet we shall persevere to ensure that the people of Iraq will prevail, with the support of the new and strengthening Iraqi security forces: the police, the Iraqi Civil Defense Corps, the Facility Protection Service, the border police, and the New Iraqi Army. We salute the courage of those Iraqis and the coalition forces engaged in the struggle against reactionary elements in Iraq who want to turn back the clock to the dark days of Saddam's regime.

We reaffirm the resolve of our two countries, with many friends and allies, to complete the process of bringing freedom, security, and peace to Iraq.

We warmly welcome the Iraqi Governing Council's announcement of a timetable for the creation of a sovereign Iraqi Transitional Administration by the end of June 2004, and for a process leading to the adoption of a permanent constitution and national elections for a new Iraqi government by the end of 2005.

This announcement is consistent with our long-stated aim of handing over power to Iraqis as quickly as possible. It is right that Iraqis are making these decisions and for the first time in generations determining their own future. We welcome the Governing Council's commitment to ensuring the widest possible participation in the Transitional Assembly and constitutional process.

We reaffirm our long-term commitment to Iraq. The United States and United Kingdom stand ready to support the Transitional Administration in its task of building a new Iraq and its democratic institutions. Our military participation in the multinational force in Iraq will serve the Iraqi people until the Iraqis themselves are able to discharge full responsibility for their own security. At the same time, we hope that international partners will increasingly participate in the multinational force.

Our long-term political, moral, and financial commitment to the reconstruction of Iraq was underlined at the Madrid Donors Conference last month. Although the Coalition Provisional Authority will come to an end once the Transitional Administration is installed, the United States and United Kingdom will continue to provide assistance as part of the international support effort. In these tasks, we welcome the involvement of other nations, regardless of earlier differences; of the United Nations and the International Financial Institutions; and of the many non-governmental organizations who are able to make an important contribution.

Great challenges remain in Iraq. But the progress we have made this year has been enormous. Iraqis no longer live in fear of their own government, and Iraq's neighbors no long feel threatened. Our resolve to complete the task we set ourselves remains undiminished. Our partnership with the Iraqi people is for the long-term.

NOTE: An original was not available for verification of the content of this joint statement.

Interview With Abdul Rahman Al-Rashed of Al-Sharq Al-Awsat in London
November 19, 2003

Mr. Al-Rashed. I know you are the busiest person——

The President. Thanks for coming by. I appreciate your interest. I'm honored you'd come by.

Timetable for Transition in Iraq

Mr. Al-Rashed. Mr. President, I think the question, number one, I have to ask is, now you're talking about transferring the power from the coalition now to the Governing Council sometime in the summer. What is exactly your timetable for that?

The President. Well, it really depends upon the Governing Coalition. They've expressed a desire for the transfer of authority in June. There are certain benchmarks that must be achieved. But let me just give you a kind of a broader assessment.

We—Ambassador Bremer came to the United States, as you know, gosh, I think it must have been a week ago or 10 days ago. And we sat down and made a conscious decision to listen to the voices on the Governing Council that were interested in accelerating the transfer of sovereignty, and we decided to—obviously if that's what they're interested in, that we needed to assess whether or not it was possible. The assessment was positive. And therefore, Jerry Bremer went back to the Governing Council and worked out a timetable that they're comfortable with. And that's very important.

As you know, one of the—initially the thought was to have a constitution written, then elections, then sovereignty. It was going to take a while to write the constitution, because there was a sentiment amongst the people that there needed to be elections to a constitutional assembly. And yet, because certain things had happened, the transfer of sovereignty seemed more realistic at this point in time than it did initially. And I could cite some of those in a minute. And so the idea was to have kind of a standard law under which the Iraqi people would operate, transfer of sovereignty, and then a constitution be written.

And as you know, the Governing Council is now in the process of—you asked the timetable—one of the decisions they must make is what will be the form of the kind of the local elections or caucuses that will then determine the makeup of the initial kind of representative body. That's their decision. And it's important for me to emphasize "their" decision, because we believe—and still believe—believed and believe that the Iraqi people are plenty capable of running their own country, a free country.

Mr. Al-Rashed. But who are we going to hand it over to—let's say, if you start in the summer, are we saying the summer is accurate?

The President. Yes, I think so. That's exactly what we're aiming for now.

Mr. Al-Rashed. Who is going to go for without, of course, the constitution, without a——

The President. Well, there's going to be kind of a general law that will be agreed upon before by the Governing Council so that people know that their rights will not be trampled, that there will be—that the minority populations will have a voice in the future Government. In other words, there has to be something other than a constitution, because the constitution it looked like was going to take a long time to write—but something that would have basic rights guaranteed, a preceding docu-ment to what eventually will be the constitution. And so that's part of what the Governing Council agreed to do.

Mr. Al-Rashed. But your vision, you think it's going to be one person, a President would be——

The President. My vision doesn't matter. That's important for you and your readers to know. What matters is the vision of the Iraqi people. And I've said in my speeches that I believe in democracy, but I recognize that democracy can come in different forms and democracies will not look like America's democracy necessarily. So there's ways to get to a system in which minority rights are represented, a rule of law prevails, all the systems inherent in democratic form. And they come in different ways, as you know, in particular in the Middle East or throughout the Arab world.

In my speech today, which I don't know if you heard it or not——

Mr. Al-Rashed. Not yet.

The President. You've got to hear it—please.

Mr. Al-Rashed. I will, indeed.

The President. Okay, because it's important for you to hear because I think it gives you some insights into my thinking in my heart about the Arab people and the Muslim people. I said in my speech, there are—I said one of the things that the Western world has to do is change its way of thinking about the Muslim world or the Arab world. And that is that—some will say, "Oh, these kind of people can't manage, can't govern themselves." I completely disagree. And one of the points I point out is that half the Muslims live under democratic societies, and they're contributing citizens. And those societies have got different ways of dealing with democracy. And Iraq's democracy will emerge in a uniquely Iraqi fashion. And that's what I'm trying to say.

Mr. Al-Rashed. So we don't know in the summer it's one President or a governing council, elected——

The President. And that's fine. Because a system is emerging. And that's what's important to know. But the Iraqi Governing Council, the Iraqi people will make that decision.

Withdrawal of Coalition Forces/Coalition Strategy

Mr. Al-Rashed. Are we saying—will that follow by withdrawing troops, American troops from——

The President. No—two separate courses. I'm sorry to interrupt you; I'm anticipating your questions in the name of time.

Mr. Al-Rashed. No, that's the question——

The President. We're talking two separate tracks. The political track is developing, and it's developing well, because certain things didn't happen. One, there was no great huge refugee flows. Two, there wasn't the sectarian violence. Remember, these were all—some of the predictions. I'm not suggesting you were making these predictions, but others might have been making predictions about sectarian violence—you remember that prediction—or refugee flows or hunger, food shortages throughout the country. And none of that happened.

But obviously, what is happening is violence that we're dealing with, and that's a security issue. But the political process is moving forward, and the ministries are now being staffed. There is a local region—local governments up and running. There's a variety of indicators that the system is moving toward this democratic transition, which the Governing Council recognizes and supports. So that's happening.

The other track, of course, is the security track. They're not mutually exclusive, of course. But in terms of our participation, we will stay until Iraq is allowed to emerge as a free society, which we know will happen.

Let me give you kind of the strategy. See, I said in my speech today, the Iraqi people will not reject freedom, and I believe that. And one way that they will protect their freedoms is to develop the forces necessary, internally, to work with coalition forces to deal with the few that are trying to destroy the hopes of the many. And I think we have over 130,000 now, Iraqis, in one kind of uniform or another. That would be your border guards, your facilities protection services, the police. And we've got a battalion in the army, and we're growing the army. I think they think it will be up around 30,000 by the end of next year, a trained, capable Iraqi army. And the first task, of course, for these uniformed Iraqi personnel is to rout out the killers, people willing to destroy.

I had a very interesting meeting—I'm sure you read about the 17 Iraqi women who came, that came to the White House. It was really, really interesting, a hopeful meeting, very capable women, anxious for a free society to emerge. And one lady made it clear to me that, "Yes, you've lost people, but we've lost a lot." And the Iraqi people are suffering and are dying, because people are trying to terrorize their society by killing them. And the Iraqi people will reject this because they yearn for freedom, just like you yearn for freedom and I yearn for freedom.

Mr. Al-Rashed. Mr. President, am I getting this right, you will not have any withdrawal of any troops by the summer?

The President. No. We will have troops on the ground that will match the security needs, is the best way to put that.

Mr. Al-Rashed. So you're not saying more or less?

The President. I'm saying I'm going to listen to the generals who say, Mr. President, we need more; we need less; we've got exactly the right number. They will tell me the number. Their job is to secure—is to work with the Iraqis to deal with the terrorists. And there are the Ba'athist terrorists; there jihadists; there are Al Qaida types, Ansar Islam types. And their job is to help the Iraqis secure their country, and they assess all the time, the commanders, and they say, we need this number here;

we need that number here. And it's their decision to make. I set the goal; they decide the tactics.

So General Abizaid—if you want to know what the troop strength will look like in June, go find General Abizaid, and he'll tell you.

Timetable for Transition in Iraq

Mr. Al-Rashed. Are we saying that you are doing the transfer of power earlier than planned because the pressure, because of the loss of life, the French, everybody——

The President. No, no, no, no, no, no, no, no, no. Because what I told you, that the Governing Council—the circumstances—the situation in Iraq and the Governing Council's progress led us to believe that this transfer of sovereignty could take place in a realistic and helpful way.

Mr. Al-Rashed. So do you expect the violence—do you have a number, like, of loss of life will determine how you will run your——

The President. Of course not. We're not leaving until we get the job done.

Mr. Al-Rashed. How long is that and how——

The President. That's like if you were interviewing me before the attack on Baghdad, you would have said, "How long is it going to take?" And I would have said, "However long," you know. I mean, you're asking me to put calendars on things—this is the second calendar question you've asked me.

Iraq and Vietnam

Mr. Al-Rashed. Some people make a parallel between Iraq and Vietnam. Do you see it?

The President. I know that people are anxious to be free. They were glad to get rid of Saddam Hussein. They were pleased when his sons met their demise. This person tortured, brutalized an entire population. And it's a different situation.

Mr. Al-Rashed. I didn't hear the word "Vietnam" in your answer.

The President. No, because—I gave you the answer; you asked the question. You asked me if there's parallel. I said it's a different situation. You understand the difference here, the people——

Mr. Al-Rashed. Yes.

The President. Okay. You know what I'm talking about. The people are pleased to get rid of Saddam.

Progress in Iraq

Mr. Al-Rashed. Mr. President, is it accurate to say that your military did a good job and they won the war in a very quite short and surprising matter, but your civilian managers did not manage the country very well?

The President. I think what's safe to say is that the initial phase of the war went well, and the second phase of the war is going as expected, because Ba'athists—there are some people who refuse to give up and yield to freedom because they were the ruling elite. And we're making, in many phases, very strong progress.

For example, the currency—I think if you were to go back and look at the history of currency replacements or issuing new currencies, that's not an easy task. And yet——

Mr. Al-Rashed. ——President Saddam, his face on the currency——

The President. No, they've got new currencies, and that's hard to do. And yet, we're making good, steady progress in replacing the currency.

The oil revenue is an interesting question. Again, this was an issue, if you remember, before the—when the ultimatum was reached, there was a lot of speculation that if we went to war, the Iraqi—the main asset of the Iraqi people would be destroyed, and it would take years to bring the oil production back up. But in fact, the oil is flowing, up to about 2.1 million barrels a day, to the benefit of the Iraqi people.

In other words—and we got that ministry stood up very quickly, and it's functioning well. The school system—I think there's 1,500 elementary schools up and running with new textbooks and supplies. The hospitals—I mean, there's example after example on the civil society side where we've made good progress.

Obviously, what is—what's tough are the terrorists who kill, and they kill Iraqis. They kill international aid workers. They kill because they're trying to shake our will. And they're not going to shake—they're not going to shake our will.

Possible Visit to Iraq

Mr. Al-Rashed. Are you going to visit Baghdad?

The President. I don't know yet. Will I at some point in time? I certainly hope so.

Mr. Al-Rashed. Before election or——

The President. [*Laughter*] I don't know. I'm just trying to finish my trip here to England.

Roadmap for Peace/Reform of Palestinian Authority

Mr. Al-Rashed. What about the roadmap? It's your project, but nothing has——

The President. No, it's our project.

Mr. Al-Rashed. Nothing has happened so far.

The President. Well, that's not exactly correct. I mean, it's—first of all, the roadmap exists—let me tell you, this was U.S., EU, U.N., and Russia. So it's kind of an international strategy toward saying to parties, "Take responsibility, be responsible citizens."

I gave a speech on June 24th, '02, in the Rose Garden, which—get on the web page and look at it, because it will give you my sense of—I hate to keep directing you to my speeches, but it will give you a sense for—and I reiterated that today. I spent quite a bit of time in the speech today on the Arab-Israeli issue. And I called on all parties to adhere to responsibility.

I said the best way for—see, I believe that the Palestinians deserve a state. As a matter of fact, I'm the first United States President to stand up and call for that. And I believe it, and I mean it. But that state must be democratic in order for it to survive, with institutions that will survive the test of time. And it needs leadership that will not steal money, that will not deal with terrorists, that will not continually dash the hopes of the Palestinian people.

And I found such a leader, I thought, in Abu Mazen. And I stood with him in Aqaba, Jordan, and as you might recall—and Israel has got responsibilities, and the Arab states have got responsibilities. And I delineated Israel's responsibilities, end the settlements and not prejudice final negotiations on states with walls, to end the daily humiliation of the Palestinians. This was all clearly enunciated today, by the way, in the public arena.

Anyway, I was with Abu Mazen. He convinced me that he believes in the aspirations of the Palestinians, and he wanted to work on the security issue. He wanted to dismantle the security—these terrorist organizations, which are destroying any chance for peace. And guess what happens to him? He gets shoved aside, and I thought it was an interesting lesson.

We hope this new Prime Minister will stand up and do what is right, which is to work to dismantle the terrorist organizations and put the institutions in place that are larger than the people, institutions which will survive the test of time, so Palestine can emerge as a peaceful, viable, democratic state.

Anyway, so therefore—that's it, the roadmap—there is a roadmap. The roadmap calls for mutual responsibilities. I just laid the division at the end of the road, which I believe in.

Saudi Arabia/Iran/Syria

Mr. Al-Rashed. Can I ask about now, a loaded question, which is, I know it's——

The President. Well, you've already asked about five loaded questions. [*Laughter*]

Mr. Al-Rashed. It's about three countries. I'd like to hear your—exactly how you're going to treat the end of this crisis. One is Iran, how you're going to——

The President. Well, it depends on Iran's decision——

Mr. Al-Rashed. ——on Syria, and finally your friends in Saudi Arabia.

The President. Yes. Well, first of all, let's start with Saudi Arabia. Crown Prince Abdullah is an honest man, and he is a friend of mine. I like him and respect him. And he has told me that we are joined at fighting off the terrorist organizations which threatened the Kingdom and they threaten the United States, and he's delivering. He also has told me that he's going to work on reform, and I believe him.

Iran: The choice is theirs. They must adhere to the Non-Proliferation Treaty that they agreed to. And they must be transparent and open and honest with the world about their ambitions. It looks like we're making some progress. The Secretary of State, as you know, yesterday met with ministers from European countries with this message, that we all need to speak with a unified voice that says to the Iranians, "Get rid of your nuclear weapons ambitions." And hopefully the—not hopefully—and work with the IAEA to develop a open and transparent regime with the Iranians.

Syria: Again, it's the leader of Syria's choice to make. The most important thing that he can do—oh, by the way, on the Iranians, one other point I want to make to you is that they hold Al Qaida operatives. And we would hope that those Al Qaida operatives were sent back to their countries of origin.

Mr. Al-Rashed. From Iran.

The President. In Iran, yes.

Syria: We have talked to Syria before, and we still feel very strongly about the same thing, that they need to shut down the Hezbollah offices in their country, Syria.

Mr. Al-Rashed. ——jihad——

The President. Hezbollah and JI, absolutely; Hamas, if there are such offices there. And they need to do a better job on their border to stop any infiltration going from Syria into Iraq with weapons and terrorists and jihadists. A peaceful Iraq is in Syria's interest. A free and peaceful Iraq is in the interest of the neighborhood. And we would hope that Syria would be cooperative in the development of a free and peaceful Iraq and not turn away from any infiltrations that might be taking place—that are taking place—from Syria into Iraq.

Mr. Al-Rashed. Does that mean you will—on Syria, is there negotiation now taking place?

The President. Well, there's—there's not much negotiation. How do you mean, negotiations?

Mr. Al-Rashed. Discussions.

The President. It's hard to negotiate—stop terror. You either stop terror or you don't stop terror. It's not—oh, yes, they understand. They know our feelings. They do, yes.

Mr. Al-Rashed. They know it by—there is someone in between?

The President. Well, they know it because they—first, they're going to read their story, and since I'm speaking directly to you and there's nobody in between, they will hear that. Secondly, that Secretary of State Powell talked to President Asad last—early last summer, I think it was, and delivered some of this message. This is before—I say "some of it" because this is before the—well, I think he delivered all the message, if I'm not mistaken. I mean, he is—in other words, if you're saying, has anybody—has President Asad heard from my Government? Yes, Secretary of State Powell had a good talk with him.

Discussions With Prime Minister Blair of the United Kingdom

Mr. Al-Rashed. Did you promise Blair anything about the roadmap? Because there's a story yesterday about it.

The President. What do you mean, promise him anything?

Mr. Al-Rashed. Prime Minister Blair, about the roadmap. There was a story yesterday that came out—to be activated or some——

The President. We haven't talked about the roadmap. I mean, we talk about the Middle East all the time, but he hasn't said—I'm not sure what you're referring to. It seems like a lot of things are printed in the newspapers here. [*Laughter*] Not yours.

Mr. Al-Rashed. Can I just have your signature here, please?

The President. I'd love to. Thank you. Thanks for the interview.

Mr. Al-Rashed. Thank you.

The President. And what you need to do is get stationed in America again. [*Laughter*]

NOTE: The interview began at 2:50 p.m. on November 19 at the American Embassy. The transcript was released by the Office of the Press Secretary on November 21. In his remarks, the President referred to L. Paul Bremer III, Presidential Envoy to Iraq; Gen. John P. Abizaid, USA, combatant commander, U.S. Central Command; former President Saddam Hussein of Iraq; Uday and Qusay Hussein, sons of former President Hussein, who were killed July 22 by U.S. military forces in Mosul, Iraq; former Prime Minister Mahmoud Abbas (Abu Mazen) and Prime Minister Ahmed Korei of the Palestinian Authority; Crown Prince Abdullah of Saudi Arabia; and President Bashar al-Asad of Syria. A tape was not available for verification of the content of this interview.

Exchange With Reporters at Sedgefield Community College in Sedgefield, United Kingdom
November 21, 2003

Terrorist Attacks in Turkey

President Bush. It was a sad day yesterday, but it's a day that reminds us all that we've got a job to do; that is to defeat terror.

Q. What did you tell Erdogan, sir?

President Bush. What?

Q. What did you tell the Turkish leader?

President Bush. I told him our prayers are with his people. I told him that we will work with him to defeat terror and that the terrorists have decided to use Turkey as a front.

Q. [*Inaudible*]—specific aid, like sending FBI agents or investigators?

President Bush. You'll see as time goes on. Both countries want to help. Obviously, we need to share intelligence. The best way to defeat Al-Qaida-type killers is to share intelligence and then work with local authorities to hunt these killers down.

Great Britain has got a fantastic intelligence service, and we've got a good one as well. And we want to work with countries like Turkey to anticipate and to find killers.

War on Terror

Q. Is Turkey a new front in this war on terror?

President Bush. It sure is, two major explosions. And Iraq is a front. Turkey is a front. Anywhere where the terrorists think they can strike is a front.

Q. [*Inaudible*]—Turkish officials wanted to go and strike Al Qaida in perhaps another country or another site?

President Bush. We'll work with any country willing to fight off terror, just like Great Britain. This country is fortunate to have a Prime Minister who is clear-sighted about the threats of the 21st century, and America is lucky to have a friend as strong as Tony Blair.

The Press

Q. Do you like having all these press around you?

President Bush. Do I like having all the press around me? Let me see here. [*Laughter*] Now, who has the final—let me ask, who has the final word, I wonder, me

or the press? I love the press around me. Just take a look at this lot. Take, for example, Scott [Scott Lindlaw, Associated Press]. He thinks he's a fine runner—until he came out to the ranch—never mind. [*Laughter*]

Prime Minister Blair. I'll tell you the truth a bit later, okay? [*Laughter*]

President Bush. Yes, we like the press. A vibrant society is a society with a free press.

Thank you all.

NOTE: The exchange began at 2:22 p.m. at the All-Weather Pitch. During the exchange, the President referred to Prime Minister Recep Tayyip Erdogan of Turkey.

Remarks With Prime Minister Blair at Sedgefield Community College and an Exchange With Reporters in Sedgefield
November 21, 2003

Prime Minister Blair. I'd just like to say, first of all, how delighted we both are to be at Sedgefield School here, and how wonderful the welcome has been from all the teachers and pupils, and what a magnificent job of work they do here. I also want to express my real pride that the President of the United States of America is here in my constituency and in the northeast of England. And everyone is really thrilled to see him here and delighted at the honor his presence here does us.

The last 2 or 3 days have been an interesting time, I think, to reflect. It's been a time when—with some fairly tragic things going on in the world. It's been an opportunity for us to reflect and know that amongst the tragedy, the alliance between Great Britain—between the United States of America is an alliance that is strong and enduring, of immense importance to our two countries. And we've got to continue that alliance now.

And these terrible attacks that happen, the terrorism that we see, the destruction, the intent to take innocent life that we see around us in our world today should make us just all the more determined to do what we need to do to restore order and justice, to bring peace and freedom and democracy to people all over the world.

It's been a fantastic opportunity these last few days just to—as I say, to think about this relationship between Britain and the United States, to reflect on its history, to assess the strength of it today, and to use that strength for a better future for our two countries but also for the wider world.

Mr. President, George, you and the First Lady, Laura, have been really welcome here in the northeast. And as I say, it's been a fantastic day for people here, and we can't tell you how delighted we are to see you.

President Bush. Mr. Prime Minister, it's been a great trip. Thanks for the invitation. Thanks for the hospitality. You and Her Majesty The Queen have made this a special part of our life. And it's really good to be in your own constituency. It's clear they love you up here, which is always a good sign. [*Laughter*]

We—being with the school—the schoolkids here reminds us of our solemn responsibility to protect our people and to create the conditions necessary for peace to prevail when they become older. That's our biggest job, and yesterday's attack in Turkey reminded us that we hadn't completed our job yet.

You know, as the Prime Minister so eloquently said yesterday, the terrorists are trying to intimidate the free world. And this man will not be intimidated, and neither will I. But more importantly, the people of Great Britain won't be intimidated, and neither will the people of America. And working together, we will make the world safer and freer for boys and girls all across the world, starting with these right here.

And so, Mr. Prime Minister, it's been a fantastic trip, and we're so thrilled to have been here. Thank you for your wonderful hospitality. And we look forward to—I look forward to our weekly phone calls to stay on the offensive against the enemy. Thank you.

I've already answered your questions, but if you've got another one——

The West's Response to Terrorism

Q. Sure, if I may. In light of the tragedy of these terrorist attacks, have your—the leaders from either Germany or France, do you find there are any indications that they're more empathetic or sympathetic to your cause? Do you feel as if there might be more aid or troops or even a stronger political alliance with those who have not agreed with you?

Prime Minister Blair. I think the important thing is that when these terrible terrorist attacks occur, there's one of two responses. People can respond either by being intimidated by it, by feeling, "Let's reduce our profile in this struggle." That's one response. Or people can respond by saying, "When we're under attack, we defend ourselves, and we go out and fight with renewed strength and determination for what we believe in."

Because when you look at what we're trying to do and trying to make sure that the world—it's not just about security; it's actually about recognizing that a world that is more free and stable and prosperous is a world that is more secure. When you recognize that that's what we're trying to do, and these people are trying by these appalling acts of terrorism against wholly innocent people, trying to prevent that world happening, then I think the response from everyone is very clear.

And I believe and hope that that is true, not just in Britain but all over Europe. Because, after all, what did we learn in Europe in our history, in the history that we share with the United States of America? And that is, when freedom is threatened in Europe, we have to fight. And the reason why you have a European Union today and we have democracy and stability and freedom in Europe is because in the face of attacks upon that freedom, we, with our allies, the United States, defended that freedom.

And so I'm sure that people in other countries in Europe will feel the same way about that. And I think you saw from the reaction, for example, in Italy, when that terrible act of terrorism killed Italian citizens who were over in Iraq trying to make that country better, I think you could see by that reaction from people in Italy that I think there is an instinctive knowledge that when you're attacked by people, by these wicked acts, there is only one response that is possible to make, and that is to get out there and be absolutely up front and say, "We are not tolerating this. We're going to fight back."

Germany's Contribution in Afghanistan

Q. Chancellor Schroeder has said that it's nice that we're going to speed up the timetable for handing over power to the Iraqi people, but he's still not going to contribute troops or any more money. Is that a disappointment?

President Bush. Chancellor Schroeder is committing troops to Afghanistan. And it is very helpful for our coalition. Afghanistan is—obviously been a—is a recently liberated country from a barbaric regime. And Chancellor Schroeder understands that it is essential that Afghanistan be free and democratic and peaceful. And I thank him for his significant and strong contribution.

U.K.-U.S. Alliance

Q. Mr. Prime Minister, you've talked a lot about the alliance between the two countries. A lot of your critics this week have said that Britain is not getting enough out of this alliance. What do you say to that? And do you feel that you've accomplished a lot this week for Britain?

Prime Minister Blair. What I say to that is that people sometimes talk about this alliance between Britain and the United States of America as if it were some scorecard. It isn't. It's an alliance of values. It's an alliance of common interests. It's an alliance of common convictions and beliefs. And the reason why we are standing side by side with America is not because we feel forced to; it is because we want to, because we believe that is the right place to be.

And as I was saying to you—I was discussing this with—last night and was just reflecting, when September the 11th happened, remember—obviously many, many American citizens lost their lives—this was the worst terrorist attack against British citizens. We're in this together. And we didn't—Britain didn't go off and attack Al Qaida. We didn't start a war against these people. They came to us. And if you look right around the world at the moment, there are something like nationals from 60 different nations in the world who have lost citizens in these terrorist attacks. And it doesn't matter whether you're up front or at the back, whether you're people who have got big profile on this or a low profile. These people aren't interested in that. This is a fundamental struggle.

And so the reason we have this alliance with the United States, the reason I'm proud to have the President here, the reason why I believe the vast majority of my country is proud of the alliance with the United States, is not because there's some payback that's going to be given to us. It's not about that. It's about knowing that this is a struggle in which we're both engaged, just as in my father's generation—they knew there was a struggle in which we both had to be engaged. And thank goodness both of us were, because that's the reason we're standing in a free country today.

President Bush. Listen, thank you. One comment on that. This leader and this country are willing to take on hard tasks in the name of freedom and peace, and so is America. And by working together, we will be able to accomplish a lot in these hard things.

As I said in my comments, that we are fortunate to have friends—I'm fortunate to have a friend like Tony Blair. America is fortunate to have friends like the people of Great Britain, because the people of Great Britain have got grit and strength and determination and are willing to take on a challenge. And we're being challenged. We're challenged by killers, cold-blooded killers. And we're going to prevail. And we're more likely to prevail working together, and that's the importance of the relationship.

Listen, thank you all. It's been a wonderful time being here in this great country.

NOTE: The President spoke at approximately 2:56 p.m. In his remarks, he referred to Queen Elizabeth II of the United Kingdom;

and Chancellor Gerhard Schroeder of Germany.

Statement on the 40th Anniversary of the Death of President John F. Kennedy
November 21, 2003

This weekend the American people turn our thoughts to images of 40 years ago and to the good and graceful life that ended on November 22, 1963. John F. Kennedy has been gone nearly as long as he lived, yet the memory of him still brings pride to our Nation and a feeling of loss that defies the passing of years.

We remember a man who welcomed great responsibilities and had a gift for awakening the idealism and sense of duty in others. We remember a leader who called our Nation to high purpose and saw America through grave dangers with calm, discernment, and personal courage. We recall, with much affection and respect, the charming and dignified manner that became familiar to us all in the years of President Kennedy's service.

On this day especially, we think of a young father whose wife and family faced sorrow with dignity and a courage of their own. America still misses our 35th President, and Laura and I join our fellow citizens in honoring the memory of John Fitzgerald Kennedy.

Remarks on Arrival From the United Kingdom
November 21, 2003

Good evening. Laura and I have just returned from Great Britain, where we had a fantastic trip. Her Majesty the Queen was a great host. Of course, we spent some time today in Tony Blair's constituency, which was not only a lot of fun, but it was a chance to continue our dialog about how to fight and defeat terror. We've got a special relationship with Great Britain. That relationship was reaffirmed during the last 3 days.

Back here at home, I'm pleased that the Congress passed the Healthy Forests Initiative, which will help us maintain our national treasure, our forests, again providing a commonsense strategy and making sure that the fire hazards that we've seen over the last couple of summers are mitigated as best as possible.

Secondly, I was pleased that House of Representatives passed an energy bill. This Nation needs an energy bill. It needs an energy plan. A minority of Senators are holding it up. For the sake of our national security and economic security, the Senate has got to pass this bill.

And finally, as you know, the Medicare legislation is—will be debated tonight in the House of Representatives and eventually in the Senate. It is an important time for Members of the U.S. Congress to honor our obligations to our seniors by providing a modern Medicare system, a system that includes prescription drugs and choices for our seniors. I urge the House and the Senate to pass this good piece of legislation.

We're glad to be home. It's good to see you all. Good night. Thank you.

NOTE: The President spoke at 6:27 p.m. on the South Lawn at the White House. In his remarks, he referred to Queen Elizabeth II and Prime Minister Tony Blair of the United Kingdom.

The President's Radio Address
November 22, 2003

Good morning. This week Congress made significant progress toward improving the lives of America's senior citizens. The House of Representatives passed legislation that would bring prescription drug coverage to Medicare and lead to health care choices for our seniors. This legislation, if also passed by the Senate, would represent the greatest improvement in senior health care since Medicare was enacted in 1965.

When these reforms take full effect, our seniors would see real savings in their health care costs. Within 6 months, seniors would be eligible for a drug discount card that would save them between 10 and 25 percent off the retail price of most drugs. When the full drug benefit arrives in 2006, all seniors become eligible for drug coverage for a monthly premium of about $35. For most seniors without coverage today, the Medicare drug plan would cut their annual drug bills roughly in half.

Seniors with the highest drug bills would save the most, and seniors with the greatest need would get the most help. Low-income seniors would pay a reduced premium or no premium at all for the new drug coverage. And low-income seniors would also have lower copayments for their medicines.

Here is an example of how this benefit would work. A senior taking drugs to treat arthritis, high cholesterol, and migraines has a typical drug bill of about $250 a month, or $3,000 a year. With this legislation, this retiree would save $1,680 after paying her insurance premiums—more than half her current drug costs.

Under the new reforms, seniors would have more choices of health care coverage.

Should seniors want to stay in traditional Medicare and receive a prescription drug benefit, they would be able to do so. Some seniors may want expanded coverage for extended hospital stays or protection against high out-of-pocket medical expenses, or they may want the coverage that comes with managed care plans. Under the new law, all those choices would be available. With choice, seniors would have more control over their health care options, and health plans would compete for the business with better coverage.

We're on the verge of success because of bipartisan leadership and because of the support of many advocates for seniors, including the AARP. Throughout many months of discussion and debate, we've remained focused on the clear objective: to modernize and strengthen the Medicare system. And by working together, we're close to meeting that goal.

In the nearly 40 years since Medicare was launched, this is the most significant opportunity for any Congress to improve health coverage for our seniors. Now we're down to the final stages. This Congress will decide whether or not seniors will have prescription drug coverage under Medicare, and this Congress will decide whether America's seniors will have better health care choices.

I urge all Members of Congress to remember what is at stake and to remember the promise we have made to America's seniors. The quality of their health care and the future strength of Medicare depends on the passage of this much needed legislation.

Thank you for listening.

NOTE: The address was recorded at 4:35 p.m. on November 21 for broadcast at 10:06 a.m. on November 22. The transcript was made available by the Office of the Press Secretary on November 21 but was embargoed for release until the broadcast. The Office of the Press Secretary also released a Spanish language transcript of this address.

Statement on House of Representatives Action on Medicare Reform Legislation
November 22, 2003

The House's historic passage of the bipartisan Medicare bill brings seniors one step closer to a modern Medicare system, one that includes prescription drugs and choices for seniors. I applaud the House for meeting our obligations to America's seniors. Now it is time for the Senate to act. I urge the Senate to pass this good piece of legislation so that I can sign it into law.

NOTE: The Office of the Press Secretary also released a Spanish language version of this statement.

Statement on Signing the Military Construction Appropriations Act, 2004
November 22, 2003

Today, I have signed into law H.R. 2559, the "Military Construction Appropriations Act, 2004." The Act appropriates funds for construction to support the operations of the U.S. Armed Forces and for military family housing.

Sections 107, 110, and 113 provide for notice to the Congress of relocation of activities between military installations, initiation of a new installation abroad, or U.S. military exercises involving $100,000 in construction costs. The Supreme Court of the United States has stated that the President's authority to classify and control access to information bearing on national security flows from the Constitution and does not depend upon a legislative grant of authority. Although notice can be provided in most situations as a matter of comity, situations may arise, especially in wartime, in which the President must act promptly under his constitutional grants of executive power and authority as Commander in Chief while protecting sensitive national security information. The executive branch shall construe these sections in a manner consistent with the constitutional authority of the President.

Section 119 provides for the Secretary of Defense to submit a report to Congress with details of proposed actions to encourage certain cooperating nations to assume a greater share of the common defense burden. Section 128 of the Act establishes a commission of eight congressionally-designated members to study the U.S. military facility structure overseas and provides for commission access to information. The executive branch shall construe sections 119 and 128 in a manner consistent with the President's constitutional authority to withhold information the disclosure of which could impair foreign relations, the national security, the deliberative processes of the

Executive, or the performance of the Executive's constitutional duties.

GEORGE W. BUSH

The White House,

November 22, 2003.

NOTE: H.R. 2559, approved November 22, was assigned Public Law No. 108–132.

Remarks at the Thanksgiving Turkey Presentation Ceremony
November 24, 2003

Thank you all. Welcome. Thanks for coming. Good morning, and welcome to the Rose Garden. In a moment you can come up and welcome our guest of honor, Stars the turkey. He looks pretty friendly. He actually looks well rested. You'd be well rested, too, if you had your own room in Hotel Washington here in Washington, DC. [*Laughter*] It sounds like Stars wants to give the speech.

I appreciate you joining me to give this turkey a Presidential pardon. Stars is a very special bird with a very special name. This year, for the first time, thousands of people voted on the White House web site to name the national turkey and the alternate turkey. "Stars" and "Stripes" beat out "Pumpkin" and "Cranberry." And it was a neck-to-neck race. [*Laughter*]

Under the official rules, the alternate turkey has an important role, not to be taken lightly. The rulebook states that an alternate turkey is chosen in case the national Thanksgiving turkey cannot fulfill his role in this ceremony. It's kind of like being the Vice President. [*Laughter*]

Our Nation's sense of gratitude is the source of great generosity of our people. Some of the boys and girls here today have done their part this year. Fifth graders from Flint Hill School collected the fixings and made sandwiches for people at the local homeless shelter. Through your compassion, you're showing the goodness of America, and we are really proud of you. Thanks for doing that.

I want to thank our Secretary of Agriculture for joining us today. Secretary Ann Veneman is doing a great job for our country. I want to thank Bob Wright, who's the chairman of the National Turkey Federation, for joining today. I appreciate Dr. Alice Johnson, who's the president. Thanks for coming, Alice.

Today marks a—and continues a long White House tradition. We're honoring the beginning of a holiday season. It speaks well for America that one of our most important holidays is set aside for sharing and appreciating our blessings. Our Nation was founded by people of great accomplishment, great courage, and great humility. They believed not only in themselves but also in the goodness of God's wisdom and God's plan for every life. This American quality has endured throughout the generations. Americans are, at our best, are a reverent and a grateful people. Even in times of hardship, we see all around us gifts to be thankful for, our families and friends, the beautiful land we call home, and the freedom granted to us all.

This year, as in other times in our history, we can be especially grateful for the courage and faithfulness of those who defend us. Every man and woman who wears our country's uniform is a volunteer, facing hardships and sometimes peril, because they believe in this country and our cause. We're thinking of them and their families. We think of the military families that have suffered loss. We can be grateful to live in a country that has produced such good and brave people who stand between us and the dangers of the world.

On this holiday, we're reminded of our blessings. We're reminded of our responsibilities. Our Nation's sense of gratitude is the source of the great generosity and compassion of our people.

And now it's time to grant a little compassion to our guest of honor. I'm not sure why any turkey would want to reside at a place called Frying Pan Park. [*Laughter*] Maybe they explained the alternatives to him. [*Laughter*] In any case, off he goes.

By virtue of the Presidential pardon, Stars will live out his days there at Kidwell Farm in Virginia. And so he won't be alone, I hereby pardon Stripes as well.

Happy Thanksgiving to you. May God bless you and your families. Thanks for coming.

NOTE: The President spoke at 9:25 a.m. in the Rose Garden at the White House. The Thanksgiving Day proclamation of November 21 is listed in Appendix D at the end of this volume.

Remarks on Signing the National Defense Authorization Act for Fiscal Year 2004 in Arlington, Virginia
November 24, 2003

Thank you for the warm welcome, and good morning. I'm honored to be here at the Pentagon with the men and women who are defending America and who are fighting the war on terror. America is counting on your skill and courage.

People in our military depend upon the support of the Congress and the President and the administration. Today, with the National Defense Authorization Act, our Government is meeting its obligations. We're sending a clear message: In a time of conflict and challenge, America stands with the United States military.

Mr. Secretary, you are doing a fantastic job for America. You lead with courage; you lead with clear vision; and you lead with strength. I appreciate General Dick Myers and the members of the Joint Chiefs who are with us. Thank you for your great service to our country. I want to thank the ranking enlisted personnel who are with us today, Sergeant Major John Estrada and Master Chief Petty Officer Terry Scott. I appreciate you all being up here as well. Thank you for your fine service. I want to thank the Department of Defense personnel who are with us today. Thank you

for working with the Secretary and Deputy Secretary Wolfowitz and others for making sure the Pentagon does its job and does its job well.

I want to thank the Members of Congress who are here. I particularly want to single out Chairman Warner and Chairman Hunter: John Warner of Virginia, United States Senate; Duncan Hunter of California, the House of Representatives. I want to thank both of you for working on this important piece of legislation, for solving issues inside the bill, and getting a good bill to this desk. Thank you—[*inaudible*].

I also thank Senator Carl Levin, who's the ranking member, Senator Susan Collins from Maine, and Congressman Tom Davis for joining us on this stage and for their leadership in this important piece of legislation. I want to thank the other Members of the United States Senate and the House of Representatives who have joined us. Thank you for supporting this piece of legislation.

It's an important signal we're sending, because, you see, the war on terror is different than any war America has ever fought. Our enemies seek to inflict mass casualties without fielding mass armies. They hide in the shadows, and they're often hard to strike. The terrorists are cunning and ruthless and dangerous, as the world saw on September the 11th, 2001, and again in Istanbul last week. Yet these killers are now facing the United States of America and a great coalition of responsible nations, and this threat to civilization will be defeated.

In this new kind of war, our military needs to be fast and smart and agile, and it is. Right now, America's Armed Forces are the best trained, best equipped, and best prepared in the world, and this administration will keep it that way. The bill I sign today authorizes $400 billion over the next fiscal year to prepare our military for all that lies ahead. We will do whatever it takes to keep our Nation strong, to keep the peace, and to keep the American people secure.

First, this legislation respects and supports the men and women of our military and their families, all of whom are a vital source of our national strength. For more than three decades, America has been well served and well defended by our All Volunteer Force. The quality and professionalism of that force has never been higher. Whether you wear four stars or one stripe, our military is making America proud.

In this time of war, our military is facing greater sacrifice. Our men and women in uniform are facing longer separations. Your families are feeling great pride, and sometimes they worry. America is grateful for your willingness to serve, and we are showing our gratitude. This bill authorizes an across-the-board pay increase averaging 4.15 percent. It extends through next year the increase of extra pay earned by servicemembers who volunteer for hazardous duty and who endure long separations from their families. The bill further reduces housing costs for those living off posts. It reauthorizes bonus pay for those with specialized skills. Those who risk their lives for our liberty deserve to be fairly paid and fairly treated, and this bill keeps those commitments.

Second, this legislation helps America remain prepared and fully equipped for the challenges of our time. In our new struggle, threats can emerge suddenly, and so we must always be ready. This bill authorizes funds for realistic training, because battles are won with the effective training of our people.

The Congress has authorized the full $9.1 billion that I requested for ballistic missile defense. The spread of ballistic missile technology, along with the spread of weapons of mass destruction, is a terrible danger to America and to the world, and we must have the tools and the technologies to properly protect our people.

This bill also advances the vital work of transforming the personnel system for civilian defense workers, so that we can place the right person in the right job to meet the challenges we face. Nearly 700,000 civilian defense workers have been laboring under a cumbersome, inefficient system designed for another century. The bill I sign today reforms this system. It gives DOD managers the flexibility to place civilian workers where they are most needed, without needless delay. It speeds up the hiring process so that new employees will not have to face a wait of many months before beginning their service to our country. It introduces pay-for-performance bonuses and streamlines the promotion process, making a career at the Defense Department more attractive to talented workers.

These are landmark reforms, the most ambitious of their kind in a quarter-century and similar in scope and purpose to those enacted for the Department of Homeland Security. To win the war on terror, America must fully utilize the skills and talents of everyone who serves our country, and this bill will help us achieve that goal.

Every member of the United States military is now involved in a great and historic task, and the stakes for our country could

not be higher. We face enemies that measure their progress by the chaos they inflict,
the fear they spread, and the innocent lives
they destroy.

America's military is standing between
our country and grave danger. You're standing for order and hope and democracy in
Afghanistan and Iraq. You're standing up
for the security of all free nations and for
the advance of freedom. The American
people and your Commander in Chief are
grateful, and we will support you in all
your essential missions.

And now it is my honor to sign the National Defense Authorization Act for Fiscal
Year 2004.

May God bless you all.

NOTE: The President spoke at 10:10 a.m. at
the Pentagon. In his remarks, he referred to
Secretary of Defense Donald H. Rumsfeld;
Sgt. Maj. John L. Estrada, USMC, Sergeant
Major of the Marine Corps; and Master
Chief Petty Officer of the Navy Terry D.
Scott, USN. H.R. 1588, approved November
24, was assigned Public Law No. 108–136.

Statement on Signing the National Defense Authorization Act for Fiscal Year 2004
November 24, 2003

Today, I have signed into law H.R. 1588,
the National Defense Authorization Act for
Fiscal Year 2004. The Act authorizes funding to defend the United States and its
interests abroad and provides much-needed
flexibility to manage effectively the personnel and taxpayer resources devoted to
the national defense.

Section 541(a) of the Act amends section
991 of title 10 of the United States Code
to purport to place limits on the number
of days on which a member of the Armed
Forces may be deployed, unless the Secretary of Defense or a senior civilian or
military officer to whom the Secretary has
delegated authority under section 541(a)
approves the continued deployment. Section 1023 purports to place restrictions on
use of the U.S. Armed Forces in certain
operations. The executive branch shall construe the restrictions on deployment and
use of the Armed Forces in sections 541(a)
and 1023 as advisory in nature, so that the
provisions are consistent with the President's constitutional authority as Commander in Chief and to supervise the unitary executive branch.

Section 903 amends section 153 of title
10 to require the Secretary of Defense to
provide for a report to the Congress by
the Chairman of the Joint Chiefs of Staff
of a plan for mitigating risks identified by
the Chairman. The executive branch shall
construe this provision in a manner consistent with the President's constitutional
authority to supervise the unitary executive
branch and as Commander in Chief.

Section 924 places restrictions upon the
exercise of certain acquisition authority by
the Director of the National Security Agency (NSA). The reference in section 924(b)
to section 2430 of title 10, United States
Code, authorizes the Secretary of Defense
to exclude from the scope of section 924(b)
highly sensitive classified programs as determined by the Secretary of Defense.
Moreover, the exercise by the Under Secretary of Defense for Acquisition, Technology, and Logistics of authority described
in section 924 remains subject to the statutory authority of the Secretary of Defense
to exercise authority, direction, and control
of the Department of Defense under section 113(b) of title 10. The executive
branch shall construe and execute section

924 in a manner consistent with these statutory authorities of the Secretary of Defense, the authority of the Director of Central Intelligence under section 103(c)(7) of the National Security Act to protect intelligence sources and methods from unauthorized disclosure, and the constitutional authority of the President to supervise the unitary executive branch and as Commander in Chief.

Section 1442(b)(2)(C) requires executive agency heads to furnish certain reports to the chairman and ranking minority member of "[e]ach committee that the head of the executive agency determines has legislative jurisdiction for the operations of such department or agency to which the information relates." The executive branch shall, as a matter of comity and for the very narrow purpose of determining to whom a department or agency will submit a report under this provision, determine the legislative jurisdiction of congressional committees.

Section 3622 purports to establish an interparliamentary working group involving up to 40 Members of Congress and the legislature of the Russian Federation on nuclear nonproliferation and security. Consistent with the President's constitutional authority to conduct the Nation's foreign relations and as Commander in Chief, the executive branch shall construe section 3622 as authorizing neither representation of the United States nor disclosure of national security information protected by law or Executive Order.

Several provisions of the Act, including sections 320(b)(5) and (e), 335, 528, 647(c)(2), 923(d)(1)(F), and 1051, call for executive branch officials to submit to the Congress proposals for legislation. These provisions shall be implemented in a manner consistent with the President's constitutional authority to supervise the unitary executive branch and to recommend for the consideration of the Congress such measures as the President judges necessary and expedient.

A number of provisions of the Act, including sections 111(c), 903, 924, 1202, 1204, 1442(b)(2)(C), 1504(b), and 2808, require the executive branch to furnish information to the Congress or other entities on various subjects. The executive branch shall construe such provisions in a manner consistent with the President's constitutional authority to withhold information the disclosure of which could impair foreign relations, national security, the deliberative processes of the Executive, or the performance of the Executive's constitutional duties.

GEORGE W. BUSH

The White House,
November 24, 2003.

NOTE: H.R. 1588, approved November 24, was assigned Public Law No. 108–136.

Remarks to Military Personnel at Fort Carson, Colorado
November 24, 2003

The President. Thank you all.

Audience members. U.S.A.! U.S.A.! U.S.A.!

The President. Thank you all very much. Thank you for the warm welcome. I'm honored to be in the Rocky Mountain State. I'm honored to be in Fort Carson. More importantly, I'm honored to be in the presence of so many fine Americans, so many great citizens who proudly wear our Nation's uniform.

The soldiers of Fort Carson are now engaged in the largest deployment from this post since World War II. You reflect tremendous credit to the United States Army. You bring great pride to the people of the United States of America.

The people of our Armed Forces are serving at a crucial period for America and for all free nations. We're at war with terrorists who hate what we stand for, liberty, democracy, tolerance, and the rights and dignity of every person. We're a peaceful nation, yet we are prepared to confront any danger. We are fighting the terrorists in Iraq and Afghanistan and in other parts of the world so we do not have to fight them on the streets of our own cities. And we will win.

In this war, America depends on our people in uniform to protect our freedom and to keep our country safe, and all who serve depend every day on the support of your families. These are challenging times for military families. You in the Pikes Peak community know that very well. Military life makes many demands on wives and husbands and sons and daughters. You have faced hardships, and you have faced them together. And I want you to know, our whole Nation is grateful to our military families.

America is also indebted to the men and women of the Guard and Reserve who are serving abroad and to those who are called for homeland security assignments. Hundreds of Reserve units across America have been activated in this time of war. Our country thanks these fine citizens, and we thank their employers for putting duty first.

I want to thank Major General Bob Wilson for his leadership and his strength of character. I want to thank General Larry Ellis as well for greeting me here today. It's my honor to have met General Lance Lord, Commander of the Air Force Space Command. I appreciate Colonels Orr, Terry, Wininger, and Resty for being such strong leaders and for greeting me here. It was my privilege to have lunch with Sergeant Major Mac McWilliams. He's the kind of guy you don't want to cross.

[*Laughter*] He's the kind of guy you want on your side. I'm glad he's on my side, and I'm glad you're on my side. I appreciate Bill Hybl, who is the Civilian Aide to the Secretary of the Army.

I want to thank the families of the fallen soldiers who are here with us today. Our prayers are with you. We ask for God's strength and God's guidance.

I'm honored that the great Governor of the great State of Colorado is with us today, Governor Bill Owens. We've got some members of the United States Congressional delegation here who are strong supporters of our military and our military families, Congressman Hefley and McInnis, Tancredo, Beauprez, and Musgrave. Thank you all for coming. I'm honored you're here.

The speaker of the house is here; Madam Speaker, thank you for coming, Lola Spradley. The mayor of Colorado Springs and the mayor of Fountain, Mayor Rivera and Mayor Barela, are with us as well. Thank you all for coming. I thank all State and local officials for being here. But most of all, I want to thank you all for coming. It's my honor to be here.

When I landed, when I got off that magnificent bird, Air Force One, I was greeted by a lady named Diane Campbell. She brought her family with her. She's an active volunteer with the Army Family Team Building program. [*Applause*] As I said, she brought her family with her. [*Laughter*]

The reason I bring up Diane Campbell is, oftentimes people measure the strength of America based upon the number of tanks and airplanes we have or the size of our wallets. No, the strength of America lies in the hearts and souls of our citizens. You see, people like Diane Campbell are providing training and information to military spouses and families to help them adjust to the life in the Army. See, they're reaching out. They've heard the universal call to love a neighbor just like they would like to be loved themselves. The true strength of America is the American people, because we're a compassionate, decent, caring, loving people, just like Diane Campbell.

I want to thank Diane and all the Army Family Team Building members for your service. I ask you all to reach out a hand to somebody who hurts. I ask you to help us change our country one lonely soul at a time.

For more than 60 years, the units of Fort Carson have been known for training hard and being prepared at all times. Men and women have gone forth from this base to make history, from the Pacific theater in World War II to Korea, Vietnam, and Desert Storm. Many thousands who served in these causes still live here in this area. I don't blame you. [*Laughter*] It's a beautiful part of our country. Our veterans and military retirees played their part in maintaining the greatest fighting force in the world. They kept our country free, and we are grateful to the veterans who are with us here today.

Today, a new generation has been called to great challenges. The soldiers of the Mountain Post have been called to serve in the first war of the 21st century. This war began more than 2 years ago, on September the 11th, 2001, when America was attacked and thousands of our fellow citizens were murdered. The events of that morning changed our Nation. We awakened to new dangers, and we accepted new responsibilities. That day we saw the harm that our enemies intend for us. And last week we saw their cruelty again, in the murders in Istanbul. Today, America, Britain, and Turkey and all responsible nations are united in a great cause: We will not rest until we bring these committed killers to justice.

These terrorists will not be stopped by negotiations or by appeals to reason or by the least hint of conscience. We have only one option: We must and we will continue to take the fight to the enemy.

We fight this war against terror on many fronts. Terrorists hide and strike within free societies, so we're draining their bank accounts, disrupting their plans. We're hunting them down one by one until they can no longer threaten America and other free peoples.

Terrorists need places to hide, to plot, and to train, so we're holding their allies, the allies of terror, to account. Working with a fine coalition, our military went to Afghanistan, destroyed the training camps of Al Qaida, and put the Taliban out of business forever.

In Iraq, where a dictator defied the world, cultivated ties to terror, armed with deadly weapons, America led a mission to make the world safer and to liberate the Iraqi people, and that brutal dictator's regime is no more. Thanks to our great military, Iraqi citizens do not have to fear the dictator's secret police or ending in a mass grave. Thanks to our military, the torture chambers are closed, and the prison cells for children are empty. Thanks to our military, we have captured many members of the former regime, and the rest of them have a lot to worry about.

Recently, in Operation Iron Hammer, our coalition worked with the Iraqi Civil Defense Corps and police to strike hard against the forces of murder and chaos. We countered attacks. We seized weapons. We brought coldblooded killers to justice. We're proud of all who participated in these forceful and successful operations. And we're sending a clear message: Anyone who seeks to harm our soldiers can know that our great soldiers are hunting for them.

Our mission in Iraq and Afghanistan is clear to our servicemembers, and it's clear to our enemies. America's military is fighting to secure the freedom of more than 50 million people who recently lived under two of the cruelest dictatorships on Earth. America's military is fighting to help democracy and peace and justice rise in a troubled and violent region. And because we're fighting terrorist enemies thousands of miles away, in the heart and center of their power, we are making the United States of America more secure.

Units from this base have been vital to our campaigns in Afghanistan and Iraq. The 7th Infantry Division has done fine work preparing Guard brigades for combat duty overseas, with one battalion in Iraq from the start of Operation Iraqi Freedom; preparing a brigade to deploy and a brigade now in Afghanistan; helping to train the Afghan National Army. We're grateful for the 3d Brigade Combat Team, the 3d Armored Calvary Regiment, the 10th Special Forces Group, the 43d Area Support Group. These and other units are showing the skill and the discipline that define Fort Carson, and you're showing the courage that defines the United States Army.

Today, American forces in Iraq are joined by about 24,000 troops from 32 other countries. Together, we're helping the Iraqi people move steadily toward a free and democratic society. Economic life is being restored to cities of Iraq. A new Iraqi currency is circulating. Local governments are up and running. Iraq will soon begin the process of drafting a constitution, with free elections to follow. As Iraq rejoins the world, it will demonstrate the power of freedom and hope to overcome resentment and hatred. And this transformation will help make America more secure.

The work we are in is not easy, yet it is essential. The failure of democracy in Iraq would provide new bases for the terrorist network and embolden terrorists and their allies around the world. The failure of democracy in those countries would convince terrorists that America backs down under attack. Yet democracy will succeed in Iraq, because our will is firm and our word is good. Democracy will succeed because every month, more and more Iraqis are fighting for their own country. People we have liberated will not surrender their freedom. Democracy will succeed because

the United States of America will not be intimidated by a bunch of thugs.

This community knows firsthand that the mission in Iraq is difficult and the enemy is dangerous. Saddam loyalists and foreign terrorists are attacking the symbols of order and freedom, from international aid workers to coalition forces to innocent Iraqi citizens. Terrorists have chosen to make a stand and test our resolve. Our resolve will not be shaken.

It is the nature of terrorism that a small number of people can inflict terrible grief, and here, you felt loss. Every person who dies in the line of duty leaves a family that lives in sorrow and comrades who must go on without them. The Fort Carson community said farewell to some of your best. One of them was Staff Sergeant Daniel Bader. This good man left behind his wife, Tiffany, and their 14-month-old daughter. Tiffany Bader said this to a reporter recently: "I'm going to wait until she is old enough to realize what happened, and I will tell her exactly what her daddy did for her. He died serving his country so that my little girl could grow up free."

The courage of that soldier and the courage of that wife show the spirit of this country in the face of great adversity. And all our military families that mourn can know this: Our Nation will never forget the sacrifice their loved one made to protect us all.

By the unselfish dedication of Americans in uniform, children in our own country and in lands far away will be able to live in freedom and know the peace that freedom brings. As Americans, we believe that freedom is not America's gift to the world; freedom is the Almighty God's gift to every person who lives in the world.

As men and women who serve the cause of freedom, each one of you has answered a great calling. You live by a code of honor, in service to your Nation, for the safety and security of your fellow citizens. You and I have taken an oath to defend America. We're meeting that duty together, and

I'm proud to be the Commander in Chief of the greatest military, full of the finest people on the face of this earth.

God bless you all. God bless America.

NOTE: The President spoke at 1:28 p.m. in a hangar at Butts Army Airfield. In his remarks, he referred to Maj. Gen. Robert Wilson, USA, commander, Fort Carson; Gen. Larry R. Ellis, USA, commanding general, U.S. Army Forces Command; General Lance W. Lord, USAF, commander, Air Force Space Command; Col. Joseph E. Orr, USA, deputy commanding general, and Col. Michael J. Terry, USA, assistant division commander for support, 7th Infantry Division (Light) and Fort Carson; Col. Walter Wininger, USA, chief of staff, 7th Infantry Division and Fort Carson; Col. Michael Resty, Jr., USA, garrison commander, Fort Carson; Command Sgt. Maj. Terrance McWilliams, USA, Fort Carson; Lola Spradley, speaker of the Colorado House of Representatives; Mayor Lionel Rivera of Colorado Springs, CO; Mayor Ken Barela of Fountain, CO; and former President Saddam Hussein of Iraq.

Remarks to Reporters in Colorado Springs, Colorado, on Medicare Reform Legislation
November 24, 2003

Because of key votes in the United States Senate today, we're moving closer to Medicare reform, a reform package that will make the system modern, make sure our seniors have prescription drug coverage, better choices. I want to commend the Senate for moving the modernization bill forward. I look forward to them completing their work and getting a bill to my desk that I can sign. Modernizing Medicare will make the system better and will enable us to say to millions of seniors, we've kept our promise to America's seniors.

Thank you all.

NOTE: The President spoke at 4:34 p.m. at Peterson Air Force Base, prior to departure for the Bush Ranch in Crawford, TX. A tape was not available for verification of the content of these remarks.

Message on the Observance of Eid al-Fitr
November 24, 2003

I send greetings to Muslims celebrating Eid al-Fitr, the Festival of Breaking the Fast.

This festival marks the end of the month-long fast of Ramadan, the holiest period of the Islamic year. Eid al-Fitr is a time to give thanks to God for the blessings of renewed faith, to perform acts of charity, and to share traditional food and good wishes with family and friends. Islam is a religion that inspires its followers to lead lives based on justice, compassion, and personal responsibility.

During this joyful season, I encourage people of all faiths to reflect on our shared values: love of family, gratitude to God, a commitment to religious freedom, and respect for the diversity that adds to our Nation's strength. By working together to advance peace and mutual understanding, we help build a future of promise and compassion for all.

Laura joins me in sending our best wishes for a joyous celebration. Eid mubarek.

GEORGE W. BUSH

NOTE: An original was not available for verification of the content of this message.

Message to the Senate Transmitting the Japan-United States Treaty on Mutual Legal Assistance in Criminal Matters
November 24, 2003

To the Senate of the United States:

With a view to receiving the advice and consent of the Senate to ratification, I transmit herewith the Treaty Between the United States of America and Japan on Mutual Legal Assistance in Criminal Matters, signed at Washington on August 5, 2003. I transmit also, for the information of the Senate, a related exchange of notes and the report of the Department of State with respect to the Treaty.

The Treaty is one of a series of modern mutual legal assistance treaties negotiated by the United States in order to counter criminal activities more effectively. The Treaty should be an effective tool to assist in the investigation and prosecution of a wide variety of crimes. The Treaty is self-executing.

The Treaty provides for a broad range of cooperation in criminal matters. Mutual assistance available under the Treaty includes: taking testimony, statements, or items; examining persons, items, or places; locating or identifying persons, items, or places; providing items from governmental departments or agencies; inviting persons to testify in the requesting Party; transferring persons in custody for testimony or other purposes; assisting in proceedings related to forfeiture and immobilization of assets; and any other form of assistance permitted under the laws of the requested Party and agreed upon by the Central Authorities of the two Contracting Parties.

I recommend that the Senate give early and favorable consideration to the Treaty, and give its advice and consent to ratification.

GEORGE W. BUSH

The White House,
November 24, 2003.

Remarks at Spring Valley Hospital in Las Vegas, Nevada
November 25, 2003

Thank you for the warm welcome. It's great to be here in Las Vegas, the great State of Nevada. I'm sorry I don't get to spend the night here. [*Laughter*] They say the nightlife is pretty active. [*Laughter*] It's a great part of our country. Thanks for your welcome.

I also appreciate the Spring Valley Hospital Medical Center team for hosting us.

It's not easy to have the President of the United States come. It seems like the entourages are quite large these days. [*Laughter*] So I appreciate the hard work in facilitating my visit.

It's amazing that this facility is not only— is not yet 2 months old, yet it is providing a really good record of care and compassion, thanks to the good docs and nurses and CEOs and aides who work here. I want to thank you for caring about your fellow citizens with good, decent health care.

Today—speaking about good, decent health care—today we had a major victory to improve the health care system in America. The United States Senate has joined the House of Representatives in passing historic reform of Medicare that will strengthen the system, that will modernize the system, that will provide high-quality care for the seniors who live in America.

I want to thank and congratulate the Members of Congress for their hard work. You see, we have a responsibility in Washington, DC, to solve problems, not to pass them on. And today the United States Congress met its responsibility. We inherited a good Medicare system. It has worked, but it was becoming old and needed help. Because of the actions of the Congress, because of the actions of members of both political parties, the Medicare system will be modern, and it will be strong.

I appreciate Karla Perez for hosting us here. She had a very good visit about health care needs in this community and around our country. Karla is an impressive CEO and managing director, and I'm really glad she invited me here. I want to thank Alan Miller, Mike Marquez, and Dan McBride for their leadership as well.

I appreciate so very much your fine Governor, Kenny Guinn, for showing up today. Governor, it's great to see you. He's a close friend, as is Dema. The Governor and I both married very well. [*Laughter*] Laura sends her love to both of you. [*Laughter*]

Two Members of the United States Congress from Nevada are with us today, Congressman Jim Gibbons and Congressman Jon Porter. They supported this piece of legislation. They support a lot of good legislation. And I'm proud of your work, and I appreciate your courage in doing the right thing for America's seniors—by the way, not only the seniors today but those of us who are going to be seniors. I also want to welcome Trent Franks from the great

State of Arizona, friend, a man who also supported Medicare reform. He and his wife Josie are here to join us today, and I'm honored that you all would come over from Arizona to say hello.

I want to thank the Nevada attorney general for joining us, Brian Sandoval. I appreciate members of the statehouse for being here. I'm glad Darlene Ensign is with us, the Senator's good wife—for joining us. Most of all, I'm really glad you all are here, and thanks for letting me come by to say hello.

Today when I landed, I met Maria Konold-Soto. She's a—where is Maria? Oh, there's Maria, yes. What Maria does is she volunteers in your community on the Medical Reserve Corps. Perhaps you've heard about it. It is a chance to help our communities prepare for a potential emergency. Notice I said "volunteers." A lot of times people talk about the strength of the country in terms of our military might or the size of our wallets. The strength of America is the heart and souls of our fellow citizens who are willing to volunteer to make their communities a better place.

I know a lot of the docs here provide a lot of care for people who hurt. That's part of making America a compassionate place. Maria is part of making America a compassionate place. All of you who volunteer, I want to thank you very much for the job you do. If you're interested in being a patriotic American, love a neighbor just like you'd like to be loved yourself, and you'll make a significant contribution to our country.

This Nation's health care is great. We've got the best health care in the world, and we need to keep it that way. We've got a great health care system because of our docs—well trained, decent, caring people who practice medicine. We've got a great health care system because of our nurses who work hard to provide compassionate care. We've got the best research in the world. We're on the leading edge of change in America.

But we've got to keep the system vibrant. And we must keep it the best in the world, which we intend to do in Washington, DC. We started that by making sure our seniors have got a modern system. The Medicare system, first of all, is an essential commitment of the Federal Government. Our Federal Government has made a commitment to our seniors that we will provide them an up-to-date, decent health care system. It's a basic trust that has been upheld throughout the generations. And we're keeping that trust by making sure the system works, by making sure that our seniors are well treated.

In recent years, Medicare has not kept up with the advances of modern medicine. In other words, it hasn't met the trust that the Federal Government has promised to our seniors. Remember, when Medicare was passed in 1965, health care meant house calls and surgery and long hospital stays. And the system was designed to meet the health care delivery systems of the day.

Modern medicine today now includes preventative care, outpatient procedures, and at-home care. Many invasive surgeries are now unnecessary because of the new prescription drugs which are being developed. Many Americans have coverage for these new forms of health care, and that's positive, and we need to keep it that way. Yet seniors who rely exclusively on Medicare do not have the coverage for many of the new treatments and do not have coverage for prescription drugs. In other words, medicine changed, and Medicare didn't. And as of today, Medicare is changing.

Let me give you an example of the need for modernization. The health care providers here know these examples only too well. Medicare is willing to pay $28,000 for a hospital stay for ulcer surgery. But it won't pay the $500 for the anti-ulcer drugs that would keep the senior out of the hospital in the first place. Those examples—or that example, like many others, says to me we had a problem with the

Medicare system. It doesn't make any sense to pay the 28,000 at the end of the process but not the 500 up front to keep the 28,000 from happening in the first place.

Medicare should cover medications to keep our seniors out of the hospitals. The new bill does this. The important part of the reform is to recognize that medicine has changed. It will save our Government and the taxpayers money by providing prescription drugs early so we don't have to pay for it in long hospital stays or invasive surgeries.

Most seniors have got some form of prescription drug coverage from a private plan, and that's important. It's a fact of life here in America. Those plans, however, are becoming less available. We've got to make sure the private sector remains vibrant. The bill I'm about to describe to you does that.

Medicare was very slow to take advantage of new medical advances, besides prescription drugs. In other words, you had to go through a bureaucracy in order to get certain procedures covered. Bureaucracies don't move very quickly. They tend not to be very sympathetic organizations. They're not consumer-driven. They're process-driven. They're hidebound by rules and regulations. The docs here know what I'm talking about. You get to deal with bureaucracies. It must be a frustrating experience. Sometimes it's a frustrating experience to try to change bureaucracies.

The Medicare plan that I'm going to sign understands that a lack of competition meant that there was no real need to provide innovation. And so we're helping to change the system by giving seniors more options and more choices. See, Members of Congress have got choices. They get to choose from a health care plan, and it works quite well. The three Congressmen here would tell you they're probably pretty satisfied with the plan, if they've chosen to be in it. In other words, you get to choose.

This new Medicare bill I'm going to sign says seniors are plenty capable of making choices themselves. I used to say, "If it's good enough for the Members of Congress to have choice, it ought to be good enough for the seniors in America to have choice." Now they're going to have choice, thanks to the bill I'm going to sign.

It's going to take a while for this piece of legislation to kick in. It's going to take about 2 years to get all the reforms in place. But within 6 months of the law being signed, our seniors will start to see real savings in health care costs because seniors will be eligible for a drug discount card that will save them between 10 to 25 percent off their regular drug costs. And low-income seniors will receive up to $600 a year to help them with their drug costs in addition to the card. Their card will serve as a transition to the reforms that are inherent in the Medicare legislation.

When the full drug benefit arrives in 2006, all seniors will be eligible for prescription drug coverage for a monthly premium of about $35. The result is that for most seniors without coverage today, the Medicare drug plan will cut their annual drug bills roughly in half. That's positive news for America's seniors.

It's positive news for Joyce and J.C. Pearson. J.C.'s from Tennessee, by the way, and he reminded me that without Tennessee, Texas wouldn't have been much. [*Laughter*] He reminded me more than once, I might add. [*Laughter*] The Pearsons are—live on a tight budget. They spend about $300 a month for prescription drugs. Under the new Medicare reform bill passed today, they will save $1,800 a year. Joyce said they can use that money. She said it's going to come in handy in their retirement years.

Seniors with the highest drug bills will save the most. Seniors with the greatest need will get the most help. Low-income seniors will pay a reduced premium or no premium at all and lower or no copayments for their medications.

Under the new reforms, seniors, as I mentioned, will have choices. You see, some seniors don't want to choose, and I can understand that. In other words, people who are on Medicare just don't want to be confronted with a choice, and the system in the bill we passed recognizes that. You can understand why. The person is up in years, and it's pretty comfortable. They don't want to have to change. Change makes some people nervous, and we understand that. And so, should seniors want to stay in traditional Medicare and receive a prescription drug benefit, they will now be able to do so. That's one of the key reforms in the bill.

But other seniors want to choose. They want to be able to make a selection based upon their own particular needs. Some might want protection from high out-of-pocket medical expenses. Some might want expanded coverage for hospital stays. Some might want to be able to pick a plan that better meets their own individual needs. And under this law, choices will be readily available for our seniors, and that's an important part of reform. Because, you see, when seniors or any citizen makes a demand, the system responds. If there is a demand-driven system, it means the doctor-patient relationship is going to be more firm, and it means people will have better choices to meet their own particular needs. Some seniors may want the coverage that comes with managed care plans, Medicare+Choice.

Bob May is with us today. Bob is a World War II veteran. He is what I would call a solid citizen. Bob said, you know, his wife—who unfortunately passed away recently—and he sat down and analyzed, made a choice. He said, "We weighed the pros and the cons about what health care plan would fit our needs." I want you to hear that carefully. Bob and his wife sat down and said, "Here's the pluses and the minuses." In other words, he's plenty capable of making a choice. He didn't need the Government telling him how to choose what health care plan best met his needs. And so he chose Medicare+Choice, and it works, he said. Under the law,

Medicare+Choice will be strengthened, not starved. It is a viable option for our seniors around the country. In other words, people will have more control over their health care options, and health care plans will start competing for their business. And that's positive, positive for the consumers, positive for the seniors of America.

There are other important reforms in this bill. When seniors sign up for Medicare, they will get a complete health examination so that doctors can know their health needs from the start. We're finally beginning to focus on preventative care. It makes sense to include preventative care in any health care reforms. The health care providers here know that better than anybody.

The bill provides incentives for companies to keep the existing coverage they provide for senior retirees. There was some concern in Washington—a legitimate concern, as far as I'm concerned—that a Medicare reform plan would encourage employers to not do their responsibility to their former retirees. This bill addresses that. Two out of every three seniors is now covered by some form of private coverage, and the bill addressed the issue to make sure that that coverage is still a viable alternative in the marketplace.

Every American, old and young, will be able to have a health savings account. They will be able to put money aside tax-free to help their families with medical expenses. Medical savings accounts are important part of reform. Medical savings accounts trust the consumers, provides incentives for people to make wise choices, and helps to maintain the doctor-patient relationship.

This bill helps rural hospitals. This would not qualify as a rural hospital here. [*Laughter*] But rural hospitals need help to continue to serve our country. This bill sets fair reimbursement rates for doctors serving Medicare patients. This is a good bill, and I'm looking forward to signing it.

Last Saturday's vote in the House and today's vote in the Senate marks an historic moment, a bipartisan achievement that all Americans can be proud of. Year after year, the problems in Medicare system were studied and debated, and yet nothing was done. As a matter of fact, they used to call Medicare "Medi-scare" for people in the political process. Some said Medicare reform can never be done. For the sake of our seniors, we've gotten something done. We're acting. We acted on principle in Washington, DC. We'll provide new treatments and new choices. We'll get prescription drug coverage they deserve. We'll keep our commitment to Medicare to better the lives of the American seniors for generations to come.

I appreciate the hard work of the Members of the Congress. It's a tough bill. People worked hard on it. A lot of people searched their soul on this complex and important piece of legislation, but they stayed after it, stayed focused on the people. A lot of Members put politics aside, which we need to do in Washington, DC, when we're talking about the people's business.

I appreciate the seniors and the seniors' groups, such as the AARP, who lobbied hard on behalf of a modern Medicare system. People made their opinions known. They let the Members know where they stand. And it worked, and it helped. And I'm honored to put my signature on this historic piece of legislation.

Another topic of conversation came up at our roundtable discussion, and that was the effect of junk lawsuits on the delivery of health care in America and in Nevada. You see, one of the things we must work for is a health care system which is affordable and available. Junk lawsuits, the threat of junk lawsuits, drive up the cost of health care and run good docs out of the system.

It's important for our fellow citizens to understand the effect of junk lawsuits. You see, docs who are threatened and are constantly sued, even though their practice is a good, strong, excellent practice, resort to what's called defensive medicine. They order procedures and tests that may not be needed but are—provide protection in the court of law. You see, if you think a lawyer is simply fishing for a rich settlement, is constantly looking over your shoulder, you'll end up practicing what's called defensive medicine. Docs are afraid to give their patients certain advice. In other words, the doctor-patient relationship is disrupted for fear that that advice will be used against them in the court of law. This problem not only affects the doctors; it affects the patients as well. See, it's running up the cost of medicine. It affects a person's ability to deliver good, quality health care.

Donna Miller is an ob-gyn specialist here in Vegas. Dr. Miller has seen her premiums go up about $28,000 last year, to about $72,000 this year. She thinks they're headed to about $100,000 this year. You know what I'm talking about, about premium increases. It's a system that reflects lawsuit after lawsuit after lawsuit. And Dr. Miller's patients pay the price. These junk lawsuits are driving up the cost of medicine.

Here's what she says. She says, "You got into medicine to take care of people and to spend time with your patients. With the premiums going up the way they are, you can't do that." She told me about the colleagues who have left Nevada. I remember when your trauma center shut down here. It made national news. It's a clear sign that you've got an issue here that must be dealt with, because the people who are affected are the people of Nevada.

It means that women who want to have their babies delivered in Nevada are having a hard time finding a doc; that's what it means. And I met Jill Forte today, a proud mother. She found out she was pregnant with her second child. She called her doctor. The doctor told her that because of insurance costs, she could no longer deliver her baby. So she started calling around. She was told the same thing—I think she told me, about five different docs. She considered going to California. Fortunately, she was able to make a connection through a

friend for a local doc to take her case. But you see—and let me tell you what she said. She said she was in total shock. She didn't know what was going on until it happened.

Looking for a doctor, worried about finding a doctor when you're pregnant, is a stress that is an unnecessary stress. It's a stress caused by frivolous and junk lawsuits. It doesn't make any sense to have a society that sues so often that expectant mothers are worried about finding a doctor. We've got to do something about this in America.

There's a cost to the Federal Government because of the frivolous and junk lawsuits and the defensive practice of medicine. It is estimated that the defensive practice of medicine raises the Federal budget by $28 billion a year. You see it from Medicare, Medicaid, veterans' health benefits, for example. The junk lawsuits affect our budget. Therefore, I view this as a national problem which requires a national solution. We need a system where patients who are harmed have their day in court, where they can collect damages to cover their injuries or recovery or rehabilitation and loss of income. If you've been harmed by a bad doc, you deserve your day in court. Frivolous lawsuits, by the way, that clog the courts make it very difficult for someone with a legitimate claim to get into the court. When patients can prove they were harmed by a doctor's egregious behavior, they should be able to collect reasonable punitive damages.

There needs to be a $250,000 cap on noneconomic damages. I laid out this proposal to the Congress. The House of Representatives responded in a positive way, and I want to thank the Members here for voting the right way. The bill is stuck in the Senate. You need to contact a Senator in the State of Nevada and let them know you're interested in national medical liability reform. The Senators must understand that nobody in America has ever been healed by a frivolous lawsuit. For the sake of the patients in this State and for the doctors in this State and for the patients and docs around the country, we need medical liability reform now. And the Members of the Senate must understand, this is a compelling national issue, and I will keep it on the front burner until we get the problem solved.

Finally, yesterday I was in Fort Carson, Colorado, where I had the honor of addressing men and women who wear the Nation's uniform. I just want to share with you right quick our country's foreign policy. In a nutshell, it's "We'll do everything we can to keep America secure." I will not forget the lessons of September the 11th, 2001. My duty as the President, obviously, is to deal with domestic issues and to tackle tough problems. My duty as your President as well is to keep this country secure. And I had the honor of meeting with men and women who wear the Nation's uniform who are doing just that.

We'll protect our homeland as best as we possibly can. But the best way to protect the homeland is to chase the killers down one at a time and bring them to justice, which is exactly what we intend to do.

Freedom equals peace, as far as I'm concerned. And when you hear us working for freedom in troubled parts of the world, you've just got to know it will lead to peace. We'll deal with the short-term security needs by staying on the offensive. We'll help our children grow up in a free society by bringing freedom to parts of the world that desperately need freedom. Our soldiers—as we head into Thanksgiving, we

need to give thanks to our soldiers for their sacrifice, for the honor they bring to our country, for the service they render by bringing freedom to troubled parts of the world. You see, we're bringing freedom in the heart of the Middle East.

Free countries don't develop weapons of mass destruction. Free countries don't attack their neighbors. Free countries listen to the hopes and aspirations of the people who live in those countries. No, America also believes that freedom is not America's gift to the world; freedom is the Almighty's gift to every person who lives in this world. And this Nation will stay the course to bring democracy and freedom to Afghanistan and Iraq. And by doing so, we will not only help the long-suffering people in those countries; we will make America more secure and the world more peaceful.

Thank you for letting me come today. May God bless you all, and may God bless America.

NOTE: The President spoke at 10:32 a.m. In his remarks, he referred to Karla Perez, chief executive officer and managing director, and S. Daniel McBride, chief of staff, Spring Valley Hospital; Alan B. Miller, president and chief executive officer, and Michael Marquez, vice president of acute care, Universal Health Services; Gov. Kenny C. Guinn of Nevada and his wife, Dema; Josephine Franks, wife of Representative Trent Franks; and Darlene Ensign, wife of Senator John Ensign of Nevada. The Office of the Press Secretary also released a Spanish language transcript of these remarks.

Remarks at a Bush-Cheney Luncheon in Las Vegas
November 25, 2003

Thanks for coming. Go ahead and please be seated. I appreciate you coming. Thanks for the warm welcome. It's great to be in one of America's greatest cities, Las Vegas.

The Governor was saying, "Don't you want to spend a little time here, a little quality time?" And I said, "Well, I'm on Government pay"—[*laughter*]—if you know what

I mean. But this is a dynamic part of our country. The growth is amazing. The spirit is great. It's such an honor to be here. We did really well in the year 2000 here in Nevada. We're going to do great in 2004 too.

I appreciate you coming. As the Governor said, this is a successful fundraiser. I'll tell you what we're doing: We're laying the foundation for what is going to be a great national victory in November 2004. I'm loosening up. I'm getting ready. But politics will come in its own time. See, I've got a job to do. I want you to tell your fellow citizens, this President is going to work on behalf of everybody to keep this country safe and secure, prosperous and free.

I appreciate Kenny, who's a good friend, and Dema. They've been friends of Laura and mine for a while. We both married above ourselves. [*Laughter*] Dema is doing a great job as the first lady of this State. Laura is doing a great job as the First Lady of our country. She sends her best. I left her this morning in Crawford. We went for about a 3½ mile walk together across the countryside, had a little time to visit outside the bubble in Washington, DC, and we're going to spend Thanksgiving together. She's a great wife, a wonderful mother, and I'm really proud of the tone she has set and the job she's doing as our Nation's First Lady.

Darlene Ensign is here. I'm proud to call John Ensign, Senator John Ensign, a friend and an ally. I appreciate so very much members from the congressional delegation who are here. You've sent some fine people from Nevada to Washington, DC, starting with Congressman Jim Gibbons. Jim, I thank you, appreciate you. Dawn is with him. Congressman Jon Porter, appreciate you coming, Jon. Laurie is with Jon.

Nevada is such a powerful attraction for people around the country that you've been able to attract some people from the United States House of Representatives who aren't from your great State. [*Laughter*] Trent Franks and Josie Franks came over from the State of Arizona. I want to thank Congressman Franks for joining us today. Frank LoBiondo from New Jersey is with us. I'm honored that Frank is with us. Thank you for coming, Frank. I told old Frank, I said, "Gosh, it's great to see you. Thanks for coming to see me." He said, "I didn't come to see you." [*Laughter*] "I came to be with my fiancee, Tina." [*Laughter*] Happens to live here in Las Vegas.

I'm honored that the Lieutenant Governor is here, Lorrie Hunt—Lorraine Hunt. I appreciate you coming, Lorraine. The chairman of the campaign, chairman of the Bush-Cheney '04 campaign, is your great attorney general, Brian Sandoval. Thanks for coming, Brian. I'm honored that Secretary of State Dean Heller is with us today. Dean, thank you for coming. I appreciate you being here. State Controller Kathy Augustine is with us. Thank you for coming, Kathy. Got a lot of other State and local officials. I'm grateful you're here. I appreciate your service to your State and to your county and to your city.

I'm honored that my friend Mercer Reynolds, who's the national finance chairman, is with us. He's from Cincinnati, Ohio. He's a business person taking time out of his life to help make sure this campaign is adequately funded. He's doing a really good job, thanks to you all. Larry and Camille Ruvo have done—a lot to do with this event. I'm honored you all are here. Thank you. Appreciate you, Larry.

I want to thank all the grassroots activists who are here with us today. See, it's important to make sure that we're well funded. It's also important to make sure people get on the phones and put up the signs and go to the coffee shops and put out the word that this is an optimistic and hopeful administration who's getting the job done for the American people.

In the last 3 years, our Nation has acted decisively to confront great challenges. I came to this office to solve problems instead of passing them on to future Presidents and future generations. I came to seize opportunities instead of letting them slip away. This administration is meeting the tests of our time.

Declare—terrorists declared war on the United States of America, and war is what they got. We've captured or killed many of the key leaders of the Al Qaida network, and the rest of them know we're on their trail. In Afghanistan and Iraq, we gave ultimatums to terror regimes. Those regimes chose defiance, and those regimes are no more. Fifty million people in those two countries once lived under tyranny, and now they live in freedom.

Three years ago, our military was not receiving the resources it needed, and morale was beginning to suffer. So we increased the defense budgets to prepare for the threats of a new era, and today, no one in the world can question the skill and the strength and the spirit of the United States military.

Three years ago, this economy of ours was in trouble, and a recession was beginning. And then our country was attacked, and we had scandals in corporate America as well as the war to make America more secure and the world more peaceful. All of that affected the people's confidence, but we acted. We passed tough new laws to hold corporate criminals to account. And to get this economy going again, I have twice led the United States Congress to pass historic tax relief for the American people.

I believe that when Americans have more take-home pay to spend, to save, or invest, the whole economy grows, and people are more likely to find a job. And so we're returning more money to the people, returning money to help them raise their families. We've reduced taxes on dividends and capital gains to encourage investment. We've given small businesses incentives to expand and to hire new people. With all these actions, we're laying the foundation

for greater prosperity and more jobs across America, so that every single person has a chance to realize the American Dream.

This economy of ours is reacting to our policy. The American economy is strong, and it is getting stronger. The third quarter figures were just revised upward to 8.2 percent, the fastest pace in nearly 20 years. Productivity is high. Business investment is rising. Housing construction is strong. The job base is expanding. The tax relief we passed is working.

Three years ago there was a lot of talk about education reform, but there wasn't much action. So I acted. I called for and the Congress passed the No Child Left Behind Act. With a solid bipartisan majority, we delivered the most dramatic education reforms in a generation. We're now bringing high standards and strong accountability measures to every public school in America. We've increased the education budgets at the Federal level. But for the first time in our Nation's history, we now expect results in return for the increased funding. This administration is challenging the soft bigotry of low expectations. We're raising the bar. We're raising the standards, because we believe every child can learn, and we expect every school to teach, so not one single child is left behind in America.

We reorganized this Government of ours to create the Department of Homeland Security, safeguard the borders and ports of America, and to better protect the American people. We passed trade promotion authority to open up new markets for our country's entrepreneurs and farmers and ranchers. We passed budget agreements to bring much needed spending discipline to Washington, DC. On issue after issue, this administration has acted on principle, has kept its word, and has made progress for the American people.

The United States Congress deserves a lot of the credit. I appreciate working with Speaker Denny Hastert, Senate Majority

Leader Bill Frist, the good folks from Nevada who are working with this administration. You see, what we're doing in Washington, DC, is we're trying to change the tone of the Nation's Capital. There's too much needless backbiting and endless politics. Instead of focusing on political process, we're focusing on the people's business by focusing on results.

And those are the kind of people I've assembled in my administration. I've put together one of the greatest teams ever to serve the American people. We've got people from all walks of life, strong, dedicated, honorable Americans who have come to Washington, DC, to serve the people of this country. Our country has had no finer Vice President than Dick Cheney. Mother may have a different opinion. [*Laughter*]

In 3 years, we have come far, but our work is only beginning. I've set great goals worthy of this great Nation. First, America is committed to expanding the realm of freedom and peace for our own security and for the benefit of the world. And second, in our own country, we must work for a society of prosperity and compassion so that every citizen has a chance to work and to succeed and to realize the promise of America.

It is clear that the future of freedom and peace depend on the actions of America. This Nation is freedom's home and freedom's defender. We welcome this charge of history, and we are keeping it. The war on terror continues. The enemies of freedom are not idle, and neither are we. This country will not rest; we will not tire; we will not stop until this danger to civilization is removed.

We are confronting that danger in Iraq, where Saddam holdouts and foreign terrorists are desperately trying to throw Iraq into chaos by attacking coalition forces and aid workers and innocent Iraqi citizens. You see, they know that the advance of freedom in Iraq would be a major defeat for their cause of terror. A collection of killers is trying to shake the will of the United States. The United States of America will never be intimidated by a bunch of thugs. We're on the offensive. We're aggressively striking the terrorists in Iraq. We will defeat them there so we do not have to face them in our own country.

Other nations are helping. They're helping to build a free country, because they understand a free Iraq will make us all more secure. We're standing with the Iraqi people as they assume more of their own defense and move toward self-government. These are not easy tasks, but they are essential tasks. The United States of America will finish what we have begun, and we will win this essential victory in the war on terror.

Our greatest security comes from the advance of human liberty, because free nations do not support terror. Free nations do not attack their neighbors. Free nations do not threaten the world with weapons of mass terror. Americans believe that freedom is the deepest need and hope of every human heart. We believe that freedom is the future of every nation. And we know that freedom is not America's gift to the world; freedom is the Almighty's—God's gift to every person who lives in the world.

Also understand that unprecedented influence brings tremendous responsibilities. We have duties in this world, and when we see disease and starvation and hopeless poverty, we will not turn away. On the continent of Africa, America is now committed to bringing the healing power of medicine to millions of men and women and children suffering from AIDS. This great, strong, compassionate land is leading the world in this incredibly important work of human rescue.

We've got challenges here at home as well, and we're equal to those challenges. I just mentioned some nice economic numbers, but we're going to stay focused on a progrowth economic agenda until everyone who wants to work can find a job. And we're keeping our commitment to America's seniors. Today the United States

Senate joined the House of Representatives and passed strong reform that will modernize and strengthen Medicare.

For years, seniors have called for a modern Medicare system that provides coverage for prescription drugs and more health care choices. For years, Washington simply listened and did nothing. Finally, the House and the Senate have acted. This historic legislation is the greatest improvement in senior health care coverage since the enactment of Medicare in 1965. And I look forward to signing this important piece of legislation.

For the sake of our health care system, we need to cut down on the frivolous lawsuits which increase the cost of medicine. People who have been harmed by a bad doctor deserve their day in court, yet the system should not reward lawyers who are simply fishing for a rich settlement. Frivolous lawsuits drive up the cost of health care, and they therefore affect the Federal budget. Medical liability reform is a national issue that requires a national solution. I have proposed such a solution. I proposed such a solution, and the U.S. House of Representatives, thanks to the Members here, voted for medical liability reform. The bill is stuck in the Senate. It is time for your Senator to understand that no one has ever been healed by a frivolous lawsuit. We need medical liability reform now.

I have a responsibility as the President to make sure the judicial system runs well, and I have met that duty. I have nominated superb men and women for the Federal courts, people who will interpret the law, not legislate from the bench. Some Members of the Senate are trying to keep my nominees off the bench by blocking up-or-down votes. Every judicial nominee deserves a fair hearing and an up-or-down vote on the Senate floor. It is time for some of the Members of the United States Senate to stop playing politics with American justice.

The Congress needs to complete work on a comprehensive energy plan. Our Nation must promote energy efficiency and conservation. We must work to develop cleaner technologies. We must explore for energy in environmentally sensitive ways. For the sake of our economic security and for the sake of national security, this country must become less dependent on foreign sources of energy.

A strong and prosperous nation must also be a compassionate nation. I'm going to continue to advance our agenda of compassionate conservatism, which means we'll apply the best and most innovative ideas to the task of helping our fellow citizens in need. There's still millions of men and women who want to end their dependence on Government and become independent through hard work. The Congress must work with the administration to continue to build on the success of welfare reform, to bring work and dignity into the lives of more of our citizens.

The Congress should complete the "Citizen Service Act" so more Americans can serve their communities and our country. Both Houses should reach agreement on my Faith-Based Initiative to support the armies of compassion that are mentoring our children and caring for the homeless and offering hope to the addicted. One of the great strengths of our country, the people of faith from all religions—people have heard a universal call to help somebody in need. This Government of ours must not fear faith, but it must welcome the good works of our faith-based institutions as we reach out as a society to heal broken hearts, to help the lonely, to say to somebody who wonders about the future of this country, "I love you."

A compassionate society must also promote opportunity for all of us, and that means the independence and dignity that come from ownership. You see, this administration is working for and will constantly strive to promote an ownership society in America. We want more people owning their own home. We've got a minority homeownership gap in America. I presented a plan to Congress to close that gap. We want people owning and managing their own retirement accounts, owning and managing their own health care accounts. We want more people owning their own small business in America, because we understand that when a person owns something, he or she has a vital stake in the future of our country.

A compassionate society is one in which people respect one another and take responsibility for the decisions they make in life. The culture of America is changing from one that has said, "If it feels good, do it," and "If you've got a problem, blame somebody else," to one in which each of us understands we're responsible for the decisions we make in life. If you're fortunate enough to be a mother or a father, you're responsible for loving your child with all your heart. If you're worried about the quality of the education in the community in which you live, you're responsible for doing something about it. If you're a CEO in corporate America, you are responsible for telling the truth to your shareholders and your employees. And in a responsibility society, each of us is responsible for loving our neighbor just like we'd like to be loved ourself.

The culture of service and responsibility is strong in this country. It's truly one of the strengths of America. You know, I started what's called the USA Freedom Corps to encourage Americans to extend a compassionate hand to neighbors in need, and the response has been strong. A lot of people are interested in helping, helping our country by helping somebody who hurts. Our charities are strong, and thank you for helping them. Our faith-based organizations are vibrant.

Policemen and firefighters and people who wear this country's uniform are reminding us what it means to sacrifice for something greater than ourself in life. Once again, the children of America believe in heroes, because they see them every day. In these challenging times, the world has seen the resolve and the courage of America. And I've been privileged to see the compassion and the character of the American people.

All the tests of the last 3 years have come to the right nation. We're a strong country, and we use that strength to defend the peace. We're an optimistic country, confident in ourselves and in ideals bigger than ourselves. Abroad, we seek to lift up whole nations by spreading freedom. At home, we seek to lift up lives by spreading opportunity to every corner of America. This is the work that history has set before us. We welcome it, and we know that for our country, the best days lie ahead.

Thank you for coming, and may God bless America. Thank you all.

NOTE: The President spoke at 12:20 p.m. at the Venetian Resort Hotel and Casino. In his remarks, he referred to Gov. Kenny C. Guinn of Nevada and his wife, Dema; Darlene Ensign, wife of Senator John Ensign; Dawn Gibbons, wife of Representative Jim Gibbons; Laurie Porter, wife of Representative Jon Porter; Josephine Franks, wife of Representative Trent Franks; Brian Sandoval, Nevada campaign chairman, Mercer Reynolds, national finance chairman, and Larry Ruvo, Nevada finance chairman, Bush-Cheney '04, Inc.; and Mr. Ruvo's wife, Camille.

Remarks at the Los Olivos Senior Center in Phoenix, Arizona
November 25, 2003

Thanks for coming. I'm thrilled to be at Los Olivos Center. You're kind to have me. And I'm here to talk about some issues facing our Nation, probably an issue you'd like to hear about, which is Medicare. I think you probably have heard of Medicare. [*Laughter*] I think you probably recognize that Medicare needs to be modernized and reformed so it works better for you.

The United States House of Representatives, the United States Senate recently took historic action to modernize and to strengthen the Medicare system so it works for you. I'm here to tell you, I look forward to signing a good piece of legislation which says that our country will keep our commitment to today's seniors and prepare to receive tomorrow's seniors into Medicare— people like me—[*laughter*]—with a system that's modern and strong.

You know, our job in Washington is to tackle problems when we see them, not to pass them on to future Congresses or future Presidents or future generations. I want to thank the Members of Congress for taking on this very difficult issue. I appreciate them for their hard work. Medicare has worked for many people. It got a little old. It got a little tired. It needed to be changed. We changed it, and the system is better for it.

The Members of Congress who are here, I appreciate them coming. Senator Jon Kyl is one of the fine Members of the United States Senate. Congressman Rick Renzi, he's from the north; Trent Franks is from the north—Congressman Franks, and Josie, his wife, is with him; J.D. Hayworth—I don't know if you've ever heard of J.D., but—[*applause*]. They're fixing to call J.D. "Slim," "Slim" Hayworth. [*Laughter*] Jeff Flake is with us. Jeff, I'm honored you're here. Congressman Jim Kolbe from Tucson, Arizona, is with us. I'm honored. These are all fine Members of the United States

Congress. I've enjoyed working with them all. They're good, honest men who care deeply about the citizens of the State of Arizona.

I appreciate Jan Brewer, who is the secretary of state of the great State of Arizona, with us. Your mayor is with us, Skip Rimsza. I'm honored, Mr. Mayor, that you're here. My only advice to the mayor is to make sure you fill the potholes. [*Laughter*] He's been doing a great job of filling the potholes for the people of Phoenix, Arizona. It's a—I know he's fixing to leave office, but I—the people of this city owe him a debt of gratitude for nearly 10 years of great service, great honest public service.

I want to thank Cindy McCabe, who is the executive director of this fine center. I really appreciate you and your staff putting on this event. It's not easy to have the President come. You know, these entourages are quite big—[*laughter*]—a lot of people roaming around when the President is here. But the center has done a fabulous job of welcoming us, and I'm really glad I came.

Mark McClellan is with me. He's a Texan, kind of like I am. And he's the Commissioner of the Food and Drug Administration, the FDA. He's got a huge responsibility, and he's doing a really good job. I appreciate you coming, Commissioner. I'm honored you're here.

You know, a lot of times people talk about the strength of America, and they think in terms of the number of airplanes we might have or, you know, look, the number of soldiers in uniform or the size of our wallets, but that's really not the strength of our country. The strength of America is the hearts and souls of the American people. You think about it. That's what makes this country incredibly strong. It's the fact that people are willing to reach out to a neighbor in need. I call them soldiers in the army of compassion. That's the most important army here in America, in many ways, when you think about it.

I met a soldier. She's probably a general, although she would call herself a simple private. That would be Maybelle Harris. Maybelle, where are you? There she is, Maybelle. She's a Sunshine Lady for AARP. She sends cards to people who are celebrating and/or mourning the loss of a loved one. In other words, she understands that there's a special responsibility for those of us who are fortunate in this country to help people who might have a hurt in their heart.

Maybelle is, since '82—has been a member of the Gold Star Wives club. This is an organization dedicated to assisting widows of military servicemen. Maybelle, I want to thank you for your compassion. I want to thank you for the example you have set. You make it clear that America can change, one heart, one soul, one conscience at a time. And you set a fine example for—particularly people coming up here in America—that in order to be a solid citizen, love your neighbor just like you'd like to be loved yourself. I appreciate your example, Maybelle.

We've got the world's greatest health care system. I hope you understand that. I say that with certainty. We've got the best docs in the world. We've got fabulous nurses. We've got wonderful facilities for people to go to. We've got wonderful research in America. I mean, if you really think about the research we do in this country, the lifesaving research, the pharmaceutical drugs that change people's lives in a positive way, it is—you understand when I say we've got the best health care system in the world.

And we need to keep it that way. We need to make sure it continues to be the best health care system in the world. A lot of that has to do with honoring our obligation to our seniors and to make sure the Medicare system works well. Some it

has to do with making sure that we don't have too many lawsuits in our society, which runs good doctors out of practice and runs up the cost of medicine, that makes it hard for people to get good health care.

I believe we need medical liability reform at the Federal level, medical liability reform which will say, "If you get harmed by a bad doctor, you ought to have your day in court." Of course you ought to be able to sue. But we've got to get rid of these frivolous lawsuits that cause our docs to practice defensive medicine, which runs up your cost of medicine and runs some doctors out of practice. This country needs national medical liability reform.

I want to thank Kyl and the Members of the House for supporting these measures. We got a good bill out of the House. It's stuck in the Senate. [*Laughter*] Some Members of the Senate must understand— and by the way, your Senators don't need this message, but some—maybe in some neighboring States they need it. No one has ever been healed by a frivolous lawsuit in our society. For the sake of good health care, for the sake of keeping our docs in practice, and for the sake of making sure our customers, the patients of America, have health care that's available and affordable, we need medical liability reform at the Federal level.

We need to make sure we've got a Medicare system that works. It's first important to recognize that Medicare is a basic trust between our Federal Government and our citizens. The Federal Government said, starting in 1965, this is our responsibility to make sure our seniors get a health care system that works. And therefore, we have a Federal responsibility to make sure that the health care system is the best we can possibly come up with through law for our seniors.

Part of making sure American health care works is to make sure Medicare is modern, and that's what the bill I am going to sign does. It changes the Medicare system, which needed to be changed. Medicare has not kept up with the advances of modern medicine. That's a fact. And we have a choice in Washington to ignore that fact or to deal with that fact.

When Medicare was passed in '65, health care meant house calls, surgery, and long hospital stays. And that's how the Medicare system was designed, to deal with that type of medicine. Medicine has changed. Modern medicine now means preventative care, which is not a part of Medicare, outpatient procedures, at-home care. In other words, medicine changed. Invasive surgeries are now unnecessary because of miraculous new prescription drugs that have been developed. Think about how much medicine changed since 1965. Medicare didn't change with it.

You know, most Americans have coverage for new forms of health care. That's the fact. But seniors who rely exclusively on Medicare do not, and that's why we needed to change the system. Medicine changed. Medicare hadn't. The Congress dealt with it, and now we can say Medicare is modern. And that's important change for the health care and for quality of life for our citizens.

I'm sure you've heard some question the need to change the system. I will give you an example of why we needed to change it. It's a clear example of why we need to change it. Medicare will pay $28,000 for a needed hospital stay for ulcer surgery. Yet it will not pay for the $500 for the anti-ulcer drugs that would keep the senior out of the hospital in the first place. Now, that doesn't make any sense to me. See, we'll pay the $28,000, but we won't pay the $500 to keep from having to pay the $28,000 in the first place, see. We needed to change the system. Medicare ought to cover medications that will keep our seniors from getting sick in the first place. And yet it doesn't for those who rely exclusively on Medicare.

Medicare was not quick to change as medicine changed. After all, there was a bureaucracy that had to make the decisions. Bureaucracies don't move very fast; they're slow. Bureaucracies are cumbersome. Many times, it took a law from the Congress to change what was covered under Medicare, and getting laws out of Congress sometimes aren't easy either. It's a cumbersome process. It's not a very good system. Private plans were able to adjust quickly. Private plans were able to meet a consumer's demand. Medicare was stuck, see. It just wouldn't change.

And so one of the things we've done in this new bill and this new system is we recognize that seniors are plenty capable of making choices, that a senior is able to choose. A senior is plenty capable of being able to say, "Here are the pros and cons of these very plans, and I want to take this plan that matches my needs."

One way to get Medicare to change is to give seniors choices. See, Congress has got choices. If you've got a health care plan for the Congress, you can say, "I like this plan," or "I like that plan," or "I might want this." But in Medicare, the old Medicare system, you didn't have that choice. And therefore, the delivery of certain procedures and technologies were slow in coming, and that's not right. The system was stuck in the past, and we needed to do something about it.

And our job in Washington is to solve problems, not pass them on. And that's what we did. This is a good piece of legislation, important reform. It will take about 2 years to get the reforms in place. It's a complex—listen, when you change something that's been in effect since 1965 by legislation, it's—there's a lot of print, a lot of pages. It was a hard piece of work, don't get me wrong. And so it's going to—there's going to be a transition period.

But Congress wisely said, "We've got to do something during the transition period," and what that is, is that seniors will be given a health care card, a prescription drug card that you'll be able to use and be able to get a discount of up to 10 to

25 percent on the drugs you now currently take. That's a positive development. You will get a card within 6 months, a discount card that will allow you to take it to where you're buying your drugs, and you'll get a discount. Plus, if you're a low-income senior, you'll get $600 a year as a credit on that card to help you buy drugs.

Congress was wise in helping with the transition. Congress was smart to enable people to better afford prescription drugs, since prescription drugs is the newest form of medicine relative to the past. When the full drug benefit arises in 2006, all seniors will be eligible for prescription drug coverage for a monthly premium of about $35. The result is that for most seniors without coverage today, the Medicare drug plan will cut their annual drug bills roughly in half. That's positive for our seniors who are relying upon prescription drugs. Seniors with the highest drug bills, of course, will save the most. Seniors with the greatest need will get the most help.

Low-income seniors will pay a reduced premium or no premium at all and lower or no copayments for their medicines. Congress wisely said, "We want to help the lowest-of-income seniors have a modern Medicare system with no premium and no copayments in certain cases." And I appreciate Congress for the compassion.

John Bajusz is with us. He's on the stage. I just had a—by the way, some of these people here and I had a wonderful visit about their current desires and needs and frustrations and worries about their status, particularly with health care. John has high prescription drug costs. He's on a Medicare HMO that provides about $100 in drug coverage a month. But he spends about $500 to $600 a month. That probably sounds familiar to some of you all. You're on a program that helps a little bit. Under the law that I'm going to sign, he will save up to about $2,000 a year in his drug costs. That helps John, at least that's what John told me. [*Laughter*] I take his word for it.

See, we're helping John. We're helping John with a modern Medicare system. He's out of pocket $500 to $600 a month. If you say he spends 6 and nets 100, it's about $500 a month. He's going to save $2,000. That will come in plenty handy. There's a lot of Johns around America who this bill will help in a very positive way.

Under the new reforms, as I told you, seniors will have choices. That's an important part of the bill. We want you to have choices. Earlier today I was in Las Vegas, and I met with a couple. The man said, "You know, my wife and I, before we chose our Medicare+Choice plan"—maybe some of you are on that plan—"before we chose that plan, we weighed out the pros and the cons. I listed the pros and the cons for a variety of policies, and we picked Medicare+Choice." My point to you is, is that he spent a lot of time trying to figure out what was best for him and his wife. I'm sure some of you do that as well. That's what we want. We want people to be able to have that choice.

Now, I fully understand some on Medicare don't want to choose at all. Some people that are on the current system like where they are, and they're frightened by change. And that's realistic. That's reasonable. I can understand that. And so could the Congress. And so we said that if you want to stay on Medicare, you can, traditional Medicare. But now we'll have a prescription drug benefit for the first time. And that's important. It's important to recognize that change sometimes isn't a part of somebody's future.

But a lot of people want to choose. And choice is important. See, some people will want expanded coverage for hospital stays or protection against high out-of-pocket medical expenses. People ought to be able to pick a plan. And when people pick a plan and they start choice, then it's amazing what happens. The plans start meeting the needs of the consumer, not the whims of somebody in Washington, DC, who gets to make the decision for you. That's an important part of this bill. This bill introduces choice for our seniors.

I met with the Weavers today, Glenn and Marjorie, from Sun City. They are on Medicare+Choice. They like the plan. See, they picked it out. They said, "This plan meets our needs." They want to stay on it. The Government was starving Medicare+Choice for awhile. One of the positive aspects about the bill I'm going to sign funds Medicare+Choice so people like the Weavers have got this plan available for them.

I met with Dick and Willa Key. They were here. They are not retired. They are near retired. They want prescription drug coverage. They want choices. See, they like the way this bill is modeled, because their view is—and I share this view—the more choices available for our American citizens, the more likely it is the health care system will meet their needs, and this bill provides that. Make no mistake about it, it recognizes that the decisionmaker in this process should be you, the American consumer.

There are other reforms I want to mention briefly. Under the new law, when seniors sign up for Medicare, they will get a complete health examination so doctors can know their health needs right from the start. That was very practical by Congress to do that. It seems like to make sense to me that it's very important to diagnose problems early so you can solve them. And so Medicare now, for the first time, will have a complete health examination available for people who sign up. There's obviously an emphasis on preventative care, and that's important.

The bill provides incentives for companies to keep existing coverage for their retirees. I'm sure some of you have worked hard and worked for a private concern, and you've got a health care plan now. And the bill makes sure that that's a health care plan is still available for you, as best as we possibly can. We don't want people saying, "Well, gosh, the Federal Government

has now modernized Medicare; we don't have an obligation any more. Go to the Government." So Congress did a good job of addressing this issue, and I appreciate that.

Every American, old and young, will be able to have what's called a health savings account. That makes a lot of sense. People ought to be able to put money aside tax-free to help their families with medical expenses, not only current medical expenses but future medical expenses. The health savings accounts will be set up to encourage people to choose healthy lifestyle choices. When you've got your own money out there for your health care that you can see on a daily basis, all of a sudden, you start making better choices with your life.

And these health savings accounts are not only important for seniors, but they're also important for younger workers as well to be able to utilize. Congress wisely put these in place. Health savings accounts not only will encourage people to make right choices but will make—will help maintain the doctor-patient relationship, which is a vital part of a effective and excellent health care system.

The bill helps rural hospitals. Hospitals in Phoenix don't qualify as rural—[laughter]—but some of these Congressmen represent rural hospitals. And this bill wisely helps them continue to be a vital part—to serve the vital part of our country, which is the good folks living in rural America. The bill sets up fair reimbursement rates for doctors serving Medicare patients. This is a good bill, is what I'm telling you. It's an historic achievement. It's a bipartisan achievement.

See, year after year, the problems in the Medicare system were studied and debated, and then nothing ever got done. As a matter of fact, Medicare in the political parlance wasn't "Medicare"; it's called "Mediscare." [Laughter] People were scared to talk about Medicare for fear of a political backlash. And so the problems just festered, and the system got out of date, and people weren't getting the health care that they deserved. And the Federal Government was not fulfilling its obligation to our seniors, and that was wrong.

And so we moved. We moved in spite of the fact that some up there in Washington said that nothing could get done, that it was impossible to make reforms. But we acted. And we acted on some solid principles, providing new treatments and choices for our seniors, provide prescription drug coverage, keep the commitment of Medicare to better the lives of America's seniors for not only this generation but generations to come.

That's what we're doing in Washington, DC, and it was hard work. It really was. It was a lot of debate and sharp elbows and a lot of political dialog. But the Members focused on the most important job of all, and that was working for the people, working to make sure that we fulfilled our promise. I'm honored to sign this bill. I'm looking forward to it. It's a historic piece of legislation. It wasn't perfect, but I haven't found a piece of legislation that's perfect yet. [*Laughter*] But we're improving the system, and I can say to the Members, "Job well done."

I also want to talk a little bit about our national defense. My job is to address problems at home, whether it be the economy or health care, whether it be medical liability reform, and to work with the Congress to get things done. My job as well is to protect the American people. It's a solemn responsibility, and I accept it. And I want to thank the Members of Congress for joining me in this important task. See, I'm not going to forget the lessons of September the 11th, 2001. Our life changed that day, didn't it? It really did.

When we were growing up—when old Senator Kyl and I were growing up, we used to think oceans could protect us. We used to think America could pick or choose where we—how to deal with a gathering threat. You know, if we saw a threat here, we may choose to deal with it or ignore

it, because we felt pretty safe here at home. We felt like the enemy could never get to us. They tried on—they hit us pretty hard on Pearl Harbor, but kind of—in our own mind, if the truth be known, we thought that it isn't going to happen again.

And September the 11th, 2001, came, and it happened. It happened in one of our great cities. Thousands of people lost their life. I vowed that day to never forget the lessons. We will do everything we can to protect our people at home, but the best way to protect our people is to chase these killers down and to bring them to justice. The best way to protect our homeland is to deny them sanctuary in countries that might allow them to train or provide them with weapons or training. The best way to protect our homeland is to work with allies and friends who understand the call to history and to share intelligence and to find them.

And that's what we're doing. Yesterday I went to Fort Carson, Colorado. I had the honor of addressing about 6,000 members of our military and their families. The military spirit is high. They understand their responsibilities. I had the chance to thank them for their service to our country, to stand in harm's way. I appreciated so very much their sacrifices in Afghanistan and Iraq.

You see, the issue in Iraq is not only our own security short-term. By removing Saddam Hussein, America is safer. So is the neighborhood. But the long-term issue is to make sure, in the heart of the Middle East, democracy and freedom reign. And that's important for peace. It's essential for peace in the world. Free countries are peaceful countries. People who live in freedom are people that are peaceful people. Free countries don't develop weapons to hurt their neighbors. Free countries focus on the aspirations of their citizens, the hopes of their citizens.

And so we've got a hard task ahead of us in Iraq. But I just want to assure you that we will stay the course; we will do the job; we will not be intimidated by thugs and killers who will kill innocent Iraqis or try to kill our coalition troops to force us out, because I truly believe that when we succeed, we will leave behind a more peaceful world.

Many of you have served our country, and you can understand what I'm about to tell you: Freedom is precious. Freedom is inherent in our soul. Freedom is not America's gift to the world; freedom is the Almighty's—Almighty God's gift to every person who lives in this world. We will work to protect ourselves, but we'll also work to free people who have been enslaved by tyranny, free those who live in a country where they get tortured if they speak out. We love freedom in America. We will never forget our love for freedom. Our foreign policy is based upon freedom and peace, and we'll succeed.

Thank you all very much. God bless.

NOTE: The President spoke at 4:33 p.m. In his remarks, he referred to Mayor Skip Rimsza of Phoenix, AZ; and former President Saddam Hussein of Iraq.

Statement on the Ongoing Review of the Overseas Force Posture
November 25, 2003

Since the end of the cold war, the once-familiar threats facing our Nation, our friends, and our allies have given way to the less predictable dangers associated with rogue nations, global terrorism, and weapons of mass destruction. We have been actively transforming our defenses to address these changes. While we continue to make progress in the transformation of our uniformed military, it remains for us to realign the global posture of our forces to better address these new challenges.

Beginning today, the United States will intensify our consultations with the Congress and our friends, allies, and partners overseas on our ongoing review of our overseas force posture. We will ensure that we place the right capabilities in the most appropriate locations to best address the new security environment.

U.S. national security is closely linked to the security of our friends, allies, and global partners, and this review will serve to strengthen existing relationships and in-crease our ability to carry out our defense commitments more effectively. To meet this objective, we will invite the full participation of our friends and allies. And because any initiatives and adjustments resulting from this review must necessarily be comprehensive and affordable, it will be conducted in close consultation with the Congress of the United States. Secretary Powell and Secretary Rumsfeld will describe further our efforts at the NATO ministerial meetings in early December. High-level U.S. teams will begin consultations in foreign capitals in Europe, Asia, and elsewhere following those meetings.

The collective security of free nations depends now more than ever on modern capabilities and security cooperation. A fully transformed and strengthened overseas force posture will underscore the commitment of the United States to effective collective action in the common cause of peace and liberty.

Remarks at a Bush-Cheney Reception in Phoenix
November 25, 2003

The President. Thank you all very much. Thank you for coming. I'm honored that so many people showed up tonight. Jon said, "If you come to Arizona, we may be able to get a couple of folks to come." [*Laughter*] This is a fantastic event. You know what we're doing? We're laying the foundation for what is going to be a great national victory in 2004.

I'm honored you're here, I really am. I want to thank you all for coming. It's a big deal that you showed up. It means a lot. You know, I'm getting ready. I'm kind of loosening up. [*Laughter*] But politics will come in its own time. I've got a job to do. I've got a job to do in our Nation's Capital. And as you circulate around this important State, when you go to your coffee shops or your community centers or your houses of worship, you tell them President Bush and his administration is focused on the people's business. We're working on behalf of everybody to keep this country strong and secure and prosperous and free.

My one regret for this evening, Senator, is the fact that Laura isn't with me.

Audience members. Aw-w-w.

The President. No, I know it. I know it. A lot of you would rather have had her than me. [*Laughter*] It shows how wise you are. [*Laughter*] She is a fabulous lady. She is a great wife, a wonderful mother, and she's doing a heck of a good job as the First Lady of this country.

Kyl married well too; I'm honored Caryll is here. I picked two fine people to be the State cochairmen of this campaign, and that's Senator Jon Kyl and Senator John McCain. You've sent two fine Americans to the United States Senate.

We've also got a great congressional delegation, some of whom are here tonight. I'm so honored that Congressman Jim Kolbe is here. Congressman J.D. Hayworth

and his wife, Mary, is here. As I mentioned a little while ago, they're starting to call him "Slim" Hayworth. [*Laughter*] He's looking quite pretty these days. [*Laughter*] John and Shirley Shadegg are here with us today. John, thank you for coming. Cheryl and Jeff Flake are with us today. Josie and Trent Franks are with us today. And finally, Congressman Rick Renzi is with us today. I'm honored that they're—thank you all for coming.

I appreciate working with these fine folks from Arizona. They care deeply about our country. They're strong leaders. They love the people of Arizona. I know you're proud of them. I'm proud to call them friends and allies.

I also want to thank statehouse members who are here. Jan Brewer, the secretary of state, is with us. Jan, thank you for coming. Speaker Jake Flake asked me to watch Congressman Jeff Flake in Washington to make sure he behaved himself. [*Laughter*] But Mr. Speaker, I'm glad you're here. As Jeff came through, he said he's a real, live cowboy. I like coming to States where they have real, live cowboys. You know, Senator, we're keeping pretty good company when people show up to fundraisers in cowboy hats. [*Laughter*]

I appreciate the mayor of this fine city, Skip Rimsza, for being here. Mr. Mayor, you've done a fine job, but most of all, thank you for coming. I do know that the former Governor, Fife Symington, is here. I saw him up close. He's a great Governor for the State of Arizona.

I appreciate my buddy from down south, Jim Click, for being such a great friend—[*inaudible*]—and Jim Simmons. Both of you all have worked hard to make sure this has been a fantastic evening, and I want to thank you. I want to thank the chairman of the Republican Party, Bob Fannin, and I want to thank Mike Hellon, the national committeeman. I want to thank the grassroots activists who are here. It's important to have a successful fundraising operation. Evelyn, thank you for coming. [*Laughter*] It's important to have a active fundraising effort, and we've done well tonight. It's equally important to have an active grassroots effort. You see, you win campaigns when you go and you put up the signs and you get on the telephone and you write the letters. For the grassroots activists here, I want to thank you for what you're going to do on behalf of the Bush-Cheney ticket in '04.

In the last 3 years, our Nation has acted decisively to confront great challenges. I came to this office to solve problems instead of passing them on to future Presidents and future generations. I came to seize opportunities instead of letting them slip away. My administration is meeting the tests of our time.

Terrorists declared war on the United States of America, and war is what they got. We've captured or killed many of the key leaders of the Al Qaida network, and the rest of them know we're on their trail. In Afghanistan and Iraq, we gave ultimatums to terror regimes. Those regimes chose defiance, and those regimes are no more. Fifty million people in those two countries once lived under tyranny, and today they live in freedom.

Three years ago, our military was not receiving the resources it needed, and morale was beginning to suffer. So we increased the defense budgets to prepare for the threats of a new era. And today, no one in the world can question the skill, the strength, and the spirit of the United States military.

Three years ago, our economy was in trouble, and recession was beginning. And then our country was attacked, and we had scandals in corporate America, and we went to war to make our country more secure and the world more peaceful. And all those actions affected the people's confidence. But we acted. We passed tough new laws to hold corporate criminals to account. And to get the economy going again, I have twice led the United States Congress to pass historic tax relief for the American people.

Here is what we believe, that when Americans have more take-home pay to spend, to save, or invest, the whole economy grows, and someone is more likely to find a job. We're returning money to the people. To help them raise their families, we've reduced taxes on dividends and capital gains to encourage investment. We've given small businesses incentives to expand and to hire new people. With all these actions, we're laying the foundation for greater economic prosperity and more jobs across America, so that every single citizen in this country has a chance to realize the American Dream.

Today, this economy of ours is strong, and it is getting stronger. They just released some new figures on the revised third-quarter growth. It turns out the third quarter grew at an annual rate of 8.2 percent. That's the fastest growth in nearly 20 years. You see, productivity is high; business investment is rising; housing construction is strong. The tax relief we passed is working.

Three years ago, there was a lot of talk in Washington about education reform, and there wasn't much action. So I acted. I called for and the Congress passed the No Child Left Behind Act. With a solid bipartisan majority, we delivered the most dramatic education reforms in a generation. We increased spending for Title I students. But for the first time, the Federal Government has asked a simple question: Are the children learning to read and write and add and subtract? In return for Federal money, we now expect results. You see, we believe every child can learn. This administration is challenging the soft bigotry of low expectations. Not only do we believe every child can learn, we expect every school to teach, so that not one single child is left behind.

We reorganized our Government and created the Department of Homeland Security to better safeguard our borders and ports and to better protect the American people. We passed trade promotion authority to open up new markets for Arizona's farmers and ranchers and entrepreneurs. We passed budget agreements, much needed budget agreements, to bring spending discipline to Washington, DC. On issue after issue, this administration has acted on principle, has kept its word, and has made progress for the American people.

And the Congress gets a lot of credit. As I told you, I've enjoyed working with the Members from the great State of Arizona, good, honorable, and decent people. I've got a great relationship with Senate Majority Leader Bill Frist from Tennessee and Speaker Denny Hastert from Illinois. These are fine people.

We're working hard on behalf of the American people. We're working hard to change the tone in Washington. There's too much needless backbiting and petty politics in the Nation's Capital. We're working hard to focus on results to do the people's work, and those are the kind of people I've attracted to my administration. I brought people from all walks of life, all backgrounds to serve the people of America. There has never been a finer administration than the one I put together for the people of this country, and we've had no finer Vice President than Dick Cheney. Mother may have a second opinion, Senator. [*Laughter*]

In 3 years, we've come far. If you look at the results, we've done a lot. But our work is only beginning. See, I've set great goals worthy of this great Nation. First, America is committed to expanding the realm of freedom and peace for our own security and for the benefit of the world. And second, in our own country, we must work for a society that is prosperous and compassionate so that every single citizen has a chance to work and to succeed and realize the great promise of America. It is clear that the future of freedom and peace depend on the actions of America. This Nation is freedom's home and freedom's defender. We welcome this charge of history, and we are keeping it.

The war on terror continues. The enemies of freedom are not idle, and neither are we. This country will not rest; we will not tire; we will not stop until this danger to civilization is removed.

We are confronting that danger in Iraq, where Saddam holdouts and foreign terrorists are desperately trying to throw Iraq into chaos by attacking coalition forces, international aid workers, and innocent Iraqi citizens. You see, they know that the advance of freedom in Iraq would be a major defeat in the cause of terror. This collection of coldblooded killers is trying to shake the will of the civilized world and trying to shake the will of America. America will never be intimidated by a bunch of thugs.

We're on the offensive in Iraq. We're aggressively after them. We're striking the terrorists in Iraq. We will defeat them there so we will not have to face them in our own cities. Other nations are helping, and there is a simple reason: They understand that a free Iraq will make the world more secure. And we're standing with the Iraqi people as they assume more of their own defense and move toward self-government. These are not easy tasks, but they are essential tasks. And we will finish what we have begun, and we will win this essential victory in the war on terror.

Our greatest security comes from the advance of human liberty, because free nations do not support terror. Free nations do not attack their neighbors. Free nations do not threaten the world with weapons of mass terror. Americans believe that freedom is the deepest need and hope of every human heart. We believe that freedom is the future of every nation. And we know that freedom is not America's gift to the world; freedom is the Almighty's gift to every person who lives in the world.

America also understands that unprecedented influence brings tremendous responsibilities. We have duties in this world, and when we see disease and starvation and hopeless poverty, we will not turn away. On the continent of Africa, America is now committed to bringing the healing power, the healing power of medicine, to millions of men and women and children suffering with AIDS. This incredibly strong and powerful Nation is a compassionate nation, and we are leading the world in this very important work of human rescue.

We face challenges here at home as well, and we will be equal to those challenges. This administration will stay focused on a progrowth economic agenda until everyone who wants to work can find a job.

We are keeping our commitment to America's seniors by strengthening and modernizing Medicare. For years, seniors have asked that the Federal Government keep its commitment, its solemn promise, by having a modern Medicare system that provides preventative care and prescription drugs and health care choices for our seniors. And Washington listened to those seniors but didn't do anything. Finally, the House and the Senate have acted. They've approved legislation that will bring modern medicine to our seniors. This historic legislation is the greatest improvement in senior health care coverage since the enactment of Medicare in 1965. I look forward to signing this bill.

For the sake of our health care system, we need to cut down on the frivolous lawsuits which increase the cost of medicine. People who have been harmed by a bad doctor deserve their day in court, yet the system shouldn't reward lawyers who are simply fishing for a rich settlement. Frivolous lawsuits drive up the cost of health care. They affect the Federal budget, and therefore, medical liability reform is a national issue that requires a national solution. I submitted a good plan to the Congress. The House of Representatives acted. The bill is stuck in the United States Senate.

I want to thank Senator Kyl and Senator McCain for working for this important legislation. Certain Members of the Senate must understand, however, that no one has ever been healed by a frivolous lawsuit. We need medical liability reform now.

I have a responsibility as your President to make sure the judicial system runs well, and I have met that duty. I have nominated superb men and women for the Federal courts, people who will interpret the law, not legislate from the bench. Some Members of the Senate—not this Senator, not Senator McCain—are trying to keep my nominees off the bench by blocking up-or-down votes. Every judicial nominee deserves a fair hearing and an up-or-down vote on the Senate floor. It is time for some Members to stop playing politics with American justice.

Congress needs to get an energy bill to my desk. We need a comprehensive energy plan in this country. We need to encourage conservation, develop cleaner technology. We need to do a lot of things. But one thing we need to do is to become less dependent on foreign sources of energy. For the sake of economic security and for the sake of national security, I need an energy bill to my desk.

Our strong and prosperous Nation must also be a compassionate nation. I'll continue to advance our agenda of compassionate conservatism, which means we'll apply the most effective and innovative ideas to the task of helping our fellow citizens who hurt. See, there's still millions of men and women who want to end their dependence on our Government and become independent through work. I want to work with Congress to build on the success of welfare reform, to bring work and dignity into the lives of more of our citizens.

Congress needs to complete the "Citizen Service Act" so that we can encourage more Americans to serve their communities and their country. We need to get the Faith-Based Initiative finished. I proposed a Faith-Based Initiative which will empower the armies of compassion which exist all across America to help the homeless, to mentor the children, to offer hope to the addicted. This is a great nation because we're a nation of many faiths. People are free to worship any way you see fit. But there's a commonality to our faiths, the call to help somebody—hurt. Our Government should not fear faith. We ought to welcome faith into helping cure some of the intractable problems of our society.

A compassionate society must promote opportunity for everyone, including the independence and dignity from ownership. My administration will constantly strive to promote an ownership society in America. We want more people owning their own home. We have a minority homeownership gap in America. I proposed a plan to the Congress to close that gap. We want people owning and managing their own retirement accounts. We want people owning and managing their own health care plans. We want more people owning their own small business. This administration understands that when a person owns something, he or she has a vital stake in the future of this country.

In a compassionate society, people respect one another, respect their opinions and respect their beliefs. And people take responsibility for the decisions they make in life. America's culture is changing from one that has said, "If it feels good, just go ahead and do it," and "If you've got a problem, blame somebody else," to a culture in which each of us understands that we're responsible for the decisions we make in life. If you're lucky enough to be a mom or a dad, you're responsible for loving your child with all your heart. If you're concerned about the quality of the education in the community in which you live, you're responsible for doing something about it. If you're a CEO in corporate America, you're responsible for telling the truth to your shareholders and your employees. In a responsibility society, each of us is responsible for loving our neighbor just like we'd like to be loved ourself.

The culture of service and responsibility is strong in this great country. It's truly one of the great strengths of America. I started what's called the USA Freedom Corps right after September the 11th. It was a chance to give people a web portal in which to find out how to volunteer in their communities, and the response has been really strong. Americans care about their neighbors. Our charities are vibrant. If you're involved in a charity or a faith-based group, thanks for what you're doing. You're making America a better place.

Our policemen and firefighters and people who wear our Nation's uniform—[*applause*]—you haven't even got the punch line yet. [*Laughter*] People who wear the uniform remind us what it means to sacrifice for something greater than yourself. You know, once again, the children of America believe in heroes, because they see them every day. In these challenging times, the world has seen the resolve and the courage of America. And I've been privileged to see the compassion and the character of the American people.

All the tests of the last 3 years have come to the right nation. We're a strong country, and we use that strength to defend the peace. We're an optimistic country, confident in ourselves and in ideals bigger than ourselves. Abroad, we seek to lift whole nations by spreading freedom. At home, we seek to lift up lives by spreading opportunity to every corner of our country. This is the work that history has set before us. We welcome it. And we know that for our country, the best days lie ahead.

May God bless you all. Thank you for coming. I appreciate it.

NOTE: The President spoke at 6:36 p.m. at the Arizona Biltmore Resort & Spa. In his remarks, he referred to Franklin "Jake" Flake, speaker pro tempore, Arizona State House of Representatives; Mayor Skip Rimsza of Phoenix, AZ; former Gov. Fife Symington of

Arizona; Robert Fannin, Arizona State chairman, and Mike Hellon, Arizona national committeeman, Republican National Committee; and former President Saddam Hussein of Iraq.

Remarks to the Troops at a Thanksgiving Dinner in Baghdad, Iraq
November 27, 2003

Thank you. I was just looking for a warm meal somewhere. [*Laughter*] Thanks for inviting me to dinner. General Sanchez, thank you, sir, for your kind invitation and your strong leadership. Ambassador Bremer, thank you for your steadfast belief in freedom and peace. I want to thank the members of the Governing Council who are here, pleased you are joining us for one of our Nation's great holidays. It's a chance to give thanks to the Almighty for the many blessings we receive.

I'm particularly proud to be with the 1st Armored Division, the 2d ACR, and the 82d Airborne. I can't think of a finer group of folks to have Thanksgiving dinner with than you all. We're proud of you. Today Americans are gathering with their loved ones to give thanks for the many blessings in our lives, and this year we are especially thankful for the courage and the sacrifice of those who defend us, the men and women of the United States military.

I bring a message on behalf of America: We thank you for your service; we're proud of you; and America stands solidly behind you. Together, you and I have taken an oath to defend our country. You're honoring that oath. The United States military is doing a fantastic job. You are defeating the terrorists here in Iraq so that we don't have to face them in our own country. You're defeating Saddam's henchmen so that the people of Iraq can live in peace and freedom.

By helping the Iraqi people become free, you're helping change a troubled and violent part of the world. By helping to build a peaceful and democratic country in the heart of the Middle East, you are defending the American people from danger, and we are grateful.

You're engaged in a difficult mission. Those who attack our coalition forces and kill innocent Iraqis are testing our will. They hope we will run. We did not charge hundreds of miles into the heart of Iraq, pay a bitter cost in casualties, defeat a brutal dictator, and liberate 25 million people only to retreat before a band of thugs and assassins.

We will prevail. We will win because our cause is just. We will win because we will stay on the offensive. And we will win because you're part of the finest military ever assembled. And we will prevail because the Iraqis want their freedom. Every day, you see firsthand the commitment and sacrifice that the Iraqi people are making to secure their own freedom.

I have a message for the Iraqi people: You have an opportunity to seize the moment and rebuild your great country based on human dignity and freedom. The regime of Saddam Hussein is gone forever. The United States and our coalition will help you, help you build a peaceful country so that your children can have a bright future. We'll help you find and bring to justice the people who terrorized you for years and are still killing innocent Iraqis. We will stay until the job is done. I'm confident we will succeed because you, the Iraqi people, will show the world that you're not only courageous but that you can govern yourself wisely and justly.

On this Thanksgiving, our Nation remembers the men and women of our military, your friends and comrades, who paid the ultimate price for our security and freedom. We ask for God's blessings on their families, their loved ones, and their friends, and we pray for your safety and your strength as you continue to defend America and to spread freedom.

Each one of you has answered a great call, participating in an historic moment in world history. You live by a code of honor: service to your Nation for the safety and the security of your fellow citizens. Our military is full of the finest people on the face of the Earth. I'm proud to be your Commander in Chief. I bring greetings from America.

May God bless you all.

NOTE: The President spoke at approximately 6 p.m. at Baghdad International Airport. In his remarks, he referred to Lt. Gen. Ricardo S. Sanchez, USA, commander, Coalition Joint Task Force Seven; L. Paul Bremer III, Presidential Envoy to Iraq; and former President Saddam Hussein of Iraq. The Office of the Press Secretary also released a Spanish language transcript of these remarks. The Thanksgiving Day proclamation of November 21 is listed in Appendix D at the end of this volume.

Remarks and an Exchange With Reporters Aboard Air Force One
November 27, 2003

President's Visit to Iraq

The President. I thank you for honoring the confidentiality necessary to pull this off. I made the decision to go because I wanted our troops not only that were there to have dinner but the troops in harm's way to know that their Commander in Chief and, more importantly, their country support. And I thought the best way to do that would be to spend time with them on Thanksgiving to thank them and to send a message—you know, the message I sent, which is we appreciate their sacrifices.

You know, Thanksgiving has got to be hard for young troops, to know that their families are gathered, having dinner, a turkey feast and everything. That's got to be a lonely moment for them. And I felt like at this point that it would be—hopefully, it would help them to see their President. And I recognize that I didn't see every troop in harm's way scattered throughout the region, but the word will get out, thanks to you all.

The idea first came up in mid-October. Andy said, "Would you be interested in going to Baghdad?" And I said, "Yes, I would, except I don't want to go if it puts anybody in harm's way. It's very essential that I fully understand all aspects of the trip, starting with whether or not we could get in/out safely, whether or not my presence there would in any way cause the enemy to react and therefore jeopardize somebody else's life."

I felt it was important to send a message that we care for them and we support them strongly and that we erase any doubt in their minds as to whether or not the people stand with them. You know, I understood the consequences and risks. And over time, I was assured by the planners and, as importantly, our military people and the pilot here of this airplane that the risk could be minimized if we were able to keep the trip quiet. I was fully prepared to turn this plane around.

I thought a crucial moment yesterday was when I saw you all. That's why I said, you know, no phones. A crucial moment in this trip, frankly, was in between changing planes, and I wasn't sure whether or not—and the circle is pretty tight—I wasn't sure whether or not people would be able to tell their loved ones, "I can't see you on Thanksgiving, and I can't tell you why." So I was worried about that, but I was fully prepared to turn this baby around and come home.

And 3 hours out, I checked with our Secret Service, who checked with people on the ground. They assured me that it was still a tight hold on the information and that the conditions on the ground were as positive as could possibly be. I even went up to the cockpit and watched Tillman bring it in—which, had the security been broken, there would have been the time that we would have been most vulnerable. However, the plane—that's why Colonel Tillman's judgment was so important to this—this plane is protected; it's protected against the kinds of things that could be used against it. It also—we obviously flew in in the dark; precautions were taken.

At any rate, it was an emotional moment to walk in that room. The energy level was beyond belief. I mean, I've been in front of some excited crowds before, but this was—the place truly erupted, and I could see the, first, look of amazement and then look of appreciation on the kids' faces. Working the crowd, a soldier said to me, "I'm so glad you came. Thanks for coming. It's important for us to know that the people of America support us, and the fact that the President would come confirms that in this soldier's mind." And I think it confirmed in a lot of soldiers' minds.

Anyway, I'd be glad to answer any questions.

Q. How'd you slip out of Crawford?

The President. How'd I get out of Crawford, was the question. The agents, the Secret Service—well, first of all, I didn't slip out, because I had to tell my family—that would be my wife and daughters—that I would not be there for Thanksgiving today. My mother and dad came over from College Station, thinking they

would see me. They did not know I was not going to be there.

So they knew—Laura knew, and the girls knew. I assured them that I wouldn't be going if it wasn't well thought out and well planned. They understood. I think the girls thought it was a great thing to do, to go see the—go thank our troops. A lot of the kids are their age, 22 years old, and younger. And Laura was pleased that I had decided to go. I comforted her about the—you know, I assured her that I wouldn't be doing this if I wasn't confident we could get in and out of there safely. That was very important.

They pulled up kind of a plain-looking vehicle with tinted windows, and I slipped on a baseball cap and pulled her down, as did Condi. We looked like a normal couple. [*Laughter*]

Q. On your way to the Wal-Mart. [*Laughter*]

The President. To buy some Berkeley Power worms. [*Laughter*]

Q. Pulling a bass boat behind you? [*Laughter*]

The President. Yes, exactly. [*Laughter*] We encountered some traffic. I–35, as you know, if you're a Texan—well, you know. Anyway, Thanksgiving traffic, a lot of people heading up to Dallas, so we were about, I guess, 10 minutes late to the plane. But he kept moving. There were plenty of vehicles out there; there just were. There were people out there.

Then we got here, to TSTC. They had a bunch of people go in the front, and I came up the back.

Q. The footman's entrance.

The President. The footman's entrance. Glad to know how the people live. [*Laughter*]

Q. Well, do you think Americans mind that you just slipped——

The President. I think Americans understand that we've got a bunch of kids in harm's way and that the President, if it can be done safely, owes an explanation of thanks and thanksgiving to these kids.

Had I not been convinced it could be done and done properly, I wouldn't have gone. I think Americans also understand that, had we announced this, had I gone in to thank our troops with the flurry of announcement and all the analysts talking about it ahead of time, it would have put me in harm's way, and it would have put others in harm's way, including yourselves.

So I think the American people appreciate me going to express their sentiments to these kids. These people are sacrificing for our freedom and our peace. We are at war with terror, and we are in the process of changing Iraq, which will make America more secure, and Americans appreciate that a lot.

Meeting With Members of Iraq's Governing Council

Q. Mr. President, we were told you got to see Mr. Chalabi today?

The President. I did see Chalabi. I met with—well, let's see, I had the dinner. You saw that. I wasn't sure how long you were there. You probably timed it, but an hour or so—are these the times? Oh, these are the people there.

I shook a lot of hands, saw a lot of kids, took a lot of pictures, served a lot of food, and we moved on to see four members of the Governing Council—the names are here. Talabani is the head of it right now, so he was the main spokesman. But Chalabi was there, as was Dr. Khuzai, who had come to the Oval Office—I don't know if you all were in the pool that day, but she was there—she was there with him and one other fellow, and I had a good talk with them.

We were there for about maybe a little less than 30 minutes. I was able to assure them that we were going to stay the course and get the job done, but I also reminded them what I said publicly, that it's up to them to seize the moment, to have a Government that recognizes all rights, the rights of the majority and the rights of the minority, to speak to the aspirations and hopes of the Iraqi people. I assured them that I believe in the future of Iraq, because I believe in the capacity of the people to govern—as I said, govern wisely and justly. I meant what I said. I told them that privately. I told them I back Jerry Bremer 100 percent. He's got my full confidence. He was sitting right there as well. We had a nice visit.

They assured me that they were making good progress, that the Iraqi people are overwhelmingly pleased that Saddam is gone, that they do see a bright future, and they want us to—they want to work with us.

Q. What do you make of what some of the ayatollahs have said lately about the need to have elections sooner and some of the concerns they've expressed about the process?

The President. Well, I think that—as I explained to these Governing Council members, to get where they need to be is going to require debate and discussion, and that's healthy. You know, the fact that there are different opinions being discussed is positive. It's a positive sign that things are different inside of Iraq.

It took us a while to get from the Articles of Confederation to the Constitution. So we've got to be realistic and patient about how they proceed. I think the game plan they've got now in place is a good plan. The Governing Council came up with the plan. I supported it. We discussed the overarching flaw that they're discussing. They understand the basic—the notion of human rights and the dignity of each person. I'm confident they'll get to where they've got to be.

President's Visit to Iraq

Q. Was there any point along in the planning for this trip that you looked at it and thought, you know, "This might be too risky; maybe we should"——

The President. Yes, all along. I mean, I was the biggest skeptic of all.

Chief of Staff Andrew H. Card. Yes, he was. [*Laughter*]

The President. Our planners worked hard to answer every question, and I had a lot of questions. John Abizaid, who I just spoke to by phone, thanking him for the trip— he chose not to come here because he wanted to be with his troops. And I understand that and appreciate that. But he was a very enthusiastic backer of this idea. But I also made sure that people interfacing with Abizaid knew that at any time he wanted us to pull out, I would do so. It was very important for John Abizaid and Jerry Bremer to be comfortable—John— Sanchez, General Sanchez, to be comfortable with this trip. And they were comfortable all the way through.

I think we addressed every issue. Hagin is the point man in the administration for this. He did a fabulous job of addressing the details. I sat down with Colonel Tillman on one of our trips recently and just said, "Look, I need to know, what does it take to get into Baghdad now, and how risky is it?" And he said, "Sir, I wouldn't take you in there if I wasn't convinced that we could do this in a way that would safely bring you to the troops."

I wouldn't have asked you to come if I didn't think it was safe. I would not have put you in this position.

Q. Was there a moment when you thought it wasn't going to happen——

The President. No, no. It was moving all along, but I was pretty tough. In Vegas, I called in and still had more questions about how this was going to happen. Andy was there, and I was pushing hard. Yesterday I sat down on CIVITS out of Crawford with Condi and Andy and the Vice President, went around one more time just to make sure everybody knew all the details. People knew different aspects of it, but these three knew all the details and were confident that it was the right thing to do.

It is the right thing to do. Having seen the reaction of those troops, you know it was the right thing to do, and the word

will get out. And their parents will appreciate it, and their loved ones will appreciate it. I went over there to thank them and not only thank them but to remind them our country stands with them and that we will stay the course until the job is done.

I met with—then we went from the Governing Council—I met with the key generals and colonels, the commanders in the field. They reported to me that we're on the offensive, that we're using the tools necessary to suppress the handful of the killers, and we're making good progress, and that the spirit of the troops is high; they understand the mission and the goal. And I was pleased to be able to talk with these men and women as well. It's an important moment. They needed to see me. They needed to see—because they don't read—they don't get to see me all the time. Sometimes they read things. And they got to see me. They saw my determination and my support and respect for what they're doing.

Meeting With Baghdad Area Leaders

Communications Director Dan Bartlett. You might want to remind them about the Baghdad officials.

The President. What?

Director Bartlett. Two Baghdad officials.

The President. Oh, met the chiefs—head of the—two council members, the chief of the council and one of his compatriots— Baghdad. Bremer tells me crime in Baghdad is down by something like 38 percent. The chairman was very positive and optimistic and very thankful, by the way. To a person, the Iraqi leadership I met with are incredibly thankful and generous with their praise of what America has done for them.

But that was a good meeting. It was getting down to the grassroots level, to— you've seen me enough to know when I see these mayors, I tease them about filling the potholes. That's what—you know, they've got a job to do, and they're doing it. I didn't say, "Fill the potholes," by the way. [*Laughter*] But I did encourage them, to let them know that we have confidence in their ability to self-govern and we respect their culture and we want to help them.

President's Visit to Iraq

Q. Did you tell any Members of Congress that you were going to make——

The President. Do what now?

Q. Did you inform any Members of Congress or anything?

The President. No.

Q. We're still a little unclear about when you told the First Lady.

The President. Oh. Well, I told her that—she knew all along—actually, I didn't mean Laura and the girls. I meant the girls. Laura knew from—we first started talking about this seriously on the trip to Asia. She was on the trip. I said, "Look, I'm thinking about going to Baghdad." And as the planning got more and more in place, I informed her more and more in place— that it was more and more in place. I was more and more comfortable.

And she asked me yesterday morning, am I going? I said, "Yes, I'm going." And so I told her yesterday—she knew I was going, or planning on going, because I told you I'd pull the plug if I needed to. And I said, "It looks like we're on." And then the girls came up from Austin in the afternoon, and that's when I told Barbara and Jenna, with Laura there, that I was going to Baghdad.

Q. Mr. President, you talked about talking to the generals and the colonels and about the more aggressive stance they've taken recently. You know, Secretary Rumsfeld said recently it's hard to get a grasp for whether or not we're making progress. Did you get a sense of what they're doing and how we can actually measure whether or not we're making headway?

The President. Well, one way you measure is how many people you bring to justice. And they feel like they're making good progress. You can measure based upon feedback from the ground. That's what they get. And that's—they're upbeat. They just said, "Mr. President, we'll stay the—you stay the course. We'll succeed." And my message was, "I know you'll succeed, and I'm here to tell you we're going to stay the course."

And I asked the General Sanchez about the recruitment of Iraqi citizens into these different security elements. He said, "It's strong. Training is going well." The Iraqi people and the Governing Council all thought the same. They want to be on the frontline of their own security, and that's a positive development. And so I was pleased with the report.

Personal Aide Blake Gottesman. Thank you, everyone.

The President. Good job.

Q. What kind of ball cap was it? What did it say on it?

National Security Adviser Condoleezza Rice. Mine was in my bag, it was——

Q. A Cleveland Browns hat?

Q. It was actually—I didn't have a Cleveland Browns hat.

Q. That would have been a dead giveaway.

Dr. Rice. That would have been a dead giveaway.

The President. Here are the names of the people here.

Q. We would love to get some video of you up here sometime, sir.

Q. What does it say, Blake?

The President. ——something like this.

Q. Did you really pull it down that low?

The President. No. We had pretty tinted windows. We went through a gate where——

Q. They thought, "Who in the world is that?"

The President. Eddie said, "We're coming to a gate."

Q. [*Inaudible*]

The President. Well, I'm telling you, this is—again, had this been jeopardized in any way, we wouldn't put myself and/or you all in this position. And we were very—

we were cautious, and we needed to be. And I want to thank you for honoring that. This is an historic trip. And it'll reverberate in such positive ways for these kids who are—and these soldiers who are far away from home serving us. And it's exactly what I wanted to do.

Q. Thank you.

Historic Presidential Visits to Combat Areas

Q. Did you look back at any precedents of any other President's trips?

The President. There is no precedent in the war on terror. This is the first war of the 21st century, unique in its nature. But I don't know. I guess you all need to do that. I don't know whether or not— I think Lyndon Johnson went as a Vice President or as President. I don't know.

Q. He was in Asia, and he made an unscheduled trip.

The President. Into Vietnam as President?

Q. Eisenhower went to Korea as a——

The President. Franklin Roosevelt went to north Africa, but the front was in Tunisia, I think, but maybe not.

Q. Abraham Lincoln went to Richmond a couple of days after——

The President. He sure did. I got the picture of the White House of the—Lincoln with his generals and Admiral Porter talking about the peace. I think that's what you're talking about.

Q. But he was mobbed by people when he went to—this was a couple of days after he fell.

The President. Right. And he was on a boat outside of Richmond—unfortunately called "The Peacemakers." It had a wonderful rainbow behind he and his generals. That's where he's talking about making sure the peace was fair and generous so that the United States would stay united.

And, interestingly enough, the original is in the—upstairs in the Treaty Room in the White House. And it is in the Pentagon as well, a copy of it, which I found to be very—so I remember going into the Pentagon and—somebody took—*[laughter]*.

But thanks for honoring it.

Q. I appreciate it.

The President. You're a credit to your Nation, a credit to your profession.

NOTE: The President spoke aboard Air Force One en route to Andrews Air Force Base following his departure from Baghdad at approximately 8 p.m. In his remarks, he referred to Col. Mark Tillman, USAF, commander, Presidential Airlift Group; Jalal Talabani, president, and Ahmad Chalabi, Raja Habib al-Khuzai, and Muwafaq Rubai, members, Iraqi Governing Council; L. Paul Bremer III, Presidential Envoy to Iraq; former President Saddam Hussein of Iraq; Gen. John P. Abizaid, USA, combatant commander, U.S. Central Command; Lt. Gen. Ricardo S. Sanchez, USA, commander, Coalition Joint Task Force Seven; and Joe Hagin, Assistant to the President and White House Deputy Chief of Staff. A tape was not available for verification of the content of these remarks.

The President's Radio Address
November 29, 2003

Good morning. On Thursday, I was honored to travel to Iraq to spend Thanksgiving with some of the finest men and women serving in our military.

My message to the troops was clear: Your country is thankful for your service; we are proud of you; and America stands with you in all that you are doing to defend America. I'm pleased to report back from the frontlines that our troops are strong. Morale is high, and our military is confident we will prevail.

Many members of our Armed Forces, Guard, and Reserve observed Thanksgiving in places far from home. In Afghanistan, Iraq, and elsewhere, our military is confronting the terrorist enemy so we don't meet that enemy in our own country. They're serving the cause of freedom. They're helping millions of people in newly liberated countries to build lives of dignity and hope. They are protecting the lives and security of the American people. All of us can be grateful to live in a country that has produced such brave men and women who stand between us and the dangers of the world.

This holiday weekend is also a time when many proud military families are also feeling separation and worry. Long deployments in dangerous places have added hardships in military communities across the country. Many parents are dealing with the burdens of raising families while praying for the safe return of a loved one. Our whole Nation respects and appreciates the commitment and sacrifice of our military families.

Americans are also thinking of the military families that must face this holiday with sorrow of recent loss. It is the nature of terrorism that a small number of people can inflict such terrible grief. Every person who dies in the line of duty commands the special gratitude of the American people. And the military families that mourn can know this: Our Nation will not forget their loved ones and the sacrifice they made to protect us all.

The courage of our soldiers and their families show the spirit of this country in great adversity. And many citizens are showing their appreciation by helping military families here at home. Members of the VFW have started an Adopt-A-Unit program, so veterans and their families can support military units in Iraq and Afghanistan. Volunteers from a group called Rebuilding Together have repaired homes for military families while their spouses are deployed.

Citizens interested in finding volunteer opportunities to support our military should visit the USA Freedom Corps web site at usafreedomcorps.gov.

Our Nation owes a debt of gratitude to every member of the United States military and to their families. It was a privilege to offer that gratitude in person to some of our troops serving in Iraq. May God bless them all, and may He continue to bless the United States of America.

Happy Thanksgiving, and thank you for listening.

NOTE: The address was recorded at 9:55 a.m. on November 28 at the Bush Ranch in Crawford, TX, for broadcast at 10:06 a.m. on November 29. The transcript was made available by the Office of the Press Secretary on November 28 but was embargoed for release until the broadcast. The Office of the Press Secretary also released a Spanish language transcript of this address.

Remarks at a Bush-Cheney Luncheon in Dearborn, Michigan
December 1, 2003

Thank you all very much. Thanks for coming. I appreciate you joining our campaign. You know what this means? It means we're laying the foundation for what is going to be a victory in Michigan and a nationwide victory in '04.

I want to thank you for your help, and I want to thank you for your support. I'm getting ready, and I'm loosening up. [*Laughter*] But the political season will come in its own time. There will be plenty of time for politics, plenty of time for all the balloon drops and political speeches. See, I've got a job to do. I've got a job to do for everybody who lives in this country. So when you go to your coffee shops and your community centers, you tell them, "The politics will come, but right now the President is working hard to make sure America is secure and strong and prosperous and free."

Laura sends her best. I know, you wish she were here instead of me. I understand. [*Laughter*] She's a fabulous First Lady. I really am a lucky man that she agreed to marry me, and the country, I think, is lucky that she is the First Lady.

I appreciate State campaign chair Candice Miller. I thank her for her introduction. I thank her for her service to this State. I look forward to working with her to carry Michigan. I want to thank Michael, Michael Kojaian, for his leadership as the State finance chairman for Bush-Cheney. I'm honored that Michael has taken on this responsibility.

I want to thank the Members of the United States Congress other than Candice Miller who have shown up today, Congressmen Upton, Camp, Knollenberg, Smith, Rogers, and McCotter. I'm honored they are here. I want to thank you all for coming.

I appreciate Secretary of State Terri Lynn Land for joining us today, as well as Attorney General Mike Cox. I know the speaker is here, Rick Johnson. Mr. Speaker, thank you for coming. And I appreciate all the members of the house and the State senate who have joined us. Go back to your districts and work hard—[*laughter*]—for Bush-Cheney '04.

I want to thank Betsy DeVos and Sharon Wise for taking a leadership position. I want to thank my friend Mercer Reynolds, who is the national finance chairman. Mostly I want to thank the activists who are

here. You see, you win a campaign not only by helping to raise money; you win a campaign by putting up the signs and licking the envelopes and making the phone calls to turn out the vote. I want to thank you for what you're going to do as we come down the stretch in 2004.

And as you do so, I want you to remind people that during the last 3 years, our Nation has acted decisively to confront great challenges. You see, I came to this office to solve problems, not to pass them on to future Presidents and future generations. I came to seize opportunities instead of letting them slip away. My administration is meeting the tests of our time.

Terrorists declared war on the United States of America, and war is what they got. We've captured or killed many of the key leaders of the Al Qaida network, and the rest of them know we're on their trail. In Afghanistan and Iraq, we gave ultimatums to terror regimes. Those regimes chose defiance, and those regimes are no more. Fifty million people in those two countries once lived under tyranny, and today they live in freedom.

Three years ago, our military was not receiving the resources it needed, and morale was beginning to suffer. So we increased the defense budgets to prepare for the threat of a new era. And today, no one in the world can question the skill, the strength, and the spirit of the United States military.

Three years ago, the economy was in trouble and a recession was just beginning. And then our country was attacked, and we had corporate scandals and war—all affected the people's confidence. But we acted. We acted. We passed tough new laws to hold corporate criminals to account. And I have twice led the United States Congress to pass historic tax relief for the American people. When Americans have more take-home pay to spend, to save, or invest, the whole economy grows, and someone is more likely to find a job. So we're returning more money to the people to help them raise their families, reduce taxes on dividends and capital gains to encourage investment, giving small businesses incentives to expand and to hire new people. With all these actions—with all these actions, we're laying the foundation for greater prosperity and more jobs across America so that every single citizen has a chance to realize the American Dream.

Our economy is strong, and it is getting stronger. Figures for the third quarter were recently revised upward to an annual growth rate of 8.2 percent. That's the fastest growth rate in nearly 20 years. Today the purchasing manager's index came out, which shows that our manufacturing sector is getting stronger. It's the highest numbers in nearly 20 years. Productivity is high. Business investment is getting strong. Housing construction is strong. The tax relief we passed is working.

Three years ago, there was a lot of talk about education reform; there wasn't much action at the Federal Government. So I acted. I called for and Congress passed, with a solid bipartisan majority, the No Child Left Behind Act. This was the most dramatic education reform in a generation. It said we will spend money at the Federal level, particularly on Title I students, but for the first time, the Federal Government is demanding results, high standards and results. You see, we believe every child can learn the basics of reading and math. We expect every school to teach the basics of reading and math. This administration is challenging the soft bigotry of low expectations. In return for Federal money, we now expect results in every single classroom in America so not one single child is left behind.

During this period, we reorganized our Government and created the Department of Homeland Security to better safeguard our borders and ports and to better protect the American people. We passed trade promotion authority to open up new markets for Michigan's farmers and entrepreneurs and manufacturers. We passed budget agreements to help maintain spending discipline in Washington. On issue after issue, this administration has acted on principle, has kept its word, and has made progress for the American people.

The Congress shares in these achievements. We've done a lot because we've worked together. I appreciate Speaker Hastert and Leader Frist. Again, I want to thank the Members of the U.S. Congress who are here today. See, we're working hard to get rid of the needless politics that tends to dominate the political landscape in Washington, DC, the backbiting and name calling. The best way to do that is to focus on results for the American people, and that's exactly what we're doing. We're delivering for the American people.

And those are the kind of people I've attracted to my administration. A mark of the administration is the capacity of fine, good, honorable people from all walks of life to serve America, and I have done just that. I put together a great group of Americans to serve. This country has had no finer Vice President than Dick Cheney. Mother has a second opinion. [*Laughter*]

In 3 years, we have come far. We've done a lot, but our work is only beginning. I've set great goals worthy of this great Nation. First, America is committed to expanding the realm of freedom and peace for our own security and for the benefit of the world. And second, in our own country, we must work for a society that is prosperous and compassionate so that every citizen has a chance to work and to succeed and realize the tremendous promise of our country. It is clear that the future of freedom and peace depend on the actions of America. This Nation is freedom's home and freedom's defender. We welcome this charge of history, and we are keeping it.

The war on terror continues. The enemies of freedom are not idle, and neither are we. This country will not rest; we will not tire; we will not stop until this danger to civilization is removed. We are confronting that danger in Iraq, where Saddam holdouts and foreign terrorists are desperately trying to throw the country into chaos by attacking coalition forces and aid workers and innocent Iraqi citizens. They know that the advance of freedom in Iraq, in the heart of the Middle East, would be a major defeat for the cause of terror. The coalition of killers—the collection of killers is trying to shake the will of America. America will not be intimidated by a bunch of thugs and assassins. We are aggressively striking the terrorists in Iraq. We will defeat them there so we do not have to face them in our own country.

Other nations are helping. They're helping to build a free country in Iraq because they know a free Iraq will make us all more secure. We're standing with the Iraqi people, the brave Iraqi people, as they assume more of their own defense and more of their own self-government. These are not easy tasks, but they are essential tasks. And the United States of America will finish what we have begun, and we will win this essential victory in the war on terror.

Our greatest security comes from the advance of human liberty, because free nations do not support terror. Free nations do not attack their neighbors. Free nations do not develop weapons of mass terror to threaten the world. Americans believe that freedom is the deepest need and hope of every human heart. We believe that freedom is the future of every nation. And we know that freedom is not America's gift to the world. Freedom is the Almighty God's gift to every man and woman living in this world.

America also understands that unprecedented influence brings tremendous responsibilities. When we see disease and starvation and hopeless poverty, we will not turn away. And that's why, on the continent of Africa, America is now committed to bringing the healing power of medicine to millions of men, women, and children now suffering with AIDS.

We face challenges here at home. Our actions will prove that we're equal to those challenges. I'm leaving here to go to a small business to talk about the entrepreneurial spirit in America, about the need to create—continue to create a progrowth environment so their businesses, large and small, can remain vibrant and can grow, so that people can find a job.

We're keeping our commitment to America's seniors by strengthening and modernizing Medicare. See, for years, seniors have called for a modern Medicare system, one that provides coverage for prescription drugs and a system that gives seniors more choices. Washington listened. Washington didn't do anything. Finally, Washington has acted. I want to thank the House and the Senate for passing a bill I will shortly sign that will modernize the Medicare system and keep a promise to this country's seniors.

For the sake of our health care system, we need to cut down on the frivolous lawsuits which increase the cost of medicine. People who have been harmed by a bad doc deserve their day in court. Yet the system should not reward lawyers who are simply fishing for a rich settlement. Frivolous lawsuits drive up the cost of health care. They therefore affect the Federal budget. Medical liability reform is a national issue which requires a national solution. I proposed a good bill for the Congress to look at. The House of Representatives passed the bill. The bill is stuck in the United States Senate. The Senators from this State must act on behalf of the American people and support medical liability reform. No one has ever been healed by a frivolous lawsuit. We need reform now.

I have the responsibility as the President to make sure the judicial system runs well, and I have met that duty. I've nominated superb men and women for the Federal courts, people who will interpret the law, not legislate from the bench. A small group of Senators is willfully obstructing the process. Some appeals court nominees, including four from the great State of Michigan, four outstanding jurists from this State, are being forced to wait months or even years for an up-or-down vote. The needless delays in the system are harming the administration of justice. They're deeply unfair to the nominees themselves. It is time for some Members of the United States Senate to stop playing politics with American justice.

This country needs an energy policy. We need a policy that encourages more conservation and energy efficiency. We need an energy policy which will help modernize the infrastructure, the capacity to deliver much needed power to homes and businesses. We need to explore in environmentally friendly ways for more energy. What we really need is, for the sake of economic security and national security, to become less dependent on foreign sources of power.

A strong and prosperous nation must be a compassionate nation as well. I'm going to continue to advance our agenda of what I call compassionate conservatism, which means we'll apply the most effective, the best, the most innovative ideas to the task of helping our fellow citizens in need. We'll promote social entrepreneurship all across our country. There's still millions of men and women who want to end their dependence on Government and become independent through hard work. We must build on the success of welfare reform by training and help, so more of our fellow citizens can find work and dignity.

Congress should pass what's called the "Citizen Service Act" so more Americans can serve their communities and their countries. Both Houses should reach agreement on my Faith-Based Initiative. Government can hand out money, can write checks, but it cannot put hope in people's hearts or a sense of purpose in people's lives. Many of the seemingly intractable problems of our society can only be solved through love. And we find love in our houses of worship. We find love where there's faith, faith of all walks of life, faith of all religions. Our Government should not fear faith. We ought to welcome faith in the helping to heal the broken hearts of America.

A compassionate society is one that promotes opportunity for all, including the independence and dignity that come from ownership. This administration will constantly strive to promote an ownership society in America. See, we want more people owning their own home. We have a minority homeownership gap in this country. I've submitted a plan to Congress to help close that gap. We want people owning and controlling their own health care plans, their own retirement accounts. We want more people owning their own small business. You see, we understand that when a person owns something in America, he or she has a vital stake in the future of this country.

A compassionate society is one in which people respect one another, respect their points of view, respect their opinions, respect their religion, and also a society in which people take responsibility for the decisions they make. The culture is changing in America from one that said, "If it feels good, just go ahead and do it," and "If you've got a problem, blame somebody else," to a culture in which each of us understands we are responsible for the decisions we make in life.

If you're fortunate enough to be a mother or a father, you're responsible for loving your child with all your heart. If you're concerned about the quality of the education in the community in which you live, you're responsible for doing something about it. If you're a CEO in corporate America, you're responsible for telling the truth to your shareholders and your employees. And in a responsibility society, each of us is responsible for loving our neighbor just like we'd like to be loved ourself.

The culture of service is strong in America. People are accepting responsibility for the decisions they make. I started what's called the USA Freedom Corps. It was a chance for people to extend a compassionate hand to people in need, and the response has been strong. Our neighborhood healers are vibrant and strong. The armies of compassion are growing all across America. Policemen and firefighters and people who wear our Nation's uniform are reminding us what it means to sacrifice for something greater than yourself in life. Once again, the children of America believe in heroes, because they see them every day.

And in these challenging times, the world has seen the resolve and the courage of America. I've been privileged to see the compassion and the character of the American people. All the tests of the last 3 years have come to the right nation. We're a strong country, and we use that strength to defend the peace. We're an optimistic country, confident in ourselves and in ideals bigger than ourselves. Abroad, we seek to lift whole nations by spreading freedom. At home, we seek to lift up lives by spreading opportunity to every corner of this country. This is the work that history has set before us. We welcome it, and we know that for our country, the best days lie ahead.

May God bless you all. Thank you for coming. Glad you're here.

NOTE: The President spoke at 12:05 p.m. at the Hyatt Regency Hotel. In his remarks, he referred to Secretary of State Terri Lynn Land and State Attorney General Mike Cox of Michigan; Rick Johnson, speaker of the Michigan State House of Representatives; Betsy DeVos, Michigan State chairman, and Sharon A. Wise, Michigan national committeewoman, Republican National Committee; and former President Saddam Hussein of Iraq.

Remarks in a Discussion With Employers and Employees at Dynamic Metal Treating, Inc., in Canton, Michigan
December 1, 2003

The President. Loren, thanks for having us. Let me say a couple things before we get started here. First, thanks for coming out to say hello. We're here, obviously, to talk about one of the great strengths of America, which is the entrepreneurial spirit of our country, the small-business men and women who create the new jobs. And we're talking about jobs. And I want to thank you all for being here today to talk about your businesses and/or your personal lives.

Just a couple of things I want to remind our fellow citizens about. We've done a lot; we've overcome a lot, when you think about what this country has been through in a short period of time. First of all, as Loren mentioned, things starting going bad in 2000 for this business. In other words, we were headed into a recession. And that's tough, when there's a recession. That means negative growth. It means businesses, in order to survive, sometimes lay people off, which, worse, means that some of our fellow citizens are looking for work and are having trouble feeding their family.

And then the enemy hit us. Just as things were getting a little better, we got attacked. And let me take a step back. I'm never going to forget the lessons of September the 11th, 2001. The only way to deal with these coldblooded killers is to stay on the offensive and bring them to justice, which is precisely what America will do.

And then we had some CEOs in corporate America forget what it means to be a responsible citizen. You might remember, right after the attacks, when the great resiliency of America came forth and the country began to recover from this unbelievable period of time, it turned out that we found—there were some corporate scandals, and that affected our confidence. We acted there. We passed some tough laws that sent a pretty clear message that if you betray the trust, if you don't tell the truth to your shareholders and employees, you need to be held to account. That means justice needs to be sent your way, and that's what's happening. And then we had a march to war. And that all affected the people's confidence.

And so when we talk about job creation and job growth, it's important to understand we have come through a lot, which speaks really to the greatness of America, doesn't it? It speaks to the greatness of the entrepreneurial spirit, to the high productivity of the American workforce. We're the best workers in the world. I think it speaks a little bit as well to the policies we put forth.

I want to thank the Members of the United States Congress who are here from the great State of Michigan. A lot of them have come over here, for which I am grateful. We passed tax relief, and I want to talk a little bit about tax relief, as we go through the panel, and its effect on economic recovery. Because when people have more money in their pocket, it means they're going to demand an additional good or a service, or likely demand a good or a service. And when that happens in our economy, somebody will produce it. And when somebody produces the good or a service to meet the demand, somebody is more likely to find a job. And so not only did the tax relief help hard-working Americans, with their pressures on their families and education needs, but it also helped the economy.

And the other thing I want to remind people about is that the tax relief was also geared toward small businesses. Most new jobs in America are created by small-business owners. You just heard Loren talk about—they laid off workers; they replaced those workers; and they've added workers. Well, there's all kinds of companies like

Dynamic Metal across the country that are adding workers, one or two or three at a time, and that's the vibrancy of our economy. And the Congress wisely cut the—made it—provided the incentive for small businesses to invest. And if the proper incentive is in place, it means people will buy equipment and computer software, and that means somebody is likely to find a job as they provide that equipment for small businesses.

The other thing is, most small businesses do not pay corporate income tax. They pay tax at the individual level because they're a Subchapter S or a limited liability partnership. And therefore, when you hear us talking about reducing all taxes on individuals, you really hear also the message that we're reducing taxes on small businesses. And when small business has got more money in their coffers, they're more likely to expand, and someone will find a job.

So what we're here today is talk about good economic policy. But really what we're here about is to make sure people can find a job. I mean, things look pretty good; the growth is high. Today the Purchasing Managers Index was released, which shows the manufacturing sector of the American economy is coming back pretty strong. But my attitude is, so long as we have one of our fellow citizens out of work and who wants to work, it says we've got a problem. So let's keep a progrowth policy in place. We're here to emphasize the role of the small business in providing that job opportunity.

I want to thank both the small-business managers as well as the employees for joining us. And Loren, after that kind of long-winded explanation of why I'm here—[*laughter*]—take over.

[*The discussion continued.*]

The President. Yes. I appreciate the story. It's indicative of how small businesses work. You'd better be light on your feet and willing to change in order to survive, be flexible and fast, and to meet the needs of your consumer. Listen, Government can create an environment in which the entrepreneurial spirit remains strong, but we can't make you successful. That's up to you. And I appreciate the—you just laid out your strategy. I hope your competitor isn't listening. [*Laughter*]

Loren Epler. We're up to the challenge. [*Laughter*]

The President. That's good. But anyway, thank you for sharing that.

Sam, how about yourself?

[*The discussion continued.*]

The President. A couple of points that Sam made: One, we need an energy policy. If you noticed, he said energy costs are high. And we need clean coal technology. We need an energy policy. We need to encourage conservation and certainly efficiencies. But in order for manufacturing concerns to be vibrant and vital, they need reliable sources of energy. And I appreciate you bringing that up.

The other thing is, Sam, is I understand these tax cuts save you and your family about $2,000.

Sam Domke. For this next tax year, yes. And that's great. I can really use the money, I'm sure.

The President. The other thing, as I understand—we had a little visit beforehand—that Sam had a chance to refinance his home. Maybe some of you have done that as well. Part of the vitality of the economy is the fact that people are able to refinance because of lower interest rates, which puts a little money in the pocket because you've got lower monthly payments. But the $2,000 is important part of an economic recovery package. You see, it's his money to begin with. And we hear people say, well, the Government is giving Government money. It's not Government money; it's the people's money we're talking about. It's the hard-working people that make this economy grow.

My attitude is, the more money you've got in your pocket, the more likely it is

your family is going to be okay, but more importantly, the more likely it is it will increase the demand for a good or a service.

Mr. Domke. I know we had the $800 checks that came back for the child credit, and that came in quite useful——

The President. Yes.

Mr. Domke. ——to help me pay some bills and——

The President. Actually, when the Government said, "The check's in the mail," it actually was. [*Laughter*]

Mr. Domke. Well, I got mine, so—[*laughter*].

The President. One of the things about the tax cuts that's important for people to understand is, they're not permanent. They're temporary because of a quirk in the law, particularly in the United States Senate. After a period of time, the tax cuts go away. And so one thing we need to do and make sure this economy stays strong is to make the tax cuts permanent. We don't want the child credit to go down. That will affect you. It's like a tax increase. We don't want the marriage penalty to be as onerous as it used to be. We want the tax cuts to stay permanent, so that people—small businesses can plan and citizens can plan their lives.

And so one of the ways that Congress can respond to the economic recovery and to make sure that this recovery keeps going is to make these tax cuts real and long-lasting. I'm for it. I think it's essential that we do this. And I hope Congress joins.

[*The discussion continued.*]

The President. Again, Government can create an environment to encourage investment; it's up to you to produce the product so people want to invest with you, want to buy your stuff. And I presume the reason why you're doing good is you've got a good workforce.

Tom Zimmerman. Yes, we do. In fact this is a——

The President. Two of them happen to be here.

Mr. Zimmerman. Let me put them on here. This is John Krynak and Cliff Daniels. Pass it on to John.

John Krynak. Mr. President, it's good to be here. It's an honor and a privilege to have you here. I'm a family man myself. I was fortunate enough not to be one of the 10 percent that was laid off. I'm very thankful for that. Spectrum is a wonderful company. I'm blessed to have a wonderful wife, Krystal, and I have four children, two daughters, 7 and 9, and two boys, 11 years old.

The President. Twins?

Mr. Krynak. No, we're a blended family.

The President. Good.

Mr. Krynak. So we got $1,600 back——

The President. That's good. [*Laughter*]

Mr. Krynak. ——$1,600 back credit this year. And it came in handy. Went down to Myrtle Beach and—[*laughter*].

The President. Yes? Somebody had to feed you when you were down there, so you helped that person keep a job. But you also got some tax relief from the reduction of the rates, as I understand it——

Mr. Krynak. Yes, this year, I——

The President. ——$2,700, somebody told me.

Mr. Krynak. Yes.

The President. I'm not putting numbers in your mouth. [*Laughter*]

Mr. Krynak. Yes, the tax relief can be a big help this year. Income is still not quite where it was, but I'm thankful that it is on the rise. Overtime is back, kicking right now. I'm ready to put my shoulders to the wheel, keep it going.

The President. I suspect old Tom is happy to have you working with him.

Mr. Zimmerman. Very much so. A good person. Same with Cliff.

[*The discussion continued.*]

Cliff Daniels. I want to retire. Your plan that you're going to sign, your Medicare prescription bill, is going to help me immensely.

The President. Yes. It is going to help you.

Mr. Daniels. And I'm figuring that I'm paying about $900 right now. And with this plan, I should save about $5,000 a year. And I do want to thank you for that very much.

The President. Well, thanks. Thank the Congress. They finally got moving.

Mr. Daniels. One more thing, sir. Can you make it a Presidential order that our local football team, the Detroit Lions, win a road game? [*Laughter*]

The President. No. [*Laughter*] If I could, I might be thinking about some of those Texas teams. [*Laughter*]

I appreciate you bringing up health care. Small businesses have got an issue with health care. I think if you were to talk to these owners, they'll tell you. Small businesses need to be able to pool risk in what's called associated health care plans. Congress needs to allow this to happen so that you can share risk across jurisdictional boundaries. And that will help with health care costs.

I appreciate you bringing up Medicare. The people in the Congress worked hard to get a good bill out. And I think it's going to make a difference in a lot of seniors' lives. It will mean we've kept our promise. It's also going to make a difference in the lives of those of us who are fixing to be seniors. It means you're going to have more choice in the marketplace, plus prescription drugs will be available as part of the basic Medicare package. And those who can least afford it will get the most help, of course, from the Government. So I thank you for bringing that up.

The other thing for health care, by the way, is it's very important that we have a society that allows a person to sue a bad doc if they get hurt. But we don't need a society in which there's junk and frivolous lawsuits being filed all the time which raise the cost of medicine, particularly to these businesses. It hurts these small-business owners when these people file these lawsuits over and over and over again. And therefore, for a while—I looked at this issue for a while, and then I decided it was a national issue because it affected our Medicare budgets, the Medicaid budgets, the veteran health care costs, because docs practice what's called defensive medicine. If they think they're going to get sued, they'll provide more medicine than needed. And you would too, if you were a doctor who thought you were going to get sued. And that then makes medicine more expensive, and it runs the cost up for you as well as the employers all around the country.

And then the other thing that happens is, docs have to pay a high premium for liability reform—insurance, and they're starting to quit the practice of medicine, which means now medicine is more expensive and less available. And so we need medical liability reform.

I want to thank the Members of the House who are here who voted with us on that bill. It was a good piece of legislation. It's stuck in the Senate, however. We need to get it out of the Senate.

And so that can help us as well. I'll tell you the other thing that I think is important for these small-business owners to hear is, at the State level—and I know that Terri Lynn is here and the attorney general is here and others from the State of Michigan are here—we need less paperwork requirements on small business, less regulations and the paperwork that these owners have to file—same, by the way, at the Federal level. It's one thing to regulate; it's another thing to overregulate. And a lot of times Government has a tendency to overregulate, which is a nonproductive cost to these small-business owners who would rather be employing people and making it easier for somebody to find work than filling out reams of paperwork that probably doesn't get read anyway.

Finally, I know there's a lot of talk about trade. I just want you to understand my position on trade. If you're good at something, we ought to try to find more markets. And we're good at a lot of things. We've got the most productive workforce in America. And we've got some of the greatest farmers in America. And we've got some of the greatest entrepreneurs in America. And therefore, it seems like to make sense to me that we ought to be opening up markets for us to sell our goods. But the other thing I want you to understand is, we're going to make sure it's fair. We want the playing field to be level so we can compete in a fair way.

But those are some of the things that we can do to keep the economy growing. And that's important. We're really here to talk about how to sustain the economic growth. About 286,000 new jobs were created over the last 3 months, and we need more. I think the foundation is laid. You've heard these two business owners talk in terms of their hiring new people and how confident they are, and that's good. We've just got to keep it going. We want everybody in the country working. We want the people who have the responsibility to put food on the table to be able to find a job to do so. We want to answer that human desire of a responsible dad to be able to say to his four children, in this case, "Here's something not only for you to eat but something for you to maybe put aside for your education." That's what we want.

And a vibrant economy will provide that opportunity for people to seize the moment. And we've got some people up here who have—one has already seized the moment. He kind of looks like he's going to try to quit seizing it. But you never retire, by the way. [*Laughter*] You never retire. And we've got some great workers and great owners up here.

I want to repeat to you that the entrepreneurial spirit of America is strong. And we aim to keep it that way. We want people owning their own business. We want people to feel like if you want to be a small-business owner, there's a chance for you. No guarantees of success, but the opportunity is available for people from all walks of life, I might add, all throughout our society. You know, one of the great strengths of America is the fact that we've got a lot of people that say, "I want to own my own company," and feel confident in trying to start that business and making it work. It's really what makes our society such a vibrant and wholesome place.

We're looking at two people right here who have taken on the tough task of running a small business. It's not easy. It may look simple when you hear them talk about it, but it's hard work. But it's the creativity and the spirit of the entrepreneur in America that I think sets us apart, and kind of the backbone and vibrancy of our society.

I want to say one other thing, and then I promise to be quiet. I met a guy at the airport today. Where is he? Did he come out? There he is. This is a good man. This is Brad Simmons. You probably never heard of Brad; I hadn't either until I landed. The reason I mention Brad is he works for Ford, but more importantly, he is in charge of encouraging Ford employees to volunteer in your communities. See, he's taken it upon himself to tap into the true spirit of the American soul, and that is that spirit that says, "I want to help a neighbor in need." And Brad's particular focus has

been on Boy Scouts. But he's got a broader job at Ford, and that is to say—to encourage voluntarism.

You know, the reason I like to talk about people like Brad—as I told Brad, he is a soldier in the army of compassion in our country. It's the Brad Simmonses of the world who really define the true character of America. You see, our strength is not measured by the size of our military or the size of our Treasury. Our strength is measured by the size of the hearts and souls of our fellow citizens, people who are willing to love a neighbor just like they'd like to be loved themselves. Brad reflects the true spirit of America. He's a great credit upon the country.

And for those of you who are doing your duty as responsible citizens, whether it being a good mom or a dad or helping a neighbor in need, I want to thank you on behalf of a grateful nation. The strength of America is the people of this country. And it's my privilege to be the President of such a great country.

God bless you all. Thank you for coming.

NOTE: The President spoke at 1:24 p.m. In his remarks, he referred to Secretary of State Terri Lynn Land and State Attorney General Mike Cox of Michigan; Loren Epler, president, and Sam Domke, quality manager, Dynamic Metal Treating, Inc.; and Tom Zimmerman, secretary and treasurer, Spectrum Automation Co.

Remarks at a Bush-Cheney Reception in Whippany, New Jersey
December 1, 2003

The President. Thank you all very much. I appreciate the warm welcome. I'm so thankful so many friends have come tonight. You know, earlier this fall, I had the honor of welcoming a fine hockey team from this State to the White House to celebrate their championship. But the start the

Devils have had this season looks like they need to repeat their trip back to the White House. I'm making similar plans myself. And with your help tonight, we are laying the foundation for what will be a victory in New Jersey in '04 and a nationwide victory in '04.

I'm getting ready. I'm loosening up. But the truth of the matter is, politics will come in its own time. See, I've got a job to do. What I would like for you to do is to remind your friends and neighbors that this administration and this President is working hard to keep America secure and strong and peaceful and free.

My only regret tonight is that Laura is not traveling with me.

Audience members. Aw-w-w.

The President. No, I know. Yes. [*Laughter*] You'd rather have her. I don't blame you. [*Laughter*] She's a fabulous wife, a great mother, and she's doing a wonderful job as our country's First Lady. And somebody who did a great job for our country, a valued member of my Cabinet, a person whose judgment I trust, that would be Christie Todd Whitman. I'm proud—[*applause*]. I miss her. But she did leave behind a little something there in Washington, DC; his name is Barney. [*Laughter*] I know——

Audience member. I love you!

The President. Gracias. [*Laughter*] I appreciate the fact that Christie Todd is our State chairman. And I want to thank my friend Lew Eisenberg for being the State campaign cochairman and finance chairman for the great State of New Jersey. I understand that some of Lew's grandchildren gave the Pledge of Allegiance. They're raising them right in his family. [*Laughter*]

I want to thank Congressman Rodney Frelinghuysen for being here. Rodney is a friend and an ally. He's doing a great job for the people of New Jersey. I'm also pleased that his wife, Virginia, is with him. I also want to thank my friend and ally Mike Ferguson—Congressman Mike Ferguson.

I know we've got members of the statehouse here. I particularly want to thank Senator Joe Kyrillos, who is the party chairman; State Senator Leonard Lance, who is the new minority leader for the State senate; State Assemblyman Alex DeCroce is the new minority leader.

I know we've got a lot of mayors here. I want to thank the mayors for coming. My only advice is to make sure you fill the potholes—[*laughter*]—and pick up the garbage. [*Laughter*] I thank the mayors for being here. Thank you for serving your towns and your communities.

I particularly want to thank my friend Mercer Reynolds, who's the national finance chairman. And he's from Cincinnati, Ohio. He's joined us today.

I want to thank all the grassroot activists who are here. You win campaigns by convincing your neighbor to go to the poll. So I want to thank you for what you're going to do, which is put up the signs and get on the phones and mail out the letters and convince your fellow citizens to do their duty and to show up to vote in November of 2004. You might just convince them, when they show up to vote, to vote for Bush-Cheney.

Remind them that during the last 3 years, our Nation has acted decisively to confront great challenges. I came to this office to solve problems and not pass them on to future Presidents and future generations. I came to seize opportunities instead of letting them slip away. My administration is meeting the tests of our time.

Terrorists declared war on the United States of America, and war is what they got. We captured or killed many of the key leaders of the Al Qaida network, and the rest of them know we're on their trail. In Afghanistan and Iraq, we gave ultimatums to terror regimes. Those regimes chose defiance, and those regimes are no more. Fifty million people in those two countries once lived under tyranny, and today, they live in freedom.

Three years ago, our military was not receiving the resources it needed, and morale was beginning to suffer, so we increased the defense budgets to prepare for the threats of a new era. And today, no one in the world can question the skill, the strength, and the spirit of the United States military.

Three years ago, the economy was in trouble and a recession was beginning. And then our country was attacked, and we had scandals in corporate America, and war—all affected the people's confidence. But we acted. We passed up new laws to hold corporate criminals to account. And to get the economy going again, I have twice led the United States Congress to pass historic tax relief for the American people. We know that when Americans have more take-home pay to spend, to save, or invest, the whole economy grows, and people are more likely to find a job. That's why we're returning more money to the people to help them raise their families, why we reduced taxes on dividends and capital gains to encourage investment. And that's why we're giving small businesses incentives to expand and to hire new people. With all these actions, this administration has laid the foundation for greater prosperity across America so that every single person in this country has a chance to realize the American Dream.

Today, the American economy is strong, and it is getting stronger. Perhaps you noticed that the third quarter annualized rate of growth numbers were increased to 8.2 percent, the fastest pace in nearly 20 years. Today the Purchasing Managers Index came out, showing that our manufacturing sector is recovering strongly. Productivity is high. Housing constructing is booming. The tax relief we passed, the economic stimulus plan that we passed, is working.

Three years ago, there was a lot of talk about education reform in Washington, DC, but there wasn't much action. So I acted. I called for and the Congress passed the No Child Left Behind Act. With a solid bipartisan majority, we delivered the most dramatic education reform in a generation. We believe that every child in America can learn the basics of reading and math, and we believe that every school in America should teach the basics. This administration is challenging the soft bigotry of low expectations. In return for increased Federal dollars, we now expect results. The days of excuse-making are over. We want every child to learn to read and write and add and subtract so that not one single child is left behind in America.

We reorganized our Government and created the Department of Homeland Security to better safeguard the borders and ports of America and to better protect the American people. We passed trade promotion authority to open up new markets for New Jersey's farmers and entrepreneurs and manufacturers. We passed budget agreements to help bring spending discipline to Washington, DC. On issue after issue, this administration has acted on principle, has kept its word, and has made progress for the American people.

The United States Congress has shared in these great achievements. I appreciate working with Speaker Denny Hastert and Majority Leader Bill Frist. I want to thank Rodney and Mike for working with us to focus on results. The tone in Washington needs to be changed. There's too much needless partisanship, backbiting, and bickering. The best way to do that is to focus on results, and that's what we'll continue to do. We'll work with Congress to focus on results, to do the people's business.

And those are the kind of people I've attracted to my administration. I've put together a superb group of men and women from all walks of life to serve the American people. And we've had no finer Vice President than Dick Cheney. Mother may have a second opinion. [Laughter]

In 3 years, we have done a lot. In 3 years, we've come far, but our work is only beginning. I have set great goals worthy of a great nation. First, America is committed to expanding the realm of freedom and peace for our own security and for the benefit of the world. And second, in our own country, we must work for a society that is prosperous and compassionate so every single citizen has a chance to work and to succeed and realize the great promise of America.

It is clear that the future of freedom and peace depend on the actions of America. This Nation is freedom's home and freedom's defender. We welcome this charge of history, and we are keeping it. The war on terror continues. The enemies of freedom are not idle, and neither are we. This country will not rest, we will not tire, we will not stop until this danger to civilization is removed.

We're confronting that danger in Iraq, where Saddam holdouts and foreign terrorists are desperately trying to throw Iraq into chaos by attacking coalition forces and international aid workers and innocent Iraqi citizens. They know that the advance of freedom in the heart of the Middle East would be a major defeat for the cause of terror. This collection of coldblooded killers is trying to shake the will of the United States. The United States will never be intimidated by a bunch of thugs and assassins.

We are aggressively striking the terrorists in Iraq, defeating them there so we do not have to face them in our own country. And other nations are helping, because they understand a free Iraq will make us all more secure. And we're standing with the brave Iraqi people as they assume more of their own defense and move toward self-government. These are not easy tasks, but they are essential tasks. We will finish what we have begun, and we will win this essential victory in the war on terror.

Our greatest security comes from the advance of human liberty, because free nations do not support terror. Free nations do not attack their neighbors. Free nations do not threaten the world with weapons of mass terror. Americans believe that freedom is the deepest need and hope of every human heart. I believe that freedom is the future of every nation. And I know that freedom is not America's gift to the world; freedom is the Almighty's gift to each man and woman who lives in the world.

America understands that unprecedented influence brings tremendous responsibilities. We have duties in this world. When we see disease and starvation and hopeless poverty, we will not turn away. And that is why, on the continent of Africa, America is now committed to bringing the healing power of medicine to millions of men, women, and children now suffering with AIDS. This great, powerful nation is leading the world in this incredibly important work of human rescue.

We face challenges at home as well, and our actions will prove that we're equal to the challenges. Even though the economic numbers look good, there are still people who are trying to find a job. I will continue to promote a progrowth, entrepreneurially friendly growth package so that the people of America can find work.

As Christie Todd has mentioned, we are keeping our commitment to America's seniors by strengthening and modernizing Medicare. For years, seniors have called for a modern Medicare system that provides health care choices and prescription drug coverage. For years, the Congress did nothing. Finally, the House and the Senate have both approved legislation, which I will soon sign, that will keep our promise to America's seniors.

For the sake of our health care system, we need to cut down on the frivolous lawsuits which increase the cost of medicine. People who have been harmed by a bad doc deserve their day in court, yet the system should not reward lawyers who are simply fishing for a rich settlement. Frivolous lawsuits drive up the cost of health care and, therefore, they affect the Federal budget. Medical liability reform is a national issue which requires a national solution. I submitted a good plan to the Congress. The House of Representatives passed the plan. It is stuck in the United States Senate. Perhaps you ought to write your United States Senators and remind them that nobody in America has been healed by a frivolous lawsuit. We need medical liability reform now.

I have a responsibility as your President to make sure the judicial system runs well, and I have met that duty. I have nominated superb men and women to the Federal bench, people who will interpret the law, not legislate from the bench. Some Members of the United States Senate are trying to keep my nominees off the bench by blocking up-or-down votes. Every judicial nominee deserves a fair hearing and an up-or-down vote on the Senate floor. It is time for some of the Members of the U.S. Senate to stop playing politics with American justice.

Congress needs to get an energy bill to my desk. This country needs a comprehensive energy plan that will encourage conservation, that will enable us to develop new technologies that will enable us to find energy in environmentally friendly ways. For the sake of economic security and for the sake of national security, this country must become less dependent on foreign sources of energy.

A strong and prosperous nation must also be a compassionate nation. I will continue to advance our agenda of what I call compassionate conservatism, which means we'll find the most innovative, effective ideas to help neighbors who hurt. There are still millions of men and women who want to end their dependence upon Government and become independent through hard work. Congress must continue to build on the success of welfare reform, provide job training money to help our fellow citizens find a job. Congress should complete the "Citizen Service Act" so more Americans can serve their communities and their country. Both Houses should reach agreement on my Faith-Based Initiative to support the armies of compassion that are mentoring children and caring for the homeless and offering hope for the addicted. One of the great strengths of our country is the fact that we are a nation of many faiths and the fact that faith-based people, whether they be Christian, Jewish, or Muslim, have had a universal call to

help somebody in need. Government should not fear faith; we ought to welcome faith and to help healing—to help to heal hurting hearts and people who need help in America.

A compassionate society must promote opportunity for all, including the independence and dignity that come from ownership. This administration will constantly strive to promote an ownership society in America. We want more people owning their own home. We have a minority homeownership gap in America. I presented plans to the Congress to close that gap. We want more people owning and managing their own retirement accounts and their own health care plans. We want more people owning their own small business in America, because this administration understands that when a person owns something, he or she has a vital stake in the future of our country.

In a compassionate society, people respect one another, respect their point of view, respect their religious beliefs, and take responsibility for the decisions they make. The culture of America is changing from one that has said, "If it feels good, do it," and "If you've got a problem, blame somebody else," to a new day, a culture in which each of us understands that we're responsible for the decisions we make in life. If you are fortunate enough to be a mother or a father, you're responsible for loving your child with all your heart. If you're worried about the quality of the education in the community in which you live, you're responsible for doing something about it. If you're a CEO in corporate America, you're responsible for telling the truth to your shareholders and your employees. And in a new responsibility society, each of us is responsible for heeding a universal call to love a neighbor just like we'd like to be loved ourself.

The culture of service is strong in America. People are responding to the call to serve their country. I started what's called the USA Freedom Corps to encourage

Americans to extend a compassionate hand to a neighbor in need. The response has been strong. People are serving their Nation by supporting charities, faith-based groups, neighborhood healers that are changing America one life at a time. Policemen and firefighters and the people who wear our Nation's uniform remind us what it means to sacrifice for something greater than ourselves. Once again, the children of America believe in heroes, because they see them every day.

In these challenging times, the world has seen the resolve and the courage of America. I've been privileged to see the compassion and the character of the American people. All the tests of the last 3 years have come to the right nation. We're a strong country, and we use that strength to defend the peace. We're an optimistic country, confident in ourselves and in ideals bigger than ourselves.

Abroad, we seek to lift whole nations by spreading freedom. At home, we seek to lift up lives by spreading opportunity to every corner of America. This is the work that history has set before us. We welcome it. And we know that for our country, the best days lie ahead.

Thank you for coming. God bless.

NOTE: The President spoke at 5:55 p.m. at the Hanover Marriott. In his remarks, he referred to Christine Todd Whitman, former Administrator, Environmental Protection Agency.

Statement on Signing the Energy and Water Development Appropriations Act, 2004
December 1, 2003

Today, I have signed into law H.R. 2754, the "Energy and Water Development Appropriations Act, 2004." The Act funds programs of the Department of Energy, the Department of the Interior's Bureau of Reclamation, the Army Corps of Engineers, and several other agencies, and provides funds to help protect the Nation's environment.

The executive branch shall construe provisions of the Act that direct the Secretary of a military department to perform the Secretary's duties through a particular military officer in a manner consistent with the statutory authority of the Secretary of Defense to exercise authority, direction, and control of the Department of Defense and the constitutional authority of the President to supervise the unitary executive branch and as Commander in Chief.

Provisions in sections 209 and 303 and under the heading "Construction, General" in title I purport to require the approval of committees of the Congress before executive branch execution of aspects of the Act or to preclude executive branch execution of a provision of the Act upon the written disapproval of such a committee. The executive branch shall construe such provisions to require only notification to the Congress, as any other construction would contravene the constitutional principles set forth by the Supreme Court in *INS* v. *Chadha*.

GEORGE W. BUSH

The White House,

December 1, 2003.

NOTE: H.R. 2754, approved December 1, was assigned Public Law No. 108–137.

Remarks on Signing the Adoption Promotion Act of 2003
December 2, 2003

The President. Good to see you all. Thank you. Thanks. Please be seated. Hi, Mary. Thank you, Jim. Thanks for coming. Thank you all for coming. Gosh, we got a lot of great families with us today. We're really proud you all are here. I want to thank you for coming to the Roosevelt Room. I'm delighted you're here.

The adoption of a boy or a girl is a moment of joy for a family, and it's a act of great generosity. When parents share their homes and all they have with a child, the child they adopt and love as their own, all their lives are transformed forever. Isn't that right?

Diana Martin. Yes.

Christopher Martin. Yes. [*Laughter*]

The President. In every young life, there is a great need to belong. For the sake of our children, this Nation has a responsibility to encourage adoption of children at all ages, from infants to adolescents. The legislation I'm about to sign today sends a clear message: Our society is building a culture that values every life, and our Government strongly supports adoption.

I appreciate Deputy Secretary Claude Allen from the Department of Health and Human Services for joining us. I want to thank three Members of the Congress who have been instrumental in this legislation, and I appreciate their good, hard work. Senator Mary Landrieu of the great State of Louisiana is with us, Jim Oberstar of Minnesota, and Dave Camp of Michigan. Thank you all for coming. I appreciate you taking time to come to herald this important piece of legislation. I'm honored you all are here.

Bruce Willis is not with us, but I do want to thank him for being the national spokesperson on foster care and adoption. His message is helpful. It's important to help spread the word about the joys of adoption, and Bruce has been mighty helpful in doing just that.

I want to thank the parents of adoptive children who are with us today. The Martin family, the Hendrix family are with us, the Morris family and the Schwarzwalder family. I'm honored you all are here. I want to thank you for giving me a chance and the Members of Congress a chance, after the bill signing, to personally thank you for showing America the generosity of spirit that makes our country such a wonderful place. We're really glad you're here.

Thanks to the Congress and thanks to the groups that work on behalf of foster children and to moms and dads across America, these last few years have brought real progress in the cause of adoption. We're making progress here in America.

Six years ago, Congress provided new incentives to the States to promote foster care adoptions, and those incentives have worked. I suspect these Members of Congress worked on that important legislation. In just 5 years, from 1998 to 2002, the States placed more than 230,000 children in adoptive homes—about the same number that had been adopted in the previous 10 years. We're making some progress here in America.

In the same period, 33 States and the District of Columbia have at least doubled foster care adoptions. To further promote adoption, we increased the adoption tax credit in 2001 from $5,000 to $10,000. I want to thank the Members for working on that important piece of legislation. I hope it helps families.

In 2002, my administration created a new web site called AdoptUSKids.org, which has already helped to join nearly 2,000 children with adoptive parents. In other words, if you want to be a part of this movement of love in America, go to the web site, and the web site will help you understand how best to become an adoptive parent. Many more still await their chance and their home, and we are determined to help all children in America.

Today in America, more 126,000 foster children still need an adoptive family. And nearly half of these children are past the age of 9. Foster parents bring help and kindness at a crucial point in a child's life, yet foster care is by nature temporary. And the aim of the system and the desire of every child is a permanent home.

The bill I sign this morning will help bring that opportunity to many more children of all ages. The Adoption Promotion Act of 2003 will continue all the current incentives that have created new momentum for the adoption process in our States. In addition, we will begin monitoring the adoptions of foster children age 9 and older and provide extra incentives for States to increase adoption of older children. This is a proven way to increase the placement of children from foster care to permanent homes, and each one of those homes will be richer for the addition of new family members.

Here's one example standing with me. It's what we call a good-size American family. [*Laughter*]

Mrs. Martin. Amen.

Mr. Martin. Yes.

The President. Diana and Chris Martin, good, solid Americans, good, loving mom and dad, are with us with seven children, four of them adopted at ages 6, 8, 10, and 11 years old.

You were 6.

Mrs. Martin. That's right.

The President. How old are you?

Terrance Martin. Seven.

The President. Okay, 7. [*Laughter*] I'll take it up with the fact-checker. [*Laughter*] Children who, at one time, were 6, 8, 10, and 11. [*Laughter*]

Chris says, "Besides having to add a whole new wing on the house"—maybe the tax credit helps—[*laughter*]—"it can be emotionally trying. They have a sense of

abandonment, and they came with the fear of bonding to you because they've been let down, and they're afraid." He also said, "It's been rewarding because you can see the love in their eyes when they finally realize they have a place, they have a home, and that I am their dad."

Adoptive parents are giving much, and they are gaining much. The future of many thousands of children depend on the willingness of caring parents to make that personal commitment. It would take less than 1 percent of the American population to provide a home to every child awaiting adoption. Welcoming a child into your home and calling that child your son or daughter is a major decision. It is never to be made lightly. Yet so many parents who have made that decision count it among life's greatest and happiest turning points. And so I hope more Americans, after careful thought and prayer, will make the decision to adopt a boy or girl of their own.

The act of Congress strongly affirms our national commitment to adoption and will encourage adoption in every part of our land. I want to thank you all for coming. We're honored to be with such loving parents and great Americans.

And now I'd like to ask the Members of Congress to join me as I sign this important piece of legislation, and maybe this great family would like to join us as well. Thanks for coming.

Here, Mary, get in here. All right, is everybody ready?

Audience members. Yes.

Child. Can I come in there too?

The President. You want to come in here? [*Laughter*]

Children. Yes.

The President. Sure, come on. All right. They won't ask her any questions. [*Laughter*] You ready?

NOTE: The President spoke at 9:25 a.m. in the Roosevelt Room at the White House. In his remarks, he referred to actor Bruce Willis, spokesman for Children in Foster Care.

H.R. 3182, approved December 2, was assigned Public Law No. 108–145.

Remarks at a Bush-Cheney Luncheon in Pittsburgh, Pennsylvania
December 2, 2003

I appreciate you coming. Thanks for being here. It's great to be back in Knowledge City—Pittsburgh, Pennsylvania. Thanks for the warm welcome. I thought I'd start off by talking a little bit about Texas football. [*Laughter*] Then I ran into Jerome Bettis. [*Laughter*] I'm a man who listens to good advice. [*Laughter*] So I'd better talk about thanking you for coming. [*Laughter*]

I appreciate your strong support. I'm proud to be back in Pennsylvania. We're laying the foundation for what is going to be a victory in Pennsylvania in 2004 and a nationwide victory in 2004.

I'm getting ready. I'm loosening up. [*Laughter*] But politics will come in its own time. I've got a job to do. I've got a job to do for every single American. I want you to remind your friends as the political season unwinds that I will continue to work hard to earn the confidence of every American by keeping this Nation secure and strong and prosperous and free.

I regret one thing about today, and that is that Laura is not traveling with me. Yes. You probably regret the fact that she's not the headline speaker. [*Laughter*] She is a fabulous lady. I love her dearly. She's a great wife, a wonderful mother, and she's doing a wonderful job for the people of this country as the First Lady.

I appreciate Evans Rose's leadership and short introduction. [*Laughter*] Evans has done a fine job. He's been a friend for a long time. I want to thank you for responding to his call. I want to thank Arlen Specter, who is the State campaign cochairman for Bush-Cheney '04. I'm proud that he's traveling with me today on Air Force One. He'll attest to the fact there's not much air rage on Air Force One. [*Laughter*] But I'm proud of his leadership for the State of Pennsylvania. I look forward to working with him as the chairman of the Judiciary Committee in the United States Senate to make sure my judges get through and get appointed.

I want to thank Congresswoman Melissa Hart and Congressman Tim Murphy for joining us today. Both are doing a fine job and are strong members of the mighty Pennsylvania delegation. I understand my friend Rob Portman has snuck across the border from the State of Ohio. I appreciate so very much Rob being here. He's one of the rising stars in the United States House of Representatives and is a strong ally.

I'm honored that the Attorney General Mike Fisher has joined us. General, I'm glad you're here. I appreciate you coming.

I want to thank the local and State officials who are here. I know we've got the—Roddey is with us, and other mayors might be with us. If you're a mayor who is here, my only advice is to make sure you fill the potholes—[*laughter*]—maybe pick up the garbage too. Thanks for serving.

My friend Mercer Reynolds, who is the Bush-Cheney '04 national finance chairman, is here today. And I appreciate Mercer's strong support and hard work. David Girard-diCarlo is here, and Manny Stamatakis is here. They're both great friends. They're not from this part of the State; they're from down there in the Philadelphia area, like Arlen, but they're strong supporters and they're taking a leadership role to help us raise money. I appreciate Leslie Gromis Baker for her hard work.

And I want to thank all the grassroots politicians who are here, the people who are turning out the vote. I'm counting on you. I'm counting on you to go to your coffee shops and community centers, and I'm counting on you to put up the signs and to make the phone calls and to mail the letters. I'm counting on you to find the people and get them to the polls. That's how you win elections. And that's how we're going to win in Pennsylvania, because of your hard work and strong support.

And finally, I'm proud to be here with Lynn Swann, my friend who is the chairman of the President's Council on Physical Fitness. What you need to do—[applause]—you need to exercise. [Laughter] And Lynn is helping us send the message to young and old alike in this country that a healthy America is a country that takes care of its physical fitness needs. As a matter of fact, when I get back this evening, I think I'll just get a good jog in. I appreciate Lynn's friendship.

In the last 3 years, our Nation has acted decisively to confront great challenges. I came to this office to solve problems instead of passing them on to future Presidents and future generations. I came to seize opportunities instead of letting them slip away. My administration is meeting the tests of our time.

Terrorists declared war on the United States of America, and war is what they got. We have captured or killed many key leaders of the Al Qaida network, and the rest of them know we're on their trail. In Afghanistan and in Iraq, we gave ultimatums to terror regimes. Those regimes chose defiance, and those regimes are no more. Fifty million people in those two countries once lived under tyranny, and today, they live in freedom.

Three years ago, our military was not receiving the help it needed, and morale was beginning to suffer, so we increased the defense budget to prepare for the threats of a new era. And today, no one in the world can question the skill and the strength and the spirit of the United States military.

Three years ago, the economy was in trouble, and a recession was beginning. And then our country was attacked, and we had some scandals in corporate America, and we marched to war for our own security and for the peace of the world. All that affected the people's confidence. But we acted. We passed tough new laws to hold corporate criminals to account. And to get the economy going again, I have twice led the United States Congress to pass historic tax relief for the American people. When Americans have more take-home pay to spend, to save or invest, the whole economy grows, and some people are more likely to be able to find a job. So we're returning money to the American people to help them raise their families, reducing taxes on dividends and capital gains to encourage investment. We're giving small businesses incentives to expand so they can hire new people. With all these actions, this administration has laid the foundation for greater prosperity and more jobs across America, so every single citizen has a chance to realize the American Dream.

The American economy is strong, and it is getting stronger. Perhaps you saw the fact that the third quarter annualized growth numbers were increased to 8.2 percent, the fastest pace in nearly 20 years. Yesterday, the Purchasing Managers Index was released, which shows strong growth in the manufacturing sector of the U.S. economy. Productivity is high. Business investment is rising. Housing construction is strong. The economic stimulus package that we passed out of the United States Congress is working.

Three years ago, there was a lot of talk about education reform, but there wasn't much action. So I acted. I called for and the Congress passed the No Child Left Behind Act. With a solid bipartisan majority, we delivered the most dramatic education reforms in a generation. This administration is challenging the soft bigotry of low expectations. We believe every child can learn the basics of reading and math. We expect every school to teach the basics of reading and math. In return for increased Federal money for Title I students, we want States to measure so that not one single child is left behind in America.

We reorganized the Government and created the Department of Homeland Security, ably headed by former Governor of Pennsylvania Tom Ridge. We did so to better safeguard our borders and our ports and to better protect the American people. We passed trade promotion authority to open up new markets for America's entrepreneurs and farmers and ranchers and manufacturers. We passed much needed budget agreements to maintain spending discipline. In Washington, DC, on issue after issue, this administration has acted on principle, has kept its word, and has made progress for the American people.

The Congress gets a lot of credit. I enjoy working with Speaker Denny Hastert and Senate Majority Leader Bill Frist. I enjoy working with the Pennsylvania Senators and the Members of the House. I enjoy working on the people's business. We're working hard to change the tone in Washington, DC. It's—there's just too much backbiting and endless politics. And the best way to change the tone is to focus on results, is to do the work on behalf of the American people. And that's exactly what we're doing.

And those are the kind of people I've attracted to my administration. I've assembled a fine group of Americans, people from all walks of life, people from different backgrounds, who have come to Washington, DC, with one thing in mind, and that is to serve the greatest nation on the face of the Earth. Our country has had no finer Vice President than Dick Cheney. Mother has a second opinion. [Laughter]

In 3 years, we have come far. We have done a lot for the people, but our work is only beginning. We have great—I have

set great goals worthy of a great nation. First, America is committed to expanding the realm of freedom and peace for our own security and for the benefit of the world. And second, in our own country, we must work for a society that is prosperous and compassionate so that every single citizen has a chance to realize the great promise of America.

It is clear that the future of freedom and peace depend on the actions of America. This Nation is freedom's home and freedom's defender. We welcome this charge of history, and we are keeping it. The war on terror continues. The enemies of freedom are not idle, and neither are we. This country will not rest, we will not stop, we will not tire until this danger to civilization is removed.

We are confronting that danger in Iraq, where Saddam holdouts and foreign terrorists are desperately trying to throw Iraq into chaos by attacking coalition forces or international aid workers and innocent Iraqi citizens. See, they know that the advance of freedom in the heart of the Middle East would be a major defeat for the cause of terror. This collection of coldblooded killers is trying to shake the will of the United States. America will never be intimidated by a bunch of thugs and assassins.

We are aggressively striking the terrorists in Iraq, defeating them there so we do not have to face them in our own cities. Other nations are helping in Iraq, because they understand a free Iraq will make us all more secure. And we're standing with the brave Iraqi citizens as they assume more of their own defense and move towards self-government. These are not easy tasks, but they are essential tasks. We will finish what we have begun, and we will win this important victory in the war against terror.

Our greatest security comes from the advance of human liberty, because free nations do not support terror, free nations do not attack their neighbors, free nations do not threaten the world with weapons of mass terror. Americans believe that freedom is the deepest need and hope of every human heart. I believe that freedom is the future of every nation. I know that freedom is not America's gift to the world; freedom is God's gift to every man and woman in this world.

America also understands that unprecedented influence brings tremendous responsibilities. We have duties in the world. When we see disease and starvation and hopeless poverty, we will not turn away. And that is why, on the continent of Africa, America is committed to bringing the healing power of medicine to the millions of men and women and children suffering with AIDS. This great, powerful nation is leading the world in this incredibly important work of human rescue.

We face challenges here at home, and our actions will prove we're equal to the challenges. I'm going to stay focused on a progrowth economic agenda, one that elevates the entrepreneurial spirit of America, until everybody who wants to work can find a job.

We're keeping our commitment to our country's seniors by strengthening and modernizing Medicare. For years, our seniors have called for a modern Medicare system that provides more choices and prescription drug coverage. For years, the United States Congress did nothing. Finally, the Congress acted. The House and the Senate have approved historic legislation that I look forward to signing soon that will keep this country's promise to our Nation's elderly citizens.

For the sake of our health care system, we need to cut down on the frivolous lawsuits which increase the cost of medicine. People who have been harmed by a bad doc deserve their day in court, yet the system should not reward lawyers who are fishing for a rich settlement. Frivolous lawsuits drive up the cost of health care. They therefore affect the Federal budget. Medical liability reform is a national issue that requires a national solution.

I proposed a good plan to the Congress. The House of Representatives passed a good bill to reform the system. The bill is stuck in the United States Senate. I appreciate the hard work of Senator Specter and Senator Santorum to get the bill to the floor of the United States Senate. Yet it is being blocked. It is time for some of the Members of the United States Senate to understand that no one has ever been healed by a frivolous lawsuit in America. We need medical liability reform now.

I have a responsibility as the President to make sure the judicial system runs well, and I have met that duty. I have nominated superb men and women for the Federal courts, people who will interpret the law, not legislate from the bench. My nominees have been strongly supported by your two United States Senators, yet some Members of the Senate are trying to keep my nominees off the bench by blocking up-or-down votes. Every judicial nominee deserves a fair hearing and an up-or-down vote on the floor of the Senate. It is time for some members of the United States Senate to stop playing politics with American justice.

This country needs a national energy policy. We need an energy bill out of the United States Congress. I appreciate the hard work in both bodies, but they need to get a bill to my desk. We need to encourage conservation. We need energy efficiency. We need new technologies to help us explore for energy in environmentally friendly ways. But for the sake of economic security and for the sake of national security, this country must become less dependent on foreign sources of energy.

A strong and prosperous nation must also be a compassionate nation. I will continue to advance what I call compassionate conservation, which means we'll apply the best, most efficient, and most innovative ideas to the task of helping our fellow citizens who are in need. There are still millions of men and women who want to end their dependence on the Government and become independent through hard work. I look forward to working with Congress to expand on the success of welfare reform and to help people better prepare themselves and to better find a job and the dignity that comes from working.

Congress should complete the "Citizen Service Act" so more of our citizens can serve their communities and their country. Both Houses should reach agreement on my Faith-Based Initiative. It will help support the armies of compassion that are mentoring our children, caring for the homeless, offering hope to the addicted. America's strength is based upon our religious diversity. People of all faiths have heard a call to help somebody who hurts. Our Government must not fear faith; we must welcome faith into helping solve the intractable problems that face our country.

A compassionate society is one that promotes opportunity for everybody, including the independence that comes from owning something. This administration is working hard to promote an ownership society in America. We want more people owning their own home. We have a minority home-ownership gap in America, and I presented plans to help close that gap. We want people owning and managing their own retirement accounts, owning and controlling their own health care accounts. We want more people owning their own small business. This administration understands that when a person owns something, he or she has a vital stake in the future of our country.

A compassionate society is one in which people respect one another, respect their opinions, respect their religious beliefs, and a society in which people take responsibility for the decisions they make. The culture of this country is changing from one that has said, "If it feels good, just go ahead and do it," and "If you've got a problem, blame somebody else," to a culture in which each of us is responsible for the decisions we make. If you're a mom or a dad, you're responsible for loving your child with all your heart. If you don't like the quality of the education in the community

in which you live, you're responsible for doing something about it. If you're a CEO in corporate America, you are responsible for telling the truth to your shareholders and your employees. In a responsibility society, each of us is responsible for loving our neighbor just like we'd like to be loved ourselves.

The culture of service is strong in America. The culture of responsibility is growing. You know, I started what's called the USA Freedom Corps; it's a chance to encourage Americans to extend a compassionate hand to somebody who hurts. And the response is strong. The charitable organizations in America are growing. I want to thank you for supporting our local charities, thank you for helping people who hurt. You know, the true strength of the country is found in the heart and souls of the American citizens. Policemen and firefighters and people who wear our Nation's uniform are reminding us what it means to sacrifice for something greater than ourselves. Once again the children of America believe in heroes, because they see them every day.

In these challenging times, the world has seen the resolve and the courage of America. And I have been privileged to see the compassion and the character of the American people. All the tests of the last 3 years have come to the right nation. We're a strong country, and we use that strength to defend the peace. We're an optimistic country, confident in ourselves and in ideals bigger than ourselves. Abroad, we seek to lift up whole nations by spreading freedom. At home, we seek to lift up lives by spreading opportunity to every corner of this country. This is the work that history has set before us. We welcome it, and we know that for our country, the best days lie ahead.

God bless you all. Thank you for coming. Proud you're here.

NOTE: The President spoke at 11:58 a.m. at the Westin Convention Center Hotel. In his remarks, he referred to Pittsburgh Steelers running back Jerome Bettis; Pennsylvania State Attorney General Mike Fisher; Allegheny County Chief Executive Jim Roddey; and David Girard-diCarlo, Pennsylvania State cochairman, and Leslie Gromis Baker, campaign chairperson for the mid-Atlantic region, Bush-Cheney '04, Inc.

Remarks Honoring 2003 NASCAR Drivers
December 2, 2003

The President. Good to see you all. Thanks for coming. Welcome. Please be seated. Thanks for coming. Welcome to the White House, and congratulations on a great NASCAR Winston Cup Series. We're honored you all are here. I see a lot of the "Bubbas" who work in my administration who have shown up. [*Laughter*] I wonder why. I've hosted champions from many sports here at the White House—first time, however, we ever parked stock cars in the South Lawn. [*Laughter*] We're proud you all are here.

I'm proud to be here with such an outstanding group of NASCAR drivers. I didn't realize you all dressed up so well—[*laughter*]—with the NASCAR owners, the crew members, and the executives of this fine sport.

I appreciate the Members of Congress who are here. I see Senator Jon Kyl of Arizona. I didn't realize you were such a race fan, Senator—helped us get the Medicare bill through the Senate, by the way. I appreciate Bart Gordon of Tennessee for joining us. Congressman Mac Collins—I knew he was a race car fan. It's good to see you, Mac.

Representative Collins. [*Inaudible*]

The President Yes, you are a "Bubba." [*Laughter*] I'm glad you all are here. I thought you might be here just because you were looking for a fast ride back up to the Capitol.

I want to congratulate Matt Kenseth, the 2003 Winston Cup points champion. Like all champs, he succeeded because of his dedication and his hard work. He started racing late-model cars in his home State of Wisconsin before he was 20 years old. He worked his way up the ranks to the Busch Series. I kind of like the name of that series. [*Laughter*] This year, he drove his number 17 Ford all the way to the Winston Cup title. He's a great driver, and, like me, he married well. We appreciate Katie coming here today. Thanks for being here, Katie.

But every NASCAR fan knows that behind the—the talent behind the wheel is not just enough, that NASCAR is a team sport. When you hear these drivers talk after a victory, they're always talking about how well their team performed, how well the team did. He had a great group in the pit, obviously—otherwise, he wouldn't be the champion—starting with the cat in the hat, the team owner, Jack Roush. Thank you for coming, Jack, and congratulations. Every team needs a strong crew chief, and Matt had a great one in Robbie Reiser. Robbie, thank you for coming. I appreciate you being here. Some of the other members of the crew are here as well. Where are they, Robbie? Where are the members of your crew? Well, they must have—couldn't pass the security check. Let them in the gate. [*Laughter*] But all of you have earned your right— earned the right to call yourselves champs. I congratulate you. We welcome you to the White House. I'm really proud of the job you've done.

One of the reasons for the success of NASCAR is the strength of its leadership. I want the thank Mike Helton, who is the president of NASCAR, for coming today. Mike, you're doing a great job.

But there's no doubt NASCAR is where it is today because of a great entrepreneur, a person who understands the consumer, the customer, and built this sport up to what it is, and that is Bill France, Jr. We're honored you're here, Bill. Thank you for coming. I appreciate Betty Jane coming as well. It's great to see you again, Betty Jane. I'm also so pleased that Lesa Kennedy, who is the president of the Daytona International Speedway, is with us; Brian France, who's taken over his dad's position at NASCAR. You know, there's nothing wrong, Brian, with following your father's footsteps. [*Laughter*] The France family is a great American family, and we're really proud you're here.

We're proud some of the members of the board from NASCAR are with us today. I'm glad my friend, former Governor Bill Graves, is here. Thank you all for coming.

We also have some former Winston Cup champs—Tony Stewart—I had the honor of greeting Tony at the Oval Office last year. Bill Elliott is with us. Some pretty fine Texans are up here too—the Labonte boys, Bobby and Terry—from Corpus, right? That's what I thought. You still from Corpus? They still claim you in Corpus. Yes. [*Laughter*]

Mark Martin is not on the stage with us, but he's one of the fine drivers on the NASCAR circuit. Mark, we're proud you're here. Thank you for coming. Some of the young drivers are with us today. These are the ones that are attracting some of the young fans to this fantastic sport—Jimmie Johnson and Dale Earnhardt, Jr., Kevin Harvick, and Ryan Newman. I'm really glad you all are here. Thanks for coming. It's such a thrill to have you on the South Lawn.

NASCAR is one of the fastest growing sports in America today; 75 million Americans now count themselves as fans. And NASCAR has followers around the world who listen to your races in 21 languages

and a hundred different countries. It's a fantastic international sport. And it's easy to figure out why the sport is so popular. The competition is intense, the drivers and their crews are skillful, the finishes are oftentimes dramatic.

NASCAR has a proud history dating back to 1948. And today, you're carrying on the tradition set by some of the great legends of American sport, Richard Petty and Cale Yarborough and Dale Earnhardt.

It's a time of change for NASCAR. It's one of the reasons why the sport is continuing to attract a lot of fans. Yet the values long held by the drivers in this sport endure. It's one of the things I like most about NASCAR. You know the work you do away from the track is really what makes the NASCAR drivers the true champs. After Hurricane Isabelle and the California wildfires, Jimmie Johnson worked with Lowe's and the American Red Cross to raise money for the victims for those disasters. Tony Stewart donated $1 million to the Petty family for the Victory Junction Gang Camp, which is a great facility in North Carolina where seriously ill children can have fun while undergoing treatment. Jeff Gordon has run a foundation to benefit children and families in need. These champs are champs on the racetrack, and they're champs off the racetrack, for which this country is grateful.

I also appreciate the strong support that NASCAR's drivers and crew members and executives continue to give to our Armed Forces. By reminding your millions of fans that America's heroes are the men and women who defend our Nation, you're reminding us all about the importance of serving a cause greater than ourself.

I want to thank you all for coming today. I want to congratulate you all for being such great champs. Good luck in the upcoming year. May God bless you all, and may God continue to bless our great country. Thanks for coming.

NOTE: The President spoke at 3:05 p.m. on the South Lawn at the White House. In his remarks, he referred to Jack Roush, owner, Roush Racing; Bill France, Jr., co-vice chairman, NASCAR, his wife, Betty Jane, and their children, Brian France, chief executive officer and chairman of the board, NASCAR, and Lesa France Kennedy, president, International Speedway Corp.; and Bill Graves, member, board of directors, International Speedway Corp.

Remarks on Signing the Healthy Forests Restoration Act of 2003
December 3, 2003

Thanks for coming. Thanks for finally inviting me to the Department of Agriculture. [*Laughter*] It's an honor to be here. I'm really glad to be here as our Government takes a major step forward in protecting America's forests.

Almost 750 million acres of forest stand tall and beautiful across the 50 States. We have a responsibility to be good stewards of our forests. That's a solemn responsibility. And the legislation I sign today carries forward this ethic of stewardship. With the Healthy Forest Restoration Act, we will help to prevent catastrophic wildfires; we'll help save lives and property; and we'll help protect our forests from sudden and needless destruction.

I appreciate so very much Secretaries Veneman and Norton for working hard on this issue. These two members of my Cabinet are doing a great job, and I'm proud that they're in my Cabinet. I want to thank Mark Rey. I also want to thank Dale Bosworth, who is the Chief of the Forest Service. From the Interior Department, I want to thank Rebecca Watson and Lynn Scarlett for their hard work and their good work for these important issues. I want to thank the officials and employees of the Department of Agriculture and the Department of Interior for doing a great job on behalf of the American citizens. Thank you for your dedication and your work on behalf of all of us.

I appreciate the Hotshot team members from the great State of California. These are the folks in the yellow shirts. I spent some time with the Hotshot members as a—this summer in California, last summer in Arizona, a time in Oregon, Washington State. These are brave, brave citizens. These are fantastic citizens in the country. We're proud to be standing with them up here.

I appreciate the Members of Congress who have joined us, strong Members who brought some common sense to what had been an acrimonious debate, who listened to the people—[*applause*]—Members who listen to the people, who know what they're talking about, and came up with a good piece of legislation, starting with Senator Thad Cochran, who's the chairman of the Committee of Agriculture, Nutrition, and Forestry. Thad has done a fabulous job of getting this bill out of the United States Senate, along with Max Baucus and Mike Crapo—Baucus being of—from Montana and Crapo being from Idaho, great Members of the Senate, and thank you all for coming. I appreciate your coming. We have two other Members of the Senate with us here. From the West, Kyl and Smith—Gordon Smith from Oregon. I appreciate you two coming.

From the House, onstage are three Members: the chairman of the Committee of Agriculture, Bob Goodlatte, from the great State of Virginia; Scott McInnis, who is the sponsor of the Healthy Forest bill—[*applause*]—McInnis is having a family reunion in Washington. [*Laughter*] Richard

Pombo is the chairman of the Committee on Resources. We've got Greg Walden and Sherry Boehlert. We've got the finest fighter pilot in Navy history with us, Duke Cunningham. We've got Renzi from Arizona. Thank you all for coming, fine Members, and appreciate you getting this bill out.

I want to thank all the State and local officials who have come here. You understand the importance of getting a good piece of legislation out of the Congress. See, you live right there where the fires occur, and I want to thank you for your help, thank you for helping bring some common sense to Washington, DC. I appreciate the representatives of the conservation groups who have worked in a constructive way to help change the attitude inside the halls of the United States Congress so we can work together to get some good legislation out to protect our forests. I want to thank the business groups who are here, who spent time making sure this legislation makes sense.

I understand Chuck Leavell is here, of the Rolling Stones. I appreciate Chuck being here. He's the keyboard player. And he also has—they tell me he's a tree raiser, a tree farmer, whatever you call them. [*Laughter*] Glad you're here. Thanks for coming, Chuck. I appreciate you being here.

For decades, Government policies have allowed large amounts of underbrush and small trees to collect at the base of our forests. The motivations of this approach were good. But our failure to maintain the forests has had dangerous consequences and devastating consequences. The uncontrolled growth left by years of neglect chokes off nutrients from trees and provides a breeding ground for insects and disease.

As we have seen this year and in other years, such policy creates the conditions for devastating wildfires. Today, about 190 million acres of forest and woodlands around the country are vulnerable to destruction.

Overgrown brush and trees can serve as kindling, turning small fires into large, raging blazes that burn with such intensity that the trees literally explode.

I saw that firsthand when we were flying over Oregon, magnificent trees just exploding as we choppered by. The resulting devastation damages the habitats of endangered species, causes flooding and soil erosion, harms air quality, oftentimes ruins water supplies. These catastrophic fires destroy homes and businesses. They put lives at risk, especially the lives of the brave men and women who are on the frontline of fighting these fires.

In 2 years' time, fires throughout the country have burned nearly 11 million acres. We've seen the cost that wildfires bring in the loss of 28 firefighters this year alone. In the fires that burned across southern California this fall, 22 civilians also lost their lives as whole neighborhoods vanished into flames. And we ask for God's blessings on the family members who grieve the loss and on the friends who mourn for their comrades.

We're seeing the tragic consequences brought by years of unwise forest policy. We face a major national challenge, and we're acting together to solve the challenge. The Healthy Forest Initiative I announced last year marked a clear and decisive change in direction. Instead of enduring season after season of devastating fires, my administration acted to remove the causes of severe wildfires. We worked within our existing legal authority to thin out and remove forest undergrowth before disaster struck. We emphasized thinning projects in critical areas. And since the beginning of 2002, we've restored almost 5 million acres of overgrown forest and rangeland.

And that's pretty good progress. But it's not enough progress. And so, thanks to the United States Congress, thanks to their action, and thanks for passing the Healthy Forest Restoration Act—we now can expand the work to a greater scale that the dangers of wildfires demand. In other words, we were confined. The Congress acted in a bipartisan spirit in order to enable this administration to work harder to do what we can do to prevent wildfires from taking place.

The bill expedites the environmental review process so we can move forward more quickly on projects that restore forests to good health. We don't want our intentions bogged down by regulations. We want to get moving. When we see a problem, this Government needs to be able to move. Congress wisely enabled a review process to go forward but also wisely recognizes sometimes the review process bogs us down and things just don't get done.

The new law directs courts to consider the long-term risks that could result if thinning projects are delayed. And that's an important reform, and I want to thank you all for that. It places reasonable time limits on litigation after the public has had an opportunity to comment and a decision has been made. You see, no longer will essential forest health projects be delayed by lawsuits that drag on year after year after year.

This act of Congress sets the right priorities for the management of our Nation's forests, focusing on woodlands that are closest to communities and on places where the risk to wildlife and the environment is the greatest. It enforces high standards of stewardship so that we can ensure that we're returning our forests to more natural conditions and maintaining a full range of forest types. It enables collaboration between community groups and private stewardship organizations and all levels of government before projects are chosen. This law will not prevent every fire, but it is an important step forward, a vital step to

make sure we do our duty to protect our Nation's forests.

The principles behind the Healthy Forest Initiative were not invented in the White House and, truthfully, not invented in the Congress. They are founded on the experience of scientists, forestry experts, and, as importantly, the firefighters who know what they're talking about. Chief Tom O'Keefe of the California Department of Forestry is among those who have seen the consequences of misguided forest policy. He put it this way: "A lot of people have been well-intentioned. They saved trees, but they lost the forest." We want to save the forest.

This bill was passed because Members of Congress looked at sound science, did the best they could to get all the politics out of the way for good legislation. Members from both parties came together, people from different regions of the country. A broad range of people who care about our forests were listened to, whether they be conservationists or resource managers, people from the South, people from the West, people from New York. You see, we all share duties of stewardship. And today we shared in an important accomplishment.

For the good of our forests and for the good of our people, I'm honored to sign this important piece of legislation. I'm honored to be here to sign the Healthy Forest Restoration Act of 2003.

NOTE: The President spoke at 10:40 a.m. at the U.S. Department of Agriculture. In his remarks, he referred to Under Secretary of Agriculture for Natural Resources and Environment Mark Rey. The Office of the Press Secretary also released a Spanish language transcript of these remarks. H.R. 1904, approved December 3, was assigned Public Law No. 108–148.

Statement on Signing the 21st Century Nanotechnology Research and Development Act
December 3, 2003

Today, I have signed S. 189, the "21st Century Nanotechnology Research and Development Act." The Act authorizes appropriations for research in nanoscience, nanoengineering, and nanotechnology research and other related activities.

Several provisions of the Act, including sections 2(d)(2), 3(c)(1), 4(d), and 5(d), purport to call for executive branch officials to submit to the Congress proposals for legislation, including funding legislation. The executive branch shall implement these provisions in a manner consistent with the President's constitutional authority to supervise the unitary executive branch and to recommend for the consideration of the Congress such measures as the President judges necessary and expedient.

The executive branch shall construe section 2(b)(4)(E) of the Act in a manner consistent with the Government's obligation under the Due Process Clause of the Fifth Amendment to the Constitution to ensure equal protection of the laws.

GEORGE W. BUSH

The White House,
December 3, 2003.

NOTE: S. 189, approved December 3, was assigned Public Law No. 108–153. An original was not available for verification of the content of this statement.

Remarks Prior to Discussions With King Abdullah II of Jordan and an Exchange With Reporters
December 4, 2003

President Bush. We're going to have some opening statements, and then I'll take a couple of questions—two questions. The Jordanian press may want to ask a question.

First, Your Majesty, thanks for coming. It's great to have you back. I view His Majesty as one of our really close friends in the world. You know, I went to London recently and gave a speech about reform and reform in the Middle East and the possibilities of governments that adhere to rule of law and transparency and women's rights and economic freedom. And Your Majesty, you're doing just that. I'm proud of your leadership. It's—you're a modern leader with a big heart and a vision for what is best for your people.

I also want to thank you for your very strong support in our mutual desire to bring peace to the Middle East. We made a tough decision when it came to Iraq, and Your Majesty, you stood with us. And we made the right decision when it came to Iraq, because Iraq will be free and will be peaceful. And that's in your interests, and it's in our interests, and it's in the world's interests that we succeed.

I look forward to discussing with you a wide range of issues of our—of mutual concern. And I look forward to your wise counsel and advice.

King Abdullah II. Thank you, sir. Well, Mr. President, again, it's always a pleasure to see you and to be back here in Washington. I'm very grateful for your support for the region, what you're trying to do to bring peace and stability for all of us in the Middle East—Iraq, the Israelis, the

Palestinians. And so I'm looking forward to our discussions today, and see how we can best bring hope to all of the people of our part of the world.

And the President has always been very courageous in trying to do the right thing and to push for a dialog and hope for all of us in the Middle East. And I'm very appreciative.

President Bush. Thanks for coming.

We'll answer a couple of questions, starting with this fellow right there, Scott [Scott Lindlaw, Associated Press].

Steel Tariffs

Q. Thank you, Mr. President. Are you going to repeal all the steel tariffs today?

President Bush. I am making a decision—let me—the decision I make will be based upon my strong belief that America's consumers, the American economy is better off with a world that trades freely and a world that trades fairly. And I listened to an International Trade Commission report about the effects that steel imports were having upon our important industry. I acted. I acted to give the steel industry time to adjust. I acted in time for us to say to the world that we will trade, but we want to trade in a fair way. And the decision will be announced here shortly.

Discussion With Prime Minister Blair

Q. Did you talk to Mr. Blair about it today?

President Bush. No, it didn't come up today with Prime Minister Blair. I did talk with the Prime Minister today. Let's see, you're not the only guy asking questions throughout this thing, but——

Q. No.

President Bush. ——it's good that you recognize that. I did talk to the Prime Minister. We talked about our—we talked about Iraq. We talked about NATO, and we had a good discussion. I talk to him about once a week, maybe once every 2 weeks. His Majesty just was with the Prime Minister.

King Abdullah II. Yes, the day before yesterday.

President Bush. Steady friend of ours, a steady friend of Jordan's as well.

Anybody here from the Jordanian press that you would like to call on?

Middle East Peace Process

Q. Your Majesty, given some of the recent events, such as the Palestinians' factions are meeting in Cairo, Geneva Accords, and the Palestinian—proposals, do you feel that there is hope to revive the negotiations? What is your next step to revive the roadmap?

King Abdullah II. Well, the President has always been out front in trying to move the process forward. There is a lot of difficulties on the ground at the moment, as we know, but we've all been working very hard behind the scenes to encourage the Palestinian Prime Minister to be able to have the dialog with the Israelis. We believe that there will be, I hope, some small steps on the ground that move the process forward. We haven't given up on the peace process. The President has been very dedicated from day one. We appreciate his support. But it's going to be a tough road ahead for all of us.

President Bush. Steven [Steve Holland, Reuters].

Q. The Geneva Accord, do you think some of these proposals should be included in an overall peace agreement? And why is Secretary Powell meeting with these people?

President Bush. Everybody knows where I stand. I gave a speech right here in Rose Garden in June of 2002. I laid out what I believe is necessary to achieve peace in the Middle East. It starts with having a Palestinian state that is at peace with Israel, a Palestinian state based upon democratic principles, a Palestinian state which recognizes the hopes and aspirations of the Palestinian people, and a Palestinian state with leadership which is committed to defeating and dismantling the terrorist organizations who are trying to prevent a Palestinian state from emerging.

I also talked about the need for the Israelis to keep in mind that if they support a Palestinian state, which they have told me they do, that the conditions on the ground must be such for a Palestinian state to be able to emerge. And that's why we're continuing to talk to them about the illegal settlements and outposts—illegal outposts and settlements as well as the fence.

As well, nations in the neighborhood must take responsibility. The King and I have spent a lot of time talking about this subject. He understands fully what I'm talking about. I want to remind you that it was in Jordan where His Majesty hosted us. I stood up with His Majesty as well as Prime Minister Sharon and then Prime Minister Abu Mazen. and made a public declaration that we were prepared to work together for the creation of a Palestinian state. Abu Mazen has since been shoved aside, and the process stalled. What the Palestinians need is leadership willing to remain committed to the aspirations of their people and bold enough to stand up and fight off the terrorists' organizations. And His Majesty and I will be glad to work with such leaders as they emerge.

Q. This is a productive process, the Geneva Accords and Secretary Powell's meeting?

President Bush. Well, I think it's productive, so long as they adhere to the principles I have just outlined. And that is, we must fight off terror, that there must be security, and there must be the emergence of a Palestinian state that is democratic and free.

And it's—the position of this Government is clear, and it's firm. We appreciate people discussing peace. We just want to make sure people understand that the principles to peace are clear.

Thank you all for coming.

NOTE: The President spoke at 10:07 a.m. in the Oval Office at the White House. In his remarks, he referred to Prime Minister Tony Blair of the United Kingdom; Prime Minister Ariel Sharon of Israel; and former Prime Minister Mahmoud Abbas (Abu Mazen) of the Palestinian Authority. King Abdullah II referred to Prime Minister Ahmed Korei of the Palestinian Authority. A tape was not available for verification of the content of these remarks.

Remarks on Signing the Fair and Accurate Credit Transactions Act of 2003
December 4, 2003

Thank you all for coming. Please be seated. Thanks. Good morning, everybody. Thanks for coming to the Roosevelt Room. Today we're taking important steps to ensure that all Americans of every income and background have fair access to credit.

For our economy, reliable access to credit and capital is essential to growth and prosperity. For individuals, a chance to get ahead and to make a better life often depends on building credit. So many decisions, like buying a home or financing a

car or owning a small business, are made easier by good credit. The bill I'm about to sign will help make sure that hard-working, law-abiding citizens are treated fairly when they apply for credit.

This bill also confronts the problem of identity theft. A growing number of Americans are victimized by criminals who assume their identities and cause havoc in their financial affairs. With this legislation, the Federal Government is protecting our citizens by taking the offensive against identity theft.

I appreciate the fact that I'm joined up here by the Secretary of the Treasury, John Snow, and Tim Muris, who is the Chairman of the Federal Trade Commission. Muris is responsible for writing the regulations to make sure that the intention of the Congress is met.

And speaking about the Congress, I want to thank the Members of the Congress, both Republicans and Democrats, who are here to join in the bill signing, good, honorable Members who have worked hard to protect our citizens. I appreciate Senator Paul Sarbanes for joining us today. I'm honored that Senator Bob Bennett has joined us as well, as well as Maria Cantwell and Elizabeth Dole. Thank you, Senators, for coming. Thanks for your good work on this. I also want to thank Richard Shelby for his good work. He's not with us today, but Shelby gets some credit. [*Laughter*] From the House—[*laughter*]— Congressman Oxley—I appreciate you, Mr. Chairman—Paul Gillmor, Spencer Bachus—thanks for coming, Spence. I appreciate you sponsoring this piece of legislation. Steve LaTourette and Darlene Hooley are here. Thank you all for coming.

Again, I want to again congratulate the Congress for working on this important piece of legislation and exceeding expectations, I might add. At least you've exceeded the expectations of the administration on this bill. [*Laughter*]

The legislation, the Fair and Accurate Credit Transactions Act of 2003, carries forward the progress this Nation has made in recent years to help qualified Americans get fair access to credit. Before 1996, there were no uniform rules on borrower information and credit reports. Lenders did not always have consistent and full information about potential borrowers. Lenders too often made broad assumptions and decisions about categories of people rather than looking at individuals and their personal credit histories.

Too often, lenders assumed the worst. And therefore, people with lower incomes and immigrants with little or no credit history, people who lived in certain neighborhoods had a more difficult time getting affordable loans. And that's not fair, and it's not right, and it does not reflect the spirit of this country.

And so the Congress wisely acted. In 1996, Congress set uniform national standards on credit reporting. Credit histories are now more complete and thorough, and the lending process is fairer. Many Americans have been able to obtain loans that they would not have had otherwise, and that's important. According to estimates, over the last 7 years, more than 1 million men and women have obtained new or refinanced mortgages that would have been denied if there had not been a fair national standard.

One of them is here today. I appreciate Shonelle Blake coming. She's got the toughest job in America. She's a single mom. She has two 4-year-olds, mom of twins. I know something about twins. [*Laughter*] In the early 1990s, Shonelle set herself two goals—she set high goals. One was to buy a house, and the other was to start a business. She made sure her credit was in order. She went to the HOPE Center in Los Angeles—I know something about there since I've been there myself— to help get a downpayment on a home. One year later, she got another loan to start her own insurance business.

Shonelle is building a life of independence and success, in part because a loan was given to her based on her own merit. Because we had a national standard, she was able to get a loan. Because Congress did the right thing in 1996, this entrepreneur and mother was able to realize a dream. The national credit standards that help ensure that the lenders considered each applicant on her merits are what made the loan possible.

John Bryant, who's with us—and it's good to see you again, John—of Operation

HOPE, he's what we call a social entre-preneur, by the way. [*Laughter*] He has heard the call to help people like Shonelle realize her dreams—said this: He said, "Shonelle would have been rejected. She wouldn't have been a homeowner, and she wouldn't have been a businessowner." That's what John said. And so the fair standards are important. The national standard was an important act that you all did, and I want to thank you for working on it in 1996.

See, the bill I sign today will make the national fair credit standards permanent. Those standards were set to expire, the '96—the good of the '96 act was going away. And then the Congress stepped up and acted for the sake of the Shonelles of the world. And now the credit standards are a permanent part of the legislative his-tory of the country. And I want to thank you for that. It's the right thing to do, and I appreciate your leadership. See, we're ensuring that lenders make decisions based upon the full and fair credit histories of each person and not on the categories that can lead to discrimination.

And as we help people gain access to credit, we're strengthening the protections that help consumers build and keep a good credit history. That good record is ruined when criminals steal identities and run up purchases under stolen names. Like other forms of stealing, identity theft leaves the victim feeling terribly violated, and undoing the damage caused by identity theft can take months.

Michael Berry is with us today. Thank you for coming, Michael. In January of 2002, Michael was applying for a credit line increase. He'd always paid his bills in a timely manner. He's a good citizen. But his application was rejected. They told him that he had taken out too many credit cards recently. It came as quite a surprise to Mi-chael, since it wasn't true. He discovered that someone had stolen his financial iden-tity. He made countless calls to credit bu-reaus and tracked down credit card pur-chases he had not made. He even found

the address of the person who had taken out the cards. He closed the credit card accounts as fast as he could, but applica-tions for more credit in his name were being made every day. And many were get-ting approved. He had to call every credit card company to get each card canceled before it was issued.

Nearly 2 years later, Michael is still fight-ing the effects of the fraud. The system was broken. Michael is living testimony to what I'm saying when I said the system was broken, and Congress acted. I want to thank you all for stepping up and doing the right thing here.

See, in an age when information about individuals can be found easily, sold easily, abused easily, Government must act to pro-tect individual privacy. And with this new law, we're taking action. First, under this law, we're giving every consumer the right to get a copy of his or her credit report free of charge every year. That's important. The credit report is more than a record of past actions; it has great influence over a person's financial future. People should be able to check their credit report for accuracy and to challenge any errors. The bill does just that.

Second, this law will help prevent iden-tity theft before it occurs, by requiring mer-chants to delete all but the last five digits of a credit card number on store receipts. Many restaurants and merchants have al-ready adopted this practice. All will now do so.

Won't they, Tim? [*Laughter*] Just making sure he was awake. [*Laughter*]

Chairman Timothy J. Muris. Always. [*Laughter*]

The President. Slips of paper that most people throw away should not hold the key to their savings and financial secrets.

Third, this law will create a national sys-tem of fraud detection so that identity theft can be traced and dealt with earlier. Up to now, victims of identity theft have been left to manage the problem themselves—ask Michael—by calling all their credit card companies to shut down each of their accounts. And then the victims must call each of the three major credit rating agencies to report the crime and to protect their credit rating. Under this legislation, victims will only have to make one phone call to receive advice and to set off a nationwide fraud alert. It's an important reform. I appreciate you all for putting this into law. Credit bureaus will then take immediate measures to protect the consumer's credit standing.

And fourth, this law will encourage lenders and credit agencies to take action before a victim even knows an identity crime has occurred. In many cases, identity thieves follow predictable patterns. Bank regulators working with credit agencies will draw up guidelines to identify these patterns and develop methods to stop identity theft before it ever happens.

These practical steps will help consumers protect their credit and their good name. People work hard to build up good credit histories and rely on their credit to move forward in life. Today we're helping to make our credit system fair, fair to all, and to better protect those—better protect people from those who would abuse it.

I'm pleased to sign into law the Fair and Accurate Credit Transactions Act of 2003, a good, solid piece of legislation.

NOTE: The President spoke at 11 a.m. in the Roosevelt Room at the White House. In his remarks, he referred to John Bryant, chairman and chief executive officer, Operation HOPE, Inc. H.R. 2622, approved December 4, was assigned Public Law No. 108–159.

Remarks on Lighting the National Christmas Tree
December 4, 2003

Thank you all very much. Welcome to the Christmas Pageant of Peace. This evening we continue a tradition in Washington as we gather to light the National Christmas Tree. Tonight and throughout the Christmas season our thoughts turn to a star in the east, seen 20 centuries ago, and to a light that can guide us still. Laura and I are so pleased to join you in this ceremony, and we thank you all for being here.

It's always good to see Santa. I know you've got a lot of commitments this time of year. [*Laughter*] We also know how Santa gets around: He travels in the dark of night; he arrives unannounced—[*laughter*]—and he's gone before you know he was there. [*Laughter*] Santa, I can assure you, it's a lot easier on a flying sled than it is on Air Force One. [*Laughter*]

I want to thank Peter Nostrand, the chairman of the Christmas Pageant of Peace, and John Betchkal, the president. I want to thank very much Secretary of the Interior Gale Norton and her staff for helping put this fine event on. I want to thank all the members of my Cabinet who are here. I appreciate Fran Mainella, who's the Director of the National Park Service. I want to thank all the National Park Service employees who work so hard on behalf of the American people.

I want to thank Father Kleinweber for his gracious offering of prayer. I appreciate the musicians—fantastic job tonight. Thank you all for coming. I want to thank the members of the board of the Christmas Pageant of Peace. I want to welcome all the children from the Boys and Girls Clubs from this region for being here.

Also with us this evening are military personnel, including some who have recently returned from duty in Iraq and Afghanistan. I know your families are glad to have you back. They're proud of your service, and so is our country. On behalf of all Americans, welcome home, and job well done.

We also honor all of our fellow Americans serving far away from home during the holidays. Separation from loved ones is especially difficult this time of year. Our people in uniform can know that their families miss them and love them, that millions are praying for them, and that America is grateful for the men and women who serve and defend our country.

The story of Christmas is familiar to us all, and it still holds a sense of wonder and surprise. When the good news came first to a young woman from Nazareth, her response was understandable. She asked, "How can this be?" The news would bring difficulty to her family and suspicion upon herself. Yet, Mary gave her reply, "Be it unto me according to Thy word." The wait for a new king had been long, and the manner of his arrival was not as many had expected. The king's first cries were heard by shepherds and cattle. He was raised by a carpenter's son.

Yet this one humble life lifted the sights of humanity forever. And in His words we hear a voice like no other. Across the generations, the poor have heard words of hope, the proud have heard words of challenge, and the weak and the dying have heard words of assurance. And mankind has been given a message first delivered by angels on a shepherd's field: "Fear not."

As we near Christmas in a time of war, these words bring comfort. We don't know all of God's ways, yet the Christmas story promises that God's purpose is justice and His plan is peace. At times this belief is tested. During the Civil War, Longfellow wrote a poem that later became a part of a Christmas carol, "Hate is strong and mocks the song of peace on Earth, good will to men."

That poem also reminds us that hate is not the final word: "Then pealed the bells more loud and deep, 'God is not dead, nor doth He sleep, the wrong shall fail, the right prevail, with peace on Earth, good will to men.'"

And now as an expression of our own hope for peace in this Christmas season, we light the national tree. Maggie Stuempfle and Andre Joyner are with us here. They're members of the Boys and Girls Clubs of America. Laura and I would like to ask Maggie and Andre to come up, and we'll turn on the lights. But I ask you all to join us in a national count down, starting with five, four, three, two, one.

NOTE: The President spoke at 5:55 p.m. on the Ellipse during the annual Christmas Pageant of Peace. In his remarks, he referred to Father Dennis Kleinweber, pastor, St. Philomena Catholic Church, East Cleveland, OH.

Statement on the Decision To Terminate Temporary Safeguards To Help the Domestic Steel Industry
December 4, 2003

Today, I signed a proclamation ending the temporary steel safeguard measures I put in place in March 2002. Prior to that time, steel prices were at 20-year lows, and the U.S. International Trade Commission found that a surge in imports to the U.S. market was causing serious injury to our domestic steel industry. I took action to give the industry a chance to adjust to the surge in foreign imports and to give relief to the workers and communities that depend on steel for their jobs and livelihoods.

These safeguard measures have now achieved their purpose, and as a result of changed economic circumstances it is time to lift them.

The U.S. steel industry wisely used the 21 months of breathing space we provided to consolidate and restructure. The industry made progress increasing productivity, lowering production costs, and making America more competitive with foreign steel producers. Steel producers and workers have negotiated new groundbreaking labor agreements that allow greater flexibility and increase job stability. The Pension Benefit Guaranty Corporation has guaranteed the pensions of eligible steelworkers and retirees and relieved the high pension costs that burdened some companies. My jobs-and-growth plan has also created more favorable economic conditions for the industry, and the improving economy will help further stimulate demand.

To keep the positive momentum going, we will continue our steel import licensing and monitoring program so that my administration can quickly respond to future import surges that could unfairly damage the industry. We will continue negotiations with our trading partners through the Organiza-

tion of Economic Cooperation and Development to establish new and stronger disciplines on subsidies that governments grant to their steel producers. We will continue to pursue economic policies that create the conditions for steel producers, steel consumers—who rely on steel to produce goods ranging from refrigerators to auto parts—and other U.S. manufacturers to succeed.

I strongly believe that America's workers can compete with anyone in the world as long as we have a fair and level playing field. Free trade opens foreign markets to American products and creates jobs for American workers, and an integral part of our commitment to free trade is our commitment to enforcing our trade laws. I am pleased the steel industry seized the opportunity we provided to regain its competitiveness and assist steelworkers and their communities. As a result, U.S. steel companies are now once again well-positioned to compete both at home and globally.

NOTE: The proclamation of December 4 is listed in Appendix D at the end of this volume.

Remarks at a Bush-Cheney Luncheon in Baltimore, Maryland
December 5, 2003

Thank you all very much. Thanks for coming. Thanks for the warm welcome. Thanks for the bumper sticker. [*Laughter*] Thanks for making this such a successful event. Thanks for laying the foundation for what is going to be a victory in the State of Maryland in 2004.

I want to thank you for your contributions. I also want to thank you for the contribution of time you're going to make. [*Laughter*] We want you to help energize the grassroots, to put up the signs, and to get on the phones and to mail the let-

ters, all reminding your fellow citizens that we have a duty to vote in America; we have an obligation in a democracy to participate.

You know, the political season is going to come in its own time, and I'm getting ready. I'm loosening up. [*Laughter*] But I've got a job to do. Right now, I'm focused on the people's business, and there's a lot on the agenda. I will continue to work hard to earn the confidence of all Americans by keeping this Nation secure and strong and prosperous and free.

Laura sends her best. I'm sorry she's not with me. She is a fabulous wife and mom. She's doing a great job as our First Lady. I'm incredibly proud of her.

Fortunately, my favorite sister came—[*laughter*]—well, my only sister. I love Doro. A brother could have no finer sister than Dorothy Koch. Thank you for coming.

I appreciate your Governor. He is a livewire—[*laughter*]—which is what this State needed. I love his attitude. He never forgot his roots, but he's an incurable optimist as well, because he brings some common sense to the Governor's office. He's doing a fine job. I'm proud to be here with the first lady, Kendel, as well. Thank you, Kendel.

I'm also proud to be with Michael—Michael Steele, the Lieutenant Governor, and Andrea. I thank them for their service and for working with the Ehrlichs to set such a positive tone for the great State of Maryland. Thank you, Lieutenant Governor, for coming.

Congressman Roscoe Bartlett is with us today. Congressman, thank you for coming. I know there's a lot of State and local officials who are here. Thank you all for coming today. I appreciate you coming. When I'm talking about energizing the grassroots, I'm talking to you. [*Laughter*] We need you to get into your districts and to energize people and get them to vote. If you happen to be a mayor, my only advice is to fill the potholes. [*Laughter*]

My campaign is going to be run by a fellow named Ken Mehlman. I just had to mention him. You know why? Because his mother and dad are here, and I appreciate them coming. You raised a good man in Ken Mehlman. My friend Mercer Reynolds is with us. He's the national finance chairman. Dick Hug is the State finance chairman, and Dick, I want to thank you and the team that made this event so successful. Thanks for working very hard, for what you're doing.

Shelly Kamins gets a lot of credit for working hard as well. Shelly, I'm honored to have your friendship and to have your hard work, along with Dick, to make this work. I want to thank all of you all for being here. I really appreciate you taking time to come. I'm proud to have your support.

I want you to tell your friends and neighbors, in the last 3 years, our Nation has acted decisively to confront great challenges. I came to this office to solve problems, not to pass them on to future Presidents and to future generations. I came to seize opportunities, instead of letting them slip away. My administration is meeting the tests of our time.

Terrorists declared war on the United States of America, and war is what they got. We have captured or killed many of the key leaders of the Al Qaida network, and the rest of them know we're on their trail. In Afghanistan and in Iraq, we gave ultimatums to terror regimes. Those regimes chose defiance, and those regimes are no more. Fifty million people in those two countries once lived under tyranny, and today they live in freedom.

Three years ago, our military was not receiving the resources it needed, and morale was beginning to suffer. So we increased the defense budgets to prepare for the threats of a new era. And today, no one in the world can question the skill and the strength and the spirit of the United States military.

Three years ago, the economy was in trouble, and a recession was beginning. And then our country was attacked, and some of our fellow citizens in corporate America forgot to tell the truth, and war came upon us, which all affected the people's confidence. But we acted. We passed tough new laws to hold corporate criminals to account. And to get the economy going again, I have twice led the United States Congress to pass historic tax relief for the American people.

When Americans have more take-home pay to spend, to save, or invest, the whole economy grows, and people are more likely to find a job. And so that's why we're returning more money to the people, to help them raise their families. That's why we've reduced taxes on dividends and capital gains, to encourage investment. That is why we're giving small businesses incentives to expand and to hire new people. With all these actions, this administration has laid the foundation for greater prosperity and more jobs across America so every single citizen has a chance to realize the American Dream.

The American economy is strong, and it is getting stronger. Today they've released some more statistics that show the economy is strong. Unemployment dropped from 6 percent to 5.9 percent. More jobs are being created. In the third quarter, our economy grew at an annual rate of 8.2 percent, the fastest pace in nearly 20 years. The Purchasing Managers Index indicates that our manufacturing sector is getting stronger and is growing. The productivity is high. Investment is strong. The home industry is vibrant. The tax relief we passed is working for the American people.

Three years ago, there was a lot of talk about education reform, but there wasn't much action in Washington, DC. So I acted, and called for and the Congress passed the No Child Left Behind Act. With a solid bipartisan majority, we delivered the most dramatic education reforms in a generation. We've increased spending on Title I students at the Federal level. But for the first time, we're asking schools to prove that our children are learning to read and write and add and subtract. We are challenging the soft bigotry of low expectations. We're raising the standards, because we believe very child can learn the basics of reading and math, and we expect every school to teach the basics of reading and math, so not one single child is left behind.

We reorganized the Government and created the Department of Homeland Security to better safeguard our borders and our ports and to better protect the American people. We passed trade promotion authority to open up new markets for Maryland's entrepreneurs and manufacturers and farmers. We passed budget agreements to help maintain spending discipline in Washington, DC. On issue after issue, this administration has acted on principle, has kept its word, and has made progress for the American people.

The Congress gets a lot of credit for the achievements. I appreciate working with the Speaker and Majority Leader Frist. These are two fine men, good leaders. We're working hard to change the tone in Washington. There's too much needless politics and endless backbiting and the zero-sum attitude. The best way to defeat that attitude is to focus on results, is to do the people's business and deliver. And that's what we're working hard to do.

And those are the kind of people I've asked to serve in my administration, by the way. I've attracted fine, fine people to serve the American people, good, honorable, decent Americans from all walks of life. Our country has had no finer Vice President than Dick Cheney. Mother may have a second opinion. [*Laughter*]

In 3 years, we have come far. In 3 years, we've done a lot for the people, but our work is only beginning. I have set great goals worthy of this great Nation. First, America is committed to expanding the realm of freedom and peace for our own security and for the benefit of the world. And second, in our own country, we must work for a society that is prosperous and compassionate so every single citizen can realize the great potential, the human potential, the God-given potential, and the great promise of this country. It is clear that the future of freedom and peace depend on the actions of America. This Nation is freedom's home and freedom's defender. We welcome this charge of history, and we are keeping it.

The war on terror continues. The enemies of freedom are not idle, and neither are we. This country will not rest; we will not stop; we will not tire until this danger to civilization is removed. We are confronting that danger in Iraq, where Saddam holdouts and foreign terrorists are desperately trying to throw Iraq into chaos by attacking our forces, by attacking international aid workers, by attacking innocent Iraqi citizens. They know that the advance of freedom in Iraq would be a major defeat for the cause of terror. This collection of killers and assassins is trying to shake the will of the United States of America. America will never be intimidated by a bunch of thugs.

We are aggressively striking the terrorists in Iraq, defeating them there so we will not have to face them in our own cities. We're calling other nations to help, and they are, because they understand that a free Iraq will make their own countries more secure. We're standing with the brave Iraqi people as they assume more of their own defense and move toward self-government. This isn't easy work, but it is essential work. The United States of America will finish what we have begun, and we will win this essential victory in the war against terror.

Our greatest security comes from the advance of human liberty, because free nations do not support terror, free nations do not attack their neighbors, free nations do not threaten the world with weapons of mass terror. Americans believe that freedom is the deepest need and hope of every human heart. I believe that freedom is the future of every nation, and I know that freedom is not America's gift to the world. Freedom is God's gift to every man and woman who lives in this world.

America also understands that unprecedented influence brings tremendous responsibilities. We have duties in this world, and when we see disease and starvation and hopeless poverty, we will not turn away. And that is why, on the continent of Africa, America is now committed to bringing the healing power of medicine to millions of men and women and children suffering from AIDS.

We face challenges at home, and our actions will prove equal to those challenges. I want everybody working. I worry when someone who wants to work can't find a job. That is why I'm going to continue to push a progrowth, pro-entrepreneurial spirit agenda.

We must make our health care system work better, and that is why we are keeping our commitment to America's seniors by strengthening and modernizing Medicare. For years, seniors have called for a modern Medicare system that provides coverage for prescription drugs and more health care choices. For years, Washington listened but did nothing. Finally, the Congress has acted. I look forward to signing this important piece of legislation. I look forward to signing a piece of legislation that says clearly, when America makes a commitment to our elderly, we will keep that commitment.

For the sake of our health care system, we need to cut down on the frivolous lawsuits which are increasing the cost of medicine. People who have been harmed by a bad doc deserve their day in court. But this system shouldn't reward lawyers who are simply fishing for a rich settlement. Because frivolous lawsuits—frivolous lawsuits drive up the cost of health care, they therefore affect the Federal budget.

Medical liability reform is a national issue which requires a national solution. I submitted a plan to the United States Congress. I want to thank the House of Representatives for passing a good reform bill. It is stuck in the United States Senate. It is time for your Senators from the State of Maryland to understand that no one has ever been healed by a frivolous lawsuit.

I have a responsibility as your President to make sure the judicial system runs well, and I have met that duty. I have nominated superb men and women for the Federal courts, people who will interpret the law, not legislate from the bench. Some Members of the Senate are trying to keep my nominees off the bench by blocking up-

or-down votes. Every judicial nominee deserves a fair hearing and an up-or-down vote on the Senate floor. It is time for some of the Members of the United States Senate to stop playing politics with American justice.

The Congress needs to complete work on a comprehensive energy plan. We need to modernize our electricity systems. We need to encourage conservation, promote energy efficiency. We need to develop cleaner technologies to help us find energy in environmentally friendly ways. For the sake of economic security, for the sake of national security, this country must become less dependent on foreign sources of energy.

A strong and prosperous nation must also be a compassionate nation. I will continue to advance what I call compassionate conservatism, which means we'll apply the best and most innovative ideas to the task of helping fellow citizens who hurt. There's still millions of men and women who want to end their dependence on Government and become independent through work. We must continue to advance the successes of the welfare reform program in a decent way, a compassionate way. We must train people for jobs which actually exist. We must bring more work and dignity into the lives of more of our citizens. Congress should complete the "Citizen Service Act" so more Americans can serve their communities and their country.

Both Houses should reach agreement on my Faith-Based Initiative to support the armies of compassion, the armies of compassion that are mentoring children and caring for the homeless and offering hope to the addicted. This great Nation has got all kinds of fabulous religions, Christian, Jewish, and Muslim. And out of that religion comes a universal call for people to help those who suffer, to those who need help. Our Government must understand that some problems are so intractable, the only thing that will matter, the only thing that will help, is for a faith-based program

to intercede in their lives. Our country should never fear faith. We should welcome faith into the compassionate delivery of human help.

A compassionate society must promote opportunity for all, including the independence and dignity that come from ownership. This administration will constantly strive to promote an ownership society in America. We want more people owning their own home. There is a minority home-ownership gap in America that must be closed, and I've submitted a plan to Congress to do so. We want people to own and manage their own retirement accounts. We want people to own and manage their own health care accounts. We want people—more people to own their own small business. You see, this administration understands that when a person owns something, he or she has a vital stake in the future of our country.

A compassionate society is one in which people respect each other, respect their opinions, respect their religious beliefs. It is a society in which each of us take responsibility for the decisions we make in life. The culture of this country is changing from one that has said, "If it feels good, do it," and, "If you've got a problem, blame somebody else," to a culture in which each of us understands we're responsible for the decisions we make. If you're a mother or a dad, if you're fortunate enough to be a mother or a dad, you're responsible for loving your child with all your heart. If you're worried about the quality of the education in the community in which you live, you're responsible for doing something about it. If you're the CEO—a CEO in corporate America, you're responsible for telling the truth to your shareholders and your employees. And in a responsibility society, each of us is responsible for loving our neighbor just like we'd like to be loved ourself.

The culture of service is strong in America. It's one of the things that makes this country so great and so unique. There is a willingness for people to serve our country by helping somebody in need. That's a powerful part of the American culture. And it's strong today, and I can tell you why. We started the USA Freedom Corps, and the response has been magnificent. People from all walks of life have signed up to help, to help make this country strong by helping to save lives. Policemen and firefighters and the people who wear our Nation's uniform are reminding us what it means to sacrifice for something greater than ourselves. Once again, the children of America believe in heroes, because they see them every day.

In these challenging times, the world has seen the resolve and the courage of America. And I've been privileged to see the compassion and the character of the American people. All the tests of the last 3 years have come to the right nation. We're a strong country, and we use the strength to defend the peace. We're an optimistic country, confident in ourselves and in ideals bigger than ourselves. Abroad, we seek to lift whole nations by spreading freedom. At home, we seek to lift up lives by spreading opportunity to every corner of America. This is the work that history has set before us. We welcome it. And we know that for our country, the best days lie ahead.

God bless. Thanks for coming. Glad you all are here. Thank you.

NOTE: The President spoke at 12:17 p.m. at the Hyatt Regency Hotel. In his remarks, he referred to Gov. Robert L. Ehrlich, Jr., of Maryland and his wife, Kendel; Lt. Gov. Michael Steele of Maryland and his wife, Andrea; Ken Mehlman, campaign manager, Mercer Reynolds, national finance chairman, and Richard E. Hug, Maryland State finance cochairman, Bush-Cheney '04, Inc.; and Sheldon B. Kamins, member, board of directors, Republican Jewish Coalition.

Remarks in a Discussion With Staff Members at the Home Depot in Halethorpe, Maryland
December 5, 2003

The President. Thank you all. I left my credit card at home. [*Laughter*] Thanks for having me. I'm honored to be here at a great company. I really appreciate the spirit of the company. I appreciate the fact that this company cares about the people who work here. And that's really what we're here to talk about, is people working and realizing their dream. I want people working in the country.

I want you to know, I'm an optimistic guy for a lot of reasons. I've seen what we've been through. I want to remind you what this country has been through in order to get to where we are today.

First, we were in recession. You know that better than me, what that means. It means fewer people coming in to buy things, as far as you're concerned. And the recession started in 2001, early 2001. We started to come out of the recession a little bit; you probably felt it around the summer of 2001, maybe fall of 2001. And then the enemy hit us, and that hurt.

Again, those of you on the frontlines of the retail business know what I'm talking about. The cash registers weren't ringing quite as much, and people weren't coming through the aisles quite as much. And it hurt us. It hurt the country a lot. It kind of changed our attitude, and it should change your attitude. We should never forget the lessons of September the 11th, 2001. I have an obligation; the Congressmen who are here have an obligation. I want to thank Roscoe Bartlett and Dutch

Ruppersberger and Ben Cardin, whose district this is. We have an obligation to do everything we can to keep this country secure, to never forget the lessons of September the 11th, 2001, to find the enemy before they come again, to stay on the offensive, and to bring these killers to justice, which is what we're going to do.

But it hurt our economy when they attacked us, of course. Not only did it change foreign policy—in other words, we can't sit there and pick and choose what threat we deal with. Now that we have become vulnerable, we're going to have deal with the threats before they mature and come upon us. But it hurt our economy. It hurt us pretty bad.

And then we started to recover, and I just wanted to remember another thing we've overcome. Some of the corporate citizens of America forgot what it meant to be a responsible citizen. This guy's a responsible guy. See, some of them didn't tell the truth, though. We had some of our citizens not tell the truth. They forgot what it meant to be a leader, and it hurt the confidence of the people. You might remember that period of time. There were these scandals, and people began to wonder whether or not there was honesty in the system. By the way, the way you deal with that, of course, is you find them and you put them into jail. Those who lie, cheat, and steal go to jail.

And then, as you know, I made the decision to deal with threats. As we saw, we put the doctrine out that said, "If you harbor a terrorist, you're just as guilty as the terrorists." And the Taliban, we took them down for the sake of our own security and for the sake of the long-suffering people of Afghanistan.

And then I obviously made the decision to go into Iraq—and by the way, a free and peaceful Iraq is in our Nation's interest; it's in our security interest—that affected the economy. When you turned on your TV, it said, "America is marching to war." That's not very conducive for—that's

not a very positive statement. It doesn't build a lot of confidence—people, you know, marching to war, why would I want to invest in my home? Or why would I want to come to Home Depot if we're fixing to go to war?

So we've overcome a lot, when you think about it. Today the unemployment rate dropped, as you may know, from 6 percent to 5.9 percent. More workers are going to work. Over 380,000 have joined the workforce in the last couple of months. We've overcome a lot. We're a strong country, a strong economy. A lot of it has to do with the fact that we got the best workers in the world. Our productivity is high. I hope some of it has to do—I know some of it has to do—I hope you understand some of it has to do with the fact that the role of Government can help create growth. See, when a person has more money in their pocket, they're likely to come to Home Depot.

Participant. Right.

The President. If they have less money in their pocket, they may not come here. And so I worked with the Congress—I want to thank Congressman Ehrlich, when he was in the Congress, now Governor Ehrlich. We cut taxes on people. It's your money to begin with, by the way. You've got more money to spend. And when you have more money to spend, it increases demand for a good or a service. And when that demand increases for a good or a service, somebody has to produce it.

And so the tax relief went for everybody, not just the favorite few. Everybody got tax relief. And it helped the economy. It also helped small business. You're going to hear from some entrepreneurs here. And by the way, most new jobs in America are created by small businesses. We're happy to have the Home Depot job, don't get me wrong. [*Laughter*] But the truth is, most new jobs are started by the entrepreneurs. And so you're wondering why we've got small-business owners here, because I want you to hear from them. I want you to hear what it means to have a little more money in your pocket.

Most small businesses pay tax at the individual income tax level. See, these two small businesses do—you're Subchapter S's, which means when the taxes come out, you pay like you're an individual, your business does. Which means when you reduce individual taxes, really what you're doing is you're making a big difference for small businesses across America so that they can grow and hire new people. If small businesses create most new jobs, then it makes sense to reward small businesses for labor and risk by reducing their taxes, which we did.

And we did a couple of other smart things. If you're married, you ought not to be penalized in the Tax Code. It seems like the Tax Code ought to encourage people to be married, not discourage them from being married.

We know how hard it is to raise a child, and therefore, we increased the child credit to $1,000 per child. That helps if you're a mom or a dad. And actually, this summer I remember going—I think it was to Philadelphia, where they were making the checks. I said, "The check is in the mail." After I said it, I felt a little nervous. [*Laughter*] Fortunately, it was in the mail. And so you got the difference between the child credit today and the new child credit of $1,000 per child. That's important— that's important relief. That's part of the money going into your pocket.

We also provided incentives for small businesses to make investment. When small businesses invest in machinery or computer equipment, somebody has to build it, see. And when somebody builds that machine, somebody is more likely to find work. And so, in other words, we passed a plan that makes sense.

Part of the things you'll hear me talk about is how to continue the growth. I mean, we're growing. This economy is good. It can be better, so more people find work. One of the ways to make sure

this economy continues to grow is to make all the tax relief we passed permanent. See, it's about to—it's going to go away in phases. The child credit is going to go back down. The marriage penalty will go back up. Taxes will go back up unless we make this permanent. It doesn't make any sense to have a Tax Code that gyrates like that. You need stability in your Tax Code, particularly for the small-business owners and planners.

So one thing that I want you to take away from here is that if you're interested in job creation and job growth for the future, the tax relief we passed must become permanent.

I want to thank all the local officials who have come, by the way. I know the Lieutenant Governor is here. I want to thank the Members of the House and the Senate. It turns out when a President shows up, all kinds of people come. [*Laughter*] And I want to thank you for being here. It's an honor to be here. I look forward to maybe shaking a couple of hands on the way out and—yes. Pretty soon. Yes, pictures, we'll get a picture. Maybe buy a chainsaw. [*Laughter*]

Participant. We carry your brand. [*Laughter*]

The President. Why don't we start off— we've got a man here who is building homes. One of the interesting things about our policy is that when interest rates go low, it provides incentive for people to buy a home; you know, it pushes mortgages down. We want a lot of people owning homes. We've got a minority homeownership gap in America, by the way, we've got to close. See, we just don't want one segment of our population owning homes. We want everybody owning a home. We want everybody to feel comfortable.

I put a plan up to the Congress to do that, help with downpayments, to make sure the fine print in the contract becomes a little larger so everybody understands what they're signing before they go in. It makes people a little nervous when you—

particularly the first-time homebuyer, if you know what I mean. So we've got programs to help educate. We've got programs to simplify the process. We've got programs to help with the downpayment. Low interest rates help.

And our man here, Jim Montgomery, is an owner. He's an entrepreneur. By the way, he is at one of these companies, a Subchapter S, it's called, that pays taxes at the individual rate. So when we cut his taxes individually, we also cut taxes on his business, so he can more likely be able to hire somebody else. He wants to hire and expand. But Jim, welcome. Tell us about your business. Tell us what's on your mind. It's your chance to tell the Governor and Lieutenant Governor if you don't like things here in Maryland. [*Laughter*] If you don't like things at the Federal level, write your Congressman. [*Laughter*]

[*The discussion continued.*]

The President. Yes. Well, that is a tax cut. That was part of it. In other words, when you provide an incentive for somebody to buy equipment—that's what Jim is talking about—it means somebody has to make the equipment or somebody has got to sell the equipment, in your case. And I appreciate you bringing that up, because it's an integral part of the tax plan, to encourage investment. And investment means jobs. And that's what we're really talking about, jobs. See, I'm glad he's building homes. I'm glad people are owning homes, but I'm also glad there's an incentive for him to go out and buy additional equipment. Somebody has got to make that equipment. And when somebody makes that equipment, somebody is working, and that's what we're really talking about. We're talking about the human dignity that comes from people being able to find a job.

Thank you for being an entrepreneur.

James Montgomery. You're welcome.

The President. Yes, I appreciate your spirit. See, one of the great strengths of America is what we call the entrepreneurial

spirit. It's a chance for—to create an environment so people like Jim feel comfortable about building their own business. And it's an exciting part of our economy and a vibrant part, just like the Bell Nursery folks here. We've got an owner; we've got a regional manager. Tell us about your business, Gary.

[*The discussion continued.*]

The President. A couple of points she made. One of the things that's interesting, low interest rates allow people to refinance their homes. You all know better than a lot the effects of refinancing. I mean, people refinance, come in with a little cash, it gives them a chance to remodel.

Secondly, I do want to mention a couple of things that are important for small businesses. One, health care, it's important for large businesses, really important for small businesses. It's difficult for a small business to provide health care, because they don't have any purchasing power. What we need to do is allow small businesses to accumulate purchasing power. It's called associated health care plans. If you've got more people demanding, it means you can reduce the price. We need the associated health care plans.

Another thing that affects all business, by the way, but especially hurts small businesses, are excessive regulations. I mean, if you've got four employees, you don't want to be spending a lot of time filling out paperwork. The Governor, I know, is working hard to reduce excessive paperwork at the State level. We're doing so at the Federal level. Look, I readily concede we've got a lot more to do. There's a lot of paperwork, a lot of regulation.

Another thing that's a problem is lawsuits. They get to be a problem on these small-business owners and large-business owners. Medical liability reform is an issue we need. I'll tell you why. They're driving up the cost of your medicine, and it's making fewer doctors practice medicine. Medicine ought to be affordable and ought to be available. And these lawsuits—everybody ought to be able to sue, don't get me wrong. We just don't want the junk lawsuits and the frivolous lawsuits and the lawyers who are simply fishing for a rich settlement to be prevalent.

Anyway, I'm interested in hearing how this great company works. Obviously, I heard the enthusiasm—[*laughter*]—when I was coming in. But John, why don't you start off, and then you can introduce your fellow workers.

[*The discussion continued.*]

The President. Let me ask you a question. So what's your feel? You're hearing from people when they're coming through, shopping, and——

John Ferraiuolo. I've got to tell you, our business in this store, this year, is about 18 percent better than last year. So where last year things were a little bit of a struggle—I think the enthusiasm and interest in people, the confidence level as people came in shopping wasn't quite there—people are now going from last year, I think, doing projects that were maybe necessities, I see people doing a little dreaming again and wanting to step themselves up and move forward and doing some wanting in their purchasing as opposed to just necessities.

The President. That's good, yes. John, by the way—he probably doesn't want me to tell you this, but I'm going to tell you anyway. He got $1,200 of tax relief as a result of the tax reductions. Probably considered a fair amount of money, I would guess.

Mr. Ferraiuolo. That's an awfully great amount of money. What happened there, I think last year—a few months ago, when my wife came home, she found a check in the mail, and you know what——

The President. Thank goodness. [*Laughter*]

Mr. Ferraiuolo. I'm going to—basically, she said, "Sign here. I'll do it for you."

The President. That's right. Yes. [*Laughter*]

Mr. Ferraiuolo. And then she went shopping, and she took the chance to buy herself a few treats. And I think with the rest of it, one of the things I've been able to do is up my 401(k) contributions——

The President. That's good.

Mr. Ferraiuolo. ——as opposed to—so I keep a little bit more of that money for my future.

The President. That's wonderful. Brandy, you're a manager, store manager. Tell us your history here, and——

[*The discussion continued.*]

The President. One of the things I like to talk about is the need for us to be a responsible society; people take responsibility for the decisions they make in life; people take responsibility—people seize opportunity. The thing I like about Jessica's story is she's willing to seize an opportunity. If you notice, she came looking, she worked hard to find a position, and now she's found a company that is doing its responsibility—in other words, helping people realize their dreams. And that's a very important part of corporate America. It's one of the reasons I like Bob, is he understands that, see.

One of the things that this company does is it provides volunteer time and encourages people to help—love your neighbor like you'd like to be loved yourself. One of the things about America is—look, we've just gone through an interesting story, that says to me that things look pretty good for the economy, and we've been through a lot. In other words, it's a fabulous country, because we'll handle every challenge put in front of us, every challenge, because we've got wonderful people.

The strength of this country, though, is not our military, although we'll keep it strong. It's strong. It needs to stay strong and will. It's not a—thank you, sir. And by the way, thanks for supporting the military. And if you've got a loved one over there, you tell them the Commander in

Chief is incredibly proud, proud of what they're doing.

Participant. They're right out there.

The President. Where?

Participant. This young man right here.

The President. Thank you for your service. I appreciate you, thanks.

Participant. He just came home.

The President. Yes. That's great. It's not—strength is not our military. It's not our wallet. It's the heart and soul of the American people. That's the strength. And the fact that this company is willing to say, you know, "Follow your heart and go help somebody who hurts," is an important part of keeping this country strong. It really is. The fact that people are willing to hear the universal call to love a neighbor like you'd like to be loved yourself is really an important part of this Nation. And it's a vital part of the Nation. So for those of you who are dreaming big dreams and working for them, like Jessica is, thanks for doing that—like our business owners— I appreciate that. It's important that you dream big dreams and work hard.

For those of you who are helping people realize their dreams, I thank you as well. It's just an incredibly vital part of a bright future for our country. There's nothing America can't achieve—nothing we can't achieve. You know why? Because this country is full of fabulous people. It's my honor to be with a lot of them here today.

Thank you for coming. God bless. Thank you for your time.

NOTE: The President spoke at 1:20 p.m. at the Lansdowne Home Depot. In his remarks, he referred to Gov. Robert L. Ehrlich, Jr., and Lt. Gov. Michael Steele of Maryland; James Montgomery, owner, James S. Montgomery & Sons; Gary Mangum, co-owner, and Alison Anderson, regional manager, Bell Nursery; John Ferraiuolo, store manager, and Jessica Adamson, paint associate, Lansdowne Home Depot; Brandy Foble, store manager, Ellicott City Home Depot; and Robert Nardelli, chairman, president, and chief executive officer, The Home Depot, Inc.

Statement Announcing the Appointment of James A. Baker III as the President's Personal Envoy on the Issue of Iraqi Debt
December 5, 2003

Iraq is moving toward freedom, stability, and prosperity. In order to support this effort, I am pleased to announce today that in response to a request from the Iraqi Governing Council for assistance, I have appointed James A. Baker III to be my personal envoy on the issue of Iraqi debt. Secretary Baker will report directly to me and will lead an effort to work with the world's Governments at the highest levels with international organizations and with the Iraqis in seeking the restructuring and reduction of Iraq's official debt. The future of the Iraqi people should not be mortgaged to the enormous burden of debt in-

curred to enrich Saddam Hussein's regime. This debt endangers Iraq's long-term prospects for political health and economic prosperity. The issue of Iraq debt must be resolved in a manner that is fair and that does not unjustly burden a struggling nation at its moment of hope and promise. James Baker's vast economic, political, and diplomatic experience as a former Secretary of State and Secretary of the Treasury will help to forge an international consensus for an equitable and effective resolution of this issue.

The President's Radio Address
December 6, 2003

Good morning. This week we received additional reports that America's economy is gaining strength.

In November, our Nation added 57,000 new jobs, and the unemployment rate fell to 5.9 percent. In the past 4 months, 328,000 Americans started work at new jobs.

In the third quarter of 2003, worker productivity rose at a 9.4 percent annual rate, the fastest pace since 1983. Rising productivity means rising wages, and productivity gains help companies keep prices low, which allows American families to stretch their paychecks further.

Other economic signs are positive. Surveys show manufacturing activity to be at its strongest level in 20 years. Automobile sales rose in November. Home construction continues to expand.

During this season, America's families are planning for the year ahead, and they have reason to be optimistic. The American economy continues on a solid path of recovery. With strong sales and improving profits, companies will continue to hire new workers in the coming year. And because of tax relief, all workers will get to keep more of what they earn, and small businesses will be able to create more jobs.

Since 2001, we have cut taxes for everyone who pays income taxes. We reduced the marriage penalty in our Tax Code. We raised the child credit to $1,000 per child, and we have reduced taxes on dividends and capital gains. This tax relief is critical because it keeps more money in the hands of workers and small-business owners and others who move this economy forward.

Here in Washington, our responsibility is to make sure this economy keeps its momentum, and I will not be satisfied until every person who wants to work can find a job. I have proposed a six-point plan to strengthen this recovery and bring prosperity to every corner of America. In the coming months, I will continue to work with Congress to achieve these important measures.

First, businesses are more likely to hire people if health care for workers is affordable. We need to allow small-business owners to join together in association health plans, giving them the purchasing power of large companies when they shop for health insurance. And we must reform the medical liability system so that health care dollars serve the interest of patients, not the interests of trial lawyers.

Second, we need broad legal reforms so frivolous lawsuits don't put good companies out of business and good people out of work. The Congress should start by enacting class action reform.

Third, we must reduce unnecessary Government regulation and redtape, so businesses can focus on consumers and customers, not paperwork.

Fourth, Congress should enact a national energy policy so that businesses and farms and homeowners can count on a reliable and affordable supply of energy and our Nation is less dependent on foreign sources of energy.

Fifth, my administration is pursuing free and fair trade agreements so that our products and services can reach new markets and new customers overseas.

Sixth, we should make all the tax relief we have passed permanent. The tax relief is scheduled to phase out in coming years if Congress does not take action. Tax relief set our economy on the right track, and permanent tax relief will keep it on the right track.

By moving forward on this agenda, we can build on the great progress our economy is making. With the confidence and hard work of the American people and with the right policies in Washington, there are even brighter days ahead for the American economy.

Thank you for listening.

NOTE: The address was recorded at 8:58 a.m. on December 5 in the Cabinet Room at the White House for broadcast at 10:06 a.m. on December 6. The transcript was made available by the Office of the Press Secretary on December 5 but was embargoed for release until the broadcast. The Office of the Press Secretary also released a Spanish language transcript of this address.

Remarks at the Kennedy Center Honors Reception
December 7, 2003

Thank you all very much. Good evening, and welcome to the White House. Laura and I are pleased to have you all here, and we are so honored to be a part of this annual tradition. We especially welcome the 2003 Kennedy Center honorees and their family and their friends.

Every year, the Kennedy Center pays tribute to five outstanding artists. Each group of honorees is an interesting mix. [*Laughter*] This year, for example, we have a director whose best films are known to all. We have an actress who has created characters we all remember, who, I'm told, still does a mighty good Tarzan yell. [*Laughter*] And the three musicians with us are among the most recognized in the world. They're not known to have performed together—[*laughter*]—but the sight of all three on the same stage is a picture to remember.

The Kennedy Center Honors recognize great contributions to American culture. Each of the honorees is here because of their hard effort and superior performance through an entire career.

Only one honoree was born in Texas. [*Laughter*] That person is Carol Burnett, who spent her early years in San Antonio. Young Carol went off into the world, and the world took a liking to her from the start. She is today one of the most recognized and warmly regarded entertainers in America.

For her first performance in acting class at UCLA, the teacher gave Carol Burnett a "D-". [*Laughter*] But Carol found, as have I—[*laughter*]—that one bad grade or two—[*laughter*]—is not the end of the road. [*Laughter*]

By the end of her freshman year, she was named "Most Outstanding Newcomer." Within a few years, she became a star on Broadway and a television favorite on the Winchell-Mahoney Show and the Garry Moore Show. In the sixties and seventies, Carol's own variety show ran 11 years and received more than 20 Emmys. Every week, Carol performed one of the most difficult feats in all of show business, playing it straight with Tim Conway. [*Laughter*]

To this day, millions of Americans can instantly recall sketches and characters from the Carol Burnett Show. Whether she was playing Eunice or the Scrub Woman or Starlett O'Hara in "Went With The Wind"—[*laughter*]—viewers could always sense the person behind the character, the sweetness, the sincerity, and the wonderful spirit of Carol Burnett.

Through the years in such performances as "Same Time Next Year," Carol has also shown the depth and range of her talent. In her good life, she has been a beloved entertainer, a devoted mom, and a faithful friend. She is a cheerful and graceful presence in American life, and America honors Carol Burnett.

All great performances in front of a camera involve an artistic vision behind the camera, and few have spent more years at the top of the directing profession than Mike Nichols. His name on a production signifies quality, intelligence, and high artistic standards. His credits include some of the most memorable films of the last two generations. "The Graduate" was a hit movie and a triumph that has held up over time.

The best directors are always extending themselves, and Mike Nichols has turned his gifts to films as varied as "Catch-22," "Who's Afraid of Virginia Woolf?" and "Working Girl." He is equally respected for his career on Broadway, first as a performer, then as director of the original "Odd Couple" and "Barefoot in the Park." The medal Mike Nichols wears this evening is the latest in a collection of other well-deserved honors, including the Oscar, the Emmy, the Tony, and the Grammy.

A movie critic once said that Mike Nichols' greatest talent may be his ability to bring out the best in performers, and that is another reason why Mike Nichols is among the finest.

Mike has summed up his career this way: "I have been in love with movies all my life. Directing them is like getting to marry this girl you followed around for years and years." I don't know how long he followed around Diane Sawyer—[*laughter*]—but she is here to share in this very proud moment.

And Mike's parents, who brought their little boy to America from Nazi Germany, would also be proud of their son. And tonight we are really proud to honor this fine man, Mike Nichols.

During this evening's reception, we will hear music from the Marine Band. I suspect that these fine musicians are thrilled to be in the presence of one of the greatest violinists of his age or any other.

As it happens, Laura and I were guests in this very room when Itzhak Perlman performed for President and Mrs. Reagan. That audience, like every audience to hear this man, was captivated by his music and charmed by his presence. According to a review of a recent concert in Minneapolis, "Perlman maintained an intimate rapport with the audience. For instance, he kept them updated on the score of the World Series between pieces." [*Laughter*] He was clearly having fun, and so was his audience.

The sound of a violin first called to him over the radio when he was just 3 years old. The Perlmans gave their boy a toy fiddle. He soon exhausted the possibilities of that instrument. Armed with a real violin, he was onstage with orchestras in Tel Aviv and Jerusalem and by the age 10 had given his first solo recital. America first came to know him 3 years later, when in 1958 he played "Flight of the Bumblebee" on the Ed Sullivan show. From that day to this, Itzhak Perlman has had a unique hold on the respect and affection of all who love classical music. He has played with every major orchestra in the world. He's collected more than a dozen Grammys, enthralled listeners with a repertoire stretching from baroque to contemporary, and touched millions of filmgoers with the pure and haunting solos in "Schindler's List."

Critics have written of Perlman's technical mastery, the rich tone and faultless intonation. And all who have seen him play are struck by the apparent ease with which he plays the most demanding of instruments. This good soul has been given a singular talent, and in sharing it he has brought much beauty into the world. For that, we are all honored to be in the presence of Maestro Itzhak Perlman.

Speaking of soul—[*laughter*]—James "Butane" Brown is in the house. Of course, he goes by other titles. Some men are too cool to only have one nickname. James Brown has been called "Mr. Dynamite," "Soul Brother Number One," and of course, "The Godfather of Soul." Many names fit him, but there's no one else like him. And in a career of more than 50 years, he has earned the reputation as a live performer with no equal and as an institution of rock and roll.

He grew up in Georgia, knowing many of the toils and struggles of an earlier time. He worked hard and took his own path. He received guidance along the way from many sources, from his Aunt Honey, who raised him, to the first preachers and gospel musicians he heard. He joined a band that called itself "The Famous Flames." It took only a short while before the name was changed, by general agreement, to "James Brown and the Famous Flames." [*Laughter*] When you hear the title of a James Brown song, right away you can picture him singing it: "I Feel Good," "Please, Please, Please," "Papa's Got a Brand New Bag," "Living in America."

Since he first achieved fame in the 1950s, James has posted 98 entries on Billboard's Top 40 R&B Singles Chart, more than any other performer. Bonnie Raitt has described James Brown's place in music history this way, "You couldn't even list how many people have been influenced by him. In the Mount Rushmore of musical figures, he definitely would be on it."

Of course, on that Mount Rushmore of music, the sculptor would have to pay particular attention to the hair. [*Laughter*] James is the first to tell you that the look is important to his success. Here's what he says, "Hair is the first thing, and teeth are the second." [*Laughter*] "Hair and teeth, a man got these two things, he's got it all." [*Laughter*]

The truth is, James Brown was being awfully modest. Along with the look, this man is blessed with incredible talent, undeniable stage presence, and the discipline of a true professional. He's still on the road and living it up—living up to that other nickname, "the hardest working man in show business." Our congratulations to James Joe Brown, Junior.

We are delighted to welcome our final honoree to the White House. Loretta Lynn even mentioned the White House in one of her songs. Since I don't have a band right here and since I can't sing—[*laughter*]—I'll just say the words, and you can imagine Loretta singing them: "The White House social season should be glittering and gay, but here in Topeka the rain is a-falling, the faucet is a-dripping, and the kids are a-bawling"—[*laughter*]—"one of them a-toddling, and one is a-crawling, and one's on the way." [*Laughter*]

Many of Loretta Lynn's songs are about the challenges, the dreams, and the joys of everyday life. She's known them all, and she has sung about them with style and feeling. More than four decades after she first sang at the Grand Ole Opry, there is no better known voice in country music and no lady more admired than Loretta Lynn.

Her song and the film "Coal Miner's Daughter" tell a true story that began in Butcher Hollow, Kentucky. Loretta grew up believing, in her words, that "from the Holler down to the mine was the whole world."

Her world changed when she met a soldier named Mooney Lynn. He made a strong impression on people. See, Mooney was the kind of man who wore a cowboy hat with a label inside that said, "Like hell it's yours." [*Laughter*] But as Loretta remembers, "I wasn't scared of Mooney. He was real nice. I was scared because I had never seen a car before." [*Laughter*] They married and moved away and were living in the State of Washington when Mooney got an idea. He knew that the voice singing lullabies to their children was better than any he had ever heard from a jukebox or in a saloon. And just maybe if Loretta cut a record, radio stations might play it.

That notion has been proven correct in more than 70 record albums, 27 number one singles, and 80 chart hits, from "Coal Miner's Daughter" to "Love is the Foundation" to "Don't Come Home A Drinkin' With Lovin' on Your Mind." [*Laughter*]

Loretta has received every top honor in country music and is loved for her own songs and for her wonderful duets with the late Conway Twitty. Her appeal has been explained this way, "She's straightforward, down home, innocent, and perfectly charming. Everyone loves her." And this evening, that unanimous opinion is expressed once again, and the Nation pays tribute to Loretta Lynn.

Americans are grateful to these Kennedy Center honorees because you have all given us wonderful memories. You have given your peers a high mark to aim for. Each of you in your own way has given America a body of work that reflects so very well on our Nation. Thank you for contributions to America. May God continue to bless you. Thank you for coming.

NOTE: The President spoke at 5:05 p.m. in the East Room at the White House. In his remarks, he referred to musician Bonnie Raitt.

Remarks on Signing the Medicare Prescription Drug, Improvement, and Modernization Act of 2003
December 8, 2003

Good morning. Thanks for the warm welcome. In a few moments I will have the honor of signing an historic act of Congress into law. I'm pleased that all of you are here to witness the greatest advance in health care coverage for America's seniors since the founding of Medicare.

With the Medicare Act of 2003, our Government is finally bringing prescription drug coverage to the seniors of America. With this law, we're giving older Americans better choices and more control over their health care, so they can receive the modern medical care they deserve. With this law, we are providing more access to comprehensive exams, disease screenings, and other preventative care, so that seniors across this land can live better and healthier lives. With this law, we are creating Health Savings Accounts. We do so so that all Americans can put money away for their health care tax-free.

Our Nation has the best health care system in the world, and we want our seniors to share in the benefits of that system. Our Nation has made a promise, a solemn promise to America's seniors. We have pledged to help our citizens find affordable medical care in the later years of life. Lyndon Johnson established that commitment by signing the Medicare Act of 1965. And today, by reforming and modernizing this vital program, we are honoring the commitments of Medicare to all our seniors.

The point man in my administration on this issue was Secretary Tommy Thompson, and he and his team did a fabulous job of working with the Congress to get this important piece of legislation passed. Tommy, I want to thank you for your leadership.

This bill passed the Congress because of the strong leadership of a handful of Members, starting with the Speaker of the House, Denny Hastert. Mr. Speaker was joined by Senator Bill Frist, the Senate majority leader of the Senate, in providing the leadership necessary to get this bill done. I want to thank you both.

I appreciate the hard work of the House majority leader, Tom DeLay, in seeing that this bill was passed. I also appreciate the hard work of the chairman of the Ways and Means Committee, Chairman Bill Thomas, for his good work. The chairman of the Finance Committee in the Senate, Senator Chuck Grassley, did a noble job, and he was joined in this task by the ranking member of the Finance Committee, Senator Max Baucus of Montana.

And the entire Senate effort was boosted by the efforts of a man from Louisiana, Senator John Breaux. And speaking about Louisiana, Billy Tauzin of the House of Representatives did great work on this bill. Senator Orrin Hatch from Utah made a significant contribution. Nancy Johnson, the House Member from Connecticut, did a great job. Mike Bilirakis from Florida worked hard on this piece of legislation. I want to thank all the other Members of the Congress and the Senate who have joined us. Thank you all for taking time out of your busy schedules to share in this historic moment.

I appreciate Tom Scully, the Administrator of the Centers for Medicare & Medicaid Services, for his good work. The Director of the CDC, Julie Gerberding, is with us today. Julie, thank you for coming. The Food and Drug Administration Commissioner, Mark McClellan, is here. Jo Anne Barnhart, the Commissioner of the Social Security Administration, is with us. Thank you for coming, Jo Anne. Kay James, who is the Director of the Office of Personnel Management, is with us. Thank you for coming, Kay.

A lot of this happened—this bill happened because of grassroots work. A lot of our fellow citizens took it upon themselves to agitate for change, to lobby on behalf of what's right. We had some Governor support around the country. Governor Craig Benson from New Hampshire is with us today. Governor, thank you for coming.

But the groups that speak for the elderly did fantastic work on this legislation. See, there was a lot of pressure not to get something done—for the wrong reasons, I might add. But Bill Novelli, the CEO of AARP, stood strong in representing the people he was supposed to represent and worked hard to get this legislation passed. And Bill, I want to thank you for your leadership. And you were joined by Jim Parkel, who is the president of the AARP. Jim, I want to thank you as well for doing what was right,

for focusing on the needs of the seniors of our country.

Jim Martin, the president of 60 Plus Association, worked hard. Charlie Jarvis, the chairman and CEO of United Seniors Association, worked hard. Mike Maves, the executive vice president and CEO of the AMA, worked hard on this piece of legislation. Mary Martin, the chairman of the board of the Seniors Coalition, worked hard. The truth of the matter is, a lot of good people worked hard to get this important legislation done, and I thank you for your work.

Medicare is a great achievement of a compassionate Government, and it is a basic trust we honor. Medicare has spared millions of seniors from needless hardship. Each generation benefits from Medicare. Each generation has a duty to strengthen Medicare, and this generation is fulfilling our duty.

First and foremost, this new law will provide Medicare coverage for prescription drugs. Medicare was enacted to provide seniors with the latest in modern medicine. In 1965, that usually meant house calls or operations or long hospital stays. Today, modern medicine includes outpatient care, disease screenings, and prescription drugs. Medicine has changed, but Medicare has not—until today.

Medicare today will pay for extended hospital stays for ulcer surgery; that's at a cost of about $28,000 per patient. Yet Medicare will not pay for the drugs that eliminate the cause of most ulcers, drugs that cost about $500 a year. It's a good thing that Medicare pays when seniors get sick. Now, you see, we're taking this a step further: Medicare will pay for the prescription drugs so that fewer seniors will get sick in the first place.

Drug coverage under Medicare will allow seniors to replace more expensive surgeries and hospitalizations with less expensive prescription medicine. And even more important, drug coverage under Medicare will save our seniors from a lot of worry. Some older Americans spend much of their Social Security checks just on their medications. Some cut down on the dosage to make a bottle of pills last longer. Elderly Americans should not have to live with those kinds of fears and hard choices. This new law will ease the burden on seniors and will give them the extra help they need.

Seniors will start seeing help quickly. During the transition to the full prescription benefit, seniors will receive a drug discount card. This Medicare-approved card will deliver savings of 10 to 25 percent off the retail price of most medicines. Low-income seniors will receive the same savings plus a $600 credit on their cards to help them pay for the medications they need.

In about 2 years, full prescription coverage under Medicare will begin. In return for a monthly premium of about $35, most seniors without any prescription drug coverage can now expect to see their current drug bills cut roughly in half. This new law will provide 95-percent coverage for out-of-pocket drug spending that exceeds $3,600 a year. For the first time, we're giving seniors peace of mind that they will not have to face unlimited expenses for their medicine.

The new law offers special help to one-third of older Americans with low incomes, such as a senior couple with low savings and an annual income of about $18,000 or less. These seniors will pay little or no premium for full drug coverage. Their deductible will be no higher than $50 per year, and their copayment on each prescription will be as little as $1. Seniors in the greatest need will have the greatest help under the modernized Medicare system.

I visited with seniors around the country and heard many of their stories. I'm proud that this legislation will give them practical and much needed help. Mary Jane Jones from Midlothian, Virginia, has a modest income. Her drug bills total nearly $500 a month. Things got so tight for a while she had to use needles twice or 3 times for her insulin shots. With this law, Mary Jane won't have to go to such extremes. In exchange for a monthly premium of about $35, Mary Jane Jones would save nearly $2,700 in annual prescription drug spending.

Hugh Iverson from West Des Moines, Iowa, just got his Medicare membership. And that's a good thing, because he hasn't had health insurance for more than 3 years. His drug bills total at least $400 a month. Within 2 years, with the $35-a-month coverage, he will be able to cut those bills nearly in half, saving him about $2,400 a year.

Neil LaGrow from Culpeper, Virginia, takes 15 medications, costing him at least $700 a month. To afford all those medications, Neil has to stay working. And thanks to this law, once he is enrolled in the drug benefit, he will be able to cut back his work hours and enjoy his retirement more because he'll have coverage that saves him about $4,700 a year.

I promised these seniors when I met with them that we would work hard to give them the help they need. They are all here today. So I am happy to report to them in person: Mary Jane, Hugh, and Neil, we are keeping our promise.

In addition to providing coverage for prescription drugs, this legislation achieves a second great goal. We're giving our seniors more health care choices, so they can get the coverage and care that meets their needs. Every senior needs to know, if you don't want to change your current coverage, you don't have to change. You're the one in charge. If you want to keep your Medicare the way it is, along with the new prescription benefit, that is your right. If you want to improve benefits, maybe dental coverage or eyeglass coverage or managed care plans that reduce out-of-pocket costs, you'll be free to make those choices as well.

And when seniors have the ability to make choices, health care plans within

Medicare will have to compete for their business by offering higher quality service. For the seniors of America, more choices and more control will mean better health care. These are the kinds of health care options we give to the Members of Congress and Federal employees. They have the ability to pick plans to—that are right for their own needs. What's good for Members of Congress is also good for seniors. Our seniors are fully capable of making health care choices, and this bill allows them to do just that.

A third purpose achieved by this legislation is smarter medicine within the Medicare system. For years, our seniors have been denied Medicare coverage—have been denied Medicare coverage for a basic physical exam. Beginning in 2005, all newly enrolled Medicare beneficiaries will be covered for a complete physical.

The Medicare system will now help seniors and their doctors diagnose health problems early, so they can treat them early and our seniors can have a better quality life. For example, starting next year, all people on Medicare will be covered for blood tests that can diagnose heart diseases. Those at high risk for diabetes will be covered for blood sugar screening tests. Modern health care is not complete without prevention, so we are expanding preventive services under Medicare.

Fourth, the new law will help all Americans pay for out-of-pocket health costs. This legislation will create health savings accounts, effective January 1, 2004, so Americans can set aside up to $4,500 every year, tax-free, to save for medical expenses. Depending on your tax bracket, that means you'll save between 10 to 35 percent on any costs covered by money in your account. Our laws encourage people to plan for retirement and to save for education. Now the law will make it easier for Americans to save for their future health care as well.

A health savings account is a good deal, and all Americans should consider it. Every year, the money not spent would stay in the account and gain interest tax-free, just like an IRA. And people will have an incentive to live more healthy lifestyles because they want to see their health savings account grow. These accounts will be good for small-business owners and employees. More businesses can focus on covering workers for major medical problems such as hospitalization for an injury or illness. And at the same time, employees and their families will use these accounts to cover doctors visits or lab tests or other smaller costs. Some employers will contribute to employee health accounts. This will help more American families get the health care they need at the price they can afford.

The legislation I'm about to sign will set in motion a series of improvements in the care available to all America's senior citizens. And as we begin, it is important for seniors and those approaching retirement to understand their new benefits. This coming spring, seniors will receive a letter to explain the drug discount card. In June, these cards, including the $600 annual drug credit for low-income seniors, will be activated. This drug card can be used through the end of 2005. In the fall of that year, seniors will receive an information booklet giving simple guidance on changes in the program and the new choices they will have. Then in January of 2006, seniors will have their new coverage, including permanent coverage for prescription drugs.

These reforms are the act of a vibrant and compassionate Government. We show our concern for the dignity of our seniors by giving them quality health care. We show our respect for seniors by giving them more choices and more control over their decisionmaking. We're putting individuals in charge of their health care decisions. And as we move to modernize and reform other programs of this Government, we will always trust individuals and their decisions and put personal choice at the heart of our efforts.

The challenges facing seniors on Medicare were apparent for many years, and those years passed with much debate and a lot of politics and little reform to show for it. And that changed with the 108th Congress. This year we met our challenge with focus and perseverance. We confronted problems, instead of passing them along to future administrations and future Congresses. We overcame old partisan differences. We kept our promise and found a way to get the job done. This legislation is the achievement of Members in both political parties. And this legislation is a victory for all of America's seniors.

Now I'm honored and pleased to sign this historic piece of legislation, the Medicare Prescription Drug, Improvement, and Modernization Act of 2003.

NOTE: The President spoke at 11:10 a.m. at DAR Constitution Hall. H.R. 1, approved December 8, was assigned Public Law No. 108–173. The Office of the Press Secretary also released a Spanish language transcript of these remarks.

Statement on Signing the Medicare Prescription Drug, Improvement, and Modernization Act of 2003
December 8, 2003

Today, I have signed into law H.R. 1, the "Medicare Prescription Drug, Improvement, and Modernization Act of 2003." The Act helps achieve a more modern Medicare system that includes prescription drug coverage and choices for seniors.

Sections 1012 and 1014 of the Act create a commission and a working group, both with most of their members designated by Members of Congress or the Comptroller General, a legislative agent. Sections 1012(h)(3) and 1014(j)(3) purport to give the commission and the working group a right to secure directly from executive departments and agencies information they seek to perform their duties. The executive branch shall construe these provisions in a manner consistent with the constitutional authorities of the President to supervise the unitary executive branch and to withhold information the disclosure of which could impair the deliberative processes of the Executive or the performance of the Executive's constitutional duties.

Section 802 of the Act calls for the President to submit to the Congress proposals for legislation in the event that a Medicare funding warning is issued under section 801(a)(2). Many other provisions in the Act, including sections 101(b), 109(d)(2), 410A(e), 434(f), 507(c)(3), 645(a)(2), 649(g), 651(d)(2), 911(f), and 1014(o), also call for executive branch officials to submit to the Congress proposals for legislation. The executive branch shall construe these provisions in a manner consistent with the President's constitutional authority to supervise the unitary executive branch and to recommend for the consideration of the Congress such measures as the President judges necessary and expedient.

GEORGE W. BUSH

The White House,
December 8, 2003.

NOTE: H.R. 1, approved December 8, was assigned Public Law No. 108–173.

Statement on the Death of Joe Skeen
December 8, 2003

Joe Skeen was a dedicated public servant who worked tirelessly for the people of New Mexico. He led an extraordinary life, from his service in the Navy and the Air Force Reserves to his work and many contributions in the New Mexico State senate and the United States House of Representatives. He was a strong leader of conviction and principle. A good man, he will be missed by his many friends. Laura and I send our condolences to his wife, Mary, and their family and friends.

Message to the Congress Transmitting a Report of the Railroad Retirement Board
December 8, 2003

To the Congress of the United States:

I transmit herewith the Annual Report of the Railroad Retirement Board presented for forwarding to you for the fiscal year ending September 30, 2002, consistent with the provisions of section 7(b)(6) of the Railroad Retirement Act and section 12(1) of the Railroad Unemployment Insurance Act.

GEORGE W. BUSH

The White House,
December 8, 2003.

Remarks at a Welcoming Ceremony for Premier Wen Jiabao of China
December 9, 2003

Mr. Premier, members of the delegation, it is my honor to welcome you to the White House. Your visit reflects the increasing ties of cooperation and commerce between our two nations.

America and China share many common interests. We are working together in the war on terror. We are fighting to defeat a ruthless enemy of order and civilization. We are partners in diplomacy working to meet the dangers of the 21st century. We are full members of a world trading system that rewards enterprise and lifts nations.

Our two nations seek a Korean Peninsula that is stable and at peace. The elimination of North Korea's nuclear programs is essential to this outcome. Realizing this vision will require the strong cooperation of all North Korea's neighbors. I am grateful for China's leadership in hosting the six-party talks which are bringing us closer to a peaceful resolution of this issue. And my Government will continue to work with China as it plays a constructive role in Asia and in the world.

The rapid rise of China's economy is one of the great achievements of our time. China's increasing prosperity has brought great benefits to the Chinese people and to China's trading partners around the world. We recognize that if prosperity's power is to reach in every corner of China, the Chinese Government must fully integrate into the rules and norms of the international trading and finance system.

China has discovered that economic freedom leads to national wealth. The growth of economic freedom in China provides reason to hope that social, political, and religious freedoms will grow there as well. In the long run, these freedoms are indivisible and essential to national greatness and national dignity.

As our two nations work constructively across areas of common interest, we are candid about our disagreements. The growing strength and maturity of our relationship allows us to discuss our differences, whether over economic issues, Taiwan, Tibet, or human rights and religious freedom, in a spirit of mutual understanding and respect.

China is a great civilization, a great power, and a great nation. Premier Wen,

when my country looks forward to—my country looks forward to working with you as China increasingly takes its place among the leading nations of the world.

The United States and China have made great progress in building a relationship that can address the challenges of our time, encourage global prosperity, and advance the cause of peace. It is my hope that your visit will further that progress.

Welcome, and thank you for coming.

NOTE: The President spoke at 10 a.m. on the South Portico at the White House, where Premier Wen was accorded a formal welcome with full military honors. The transcript released by the Office of the Press Secretary also included the remarks of Premier Wen.

Remarks Following Discussions With Premier Wen Jiabao of China and an Exchange With Reporters
December 9, 2003

President Bush. Welcome. I will make a statement; the Premier will make a statement. We'll answer questions, one from the American side, one from the Chinese side, one from the American side, and one from the Chinese side.

Mr. Premier, welcome. We're going to have extensive discussions today on a lot of issues. We've just had a very friendly and candid discussion. There's no question in my mind that when China and the United States works closely together, we can accomplish a lot of very important objectives. Our relationship is good and strong, and we are determined to keep it that way for the good of our respective peoples and for the sake of peace and prosperity in the world.

So, welcome. Glad you're here.

Premier Wen. I'm very grateful towards President Bush and the U.S. Government for the kind invitation and warm hospitality.

Just now, President Bush and I had an indepth exchange of views on China-U.S. relationship and on international and regional issues of mutual interest. The discussion took place under very friendly, candid, cooperative, and constructive atmosphere, and we reached consensus on many issues.

President Bush and I both believe that the further improvement and growth of the bilateral ties between China and the U.S. will not only bring benefits for the people of the two countries but also in the interest of world peace and stability.

Thank you.

President Bush. AP man.

Taiwan

Q. Mr. President, George Gedda of AP. Given the sensitivity of the issue, do you believe the referendum planned by the Taiwanese on March 20th should be canceled?

President Bush. Someone needs to interpret that.

Let me tell you what I've just told the Premier on this issue. The United States Government's policy is "one China," based upon the three communiques and the Taiwan Relations Act. We oppose any unilateral decision by either China or Taiwan to change the status quo. And the comments and actions made by the leader of Taiwan indicate that he may be willing to make decisions unilaterally to change the status quo, which we oppose.

Why don't you call on somebody from your press.

Q. Premier Wen, what is the position of the Chinese Government on the question of Taiwan?

Premier Wen. Our fundamental policy on the settlement of the question of Taiwan is peaceful reunification and one country, two systems. We would do our utmost with utmost sincerity to bring about national unity and peaceful reunification through peaceful means.

The Chinese Government respects the desire of people in Taiwan for democracy, but we must point out that the attempts of Taiwan authorities, headed by Chen Shui-bian, are only using democracy as an excuse and attempt to resort to defensive referendum to split Taiwan away from China. Such separatist activities are what the Chinese side can absolutely not accept and tolerate.

We also want to say that so long as there is a glimmer of hope, we would not give up our efforts for peaceful reunification. We have expressed our will and determination to uphold national unity. This is for the very purpose of maintaining peace and stability in the Taiwan Straits. And such stability can only be maintained through unswerving opposition and firm opposition to pro-independence activities.

On many occasions and just now in the meeting as well, President Bush has reiterated the U.S. commitment to the three Sino-U.S. Joint Communiques, the "one China" principle, and opposition to Taiwan independence. We appreciate that. In particular, we very much appreciate the position adopted by President Bush toward the latest moves and developments in Taiwan, that is, the attempt to resort to referendum of various kinds as excuse to pursue Taiwan independence. We appreciate the position of the U.S. Government.

President Bush. Steve [Steve Holland, Reuters].

North Korea

Q. Mr. President, thank you. North Korea is saying they will freeze their nuclear program if the U.S. takes them off the terrorism list and provides fuel aid. Is this a worthwhile idea? And how are you going to get the six-party talks going again?

President Bush. Yes, well, we spent a lot of time talking about North Korea here. We share a mutual goal, and that is for the Korean Peninsula to be nuclear-weapons-free. I thank the Premier for China starting the six-party talks, and I will continue those talks. I think they're very important.

The goal of the United States is not for a freeze of the nuclear program. The goal is to dismantle a nuclear weapons program in a verifiable and irreversible way, and that is a clear message that we are sending to the North Koreans. And we will continue to work with China and the other countries involved to resolve this issue peacefully.

China-U.S. Relations

Q. Premier Wen, what's your reading of the status quo and the future development of China's economic relationship and trade with the United States?

Premier Wen. The expansion of China's economic cooperation and trade with the United States, as we see today, has not come by easily. Just imagine, 25 years ago, our trade was less than 2.5 billion U.S. dollars, and now the volume has exceeded 100 billion U.S. dollars. Our economic and trade links have been conducive to the interest of our two people and two countries.

We have to admit, though, in our economic and trade relationship, problems do exist, and mainly, the U.S. trade deficit with China. The Chinese Government takes this problem seriously and has taken measures to improve the situation. Soon, in a few minutes, we will have a large group meeting with the U.S. side, and in that setting, I would make one proposal, and I will also share with President Bush five principles we think that should guide the develop-

ment of economic cooperation and trade between China and the U.S.

President Bush. Thank you, sir. Thank you.

NOTE: The President spoke at 11:05 a.m. in the Oval Office at the White House. In his remarks, he referred to President Chen Shui-bian of Taiwan. Premier Wen spoke in Chinese, and his remarks were translated by an interpreter. A tape was not available for verification of the content of these remarks.

Statement on the Resignation of Mel R. Martinez as Secretary of Housing and Urban Development
December 9, 2003

Mel Martinez is a good friend and an exceptional public servant. As a refugee from Cuba, Mel came to America in search of freedom and opportunity as one of the many young children sent by their parents as part of a Catholic relief program known as Pedro Pan. As Secretary of Housing and Urban Development, he has worked tire-

lessly to help every American realize the promise of our country for themselves and their families. I appreciate the energy, optimism, and compassion he brought to my administration. I thank him for serving our Nation so selflessly, and Laura and I wish Mel, his wife, Kitty, and their family well.

Statement on the Resignation of John Bridgeland as Assistant to the President and Director of the USA Freedom Corps
December 9, 2003

John Bridgeland has been a valuable advisor to me for nearly 4 years. He started on the policy staff of my Presidential campaign in early 2000. Since January 20, 2001, he has faithfully served in my administration, first as Deputy Assistant to the President for Domestic Policy and Director of the Domestic Policy Council and then as Assistant to the President and the first Director of the USA Freedom Corps Office. He has worked tirelessly to strengthen a culture of service in America and to ensure

that we all love our neighbors as we want to be loved ourselves. His work has had a positive and vitally important impact on government, nonprofit and community service organizations, businesses, and many men, women, and children who need a helping hand. I appreciate and thank John for his friendship and wise counsel. This good man has touched many people through his dedicated public service, and I wish him, Maureen, and their three children all the best.

Message to the Senate Transmitting the Additional Protocol to the Romania-United States Investment Treaty
December 9, 2003

To the Senate of the United States:

With a view to receiving the advice and consent of the Senate to ratification, I transmit herewith the Additional Protocol between the Government of the United States of America and the Government of Romania Concerning the Reciprocal Encouragement and Protection of Investment of May 28, 1992, signed at Brussels on September 22, 2003. I transmit also, for the information of the Senate, the report of the Department of State with respect to this Additional Protocol.

My Administration expects to forward to the Senate shortly analogous Additional Protocols for Bulgaria, the Czech Republic, Estonia, Latvia, Lithuania, Poland, and the Slovak Republic. Each of these Additional Protocols is the result of an understanding the United States reached with the European Commission and six countries that will join the European Union (EU) on May 1, 2004 (the Czech Republic, Estonia, Latvia, Lithuania, Poland, and the Slovak Republic), as well as with Bulgaria and Romania, which are expected to join the EU in 2007.

The understanding is designed to preserve U.S. bilateral investment treaties (BITs) with each of these countries after their accession to the EU by establishing a framework acceptable to the European Commission for avoiding or remedying present and possible future incompatibilities between their BIT obligations and their future obligations of EU membership. It expresses the U.S. intent to amend the U.S. BITs, including the BIT with Romania, in order to eliminate incompatibilities between certain BIT obligations and EU law. It also establishes a framework for addressing any future incompatibilities that may arise as European Union authority in the area of investment expands in the future, and endorses the principle of protecting existing U.S. investments from any future EU measures that may restrict foreign investment in the EU.

The United States has long championed the benefits of an open investment climate, both at home and abroad. It is the policy of the United States to welcome market-driven foreign investment and to permit capital to flow freely to seek its highest return. This Additional Protocol preserves the U.S. BIT with Romania, with which the United States has an expanding relationship, and the protections it affords U.S. investors even after Romania joins the EU. Without it, the European Commission would likely require Romania to terminate its U.S. BIT upon accession because of existing and possible future incompatibilities between our current BIT and EU law.

I recommend that the Senate consider this Additional Protocol as soon as possible, and give its advice and consent to ratification at an early date.

GEORGE W. BUSH

The White House,
December 9, 2003.

Message to the Senate Transmitting the Japan-United States Tax Convention
December 9, 2003

To the Senate of the United States:

I transmit herewith, for Senate advice and consent to ratification, the Convention between the Government of the United States of America and the Government of Japan for the Avoidance of Double Taxation and the Prevention of Fiscal Evasion with respect to Taxes on Income, signed at Washington on November 6, 2003, together with a Protocol and an exchange of notes (the "Convention"). I also transmit, for the information of the Senate, the report of the Department of State concerning the Convention.

This Convention would replace the Convention between the United States of America and Japan for the Avoidance of Double Taxation and the Prevention of Fiscal Evasion with respect to Taxes on Income, signed at Tokyo on March 8, 1971.

This Convention, which is similar to tax treaties between the United States and other developed nations, provides rules specifying the circumstances under which income that arises in one of the countries and is derived by residents of the other country may be taxed by the country in which income arises, providing for maximum source-country withholding tax rates that may be applied to various types of income and providing for protection from double taxation of income. The proposed Convention also provides rules designed to ensure that the benefits of the Convention are not available to persons that are engaged in treaty shopping. Also included in the proposed Convention are rules necessary for administering the Convention.

I recommend that the Senate give early and favorable consideration to this Convention, and that the Senate give its advice and consent to the ratification of the Convention.

GEORGE W. BUSH

The White House,
December 9, 2003.

Remarks Following a Meeting With Members of the Iraqi National Symphony
December 10, 2003

Last night Laura and I had the honor of going to hear the Iraqi National Symphony play with the Washington Symphony at the Kennedy Center. It was an extraordinary event. And today I've had the honor of welcoming members of the symphony here at the White House. Maestro, you did a superb job. Thank you very much.

I'm also honored to be here with Rend al-Rahim, who is the Iraqi representative to the United States. Rend is an articulate defender of freedom and peace. I'm so honored you're here, Rend, and we look forward to working with you.

We've had a very positive discussion here about freedom and hopes and aspirations of young and old alike. And I am so impressed by the spirit of these musicians. I'm so honored you would come to our country.

It's very interesting that the Iraqi Symphony is made up of people who are Shi'a and Sunni and Armenian and Kurdish. They work for one thing, and that is a unified sound, a beautiful sound. And that's the country that is now emerging in Iraq, a country that will work together and recognize everybody's rights. We're making good progress in Iraq. There's more to do, obviously, but the fact that the Iraqi Symphony is here and entertaining Americans is a sign of that progress.

And we thank you all for coming. We wish you Godspeed.

NOTE: The President spoke at 2:01 p.m. in the Roosevelt Room at the White House. In his remarks, he referred to Mohammed Amin Ezzat, conductor, Iraqi National Symphony; and Rend Rahim Francke, head of Iraq's Interest Section in the U.S. A tape was not available for verification of the content of these remarks.

Statement on the Death of Paul Simon
December 10, 2003

Laura and I were saddened to learn of the death of former Senator Paul Simon. Paul Simon contributed significantly to America as an Army special agent, newspaper publisher, Member of the United States Senate and House of Representatives, and author and teacher. He will be missed by the many people in Illinois and throughout the country whose lives he touched and improved. Laura and I send our condolences to his family and many friends.

Statement on the Death of Bob Bartley
December 10, 2003

Bob Bartley was a giant of journalism. His extraordinary contributions to America as an author, editor, and columnist helped shape our times. I was pleased to award him the Presidential Medal of Freedom, our highest civil honor, in recognition of his enormous impact on the intellectual and political life of our Nation. Laura joins me in sending condolences to Edith and his daughters, family, colleagues, and friends.

Remarks Following a Cabinet Meeting and an Exchange With Reporters
December 11, 2003

The President. I want to thank the members of my Cabinet for coming for what will be the last Cabinet meeting of the year 2003. I've just heard from each Cabinet member about the accomplishments in the year 2003. This has been an historic year. America is safer. America is more prosperous. America is a better place because of the actions this administration has taken.

In order to secure America, we liberated the people of Iraq from a brutal tyrant, and now we're in the process of rebuilding that country, along with others, and we're making good progress.

In order to make sure people could find work in America, we proposed and Congress passed an economic stimulus package, and that package is making a significant difference on our economy. Our economy is strong; it is vibrant. People are finding work, but we won't rest until everybody who wants to find a job can find one.

The country is better off for a lot of reasons. A significant piece of legislation was passed by the Congress, which I recently signed, and that is the Medicare reform bill. We took on a tough issue; we worked with Congress to make sure that we fulfilled a promise to America's seniors by modernizing and strengthening Medicare.

This has been a year of accomplishment. We also recognize we've got a job to do, to continue to do for the American people, to keep this country safe and prosperous and strong and a better place for all our citizens. And we look forward to working with the Congress in the year '04 to accomplish those objectives.

Today is Mel Martinez's, the fine Secretary of HUD, last meeting. Mel has served our country with class and distinction. I'm proud, Mel, to have had you on this team. Good job.

Secretary Martinez. Thank you, sir.

The President. I'll answer a couple of questions—that would be two questions. Terry [Terence Hunt, Associated Press].

Iraqi Reconstruction Contracts

Q. Mr. President, what did the leaders of France, Russia, and Germany say to you yesterday about being excluded from contracts, reconstruction contracts in Iraq? And can those countries be considered for the contract if they forgive debt that's owed by Iraq?

The President. Let me make sure everybody understands that men and women from our country, who proudly wear our uniform, risked their life to free Iraq. Men and women from other countries in a broad coalition risked their lives to free Iraq. And

the expenditure of U.S. dollars will reflect the fact that U.S. troops and other troops risked their life.

Now, we want to work with all countries. We have a common goal, and that is to see that Iraq is free and peaceful. It is in every nation's interest that Iraq be free and peaceful, and we welcome contributions. We welcome people's willingness to participate in this difficult yet important job of rebuilding Iraq.

Holland [Steve Holland, Reuters].

Q. Sir, Chancellor Schroeder says international law must apply in this case. What's your understanding of the law?

The President. International law? I better call my lawyer. He didn't bring that up to me. I asked President Chirac and Chancellor Schroeder and President Putin to see Jim Baker to talk about debt restructuring. If these countries want to participate in helping the world become more secure by enabling Iraq to emerge as a free and peaceful country, one way to contribute is through debt restructuring. And so Jim Baker, with the consent of the Secretary of State, is going to go over and talk to these leaders about that. But I don't know what you're talking about, about international law. I've got to consult my lawyer.

Iraqi Debt Relief

Q. Can I clarify one thing?

The President. Yes, you may clarify something.

Q. Thank you very much.

The President. Depends on what it is, though. [*Laughter*]

Q. Same issue.

The President. Okay.

Q. You seem to be saying that the boots on the ground are the only qualifications for—but what about the forgiveness of debt? Isn't that a fairly substantial——

The President. It is. It would be a significant contribution for which we would be very grateful. What I'm saying is, in the expenditure of taxpayers' money—and that's what we're talking about now—the

U.S. people, the taxpayers, understand why it makes sense for countries that risk lives to participate in the contracts in Iraq. It's very simple. Our people risk their lives; coalition—friendly coalition folks risk their lives; and therefore, the contracting is going to reflect that. And that's what the U.S. taxpayers expect.

Thank you all.

NOTE: The President spoke at 10:51 a.m. in the Cabinet Room at the White House. In his remarks, he referred to former President Saddam Hussein of Iraq; President Jacques Chirac of France; Chancellor Gerhard Schroeder of Germany; President Vladimir Putin of Russia; and James A. Baker III, the President's personal envoy on the issue of Iraqi debt. A tape was not available for verification of the content of these remarks.

Remarks at a Bush-Cheney Luncheon in McLean, Virginia
December 11, 2003

Thanks for the warm welcome. Thanks for coming. Thanks for your strong support. I tell you what we're doing here: We're laying the foundation to make sure that we carry Virginia again in 2004, and we're laying the foundation for what is going to be a great nationwide victory in 2004. And I really appreciate your help. I also appropriate you letting some Oklahoma folks come today too. [*Laughter*] Yes, that's what—[*inaudible*]. Tell them hello in Tulsa.

I want you to know that I am—I'm getting ready for the campaign. I'm loosening up. [*Laughter*] But politics is going to come in its own time. See, I've got a job to do. I'm focusing on the people's business. I want you to remind your neighbors and your friends that this administration will continue to work hard to earn the confidence of every single citizen by keeping this Nation secure and strong and prosperous and free.

I want to thank the attorney general for his kind introductory remarks. I appreciate you, General. I appreciate the fact that you're going to be the campaign chairman of the Bush-Cheney '04 campaign. I'm counting on you to energize the grassroots. And for those of you who are involved in the party like Kate Griffin, who's the party chairman, and other folks who are out in the precincts, thank you for what you are going to do.

I'm so proud that I married above myself. I'm sorry the First Lady is not here with me. Laura is a great wife, a great mother, and a great First Lady for our country. She sends her very best, and she sends her warm regards to all our friends here in northern Virginia.

Speaking about great family members, I am lucky to have a great brother who's from the great State of Virginia. He is my friend. He is—he comes to the White House; he helps remind me about what is important in life, and what is important is family. And Marvin Bush, I want to thank you for your love.

I'm also proud to be closely working with the chairman—I call him the chairman—one of the great leaders in the United States Senate, somebody who has stood strong for the State of Virginia and, more importantly, has stood strong for America by making sure we are a strong nation, and that is Senator John Warner. I know your former Governor is here with us today, my good friend Jim Gilmore. Thank you for coming, Jim. I appreciate your support.

I want to thank my friend Dwight Schar, who is the State finance chairman for Bush-

Cheney '04. Thank you, Dwight, for helping make this event such a good event. I appreciate all the event chairmen for working so hard. It's been an incredibly successful day today, and I want to thank you. I know how much work goes into organizing and planning and rallying the folks to come to this type of event. I want to thank my friend Mercer Reynolds, who is the national finance chairman, for being here. But most of all, thank you all.

I want you to remind your friends and neighbors that in the last 3 years, our Nation has acted decisively to confront great challenges. I came to this office to solve problems instead of passing them on to future Presidents and future generations. I came to seize opportunities instead of letting them slip away. This administration is meeting the tests of our time.

Terrorists declared war on the United States of America, and war is what they got. We have captured or killed many of the key leaders of the Al Qaida network, and the rest of them know we're on their trail. In Iraq and Afghanistan, we gave ultimatums to terror regimes. Those regimes chose defiance, and those regimes are no more. Fifty million people in those two countries once lived under tyranny, and today they live in freedom.

Three years ago, our military was not receiving the resources it needed, and morale was beginning to suffer. So we increased the defense budgets to prepare for the threats of a new era. And nobody in the world today can question the skill, the strength, and the spirit of the United States military.

Three years ago, the economy was in trouble, and a recession was beginning. And then our country was attacked, and we had some citizens who didn't tell the truth, and war came upon us in order to make us the—America more secure and the world more peaceful. And all that affected the people's confidence. But this administration acted. We passed tough new laws to hold corporate criminals to account. And to get the economy going again, I have twice led the United States Congress to pass historic tax relief for the American people.

This administration understands that when Americans have more take-home pay to spend, to save, or to invest, the whole economy grows, and people are more likely to find a job. And that is why we are returning more money to people to help them raise their families. That is why we reduced taxes on dividends and capital gains to encourage investment. That is why we've given small businesses incentives to expand and to hire new people. With all these actions, we have laid the foundation for greater prosperity and more jobs across America, so every single citizen has a chance to realize the American Dream.

And this economy of ours is strong, and it is getting stronger. The figures for the third quarter show that our economy grew at an annual rate of 8.2 percent, the fastest rate in 20 years. Productivity is high. Business investment is rising. Housing construction is expanding. Manufacturing activity is increasing. We've added 300,000 new jobs in the last 4 months. The tax relief plan we passed is working.

Three years ago, there was a lot of talk about education reform in Washington, but there wasn't much action. So I acted, and I called for and the Congress passed the No Child Left Behind Act. With a solid bipartisan majority, we delivered the most dramatic education reforms in a generation. We've increased spending at the Federal level, particularly for Title I students, but for the first time, the Federal Government is asking whether or not our children can read and write and add and subtract. See, we believe every child can read and write and add and subtract. We expect every school in America to teach every child, so that not one single child is left behind.

We reorganized our Government and created the Department of Homeland Security to better safeguard our borders and ports and the American people. We passed trade promotion authority to open up new markets for Virginia's entrepreneurs and manufacturers and farmers. We passed much needed budget agreements to help maintain spending discipline in Washington, DC.

And this week, we completed the greatest advance in health care coverage for America's seniors since the founding of Medicare. The new Medicare law will give older Americans the option of prescription drug benefits and more control over their health care so they can receive the modern medical care they deserve. The new bill will provide more access to comprehensive exams and disease screenings and offer preventative care so seniors across this land can live better and healthier lives. The bill I signed creates health savings accounts so all Americans could put money away for their health care, tax-free. We confronted a big issue, and we made progress on behalf of today's seniors and tomorrow's seniors.

On issue after issue, this administration has acted on principle, has kept its word, and has made progress for the American people. And the Congress gets a lot of credit. We've done a lot, working together. I appreciate my relationship with Senate Majority Leader Bill Frist and, of course, Chairman Warner and Senator Allen from this State as well. Got a great relationship with Speaker Hastert. We're working hard to try to change the tone in Washington. There's too much needless politics, endless backbiting, constant posturing. See, the best way to deal in that kind of environment— or with that environment—is to elevate the discourse and to focus on the people's business by delivering. And that's what we have done. We've delivered on behalf of all people who live in this country.

And by the way, that's the kind of people I've attracted to my administration. I've put together a superb team of men and women from all walks of life to represent the United States of America. Our country has had no finer Vice President than Dick Che-

ney, although Mother may have a second opinion. [*Laughter*]

In 3 years—in 3 years, we've done a lot. We have come far, but our work is only beginning. I have set great goals worthy of a great nation. First, America is committed to expanding the realm of freedom and peace for our own security and for the benefit of the world. And second, in our own country, we must work for a society that is prosperous and compassionate, so every single citizen has a chance to work and to succeed and to realize the great promise of America.

It is clear that the future of freedom and peace depend on the actions of America. This Nation is freedom's home and freedom's defender. We welcome this charge of history, and we are keeping it. The war on terror continues. The enemies of freedom are not idle, and neither are we. This country will not rest; we will not tire; we will not stop until this danger to civilization is removed.

We are confronting that danger in Iraq, where Saddam holdouts and foreign terrorists are desperately trying to throw Iraq into chaos by attacking coalition forces, international aid workers, and innocent Iraqis. You see, they know that the advance of freedom in Iraq will be a major defeat in the cause of terror. This collection of coldblooded killers is trying to shake the will of the United States of America. America will never be intimidated by thugs and assassins.

We are aggressively striking the terrorists in Iraq. We will defeat them there so we do not have to face them in our own country. Other nations are helping, and the reason they are is because they understand that a free Iraq will make the world more secure.

And we're standing with the Iraqi people. I was so touched when the symphony, the Iraqi Symphony, played in Kennedy Center the other night. These are brave, decent people who love freedom like we love freedom. And we're standing with them and encouraging them to assume more of their own self-defense and to take the steps necessary for self-government.

I understand and you know these are not easy tasks. But they are essential tasks. And we will finish what we have begun, and we will win this essential victory in the war on terror.

Our greatest security comes from the advance of human liberty, because free nations do not support terror, free nations don't attack their neighbors, free nations do not threaten the world with weapons of mass terror. Americans believe that freedom is the deepest need and hope of every human heart. And I believe that freedom is the future of every nation. I also know that freedom is not America's gift to the world. Freedom is God's gift to every man and woman in this world.

This country also understands that unprecedented influence brings tremendous responsibilities. We have duties in this world, and when we see disease and starvation and hopeless poverty, we will not turn away. And that is why, on the continent of Africa, America is now committed to bringing the healing power of medicine to millions of men and women and children suffering from AIDS. This great, strong, compassionate Nation is leading the world in this incredibly important work of human rescue.

We face challenges here at home. Our actions will prove that we're equal to those challenges. This administration will stay focused on a progrowth agenda. We'll stay focused on making sure this economy continues to grow so that everyone who wants to work can find a job.

For the sake of our health care, we've got more to do. We need to cut down on the frivolous lawsuits which increase the cost of medicine. People who have been harmed by a bad doc deserve their day in court. Yet the system should not reward lawyers who are simply fishing for a rich settlement. Frivolous lawsuits drive up the cost of health care, and they, therefore,

affect the Federal budget. Medical liability reform is a national issue that requires a national solution.

I submitted a good bill to the Congress. The House of Representatives passed that bill. Senator Warner is working hard to get the bill out of the United States Senate, but it is stuck. The Senate must act. And some Senators must understand that no one has ever been healed by a frivolous lawsuit. We need medical liability reform.

I have a responsibility as the President to make sure the judicial system runs well, and I have met that duty. I have nominated superb men and women for the Federal courts, people who will interpret the law, not legislate from the bench. I appreciate so very much the strong support of Senator Warner and Senator Allen on this very important issue. See, some Members of the Senate are trying to keep nominees off the bench by blocking up-or-down votes. Every judicial nominee deserves a fair hearing and an up-or-down vote on the floor of the United States Senate. It is time for some Members of the Senate to stop playing politics with American justice.

This country needs a comprehensive energy plan. Congress needs to complete work on the plan when you come back. You see, we need to promote energy efficiency and conservation and clean coal technology. We need to develop better technologies to explore for energy in environmentally sensitive ways. But for the sake of economic security and for the sake of national security, this Nation must become less dependent on foreign sources of energy.

A strong and prosperous nation must also be a compassionate nation. I will continue to advance what I call compassionate conservatism, which means we'll apply the best and most innovative ideas to the task of helping fellow citizens who are in need. There's still millions of men and women who want to end their dependence on the Government and become independent through hard work. I look forward to working with the Congress to build on the success of welfare reform, to bring more work and dignity into lives of our fellow citizens. We should complete the "Citizen Service Act," so more Americans can serve their communities and their country. Congress should finally reach agreement on my Faith-Based Initiative, which will help us support the armies of compassion that are mentoring our children and caring for the homeless, offering hope to the addicted.

One of the great strengths of America is the fact that we worship the Almighty in different ways. We value religious diversity in America. We also understand that many of the problems, seemingly intractable problems in our society, can be solved by helping a soul change their heart. Our Government should never fear the influence of faith in the lives of our average citizens. We ought to encourage faith-based programs to help solve problems.

A compassionate society must promote opportunity for all citizens, including the independence and dignity that come from ownership. This administration will constantly strive to promote an ownership society in America. We want more people owning their own home. We have a minority homeownership gap in America that must be closed. Next week, I'm signing a bill to help people with their downpayment so they can realize the great American Dream of owning their own home. We want people owning and managing their own retirement accounts. We want people owning and managing their own health care plans. We want more people owning their own small business. When a person owns something, he or she has a vital stake in the future of this great land.

In a compassionate society, people respect one another. They respect their religions. They respect their backgrounds. They respect their opinions. And they take responsibility for the decisions they make in life. The culture of America is changing from one that has said, "If it feels good,

do it," and "If you've got a problem, blame somebody else," to a culture in which each of us understands we are responsible for the decisions we make in life. If you're fortunate enough to be a mom or a dad, you're responsible for loving your child with all your heart. If you're worried about the quality of the education in the community in which you live, you're responsible for doing something about it. If you're a CEO in corporate America, you're responsible for telling the truth to your shareholders and your employees.

And in a responsibility society, each of us is responsible for loving our neighbor just like we'd like to be loved ourself. The culture of service is strong in America. I started what's called the USA Freedom Corps to encourage our fellow citizens to extend a hand to a neighbor in need, and the response has been great. People are responding in America to the needs of others. It's truly the great strength of our country. Policemen and firefighters and people who wear our Nation's uniform remind us on a daily basis what it means to sacrifice for something greater than yourself. You see, once again the children of America see heroes—believe in heroes, because they see them every day.

In these challenging times, the world is seeing the resolve and the courage of America. And I have been privileged to see the compassion and the character of the American people. All the tests of the last 3 years have come to the right nation. We're a strong country, and we use that strength to defend the peace. We're an optimistic country, confident in ourselves and in ideals bigger than ourselves.

Abroad, we seek to lift whole nations by spreading freedom. At home, we seek to lift up lives by spreading opportunity to every corner of America. This is the work that history has set before us. We welcome it, and we know that for our country, the best days lie ahead.

May God bless you all. Thank you very much.

NOTE: The President spoke at 12:14 p.m. at the Hilton McLean Tysons Corner. In his remarks, he referred to Virginia State Attorney General Jerry W. Kilgore; Kate Obenshain Griffin, Virginia State chairman, Republican National Committee; and former President Saddam Hussein of Iraq.

Remarks Announcing the Nomination of Alphonso Jackson To Be Secretary of Housing and Urban Development and an Exchange With Reporters
December 12, 2003

The President. Good afternoon. I am pleased to announce that I will nominate Alphonso Jackson of Dallas, Texas, to serve as Secretary of Housing and Urban Development.

Since 2001, Alphonso Jackson has given fine service as Deputy Secretary of the Department, responsible for many of the day-to-day operations of HUD. In his career, Alphonso has been a senior administrator of housing agencies in three cities, St. Louis and Washington and Dallas. He's an experienced executive in the public and private sectors, a man who knows the issues facing HUD and knows how to get things done.

I can tell you from personal experience that Alphonso is a man of great integrity and compassion. We used to live in the same neighborhood in Dallas. [*Laughter*] I used to drop by for an occasional cup of coffee, sometimes unannounced. [*Laughter*] I'm pleased that he has agreed to join my Cabinet.

I'm also grateful to former Secretary Martinez, Mel Martinez, for his outstanding leadership of HUD over the past 3 years. These have been years of important progress for the Department, for its mission, and for the families across America that benefit from its good work. Over the last 3 years, homeownership in America has reached its highest level ever, and in the last 18 months, more than a million minority citizens have become homeowners.

As leader of HUD, Mel has repaid my confidence many times over. He is a good man and a good friend, and I thank him for his service to our Nation, and I wish Mel and Kitty all the very best.

With the Senate's approval, Mel Martinez will be succeeded by another man who understands the struggles and hopes of urban America. Alphonso Jackson grew up in a family with 12 children, a housing challenge unto itself. [*Laughter*] His dad, Arthur, worked three jobs, educated his children, and instilled the values that have carried his son far in life.

These values and experiences have also shaped the priorities Alphonso brings to his new assignment. He believes, as I do, that homeownership is a source of stability for our communities and a source of dignity for our families. He believes our Government can provide effective help to our fellow citizens who are homeless, and he has seen how entire neighborhoods can turn themselves around with strong local leadership and the help of our Federal Government. Alphonso is just the man to carry on the work of compassionate conservatism in America's cities.

Laura and I have known Alphonso and Marcia for many years. They're close friends, and I appreciate you coming, Marcia. I also want to welcome the other members of your family who are here.

Alphonso is a friend, and he's one of the most experienced and respected authorities on housing policy in America. He will be a superb Secretary of Housing and Urban Development. I want to thank you for accepting this assignment and congratulate you, my friend.

[*At this point, Deputy Secretary Jackson made brief remarks.*]

The President. I thought I would answer a couple of questions. Jennifer [Jennifer Loven, Associated Press].

Halliburton Contract in Iraq

Q. Yes, sir, thank you. With the Pentagon looking into the Halliburton contract, are you concerned that that gives some fuel to your critics that the contract was inappropriate in the first place?

The President. I appreciate the Pentagon looking out after the taxpayers' money. They felt like there was an overcharge issue. They put the issue right out there on the table for everybody to see, and they're doing good work. We're going to watch—we're going to make sure that as we spend the money in Iraq that it's spent well and spent wisely. And their investigation will lay the facts out for everybody to see. And if there's an overcharge, like we think there is, we expect that money to be repaid.

Randy [Randall Mikkelsen, Reuters].

Middle East Peace Process

Q. Mr. President, Secretary Powell has been meeting with unofficial Middle East peace negotiators, despite Israel's objections. And there's other signs of U.S. dissatisfaction with Israel. My question is, what does Israel need to do to convince you that it's doing its part in the peace process?

The President. Randy, you may remember I gave the speech on June 24, 2002. I laid out exactly what I think must happen in order for us to achieve peace in the Middle East, in order for the Palestinian state to emerge that is at peace with Israel. And I haven't changed my opinion. Step one is for all parties to fight off terror, to stop the few from destroying the hopes of the many. Step two is for the Palestin-

ians to find leadership that is willing to reject the tired old policy of the past and lead the Palestinian people to not only a democratic state but a peaceful solution of differences.

Israel must be mindful that the decisions they make today will make it difficult to create—must be mindful that they don't make decisions that make it hard to create a Palestinian state. It's in Israel's interests there be a Palestinian state. It's in the poor, suffering Palestinian people's interest there be a Palestinian state. The Arab world has got responsibilities to see that this vision be implemented.

Q. But why these contacts with the unofficial negotiators?

The President. I'm sure the Secretary of State meets with all kinds of people all the time. But the policy of this administration was laid out in the Rose Garden for everybody to see, everybody to listen to.

You might remember I took that policy to Aqaba, Jordan. I stood up in front of the world and said this man has—he, Abu Mazen, came to the Oval Office and said, "I'm willing to join you, Mr. President, to help fight off terror," because he understood that terror was what was preventing progress from being made. He said, "I'm willing to work to put the institutions in place for a Palestinian state." And as we began to make progress, he got shoved aside, and that's why we're stalled where we are today.

It is time for Palestinian leadership to emerge that believes in peace and believes in the aspirations of the Palestinian people.

April [April Ryan, American Urban Radio Networks], I see you've got something that you'd like to ask. First, let me ask you a question. As you're heading into—my turn to ask you a question. [*Laughter*] So this is your first Christmas season as a mom.

Q. Second, actually, 18 months.

The President. Exactly right. [*Laughter*] Good answer. I was just trying to check and see if you knew—if you and I both knew how old your child was. [*Laughter*] Do you have a question to the President?

Halliburton Contract in Iraq

Q. Yes, I do, sir. Mr. President——

The President. Do you remember what it is? [*Laughter*]

Q. You can throw a person, you know that. [*Laughter*] Mr. President, many of your critics are saying that you should distance yourself from Halliburton, and they say it's an albatross around this administration's neck, particularly the Vice President and you. What are your thoughts about that?

The President. My thoughts are, is that I expect anybody doing business with the United States Government to be transparent and to give the taxpayers a good return on their money. That's what I expect. And if anybody is overcharging the Government, we expect them to repay that money.

Wendell [Wendell Goler, FOX News].

Iraqi Debt Relief

Q. Mr. President, in light of the New York Times editorial today, tell me why——

The President. Right. Let me stop you, Wendell. I don't read those editorials—[*laughter*]—so you're going to have to—maybe you ought to ask the question not in that context, but in another context. Sorry to interrupt you.

Q. All right, sir. Tell me why former Secretary of State Baker's ties with Carlyle Group and with Baker Botts don't pose a conflict of interest in this new task you have given him of restructuring Iraq's debt?

The President. Jim Baker is a man of high integrity. He's a man of enormous experience. And it makes sense for him to serve our country on an important mission. And that mission is to encourage countries to forgive debt so the Iraqi people can more easily grow a nation that is prosperous and peaceful.

And Jim Baker is—we're fortunate to have Jim Baker agree to serve our country. We're fortunate he decided to take time out of what is an active life but one out of the press and one that's probably not nearly as stressful as it has been when he's been involved in public service, to step forward and serve America. We're fortunate that he is willing to do that, and I thank him for that.

And I'm really happy that he has agreed to serve. His mission is to go to Paris and Berlin and Moscow and London to convince these countries to forgive debt. And I'm hopeful they do forgive debt. I'm hopeful that they're willing, in some cases, to contribute for the first time to the efforts of the Iraqi citizens. See, it's in the interest of their countries that Iraq be free and peaceful. Matter of fact, it's in the interest of all countries that Iraq be peaceful and free. It makes us all more secure. Imagine what the effect is going to have—a peaceful and free Iraq is going to have in the heart of the Middle East, where there's so much violence and hatred.

And so Jim Baker is on a noble mission. He'll do a great job. I didn't mean to dis the New York Times editorial page, but I just didn't—I'm not reading it a lot these days. [*Laughter*]

Yes, sir.

Q. Mr. President——

The President. Or anybody else's, for that matter.

Q. I have no ties with the New York Times. [*Laughter*]

The President. You didn't mean to dis it either, then. [*Laughter*]

Strength of the Dollar

Q. Mr. President, the dollar fell again against the euro. Mr. Snow, your Treasury Secretary, says that the decline has been orderly, boosting exports. Do you plan any intervention to stop the slide in the dollar?

The President. My answer to that question about the dollar is that this Government is for a strong dollar and that the dollar's value ought to be set by the market and by the conditions inherent in our respective economies. And our economy is very strong and is getting stronger. But the policy, the stated policy—and not only the stated policy but the strong belief of this administration is that we have a strong dollar.

Well, listen, thank you all. Alphonso, congratulations.

Deputy Secretary Jackson. Thank you, Mr. President.

The President. I appreciate you coming.

NOTE: The President spoke at 2:40 p.m. in the Roosevelt Room at the White House. In his remarks, he referred to former Prime Minister Mahmoud Abbas (Abu Mazen) of the Palestinian Authority; and James A. Baker III, the President's personal envoy on the issue of Iraqi debt.

Statement on Signing the Syria Accountability and Lebanese Sovereignty Restoration Act of 2003
December 12, 2003

Today, I have signed into law H.R. 1828, the "Syria Accountability and Lebanese Sovereignty Restoration Act of 2003." The Act is intended to strengthen the ability of the United States to conduct an effective foreign policy.

Section 5 of the Act purports to impose upon the President requirements to take certain actions against Syria unless the President either determines and certifies to the Congress that the Government of Syria has taken specific actions, or determines that it is in the national security interest of the United States to waive such requirements and reports the reasons for that determination to the Congress. A law cannot burden or infringe the President's exercise of a core constitutional power by attaching conditions precedent to the use of that power. The executive branch shall construe and implement section 5 in a manner consistent with the President's constitutional authority to conduct the Nation's foreign affairs and as Commander in Chief, in particular with respect to the conduct of foreign diplomats in the United States, the conduct of United States diplomats abroad, and the exportation of items and provision of services necessary to the performance

of official functions by United States Government personnel abroad.

Section 6 of the Act requires an officer in the executive branch to furnish information to the Congress on various subjects involving Syria and terrorism. The executive branch shall construe section 6 in a manner consistent with the President's constitutional authority to withhold information the disclosure of which could impair foreign relations, national security, the deliberative processes of the Executive, or the performance of the Executive's constitutional duties.

My approval of the Act does not constitute my adoption of the various statements of policy in the Act as U.S. foreign policy. Given the Constitution's commitment to the Presidency of the authority to conduct the Nation's foreign affairs, the executive branch shall construe such policy statements as advisory, giving them the due weight that comity between the legislative and executive branches should require, to the extent consistent with U.S. foreign policy.

GEORGE W. BUSH

The White House,
December 12, 2003.

NOTE: H.R. 1828, approved December 12, was assigned Public Law No. 108–175.

Statement on Signing the Vision 100—Century of Aviation Reauthorization Act
December 12, 2003

Today, I have signed into law H.R. 2115, the "Vision 100—Century of Aviation Reauthorization Act." The Act is designed to strengthen America's aviation sector, provide needed authority to the Federal Aviation Administration (FAA), and enhance the safety of the traveling public.

Subtitle A of title II of the Act amends section 106 of title 49 of the United States Code to abolish the Air Traffic Services Subcommittee of the Federal Aviation Management Advisory Council and creates, separate from the Council, an Air Traffic Services Committee (ATSC). Section 106 as amended vests in the ATSC substantial governmental authority, including the power to approve the FAA's strategic plan for the air traffic control system, certain large procurements, appointment and pay of the FAA Chief Operating Officer, FAA major reorganizations, and the FAA cost accounting and financial management structure. Under section 106(p)(6)(C), as amended, the members of the abolished Air Traffic Services Subcommittee of the Council automatically become the members of the ATSC, but only to "serve in an advisory capacity," with the ATSC beginning to exercise non-advisory authority when the ATSC members have been appointed by the President by and with the advice and consent of the Senate. Accordingly, in light of section 106(p)(6)(C), the executive branch shall construe the provisions of section 106(p) and 106(r) that refer to approval or other non-advisory functions of the ATSC to require, from the date of enactment of the Act through the date on which the last Senate-confirmed Presidential appointment is made to the ATSC, only notice to the ATSC and an opportunity for the ATSC to express its views.

Section 106(p)(7)(B)(iii) of title 49, as enacted by section 202 of the bill, purports to limit the qualifications of the pool of persons from whom the President may select ATSC members in a manner that rules out a large portion of those persons best qualified by experience and knowledge to fill the office. Congressional participation in such appointments is limited by the Appointments Clause of the Constitution to the Senate's provision of advice and consent with respect to Presidential nominees. The executive branch shall construe the provisions concerning qualifications in section 106(p)(7)(B)(iii) as advisory, as is consistent with the Appointments Clause.

Section 47171 of title 49, as enacted by section 304(a) of the Act, purports to mandate the process for cooperation among agencies in the executive branch in conducting environmental reviews for certain airport projects. In particular, section 47171(i) purports to require one part of the executive branch to report to committees of Congress when a second part of the executive branch has not met the first part's deadlines for action on certain environmental reviews, and then requires the second part to explain to the committees why it did not meet the deadline and what actions it intends to take to complete the relevant matter. The executive branch shall implement section 47171 in a manner and to the extent consistent with the President's constitutional authority to supervise the unitary executive branch.

The executive branch shall construe and implement section 323(b)(2) of the Act, relating to certain disputes, in a manner consistent with the constitutional authority of the President to supervise the unitary executive branch.

The executive branch shall construe the provisions of section 411(i) of the Act, concerning the provision of executive branch information and records to the National Commission on Small Community Air Service, in a manner consistent with the President's constitutional authority to withhold information the disclosure of which could impair the foreign relations, the national security, the deliberative processes of the Executive, or the performance of the Executive's constitutional duties.

The executive branch shall construe and implement section 46111 of title 49, as enacted by section 601(a) of the Act, relating to access to and use of classified information, in a manner consistent with the President's constitutional authority to classify and control access to information bearing on the national security.

The executive branch shall implement sections 702 and 703 of the Act, which relate to the award of certain government scholarships, in a manner consistent with the equal protection requirements of the Due Process Clause of the Fifth Amendment to the Constitution.

Section 44511(f) of title 49, as enacted by section 712 of the Act, requires the Secretary of Transportation to appoint "an independent governing board" for a 4-year airport cooperative research pilot program. The executive branch shall construe the reference to the board as "independent" to mean independence within the Department of Transportation from the FAA, while the board remains subject to the statutory authority of the Secretary as the head of the Department and the President's constitutional authority to supervise the unitary executive branch. Moreover, the executive branch shall construe the provisions for nomination of candidates for the board by particular officials or organizations as advisory, as is consistent with the Appointments Clause of the Constitution.

The executive branch shall construe as advisory the provisions of section 812(a) of the Act that purport to direct or burden the conduct of negotiations by the executive branch with foreign governments, international organizations, or other entities abroad. Such provisions, if construed as mandatory rather than advisory, would impermissibly interfere with the President's constitutional authority to conduct the Nation's foreign affairs, participate in international negotiations, and supervise the unitary executive branch.

GEORGE W. BUSH

The White House,
December 12, 2003.

NOTE: H.R. 2115, approved December 12, was assigned Public Law No. 108–176.

The President's Radio Address
December 13, 2003

Good morning. This week I was honored to sign the Medicare Act of 2003, the greatest advance in health coverage for America's seniors since Medicare was founded nearly four decades ago. This new law will give seniors better choices and more control over their health care and provide a prescription drug benefit.

Beginning in 2006, most seniors now without prescription coverage can expect to see their current drug bills cut roughly in half in exchange for a monthly premium of about $35. And for the first time, seniors will have peace of mind that they will not face unlimited expenses for their Medicare.

These and other major improvements in Medicare came about because Republicans and Democrats in Congress were willing to work together for the interests of our senior citizens. We were able to pass this law because we listened to the people, set the right priorities, and worked hard until we finished the job.

The reform and modernization of Medicare was one milestone in a year of accomplishment. We worked with Congress to take action in a number of areas on behalf of the American people. Last May, the House and Senate passed my jobs-and-growth package into law, delivering substantial tax relief to 91 million Americans. We reduced taxes for everyone who pays income taxes, increased the child tax credit, cut the taxes on dividends and capital gains, and gave 23 million small-business owners incentives to invest for the future.

And now we are seeing the results. In the third quarter, the economy grew at the fastest pace in almost 20 years. Productivity, manufacturing, and housing construction are expanding, and we have added over 300,000 jobs since August. The tax relief we passed is working, and our economy is gaining strength.

Legislation passed this year also showed the compassion and the good heart of America. We created the American Dream Downpayment Fund to help low-income citizens afford the downpayment on homes of their own. We defended children from the violence of partial-birth abortion and passed new incentives to promote the adoption of children in foster care. And we acted to fight the global spread of AIDS by launching a multiyear emergency effort to prevent millions of new infections in Africa and the Caribbean and to provide medicine and humane care to millions more who suffer.

This year we took important action to protect the environment. Our whole Nation saw the devastation left by wildfires in the West, and we passed healthy forest legislation to thin the underbrush that fuels catastrophic blazes.

Our Government also took urgent action on every front in the war on terror. Congress appropriated more than $31 billion for the Department of Homeland Security to prepare first-responders and safeguard our ports and infrastructure and help scientists develop vaccines against dangerous biological threats. Our country stood behind the men and women of our Armed Forces as they liberated Iraq and helped carry out the work of reconstruction there and in Afghanistan. In Congress, members of both parties worked together to provide vital resources for our troops, who are fulfilling their responsibility to defend the Nation.

All these actions have made us safer, more prosperous, and a better country. We confronted problems with determination and bipartisan spirit. Yet our work is not done. There will be pressing business in the new year on issues from job creation to health care to public schools. And above all, we will continue to fight the war on terror until the war is won.

On behalf of all Americans, I thank the Congress for a productive year. Working together, we can add to this progress in the year to come.

Thank you for listening.

NOTE: The address was recorded at 10:35 a.m. on December 12 in the Cabinet Room at the White House for broadcast at 10:06 a.m. on December 13. The transcript was made available by the Office of the Press Secretary on December 12 but was embargoed for release until the broadcast. The Office of the Press Secretary also released a Spanish language transcript of this address.

Statement on Signing the Intelligence Authorization Act for Fiscal Year 2004
December 13, 2003

Today, I have signed into law H.R. 2417, the "Intelligence Authorization Act for Fiscal Year 2004." The Act authorizes funding for United States intelligence activities, including activities in the war against terrorists of global reach.

Section 506A(c) of the National Security Act of 1947, as enacted by section 312(b) of the Act, purports to require the President to request that the Congress enact laws appropriating funding for a major intelligence system procurement in an amount set as a cost estimate by an entity subordinate to the President or to explain why the President instead requests amounts below those levels. Moreover, beginning with the submittal to the Congress of the President's budget for FY 2006, section 312(d)(2) of H.R. 2417 purports to condition the obligation or expenditure of funds for development or procurement of a major intelligence system on the President's compliance with the requirements of section 506A. The executive branch shall construe these provisions in a manner consistent with the Constitution's commitment to the President of exclusive authority to submit for the consideration of the Congress such measures as the President judges necessary and expedient and to supervise the unitary executive branch, and to withhold information the disclosure of which could impair the deliberative processes of the Executive or the performance of the Executive's constitutional duties.

Section 341(b) purports to require the Attorney General and the Director of Central Intelligence, acting through particular offices subordinate to them respectively, to establish certain policies and procedures relating to espionage prosecutions. The executive branch shall implement this provision in a manner consistent with the authority committed exclusively to the President by

the Constitution to faithfully execute the laws and to supervise the unitary executive branch. Similarly, sections 1102(a) and 1102(c) of the National Security Act, as enacted by section 341(a) of the Act, purport to mandate that the Director of Central Intelligence use or act through the Office of National Counterintelligence Executive to establish and implement an inspection process for all agencies and departments of the U.S. Government that handle classified information. The executive branch shall implement this provision in a manner consistent with the President's constitutional authority to supervise the unitary executive branch.

The executive branch shall construe and implement section 376 of the Act, relating to making available classified information to courts, in a manner consistent with the President's constitutional authority to classify and control access to information bearing on the national security and consistent with the statutory authority of the Attorney General for the conduct of litigation for the United States.

Many provisions of the Act, including section 106 and subtitle D of title III of the Act, seek to require the executive branch to furnish information to the Congress on various subjects. The executive branch shall construe the provisions in a manner consistent with the President's constitutional authority to withhold information the disclosure of which could impair foreign relations, national security, the deliberative processes of the Executive, or the performance of the Executive's constitutional duties.

The executive branch shall implement section 319 of the Act in a manner consistent with the requirement to afford equal protection of the laws under the Due Process Clause of the Fifth Amendment to the Constitution.

Section 502 purports to place restrictions on use of the U.S. Armed Forces and other personnel in certain operations. The executive branch shall construe the restrictions in section 502 as advisory in nature, so that the provisions are consistent with the President's constitutional authority as Commander in Chief, including for the conduct of intelligence operations, and to supervise the unitary executive branch.

Section 106 enacts by reference certain requirements set forth in the joint explanatory statement of the House-Senate committee of conference or in a classified annex. The executive branch continues to discourage this practice of enacting secret laws and encourages instead appropriate non-binding uses of classified schedules of authorizations, classified annexes to committee reports, and joint statements of managers that accompany the final legislation.

GEORGE W. BUSH

The White House,
December 13, 2003.

NOTE: H.R. 2417, approved December 13, was assigned Public Law No. 108–177.

Address to the Nation on the Capture of Saddam Hussein
December 14, 2003

Good afternoon. Yesterday, December the 13th, at around 8:30 p.m., Baghdad time, United States military forces captured Saddam Hussein alive. He was found near a farmhouse outside the city of Tikrit, in a swift raid conducted without casualties, and now the former dictator of Iraq will face the justice he denied to millions.

The capture of this man was crucial to the rise of a free Iraq. It marks the end of the road for him and for all who bullied and killed in his name. For the Ba'athist holdouts largely responsible for the current violence, there will be no return to the corrupt power and privilege they once held. For the vast majority of Iraqi citizens who wish to live as free men and women, this event brings further assurance that the torture chambers and the secret police are gone forever.

And this afternoon, I have a message for the Iraqi people: You will not have to fear the rule of Saddam Hussein ever again. All Iraqis who take the side of freedom have taken the winning side. The goals of our coalition are the same as your goals: Sovereignty for your country; dignity for your great culture; and for every Iraqi citizen, the opportunity for a better life. In the history of Iraq, a dark and painful era is over. A hopeful day has arrived. All Iraqis can now come together and reject violence and build a new Iraq.

The success of yesterday's mission is a tribute to our men and women now serving in Iraq. The operation was based on the superb work of intelligence analysts who found the dictator's footprints in a vast country. The operation was carried out with skill and precision by a brave fighting force. Our service men and women and our coalition allies have faced many dangers in the hunt for members of the fallen regime and in their effort to bring hope and freedom to the Iraqi people. Their work continues, and so do the risks. Today, on behalf of the Nation, I thank the members of our Armed Forces, and I congratulate them.

I also have a message for all Americans: The capture of Saddam Hussein does not mean the end of violence in Iraq. We still face terrorists who would rather go on killing the innocent than accept the rise of liberty in the heart of the Middle East. Such men are a direct threat to the American people, and they will be defeated.

We've come to this moment through patience and resolve and focused action, and that is our strategy moving forward. The war on terror is a different kind of war, waged capture by capture, cell by cell, and victory by victory. Our security is assured by our perseverance and by our sure belief in the success of liberty, and the United States of America will not relent until this war is won.

May God bless the people of Iraq, and may God bless America. Thank you.

NOTE: The President spoke at 12:15 p.m. in the Cabinet Room at the White House. The Office of the Press Secretary also released a Spanish language transcript of this address.

Statement on the Death of William V. Roth, Jr.
December 14, 2003

During his extraordinary career as a United States Senator, Bill Roth was the taxpayer's friend and the people's champion. He worked to cut wasteful Government spending and was one of the first to argue that lower taxes would lead to greater economic growth. Among his many other legislative achievements, he helped create the retirement account that bears his name and that has benefited millions of American families. He was an American hero, earning a Bronze Star for his service in World War II. Bill Roth was loved and respected by the people of Delaware and by his colleagues in the United States Congress. Laura and I send our condolences to his wife, Jane, herself a dedicated public servant and superb Federal judge; to the Roth family; and to the Roths' many friends in Delaware and throughout the country.

The President's News Conference
December 15, 2003

The President. Thank you all. Please be seated. Thank you for coming to this, the last press conference of the year 2003.

Before I begin, I do want to talk a little bit about a meeting I just attended. Rend al-Rahim is here—she's the representative from the Iraqi Government, the interim Government, to the United States—as well as Dr. Khadir Abbas, who is the interim Minister of Health. We just had an interesting discussion in the Roosevelt Room about the health needs of Iraq, about the future of the health care system in Iraq. And we were joined by doctors, Iraqi doctors who were anxious to work with their fellow counterparts here in America to enhance educational opportunities and to get caught up on the latest technologies in health care. The thing that struck me about the meeting was the kind of joy that they expressed about being free. It was a touching meeting, and I want to thank you all for coming.

And Doc, I want to thank you for your good work. We are making progress together in improving the lives of your citizens with better health care. Immunization rates are up. People are getting better health care. He was reminding me, I think the budget of Saddam Hussein's Government for health was, like, $16 million, less than a dollar per person. And of course, we're spending a lot more than that now on health care in Iraq. But it was a very meaningful meeting. I want to thank you—please thank those good docs for being there.

This weekend's capture of Saddam Hussein was a great moment for the people of Iraq. Iraqi citizens have lost a source of fear, and they can now focus with confidence on the task of creating a hopeful and self-governing nation. With the capture of the former dictator, the enemies of a free Iraq have lost their leader, and they've lost any hope of regaining power. The nightmare of the Ba'athist tyranny is finally over.

The terrorists in Iraq remain dangerous. The work of our coalition remains difficult and will require further sacrifice. Yet, it should now be clear to all, Iraq is on the path to freedom, and a free Iraq will serve the peace and security of America and the world.

This achievement comes at the end of an extraordinary year for our country, abroad and here at home. In 2003, we have become a safer, more prosperous, and better nation. Our Armed Forces, joined by our allies, continue on the offensive against terrorist enemies around the world. We continue our systematic hunt for Al Qaida leaders and Al Qaida cells in many countries. I want to thank the Congress for standing behind our military with needed resources and for giving vital support to the work of reconstruction in Iraq and Afghanistan.

America's economy is growing at a robust pace and beginning to generate new jobs for America, American workers. I want to thank the Congress for passing my jobs-and-growth package, which is doing just what it was supposed to do. And we will continue pursuing a progrowth agenda next year.

In this year of accomplishment, we passed Medicare reform. American seniors can now look forward to prescription drug coverage, more choices, and a stronger Medicare system. I want to thank the Congress for coming together to get the job done.

This session of Congress has also produced vital action on homeland security, healthy forests, global AIDS relief, housing assistance, adoption, Amber alerts to capture kidnapers and rescue their victims, and protection of children from partial-birth abortion. Members of both political parties can take pride in the important goals we have met by working together.

We have a great deal to show for our efforts in 2003. Yet, unfinished business remains. The majority in both Houses support a comprehensive energy bill as well as reforms in class action to curtail junk lawsuits. The House also passed a medical liability reform bill. It is stuck in the Senate. These measures were blocked, and they are needed. They are needed to help America become more prosperous, and they're needed to help America be a better place. When the House and Senate return in January, there will be more to do, and I look forward to working with them. I've got a few ideas about what we can do together in the year 2004.

As we end 2003, we have a lot to be thankful for, especially for the fine men and women who wear our country's uniform and who will spend their holidays far from home. I hope all Americans will keep these brave men and women in their thoughts and prayers during this blessed season.

I will take some questions, starting with AP man [Terence Hunt, Associated Press].

Trial of Saddam Hussein

Q. Thank you, Mr. President. What's the United States going to do with Saddam Hussein after questioning him? Will he be turned over to Iraqis for trial? And based on what you know now about mass executions and hundreds of thousands of graves, do you think that execution should be an option?

The President. He will be detained. We will work with the Iraqis to develop a way to try him in a—that will stand international scrutiny, I guess is the best way to put it.

I shared my sentiments today with Prime Minister Martin of Canada. He asked me about Saddam Hussein and his trial. I said, "Look, the Iraqis need to be very much involved. He was the person that—they were the people that were brutalized by this man." He murdered them. He gassed them. He tortured them. He had rape rooms. And they need to be very much involved in the process, and we'll work with the Iraqis to develop a process.

And of course we want it to be fair. And of course we want the world to say, "Well, this—he got a fair trial," because whatever justice is meted out needs to stand international scrutiny. I've got my own personal views of how he ought to be treated, but that's—I'm not an Iraqi citizen. It's going to be up to the Iraqis to make those decisions.

Q. And the question of execution?

The President. Yes, I said I have my personal views, and this is a brutal dictator. He's a person who killed a lot of people. But my views, my personal views, aren't important in this matter. What matters is the views of the Iraqi citizens. And we need to work, of course, with them to develop a system that is fair and—where he will be put on trial and will be brought to justice, the justice he didn't, by the way, afford any of his own fellow citizens.

Steve [Steve Holland, Reuters].

U.S. Policy in Iraq

Q. Thank you, sir. Will Saddam's capture accelerate the timetable for pulling U.S. troops out and increase the likelihood of getting more foreign troops involved?

The President. We will stay the course until the job is done, Steve. And the temptation is to try to get the President or somebody to put a timetable on the definition of getting the job done. We're just going to stay the course. And it's very important for the Iraqi people to know that. I've expressed that to Rend; I've told that to the Iraqi citizens with whom I have met on a regular basis.

I tell them two things: One, you can count on America remaining until the job is done. And it's important for them to hear that, because there will probably be some that will continue to test our will. They'll try to kill in hopes that we will flee, and the citizens of Iraq need to know we will stay the course. I also tell them that now is a chance to seize the opportunity and show the world that which this Government believes, and that is, you're plenty capable of governing yourself.

And the level of the troops in Iraq will depend upon the security situation on the ground, and those decisions will be made by our commanders. I have not changed my philosophy of how a President ought to act during wartime, which is to set the strategy, lay out the goals, and empower the military people, both civilian and uniform, to make the decisions necessary to achieve the objective. And they will make those recommendations about troop levels and what is necessary to—go ahead—you've got a followup? This is part of the holiday spirit, to give you a followup. [*Laughter*]

Possible Expansion of Coalition in Iraq

Q. [*Inaudible*]—opportunity to get more foreign troops involved?

The President. Well, listen, we're constantly working to get foreign countries involved, but I want to remind you we've got over 60 nations involved now. When you hear me talk about "our" efforts, I'm talking about the efforts of a lot of countries. We've got a large coalition involved, and of course we will accept the willingness of nations to put troops on the ground.

We're continuing to work, whether it be troops on the ground or construction contracts or loans. We're constantly reaching out to more nations to get them involved in the process.

And after all, there is a reason why nations should be involved in the process. A secure and free Iraq is in their national interest. A free country, a peaceful country in the heart of the Middle East is in the interest of all nations. This is a transforming event. The emergence of a peaceful Iraq will transform the region in a positive way that will make it more likely that the world is peaceful. And that we're constantly talking about that message and encouraging people to participate.

Gregory [David Gregory, NBC News].

Saddam Hussein

Q. Mr. President, good morning. When Saddam emerged from his hole on Saturday, he told a U.S. soldier that he was willing to negotiate. Might there be room for negotiation, perhaps in exchange for a public statement to the Iraqi people that may serve your interest? And secondly, this soldier also said to Saddam, reportedly, that President Bush sends his greetings. You say this is not personal, but you've also pointed out this was a man who tried to murder your father. What is your greeting to him?

The President. Good riddance. The world is better off without you, Mr. Saddam Hussein. I find it very interesting that when the heat got on, you dug yourself a hole, and you crawled in it. And our brave troops, combined with good intelligence, found you. And you'll be brought to justice, something you did not afford the people you brutalized in your own country.

And what was the first part of the question?

Q. I know you'd scoffed at the idea of negotiation. What I'm asking you——

The President. Oh, yes, yes. How do you know I scoffed at it? Laughing does not mean scoffing, but—[*laughter*].

Q. Oh, I know, I'm just saying——

Q. There were others who were scoffing. [*Laughter*]

The President. Okay.

Q. If you were to do something that you might view as constructive, like making a public statement, a video statement?

The President. David, it's just way too early to tell. First of all, I don't trust Saddam Hussein. I don't believe he'll tell the truth. He didn't tell the truth for over a decade. I just can't believe he's going to change his ways just because he happens to be captured. And so I don't think we ought to trust his word.

I think what needs to happen is, he needs to be brought to justice, and the Iraqi citizens need to be very much involved in the development of a system that brings him to justice. And there needs to be a public trial, and all the atrocities need to come out, and justice needs to be delivered. And I'm confident it will be done in a fair way.

Terry [Terry Moran, ABC News].

France and Germany

Q. Mr. President, do you believe that the capture of Saddam Hussein will bridge some of the differences, the bitter differences that have arisen in the world over Iraq? Or do you believe that the Iraq war marks a dividing line, perhaps a long-term dividing line, between those countries which fought to topple Saddam Hussein and those which did not?

The President. Interesting question. I think that—well, first of all, as I want to repeat, there's over 60 nations involved in the reconstruction of Iraq now. So there's a—a lot of people are participating, and we're out working to encourage others to participate.

You're talking—what you're talking about is France and Germany, if the truth be known, if I might clarify your question to me. Look, France and Germany—I have reached out to them. They've reached out to us. It's in our national interests we work together. A whole and united and peaceful

Europe is in this country's interest, and we look forward to working with them on a wide range of issues, whether it be intelligence sharing or in the reconstruction of Afghanistan. I want to remind you, Germany has committed troops to Afghanistan. It's in this country's interest that Afghanistan emerge as a peaceful country. Germany is contributing to that effort. There's a lot of areas where we do work together.

We had a disagreement on this issue about Saddam Hussein and his threat. I obviously felt like September the 11th changed the equation to the point where we needed to deal with emerging threats and deal with them in a way that would make America more secure. And they didn't see that; they didn't agree with that point of view. I can understand that. And we are now reaching out to them, by the way—Jim Baker, as you know, will be going to both those two countries tomorrow, I think it is, to encourage them to work with us on debt relief, all aimed at encouraging the development of a free and peaceful Iraq.

So, no, I don't agree that this is a dividing line. I think this is a disagreement on this particular issue. And I know that we can work together on a variety of other issues, and I'll cite one example, Iran. I was most pleased that the French and Germans as well as the Brits delivered a very strong message to the Iranian Government about the development of a nuclear weapon. It was a message that we agree with, and that is: Don't do so; otherwise there will be international consequences at the United Nations. And it was a very important message to be delivered. We agreed on that. And working together, it made it easier for us to send that message.

John [John Roberts, CBS News]. Working my way across here.

President's Course of Action/2004 Elections

Q. Thank you, Mr. President. The capture of Saddam Hussein is something that has been universally applauded. But there still remain a lot of lingering questions about the postwar phase of Iraq. This administration has stated that it would like to see an interim Iraqi Government stood up by next June, the ability to be able to begin to draw down troops if that's possible. Even a political novice would have to say, well, there appears to be some political component to all this, some way of making real progress ahead of the November elections.

The President. Yes, well, people can read whatever they want to read into it. My job is to keep America secure. That's my job. I've got a solemn duty to do everything I can to protect the American people. I will never forget the lessons of September the 11th, 2001. Terrorists attacked us. They killed thousands of our fellow citizens. And it could happen again, and therefore, I will deal with threats, threats that are emerging and real.

We gave Saddam Hussein plenty of time to heed the demands of the world, and he chose defiance. He did. He said, "Forget it. I don't care what the United Nations has said over a decade. I don't care about all the resolutions passed." He chose defiance. We acted. And I acted because I— I repeat—I have a duty to protect this country. And I will continue to protect the country, so long as I'm the President of the United States.

A free and peaceful Iraq is part of protecting America, because, I told you before, and I truly believe this, this will be a transforming event in a part of the world where hatred and violence are bred, a part of a world that breeds resentment.

And you know, look, we're going into an election; there's going to be plenty of time for politics. And people can debate all they want. I'm going to do my job. That's what I'm going to do. I'm going to do my job to make this country safer, and I believe we're making good progress toward that objective.

Angle [Jim Angle, FOX News].

Q. Thank you, Mr. President. Until recently, a growing number of Americans and a couple of Presidential candidates were saying it might be time to think about getting out of Iraq. I know you said that you intend to stay the course, but I wonder what your view is of such sentiments, how concerned you are about that view among the public, and whether or not you think Saddam's capture should change people's thinking?

The President. You know, I think Saddam's capture should make it clear to the people of Iraq, most importantly, that he's through, that people can no longer— no longer have to hold back their sentiments and their feelings toward living in a free society because he might reemerge. That's the most important thing about this capture, is that he can no longer provide any excuse for some who were afraid to act.

And I can understand why people would be afraid to act in Iraq, afraid that Saddam might come back. After all, he's a torturer and a killer. I met with a doctor today. The guy took me aside and he said, "I want to thank you. My dad was murdered by Saddam Hussein." A lot of people share that sentiment, by the way, because it's happened to them. And you can understand why people feared him. After all, he stayed in power by fear, by ruling through fear.

And you know, Jim, I will make the decisions based upon what I think is right to achieve the objectives I've outlined, the objectives I outlined prior to freeing Iraq from Saddam Hussein, and that is to make this country more secure and the world more free.

And I'm confident people aren't going to agree with every decision I make. I understand that, and I don't expect people to agree with every decision I make. But regardless of whether they do or not, I'm going to continue making the decisions in the way that I think is best for the country. And there will be ample time to have the debate about whether or not it's the right

strategy or not. I look forward to the debate. I look forward to making my case to the American people about why America is more secure today based upon the decisions that I've made.

As I said, there's ample time for politics. I know you all want to jump the gun. It makes exciting news. It makes the stories more interesting and more vital from your perspective. Let me just—so that we can get this straight early in the process, I take my job seriously. I will do my job, and I look forward to the political debate later on. So I'm confident during the numerous press conferences I'll be having next year, just like I had this year, that you'll be asking me questions about this political statement or that political statement. And my answer is going to be the same until I'm ready to engage, and that is—let me just tell you what the strategy is of this administration—forget politics—the strategy that I've outlined in order to do my solemn duty, and my duty is not only to keep the country more secure but more prosperous and a better country as well.

Dana [Dana Milbank, Washington Post].

Federal Deficit

Q. Thank you, Mr. President. The dollar has fallen quite sharply. Wall Street is increasingly worried about the deficit— sorry—Wall Street is increasingly worried about the deficit. Will you have a specific plan for reducing the deficit, or will economic growth alone take care of the problem?

The President. Yes. No, I appreciate that question. Josh Bolten laid out a plan that will shrink the deficit in half in a 5-year period, and that's based upon reasonable growth assumptions. And it's a plan that depends upon Congress to continue to hold the line on spending.

We have a deficit because of, one, a recession, two, a war. I want to remind you all that in order to fight and win the war, it requires a expenditure of money that is commiserate with keeping a promise to our troops to make sure that they're well-paid, well-trained, well-equipped. And so we've exceeded—we've spent a lot on defense budgets in order to win the war. We've also spent a lot of money to secure our homeland.

And then of course, there was the tax relief, a stimulus package which was necessary to make sure that we had ample revenues coming into the Treasury in the first place. See, without the tax relief package, there would have been a deficit, but there wouldn't have been the commiserate—not "commiserate"—the kick to our economy that occurred as a result of the tax relief. And the tax relief is working.

When the Senate finishes its work on the appropriations bill, we will have held discretionary spending to 4 percent, and that's what we agreed to with the Congress during the budget negotiations.

I want to remind you of a fact that I think you'll find interesting—or maybe you won't find interesting, but I find it interesting—that non-military, non-homeland-security discretionary spending was at 15 percent—increase from year to year was at 15 percent prior to our arrival; then it was at 6 percent, 5 percent, and 3 percent. So we're working with Congress to hold the line on spending. And we do have a plan to cut the deficit in half.

Sanger [David Sanger, New York Times].

Iraqi Weapons of Mass Destruction/North Korea

Q. Thank you, Mr. President. Mr. President, it's been 9 months now, and still there is relatively little evidence of WMD in Iraq. In retrospect, if you think back over the year, would you have been better to make more of your—of the argument that you've made in recent times, that democratization in the Middle East was the reason to go to war, rather than WMD? And since the CIA has been telling you that North Korea does have two or more weapons, what lesson should Kim Chong-il draw from the capture of Saddam Hussein?

The President. Very deft at weaving in two questions there. Here's what I took away from September the 11th, 2001, that any time a President sees a gathering threat to the United States, we must deal with it. We can't pick or choose like we used to, could in the past. In the old days, oceans protected us from harm's way, and a President could stand back and say, "Well, maybe this gathering threat is an issue. Maybe it's not." After September the 11th, that complacency, I guess may be the right word, no longer is relevant. And therefore, I began to assess threats.

And the threat of Saddam Hussein was a unique threat in this sense: The world recognized he was a threat for 12 years and 17 resolutions, I think it is—I believe it was 17 resolutions—for the resolution counter, give me a hand here—17? Seventeen resolutions. And he ignored them. He just treated the U.N. as an empty debating society, as if their resolutions meant nothing. This is a person who has used chemical weapons before, which indicated to me he was a threat. He invaded his neighbors before. This is a person who was defiant. He's a deceiver, and he was a murderer in his own country. He was a threat.

And so I went to the United Nations, as you recall, September the 12th, 2002, and said to the United Nations, "Let's work together to disarm this man. You recognized he had arms. We recognize he's got arms. Let's disarm him." And 1441 came about. It's when the world spoke in—through the United Nations Security Council with one voice and in a unanimous voice said, "Disarm, or there will be serious consequences." In other words, they agreed that Saddam was a threat, and so we moved to disarm him. In other words, there were serious consequences because he was defiant.

Since then, David Kay has reported back that he had weapons programs that would have put him in material breach of 1441.

What that means, of course, is that had David Kay been the lead inspector and had done the work that he did prior to our removal of Saddam, he would have reported back to the U.N. Security Council that Saddam was, in fact, in breach of the Council resolutions that were passed.

Secondly, North Korea—one of the things, David, I think you've seen about our foreign policy is that I'm reluctant to use military power. It's the last choice. It's not our first choice. And in Iraq, there was a lot of diplomacy that took place before there was any military action. There was diplomacy prior to my arrival, diplomacy during my time here, and we tried all means and methodologies to achieve the objective, which was a more secure America, by using diplomatic means and persuasion.

In North Korea, we're now in the process of using diplomatic means and persuasion to convince Kim Chong-il to get rid of his nuclear weapons program. And that's changed by altering the dynamics between the United States and North Korea this way, by inviting other parties to be stakeholders in the process. And that's been successful thus far, of convincing others that they have a stake in the process.

This started in Crawford with Jiang Zemin, where we held a joint press conference, and he stepped out and said that we share a common goal, and that is a nuclear-weapons-free Peninsula—and as you know full well, that the relationship has evolved beyond just a statement, where we're now coparticipants in the process of convincing Kim Chong-il to change his ways. And that's exactly where we are in the process. And I'm pleased with the progress we're making, and I hope, of course, he listens.

Suzanne [Suzanne Malveaux, Cable News Network].

Iraqi Reconstruction Contracts

Q. Mr. President, you have justified your policy in awarding prime Iraq contracts to members of the Coalition Authority because of their sacrifice with the war in Iraq. At the same time, your administration has indicated some room for negotiation. Your critics have called this retaliation and even blackmail. How do you respond to that, and how is this policy helpful in generating international support?

The President. There are over 60 nations involved in Iraq. Let's make sure everybody—let's all start from the same basis, if you don't mind. So there is international support. When you say there's over 60 nations involved in Iraq, that means that there's international support in Iraq. Again, I think you're talking about one or two countries, if I'm not mistaken. And we're reaching out to them, and we want them to participate. But the idea of spending taxpayers' money on contracts to firms that did not participate in the initial thrust is just something I wasn't going to do. And you know what? The American taxpayers understand that. They understand that clearly. That's not to say there's not other ways to participate, and we look forward to including them in the process.

Stretch—Big Stretch [Bill Sammon, Washington Times]. I'm sorry. [*Laughter*]

Howard Dean

Q. I know you said there will be a time for politics. But you've also said you wanted to change the tone in Washington. Howard Dean recently seemed to muse aloud whether you had advance knowledge of 9/11. Do you agree or disagree with the RNC that this kind of rhetoric borders on political hate speech?

The President. There's time for politics. And, you know—there's time for politics, and I—it's an absurd insinuation.

Immigration Policy

Q. In that case, sir, can I follow up on something unrelated? [*Laughter*] Tom Ridge recently seemed to discuss something you had talked about pre-9/11, and that is finding a way to legalize some of the illegal immigrants in this country. Could you clarify your policy, what it is, short of blanket amnesty?

The President. Yes. Well, first of all, I have constantly said that we need to have a immigration policy that helps match any willing employer with any willing employee. It makes sense that that policy go forward. And we're in the process of working that through now so I can make a recommendation to the Congress.

Let me also clarify something. This administration is firmly against blanket amnesty.

Let's see here. Judy [Judy Keen, USA Today].

Situation in Iraq/War on Terror

Q. Mr. President, do you have a sense yet of how involved Saddam Hussein was in planning and directing attacks on coalition troops? Should the American people expect that those attacks will now decrease, or should they be prepared that they might, in the short term, get worse?

The President. To answer your question, we're—the Defense Department will try to learn more from Saddam Hussein as time goes on. And secondly, I believe there will be more violence, because I believe there's holdovers of Saddam that are frustrated, and I believe there are foreign terrorists that cannot stand the thought of a free Iraq emerging in the Middle East. This is a—a free Iraq will be a defeat for those who believe in violence and murder and mayhem. And they will try to resist us there.

And that's—I do believe that there are going to be some people who are persuaded that since Saddam Hussein has been captured, that he will never return, and therefore, they need to be a part of the emergence of a free Iraq and a free society and that there—and it's going to be very important for the Iraqi authorities to reach out to those people and talk about a system that guarantees minority rights

and a system which says that for some the future is bright.

And I think when people begin to realize that, when people begin—that were—I would call them fence-sitters—when people begin to realize that the Saddam regime is gone forever and that the new society that will emerge will be a fair society, it will protect people, and protect people from the—protect them based upon their own religious views, for example, guarantee them rights—that's what I mean by "protect"—that it's more likely people will begin to sign on to the future of Iraq. And that's positive. It's a very hopeful thing.

But there will be terrorists, and they want to fight us. Remember this is—Iraq is a battle in the war on terror. The war on terror is being fought on many fronts, and some of them obviously more visible than others. Obviously, the Afghanistan front was a visible front. Iraq is a visible front. The Philippines, for example, is a front in the war on terror against Abu Sayyaf, and we've had fairly stealthy operations there to bring the leadership of Abu Sayyaf to justice.

The war on terror encompasses more than just military action, of course, or the use of special force strike teams. Cutting off money is an important part in the war on terror. And so, Judy, it's very important for people to put this—Iraq in a broader context about a war that will continue on.

The reason I bring that up is that these—the enemy, the terrorists, the killers may continue to try to strike in Iraq. They think they may be able to defeat us there. Yesterday was a clear signal to them that they won't be able to.

The other thing that's happening in Iraq that's positive, and I think this—some of you, your papers and broadcasts have picked this up—is that the intelligence on the ground is getting better. It's getting richer. There's—what they call actionable intelligence, to which our military's responding on a quick basis, is improving. And that's a very important development because, as you notice, when there's a hole in the ground and a person is able to crawl into it, in a country the size of California, it means we're on a scavenger hunt for terror. And the best way to find these terrorists who hide in holes is to get people coming forth to describe the location of the hole, is to give clues and data.

And we're on it. Our military is responding, and our intelligence services are doing very good work. And it's just a long process that requires patience and perseverance. And yesterday's arrest of this tyrant and killer was a good example of persistence and fine tuning intelligence and gathering information and the hard work necessary to find people who are willing to hide in holes.

Other Stretch [Richard Keil, Bloomberg News].

Economic Growth/Monetary Policy

Q. Thank you, Mr. President. At the outset you said that you will pursue next year, the election year, a progrowth agenda. Up until now, "progrowth" in this administration has largely been synonymous with tax cuts. Can you rule out the possibility of further tax cut proposals next year?

The President. You know, Stretch, it's a trick question. [*Laughter*] It's not very generous of you during the holiday season. [*Laughter*]

First of all, I'm pleased with the economic growth that we've seen. I believe the economy is strong. I believe it's getting stronger. I'm pleased with the productivity numbers. I appreciate the fact that durable—orders for durable goods are up. It looks like the manufacturing sector is strengthening.

And what I've been referring to, in terms of progrowth, are an energy bill, good tort reform coming out of the Congress. I thought we had a chance to get some this year. It got stuck, unfortunately, in the Senate. In my judgment, it was a mistake. It was a mistake not to let class-action lawsuit reform go forward. It was a mistake not to get asbestos reform, a mistake not to get medical liability reform. All three of those measures, in my judgment, obviously, are justifiable reforms at the Federal level which would have made a difference in terms of a progrowth environment. We need more regulatory relief. We certainly need to send a signal to the capital markets that we're going to maintain spending discipline. Dana talked about the deficit. He also mentioned the strong dollar.

And by the way, I didn't answer that part of your question. I'll get back there right now. Part of the economic policy of this administration is a strong dollar policy. We fully expect markets to set the dollar. But we have a strong dollar policy, which is, in our judgment, good for the economic vitality of this country. And so we'll see, is the answer to your question.

Yes, Ed [Ed Chen, Los Angeles Times].

Trial of Saddam Hussein

Q. Mr. President, you said earlier this morning that in a trial, that all of Saddam's atrocities be brought up. He was in power more than 30 years—probably would make for a long rap sheet. Do you believe——

The President. Well, Ed, you're not supposed to prejudge.

Q. I'm just counting the years.

The President. Okay, good.

Q. Do you believe that the invasion of Kuwait in 1990 should be included, as well as his assassination attempt against former President Bush?

The President. Ed, that will all be decided by the lawyers. And I will instruct this Government to make sure the system includes the Iraqi citizens and make sure the process stands in—withstands international scrutiny. But we'll let the lawyers handle all that, and as you know, I'm not a lawyer. And I delegate, and I'm going to delegate this to the legal community, which will be reviewing all this matter.

Tamara [Tamara Lipper, Newsweek].

Iraqi Weapons of Mass Destruction

Q. Thank you, sir. Given your skepticism about Saddam Hussein's ability to tell the truth, do you think his interrogation might help resolve any lingering questions about what he did with his weapons of mass destruction and his ties to terrorist groups?

The President. I don't know. I would think not. I mean, he's a deceiver. He's a liar. He's a torturer. He's a murderer. I can't imagine why he would change his attitude, since he'll be treated humanely by the U.S. coalition—U.S. troops. And you know, I would be very skeptical of anything he said, one way or the other, I might add. You just don't know. He's a—he's just—he is what he is. He's a person that was willing to destroy his country and to kill a lot of his fellow citizens. He's a person who used weapons of mass destruction against citizens in his own country. And so it's—he is the kind of person that is untrustworthy, and I'd be very cautious about relying upon his word in any way, shape, or form.

Yes.

Q. Mr. President——

The President. Yes, Bob [Bob Deans, Cox Newspapers].

The Presidency/Capture of Saddam Hussein

Q. ——when you asked the American people for their support 3 years ago, there was no way anyone could have imagined the nature of the job you would have before you. If you had known then what you know now, sir, would you have wanted the job? Would you have had any hesitation——

The President. That's an interesting question.

Q. ——about asking the American people for it? Now, I have to ask you since we're here, sir, have you chatted with your dad since Saddam was captured?

The President. He called me—let me answer your first question. I absolutely would have wanted the job. I have come to realize this job is a magnificent job because you

have a chance to use the position of the United States of America to achieve peace and freedom. And that is a rare opportunity for any person. I put together a fantastic administration to help me with this task. I feel very comfortable in the job because I've got great advice and advisers to whom I—get good advice from great advisers to whom I listen. I am comfortable delegating the awesome responsibilities of, in this administration's case, war two times to incredibly capable and brave people.

At home, this job affords the opportunity to capture what I call the American spirit and to call people to serve in their communities and their neighborhoods and to help people who hurt. It's a fantastic opportunity to try to lift up this country so everybody can realize its full potential. I absolutely would seek the office again, and I intend to do so in '04, by the way. [*Laughter*]

I talked to my Dad. He called me Sunday morning. I got the call from Donald Rumsfeld Saturday afternoon and made the decision there, until I was more certain about the facts, that I would talk to very few people. I talked to Condi and asked her to call Andy, and I talked to Vice President Cheney. Because what I didn't want to have happen is that there would be this rush of enthusiasm and hope and then all of a sudden it would turn out not to be the person that we would hope it would be. So I didn't talk to my family. I told Laura, of course, and pretty much went to bed early Saturday night.

And Condi woke me at 5:15 in the morning, which was okay this time. [*Laughter*] Just don't do it again. [*Laughter*] But she said that Jerry Bremer had just called her and they were prepared to say this was Saddam Hussein, in which case we got dressed and hustled over to the Oval Office to start making calls. One of the calls I did receive was from my dad, and it was a very brief conversation. He just said, "Congratulations. It's a great day for the country." And I said, "It's a greater day for the Iraqi people."

And that's what I believe. I believe that yesterday was a day—or Saturday, when we captured Saddam, it was a day where America is more secure as a result of his capture. But more importantly, Saturday was a great day for the people who have suffered under this tyrant.

He is—I believe, firmly believe—and you've heard me say this a lot, and I say it a lot because I truly believe it—that freedom is the Almighty God's gift to every person, every man and woman who lives in this world. That's what I believe. And the arrest of Saddam Hussein changed the equation in Iraq. Justice was being delivered to a man who defied that gift from the Almighty to the people of Iraq. And justice will be delivered to him in a way that is transparent and for the world to see. And so I told my dad, I said, "It's a great day for America, but it's a better day for the people of this country," and that's why.

Thank you all for coming. I'll see you Thursday, coats and ties. [*Laughter*] This year, Gregory, don't take any silverware. [*Laughter*]

NOTE: The President's news conference began at 11:15 a.m. in Room 450 of the Dwight D. Eisenhower Executive Office Building. In his remarks, he referred to Rend Rahim Francke, head of Iraq's Interest Section in the U.S.; Prime Minister Paul Martin of Canada; James A. Baker III, the President's personal envoy on the issue of Iraqi debt; Joshua Bolten, Director, Office of Management and Budget; David Kay, CIA Special Advisor for Strategy Regarding Iraqi Weapons of Mass Destruction Programs; Chairman Kim Chong-il of North Korea; former President Jiang Zemin of China; National Security Adviser Condoleezza Rice; Assistant to the President and Chief of Staff Andrew H. Card, Jr.; and L. Paul Bremer III, Presidential Envoy to Iraq. A reporter referred to Democratic Presidential candidate Howard Dean.

Statement on Senator John Breaux's Decision Not To Seek Reelection
December 15, 2003

John Breaux is a distinguished public servant. His tenure in the Senate has been marked by bipartisan statesmanship, results for the people of Louisiana, and dedicated service for America.

During more than 30 years in the Congress, John Breaux has put party politics aside to get things done for the American people. His leadership in getting the 2001 tax cut passed helped spur economic growth and job creation, and his vision and tenacity on Medicare reform have now helped provide senior citizens with long-awaited prescription drug benefits and more choices in health care. He also has been a leader in the effort to pass comprehensive energy legislation, among many other legislative achievements.

It is with deep respect that Laura and I extend our gratitude and best wishes to John, his wife, Lois, and their children.

Letter to Congressional Leaders Transmitting a Report on Iraq
December 15, 2003

Dear Mr. Speaker: (Dear Mr. President:)

Consistent with the Authorization for Use of Military Force Against Iraq Resolution of 2002 (Public Law 107–243), the Authorization for the Use of Force Against Iraq Resolution (Public Law 102–1), and in order to keep the Congress fully informed, I am providing a report prepared by my Administration. This report includes matters relating to post-liberation Iraq

under section 7 of the Iraq Liberation Act of 1998 (Public Law 105–338).

Sincerely,

GEORGE W. BUSH

NOTE: Identical letters were sent to J. Dennis Hastert, Speaker of the House of Representatives, and Richard B. Cheney, President of the Senate.

Remarks on Signing the American Dream Downpayment Act
December 16, 2003

Thank you all. Thank you for coming. Thanks for the warm welcome. It's great to be back at the Department of Housing and Urban Development. This is not my first time here, nor will it be my last.

I am here today because we are taking action to bring many thousands of Americans closer to owning a home. Our Government is supporting homeownership because it is good for America; it is good for our families; it is good for our economy. One of the biggest hurdles to homeownership is getting money for a downpayment. This administration has recognized that, and so today I'm honored to be here to sign a law that will help many low-income buyers to overcome that hurdle and to achieve an important part of the American Dream.

I appreciate Alphonso Jackson agreeing to step up and become the Acting Secretary of the Housing and Urban Development. I look forward to his Senate confirmation, a hasty confirmation.

I also want to thank Mel Martinez for doing such a fine job as the Secretary of this important organization. Mel brought integrity and honor to the office. He did

a fine job on behalf of all Americans. And we honor you, Mel.

I want to thank all the hard-working officers and employees of HUD. I appreciate your focus and your dedication, your willingness to work on behalf of a better America.

I thank very much Members of the Congress who have taken time to come and join us for this important bill signing. Senator Wayne Allard from Colorado is with us. Senator Allard, thank you for your work on the floor of the Senate. Chairman of the Financial Services Committee Mike Oxley is with us. Congressman, thank you for coming. Congressman Jim Leach from Iowa is with us today. Congressman, thank you for being here. Congresswoman Katherine Harris, who had a lot to do with this bill getting passed, is here with us. Katherine, thank you for coming. Delegate Madeleine Bordallo of Guam is with us today. I'm honored you are here. Thank you for coming, Madeleine. I appreciate you coming.

I too want to pay homage to a man I call Little Woody; that would be Rob

Woodson. He worked hard in the development of this policy. I think it is safe to say that he was the—he developed the concept for this policy, a concept embraced by my administration. I'm appreciative that Michelle is here. I also want to thank Dad for coming, Bob Woodson, who is a social entrepreneur, a person who cares deeply about every American having the right and a chance to own a home. Thank the Woodson family. God bless you all.

I want to thank the representatives of consumer and housing groups that worked hard on this piece of legislation. I want to thank leaders of the national community organizations that are with us, members of the real estate industry.

This administration will constantly strive to promote an ownership society in America. We want more people owning their own home. It is in our national interest that more people own their own home. After all, if you own your own home, you have a vital stake in the future of our country.

And this is a good time for the American homeowner. Today we received a report that showed that new home construction last month reached its highest level in nearly 20 years. The reason that is so is because there is renewed confidence in our economy. Low interest rates help. They have made owning a home more affordable for those who refinance and for those who buy a home for the first time. Rising home values have added more than $2½ trillion to the assets of the American families since the start of 2001.

The rate of homeownership in America now stands at a record high of 68.4 percent. Yet there is room for improvement. The rate of homeownership amongst minorities is below 50 percent. And that's not right, and this country needs to do something about it. We need to close the minority homeownership gap in America so more citizens get the satisfaction and mobility that comes from owning your own home,

from owning a piece of the future of America.

Last year I set a goal to add 5.5 million new minority homeowners in America by the end of the decade. That is an attainable goal; that is an essential goal. And we're making progress toward that goal. In the past 18 months, more than 1 million minority families have become homeowners. And there's more that we can do to achieve the goal.

The law I sign today will help us build on this progress in a very practical way. Many people are able to afford a monthly mortgage payment but are unable to make the downpayment, and so this legislation will authorize $200 million per year in downpayment assistance to at least 40,000 low-income families. These funds will help American families achieve their goals and, at the same time, strengthen our communities.

And there's more to do as well. We'll continue to pursue a broad agenda to help people own a home. There are three steps I want to describe to you right quickly about what we intend to do.

First, those who apply for mortgages should be made aware of all the costs and warned about predatory lenders who take advantage of inexperienced buyers. So we've doubled the funds for housing counseling services, including those run by faith-based and community groups. We understand that buying a home for the first time is complicated, and we want to simplify the process. We want to help people understand the pros and cons of buying a home. We want people to be fully aware of what it means to buy a home and what it takes. And we want people as best protected as possible from those shysters who would take advantage of first-time buyers.

Second, we need to make the homebuying process more affordable. Some of the biggest upfront costs in a home purchase are the closing costs. Sometimes they catch you by surprise. [*Laughter*] Many homebuyers do not have the time to shop around looking for a better deal on closing costs. You're kind of stuck with what you're presented with. And so they end up paying more than they should. So we've proposed new rules to make it easier for buyers to shop around and to compare prices on closing costs, so they can get the best deal and the best service possible.

And thirdly, we want to make buying a home simpler. Many first-time buyers look at the paperwork from a loan application and, frankly, get a little nervous about all the fine print. Those forms can be intimidating to the first-time homebuyer. They can be intimidating to the second- or third-time homebuyer too. [*Laughter*] So this administration has proposed new rules to simplify the forms homebuyers and homeowners fill out when they apply for a loan or close on a mortgage.

We understand that buying a home is a big step, and so these three recommendations we're making, these three changes in the rules, will make that step easier, will enable people to make the step to buying a home—they'll be able to do so with more confidence. These are practical ways that we are working to expand homeownership across the country.

The dream of homeownership should be attainable for every hard-working American. That's what we want. And this act of Congress I'm going to sign, the regulations that I hope are finalized soon will help thousands of families fulfill the dream.

And so now it is my honor, right here at this important Department, the Department responsible for encouraging homeownership in America, to sign the American Dream Downpayment Act.

NOTE: The President spoke at 1:57 p.m. at the Department of Housing and Urban Development. In his remarks, he referred to the late Robert Woodson, Jr., former Chief of Staff, Department of Housing and Urban Development, and his widow, Michelle; and Robert Woodson, Sr., founder and president, National Center for Neighborhood Enterprise. S. 811, approved December 16, was assigned Public Law No. 108–186. The Office of the Press Secretary also released a Spanish language transcript of these remarks.

Statement on Completion of the Kabul-Kandahar Highway
December 16, 2003

More than a year ago, Afghan President Hamid Karzai broke ground on the reconstruction of a highway that—when completed—will run through the heart of Afghanistan, helping to unify that great nation. The United States and Japan pledged to provide financing and personnel to the project, and we further pledged that the first leg—the 300 miles from the capital of Kabul to the important city of Kandahar—would be completed by the end of this year.

Today we have met that pledge, as the first phase of paving the Kabul-Kandahar leg of the highway is completed under budget and ahead of schedule. This new road reduces travel time between Kabul to Kandahar to 5 hours. It will promote political unity between Afghanistan's provinces, facilitate commerce by making it easier to bring products to market, and provide the Afghan people with greater access to health care and educational opportunities.

I am grateful for the enormous efforts of engineers and laborers from many countries who worked tirelessly and often in the face of hardship and danger to finish this leg of the road on time. This accomplishment underscores the firm commitment of the United States and coalition to support the Afghan people as they build a democratic, stable, and thriving Afghanistan.

Joint Statement Agreed to by President Bush, President Chirac, and Chancellor Schroeder
December 16, 2003

Debt reduction is critical if the Iraqi people are to have any chance to build a free and prosperous Iraq. Therefore, France, Germany, and the United States agree that there should be substantial debt reduction for Iraq in the Paris Club in 2004, and will work closely with each other and with other countries to achieve this objective. The exact percentage of debt reduction that would constitute "substantial" debt reduction is subject to future agreement between the parties.

NOTE: An original was not available for verification of the content of this joint statement.

Remarks on the 100th Anniversary of the Wright Brothers' First Flight at Kill Devil Hills, North Carolina
December 17, 2003

Thank you all very much. Rain will never dampen our spirits. I'm honored to be here, and I'm honored to be in the great State of North Carolina.

Madam Secretary, thank you for your fine leadership and your friendship. Secretary Mineta, thank you for your great leadership, as well. I'm proud that you're serving in my Cabinet. Mr. Governor, I appreciate your kind comments. I appreciate the values you hold dear to your heart, and I thank you for leading this great State.

To John Travolta, we shall call him "Moon Man" from now on. I appreciate your friendship. I appreciate your love of flight. Thank you for being such a fine entertainer for millions of Americans, but most importantly, thanks for being a great American. I'm proud you're here.

I appreciate the fact that the Secretary of the Navy, Gordon England, is here. The Secretary of the Air Force, James Roche, is traveling with me today. I appreciate Sean O'Keefe, who is the Administrator of NASA, who has come today. I thank all members of my administration who have joined us. I hope you were smart enough to have brought an umbrella. [*Laughter*]

I know we've got Members of the Congress who are here. Senate Majority Leader Bill Frist from Tennessee is with us today. Senator Frist, thank you for coming. Senator Elizabeth Dole from the great State of North Carolina is with us. Senator Dole, thank you for being here. All Members of Congress from North Carolina and from other States, thank you for being here. I know we've got mayors and State officials.

I appreciate so very much American heroes who are here, well-known and not so well-known heroes. Let me name four of the well-known heroes who are here: Neil Armstrong; Buzz Aldrin; John Glenn; one of the great fighter pilots ever, Chuck Yeager, is with us today. We're honored to be in your presence. Thank you for being pioneers.

I'm also pleased that we're joined by Stephen Wright and Amanda Wright Lane, who both bear one of the great American names.

Powered flight has advanced in ways that could not have been imagined on December 17, 1903. And in the future, flight will advance in ways that none of us can imagine as we stand here today. Yet always, for as long as there is human flight, we will honor the achievement of a cold morning on the Outer Banks of North Carolina by two young brothers named Orville and Wilbur Wright.

Orville Wright lived to see the days of barnstorming and military aviation, the jet engine, commercial airlines, and the DC–3. The thrill of his life, however, was surely right here when he felt that first lift of the wing. He flew just 12 seconds and 40 yards, moving so slowly that his older brother ran alongside. And later in the day, with Wilbur at the controls, the machine stayed in the air for 59 seconds and traveled 852 feet. Yet everyone who was here at that hour sensed that a great line had been crossed and the world might never be the same. A local boy named Johnny Moore was one of the witnesses. He ran down the beach and said, "They done it. They done it. Damned if they ain't flew!"

The anniversary now observed might have fallen a few days earlier, on the 13th. But December the 13th, 1903, was a Sunday, and the brothers had promised their dad they wouldn't attempt to fly on the Sabbath. And on the day they did fly, just like today, the conditions were not ideal. But they went ahead anyway, so they could get home to Dayton, Ohio, for Christmas.

Orville and Wilbur were, in so many ways, ordinary Americans, and hearing of their plans, a lot of folks must have thought those boys should have stayed in the bicycle business. The story is told of a newspaper editor who heard what the Wright brothers had been up to. He said, "Man will never fly, and if he does, he won't be from Dayton." [*Laughter*]

The United States Patent Office also had its doubts. So many others had submitted plans and models of flying machines that when the brothers sent in theirs, patent officials had a ready response. The office concluded the plans were inadequate and the machine could never function as intended. The New York Times once confidently explained why all attempts at flight were doomed from the start. To build a flying machine, declared one editorial, would require "the combined and continuous efforts of mathematicians and mechanicians from 1 million to 10 million years." As it turned out, the feat was performed 8 weeks after the editorial was written. And not only did the machine perform its function, that little wood and canvas aircraft had brought together all the essentials that still give flight to every modern aircraft, from a single-prop plane to Air Force One.

The Wright brothers had some disappointments along the way, and there must have been times when they had to fight their own doubts. They pressed on, believing in the great work they had begun and in their own capacity to see it through. We would not know their names today if these men had been pessimists. And when it was over, they marveled at their own achievement. As Orville wrote in a letter to a friend, "Isn't it astounding that all these secrets have been preserved for so many years just so we could discover them."

The Wright brothers' invention belongs to the world, but the Wright brothers belong to America. We take special pride in their qualities of discipline and persistence, optimism and imagination—of people like them and a lot of other people throughout our history. So many great inventions arose in this country, and so many of the great inventors came from unlikely backgrounds. The Wright brothers had their storefront bicycle shop. Thomas Edison was a newsboy. Eli Whitney and Henry Ford worked as farm hands. George Washington Carver was born a slave. There is something in the American character that always looks for a better way and is unimpressed when others say it cannot be done. Those traits still define our Nation. We still rely on men and women who overcome the odds and take the big chance with no advantage but their own ingenuity and the opportunities of a free country.

A great American journey that began at Kitty Hawk continues in ways unimaginable to the Wright brothers. One small piece of their Flyer traveled far beyond this field. It was carried by another flying machine, on *Apollo 11*, all the way to the Sea of Tranquility on the Moon. These past 100 years have brought supersonic flights, frequent space travel, the exploration of Mars, and the *Voyager One* spacecraft, which right now is moving at 39,000 miles per hour toward the outer edge of our solar system. By our skill and daring, America has excelled in every area of aviation and space travel. And our national commitment remains firm: By our skill and daring, we will continue to lead the world in flight.

This day, however, is one for recalling an heroic event in the history of our Nation and in the story of mankind. Here at the Wright Brothers National Memorial, we remember one small machine, and we honor the giants who flew it.

May God bless you all, and may God continue to bless America.

NOTE: The President spoke at 9:37 a.m. at the Wright Brothers National Memorial. In his remarks, he referred to Secretary of the Interior Gale A. Norton; Secretary of Transportation Norman Y. Mineta; Gov. Michael F. Easley of North Carolina; and actor John Travolta, who served as master of ceremonies. The Wright Brothers Day proclamation of December 17 is listed in Appendix D at the end of this volume.

Letter to Congressional Leaders Transmitting the Executive Order on Appointments During National Emergency
December 17, 2003

Dear Mr. Speaker: (*Dear Mr. President:*)

Consistent with section 301 of the National Emergencies Act (50 U.S.C. 1631), I hereby report that I have taken additional steps with respect to the national emergency I declared in Proclamation 7463 of September 14, 2001, by invoking and making available to the Secretary of Defense the emergency appointments authority of section 603 of title 10 of the United States Code, consistent with the terms of that statute and of Executive Order 12396 of December 9, 1982.

I am enclosing a copy of the Executive Order I have issued, which is effective immediately.

Sincerely,

GEORGE W. BUSH

NOTE: Identical letters were sent to J. Dennis Hastert, Speaker of the House of Representatives, and Richard B. Cheney, President of the Senate. The Executive order of December 17 is listed in Appendix D at the end of this volume.

Homeland Security Presidential Directive/HSPD–7—Critical Infrastructure Identification, Prioritization, and Protection
December 17, 2003

Subject: Critical Infrastructure Identification, Prioritization, and Protection

Purpose

(1) This directive establishes a national policy for Federal departments and agencies to identify and prioritize United States critical infrastructure and key resources and to protect them from terrorist attacks.

Background

(2) Terrorists seek to destroy, incapacitate, or exploit critical infrastructure and key resources across the United States to threaten national security, cause mass casualties, weaken our economy, and damage public morale and confidence.

(3) America's open and technologically complex society includes a wide array of critical infrastructure and key resources that are potential terrorist targets. The majority of these are owned and operated by the private sector and State or local governments. These critical infrastructures and key resources are both physical and cyber-based and span all sectors of the economy.

(4) Critical infrastructure and key resources provide the essential services that underpin American society. The Nation possesses numerous key resources, whose exploitation or destruction by terrorists could cause catastrophic health effects or mass casualties comparable to those from the use of a weapon of mass destruction, or could profoundly affect our national prestige and morale. In addition, there is critical infrastructure so vital that its incapacitation, exploitation, or destruction, through terrorist attack, could have a debilitating effect on security and economic well-being.

(5) While it is not possible to protect or eliminate the vulnerability of all critical infrastructure and key resources throughout the country, strategic improvements in security can make it more difficult for attacks to succeed and can lessen the impact of attacks that may occur. In addition to strategic security enhancements, tactical security improvements can be rapidly implemented to deter, mitigate, or neutralize potential attacks.

Definitions

(6) In this directive:
(a) The term "critical infrastructure" has the meaning given to that term in section 1016(e) of the USA PATRIOT Act of 2001 (42 U.S.C. 5195c(e)).
(b) The term "key resources" has the meaning given that term in section 2(9) of the Homeland Security Act of 2002 (6 U.S.C. 101(9)).
(c) The term "the Department" means the Department of Homeland Security.
(d) The term "Federal departments and agencies" means those executive departments enumerated in 5 U.S.C. 101, and the Department of Homeland Security; independent establishments as defined by 5 U.S.C. 104(1); Government corporations as defined by 5 U.S.C. 103(1); and the United States Postal Service.
(e) The terms "State," and "local government," when used in a geographical sense, have the same meanings given to those terms in section 2 of the Homeland Security Act of 2002 (6 U.S.C. 101).
(f) The term "the Secretary" means the Secretary of Homeland Security.

(g) The term "Sector-Specific Agency" means a Federal department or agency responsible for infrastructure protection activities in a designated critical infrastructure sector or key resources category. Sector-Specific Agencies will conduct their activities under this directive in accordance with guidance provided by the Secretary.

(h) The terms "protect" and "secure" mean reducing the vulnerability of critical infrastructure or key resources in order to deter, mitigate, or neutralize terrorist attacks.

Policy

(7) It is the policy of the United States to enhance the protection of our Nation's critical infrastructure and key resources against terrorist acts that could:

(a) cause catastrophic health effects or mass casualties comparable to those from the use of a weapon of mass destruction;

(b) impair Federal departments and agencies' abilities to perform essential missions, or to ensure the public's health and safety;

(c) undermine State and local government capacities to maintain order and to deliver minimum essential public services;

(d) damage the private sector's capability to ensure the orderly functioning of the economy and delivery of essential services;

(e) have a negative effect on the economy through the cascading disruption of other critical infrastructure and key resources; or

(f) undermine the public's morale and confidence in our national economic and political institutions.

(8) Federal departments and agencies will identify, prioritize, and coordinate the protection of critical infrastructure and key resources in order to prevent, deter, and mitigate the effects of deliberate efforts to destroy, incapacitate, or exploit them. Federal departments and agencies will work with State and local governments and the private sector to accomplish this objective.

(9) Federal departments and agencies will ensure that homeland security programs do not diminish the overall economic security of the United States.

(10) Federal departments and agencies will appropriately protect information associated with carrying out this directive, including handling voluntarily provided information and information that would facilitate terrorist targeting of critical infrastructure and key resources consistent with the Homeland Security Act of 2002 and other applicable legal authorities.

(11) Federal departments and agencies shall implement this directive in a manner consistent with applicable provisions of law, including those protecting the rights of United States persons.

Roles and Responsibilities of the Secretary

(12) In carrying out the functions assigned in the Homeland Security Act of 2002, the Secretary shall be responsible for coordinating the overall national effort to enhance the protection of the critical infrastructure and key resources of the United States. The Secretary shall serve as the principal Federal official to lead, integrate, and coordinate implementation of efforts among Federal departments and agencies, State and local governments, and the private sector to protect critical infrastructure and key resources.

(13) Consistent with this directive, the Secretary will identify, prioritize, and coordinate the protection of critical infrastructure and key resources with an emphasis on critical infrastructure and key resources that could be exploited to cause catastrophic health effects or mass casualties comparable to those from the use of a weapon of mass destruction.

(14) The Secretary will establish uniform policies, approaches, guidelines, and methodologies for integrating Federal infrastructure protection and risk management activities within and across sectors along with metrics and criteria for related programs and activities.

(15) The Secretary shall coordinate protection activities for each of the following critical infrastructure sectors: information technology; telecommunications; chemical; transportation systems, including mass transit, aviation, maritime, ground/surface, and rail and pipeline systems; emergency services; and postal and shipping. The Department shall coordinate with appropriate departments and agencies to ensure the protection of other key resources including dams, government facilities, and commercial facilities. In addition, in its role as overall cross-sector coordinator, the Department shall also evaluate the need for and coordinate the coverage of additional critical infrastructure and key resources categories over time, as appropriate.

(16) The Secretary will continue to maintain an organization to serve as a focal point for the security of cyberspace. The organization will facilitate interactions and collaborations between and among Federal departments and agencies, State and local governments, the private sector, academia and international organizations. To the extent permitted by law, Federal departments and agencies with cyber expertise, including but not limited to the Departments of Justice, Commerce, the Treasury, Defense, Energy, and State, and the Central Intelligence Agency, will collaborate with and support the organization in accomplishing its mission. The organization's mission includes analysis, warning, information sharing, vulnerability reduction, mitigation, and aiding national recovery efforts for critical infrastructure information systems. The organization will support the Department of Justice and other law enforcement agencies in their continuing missions to investigate and prosecute threats to and attacks against cyberspace, to the extent permitted by law.

(17) The Secretary will work closely with other Federal departments and agencies, State and local governments, and the private sector in accomplishing the objectives of this directive.

Roles and Responsibilities of Sector-Specific Federal Agencies

(18) Recognizing that each infrastructure sector possesses its own unique characteristics and operating models, there are designated Sector-Specific Agencies, including:
  (a) Department of Agriculture—agriculture, food (meat, poultry, egg products);
  (b) Health and Human Services—public health, healthcare, and food (other than meat, poultry, egg products);
  (c) Environmental Protection Agency—drinking water and water treatment systems;
  (d) Department of Energy—energy, including the production refining, storage, and distribution of oil and gas, and electric power except for commercial nuclear power facilities;
  (e) Department of the Treasury—banking and finance;
  (f) Department of the Interior—national monuments and icons; and
  (g) Department of Defense—defense industrial base.

(19) In accordance with guidance provided by the Secretary, Sector-Specific Agencies shall:
  (a) collaborate with all relevant Federal departments and agencies, State and local governments, and the private sector, including with key persons and entities in their infrastructure sector;
  (b) conduct or facilitate vulnerability assessments of the sector; and
  (c) encourage risk management strategies to protect against and mitigate the effects of attacks against critical infrastructure and key resources.

(20) Nothing in this directive alters, or impedes the ability to carry out, the authorities of the Federal departments and agencies to perform their responsibilities under law and consistent with applicable legal authorities and presidential guidance.

(21) Federal departments and agencies shall cooperate with the Department in implementing this directive, consistent with the Homeland Security Act of 2002 and other applicable legal authorities.

Roles and Responsibilities of Other Departments, Agencies, and Offices

(22) In addition to the responsibilities given the Department and Sector-Specific Agencies, there are special functions of various Federal departments and agencies and components of the Executive Office of the President related to critical infrastructure and key resources protection.

(a) The Department of State, in conjunction with the Department, and the Departments of Justice, Commerce, Defense, the Treasury and other appropriate agencies, will work with foreign countries and international organizations to strengthen the protection of United States critical infrastructure and key resources.

(b) The Department of Justice, including the Federal Bureau of Investigation, will reduce domestic terrorist threats, and investigate and prosecute actual or attempted terrorist attacks on, sabotage of, or disruptions of critical infrastructure and key resources. The Attorney General and the Secretary shall use applicable statutory authority and attendant mechanisms for cooperation and coordination, including but not limited to those established by presidential directive.

(c) The Department of Commerce, in coordination with the Department, will work with private sector, research, academic, and government organizations to improve technology for cyber systems and promote other critical in-

frastructure efforts, including using its authority under the Defense Production Act to assure the timely availability of industrial products, materials, and services to meet homeland security requirements.

(d) A Critical Infrastructure Protection Policy Coordinating Committee will advise the Homeland Security Council on interagency policy related to physical and cyber infrastructure protection. This PCC will be chaired by a Federal officer or employee designated by the Assistant to the President for Homeland Security.

(e) The Office of Science and Technology Policy, in coordination with the Department, will coordinate interagency research and development to enhance the protection of critical infrastructure and key resources.

(f) The Office of Management and Budget (OMB) shall oversee the implementation of government-wide policies, principles, standards, and guidelines for Federal government computer security programs. The Director of OMB will ensure the operation of a central Federal information security incident center consistent with the requirements of the Federal Information Security Management Act of 2002.

(g) Consistent with the E-Government Act of 2002, the Chief Information Officers Council shall be the principal interagency forum for improving agency practices related to the design, acquisition, development, modernization, use, operation, sharing, and performance of information resources of Federal departments and agencies.

(h) The Department of Transportation and the Department will collaborate on all matters relating to transportation security and transportation infrastructure protection. The Department of Transportation is responsible for operating the national air space system. The Department of Transportation and the Department will collaborate in regulating the transportation of hazardous materials by all modes (including pipelines).

(i) All Federal departments and agencies shall work with the sectors relevant to their responsibilities to reduce the consequences of catastrophic failures not caused by terrorism.

(23) The heads of all Federal departments and agencies will coordinate and cooperate with the Secretary as appropriate and consistent with their own responsibilities for protecting critical infrastructure and key resources.

(24) All Federal department and agency heads are responsible for the identification, prioritization, assessment, remediation, and protection of their respective internal critical infrastructure and key resources. Consistent with the Federal Information Security Management Act of 2002, agencies will identify and provide information security protections commensurate with the risk and magnitude of the harm resulting from the unauthorized access, use, disclosure, disruption, modification, or destruction of information.

Coordination with the Private Sector

(25) In accordance with applicable laws or regulations, the Department and the Sector-Specific Agencies will collaborate with appropriate private sector entities and continue to encourage the development of information sharing and analysis mechanisms. Additionally, the Department and Sector-Specific Agencies shall collaborate with the private sector and continue to support sector-coordinating mechanisms:

(a) to identify, prioritize, and coordinate the protection of critical infrastructure and key resources; and

(b) to facilitate sharing of information about physical and cyber threats, vulnerabilities, incidents, potential

protective measures, and best practices.

National Special Security Events

(26) The Secretary, after consultation with the Homeland Security Council, shall be responsible for designating events as "National Special Security Events" (NSSEs). This directive supersedes language in previous presidential directives regarding the designation of NSSEs that is inconsistent herewith.

Implementation

(27) Consistent with the Homeland Security Act of 2002, the Secretary shall produce a comprehensive, integrated National Plan for Critical Infrastructure and Key Resources Protection to outline national goals, objectives, milestones, and key initiatives within 1 year from the issuance of this directive. The Plan shall include, in addition to other Homeland Security-related elements as the Secretary deems appropriate, the following elements:

(a) a strategy to identify, prioritize, and coordinate the protection of critical infrastructure and key resources, including how the Department intends to work with Federal departments and agencies, State and local governments, the private sector, and foreign countries and international organizations;

(b) a summary of activities to be undertaken in order to: define and prioritize, reduce the vulnerability of, and coordinate the protection of critical infrastructure and key resources;

(c) a summary of initiatives for sharing critical infrastructure and key resources information and for providing critical infrastructure and key resources threat warning data to State and local governments and the private sector; and

(d) coordination and integration, as appropriate, with other Federal emergency management and preparedness activities including the National Response Plan and applicable national preparedness goals.

(28) The Secretary, consistent with the Homeland Security Act of 2002 and other applicable legal authorities and presidential guidance, shall establish appropriate systems, mechanisms, and procedures to share homeland security information relevant to threats and vulnerabilities in national critical infrastructure and key resources with other Federal departments and agencies, State and local governments, and the private sector in a timely manner.

(29) The Secretary will continue to work with the Nuclear Regulatory Commission and, as appropriate, the Department of Energy in order to ensure the necessary protection of:

(a) commercial nuclear reactors for generating electric power and non-power nuclear reactors used for research, testing, and training;

(b) nuclear materials in medical, industrial, and academic settings and facilities that fabricate nuclear fuel; and

(c) the transportation, storage, and disposal of nuclear materials and waste.

(30) In coordination with the Director of the Office of Science and Technology Policy, the Secretary shall prepare on an annual basis a Federal Research and Development Plan in support of this directive.

(31) The Secretary will collaborate with other appropriate Federal departments and agencies to develop a program, consistent with applicable law, to geospatially map, image, analyze, and sort critical infrastructure and key resources by utilizing commercial satellite and airborne systems, and existing capabilities within other agencies. National technical means should be considered as an option of last resort. The Secretary, with advice from the Director of Central Intelligence, the Secretaries of Defense and the Interior, and the heads of other appropriate Federal departments and agencies, shall develop mechanisms for accomplishing this initiative. The Attorney General shall provide legal advice as necessary.

(32) The Secretary will utilize existing, and develop new, capabilities as needed to model comprehensively the potential implications of terrorist exploitation of vulnerabilities in critical infrastructure and key resources, placing specific focus on densely populated areas. Agencies with relevant modeling capabilities shall cooperate with the Secretary to develop appropriate mechanisms for accomplishing this initiative.

(33) The Secretary will develop a national indications and warnings architecture for infrastructure protection and capabilities that will facilitate:

(a) an understanding of baseline infrastructure operations;

(b) the identification of indicators and precursors to an attack; and

(c) a surge capacity for detecting and analyzing patterns of potential attacks.

In developing a national indications and warnings architecture, the Department will work with Federal, State, local, and nongovernmental entities to develop an integrated view of physical and cyber infrastructure and key resources.

(34) By July 2004, the heads of all Federal departments and agencies shall develop and submit to the Director of the OMB for approval plans for protecting the physical and cyber critical infrastructure and key resources that they own or operate. These plans shall address identification, prioritization, protection, and contingency planning, including the recovery and reconstitution of essential capabilities.

(35) On an annual basis, the Sector-Specific Agencies shall report to the Secretary on their efforts to identify, prioritize, and coordinate the protection of critical infrastructure and key resources in their respective sectors. The report shall be submitted within 1 year from the issuance of this directive and on an annual basis thereafter.

(36) The Assistant to the President for Homeland Security and the Assistant to the

President for National Security Affairs will lead a national security and emergency preparedness communications policy review, with the heads of the appropriate Federal departments and agencies, related to convergence and next generation architecture. Within 6 months after the issuance of this directive, the Assistant to the President for Homeland Security and the Assistant to the President for National Security Affairs shall submit for my consideration any recommended changes to such policy.

(37) This directive supersedes Presidential Decision Directive/NSC–63 of May 22, 1998 ("Critical Infrastructure Protection"), and any Presidential directives issued prior to this directive to the extent of any inconsistency. Moreover, the Assist-

ant to the President for Homeland Security and the Assistant to the President for National Security Affairs shall jointly submit for my consideration a Presidential directive to make changes in Presidential directives issued prior to this date that conform such directives to this directive.

(38) This directive is intended only to improve the internal management of the executive branch of the Federal Government, and it is not intended to, and does not, create any right or benefit, substantive or procedural, enforceable at law or in equity, against the United States, its departments, agencies, or other entities, its officers or employees, or any other person.

GEORGE W. BUSH

Homeland Security Presidential Directive/ HSPD–8—National Preparedness
December 17, 2003

Subject: National Preparedness

Purpose

(1) This directive establishes policies to strengthen the preparedness of the United States to prevent and respond to threatened or actual domestic terrorist attacks, major disasters, and other emergencies by requiring a national domestic all-hazards preparedness goal, establishing mechanisms for improved delivery of Federal preparedness assistance to State and local governments, and outlining actions to strengthen preparedness capabilities of Federal, State, and local entities.

Definitions

(2) For the purposes of this directive:
(a) The term "all-hazards preparedness" refers to preparedness for domestic terrorist attacks, major disasters, and other emergencies.

(b) The term "Federal departments and agencies" means those executive departments enumerated in 5 U.S.C. 101, and the Department of Homeland Security; independent establishments as defined by 5 U.S.C. 104(1); Government corporations as defined by 5 U.S.C. 103(1); and the United States Postal Service.
(c) The term "Federal preparedness assistance" means Federal department and agency grants, cooperative agreements, loans, loan guarantees, training, and/or technical assistance provided to State and local governments and the private sector to prevent, prepare for, respond to, and recover from terrorist attacks, major disasters, and other emergencies. Unless noted otherwise, the term "assistance" will refer to Federal assistance programs.
(d) The term "first responder" refers to those individuals who in the early

stages of an incident are responsible for the protection and preservation of life, property, evidence, and the environment, including emergency response providers as defined in section 2 of the Homeland Security Act of 2002 (6 U.S.C. 101), as well as emergency management, public health, clinical care, public works, and other skilled support personnel (such as equipment operators) that provide immediate support services during prevention, response, and recovery operations.

(e) The terms "major disaster" and "emergency" have the meanings given in section 102 of the Robert T. Stafford Disaster Relief and Emergency Assistance Act (42 U.S.C. 5122).

(f) The term "major events" refers to domestic terrorist attacks, major disasters, and other emergencies.

(g) The term "national homeland security preparedness-related exercises" refers to homeland security-related exercises that train and test national decision makers and utilize resources of multiple Federal departments and agencies. Such exercises may involve State and local first responders when appropriate. Such exercises do not include those exercises conducted solely within a single Federal department or agency.

(h) The term "preparedness" refers to the existence of plans, procedures, policies, training, and equipment necessary at the Federal, State, and local level to maximize the ability to prevent, respond to, and recover from major events. The term "readiness" is used interchangeably with preparedness.

(i) The term "prevention" refers to activities undertaken by the first responder community during the early stages of an incident to reduce the likelihood or consequences of threat-

ened or actual terrorist attacks. More general and broader efforts to deter, disrupt, or thwart terrorism are not addressed in this directive.

(j) The term "Secretary" means the Secretary of Homeland Security.

(k) The terms "State," and "local government," when used in a geographical sense, have the same meanings given to those terms in section 2 of the Homeland Security Act of 2002 (6 U.S.C. 101).

Relationship to HSPD–5

(3) This directive is a companion to HSPD–5, which identifies steps for improved coordination in response to incidents. This directive describes the way Federal departments and agencies will prepare for such a response, including prevention activities during the early stages of a terrorism incident.

Development of a National Preparedness Goal

(4) The Secretary is the principal Federal official for coordinating the implementation of all-hazards preparedness in the United States. In cooperation with other Federal departments and agencies, the Secretary coordinates the preparedness of Federal response assets, and the support for, and assessment of, the preparedness of State and local first responders.

(5) To help ensure the preparedness of the Nation to prevent, respond to, and recover from threatened and actual domestic terrorist attacks, major disasters, and other emergencies, the Secretary, in coordination with the heads of other appropriate Federal departments and agencies and in consultation with State and local governments, shall develop a national domestic all-hazards preparedness goal. Federal departments and agencies will work to achieve this goal by:

(a) providing for effective, efficient, and timely delivery of Federal preparedness assistance to State and local governments; and

(b) supporting efforts to ensure first responders are prepared to respond to major events, especially prevention of and response to threatened terrorist attacks.

(6) The national preparedness goal will establish measurable readiness priorities and targets that appropriately balance the potential threat and magnitude of terrorist attacks, major disasters, and other emergencies with the resources required to prevent, respond to, and recover from them. It will also include readiness metrics and elements that support the national preparedness goal including standards for preparedness assessments and strategies, and a system for assessing the Nation's overall preparedness to respond to major events, especially those involving acts of terrorism.

(7) The Secretary will submit the national preparedness goal to me through the Homeland Security Council (HSC) for review and approval prior to, or concurrently with, the Department of Homeland Security's Fiscal Year 2006 budget submission to the Office of Management and Budget.

Federal Preparedness Assistance

(8) The Secretary, in coordination with the Attorney General, the Secretary of Health and Human Services (HHS), and the heads of other Federal departments and agencies that provide assistance for first responder preparedness, will establish a single point of access to Federal preparedness assistance program information within 60 days of the issuance of this directive. The Secretary will submit to me through the HSC recommendations of specific Federal department and agency programs to be part of the coordinated approach. All Federal departments and agencies will cooperate with this effort. Agencies will continue to issue financial assistance awards consistent with applicable laws and regulations and will ensure that program announcements, solicitations, application instructions, and other guidance documents are consistent with other Federal preparedness programs

to the extent possible. Full implementation of a closely coordinated interagency grant process will be completed by September 30, 2005.

(9) To the extent permitted by law, the primary mechanism for delivery of Federal preparedness assistance will be awards to the States. Awards will be delivered in a form that allows the recipients to apply the assistance to the highest priority preparedness requirements at the appropriate level of government. To the extent permitted by law, Federal preparedness assistance will be predicated on adoption of Statewide comprehensive all-hazards preparedness strategies. The strategies should be consistent with the national preparedness goal, should assess the most effective ways to enhance preparedness, should address areas facing higher risk, especially to terrorism, and should also address local government concerns and Citizen Corps efforts. The Secretary, in coordination with the heads of other appropriate Federal departments and agencies, will review and approve strategies submitted by the States. To the extent permitted by law, adoption of approved Statewide strategies will be a requirement for receiving Federal preparedness assistance at all levels of government by September 30, 2005.

(10) In making allocations of Federal preparedness assistance to the States, the Secretary, the Attorney General, the Secretary of HHS, the Secretary of Transportation, the Secretary of Energy, the Secretary of Veterans Affairs, the Administrator of the Environmental Protection Agency, and the heads of other Federal departments and agencies that provide assistance for first responder preparedness will base those allocations on assessments of population concentrations, critical infrastructures, and other significant risk factors, particularly terrorism threats, to the extent permitted by law.

(11) Federal preparedness assistance will support State and local entities' efforts including planning, training, exercises, interoperability, and equipment acquisition for major events as well as capacity building for prevention activities such as information gathering, detection, deterrence, and collaboration related to terrorist attacks. Such assistance is not primarily intended to support existing capacity to address normal local first responder operations, but to build capacity to address major events, especially terrorism.

(12) The Attorney General, the Secretary of HHS, the Secretary of Transportation, the Secretary of Energy, the Secretary of Veterans Affairs, the Administrator of the Environmental Protection Agency, and the heads of other Federal departments and agencies that provide assistance for first responder preparedness shall coordinate with the Secretary to ensure that such assistance supports and is consistent with the national preparedness goal.

(13) Federal departments and agencies will develop appropriate mechanisms to ensure rapid obligation and disbursement of funds from their programs to the States, from States to the local community level, and from local entities to the end users to derive maximum benefit from the assistance provided. Federal departments and agencies will report annually to the Secretary on the obligation, expenditure status, and the use of funds associated with Federal preparedness assistance programs.

Equipment

(14) The Secretary, in coordination with State and local officials, first responder organizations, the private sector and other Federal civilian departments and agencies, shall establish and implement streamlined procedures for the ongoing development and adoption of appropriate first responder equipment standards that support nationwide interoperability and other capabilities consistent with the national preparedness goal, including the safety and health of first responders.

(15) To the extent permitted by law, equipment purchased through Federal preparedness assistance for first responders shall conform to equipment standards in place at time of purchase. Other Federal departments and agencies that support the purchase of first responder equipment will coordinate their programs with the Department of Homeland Security and conform to the same standards.

(16) The Secretary, in coordination with other appropriate Federal departments and agencies and in consultation with State and local governments, will develop plans to identify and address national first responder equipment research and development needs based upon assessments of current and future threats. Other Federal departments and agencies that support preparedness research and development activities shall coordinate their efforts with the Department of Homeland Security and ensure they support the national preparedness goal.

Training and Exercises

(17) The Secretary, in coordination with the Secretary of HHS, the Attorney General, and other appropriate Federal departments and agencies and in consultation with State and local governments, shall establish and maintain a comprehensive training program to meet the national preparedness goal. The program will identify standards and maximize the effectiveness of existing Federal programs and financial assistance and include training for the Nation's first responders, officials, and others with major event preparedness, prevention, response, and recovery roles. Federal departments and agencies shall include private organizations in the accreditation and delivery of preparedness training as appropriate and to the extent permitted by law.

(18) The Secretary, in coordination with other appropriate Federal departments and agencies, shall establish a national program

and a multi-year planning system to conduct homeland security preparedness-related exercises that reinforces identified training standards, provides for evaluation of readiness, and supports the national preparedness goal. The establishment and maintenance of the program will be conducted in maximum collaboration with State and local governments and appropriate private sector entities. All Federal departments and agencies that conduct national homeland security preparedness-related exercises shall participate in a collaborative, interagency process to designate such exercises on a consensus basis and create a master exercise calendar. The Secretary will ensure that exercises included in the calendar support the national preparedness goal. At the time of designation, Federal departments and agencies will identify their level of participation in national homeland security preparedness-related exercises. The Secretary will develop a multi-year national homeland security preparedness-related exercise plan and submit the plan to me through the HSC for review and approval.

(19) The Secretary shall develop and maintain a system to collect, analyze, and disseminate lessons learned, best practices, and information from exercises, training events, research, and other sources, including actual incidents, and establish procedures to improve national preparedness to prevent, respond to, and recover from major events. The Secretary, in coordination with other Federal departments and agencies and State and local governments, will identify relevant classes of homeland-security related information and appropriate means of transmission for the information to be included in the system. Federal departments and agencies are directed, and State and local governments are requested, to provide this information to the Secretary to the extent permitted by law.

Federal Department and Agency Preparedness

(20) The head of each Federal department or agency shall undertake actions to support the national preparedness goal, including adoption of quantifiable performance measurements in the areas of training, planning, equipment, and exercises for Federal incident management and asset preparedness, to the extent permitted by law. Specialized Federal assets such as teams, stockpiles, and caches shall be maintained at levels consistent with the national preparedness goal and be available for response activities as set forth in the National Response Plan, other appropriate operational documents, and applicable authorities or guidance. Relevant Federal regulatory requirements should be consistent with the national preparedness goal. Nothing in this directive shall limit the authority of the Secretary of Defense with regard to the command and control, training, planning, equipment, exercises, or employment of Department of Defense forces, or the allocation of Department of Defense resources.

(21) The Secretary, in coordination with other appropriate Federal civilian departments and agencies, shall develop and maintain a Federal response capability inventory that includes the performance parameters of the capability, the timeframe within which the capability can be brought to bear on an incident, and the readiness of such capability to respond to domestic incidents. The Department of Defense will provide to the Secretary information describing the organizations and functions within the Department of Defense that may be utilized to provide support to civil authorities during a domestic crisis.

Citizen Participation

(22) The Secretary shall work with other appropriate Federal departments and agencies as well as State and local governments and the private sector to encourage active citizen participation and involvement in

preparedness efforts. The Secretary shall periodically review and identify the best community practices for integrating private citizen capabilities into local preparedness efforts.

Public Communication

(23) The Secretary, in consultation with other Federal departments and agencies, State and local governments, and non-governmental organizations, shall develop a comprehensive plan to provide accurate and timely preparedness information to public citizens, first responders, units of government, the private sector, and other interested parties and mechanisms for coordination at all levels of government.

Assessment and Evaluation

(24) The Secretary shall provide to me through the Assistant to the President for Homeland Security an annual status report of the Nation's level of preparedness, including State capabilities, the readiness of Federal civil response assets, the utilization of mutual aid, and an assessment of how the Federal first responder preparedness assistance programs support the national

preparedness goal. The first report will be provided within 1 year of establishment of the national preparedness goal.

(25) Nothing in this directive alters, or impedes the ability to carry out, the authorities of the Federal departments and agencies to perform their responsibilities under law and consistent with applicable legal authorities and presidential guidance.

(26) Actions pertaining to the funding and administration of financial assistance and all other activities, efforts, and policies in this directive shall be executed in accordance with law. To the extent permitted by law, these policies will be established and carried out in consultation with State and local governments.

(27) This directive is intended only to improve the internal management of the executive branch of the Federal Government, and it is not intended to, and does not, create any right or benefit, substantive or procedural, enforceable at law or in equity, against the United States, its departments, agencies, or other entities, its officers or employees, or any other person.

GEORGE W. BUSH

Letter to the Speaker of the House of Representatives on Funding for the Department of the Treasury's Counterterrorism Fund
December 17, 2003

Dear Mr. Speaker:

In accordance with provisions of the Consolidated Appropriations Act, 2001 (Public Law 106–554), I hereby request and make available $7 million for the Department of the Treasury's Counterterrorism Fund. I hereby designate this $7 million as an emergency requirement pursuant to Public Law 106–554.

These funds would support Internal Revenue Service Criminal Investigation Service Agents in overseas and domestic counterterrorism efforts.

The details of this action are set forth in the enclosed letter from the Director of the Office of Management and Budget.

Sincerely,

GEORGE W. BUSH

Remarks to Medical Personnel at Walter Reed Army Medical Center
December 18, 2003

Thank you all very much. Thanks for the warm welcome. Laura and I are thrilled to be here at the Army Medical Center. We're thrilled because this is a place of love and healing and great compassion. This Center has a great history and an important mission, and that is, you are serving those who serve our country. In this time of war—and we are at war with an enemy that hates what America stands for—the good people of Walter Reed are giving the best of care to the men and women who have been wounded in action. During a difficult time in their lives, they count on you. You give them the kind, professional care and decency and hope they deserve. And on behalf of America, I thank you for your service.

Laura and I have had a great visit here. I know I'm not supposed to get out of my lane and give medical reports—[*laughter*]—but I can report that Colin Powell received great health care here and he is doing very well.

I want to thank General Kiley and Babs for your hospitality again. I appreciate Colonel Jaffin. I appreciate Colonel B.J. Mielcarek. She is—she's been kind of looking after my body on occasion too. [*Laughter*] Fortunately, she's got a lot to work with. [*Laughter*] But she's in charge of the physical therapy services. We've just come from her department, where we saw some incredible work being done and some brave soldiers who are working hard to get to 100 percent.

I appreciate Colonel Saulsbery, deputy commander for nursing; Colonel Greenwood; Colonel Fitzpatrick. And thank you all. I really appreciate the hard-working staff, the docs, the nurses, the people who make this fantastic facility operate in a way that makes me proud and in a way that will make every American proud when they learn your story.

Each one of you has got a demanding job, and it's a tough job here. I've seen your work firsthand. I know how tough it is. But I also know that you count it as a privilege to look after some exceptional Americans, people who are willing to sacrifice for their country.

When I spend time with members of our military, I'm impressed by the idealism and the concern for each other and the strong sense of duty that our soldiers feel. Members of the Armed Forces are now serving in a great cause, serving in an historic time. Peace and security of our fellow citizens depend upon their bravery and their willingness to serve. In so doing, our soldiers accept the dangers and the hardships that this cause sometimes requires. You know them well. I'm coming to know them. They're the finest of our citizens.

If you spend any time with these young men and women, you know that whether it's on the battlefield or in the hospital, our men and women are always thinking of one another. Even after being wounded, they often speak about returning to their units. And these aren't idle words. These are words that come from people who have seen the true nature of combat. I'm proud to be their Commander in Chief. I'm proud to lead such fine men and women who are willing to sacrifice for their country.

There's something else the wounded say, and they say it often, and they say it clearly. They praise you all, and they praise the incredible health care they receive here at Walter Reed. The doctors and nurses here are superb and dedicated and tireless. The administrative staff and the patient advocates and the chaplains are incredibly committed Americans and compassionate souls. You show concern for the patients, and you love their families as well. You give attention to the medical needs, to the emotional needs, and to the spiritual needs of those recently removed from the battlefield.

I want to thank the volunteers at Walter Reed. Many of you are veterans. Many of you have known war injuries of your own. You're a source of inspiration and your good advice for people who are in recovery. The country is grateful for your service in the past, and your country is very grateful for your continued service to help lift the spirits of those who have been wounded on the battlefield.

Military medicine is a model of professionalism and organization. It starts with the combat medic, the combat medic who is on the scene, the first health care a wounded soldier receives within moments of the injury. Patients are then treated by forward surgical teams and at combat support hospitals. I found it interesting that Walter Reed has more than 60 of its staff serving in the Iraqi theater today. You've moved your great medicine from this fantastic facility to the battlefront so that our soldiers get instant professional care.

Our wounded troops might next go to Landstuhl Medical Center in Germany, where they receive fine medical treatment before being delivered into your hands. Our fellow citizens must understand that every stop that a soldier makes from battlefield to Walter Reed is manned by a staff trained in every skill of trauma medicine.

This morning, I had a chance to visit, as I said, B.J.'s shop, which is the physical and occupational therapy facilities. Walter Reed is second to none in this kind of medicine. You're using the latest prosthetic technology to help patients overcome great challenges and resume their lives. I know firsthand—I remember coming here a couple of months ago to pin the Purple Heart on a fellow who lost both legs and one arm. Today I saw him walking. What makes this story even more profound is, he lost both legs and one arm not as a citizen of the United States but as a soldier fighting for the United States. Today I saw a citizen of the United States walking.

Americans would be surprised to learn that a grievous injury such as the loss of a limb no longer means forced discharge. In other words, the medical care is so good, and the recovery process is so technologically advanced, that people are no longer forced out of the military. When we're talking about forced discharge, we're talking about another age and another army. This is a new age, and this is a new army. And today, if wounded servicemembers want to remain in uniform and can do the job, the military tries to help them stay.

This country takes—asks a great deal of the men and women who serve our military. We're asking a lot of them, particularly in the first war of the 21st century. We put a lot of fine troops into harm's way to make this country more secure and the world more free and the world more peaceful. We ask them to face great dangers to meet a national need. In return, we have made a commitment. We have made a commitment to the troops, and we have made a commitment to their loved ones, and that commitment is that we will provide excellent health care—excellent care—to anybody who is injured on the battlefield.

Here at Walter Reed, all of you are making good on that commitment. You're saving the lives of liberators. You're healing the defenders of our country. You're comforting the champions of freedom. For that, every single person who works here has the respect and the gratitude of our entire Nation.

All of you here today are engaged in a great cause, a noble cause, an important cause for our country and for freedom and peace. By your good work, you're helping to protect America. And for that, your Commander in Chief says God bless, and thank you.

Happy holidays. Thank you all.

NOTE: The President spoke at noon in the Lawrence Joel Auditorium. In his remarks, he referred to Maj. Gen. Kevin Kiley, USA, commanding general, North Atlantic Regional Medical Command and Walter Reed Army Medical Center, and his wife, Babs; Col. Jonathan Jaffin, USA, commander, Walter Reed Health Care System; and Col. Billie Mielcarek, USA, chief of physical therapy, Col. Patricia A.H. Saulsbery, USA, deputy commander for nursing, Col. Jim Greenwood, USA, deputy commander for administration, and Col. Thomas M. Fitzpatrick, USA, deputy commander for clinical services, Walter Reed Army Medical Center. The Office of the Press Secretary also released a Spanish language transcript of these remarks.

Remarks on the Decision by Colonel Muammar Abu Minyar al-Qadhafi of Libya To Disclose and Dismantle Weapons of Mass Destruction Programs
December 19, 2003

Good evening. I have called you here today to announce a development of great importance in our continuing effort to prevent the spread of weapons of mass destruction. Today in Tripoli, the leader of Libya, Colonel Muammar al-Qadhafi, publicly confirmed his commitment to disclose and dismantle all weapons of mass destruction programs in his country. He has agreed immediately and unconditionally to allow inspectors from international organizations to enter Libya. These inspectors will render an accounting of all nuclear, chemical, and biological weapons programs and will help oversee their elimination. Colonel Qadhafi's commitment, once it is fulfilled, will make our country more safe and the world more peaceful.

Talks leading to this announcement began about 9 months ago when Prime Minister Tony Blair and I were contacted, through personal envoys, by Colonel Qadhafi. He communicated to us his willingness to make a decisive change in the policy of his Government. At the direction of Colonel Qadhafi himself, Libyan officials have provided American and British intelligence officers with documentation on that country's chemical, biological, nuclear, and ballistic missile programs and activities. Our experts in these fields have met directly with Libyan officials to learn additional details.

Opposing proliferation is one of the highest priorities of the war against terror. The attacks of September the 11th, 2001, brought tragedy to the United States and revealed a future threat of even greater magnitude. Terrorists who kill thousands of innocent people would, if they ever gained weapons of mass destruction, kill hundreds of thousands without hesitation and without mercy. And this danger is dramatically increased when regimes build or acquire weapons of mass destruction and maintain ties to terrorist groups.

The United States and our allies are applying a broad and active strategy to address the challenges of proliferation, through diplomacy and through the decisive actions that are sometimes needed. We've enhanced our intelligence capabilities in order to trace dangerous weapons activities. We've organized a Proliferation Security Initiative to interdict dangerous materials and technologies in transit. We've insisted on multilateral approaches, like that in North Korea, to confront threats. We are supporting the work of the International Atomic Energy Agency to hold the Iranian regime to its treaty obligations. We obtained an additional United Nations Security Council resolution requiring Saddam Hussein to prove that he had disarmed, and when that resolution was defied, we led a coalition to enforce it.

All of these actions by the United States and our allies have sent an unmistakable message to regimes that seek or possess weapons of mass destruction: Those weapons do not bring influence or prestige. They bring isolation and otherwise unwelcome consequences.

And another message should be equally clear: Leaders who abandon the pursuit of chemical, biological, and nuclear weapons and the means to deliver them will find an open path to better relations with the United States and other free nations.

With today's announcement by its leader, Libya has begun the process of rejoining the community of nations. And Colonel Qadhafi knows the way forward. Libya should carry out the commitments announced today. Libya should also fully engage in the war against terror. Its Government, in response to the United Nations Security Council's Lockerbie demands, has already renounced all acts of terrorism and pledged cooperation in the international fight against terrorism. We expect Libya to meet these commitments as well.

As the Libyan Government takes these essential steps and demonstrates its seriousness, its good faith will be returned. Libya can regain a secure and respected place among the nations and, over time, achieve far better relations with the United States. The Libyan people are heirs to an ancient and respected culture, and their country lies at the center of a vital region. As Libya becomes a more peaceful nation, it can be a source of stability in Africa and the Middle East. Should Libya pursue internal re-form, America would be ready to help its people to build a more free and prosperous country.

Great Britain shares this commitment, and Prime Minister Blair and I welcome today's declaration by Colonel Qadhafi. Because Libya has a troubled history with America and Britain, we will be vigilant in ensuring its Government lives up to all its responsibilities. Yet, as we have found with other nations, old hostilities do not need to go on forever. And I hope that other leaders will find an example in Libya's announcement today.

Our understanding with Libya came about through quiet diplomacy. It is a result, however, of policies and principles declared to all. Over the last 2 years, a great coalition of nations has come together to oppose terror and to oppose the spread of weapons of mass destruction. We've been clear in our purposes. We have shown resolve. In word and in action, we have clarified the choices left to potential adversaries. And when leaders make the wise and responsible choice, when they renounce terror and weapons of mass destruction, as Colonel Qadhafi has now done, they serve the interest of their own people, and they add to the security of all nations.

Thank you.

NOTE: The President spoke at 5:32 p.m. in the James S. Brady Briefing Room at the White House. In his remarks, he referred to Prime Minister Tony Blair of the United Kingdom; and former President Saddam Hussein of Iraq.

Statement on Signing the Defense Production Reauthorization Act of 2003
December 19, 2003

Today, I have signed into law S. 1680, the "Defense Production Reauthorization Act of 2003". The Act extends production-related authorities available to the President to provide support for the Armed Forces and meet important civil needs.

Section 123(c) of the Defense Production Act Amendments of 1992, as enacted by section 7(c) of the Act, purports to require the executive branch to undertake consultations with foreign nations on specific matters and to report thereon to the Congress. The executive branch shall construe section 123(c) in a manner consistent with the constitutional authorities of the President to conduct the Nation's foreign relations and to withhold information the disclosure of which could impair foreign relations, the national security, the deliberative processes of the Executive, or the performance of the Executive's constitutional duties.

GEORGE W. BUSH

The White House,
December 19, 2003.

NOTE: S. 1680, approved December 19, was assigned Public Law No. 108–195.

Statement on Signing the Federal Law Enforcement Pay and Benefits Parity Act of 2003
December 19, 2003

Today, I have signed into law S. 1683, the "Federal Law Enforcement Pay and Benefits Parity Act of 2003." The Act provides for a report on the pay and benefits of Federal law enforcement officers and for a program of law enforcement officer exchanges between the Federal Government and States or localities.

To the extent that section 2(b)(2) of the Act calls for submission by the executive branch of legislative recommendations, the executive branch shall implement the provision in a manner consistent with the President's constitutional authority to supervise the unitary executive branch and to submit for the consideration of the Congress such measures as the President judges necessary and expedient.

GEORGE W. BUSH

The White House,
December 19, 2003.

NOTE: S. 1683, approved December 19, was assigned Public Law No. 108–196.

Message on the Observance of Christmas 2003
December 19, 2003

Glory to God in the highest, and on earth peace, good will toward men.

LUKE 2:14

As families and friends gather to celebrate Christmas, we remember all the blessings that fill our lives, beginning with the great blessing that came on a holy night in Bethlehem. For Christians around the world, the birth of Jesus is a central religious event; an example of God's profound love for humanity; and the pathway to hope and to new life. Today, the Christmas story still speaks to every generation.

This holiday season, as we share in the spirit of giving and enjoy familiar Christmas traditions, we give thanks for the wonder of God's love and rededicate ourselves to helping those in need. We also pray for our brave men and women in uniform, many of whom will spend the holidays far from home. Their courage and dedication is helping keep us safe and extending free-dom and peace. We are grateful for their service to our country, and for the support and sacrifice of their families.

Laura joins me in wishing you a Merry Christmas and a Happy New Year. May the peace and goodwill of the season fill every heart and warm every home.

GEORGE W. BUSH

NOTE: An original was not available for verification of the content of this message. The Office of the Press Secretary also re-leased a Spanish language version of this message.

Message on the Observance of Hanukkah 2003
December 19, 2003

I send greetings to all those celebrating Hanukkah, the festival of lights.

During Hanukkah, people of the Jewish faith around the world mark the triumph of Jews against tyranny and oppression more than two millennia ago. With courage and unfailing faith, the Maccabees secured the Jewish people's freedom and reclaimed the Holy Temple in Jerusalem. As they pre-pared to rededicate the Temple, there was only enough oil for one day, but the light continued to burn for eight days. Today, the lighting of the Menorah represents this ancient miracle and brings a message of hope and freedom to the Jewish people.

As families and friends share in the joy-ous traditions of Hanukkah, we recognize the power of faith to accomplish miracles and bring light from the darkness. We join in giving thanks for the blessings God has granted to our Nation. May the joy of Ha-nukkah and the peace and goodwill of the season fill our hearts and inspire us to lead lives of compassion.

Laura joins me in wishing you a blessed and Happy Hanukkah.

GEORGE W. BUSH

NOTE: An original was not available for verification of the content of this message.

Message on the Observance of Kwanzaa 2003
December 19, 2003

I send greetings to those observing Kwanzaa.

Celebrated by millions across the world, Kwanzaa honors the history and heritage of Africa. This seven-day observance is an opportunity for individuals of African de-scent to remember the sacrifices of their ancestors and reflect on the *Nguzo Saba*. Kwanzaa's seven social and spiritual prin-ciples offer strength and guidance to meet the challenges of each new day.

During this joyous time of year, Ameri-cans renew our commitment to hope, un-derstanding, and the great promise of our Nation. In honoring the traditions of Africa, Kwanzaa strengthens the ties that bind in-dividuals in communities across our country and around the world.

Laura joins me in sending our best wish-es for a joyous Kwanzaa.

GEORGE W. BUSH

NOTE: An original was not available for verification of the content of this message.

The President's Radio Address
December 20, 2003

Good morning. Every year during the holidays, families across America gather to celebrate our blessings, and we unite to share those blessings with others. Particularly in this time of giving, our thoughts turn to fellow citizens who face hardship or illness or loneliness. Their burden often seems even greater at Christmastime, yet the hope of this season was meant for them as well.

The American people see these needs, and they are responding, as always, with great generosity. Just this week, a Government report found that more than 63 million Americans volunteered over the past year, about 4 million more than in the year before. On average, volunteers gave 52 hours—more than a full week of work—of their year in service to others. This increase in volunteering is evidence of the new culture of service we are building in America, especially among young people.

Nearly 2 years ago, I created the USA Freedom Corps to continue the momentum generated by the countless acts of kindness we saw after the attacks of September the 11th, 2001. I asked every person in America to commit 4,000 hours over a lifetime— or about 100 hours a year—to serving neighbors in need. The response was immediate and enthusiastic and has remained strong. Over 75,000 service organizations now work with USA Freedom Corps, and a growing percentage of Americans have answered the call to service.

Americans are volunteering in every region of the country and in nearly every part of the world. Many communities have formed Citizen Corps Councils to train neighborhoods in emergency response.

About 50,000 people are enrolled in AmeriCorps, which carries out vital work in education, the environment, and homeland security. And the Peace Corps expanded to over 7,500 volunteers in 2003, the highest level of participation in almost 3 decades.

Every time I travel in America, I have the honor to meet some of our country's most dedicated volunteers. They include people like Phuong Nguyen, a high school student in Denver who gives hours of her free time to lead service projects for the American Red Cross, and Ana Cooper of Miami, who helps senior citizens with daily needs like grocery shopping, and Bill Sellers, an 83-year-old man from Houston who has dedicated almost half his life to feeding the hungry. Some of the men and women I have met are members of the Armed Forces who volunteer time in their communities on top of their service to the Nation. And next week, I look forward to helping a generous group from Virginia distribute Angel Tree gifts to children whose parents are in prison.

America's 63 million volunteers are setting a fine example for our Nation. They are meeting essential needs in their communities, and they know the fulfillment that only comes from serving a cause greater than self. And many volunteers got started in the same way, because someone asked them.

This holiday season, I ask every American to look for a challenge in your own community and step forward to lend a hand. You can learn about thousands of service opportunities by visiting the USA Freedom Corps web site, usafreedomcorps.gov. Many Americans volunteer with their families, allowing them to spend time together while improving the lives of others. And if you find a need that no one else is meeting, you might want to start a group of your own.

The high level of voluntarism in our country is encouraging, though not surprising. America is a compassionate and generous land. With their good works, volunteers are living out the spirit of this season, and year-round they are showing the heart and soul of our people, which is the greatest strength of our Nation.

Thank you for listening.

NOTE: The address was recorded at 11:26 a.m. on December 19 in the Cabinet Room at the White House for broadcast at 10:06 a.m. on December 20. The transcript was made available by the Office of the Press Secretary on December 19 but was embargoed for release until the broadcast. The Office of the Press Secretary also released a Spanish language transcript of this address.

Remarks in a Visit With Angel Tree Children in Alexandria, Virginia
December 22, 2003

The President. Hey everybody.

Rev. Lee A. Earl. Mr. President.

The President. Thank you very much, Reverend Lee. Thank you so much for having us here. Lee, thank you very much. Merry Christmas to everybody.

Audience members. Merry Christmas.

The President. We are so honored to be here to celebrate the Angel Tree Christmas. This is a program in which people who love you a lot want you to have a merry Christmas. And I want to thank you. I want to thank Chuck Colson and Mark Earley of the Prison Fellowship program, which has been hosting and organizing the Angel Tree program since 1982. Six million boys and girls have received a gift on Christmas, and I want to thank you very much for doing that.

Our attitude is—I know that the reverend here at Shiloh shares this attitude—that we change America one heart and one soul at a time; that everybody matters, everybody counts; that every child has got a hopeful and bright future; and each of us has a responsibility of loving that child with all our heart and all our soul. And it's important that all of us during this time of—joyous time, this holiday, recognize that probably the greatest gift you can possibly give is to love a neighbor just like you'd like to be loved yourself.

And that's what we're doing today. We're honoring that call to love and the call to service. And so Laura and I are thrilled that you're here. We look forward to joining the good reverend here as we pass out some of the gifts to the boys and girls.

Reverend Earl. Absolutely. And thank you for the gifts that you've provided.

The President. Well, thank you very much. We're honored to be here.

We want to wish you a merry Christmas, and we've got some gifts to give out. Don't we, Laura?

The First Lady. Yes, we have a lot of gifts to give out.

The President. Where do we want to start?

The First Lady. I don't know where to start. [*Laughter*]

The President. Right over here? Okay, good.

NOTE: The President spoke at 3:20 p.m. at the Shiloh Baptist Church. In his remarks, he referred to Rev. Lee A. Earl, senior pastor, Shiloh Baptist Church; and Charles W.

Colson, founder, and Mark Earley, president, Prison Fellowship Ministries.

Remarks on Lighting the Hanukkah Menorah and an Exchange With Reporters
December 22, 2003

The President. Thank you all. Welcome.

Hanukkah celebrates a great miracle and a great victory, the triumph of faith over tyranny. More than 2,000 years ago, the land of ancient Israel had been conquered, and the practice of Judaism was outlawed. Yet a patriot named Judah Maccabee and his followers courageously captured Jerusalem. As the Maccabees prepared to rededicate the holy temple, they found enough oil to last for only one day. But the oil lasted for 8 days, a miracle that we remember by lighting the menorah.

The Jewish tradition calls on us to honor every commandment with works of beauty. This beautiful menorah, more than two centuries old, is from the Spertus Museum in Chicago, and Laura and I are honored to have it here at the White House.

I want to thank the Kol Sasson from the great University of Maryland for joining us today, and thank you for lending your beautiful voice for this occasion.

Tonight as we prepare to light the candles, we hope and pray that all who live under tyranny will see their day of freedom and that the light of faith will always shine through the darkness. We also pray for the brave men and women of our Armed Forces, many of whom are spending the holiday season far from home and their loved ones. We are grateful for their service

to America. We're grateful for the support and sacrifice of their families.

And now, Jacob Murphy and Sidney Hallem will help us light the candles. Their fathers are serving in our United States Armed Forces with distinction and with honor.

[At this point, the menorah was lit.]

Holiday Travel

Q. Mr. President, do you have any words for Americans who are worried about traveling this holiday season?

The President. My words are these: Our Government is doing everything we can to protect our country. We've got a lot of really decent, hard-working Americans who will be working over the holiday season to do everything we can to protect Americans from harm. And I want to thank them for their efforts, thank them for their hard work. American citizens need to go about their lives, but as they do so, they need to know that governments at all levels are working as hard as we possibly can to protect the American citizens.

Thank you all.

NOTE: The President spoke at 4:32 p.m. in the Bookseller's Area in the East Wing at the White House. In his remarks, he referred to a cappella singing group Kol Sasson.

Christmas Message to the Members of the Armed Forces
December 24, 2003

Laura and I send greetings to the men and women of our military. Many of you are far from home during the holidays. We know you miss the people you love, especially this time of year. Your family and friends and fellow citizens miss you too—and our whole country is proud of you.

All who serve in our military are protecting the American people in a time of challenge and danger. You are confronting terrorists abroad so that we don't have to face them in our own country, and so that people around the world can live in peace. By spreading freedom and democracy, you are making our future more secure.

As your Commander in Chief, I am proud of every one of you. Some of your comrades have been wounded, and we pray for their recovery. Some have given their lives. This Nation will never forget their service and sacrifice, and in this holiday season we pray that God will comfort the families they left behind.

The liberty we prize is not America's gift to the world; it is God's gift to humanity. Americans are blessed to have men and women like you protecting us, and defending the cause of freedom across the world. May God bless you, and may He watch over our country.

GEORGE W. BUSH

NOTE: This message was made available by the Office of the Press Secretary on December 25 and follows the text as printed in the December 24 edition of USA Today. An original was not available for verification of the content of this message.

Statement on the Earthquake in Iran
December 26, 2003

Laura and I heard this morning of the earthquake centered in the city of Bam, Iran. We are greatly saddened by the loss of life, injuries, and widespread damage to this ancient city. I extend my condolences to all those touched by this tragedy. The thoughts of all Americans are with the victims and their families at this time, and we stand ready to help the people of Iran.

The President's Radio Address
December 27, 2003

Good morning. In this week of Christmas, Laura and I send good wishes to the families of America. We hope this season has brought happy reunions, celebration, and new memories to cherish as we approach the new year.

Christmas centers on the birth of a child and on the message of hope and peace. We hear that message in many ways at Christmas, and it never loses the power to lift our hearts. The holidays can also deepen our sense of gratitude for life and for all the family and friends who fill our lives. In this great and prosperous land, we remember how much we have been given and how much we have to share.

We think of those among us who spend the holidays in sadness or solitude. We think of those facing illness or the loss of a loved one or the hardships of poverty or unemployment. And across our country, caring citizens are reaching out to those in need by volunteering their time. By serving a cause greater than themselves, Americans spread hope in our country, and they make our Nation better, one life at a time.

At Christmas, we also think of the men and women of our Armed Forces who are defending freedom around the world. These brave Americans are fighting terrorists in Afghanistan, Iraq, and elsewhere so that we do not meet these killers on our own streets. We are grateful for the courage and commitment of our troops, and we are safer because of their skill and sacrifice. Separation from loved ones is always difficult, especially at this time of year. All our men and women serving abroad can know that their families miss them, millions are praying for them, and their Nation is proud of them.

All who serve others are living out the spirit of the Christmas season. The story of Christmas is familiar to us all, yet it still brings inspiration and comfort and love to people everywhere. The voice first heard 20 centuries ago in Bethlehem stirs churches and communities to open homeless shelters and food pantries and job training centers to help those in need.

This Christmas season comes at a time of great challenge for our country. Yet the story of this holiday reminds us of an eternal promise, that God's purpose is justice and His plan is peace.

Thank you for listening.

NOTE: The address was recorded at 11:40 a.m. on December 22 in the Cabinet Room at the White House for broadcast at 10:06 a.m. on December 27. The transcript was made available by the Office of the Press Secretary on December 26 but was embargoed for release until the broadcast. The Office of the Press Secretary also released a Spanish language transcript of this address.

Letter to the Speaker of the House of Representatives Transmitting a Subsidy Budget Request for World Airways, Inc.
December 30, 2003

Dear Mr. Speaker:

Consistent with provisions of Public Law 107–42, the Air Transportation Safety and System Stabilization Act, 2001, I hereby notify the Congress of a $30 million Federal credit instrument for World Airways, Inc.

The details of this request are set forth in the enclosed letter from the Director of the Office of Management and Budget.

Sincerely,

GEORGE W. BUSH

Message on the Observance of New Year's Day, 2004
December 31, 2003

The past year has been a time of accomplishment and progress. Working together, our citizens have made America a safer, more prosperous, and better country. In the New Year, we will build on these successes, embracing the challenges and opportunities ahead.

We have seen our brave men and women in uniform defend America and liberate the oppressed. We pray for their safety, and we are grateful for their service and the support of their families.

In the past year, millions of people have answered the call to serve their neighbors in need. Americans from every walk of life are building a culture of compassion by devoting their time and talents to help others. In the New Year, I ask all Americans to answer the call to bring hope to those who are less fortunate.

I encourage every American to give thanks to God for His many blessings and to reaffirm our commitment to peace and freedom around the world. Laura joins me in wishing all Americans a Happy New Year. May God bless you, and may God continue to bless the United States of America.

GEORGE W. BUSH

NOTE: An original was not available for verification of the content of this message.

Appendix A—Digest of Other White House Announcements

The following list includes the President's public schedule and other items of general interest announced by the Office of the Press Secretary and not included elsewhere in this book.

July 1

In the morning, the President had an intelligence briefing and met with the National Security Council.

The President announced his intention to nominate Gwendolyn Brown to be Chief Financial Officer for the National Aeronautics and Space Administration.

The President announced his intention to nominate Jeane J. Kirkpatrick for the rank of Ambassador during her service as U.S. Representative on the Human Rights Commission of the Economic and Social Council of the United Nations.

The President announced his intention to appoint Joan Avalyn Dempsey as Executive Director of the President's Foreign Intelligence Advisory Board.

July 2

In the morning, the President had a telephone conversation with President Vladimir Putin of Russia to discuss the situations in Iran and North Korea. He then had intelligence and FBI briefings.

Later in the morning, the President met with Secretary of the Interior Gale A. Norton to discuss the National Park System. He then had separate telephone conversations with President Hosni Mubarak of Egypt and King Abdullah II of Jordan to discuss the peace process in the Middle East. Later, he met with Randall Tobias, his nominee to be Global AIDS Coordinator.

In the afternoon, the President had a telephone conversation with Prime Minister Ariel Sharon of Israel to discuss the peace process in the Middle East.

The President announced his intention to nominate Joel David Kaplan to be Deputy Director of the Office of Management and Budget.

The President announced his intention to nominate Donald K. Steinberg to be Ambassador to Nigeria.

The President declared a major disaster in Kentucky and ordered Federal aid to supplement Commonwealth and local recovery efforts in the area struck by severe storms, flooding, mud and rock slides, and tornadoes on June 14 and continuing.

July 3

In the morning, the President had intelligence and FBI briefings. Later, he had a telephone conversation with Prime Minister Mahmoud Abbas (Abu Mazen) of the Palestinian Authority to discuss the peace process in the Middle East.

July 4

In the morning, the President had an intelligence briefing and met with the National Security Council. Later, he traveled to Dayton, OH.

In the afternoon, the President returned to Washington, DC. Later, he attended a party hosted by Mrs. Bush to celebrate his upcoming 57th birthday.

In the evening, the President and Mrs. Bush viewed the Independence Day fireworks display on the National Mall from the Truman Balcony.

July 5

In the morning, the President had an intelligence briefing.

July 6

In the morning, the President and Mrs. Bush attended church services at St. John's Church in Lafayette Square.

July 7

In the morning, the President had intelligence and FBI briefings. Later, he traveled to Landover, MD.

In the afternoon, the President returned to Washington, DC.

In the evening, the President and Mrs. Bush traveled to Dakar, Senegal, arriving the next morning.

July 8

In the morning, the President had an intelligence briefing. Later, at the Presidential Palace, he and Mrs. Bush participated in a welcoming ceremony with President Abdoulaye Wade of Senegal and his wife, Viviane. Later, the two Presidents participated in a meeting followed by a photo opportunity with leaders of West African democracies, including President Mathieu Kerekou of Benin, President Pedro Pires of Cape Verde, President Yahya Jammeh of The Gambia, President John Agyekum Kufuor of Ghana, President Amadou Toumani Toure of Mali, President Mamadou Tandja of Niger, and President Ahmad Tejan Kabbah of Sierra Leone.

Later in the morning, the President and Mrs. Bush, with President Wade and Mrs. Wade, traveled to Goree Island, where they toured the House of Slaves.

In the afternoon, the President and Mrs. Bush traveled to Pretoria, South Africa, arriving in the evening.

The President announced his intention to nominate James Casey Kenny to be Ambassador to Ireland.

July 9

In the morning, the President had an intelligence briefing. Later, at Union House, he and Mrs. Bush participated in a welcoming ceremony with President Thabo Mbeki of South Africa and his wife, Zanele Dlamini.

In the afternoon, at the Presidential Guest House, the President and Mrs. Bush attended a luncheon hosted by President Mbeki and Mrs. Mbeki. Later, the President toured a Ford Motor Co. automobile assembly plant in Mamelodi, Pretoria, and participated in a roundtable discussion on AIDS prevention with Ford employees.

In the evening, at the U.S. Ambassador's residence, the President and Mrs. Bush attended a dinner with South African and U.S. business executives hosted by Ambassador Cameron R. Hume and his wife, Rigmor.

The President announced his intention to nominate Susan C. Schwab to be Deputy Secretary of the Treasury.

The President announced his intention to nominate Kenneth Leet to be Under Secretary of the Treasury for Domestic Finance.

July 10

In the morning, the President had an intelligence briefing. Later, at the Sheraton Pretoria Hotel, he met with U.S. Embassy employees and their families.

Later in the morning, the President and Mrs. Bush traveled to Gaborone, Botswana, where they participated in an arrival ceremony with President Festus Gontebanye Mogae of Botswana at Sir Seretse Khama International Airport. Later, at the Gaborone International Convention Centre, the President and Mrs. Bush, with President Mogae and his wife, Barbara, viewed Southern African Global Competitiveness Hub exhibits on trade between southern Africa and the U.S. and met with Botswanan businesspeople, including women business entrepreneurs.

In the afternoon, the President and Mrs. Bush toured the Mokolodi Nature Reserve.

Later in the afternoon, the President greeted U.S. Embassy employees and their families at Sir Seretse Khama International Airport. He and Mrs. Bush then traveled to Pretoria, South Africa.

The White House announced that the President will meet with United Nations Secretary-General Kofi Annan at the White House on July 14.

The President announced his intention to nominate Karan K. Bhatia to be Assistant Secretary of Transportation for Aviation and International Affairs.

The President announced his intention to nominate Cynthia R. Church to be Assistant Secretary of Veterans Affairs for Public and Intergovernmental Affairs.

The President announced his intention to nominate Domingo S. Herraiz to be Director of the Bureau of Justice Assistance.

The President announced his intention to nominate Leslie Silverman to be a member of the Equal Employment Opportunity Commission.

The President announced his intention to nominate Mauricio J. Tamargo to be Chairman of the Foreign Claims Settlement Commission of the United States.

The President announced his intention to designate Marianne Lamont Horinko as Acting Administrator of the Environmental Protection Agency.

The President announced his intention to designate Stephen L. Johnson as Acting Deputy

Administrator of the Environmental Protection Agency.

July 11

In the morning, the President had an intelligence briefing. Later, he and Mrs. Bush traveled to Entebbe, Uganda, arriving in the afternoon.

In the afternoon, the President and Mrs. Bush participated in an arrival ceremony with President Yoweri Kaguta Museveni of Uganda at Entebbe International Airport. Later, at the Imperial Botanical Beach Hotel, the President met with U.S. Embassy employees and their families.

Later in afternoon, at The AIDS Support Organisation (TASO) Centre, the President and Mrs. Bush, with President Museveni and his wife, Janet, toured facilities and listened to a performance of the Watoto Children's Choir. Later, the President and Mrs. Bush traveled to Abuja, Nigeria, arriving in the evening.

The White House announced that the President will welcome Prime Minister Tony Blair of the United Kingdom to the White House for a meeting and dinner on July 17.

The President announced his intention to nominate David Eisner to be Chief Executive Officer of the Corporation for National and Community Service.

The President announced his intention to nominate Constance A. Morella to be Representative of the U.S. to the Organization for Economic Cooperation and Development, with the rank of Ambassador.

The President declared a major disaster in Indiana and ordered Federal aid to supplement State and local recovery efforts in the area struck by severe storms, tornadoes, and flooding on July 4 and continuing.

July 12

In the morning, in Abuja, Nigeria, the President had an intelligence briefing. Later, in the courtyard of the Nicon Hilton Hotel, the President and Mrs. Bush met with U.S. Embassy employees and their families.

Later in the morning, at the Abuja National Hospital, the President and Mrs. Bush had a briefing on HIV/AIDS programs, toured laboratories, and participated in a roundtable discussion with medical staff and beneficiaries of HIV/AIDS mother-to-child transmission prevention programs.

Also in the morning, at Aso Presidential Villa, the President and Mrs. Bush participated in a welcoming ceremony with President Olusegun Obasanjo of Nigeria.

In the afternoon, the President and Mrs. Bush returned to Washington, DC, arriving in the evening.

July 14

In the morning, the President had intelligence and FBI briefings and met with the National Security Council. Later, in the Oval Office, he met with Secretary of Defense Donald H. Rumsfeld.

In the afternoon, the President had lunch with Gen. Tommy R. Franks, USA, former combatant commander, U.S. Central Command, and his wife, Cathryn, in honor of General Franks' retirement.

The White House announced that the President will host Prime Minister Silvio Berlusconi of Italy at the Bush Ranch in Crawford, TX, on July 20–21.

The President declared a major disaster in Arizona and ordered Federal aid to supplement State and local recovery efforts in the area struck by the Aspen fire on June 17 and continuing.

July 15

In the morning, the President had an intelligence briefing. Later, in the Oval Office, he met with Prime Minister Vladimir Spidla of the Czech Republic to discuss the situation in Iraq and Europe-U.S. relations.

Later in the morning, he met with Secretary of State Colin L. Powell.

In the afternoon, the President participated in a photo opportunity with teenagers involved in the Seeds of Peace camp program. Later, he met with bipartisan congressional leaders to discuss Medicare reform.

The White House announced that the President will host the G–8 Summit in Sea Island, GA, on June 8–10, 2004.

The President announced his intention to nominate Robert B. Charles to be Assistant Secretary of State for International Narcotics and Law Enforcement Affairs.

The President announced his intention to nominate Thomasina V. Rogers to be a member of the Occupational Safety and Health Review Commission.

The President declared a major disaster in Ohio and ordered Federal aid to supplement State and local recovery efforts in the area struck by severe storms and flooding on July 4 and continuing.

July 16

In the morning, the President had an intelligence briefing. Later, he made brief remarks to U.S. Attorneys at the Department of Justice headquarters building.

Later in the morning, the President met with economists.

In the afternoon, the President participated in the ceremonial swearing-in of Office of Management and Budget Director Joshua B. Bolten.

Later in the afternoon, the President met with Members of Congress to discuss African affairs.

In the evening, the President and Mrs. Bush hosted a reception in the Residence followed by a dinner on the State Floor for former President Gerald Ford and his wife, Betty, in honor of former President Ford's 90th birthday.

The President announced his intention to nominate George H. Walker to be Ambassador to Hungary.

July 17

In the morning, the President had an intelligence briefing and met with the National Security Council. Later, he met with Secretary of Defense Donald H. Rumsfeld.

In the afternoon, in the Oval Office, the President met with Veterans of Foreign Wars commander in chief Raymond C. Sisk. Later, he participated in an interview with a journalist from Leaders magazine.

Later in the afternoon, the President met with U.S. Ambassador to Japan Howard H. Baker, Jr. Later, in the Oval Office, he met with Prime Minister Tony Blair of the United Kingdom.

In the evening, the President and Mrs. Bush traveled to the Bush Ranch in Crawford, TX.

The White House announced that the President will welcome President Nestor Kirchner of Argentina to the White House on July 23.

The White House announced that the President will welcome Prime Minister Mahmoud Abbas (Abu Mazen) of the Palestinian Authority to the White House for a meeting and working lunch on July 25.

The White House announced that the President will welcome Prime Minister Ariel Sharon of Israel to the White House for a meeting and working lunch on July 29.

July 18

In the morning, the President had an intelligence briefing.

In the afternoon, the President and Mrs. Bush traveled to Dallas, TX, and in the evening, they returned to the Bush Ranch in Crawford, TX.

The White House announced that the President will award the Presidential Medal of Freedom to the following individuals in a ceremony at the White House on July 23:

Jacques Barzun;
Julia Child;
Roberto Clemente Walker;
Van Cliburn;
Vaclav Havel;
Charlton Heston;
Edward Teller;
R. David Thomas;
Byron Raymond White;
James Q. Wilson; and
John R. Wooden.

The President announced his intention to nominate John Joseph Grossenbacher to be a member of the Nuclear Regulatory Commission.

The President announced his intention to nominate Peter Lichtenbaum to be Assistant Secretary of Commerce for Export Administration.

The President announced his intention to designate Joan Ridder Challinor as Chairman of the National Commission on Libraries and Information Science.

The President declared a major disaster in Texas and ordered Federal aid to supplement State and local recovery efforts in the area struck by Hurricane Claudette on July 15 and continuing.

July 19

In the morning, the President had an intelligence briefing.

In the afternoon, the President and Mrs. Bush traveled to Houston, TX, and in the evening, they returned to the Bush Ranch in Crawford, TX.

July 20

In the afternoon, the President and Mrs. Bush welcomed Prime Minister Silvio Berlusconi of Italy to the Bush Ranch in Crawford, TX.

July 21

In the morning, the President had an intelligence briefing.

In the afternoon, the President and Mrs. Bush returned to Washington, DC.

The President declared a major disaster in Nebraska and ordered Federal aid to supplement State and local recovery efforts in the area struck by severe storms and tornadoes on June 9 through July 14.

July 22

In the morning, the President had an intelligence briefing. Later, he met with his Corporate Fraud Task Force to discuss progress in combating corporate fraud.

Later in the morning, the President met with his National Infrastructure Assurance Council to discuss progress in enhancing cybersecurity and the war on terrorism.

Also in the morning, the President communicated with Secretary of Defense Donald H. Rumsfeld concerning military operations in Iraq.

In the afternoon, at the Willard Intercontinental Hotel, the President made remarks at the Bush-Cheney '04, Inc., national finance committee meeting.

Later in the afternoon, the President hosted Members of Congress at the White House to discuss constituent concerns and other issues.

In the evening, the President hosted a reception for Republican Members of Congress.

The President announced his intention to nominate Kerry N. Weems to be Assistant Secretary of Health and Human Services for Management and Budget.

July 23

In the morning, the President had an intelligence briefing. Later, he met with L. Paul Bremer III, Presidential Envoy to Iraq, and Secretary of Defense Donald H. Rumsfeld to discuss the situation in Iraq.

Later in the morning, in Room 450 at the Dwight D. Eisenhower Executive Office Building, the President made brief remarks to State and national student leaders of the National FFA Organization. Later, in the Oval Office, he met with former President Vaclav Havel of the Czech Republic.

In the afternoon, in the Oval Office, the President met with President Nestor Kirchner of Argentina. Later, he met with the congres-

sional conference committee on Medicare reform.

In the evening, the President hosted a reception for Republican Members of Congress.

The President announced his intention to nominate Cristina Beato to be Assistant Secretary of Health and Human Services for Health.

The President announced his intention to nominate Jennifer Young to be Assistant Secretary of Health and Human Services for Legislation.

The President announced his intention to nominate Michael O'Grady to be Assistant Secretary of Health and Human Services for Planning and Evaluation.

The President announced his intention to designate Eugene Hickok as Acting Deputy Secretary of Education.

The President announced his intention to designate Ronald Tomalis as Acting Assistant Secretary for Elementary and Secondary Education.

July 24

In the morning, the President had an intelligence briefing. He also had a telephone conversation with President Roh Moo-hyun of South Korea to discuss the situation in North Korea.

Later in the morning, the President traveled to Philadelphia, PA, where he toured the Treasury Department's Philadelphia Financial Management Service regional center.

In the afternoon, the President traveled to Livonia, MI. Later, he traveled to Dearborn, MI.

In the evening, the President returned to Washington, DC.

The President announced his intention to appoint Michelle Van Cleave as National Counterintelligence Executive.

July 25

In the morning, the President had an intelligence briefing. Later, he met with Secretary of State Colin L. Powell.

In the afternoon, the President had lunch with Prime Minister Mahmoud Abbas (Abu Mazen) of the Palestinian Authority. Later, in Room 450 at the Dwight D. Eisenhower Executive Office Building, he made remarks to 2003 Boys and Girls Nation participants.

Later in the afternoon, the President traveled to Camp David, MD.

The President announced his intention to nominate Barbara McConnell Barrett to be Secretary of the Air Force.

July 26
In the morning, the President had an intelligence briefing.

July 27
In the afternoon, the President returned to Washington, DC. Later, he hosted a White House tee-ball game on the South Lawn and made welcoming remarks to the participants.

Also in the afternoon, the President had a telephone conversation with American cyclist Lance Armstrong to congratulate him on winning his fifth Tour de France earlier in the day.

July 28
In the morning, the President had an intelligence briefing. Later, he had a telephone conversation with Prime Minister Junichiro Koizumi of Japan to discuss the situations in Iraq and North Korea and economic development in Japan.

Later in the morning, the President traveled to Pittsburgh, PA.

In the afternoon, the President returned to Washington, DC.

July 29
In the morning, the President had an intelligence briefing.

In the afternoon, in the Old Family Dining Room, the President had lunch with Prime Minister Ariel Sharon of Israel. Later, he met with Foreign Minister Saud al-Faysal al Saud and Ambassador to the U.S. Prince Bandar of Saudi Arabia to discuss the recent congressional report on the September 11, 2001, terrorist attacks.

Later in the afternoon, the President met with a bipartisan group of Senators to discuss proposed energy legislation.

The President announced his intention to appoint Duane Acklie as a member of the Board of Directors of the Student Loan Marketing Association and, upon appointment, to designate him as chairman.

The President declared a major disaster in Florida and ordered Federal aid to supplement State and local recovery efforts in the area struck by severe storms and flooding on June 13 and continuing.

The President declared a major disaster in Tennessee and ordered Federal aid to supplement State and local recovery efforts in the area struck by severe storms, high winds, and heavy rain on July 21–22.

July 30
In the morning, the President had an intelligence briefing. He also had a telephone conversation with President Hu Jintao of China to discuss the situation in North Korea.

The President announced his intention to reappoint William K. Sessions III as a Vice Chair of the U.S. Sentencing Commission.

The President announced his intention to nominate Pamela P. Willeford to be Ambassador to Switzerland and concurrently to Liechtenstein.

The President announced his designation of William H. Campbell as Acting Assistant Secretary of Veterans Affairs for Human Resources and Administration.

July 31
In the morning, the President had an intelligence briefing. Later, he met with Secretary of State Colin L. Powell.

In the afternoon, the President had lunch with Vice President Dick Cheney.

The President announced his intention to nominate Michele M. Leonhart to be Deputy Administrator of Drug Enforcement at the Drug Enforcement Administration.

The President announced his designation of Karen P. Tandy as Acting Administrator of Drug Enforcement at the Drug Enforcement Administration.

August 1
In the morning, the President had an intelligence briefing.

The President announced his intention to nominate Richard Eugene Hoagland to be Ambassador to Tajikistan.

The President declared a major disaster in North Dakota and ordered Federal aid to supplement State and local recovery efforts in the area struck by severe storms and high winds on June 24–25.

The President declared a major disaster in Ohio and ordered Federal aid to supplement State and local recovery efforts in the area struck by tornadoes, flooding, severe storms, and high winds on July 21 and continuing.

August 2

In the morning, the President had an intelligence briefing. Later, he traveled to the National Naval Medical Center in Bethesda, MD, where he had his annual physical examination and visited U.S. military personnel injured in operations in Iraq.

Later in the morning, the President traveled to the Bush Ranch in Crawford, TX.

August 3

In the morning, the President had a telephone conversation with members of the U.S. women's gymnastics team to congratulate them on winning a gold medal at the Pan American Games in the Dominican Republic.

August 4

In the morning, the President had an intelligence briefing.

August 5

In the morning, the President had an intelligence briefing.

In the evening, the President had dinner with Secretary of State Colin L. Powell and Deputy Secretary of State Richard L. Armitage.

The President announced his intention to nominate David L. Lyon to be Ambassador to Kiribati.

The President announced his intention to nominate William A. Chatfield to be the Director of Selective Service.

August 6

In the morning, the President had an intelligence briefing. Later, he had a meeting and then lunch with Secretary of State Colin L. Powell and Deputy Secretary of State Richard L. Armitage.

August 7

In the morning, the President had intelligence and national security briefings.

August 8

In the morning, the President had an intelligence briefing. Later, he met with Vice President Dick Cheney, Secretary of Defense Donald H. Rumsfeld, Chairman of the Joint Chiefs of Staff Gen. Richard B. Myers, USAF, National Security Adviser Condoleezza Rice, and other officials to discuss military issues.

August 9

In the morning, the President had an intelligence briefing.

In the afternoon, the President hosted a barbecue for Bush-Cheney '04, Inc., fundraisers at a neighboring ranch in Crawford.

August 11

In the morning, the President had intelligence and national security briefings aboard Air Force One en route to Tucson, AZ. Upon his arrival in Tucson, he met with USA Freedom Corps volunteer Deborah Toland. Later, he traveled to Coronado National Forest. En route, he took an aerial tour of areas damaged by wildfire near Summerhaven, AZ.

Later in the morning, the President traveled to Denver, CO, where he met with USA Freedom Corps volunteer Phuong Nguyen.

In the evening, the President returned to the Bush Ranch in Crawford, TX.

August 12

In the morning, the President had intelligence and national security briefings.

The President announced his designation of the following individuals as members of the Presidential delegation to the inauguration of President Nicanor Duarte Frutos of Paraguay on August 15: Anthony J. Principi (head of delegation), John F. Keane, and Robert L. Peeler.

August 13

In the morning, the President had intelligence and national security briefings, during which he had a video conference call to discuss the capture of Al Qaida terrorist Nurjaman Riduan Isamuddin (also known as Hambali).

Later in the morning, the President met with members of his economic team.

The President announced his intention to appoint Duane H. Laible as a member of the Arctic Research Commission.

The President announced his intention to appoint Sandra O. Sieber as a member of the Committee for Purchase From People Who Are Blind or Severely Disabled.

The President announced his intention to appoint Peter Field as Federal Commissioner and Alternate Federal Commissioner of the Apalachicola-Chattahoochie-Flint River (ACF) Basin Commission.

The President announced his intention to appoint Charles J. Chaput, Khaled Abou El Fadl, and Richard D. Land as members of the U.S.

Commission on International Religious Freedom.

August 14

In the morning, the President had an intelligence briefing. Later, he traveled to the Marine Corps Air Station in Miramar, CA.

In the afternoon, the President had lunch with U.S. military personnel. During lunch, he was informed by White House Deputy Chief of Staff Joseph W. Hagin of the power blackout in portions of the Northeastern and Midwestern United States and Canada. Later, he received updates on the blackout from Deputy Hagin and Deputy National Security Adviser Stephen J. Hadley.

Later in the afternoon, the President participated in an interview with Armed Forces Radio and Television journalists. Later, he had a telephone conversation with Secretary of Homeland Security Tom Ridge to discuss the blackout. He also received updates on the blackout from Deputies Hagin and Hadley and White House Chief of Staff Andrew H. Card, Jr.

Later in the afternoon, the President traveled to San Diego, CA.

In the evening, the President traveled to Newport Beach, CA.

August 15

In the morning, the President had intelligence and national security briefings. He then had a telephone conversation with Secretary of the Treasury John Snow to discuss the status of the stock markets during the blackout. Later, he traveled to Thousand Oaks, CA, where he toured the Santa Monica Mountains National Recreation Area.

Later in the morning, the President traveled to Irvine, CA, where he had telephone conversations from the Hyatt Regency Irvine with Governors George E. Pataki of New York, John G. Rowland of Connecticut, Jennifer Granholm of Michigan, and Bob Taft of Ohio and Mayor Michael Bloomberg of New York City to discuss the blackouts.

In the afternoon, the President returned to the Bush Ranch in Crawford, TX. While en route aboard Air Force One, he had a telephone conversation with Prime Minister Jean Chretien of Canada to discuss the blackout.

During the day, the President received updates on the blackout from Deputies Hagin and Hadley and other officials.

August 16

In the morning, the President had an intelligence briefing.

August 18

In the morning, the President had an intelligence briefing. Later, he had a telephone conversation with Energy Secretary Spencer Abraham to discuss the recent power blackout in portions of the Northeastern and Midwestern United States and Canada.

August 19

In the morning, the President had an intelligence briefing.

In the evening, the President had a telephone conversation with President Luiz Inacio Lula da Silva of Brazil to express his condolences concerning the death of Brazilian citizen Sergio Vieira de Mello, Special Representative of the United Nations Secretary-General to Iraq, who died in the August 18 terrorist bombing of the U.N. headquarters in Baghdad. Later, he had a telephone conversation with Prime Minister Tony Blair of the United Kingdom to discuss the Baghdad terrorist attack.

August 20

In the morning, the President had a telephone conversation with Prime Minister Ariel Sharon of Israel to discuss the August 18 terrorist attack in Jerusalem. He then had an intelligence briefing.

Later in the morning, the President participated in a video conference call with the National Security Council, including Ambassador L. Paul Bremer III, Presidential Envoy to Iraq, and Gen. John P. Abizaid, USA, combatant commander, U.S. Central Command.

August 21

In the morning, the President had an intelligence briefing. Later, he traveled to Portland, OR.

In the afternoon, the President traveled to Redmond, OR, where he participated in a briefing on the Bear Butte and Booth fires in Deschutes National Forest. Later, aboard Marine One, he took an aerial tour of the forest fires.

Later in the afternoon, the President traveled to Bend, OR.

The President announced his intention to nominate Hugh Douglas Barclay to be Ambassador to El Salvador.

The President announced his intention to nominate Michael David Gallagher to be Assistant Secretary of Commerce for Communications and Information.

The President announced his intention to appoint Lydia Irene Beebe, William Wilson III, and Joseph Thomas Yew, Jr., as members of the Board of Directors of the Presidio Trust.

The President announced his intention to appoint Carl Michael Morgan, Jr., and Deborah Doris Wetsit as members of the President's Board of Advisors on Tribal Colleges and Universities.

August 22

In the morning, the President traveled to Burbank, WA. While en route aboard Air Force One, he had an intelligence briefing. Following his arrival, he participated in a briefing and tour of Ice Harbor Lock and Dam. Later, he traveled to Seattle, WA.

In the afternoon, the President attended a Bush-Cheney luncheon at a private residence. Later, he returned to the Bush Ranch in Crawford, TX.

The President announced his intention to nominate Gordon England to be Secretary of the Navy.

August 23

In the morning, the President had an intelligence briefing.

The President declared a major disaster in Pennsylvania and ordered Federal aid to supplement Commonwealth and local recovery efforts in the area struck by severe storms, tornadoes, and flooding on July 21 and continuing.

The President declared an emergency in New York and ordered Federal aid to supplement State and local response efforts in the area impacted by a statewide power outage on August 14–16.

August 25

In the morning, the President had intelligence and FBI briefings.

The White House announced that the President will welcome Prime Minister Sabah al-Ahmad al-Jabir al-Sabah of Kuwait to the White House on September 10.

The President announced the recess appointments of Charlotte A. Lane and Daniel Pearson as members of the U.S. International Trade Commission.

The President announced the recess appointment of A. Paul Anderson as a Federal Maritime Commissioner.

The President announced the recess appointment of Daniel Pipes as a member of the Board of Directors of the U.S. Institute of Peace.

The President announced the recess appointment of John Paul Woodley, Jr., as Assistant Secretary of the Army for Civil Works.

The President announced the recess appointments of David W. Fleming, Jay Phillip Greene, and John Richard Petrocik as members of the Board of Trustees of the James Madison Memorial Fellowship Foundation.

The President announced the recess appointments of Juanita Alicia Vasquez-Gardner and Patrick Lloyd McCrory as members of the Board of Trustees of the Harry S. Truman Scholarship Foundation.

The President announced the recess appointments of Jose A. Fourquet, Adolfo A. Franco, and Roger Francisco Noriega as members of the Board of Directors of the Inter-American Foundation.

The President announced the recess appointments of Ephraim Batambuze and Walter H. Kansteiner as members of the Board of Directors of the African Development Foundation.

August 26

In the morning, the President had an intelligence briefing. Later, he traveled to Minneapolis, MN. While en route aboard Air Force One, he had a telephone conversation with Prime Minister Atal Bihari Vajpayee of India to express his condolences and offer assistance concerning the August 25 terrorist attacks in Mumbai, India. Upon his arrival in Minneapolis, he met with USA Freedom Corps volunteers Edward and Jane Bardon.

In the afternoon, the President traveled to St. Louis, MO, where he met with American Legion member and volunteer James Mareschal.

In the evening, the President returned to the Bush Ranch in Crawford, TX.

The White House announced that the President will welcome Prime Minister Jan Peter Balkenende of the Netherlands to the White House on September 3 for a working breakfast.

August 27

In the morning, the President had intelligence and FBI briefings. Later, he had a videoconference with senior national security advisers.

In the evening, at the Bush Ranch, the President and Mrs. Bush hosted a tour and barbecue for members of the White House press corps.

August 28

In the morning, the President had intelligence and FBI briefings.

August 29

In the morning, the President had intelligence and FBI briefings.

The President declared a major disaster in New York and ordered Federal aid to supplement State and local recovery efforts in the area struck by severe storms, flooding, and tornadoes on July 21–August 13.

August 30

In the morning, the President had an intelligence briefing. Later, he and Mrs. Bush returned to Washington, DC. Before departing from the Texas State Technical College Waco Airport in Waco, TX, they greeted members of the Midway All-Stars Little League girls softball team.

September 1

In the morning, the President had an intelligence briefing. Later, he traveled to Cleveland, OH, where he met with USA Freedom Corps volunteer Shirley Moore. He then traveled to Richfield, OH.

In the afternoon, the President returned to Washington, DC.

September 2

In the morning, the President had intelligence and FBI briefings. Later, in the Oval Office, he met with Mississippi State officials who recently switched to the Republican Party.

In the afternoon, the President had lunch with Federal Reserve Chairman Alan Greenspan. Later, in the Oval Office, he participated in the presentation of the game football for the opening game of the 2003 National Football League season to be held September 4. He then met with Secretary of State Colin L. Powell.

The White House announced that beginning September 16 the White House will be open to tours on an expanded basis to parties through their Members of Congress.

September 3

In the morning, the President had breakfast and a meeting with Prime Minister Jan Peter Balkenende and Minister of Foreign Affairs Jakob Gijshert "Jaap" de Hoop Scheffer of the Netherlands. Later, he had intelligence and FBI briefings.

Later in the morning, the President met with Secretary of Defense Donald H. Rumsfeld.

In the afternoon, the President met with Speaker of the House of Representatives J. Dennis Hastert and Senate Majority Leader Bill Frist. He then met with Republican congressional leaders to discuss the congressional agenda.

The White House announced that the President will meet with Prime Minister Mir Zafarullah Khan Jamali of Pakistan at the White House on October 1.

The President announced his intention to nominate William J. Hudson to be Ambassador to Tunisia.

The President announced his intention to nominate Hector Elias Morales to be U.S. Alternate Executive Director of the Inter-American Development Bank.

The President announced his intention to nominate Jeffrey Adam Rosen to be General Counsel of the Department of Transportation.

The President announced his intention to nominate Susan Krouner Sclafani to be Assistant Secretary for Vocational and Adult Education and to designate her as Acting Assistant Secretary for Vocational and Adult Education.

The President announced his intention to nominate Michael Walter Wynne to be Under Secretary of Defense for Acquisition, Technology, and Logistics.

The President announced his intention to designate Michele Marie Leonhart as Acting Deputy Administrator of Drug Enforcement.

The President announced his intention to nominate Bradley Deck Belt to be a member of the Social Security Advisory Board.

The President announced his intention to nominate James McBride to be a member of the National Council on the Arts.

The President announced his intention to appoint the following individuals as members of the J. William Fulbright Foreign Scholarship Board:

Robert H. Bruininks;
John S. Butler;
Shirley M. Green; and
Thomas T. Lyons.

The President announced his intention to appoint Karen S. Evans as Administrator of the Office of Electronic Government, Office of Management and Budget.

September 4

In the morning, the President had intelligence and FBI briefings. Later, in the Oval Office, he participated in a signing ceremony for the Prison Rape Elimination Act of 2003.

Later in the morning, the President traveled to Kansas City, MO.

In the afternoon, the President returned to Washington, DC. Later, he participated in an interview with journalist Ron Insana from the CNBC television network.

September 5

In the morning, the President had intelligence and FBI briefings.

In the afternoon, the President traveled to Indianapolis, IN, where he met with families and small-business owners.

In the evening, the President traveled to Camp David, MD.

The President declared a major disaster in Indiana and ordered Federal aid to supplement State and local recovery efforts in the area struck by severe storms, tornadoes, and flooding on August 26 and continuing.

September 6

In the morning, the President had an intelligence briefing.

September 7

In the afternoon, the President and Mrs. Bush returned to Washington, DC. Later, they attended a White House tee-ball game on the South Lawn.

September 8

In the morning, the President had separate telephone conversations with President Luiz Inacio Lula da Silva of Brazil to discuss the upcoming World Trade Organization (WTO) ministerial meeting in Cancun, Mexico; and President Aleksander Kwasniewski of Poland to discuss the situations in Iraq and the Middle East and the war on terror. Later, he had intelligence and FBI briefings.

Later in the morning, the President had separate telephone conversations with Prime Minister Atal Bihari Vajpayee of India to discuss the upcoming WTO meeting and a potential

United Nations Security Council resolution on Iraq; and President Pervez Musharraf of Pakistan to discuss the WTO meeting.

Later, in an Oval Office ceremony, the President received diplomatic credentials from Ambassadors Mikhail M. Khvostov of Belarus, Abdoulaye Diop of Mali, Raul Gangotena Rivadeneira of Ecuador, Jose Octavio Bordon of Argentina, Rastislav Kacer of the Slovak Republic, Evan Jeremy Paki of Papua New Guinea, Barbara Joyce Masekela of South Africa, Juri Luik of Estonia, and Sir David Manning of the United Kingdom.

In the afternoon, the President traveled to Nashville, TN. While en route aboard Air Force One, he had a telephone conversation with President Thabo Mbeki of South Africa to discuss the upcoming WTO meeting.

Upon arrival, he met with USA Freedom Corps volunteer Brenda Wilson. Later, he toured the Tutoring Center at Kirkpatrick Elementary School.

In the evening, the President returned to Washington, DC.

The President announced his designation of Robert D. McCallum, Jr., as Acting Deputy Attorney General.

September 9

In the morning, the President had intelligence and FBI briefings. Later, he traveled to Jacksonville, FL, where, upon arrival, he met with USA Freedom Corps volunteer Daniel Trifiletti.

In the afternoon, the President participated in a briefing on educational tools available to parents and teachers at Hyde Park Elementary School.

In the evening, the President returned to Washington, DC.

The President announced his intention to nominate Roger Walton Ferguson, Jr., to be Vice Chairman of the Board of Governors of the Federal Reserve System.

The President announced his intention to nominate Ben S. Bernanke to be a member of the Board of Governors of the Federal Reserve System for the Sixth District.

September 10

In the morning, the President had intelligence and FBI briefings and then met with Secretary of Defense Donald H. Rumsfeld. Later, he met with the Dalai Lama of Tibet to discuss Tibetan-Chinese relations.

In the afternoon, the President had lunch with Prime Minister Sabah al-Ahmad al-Jabir al-Sabah of Kuwait, following their meeting in the Oval Office. Later, he traveled to Quantico, VA, where he toured the FBI laboratory.

In the evening, at the White House, the President hosted a dinner and screening of "Twin Towers," a documentary film on the terrorist attacks on the World Trade Center on September 11, 2001.

September 11

In the morning, at St. John's Episcopal Church in Washington, DC, the President and Mrs. Bush attended a prayer service commemorating the September 11 terrorist attacks. Later, on the South Lawn, they observed a moment of silence with Vice President Dick Cheney and Mrs. Cheney and White House staff for victims of the September 11 attacks.

Later in the morning, the President had intelligence and FBI briefings and then met with Secretary of State Colin L. Powell.

In the afternoon, the President went to Walter Reed Army Medical Center, where he visited U.S. military personnel injured in Iraq and their family members. He also presented Purple Heart awards to certain personnel.

The White House announced that the President will host King Abdullah II and Queen Rania of Jordan at Camp David, MD, on September 18–19.

September 12

In the morning, the President had an intelligence briefing. Later, he traveled to Fort Stewart, GA. While en route aboard Air Force One, he had a telephone conversation with President Nestor Kirchner of Argentina to discuss the International Monetary Fund agreement that was reached earlier in the week. He also had a telephone conversation with Prime Minister Goran Persson of Sweden to extend his condolences concerning the death of Swedish Foreign Minister Anna Lindh. Also en route, he met with Senators Zell Miller and Saxby Chambliss and Representatives Jack Kingston and Max Burns of Georgia.

In the afternoon, at Fort Stewart, the President presented the Presidential Unit Citation to the 3d Infantry Division of the U.S. Army.

Later in the afternoon, the President traveled to Jackson, MS. Later, he traveled to Houston, TX.

In the evening, the President traveled to Camp David, MD.

The White House announced that the President will visit the United Nations in New York on September 23–24 to address the General Assembly on the opening day of the General Debate, and that he will meet with U.N. Secretary-General Kofi Annan, Foreign Minister Julian Hunte of Saint Lucia, who is the incoming General Assembly President, and other foreign leaders.

The White House announced that the President will host President Mwai Kibaki of Kenya for a state visit on October 6.

The President announced his intention to nominate Robert L. Crandall, Louis S. Thompson, and Floyd Hall to be members of the Amtrak Reform Board.

The President announced his intention to nominate Gracia M. Hillman and Raymundo Martinez III to be members of the Election Assistance Commission.

The President announced his intention to nominate David Wayne Anderson to be Assistant Secretary of the Interior for Indian Affairs.

The President announced his intention to nominate W. Robert Pearson to be Director General of Foreign Service, and to appoint him as Chairman of the Board of the Foreign Service.

The President announced his intention to nominate Read Van de Water to be a member of the National Mediation Board.

The President declared a major disaster in Vermont and ordered Federal aid to supplement State and local recovery efforts in the area struck by severe storms and flooding on July 21 through August 18.

The President declared a major disaster in New Hampshire and ordered Federal aid to supplement State and local recovery efforts in the area struck by severe storms and flooding on July 21 through August 18.

September 13

In the morning, the President had an intelligence briefing.

September 14

In the afternoon, the President returned to Washington, DC.

September 15

In the morning, the President had an intelligence briefing. Later, he traveled to Monroe,

MI, where, upon arrival, he met with USA Freedom Corps volunteer Claire Jennings. Later, he toured the Detroit Edison Powerplant.

In the afternoon, the President traveled to Drexel Hill, PA, where, upon arrival, he met with USA Freedom Corps volunteer David Richman.

In the evening, the President returned to Washington, DC.

The White House announced that the President and Mrs. Bush will welcome President Vladimir Putin of Russia and Mrs. Putin to Camp David, MD, on September 26–27.

September 16

In the morning, the President had a telephone conversation with Prime Minister Tony Blair of the United Kingdom to discuss the situation in Iraq. He then had intelligence and FBI briefings. Later, he participated in a roundtable interview with regional media.

Later in the morning, in the Oval Office, the President met with musician and activist Bono to discuss U.S. contributions to AIDS relief in Africa.

In the afternoon, in the Roosevelt Room, the President participated in a roundtable discussion on the Clear Skies Initiative legislation with State, local, and community leaders.

Later in the afternoon, in the Residence, the President hosted Republican Senators.

The White House announced that the President has invited President Nicanor Duarte Frutos of Paraguay to meet with him at the White House on September 26.

September 17

In the morning, the President had an intelligence briefing and then met with the National Security Council. Later, he met with Secretary of Defense Donald H. Rumsfeld.

Later in the morning, in the Roosevelt Room, the President had a briefing on Hurricane Isabel.

In the afternoon, the President met with Secretary of State Colin L. Powell.

In the evening, the President traveled to Camp David, MD.

The President announced his intention to nominate Benjamin A. Gilman to be U.S. Representative to the General Assembly of the United Nations.

The President announced his intention to nominate Ann M. Corkery and Walid Maalouf to be U.S. Alternate Representatives to the General Assembly of the United Nations.

The President announced his intention to nominate William Cabaniss to be Ambassador to the Czech Republic.

The President announced his intention to nominate Roderick R. Paige and Louise V. Oliver to be U.S. Representatives to the General Conference of the United Nations Educational, Scientific, and Cultural Organization.

The President announced his intention to nominate Bernice Phillips to be a member of the Board of Directors of the Legal Services Corporation.

The President announced his intention to nominate Kirk Van Tine to be Deputy Secretary of Transportation.

September 18

In the morning, the President had an intelligence briefing. Later, he and Mrs. Bush welcomed King Abdullah II and Queen Rania of Jordan to Camp David for an overnight visit.

The President declared a major disaster in North Carolina and ordered Federal aid to supplement State and local recovery efforts in the area struck by Hurricane Isabel on September 18 and continuing.

The President declared a major disaster in Virginia and ordered Federal aid to supplement Commonwealth and local recovery efforts in the area struck by Hurricane Isabel on September 18 and continuing.

September 19

In the morning, the President had an intelligence briefing.

The President declared a major disaster in Maryland and ordered Federal aid to supplement State and local recovery efforts in the area struck by Hurricane Isabel on September 18 and continuing.

September 20

In the morning, the President had an intelligence briefing.

The President declared a major disaster in the District of Columbia and ordered Federal aid to supplement the District's recovery efforts in the area struck by Hurricane Isabel on September 18 and continuing.

The President declared a major disaster in Delaware and ordered Federal aid to supplement State and local recovery efforts in the area struck by Hurricane Isabel on September 18 and continuing.

September 21

In the afternoon, the President returned to Washington, DC.

September 22

In the morning, the President had an intelligence briefing. Later, he met with Special Presidential Envoy for Afghanistan Zalmay Khalilzad. He then met with Minister of Foreign Affairs Li Zhaoxing of China to discuss the situation in North Korea.

Later in the morning, the President met with Labor Secretary Elaine L. Chao, Housing and Urban Development Secretary Mel R. Martinez, Deputy Education Secretary Eugene Hickok, Deputy Veterans Affairs Secretary Leo S. Mackay, Jr., Assistant Attorney General Daniel J. Bryant, Deputy Secretary of Health and Human Services Claude A. Allen, USA Freedom Corps Director John Bridgeland, and Office of Faith-Based and Community Initiatives Director Harry James "Jim" Towey to discuss his Faith-Based Initiative.

In the afternoon, the President traveled to Richmond, VA, where he toured the Temporary Virginia Emergency Operations Center at the Virginia State Police Academy. Later, he returned to Washington, DC.

The President announced his intention to nominate Zalmay Khalilzad to be Ambassador to Afghanistan.

The President announced his intention to nominate Raymond Simon to be Assistant Secretary for Elementary and Secondary Education.

The President announced his intention to nominate Cynthia Boich, Dorothy A. Johnson, and Henry Lozano to be members of the Board of Directors of the Corporation for National and Community Service.

September 23

In the morning, the President and Mrs. Bush traveled to New York City. While en route aboard Air Force One, he had an intelligence briefing.

Later in the morning, at the United Nations Headquarters, the President met with U.N. General Assembly President Julian Hunte.

In the afternoon, at the U.S. Mission to the United Nations, the President met with President Jacques Chirac of France. Later, at the Waldorf-Astoria Hotel, he met separately with President Megawati Sukarnoputri of Indonesia, King Mohamed VI of Morocco, and President Hamid Karzai of Afghanistan.

The White House announced that the President will host President Carlo Azeglio Ciampi of Italy for a meeting and working luncheon on November 14.

September 24

In the morning, at the Waldorf-Astoria Hotel, the President had an intelligence briefing. Later, he had a breakfast meeting with Caribbean leaders, including Prime Minister Perry Christie of the Bahamas, Prime Minister Keith Mitchell of Grenada, President Bharrat Jagdeo of Guyana, and Prime Minister Kenny Davis Anthony of Saint Lucia.

Later in the morning, the President had separate meetings with President John Agyekum Kufuor of Ghana, President Pervez Musharraf of Pakistan, President Joaquim Alberto Chissano of Mozambique, and Prime Minister Atal Bihari Vajpayee of India.

In the afternoon, the President and Mrs. Bush returned to Washington, DC.

The President declared an emergency in Michigan and ordered Federal aid to supplement State and local response efforts in the area impacted by that power outage that occurred August 14–17.

The President declared an emergency in New Jersey and ordered Federal aid to supplement State and local response efforts in the area impacted by the power outage that occurred on August 14–17.

The President declared an emergency in Ohio and ordered Federal aid to supplemental State and local response efforts in the area impacted by the power outage that occurred on August 14–17.

The President declared a major disaster in Delaware and ordered Federal aid to supplement State and local recovery efforts in the area struck by Tropical Storm Henri on September 15.

The President declared a major disaster in West Virginia and ordered Federal aid to supplement State and local recovery efforts in the area struck by Hurricane Isabel on September 18 and continuing.

September 25

In the morning, the President had an intelligence briefing.

In the afternoon, the President had lunch with Vice President Dick Cheney.

The White House announced that the President will make a state visit to the United Kingdom on November 18–21.

September 26

In the morning, the President had an intelligence briefing. Later, he met separately with Secretary of Defense Donald H. Rumsfeld and Ambassador L. Paul Bremer III, Presidential Envoy to Iraq.

Later in the morning, in the Oval Office, the President met with President Nicanor Duarte Frutos of Paraguay.

In the afternoon, the President and Mrs. Bush traveled to Camp David, MD, where they hosted President Vladimir Putin of Russia and his wife, Lyudmila Putin, for an overnight visit.

September 27

In the morning, the President had an intelligence briefing.

In the afternoon, the President returned to Washington, DC.

The White House announced that on September 26 the President declared a major disaster in Pennsylvania and ordered Federal aid to supplement State and local recovery efforts in the area struck by Tropical Storms Henri and Isabel and related severe storms and flooding on September 15–23.

September 29

In the morning, the President had intelligence and FBI briefings.

In the afternoon, in the Eisenhower Executive Office Building, the President met with congregational rabbis.

September 30

In the morning, the President had intelligence and FBI briefings. Later, he traveled to Chicago, IL.

In the afternoon, the President traveled to Cincinnati, OH, where, in the evening, he attended a Bush-Cheney '04 reception at a private residence.

Later in the evening, the President returned to Washington, DC.

October 1

In the morning, the President had intelligence and FBI briefings. Later, he met with Secretary of Defense Donald H. Rumsfeld.

Later in the morning, in the Oval Office, the President met with President Alvaro Uribe of Colombia.

In the afternoon, the President had a briefing at the Department of Homeland Security.

Later in the afternoon, in the Oval Office, the President participated in a photo opportunity with members of the International Space Station Expedition 6 crew and NASA Administrator Sean O'Keefe.

The President announced his intention to nominate Mary Kramer to be Ambassador to Barbados and to serve concurrently and without additional compensation as Ambassador to St. Kitts and Nevis, St. Lucia, Antigua and Barbuda, Dominica, Grenada, and St. Vincent and the Grenadines.

The President announced his intention to appoint Charles A. Calhoun as Commissioner of the Pecos River Commission for New Mexico and Texas.

The President announced his intention to appoint Maria Pilar Aristigueta as a member of the Board of Trustees of the Christopher Columbus Fellowship Foundation.

The President announced his intention to nominate the following individuals to be members of the National Commission on Libraries and Information Science:

Jose Antonio Aponte;
Sandra Frances Ashworth;
Edward Louis Bertorelli;
Carol L. Diehl;
Allison Druin;
Beth Fitzsimmons;
Patricia M. Hines;
Colleen Ellen Huebner;
Stephen M. Kennedy;
Herman Lavon Totten;
Bridget L. Lamont; and
Mary H. Perdue.

October 2

In the morning, the President had intelligence and FBI briefings.

In the afternoon, the President had lunch with Vice President Dick Cheney. Later, he met with Secretary of State Colin L. Powell.

The President announced his intention to nominate Edward Baxter O'Donnell for the rank of Ambassador during his tenure of service as Special Envoy for Holocaust Issues.

The President announced his intention to designate Rita E. Hauser as a member of the Intelligence Oversight Board, a standing committee of the President's Foreign Intelligence Advisory Board.

October 3

In the morning, the President had intelligence and FBI briefings. Later, he traveled to Milwaukee, WI.

In the afternoon, the President returned to Washington, DC.

In the evening, the President and Mrs. Bush attended the National Book Festival Gala at the Library of Congress.

The President announced his intention to nominate James B. Comey to be Deputy Attorney General.

October 4

In the morning, the President had an intelligence briefing.

October 6

In the morning, the President had an intelligence briefing. Later, on the South Lawn, he participated in a state arrival ceremony for President Mwai Kibaki of Kenya and his wife, Lucy.

In the afternoon, the President met with U.S. officials returning from Iraq to discuss reconstruction efforts there. Later, he met with former Senator John C. Danforth, Special Envoy for Peace in the Sudan, to discuss peace efforts in that country.

In the evening, in the Cross Hall, the President and Mrs. Bush participated in a photo opportunity with President Kibaki and Mrs. Kibaki. Later, in the State Dining Room, they hosted a state dinner for President and Mrs. Kibaki.

The President announced his intention to nominate Jon Robert Purnell to be Ambassador to Uzbekistan.

The President announced his intention to nominate Thomas Riley to be Ambassador to Morocco.

The President announced his intention to designate Brian Carlton Roseboro as Acting Under Secretary of the Treasury (Domestic Finance).

October 7

In the morning, the President had an intelligence briefing.

The President announced his intention to nominate Stuart Ishimaru to be a member of the Equal Employment Opportunity Commission.

The President announced his intention to appoint the following individuals as members of the U.S. Section of the U.S.-Mexico Border Health Commission:

Jose Manual de la Rosa;
Lawrence Edward Kline;
Tom G. Lindsey II; and
Emma Torres.

October 8

In the morning, the President had an intelligence briefing.

In the afternoon, the President had a telephone conversation with Governor-elect Arnold Schwarzenegger of California to congratulate him on his October 7 election victory.

Also in the afternoon, the President met with Republican Members of Congress to discuss proposed legislation on reconstruction aid to Iraq.

The White House announced that the President will attend the APEC Leaders' Meeting in Bangkok, Thailand, on October 20–21, and that he has accepted invitations from Prime Minister Junichiro Koizumi to visit Japan on October 17–18, from Prime Minister Goh Chok Tong to visit Singapore on October 21–22, from President Megawati Sukarnoputri to visit Indonesia on October 22, and from Prime Minister John Howard to visit Australia on October 22–23.

The President announced his intention to nominate April Hoxie Foley to be First Vice President of the Export-Import Bank.

The President announced his intention to nominate Gary Lee Visscher to be a member of the Chemical Safety and Hazard Investigation Board.

The President announced his appointment of Kristen Lee Silverburg as Deputy Assistant to the President for Domestic Policy.

The President announced his intention to appoint William O. DeWitt, Jr., as a member of the President's Foreign Intelligence Advisory Board.

October 9

In the morning, the President had an intelligence briefing. Later, he traveled to Portsmouth, NH, where, upon arrival, he met with USA Freedom Corps volunteer Cathy Rice.

Later in the morning, the President traveled to Manchester, NH, where, upon arrival, he met with USA Freedom Corps volunteer Robert Perkins.

In the afternoon, the President traveled to Lexington, KY.

In the evening, the President returned to Washington, DC.

October 10

In the morning, the President had an intelligence briefing. Later, he met with Secretary of State Colin L. Powell.

In the afternoon, the President had lunch with Vice President Dick Cheney. Later, in the Roosevelt Room, he met with members of the U.S. Commission on International Religious Freedom, who presented him with the fourth annual report of the Commission.

Later in the afternoon, the President traveled to Camp David, MD.

October 11

In the morning, the President had an intelligence briefing.

October 12

During the day, the President returned to Washington, DC.

October 13

In the morning, the President had an intelligence briefing. Later, he participated in interviews with regional television stations.

October 14

In the morning, the President had an intelligence briefing and later met with the National Security Council.

In the afternoon, the President participated in television and radio interviews with Asian journalists. He also dropped by a meeting between Secretary of State Colin L. Powell, Office of Management and Budget Director Joshua B. Bolten, and other officials and bipartisan Senators to discuss proposed legislation concerning reconstruction aid to Iraq.

The President announced his designation of the following individuals as members of a Presidential delegation to celebrations on October 16–20 at the Vatican in Rome, Italy, marking the 25th anniversary of Pope John Paul II's pontificate and the beatification of Mother Teresa:

Columba Bush (head of delegation);
Jim Nicholson;
Jim Towey;
Mary Ellen Bork;
Frances Winfield Bremer;
Joseph C. Canizaro;
Mother Agnes Mary Donovan, SV;
Raymond L. Flynn;
Mary Ann Glendon;
Deal W. Hudson;
John M. Klink;
Sister Mary Rose McGeady, DC;
Peggy Noonan;
Kate O'Beirne; and
Gabrielle Reynolds.

October 15

In the morning, the President had an intelligence briefing. Later, he traveled to Dinuba, CA.

In the afternoon, the President traveled to Fresno, CA. Later, he traveled to Riverside, CA.

The President announced the nomination of Robert McFarland to be Assistant Secretary of Veterans Affairs for Information and Technology.

The President announced the nomination of Susan Johnson Grant to be Chief Financial Officer for the Department of Energy.

The President announced the nomination of Marguerita Dianne Ragsdale to be Ambassador to Djibouti.

The President announced the nomination of Margaret Scobey to be Ambassador to Syria.

The President announced the nomination of Margaret DeBardeleben Tutwiler to be Under Secretary of State for Public Diplomacy.

The President announced the nomination of Drew R. McCoy to be a member of the Board of Trustees of the James Madison Memorial Fellowship Foundation.

The President announced his intention to designate Jeffrey E. Phillips as Acting Assistant Secretary of Veterans Affairs for Public and Intergovernmental Affairs.

October 16

In the morning, the President had an intelligence briefing. Later, he met with Governor-elect Arnold Schwarzenegger of California and then traveled with him to San Bernardino, CA.

Later in the morning, the President returned to Riverside. Later, he was joined by Mrs. Bush at March Air Reserve Base, and they then traveled to Tokyo, Japan, arriving in the afternoon of October 17.

The White House announced that the President will welcome President Ion Iliescu of Romania to the White House on October 28.

The President announced his intention to nominate Timothy J. Dunn for the rank of Ambassador during his tenure as Deputy Permanent Representative of the U.S. Permanent Mission to the Organization of American States.

The President announced his intention to nominate Adam Marc Lindemann to be a member of the Advisory Board for Cuba Broadcasting.

The President announced his intention to nominate James C. Struble to be Ambassador to Peru.

October 17

In the evening, the President met with Prime Minister Junichiro Koizumi of Japan at Akasaka Palace. Later, also at Akasaka Palace, he and Mrs. Bush had dinner with Prime Minister Koizumi.

The President announced his intention to nominate Stuart Holliday to be Alternate Representative of the U.S. for Special Political Affairs in the United Nations, with the rank of Ambassador.

October 18

In the morning, at the U.S. Ambassador's residence in Tokyo, Japan, the President had an intelligence briefing. Later, he and Mrs. Bush traveled to Manila, Philippines, where they greeted U.S. Embassy personnel and members of the American community at the Embassy.

In the afternoon, at the Rizal Monument, the President and Mrs. Bush participated in a wreath-laying ceremony with President Gloria Macapagal-Arroyo of the Philippines. Later, at Malacanang Palace, he and Mrs. Bush participated in a welcoming ceremony with President Macapagal-Arroyo and her husband, Jose Miguel Arroyo. The two Presidents then had a meeting.

In the evening, in the Ceremonial Hall at Malacanang Palace, the President and Mrs. Bush attended a state dinner hosted by President Macapagal-Arroyo.

October 19

In the morning, the President and Mrs. Bush traveled to Bangkok, Thailand. Later, at the Grand Hyatt Erawan Bangkok, he met with Prime Minister Thaksin Chinnawat of Thailand.

In the afternoon, the President participated in a review of Thai troops recently returned from Afghanistan. Later, he and Mrs. Bush toured the Grand Palace.

Later in the afternoon, at the Grand Hyatt Erawan Bangkok, the President met with President Hu Jintao of China.

In the evening, at the Grand Palace, the President and Mrs. Bush attended a state dinner hosted by King Phumiphon Adunyadet and Queen Sirikit of Thailand.

October 20

In the morning, the President had an intelligence briefing. Later, at the Grand Hyatt Erawan Bangkok, he had a breakfast meeting with President Roh Moo-hyun of South Korea. He then met with President Vicente Fox of Mexico.

In the afternoon, at the Government House, the President participated in the first session of the Asia-Pacific Economic Cooperation (APEC) Leaders' Retreat. Later, he attended an APEC Business Advisory Council reception.

In the evening, at the Grand Palace, the President and Mrs. Bush and other APEC leaders and their spouses had an audience with King Phumiphon Adunyadet and Queen Sirikit of Thailand. Later, the President participated in a photo opportunity with APEC leaders.

Later in the evening, the President and Mrs. Bush attended the APEC leaders' gala dinner at the Royal Thai Navy Conference Hall and a cultural performance at the Royal Thai Navy Institute.

The President announced his intention to nominate James M. Strock to be a member of the U.S. Advisory Commission on Public Diplomacy.

October 21

In the morning, the President had an intelligence briefing. Later, in the Old Parliament Building, he participated in a photo opportunity with APEC leaders and the second session of the APEC Leaders' Retreat.

In the afternoon, he attended a reception for APEC leaders.

Later in the afternoon, the President and Mrs. Bush traveled to Singapore.

In the evening, the President greeted U.S. Embassy personnel at the Shangri-La Singapore Hotel. Later, at the Istana, he paid a courtesy call on President Sellapan Rama Nathan of Singapore and his wife, Urmila Nandey. Then, also at the Istana, he met with Prime Minister Goh Chok Tong of Singapore.

The President announced his intention to nominate Edward McPherson to be Under Secretary of Education.

October 22

In the morning, the President had an intelligence briefing. Later, he and Mrs. Bush traveled to Bali, Indonesia, where, at Bali International Airport, he met with President Megawati Sukarnoputri of Indonesia.

In the afternoon, at the airport, the President met with religious leaders. Later, he and Mrs. Bush traveled to Canberra, Australia.

The President announced the laureates of the 2002 National Medals of Science and National Medals of Technology, which will be presented at a White House ceremony on November 6.

The President announced his intention to nominate Carol Kinsley to be a member of the Board of Directors of the Corporation for National and Community Service.

October 23

In the morning, the President had an intelligence briefing. Later, he and Mrs. Bush paid a courtesy call on Governor-General Michael Jeffery of Australia and his wife, Marlena, at Australia's Government House.

Later in the morning, at Australia's Parliament House, the President met with Prime Minister John Howard of Australia.

In the afternoon, the President and Mrs. Bush participated in a wreath-laying ceremony at the Australian War Memorial.

In the evening, the President and Mrs. Bush traveled to Hickam Air Force Base on the island of Oahu, HI, crossing the international date line and arriving Thursday morning, October 23.

Upon arriving at Hickam Air Force Base, the President and Mrs. Bush greeted Gov. Linda Lingle and Lt. Gov. James "Duke" Aiona of Hawaii, U.S. military leaders, and National Park Service volunteer Hilma Chang.

Later in the morning, the President and Mrs. Bush traveled to Pearl Harbor, where they participated in a wreath-laying ceremony at the U.S.S. *Arizona* (BB–39) Memorial and met with eight survivors of the 1941 Japanese attack on Pearl Harbor. Later, aboard the U.S.S. *Missouri*, the President participated in a briefing by Adm. Thomas Boulton Fargo, USN, combatant commander, U.S. Pacific Command. He then toured

the U.S.S. *Missouri* and greeted veterans and former *Missouri* crewmembers. Later, he and Mrs. Bush visited second-grade students at Pearl Harbor Elementary school.

In the afternoon, the President and Mrs. Bush traveled to Honolulu, HI, where, at the Kahala Mandarin Oriental Hotel, he attended a Hawaii Republican Party reception. Later, he met with delegates of 13 Pacific Island nations attending the Pacific Islands Conference of Leaders.

In the evening, the President and Mrs. Bush departed for Washington, DC.

The President announced his intention to nominate James M. Loy to be Deputy Secretary of Homeland Security and to designate him as Acting Deputy Secretary of Homeland Security.

October 24

In the morning, the President and Mrs. Bush arrived in Washington, DC. Later in the day, they traveled to Camp David, MD.

The White House announced that the President will welcome Prime Minister Ranil Wickremesinghe of Sri Lanka to the White House on November 4.

The White House announced that the President will welcome President Joseph Kabila of the Democratic Republic of the Congo to the White House on November 5.

The White House announced that the President will welcome President Rolandas Paksas of Lithuania to the White House on December 8.

The President announced his intention to appoint the following individuals as members of the Benjamin Franklin Tercentenary Commission:

Ralph F. Archbold;
Wayne A. Budd;
John Anderson Fry;
Charles R. Gerow;
Judith Rodin; and
Jeffrey L. Sedgwick.

The President announced his intention to nominate Edward E. Kaufman, Fayza Veronique Boulad Rodman, and Steven J. Simmons to be members of the Broadcasting Board of Governors.

The President announced his designation of the following individuals as members of a Presidential delegation to attend the ceremony commemorating the 20th anniversary of the restoration of democracy to Grenada in St. George's:

Otto J. Reich (head of delegation);
Marcia Bernicat;
Adm. Joseph Metcalf III;
Langhorne Anthony Motley; and
Ken Tomlinson.

October 25
In the morning, the President had an intelligence briefing.

October 26
In the evening, the President returned to Washington, DC.

October 27
In the morning, the President had an intelligence briefing.

The President announced his intention to nominate Arnold I. Havens to be General Counsel for the Department of the Treasury.

The President declared a major disaster in California and ordered Federal aid to supplement State and local recovery efforts in the area struck by wildfires on October 21 and continuing.

October 28
In the morning, the President had an intelligence briefing. Later, in the Oval Office, he met with President Ion Iliescu of Romania.

In the afternoon, in the Oval Office, the President met with economic advisers.

The White House announced that the President will host NATO Secretary General Lord Robertson for a meeting and working luncheon on November 12.

October 29
In the morning, the President had a breakfast meeting with Speaker of the House of Representatives J. Dennis Hastert, Senate Majority Leader Bill Frist, Senate Minority Leader Thomas A. Daschle, House Minority Leader Nancy Pelosi, and House Majority Leader Tom DeLay to discuss legislative priorities. Later, he had an intelligence briefing. He then met with the National Security Council and later with Secretary of Defense Donald H. Rumsfeld.

Later in the morning, in Room 472 of the Dwight D. Eisenhower Executive Office Building, the President participated in a roundtable discussion on Medicare with Secretary of Health and Human Services Tommy G. Thompson, AARP President James G. Parkel, and a group of senior citizens.

In the afternoon, on the South Steps, the President participated in a photo opportunity with White House interns. Later, he traveled to Dallas, TX, where, upon arrival, he met with USA Freedom Corps volunteer Laura Wheat.

In the evening, the President traveled to the Bush Ranch in Crawford, TX.

October 30
In the morning, the President traveled to Columbus, OH. While en route aboard Air Force One, he had an intelligence briefing. Upon arrival, he met with USA Freedom Corps volunteer Leslie Gagne.

In the afternoon, the President traveled to San Antonio, TX, where, upon arrival, he met with USA Freedom Corps volunteer Thom Ricks.

In the evening, the President returned to the Bush Ranch in Crawford, TX.

October 31
In the morning, the President had a telephone conversation with Prime Minister Silvio Berlusconi of Italy to discuss reconstruction in Afghanistan and Iraq. Later, he had an intelligence briefing.

The President announced his intention to nominate Samuel Wright Bodman to be Deputy Secretary of the Treasury.

The President announced his intention to nominate Eugene Welch Hickok, Jr., to be Deputy Secretary of Education.

The President announced his intention to nominate Brian Carlton Roseboro to be Under Secretary of the Treasury for Domestic Finance.

November 1
In the morning, the President had an intelligence briefing.

Later in the morning, the President traveled to Southaven, MS, and then to Paducah, KY.

In the afternoon, the President traveled to London, KY, and later to Gulfport, MS.

In the evening, the President returned to the Bush Ranch in Crawford, TX.

November 3
In the morning, the President traveled to Birmingham, AL. While en route aboard Air Force One, he had an intelligence briefing. Upon arrival in Birmingham, he met with USA Freedom Corps volunteer Jason Nabors. Later, he met with small-business owners at CraneWorks.

In the afternoon, the President returned to the Bush Ranch in Crawford, TX.

The President announced his intention to nominate Francis Joseph Harvey to be Assistant Secretary of Defense for Networks and Information Integration.

The President announced his intention to nominate William Douglas Buttrey and Francis Patrick Mulvey to be members of the Surface Transportation Board.

The President announced his intention to nominate Gordon Hall Mansfield to be Deputy Secretary of Veterans Affairs.

The President announced his intention to nominate David Hossein Safavian to be Administrator for Federal Procurement Policy at the Office of Management and Budget.

The President announced his intention to nominate Laurie Susan Fulton to be a member of the Board of Directors of the U.S. Institute of Peace.

November 4

In the morning, the President traveled to Miramar, CA. While en route aboard Air Force One, he had an intelligence briefing. Upon arrival at the Marine Corps Air Station, he met with USA Freedom Corps volunteer Suellen Mayberry.

Later in the morning, the President, joined by Governor Gray Davis and Governor-elect Arnold Schwarzenegger of California, California Department of Forestry Division Chief Bill Clayton, and Under Secretary for Emergency Preparedness and Response Mike Brown, took an aerial tour of the San Diego area affected by wildfires. Later, he participated in a walking tour of the Harbison Canyon community damaged by wildfires. He then traveled to El Cajon, CA, where, at Gillespie Field, he participated in a briefing by area fire chiefs on the wildfires.

In the afternoon, the President returned to Washington, DC.

In the evening, the President had separate telephone conversations with Governors-elect Haley Barbour of Mississippi and Ernie Fletcher of Kentucky to congratulate them on their electoral victories earlier in the day.

November 5

In the morning, the President had an intelligence briefing. Later, he met with Secretary of Defense Donald H. Rumsfeld.

Later in the morning, in the Oval Office, the President met with President Joseph Kabila of the Democratic Republic of the Congo. Later, also in the Oval Office, he met with Prime Minister Ranil Wickremesinghe of Sri Lanka to discuss peace efforts in Sri Lanka and free trade.

In the afternoon, the President met with Polish philosopher and writer Leszek Kolakowski to congratulate him on winning the John W. Kluge Prize in Human Sciences.

November 6

In the morning, the President had an intelligence briefing.

In the afternoon, the President met with Secretary of State Colin L. Powell.

The President announced his intention to nominate Kiron Kanina Skinner to be a member of the National Security Education Board.

November 7

In the morning, the President had separate telephone conversations with President Carlos Diego Mesa Gisbert of Bolivia to discuss democracy in Bolivia, President Mesa's plans for a national referendum on Bolivian natural gas resources, and cooperation in counternarcotics efforts; President Jose Maria Aznar of Spain to discuss the situation in Iraq and transatlantic relations; and President Aleksander Kwasniewski of Poland to express his condolences concerning the death of a Polish officer in Iraq on November 6 and to discuss other issues.

Later in the morning, the President had an intelligence briefing. Later, he traveled to Winston-Salem, NC, where, upon arrival, he met with USA Freedom Corps volunteer Brian Koontz.

In the afternoon, the President traveled to Camp David, MD.

The President announced his intention to nominate Linda Morrison Combs to be Assistant Secretary of Transportation and, upon confirmation, to designate her as Chief Financial Officer.

The President announced his intention to nominate Steven J. Law to be Deputy Secretary of Labor.

The President announced his intention to nominate J. Robinson West to be a member of the Board of Directors of the U.S. Institute of Peace.

The President declared a major disaster in Washington and ordered Federal aid to supplement State and local recovery efforts in the area struck by severe storms and flooding on October 15–23.

November 8

In the morning, the President had an intelligence briefing.

November 9

In the afternoon, the President returned to Washington, DC.

November 10

In the morning, the President had an intelligence briefing. Later, he traveled to Little Rock, AR, where, upon arrival, he met with USA Freedom Corps volunteer Dr. Michael Quick.

In the afternoon, the President traveled to Greer, SC, where, upon arrival, he met with USA Freedom Corps volunteer Robin Longino and high school athlete Ben Comen. Later, he traveled to Greenville, SC.

In the evening, the President returned to Washington, DC.

The White House announced that the President will award the Medal of Freedom to NATO Secretary General Lord Robertson in a ceremony at the White House on November 12.

The President announced his intention to appoint Patrick Marshall Hughes to be Assistant Secretary for Information Analysis at the Department of Homeland Security.

November 11

In the morning, the President had an intelligence briefing. Later, in an Oval Office ceremony, he signed the Military Family Tax Relief Act of 2003.

Later in the morning, the President and Mrs. Bush traveled to Arlington, VA, where they participated in a Veterans Day wreath-laying ceremony at the Tomb of the Unknowns in Arlington National Cemetery. In the afternoon, they returned to Washington, DC.

Later in the afternoon, in an Oval Office ceremony, the President signed the National Cemetery Expansion Act.

November 12

In the morning, the President had an intelligence briefing followed by a National Security Council meeting. He then met with Secretary of Defense Donald H. Rumsfeld and L. Paul Bremer III, Presidential Envoy to Iraq. Later,

in the Oval Office, he participated in a photo opportunity with Environmental Protection Agency Administrator Michael O. Leavitt and members of Mr. Leavitt's family.

Later in the morning, the President met with NATO Secretary General Lord Robertson.

In the afternoon, in the Oval Office, the President and Mrs. Bush participated in the presentation of the National Medal of Arts awards.

November 13

In the morning, the President had an intelligence briefing. Later, he traveled to Orlando, FL. While en route aboard Air Force One, he had a telephone conversation with Prime Minister Silvio Berlusconi of Italy to express his condolences to the families of the Italians killed in the suicide bombing in Nasiriyah, Iraq, on November 12 and to discuss reconstruction efforts in Iraq and Europe-U.S. relations. Upon arrival in Orlando, he met with USA Freedom Corps volunteer Matilda Walther.

In the afternoon, the President traveled to Fort Myers, FL, where, upon arrival, he met with USA Freedom Corps volunteer Mark Asperilla.

In the evening, the President attended a Bush-Cheney '04 reception at a private residence. Later, he returned to Washington, DC.

The President announced his intention to nominate Rhonda Newman Keenum to be an Assistant Secretary of Commerce and Director General of the U.S. and Foreign Commercial Service.

The President announced his intention to nominate David Campbell Mulford to be Ambassador to India.

November 14

In the morning, the President had an intelligence briefing. Later, in the Oval Office, he and Mrs. Bush participated in the presentation of the National Humanities Medal awards.

In the afternoon, in the Residence, the President had lunch with President Carlo Azeglio Ciampi of Italy. Later, he traveled to Camp David, MD.

November 15

In the morning, the President had an intelligence briefing.

During the day, the President had a telephone conversation with Prime Minister Recep Tayyip Erdogan of Turkey to express condolences for the terrorist attacks in Istanbul earlier in the day.

November 16

In the afternoon, the President returned to Washington, DC.

November 17

In the morning, the President had intelligence and FBI briefings. Later, he participated in a photo opportunity with 2003 Nobel laureates.

The President announced his intention to nominate Glyn Townsend Davies for the rank of Ambassador during his tenure of service as the Political Director for the U.S. Presidency of the G–8.

The President announced his intention to nominate William Douglas Buttrey and Francis Patrick Mulvey to be members of the Surface Transportation Board.

The President announced his intention to nominate James Curtis Oberwetter to be Ambassador to Saudi Arabia.

The President announced his intention to nominate Gay Hart Gaines to be a member of the Board of Directors of the Corporation for Public Broadcasting.

November 18

In the morning, the President had an intelligence briefing. Later, he and Mrs. Bush traveled to London, United Kingdom, arriving in the evening at Heathrow Airport, where they participated in a greeting with Charles, Prince of Wales.

In the evening, at Buckingham Palace, the President and Mrs. Bush were welcomed privately by Queen Elizabeth II and her husband, Prince Philip, Duke of Edinburgh, who escorted them to their suite in the palace, their residence during their visit to London.

November 19

In the morning, the President had an intelligence briefing. Later, he and Mrs. Bush participated in a welcoming ceremony with Queen Elizabeth II and Prince Philip, Duke of Edinburgh. Later, in the Bow Room of Buckingham Palace, they participated in the presentation of delegations and then viewed the royal collection of American memorabilia in the Picture Gallery.

In the afternoon, at the American Embassy, the President and Mrs. Bush met with family members of British victims of the September 11, 2001, terrorist attacks. Later, the President

met with U.S. Embassy employees and their family members.

Later in the afternoon, at Buckingham Palace, the President met separately with Conservative Party leader Michael Howard and Liberal Democrat leader Charles Kennedy.

The President announced his intention to nominate Joey Russell George to be Inspector General for Tax Administration at the Department of the Treasury.

The President announced his intention to nominate the following individuals to be members of the Board of Directors of the National Board for Education Sciences:

Jonathan Baron;
Elizabeth Ann Bryan;
James R. Davis;
Robert C. Granger;
Frank Philip Handy;
Eric Alan Hanushek;
Caroline M. Hoxby;
Gerald Lee;
Roberto Ibarra Lopez;
Richard James Milgram;
Sally Epstein Shaywitz;
Joseph K. Torgesen; and
Herbert John Walberg.

The President announced his intention to appoint Sara Gear Boyd, Maria Elena Lagomasino, and Donald L. Pilling as members of the President's Commission on White House Fellowships.

The President announced his intention to designate James B. Comey as Acting Deputy Attorney General.

November 20

In the morning, the President had an intelligence briefing. Later, at Westminster Abbey, he participated in a wreath-laying ceremony at the Tomb of the Unknown Warrior, followed by a tour of the abbey. He then met with families of British servicemembers who died in Iraq.

In the afternoon, the President and Mrs. Bush participated in a photo opportunity with Prime Minister Tony Blair of the United Kingdom and his wife, Cherie, at 10 Downing St., the Prime Minister's official residence. The President and Prime Minister Blair then had a meeting and a working lunch and later participated in a roundtable discussion on HIV/AIDS.

Later in the afternoon, at 10 Downing St., the President and Mrs. Bush participated in a visit with Prime Minister Blair and his family.

In the evening, at Winfield House, the U.S. Ambassador's residence, the President and Mrs. Bush hosted a reciprocal dinner for Queen Elizabeth II; Prince Philip, Duke of Edinburgh; and Charles, Prince of Wales.

The President announced his intention to nominate Ronald Edward Meisburg to be a member of the National Labor Relations Board.

The President announced his intention to nominate Stuart Wadlington Holliday to be an Alternate U.S. Representative to the Sessions of the United Nations General Assembly during his tenure of service as Alternate U.S. Representative for Special Political Affairs in the United Nations.

November 21

In the morning, the President had an intelligence briefing. Later, he and Mrs. Bush participated in a farewell ceremony with Queen Elizabeth II and Prince Philip, Duke of Edinburgh. They then traveled to Sedgefield, United Kingdom. While en route aboard Air Force One, the President had a telephone conversation with Prime Minister Recep Tayyip Erdogan of Turkey to express condolences for the November 20 terrorist attacks in Istanbul. In Sedgefield, the President and Mrs. Bush had tea with Prime Minister and Mrs. Blair at their home, Myrobella House.

In the afternoon, at the Dun Cow Inn, the President and Mrs. Bush had lunch with Prime Minister and Mrs. Blair and a group of the Prime Minister's constituents. Later, the President and Prime Minister Blair met with teachers and students and viewed an athletic display at Sedgefield Community College.

Later in the afternoon, the President and Mrs. Bush departed for Washington, DC, arriving in the evening.

The President announced his intention to nominate Jaymie Alan Durnan to be Assistant Secretary of the Army (Installations and Environment).

The President announced his intention to nominate Lawrence Thomas Di Rita to be Assistant Secretary of Defense (Public Affairs).

The President announced his intention to nominate Robert Hurley McKinney to be a member of the Advisory Board for Cuba Broadcasting.

The President announced his intention to nominate Sanford Gottesman, Diane M. Ruebling, and C. William Swank to be members

of the Board of Directors of the Overseas Private Investment Corporation.

The President declared a major disaster in Puerto Rico and ordered Federal aid to supplement Commonwealth and local recovery efforts in the area struck by severe storms, flooding, mudslides, and landslides on November 10 and continuing.

The President declared a major disaster in West Virginia and ordered Federal aid to supplement State and local recovery efforts in the area struck by severe storms, flooding, and landslides on November 11 and continuing.

November 22

In the morning, the President had an intelligence briefing.

November 24

In the morning, the President had an intelligence briefing. Later, he traveled to Colorado Springs, CO. Upon his arrival in the afternoon at Peterson Air Force Base, he met with USA Freedom Corps volunteer Diane Campbell. He then traveled to Fort Carson, CO, where he had lunch with members of the U.S. military.

Later in the afternoon, the President returned to Peterson Air Force Base and met with families of U.S. servicemembers who died in Iraq. He then traveled to the Bush Ranch in Crawford, TX.

November 25

In the morning, the President traveled to Las Vegas, NV. While en route aboard Air Force One, he had an intelligence briefing. Upon arrival, he met with USA Freedom Corps volunteer Maria Konold-Soto. Later, at Spring Valley Hospital, he met with health care professionals and seniors to discuss Medicare and medical liability reform.

In the afternoon, the President traveled to Phoenix, AZ, where, upon arrival, he met with USA Freedom Corps volunteer Maybelle Harris. Later, at the Los Olivos Senior Center, he met with seniors to discuss Medicare reform.

In the evening, the President returned to the Bush Ranch in Crawford, TX.

The President announced his intention to nominate Dennis C. Shea to be Assistant Secretary of Housing and Urban Development for Policy, Development, and Research.

The President announced his intention to nominate Mark J. Warshawsky to be Assistant Secretary of the Treasury for Economic Policy.

The President announced his intention to nominate Roger W. Wallace to be a member of the Board of Directors of the Inter-American Foundation.

The President announced his intention to nominate Jack Edwin McGregor and Scott Kevin Walker to be members of the Advisory Board of the St. Lawrence Seaway Development Corporation.

The President announced the appointment of James R. Wilkinson as Deputy Assistant to the President and Deputy National Security Advisor for Communications.

The President announced the appointment of Sean McCormack as Special Assistant to the President and Senior Director of the National Security Council Press Office.

November 26

In the morning, the President had a telephone conversation with interim President Nino Burjanadze of Georgia to discuss political reforms in Georgia. He then had an intelligence briefing.

In the evening, the President traveled to Baghdad, Iraq, arriving the following afternoon.

The White House announced that the President will welcome Premier Wen Jiabao of China to the White House for an official visit on December 9.

November 27

In the late afternoon, at Baghdad International Airport, the President had Thanksgiving dinner with members of the U.S. military stationed in Baghdad. Later, he met with four members of the Iraqi Governing Council and then senior U.S. military personnel stationed in Baghdad.

In the evening, the President traveled to the Bush Ranch in Crawford, TX, arriving early the next morning.

November 28

In the morning, the President had an intelligence briefing.

November 29

In the morning, the President had an intelligence briefing.

November 30

In the afternoon, the President and Mrs. Bush returned to Washington, DC.

December 1

In the morning, the President had an intelligence briefing. Later, he traveled to Detroit, MI, where, upon arrival, he met with USA Freedom Corps volunteer Bradley Simmons. He then traveled to Dearborn, MI.

In the afternoon, the President traveled to Canton, MI. Later, he traveled to Newark, NJ, where, upon arrival, he met with USA Freedom Corps volunteer Patricia Fields. He then traveled to Whippany, NJ.

In the evening, the President returned to Washington, DC.

The President announced his intention to nominate M. Teel Bivins to be Ambassador to Sweden.

December 2

In the morning, the President had a telephone conversation with President Hosni Mubarak of Egypt to discuss peace efforts in the Middle East and the situation in Iraq. Later, he had an intelligence briefing.

Later in the morning, the President traveled to Pittsburgh, PA, where, upon arrival, he met with USA Freedom Corps volunteer Mila Nguyen.

In the afternoon, the President returned to Washington, DC.

During the day, the President informed Robert L. Bartley that he would receive the Presidential Medal of Freedom.

December 3

In the morning, the President had an intelligence briefing.

In the afternoon, in an Oval Office ceremony, the President signed the 21st Century Nanotechnology Research and Development Act. Later, he met with the President's Council of Advisors on Science and Technology.

In the evening, on the State Floor, the President hosted a holiday reception.

The White House announced that the President will meet with King Abdullah II of Jordan at the White House on December 4.

The President announced his intention to nominate B. Francis Saul II and Ruth Sharp Altshuler to be members of the Library of Congress Trust Fund Board.

The President announced his intention to appoint Arturo Duran as Commissioner of the U.S. Section of the International Boundary and Water Commission, United States and Mexico.

The President announced his intention to appoint Victor Rodriguez and Bray Bruce Barnes as members of the Coordinating Council on Juvenile Justice and Delinquency Prevention.

December 4
In the morning, the President had a telephone conversation with Prime Minister Tony Blair of the United Kingdom to discuss the situation in Iraq and the NATO Alliance. He then had an intelligence briefing.

In the afternoon, in an Oval Office ceremony, the President received diplomatic credentials from Ambassadors Eva Nowotny of Austria, Feturi Elisaia of Samoa, Euripides L. Evriviades of Cyprus, Abdulaziz Kamilov of Uzbekistan, Said Tayeb Jawad of Afghanistan, Salvador Stadthagen of Nicaragua, Bayney Karran of Guyana, and Mikhailo Reznyk of Ukraine.

Later in the afternoon, the President and Mrs. Bush attended the Pageant of Peace on the Ellipse.

December 5
In the morning, the President had a telephone conversation with President Mireya Elisa Moscoso of Panama to discuss a possible Panama-U.S. free trade agreement. He then had an intelligence briefing.

Later in the morning, the President traveled to Baltimore, MD.

In the afternoon, the President traveled to Halethorpe, MD. Later, he returned to Washington, DC.

Later in the afternoon, in the Residence, the President participated in an interview with People magazine.

In the evening, on the State Floor, the President hosted a holiday dinner.

The White House announced the members of the President's Task Force on Puerto Rico's Status:

Gilbert G. Gonzalez, Jr.;
Elizabeth Dial;
Victor E. Bernson, Jr.;
Kathleen Leos;
Theresa Speake;
Regina Schofield;
Joshua Filler;
Frank Jimenez;
David P. Smith;
Noel J. Francisco;
Chris Spear;
Leo DiBenigno;

Sam Reid;
Tony Fratto;
William McLemore; and
Ruben Barrales.

December 6
In the morning, the President had an intelligence briefing.

December 8
In the morning, the President had separate telephone conversations with President Umar Hasan Ahmad al-Bashir of Sudan and Sudan People's Liberation Movement Chairman Dr. John Garang to discuss the Sudan peace process. Later, he had an intelligence briefing.

Later in the morning, the President made a surprise drop-by visit during Mrs. Bush's interview with Larry King of CNN.

In the afternoon, the President met with Secretary of the Treasury John W. Snow, Postmaster General John E. Potter, and members of the President's Commission on the U.S. Postal Service to discuss postal reform. Later, on the State Floor, the President and Mrs. Bush hosted a Christmas reception and program for children of U.S. military personnel.

In the evening, on the State Floor, the President hosted the Congressional Ball.

December 9
In the morning, the President had an intelligence briefing. Later, in the Oval Office, he met with Premier Wen Jiabao of China. Later in the morning, in the Cabinet Room, the President and Premier Wen met with U.S. and Chinese economic officials to discuss economic and trade issues.

In the afternoon, in the Residence, the President had lunch with Premier Wen. Later, in Room 450 at the Dwight D. Eisenhower Executive Office Building, he dropped by a meeting between National Security Adviser Condoleezza Rice and the U.S.-Sub-Saharan Africa Trade and Economic Cooperation Forum to discuss the African Growth and Opportunity Act.

In the evening, at the John F. Kennedy Center for the Performing Arts, the President and Mrs. Bush attended a joint performance by the National Symphony Orchestra and the Iraqi National Symphony Orchestra.

The President announced his intention to nominate Lisa Marie Kruska to be Assistant Secretary of Labor for Public Affairs.

The President announced his intention to nominate Donald Lee Korb to be Chief Counsel for the Internal Revenue Service and Assistant General Counsel in the Department of the Treasury.

The President announced his intention to nominate Robert Scott Jepson, Jr., Paul Byron Jones, and Charles Leon Kolbe to be members of the Internal Revenue Service Oversight Board.

The President announced his intention to appoint Robert A. Martinez as a member of the Board of Governors of the United Service Organizations, Inc.

The President declared a major disaster in the U.S. Virgin Islands and ordered Federal aid to supplement Territory recovery efforts in the area struck by severe storms, flooding, landslides, and mudslides on November 10–16.

The President declared a major disaster in Virginia and ordered Federal aid to supplement Commonwealth and local recovery efforts in the area struck by severe storms and flooding on November 18–19.

December 10

In the morning, the President had an intelligence briefing followed by a National Security Council meeting. Later, he met with Secretary of Defense Donald H. Rumsfeld.

During the day, the President had separate telephone conversations with President Vladimir Putin of Russia, Chancellor Gerhard Schroeder of Germany, and President Jacques Chirac of France, to discuss his appointment of James A. Baker III as his personal envoy on the issue of Iraqi debt.

December 11

In the morning, the President had an intelligence briefing. He also had separate telephone conversations with outgoing Prime Minister Jean Chretien of Canada, to congratulate him on his service to the Canadian people; and with Prime Minister Silvio Berlusconi of Italy, to discuss the situation in Iraq and the President's appointment of James A. Baker III as his personal envoy on the issue of Iraqi debt.

Later in the morning, the President traveled to McLean, VA.

In the afternoon, the President returned to Washington, DC.

In the evening, the President attended a holiday dinner.

The President announced his designation of Kirk Van Tine as Acting Deputy Secretary of Transportation.

The President announced his designation of Neil McPhie as Vice Chairman of the Merit Systems Protection Board.

December 12

In the morning, the President had an intelligence briefing and then met with Secretary of State Colin L. Powell. Later, he dropped by a meeting in the Roosevelt Room between Secretary of the Interior Gale A. Norton, Secretary of Agriculture Ann M. Veneman, Council on Environmental Quality Chairman James L. Connaughton, and wildlife conservation leaders.

In the afternoon, in the Oval Office, the President greeted winners of the 2003 MATHCOUNTS National Competition. Later, on the State Floor, he attended a holiday reception for members of the U.S. Secret Service.

In the evening, on the State Floor, the President attended a holiday reception for members of the U.S. Secret Service. Later, he traveled to Camp David, MD.

December 13

In the morning, the President had an intelligence briefing.

In the afternoon, in a telephone conversation with Secretary of Defense Donald H. Rumsfeld, the President received notice of the possible capture of former President Saddam Hussein of Iraq by U.S. military personnel in Tikrit, Iraq. Later, he had another telephone conversation with Secretary Rumsfeld to discuss further information on the possible capture. He then had separate telephone conversations with Vice President Dick Cheney and National Security Adviser Condoleezza Rice to notify them of the possible capture.

In the evening, the President and Mrs. Bush returned to Washington, DC.

December 14

In the early morning, in a telephone conversation with National Security Adviser Condoleezza Rice, the President received confirmation of the capture of former President Saddam Hussein of Iraq. Later, in the Residence, the President and Mrs. Bush watched television coverage of the briefing in Baghdad by L. Paul Bremer III, Presidential Envoy to Iraq, announcing the capture.

Also in the morning, the President had a briefing on the details of the capture and had separate telephone conversations with the following individuals to discuss the capture: Senate Majority Leader Bill Frist; Prime Minister Tony Blair of the United Kingdom; Central Intelligence Agency Director George J. Tenet; Adnan Pachachi, Acting President of the Governing Council of Iraq; Secretary of Defense Donald H. Rumsfeld; Gen. John P. Abizaid, USA, combatant commander, U.S. Central Command; Secretary of State Colin L. Powell; and President Jose Maria Aznar of Spain.

In the evening, at the National Building Museum, the President and Mrs. Bush participated in the taping of the annual "Christmas in Washington" concert for later television broadcast.

December 15

In the morning, the President had a telephone conversation with Prime Minister Paul Martin of Canada to discuss Canada-U.S. relations. He then had an intelligence briefing.

Later in the morning, the President met with Iraqi Minister of Health Khadir Abbas; Rend Rahim Francke, Head of the Iraq Interests Section in the U.S.; and a group of Iraqi doctors to discuss health care in Iraq.

The President announced his designation of the following individuals as members of a Presidential delegation to attend the funeral of former President Heydar Aliyev of Azerbaijan:

Brent Scowcroft (head of delegation);
Sam Brownback;
A. Elizabeth Jones; and
Reno L. Harnish.

December 16

In the morning, the President had a telephone conversation with President Hamid Karzai of Afghanistan to discuss the completion of the Afghan national highway from Kabul to Kandahar and other developments in Afghanistan. He then had an intelligence briefing.

Later in the morning, in the Oval Office, the President participated in a photo opportunity for the Pediatric Equity Research Act of 2003 and a signing ceremony for the Controlling the Assault of Non-Solicited Pornography and Marketing Act of 2003. Later, he participated in an interview with Diane Sawyer of ABC News.

In the afternoon, in the Oval Office, the President participated in separate signing ceremonies for the National Museum of African American History and Culture Act and the Veterans Benefits Act of 2003. He then participated in separate photo opportunities for the Vision 100—Century of Aviation Reauthorization Act and the Hometown Heroes Survivors Benefits Act of 2003.

Later in the afternoon, at Blair House, the President and Mrs. Bush attended the diplomatic corps holiday reception.

During the day, the President had a telephone conversation with James A. Baker III, his personal envoy on the issue of Iraqi debt, concerning Secretary Baker's discussions with President Jacques Chirac of France and Chancellor Gerhard Schroeder of Germany.

In the evening, the President attended a holiday reception on the State Floor.

December 17

In the morning, the President had an intelligence briefing. Later, he traveled to Kill Devil Hills, NC.

In the afternoon, the President returned to Washington, DC.

In the evening, the President attended holiday receptions.

December 18

In the morning, the President had an intelligence briefing. Later, at Walter Reed Army Medical Center, he had an MRI examination of his knees, followed by a brief visit with Secretary of State Colin L. Powell, who was recovering from surgery. He then visited U.S. military personnel injured in Iraq and Afghanistan and awarded Purple Hearts to several of them.

In the afternoon, the President had a telephone conversation with President Alvaro Uribe of Colombia to discuss the capture of former President Saddam Hussein of Iraq, Colombia's fight against drugs and terrorism, and bilateral and regional issues. Later, he had a telephone conversation with President Vicente Fox of Mexico to discuss the capture and bilateral and regional issues.

In the evening, on the State Floor, the President and Mrs. Bush attended a holiday reception for members of the press.

December 19

In the morning, the President had an intelligence briefing. Later, he had a telephone conversation with Secretary-General Kofi Annan of the United Nations to exchange holiday greetings. He then met with Secretary of Health and

Human Services Tommy G. Thompson and Director of National Drug Control Policy John P. Walters to discuss progress toward the President's goals for reducing drug use.

In the afternoon, the President met with James A. Baker III, his personal envoy on the issue of Iraqi debt.

In the evening, the President hosted a holiday dinner for senior White House staff.

The White House announced that the President will travel to Monterrey, Mexico, on January 12–13, 2004, to attend the Special Summit of the Americas.

The President announced his intention to designate Mark J. Warshawsky as Acting Assistant Secretary of the Treasury for Economic Policy.

The President announced his intention to designate Gordon H. Mansfield as Acting Deputy Secretary of Veterans Affairs.

The President declared a major disaster in the Federated States of Micronesia and ordered Federal aid to supplement national and State recovery efforts in the area struck by Typhoon Lupit on November 22–26.

December 20

In the morning, the President had a telephone conversation with President Abdoulaye Wade of Senegal to discuss the capture of former President Saddam Hussein of Iraq. He then had a telephone conversation with Prime Minister Junichiro Koizumi of Japan to discuss the situations in Iraq, North Korea, and Libya, and the upcoming visit to Japan of James A. Baker III, the President's personal envoy on the issue of Iraqi debt. The President then had an intelligence briefing.

Later in the morning, the President had a telephone conversation with President Hu Jintao of China to discuss the situations in Taiwan, Iraq, and North Korea, and Presidential Envoy Baker's upcoming visit to China.

December 22

In the morning, the President had a telephone conversation with President Roh Moo-hyun of South Korea to discuss the situations in Iraq and North Korea and Presidential Envoy Baker's upcoming visit to South Korea. He then had an intelligence briefing and met with the Homeland Security Council. Later, he met with Secretary of Defense Donald H. Rumsfeld and then with L. Paul Bremer III, Presidential Envoy to Iraq, to discuss the situation in Iraq.

In the afternoon, the President met with rabbis and Jewish community leaders in the Roosevelt Room. Later, he and Mrs. Bush traveled to Alexandria, VA, and then returned to Washington, DC.

Later in the afternoon, the President and Mrs. Bush hosted a Hanukkah reception on the State Floor.

In the evening, the President and Mrs. Bush went to Camp David, MD.

December 23

In the morning, the President had an intelligence briefing.

The President announced his intention to appoint Eloise Anderson as a member of the Board of Directors of the Student Loan Marketing Association.

December 24

In the morning, the President had an intelligence briefing. Later, he had telephone conversations with members of the U.S. Armed Forces.

December 25

In the morning, the President had an intelligence briefing.

During the day, the President celebrated Christmas with family members.

December 26

In the morning, the President had an intelligence briefing. Later, he and Mrs. Bush traveled to the Bush Ranch in Crawford, TX.

The President announced the recess appointment of Albert Casey as a Governor of the U.S. Postal Service.

The President announced the recess appointment of Bradley D. Belt as a member of the Social Security Advisory Board.

The President announced the recess appointment of Raymond Simon as Assistant Secretary of Education for Elementary and Secondary Education.

The President announced the recess appointments of Gay Hart Gaines and Claudia Puig as members of the Board of Directors of the Corporation for Public Broadcasting.

The President announced the recess appointment of Fayza Veronique Boulad Rodman as a member of the Broadcasting Board of Governors.

The President announced the recess appointments of Cynthia Boich, Dorothy A. Johnson, and Henry Lozano as members of the Board of Directors of the Corporation for National and Community Service.

The President announced the recess appointment of Ronald E. Meisburg as a member of the National Labor Relations Board.

The President announced the recess appointment of Clark Kent Ervin as Inspector General at the Department of Homeland Security.

The President announced the recess appointment of Robert Lerner as Commissioner of Education Statistics at the Department of Education.

December 27

In the morning, the President had an intelligence briefing.

December 28

During the day, the President had a telephone conversation with Secretary of Agriculture Ann M. Veneman concerning the recent incidence of bovine spongiform encephalitis (also known as mad cow disease) in Washington State.

December 29

In the morning, the President had an intelligence briefing.

December 30

In the morning, the President had an intelligence briefing. Later, he participated in an interview with author Ken Walsh.

December 31

In the morning, the President had an intelligence briefing.

Appendix B—Nominations Submitted to the Senate

The following list does not include promotions of members of the Uniformed Services, nominations to the Service Academies, or nominations of Foreign Service officers.

Submitted July 7

Jeane J. Kirkpatrick,
of Maryland, for the rank of Ambassador during her tenure of service as Representative of the United States of America on the Human Rights Commission of the Economic and Social Council of the United Nations.

Federico Lawrence Rocha,
of California, to be U.S. Marshal for the Northern District of California for the term of 4 years, vice James J. Molinari, resigned.

James G. Roche,
of Maryland, to be Secretary of the Army, vice Thomas E. White, resigned.

Donald K. Steinberg,
of California, a career member of the Senior Foreign Service, class of Minister-Counselor, to be Ambassador Extraordinary and Plenipotentiary of the United States of America to the Federal Republic of Nigeria.

Submitted July 8

Daniel J. Bryant,
of Virginia, to be an Assistant Attorney General, vice Viet D. Dinh, resigned.

Submitted July 11

Cynthia R. Church,
of Virginia, to be an Assistant Secretary of Veterans Affairs (Public and Intergovernmental Affairs), vice Maureen P. Cragin, resigned.

Joel David Kaplan,
of Massachusetts, to be Deputy Director of the Office of Management and Budget, vice Nancy Dorn.

Constance Albanese Morella,
of Maryland, to be Representative of the United States of America to the Organization for Economic Cooperation and Development, with the rank of Ambassador.

Leslie Silverman,
of Virginia, to be a member of the Equal Employment Opportunity Commission for a term expiring July 1, 2008 (reappointment).

Mauricio J. Tamargo,
of Florida, to be Chairman of the Foreign Claims Settlement Commission of the United States for a term expiring September 30, 2006 (reappointment).

Submitted July 14

Craig S. Iscoe,
of the District of Columbia, to be Associate Judge of the Superior Court of the District of Columbia for the term of 15 years, vice Frederick D. Dorsey, retired.

Margaret Catharine Rodgers,
of Florida, to be U.S. District Judge for the Northern District of Florida, vice Lacey A. Collier, retiring.

Paul Michael Warner,
of Utah, to be U.S. Attorney for the District of Utah for the term of 4 years (reappointment).

Submitted July 15

Robert B. Charles,
of Maryland, to be an Assistant Secretary of State (International Narcotics and Law Enforcement Affairs), vice R. Rand Beers, resigned.

Kristin J. Forbes,
of Massachusetts, to be a member of the Council of Economic Advisers, vice Randall S. Kroszner, resigned.

Thomasina V. Rogers,
of Maryland, to be a member of the Occupational Safety and Health Review Commission

for a term expiring April 27, 2009 (reappointment).

Harvey S. Rosen,
of New Jersey, to be a member of the Council of Economic Advisers, vice Mark B. McClellan.

Withdrawn July 15

William Preston Graves,
of Kansas, to be a member of the Board of Trustees of the Harry S. Truman Scholarship Foundation for the remainder of the term expiring December 10, 2005, vice Mel Carnahan, which was sent to the Senate on January 9, 2003.

Submitted July 17

Gwendolyn Brown,
of Virginia, to be Chief Financial Officer, National Aeronautics and Space Administration, vice Arnold Gregory Holz, resigned.

Susan C. Schwab,
of Maryland, to be Deputy Secretary of the Treasury, vice Kenneth W. Dam, resigned.

George H. Walker,
of Missouri, to be Ambassador Extraordinary and Plenipotentiary of the United States of America to the Republic of Hungary.

Submitted July 22

Peter Lichtenbaum,
of Virginia, to be an Assistant Secretary of Commerce, vice James J. Jochum.

Kerry N. Weems,
of Virginia, to be an Assistant Secretary of Health and Human Services, vice Janet Hale, resigned.

Submitted July 25

Janice R. Brown,
of California, to be U.S. Circuit Judge for the District of Columbia Circuit, vice Stephen F. Williams, retired.

John Joseph Grossenbacher,
of Illinois, to be a member of the Nuclear Regulatory Commission for the remainder of the term expiring June 30, 2004, vice Richard A. Meserve, resigned.

John Joseph Grossenbacher,
of Illinois, to be a member of the Nuclear Regulatory Commission for a term expiring June 30, 2009 (reappointment).

Brett M. Kavanaugh,
of Maryland, to be U.S. Circuit Judge for the District of Columbia Circuit, vice Laurence H. Silberman, retired.

Submitted July 30

Cristina Beato,
of New Mexico, to be Medical Director in the Regular Corps of the Public Health Service, subject to the qualifications therefor as provided by law and regulations, and to be an Assistant Secretary of Health and Human Services, vice Eve Slater, resigned.

James Casey Kenny,
of Illinois, to be Ambassador Extraordinary and Plenipotentiary of the United States of America to Ireland.

George W. Miller,
of Virginia, to be a Judge of the U.S. Court of Federal Claims for the term of 15 years, vice James T. Turner, term expired.

F. Dennis Saylor IV,
of Massachusetts, to be U.S. District Judge for the District of Massachusetts, vice Robert E. Keeton, retired.

Pamela P. Willeford,
of Texas, to be Ambassador Extraordinary and Plenipotentiary of the United States of America to Switzerland, and to serve concurrently and without additional compensation as Ambassador Extraordinary and Plenipotentiary of the United States of America to the Principality of Liechtenstein.

Submitted August 1

Richard Eugene Hoagland,
of the District of Columbia, a career member of the Senior Foreign Service, class of Minister-Counselor, to be Ambassador Extraordinary and Plenipotentiary of the United States of America to the Republic of Tajikistan.

Sandra L. Townes,
of New York, to be U.S. District Judge for the Eastern District of New York, vice Sterling Johnson, Jr., retired.

Submitted September 2

David L. Lyon,
of California, a career member of the Senior
Foreign Service, to serve concurrently and without additional compensation as Ambassador Extraordinary and Plenipotentiary of the United
States of America to the Republic of Kiribati.

Submitted September 3

Paul S. Atkins,
of Virginia, to be a member of the Securities
and Exchange Commission for a term expiring
June 5, 2008 (reappointment).

Bradley D. Belt,
of the District of Columbia, to be a member
of the Social Security Advisory Board for a term
expiring September 30, 2008, vice Stanford G.
Ross, term expired.

Karan K. Bhatia,
of Maryland, to be an Assistant Secretary of
Transportation, vice Read Van de Water.

William A. Chatfield,
of Texas, to be Director of Selective Service,
vice Alfred Rascon, resigned.

Gordon England,
of Texas, to be Secretary of the Navy (reappointment).

William J. Hudson,
of Virginia, a career member of the Senior Foreign Service, class of Minister-Counselor, to be
Ambassador Extraordinary and Plenipotentiary
of the United States of America to the Republic
of Tunisia.

Michael O. Leavitt,
of Utah, to be Administrator of the Environmental Protection Agency, vice Christine Todd
Whitman, resigned.

James McBride,
of New York, to be a member of the National
Council on the Arts for a term expiring September 3, 2008, vice Nathan Leventhal, term
expired.

Hector E. Morales,
of Texas, to be U.S. Alternate Executive Director of the Inter-American Development Bank,
vice Jorge L. Arrizurieta, resigned.

Michael W. Wynne,
of Florida, to be Under Secretary of Defense
for Acquisition, Technology, and Logistics, vice
Edward C. Aldridge, resigned.

Jennifer Young,
of Ohio, to be an Assistant Secretary of Health
and Human Services, vice Scott Whitaker.

Withdrawn September 4

Miguel A. Estrada,
of Virginia, to be U.S. Circuit Judge for the
District of Columbia Circuit, vice Patricia M.
Wald, which was sent to the Senate on January
7, 2003.

Kerry N. Weems,
of Virginia, to be an Assistant Secretary of
Health and Human Services, vice Janet Hale,
resigned, which was sent to the Senate on July
22, 2003.

Submitted September 10

Ben S. Bernanke,
of New Jersey, to be a member of the Board
of Governors of the Federal Reserve System
for a term of 14 years from February 1, 2004
(reappointment).

Roger Walton Ferguson, Jr.,
of Massachusetts, to be Vice Chairman of the
Board of Governors of the Federal Reserve System for a term of 4 years (reappointment).

Submitted September 15

David Wayne Anderson,
of Minnesota, to be an Assistant Secretary of
the Interior, vice Neal A. McCaleb, resigned.

H. Douglas Barclay,
of New York, to be Ambassador Extraordinary
and Plenipotentiary of the United States of
America to the Republic of El Salvador.

David Eisner,
of Maryland, to be Chief Executive Officer of
the Corporation for National and Community
Service, vice Leslie Lenkowsky, resigned.

W. Robert Pearson,
of Tennessee, a career member of the Senior
Foreign Service, class of Minister-Counselor, to
be Director General of the Foreign Service, vice
Ruth A. Davis.

Randall L. Tobias,
of Indiana, to be Coordinator of U.S. Government Activities To Combat HIV/AIDS Globally, with the rank of Ambassador.

Read Van de Water,
of North Carolina, to be a member of the National Mediation Board for a term expiring July 1, 2006, vice Francis J. Duggan, term expired.

Submitted September 17

William Cabaniss,
of Alabama, to be Ambassador Extraordinary and Plenipotentiary of the United States of America to the Czech Republic.

Louise V. Oliver,
of the District of Columbia, to be a Representative of the United States of America to the 32d Session of the General Conference of the United Nations Educational, Scientific, and Cultural Organization.

Louise V. Oliver,
of the District of Columbia, for the rank of Ambassador during her tenure of service as the U.S. Permanent Representative to the United Nations Educational, Scientific, and Cultural Organization.

Roderick R. Paige,
of Texas, to be a Representative of the United States of America to the 32d Session of the General Conference of the United Nations Educational, Scientific, and Cultural Organization.

Submitted September 18

Kenneth M. Karas,
of New York, to be U.S. District Judge for the Southern District of New York, vice Allen G. Schwartz, deceased.

Kirk Van Tine,
of Virginia, to be Deputy Secretary of Transportation, vice Michael P. Jackson, resigned.

Submitted September 22

Raymond Simon,
of Arkansas, to be Assistant Secretary for Elementary and Secondary Education, Department of Education, vice Susan B. Neuman, resigned.

Submitted September 23

Cynthia Boich,
of California, to be a member of the Board of Directors of the Corporation for National and Community Service for a term expiring October 6, 2007, vice Thomas Ehrlich, term expired.

Louis Guirola, Jr.,
of Mississippi, to be U.S. District Judge for the Southern District of Mississippi, vice Walter J. Gex III, retiring.

Judith C. Herrera,
of New Mexico, to be U.S. District Judge for the District of New Mexico, vice James A. Parker, retired.

David L. Huber,
of Kentucky, to be U.S. Attorney for the Western District of Kentucky for the term of 4 years, vice Stephen Beville Pence, resigned.

Dorothy A. Johnson,
of Michigan, to be a member of the Board of Directors of the Corporation for National and Community Service for a term expiring October 6, 2007 (reappointment).

Henry Lozano,
of California, to be a member of the Board of Directors of the Corporation for National and Community Service for a term expiring October 6, 2008, vice Christopher C. Gallagher, term expiring.

Bernice Phillips,
of New York, to be a member of the Board of Directors of the Legal Services Corporation for a term expiring July 13, 2005, vice Maria Luisa Mercado, term expired.

Submitted September 25

Gregory E. Jackson,
of the District of Columbia, to be an Associate Judge of the Superior Court of the District of Columbia for the term of 15 years, vice Mildred M. Edwards, retired.

Submitted September 29

Raymond W. Gruender,
of Missouri, to be U.S. Circuit Judge for the Eighth Circuit, vice Pasco M. Bowman II, retired.

William James Haynes II,
of Virginia, to be U.S. Circuit Judge for the Fourth Circuit, vice H. Emory Widener, Jr., retiring.

Submitted September 30

William K. Sessions III,
of Vermont, to be a member of the U.S. Sentencing Commission for a term expiring October 31, 2009 (reappointment).

Submitted October 1

Charlotte A. Lane,
of West Virginia, to be a member of the U.S. International Trade Commission for a term expiring December 16, 2009, vice Dennis M. Devaney, to which position she was appointed during the last recess of the Senate.

Daniel Pearson,
of Minnesota, to be a member of the U.S. International Trade Commission for the term expiring June 16, 2011, vice Lynn M. Bragg, term expired, to which position he was appointed during the last recess of the Senate.

A. Paul Anderson,
of Florida, to be a Federal Maritime Commissioner for the term expiring June 30, 2007, vice Delmond J.H. Won, term expired, to which position he was appointed during the last recess of the Senate.

Daniel Pipes,
of Pennsylvania, to be a member of the Board of Directors of the U.S. Institute of Peace for a term expiring January 19, 2005, vice Zalmay Khalilzad, term expired, to which position he was appointed during the last recess of the Senate.

John Paul Woodley, Jr.,
of Virginia, to be an Assistant Secretary of the Army, vice Michael Parker, to which position he was appointed during the last recess of the Senate.

David Wesley Fleming,
of California, to be a member of the Board of Trustees of the James Madison Memorial Fellowship Foundation for a term expiring May 29, 2007, vice Alan G. Lowy, term expired, to which position he was appointed during the last recess of the Senate.

Jay Phillip Greene,
of Florida, to be a member of the Board of Trustees of the James Madison Memorial Fellowship Foundation for a term expiring November 17, 2005, vice Louise L. Stevenson, term expired, to which position he was appointed during the last recess of the Senate.

John Richard Petrocik,
of Missouri, to be a member of the Board of Trustees of the James Madison Memorial Fellowship Foundation for a term expiring September 27, 2008, vice Elizabeth Griffith, term expired, to which position he was appointed during the last recess of the Senate.

Juanita Alicia Vasquez-Gardner,
of Texas, to be a member of the Board of Trustees of the Harry S. Truman Scholarship Foundation for a term expiring December 10, 2003, vice Steven L. Zinter, term expired, to which position she was appointed during the last recess of the Senate.

Juanita Alicia Vasquez-Gardner,
of Texas, to be a member of the Board of Trustees of the Harry S. Truman Scholarship Foundation for a term expiring December 10, 2009 (reappointment).

Patrick Lloyd McCrory,
of North Carolina, to be a member of the Board of Trustees of the Harry S. Truman Scholarship Foundation for a term expiring December 10, 2005, vice Richard C. Hackett, term expired, to which position he was appointed during the last recess of the Senate.

Jose A. Fourquet,
of New Jersey, to be a member of the Board of Directors of the Inter-American Foundation for a term expiring September 20, 2004, vice Mark L. Schneider, term expired, to which position he was appointed during the last recess of the Senate.

Adolfo A. Franco,
of Virginia, to be a member of the Board of Directors of the Inter-American Foundation for a term expiring September 20, 2008, vice Jeffrey Davidow, resigned, to which position he was appointed during the last recess of the Senate.

Roger Francisco Noriega,
of Kansas, to be a member of the Board of Directors of the Inter-American Foundation for

a term expiring September 20, 2006, vice Harriett C. Babbitt, term expired, to which position he was appointed during the last recess of the Senate.

Ephraim Batambuze,
of Illinois, to be a member of the Board of Directors of the African Development Foundation for a term expiring February 9, 2008, vice Henry McKoy, term expired, to which position he was appointed during the last recess of the Senate.

Mary Kramer,
of Iowa, to be Ambassador Extraordinary and Plenipotentiary of the United States of America to Barbados, and to serve concurrently and without additional compensation as Ambassador Extraordinary and Plenipotentiary of the United States of America to St. Kitts and Nevis, St. Lucia, Antigua and Barbuda, the Commonwealth of Dominica, Grenada, and St. Vincent and the Grenadines.

Submitted October 2

Jose Antonio Aponte,
of Colorado, to be a member of the National Commission on Libraries and Information Science for a term expiring July 19, 2007, vice Martha B. Gould, term expired.

Sandra Frances Ashworth,
of Idaho, to be a member of the National Commission on Libraries and Information Science for a term expiring July 19, 2004, vice Paulette H. Holahan.

Edward Louis Bertorelli,
of Massachusetts, to be a member of the National Commission on Libraries and Information Science for a term expiring July 19, 2005, vice C. E. Abramson, term expired.

Carol L. Diehl,
of Wisconsin, to be a member of the National Commission on Libraries and Information Science for a term expiring July 19, 2005, vice Walter Anderson, term expired.

Allison Druin,
of Maryland, to be a member of the National Commission on Libraries and Information Science for a term expiring July 19, 2006, vice Rebecca T. Bingham, term expired.

Beth Fitzsimmons,
of Michigan, to be a member of the National Commission on Libraries and Information Science for a term expiring July 19, 2006, vice Jose-Marie Griffiths, term expired.

Patricia M. Hines,
of South Carolina, to be a member of the National Commission on Libraries and Information Science for a term expiring July 19, 2005, vice LeVar Burton, term expired.

Colleen Ellen Huebner,
of Washington, to be a member of the National Commission on Libraries and Information Science for a term expiring July 19, 2007, vice Jeanne Hurley Simon.

Stephen M. Kennedy,
of New Hampshire, to be a member of the National Commission on Libraries and Information Science for a term expiring July 19, 2007, vice Donald L. Robinson.

Bridget L. Lamont,
of Illinois, to be a member of the National Commission on Libraries and Information Science for a term expiring July 19, 2008, vice Marilyn Gell Mason, term expired.

Mary H. Perdue,
of Maryland, to be a member of the National Commission on Libraries and Information Science for a term expiring July 19, 2008, vice Frank J. Lucchino, resigned.

Herman Lavon Totten,
of Texas, to be a member of the National Commission on Libraries and Information Science for a term expiring July 19, 2008, vice Bobby L. Roberts, term expired.

Submitted October 3

Paul S. DeGregorio,
of Missouri, to be a member of the Election Assistance Commission for a term of 2 years (new position).

Gracia M. Hillman,
of the District of Columbia, to be a member of the Election Assistance Commission for a term of 2 years (new position).

Michele M. Leonhart,
of California, to be Deputy Administrator of Drug Enforcement, vice John B. Brown III, resigned.

Raymundo Martinez III,
of Texas, to be a member of the Election Assistance Commission for a term of 4 years (new position).

Edward B. O'Donnell, Jr.,
of Tennessee, a career member of the Senior Foreign Service, class of Counselor, for the rank of Ambassador during his tenure of service as Special Envoy for Holocaust Issues.

Jeffrey A. Rosen,
of Virginia, to be General Counsel of the Department of Transportation, vice Kirk Van Tine.

Deforest B. Soaries, Jr.,
of New Jersey, to be a member of the Election Assistance Commission for a term of 4 years (new position).

Submitted October 14

Robert L. Crandall,
of Texas, to be a member of the Reform Board (Amtrak) for a term of 5 years, vice Michael S. Dukakis, term expired.

Michael D. Gallagher,
of Washington, to be Assistant Secretary of Commerce for Communications and Information, vice Nancy Victory, resigned.

Susan Johnson Grant,
of Virginia, to be Chief Financial Officer, Department of Energy, vice Bruce Marshall Carnes, resigned.

Virginia E. Hopkins,
of Alabama, to be U.S. District Judge for the Northern District of Alabama, vice Edwin L. Nelson, deceased.

Stuart Ishimaru,
of the District of Columbia, to be a member of the Equal Employment Opportunity Commission for a term expiring July 1, 2007, vice Paul M. Igasaki, term expired.

Ricardo S. Martinez,
of Washington, to be U.S. District Judge for the Western District of Washington, vice an additional position in accordance with 28 U.S.C. 133(b)(1).

Drew R. McCoy,
of Massachusetts, to be a member of the Board of Trustees of the James Madison Memorial Fellowship Foundation for a term of 6 years, vice Lance Banning.

Robert N. McFarland,
of Texas, to be an Assistant Secretary of Veterans Affairs (Information and Technology), vice John A. Gauss, resigned.

Jon R. Purnell,
of Massachusetts, a career member of the Senior Foreign Service, class of Counselor, to be Ambassador Extraordinary and Plenipotentiary of the United States of America to the Republic of Uzbekistan.

Thomas Thomas Riley,
of California, to be Ambassador Extraordinary and Plenipotentiary of the United States of America to the Kingdom of Morocco.

Margaret Scobey,
of Tennessee, a career member of the Senior Foreign Service, class of Minister-Counselor, to be Ambassador Extraordinary and Plenipotentiary of the United States of America to the Syrian Arab Republic.

Louis S. Thompson,
of Maryland, to be a member of the Reform Board (Amtrak) for a term of 5 years, vice John Robert Smith, term expired.

Margaret DeBardeleben Tutwiler,
of Alabama, to be Under Secretary of State for Public Diplomacy, vice Charlotte L. Beers, resigned.

Gary Lee Visscher,
of Maryland, to be a member of the Chemical Safety and Hazard Investigation Board for a term of 5 years, vice Isadore Rosenthal, term expiring.

Submitted October 15

Marguerita Dianne Ragsdale,
of Virginia, a career member of the Senior Foreign Service, class of Counselor, to be Ambassador Extraordinary and Plenipotentiary of the United States of America to the Republic of Djibouti.

Submitted October 16

Timothy John Dunn,
of Illinois, a career member of the Senior Foreign Service, class of Counselor, for the rank of Ambassador during his tenure of service as Deputy Permanent Representative of the United States of America to the Organization of American States.

Stuart W. Holliday,
of Texas, to be Alternate Representative of the United States of America for Special Political Affairs in the United Nations, with the rank of Ambassador.

Zalmay Khalilzad,
of Maryland, to be Ambassador Extraordinary and Plenipotentiary of the United States of America to the Transitional Islamic State of Afghanistan.

Adam Marc Lindemann,
of New York, to be a member of the Advisory Board for Cuba Broadcasting for a term expiring October 27, 2005, vice Christopher D. Coursen, term expired.

James Curtis Struble,
of California, a career member of the Senior Foreign Service, class of Minister-Counselor, to be Ambassador Extraordinary and Plenipotentiary of the United States of America to the Republic of Peru.

Withdrawn October 16

Thomas Thomas Riley,
of California, to be a member of the Board of Directors of the African Development Foundation for the remainder of the term expiring September 22, 2005, vice Claude A. Allen, which was sent to the Senate on February 27, 2003.

Submitted October 17

James B. Comey,
of New York, to be Deputy Attorney General, vice Larry D. Thompson, resigned.

Submitted October 22

Neil Vincent Wake,
of Arizona, to be U.S. District Judge for the District of Arizona, vice Paul G. Rosenblatt, retiring.

Submitted October 23

Carol Kinsley,
of Massachusetts, to be a member of the Board of Directors of the Corporation for National and Community Service for a term expiring October 6, 2006, vice Toni G. Fay.

Submitted October 24

Floyd Hall,
of New Jersey, to be a member of the Reform Board (Amtrak) for a term of 5 years, vice Amy M. Rosen, term expired.

Edward E. Kaufman,
of Delaware, to be a member of the Broadcasting Board of Governors for a term expiring August 13, 2006 (reappointment).

Fayza Veronique Boulad Rodman,
of the District of Columbia, to be a member of the Broadcasting Board of Governors for a term expiring August 13, 2006, vice Robert M. Ledbetter, Jr., term expired.

Steven J. Simmons,
of Connecticut, to be a member of the Broadcasting Board of Governors for a term expiring August 13, 2006 (reappointment).

Submitted October 29

Arnold I. Havens,
of Virginia, to be General Counsel for the Department of the Treasury, vice David Aufhauser.

Susan K. Sclafani,
of the District of Columbia, to be Assistant Secretary for Vocational and Adult Education, Department of Education, vice Carol D'Amico, resigned.

Submitted October 31

Walter D. Kelley, Jr.,
of Virginia, to be U.S. District Judge for the Eastern District of Virginia, vice Henry C. Morgan, Jr., retiring.

Submitted November 3

Gordon H. Mansfield,
of Virginia, to be Deputy Secretary of Veterans Affairs, vice Leo S. Mackay, Jr., resigned.

Gene E.K. Pratter,
of Pennsylvania, to be U.S. District Judge for the Eastern District of Pennsylvania, vice William H. Yohn, Jr., retiring.

Submitted November 5

William S. Duffey, Jr.,
of Georgia, to be U.S. District Judge for the Northern District of Georgia, vice J. Owen Forrester, retiring.

Laurie Susan Fulton,
of Virginia, to be a member of the Board of Directors of the U.S. Institute of Peace for a term expiring January 19, 2007, vice Harriet M. Zimmerman, term expired.

James M. Loy,
of Virginia, to be Deputy Secretary of Homeland Security, vice Gordon England, resigned.

Peter G. Sheridan,
of New Jersey, to be U.S. District Judge for the District of New Jersey, vice Stephen M. Orlofsky, resigned.

Submitted November 6

Francis J. Harvey,
of California, to be an Assistant Secretary of Defense, vice John P. Stenbit.

Lawrence F. Stengel,
of Pennsylvania, to be U.S. District Judge for the Eastern District of Pennsylvania, vice Ronald L. Buckwalter, retiring.

Submitted November 7

Steven J. Law,
of the District of Columbia, to be Deputy Secretary of Labor, vice Donald Cameron Findlay, resigned.

Kiron Kanina Skinner,
of Pennsylvania, to be a member of the National Security Education Board for a term of 4 years, vice Herschelle S. Challenor.

J. Robinson West,
of the District of Columbia, to be a member of the Board of Directors of the U.S. Institute

of Peace for a term expiring January 19, 2007, vice Marc E. Leland, term expired.

Submitted November 14

David C. Mulford,
of Illinois, to be Ambassador Extraordinary and Plenipotentiary of the United States of America to India.

Diane S. Sykes,
of Wisconsin, to be U.S. Circuit Judge for the Seventh Circuit, vice John L. Coffey, retiring.

Submitted November 17

W. Douglas Buttrey,
of Tennessee, to be a member of the Surface Transportation Board for a term expiring December 31, 2008, vice Linda Joan Morgan, resigned.

Glyn T. Davies,
of the District of Columbia, a career member of the Senior Foreign Service, class of Minister-Counselor, for the rank of Ambassador during his tenure of service as the Political Director for the U.S. Presidency of the G–8.

Gay Hart Gaines,
of Florida, to be a member of the Board of Directors of the Corporation for Public Broadcasting for a term expiring January 31, 2010, vice Ritajean Hartung Butterworth, term expiring.

Francis Mulvey,
of Maryland, to be a member of the Surface Transportation Board for a term expiring December 31, 2007, vice Wayne O. Burkes, resigned.

James C. Oberwetter,
of Texas, to be Ambassador Extraordinary and Plenipotentiary of the United States of America to the Kingdom of Saudi Arabia.

Submitted November 19

J. Russell George,
of Virginia, to be Inspector General for Tax Administration, Department of the Treasury, vice David C. Williams.

Submitted November 20

Jonathan Baron,
of Maryland, to be a member of the Board of Directors of the National Board for Education Sciences for a term of 3 years (new position).

Elizabeth Ann Bryan,
of Texas, to be a member of the Board of Directors of the National Board for Education Sciences for a term of 4 years (new position).

James R. Davis,
of Mississippi, to be a member of the Board of Directors of the National Board for Education Sciences for a term of 2 years (new position).

Robert C. Granger,
of New Jersey, to be a member of the Board of Directors of the National Board for Education Sciences for a term of 4 years (new position).

Frank Philip Handy,
of Florida, to be a member of the Board of Directors of the National Board for Education Sciences for a term of 3 years (new position).

Eric Alan Hanushek,
of California, to be a member of the Board of Directors of the National Board for Education Sciences for a term of 2 years (new position).

Caroline M. Hoxby,
of Massachusetts, to be a member of the Board of Directors of the National Board for Education Sciences for a term of 4 years (new position).

Gerald Lee,
of Pennsylvania, to be a member of the Board of Directors of the National Board for Education Sciences for a term of 4 years (new position).

Roberto Ibarra Lopez,
of Texas, to be a member of the Board of Directors of the National Board for Education Sciences for a term of 2 years (new position).

Richard James Milgram,
of New Mexico, to be a member of the Board of Directors of the National Board for Education Sciences for a term of 3 years (new position).

Sally Epstein Shaywitz,
of Connecticut, to be a member of the Board of Directors of the National Board for Education Sciences for a term of 3 years (new position).

Joseph K. Torgesen,
of Florida, to be a member of the Board of Directors of the National Board for Education Sciences for a term of 4 years (new position).

Herbert John Walberg,
of Illinois, to be a member of the Board of Directors of the National Board for Education Sciences for a term of 3 years (new position).

Stuart W. Holliday,
of Texas, to be an Alternate Representative of the United States of America to the Sessions of the General Assembly of the United Nations during his tenure of service as Alternate Representative of the United States of America for Special Political Affairs in the United Nations.

Ronald E. Meisburg,
of Virginia, to be a member of the National Labor Relations Board for the term of 5 years expiring August 27, 2008, vice Rene Acosta, resigned.

Submitted November 21

Joseph Max Cleland,
of Georgia, to be a member of the Board of Directors of the Export-Import Bank of the United States for a term expiring January 20, 2007, vice Dorian Vanessa Weaver, term expired.

Ann M. Corkery,
of Virginia, to be an Alternate Representative of the United States of America to the 58th Session of the General Assembly of the United Nations.

Lawrence T. Di Rita,
of Michigan, to be an Assistant Secretary of Defense, vice Victoria Clarke.

Jaymie Alan Durnan,
of New Hampshire, to be an Assistant Secretary of the Army, vice Mario P. Fiori.

April H. Foley,
of New York, to be First Vice President of the Export-Import Bank of the United States for the remainder of the term expiring January 20, 2005, vice Eduardo Aguirre, Jr., resigned.

Benjamin A. Gilman,
of New York, to be a Representative of the United States of America to the 58th Session of the General Assembly of the United Nations.

Sanford Gottesman,
of Texas, to be a member of the Board of Directors of the Overseas Private Investment Corporation for a term expiring December 17, 2005, vice Gary A. Barron, term expired.

Walid Maalouf,
of Virginia, to be an Alternate Representative of the United States of America to the 58th Session of the General Assembly of the United Nations.

Robert Hurley McKinney,
of Indiana, to be a member of the Advisory Board for Cuba Broadcasting for a term expiring October 27, 2004, vice William A. Geoghegan, term expired.

Diane M. Ruebling,
of California, to be a member of the Board of Directors of the Overseas Private Investment Corporation for a term expiring December 17, 2005 (reappointment).

James M. Strock,
of California, to be a member of the U.S. Advisory Commission on Public Diplomacy for a term expiring July 1, 2006, vice Penny Percy Korth, term expired.

C. William Swank,
of Ohio, to be a member of the Board of Directors of the Overseas Private Investment Corporation for a term expiring December 17, 2005 (reappointment).

Franklin S. Van Antwerpen,
of Pennsylvania, to be U.S. Circuit Judge for the Third Circuit, vice Edward R. Becker, retired.

Withdrawn November 21

April H. Foley,
of New York, to be a member of the Board of Directors of the Export-Import Bank of the

United States for a term expiring January 20, 2007, vice Dan Herman Renberg, term expired, which were sent to the Senate on April 10, 2003, and May 14, 2003.

Submitted November 24

Jane J. Boyle,
of Texas, to be U.S. District Judge for the Northern District of Texas, vice Jerry L. Buchmeyer, retired.

Submitted November 25

Linda Morrison Combs,
of North Carolina, to be an Assistant Secretary of Transportation, vice Donna R. McLean, resigned.

Marcia G. Cooke,
of Florida, to be U.S. District Judge for the Southern District of Florida, vice Wilkie D. Ferguson, Jr., deceased.

Curtis V. Gomez,
of Virgin Islands, to be Judge for the District Court of the Virgin Islands for a term of 10 years, vice Thomas K. Moore, term expired.

Jack Edwin McGregor,
of Connecticut, to be a member of the Advisory Board of the Saint Lawrence Seaway Development Corporation, vice Vincent J. Sorrentino.

Scott Kevin Walker,
of Wisconsin, to be a member of the Advisory Board of the Saint Lawrence Seaway Development Corporation, vice Anthony S. Earl.

Roger W. Wallace,
of Texas, to be a member of the Board of Directors of the Inter-American Foundation for a term expiring October 6, 2008, vice Fred P. DuVal.

Mark J. Warshawsky,
of Maryland, to be an Assistant Secretary of the Treasury, vice Richard Clarida, resigned.

Juan R. Sanchez,
of Pennsylvania, to be U.S. District Judge for the Eastern District of Pennsylvania, vice Jay C. Waldman, deceased.

Submitted December 9

Samuel W. Bodman,
of Massachusetts, to be Deputy Secretary of the Treasury, vice Kenneth W. Dam, resigned.

LaFayette Collins,
of Texas, to be U.S. Marshal for the Western District of Texas for the term of 4 years, vice Jack O. Dean.

Peter W. Hall,
of Vermont, to be U.S. Circuit Judge for the Second Circuit, vice Fred I. Parker, deceased.

Robert Jepson,
of Georgia, to be a member of the Internal Revenue Service Oversight Board for a term expiring September 14, 2008, vice Karen Hastie Williams, term expired.

Paul Jones,
of Colorado, to be a member of the Internal Revenue Service Oversight Board for a term expiring September 14, 2008, vice Charles L. Kolbe, term expired.

Rhonda Keenum,
of Mississippi, to be Assistant Secretary of Commerce and Director General of the United States and Foreign Commercial Service, vice Maria Cino, resigned.

Charles L. Kolbe,
of Iowa, to be a member of the Internal Revenue Service Oversight Board for the remainder of the term expiring September 14, 2004, vice Steve H. Nickles, resigned.

Donald Korb,
of Ohio, to be Chief Counsel for the Internal Revenue Service and an Assistant General Counsel in the Department of the Treasury, vice B. John Williams, Jr.

Lisa Kruska,
of Virginia, to be an Assistant Secretary of Labor, vice Kathleen M. Harrington.

James L. Robart,
of Washington, to be U.S. District Judge for the Western District of Washington, vice Thomas S. Zilly, retiring.

Brian Carlton Roseboro,
of New Jersey, to be an Under Secretary of the Treasury, vice Peter R. Fisher, resigned.

Ronald J. Tenpas,
of Illinois, to be U.S. Attorney for the Southern District of Illinois for the term of 4 years, vice Miriam F. Miquelon, resigned.

Withdrawn December 9

Susan C. Schwab,
of Maryland, to be Deputy Secretary of the Treasury, vice Kenneth W. Dam, resigned, which was sent to the Senate on July 17, 2003.

Appendix C—Checklist of White House Press Releases

The following list contains releases of the Office of the Press Secretary which are not included in this book.

Released July 1

Transcript of a press briefing by Press Secretary Ari Fleischer

Statement by the Press Secretary announcing that the President signed H.R. 389, H.R. 519, and H.R. 788

Fact sheet: Progress in the Global War on Terrorism

Announcement of nomination for U.S. District Judge for the Eastern District of New York

Announcement of nomination of U.S. Marshal for the Northern District of California

Released July 2

Transcript of a press briefing by Press Secretary Ari Fleischer

Statement by the Press Secretary on disaster assistance to Kentucky

Fact sheet: The President's Emergency Plan for AIDS Relief

Released July 3

Transcript of a press briefing by National Security Adviser Condoleezza Rice on the President's upcoming visit to Africa

Statement by the Press Secretary announcing that the President signed H.R. 658

Statement by the Press Secretary: Visit by Presidential Envoy James Baker to Tbilisi, Georgia

Fact sheet: USA Freedom Corps Launches "How I Spent My Summer"

Released July 4

Transcript of a press gaggle by Press Secretary Ari Fleischer

Transcript of an interview of the Press Secretary by the TV pool

Released July 5

Statement by the Press Secretary on the terrorist attack in Moscow

Released July 9

Transcript of a press gaggle by Press Secretary Ari Fleischer

Released July 10

Transcript of a press gaggle by Press Secretary Ari Fleischer

Transcript of a press briefing by Secretary of State Colin L. Powell on the President's visit to Africa

Statement by the Press Secretary: Visit by United Nations Secretary-General Kofi Annan

Released July 11

Transcript of a press gaggle by Press Secretary Ari Fleischer and National Security Adviser Condoleezza Rice

Statement by the Press Secretary: Visit of British Prime Minister Tony Blair

Statement by the Press Secretary on disaster assistance to Indiana

Announcement of nomination of U.S. Attorney for the District of Utah

Released July 12

Transcript of a press gaggle by Press Secretary Ari Fleischer

Released July 14

Transcript of a press briefing by Press Secretary Ari Fleischer

Statement by the Press Secretary: Visit of Prime Minister Silvio Berlusconi of Italy

Statement by the Press Secretary announcing that the President signed into law H.R. 825, H.R. 917, H.R. 925, H.R. 981, H.R. 985, H.R. 1055, H.R. 1368, H.R. 1465, H.R. 1596, H.R. 1609, H.R. 1740, H.R. 2030, and S. 858

Statement by the Press Secretary on disaster assistance to Arizona

Announcement of nomination for Associate Judge of the Superior Court of the District of Columbia

Released July 15

Transcript of a press briefing by Press Secretary Scott McClellan

Transcript of a press briefing by Office of Management and Budget Director Josh Bolten

Statement by the Press Secretary: United States Hosting 2004 Group of Eight (G–8) Summit in Sea Island, GA

Statement by the Press Secretary on disaster assistance to Ohio

Released July 16

Transcript of a press briefing by Press Secretary Scott McClellan

Statement by the Press Secretary: Passage of the Burmese Freedom and Democracy Act

Released July 17

Transcript of a press briefing by Press Secretary Scott McClellan

Statement by the Press Secretary: Visit of President Nestor Kirchner of Argentina

Statement by the Press Secretary: Visit by Palestinian Prime Minister Mahmoud Abbas

Statement by the Press Secretary: Visit by Prime Minister Ariel Sharon of Israel

Statement by the Press Secretary: Enhanced U.S.-U.K. Exchange of Defense-Related Information

Released July 18

Transcript of a press gaggle by Press Secretary Scott McClellan

Statement by the Press Secretary: U.S.-U.K. Discussions on British Detainees

Statement by the Press Secretary announcing the recipients of the Presidential Medal of Freedom, to be presented on July 23

Statement by the Press Secretary on disaster assistance to Texas

Statement by the Press Secretary announcing that the President signed S. 709 on July 17

Fact sheet: President Bush Highlights Health and Fitness Initiative

Released July 21

Transcript of a press gaggle by Press Secretary Scott McClellan

Statement by the Press Secretary on disaster assistance to Nebraska

Released July 22

Transcript of a press briefing by Press Secretary Scott McClellan

Transcript of a press briefing by Securities and Exchange Commission Chairman William H. Donaldson and Deputy Attorney General Larry D. Thompson on the status report of the Corporate Fraud Task Force

Fact sheet: One-Year Anniversary of the President's Corporate Fraud Task Force

Transcript of a press briefing by White House Communications Director Daniel Bartlett and Deputy National Security Adviser Stephen J. Hadley on Iraqi weapons of mass destruction and the State of the Union speech

Statement by the Press Secretary on U.S. military action against Uday and Qusay Hussein

Released July 23

Transcript of a press briefing by Press Secretary Scott McClellan

Transcript of remarks by National Security Adviser Condoleezza Rice at the Dole Institute of Politics on July 22

Text of the citations for the Presidential Medal of Freedom

Released July 24

Transcript of a press gaggle by Press Secretary Scott McClellan

Fact sheet: Strengthening the Economy

Released July 25

Transcript of a press briefing by Press Secretary Scott McClellan

Statement by the Press Secretary: Liberia

Fact sheet: White House South Lawn Tee Ball

Released July 28

Transcript of a press gaggle by Press Secretary Scott McClellan

Statement by the Press Secretary announcing that the President signed H.R. 2330

Released July 29

Transcript of a press briefing by Press Secretary Scott McClellan

Statement by the Press Secretary announcing that the President signed H.R. 255, H.R. 773, H.R. 1577, and S. 1399

Statement by the Press Secretary on disaster assistance to Florida

Statement by the Press Secretary on disaster assistance to Tennessee

Released July 30

Statement by the Press Secretary announcing that the President signed S. 246

Announcement of nomination for U.S. Court of Federal Claims Judge

Released July 31

Transcript of a press briefing by Press Secretary Scott McClellan

Released August 1

Transcript of a press briefing by Press Secretary Scott McClellan

Statement by the Press Secretary announcing that the President signed H.R. 74 and S. 1280

Statement by the Press Secretary: Terrorist Act in Mozdok on August 1

Statement by the Press Secretary on disaster assistance to North Dakota

Statement by the Press Secretary on disaster assistance to Ohio

Released August 2

Transcript of a press gaggle by Press Secretary Scott McClellan

Released August 4

Transcript of a press gaggle by Press Secretary Scott McClellan

Released August 5

Transcript of a press gaggle by Press Secretary Scott McClellan

Released August 7

Transcript of a press gaggle by Deputy Press Secretary Claire Buchan

Advance text of remarks by National Security Adviser Condoleezza Rice at the 28th Annual Convention of the National Association of Black Journalists

Released August 8

Statement by the Deputy Press Secretary announcing that the President signed H.R. 2859

Released August 11

Transcript of a press gaggle by Deputy Press Secretary Claire Buchan

Fact sheet: President Bush Promotes Healthy Forests

Announcement of nomination for Environmental Protection Agency Administrator

Released August 12

Transcript of a press gaggle by Deputy Press Secretary Claire Buchan

Released August 13

Announcement of nomination for U.S. District Judge for the Western District of Washington

Released August 14

Transcript of a press gaggle by Press Secretary Scott McClellan

Released August 15

Transcript of a press gaggle by Press Secretary Scott McClellan

Statement by the Press Secretary on the joint Canada-U.S. task force on the recent power outage in North America

Statement by the Press Secretary on the appointment of Deputy Assistant to the President and Coordinator for Strategic Planning at the National Security Council

Statement by the Press Secretary on Libya's letter to the U.N. Security Council stating it accepts responsibility for the actions of its officials in the 1988 Pan Am 103 bombing

Statement by the Press Secretary announcing that the President signed H.R. 1018 and H.R. 1761 on August 14

Fact sheet: Strengthening and Caring for America's National Parks

Announcement of nomination for U.S. District Judge for the District of New Jersey

Released August 16

Statement by the Press Secretary announcing that the President signed H.R. 2195, H.R. 2465, H.R. 2854, and S. 1015 on August 15

Released August 18

Transcript of a press gaggle by Press Secretary Scott McClellan

Statement by the Press Secretary: Liberian Peace Agreement Signed in Accra, Ghana

Released August 19

Statement by the Press Secretary: Presidential Determination Regarding U.S. Assistance to the Government of Colombia Airbridge Denial Program

Released August 20

Transcript of a press gaggle by Press Secretary Scott McClellan

Released August 21

Transcript of a press gaggle by Press Secretary Scott McClellan

Released August 22

Transcript of a press gaggle by Press Secretary Scott McClellan

Fact sheet: President Bush Highlights Salmon Recovery Successes

Released August 23

Statement by the Press Secretary on disaster assistance to Pennsylvania

Statement by the Press Secretary on emergency assistance to New York

Released August 25

Statement by the Press Secretary: Visit of the Prime Minister of Kuwait

Advance text of remarks by National Security Adviser Condoleezza Rice at the 104th National Convention of the Veterans of Foreign Wars

Released August 26

Transcript of a press gaggle by Deputy Press Secretary Claire Buchan

Statement by the Deputy Press Secretary: Visit of Prime Minister Jan Peter Balkenende of the Netherlands

Released August 27

Transcript of a press gaggle by Deputy Press Secretary Claire Buchan

Statement by the Deputy Press Secretary on the Presidential election in Rwanda

Released August 28

Transcript of a press gaggle by Deputy Press Secretary Claire Buchan

Transcript of an interview of National Security Adviser Condoleezza Rice by ZDF German Television on July 31

Released August 29

Statement by the Deputy Press Secretary on disaster assistance to New York

Released September 1

Transcript of a press gaggle by Deputy Press Secretary Claire Buchan

Released September 2

Transcript of a press briefing by Press Secretary Scott McClellan

Released September 3

Transcript of a press briefing by Press Secretary Scott McClellan

Statement by the Press Secretary: Visit by Pakistani Prime Minister Jamali

Released September 4

Transcript of a press gaggle by Press Secretary Scott McClellan

Statement by the Press Secretary: Principles for the Proliferation Security Initiative

Fact sheet: Proliferation Security Initiative: Statement of Interdiction Principles

Fact sheet: President Bush Outlines Six Point Plan for the Economy: "A full agenda for the creation of jobs in America"

Released September 5

Transcript of a press gaggle by Press Secretary Scott McClellan

Transcript of remarks by Press Secretary Scott McClellan to the travel pool

Statement by the Press Secretary on disaster assistance to Indiana

Released September 6

Statement by the Press Secretary: Prime Minister Abbas' Submission of His Resignation

Released September 7

Excerpts of the President's address to the Nation on the war on terror

Advance text of the President's address to the Nation on the war on terror

Fact sheet: White House South Lawn Tee Ball

Released September 8

Transcript of a press gaggle by Press Secretary Scott McClellan

Fact sheet: Request for Additional FY 2004 Funding for the War on Terror

Released September 9

Transcript of a press gaggle by Press Secretary Scott McClellan

Released September 10

Transcript of a press briefing by Press Secretary Scott McClellan

Statement by the Press Secretary: Presidential Determination Regarding the Trafficking Victims Protection Act for 2003

Statement by Press Secretary on the President's meeting with His Holiness, the XIV Dalai Lama

Released September 11

Statement by the Press Secretary: Visit of King Abdullah II and Queen Rania of Jordan

Statement by the Press Secretary on the murder of Swedish Foreign Minister Anna Lindh

Announcement of nomination for U.S. Attorney for the Western District of Kentucky

Released September 12

Transcript of a press gaggle by Press Secretary Scott McClellan

Statement by the Press Secretary: State Visit by President Kibaki of Kenya

Statement by the Press Secretary: President Bush To Participate in the 58th United Nations General Assembly

Statement by the Press Secretary on disaster assistance to Vermont

Statement by the Press Secretary on disaster assistance to New Hampshire

Released September 15

Transcript of a press gaggle by Press Secretary Scott McClellan, Acting Environmental Protection Agency Administrator Marianne Horinko, and Council on Environmental Quality Chairman James L. Connaughton

Statement by the Press Secretary: Annual Presidential Determinations of Major Illicit Drug-Producing and Drug-Transit Countries

Statement by the Press Secretary: Visit of President Vladimir Putin of the Russian Federation

Statement by the Press Secretary: Presidential Determination Regarding KEDO Funding

Fact sheet: Improving Air Quality and Increasing Energy Efficiency, Safety, and Reliability

Released September 16

Transcript of a press briefing by Press Secretary Scott McClellan

Statement by the Press Secretary: Visit of President Nicanor Duarte of Paraguay

Fact sheet: Clear Skies: A Clear Improvement for the Environment

Released September 17

Transcript of a press briefing by Press Secretary Scott McClellan

Statement by the Press Secretary announcing that the President signed H.R. 1668

Released September 18

Statement by the Press Secretary on disaster assistance to North Carolina

Statement by the Press Secretary on disaster assistance to Virginia

Released September 19

Statement by the Press Secretary on disaster assistance to Maryland

Released September 20

Statement by the Press Secretary: One Hundred Years of Diplomatic Relations With Bulgaria

Statement by the Press Secretary on disaster assistance to Delaware

Statement by the Press Secretary on disaster assistance to the District of Columbia

Released September 22

Transcript of a press briefing by Faith-Based and Community Initiatives Office Director H. James Towey, Labor Secretary Elaine L. Chao, Housing and Urban Development Secretary Mel R. Martinez, and Health and Human Services Deputy Secretary Claude Allen

Transcript of a press briefing by National Security Adviser Condoleezza Rice on the President's upcoming visit to the United Nations General Assembly

Fact sheet: White House Office of Faith-Based and Community Initiatives

Released September 23

Transcript of a press gaggle by Press Secretary Scott McClellan

Statement by the Press Secretary: Visit of President Carlo Ciampi of Italy

Advance text of the President's address to the United Nations General Assembly

Released September 24

Statement by the Press Secretary on disaster assistance to New Jersey

Statement by the Press Secretary on disaster assistance to Michigan

Statement by the Press Secretary on disaster assistance to Delaware

Statement by the Press Secretary on disaster assistance to Ohio

Statement by the Press Secretary on disaster assistance to West Virginia

Released September 25

Transcript of a press briefing by Press Secretary Scott McClellan

Statement by the Press Secretary: State Visit to the United Kingdom

Statement by the Press Secretary on the death of Akila Hashimi, member of the Governing Council of Iraq

Statement by the Press Secretary announcing that the President signed H.R. 13

Released September 26

Transcript of a press briefing by Press Secretary Scott McClellan

Released September 27

Fact sheet: U.S.-Russian Commercial Investments

Fact sheet: Export-Import Bank of the United States in Russia

Fact sheet: U.S.-Russia Cooperation in Housing and Urban Development

Fact sheet: Russian-American Banking Dialogue

Fact sheet: Russian-American Business Dialogue

Fact sheet: United States-Russia Commercial Energy Summit

Fact sheet: HIV/AIDS

Statement by the Press Secretary on disaster assistance to Pennsylvania

Released September 29

Transcript of a press briefing by Press Secretary Scott McClellan

Released September 30

Transcript of a press gaggle by Press Secretary Scott McClellan

Statement by the Press Secretary announcing that the President signed H.J. Res. 69, S. 520, and S. 678

Released October 1

Transcript of a press briefing by Press Secretary Scott McClellan

Statement by the Press Secretary announcing that the President signed H.R. 3087

Statement by the Press Secretary announcing that the President signed H.R. 3146

Released October 2

Transcript of a press briefing by Press Secretary Scott McClellan

Released October 3

Transcript of a press gaggle by Press Secretary Scott McClellan

Statement by the Press Secretary announcing that the President signed H.R. 659, H.R. 978, S. 111, S. 233, and S. 278

Released October 6

Transcript of a press briefing by Press Secretary Scott McClellan

Released October 7

Transcript of a press briefing by Press Secretary Scott McClellan

Released October 8

Transcript of a press briefing by Press Secretary Scott McClellan

Statement by the Press Secretary on the President's upcoming visit to Asia and Australia

Advance text of remarks by National Security Adviser Condoleezza Rice to the Chicago Council on Foreign Relations in Chicago, IL

Fact sheet: Preventing Domestic Violence

Released October 9

Transcript of a press gaggle by Press Secretary Scott McClellan

Fact sheet: Building Momentum for New Job Creation

Released October 10

Transcript of a press briefing by Press Secretary Scott McClellan

Statement by the Press Secretary announcing that the President signed H.R. 1925, H.R. 2826, and S. 570

Fact sheet: Cuba

Released October 14

Transcript of a press briefing by Press Secretary Scott McClellan

Transcript of a press briefing by National Security Adviser Condoleezza Rice on the President's visit to Asia and Australia

Transcript of remarks by National Security Adviser Condoleezza Rice to the Inter American Press Association on October 13

Announcement of nomination for U.S. District Judge for the Eastern District of Virginia

Excerpts of the President's roundtable interview with Asian journalists

Released October 15

Transcript of a press gaggle by Press Secretary Scott McClellan

Fact sheet: Expanding Homeownership Opportunities and Strengthening Our Economy

Released October 16

Statement by the Press Secretary: President Ion Iliescu To Visit Washington

Released October 18

Transcript of a press gaggle by Press Secretary Scott McClellan

Released October 19

Statement by the Press Secretary: Announcement of U.S.-Thailand FTA Negotiations

Advance text of the President's remarks to the Thai troops

Released October 20

Transcript of a press briefing by National Security Adviser Condoleezza Rice on the President's bilateral meetings

Fact sheet: President Bush Announces United States Intends To Negotiate a Free Trade Agreement With Thailand

Fact sheet: APEC Pledges To Improve Transparency and Fight Corruption

Fact sheet: U.S. Actions at the APEC Summit: Day One

Released October 21

Transcript of a press gaggle by Press Secretary Scott McClellan

Transcript of remarks by Press Secretary Scott McClellan on Iran

Fact sheet: Health Security Initiative

Fact sheet: New APEC Initiatives on Counterterrorism

Fact sheet: Energy Security Initiative

Statement by the Press Secretary: President Bush To Award Medal of Freedom to NATO Secretary General Lord Robertson

Statement by the Press Secretary announcing that the President signed H.R. 2691

Released November 11

Transcript of an interview of National Security Adviser Condoleezza Rice by KXAS–TV, Dallas, TX, on November 10

Transcript of an interview of National Security Adviser Condoleezza Rice by KING–TV, Seattle, WA, on November 10

Transcript of an interview of National Security Adviser Condoleezza Rice by KHOU–TV, Houston, TX, on November 10

Statement by the Press Secretary announcing that the President signed H.J. Res. 52, H.R. 1516, H.R. 3365, S. 470, S. 926, H.R. 1610, H.R. 1882, H.R. 1883, H.R. 2075, H.R. 2254, H.R. 2309, H.R. 2328, H.R. 2396, H.R. 2452, H.R. 2533, H.R. 2746, and H.R. 3011

Fact sheet: In Support of America's Veterans

Released November 12

Transcript of a press briefing by Press Secretary Scott McClellan

Announcement of the National Medal of Arts recipients

Citation for the Presidential Medal of Freedom presentation ceremony for NATO Secretary General Lord Robertson

Released November 13

Transcript of a press gaggle by Press Secretary Scott McClellan

Transcript of a press briefing by National Security Adviser Condoleezza Rice on the President's upcoming visit to the United Kingdom

Fact sheet: President Calls on Congress To "Finish the Job"—Pass a Medicare Prescription Drug Benefit for Seniors

Released November 14

Transcript of a press briefing by Press Secretary Scott McClellan

Transcript of an interview of National Security Adviser Condoleezza Rice by WAGA–TV, Atlanta, GA, on November 10

Transcript of an interview of National Security Adviser Condoleezza Rice by WTVT–TV, Tampa, FL, on November 10

Released November 17

Transcript of a press briefing by Press Secretary Scott McClellan

Statement by the Press Secretary announcing that the President signed H.R. 1442, H.R. 3288, S. 677, and S. 924

Released November 18

Statement by the Press Secretary announcing that the President signed S. 313

Released November 20

Transcript of remarks by First Lady Laura Bush in a Q & A with the press

Released November 21

Transcript of a press gaggle by Deputy Press Secretary Claire Buchan

Statement by the Deputy Press Secretary on Congressional Passage of H.R. 2115, the Federal Aviation Administration Reauthorization Bill

Statement by the Deputy Press Secretary on disaster assistance to Puerto Rico

Statement by the Deputy Press Secretary on disaster assistance to West Virginia

Released November 22

Statement by the Press Secretary announcing that the President signed H.J. Res. 79 and H.R. 2559

Statement by the Press Secretary announcing that the President signed H.R. 274, H.R. 3054, and H.R. 3232

Released November 24

Transcript of a press gaggle by Deputy Press Secretary Claire Buchan

Statement by the Deputy Press Secretary announcing that the President signed H.R. 1588

Released November 25

Transcript of a press gaggle by Deputy Press Secretary Claire Buchan

Fact sheet: A Great Day for America's Seniors: Historic Passage of a Broadly Bipartisan Medicare Modernization Bill

Released November 26

Transcript of a press gaggle by Deputy Press Secretary Claire Buchan

Statement by the Deputy Press Secretary: Official Visit by Premier Wen Jiabao of China

Released November 28

Transcript of a press gaggle by Communications Director Dan Bartlett on the President's visit to Iraq

Released December 1

Transcript of a press gaggle by Press Secretary Scott McClellan

Statement by the Press Secretary announcing that the President signed S.J. Res. 18, S.J. Res. 22, S. 1066, and H.R. 2754

Released December 2

Transcript of a press gaggle by Press Secretary Scott McClellan

Statement by the Press Secretary announcing that the President signed S. 1590

Statement by the Press Secretary announcing that the President signed S. 254, S. 867, S. 1718, and H.R. 3182

Released December 3

Transcript of a press briefing by Press Secretary Scott McClellan

Statement by the Press Secretary: King Abdullah of Jordan To Visit Washington

Statement by the Press Secretary on the President's decision to award the Presidential Medal of Freedom to Robert L. Bartley and the text of the citation

Statement by the Press Secretary announcing that the President signed H.R. 1904

Statement by the Press Secretary announcing that the President signed H.R. 23, H.R. 2744, H.R. 3175, H.R. 3379, S. 117, S. 286, S. 650, S. 189, H.R. 1683, H.R. 1685, S. 1720, and S. 1824

Fact sheet: President Bush Signs Healthy Forests Restoration Act Into Law

Fact sheet: President Bush Signs the 21st Century Nanotechnology Research and Development Act

Released December 4

Transcript of a press briefing by Press Secretary Scott McClellan

Transcript of a press briefing by U.S. Trade Representative Robert B. Zoellick on ending the temporary steel safeguards

Statement by the Press Secretary announcing that the President signed H.R. 2622

Fact sheet: President Bush Signs the Fair and Accurate Credit Transactions Act of 2003

Fact sheet: The Presidential Determination on Steel

Released December 5

Statement by the Press Secretary: Terrorist Act in Yessentuki, Stavropol Region, Russia, on December 5

Announcement of the membership of the President's Task Force on Puerto Rico's Status

Fact sheet: 57,000 Americans Find Work in November: Unemployment Rate Drops Below 6%

Released December 6

Statement by the Press Secretary announcing that the President signed H.R. 421, H.R. 1367, H.R. 1821, H.R. 3038, H.R. 3140, H.R. 3166, H.R. 3185, H.R. 3349, S. 579, S. 1152, S. 1156, S. 1768, and S. 1895

Released December 8

Transcript of a press briefing by Press Secretary Scott McClellan

Statement by the Press Secretary announcing that the President signed H.R. 1

Fact sheet: President Bush Signs the Medicare Prescription Drug, Improvement, and Modernization Act of 2003

Fact sheet: Commission for Assistance to a Free Cuba

Released December 9

Transcript of a press briefing by Press Secretary Scott McClellan

Statement by the Press Secretary announcing that the President signed H.R. 3348

Statement by the Press Secretary on disaster assistance to Virginia

Statement by the Press Secretary on disaster assistance to the U.S. Virgin Islands

Released December 10

Transcript of a press briefing by Press Secretary Scott McClellan

Released December 11

Transcript of a press briefing by Press Secretary Scott McClellan

Released December 12

Transcript of a press briefing by Press Secretary Scott McClellan

Statement by the Press Secretary announcing that the President signed H.R. 1828 and H.R. 2115

Released December 13

Statement by the Press Secretary announcing that the President signed H.R. 2417

Fact sheet: 2003: A Year of Accomplishment for the American People

Released December 14

Transcript of a press gaggle by Press Secretary Scott McClellan

Released December 15

Statement by the Press Secretary announcing that the President signed H.J. Res. 80, H.R. 1437, H.R. 1813, H.R. 3287, and S. 459

Fact sheet: Facts About the New Iraqi Healthcare System

Released December 16

Transcript of a press briefing by Press Secretary Scott McClellan

Statement by the Press Secretary on the France-Germany-U.S. agreement on debt reduction for Iraq

Statement by the Press Secretary announcing that the President signed H.J. Res. 82 and S. 877

Statement by the Press Secretary announcing that the President signed H.R. 3491, H.R. 2297, and S. 811

Fact sheet: Expanding Homeownership Opportunities for All Americans

Fact sheet: President Bush Signs Anti-Spam Law

Released December 17

Transcript of a press gaggle by Press Secretary Scott McClellan

Statement by the Press Secretary on Special Presidential Envoy James A. Baker III's meeting with Italian Prime Minister Berlusconi concerning debt reduction for Iraq

Statement by the Press Secretary announcing that the President signed H.J. Res. 63

Released December 18

Transcript of a press gaggle by Press Secretary Scott McClellan

Transcript of a press briefing by Press Secretary Scott McClellan

Medical Summary: The President's Orthopedic Exam

Released December 19

Transcript of a press briefing by Press Secretary Scott McClellan

Statement by the Press Secretary: President To Attend Special Summit of the Americas

Statement by the Press Secretary announcing that the President signed H.R. 100, H.R. 622, H.R. 1006, H.R. 1012, H.R. 2620, S. 686, S. 1680, S. 1683, S. 1929, and S. 1947

Statement by the Press Secretary on disaster assistance to the Federated States of Micronesia

Fact sheet: The President's National Security Strategy To Combat WMD

Released December 22

Transcript of a press briefing by Press Secretary Scott McClellan

Statement by the Press Secretary announcing that Special Presidential Envoy James A. Baker III will travel to Japan, South Korea, and China on December 27–30

Fact sheet: Guidance Released on Health Savings Accounts (HSAs): HSAs Are Good News for All Americans

Released December 26

Transcript of a press gaggle by Press Secretary Scott McClellan

Released December 27

Statement by the Press Secretary on the U.S. Government's deployment of humanitarian assistance to the people of Iran following the earthquake in Bam

Released December 29

Transcript of a press gaggle by Deputy Press Secretary Trent Duffy

Released December 30

Transcript of a press gaggle by Deputy Press Secretary Trent Duffy

Statement by the Deputy Press Secretary announcing that the President approved the designation of 37 sub-Saharan African countries as eligible for tariff preferences under the African Growth and Opportunity Act

Released December 31

Statement by the Deputy Press Secretary announcing that the President directed the Secretary of State and Secretary of the Treasury to take significant steps to expedite disaster relief and humanitarian aid operations in response to the earthquake in Bam, Iran

Appendix D—Presidential Documents Published in the Federal Register

This appendix lists Presidential documents released by the Office of the Press Secretary and published in the Federal Register. The texts of the documents are printed in the Federal Register (F.R.) at the citations listed below. The documents are also printed in title 3 of the Code of Federal Regulations and in the Weekly Compilation of Presidential Documents.

PROCLAMATIONS

PROCLAMATIONS—Continued

EXECUTIVE ORDERS

EXECUTIVE ORDERS—Continued

OTHER PRESIDENTIAL DOCUMENTS

OTHER PRESIDENTIAL DOCUMENTS—Continued

OTHER PRESIDENTIAL DOCUMENTS—Continued

OTHER PRESIDENTIAL DOCUMENTS—Continued

Subject Index

ABC News—1790
Acquired immune deficiency syndrome (AIDS)
   See Health and medical care
Administration. *See* other part of subject
Adoption Promotion Act of 2003—1660
Advisory. *See* other part of subject
Aeronautics and Space Administration, National—1052, 1065, 1736, 1763, 1777
Afghanistan
   Ambassador to U.S.—1788
   President—1473, 1735, 1776, 1790
   Reconstruction efforts—985, 1027, 1178, 1360, 1461, 1473, 1474, 1476, 1735
   U.S. Ambassador—1776
   U.S. assistance—1106, 1217, 1735
   U.S. Special Presidential Envoy—1776
Africa
   African Union—869
   AIDS prevention and care—827, 862, 964, 1083, 1765
   Relations with U.S.—821, 822, 864
   Teacher training program with U.S.—867
   Trade with U.S.—856
   U.S. assistance—866, 867, 964
   U.S.-Sub-Saharan Africa Trade and Economic Cooperation Forum—1788
African American History and Culture Act, National Museum of—1790
African Development Foundation—1171
Agency. *See* other part of subject
Agriculture
   International food assistance—1193
   Bovine spongiform encepholopathy—1792
Agriculture, Department of
   Forest Service—989, 991, 1039, 1669
   Secretary—989, 1039, 1081, 1270, 1604, 1669, 1789, 1792
   Under Secretary—1669
AIDS Policy, Office of National—815
AIDS. *See* Health and medical care
Air Force, Department of the
   See also Armed Forces, U.S.
   Secretary—810, 1768, 1736
Airline industry. *See* Aviation
Al Qaida terrorist group. *See* Terrorism
Alabama
   Governor—1450, 1456

Alabama—Continued
   President's visits—1449, 1456, 1782
   Republican Party event—1456
Albertson's—1542
Ambassadors. *See* specific country or region
American. *See* other part of subject
Amtrak Reform Board—1774
Angola
   National Union for the Total Independence of Angola (UNITA)—979
   U.S. national emergency—979
Animal Drug User Fee Act of 2003—1572
Antigua and Barbuda, U.S. Ambassador—1777
Apalachicola-Chattahoochie-Flint River Basin Commission—1769
Archives and Records Administration, National—1175
Arctic Research Commission—1769
Argentina
   Ambassador to U.S.—1773
   President—1766, 1767, 1774
Arizona
   Disaster assistance—990, 991, 1765
   Forest management—989
   President's visits—989, 1625, 1632, 1769, 1786
   Republican Party event—1632
Arkansas
   Governor—1492
   President's visits—1491, 1784
   Republican party event—1491
Armed Forces Radio and Television. *See* Defense, Department of
Armed Forces, U.S.
   See also specific military department; Defense and national security
   All-Volunteer Force, 30th anniversary—810
   Detention, treatment, and trial of certain noncitizen terrorists—1381
   Housing—1029, 1603
   Iraq, deployment to stabilize—955
   Kosovo, deployment to stabilize—1544
   Liberia, deployment to stabilize—932, 933, 1004, 1025, 1026
   Medical care—1752
   Military readiness—851

A–1

Fair and Accurate Credit Transactions Act of 2003—1674
Faith-Based and Community Initiatives, Office of—1776
Faith-based and community organizations initiative. *See* Government organizations and employees
FBI. *See* Justice, Department of
Federal. *See* other part of subject
Florida
Disaster assistance—1768
Engelwood Neighborhood Center in Orlando—1522
Governor—1116, 1121, 1127, 1517, 1522
Hyde Park Elementary School in Jacksonville—1121, 1773
Life support court case—1402
President's visits—1116, 1121, 1127, 1517, 1522, 1773, 1784
Republican Party events—1116, 1127, 1517, 1784
Food and Drug Administration. *See* Health and Human Services, Department of
Foreign Claims Settlement Commission—1764
Foreign Intelligence Advisory Board, President's—1763, 1778
Foreign policy, U.S.
See also specific country or region
International food assistance—1193
Forest Service. *See* Agriculture, Department of
Forsyth Technical Community College—1485
France
President—1552, 1706, 1736, 1776, 1789, 1790
Relations with U.S.—1552
Freedom Corps, USA. *See* USA Freedom Corps
Freedom, Presidential Medal of—910, 1513, 1766, 1784, 1787
Future Farmers of America Organization, National—1767

Gambia, President—1764
Georgia
Governor—1141
President's visit—1141, 1774
Georgia, Republic of, Interim President—1787
Germany
Assistance to Afghanistan—985
Chancellor—985, 1196, 1552, 1600, 1706, 1736, 1789, 1790
Relations with U.S.—1196, 1552
Ghana, President—844, 866, 993, 1776
Girls Nation—1767
Global AIDS Coordinator. *See* State, Department of

Government organizations and employees
See also specific organization
Activated military members, return to Federal civilian employment—1543
Combined Federal Campaign—1023
Faith-based and community organizations initiative—815, 878, 1153, 1154, 1268, 1416–1418, 1734
Federal contracts—1713, 1714
National emergency preparedness—1738, 1745
Pay—1070
Grenada
Prime Minister—1776
U.S. Ambassador—1777
Grenadines, U.S. Ambassador—1777
Group of Eight nations (G–8). *See* Commerce, international
Guard and Reserve, National Committee for Employer Support of the—1541
Guard and Reserve Week, National Employer Support of the—1541
Guyana, Ambassador to U.S.—1788

Hanukkah—1756, 1758
Harry S. Truman Scholarship Foundation—1771
Hawaii
Governor—1781
President's visit—1386, 1781
Head Start. *See* Health and Human Services, Department of
Health and Human Services, Department of
Assistant Secretaries—1522, 1767
Deputy Secretary—1660, 1776
Disease Control and Prevention, Centers for—966, 967, 1695
Food and Drug Administration—913, 967, 1695
Head Start—840
Health, National Institutes of—815, 967, 1297
Medicare and Medicaid—966, 967, 1198, 1409, 1410, 1522, 1545, 1547, 1549, 1570, 1603, 1612, 1625, 1652, 1694, 1698, 1782
Safe and Bright Futures for Children Program—1268
Secretary—815, 839, 967, 1015, 1238, 1265, 1410, 1466, 1522, 1572, 1782, 1791
Surgeon General—967, 1522
Health and medical care
Abortion—1235, 1380, 1402, 1466
Acquired immune deficiency syndrome (AIDS)—815, 860, 1083, 1785
Euthanasia—1402
Insurance—1652

State, Department of—Continued
1158, 1174, 1175, 1209, 1226, 1292, 1294,
1295, 1408, 1475, 1596, 1631, 1713, 1765,
1767, 1769, 1772, 1775, 1777, 1778, 1783,
1789–1791
Special Envoy for Holocaust Issues—1777
Special Envoy for Peace in the Sudan—849
Under Secretary—1779
States, Organization of American—1292, 1780
Steel industry—1515, 1585
Student Loan Marketing Association—1768,
1791
Sudan
Civil conflict—849, 1788
U.S. Special Envoy for Peace—849, 1778
U.S. national emergency—1413
Sudan People's Liberation Movement—1788
Surface Transportation Board—1785, 1783
Surgeon General. *See* Health and Human Services, Department of
Sweden
Foreign Minister—1774
Prime Minister—1774
U.S. Ambassador—1787
Switzerland, U.S. Ambassador—1768
Syria
President—1596
Relations with U.S.—1715
U.S. Ambassador—1779
Syria Accountability and Lebanese Sovereignty
Restoration Act of 2003—1715

Taiwan
President—1701
Relations with China—1701
Tajikistan
Trade with U.S.—987
U.S. Ambassador—1768
Taxation
Bilateral conventions and agreements—1409,
1704
Child tax credit—913, 955
Military tax relief—1784
Tax cuts for small and minority businesses—
1185
Tax relief legislation—1032
Tennessee
Disaster assistance—1768
Kirkpatrick Elementary School in Nashville—
1107, 1773
President's visit—1107, 1111, 1773
Republican Party event—1111
Terrorism
See also specific State, country, or region; Defense and national security

Terrorism—Continued
Al Qaida—812, 956, 957, 1140, 1177, 1397,
1435, 1493, 1769
Certain terrorist attacks, U.S. national emergency—1139
Counterterrorism efforts—849, 882, 913, 925,
956, 1000, 1001, 1005, 1006, 1103, 1106,
1138, 1174, 1183, 1217, 1224, 1335, 1381,
1385, 1475, 1739, 1750, 1759
Critical infrastructure protection—1740, 1744,
1745
Detention, treatment, and trial of certain noncitizen terrorists—888, 1345
Persons who commit, threaten to commit, or
support terrorism, U.S. national emergency—1183
September 11, 2001, terrorist attacks—925,
949, 957, 1140, 1774
Terrorist organizations, efforts to freeze assets—1053
Terrorist Attacks upon the United States, National Commission on—1395, 1398
Terrorist Threat Integration Center—1136, 1174
Texas
Disaster assistance—1766
Governor—890, 895, 900
Oak Cliff Bible Fellowship Youth Education
Center in Dallas—1414
Power Center in Houston—1151
President's visits—890, 894, 899, 904, 979,
982, 999, 1031, 1151, 1414, 1431, 1766,
1769–1772, 1774, 1782, 1783, 1786, 1787,
1791
Republican Party events—894, 899, 1431,
1769
Thailand
Assistance to Afghanistan—1360
King—1362, 1780
Nation TV—1339
President—1362
President Bush's visit—1357, 1359, 1360,
1362, 1363, 1780
Prime Minister—1339, 1340, 1357, 1359,
1780
Relations with U.S.—1339, 1360
Trade with U.S.—1360
Thanksgiving—1604
Trade agreements. *See* specific country; Commerce, international
Trade Commission, Federal—1199, 1208, 1264,
1675
Trade Commission, U.S. International—1771
Trade Representative, Office of the U.S.—973,
1081, 1323

Name Index

Abbas, Khadir—1721, 1790
Abbas, Mahmoud "Abu Mazen"—818, 884, 904, 930, 947, 949, 950, 962–964, 1179, 1180, 1320, 1374, 1377, 1400, 1556, 1557, 1595, 1674, 1713, 1763, 1766, 1767
Abbott, Greg—1431
Abdul-Jabbar, Kareem—912
Abizaid, John P.—909, 1393, 1398, 1401, 1528, 1594, 1641, 1770, 1790
Abraham, Spencer—1031, 1044, 1160, 1270, 1408, 1770
Acklie, Duane—1768
Adams, Dwight E.—1134
Adamson, Jessica—1688, 1689
Aderholt, Robert—1450, 1451, 1454, 1456
Aguirre, Eduardo, Jr.—1232, 1234
Aiona, James R. "Duke," Jr.—1387, 1781
Akin, W. Todd—1060, 1066
Albert, Cheryle—1268
Albright, Madeleine—910
Aldrin, Buzz—1736
Alexander, Lamar—1108, 1111, 1112
Alford, Harry C.—1170
Aliyev, Heydar—1790
Allard, Wayne—995, 1733
Allen, Claude A.—1660, 1776
Allen, George—1293, 1709, 1710
Allen, Richard—1040
Allred, Beverly—1524
Allred, Dick—1524
Alsammarae, Aiham—1187
Altshuler, Ruth Sharp—1787
Amos, James F.—1005
Anderson, A. Paul—1771, 1797
Anderson, Alison—1687
Anderson, David W.—1774, 1795
Anderson, Eloise—1791
Andrew, Neil—1383, 1385
Andrews, John—995
Annan, Kofi—816, 823, 827, 828, 869, 907, 909, 1033, 1141, 1158, 1189, 1190, 1195, 1764, 1774, 1790
Anthony, Bill—1042
Anthony, Kenny Davis—1776
Aponte, Jose Antonio—1777, 1798
Arafat, Yasser—1180, 1312, 1377
Arakawa, Alan M.—1387

Archbold, Ralph F.—1781
Aristigueta, Maria Pilar—1777
Armitage, Richard L.—979, 1475, 1769
Armstrong, Lance—1768
Armstrong, Neil A.—1736
Arndt, Mary Jo—1211
Arroyo, Carlos—1233
Arroyo, Jose Miguel—1351, 1356, 1780
Ashcroft, John—1065, 1134, 1466
Asher, Robert—1166
Ashworth, Sandra F.—1777, 1798
Asperilla, Mark—1784
Assemi, Farid—1301
Atkins, Paul S.—1795
Augustine, Kathy—1620
Aung San Suu Kyi—944, 945, 1326, 1357
Autry, Alan—1301, 1307
Avila, Leonardo Bruzon—1293
Awada, Patricia—1055
Ayeeri, Yousif Salih Fahad Al- —812, 956
Azdi, Abu Bakr Al—812, 822, 956
Azel, Dan—1301, 1303
Azel, Kelly—1301, 1303
Aznar, Jose Maria—1194, 1376, 1391, 1554, 1559, 1783, 1790
Azyumardi Azra—1372

Bachus, Spencer—1450, 1451, 1454, 1456, 1675
Bader, Daniel—1611
Bader, Taryn—1611
Bader, Tiffany—1611
Bailey, Cathy—1288
Bailey, Elsie—1060
Baines, Robert A.—1280
Bajusz, John—1628
Baker, Doug—1094
Baker, Estelle—1524
Baker, Howard H., Jr.—1766
Baker, James A., III—1689, 1706, 1714, 1725, 1789–1791
Baker, Josiah—1094
Baker, Leslie Gromis—1663
Baker, Mindy—1094
Balkenende, Jan Peter—1083, 1771, 1772
Baptiste, Bryan J.—1387
Barbour, Haley—1145, 1436–1439, 1446–1449, 1783
Barbour, Marsha—1146, 1436, 1446

Document Categories List